THE HOMEOWNER'S HANDBOOK

A Do-It-Yourself Home Repair and Remodeling Guide

By the Editors of *WORKBENCH* Magazine

6423610

COPYRIGHT 1994 KC PUBLISHING, INC.

Attention Schools and Business Firms:
KC PUBLISHING books are available at quantity discounts for bulk purchases for education, business or sales promotion use. For more information call our Book Department at (816) 531-5730.

Printed in the United States of America

THE HOMEOWNER'S HANDBOOK
A Do-It-Yourself Home Repair and Remodeling Guide
by the staff of WORKBENCH Magazine

ISBN # 0-86675-015-0

TABLE OF CONTENTS

Whether you live in a new home that simply needs to be maintained or in a handyman's special that needs a complete overhaul, chances are you have questions. Questions about selecting paint and siding, fixing marred countertops and keeping your house warm all winter. Or maybe you need advice on adding a deck, curing condensation problems or replacing worn windows. If so, *The Homeowner's Handbook* can help.

In 1987 the editors of *Workbench*, a how-to magazine for do-it-yourselfers interested in woodworking and home improvement, began publishing a column called *Workbench* Solver. In the column, the editors and other experts answered readers' questions on topics ranging from leaky roofs to squeaky floors and everything in between. This book is a compilation of those questions and answers plus additional information every homeowner needs to keep his house in shape.

The editors would like to thank the following people for their many contributions to *The Homeowner's Handbook:* Roy Barnhart and Gary Branson, former builders and current free-lance writers who researched answers to many of the questions; Walter F. Gozdan, technical director of the Rohm and Haas Paint Quality Institute, who contributed substantially to the paint chapter; Phil McCafferty, a free-lance writer whose articles have appeared in *Workbench* for many years; Jim Rosenau, a home improvement writer and contractor; Nancy Hill, whose photographs appear in the window chapter; and technical artists Mario Ferro, Don Mannes, James P. Sexton and Eugene Thompson, whose drawings appear throughout the book.

PAINT

Homeowners have more questions and problems regarding peeling paint and moisture than all others combined. (In fact, the two problems are often related.) This chapter offers advice on selecting the proper paint for your project, preparing and painting new and old siding and areas prone to decay, fixing peeling paint on siding, ceilings and interiors, and painting paneling and textured ceilings.

CHOOSING PAINTS

Q **What is the best way to judge paint quality in the can?**

A Within a given paint manufacturer's product line, price is your best guide (disregarding sales, of course). You tend to get what you pay for, and you can usually be sure that the more you spend within a manufacturer's line, the better the quality of paint you'll get. But choosing between brands is not so easy. One manufacturer's best quality may not be as good as another manufacturer's middle grade. You can get some idea of quality from the paint can label — manufacturers often list ingredients, although they are not required by law to do so — but labels vary and often are not comparable.

Paint consists of two basic parts: pigment and vehicle. The pigment gives the paint its color and covering power. Look for titanium dioxide (TiO2), a frequently used opaque pigment. The vehicle consists of the binder and thinner. The binder cements the pigment particles into a uniform paint film and makes the paint adhere to the surface.

The nature and amount of binder determine most of the paint's service properties — washability, toughness, adhesion and color retention. Of the two most common latex-paint binders — acrylic polymer and polyvinyl acetate (PVA) — 100 percent acrylic is best. The better-quality paints contain more solids (binder and pigment) — some have up to about 50 percent by weight. These paints adhere and cover better. Obviously, a manufacturer can cut costs (and price) by using more

These test panels at the Rohm and Haas Institute were painted in 1961 and left outdoors to weather. They show what happens to paint with poor adhesion (non-acrylic latex paint was used on the left panel). The high-quality acrylic latex on the right exhibits only natural erosion.

water. Your best bet is to buy one of the higher-priced paints from a reputable and knowledgeable paint dealer and avoid "special buys" for low-end paints. To find out more about the paint you're buying, ask your paint dealer for technical information sheets or have him explain the differences in his products.

Q In terms of application, durability and cleaning, which is better — acrylic latex or alkyd?

A The better choice for most applications is 100 percent acrylic latex paint (also called all-acrylic). It adheres well to most surfaces, including wood, galvanized metal and prefinished aluminum siding. Latex paint can breathe and allows movement of water vapor through the paint film, but it also has more elasticity — the ability to expand and contract with the substrate — so it holds up better on wood. Alkyd paint achieves its adhesion by penetration and is the best choice for priming over old, heavily chalked, weathered paint. Alkyd paint provides a better water shield, but it is very inflexible. The top coats eventually crack, peel and blister as the wood expands and contracts.

Alkyd paint is a product of vegetable oils, so it is a natural growth medium for molds and mildews.

Latex paint also has low levels of volatile organic compounds. Except for water, nearly all paint solvents are VOCs and are being scrutinized or regulated because of concern about their possible detrimental effects on the environment.

Q Can paint be mixed with water or other additives? A painting contractor told me he added acrylic to the paint to extend its life. Another contractor claims you can always add water to get five quarts of paint out of each gallon you buy.

A It is conceivable that the contractor could have added an acrylic polymer. However, paints have been carefully formulated, and any change or alteration may compromise the balance or properties. Adding water will result in a thinner film once the paint dries, which can reduce its durability. This is especially true in exterior applications.

PAINTING EXTERIORS

Q How should I prepare and paint new wood siding?

A Prime all new wood (excluding pressure-treated lumber) with an acrylic latex primer as soon as possible. Letting the wood weather, even for a few weeks, will degrade paint performance. The final paint coat can be applied later (preferably within two weeks), but get the primer on as soon as possible.

Q Are there special procedures for painting factory-manufactured hardboard sidings?

A Be sure to clean any wax or oil from the siding, or use a stain-blocking acrylic-latex primer. The presses that form the siding sometimes use wax or oil as a release agent. In addition, waxes used in the siding for water resistance can bleed through some factory-applied primers and poor-quality top coats, darkening the paint. Top-quality latex paint will minimize wax bleed-through, but applying a good stain-blocking latex primer first is the best bet.

Always prime the ends of siding as you install it, especially where cuts are made. This is where moisture is most likely to penetrate the siding and cause swelling and early paint failure.

Q What is the best product for preparing and painting over old oil-base/alkyd paint?

A If the paint is sound, the first step is to remove chalk, dirt and mildew. To test for mildew, apply a few drops of household bleach to the darkened areas. If mildew is present, it will bleach out (lighten) in a minute or two. To clean the paint and kill mildew, add fresh household bleach to a mild solution of laundry detergent and water (use a ratio of 1 part bleach to 3 parts water), and scrub with a bristle brush. You can also use a high-pressure washer; in that case use the cleaning materials recommended by the washer manufacturer. Rinse with clean water; then, when the surface is dry, lightly sand so the new paint will adhere well. Remove all cracked, blistered and peeling paint, and prime the bare wood with an alkyd primer. If the house has many coats of oil or alkyd paint, recoat with alkyd paint. If there are only a few coats of oil or alkyd, use 100 percent acrylic latex.

Q What is the best procedure for preparing and painting window sills and other areas susceptible to mildew and rot?

A Window sills are one of the first places paint peels. Because of their faceup exposure, water tends to lay on the sill. The water freezes and thaws, causing some paints to crack, blister and peel. Remove the loose paint and sand lightly. Fill voids with an exterior wood filler; then prime with an alkyd primer. Apply a top-quality 100 percent acrylic latex paint that contains a mildewcide to protect against mildew.

Q What is the most important factor in painting a house?

A Preparation! Paint will not adhere to a surface covered with chalk, dirt, oil or mildew. Painting over cracked, blistered or peeling paint is an invitation to early failure. The time spent preparing the substrate will pay off in longer paint life.

Q What are the advantages and disadvantages of spray painting? How will spraying affect paint adhesion?

A The biggest advantage of spray painting is speed. But it has its drawbacks. First of all, it's difficult to apply an even coating if you're inexperienced — the paint will be too thin in some areas and too thick in others. Second, compressed-air sprayers sometimes cause the paint to bridge over cracks, holes and corners rather than fill in those areas. This leads to early checking or peeling. Another disadvantage of compressed-air sprayers is overspray — the paint fog that covers everything nearby. You must mask windows, doors, trim, shutters, etc., and cover plants, shrubs, fences and decks, etc. For your own safety, wear a respirator while spraying.

Spray painting indoors is a lot more practical than outdoors, but if you do spray your exterior, try a technique used by many professionals: Apply paint to a relatively small area, then back-brush (go over the sprayed area with a brush) or roll out the paint before it begins to dry. Back brushing evens the paint coating and forces the paint into pores and joints to increase adhesion. Use a brush on smooth surfaces such as lap siding. A roller works best on rough masonry such as brick.

Whether you spray, brush or roll on the paint, proper surface preparation is the key to a professional-looking paint job. Make sure you clean the surface of dirt, chalk and mildew and cracked, blistered or peeling paint before you begin.

Q Why is the paint flaking off my pine siding? The siding was first painted with oil-base paint. A few years ago, in an attempt to overcome the peeling, I removed all the flaking oil paint and prepared the surfaces as recommended by a paint manufacturer; then I applied latex paint. I also installed wall-ventilation plugs to make sure there wouldn't be a moisture problem. The next year the peeling reoccurred, and the condition of the paint has gradually worsened. I'd like to remove all the paint and apply stain. Is there a good product I could use to remove the paint?

A Coating manufacturers agree that in cases like yours the culprit is most likely the original oil-base house paint buried under layers of various other paints. Because you have installed vents to deter the lifting effects of moisture migration from inside your home, it's apparent that other factors are contributing to the peeling problems.

Unlike latex paints, oil-base paints eventually dry out and become brittle, losing their integrity and adhesion. This is characterized by the fine, even cracks that go across the wood grain. Additional layers of paint add considerable weight to the original layer, which then simply falls off.

There are several methods of paint removal. But if you are seriously interested in a natural stained finish, you should invest in new wood siding. To return the original siding to a condition suitable for staining and preserving requires the removal of all the paint on the wood and in its pores. Once they've been sealed, the pores will not accept stain uniformly, and you will end up with a blotchy mess.

If new siding is out of the question, the most economical remedy is to strip and repaint. There are four methods of stripping: chemical, heat, sandblasting and water-blasting. Water-blasting is the best possibility for the do-it-yourselfer. Using high-pressure water — 1,200 to 1,800 psi — you can blast the paint free without having to resort to particulate abrasives. Gouging and surface texturing are minimal. You can rent a compressor and spray tool, but be sure to wear proper face protection when water-blasting. The lower edges of the clapboard must be scraped by hand.

Repaint the house as soon as possible after paint removal (when the surface water evaporates from the water-blasting) before the siding shows signs of graying or oxidation. For a long-lasting painted surface, use an oil-base primer followed by two or three coats of good-quality latex paint. Both will allow moisture to penetrate their film formations without deterioration.

Q Should I paint the back of clapboards before I install them? I plan to replace the siding on my house with new pine clapboards. Someone recommended that I treat the back of the new clapboards to prevent the paint from peeling. What kind of coating should I use?

A If you coat the face with acrylic latex paint, there is no need to seal or treat the back of the siding. Latex paint allows water vapor to pass through without causing paint peeling. But priming the back of the siding with acrylic latex primer will do no harm and may be beneficial under certain circumstances.

If you do not have an exterior wall vapor barrier, it is possible for warm water vapor to pass through the walls from inside your house. As the water vapor reaches the siding and cools to the dew point, it may condense or even freeze. Water trapped behind the siding can cause the wood to rot.

If you decide to prime the back of your siding, lay the boards facedown across sawhorses and apply primer to the back, ends and edges. Let the primer dry; then prime the face. When you install the siding, be sure to prime-coat newly cut ends; then apply a finish coat of good-quality exterior acrylic latex paint.

Keep in mind that replacing your siding is a good opportunity to upgrade the energy efficiency of your house. You can blow insulation into the sidewall while the old siding is off or add a layer of rigid foam insulation on the outside.

When you have upgraded the insulation in your walls, apply a weather barrier, such as Tyvek, over the sheathing to reduce drafts and air infiltration.

Q How long should I wait before painting pressure-treated wood? (My lumber dealer recommends four to six weeks.) Also, is there a way to prevent pressure-treated wood from splitting?

A To minimize splitting of any lumber used outdoors, coat it with paint or water repellent as soon as the wood is relatively dry to the touch. There is no hard-and-fast rule on the waiting period. In the same batch of lumber some boards may be very dry (judged primarily by their relative weight) and others may be so wet that a hammer blow will literally splash water from the surface of the wood. Choose lumber carefully, rejecting excessively wet pieces.

Your dealer's recommendation may be based on his judgment of how wet or dry the wood is when it leaves his yard. It is probably good advice.

PEELING PAINT

Q How can I stop the paint from peeling off my ceiling? I know that the ceiling collects moisture.

A Be sure that your attic is well ventilated (see drawing, below), and make sure you don't have any roof leaks. The humidity in your house is probably very high. Rent or borrow a humidity meter to check it; then try some of the humidity-reduction methods suggested in the chapter on condensation. Circulating air with a ceiling fan also might be helpful.

Q Why is the paint peeling from my plywood porch ceiling? The roof is flat, and I've found no source of leaks. I've painted it twice with latex acrylic paint over the past five years and it continues to peel. How can I stop it?

A Plywood absorbs and desorbs moisture, so the peeling is almost certainly caused by moisture from leaks or high humidity. When moisture reaches the wood surface it pops the paint off. Because the plywood is probably the underside of the roof sheathing, check again for leaks — flat roofs are particularly susceptible to them. Examine the caulking, flashing and drip-cap for leaks. Repair any leaks you find and wait until the wood dries. Then, wearing goggles and gloves, scrape the loose paint from the surface. Sand the edges of the firm areas that remain. Next, paint with a pig-

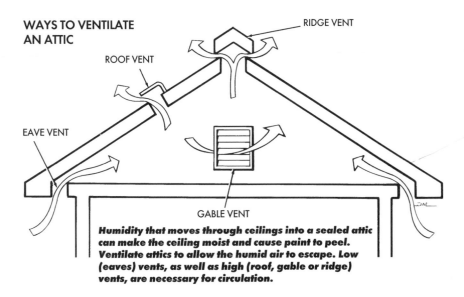

WAYS TO VENTILATE AN ATTIC

RIDGE VENT

ROOF VENT

EAVE VENT

GABLE VENT

Humidity that moves through ceilings into a sealed attic can make the ceiling moist and cause paint to peel. Ventilate attics to allow the humid air to escape. Low (eaves) vents, as well as high (roof, gable or ridge) vents, are necessary for circulation.

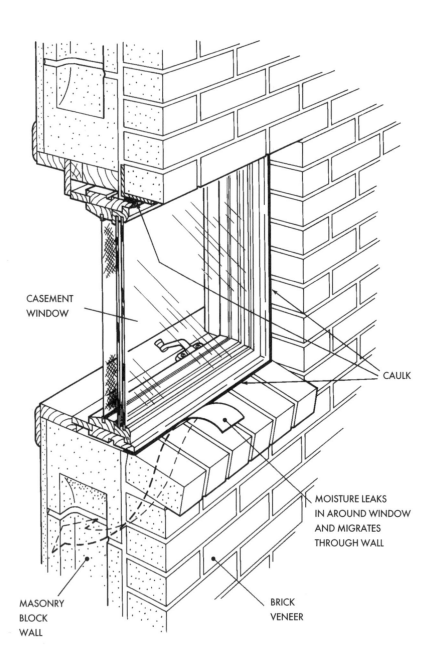

CASEMENT
WINDOW

CAULK

MOISTURE LEAKS
IN AROUND WINDOW
AND MIGRATES
THROUGH WALL

MASONRY
BLOCK
WALL

BRICK
VENEER

PAINT

mented latex acrylic primer. Finish with a top coat of acrylic latex.

If you find no leaks after rechecking, try reducing the moisture in the room by installing a dehumidifier.

Q What's causing the paint to peel beneath the windows inside my house? My 40-year-old brick and cinder block home has plastered interior walls. The paint peels and the plaster flakes off the inside of the exterior walls directly beneath thermal insulated windows. The windows have floor-length drapes and sheers. The drapes are always open but the sheers are kept closed. Is condensation the cause of my problem, and are the drapes contributing to it?

A It's doubtful the drapes or sheers are a factor in the paint peeling. Your problem is caused by water vapor inside the wall cavities under the windows (see drawing, left). The water vapor may be penetrating through the plaster from inside the house, or water may be leaking into the wall from the outside through uncaulked windows. Once inside the cold wall cavity, moisture soaks into and softens the plaster and causes the paint to peel.

Remove old caulk from around the window exterior, then apply a good-quality latex or silicone caulk around the window. Inside, scrape away the peeling paint and loose plaster. Patch as required, using a spackling compound. Cover water stains with a sealer; then apply the finish paint. If possible, do the repairs when the humidity is low and the walls are warm.

SPECIAL PREPARATIONS

Q How should I prepare dark wood paneling for painting? I want to apply a lighter color.

A Start by removing any wax or polish with mineral spirits. (Make sure the room is well ventilated before you begin working.) Next, fill any nail holes and imperfections with wood putty or spackle. Scuff-sand the paneling with 150-grit or finer sandpaper to break the shiny film surface, or apply a coat of Liquid Sandpaper (available at hardware stores). Next, coat with a good-quality shellac-based stain blocker to provide a grip for the finished coat and to prevent the dark color of the paneling from bleeding through the new paint. Finally, apply the paint.

Q How do you paint a textured ceiling? When I paint our "popcorn" textured ceiling the first stroke is fine, but when I go back over it again the texture comes off on the roller or paintbrush, leaving the drywall exposed.

A Apparently you have simulated acoustic ceiling texture, a dry spackle that is mixed with water and sprayed into place. According to the United States Gypsum Co., a manufacturer of this product, the problem you describe is not unusual, and this type of texture is typically spray-painted.

If the texture is more than 15 years old, it may contain asbestos. By the late 1970s, as awareness of asbestos-related health hazards grew, most manufacturers quit using asbestos in their products. If the texture was applied prior to that time, the United States Gypsum Co. suggests you have a sample analyzed at a laboratory approved by the Environmental Protection Agency. (See "Asbestos" or "Laboratories" in your classified telephone directory.) Do not attempt to remove texture containing asbestos yourself.

If the texture is asbestos free, rent an airless spray gun for best results. You can paint texture with a roller, but you should use a long-nap roller cover and allow each coat to dry completely before applying the next. Do not roll while the paint is wet. Semigloss or low-luster enamel is a good sealer and will make the next paint job a little easier.

REMODELING

What homeowner hasn't modified his or her home to make it more comfortable, convenient or attractive? And who hasn't dreamed of doing even more (gutting the bathroom, overhauling the kitchen, adding a new deck)? This chapter addresses diverse remodeling topics, from the basics of installing drywall, making laminate joints and altering bathtub plumbing to the intricacies of installing new flooring, attaching a mantel, building a laundry chute and adding a folding attic stairway. You'll also find advice on new additions — orienting deck boards properly, building a postless garage, constructing a floor to support a hot tub — as well as information on siding, insulation, mobile homes and more.

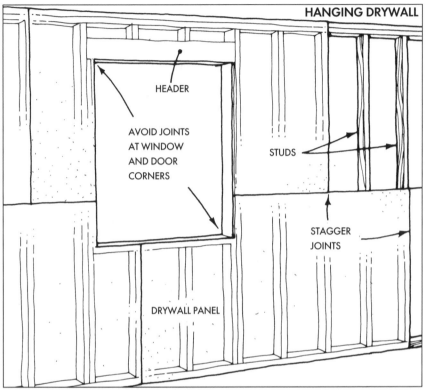

HANGING DRYWALL

HEADER

AVOID JOINTS
AT WINDOW
AND DOOR
CORNERS

STUDS

STAGGER
JOINTS

DRYWALL PANEL

Install long sheets of drywall horizontally to minimize flush joints and make taping easier.

INTERIOR RENOVATIONS

Q **How should drywall be installed — vertically or horizontally?** Does it matter?

A It matters only to the person doing the taping. Unlike plywood sheathing, which has to be oriented to provide maximum shear strength, drywall can be installed in either direction. It isn't meant to provide stiffness to the building.

Professional installers prefer to hang the panels horizontally to make the finisher's work easier. When the 4- x 8-ft. sheets are positioned verti-cally, the finisher has to use a ladder to reach the top of each vertical seam every 4 ft. along the wall. By placing the sheets horizontally, professional installers can use longer sheets (9- to 12-ft.-long sheets can be found in most areas), and most of the seams will be 4 ft. from the floor (see drawing, above). If the wall is 9 ft. high, a 1-ft.-wide strip is installed between the sheets so that both seams are easy to tape.

By hanging long sheets horizontally, the installers are doing another favor for the finisher: They're minimizing the number of flush (butt) joints. The long edges of drywall

REMODELING

panels are tapered to provide a space for the joint tape and compound, which makes it easy to hide the tape. Professional installers know that it's cheaper to use bigger sheets, even if that means more waste around doors and windows, than to put up lots of smaller pieces with more butt joints. The cutoff pieces can often be used in out-of-the-way areas such as closets, where a high-quality finish isn't demanded.

Q **How do you make a good laminate joint in an L-shaped countertop?**

A How you make the joint depends on whether you're using a prefabricated post-formed top with an integral backsplash or a square-edged top with a separate back-splash. The size of the top and the room layout also matter.

A post-formed top, which you can buy in home centers, is curved at the backsplash and front edge, so the two legs of an L-shaped counter-top must be joined with a miter. Your supplier should be able to cut the miter and provide the mechanical connectors necessary to connect the two legs on site.

Do-it-yourselfers can make their own square-edged L-shaped top (see drawing, above right). Ideally, the substrate (or blank) is fabricated in one piece and covered with a single piece of laminate. If the top is too large to get into the kitchen, however, two blanks would have to be mechanically fastened together at a 90-degree angle on site. The laminate is applied after the blanks have

SQUARE-EDGED COUNTERTOP

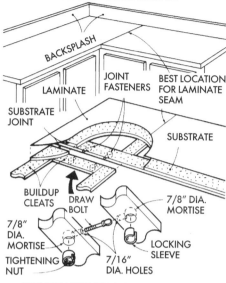

JOINT FASTENER BOTTOM VIEW

To install a two-piece L-shaped countertop on site, install joint fasteners in the underside of the countertop blanks and tighten as you carefully align the two pieces. Sand the joint before applying the laminate.

been joined and the joint between them has been sanded. If the short leg of the countertop measures more than 60 in. (the widest available laminate size), the laminate must be installed in two pieces.

Whenever you laminate a two-piece counter on site, bridge the seam in the substrate with the laminate. Place the laminate seam over a one-piece leg. If you're laminating a large two-piece top in the shop, however, the laminate joint must fall near the joint in the substrate.

To ensure that two pieces of laminate have perfectly mating edges, clamp the pieces in place over the substrate, overlapping the laminate where the joint will be. Then cut both pieces at once using a router equipped with a sharp straight bit and guided by a straightedge.

Stress cracking can be a problem with L- or U-shaped countertops. A technical booklet from the Formica Corp. for professional installers suggests that to minimize cracking, the laminate and substrate should be acclimated to the same conditions — ideally 75 degrees F and 45 to 55 percent humidity — for at least 48 hours before you apply the laminate. Industry-wide guidelines also say to leave a minimum 1/8-in. radius on the laminate at inside corners.

Q **Will I have to completely redo the plumbing to install a shower in my tub?** I recently removed the plaster from the end wall by the bathtub, and I don't see any way to hook up a shower pipe to the existing plumbing.

A There are two kind of faucet bodies used in bathtubs. If a shower is not planned when the plumbing is first installed, a faucet body with three openings — two for the incoming hot and cold water supply and a third for connecting the spout to direct water into the tub — is used. The faucet body controls the amount of hot and cold water flowing through it and the temperature of the bathwater. If a shower is planned, a faucet body with a fourth opening in the top for the shower pipe is used. It is unlikely that this type of faucet body would be used if a shower is not installed at the same time.

To add a shower, you must replace the old faucet body with a

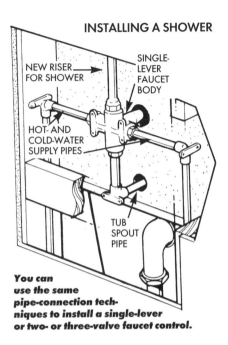

INSTALLING A SHOWER

NEW RISER FOR SHOWER

SINGLE-LEVER FAUCET BODY

HOT- AND COLD-WATER SUPPLY PIPES

TUB SPOUT PIPE

You can use the same pipe-connection techniques to install a single-lever or two- or three-valve faucet control.

new one that provides for a shower pipe (see drawing, above). You did not say what kind of pipe you have. If the house has galvanized steel pipes (threaded with fittings), unscrew the pipe to remove the old faucet body. You probably will have to cut the pipe nipples with a hacksaw; if the pipes are copper, you can use a tubing cutter. Remove the old faucet body; then install the new faucet body by threading or soldering in new couplings and elbows.

Q **How do I prepare a concrete slab to lay a new floor?** I want to convert my garage into an office and need to know how to treat the concrete slab. The slab rests on the ground with no gravel base, and it sweats in spring and fall or whenever it rains a lot.

REMODELING

COVER A SWEATING CONCRETE SLAB

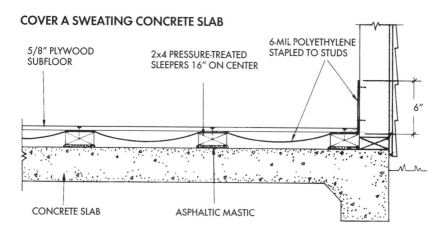

5/8" PLYWOOD SUBFLOOR

2x4 PRESSURE-TREATED SLEEPERS 16" ON CENTER

6-MIL POLYETHYLENE STAPLED TO STUDS

6"

CONCRETE SLAB

ASPHALTIC MASTIC

Pressure-treated sleepers covered with plastic and plywood will stop a concrete floor from sweating.

A The sweating can be caused by warm, humid air within the garage condensing when it comes in contact with the cold concrete slab or by water vapor passing through the concrete slab from below. In either case, your best approach is to install 2x4 sleepers (wood strips that provide a nailing surface for the plywood subfloor), a vapor barrier and a subfloor.

Wood that comes into contact with concrete should always be pressure treated to prevent decay, so set 2x4 pressure-treated sleepers 16 in. on center in a bed of mastic — construction adhesive that you can apply with a caulking gun. Place a minimum of 6-mil-thick polyethylene on the sleepers and staple it up the wall studs about 4 to 6 in. Allow some slack in the polyethylene so you won't tear it while working on the system. Next, add a 5/8-in.-thick plywood subfloor, which should be a suitable underlayment for most floors. (Check this detail with your flooring supplier.) Depending upon the type of flooring you plan to use, you may require underlayment over the plywood. Caution: Polyethylene is slippery to walk on, so watch your footing as you work.

Q Can I put down new flooring without removing old tiles? Carpetlayers refuse to put down a new vinyl sheet floor over our old 9-in.-sq. asphalt tiles because of shrinkage cracks between the tiles. They insist on adding 1/4-in. underlayment. I hesitate to do this because we have five pocket doors that may have to be cut, and because the new floor will not be even with adjoining hardwood floors. Is there anything else I can do without removing the tiles, which would be costly and possibly hazardous?

A You're right to be concerned about the hazards of tile removal. Many old tiles contain asbestos, and although they can be removed safely, it's usually better to leave them in place. Even if you remove them, underlayment might still be required to cover the mess and damage.

You need to add the underlayment for several reasons. If you install the sheet vinyl directly over the tiles, textured patterns and imperfections (such as the cracks between your tiles) most likely will telegraph through the vinyl. A perimeter bond flooring such as Armstrong's Inter Flex is less likely to show imperfections than a fully adhered flooring, but your installers are aware of this, and apparently they think the cracks are too wide.

You can buy patching compounds that fill cracks, but it is highly unlikely that such compounds would stay put in cracks that are probably filled with dirt, grease and wax. Any movement would force out the compound, and that would look like a mountain range under your new floor. Finally, you can never guarantee the bond of the old flooring.

The minor level change the new underlayment will produce is not considered a problem from a safety or appearance viewpoint. Unless all the pocket doors would have to be removed and shortened, they shouldn't present a problem.

Even if they must be cut, the first priority should be a properly installed, warranted floor.

Q How do I install a wood mantel in a stone wall? I want to install the mantel above my wood-burning fireplace insert. Can you tell me how to install the mantel so it conforms to the irregular face of the stone?

FITTING A FIREPLACE MANTEL

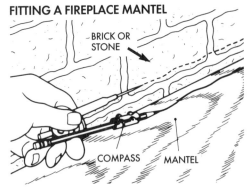

As you run the pointed leg of the compass against the wall, the pencil marks the wall profile on the wood mantel.

A You're confronted with a typical carpentry problem that can be solved by a technique known as "scribing." All you need are a pencil compass and sabre saw or band saw.

Start by temporarily mounting the mantel, either on wall brackets or with braces resting on the floor. Push the mantel against the wall so the front edge is parallel with the hearth.

Now, using a pencil compass, spread the compass legs to the widest gap between the wall and back edge of the mantel. Starting at one end, run the pointed leg against the stone. The pencil leg marks the contour of the stone on the wood mantel (see drawing, above). Let the compass move freely, following the pattern of the stones and the mortar joints between the stones.

After you have marked the wall contour on the wood, remove the mantel and carefully cut along the scribe line. If the fit is not perfect, use a wood rasp to dress the cut edge until the fit is satisfactory.

This technique can be used to

install countertops against a wall, fit scribe pieces that trim cabinet built-ins and install cabinet kick (toe) plates neatly along a floor that's contoured.

Q Do I have to modify the chimney of my house in order to install a wood heater in the fireplace? I have a large fireplace with a brick chimney lined with 12-in. x 12-in. clay tile. I plan to reduce the size of the flue for use with a wood heater. I've heard of an insulating concrete mixture that can be used for relining. Do you have any information on this process?

A Reducing the size of the chimney flue by relining it is your only sensible choice. You'll be rewarded with improved safety, less pollution, better draft and lower maintenance costs.

There are two basic relining options — cast-in-place concrete (the method you referred to) and insulated stainless steel. Cast-in-place relining is a superior approach because it significantly strengthens the chimney and is more durable. (It lasts about 60 years, compared to 20 years for steel.) But it typically costs 30 to 35 percent more.

There are two approaches to cast-in-place relining, both of which originated in Europe. In the English method (see drawing, right), a special cementitious mixture is poured around an inflated rubber former, which is removed when the cement hardens. In the German method, a similar mixture is poured into the chimney and then a vibrating bullet-

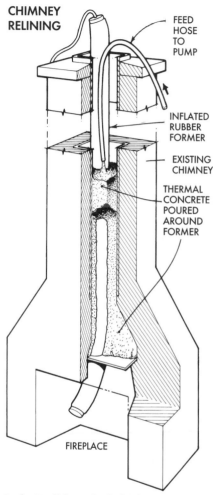

CHIMNEY RELINING

FEED HOSE TO PUMP

INFLATED RUBBER FORMER

EXISTING CHIMNEY

THERMAL CONCRETE POURED AROUND FORMER

FIREPLACE

In the English method of chimney relining, insulating cement is pumped around an inflated rubber former. After curing, the former is removed.

shaped probe is pulled up through the chimney. In both cases, the solid flue extends just to the smoke chamber. From there stainless steel connections are made to the wood-burning stove or fireplace.

A variety of stainless steel relining systems are available (no. 304 stainless steel is best for use with wood-burning devices), including some with flexible pipe for use in chimneys with offsets. The Consumer Product Safety Commission strongly recommends that you use chimney liners that comply with Underwriters Laboratory standard 1777, which states that liners can withstand a temperature of 2,100 F.

Most wood-burning appliance manufacturers require stainless steel flues to be insulated with a wrap or a poured mixture of Portland cement, vermiculite (or perlite) and water. A warm flue has better draft, is more efficient and has less creosote buildup.

According to the National Chimney Sweep Guild, it is essential that the existing flue be "squeaky clean" to avoid a fire hazard, whichever system you install. In fact, the old flue liners are usually broken out with a tile breaker (a long steel rod with an off-center triangle on the end attached to a heavy-duty drill). This provides more room for the new flue, and it's often easier to do than a proper cleaning.

Consult the heater manufacturer about flue requirements. (Warranties are often voided if the proper system is not used.) Relining systems are approved for specific applications, and using them for other purposes is unsafe. You may be required to get a permit and have the work inspected. Finally, contact your insurance company to see if it has any requirements.

Because installation instructions are often sketchy and the slightest error or oversight can have disastrous consequences, professional installation of flue liners is strongly recommended. For more information, consult the classified telephone directory under "Chimney Lining" or "Chimney Cleaning."

Q **How should I install a laundry chute?** I want to install one that leads from the first-floor hallway to the basement laundry room. What is the slickest material to use? I must angle the chute to get past a beam and into the laundry room. What angle can I use? What kind of self-closing cover would let laundry through but keep out cold air, dust, etc.?

A Let's make sure your laundry chute is a pleasant addition. A laundry chute can be a hazard to young children, and it could speed the spread of a fire originating in the basement.

Although the National Fire Protection Association (the organization that produces the National Fire Codes, including the National Electrical Code, which are used as references by the various model building codes) has no fire-rating requirements for single-family dwellings, you should have smoke detectors connected to your house wiring and have a battery backup.

Some communities follow codes written by the Council of American Building Officials, which exempts single-family dwellings from safety requirements for laundry chutes. But it's still advisable to have a building inspector review your plan and make safety suggestions.

In other municipalities, building

REMODELING

codes may apply. For example, the Uniform Building Code, one of three national model building codes used in the United States, requires laundry chutes to have fire-resistant walls made of 5/8-in. type-X drywall (gypsum panels with a fire-retardant core) or a metal lining (26-gauge minimum) and a self-closing 1-3/8-in.-thick solid-wood inlet door. Other requirements may include specific hinge locations and a fire stop (a concealed device that prevents the spread of fire through an open space) at the top of the chute. To prevent small children from falling into the chute, the bottom of the inlet door should be at least 42 in. above the floor.

Most residential laundry chutes are constructed of galvanized steel or aluminum with interlocking connections. A round 16-in.-dia. shaft is ideal, but because the open space between floor joists is typically 14-1/2 in., smaller 12- or 14-in.-dia. shafts are often substituted.

Offsets (jogs or deviations from a straight line usually achieved with elbows that twist out to any angle) should be avoided if possible and may even be prohibited by local codes. If offsets are allowed, they should be at a steep angle to the floor (no less than 30 degrees) unless you're able to reach in to free a clog.

The chute should terminate in an enclosed counter-height compartment with a self-closing weather-stripped door.

Q **Can I replace the small access panel in my attic with a folding stairway?** Because I live in an old

DISAPPEARING STAIRWAY

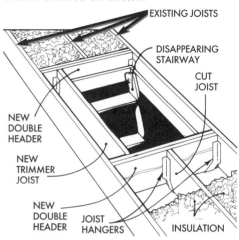

To install a folding stairway, cut and frame the ceiling joists to fit the stairway frame. Install the new framing with joist hangers.

house in a remote area, getting a contractor to do the work would be expensive, so I want to do it myself. The ceiling joists are parallel to the hall.

A The system you describe is widely available. Preassembled disappearing (folding) stairways can be found in home centers and building supply outlets. Most disappearing stairways are made of wood and fold down when the door is opened. They're compact and relatively easy to install (see drawing, above).

Cutting the opening is easy if the ceiling is made of drywall. Cutting a ceiling constructed of plaster on metal or wood lath is harder and messier, but it can be done. Reframing is minimal. Cut one joist, add double headers at either end and add a new trimmer joist. Installation of the stairway is a snap if you have a helper. Complete instructions should come with the unit, but basically here's what's involved.

First, go into the attic and remove insulation; then check for obstacles (electric wiring, etc.). Using a chalkline, mark the cutout, placing one side along an existing joist if possible. Check squareness by measuring diagonals. (If the measurements are equal, the cutout is square.) Cut out the drywall or plaster with a reciprocating saw or sabre saw. Cut two sides and then brace the cutout before cutting the ends. Even if you exercise care, plaster often cracks outside of the cut. If this happens, use drywall patching compound to repair the crack. Brace the ceiling joists before cutting them and removing the interfering joist. Use joist hangers to install the headers and trimmer joist.

Before you raise the stairway into the opening, tack some scrap lumber on one end of the opening to help support the unit while you and a helper lift it into place. You can also make a T-support to help hold the unit in place while you fasten it from above.

Shim and attach the stairway with screws according to the instructions provided with the unit. Lower the ladder and cut the lower section to length. Finally, trim the opening with casing; then paint.

Folding stairways are not as sturdy or as safe as a permanently placed stairway. Periodically check the condition of the wood and the tightness of the various fittings and fasteners.

ADDING ON

Q **How should deck boards be oriented?** I've read that they should be installed bark-side up, and a contractor I trust confirmed this. But I've seen some decks in my neighborhood where this has created ridges, which I'd like to avoid.

A To answer your question, we'd need to know what kind of wood you are using. Assuming the boards are straight and not warped or cupped when you receive them, the primary factors are whether the boards are wet or dry and how they are sawn. If possible, obtain vertical-grain material as there will be little cupping. Cupping occurs more readily with flat-grained (flat-sawn) boards. If a board has been kiln dried and then absorbs moisture, it will cup toward the pith side. If the board is wet, it will cup toward the bark side when it dries.

Most publications recommend that deck boards be placed bark-side up, but they were written when most of the lumber used for decks came from western forests. A secondary reason was to minimize splintering or slivering that can occur on the pith side. Today, however, much of the wood used for decks is pressure treated and is installed wet. These boards will cup toward the bark side when they dry.

Cupping will be more pronounced on a wider board (2x6s will cup more than 2x4s). A crown is more desirable than edge ridges, and pressure-treated lumber should be laid bark-side down. Kiln-dried lumber should be installed bark-side up.

In actual practice, the boards will successively dry and absorb moisture and dry again. This constant flexing eventually will cause standard nails to pull. Therefore you should use spiral nails, which have superior holding power.

Q **What's the proper construction technique for building a postless garage?** I plan to build a 24- x 36-ft. detached garage/workshop without any interior bearing walls or posts. Can I use engineered wood beams to span the 24-ft. width?

A The least expensive approach is to use roof trusses, which are routinely used to span 24-ft. widths. Fabricators of trusses are listed in the classified telephone directory under "Roof & Floor Structures." Some truss designs even provide limited storage, but there are weight restrictions. If you're looking for an attic floor with full-loading capabilities

Using engineered lumber makes it possible to build a garage free of supporting posts and also provide storage space in the attic. You can use PSL, LVL or I-joists. Make your decision on what to use after you've figured the cost of materials and the labor required.

POSTLESS GARAGE

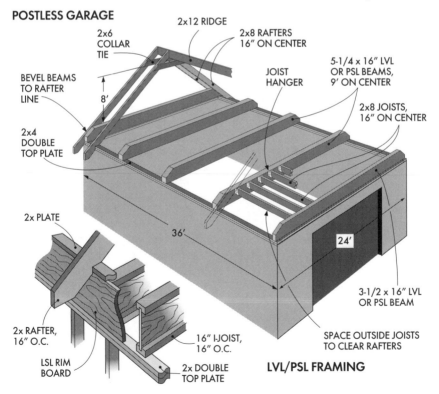

2x12 RIDGE

2x6 COLLAR TIE

2x8 RAFTERS 16" ON CENTER

BEVEL BEAMS TO RAFTER LINE

JOIST HANGER

5-1/4 x 16" LVL OR PSL BEAMS, 9' ON CENTER

8'

2x4 DOUBLE TOP PLATE

2x8 JOISTS, 16" ON CENTER

2x PLATE

36'

24'

2x RAFTER, 16" O.C.

LSL RIM BOARD

16" I-JOIST, 16" O.C.

2x DOUBLE TOP PLATE

3-1/2 x 16" LVL OR PSL BEAM

SPACE OUTSIDE JOISTS TO CLEAR RAFTERS

LVL/PSL FRAMING

OPTIONAL I-JOIST FRAMING

(50 pounds a square foot), engineered lumber (wood building products made from dried pieces of wood bonded together under heat and pressure) is the way to go.

One method is to span the 24 ft. with 16-in. laminated veneer lumber (a layered composite of wood veneers and adhesive) or parallel strand lumber (a layered composite of wood strips and adhesive) beams spaced on 9-ft. centers (see drawing, p. 23). LVL beams come in 1-3/4-in. widths only and must be doubled or tripled and joined with three rows of 16-penny nails spaced 12-in. on center to obtain the necessary width. PSL beams are available in 3-1/2- and 5-1/4-in. widths but are heavier and harder to handle. Use 3-1/2-in.-thick beams over the ends of the garage (either a single PSL beam or two LVL beams nailed together). For the remaining beams, use three LVL beams or a single 5-1/4-in. PSL beam. Complete the floor framing with 2x8s on 16-in. centers.

Use framing hardware (not nails alone) to tie the LVL beams to the sidewall plates because these four beams are all that keep the structure from spreading apart. Frame the roof with a 2x12 ridge beam and 2x8 rafters. (Use 2x12 rafters if you plan to insulate the roof.) Install 2x6 collar ties 8 ft. above the floor level on every rafter pair.

Another method is to build a conventional floor spanning the 24 ft. using either 16-in. 35SP series I-joists (prefabricated joists made from two flanges and a web assembled from engineered wood or a combination of engineered wood and dimension lumber) or, if depth is an issue, 14-in. 55SP series I-joists. Both of these products are available from Trus Joist MacMillan. Set on 16-in. centers, both I-joists would have the weight-carrying capacity that most building codes require (50 pounds a square foot). For best results, use laminated strand lumber (1-1/4-in.-thick laminated veneer lumber used as an alternative to dimension lumber) for the rim joists.

Q **What type of floor structure do you recommend for a solarium?** The 12- x 21-ft. solarium will be attached to the side of my house. It will have a tiled Gypcrete floor with in-floor radiant heating. I also plan to install a hot tub. The floor weighs 4,465 pounds and the tub (with water) weighs 5,000 pounds. After deducting the space needed for the sill plate, Gypcrete and tile, I have only 9-1/2 in. remaining for the joists and subfloor.

A To fit the floor framing into the 9-1/2-in. space you have available, you must use 2x8 (1-1/2 x 7-1/4 in. actual size) joists under a 3/4-in. subfloor. For 2x8s to support all that weight, you must build another foundation wall in the middle of the span (see drawing, right). Use 8-in. concrete block on a 1- x 2-ft. footing. If the crawl space is unvented, the footing can sit at grade on firm, undisturbed soil. If the space is vented (and therefore subject to freezing), the footing must extend below your area frost line.

The footing should contain two continuous no. 4 reinforcing rods (rebar). You should tie the footing to

REMODELING

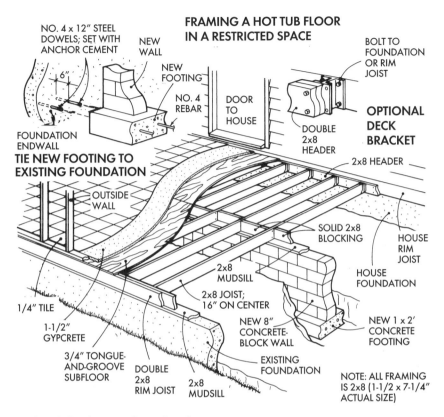

FRAMING A HOT TUB FLOOR IN A RESTRICTED SPACE

NO. 4 x 12" STEEL DOWELS; SET WITH ANCHOR CEMENT

NEW WALL

NEW FOOTING

NO. 4 REBAR

DOOR TO HOUSE

6"

FOUNDATION ENDWALL

TIE NEW FOOTING TO EXISTING FOUNDATION

OUTSIDE WALL

BOLT TO FOUNDATION OR RIM JOIST

DOUBLE 2x8 HEADER

OPTIONAL DECK BRACKET

2x8 HEADER

SOLID 2x8 BLOCKING

HOUSE RIM JOIST

HOUSE FOUNDATION

2x8 MUDSILL

2x8 JOIST; 16" ON CENTER

1/4" TILE

1-1/2" GYPCRETE

3/4" TONGUE-AND-GROOVE SUBFLOOR

DOUBLE 2x8 RIM JOIST

2x8 MUDSILL

NEW 8" CONCRETE-BLOCK WALL

EXISTING FOUNDATION

NEW 1 x 2' CONCRETE FOOTING

NOTE: ALL FRAMING IS 2x8 (1-1/2 x 7-1/4" ACTUAL SIZE)

Optional aluminum Deck Brackets (see detail) are used to attach ledgers to the house framing and prevent rot and insect damage to house sills and rim joists that often occurs when ledgers are attached directly to the house.

the existing foundation wall or footing, depending on the location of the new footing. To do that, install two 12-in.-long no. 4 steel dowels (they can be cut from rebar) in 6-in.-deep holes in the existing foundation. Use anchor cement to hold them in place. Then pour the new footing.

Be sure to use pressure-treated lumber for the floor framing. First, attach the header to the house. You can use a single 2x8 bolted to the foundation or a double 2x8 attached with Deck Brackets (made by Crawford Products). Space the brackets 6 ft. apart with an extra one installed at the hot tub location. Install double 2x8 rim joists; then attach 2x8 floor joists to the header and rim joists with joist hangers 16 in. on center. For added stiffness, install solid blocking between the joists at midspan.

The preferred underlayment for a Gypcrete in-floor heating system is 3/4-in. tongue-and-groove plywood or oriented strand board panels, such as Sturd-I-Floor, that have been rated for structural use by the American Plywood Association.

Look for the APA rating stamp showing that the panels have passed inspection.

Q **How should I polish and seal brick?** I just completed a used-brick patio. I would like the sealed brick to have a wet look.

A Different climates determine whether or not brick should be sealed, so first check with brick masons and suppliers where you live to learn what they advise. In some areas, experts advise you to leave bricks unsealed for several reasons. First, moisture trapped inside bricks or mortar joints could expand and damage the bricks in freezing weather. Next, trace salts in bricks can leach out, or effloresce, and create a chalky stain between the sealer and the bricks.

If you're advised that bricks can be successfully sealed in your area, be sure to let the bricks age; the salts tend to leach out and away in about five years. Because you made your patio of used bricks, this may not be a problem.

Next, be sure that water drains off and away from the patio so that it cannot penetrate into the brick or the mortar joints. Then apply one or more generous coats of sealer according to the manufacturer's directions. Be careful not to neglect any spots because water could soak into the brick and cause problems. Use a sealer recommended by your local masonry dealer or contractor, and ask for customer references to check the sealer before you make your choice.

SIDING

Q **What kinds of siding are available for houses?** My 40-year-old house has aluminum siding installed over stucco. The stucco is falling apart. I'd like to tear off the siding and stucco and start anew. I do not want to stucco again. I thought that there were many types of siding materials on the market, but a local supplier tells me that the only siding available is vinyl.

A It's odd that a building-supply company would not acknowledge the existence of the many types of exterior finishing systems — wood, metal, vinyl, stucco and masonry — that are available. In recent years, siding has undergone many technological and design changes. The vinyl siding manufactured today is far superior in performance and appearance to that sold five to 10 years ago. Both aluminum- and vinyl-siding manufacturers have developed a wide range of accessories that add interest and character.

If you like the look of stucco, you might consider brush-on acrylic elastomeric stucco or a system that combines foam insulation with a material similar to stucco. Both are appealing alternatives to traditional Portland cement stucco.

Plywood and hardboard sidings often offer performance and appearance comparable or superior to solid lumber sidings.

To explore the available options, contact specific manufacturers for literature and instruction manuals (if you plan to do the work yourself) and the names of local outlets.

Finally, get firm bids on material prices and installation fees so you'll know how much the system you choose will cost.

For information on siding options contact the following associations and suppliers:

Wood sidings (shingles, shakes, lap, board, etc.):
California Redwood Association, 405 Enfrente Drive, Suite 200, Novato, CA 94949; (415) 382-0662.

Cedar Shake & Shingle Bureau, 515 116th Ave. N.E., Suite 275, Bellevue, WA 98004; (206) 453-1323.

Southern Forest Products Association, Box 641700, Kenner, LA 70064-1700; (504) 443-4464.

Western Wood Products Association, Yeon Building, 522 S.W. Fifth Ave., Portland, OR 97204; (503) 224-3930.

Performance-rated plywood sidings (panel, lap):
American Plywood Association, Box 11700, Tacoma, WA 98411; (206) 565-6600.

Hardboard siding (panel, lap):
American Hardboard Association, 1210 W. Northwest Highway, Palatine, IL 60067; (708) 934-8800.

Vinyl siding:
Vinyl Siding Institute, 355 Lexington Ave., New York, NY 10017; (212) 351-5400.

Aluminum siding:
American Architectural Manufacturers Association, 1540 E. Dundee Road, Suite 310, Palatine, IL 60067; (708) 202-1350.

Brick veneer:
Brick Institute of America, 11490 Commerce Park Drive, Reston, VA 22091-1525; (703) 620-0010.

Stucco:
Portland Cement Association, 5420 Old Orchard Road, Skokie, IL 60077-1083; (708) 966-6200.

Fiber-cement siding:
Supradur, Box 908, Rye, NY 10580; (914) 967-8230.

Q **Is aluminum or vinyl siding the best choice?** We live in a cold climate. Are scalloped (fish-scale) shingles available in both aluminum and vinyl?

A Each material has advantages and disadvantages. Aluminum lies straighter on the wall than vinyl and it can bridge low spots that would require shimming if vinyl were used. Its main disadvantage is that it dents, but you may be able to purchase a hail-damage warranty. Vinyl is relatively easy to install, but if it is not done properly (it must be free to expand and contract with changes in temperature) it will have a wavy appearance. Dark colors will fade with both products, perhaps a little quicker with vinyl, but both can be refinished with paint. Don't worry about vinyl siding shrinking or cracking in your cold climate. Vinyl formulations today are more flexible and resistant than those produced in the '60s and '70s. Both products include a wide line of accessories, including fish-scale designs. Finally, although aluminum material will cost more, many contractors offer both at the same price.

Q **Where can I get the tool used for removing a single panel of vinyl siding?**

A Appropriately called the zipper or zip tool, the vinyl-siding unlocking tool allows you to remove a sin-

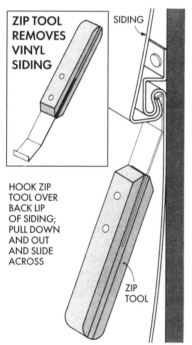

ZIP TOOL REMOVES VINYL SIDING

SIDING

HOOK ZIP TOOL OVER BACK LIP OF SIDING; PULL DOWN AND OUT AND SLIDE ACROSS

ZIP TOOL

A vinyl-siding zipper is used to unlock vinyl siding so you can replace individual courses.

gle panel of siding without removing the one above (see drawing, below left). Few hardware stores or home centers carry this tool, but it may be available from vinyl-siding dealers.

Q **What's the best way to apply siding to a small 100-year-old building?** It was constructed with 2x4 studs spaced 25 in. apart with clay tiles between them. The interior is plastered and in good shape, with few cracks. The exterior siding has many coats of peeling paint. My plan is to put a vapor barrier over the exterior and then screw 2x2 furring strips to the studs. I would insert styrofoam insulation sheets between the 2x2 furring strips and then screw aluminum siding into the 2x2s (rather than nailing, which might cause the interior plaster to crack).

A Placing tiles between 2x4 studs on 25-in. centers is not a typical construction method. Assuming the present siding is wood (because the building in 100 years old), you should not apply a vapor barrier to the exterior. A vapor barrier should be applied to the warm side, not the cold side of the wall. Sandwiching a vapor barrier between the old wall and the new insulation and siding provides a new place for moisture to be trapped and condense (this is called a dew point), which can cause future damage to the wall.

You mentioned using screws to attach the aluminum siding to avoid damage to the interior plaster from hammer vibration. If you apply lap siding, use a power nailer to reduce hammer impact and vibration that could crack the plaster. Remove the old siding first; then apply an exterior finish of wire lath covered with stucco. The cost of applying aluminum, steel, wood or stucco siding should be about the same, but consider the stucco option before making a decision.

Q **How do I remove stains from redwood siding?** My 40-year-old house is dark and discolored. How should I refinish it to prevent it from becoming discolored again?

A According to the California Redwood Association, redwood can turn nearly black from mildew growth and soot accumulation. To remove the stains, first try scrubbing the wood with a stiff-bristle brush and a solution of 1 cup trisodium phosphate (TSP) and 1 cup of bleach per gallon of warm water. Rinse with clear water. (Note: Never mix bleach with detergent containing ammonia.) If the discoloration persists, repeat and then apply a solution of 4 ounces of oxalic acid crystals (available in paint stores) per gallon of warm water, or use a commercial deck-cleaning product. When the wood is thoroughly dry, rinse with clean water. A second application may be necessary. (Wear old clothes, rubber gloves and eye protection when using oxalic acid or any deck-cleaning product.) To maintain the natural redwood color, apply a clear water repellent that contains a mildewcide. Reapplication may be required every 18 to 24 months.

Q **Must I seal redwood siding to protect it from the sun?** I'm building a cabin in the mountains, and I plan to cover it with redwood siding and build a redwood deck. The elevation is about 8,000 ft.

A According to chemists at the Forest Products Laboratory in Madison, Wisconsin, the sun's ultraviolet (UV) rays destroy unprotected wood at the rate of 1/8 to 1/2 in. per 100 years. So you can do nothing and your cabin will last a long time. In fact, in some mountain areas, owners prefer the dark gray or black color that siding or logs acquire after long exposure to the sun.

Preserving the wood, however, may extend its life so that your children and grandchildren can also enjoy the cabin. The Forest Products Laboratory recommends using a semitransparent or opaque oil-base penetrating stain that contains a water repellent — dark gray or brown are the best colors — for both the siding and the deck. Clear water repellents will not prevent UV damage; it's the stain pigment that protects the wood. You will need to reapply the stain every few years to provide continuous protection.

You used the word "seal" in your question. Technically, a sealer is a varnish-type product. A clear varnish does not provide protection from ultraviolet light and should not be used on wood that will be exposed to the elements. In a year or two, the wood underneath will be destroyed and the varnish will begin to peel, just as sunburned skin peels from your body.

STEPS FOR STAIRWAYS

Q How do I cover my L-shaped (winder) concrete stairs with oak? And is it safe? (They would be very unforgiving in a fall.) The treads are 10 in. deep. Risers are angled back 1 in. and vary from 7 in. to 7-1/2 in. except for the last step, which is 4 in. because we raised the basement floor.

A The project you propose would be feasible but costly and time consuming. Because of the riser irregularities, you ideally should use a jackhammer to remove the existing stairs. However, for most people, this is not practical. A better solution would be to carpet the stairs and invest in good graspable handrails — one on each side of the stairway. The handrails should extend all the way to the bottom of the stairway.

You also can install 5/4x12 (1-1/8- x 11-1/4-in. actual size) oak treads and 3/4-in. oak plywood risers glued to the concrete with a polyurethane construction adhesive such as PL Premium, which is made by Contech Brands. These adhesives cure fast — you can walk on the stairs after the adhesives cure overnight — and remain flexible, which is important because wood expands and contracts much more than concrete.

Clean any visible grease or oil from the concrete with mineral spirits. Wear a respirator and ventilate well with a window fan. Apply a 3/8-in.-dia. bead of adhesive at the front, middle and back of a tread and press it firmly against the concrete to seat it; then add weight until the adhesive sets. If the wood is wedged tightly in place, a weight is not necessary.

Work from the top down and find another way out of the basement.

Because the first-floor landing will not be built up, use only a 1/2-in.- thick tread for the top step. This will minimize the difference between the rise of this step and the others. You might even add a layer of 1/4-in. plywood where necessary if doing so would correct the most serious rise irregularities. (The rises ideally should be the same.) The 4-in. step at the bottom is less of a concern because it is at the bottom. You could make it marginally safer by changing that step into a wide platform, providing you have the headroom.

Q How do I build concrete steps? I plan to cover them with bricks, and I need bricklaying advice as well.

A To begin with, concrete steps are extremely heavy, and you don't want to lay the steps on the ground. To prevent sinking, dig to a depth according to the building code in your city. (In general, dig the footing between 18 and 24 in. deep or at least 6 in. deeper than the frost line.) When you lay out your steps (see drawing, above right), adjust the wooden form to allow for the bricks on the risers and treads. Treads for outdoor steps are usually 12 in. Riser height is equal to the height of two regular bricks plus the mortar joint thickness (about 6 in. total).

Select bricks designed to withstand the weather — called pavers by many manufacturers.

Forms for concrete steps need to be strong, tight and rigidly braced to

REMODELING

FORMING CONCRETE STEPS

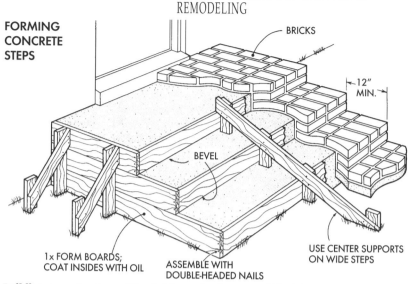

BRICKS

12" MIN.

BEVEL

1x FORM BOARDS; COAT INSIDES WITH OIL

ASSEMBLE WITH DOUBLE-HEADED NAILS

USE CENTER SUPPORTS ON WIDE STEPS

Building concrete steps with a brick overlay is accomplished in two stages: Pour the concrete base first; then lay the bricks in a bed of mortar. The riser forms are beveled so you can trowel into the corner.

prevent concrete leaks and bulging. It's OK to use 1x boards or 3/4-in. plywood, but use straight material free of knots and cracks so it will be easy to strip from the concrete and won't leave blemishes or imperfections in the finished steps. Use double-headed nails to make it easier to disassemble the forms without damaging the fresh concrete. You can coat the inside of the forms with oil to make them easier to remove.

Allow about a 1/4-in. slope on each tread for drainage. Bevel the lower edge of the riser forms to permit finishing the full width of the tread. Securely fasten the riser forms to the sidewall forms. On wide steps, use center supports and remove just before finishing the concrete. (Fill the holes left by the supports with a small hand trowel.)

Carefully consider whether you want to lay the brick yourself, particularly if this is your first experience.

A botched job can detract from your home's appearance and value. Laying the bricks uniformly (soldiering) and keeping them free of excess mortar calls for care, patience and experience. If you haven't laid brick, you'd be well advised to let an experienced bricklayer complete the job for you.

If you do plan to lay the brick, you may begin as soon as the concrete has set. (It's not necessary to let it cure.) Use a weather-resistant mortar mix — 1 part Portland cement, 1/4 part hydrated lime and 3 parts sand with enough water to bring the mix to a workable state.

For more information on concrete work and bricklaying, I suggest you read *The Complete Concrete, Masonry and Brick Handbook*, by J.T. Adams (copyright 1979), Arco Publishing Inc. This book is no longer available from the publisher, so check in your library for a copy.

INSULATION

Q How much insulation does my central-Florida home need? I'm planning to cover the exterior walls, which are concrete-block, with 1-in. foam panels and installing brick veneer. Will that be enough insulation?

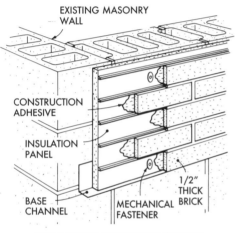

EXISTING MASONRY WALL
CONSTRUCTION ADHESIVE
INSULATION PANEL
BASE CHANNEL
MECHANICAL FASTENER
1/2" THICK BRICK

REAL BRICK PRODUCTS SYSTEM

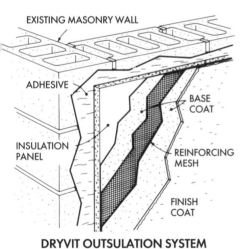

EXISTING MASONRY WALL
ADHESIVE
INSULATION PANEL
BASE COAT
REINFORCING MESH
FINISH COAT

DRYVIT OUTSULATION SYSTEM

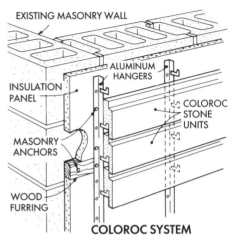

EXISTING MASONRY WALL
ALUMINUM HANGERS
INSULATION PANEL
COLOROC STONE UNITS
MASONRY ANCHORS
WOOD FURRING

COLOROC SYSTEM

A You don't need much insulation; R-5 should be fine. In central Florida, where air conditioners are common, you just need something to isolate the block from direct solar gain. The insulation will do that.

Several commercial insulated siding systems can be used on your home (see the drawings at left and above). Real Brick Products' system is brick veneer attached to foam panels with construction adhesive.

If your heart isn't necessarily set on brick, you might also look into an exterior insulation and finish system (EIFS) such as the Dryvit Outsulation System. An acrylic finish similar to stucco is available in a variety of colors and textures. It is applied over foam insulation board, which is secured to the exterior of the home with a special adhesive. Other EIFS products are made by STO and Thoro System Products.

A final alternative to consider is a veneer system called Coloroc. Overlapping precast stones are suspended on aluminum hangers, which are installed over insulation.

The company claims a wall will withstand 150-mph winds and temperatures up to 176 degrees F. Coloroc comes in a variety of colors and requires no maintenance. By the way, heat pumps are definitely the best choice for your new HVAC system. Look for a minimum seasonal energy rating of 10 or 12.

Q How should I install a radiant barrier in my attic over blown-in insulation? Is it necessary for the radiant barrier to be reflective on both sides to be effective in summer and winter? If the barrier is backed by paper, will the paper prevent it from reflecting from that side? Would it be beneficial to wrap my air conditioning/heating ductwork with this material, as the insulation on the duct is covered with plastic? I plan to install the radiant barrier myself to minimize the cost.

INSTALLING A RADIANT BARRIER

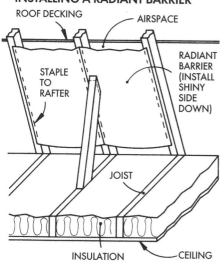

ROOF DECKING

AIRSPACE

STAPLE TO RAFTER

RADIANT BARRIER (INSTALL SHINY SIDE DOWN)

JOIST

INSULATION

CEILING

A A radiant barrier is basically aluminum foil placed in an airspace to block radiant-heat transfer from a heat-radiating surface, such as a hot roof, to a heat-absorbing material, such as conventional attic insulation. Aluminum reflects thermal radiation very well, and it emits very little heat. In other words, aluminum is a good heat reflector and a bad heat radiator. A radiant barrier in a roof is most effective as a summer cooling strategy because the aluminum will not radiate the heat it gains from the roof to the cooler insulation below. Radiant barriers are less effective during the winter because most of the upward heat transfer from the living area into the attic occurs by convection. For this reason, radiant barriers are not a substitute for insulation. To be effective, there must be an airspace on the foil side.

For attic installations, attach the material to the rafters with the foil side facing down (see drawing, left). At first, a single-sided radiant barrier will work equally well with the foil side up or down, but over a period of time, as dust accumulates on the upper surface, the foil absorbs rather than reflects thermal radiation.

Do not lay the foil directly on the insulation. It may act as a vapor barrier and trap moisture migrating from the room below and cause serious damage to the ceiling joists and insulation. By all means, wrap your plastic-covered insulated ducts foil-side out to block radiant heat transfer from the duct. It will also reduce heat transfer into the duct during the cooling season.

Several home center chains now carry radiant-barrier material. (They may call it foil insulation.) Manufacturers can provide names of local distributors.

A number of non-industry organizations, including The Florida Solar Energy Center (of the State University System of Florida), Tennessee Valley Authority (TVA), Oak Ridge National Laboratory, University of Mississippi and Tennessee Technical University, have conducted extensive tests to determine the effectiveness of radiant barriers in reducing the summer air-conditioning (cooling) load in the sunbelt states.

The tests conclude that the best attic location for a radiant-barrier retrofit is stapled to the bottom of the rafters with single-sided foils facing down. The aluminum foil reflects the radiant energy toward the heat source (roof). It will not radiate the heat it gains from the roof to the cooler airspace and insulation it faces. We've not seen any test results to support the claim that rafter-installed radiant barriers increase air-conditioning loads.

Initially there is no difference in the effectiveness of a radiant barrier attached to the rafters and one laid directly on ceiling insulation, but Tennessee Tech found that after four years of dust accumulation, performance of all radiant barriers was reduced an average of 50 percent. Condensation can accumulate under a radiant barrier laid directly on ceiling insulation in homes without a ceiling vapor barrier. The TVA found this was true even for perforated radiant barriers when attic temperatures were below freezing.

The feasibility of moving an installed radiant barrier from the ceiling joists to the rafters depends on the tightness of the attic (dust accumulation) and whether you must pay someone to do it.

Not all electric utility companies agree on placement of radiant barriers, but dust and moisture problems are not well understood. Also, application methods in the moderate- and cooler-temperature regions of the country for winter benefits are different from those in the sunbelt. Rafter-mounted radiant barriers are not particularly effective in reducing winter heat loss. A radiant barrier mounted under the ceiling joists with an unvented airspace between the foil and the drywall works better.

Claims for energy savings by some manufacturers' representatives and contractors are often too high. A radiant barrier can reduce heat gain through R-19 insulated ceilings by 40 percent. The ceiling represents about 20 percent of the total cooling load in sunbelt states. Therefore, the ceiling-installed barrier accounts for 8 percent of the total cooling load (40 percent x 20 percent). Homeowners in the sunbelt can expect to save about 8 to 12 percent on their air-conditioning bills, not the total electric bill. In short, if a salesperson's claims about energy savings sound too good to be true, don't believe the claims.

There are several satisfactory radiant-barrier products: single-sided foil with a kraft paper or polypropylene backing, double-sided foil with a reinforcement material between the foils, foil-faced rigid insulation, and multilayered foil systems that form insulating airspaces when installed. Low-emissivity paint that may be applied to the underside of the roof decking is also available, but it is not nearly as effective as aluminum foil. Neither the paint nor foil radiant barriers increase roof temperatures more than 10 degrees.

Always shop for the best price before you buy radiant barriers.

Q **How do you cover a concrete slab floor and make the floor warmer at the same time?**

A Before carpeting, lay down Homasote Comfort Base (available at home centers or building supply stores). Comfort Base is a 1/2-in.-thick high-density fiberboard panel made from recycled paper. It provides a nice, resilient base for carpet and does an excellent job at stopping heat loss.

About 24 hours before installation, separate the panels and set them inside so they can acclimatize to the humidity level in your home. Also, nail or glue 1/2- x 1-1/2-in. wood nailers along the walls where tackless carpet strips are to be installed (see drawing, below).

Apply beads of decking adhesive to the grid surface (back) of the panels along the perimeter and at 16-in. intervals crosswise. Lay the panels on the floor with a 3/16-in. gap between panels and a 3/8-in. gap at walls. Then apply pressure or weight to assure proper setting. Stay off the floor for a day or two before you have the carpet installed.

Q **Will adding plywood flooring in my attic affect the R-value of the insulation?** My 5-year-old house has an unfinished attic with blown-in insulation. The roof is truss construction. Does the truss construction affect my plans?

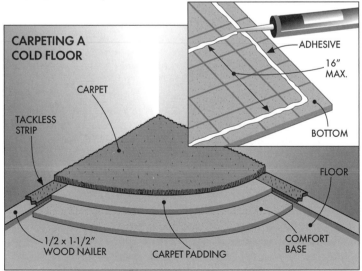

CARPETING A COLD FLOOR

ADHESIVE

16" MAX.

BOTTOM

FLOOR

CARPET

TACKLESS STRIP

1/2 x 1-1/2" WOOD NAILER

CARPET PADDING

COMFORT BASE

To make a cold concrete slab warmer, cover it with Comfort Base. Then install carpet padding and carpet. Use Comfort Base only on dry floors.

A The R-value of loose-fill insulation is reduced whenever it is compressed, as covering your attic floor with plywood would do. But there are more serious considerations concerning attic conversions when the roof is constructed with trusses. First, activity on the lower 2x4 chord of the truss, such as walking or hammering, could pop the nails or screws in the wallboard (drywall) ceiling below.

Loading the trusses with the weight of stored items also could deflect the trusses, causing ceiling cracks or nail/screw pops. You may want to look at other storage options rather than using the attic space you describe.

MOBILE HOMES

Q **Can the information in books and magazines on home remodeling and construction be applied to mobile homes?** Or is mobile-home construction different from standard house construction? Are there articles written specifically for mobile homes?

A The design ideas and most of the how-to information you gather from remodeling books and magazines can be applied to manufactured or HUD-Code houses (mobile homes). Today, most mobile-home builders use standard light-frame construction. Because roof and floor spans typically are shorter, smaller-dimension lumber may be used.

As with standard house construction, however, details will vary, especially in homes built before federal standards were established in 1976. For structural work, such as replacing an existing window or door with a wider one, or for any project that requires roof or exterior wall penetration — insulating or adding a skylight, etc.— you must first determine how your home is constructed, such as stud and joist size and spacing, and alter the how-to information to suit your home.

Whether your home is new or old, you should have a licensed contractor or your municipal building department review your plans before you proceed with any remodeling.

Two books worth looking into are *Your Mobile Home Energy and Repair Guide* by John Krigger (published by Saturn Resource Management, Helena, Mont.) and the *Foremost Mobile Home Fix-It Guide* (published by Foremost Corp. of America, Grand Rapids, Mich.).

Q **How can I better insulate my mobile home?** I want to build a shell around my mobile home with 2x4 walls extending above the existing roofline so that a new truss roof can be constructed. Should the metal siding be removed from the mobile home before installing the new shell? If not, would moisture condense on the metal between the walls?

A You're actually proposing to construct a house around a house, which may be more than you need. First, you'll need to build a foundation to support the new building. Then after you frame, seal, insulate and apply siding and roofing, you'll have to buy

REMODELING

new windows, doors, etc. Your pro-posed shell is likely to cost much more than any long-term energy savings will compensate for.

If you do decide to build this shell, you do not have to remove the exist-ing metal siding. But to avoid short-circuiting your insulation, it is critical to carefully air-seal the new wall to the old wall at the top and bottom and to fill the entire cavity with insu-lation. Any air leaks could quickly undermine your insulation efforts.

There are numerous cost-effective insulation and roofing approaches that, for an investment of about $2,500, will probably net you better savings. Many of them are spelled out in *Your Mobile Home Energy and Repair Guide* by John Krigger, a book devoted entirely to mobile home repair and energy-saving strategies.

Q How should I upgrade the insulation in my mobile home? I've been told I can remove the exte-rior siding panels and then staple faced insulation batts between the studs. Won't this put the insulation's vapor barrier on the outside, which is the cold (wrong) side of the wall? After insulating, would it be advan-tageous to staple tarpaper on the studs before reinstalling the exterior siding panels?

A Although your question focuses on wall insulation, you must con-sider the entire home (see drawing, p. 38).

To be effective, insulation must provide a continuous barrier to heat loss and should enclose the ceiling, walls and floors. Before you attempt to remove the siding, find out how much insulation is in the attic and under the floor. Attic insulation is of primary importance; the floor is sec-ond and the walls come in third. It's equally important to stop air leaks (infiltration) around doors and win-dows.

Assuming your home is already insulated to some degree, first caulk around window and door frames and other openings where cold air can enter. Replace any worn weather stripping. Walk around inside the house and feel for cold air with your hands; then seal those leaks.

Next, upgrade the insulation in the attic with unfaced fiberglass batts. Your mobile home roof is probably constructed with trusses and will be difficult to access. If so, have a professional insulation installer blow in fiberglass insula-tion. Be sure the installer adds card-board or foam baffles between the rafters at the soffits to prevent insu-lation from blocking the soffit vents.

If your mobile home is not sitting on a permanent foundation, install skirting around the bottom to keep out mice and other rodents that like to live in insulation. Then install faced fiberglass batts between the floor joists or trusses with the vapor barrier against the floor. Use metal support straps or staple chicken-wire mesh to the floor joists.

This standard insulating tech-nique for vented crawl spaces requires that you install a 6-mil-polyethylene vapor retarder on the ground or crawl space floor. Overlap the seams at least 4 in. and seal with acoustical sealant or plastic tape,

Insulate the top of your mobile home first; then insulate the floor. Install skirting (if you don't already have a foundation) to stop direct wind blasts. Caulk around windows and doors to stop infiltration before you upgrade the wall insulation.

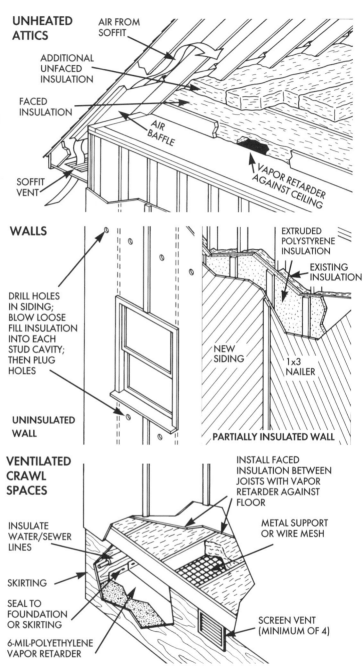

UNHEATED ATTICS

AIR FROM SOFFIT

ADDITIONAL UNFACED INSULATION

FACED INSULATION

AIR BAFFLE

SOFFIT VENT

VAPOR RETARDER AGAINST CEILING

WALLS

EXTRUDED POLYSTYRENE INSULATION

EXISTING INSULATION

DRILL HOLES IN SIDING; BLOW LOOSE FILL INSULATION INTO EACH STUD CAVITY; THEN PLUG HOLES

NEW SIDING

1x3 NAILER

UNINSULATED WALL

PARTIALLY INSULATED WALL

VENTILATED CRAWL SPACES

INSTALL FACED INSULATION BETWEEN JOISTS WITH VAPOR RETARDER AGAINST FLOOR

METAL SUPPORT OR WIRE MESH

INSULATE WATER/SEWER LINES

SKIRTING

SEAL TO FOUNDATION OR SKIRTING

6-MIL-POLYETHYLENE VAPOR RETARDER

SCREEN VENT (MINIMUM OF 4)

such as 3M Contractor's Tape. Extend the vapor retarder up the foundation walls or a skirting about 6 in. and seal. Don't forget to insulate exposed water lines. It's also important to provide adequate ventilation. Use at least four screened vents on opposite walls to encourage air circulation. You should have 1 sq. ft. of vent area for each 1,500 sq. ft. of floor space.

To determine the best way to upgrade wall insulation, first learn if you have any existing insulation in the walls. You may have to drill a small hole in the wall or remove an electrical outlet to find out. If the walls are empty and you decide to remove the siding panels, you can install faced batts with the facing against the interior wall. You won't be able to staple the facing to the studs, but recent studies indicate that a friction fit between the studs may be just as effective. Before you replace the siding, cover the insulation with building paper or similar weather-resistant barrier.

If you find that removing the siding panels is more difficult than you expected, the most practical alternative is to blow insulation into the walls. This is a job many homeowners do themselves, but doing the job right requires skill and should be done by a reliable company and an experienced installer.

If your walls already have some insulation, you cannot efficiently fill the remaining cavities by blowing in

insulation. It's still possible to upgrade by adding an inch or more of foam insulation to the outside walls, but only if you're planning to reapply siding to the house. If you use wood siding, install 1x3 nailers over the insulation at the studs to ventilate the back of the siding. Metal and vinyl siding can be installed against the insulation.

Q **How do I know whether the walls of my mobile home will support the weight of a new roof?** I'm considering adding a new trussed roof with plywood sheathing and asphalt shingles to the 20-year-old structure.

A The roof system you described will add considerable dead-load weight. While it's likely that walls could handle the load, the roof addition may require reinforcement of the wall's top plate and additional support over wide door and window openings.

Without knowing how the walls are designed, you cannot assume anything. There were no federal building standards for manufactured (mobile) homes at the time yours was built, and state standards varied widely. You should contact the manufacturer of the house (if the company is still in business), a licensed contractor or your local building department for guidance.

REPAIRS

No matter how new your home or how well you maintain it, signs of wear and tear are an inevitable part of homeownership. But that doesn't mean you have to live with marred countertops, stained shower tiles, squeaky floors and cracked stucco; you just have to learn how to make the needed repairs. This chapter helps you deal with these and other problems, including refinishing sinks and bathtubs, cleaning grout stains, removing paint spatters from flooring, cleaning old paneling, removing soot and creosote from a chimney, fixing water-hammer problems in plumbing, replacing wood shakes and more.

KITCHEN AND BATH

Q **How can I restore dull laminate?** Almost two years ago we installed new Formica countertops with a glossy finish. The laminate has numerous surface scratches and has become dull.

A Formica is made from melamine resin, one of the hardest plastics made, but it's not nearly as hard as ceramic dishes or abrasive cleansers. Kitchen designers and contractors generally do not recommend glossy laminate for kitchen countertops because it shows scratches more readily than laminate with a matte finish. Dark-colored melamine is particularly vulnerable because deep scratches reveal the lighter base material.

According to Formica technical services, a coat of furniture polish, such as Pledge or Jubilee, can restore some of the luster lost to abrasive cleansers or cleaning pads. A better and more permanent repair is to buff out the scratches with auto polishing compound. This procedure works only on glossy finishes, and it's a messy job that's best done with an electric polishing machine, which may be rented at a tool-rental store.

If the scratches are too deep to buff out, you can apply new laminate directly over the old. You may be able replace the countertop without replacing the backsplash if you're applying an identical pattern. But even if the countertop must be removed, it's usually easily done.

If you're leaving the countertop in place, first remove the sink with the faucet attached and slide out any appliances. Then sand the laminate well with medium-grit paper, being careful not to scratch the backsplash. If you remove the top, take off the backsplash before you begin sanding. Otherwise, scribe the new laminate (mark the edge outline) to match the existing backsplash and sidewalls. Sand the edge of the new laminate to match the scribe line.

After you've installed the new laminate, trim the edges with a router and laminate trimmer. Unless you have a laminate trimmer that can trim right next to a vertical surface, you'll have to trim the edges with a file where the router cannot reach, such as next to the backsplash and in sidewall corners.

You may want to finish the edge of the countertop with wood trim to help prevent the laminate edges from pulling loose.

Q **Can I remove a scorch mark from plastic laminate?**

A A scorch is next to impossible to mask. No matter what you use, the area will show as a predominantly different color or texture.

If you are handy, plastic laminate can be replaced. To remove the old, start on one edge and carefully pry the corner with a metal putty knife. It's likely the laminate was glued with contact cement. Squirt small amounts of lacquer thinner in front of the knife with a glass eye dropper. Try to remove the entire piece at once. If it breaks, you'll waste time and become frustrated removing the laminate in pieces.

Continue until the entire top has

REPAIRS

been removed. You may need to remove a fixture such as the sink before you can remove all the laminate. Be certain to ventilate the area well while working with lacquer thinner, and if you have a gas range, turn off the pilot light. When you replace the laminate, you can rent the proper laminate trimmers from a tool-rental shop.

To cover the scorch, you can install a decorative ceramic tile trivet or a cutting board over it. To do so, cut a hole in the countertop 7/8 in. smaller than the cutting board (7/16 in. on each side); then cut a 3/8-in.-deep x 3/8-in.-wide rabbet with a router and a rabbeting bit.

Q **Is there any way to patch a screw hole in a laminate countertop?**

A You should be able to order a color-matched putty from the manufacturer for any solid color laminate. To get the right color you'll either have to find the color code on your order tag, bring a sample to a dealer or bring color chips home to compare with your counter. Keep in mind that nobody can make a truly invisible repair in laminate.

You can make a waterproof patch with siliconized acrylic caulk colored with artist's acrylic paints. It will take a little experimentation to get just the right color, but the repair should be just as durable as putty.

Q **How do I refinish a sink?** The porcelain finish on my cast-iron

kitchen sink and bathroom lavatory, which were installed when the house was built in 1930, has become pitted. I'd like to use a refinishing kit and do the work myself.

A The good news in enamel and porcelain repair is that there are products and services available today that didn't exist a generation ago. The bad news is that a patch is still a patch. No repair surface is likely to be as durable as a fixture's original baked-on finish.

One kit is sold under the trade name Match-Patch. It includes an epoxy resin and hardener that you blend with a variation of five basic colors. Matching colors requires patience and a lot of tinkering, even when the color is white.

Once you've got the color, the job is easy. All you do is clean the chipped surface, apply the mixture and smooth it with alcohol. The patch blends well and appears to last.

For a more professional treatment, you might hire one of a number of glazing companies. These companies can repair a small chip or resurface an entire bathtub.

Bath Masters uses a polyester resin with a hardener and is able to match colors very well. After extensive surface preparation, the resin is sprayed onto the fixture.

Bath Masters licenses its products and services under a variety of local trade names. Match Patch is sold at retail stores.

Q **How do I fix peeling epoxy paint?** I own a motel and recently painted 12 bathtubs with epoxy paint. The paint is made by a nationally known manufacturer and is recommended for refinishing tubs and sinks. But the adhesion was very poor, and large areas of finish peeled.

A There is a high failure rate for do-it-yourself porcelain refinishing, due in large part to insufficient preparation and improper application. Professional tub refinishers often use a strong acid bath to clean and etch the old finish. (Because of the danger to your lungs, eyes, and skin associated with acid use, you're advised to let a professional refinisher apply acid baths.) They then spray the two-part epoxy or polyurethane paint products following application instructions exactly — mixing, temperature and humidity are critical.

If you decide to try again, first remove the old paint with a paint stripper such as Zip Strip or Bix. After you've removed the residue, wash the tub inside and out with a strong solution of trisodium phosphate. Wet-sand the porcelain with 80-grit sandpaper to break the glaze. When the finish is completely dull, with no missed spots, thoroughly clean the tub with mineral spirits to remove all traces of oil. (Even the oil from your fingers can cause problems.)

After you've masked and covered the areas you don't want painted, apply the new finish.

If you have spraying equipment, you can purchase professional porcelain refinishing epoxy and polyurethane paint in mix-to-match colors.

To find a professional porcelain refinisher, look in your classified telephone directory under "Bathtubs & Sinks — Repairing and Refinishing." Look for firms that warrant their work and ask for references. If you cannot find a firm in your own city, check in directories from larger cities nearby. Many of these types of firms work statewide.

CLEANING UP

Q **How can I remove stains from shower-wall tiles?** The unglazed tiles have a clear finish that has come off with cleaning and has become stained.

A Poultices often draw out stains in marble, unglazed porcelain and clay tiles. Try applying a paste of household chlorine bleach and baking soda for organic stains (food juice, etc.), and an ammonia or mineral spirits and baking soda paste for oil or grease stains. If possible, test your work first in an inconspicuous spot. Apply a layer of the paste about 1/2 in. thick over the stained area and cover with plastic wrap to retard evaporation; then allow it to sit for a couple of days. (On a shower wall, do small areas and tape the plastic to the wall.) Remove the poultice and wash with clear water. Repeat the procedure if necessary.

If the stains are caused by mineral deposits, use a powdered cleaner that contains oxalic acid, such as Zud or Barkeeper's Friend.

When the wet tile has a uniform color, wash the entire area with an oil-base cleaner such as Murphy's Oil Soap, Janitor-In-A-Drum or

Lestoil. Apply a strong solution to the poultice-treated areas first; then apply a regular-strength solution over the entire area. Repeated washings with oil-base cleaners will tend to build a protective sheen on the surface. Scrubbing the cleaner may also help remove the original finish.

Finally, avoid the use of alkaline-based soaps (most detergents). Don't use muriatic acid as it will crystallize acrylic finishes and cause white spotting.

Q **How can I remove stains from grout?** I have a relatively new quarry-tile kitchen floor. Although the tile was sealed after installation, there are some stains in the grout joints. I have been unable to remove the stains with grout cleaner or even by grinding away the grout surface. I would like to replace only the stained areas with new grout that I have. What is the proper technique to use? Can you suggest a more effective cleaning method?

A First, check the label on the grout cleaner you used. Most grout cleaners contain citric acid and other ingredients and are mild cleaners. You should be able to buy stronger cleaners at any tile store. Try a grout cleaner that contains phosphoric acid and detergents.

If the phosphoric acid cleaners don't remove the stains, you must remove and replace the stained grout. Grout can be removed with a carbide grout saw, a tool that resembles a utility knife. Grout is difficult to remove, so you might consider hiring a professional tile installer

rather than doing the job yourself.

After the grout has been cleaned or replaced, apply a sealer. Many tile sealers are silicone and last only a few months. Penetrating acrylic-latex sealer lasts much longer. You should be able to find it at stores that sell ceramic tile and flooring.

Q **How do I remove paint spatters from a ceramic-tile floor?** The spatters have apparently been there for a long time. It looks like whoever tried to remove it merely smeared the paint. How do I maintain the tile after it's clean?

A Apply paint remover to the paint spatters and smeared areas with a small brush. Give the remover time to loosen the paint by covering the area with plastic wrap or aluminum foil to slow evaporation. Carefully remove the softened paint with a putty knife. Wipe away the residue with a clean cloth soaked in paint remover. (Be sure to wear rubber gloves.) Be careful not to let the remover or softened paint get into the grout.

If the tile is unglazed ceramic, it's important not to remove the paint with a wiping action — you'll only spread the softened paint over a wider area to be absorbed by the unglazed tile. Use an up-and-down daubing action instead.

To maintain glazed ceramic tile, simply clean it with detergent and water. Coat the grout with a sealer — your local ceramic tile supplier can recommend a product. Unglazed ceramic tiles are usually cleaned with soap and water. You can coat them with a sealer, but it will impart a slight sheen to the tile.

Q How do I remove old paint spatters from a vinyl-tile floor?

A For vinyl or composition tile, try using a product called Goof Off! It can be used on everything from vinyl tile to countertops to shoes without damage. If Goof Off! isn't available in your area, try another brand of paint remover on a small, hidden spot to see how it reacts with the tile. If it softens it, don't use it. If it doesn't affect the tile, apply the remover as described in the preceding question.

Q What's the best way to clean old, dirty, unfinished knotty-pine paneling?

A Try a fast-evaporating solvent such as denatured alcohol. You need a solvent with a high evaporation rate to draw dirt out of wood. First, brush and vacuum the paneling to remove loose surface dirt. Then open all the windows, don rubber gloves and an approved respirator (not a dust mask) and clean the wood with the minimum amount of solvent that will do the job — there's no need to soak the wood. Pine darkens with age, and cleaning alone will not lighten it significantly. Lightening wood is a bleaching process, which is much more involved.

You also should apply a protective coating when you're finished cleaning. Assuming that you like the natural look, use a Danish oil finish

such as Watco or, for more protection, a low-gloss polyurethane such as Formby's Poly Hand-Rubbed Finished. To avoid the risk of spontaneous combustion, hang oil-soaked rags out to dry before throwing them away.

Q How can I remove soot from my fireplace? The floor-to-ceiling fireplace was built in 1963 of unglazed white brick. We've been unable to find a product locally that will remove the soot.

A Minor soot stains can be removed with a household cleaner, such as 409 or Fantastic, and plenty of elbow grease. For heavier soot, the Brick Institute of America recommends a cleanser that contains bleach, such as Comet. Clean 'N Brite (manufactured by August West) is a stronger cleanser that etches the surface. It's available at some hardware stores and fireplace specialty shops and from chimney sweeps. The active ingredient — sodium hydroxide — is caustic, so wear rubber gloves and eye protection when you use it.

Some brick masons recommend using muriatic acid, but it can be dangerous to use it indoors. For one thing, the surface must be thoroughly washed down, which is a problem in a home. And there have been cases when acid used on a humid day has vaporized and tarnished all the shiny metal in the house.

High-strength cleaners and acids are dangerous in the wrong hands, so if the problem requires their use, call a professional cleaning service such as Servicemaster, which specializes in fire-damage restoration. It is a national company and should be listed in the classified telephone directory under "Fire and Water Damage Restoration."

Q **How can I remove creosote from my chimney?** The chimney flue lining above the roofline of my house is coated with a glasslike layer of creosote up to 1/2 in. thick. I've tried to remove it with little success. I've even used a cold chisel. Is there a chemical that can be painted on to soften it?

A The creosote you described has been literally baked on the flue walls. Because it's only at the top of the chimney, it's less likely to ignite, but if it ever does, it will burn at an extremely high temperature and probably damage the flue.

To correct light creosote buildup, manganese-based catalysts such as Anti-Creo-Soot (ACS), made by Combustion Improvers Co. Inc., can be sprayed on wood before it is burned. Over a long period of time, the catalyst will convert the glaze to a flaky material that can be brushed off. However, the buildup you described is so extensive it would take a catalyst forever to soften it.

For heavy glaze buildup, professional chimney sweeps use motorized creosote removers, which scour the surface with rotary tools (steel cable strands, chains or metal balls), sometimes in combination with sodium hydroxide (lye), which is sprayed directly on the creosote.

Sodium hydroxide is a caustic chemical and should be used only by professional sweeps. People with respiratory problems may be adversely affected by sodium hydroxide. The creosote and soot particles that are released into the air may cause cancer, so head-to-toe skin protection, an organic-vapor respirator and goggles (or a full-face respirator mask) are required safety equipment.

You should hire a reputable chimney sweep, preferably a member of the National Chimney Sweep Guild, to clean the chimney. Then you may want to use an ACS product to help maintain a cleaner flue. You can buy ACS from chimney sweeps and wood stove retailers.

SQUEAKY FLOORS

Q **Can I inject glue between layers of flooring to stop squeaks?** I have an 80-year-old house with 1x6 tongue-and-groove pine flooring. A previous owner installed 3/8-in.-thick prefinished oak flooring over the old pine floors. The oak flooring strips are not tight against the old pine flooring, and the floor squeaks. Are there special nails that I can drive through the face of the oak flooring to stop the squeaks?

A It sounds as if someone did a poor job installing the oak flooring. Your problem points out the perils of not following the manufacturer's installation instructions to the letter, even if you do not understand the full reasons for doing so. Shortcuts or economies, such as using cheap flooring adhesives or applying adhesive with a regular trowel rather than one with a notched edge, can ruin expensive materials and make the project a detriment rather than an improvement to your home.

Be sure that it is the top 3/8-in. layer of oak flooring that is causing the squeaks. Squeaking floors can be due to flexing floor joists, loose bridging or the original 1x6 pine flooring rubbing together.

If you are sure the squeaks are coming from the oak flooring, the best remedy is to remove the oak flooring (not an easy job) and lay it properly. You cannot successfully inject adhesives between the boards, as you propose: The damage to the oak flooring from boring the holes would be objectionable, and it would be difficult to know the exact points where you should inject the adhesive.

If only a few boards are loose, you might use a power nailer to drive finishing nails through the face of the oak. The power nailer will countersink the headless nails, and you can fill the small holes with matching wood putty. If you try this approach, drive the nails into grain highlights in the oak strips, where they will be less noticeable.

Q **Must I tear up my floor to stop its squeaking?** The floors are constructed of 2x10 joists with a 1-in.-thick shiplap subfloor. The kitchen and baths have 5/8-in.-thick plywood underlayment covered with linoleum. The rest of the floors have 3/8-in.-thick particleboard underlayment with wall-to-wall carpeting. All the floors squeak severely. I have tried shimming between the exposed joists and shiplap to no avail.

A Because of the shiplap subfloor, you have unlimited places for wood movement (squeaks) to occur. The subfloors of new homes are typically 4x8 plywood or particleboard panels nailed and glued to the joists. Any movement that occurs is between the panels and the joists and is fairly easy to control.

In your house, you can have movement between the shiplap and the joists, between the shiplap and the underlayment and between the rabbeted edges of the shiplap. There probably is no way to stop all the squeaks.

When you replace your carpet or linoleum, use a power nailer to nail the underlayment and subfloor to the joists. Space the nails about 4 in. apart so you drive at least one nail into each shiplap board. This should help, but there is no guarantee that you'll eliminate all the squeaks without removing the shiplap and installing a new subfloor.

PLUMBING

Q **How do I stop corrosion in copper hot-water lines?** The lines in our 15-year-old home are plagued with tiny green formations, and all of the faucet screens must be constantly removed and cleaned. Our local plumber attributes the problem to electrolysis, saying that we must have an electrical line touching or grounded to the pipe. We have a gas water heater.

A The Copper Development Association says it's unlikely that those green deposits are the result of an errant electrical line, but your water heater may be setting up a condition for the real culprit.

The green material is probably a copper compound (salt) resulting from a soft acid water high in carbon dioxide that is reacting with the inner surface of the copper tube. High water temperature and excessive velocity through pipes can aggravate the problem. Try lowering the water heater temperature to below 140 F unless you have an older dishwasher that does not boost water temperature to the required level.

Next, have a plumber check your water distribution system design. If a small tube diameter creates high velocity, a reconfiguration is in order. If the condition persists, the pH of the water must be raised to make it less acidic. Assuming you don't have a private well, this is usually done either by removing the excess carbon dioxide through aeration or blending in a harder water at your local water-treatment facility. An analysis of your tap water is in order, especially the carbon dioxide and oxygen gas content.

Q Can I solve a water-hammer problem without opening the wall? When my house was built in 1958, the plumbing was installed without air-reservoir pipe extensions above the faucets.

HOW A SHOCK ABSORBER STOPS WATER HAMMER

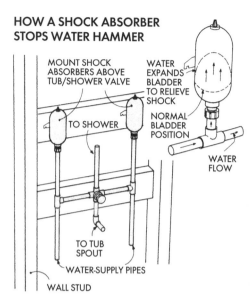

MOUNT SHOCK ABSORBERS ABOVE TUB/SHOWER VALVE

TO SHOWER

TO TUB SPOUT

WATER-SUPPLY PIPES

WALL STUD

WATER EXPANDS BLADDER TO RELIEVE SHOCK

NORMAL BLADDER POSITION

WATER FLOW

In some instances you can avoid opening the walls to prevent water hammer, but not if the problem occurs in the bathtub plumbing.

A Water hammer is caused by a sudden halt of water flow when a valve is shut. The problem is most severe at the end of long runs of pipe. Air trapped in chambers (pipe extensions) above the valves cushions the water flow, but the chambers eventually fill with water and become ineffective. A better method is to fit special shock-absorbing devices in the hot- and cold-water lines (see drawing, above). These air-filled cylinders contain bladders that expand momentarily to relieve the shock, but they never allow water to replace air.

One product, Water Hammer Muffler, is made by Genova. Another, the Mini-Trol Shock Absorber, is made by Amtrol. These devices work best when they are installed within a few feet of the valve, but according to Genova, the Water Hammer Muffler is often effective many feet away and works to a lesser degree when installed on the main incoming water line. Amtrol suggests the larger Diatrol if you must install more than a few feet from the problem valves. If you can access your water lines from a basement or crawl space, install the shock absorbers in the pipes near the faucets to see whether they'll stop the noise. If you find that they help, you may be able to totally eliminate water hammer by installing additional shock-absorbers at other faucet locations and avoid opening the walls.

Q **What kind of pipe should I use to replace my old lead water-service line?** The line runs from the street water main to the house. Should the new pipe be insulated? What are the possibilities of the water line or soil moving and causing a leak in the pipe?

A Copper and plastic are both good choices for water-service lines because, unlike galvanized steel pipe, joint-free lines up to 100 ft. long (the length of a coil of pipe) are possible.

Be sure to check with your local building codes administrator for the required type and size of pipe. Codes often require 1-in. pipe because of the increased water demand of lawn sprinklers and swimming pools, but 3/4-in. pipe is still allowed in some places.

Your best bet is polybutylene (PB) plastic pipe. It is flexible, easy to work with, non-corrosive (it will not rust or collect mineral deposits) and much cheaper than copper pipe. You can get how-to information on using PB pipe in the plumbing departments of local home centers and hardware stores. Connecting to existing house plumbing is simple because solvent welding and soldering are not required. Slip-on screw-type connectors are available to join PB to copper, galvanized and plastic (PVC) pipe.

If you decide to use copper pipe, be sure to use lead-free solder when making pipe connections. Lead solder is restricted from use for drinking water connections, but it's still available for other uses.

You need not insulate water service pipe, but you must bury it below the local frost line to keep the pipe from freezing. Lay the flexible PB pipe in the trench in a slightly wavy pattern so it will have room to contract when it gets cold.

Whichever pipe you use, cover it lightly with pulverized soil before using a tractor to backfill the trench. If you just push the soil in the trench with a tractor blade or back-hoe bucket, you may dent or damage the pipe with a rock or a hard chunk of dirt.

OUTDOOR REPAIRS

Q **What's the proper method for replacing wood shakes?** I've heard about a tool that slips under the damaged shake to pull out nails and

REPAIRS

REPLACE A BROKEN SHAKE

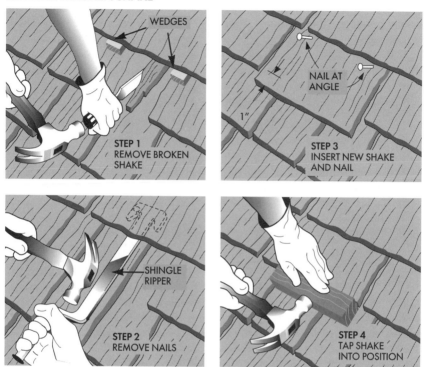

WEDGES

STEP 1
REMOVE BROKEN
SHAKE

NAIL AT
ANGLE

1"

STEP 3
INSERT NEW SHAKE
AND NAIL

SHINGLE
RIPPER

STEP 2
REMOVE NAILS

STEP 4
TAP SHAKE
INTO POSITION

Whether you're replacing a broken wood shake or shingle, the steps are the same. Use extreme caution when working on a roof. Work only on a dry roof, wear rubber-soled sneakers and use a safety rope.

free it. Where can I get one? And how do you nail the replacement shingle without exposing the nails?

A The tool you're referring to is called a shingle ripper. It is available at building-supply and tool outlets.

Installing the replacement shingle is a four-step process. First, remove the old shake using a chisel and hammer to split it into pieces you can pull out (see step 1 in drawing, above). Then use a shingle ripper or a hacksaw (wrap one end with tape)

to cut the nails (step 2). Next, slip the new shake into position until it's about 1 in. from being in line with the others in its course. Drive and set two nails into the replacement shake at an angle and just below the course above (step 3). Finally, using a hammer and wood scrap, tap the shake the rest of the way in to conceal the nail heads (step 4).

Q How can I repair cracks in stucco? We recently bought a house with a painted stucco exterior. The stucco is cracked in places and the paint is peeling. What type of paint should I use?

A To prepare stucco for repair, first remove the peeling paint and dirt. Rent a power (high-pressure) washer — the usual sanding or stripping methods won't remove the dirt stuck in the rough stucco. Nor will a hose and nozzle do the job.

If the old paint finish is chalked, apply a cleaner such as trisodium phosphate (TSP), or one of the deck-cleaning products on the market — they're excellent paint cleaners. As you apply the cleaner, scrub the stucco with a stiff brush. Remove any remaining loose paint with a wire brush or a rotary wire wheel chucked into a drill. Then wash with a power washer.

Wear goggles or a face shield when power washing or scrubbing and using cleaners, and cover your arms and wear rubber gloves as well. Also cover your plants with plastic sheet to protect them from the harsh chemicals.

When the stucco is clean, fill the cracks with a concrete patcher. A two-part patcher (Portland cement mixed with a latex hardener additive) works best. Press the mix into the cracks with a pointing trowel. For very small cracks, use Spak-Fast, a fast-drying 3M product with a low shrink factor.

After you have patched the cracks, spot-prime the repaired areas with acrylic latex primer; then coat the entire house with a high-quality acrylic latex exterior paint. Wet the stucco surface before you apply the paint to prevent the cement from wicking water from the paint.

If it's necessary to repair large areas with new stucco, let the stucco cure for 30 days before you paint.

Q **How can I seal my deck and stop it from leaking?** The second-story deck, which is above a screened patio, is surfaced with tongue-and-groove boards. The boards have shrunk and warped, and rainwater drips through the cracks onto the porch below.

A As you've learned, tongue-and-groove flooring is a poor choice for an exposed deck floor that is also a roof. Water enters the cracks between the boards and becomes trapped in the grooves, ruining the deck and allowing leaks — a problem associated with all flat roofs.

In new construction, it's better to build a separate roof a few inches below the deck if there's enough space. The roof should be sloped to allow water to run off. But because your deck and screened porch are already built, that's probably not a viable alternative.

Your next-best option is to coat the deck with an elastomeric sealer similar to those used for built-up roofs on commercial buildings. Most of these products — elastomeric sheet (EPDM) or modified bitumen roofing — must be applied by professional roofing contractors using special adhesives or heat.

The Kote-A-Deck roof-deck system (see drawing, right) is a good one. It forms a built-up seal similar to the commercial systems, can be applied by do-it-yourselfers (the liquid components are water-borne and safe to use) and forms a waterproof, wear-resistant surface. The Kote-A-Deck materials can be special-ordered through home centers and hardware stores.

Q **How do you remove stains from patio blocks?** I recently installed red patio blocks in the backyard and noticed white stains on them. I was told the stains were limestone, and vinegar or baking soda would remove them. Neither worked.

A Your blocks are probably a cement product. The staining is efflorescence, a generally harmless crystalline deposit of soluble salts that occurs when moisture interacts with the salts and brings them to the surface. The salts remain on the surface when the moisture evaporates.

Efflorescence can usually be removed with a solution of water mixed with 5 to 10 percent muriatic acid. Wet the blocks with water before you begin and experiment on a small area first. Scrub the stains with a soft-bristle brush; then follow with an application of tile or concrete sealer. Be sure to wear a long-sleeved shirt, eye goggles and rubber gloves when working with muriatic acid.

Reduce the mix to 2 percent acid for colored blocks to prevent discoloration.

If your blocks are installed on a sand or soil base and can be lifted, place a vapor barrier (a sheet of plas-

FIXING DECK LEAKS

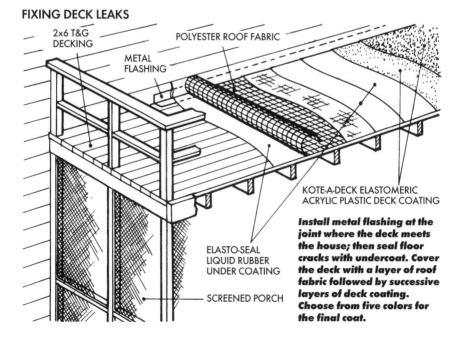

2x6 T&G DECKING

POLYESTER ROOF FABRIC

METAL FLASHING

KOTE-A-DECK ELASTOMERIC ACRYLIC PLASTIC DECK COATING

ELASTO-SEAL LIQUID RUBBER UNDER COATING

SCREENED PORCH

Install metal flashing at the joint where the deck meets the house; then seal floor cracks with undercoat. Cover the deck with a layer of roof fabric followed by successive layers of deck coating. Choose from five colors for the final coat.

tic) beneath the blocks to prevent moisture migration.

Q What can I do to stop my steel tool shed from rusting?

A First, remove loose rust and paint with a wire brush, but do not sand away all the rust. Then apply two coats of a rust converter such as Neutra Rust, made by Plasti-Kote Co. Inc. Rust converters are found in auto parts stores, auto paint stores, home centers and hardware stores. As the rust converter works, the rust will turn black. Wait 24 hours and then apply a corrosion-resistant (anti-rust) primer followed by a top-quality acrylic-latex exterior enamel.

Q How do I rebuild barn roof trusses?

A Truss design is best left to professionals. Contact a local lumberyard that offers truss fabrication and have it done. Detailed information on the span, the existing truss design and local building codes (particularly snow-load requirements) is necessary before a structural engineer can make specific recommendations.

If you insist on building the trusses yourself, you'd probably be safe to duplicate the existing trusses. The factors that affect design strength are lumber species and dimensions, truss design and type and fastening details.

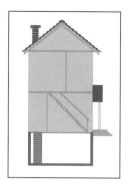

BASEMENTS

A basement shouldn't be a dank, dark pit that you dread descending into. If it's properly built and maintained, a basement can provide easily accessible storage or even add finished living space to your home. This chapter tells how to keep your basement dry and get rid of musty odors and offers advice on preparations for finishing a basement, including sandblasting, waterproofing and sealing concrete walls, fixing cracks, installing a vapor barrier and laying new flooring over concrete.

CURING WET BASEMENT WOES

Q How can I get rid of the musty odor in my basement? When I purchased my home it was not uncommon to find water in the basement after it rained. I have reduced the scope of the problem by correcting the grade (slope) around the basement. But because of a high water table, water seeps in during a heavy rain. Are there any deodorizing products available that can mask the odor problem?

A Home inspectors, builders and architects agree that most wet basement problems are due to the entry of surface water. With a little detective work, the homeowner can usually find the water source and correct it at little cost (see drawing, right).

In most cases, a high water table is not the problem. Although you have already taken steps to divert groundwater away from the basement, it would be worth your time to look around some more.

Common water sources include dirty or leaking gutters and downspouts and short ground pipes that dump rainwater next to the foundation. Make sure you clean or repair gutters and install longer ground pipes or add splash blocks.

Adjacent patios, drives or walks that slope toward the basement let rainwater run to the house and seep in next to the foundation. The joints between slabs and foundation walls should be sealed. Even a properly sloped drive or concrete entry can have a cavity underneath that allows water accumulation next to the foun-

KEEPING YOUR BASEMENT DRY

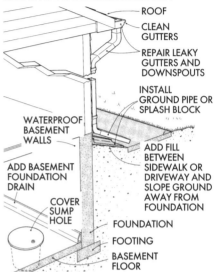

Labels: ROOF; CLEAN GUTTERS; REPAIR LEAKY GUTTERS AND DOWNSPOUTS; INSTALL GROUND PIPE OR SPLASH BLOCK; WATERPROOF BASEMENT WALLS; ADD BASEMENT FOUNDATION DRAIN; COVER SUMP HOLE; ADD FILL BETWEEN SIDEWALK OR DRIVEWAY AND SLOPE GROUND AWAY FROM FOUNDATION; FOUNDATION; FOOTING; BASEMENT FLOOR

Most wet basements are caused by runoff water entering through wall cracks and pin holes. Taking the actions shown in the drawing will keep most basements dry.

dation. Sometimes you can have a contractor fill these cavities or even lift the slab to slope away from the foundation by pumping concrete into them (mud jacking). Check under "Concrete Pumping Service" in the classified telephone directory.

Finally, have a landscape service survey the slope or grade around your house. Sometimes a few shovels of dirt can stop a bad water problem by damming a path into the basement.

Once you've done all you can to keep water away from the foundation, call your local building department to determine the average water-table depth in your area. (The water table is simply the depth at which the soil is continuously saturated by water.) If your basement is below the water table, hydrostatic water pressure may be forcing water into the basement through cracks, pinholes and utility entrance lines in the walls. If the seepage is minor, fill cracks with hydraulic cement and seal the walls with waterproofing paint.

Water can also be forced through the joint where the basement wall and floor meet. One solution, albeit a labor-intensive one, is to break up the floor around the basement perimeter, install drain tile and a sump pump, and pump the water out as it runs in. But it's easier to install hollow plastic baseboard that you seal to the wall and floor. Water drains into the plastic baseboard through holes in the back and is channeled to a sump pump where it is pumped out.

Your odor problem is due to mold and mildew, which grow where there is warmth and moisture. You must remove the moisture to stop the odor. In addition to stopping water seepage into the basement, you should install exhaust vents, open basement windows, circulate the air throughout the house or operate a dehumidifier to lower the basement humidity. No deodorizer can mask a problem of this size.

Q What can I use to seal a concrete basement wall? About 25 years ago I had a wet spot on the wall underneath the front porch steps. I covered the wall with a two-part epoxy paint named Zapp (or something similar). The wall didn't leak again until recently when we had a very heavy rain. I can't find the product I used or one similar to it.

A Some early epoxy products were difficult to work with and were discontinued, even those that performed well when properly mixed. Look into some of the newer basement waterproofing products that are available. For holes in concrete, try a hydraulic-cement patching product such as UGL Drylok Fast Plug. Then paint the wall with Drylok Masonry Waterproofer Paint. Other products include Thoro System Products Thoroseal masonry patch and seal products and Thomas Waterproof Coatings Damtite patch, paint, waterproofing and repair products. These should be available at your local home center.

You should also learn the cause of the leak. If the porch or steps are concrete, you'll probably find the soil under the concrete has settled and formed a cavity where rainwater accumulates and finds its way into your basement. If that's the case, have a concrete contractor pump (mud jack) concrete into the cavity to fill it and keep out water.

PREPARING TO FINISH A BASEMENT

Q Should I seal the walls and floor of my basement before I finish it? I'm adding studs, insulation, drywall and inlaid carpeting. The walls and floor are poured concrete, and a section of one wall has been painted by a previous owner. I have no signs of water coming in, but there is moisture.

A All traces of paint must be removed from the wall, and the only certain way to remove it is by sandblasting. Sandblasting equipment can be rented at most tool-rental shops. It's a messy job at best, and it requires complete protection of all nearby areas. A resilient material such as loosely hung plastic works best. The room must be sealed off, and you must wear goggles, gloves and a respirator. Portable sandblasters can be rented. Your dealer can fill you in on the details.

Once the walls are cleaned of all paint, apply a coat of masonry waterproofer. Although waterproofing ideally should be applied to the outside of exterior walls, a good-quality masonry waterproofer will withstand water pressure up to 4 pounds per square inch if it's applied to the inside surfaces of the walls. Once the waterproofer has been applied, don't nail or apply anything to the treated surface or you will break the waterproofing seal. Do not apply waterproofer to the floor.

As with any basement or below-grade room, make certain that the exterior grade slopes away from the wall and that all downspouts are connected by positive drainage away from the house.

Q If I clean my walls by sand-blasting, will I still need to use muratic acid or etching compound on the areas that are now efflorescent?

A Normally not. A visual inspection will dictate the action needed.

Q Do I also need to chisel out hairline cracks and pack them with hydraulic cement, or can I simply paint over them with a waterproofing paint?

A You're asking an awful lot to suggest the paint will hold with pressure from behind the crack. Definitely chisel out and pack the hairline cracks.

Q Would putting a 2- to 3-ft.-wide concrete sidewalk outside of our basement wall help prevent basement leakage?

A Yes, the sidewalk would help, providing you pour it against an asphaltic expansion joint and pitch it away from the house 1/4 in. per ft.

Q Will flashing installed behind the bottom of the siding running down to the sidewalk

ADDING A SIDEWALK

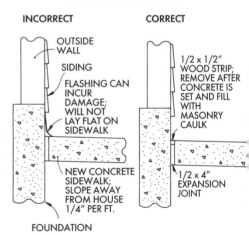

INCORRECT

OUTSIDE WALL

SIDING

FLASHING CAN INCUR DAMAGE; WILL NOT LAY FLAT ON SIDEWALK

NEW CONCRETE SIDEWALK; SLOPE AWAY FROM HOUSE 1/4" PER FT.

FOUNDATION

CORRECT

1/2 x 1/2" WOOD STRIP; REMOVE AFTER CONCRETE IS SET AND FILL WITH MASONRY CAULK

1/2 x 4" EXPANSION JOINT

cause any foreseeable problems?

A It could. It would be nearly impossible to keep the flashing tight against the sidewalk surface. Dirt and water blown behind the flashing would cause even more problems. Keep the expansion joint 1/2 in. below the sidewalk and create a soft-joint fillet using a good-quality masonry caulking compound (see drawing, below left).

Q What kind of treatment should I give a basement closet? I'm building one with drywall walls. The poured concrete walls throughout my basement are bone dry. Should I use a wall of 2x4s or 1x3s fastened to the foundation? Should I install a vapor barrier in all walls? Is there any advantage to lining the closet with cedar to avoid infestation of moths and pests?

A If space is not at a premium, go for the 2x4 stud walls. Use pressure-treated wood for the plates and any wood that comes in contact with concrete. Even though your walls are dry, keep the new closet free of the existing walls. You should place a vapor barrier on the inside face of the studs, under the drywall.

There is no advantage to lining the closet with cedar. Although the heartwood of red cedar has a volatile oil, alcohol cedar or cedroc camphor, these substances will kill only young larvae of the clothes moth; they are not repellents. Also, even if the closet is kept tightly closed, after 36 months the oils are practically useless in killing insects.

Q What steps do I need to take to lay oak flooring over a concrete floor? How do you fill and level a concrete floor? How do you install badly warped flooring boards? Will the mastic prevent future buckling of the floors in a high-humidity area?

A Hard wood flooring can be installed on grade-level concrete slabs poured over a polyethylene ground cover. Most flooring manufacturers advise against attaching wood flooring directly to below-grade concrete. You can lay pressure-treated wood sleepers in mastic over the floor and cover with 4-mil polyethylene plastic sheeting before laying the flooring.

Use a concrete patching compound to level your floor. Follow the mixing directions on the package and smear the paste over the concrete with a trowel. Level the paste with a straightedge. When the patch has set up, lay the wood flooring over the leveled concrete.

Prefinished tongue-and-groove flooring strips can be laid just as they come from the carton, and if you follow the manufacturer's instructions, they shouldn't warp after they are laid. If the strips are too warped to lay, return them to the dealer. Don't attempt to reuse old, warped flooring — it's unlikely you'll successfully glue it to the concrete.

Mastic will not prevent wood flooring from buckling where the humidity cannot be controlled, which is why manufacturers warn you against using wood-flooring products below grade.

Q **How should I insulate my basement floor and install a vapor barrier?** The basement slab was poured over a gravel bed without a vapor retarder. During the summer a dehumidifier pulls about 30 pints of water a day from the basement air. (A radon fan pulls a small amount of water from the gravel, which suggests that there is moisture below the slab.) I plan to glue the 3-1/2-in. face of pressure-treated (CCA) 2x4 sleepers to the concrete with rigid-foam insulation between them and cover it with a 4-mil-polyethylene vapor barrier. I'll install exterior-grade plywood with adhesive and screws and then finish with under-layment and vinyl tile.

A You'll get a better vapor seal if you lay the plastic vapor barrier (retarder) directly on the slab (see drawing, below). Use 6-mil poly because it's less likely to puncture or tear. Overlap the seams about 12 in. and extend the plastic up the side-walls to grade level using dabs of asphalt roofing cement and tacked-on furring strips to hold it in place. Then install 2x4 sleepers (use enough nails to hold them in place) and insulation (use a water-resistant polystyrene such as Styrofoam). Install your subfloor with screws or coated sheathing nails. It's not necessary to use adhesive. Finally, apply the underlayment and vinyl floor.

You didn't mention whether you plan to install studs or attach furring strips to the walls. In either case, when you insulate the walls, add another vapor retarder on the room-side of the studs/furring strips to limit moisture transmission from the room into the wall cavity. If you use faced fiberglass insulation, the facing is the vapor retarder.

NEW BASEMENT FLOOR

- 1/2" DRYWALL
- VINYL TILE
- FIBERGLASS INSULATION
- VAPOR RETARDER
- STUD WALL
- GRADE LEVEL
- FURRING STRIP
- 6-MIL-POLY VAPOR RETARDER
- FOUNDATION WALL
- UNDERLAYMENT
- 1/2" CDX
- 2x4 PRESSURE-TREATED SLEEPERS; 16" O.C.
- GRAVEL
- POLYSTYRENE INSULATION

To stop water vapor from moving through below-grade concrete into the house, install a 6-mil-plastic vapor retarder next to the concrete before you add insulation and install floor and wall framing. To prevent insulation from absorbing water vapor from inside of the house, install a vapor retarder on the room-side of the insulation.

HEATING & COOLING

Most of us take our heating and cooling systems for granted — that is, until they break down and leave us shivering or marinating in a pool of sweat. In this chapter you'll learn how to maintain your heating and cooling systems so they'll keep working year after year. You'll also find information on winterizing your home to keep heating costs down, choosing appliances such as pellet stoves and air-circulation systems and solving annoying heating-system problems such as noise, temperature fluctuations and dusty odors.

STAYING WARM

Q **What do I need to do to prepare my heating system for the winter?**

A That depends on what kind of heating system you have. The following list addresses the maintenance chores that need to be performed on the most common heating systems.

Forced-Air Furnaces

☞Turn on your furnace and check for air leaks. Seal any open joints with duct tape to be sure you aren't losing expensive heat in the attic or basement.

☞Clean reusable filters with soap and water. Replace the filter if necessary.

☞Clean and adjust the humidifier. (See your owner's manual for detailed instructions.)

☞Check the pilot light for a blue — not yellow — flame. A yellow flame indicates an improper fuel-air mixture. Have the burners adjusted by a serviceman.

☞Check for soot accumulation in flue pipes. Soot indicates poor combustion or draft. Call a repairman.

☞Schedule a repairman to check the heat exchanger and blower system and test safety controls.

Hydronic (Hot-Water) and Steam Heating

☞Vacuum dust from convectors and radiators. Straighten bent convector fins.

☞Check the water level, the pressure-reducing valve and the safety relief valve. (See your owner's manual.)

☞Turn the heating system on and vent air from convectors and radiators (for hot-water systems only).

☞Check for steam or water leaks. Before making repairs, turn off the heating system, close the water-feed valve and let the system cool.

☞Oil the hot-water circulator pump and motor if they're not permanently lubricated.

☞Schedule a repairman to check and clean gas- or oil-burner controls and the heat exchanger, test and adjust safety controls and check boiler operation.

All-Electric Heating

☞Vacuum dust from baseboard heaters and blowers (if installed).

☞Schedule a repairman to check the condition and operation of the heating coils and blower system in electric warm-air furnaces.

Fireplaces and Wood Stoves

☞Replace cracked and missing mortar. Coat the exterior with a clear silicone-based concrete-mortar sealer. Repair cracked chimney mortar caps with hydraulic cement.

☞Disassemble metal flue pipes and take them outdoors for cleaning. Check for cracks or holes in the pipes.

☞Check and remove chimney blockages such as bird nests.

☞Call in a professional chimney sweep to inspect the chimney and to remove creosote buildup.

☞ Clean ash from the base of the fireplace and chimney flues. Soot accumulation may signal inefficient combustion.

Q **How should I winterize my house to lower heating costs?**

A Take a caulking and weatherstripping tour at the beginning of every heating season and do the following:

☞ Ensure the windows are shut and locked for the winter.

☞ Inspect and install (if needed) storm windows.

☞ Replace loose or missing window, door and siding caulk with flexible latex, silicone or polyurethane caulk.

☞ Check exterior door thresholds and replace or repair the sealing strip if needed.

☞ Replace worn or missing weather stripping around doors and windows. Don't forget the doors on attached garages.

☞ Seal skylight frames and flashings with roofing tar to prevent melting snow from leaking in.

☞ Seal the joints between the chimney and the siding with acrylic or siliconized-acrylic multipurpose caulk.

☞ Install covers on window air-conditioning units.

☞ Check that blowing-in insula-

Replace loose, missing or cracked caulk in these areas: A. Where the chimney goes through the roof and where it joins the siding (if applicable); B. Where water faucets or utilities enter the house; C. Between the siding and the foundation; D. Between the siding and corner trim; E. Around the door frame where it joins the siding and along the bottom of the door threshold; F. Between the window frame and siding; G. Between the garage door frame and siding and where stop molding joins the door frame.

WHERE TO CAULK

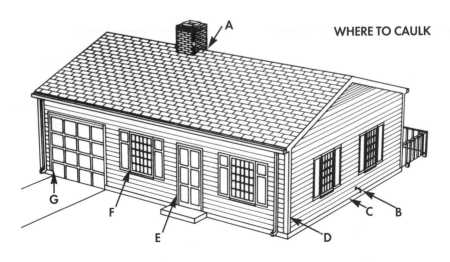

tion has equal depth across the entire attic. If not, redistribute or add more insulation.

☞ Check the attic ventilation. Do not cover turbine vents in an attempt to keep the attic warm. That only contributes to the formation of ice-dams and subsequent roof leaks.

Q How do pellet stoves compare with more traditional heating systems?

A Because they use wastes that might otherwise end up in landfills, pellet stoves are perhaps the biggest improvement in home heating since Benjamin Franklin invented the cast-iron fireplace stove.

Pellet stoves burn 1/4-in.-dia. pellets made of sawdust, cardboard or peanut shells. Some stoves can burn all kinds of pellets and shelled corn; others can burn only premium-grade low-ash wood pellets.

Compared to wood stoves, pellet stoves are superefficient and can operate unattended for many hours — something few wood stoves can do efficiently. The exteriors of pellet stoves radiate heat, but unlike wood stoves they stay relatively cool, preventing you from burning yourself if you touch the stove. Pellet stoves are more expensive than their wood-burning counterparts.

How they work

The typical pellet stove has a built-in fuel hopper that holds 40 to 80 pounds of pellets — a supply that will last up to 90 hours, depending on the brand and model of the stove. A slow-moving motor-driven corkscrew-shaped auger moves pellets to the firepot. A forced-air blower ensures a hot, clean-burning flame.

In most stoves, a separate blower circulates air over the heating chamber and into the room. Electronic controls regulate heat output to ensure maximum operating efficiency and comfort. Some stoves can be connected to a central home thermostat for precise temperature control.

Sophisticated design and combustion management make pellet appliances 75 to 85 percent efficient, compared with 60 to 80 percent for the most efficient wood-burning stoves.

Safe heat

Pellet stoves produce very little creosote, so the danger of chimney fires is virtually eliminated. The stoves can usually use an existing stove or fireplace flue. If the existing flue is unsafe, small-diameter flue liners can usually be installed. Some stoves have exhaust fans and can be vented through the wall, but most installers recommend vertical flues to provide better draft in case of power failure.

Controls on the appliances monitor heat output and ensure safe fuel feeding to prevent overheating. Because of the stoves' high efficiency and sealed doors, there is virtually no smoke or odor, a boon to allergy sufferers.

Wood ash residue is not considered hazardous, and disposing of it is not a problem. In small quantities, ash can be used as a soil conditioner or fertilizer. (Ash is alkaline and contains potash.) High-quality wood pellets leave only enough ash to fill a shoe box every month or two, but ash pans need to be emptied at least once every two weeks.

Because of the way many of the stoves are constructed, the visible flame is small and cylindrical and tends to flicker (often called a nervous flame). At least two manufacturers have modified the air flow and added ceramic logs to their stoves to produce the characteristic flame pattern found in log-burning stoves.

Pellet stoves can be installed by do-it-yourselfers, but there are good reasons for having a qualified installer do the work. The stoves are heavy — most weigh more than 300 pounds — and awkward to handle. Dealers have special handling devices. Compliance with the manufacturer's specifications, warranty requirements and local codes are critical for your safety and comfort.

Shopping for stoves

If you're interested in buying a pellet appliance (stove, fireplace or fireplace insert), first decide where you'd put it in your home and what options you have for ventilating it. Figure the square footage of the area you plan to heat and list the heat sources you currently use. When you visit dealers, try to see the stoves in operation. In addition to appearance and price, get answers to these important questions:

☞ Does the stove meet local air-quality regulations?

☞ Are pellets easily loaded without spilling?

☞ Is pellet fuel available locally?

☞ Will the stove burn a variety of pellet fuels (high-ash, corn, etc.)?

☞ What is the ash-pan capacity, and is the stove easy to clean?

☞ Does the stove have enough heat output and burn-time to suit your heating demands and lifestyle?

☞ Can you use a thermostat for remote temperature control?

☞ If you enjoy watching a fire, are ceramic logs available as an accessory to simulate a wood fire?

☞ Will do-it-yourself installation void the warranty?

Q **What are the recommended maintenance procedures for residential water-heating systems?**

A A hydronic heating system circulates heated water with a pump. The system includes a boiler (usually gas- or oil-fired), controls, a chimney/flue and hot water distribution system (circulating pump, piping and radiating elements.

These systems require annual service by qualified technicians to clean the flues in the boiler (if necessary), to clean the gas burners or oil-fired combustion chambers and to make adjustments to assure proper operating efficiency.

You may be able to perform some of the other required maintenance procedures, preferably in consulation with a service technician. You may: 1) inspect the fuel oil filter annually and replace it if it's dirty; 2) check boiler pressure periodically to ensure it is about 12 pounds per square inch; 3) vent or purge the water system if required; 4) lubricate the oil-fired burner motor and circulating pump annually; 5) replace the fuel oil filter; and 6) maintain the air-cushion tank.

Q **What kind of heating unit should I install in my woodworking shop, which is in an outbuilding?** I'm concerned about the presence of flammable products and heating efficiency.

A A gas-fired sealed-combustion boiler (see drawing, below) is probably your best bet. For the area of a typical shop, a small direct-vent wall furnace or boiler, which doesn't require a chimney, or even an instantaneous water heater would supply adequate heat. Because you

probably want quick response in your type of application, use fan convectors.

Naturally, the building should be well insulated, especially if you intend to maintain minimum temperatures. If the shop is heated only during use and there's a danger of freezing, talk to a heating contractor about having antifreeze put into the system.

Q **Is there an air-circulation system I can install that won't affect heating efficiency?** There's very little air circulation in my house during the winter. Stale air and cooking odors linger in the bedrooms at the rear of the house. I have a hot-water heating system.

A Assuming you have no major sources of air pollution, such as

DIRECT-VENT HEATING FOR A SHOP

A typical direct-vent water heater is mounted on an outside wall. A circulating pump moves hot water through distribution pipes to heat exchangers (caseboard or fan convectors) and back to the boiler. Fan convectors heat room air by blowing it through the heated, finned copper coils.

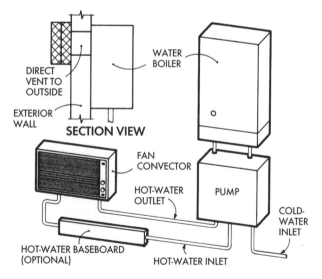

tobacco smoke or combustion by-products from an unvented gas range, the American Society of Heating Refrigeration and Air Conditioning Engineers recommends minimum ventilation of 10 cubic feet per minute (cfm) for each room, which translates to 0.2 to 0.4 air changes an hour in most houses with five or six rooms.

Natural ventilation is unreliable because of wide variations in the weather and occupant habits, and kitchen and bath fans are rarely used continuously. There is a variety of central mechanical exhaust systems that operate continuously — primarily in kitchens and bathrooms — but they are costly and occupants often disable them because of comfort and cost.

For superinsulated or very "tight" homes, an air-to-air heat exchanger (see drawing, below) is the best choice, particularly for homes in cold climates. This fan-powered heat-recovery ventilation device recovers heat from stale outgoing air and uses it to warm the incoming fresh air. But for conventional houses with numerous air leaks, whole-house air-to-air heat exchangers can be short-circuited. The U.S. Department of Energy National Appropriate Technology Assistance Service (NATAS) says that short-circuiting can cause poor air distribution as well as lowered heat-recovery efficiency. Other types of heat-recovery ventilators are being used in homes in Sweden, but they're not available in the United States.

If you own a conventional home, you may want to consider using a window air-to-air heat exchanger for an open area. The Recoup-Aerator, available from Stirling Technology Inc., is a unit with a rotary-wheel heat-exchanger core. You can also try to reduce or eliminate potential air-pollution sources: Don't allow smoking in the house; use an electric range or a vented gas stove; use kitchen and bath fans regularly; pipe outside air to heating appliances and fireplaces; and when weather permits, close bedroom doors and open bedroom windows at night.

HOW AN AIR-TO-AIR HEAT EXCHANGER WORKS

KEY

HOUSE AIR   OUTSIDE AIR

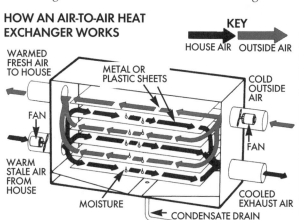

An air-to-air heat exchanger pulls stale, warm air from the house and transfers the heat in that air through thin metal or plastic sheets to the fresh, cold air being pulled into the house. The exchanger does not produce heat; it only exchanges heat from one air stream to the other. Moisture in the stale air condenses in the core and is drained away.

WARMED FRESH AIR TO HOUSE

METAL OR PLASTIC SHEETS

COLD OUTSIDE AIR

FAN

FAN

WARM STALE AIR FROM HOUSE

MOISTURE

COOLED EXHAUST AIR

CONDENSATE DRAIN

KEEPING YOUR COOL

Q How often should I have my air conditioner inspected?

A According to Carrier Corp., manufacturer of heating and cooling systems, central air conditioners should be inspected by a service technician at the beginning of every cooling season. Carrier also offers these maintenance tips to help you keep cool all summer:

☞ Make sure outdoor units and condensers are free of debris, shrubs, etc.

☞ Be careful that grass clippings and leaves are not blown toward the unit when you mow the lawn.

☞ Clean filters once a month or as needed.

☞ Never try to add refrigerant to an air conditioner yourself. Call a service technician.

☞ Do not run a central air conditioner when the outdoor temperature is below 55 degrees.

ANNOYING HEATING PROBLEMS

Q How can I get rid of the dusty smell that emanates from our heating system? There are return air registers in two bedrooms and the living room. We just changed the filter on our Space Gard air cleaner, and after three years of use it wasn't even dirty.

A Your Space Gard central air cleaner is a high-efficiency unit, which should trap 99 percent of the visible pollutants, including dust. If the filter media is not dirty after three years, something is wrong. Air is bypassing the filter as it is drawn into the furnace.

First, ensure that the air cleaner is properly installed. It should be in the return air duct next to the furnace so that return air must flow through it into the furnace. Next, be sure your furnace has a sealed floor. If not, the resistance created by the filter could be forcing air to enter through the bottom of the furnace instead of through the return air duct.

Check the return airflow by holding your hand over a return air grill and feeling for air movement. Also check for obvious air leaks in the return air ducts at the furnace and repair them as needed. Contact a reputable heating contractor (perhaps the company that installed your furnace) for help.

Q How do I control temperature fluctuations with my electric baseboard heating system? The problem is particularly annoying in my bedroom. Each electric baseboard heater is equipped with its own thermostat. Should I relocate the thermostats a few feet directly above the heater, try another type of thermostat or just get a heavier comforter?

A Your problem almost certainly lies with the thermostat — it's probably a line-voltage (in-line) bimetal unit. You should replace it with a more precise thermostat mounted on the wall opposite the heater (not above the heater as you suggest).

Fishing high-voltage wires through closed ceilings or floors is difficult, so low-voltage controls may be the best choice in finished basements or second floors. Low-voltage wiring can be run behind baseboards to the wall opposite the heater and then fished up through the wall to the new thermostat.

For more information call a licensed electrician.

Q **Why does my hot-water baseboard heating system gurgle, crackle and bang?** The system provides heat in three areas (zones) of the house.

A In all likelihood the noises you hear are the nature of the system. The crackling occurs as the aluminum-finned copper-tubing convectors expand and contract with changes in temperature. Wrapping the pipes with insulation would keep the water warmer and reduce temperature fluctuation, thus helping to quiet the system.

More noise can be caused bv excessively long runs, lack of clearance where pipes penetrate floors and inadequate tubing support.

If your system has one circulating pump with zone valves, closing the valves in two of the zones will increase water velocity and noise through the remaining loop.

Complaints often arise after people have installed setback thermostats. Cold pipes at night mean noise in the morning.

The gurgling (and sometimes loud banging) might be caused by air in the system. Check wherever pipes enter the convectors. You should find at least one air valve (it looks like a screw head set into a tee fitting) for each loop and often one at every convector. Open each valve a little to allow air to escape. If neither water nor air escapes, replace the faulty valve. If you find air and the problem peisists after bleeding the system, have a plumber check the air-water separator at the boiler.

WATER WOES

Whether from leaks, a flood or condensation, when water gets in the wrong place it can quickly cause widespread damage — mildew, peeling paint, structural wood damage and insulation deterioration — and the aftermath is often expensive to repair. This chapter addresses common condensation problems with bathrooms, plumbing, garages, crawl spaces and windows as well as other water-related problems, including flood damage, leaky roofs, rotting flooring and buckled roofing.

CONDENSATION

Q **What causes condensation, and how can it be prevented?**

A Condensation occurs in the home when water vapor in air changes to water. When warm, moist air settles on a cold surface, water droplets form, and if the surface temperature is below freezing, the water turns to ice. Sometimes condensation is only a nuisance — sweat rings on your tabletop, fogged windows, a wet toilet tank, dripping cold-water pipes or a frosty freezer — but it can cause serious problems.

In theory, there are three ways to stop condensation:
1) Don't add excessive water vapor to the air.
2) Remove excessive water vapor from the house before it condenses.
3) Warm the inside surfaces above the dew point (the temperature at which water vapor condenses).

In the "good old days" homes were poorly insulated and riddled with cracks and gaps, so water vapor escaped easily, and condensation was not a problem. In fact, homeowners once used boiling water and furnace humidifiers to keep enough humidity in the air for personal comfort. People living in homes not sealed and insulated by current standards still humidify homes that way.

Today, because of increased heating and cooling costs and greater awareness of our finite energy sources, many homes are heavily insulated and tightly sealed. Water vapor cannot escape, so the humidity is high and condensation problems are commonplace. The solutions sometimes mean changing your living habits or expending time and energy.

Q **Is there anything I can do to reduce the humidity in my superinsulated home?**

A One of the most effective devices for supplying fresh, dry air is an air-to-air heat exchanger (see drawing, right). These devices exhaust stale, humid air and replace it with fresh air. As the warm air is exhausted through the heat exchanger, the incoming cold air is warmed, thereby minimizing heat loss.

Assuming your attic ventilation is adequate and you have no roof or basement water leaks, there are several other things you can do to reduce the amount of water vapor released into your home:

☞ Run only full loads in clothes washers and dishwashers to reduce the number of uses.

☞ Vent your clothes dryer outside, and don't hang laundry to dry inside the house.

☞ Shorten the time you shower or bathe.

☞ Cover hot tubs when they're not in use.

☞ Cook with electric stoves or microwaves and keep pots and pans covered while cooking. (Gas stoves and unvented gas and kerosene heaters generate a lot of water vapor.)

SUPER-INSULATED HOUSE

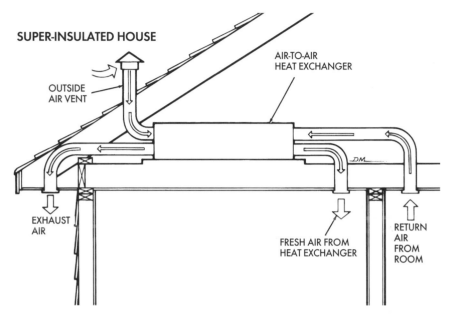

A heat exchanger replaces humid room air with dry outside air. As the air circulates through the heat exchanger, the incoming cold air absorbs heat from the warm air, minimizing the energy required to heat the incoming air.

☞ Avoid excessive watering of plants.

☞ Fix dripping faucets.

☞ Don't dry wet firewood inside the house.

☞ Circulate air to maintain even temperatures and a consistent humidity level throughout the house.

☞ Keep the temperature as low as is comfortable in the winter.

☞ Use an exhaust fan to remove water vapor in the bath while bathing and in the kitchen while cooking. (But be aware that exhaust fans remove heat as well as water vapor.)

☞ Use a dehumidifier in rooms such as basements where the humidity tends to be high.

Q **How can I stop my bathroom paint from chipping?** The upstairs bathroom was formerly an open dormer. The paint is chipping on the ceiling above the tub/shower, the highest point in the room. The room has three small windows that don't help very much. The room needs some kind of vent to force out the steam and moisture, but I am worried about electrical codes.

A Steam is one of the most effective cleaning agents, and each time you use the tub or shower, you are in effect steam cleaning the bathroom paint. Steam penetrates almost any paint barrier; the moisture accumulates at the ceiling peak because the hot air rises and is trapped there.

One way to remove the moisture is to use a power ventilator and force out the hot air. Because you expressed reservations about doing the wiring for the ventilator, have a professional electrician install the unit.

But there is another option you can try first: Reduce the amount of moisture in the room through other means. For example, assuming you have other bathrooms in the house, use only the stool and lavatory in this bathroom and do your bathing in a better-ventilated bathroom. Or open windows a crack while you bathe to let the moisture escape, and leave the bathroom door wide open when the bath is not in use so the moisture can dissipate throughout the house. Fix any leaking faucets, and keep the toilet lid down to reduce moisture caused by evaporation. Wipe the tub, tile and shower doors with your bath towel after drying yourself, and remove damp towels or shower/bath mats to eliminate their moisture from the room.

Don't use a suction-type rubber mat in the tub because water can be trapped between the mat and the tub, and when the trapped water evaporates, it adds to the moisture problem. Instead, use non-slip tub decals, which don't trap water.

In many cases, simply removing wet towels or mats and wiping the tile/tub area down after bathing will reduce moisture levels so the paint won't peel. Give these ideas a try before you install a power vent. When the moisture/peeling problem is solved, scrape all loose and peeling paint away, prime the affected area and apply at least two coats of alkyd enamel for a water-resistant finish.

Q **What can I do about pipes and ducts that sweat?**

A The sweating is a result of warm, moist air contacting a cold surface. Cover the ducts and pipes with foam or fiberglass insulation blankets (see drawing, below) and the condensation will end. Be sure to seal joints between sections of insulation with waterproof duct tape or plastic tape.

SWEATING PIPES AND DUCTS

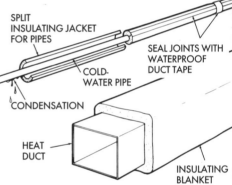

Wrap cold water pipes and heat ducts with insulation. Seal the insulation joints with waterproof tape.

Q **How should I insulate the walls of my house and cure a condensation problem?** The house has severe paint peeling and mildew problems inside, especially at exterior wall corners, under windows and at corners where the ceilings and walls meet. I do a lot of cooking and baking, and I have many houseplants. I am told these factors add to the moisture problems. The home was built without a vapor barrier, but we have removed some of the outside wall drywall and added insulation and a vapor barrier. Can we add furring strips to the walls and insulate from inside? Are there vapor control techniques other than vapor barrier paint?

A Water vapor moves through walls in an attempt to equalize pressure. When indoor air is warm and humid and outside air is cold and dry, water vapor moves through the exterior walls and ceilings. Without a vapor barrier, moisture penetrates cold spots in the walls (see drawing, below) and condenses into water or forms ice, depending on the temperature in the wall or ceiling cavities. Continuous wetting action eventually causes paint to peel. If the surface remains damp when it warms, you'll also have mildew or mold.

The first step is to insulate the wall and attic voids to eliminate cold spots and prevent condensation. You can fur out the walls to add insulation. In superinsulated homes, some builders nail 2x4s wide-face down on 24-in. centers over and perpendicular to the existing wall studs and then install batt insulation between the new 2x4s. This approach will cost you about 2 in. of interior floor space (the thickness of the 2x4 plus the drywall). You

Insulation gaps are common at attic sill plates and wall corners. Walls and ceilings are cold at these insulation voids, and moisture condenses and may even freeze on the cold areas.

will have to reset your electrical outlets and switches on the new 2x4s and replace the trim around doors, windows and floors. You also will have to add extenders equal to the new wall thickness to the window and door frames.

Staple 4-mil polyethylene plastic sheeting over the 2x4 furring before you install new drywall. As added protection, cover the drywall with a coat of vapor-barrier paint, such as Glidden's InsulAid, to prevent moisture from being trapped within the wall.

To solve your humidity problem, you can either cut down on the activities and items that contribute to the humidity — baking, showering, laundering, plants, aquariums, etc.— or use mechanical methods to remove the excess humidity. Because

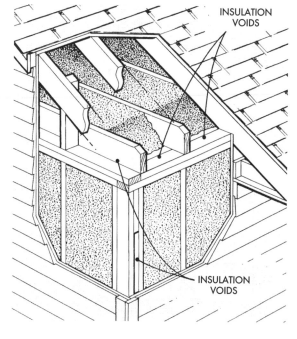

INSULATION VOIDS

INSULATION VOIDS

you live in a cold climate, installation of an air-to-air heat exchanger may be the most practical solution, or you can install humidistatically controlled exhaust vents in the laundry, kitchen and baths.

Q Do vapor-barrier paints work?

A Most new homes have vapor-barrier-backed insulation batts or a separate vapor-barrier plastic material behind the drywall on exterior walls. Older homes (those without

VAPOR-BARRIER PAINT

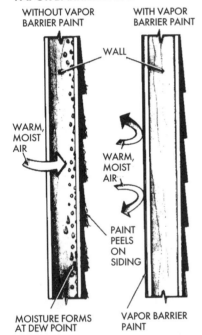

WITHOUT VAPOR BARRIER PAINT

WITH VAPOR BARRIER PAINT

WALL

WARM, MOIST AIR

WARM, MOIST AIR

PAINT PEELS ON SIDING

MOISTURE FORMS AT DEW POINT

VAPOR BARRIER PAINT

Warm moist air can move through drywall and freeze in the wall, saturating insulation and causing wood rot when it melts. Vapor-barrier paint is a relatively inexpensive and easy way to solve this problem.

insulation) were built without a barrier. A vapor-barrier paint is a viable alternative to ripping off the drywall or plaster to apply a vapor barrier and can save you considerable expense.

Vapor-barrier paints are specifically formulated to seal walls and ceilings against the passage of water vapor (see drawing, left). Some are primers that need to be covered with regular paint; others are top coats applied over regular primers. These paints can be very effective when used in conjunction with other water-vapor control techniques.

Don't forget to seal the cracks and gaps around electrical outlets and fixtures before you apply the paint. Several major paint suppliers such as Glidden, Benjamin Moore and Sears sell the paint. Check several reliable paint stores to be assured you're getting the most effective material.

Q Why does my garage sweat? I

recently built a garage with insulated 6-ft.-high frame walls on top of a 2-ft.-high concrete block foundation. I use the garage for woodworking, so I installed an unvented DESA model CGN18T (18,000-Btu) natural gas heater. When I use the heater in cold weather, condensation forms on the windows, doors and walls. I use the same type of heater in another garage that's attached to my house without any problem. Could the heater be defective or the wrong size? Would a vented heater solve my problem?

A The heater is part of the problem, but it's probably not defective.

An unvented heater burns air from the room and releases the products of combustion back into the room. One of the chief by-products of burning natural gas or propane is water. (Other sources of moisture include your respiration and drying wood.)

According to DESA International, this particular model produces about 1-1/2 cups of moisture each hour when it's operated at full capacity. Your other garage probably doesn't suffer from condensation because it leaks air fast enough to let the water vapor escape.

One solution would be to switch heaters. You could install a vented heater or a sealed-combustion heater. With either heater, the waste gases would be directed outdoors, so your working environment would be safer and you would not have the condensation problem. But because you already have the heater, you may want to ventilate your new garage.

Because unvented gas heaters reduce the supply of oxygen in a closed room, DESA International recommends that these heaters be operated with a window slightly open to provide adequate ventilation and a safe supply of oxygen. You've obviously built a reasonably tight structure, and because you're using the garage for woodworking, you should have active venting. If you do welding or soldering or work with solvents, venting is even more crucial. Current residential building codes and standards recommend a minimum of 15 cubic ft. of outdoor ventilation each hour for each occupant.

CRAWL SPACES

Q **What should I do about a damp crawl space?**

A A damp crawl space can be a major contributor to condensation problems by allowing water vapor to enter the house. First, be sure the crawl space is ventilated and has at least two window/vent openings with a minimum of 1 sq. ft. of free, open area for each 1,500 sq. ft. of crawl space area. This may require cutting more openings or altering existing openings so air can circulate freely.

If the crawl space remains damp, cover it with a vapor barrier (see drawing, below). Spread a layer of

DAMP CRAWL SPACE

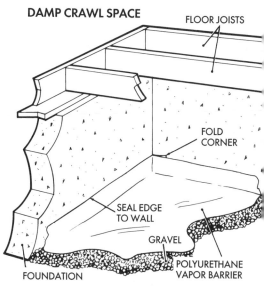

Install a 4- or 6-mil polyethylene vapor barrier in crawl spaces to stop migration of moisture through the floor into the house.

gravel over the entire earthen surface; then cover the gravel with a large sheets of heavy (4- or 6-mil) polyethelene plastic. Overlap the plastic sheets at least 6 in. and seal with plastic tape. Fold the corners and turn up about 6 in. against the foundation walls; then seal with tape or adhesive.

If the crawl space is really wet and has standing water, you may have to add tile drains and a sump pump to remove excess water.

Q How can I get rid of the condensation that forms in my crawl space during the summer? To cure moisture problems in the crawl space, I ventilated and then covered it with gravel and a plastic sheet. The crawl space is fine in winter, but during the summer moisture condenses into puddles on the plastic. Because of the high summer humidity, the water evaporates very slowly.

A First, make sure the plastic is taped or sealed tightly against the crawl space walls to prevent moisture migration from the ground below. You should also have at least two window/vent openings (preferably on opposite sides of the crawl space) that give you at least 1 sq. ft. (net) of free open air per 1,500 sq. ft. of crawl space area to provide adequate ventilation. To compensate for airflow restrictions caused by vent screens or louvers, increase the gross vent area using these factors: For 1/8-in. mesh screening, increase the area 1-1/4 times (125 percent); for 1/16-in. mesh screening or louvers and hardware cloth, two times; for

louvers and 1/8-in. mesh screening, 2-1/4 times; and for louvers and 1/16-in. screening, three times. Finally, spread an inch or two of sand or pea gravel on top of the plastic sheeting. The sand will insulate the plastic and minimize condensation.

MILDEW

Q What can I do about dampness and mildew in a closet?

A It sounds as if your closet is on an outside wall. First, check the outside closet walls for cold areas that would indicate a gap in the insulation, which could cause condensation on the wall. Also, make sure you don't have any roof or eave leaks above the area. Then remove everything from the closet and scrub the walls and ceiling with a strong mildewcide cleaner. Use a fan to thoroughly dry the room. To increase air circulation, replace the solid closet door with a louvered door, or cut openings in the top and bottom of the existing door to accept louvered panels. Finally, don't overfill the closet, and try to keep items away from the walls to allow better air circulation.

Q Why does mildew grow on the inside of many of our exterior walls, particularly near the ceiling and behind furniture? Moisture sometimes appears at drywall nail locations, too.

A Although some of the often-mentioned interior sources of excess humidify — unvented bathrooms, kitchens, dryers, etc. — could be contributing to the problem, the fact that the problem is so extensive suggests major broad-based moisture sources. First, if your home is built above an unvented crawl space or the ground is not covered wall-to-wall with a heavy plastic vapor retarder, the crawl space could be the cause. Second, foundation walls can wick moisture from the ground up into wall cavities, causing the symptoms you describe. If that is the case (it's a newly discovered phenomenon), it's possible that your foundation drainage system is clogged with silt or that the grade has settled around your house, allowing water to puddle against the foundation. This condition also can be aggravated by leaking, clogged or non-existent gutters.

If these leads don't pan out, engage a qualified house inspector to determine the cause. Find one in your classified telephone directory under "Building and Land Inspection Service."

WINDOWS

Q What can I do to stop condensation on my windows?

A In many climates windows show condensation buildup almost all winter. Reducing the amount of water vapor in the house may help, but the best way to stop the condensation is to install storm windows or replace the single-glazed windows with double- or triple-glazed windows.

Q How can I stop condensation from forming on my storm windows?

A Either your primary windows are too loose or your storm windows are too tight. The primary windows should always be tighter. Check the glazing and the fit in the frame. Replace broken or missing glazing putty and weather stripping if necessary. Seal the storm windows too, but make sure the ventilating holes (or drain holes) remain open.

Q Why is condensation forming on my double-glazed windows? I have a hard-to-heat living room on the north side of my house. Hoping to eliminate winter drafts and condensation on inside window surfaces, I replaced the single-pane windows with double-glazed ones. The condensation is worse than ever. Could the windows be defective?

A Your new windows are not defective — a sign of that would be condensation between panes. Condensation occurs on the inside of windows when warm, humid air contacts the cold glass. As the window becomes warmer or the air less humid, condensation is less of a problem.

Your new windows may actually be contributing to the increased condensation. The superior seal on these windows does not allow as much moisture to escape as your old windows did. But because the inside pane of a double-pane window is warmer than a single pane,

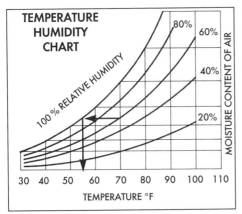

TEMPERATURE HUMIDITY CHART

100% RELATIVE HUMIDITY
80% 60% 40% 20%
MOISTURE CONTENT OF AIR
TEMPERATURE °F
30 40 50 60 70 80 90 100 110

Use this chart to determine when condensation will occur on your windows.

exhaust fans to remove excess moisture from bathrooms and kitchens. Ensure that crawl spaces have adequate ventilation or install a plastic vapor retarder. Clean clogged gutters and drains and improve the grading around the house to eliminate standing water grading.

In Northern areas, where the winter humidity and temperatures are lower, installing storm windows (to make triple-pane windows) will make the inside window glass warmer and minimize condensation problems.

condensation should occur at a lower outdoor temperature than before.

To determine when window condensation will occur, use the chart (a bove). Begin at the point that represents your indoor temperature and relative humidity — 70 F and 60 percent relative humidity, in the example. From that point, move horizontally to the 100 percent relative humidity line; then move down to the Temperature axis. Condensation will occur on a surface with a temperature of about 55 F.

If the humidity and winter temperatures in your area are relatively high, your only solution is to reduce indoor moisture. (You can do nothing about the outdoor temperature.) Typical sources of moisture are from the kitchen and bath, excess humidification, house plants, an unvented clothes dryer or gas heating appliance, unvented dirt-floor crawl space, and outdoor moisture penetrating the foundation wall. Use

Q **How can I prevent my triple-glazed windows from fogging up?**

A Water can condense on double- or triple-glazed windows when the humidity levels in the house are too high. You may need to lower the humidity in the house. If your triple-glazed windows are fogged between the glazing, the edge seals have probably failed. If so, replace the glazing or window.

Q **Is there anything I can do to stop frosting on my metal-frame windows?**

A Many of the new metal-frame windows and doors have a plastic isolation strip (thermal break) between the inner and outer frames to stop the migration of cold. This is very effective in fighting frost buildup. But on uninsulated sashes or frames without a thermal break, installing storm windows on the outside will help greatly. You can also install storm windows on the inside to keep the warm air off the cold frames.

SKYLIGHTS

Q **What can I do about moisture that collects in my skylight in the winter?** It runs down and is causing ceiling paint to peel.

A It sounds as if you have a single-glazed skylight without a condensation gutter. Single-glazed skylights are predestined to collect moisture when warm moist air rises from the room and condenses on the cold glass or acrylic glazing.

You may be able to install a window near the bottom of the frame (see drawing, below). This creates a storm window effect, with the skylight becoming the storm window. The new glass will prohibit the warm air from reaching the cold outer glass. This method is only as good as its seal, however; if warm air gets around the lower glass, it can cause condensation between the two

SWEATING SKYLIGHT

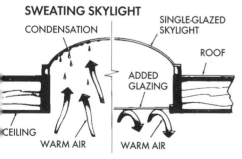

Seal sweating skylights (those without a condensation gutter) with tightly-sealed glazing installed in the light shaft below the skylight.

assemblies, which could be worse. Therefore, be sure to caulk in the grooves of the new frame before inserting the glass, and caulk between the new frame and the existing frame.

If your homemade inner "storm window" doesn't work, the most satisfactory fix is to replace the skylight with a new, high-quality double-glazed unit. Installing a ceiling fan may help by lowering the temperature at the ceiling.

Q **Why is my professinally installed skylight leaking?** The leak is somewhere near a skylight located in the cathedral ceiling of a new addition to our home. The roof and the factory-supplied flashing on the Velux skylight was professionally installed. The leak seems to be in the skylight, but I cannot pinpoint the source. Water drips from the window in varying amounts during different outdoor temperatures and sometimes not until days after a storm. The roof is properly vented with soffit and ridge vents, and an air channel is provided between the insulation and the underside of the roof sheathing.

A When properly installed, Velux skylights are guaranteed not to leak. The skylights use a step system in which each piece of flashing is interwoven with each layer of roofing material. Because there are no caulks or mastics used, the seal does not deteriorate.

According to a Velux technical representative, most skylight-related leakage problems occur because of improper installation. He suggests that you or the contractor call Velux and speak with a customer-service representative. Velux will schedule a representative to meet with you and the contractor and inspect the skylight. If the representative finds a problem with the skylight, Velux will repair or replace it. If there is an installation problem, he will point it out to the contractor. (The contractor should assume the responsibility of any repair costs).

If the skylight is properly installed, there are two other possible sources for the leaks. First, the leak may occur in the roof above the skylight because of water leaking in around a ridge vent or chimney flashing. Second, although the roof is through-vented with soffit and ridge vents to prevent condensation, the bays directly above and below the skylight often do not get adequate air movement because the horizontal framing between the rafters blocks the airflow between soffit and ridge vents. Drilling holes through the rafters to join the skylight bay to the adjacent air channels is the solution.

OTHER WATER PROBLEMS

Q How do you restore a flooded home?

A Restoring a flooded home to its original state is a long and painful process. Many homes are so badly damaged that it would cost more to repair them than to rebuild, but most flooded houses can be restored.

Flood water is laden with silt (dirt), sewage, chemicals and debris, and it leaves the house dirty, unhealthy and potentially dangerous, so enter with caution.

When you enter:
☞ Turn off gas lines at the meter or propane tank.
☞ Turn off electricity at the meter. (You can be electrocuted in water.)
☞ Ensure that the house is structurally safe to enter. Support posts that are not adequately anchored to the floor above can be dislodged by flood water.
☞ Wear goggles and a mask in homes contaminated with sewage or chemicals.
☞ Open doors and windows and let the house air out for a few minutes.
☞ Do not use the home's electrical system until the main circuit-breaker box, wiring and outlet boxes have been cleaned and inspected. You'll need an auxiliary generator and portable lighting.

Clean-up begins
☞ Remove everything that is wet as soon as possible. Moisture and humidity that remain in the house will cause more damage.
☞ Wash the mud off of salvageable furniture and personal belongings. Keep wooden items out of direct sunlight.
☞ Apply a light coat of oil or a greaseless lubricant to iron and steel to prevent rust.
☞ Shovel out mud while it is still moist.
☞ Remove and discard flooded rugs and carpet padding.

REPAIRING WATER DAMAGE

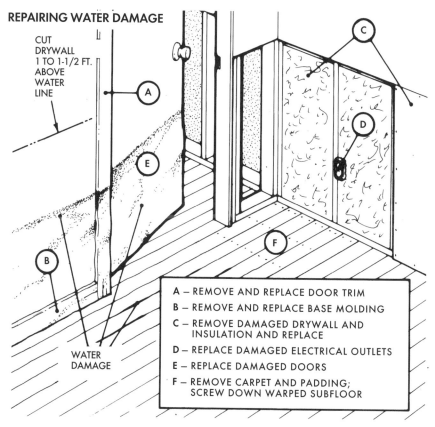

CUT DRYWALL 1 TO 1-1/2 FT. ABOVE WATER LINE

WATER DAMAGE

A – REMOVE AND REPLACE DOOR TRIM
B – REMOVE AND REPLACE BASE MOLDING
C – REMOVE DAMAGED DRYWALL AND INSULATION AND REPLACE
D – REPLACE DAMAGED ELECTRICAL OUTLETS
E – REPLACE DAMAGED DOORS
F – REMOVE CARPET AND PADDING; SCREW DOWN WARPED SUBFLOOR

☞ Remove drywall or plaster, insulation, base molding, door casings and any doors that are warped or buckled.

☞ Remove wet kitchen cabinets. Discard warped or delaminated cabinets.

☞ While everything is still wet, wash walls and floors. Power wash the basement, including the ceiling. But don't drain a flooded basement before the flood waters have receded — structural damage may occur.

☞ Disinfect every nook and cranny. Use a commercial disinfectant or a solution of equal parts of chlorine bleach and water.

☞ Before you begin repairs, let the house dry. Use fans and dehumidifiers. Some experts recommend heating the house if the furnace is working. Also operate room air conditioners; they'll remove moisture.

☞ Don't rush repairs. It will take from two to six weeks for the wood to dry. Test moisture content with a moisture meter (12 percent or less moisture is ideal) or test with cat litter: If the litter becomes damp when it is spread on the wood, the wood is too wet.

☞ Remove mildew from dry wood with a solution of 4 to 6 teaspoons of trisodium phosphate (TSP), 1 cup of chlorine bleach and 1 gallon of water.

Making repairs

☞ Flatten small buckles in plywood subfloors by driving in more screws. Replace a badly buckled subfloor.

☞ Replace oak flooring if it has been wet for more than a few hours.

☞ Repair walls, floors and trim (see drawing, p. 83).

☞ Wait a few weeks to paint. Allow plenty of time for the moisture to escape.

Appliances and utilities

☞ Electric motors usually must be replaced.

☞ Replace freezers, refrigerators and water heaters if the insulation is wet.

☞ Clean the burners in gas furnaces and water heaters and treat the metal to prevent rust. Replace damaged electronic controls.

☞ Replace damaged receptacles and switches, including the main circuit-breaker box and breakers. Copper wire will dry, but replace old knob-and-tube wiring.

☞ Replace forced-air heating and cooling ducts that cannot be cleaned.

Q How can I stop water from recirculating into my sump pump hole? The pump runs constantly and seems to move the water in an endless cycle. The pump drainpipe dumps the water just outside the house, and the water apparently soaks down to the foundation drain tiles and then into the sump hole. I have been advised to install underground downspout kits on the gutter pipes and to pipe the pumped water to a dry well 15 ft. away from the foundation.

A You have pinpointed the problem: The sump pump is acting as a recirculating pump, dumping the collected basement water just outside the foundation wall, where it runs right back down to the drain tiles at the foundation footings. You should be able to correct the problem without a great amount of work or expense.

First, attach a plastic or rubber hose to the sump pump drain pipe. The hose should be at least 15 ft. long to carry the water from the foundation area. Try to find a spot lower than the house so the water will flow away from the house.

If you're a gardener, use the water to irrigate your garden — flowers and vegetables will cause the water to evaporate faster. You can leave the hose on the surface of the lawn temporarily to see if this method helps. Later, bury it below ground a few inches to conceal the hose, but let the water run out of the hose at ground level. There should be no need to build a dry well to hold the water.

There are other measures you can take to reduce water drainage into the basement. Fill low spots around the foundation with dirt to ensure rainwater runoff flows away from the house. Make sure the gutters are clean to prevent overflow, and add extensions to your gutter drains. Anything you do to encourage water to flow away from the house will help.

After you've made these changes, watch the system for a few weeks to learn if the measures you've taken have helped. If not, have a professional engineer inspect your property. It may be necessary to grade your lot to direct water flow away from the house.

Q **What could cause water to begin dripping from the ceiling joints of our 20-year-old mobile home even though it hasn't rained for a week?** The ground under the crawl space is covered with plastic, and the roof vents are open. The only change we have made is to paint the roof with a white roof-sealing product. (We formerly used an aluminum product.)

A Don't assume the water is condensation. Condensation within the roof cavities of metal-roofed mobile homes is not usually a problem even without venting, and it's doubtful that the problem is related to the roof coating. It's possible that water from a roof leak — perhaps a very fine, age-related crack in the metal caused by stress or fatigue — could take that long to penetrate. To test the roof, cover it with heavy plastic sheeting and see whether the roof still drips after it rains or when you wet it with a garden hose. (Slit the plastic and seal plumbing or heating vents with duct tape.)

Q **How should I replace the rotting flooring in my mobile home?** What type of plywood should I use for the subfloor? Is a vapor barrier necessary? Should I paint the underside of the plywood?

A Your floors probably have warped because of the high humidity in your area. First, to stop moisture migration upward through the floor, cover the earth under your home with a layer of 6-mil polyethylene sheeting. Cover the plastic sheeting with at least 1 in. of dry sand to prevent condensation.

Second, remove skirting from around the base of your home or install lattice to allow air circulation. Then remove the old flooring and cover the joists with a 6-mil-poly vapor barrier. Overlap the joints 6 in. (Always install a barrier on the warm side of the room directly under the subfloor.) Finally, install a Marine-plywood subfloor. Exterior-grade plywood should also serve well at a lower cost. Before you install the new subfloor, coat all sides and edges with an exterior varnish or alkyd (oil-base) paint. When the coating is dry, fasten the plywood to the joists with drywall screws spaced 12 in. on center.

Q **What causes roofing to buckle?** My 3-year-old house has 1/2-in. plywood roof sheathing covered with 30-year-warranted asphalt shingles nailed directly over the plywood without roofing-felt underlayment. The plywood has buckled in four places. I was able to flatten the plywood by stepping on it and driving galvanized screws under the shingle tabs, but I'm worried that the rest of the roof may buckle. The attic floor has a vapor retarder under the insulation, and the attic is well ventilated. What causes such a problem? Would the small lake behind the house contribute to it?

A It appears your problem is caused by moisture getting to the plywood. It's possible that water from windblown rain or ice-dams could have leaked through to the plywood. Unless the exposure to water occurred on a regular basis, you probably would not have seen any leaks in the attic.

Felt underlayment is needed under asphalt roofing to adequately protect the sheathing from moisture. The Council of American Building Officials requires double-layer underlayment on one- and two-family houses with roof slopes less than four vertical units in 12 horizontal units (4:12 pitch) and single-layer underlayment for all others. Some roofing manufacturers' warranties and most building codes also require felt underlayment.

Another source of moisture may be humidity in your attic. Check your ventilation. With an attic vapor barrier, the Federal Housing Authority recommends 1 sq. ft. of free vent area for each 300 sq. ft. of attic floor area. The vent area should be divided equally between the inlet and outlet vents. If the vents are screened or louvered to keep rain and insects out, multiply the needed vent area by three.

Dampness from your backyard lake

should not have caused your problem. Neither should installation of a power attic vent create any problems.

Inadequate nailing or failure to use plywood clips on joints between rafters may be contributing to the buckling. The minimum fastening schedule for roof sheathing calls for 6d (2-in.) nails or 16-gauge staples (1-3/4-in. leg length) spaced 6 in. at the edges and 12 in. in the field. Whether the problem is widespread depends on whether the builder under-nailed in just a few places or over the entire roof.

Contact the builder and your building department to determine whether the roof was constructed according to code. If not, the builder may make it right. Otherwise, keep making needed repairs as you've done.

Q **Is there a way to harden a particleboard floor once it has been exposed to water?** My water heater leaked and left a spongy strip about 12 in. wide and 10 ft. long. I'd rather repair the floor than replace it if there's an easy solution.

A There is no way to repair water-damaged particleboard. But replacing the material with plywood is inexpensive and relatively easy to do. It sounds like you'll need one or two 4- x 8-ft. sheets.

Pull back the carpeting and cut out the damaged floor using a circular saw. Set the saw to the thickness of the floor (usually 5/8 or 3/4 in.) and cut over the center of the joists. If possible, stagger the end joints of each panel. Cut the replacement panels to allow a 1/8-in. gap on all sides. After a trial fit, put a bead of construction adhesive along the top of each joist and install the new panels with countersunk drywall screws spaced 12 in. apart.

Q How do I keep water from collecting under my greenhouse? I added a window greenhouse to the basement. On the outside, the window clears the ground by just 2 to 3 in. on one end and slightly more on the other end where the ground slopes away. I dug out a few inches under the structure and added gravel, but I'm concerned that water will collect there. When it rains, muddy water splashes on the window, necessitating frequent cleaning. What's the solution?

A The cavity or low spot now holding the gravel may collect water eventually. You're better off covering the ground with pine straw or pine bark (see drawing, below). The restricted clearance in your case would make weeding difficult, so I suggest you cover the ground under the structure and an additional 12 in. on three sides with black 6-mil polyethylene and then spread the straw or bark on the polyethylene.

To keep the material from washing away when it rains, cover the mulch material and polyethylene with 2-in.-mesh chicken wire held in place with hooks fashioned from wire coat hangers.

If it is necessary to hide the mesh, additional mulch can be sprinkled on top. The pine straw or pine bark will help prevent rain splatters on the window, and the water that does splash will be clean.

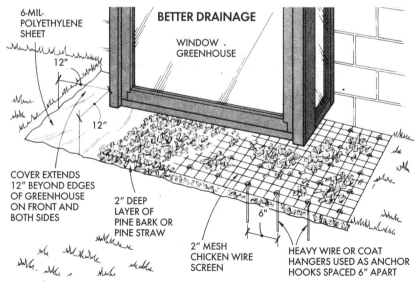

BETTER DRAINAGE

6-MIL-POLYETHYLENE SHEET

WINDOW GREENHOUSE

12"

12"

COVER EXTENDS 12" BEYOND EDGES OF GREENHOUSE ON FRONT AND BOTH SIDES

2" DEEP LAYER OF PINE BARK OR PINE STRAW

2" MESH CHICKEN WIRE SCREEN

6"

HEAVY WIRE OR COAT HANGERS USED AS ANCHOR HOOKS SPACED 6" APART

To prevent water from collecting beneath the jutting window frame, potentially causing wood rot, add a pine bark bed.

WINDOWS

Nothing affects your view of the outside world like your windows. When they're in good condition, they provide light and a view and add an open, airy feeling to the room. But when they're in bad shape, they waste energy and can detract severely from the appearance of your home. This chapter offers advice for keeping your windows looking good and operating smoothly, including replacing glass and glazing, repairing torn screens, fixing broken sash cords and making double-hung windows removable for easy cleaning.

Q **How do you decide whether to repair windows or replace them?**
I like my double-hung windows, but the sashes are in terrible shape. Most are painted shut and need new sash weight ropes. They all need to be reglazed. What little putty is left has dried and cracked. Some of the sashes need to be rebuilt, and a couple are so warped or rotten that they need to be replaced. Would it be cheaper to repair them, or should I break down and buy new windows?

WHEN WINDOWS ARE RIPE FOR REPLACEMENT

AIR LEAKS AROUND FRAME AND SASH
MUNTIN (GRILL)
INEFFICIENT SINGLE GLAZING
DRY OR MISSING GLAZING COMPOUND
UNINSULATED WEIGHT CAVITY
SASH WEIGHT
ROTTEN SILLS AND SASH

SASH STICKS OR IS PAINTED SHUT
UPPER SASH
LOOSE SASH JOINTS
LOWER SASH
PARTING STRIP
STOP
MISSING OR FAILED WEATHER-STRIPPING
FRAME
NEEDS WEIGHT-ROPE REPLACEMENT

A Your decision depends largely on how much work you're willing to do and how much money you're willing to spend, but you should definitely consider replacing your windows if:

☞ They are in poor condition. (Glazing compound is dried, cracked or missing; there are too many layers of paint, or paint is peeling; sills or sashes are rotted; sash joints are loose; sashes are painted shut; repairs are too time consuming or expensive.)

☞ They waste energy. (Windows contain single glazing; frames leak air; weight cavities are uninsulated; weather stripping is inadequate or non-existent.)

☞ They are unattractive or out of date, or you want to change the size of a window.

☞ They are inconvenient. (Old rope-weight system requires maintenance; new windows offer tilt-in sash for cleaning and easy sash removal for painting.)

In these cases, new windows will pay off. They improve energy efficiency (cost savings vary depending on climate, your heating/cooling system, overall energy efficiency of your house, etc.), increase your property value and reduce maintenance expenses.

On the other hand, if the frames and sills are generally in good condition, and if you want the same size and style as the double-hung window you have now, it's cheaper to replace only the sash (especially if you order unfinished sashes and paint them yourself), and the labor savings can be very significant. Inconvenience is minimized as well. Many sash replacement options are available, including:

☞ Wood sash or all-vinyl units

☞ Maintenance-free vinyl or aluminum-clad exterior

☞ Primed exterior

WINDOWS

☞ Prefinished (painted) exterior

☞ Primed interior

☞ Vinyl balance color (white or a neutral color)

☞ True divided-light sash

☞ Snap-in grills

☞ Single or insulating double glazing

☞ Low-E insulating glazing

☞ Argon-filled, insulating low-E glazing

☞ Locking hardware (white, brass-colored)

☞ Sash-lift hardware or handhold grooves in rails

☞ Screens (white or mill-finish aluminum)

☞ Replaceable or non-replaceable glazing

Several window manufacturers offer replacement kits that include new vinyl balances and wood sashes that tilt in for cleaning. Although they aren't quite as energy efficient as new window units, which include the sash, frame and glazing, they offer an easy way to replace the sash without disturbing the frame and trim.

To replace a sash you first have to remove the existing one, along with the rope-weight system. Then it is a matter of screwing in a few clips, snapping on balances, tilting windows in place and reinstalling the stops.

Instead of fixing broken sash-weight ropes, you can try installing new aluminum balances. They look great, but they may not work as well as the rope-weight systems.

If you want to change the window size or style, you'll have to buy a new unit. Even if you want the same style but are planning major exterior or interior remodeling, you're probably better off with new windows. Resizing can be done without too much additional trouble or expense.

Q How do I replace broken glass in windows?

A Homeowners who take care of small repairs around the house should have no trouble with glazing — installing glass in a frame. There are two basic glass-related repairs: replacing broken glass and replacing glazing.

The glass in most older windows is held in place by glazing compound. Newer insulated glass units and some storm windows use vinyl bead, and divided-light or multipane glass doors use wood stops called glazing beads. Some storm sashes have a grooved frame that must be disassembled to remove the glass.

Whether you can reglaze in place or remove the sash depends on the type of sash, how much repair is required and whether you're comfortable working from a ladder. Storm windows and storm door sashes are easily removed for repair, as are glass doors and casement windows. Removing a double-hung sash is more involved. Some of the newer insulated glass units are not designed for glass unit replacement. Instead, the whole sash usually must be replaced (which is convenient and economical, but wasteful).

To reglaze a window, first put on heavy gloves and remove any loose pieces of broken glass. If the glass is cracked, don't break it; you might damage the frame. Remove the glazing beads (wood or vinyl) or glazing compound. Glazing beads can be pried free after you run a knife blade along any paint-sealed joint to minimize damage.

Removing putty

Old glazing compound or putty is often very hard and brittle and can be difficult to remove. Professionals use heating irons to soften glazing compound, but the irons are expensive. A heat gun with a window attachment that deflects heat away from the glass will soften the compound (photo 1, right). But beware: When the compound is very hard and dry, it requires so much heat to soften that the glass can still get hot enough to crack.

To pry out heat-softened putty, draw the corner of the chisel-end of a glazing tool or stiff putty knife between the putty and frame. Then lay the tool on the glass, parallel to the muntin or frame, and chisel between the glass and putty.

You can do without heat if you exercise special care. An unconventional but effective approach is to carefully position a metal straightedge at the putty/frame joint and lightly and repeatedly draw a utility knife between the putty and the wood (photo 2). Follow by chiseling between the glass and the putty. A more conventional technique is to work the corner of a putty knife into the putty-frame joint (photo 3), separating the putty from the frame; then finish removing the putty as described above. Remove any glazier's points (triangular headless "nails" that hold glass in place) from the frame.

3 WAYS TO REMOVE OLD PUTTY

1 *If available, use a heat gun equipped with a heat deflector to soften glazing putty.*

2 *A knife and straightedge are very effective if you align the straightedge at the joint and use a light touch with the knife.*

3 *Use a glazing tool, a stiff putty knife or an old chisel to carefully pry old compound away from the frame and the glass.*

Buying glass

Standard window glass is sold in two thicknesses: single and double strength. As a rule, use double strength for glass sizes over 200 sq. in. Cutting is figured into the price. Tempered (heat-strengthened) glass — the type used in patio doors, windows that extend below 18 in. from the floor and some overhead glazing — cannot be cut. You must order it to size. Insulated glass units also must be ordered to size. Large pieces of glass require special handling, and installation is best left to a professional.

Cutting glass

Although most glass is purchased cut-to-size, a do-it-yourselfer may have some old glass around for repairs. It's fairly easy to cut glass — all you need are a glass cutter, a straightedge and a permanent marker, and gloves and eye protection for safety.

Glass is cut by scoring the surface and breaking along the score line. Lay the glass on a clean, flat surface (a piece of plywood or a workbench top) and against a wood stop screwed to the work surface (photo 4). Measure and mark the cut with a fine-point permanent marker. If you have kerosene, apply some along the cut line; then, using firm, even pressure, draw the cutter across the glass and off the end in a continuous motion. (Practice on scraps beforehand.) Never rescore. Lay the glass with the scored line over a pencil and press down at opposite edges (photo 5). Smooth any rough edges with a whetstone or a belt sander.

Before you reglaze, clean the glass and the frame. (There's a powder on

CUTTING GLASS

4 *Use the wood stop to align your straightedge; then tape the straightedge to the glass.*

5 *Place scored glass over a pencil and press lightly on both sides to break it. Wear gloves, just in case.*

REINSTALLING GLASS

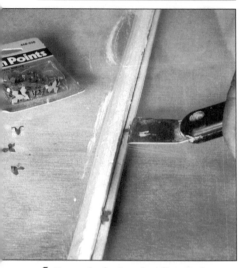

6 Press glazier's points flat against the glass and into the wood frame every 6 in. or so. Use a least two for each side.

7 Smooth the glazing compound with a single corner-to-corner pass. The wood frame should be primed before glazing.

new glass to keep sheets from sticking together.) If the frame is not primed, apply a coat of paint or linseed oil. Set the glass (which should be cut 1/16 to 1/8 in. smaller than the opening) in the frame and push glazing points into the frame (photo 6). Roll the compound into a ropelike length and press it in place with your fingers; then smooth it at the appropriate angle with a glazing tool or putty knife (photo 7). Wait a day to paint with oil- or alkyd-based paints. If you're using latex paint, wait at least a week.

Q How do I replace the seal in an aluminum-frame window?

A One of the most common types of aluminum-frame residential windows is single-hung with vinyl glazing beads holding the glass in place (see drawing, opposite page). Glass is mounted in other sliding metal-frame windows in a similar manner. If the glazing bead is relatively new, you may be able to release it from its groove by pressing down and toward the center of the glass. Otherwise the bead must be pried out or cut. Occasionally, with insulating-glass units, a leg of the bead will stick to the glazing sealant, making it difficult to remove the bead without damaging it. With older windows, the bead may be brittle and need to be replaced.

Almost every manufacturer uses a different glazing bead, and only large metropolitan glazing stores (or the window manufacturer) are likely to carry the right bead for a particular window, so bring a sample.

While you're working on your

SEALING GLASS IN ALUMINUM-FRAME WINDOWS

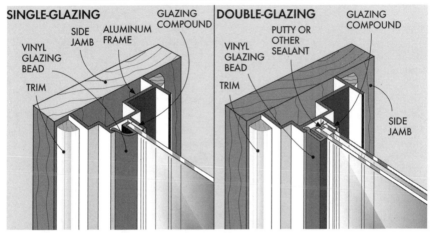

SINGLE-GLAZING

VINYL GLAZING BEAD

TRIM

SIDE JAMB

ALUMINUM FRAME

GLAZING COMPOUND

DOUBLE-GLAZING

VINYL GLAZING BEAD

TRIM

PUTTY OR OTHER SEALANT

GLAZING COMPOUND

SIDE JAMB

In most single-pane metal-frame windows (left), a glazing bead holds the glass in place in the frame. Double-pane window glass (right) is mounted in a similar manner. To install new glazing bead, carefully remove the old bead and clean the frame and glass; then install the new bead with the glass.

window, check the condition of the window-frame trim and replace or caulk as needed.

Q How do I fix holes in my screens? Can I patch them, or do I have to replace the screening?

A You can make an almost invisible patch on one or two small holes in metal and fiberglass screening with a clear-drying waterproof glue, such as epoxy or cyanoacrylate (Super Glue). To patch larger holes in metal screening, bend the end wires on a small piece of screening and push it over the hole; then crimp the ends to hold the patch in place. These patches are unsightly, however, so they should be used only until you have time to replace the screening.

Whoops! Accidents happen. But with the right tools and materials, replacing torn screening is simple and inexpensive.

Selecting screening

If you're replacing only one or two screens, choose a screening that matches your existing screening. However, if you're planning to replace many screens, you may prefer to work with a certain material. Aluminum is stronger than fiberglass and is a good choice for doors or screened porches because of the abuse they must withstand. On the other hand, fiberglass tends to return to its original shape after it has been bumped, and it's easier to install, especially when it's being rolled into a channel.

If you're replacing all of your window or porch screens, consider using metal or fiberglass solar/insect screening. It not only keeps out insects but also blocks most of the sun's heat and glare.

Screening wood frames

The only tools you'll need to replace screening on a porch or in a removable wood frame are a stapler, hammer, utility knife and tin snips (for aluminum screening). All the tools and the screening materials are available in hardware stores and home centers.

FIXED FRAME

WOOD FRAME STAPLING SEQUENCE

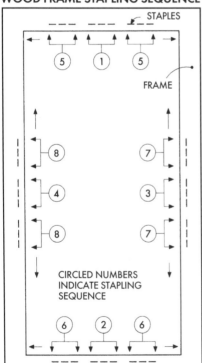

Cut the screening oversize and begin stapling at the top and bottom; then staple the sides in sequence. Work from the center outward. Drive a few staples at a time spaced 2 in. apart. Pull the screening taut as you staple it to the frame, but do not distort the weave.

REMOVABLE FRAME

Place strips of 3/4-in.-thick wood under the ends of removable wood frames; then clamp the center of the frame so it bows slightly. Staple the ends of the screening first; then staple the sides. When you release the frame, the screening will be stretched taut.

To begin, remove the old screen molding, screen and staples. If the frame needs repainting, now is the time to do it. When the paint is dry, cut the screen slightly longer than needed; then staple the screening to the face of the frame (or in a rabbet around the inside perimeter), stretching it as you go. Cover the staples with half-round molding or screen molding nailed to the frame.

Using clamps to bow the frame makes it easy to replace screening in smaller wood frames. If you prefer to leave the frame flat, use the stapling sequence shown in the drawing.

Aluminum frames

The only tools you'll need to replace screening in an aluminum frame are a screen roller, utility knife and tin snips (for aluminum screening). If the frame for an aluminum combination storm window is dam-

MAKE AN ALUMINUM FRAME

1 *Cut the channel at a 45-degree angle with a power miter saw equipped with an aluminum-cutting (carbide-tipped) blade. You can also use a hacksaw and miter box.*

2 *Smooth rough edges with a file; then snap the corner keys into the ends of the channels to hold the frame together.*

INSTALLING AN ALUMINUM WINDOW SCREEN FRAME

To install an aluminum-frame screen, slide it into friction swivel hangers (Detail 1); then secure the screen to the window sill with one or two bale latches hooked on ball-headed screws (Detail 3) or with plunger bolts installed in the sides of the screen frame (Detail 2).

FRICTION SIDE HANGER

WINDOW FRAME

STOP

DETAIL 1

SCREEN FRAME

BORE HOLE IN WINDOW FRAME

PLUNGER BOLT

DETAIL 2

DRIVE SCREW INTO WINDOW SILL

SCREEN FRAME

DETAIL 3

BALE SCREEN LATCH WITH SCREW

WINDOW SCREEN

aged, you'll probably need to take it to a repair shop because the parts are not generally available to consumers. Window and screen repair shops and many hardware stores can do this for you.

You can make your own simple aluminum screen frames with parts or kits sold in home centers and hardware stores (photos 1,2, p. 97). The screens can be installed in window frames with hardware available in hardware stores and home centers (see drawing, above).

To hold the top of the screen, attach friction side hangers to the top inside edges of the window casing (Detail 1). For side latching, bore holes through the sides of the screen frame and attach it to the window frame with plunger bolts (Detail 2). To secure the screen to the sill, attach two bale latches to the screen and hook them on ball-headed screws driven into the sill (Detail 3).

Replacing screening

To remove old screening from aluminum frames, pry the spline out of the channel. Vinyl spline should be replaced, but metal splines should be pried out carefully so they can be reused.

To replace aluminum screening, roll it into the frame beginning at one corner; then roll in the spline (photos 3-5, right). Fiberglass screening and spline are rolled into the groove simultaneously (photo 6, far right top). Except for the corners of aluminum screening, which are cut at 45 degrees as it is installed, both types of screening are cut to exact size after installation (photo 7).

SCREENING WITH ALUMINUM

3 Align the screening on the frame so that it overlaps the grooves. Cut the beginning corner at a 45-degree angle 1/8 in. past the groove. Crimp the aluminum screening into the groove with the convex end of the screening tool. Cleats keep the frame from bending.

4 Stop rolling just short of the next corner. Clip the screen at this corner at 45 degrees; then continue rolling to the next corner.

5 Next, roll in vinyl spline with the concave end of the roller (or press in a metal spline). Cut excess screening next to the spline with a utility knife (see photo 7).

SCREENING WITH FIBERGLASS

6 Cut the screening oversize; then roll it and the spline into place simultaneously. Start at the top of the frame; then roll in the bottom followed by the sides. It's not necessary to clip corners.

7 After the spline is installed, trim the excess screening with a utility knife. To avoid a mishap, hold the knife so the blade faces the outside of the frame and cut the screening at an angle.

Q Can I replace broken window-sash cords without removing the interior trim around the window units?

A Older double-hung window units have a space called a sash weight channel or pocket between the wall stud and the window frame side jamb (see drawing, right). Cast-iron weights are attached to the window sash by ropes or sash cords, which run over metal pulleys at the top of the side jambs. The weights move up and down within the pockets as the windows are opened and closed. The sash cords wear from friction and must be replaced when they break.

Often, there are small doors or covers cut into the side jambs near the bottom of the sash channel. The pocket covers may be friction-fit or held in place with a screw. Raise the lower window sash and look for a pocket cover. (It may be partially hidden with paint.) If pocket covers are present, you can replace the cords without removing the inside frame or casing from the window.

The inside stops, which hold the window in place, must always be removed to replace the sash. Before prying out the stops, use a utility knife to cut the paint film between the stops and the window frame. Then gently pry the stops away from the frame. If there is a metal weather strip, remove it so you can pull the window sash out of the frame.

When you remove the pocket cover you'll have access to the weight channel, and you can remove the old sash cord and the weight. Thread a new sash cord over the pul-

REPLACING WINDOW SASH CORDS

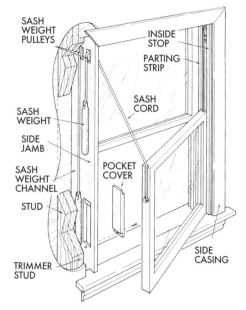

If your double-hung windows have a pocket cover, you need only remove the inside stop parting strip and sash to replace the cords. Otherwise, you must also remove the side casing to access the weights.

ley; then push the end of the sash cord into the pocket far enough for you to grasp the end.

Tie the end of the cord to the weight. Set the window sash on the sill, pull the sash cord tight and cut the cord so it reaches 3 in. past the retaining groove in the side of the window sash. Cut the cord long enough so the weight is opposite the pocket door when the lower sash is fully open. (The weight should not hit the bottom of the pocket.) Tie a knot in the end of the sash cord and push the knot into the groove in the edge of the window sash. Do this on both sides of the window.

To replace the sash cords on the upper sash, it's necessary to remove the parting strip before removing the sash. The sash cord replacement technique is the same as for the lower sash.

If there are no pocket covers, you must remove the casing from the sides of the window to gain access to the sash weights. Otherwise, the replacement procedure is the same.

When you've finished replacing the cords, replace the pocket cover or casing. Push the window sash (and any metal weather strip) into place, and replace the parting strip, inside stop and outside trim.

Q How do I keep new double-hung windows operating smoothly?

A Double-hung windows are the most common type in American homes. Because they consist of many moving parts, including two framed glass panels (sashes), vertical channels and a balance system that holds the window in any position, double-hung windows are prone to breaking down. Sashes that are painted shut or plagued by a failed balance system, especially the rope in a weighted balance, are the two most common problems.

Regular lubrication of metal parts with a spray lubricant such as WD-40 and application of paraffin or candle wax to moving wood parts helps keep these window operating smoothly for years.

Sash removal

To repair or replace a balance,

you must remove the sash. Although a stuck window can often be freed by simply breaking the paint bond between the sash and the stops and the sash and the parting strip (photos 1,2, below), more often the best repair involves removing the sash from the frame (photos 3-6, p. 102). Once the sash has been removed, you can scrape paint from it and the channel. If necessary, do any touch-up painting before reinstalling the sash.

UNSTICK A WINDOW

1 Drive a putty knife between the sash and the stops, both inside and out, to break a paint bond.

2 If the sash remains stuck, pry it up from the outside. Use a fulcrum block and pry only near the stiles, not in the center of the window.

HOW TO REMOVE A SASH

3 *To limit paint damage when removing a stop, make several light passes with a utility knife to cut through the paint.*

4 *After clearing paint from screw heads, remove stop screws or, if stops are nailed in, use a trim prybar to pry the stops off.*

5 *Pry out nails that fasten metal channel weather stripping. At least one side must be free to come out with the sash.*

6 *With the lower sash removed and the upper one fully lowered, score the paint line; then grasp the parting strip with a padded locking plier and pull it out.*

AN ALTERNATIVE BALANCE SYSTEM

7 *An alternative balance system requires that you plow a channel in the sash to accept the new balance. Use a dado head on a table saw to make the channel.*

8 *After insulating the wall cavities, set the sashes and the new balance into the frame; then replace the interior stops.*

DOUBLE-HUNG WINDOW WITH WEIGHTED BALANCE SYSTEM

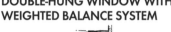

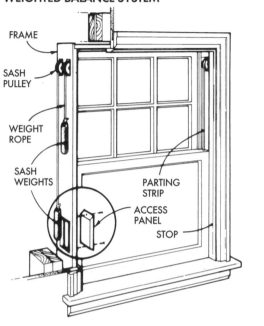

FRAME

SASH PULLEY

WEIGHT ROPE

SASH WEIGHTS

PARTING STRIP

ACCESS PANEL

STOP

SPIRAL SPRING LIFT

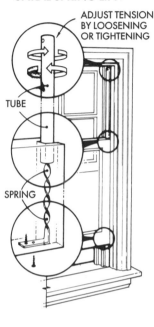

ADJUST TENSION BY LOOSENING OR TIGHTENING

TUBE

SPRING

REPLACING WEIGHTS WITH A SPRING TENSION

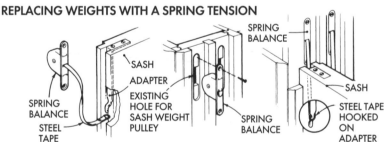

SPRING BALANCE

SASH

ADAPTER

EXISTING HOLE FOR SASH WEIGHT PULLEY

SPRING BALANCE

STEEL TAPE

SPRING BALANCE

SASH

STEEL TAPE HOOKED ON ADAPTER

Each balance system requires you to remove the sash to make repairs. Top left: When a weighted balance breaks, a broken rope is usually the culprit. It can be replaced with rope or chain. Top right: Twist the metal tube of a spiral spring lift to tighten or loosen the spring. Above: A spring balance can be installed to replace a weight system.

When you remove a window, take a little extra time for other repairs and maintenance: Clean and lubricate the metal pulley or spiral rods, replace the ropes and clean the outside of the glass.

Repairing balance systems

A balance system lets you operate a window with relative ease, but it has its drawbacks. To remove a sash so you can replace a rope that is broken or caked with paint, you have to remove the trim. No matter how careful you are, you'll either have to repaint the trim or replace it entirely if it breaks. Another problem is that the wall cavity occupied by the weights and ropes — about 50 to 100 sq. ft. of exterior wall for each window — is uninsulated.

A spring-tension channel like the one by Quaker City Manufacturing (see photos 7,8, p. 102) can replace weighted systems and allows you to stuff fiberglass insulation into the cavities, reducing energy loss. To install spring-tension channels, first remove the sash, parting strips and pulleys. Then slip the sash into the new aluminum channels and set the assembly into the window frame against the exterior stop. Tension is increased by positioning the inside stop closer to the channel.

Another option that allows you to insulate the wall cavities is replacing the weight system with spring balances. The spring balances simply replace the pulleys and are relatively easy to install (drawing, p. 103).

If you want to repair a weighted system rather than replace it, first remove the sash, disconnect the ropes and lower the weights into the cavity. Open the access panels and thread new rope or chain into the cavities through each pulley.

Attach each rope or chain to its weight. Finally, attach the rope to the sash by setting the knotted end into the hole and securing it with a couple of small common nails. Attach a chain with a screw through one link.

Spiral lifts can fail when the screws that attach the lift to the bottom of the window come loose. You'll have to remove the sash and

fill the screw holes with small-diameter dowels and then replace the screws. Adjust the tension by twisting the metal tube that houses the spring to tighten or loosen the spring before screwing the top into the window frame.

TRICKY SITUATIONS

Q Can I install combination storm windows over my vinyl replacement windows? I want to install triple-track aluminum storm windows over my vinyl replacement windows so I can improve cross-ventilation, particularly during rain storms, by leaving the storm window open at the bottom and the window open at the top. But local window installers say they cannot do it. Why not?

A First, there may be physical limitations. Combination storm windows are normally screwed to the exterior of the blind stop, and a standard-size storm and screen sash would probably be too large to fit into the vinyl window frame. In some cases the extruded track that holds the window screen may protrude too far and interfere with normal installation. Sometimes these problems can be overcome by using smaller storm windows and mounting them on the extruded screen track or by mounting the storm window on the exterior casing.

But the real problem is that excessive heat can build up between the windows and the storms and deform and ruin the vinyl. Although you might not have a problem if you have white windows and leave the storms open during the summer, some manufacturers will void the warranty if storm windows are installed. Check with your window manufacturer to learn the company's policy.

Q Can I remove just part of my steel sliding windows? The windows were made by Rusco Building Systems of Marion, Iowa. The window frame is sandwiched between an outer shell, which is nailed to the framing under the brick, and a sill-trim assembly, which overlaps the drywall. I want to remove the inner steel trim and leave the outer shell in place.

A You cannot remove only a part of the window you described; the entire window must be removed before a new wood or vinyl-frame window can be installed. It's a messy project that will involve some brick removal and possibly the installation of lintels. Although you'll probably be able to do part of the work yourself, you should consult a remodeling contractor who specializes in window replacement and a masonry contractor before deciding to tackle the job on your own.

Q Can I convert my double-hung windows to the tilt-in type?

A We don't know of a way to make your windows tilt in without replacing them. But if you don't mind replacing the channels on your old windows, you can add Quaker takeout window channels (see drawing, above right). The channels allow you

REMOVABLE DOUBLE-HUNG WINDOW

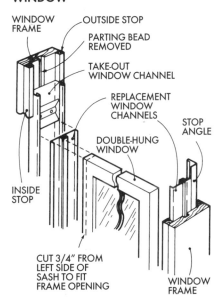

Nail the take-out channel to the left side of the window frame, flush against the outside stop; then insert the left replacement channel into the take-out channel. Nail the second replacement channel to the right side of the window frame.

to push the sash to one side and remove it. The system works only on wood windows.

Quaker take-out channels must be used with Quaker's spring-tension replacement window channels. Window preparation is the same as that described for installing the replacement channels. Then you add one take-out channel for each window. The sash must be trimmed 3/4 in. (from the left side) to fit into the new channel. To insert or remove the sash, push it against the spring tension of the take-out channel until the right side of the sash clears the trim and parting bead.

INDEX

INDEX

NOTES

NOTES

NOTES

Merrill

Physics

*Principles
and Problems*

CONTENT CONSULTANT

Frank Kokai
Physics Teacher
Upper Arlington High School
Upper Arlington, Ohio

GLENCOE

Macmillan/McGraw-Hill

New York, New York   Columbus, Ohio   Mission Hills, California   Peoria, Illinois

A Glencoe/McGraw-Hill Program

Merrill Physics: Principles & Problems

Student Edition
Teacher Wraparound Edition
Problems and Solutions Manual
Teacher Resource Package
Transparency Package
Laboratory Manual:
  Student and Teacher Editions

Study Guide, Student Edition
Lesson Plan Booklet
English/Spanish Glossary
Computer Test Bank

Four-section chapter tests correlated to student objectives are provided as a closure for each chapter. In addition, semester evaluation masters are also included in the booklet. The first semester evaluation covers chapters 1-13 and the second semester evaluation covers chapters 14-31. In each evaluation, Parts A and B test concepts qualitatively through the use of multiple-choice and brief essay questions. Parts C and D test concepts quantitatively through the use of problems. Some of the problems in Part D may apply concepts learned in previous chapters.

ISBN 0-02-826743-5

Copyright 1995, 1992, 1990 by the Glencoe Division of Macmillan/McGraw-Hill Publishing Company.

Send all inquiries to: **GLENCOE DIVISION, Macmillan/McGraw-Hill**
936 Eastwind Drive
Westerville, Ohio 43081

Printed in the United States of America

2 3 4 5 6 7 8 9 MAL 99 98 97 96 95

Contents

CHAPTER
1 Evaluation

WHAT IS PHYSICS?

A. Testing Concepts

In the space to the left, write the letter of the answer to each question.

1. _____ Which of the following are the results of the work of physicists?
   a. lasers   b. calculators   c. computers   d. all of the above

2. _____ The BCS theory was developed to explain how
   a. superconductors work   b. magnets attract matter
   c. generators work   d. to build an atomic bomb.

3. _____ Absolute zero is the
   a. highest possible temperature at which matter freezes   b. lowest possible
   temperature at which materials conduct electricity   c. highest possible temperature at
   which materials conduct electricity   d. lowest possible temperature for matter.

4. _____ Which of the following is called the language of physics?
   a. biology   b. engineering   c. mathematics   d. chemistry

5. _____ Physics is the study of
   a. matter and cells   b. energy and heat
   c. energy and atoms   d. matter and energy.

6. _____ Why is the work of theoretical physicists in superconductivity not finished?
   a. Superconductors have not yet been produced.   b. Absolute zero has not yet been
   reached.   c. There is no complete explanation of how new superconductors work.
   d. Room-temperature superconductors have not yet been produced.

7. _____ Aristotle believed that all matter was composed of
   a. atoms   b. energy   c. four elements   d. motion.

8. _____ Aristotle and his followers were mainly concerned with finding out
   a. when specific events occur   b. why specific events occur
   c. how specific events occur   d. all of the above.

9. _____ One of the first European scientists to claim publicly that knowledge must be based on
   observations and experiments was
   a. Albert Einstein   b. Aristotle   c. Heike Kamerlingh Onnes   d. Galileo Galilei.

10. _____ A surprising aspect of physics is that its results can be described by a small number of
    relationships, or
    a. laws   b. earthly elements   c. rules   d. theories.

B. Applying Concepts

Answer the following questions in two or three complete sentences.

1. What problem with early superconductors has been eliminated by the discovery of new superconductors that work at higher temperatures?

2. Explain the difference between an experimental physicist and a theoretical physicist.

3. What is the difference between a theory and a law in physics?

4. What are some personality traits that aid physicists in their work?

5. Why is an understanding of physics a benefit to all citizens?

6. Name two views held by Galileo that differed from those held by scientists who had gone before him.

7. How is the way all scientists study problems similar?

CHAPTER

2 Evaluation

A MATHEMATICAL TOOLKIT

A. Testing Concepts

In the space to the left, write the letter of the answer to each question.

1. _____ The fundamental SI unit for time is the
   a. minute   b. day   c. second   d. hour.

2. _____ In scientific notation, a number between 1 and 10 is multiplied by
   a. a whole-number power of 10   b. a fraction   c. 10   d. any whole number.

3. _____ The metric prefix that means 100 is
   a. pico   b. nano   c. centi   d. hecto.

4. _____ When multiplying quantities expressed in scientific notation ($M \times 10^n$) that have different exponents, you multiply the values of M and _____ the exponents.
   a. add   b. multiply   c. subtract   d. divide

5. _____ To avoid parallax errors, laboratory instruments should be read
   a. at eye level   b. from the side   c. below eye level   d. at all of these positions.

6. _____ The degree of exactness to which the measurement of a quantity can be reproduced is called
   a. accuracy   b. precision   c. parallax   d. none of the above.

7. _____ When adding or subtracting measurements, first perform the operation and then round off the result to correspond to the _____ value involved.
   a. most precise   b. largest   c. least precise   d. smallest

8. _____ A variable that can be manipulated in an experiment is
   a. a dependent variable   b. an independent variable
   c. a responding variable   d. none of the above.

9. _____ When constructing a graph from data, the range of the x-axis is determined by the range of the
   a. independent variable   b. dependent variable
   c. combined range of the independent variable and dependent variable   d. origin.

10. _____ What is indicated by a smooth, upward curving line on a graph?
    a. a linear relationship between x and y b. an inverse relationship between x and y
    c. a direct relationship between y and with the square of x
    d. No relationship between x and y is indicated.

11. _____ The slope of a straight-line graph is the vertical change _____ the horizontal change.
    a. minus   b. added to   c. divided by   d. multiplied by

12. _____ A graph that is a hyperbola represents _____ relationship.
    a. an inverse   b. a quadratic   c. a linear   d. no

13. _____ To solve the equation $vt = d$ for t,
    a. multiply both sides of the equation by v b. add v to both sides of the equation
    c. divide both sides of the equation by v d. divide both sides of the equation by t.

14. _____ An equation is wrong if both sides contain
    a. different variables   b. the same variable
    c. different units of measure   d. the same unit of measure.

2 Evaluation

B. Applying Concepts

Answer the following questions in two or three complete sentences.

1. Describe the relationship between fundamental units and derived units.

2. Which of the following length measurements are equivalent?
   a. 5687 nm   b. 568.7 km   c. 0.000 568 7 dag   d. 0.000 056 87 dm

3. Which of the following is a more precise measurement, the length of a car measured to the nearest meter or measured to the nearest millimeter? Explain your answer.

4. Explain the difference between accuracy and precision.

5. State the number of significant digits in each of the following measurements.
   a. 3809 m   b. 9.013 m   c. 0.0045 m

6. Which of the following measurements contains zeros that are *not* significant? Explain your answer.
   a. 3.050 × 10.5   b. 0.0053 m   c. 45.020 cm   d. 101.20 g

7. How are independent and dependent variables related? Identify the graph axis on which each type of variable would be plotted.

2 Evaluation

C. Understanding Concepts

1. Express the following measurements in scientific notation.
   a. 142 000 s   b. 0.008 09 kg   c. 501 000 000 m

2. Solve the following problems. Express your answers in scientific notation using the correct number of significant digits.

   a. $(2 \times 10^6 \text{ m})(5 \times 10^5 \text{ m})$

   b. $(12 \times 10^6 \text{ m})/(4 \times 10^2 \text{ s})$

   c. $(5.06 \times 10^2 \text{ m}) + (8.124 \text{ km})$

3. Describe the relationship between the variables shown in the graph below. Identify the general equation that is used to represent this type of relationship.

4. Identify the slope and y-intercept of the equation $y = 3x + 6$.

5. Solve each equation for x.

   a. $p = rx$ c. $b = \dfrac{x - d}{y}$

   b. $w = \dfrac{s}{x}$

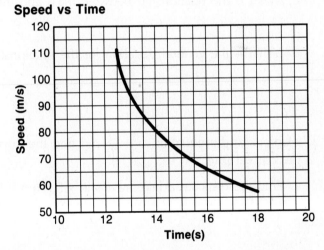

6. Write an equation using the variables M and P to represent the following sentence: "Twice Peter's age is equal to one-fourth Mary's age."

7. If $v = 15.5$ m/s and $t = 12$ s, find d using $d = vt$. Include the correct units in your answer.

D. Extending Concepts

1. The total mass of four containers is 5.000 kg. If the mass of Container **A** is 256 mg, Container **B** is 5117 cg, and Container **C** is 382 g, what is the mass of Container **D**?

2. The results of a class experiment investigating the relationship between mass and acceleration are shown in the table below. The force applied to each mass remained constant.

Mass (g)	Acceleration (m/s²)
0.5	6.0
1.0	3.0
1.5	2.0
2.0	1.5
2.5	1.25
3.0	1.0

a. Plot the values given and draw the curve that best fits the points.

b. Describe the resulting curve.

c. What is the relationship between mass and the acceleration produced by a constant force?

d. What is the general equation for the relationship shown in the graph?

3. Manipulate the equation $v = \dfrac{d}{t}$ and find the answers to each problem. Express each answer in the correct unit.

a. Find the distance a bike travels in 4.50 min if it is traveling at a constant speed of 20.0 km/h.

b. How long would it take a car to travel 6.0×10^3 m if its speed is a constant 30.0 km/h?

CHAPTER

3 Evaluation

DESCRIBING MOTION: VELOCITY

A. Testing Concepts

In the space to the left, write the letter of the answer to each question.

1. _____ A runner is 5.0 km east of another runner, who is 5.0 km east of a parking lot. Where is the first runner with respect to the parking lot?
   a. +5.0 km from the lot   b. +10.0 km from the lot   c. −5.0 km from the lot
   d. −10.0 km from the lot

2. _____ The parking lot mentioned above is
   a. a distance between the two runners   b. a position separating the two runners
   c. the displacement between the two runners   d. a reference point for the runners.

3. _____ Distance is a quantity that
   a. always needs a reference point   b. is always a vector   c. has only magnitude
   d. is always positive.

4. _____ A cyclist finishes a 100-km race in 2.7 hours. The average velocity
   a. equals the displacement divided by the total time
   b. equals the time divided by the displacement
   c. equals the greatest speed divided by the total time.

5. _____ If the average velocity of an object is the same for all time intervals, then the object moves at a(n)
   a. constant velocity   b. instantaneous velocity   c. changing speed   d. relative speed.

6. _____ On a position-time graph, the velocity equals
   a. the x-intercept   b. the y-intercept   c. the rise divided by the run
   d. the run divided by the rise.

7. _____ Using _____ rise and run will result in the most accurate slope on a position-time graph.
   a. an average   b. the smallest   c. the largest

8. _____ A runner traveled 15 km east then backtracked 11 km before stopping. The displacement from the original position is
   a. +26.0 km   b. −4.0 km   c. +4.0 km   d. −26.0 km.

9. _____ The _____ of any point on a velocity-time graph equals the instantaneous velocity at the time.
   a. slope of the tangent   b. displacement   c. horizontal value   d. vertical value

10. _____ The area under the curve on a velocity-time graph equals the
    a. rise divided by the run   b. displacement from the original position to its position at time *t*
    c. relative velocity   d. instantaneous velocity.

11. _____ A child on a bicycle rides eastward past a house, as a car, also traveling eastward, slowly passes. Which of the following people would perceive the biker as having the greatest velocity?
    a. the biker   b. the driver of the car   c. a person in the house   d. all of the above

12. _____ The slope of the tangent on a position-time graph equals the
    a. average speed   b. constant speed   c. average velocity   d. instantaneous velocity.

B. Applying Concepts

Answer the following questions in two or three complete sentences.

1. In terms of graphing, distinguish between average velocity and instantaneous velocity.

2. When does an object move at a constant velocity?

3. Show mathematically that an object can have a negative position but a positive velocity.

4. On a position-time graph, compare the instantaneous velocities of an object when the tangent to the curve slopes upward to the right, when the tangent slopes downward to the right, and when the tangent is horizontal.

5. A stunt car is driven along a flat train car. The stunt car is moving toward the engine of the train. How would you calculate the velocity of the stunt car relative to Earth?

6. Suppose a runner is running aboard an ocean liner at +12 km/h toward the southeast. What is the velocity of the ocean liner relative to the runner?

C. Understanding Concepts

1. After 16.5 s, a jogger's displacement is 200.0 m. What is the average velocity in m/s? In km/h?

2. The data shown represent a series of readings taken by a motorcyclist. Find the average velocity during each 2-second interval.

Time (s)	Position (m)
0.0	+0.0
2.0	+0.0
4.0	+2.0
6.0	+5.0
8.0	+10.0
10.0	+15.0
12.0	+20.0

3. Find the average velocity of the cyclist between 2.0 and 8.0 s.

4. Use the following data to make a velocity-time graph.

Time (s)	Velocity (m/s)
0	20
2	20
5	20
6	30
7	35
8	40
10	30
11	15
12	10

5. Describe the velocity of the object using the graph you made for Problem 4.

6. Use the graph to find the displacement in the first 5 s.

D. Extending Concepts

1. A "moving sidewalk" in a busy airport terminal moves 1.0 m/s and is 200.0 m long. A passenger steps onto one end and walks, in the same direction as the sidewalk is moving, at a rate of 2.0 m/s relative to the moving sidewalk. How much time does it take the passenger to reach the opposite end of the walkway?

2. Suppose another passenger gets on one end of the same "moving sidewalk" and walks at a rate of 2.0 m/s relative to the moving sidewalk but in a direction opposite to that of the sidewalk. How much time does it take this passenger to reach the opposite end of the walkway?

3. If the two passengers step on the moving sidewalk at the same time, how far will the second passenger have moved, relative to the sidewalk, when the first passenger steps off the sidewalk?

4. The following data show velocity readings taken every 5 s. Prepare a position-time graph for the data. Assume uniform acceleration.

Time (s)	Velocity (m/s)
0.0	0.0
5.0	6.2
10.0	12.4
15.0	22.0
20.0	22.0
25.0	18.0
30.0	18.0

CHAPTER

4 Evaluation

ACCELERATION

A. Testing Concepts

In the space to the left, write the letter of the answer to each question.

1. _____ The change in a runner's velocity with time is the runner's
   a. average velocity   b. instantaneous velocity   c. average acceleration
   d. instantaneous acceleration.

2. _____ A child lets go of a ball at the top of a driveway. The instantaneous velocity of the ball as the child lets go is
   a. zero   b. positive   c. negative.

3. _____ On a velocity-time graph, the slope of the tangent to the curve at a given point is the
   a. average velocity   b. average acceleration   c. instantaneous velocity
   d. instantaneous acceleration.

4. _____ Constant acceleration on a velocity-time graph produces a curve that is
   a. half a parabola   b. a straight line   c. parallel to the horizontal axis
   d. parallel to the vertical axis.

5. _____ The area under a curve on a velocity-time graph for an object moving with a uniform acceleration is the _____ of that object.
   a. displacement   b. position   c. velocity   d. acceleration

6. _____ The slope of a position-time graph is the _____ of an object.
   a. displacement   b. velocity   c. acceleration   d. mass

7. _____ Which of the following best describes the relationship between the final and initial velocities of a uniformly accelerating object?
   a. The final velocity increases as the initial velocity decreases.   b. The final velocity decreases as the initial velocity increases.   c. The final velocity increases as the initial velocity increases.

8. _____ Ignoring air resistance, if a 10-kg ball and a 200-kg crate were both dropped from the top of a building, the acceleration of the crate would be _____ the acceleration of the ball.
   a. greater than   b. less than   c. equal to

9. _____ In Greenland, the acceleration due to gravity is _____ the acceleration due to gravity at Earth's equator.
   a. greater than   b. less than   c. equal to

10. _____ A toy rocket is launched straight up into the air. When the rocket reaches its maximum height, its velocity is
    a. at its maximum   b. at its minimum   c. equal to its displacement multiplied by time
    d. equal to its displacement divided by time.

11. _____ The total displacement of the toy rocket upon landing is
    a. zero   b. equal to the distance it traveled up   c. equal to the distance it traveled up multiplied by 2   d. equal to the difference between the final and initial velocities divided by the acceleration due to gravity.

4 Evaluation

NAME _____

B. Applying Concepts

Answer the following questions in two or three complete sentences.

1. After making a delivery, a truck driver must maneuver the vehicle backwards down a narrow ramp. The speed of the truck increases with distance down the ramp. Describe the truck's acceleration.

2. How can you find the instantaneous acceleration of an object whose curve on the velocity-time graph is a straight line?

3. Suppose an object starts at rest. Explain how the displacement of the object, which has a constant acceleration, can be determined from a velocity-time graph.

4. Describe the curve on a position-time graph of an object with a constant velocity. How does the curve differ for an object that is accelerating constantly?

5. Derive an equation for determining displacement when velocity and acceleration are known.

6. How is the acceleration of an object in freefall related to acceleration due to gravity?

7. In your own words, state the first and last steps that are critical to solving any physics problem.

C. Understanding Concepts

1. A skateboard rider starts from rest and accelerates at a constant $+0.50$ m/s^2 for 8.4 s. What is the rider's displacement during this time?

2. A sports car can move 100.0 m in the first 4.5 s of uniform acceleration. Find the car's acceleration.

3. A cyclist passes a race check point at $+5.5$ m/s and then accelerates at a constant rate of $+0.55$ m/s^2. The cyclist forgot to check in at the check point, and after 20.0 s turns around to head back. How far did the cyclist move from the check point to the point of turning back?

4. A rolling ball has an initial velocity of -1.63 m/s.

   a. If the ball accelerates at a constant rate of -0.33 m/s^2, what is its velocity after 3.6 s?

   b. If this acceleration occurs for another 2.8 s, what is the ball's final velocity?

5. A construction worker drops a tool from a bridge and it hits the river 3.60 s later. What is the displacement of the tool?

6. A jogger accelerates constantly to a velocity of 2.3 m/s in 6.5 s. After jogging 11 m, the jogger stops. What was the initial velocity of the jogger?

D. Extending Concepts

1. A car is traveling with a velocity of +88.0 km/h. It accelerates at a constant rate of −20.0 m/s^2. If the acceleration lasts for 5.60 s, what is the final velocity of the car?

2. A toy rocket is shot straight up into the air with an initial speed of 45.0 m/s.

   a. How long does it take the rocket to reach its highest point?

   b. How high does the rocket rise above the ground?

3. A bird drops an acorn from a tree branch that is 8.00 m from the ground.

   a. How long is the acorn in the air?

   b. What is its velocity when it reaches the ground?

4. Derive an equation to determine how long it takes a runner moving at 10.2 m/s on a circular track to go completely around the track once. The radius of the track is 25.0 m.

CHAPTER
5 Evaluation

FORCES

A. Testing Concepts

In the space to the left, write the letter of the answer to each question.

1. _____ The attractive force that acts between all objects is
   a. electromagnetic force   b. gravitational force
   c. strong nuclear force   d. weak nuclear force.

2. _____ The strongest force is
   a. electromagnetic force   b. gravitational force
   c. strong nuclear force   d. weak nuclear force.

3. _____ Metals such as copper can be pounded into thin sheets due to
   a. electromagnetic force   b. gravitational force
   c. strong nuclear force   d. weak nuclear force.

4. _____ According to Newton's _____ law, an object with no net force acting on it remains at rest or in motion with a constant velocity.
   a. first   b. second   c. third

5. _____ Newton's _____ law states that the acceleration of a body is directly proportional to the net force on it and inversely proportional to its mass.
   a. first   b. second   c. third

6. _____ Losing speed as you ride your bike uphill demonstrates Newton's _____ law.
   a. first   b. second   c. third

7. _____ Two teams in a tug of war exert the same amount of force on each other and the rope does not move. Newton's _____ law explains why the rope does not move.
   a. first   b. second   c. third

8. _____ If you push against a wall, the wall pushes back against you with _____ force.
   a. no   b. less   c. equal   d. more

9. _____ The gravitational force exerted by a large body, such as Earth, is
   a. weight   b. mass   c. acceleration   d. inertial mass.

10. _____ Mass and weight are related by
    a. the force of gravity   b. newtons   c. friction   d. none of these.

11. _____ Difficulty in pushing a large crate from rest involves
    a. gravity   b. sliding friction   c. static friction   d. balanced forces.

12. _____ When the drag force on an object equals the force of gravity, _____ occurs.
    a. acceleration   b. inertial mass   c. terminal velocity   d. maximum mass

13. _____ The effect of air resistance on the tail of a kite is _____ the effect of air resistance on the body of the kite.
    a. the same as   b. less than   c. more than

14. _____ If the force of gravity on a balloon is 3000 N, and the lift force provided by the atmosphere is 3300 N, in which direction is the net force acting?
    a. upward   b. downward   c. toward the east   d. There is no net force.

B. Applying Concepts

Answer the following questions in two or three complete sentences.

1. Explain the relationship between mass and weight on Earth. Would this relationship change on Mars? Explain your answer.

2. Why is it easier to stop a compact car than a large station wagon when both are moving at the same speed?

3. An elevator is traveling from the lobby to the top of the building. As it stops on the top floor, in which direction is its acceleration? Explain.

4. In the drawing at right, use arrows to show the two horizontal and two vertical forces acting on the boat as it is pulled to the shore. Is there a net force on the boat?

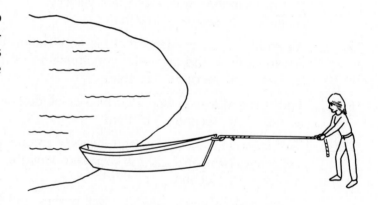

5. Explain the difference between action-reaction forces and net forces. Using the boat shown in the figure, describe an example of each.

6. What is the relationship between sliding friction and speed? Between sliding friction and normal force?

7. Suppose you try to pull a rope tied to a large carton. You cannot move the carton. What forces are acting on your hand?

C. Understanding Concepts

1. What force is required to accelerate a 6.0-kg bowling ball at +2.0 m/s²?

2. What is the mass of a cat that weighs 30.0 N?

3. Acceleration due to gravity on Mars is 3.8 m/s².

   a. Would a 5.0-kg watermelon weigh more on Earth or on Mars?

   b. How would the mass of the watermelon differ?

4. What is the inertial mass of a 75-N dog?

5. How much force is needed to keep a 78-kg box moving at a constant velocity across a warehouse floor if the coefficient of friction between the box and the floor is 0.21?

6. A 597-N cross-country skier is moving over packed snow. The coefficient of friction between the skis and the snow is 0.11. What force is required to keep the skier moving at a constant speed?

7. What is the coefficient of friction between a 65-kg roller skater and the floor of the roller rink if the skater moves at a constant speed with a force of 75 N?

NAME ─────────────────────────

D. Extending Concepts

1. An elevator has a mass of 1.10×10^3 kg. Suppose it accelerates upward at 0.45 m/s². What is the force acting on the elevator's support cable?

2. A rocket weighs 2.0×10^7 N. Its engines exert $+25 \times 10^6$ N of force at lift-off.

   a. What is the mass of the rocket?

   b. What is its acceleration when it lifts off?

   c. The average acceleration of the rocket during its 7.0 minute launch is 10.0 m/s². What velocity does it reach?

3. A 47-N box is pulled along a horizontal surface by a 25-N weight hanging from a cord along a frictionless pulley.

   a. What is the acceleration of the box and the weight?

   b. What force is exerted on the cord?

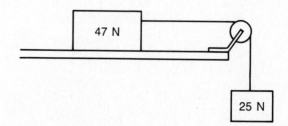

CHAPTER

6 Evaluation

VECTORS

A. Testing Concepts

In the space to the left, write the letter of the answer to each question.

1. _____ A hiker moves 15 km due east then heads due north for 8 km. What is the direction of the resultant vector?
   a. due east   b. due north   c. northeast   d. southwest

2. _____ The downstream velocity of a river that flows south _____ a boat's eastward velocity.
   a. slightly increases   b. slightly decreases   c. has no effect on

3. _____ When adding vectors graphically, the direction and length of each vector must
   a. be the same as the equilibrant   b. not be changed   c. be similar to the direction and length of the resultant   d. be reversed.

4. _____ Knowing the magnitudes of the hypotenuse of a right triangle and the side opposite angle θ, you could compute the _____ of angle θ.
   a. sine   b. cosine   c. tangent

5. _____ The effect of the resultant vector is _____ the effect of the original vectors.
   a. less than   b. greater than   c. the same as

6. _____ Suppose you pull a wagon along a horizontal sidewalk. The force that pulls the wagon forward over the sidewalk is the _____ force.
   a. resultant   b. vertical component   c. equilibrant   d. horizontal component

7. _____ If the horizontal component of a force is positive, then, by convention, the force acts
   a. upward   b. downward   c. to the right   d. to the left.

8. _____ An object is in equilibrium when
   a. the vertical component equals the horizontal component of force   b. the net sum of the forces is zero   c. the resultant force is the equilibrant.

9. _____ The equilibrant force is _____ the resultant.
   a. greater than and in the same direction as   b. less than but opposite in direction to
   c. equal in magnitude but opposite in direction to
   d. equal in magnitude and in the same direction as

10. _____ To resolve a force vector into its components, a set of perpendicular axes is drawn. Then the _____ is drawn to scale at the correct angle.
    a. resultant force   b. horizontal component   c. vertical component
    d. the equilibrant

11. _____ When vectors are resolved into components on an inclined plane, the _____ force is the one that acts along the incline.
    a. parallel   b. perpendicular   c. original   d. weight

12. _____ As the angle of an inclined plane increases, the parallel force _____ and the perpendicular force _____ .
    a. decreases, decreases   b. decreases, increases   c. increases, increases
    d. increases, decreases

B. Applying Concepts

Answer the following questions in two or three complete sentences.

1. Is a plane traveling at a constant velocity in equilibrium? Explain your answer.

2. There are four forces acting on the plane described above. Explain how you would add these vectors graphically.

3. Describe how perpendicular vectors are added.

4. Suppose the hill described above were frictionless. If a force of 150 N was needed to move the wagon uphill at a constant speed, what force is needed for the wagon to roll downhill at a constant speed?

5. Suppose you are driving due north at 15 m/s in a severe thunderstorm. The wind is blowing due east at 30 km/h. How does the wind affect your northward movement?

6. Is a person standing still on a carpeted floor in equilibrium? Explain your answer.

7. What is the relationship between the components of the weight of an object and the angle of an inclined plane on which the object rests?

6 Evaluation

C. Understanding Concepts

1. A runner jogs 8.0 km due west, turns and jogs 10.0 km south, and then jogs 7.0 km due north at a constant speed. Graphically determine the magnitude and direction of the jogger's total displacement.

2. Trigonometrically determine the magnitude and direction of the velocity of a plane that is flying toward 180° at 100.0 km/h while the wind blows toward 90° at 65.0 km/h.

3. The force exerted on a rope pulling a wagon is 49.0 N. The rope is 35° above the horizontal. Find the force that pulls the wagon over the ground.

4. A pilot wants to fly a plane at 500.0 km/h, directly north. The wind is blowing at 90.0 km/h from the east. Find the magnitude and direction of the course the pilot should fly.

5. A net force of 125 N acts due east on an object. Find the single force that will produce equilibrium.

6. A crate weighing 823 N is resting on a plank that makes a 25° angle with the ground. Find the components of the crate's weight parallel and perpendicular to the plank.

D. Extending Concepts

1. Two people pull on a wagon using two ropes. One rope is exerting a force of 200.0 N at 5° from east. The other is exerting a force of 250.0 N at 120° from east. Assume that friction is negligible. What is the net force acting on the wagon?

2. A child weighing 29.0 kg is on a swing supported by two chains. Another child is pulling the swing back so that the chains make a 30° angle with the vertical. What force is exerted by each chain?

3. A 55-N force acts on an object at 25°. A second force of 63 N acts at 90°. What is the magnitude and direction of the equilibrant?

4. A trunk with a mass of 200.0 kg is resting on a moving truck ramp that makes a 45° angle with the horizontal.

   a. Find the components of the weight of the trunk both parallel and perpendicular to the ramp.

   b. What is the acceleration of the trunk?

CHAPTER
7 Evaluation

MOTION IN TWO DIMENSIONS

A. Testing Concepts

In the space to the left, write the letter of the answer to each question.

1. _____ For an object moving along a trajectory, the horizontal acceleration of the object _____ as the position changes.
   a. increases   b. decreases   c. is constant

2. _____ The vertical change in position of an object that is dropped and that of an identical object that is thrown horizontally from the same height
   a. is the same   b. is greater for the thrown object   c. is less for the thrown object
   d. depends on the initial velocities of the objects.

3. _____ Suppose an object is dropped from a moving train. The time it takes to fall
   a. will vary depending upon the observer's position relative to the train
   b. is independent of the observer's position   c. depends upon the shape of the trajectory
   d. depends upon the speed of the train.

4. _____ In trajectory motion, the initial horizontal velocity is _____ the final horizontal velocity.
   a. greater than   b. less than   c. equal to

5. _____ In projectile motion, the rising and falling times of the object are equal if the launching position is _____ the landing position.
   a. above   b. below   c. at the same height as

6. _____ Where would a pitcher have to aim a fast ball in order to have it pass at the height of the batter's chest?
   a. exactly at the height of the batter's chest   b. slightly below the height of the batter's chest   c. just above the height of the batter's chest   d. at any height

7. _____ For an object moving with circular motion, the direction of centripetal acceleration is
   a. tangent to the circle   b. toward the center of the circle   c. away from the center of the circle   d. toward the circumference of the circle.

8. _____ An object in circular motion travels a distance of _____ during its period.
   a. r b. $4\pi r^2$ c. $2\pi r$ d. v^2/r

9. _____ When the displacement of an object with simple harmonic motion is greatest, the acceleration has a
   a. maximum value   b. minimum value   c. value between maximum and minimum.

10. _____ The period of a simple pendulum depends upon
    a. the mass of the bob   b. the length of the pendulum   c. the amplitude of the swing
    d. the stiffness of the pendulum.

11. _____ To produce mechanical resonance, the time between applied forces must equal the _____ of the object.
    a. period   b. frequency   c. length   d. mass

B. Applying Concepts

Answer the following questions in two or three complete sentences.

1. Compare the distance a ball falls during the first second after it is dropped with the distance it falls during the second second.

2. If the ball described in Problem 1 were thrown downward instead of being dropped from rest, would the average velocity for its downward motion be different? Would its being thrown affect the time required to fall to the ground? Explain both answers.

3. Two people are on a carnival ride that uses centripetal and frictional forces to hold its riders in place inside a rotating drum. How do the velocity, acceleration, and force acting on the people differ if one person has twice the mass of the other?

4. Could the equations you learned in this chapter be used to calculate the height of a building from which paper confetti was thrown? Explain your answer.

5. On a certain game show, contestants spin a large wheel to determine the prize associated with correct answers. Explain how a contestant would apply force to get the wheel to spin as rapidly as possible.

6. Hooke's law describes a relationship between force and the displacement from an equilibrium position for certain objects with simple harmonic motion. A proportionality constant k relates the other two quantities. Write an equation to represent Hooke's law. Identify the variables in the equation.

7. Explain the relationship among velocity, displacement, and acceleration of a mass suspended on a vibrating spring when the mass is at its equilibrium point.

8. Describe the force on the bob of a simple pendulum when it is pulled away from the vertical.

9. Explain how you could use the physics you learned in this chapter to break a fine crystal glass without touching it.

C. Understanding Concepts

1. A projectile is launched horizontally with a speed of 80.0 m/s. If the projectile is launched 1.5 m above the floor, how long does it take the projectile to hit the floor?

2. A soccer ball is kicked into the air at an angle of 38° above the horizontal. The initial velocity of the ball is +30.0 m/s. How long is the soccer ball in the air?

3. What is the horizontal distance traveled by the soccer ball in Problem 2?

4. What is the maximum height reached by the soccer ball mentioned in Problem 2?

5. A runner moving at a speed of 5.60 m/s rounds a curved track with a 60.0 m-radius. What is the runner's acceleration?

6. A person with a mass of 75 kg sits at a distance of 1.5 m from the pivot point on a 4-m seesaw. Where would a person with a mass of 65 kg have to sit to balance the seesaw?

7. What is the period of a simple pendulum that is 0.56 m in length?

D. Extending Concepts

1. A coin rolls along the top of a 1.33 m-high desk with a constant velocity. It reaches the edge of the desk and hits the ground +0.25 m from the edge of the desk. What was the velocity of the coin as it rolled across the desk?

2. A 0.500 kg-object attached to the end of a 0.550 m-wire revolves uniformly on a flat, frictionless surface.

   a. If the object makes three complete revolutions per second, what is the force exerted by the wire on the object?

   b. What is the speed of the object?

3. Earth's moon, which is 3.80×10^8 m from the planet, is in freefall. Acceleration due to Earth's gravity acting on the moon is 2.70×10^{-3} m/s^2.

   a. What is the moon's speed?

   b. How long does it take to complete its orbit?

4. The mass of the moon is 7.38×10^{22} kg. What is the centripetal force acting on the moon?

CHAPTER 8 Evaluation

UNIVERSAL GRAVITATION

A. Testing Concepts

In the space to the left, write the letter of the answer to each question.

1. _____ During its orbital period, as a planet moves closer to the sun, the orbital velocity of the planet
   a. increases   b. decreases   c. remains the same.

2. _____ According to Newton's law of universal gravitation, the force of attraction between any two masses is directly related to
   a. the distance between the masses   b. the product of the two masses   c. the velocity of the two masses   d. the sum of the two masses.

3. _____ As the distance between two bodies increases, the force of attraction between the bodies
   a. increases   b. decreases   c. remains the same.

4. _____ In his experiment, Cavendish was able to determine
   a. the mass of several lead spheres   b. the value of *G*   c. the period of Io
   d. the mass of Io.

5. _____ Astronauts in an orbiting space shuttle experience a sensation of weightlessness because
   a. the space shuttle is falling freely toward Earth   b. the space shuttle is not affected by Earth's gravity   c. the mass of the space shuttle decreases as the distance from Earth increases   d. the space shuttle is moving away from Earth.

6. _____ According to Einstein's general theory of relativity
   a. mass causes space to be curved   b. gravity is a contact force   c. the gravitational force between two bodies is not affected by the distance between the bodies
   d. all of the above are true.

7. _____ According to _____, an imaginary line from the sun to a planet sweeps out equal areas in equal time intervals.
   a. Newton's law of universal gravitation   b. Newton's third law of motion
   c. Kepler's second law of planetary motion   d. Cavendish's experiment

8. _____ Anything that has mass is surrounded by
   a. a satellite in orbit   b. a magnetic field   c. a gravitational field   d. all of these.

9. _____ The force of attraction will be equal between which two pairs of spheres?
   a. 1 and 2   b. 2 and 3   c. 1 and 3

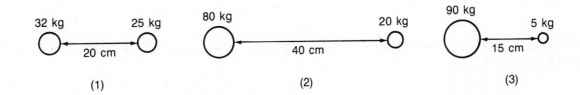

32 kg	25 kg	80 kg	20 kg	90 kg	5 kg
20 cm		40 cm		15 cm	
(1)		(2)		(3)	

8 : Evaluation

B. Applying Concepts

Answer the following questions in two or three complete sentences.

1. Explain why Kepler was able to use Tycho Brahe's data about the positions of stars and planets to develop his laws of planetary motion, while Brahe was unable to use the same data successfully.

2. Earth is closer to the sun in December than it is in July. What happens to the orbital speed of the planet between July and December? Explain your answer.

3. What would happen to the magnitude of the gravitational force between two bodies if:

   a. the mass of one of the bodies were doubled?

   b. the distance between the two bodies were doubled?

4. What information do you need to find the period of a planet?

5. The mass of Jupiter is approximately 318 times that of Earth. Yet, the surface gravity of Jupiter is less than three times the surface gravity of Earth. How do you account for this apparent discrepancy?

6. How does an artificial satellite remain in orbit at a constant distance from Earth's surface?

7. How does Einstein's general theory of relativity account for the presence of "black holes" in the universe?

C. Understanding Concepts

1. Two spheres, each having a mass of 20.0 kg, are positioned so that their centers are 8.00 m apart. What is the gravitational force between the spheres?

2. What will the force be if the spheres described in Problem 1 are positioned with their centers 4.00 m apart?

3. If the mass of one of the spheres described in Problem 1 were doubled, how far apart would the spheres have to be placed in order to maintain the same gravitational force between them?

4. At Earth's surface a 1.0-kg mass weighs 9.8 N. How much would the same mass weigh on the surface of Mercury? (The mass of Mercury is 3.2×10^{23} kg. Its mean radius is 2.43×10^6 m. The mass of Earth is 5.979×10^{24} kg. Its mean radius is 6.3713×10^8 m.)

8 Evaluation

D. Extending Concepts

1. The distance between Earth and the sun is often expressed as one astronomical unit (AU). Using this unit, find the distance between the sun and Mars, which has a period of approximately 686 Earth days.

2. The mean distance between the center of Earth and the center of the moon is 3.84×10^8 meters, and the moon has an orbital period of 27.3 days. Find the distance from Earth of an artificial satellite that has an orbital period of 9.1 days.

3. The gravitational force between two spheres is 2.50×10^{-8} N. Their centers are 105 cm apart. The larger sphere has a mass of 8.20 kg. Find the mass of the smaller sphere.

4. A body orbits the sun at a distance ten times the mean distance of Earth's orbit from the sun.

   a. Find the period of the body in years.

   b. Determine the velocity of the body.

CHAPTER

9 Evaluation

MOMENTUM AND ITS CONSERVATION

A. Testing Concepts

In the space to the left, write the letter of the answer to each question.

1. _____ Momentum can be calculated by multiplying mass by
    a. acceleration   b. velocity   c. impulse   d. time.

2. _____ If no net force acts on a body
    a. the velocity of the body is constant   b. the body is accelerating
    c. the momentum of the body is zero   d. the momentum of the body is increasing.

3. _____ The greatest change in momentum will be produced by
    a. a large force acting over a long time   b. a small force acting over a short time
    c. a large force acting over a short time.

4. _____ If an object with a velocity of 50 m/s has the same momentum as that of a 10-kg mass having
    a velocity of 20 m/s, the mass of the object is
    a. greater than 10 kg   b. less than 10 kg   c. 10 kg.

5. _____ Impulse can be represented by
    a. $\Delta v/\Delta t$ b. $F\Delta t$ c. mv d. none of these.

6. _____ When a golfer hits a golf ball, the force exerted by the ball on the club is _____ that exerted by
    the club on the ball.
    a. equal to   b. greater than   c. less than

7. _____ When a golf club hits a golf ball, the change in momentum of the ball is _____ the change in
    momentum of the club.
    a. equal to   b. greater than   c. less than

8. _____ When a golf club hits a golf ball, the change in velocity of the ball is _____ that of the club.
    a. equal to   b. greater than   c. less than

9. _____ A system is said to be closed if
    a. no net external force acts on it   b. the momentum of each object in the system remains
    constant   c. objects cannot enter or leave the system   d. objects can enter, but not leave,
    the system.

10. _____ If an object moving at a rate of 20 m/s collides with a stationary object and the two objects
    move away together, the velocity of the combined objects will be
    a. greater than 20 m/s   b. less than 20 m/s   c. 20 m/s.

11. _____ An internal force _____ the total momentum of a system.
    a. increases   b. decreases   c. does not change

12. _____ Two moving objects collide and move apart on paths that are 120° apart. The total momen-
    tum of the objects after the collision is _____ the total momentum before the collision.
    a. equal to   b. greater than   c. less than

B. Applying Concepts

Answer the following questions in two or three complete sentences.

1. Explain how it is possible for a motorcycle to have the same momentum as a locomotive.

2. In order to effectively "bunt" a baseball, at the instant the ball strikes the bat the batter moves the bat in the same direction as the moving baseball. What effect does this action have? Why?

3. In the sport of curling, players slide large 19-kg masses called "stones" along the surface of the ice toward a target. If a stone traveling 3 m/s strikes a stationary stone directly, the first stone will stop moving. Using the concept of conservation of momentum, describe what happens to the second stone. Assume there is no friction.

4. Why does a fire hose recoil, or "kick" backward, when the water is turned on?

5. Use impulse and momentum to explain why an empty pickup truck can change speed and direction more easily than an identical truck traveling at the same speed but carrying a load of gravel.

6. The drawing shows five identical metal spheres suspended from a support. What will happen if the elevated sphere is released and allowed to strike the ball adjacent to it? Explain your answer.

7. Suppose you were an astronaut drifting in space several meters from your spacecraft. The only thing you have with you is a sack filled with "moon rocks". How could you return to your ship?

C. Understanding Concepts

1. Which has the greater momentum: a 145-g baseball traveling at 40.0 m/s or a 45-g golf ball traveling at 67.0 m/s? How much greater?

2. What impulse is needed to stop a 45-g mass traveling at 42 m/s?

3. A force of 540 N is used to stop an object with a mass of 65 kg moving 175 m/s. How long will it take to bring the object to a full stop?

4. In hitting a stationary hockey puck having a mass of 180 g, a hockey player gives the puck an impulse of 6.0 N•s. At what speed will the puck move toward the goal?

5. A metal sphere with a mass of 80.0 g rolls along a frictionless surface at 20.0 m/s and strikes a stationary sphere having a mass of 200.0 g. The first sphere stops completely. At what speed does the second sphere move away from the point of impact?

6. A snowball with a mass of 85 g hits a snowman's top hat and sticks to it. The hat and the snowball, with a combined mass of 220 g, fall off together at 8.0 m/s. How fast was the snowball moving at the moment of impact?

D. Extending Concepts

1. A ball with a mass of 12 g moving at +15.0 m/s collides with a second ball of mass 36 g moving at +5.0 m/s. After the collision, the 12-g ball moves at +6.0 m/s. What is the change in momentum of the 36-g ball?

2. A 24.0-kg dog running at a speed of 3.0 m/s jumps onto a stationary skateboard that has a mass of 3.6 kg. How long will it take an average force of 9.0 N to stop the skateboard and dog?

3. A sphere of mass 5.00 kg moving at 4.00 m/s collides with an identical sphere that is at rest. If the first sphere moves off at an angle of 60° from its original path, what are the speeds of the two spheres as they separate? Assume frictionless conditions.

CHAPTER

10 Evaluation

WORK, ENERGY, AND SIMPLE MACHINES

A. Testing Concepts

In the space to the left, write the letter of the answer to each question.

1. _____ Any object that has energy has the ability to
a. burn   b. produce a change   c. fall   d. do none of these.

2. _____ When a force is exerted on an object, work is done only if the object
a. is heavy   b. remains stationary   c. moves   d. has no momentum.

3. _____ In which of the following situations is no work done on a football?
a. picking up the football   b. carrying the football down the field   c. dropping the foot-ball   d. all of the above

4. _____ In which of the following situations is work done on the football by a person?
a. picking up the football   b. carrying the football down the field   c. dropping the foot-ball   d. all of the above

5. _____ In which of the following situations is work done on the football by gravity?
a. picking up the football   b. carrying the football down the field   c. dropping the foot-ball   d. all of the above

6. _____ How much work is done if you raise a 6.0-N weight 1.5 m above the ground?
a. 0.0 J   b. 4.0 J   c. 7.5 J   d. 9.0 J

7. _____ One definition of power is
a. force exerted per unit distance   b. work done per unit time   c. the amount of energy expended   d. force applied multiplied by time interval.

8. _____ A machine with a mechanical advantage greater than one
a. increases friction   b. increases energy   c. increases effort force
d. does all of these.

9. _____ For an ideal machine,
a. the mechanical advantage is always greater than 1   b. input work is always less than output work   c. efficiency is always 100%   d. all of the above are true.

10. _____ If the mechanical advantage of a machine is less than 1,
a. effort force is greater than resistance force   b. output work is greater than input work
c. efficiency is greater than 100%   d. all of the above are true.

11. _____ Using an ideal machine, a worker exerts an effort force of 5.0 N to move a 12.0-N weight a distance of 3.0 meters. The effort distance is
a. greater than 3.0 meters   b. 3.0 meters   c. less than 3.0 meters.

12. _____ Which of the following objects is not being used as a simple machine?
a. a pulley used to lift a heavy object   b. a wedge used to split wood   c. a stick used to hold up a wilted plant   d. a screwdriver used to pry open a can of paint

13. _____ Which of the following make up a complex machine?
a. a lever and a pulley   b. a wheel and an axle   c. a pair of gears
d. All of the above are complex machines.

B. Applying Concepts

Answer the following questions in two or three complete sentences.

1. Two students are moving 80-N cartons of books from the floor up onto a platform. One student moves 12 cartons in 7 minutes. The other student moves the same number of cartons in 5 minutes. Which student does more work? Explain your answer.

2. What type of simple machine is the handle of a pencil sharpener? How does it make work easier?

3. Explain the following: When a screwdriver is used to drive a screw, the diameter of its handle is more important than its length, but when used to pry open a stuck window, its length is more important than the diameter of its handle.

4. If a machine is used to increase force, what factor is sacrificed? Cite an example.

5. Distinguish between work and power.

6. Compare the size of the effort force to the size of the resistance force in a machine that has a mechanical advantage less than 1. What can be gained by using such a machine?

7. Use mechanical advantage to explain what happens when you shift the gears of a multi-speed bike.

C. Understanding Concepts

1. An adult and a child exert a total force of 930 N in pushing a car 15 m down their driveway. The adult exerts twice as much force as the child. How much work does each person do?

2. An effort force of 200.0 N is applied to an ideal machine to move a 750.0-N resistance a distance of 300.0 cm.

   a. Through what distance must the effort force act?   b. What is the IMA of the machine?

3. How much power is developed by an electric motor that moves a 500-N load a distance of 20 m in 10 s?

4. How much work must be put into a machine that is 70.0 efficient in order to move a mass of 400.0 kg a distance of 12.5 m?

5. How much power is generated by a machine in moving a 250-kg mass a distance of 150 m in 30.0 seconds?

D. Extending Concepts

1. An adult pulls a child across the ice on a sled. The combined weight of the sled and the child is 26 N, and the adult pulls on a rope that joins the sled at an angle of 30° above horizontal. Ignoring friction, how much work is done in pulling the sled 390 m?

2. A grocer lifts an 8.0-kg carton from the floor to a height of 0.80 m, carries it 24 m across the store, and places it on a shelf 1.8 m above the floor. How much work does the grocer accomplish?

3. At what rate (speed) can a 150-W motor lift a 2500-N load?

4. A mover pushes a 260-kg piano on wheels up a ramp 7.0 m long onto a stage 1.75 m above the auditorium floor. The mover pushes the piano with a force of 680 N.

   a. How much work does the mover do?

   b. What work is done on the piano by the machine?

   c. What is the efficiency of the machine?

CHAPTER
11 : Evaluation

ENERGY

A. Testing Concepts

In the space to the left, write the letter of the answer to each question.

1. _____ The transfer of energy by mechanical means is
   a. momentum   b. work   c. effort   d. acceleration.

2. _____ An object has energy caused by its motion. This is
   a. potential energy   b. chemical energy   c. kinetic energy   d. momentum.

3. _____ Which of these is *not* needed to find the kinetic energy of an object?
   a. its shape   b. its mass   c. its velocity
   d. None of the above are needed to find kinetic energy.

4. _____ When you throw a ball up into the air, the total energy of the ball at any point in its flight
   can be expressed as kinetic energy _____ potential energy.
   a. times   b. minus   c. divided by   d. plus

5. _____ As an object falls towards Earth, the potential energy of the object
   a. increases   b. decreases   c. remains the same.

6. _____ The kinetic energy of a boulder weighing 50.0 N perched on the edge of a cliff 25.0 m high is
   a. 750.0 J   b. 0 J   c. 2.0 J   d. 25.0 J.

7. _____ The total amount of energy in an isolated, closed system
   a. is constantly increasing   b. is constantly decreasing   c. remains constant
   d. cannot be accurately measured.

8. _____ A change in the kinetic energy of an object is equal to the
   a. force exerted on the object   b. velocity of the object   c. net work done on the object
   d. change in its mass.

9. _____ The gravitational potential energy of an object close to Earth is directly related to
   a. the mass of the object   b. the height of the object   c. the velocity of the object
   d. both a and b.

10. _____ If two bodies meet in an elastic collision, the total *KE* of the bodies before the collision is
    _____ the total *KE* of the bodies after the collision.
    a. greater than   b. less than   c. equal to

B. Applying Concepts

Answer the following questions in two or three complete sentences.

1. Describe the energy changes that take place when the spring of a toy car is wound up and then released.

2. Why must the first hill of a roller coaster ride be the highest hill?

3. When a golfer drives a golf ball, is the net work done on the ball positive or negative? Explain your answer.

4. Distinguish between an elastic collision and an inelastic collision.

5. A ball is thrown up into the air. Describe the work done on the ball and the energy transformations that take place between the time the ball is released and the time it reaches its maximum height.

6. When a pitcher throws a ball, the net work done on the ball is positive. Describe the net work done on the pitched ball when a batter strikes the ball with a bat and hits it back toward the pitcher.

7. Under what condition will a marble and a baseball have the same gravitational potential energy? Under what condition will they have the same kinetic energy?

C. Understanding Concepts

1. Find the kinetic energy of an airplane traveling at a speed of 648 km/h. The mass of the airplane is 5.00×10^3 kg.

2. A diver, who has a mass of 48 kg, climbs up a ladder to a diving platform 5.0 m above the ground. How much potential energy does the diver gain?

3. How does the gravitational potential energy of a 550-g object, 20.0 m above the ground, compare with that of a 350-g object, 30.0 m above the ground?

4. An object with a mass of 10.0 kg moves toward the east along a frictionless surface at a velocity of 16.0 m/s. A net force of 20.0 N acts on the object and its velocity changes to 10.0 m/s toward the east.

   a. In what direction is the net force applied?

   b. How much does the kinetic energy of the object change?

5. A weightlifter lifts a 90.0-kg barbell from a stand 0.90 m high and raises it to a height of 1.75 m. What is the increase in the potential energy of the barbell?

6. A child having a mass of 35.0 kg is on a sled having a mass of 5.0 kg. If the child and sled traveling together have a kinetic energy of 260 J, how fast are they moving?

D. Extending Concepts

1. Two projectiles are launched horizontally at a point 1.0 m above the ground. Each has a mass of 40.0 g. One projectile lands 200.0 m away. The second projectile lands 220.0 m away. Find the potential and kinetic energy of each projectile at the time it is launched.

2. A body with a mass of 5.0 kg has the same kinetic energy as a second body. The second body has a mass of 10.0 kg and is moving at a speed of 20.0 m/s. How fast is the first body moving?

3. During a contest that involved throwing a 7.0-kg bowling ball straight up in the air, one contestant exerted a force of 810 N on the ball. If the force was exerted through a distance of 2.0 m, how high did the ball go from the point of release?

CHAPTER

12 : Evaluation

THERMAL ENERGY

A. Testing Concepts

In the space to the left, write the letter of the answer to each question.

1. _____ Which form of thermal energy transfer is most effective in fluids?
   a. convection   b. radiation   c. conduction
   d. All of the above are equally effective in fluids.

2. _____ The hotness of a body is its
   a. thermal energy   b. thermal equilibrium   c. temperature   d. specific heat.

3. _____ The amount of heat needed to melt one kilogram of a substance is called that substance's
   a. melting point   b. specific heat   c. heat of fusion   d. heat of vaporization.

4. _____ A heat engine converts
   a. thermal energy to mechanical energy   b. thermal energy to chemical energy
   c. mechanical energy to thermal energy   d. mechanical energy to chemical energy.

5. _____ The disorder in a system is known as
   a. thermodynamic   b. fusion   c. equilibrium   d. entropy.

6. _____ The energy that flows as a result of a difference in temperature is
   a. radiation   b. heat   c. temperature   d. vaporization.

7. _____ On the Kelvin temperature scale, the freezing point of water is _____ K.
   a. −273.15   b. −100   c. 0   d. 273.15

8. _____ When two objects are at thermal equilibrium,
   a. they contain the same amount of heat   b. they have the same thermal energy
   c. they are at the same temperature   d. they melt.

9. _____ If thermal energy is added to equal masses of substances, they will show different changes
   in temperature because their _____ are different.
   a. heats of fusion   b. heats of vaporization   c. specific heats   d. volumes

10. _____ If 25 g of hot water are added to 35 g of cold water, the heat lost by the hot water is _____ the
    heat gained by the cold water.
    a. greater than   b. less than   c. equal to

11. _____ Unlike work, heat is energy transferred because of
    a. mechanical action   b. a difference in temperature   c. forces acting on matter
    d. accelerating particles.

12. _____ The total increase in the thermal energy of a system is the work done on it _____ the heat
    added to it.
    a. plus   b. minus   c. multiplied by   d. divided by

13. _____ If the average kinetic energy of the particles that make up a liquid increases,
    a. the liquid changes state   b. the temperature of the liquid increases
    c. the liquid loses heat to its surroundings   d. all of the above take place.

12 Evaluation

B. Applying Concepts

Answer the following questions in two or three complete sentences.

1. Define thermal energy in terms of the kinetic-molecular theory.

2. Distinguish among thermal energy, temperature, and heat.

3. What is absolute zero? What is its value on the Celsius scale?

4. Equal masses of methyl alcohol and water are heated by the same heat source. How will the temperatures of these two substances compare after being heated for the same period of time? Explain your answer.

5. A sample of iron at a temperature of 225 K is placed in a container of water at a temperature of 350 K. Describe what takes place in terms of heat transfer and temperature.

6. What is entropy? How does the entropy of a system change when heat is removed from the system?

7. The term *latent* means "hidden." Why are heats of fusion and vaporization often referred to as latent heats?

12 Evaluation

C. Understanding Concepts

NOTE: In these exercises, assume that no energy is transferred between the system described and its surroundings unless otherwise stated.

1. The boiling point of liquid helium is −267°C, which is the lowest boiling point of all the elements. Express this temperature in Kelvins.

2. How much heat must be added to 250 g of methanol to raise its temperature by 15°C? The specific heat of methanol is 2450 J/kg•K.

3. How much heat must be absorbed by 2.0 kg of ice at −20.0°C to raise it to its melting point? The specific heat of ice is 2060 J/kg•K. The heat of fusion of ice is 3.34×10^5 J/kg.

4. How much more heat must be added to the ice in Problem 3 to change it to liquid water at 0°C?

5. How much heat must be added to 1.5 kg of water at 95.0°C to change it to steam at 100.0°C? The specific heat of water is 4180 J/kg•K. The heat of vaporization of water is 2.26×10^6 J/kg.

6. A 2.0-kg cube of iron at a temperature 300.0°C is placed on a 5-kg block of ice at 0.0°C. How much ice will change to liquid water at 0.0°C? The specific heat of iron is 450 J/kg•K.

12 Evaluation

D. Extending Concepts

1. A 4.0-kg iron ball at a temperature of 225°C is placed in a container of water at 42°C. When the system reaches thermal equilibrium, its temperature is 45°C. What is the volume of water in the container? (1 kg of water = 1 L) The specific heat of iron is 450 J/kg•K. The specific heat of water is 4180 J/kg•K.

2. How much heat is absorbed in changing 2.00 kg of ice at −5.0°C to steam at 110.0°C? The specific heat of ice is 2060 J/kg•K and of steam is 2020 J/kg•K. The heat of fusion of water is 3.34×10^5 J/kg. The heat of vaporization of water is 2.26×10^6 J/kg.

3. The melting point of lead is 327.5°C. In order to change 50.0 g of lead at room temperature (20.0°C) to a liquid at its melting point, 3150 J of heat must be added. The specific heat of lead is 130 J/kg•K. What is the heat of fusion of lead?

4. If 50.0 g of ice at 0.0°C is added to 150.0 g of water at 80.0°C, what will the temperature of the mixture be when it reaches thermal equilibrium?

CHAPTER

13 Evaluation

STATES OF MATTER

A. Testing Concepts

In the space to the left, write the letter of the answer to each question.

1. _____ At sea level, if the area of a surface increases, the pressure of the atmosphere on the surface
   a. increases   b. decreases   c. stays the same.

2. _____ Pressure can be calculated as force _____ area.
   a. plus   b. minus   c. multiplied by   d. divided by

3. _____ The SI unit of pressure is the
   a. pascal   b. atmosphere   c. millibar   d. newton.

4. _____ According to Pascal's principle, any change on a confined fluid
   a. is directly proportional to the volume of the fluid
   b. is inversely proportional to the volume of the fluid
   c. depends on the shape of the container
   d. is transmitted unchanged throughout the fluid.

5. _____ The buoyant force exerted on an object immersed in a fluid is equal to
   a. the volume of the immersed object   b. the weight of the displaced fluid
   c. the weight of the immersed object   d. the mass of the immersed object.

6. _____ According to Bernoulli's principle, as the velocity of a fluid increases,
   a. the density of the fluid decreases   b. the pressure exerted by the fluid decreases
   c. the buoyant force of the fluid increases   d. the buoyant force of the fluid decreases.

7. _____ When heated, only matter in the solid state exhibits
   a. volume expansion   b. linear expansion   c. decrease in density   d. all of these.

8. _____ The process by which matter changes state from a gas to a liquid is
   a. condensation   b. evaporation   c. sublimation   d. buoyancy.

9. _____ As heat is applied to a sample of water at 1°C, the volume of the water
   a. increases   b. decreases   c. remains the same.

10. _____ A crystal lattice is a characteristic of many
    a. solids   b. liquids   c. gases   d. solids and liquids.

11. _____ An object that is deformed by a force and returns to its original form when the force is removed
    shows the property of
    a. buoyancy   b. expansion   c. elasticity   d. contraction.

12. _____ The state of matter in which atoms become torn apart is
    a. solid   b. liquid   c. gas   d. plasma.

13. _____ Surface tension is the result of _____ forces within a liquid.
    a. adhesive   b. cohesive   c. gravitational   d. buoyant

13 Evaluation

B. Applying Concepts

Answer the following questions in one or two complete sentences.

1. Use the kinetic molecular theory of matter to explain the properties of gases.

2. Most automobile brake systems are hydraulic systems. Explain how pressing on a brake pedal inside an automobile can cause pressure to be exerted on the brakes on all four wheels.

3. An iron cube weighing 5 N is suspended from a string and lowered into a container of water until it is completely immersed. Describe what happens to the weight of the cube. Explain your answer.

4. What properties can be used to distinguish between gases and liquids? What properties do gases and liquids have in common that allow them to be classified as fluids?

5. How is matter in the plasma state similar to matter in the gas state? How is it different?

6. Explain the principle behind the operation of a bimetallic strip.

NAME ──────────────────────────────

13 Evaluation

C. Understanding Concepts

1. Atmospheric pressure at sea level is about 1.0×10^5 Pa. How much force does the atmosphere exert on a driveway that is 15.0 m long and 5.0 m wide?

2. Find the total force exerted by Earth's atmosphere on the top and sides of a rectangular can. The base of the can is 10.0 cm wide and 15.0 cm long, and the can is 12.0 cm high.

3. A force of 400.0 N is exerted on a small piston, which has an area of 8.0 cm^2. How much weight can be lifted on a large piston, which has an area of 20.0 cm^2?

4. The area of a small piston is 4.0 cm^2. A force of 150 N on the small piston will move a weight of 1200 N on a large piston. What is the area of the large piston?

5. A cube of lead, 10.0 cm on each side, is suspended from a line and immersed in water. How much force is exerted on the line holding the lead cube? The density of lead is 11.3×10^3 kg/m^3.

6. An iron bar 1.6 m long at room temperature (20°C) is heated uniformly along its entire length until its temperature reaches 1250°C. How much longer is the bar at the higher temperature? The coefficient of linear expansion of iron is 12×10^{-6} °C^{-1}.

13 Evaluation

D. Extending Concepts

1. A cylindrical water tank 30.0 m high has a diameter of 14.0 m. The tank is two-thirds full of water. What is the pressure at the bottom of the tank?

2. A rectangular solid measures 1.20 m × 0.80 m × 0.20 m. When the solid is standing on its smallest face, it exerts a pressure of 5.2×10^3 Pa.

   a. How much does the solid weigh?

   b. What is the density of the solid?

3. An open-top container with a capacity of 200.0 mL is filled to the brim with water at a temperature of 4°C. The container and its contents are heated to 95°C and then cooled. How much water is in the container when it returns to its original temperature? Explain your answer. Assume no change in the volume of the container. The coefficient of volume expansion of water is 210×10^{-6}°C^{-1}.

CHAPTER

14 Evaluation

WAVES AND ENERGY TRANSFER

A. Testing Concepts

In the space to the left, write the letter of the answer to each question.

1. _____ A(n) _____ transmits energy without transferring matter.
   a. light particle   b. sound wave   c. electron   d. proton.

2. _____ Waves on banjo strings are _____ waves.
   a. transverse   b. electromagnetic   c. longitudinal   d. surface

3. _____ Dropping a stone into water will produce a(n)
   a. single wave pulse   b. standing wave   c. longitudinal wave
   d. electromagnetic wave.

4. _____ Vibrating bells produce _____ waves.
   a. electromagnetic   b. surface   c. traveling   d. light

5. _____ The shortest time interval during which wave motion repeats is the
   a. wave pulse   b. period   c. frequency   d. wavelength.

6. _____ The number of complete vibrations per second is the
   a. wave pulse   b. period   c. frequency   d. wavelength.

7. _____ The shortest distance between two points on a wave where the wave pattern is repeated
   is the
   a. amplitude   b. period   c. frequency   d. wavelength.

8. _____ The speed of any mechanical wave depends on
   a. the medium through which it travels   b. its amplitude   c. its frequency
   d. its reflection.

9. _____ When light from the air enters a body of water, some of the energy moves back into the air as
   a(n) _____ wave.
   a. reflected   b. incident   c. transmitted   d. sound

10. _____ During constructive interference, the individual wave pulses
    a. change their shapes   b. change their sizes   c. retain their original sizes and
    shapes   d. change both their sizes and shapes.

11. _____ A(n) _____ is produced during destructive interference of waves.
    a. antinode   b. node   c. higher crest   d. lower trough

12. _____ The _____ states that the angle of incidence equals the angle of reflection.
    a. principle of superposition   b. law of standing waves   c. principle of refrac-
    tion   d. law of reflection

13. _____ The change in the direction of waves at the boundary between two different media is
    a. resonance   b. reflection   c. refraction   d. diffraction.

14. _____ When waves spread out around the edge of a barrier, _____ occurs.
    a. resonance   b. reflection   c. refraction   d. diffraction

B. Applying Concepts

Answer the following questions in two or three complete sentences.

1. Describe the relationship between the amplitude of a wave and the energy that is transferred by the wave.

2. Suppose two boats a few meters apart are subjected to passing ocean waves. Describe the motion of the boats. Will the oscillations of the two boats have the same amplitudes and frequencies?

3. How do the reflected waves produced when a wave passes into a less dense medium differ from reflected waves produced when a wave passes into a more dense medium?

4. What is the principle of superposition and how is it related to interference?

5. Contrast the amount of energy transmitted by a wave passing through two similar media with that transmitted through two very different materials.

6. How do the speed of the transmitted wave and orientation of the reflected wave pulse change when a sound wave is transmitted from the air into water?

14 Evaluation

C. Understanding Concepts

1. Middle C on a finely tuned piano vibrates 262 times per second. What is the period of the wave?

2. Sound travels at 5600 m/s through a steel rod. If the frequency of the waves is 2480 Hz, what is the wavelength?

3. Suppose the steel rod mentioned in Problem 2 was fixed at one end but attached to a taut cord at its other end. What is the frequency of a wave that originated in the rod and traveled through the cord?

4. The wavelength of a sound produced by a tuning fork is 1.30 m. The fork has a frequency of 256 Hz. What is the wave velocity?

5. The wavelength of a water wave is 4.0×10^2 m. The wave is approaching land at 25 m/s. What is the period?

6. A beam of light strikes a mirror at an angle of 43°. What is the angle between the normal and the reflected ray?

14 Evaluation

D. Extending Concepts

1. You set a cup of coffee on the kitchen counter while the dishwasher is running. You notice that the vibration of the dishwasher causes standing waves in the coffee. The crests form four concentric rings, and the diameter of the cup is 6.0 cm. The speed of the wave in water is 1.5 m/s. What is the frequency of the vibrations coming from the dishwasher?

2. The average distance between Earth and the moon is 384 790 km. If Earth's atmosphere were uniform and extended to the moon's surface, how many days would it take sound to travel to the moon?

3. Waves traveling along a string have a wavelength of 2.4 m. When the waves reach the fixed end of the string, they are reflected. How far from the end are the first two antinodes?

4. Two springs are tied together. A transverse wave is started on the heavier spring. The wavelength is 0.20 m. When the wave reaches the point where the springs are tied together, a wave with a small amplitude travels back along the heavier spring at a speed of 5.0 m/s. A wave also passes along the lighter spring at a speed of 7.5 m/s. What is the wavelength of the wave in the lighter spring?

CHAPTER
15 : Evaluation

SOUND

A. Testing Concepts

In the space to the left, write the letter of the answer to each question.

1. _____ Echoes demonstrate _____ of sound waves.
   a. refraction   b. interference   c. diffraction   d. reflection

2. _____ Sound is a(n) _____ wave.
   a. transverse   b. longitudinal   c. electromagnetic   d. electron

3. _____ As an approaching ambulance passes a stationary observer, the frequency of the sound emitted by its siren
   a. increases   b. decreases   c. stays the same.

4. _____ The frequency of the sound heard by the observer in Question 3 _____ as the approaching ambulance passes the observer.
   a. increases   b. decreases   c. stays the same

5. _____ A detected change in the frequency of a sound due to a moving source or a moving observer is
   a. refraction   b. sonar   c. the Doppler effect   d. resonance.

6. _____ Which of the following *does not* describe the pitch of a sound?
   a. frequency of vibration   b. a note on a musical scale
   c. loud or soft   d. high or low

7. _____ Two notes have frequencies the ratio of which is 2:1. The notes differ by a(n)
   a. major third   b. octave   c. fifth   d. fourth.

8. _____ A source with a sound level of 40 dB has a pressure amplitude that is _____ times greater than a source with a sound level of 20 dB.
   a. 5   b. 10   c. 20   d. 100

9. _____ The sound heard from a record album is
   a. sound that is stored on the vinyl disk   b. produced by the needle vibrating against the record   c. produced by vibrations within the turntable   d. none of the above.

10. _____ Which of the following *is not* true of closed-pipe resonators?
    a. Nodes are separated by one-half wavelength.   b. The pressure wave is reflected from the closed end without inversion.   c. A pressure wave is inverted when it is reflected from the open end.   d. The open end of the pipe is a pressure antinode.

11. _____ Which of the following *is not* true of open-pipe resonators?
    a. There are nodes at each end of the pipe.   b. The resonances are spaced by quarter wavelengths.   c. Some sound is transmitted at the open ends.
    d. Some sound is reflected at the open ends.

12. _____ The _____ of the human ear collects sound waves.
    a. auditory canal   b. eardrum   c. inner ear   d. pinna

13. _____ Sound quality of the human voice depends on
    a. tongue movements   b. nasal cavities   c. throat movements   d. all of these.

B. Applying Concepts

Answer the following questions in two or three complete sentences.

1. How are molecules in air involved in producing sound from a trumpet?

2. In terms of resonance, pitch, and frequency, describe how sound is produced in a trumpet.

3. Tornadoes can develop in only an hour and they can cause much damage in only a few minutes. Describe how the Doppler effect could be used to warn against an oncoming tornado.

4. Diagram the standing waves on plucked strings. The relationship between the length of the string and the wavelength of the note is shown for each example. Label nodes and antinodes.

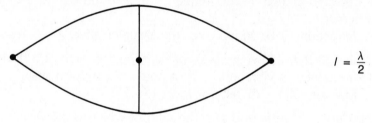

$l = \frac{\lambda}{2}$

a.

$l = \lambda$

b.

$l = \frac{3}{2}\lambda$

c.

$l = 2\lambda$

5. What is a beat and what produces it?

6. What are harmonics? Contrast the harmonics of open-pipe resonators with the harmonics of closed-pipe resonators.

15 Evaluation

C. Understanding Concepts

1. A sound wave traveling at a speed of 340 m/s has a wavelength of 1.25 m. What is the frequency of the sound?

2. What would be the wavelength of the wave in Problem 1 if it were traveling through water at 1435 m/s?

3. An A on the piano has a frequency of 55 Hz. What is the frequency of the A three octaves higher?

4. What is the wavelength of a sound made by a violin string vibrating at 640 Hz if the wave is traveling at 350 m/s?

5. What is the period of the sound wave in Problem 4?

6. A 448-Hz tuning fork and a 444-Hz tuning fork are struck at the same time. What is the frequency of the beat produced?

7. Two tuning forks are struck simultaneously to produce 2 beats/s. The frequency of one fork is 364 Hz. What are the possible frequencies of the other tuning fork?

D. Extending Concepts

1. The speed of sound through air depends on air temperature. Sound waves travel through 20°C air at 343 m/s. The velocity of sound in air increases 0.6 m/s for each increase of 1 Celsius degree. What is the temperature of the air if the speed of sound is 350 m/s?

2. A tuning fork has a frequency of 395 Hz. The fork causes resonances in an air column spaced at 45.6 cm. What is the velocity of the sound?

3. A tuning fork with a frequency of 365 Hz is held above a closed pipe. What is the spacing between resonances if the air temperature is 15°C?

4. The equation for the Doppler shift of a sound wave moving at a velocity v, approaching a moving detector, is: $f = f[(v + v_d)/(v - v_s)]$. If a whistle has a frequency of 545 Hz and the air temperature is 7°C, what frequency will you hear if you are approaching the whistle at 32 m/s?

CHAPTER

16 Evaluation

LIGHT

A. Testing Concepts

In the space to the left, write the letter of the answer to each question.

1. ＿＿＿ Light is a(n) ＿＿＿ wave.
   a. electromagnetic   b. mechanical   c. compressional   d. longitudinal

2. ＿＿＿ Violet light has a wavelength of about
   a. 0.2 μm   b. 0.4 μm   c. 500 nm   d. 700 nm.

3. ＿＿＿ The wavelength of red light is
   a. 0.2 μm   b. 0.4 μm   c. 500 nm   d. 700 nm.

4. ＿＿＿ Putting your hand into the path of light from a flashlight illustrates
   a. that light is a mechanical wave   b. that light travels in a straight line
   c. the refractive property of light   d. the candela unit of measurement.

5. ＿＿＿ The ＿＿＿ of light is a defined value.
   a. wavelength   b. speed   c. frequency   d. amplitude

6. ＿＿＿ The rate at which light is emitted is the ＿＿＿ of a light bulb.
   a. luminous flux   b. illuminance   c. candela   d. luminous intensity

7. ＿＿＿ Illuminance directly under a small light source is
   a. directly proportional to $4\pi d^2$ b. directly proportional to luminous flux
   c. indirectly proportional to luminous flux   d. indirectly proportional to luminous intensity.

8. ＿＿＿ Thin, white tissue paper can be described as
   a. transparent   b. translucent   c. opaque   d. none of the above.

9. ＿＿＿ Materials such as concrete that do not allow any transmission of light are described as
   a. transparent   b. translucent   c. opaque   d. none of the above.

10. ＿＿＿ Using primary colors of light to produce other colors is a(n) ＿＿＿ process.
    a. secondary   b. pigment   c. subtractive   d. additive

11. ＿＿＿ When yellow light and blue light are combined, ＿＿＿ light is produced.
    a. green   b. black   c. red   d. white

12. ＿＿＿ Which of the following is *not* true of primary pigments?
    a. They absorb all colors from white light.   b. They are secondary light colors.
    c. They absorb light by the subtractive process.
    d. They absorb one and reflect two primary colors.

13. ＿＿＿ The spectrum of colors produced by an oil film on water is due to the
    a. absorption of colors in a pigment   b. separation of white light into its components
    c. constructive interference of light waves   d. reflection of colors by a pigment.

14. ＿＿＿ As the thickness of a film increases, the light that is least strongly reflected is ＿＿＿ light.
    a. blue   b. green   c. orange   d. red

15. ＿＿＿ Only waves ＿＿＿ to the polarizing axis of a polarizing filter can pass through.
    a. smaller than the opening   b. larger than the opening
    c. vibrating parallel   d. vibrating perpendicular

NAME ———————————————————————————

B. Applying Concepts

Answer the following questions in two or three complete sentences.

1. What is a ray? How are rays used to study light?

2. Contrast luminous flux, luminous intensity, and illuminance.

3. Mathematically describe the relationship between illumination on a surface and the distance the surface is from the light source.

4. Explain why a dandelion appears yellow. Is the process additive or subtractive? Why?

5. How is a dye different from a pigment?

6. How can you tell whether or not light is polarized?

16 Evaluation

C. Understanding Concepts

1. What is the frequency of light with a wavelength of 7.00×10^{-7} m? What color is the light?

2. What is the illumination on a piece of paper that is on a table 3.0 m from a light source producing 1600 lumens of flux?

3. How much luminous flux must a light bulb produce if the bulb is positioned 4.1 m from the surface and the luminance required is 22 lx?

4. What is the candle power of a bulb with 2.00×10^3 lm flux?

5. The light of a sodium vapor lamp emits light waves with wavelengths of 570 nm. What is the frequency of the electromagnetic waves?

6. At what distance from a work area would the lamp in Problem 5 have to be placed in order to provide maximum illumination of the space?

D. Extending Concepts

1. The radius of Saturn's orbit is 1.43×10^9 km. How long, in minutes, will it take light to cross its orbit?

2. On the average, one watt of electromagnetic energy produces about 500 lumens of luminous flux. What is the illumination of a 40-watt fluorescent bulb that operates at 20% efficiency if the bulb is placed 2.0 m from a book it is illuminating?

3. Use the data provided in Problem 2 to compare the fluorescent bulb with an incandescent lamp, which is only about 3% efficient.

4. Suppose a lamp were placed on a desk 0.33 m above a work area. How would the illumination compare with that provided by a ceiling light fixture, with the same luminous flux of 1500 lm, which is 2.0 m from the work area?

CHAPTER
17 Evaluation

REFLECTION AND REFRACTION

A. Testing Concepts

In the space to the left, write the letter of the answer to each question.

1. _____ According to the law of reflection,
   a. the normal is parallel to the angle of reflection   b. the incident ray and the reflected ray are in different planes   c. light rays are reflected in the same direction from a smooth surface   d. the angles of reflection and incidence are equal.

2. _____ From which of the following surfaces would light rays undergo regular reflection?
   a. white construction paper   b. a telescope mirror
   c. a piece of black cloth   d. a concrete sidewalk

3. _____ Refraction occurs when
   a. light travels through two adjacent media with different optical densities   b. light strikes the boundary of two media with the same optical density   c. the angle of incidence equals zero   d. the angle of reflection equals zero.

4. _____ When light rays travel from an optically-dense medium into a less-dense medium,
   a. the rays travel more quickly   b. the angle of refraction is smaller than the angle of incidence   c. the refracted rays bend toward the normal
   d. the angle of incidence equals the angle of refraction.

5. _____ Which of the following is *not* true of Snell's law?
   a. Light moving from a substance with a smaller n to a larger n is bent toward the normal.   b. Light rays traveling between any two media are related by a constant, n.
   c. As the angle of refraction increases, the angle of incidence increases.
   d. The sines of the angles of refraction and incidence are inversely proportional to the indices of refraction of the two media.

6. _____ The incident angle for which a refracted ray emerges tangent to the surface of a medium is the _____ angle.
   a. reflected   b. zero   c. critical   d. normal

7. _____ The sine of the critical angle of a substance is
   a. directly proportional to the index of refraction of the substance   b. indirectly proportional to the index of refraction of the substance   c. indirectly proportional to the sine of 90°   d. directly proportional to the cosine of 90°.

8. _____ A rainbow is a phenomenon caused by
   a. a mirage   b. refraction   c. total internal reflection   d. b and c.

9. _____ In an optical fiber, the index of refraction of the core is _____ that of the outer layer.
   a. greater than   b. less than   c. equal to

10. _____ The index of refraction of the mineral, beryl, ranges between 1.57 and 1.61. Transparent quartz has an index of 1.54. Which of the following statements is true?
    a. Both minerals will disperse the same amount of light.   b. Quartz will disperse more light than beryl.   c. Beryl will disperse more light than the quartz.
    d. Both minerals will disperse more light than diamond.

B. Applying Concepts

Answer the following questions in two or three complete sentences.

1. Explain the difference between regular and diffuse reflection.

2. Explain the relationship between the sine of the angle of incidence and the sine of the angle of refraction of light rays traveling from a vacuum into another medium.

3. Mathematically express the relationship between indices of refraction for a light ray traveling from one medium into another.

4. How does the angle of refraction change as a light ray passes from a medium with a higher index of refraction to one with a lower index of refraction?

5. What is total internal reflection?

6. Why is the sun still visible over the horizon after sunset?

C. Understanding Concepts

1. Light rays traveling through quartz enter the quartz at an angle of 35°. The index of refraction of quartz is 1.54. At what angle do the light rays leave the substance?

2. A light ray enters a substance at an angle of 55°. The light is refracted inside the substance and leaves the substance at an angle of 35°. What is the index of refraction of the material?

3. Diamond has an index of refraction of 2.42. If it is immersed in water, which has an index of 1.33, and light rays in the water shine on the diamond at a 53° angle, what is the angle of refraction inside the diamond?

4. The index of refraction of halite, or table salt, is 1.54. What is the speed of light in this mineral?

5. What is the index of refraction of a material if light travels through the material at 2.10×10^8 m/s?

6. The mineral calcite, $CaCO_3$, has an index of refraction of 1.66. What is the critical angle of calcite?

17 Evaluation

D. Extending Concepts

1. Flint glass has an index of refraction of 1.57 for red light and 1.59 for violet light. If the red light ray is refracted at 67°, what is the angle of incidence for the violet ray?

2. A light ray in a tub of water makes an angle of incidence of 52° at the surface. The index of refraction of air is 1.00 and of water is 1.33.
   a. Prove that the ray undergoes total internal reflection.

   b. What is the value of the angle of internal reflection?

3. In some optical instruments, such as binoculars, 45°-prisms are used to produce total internal reflection at two surfaces. What is the minimum index of refraction needed for each prism?

4. The index of refraction for borate flint glass is 1.57 for red light and 1.59 for violet light. When a ray of white light nears the surface of the glass at an angle of 60.0°, what are the angles of refraction for the two wavelengths?

CHAPTER

18 Evaluation

MIRRORS AND LENSES

A. Testing Concepts

In the space to the left, write the letter of the answer to each question.

1. ____ Which of the following is *not* true of plane mirrors and the images they form?
   a. The light rays intersect at a point behind the mirror to form a real erect image.
   b. The angles of reflection and incidence are equal.   c. A virtual image is formed at the same distance behind the mirror that the object is in front of the mirror.
   d. The virtual image that forms is the same size as the actual object.

2. ____ For very small angles, the focal length of a concave mirror is
   a. equal to the radius of the mirror   b. two times the length of the principal axis
   c. half the distance between the center of curvature and the mirror's surface
   d. equal to twice the radius of the mirror.

3. ____ Parabolic mirrors are often used in
   a. department store dressing rooms   b. certain types of astronomical equipment
   c. eyeglasses   d. all of the above.

4. ____ A real image is formed when
   a. light rays converge and pass through the image   b. light rays seem to diverge from behind the mirror   c. the image cannot be projected onto a screen
   d. rays farthest from the principal axis meet at the mirror's surface.

5. ____ If an object is located between the focal point and a concave mirror, the image formed will be ____ than the object.
   a. real and smaller   b. real and larger
   c. virtual and larger   d. virtual and smaller

6. ____ Which of the following is *not* true of a convex mirror?
   a. It reflects light from its outer surface.   b. It forms real images.
   c. The focal point is behind the mirror.   d. The focal length of the mirror is negative.

7. ____ The image formed of an object located beyond the principal focus of a convex lens is ____ than the actual object.
   a. real and smaller   b. virtual and smaller
   c. virtual and larger   d. real and larger

8. ____ Which of the following is *not* true of a concave lens?
   a. It forms a virtual, erect, and reduced image.
   b. The image is formed due to divergence of the light rays.   c. It has a positive focal length.
   d. It is thinner in the middle than at the edges.

9. ____ Chromatic aberration can be reduced by cementing ____ together to form a single lens.
   a. two converging lenses   b. two diverging lenses
   c. three converging lenses   d. a converging lens and a diverging lens

10. ____ The focal length of the objective lens in a telescope is ____ the focal length of the objective lens in a microscope.
    a. greater than   b. less than   c. about the same as

B. Applying Concepts

Answer the following questions in two or three complete sentences.

1. What happens to a light ray that is parallel to the principal axis of a concave mirror after it is reflected from the mirror's surface? What happens to a ray that passes through the focal point of such a mirror before being reflected?

2. What causes spherical aberration?

3. Complete the diagram to show the size and location of the image of an object located beyond the center of curvature of a concave mirror.

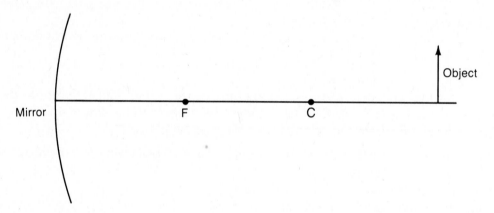

4. Contrast convex and concave lenses.

5. Contrast the image formed by a converging lens when an object is located beyond the principal focus of the lens with the image formed when the object is between the lens and the principal focus.

6. Complete the diagram to show the size and location of the image produced by a concave lens.

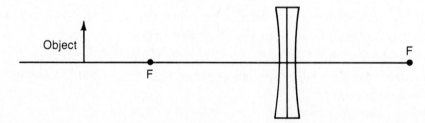

C. Understanding Concepts

1. A thimble 2.5 cm high is 32.0 cm from a concave mirror. The curvature of the mirror is 22.0 cm. Where is the image located?

2. What is the size and orientation of the thimble's image in Problem 1?

3. What is the magnification of the mirror in Problem 1?

4. What is the size of the image produced by a child 1.1 m tall who is standing 6.0 m from a convex mirror if the location of the image produced is 0.40 m behind the mirror?

5. What is the focal length of the mirror in Problem 4?

6. An object is 5.00 cm from a convex lens with a focal length of 6.00 cm. Locate and describe the image.

7. What focal length concave lens is needed to form a virtual image 10 cm from the lens when the object is 35 cm from the lens?

D. Extending Concepts

1. If a flower 1.00 m high is to have an image 35 mm high when the flower is 10.0 m from the concave mirror, what must the radius of curvature of the mirror be?

2. If a vehicle 2.0 m high is 4.6 m from your car's convex mirror, find the size and position of the image. The radius of curvature of the mirror is 80.0 cm. Is the image real or virtual? Explain.

3. Two convex lenses are positioned 52 cm apart. The first lens has a focal length of 10.0 cm and the second has a focal length of 13.0 cm. An object 1.0 cm high is placed 13 cm from the first lens. What is the size of the image produced by the second lens? Is the image real or virtual?

CHAPTER

19 Evaluation

DIFFRACTION AND INTERFERENCE OF LIGHT

A. Testing Concepts

In the space to the left, write the letter of the answer to each question.

1. _____ The destructive and constructive interference of light that passes through two closely-spaced slits produces
   a. interference fringes   b. monochromatic light sources
   c. coherent light waves   d. diffraction gratings.

2. _____ The bending of waves around the edges of barriers is
   a. diffraction   b. interference   c. refraction   d. reflection.

3. _____ What happens when monochromatic light is passed successively through a single narrow slit and then through a double slit?
   a. The double slit acts as two sources of circular waves.
   b. The waves interfere destructively where crests and troughs overlap.
   c. The light waves interfere constructively where two crests meet.
   d. all of the above

4. _____ The paths of the light waves that interfere to cause first-order lines
   a. differ in length by the wavelength of the light   b. are parallel lines
   c. are the same length   d. are curved lines.

5. _____ The wavelength of light using double-slit interference patterns is
   a. directly proportional to the distance between the screen and the slits
   b. indirectly proportional to the distance between the two slits
   c. indirectly proportional to the distance between the slits and the screen
   d. directly proportional to the distance between the two slits.

6. _____ When light passes through a single slit,
   a. a series of equally-bright bands appear
   b. a bright central band appears, with dimmer bright bands to the sides
   c. a dark central band appears, with bright bands to either side
   d. a single wide bright band appears.

7. _____ Interference patterns of diffraction gratings
   a. form in a similar way to those formed by double slits
   b. have bright bands that are narrower than those produced by double slits
   c. allow wavelengths to be measured more accurately than with double slits
   d. do all of the above.

8. _____ A binary star system can be misinterpreted as a single star because
   a. the telescope lens acts as a double slit
   b. the lens has a limited resolution
   c. the light is refracted as it enters Earth's atmosphere
   d. a binary star system contains only one star.

9. _____ The effects of diffraction on the resolving power of the telescope can be reduced by
   a. increasing the size of the lens   b. decreasing the size of the lens
   c. magnifying the images being viewed   d. using yellow filters to view the objects.

B. Applying Concepts

Answer the following questions in two or three complete sentences.

1. Why are the edges of shadows not sharp? What is this phenomenon called?

2. Complete and label this geometric representation of Young's double-slit experiment. How can wavelength be determined from the drawing?

Source

Screen

3. Explain the cause of the dark bands seen as a result of single-slit diffraction.

4. Contrast the interference patterns formed by double slits with those formed by diffraction gratings.

5. Can the values for white-light wavelengths be directly measured with a grating spectrometer? Explain your answer.

19 Evaluation

C. Understanding Concepts

1. If the slit separation is 1.72×10^{-5} m and the screen is 0.650 m from the slits, how far from the central band will the violet light of the spectrum appear? The wavelength of violet light is 4.50×10^{-7} m.

2. A red laser falls on two slits that are 1.95×10^5 m apart. A first-order line appears 4.42×10^{-2} m from the central bright line. If the screen is 1.25 m from the slits, what is the wavelength of the light?

3. Monochromatic light of a sodium vapor lamp has a wavelength of 570 nm. If two slits are separated by 1.90×10^{-5} m and the slits are 0.800 m from the screen, what is the distance from the central line to the first-order yellow line?

4. Suppose the double slit in Problem 3 were replaced by a single slit 0.0900 mm wide. What is the distance from the center of the central band to the first dark band?

5. A diffraction grating has 6.00×10^3 lines per centimeter. The screen is 0.40 m from the grating. If a red line appears on the screen 12.9 cm from the central line, what is the wavelength of the red light?

D. Extending Concepts

1. The range of wavelengths for visible light is from about 400 nm to 700 nm. What is the angular breadth of the first-order visible spectrum produced by a grating that has 1.00×10^{44} lines per cm?

2. A diffraction grating forms a number of spectra on either side of the normal. Using the equation

$$\sin \theta = (m\lambda)/d$$

spectra can be classified. Those that correspond to $m = 1$ are first order, those that correspond to $m = 2$ are second order and so on. Use this information to show that the violet of the third-order spectrum overlaps the red of the second-order spectrum. The wavelength for violet is about 400 nm; the wavelength for red light is about 700 nm.

3. Using the equation given in Problem 2, what is the longest wavelength that can be observed in the fourth order of a diffraction grating that has 5000 lines per cm?

CHAPTER

20 Evaluation

STATIC ELECTRICITY

A. Testing Concepts

In the space to the left, write the letter of the answer to each question.

1. _____ Because charged objects can attract other charged objects upward, away from Earth, the upward acceleration due to the electrical charge must be _____ the acceleration downward due to gravity.
   a. greater than   b. less than   c. equal to

2. _____ Rubbing two objects such as plastic and wool together creates a static charge because
   a. atoms are transferred from one object to another
   b. electrons are transferred from atoms in one object to atoms in the other object
   c. the electrons in one object are attracted to the nuclei in the other object
   d. electrons become more widely distributed in each object.

3. _____ Bits of paper stick to a plastic comb that has been rubbed because of
   a. electrical charge   b. nuclear forces   c. gravity   d. kinetic energy.

4. _____ When electrons are transferred from one object to another, positive and negative charges are
   a. created   b. reversed   c. separated   d. canceled.

5. _____ An important difference between insulators and conductors is that in conductors
   a. electrons can be removed from atoms easily
   b. electrons are free to move around
   c. electrons carry electric charges   d. all of the above are true.

6. _____ When an electroscope is charged, its leaves spread apart because
   a. like charges repel   b. charges exert force on other charges over a distance
   c. positive and negative charges spread over the metal surfaces
   d. of both a and b.

7. _____ Touching an electroscope with a negatively-charged rod is an example of
   a. charging by conduction   b. charging by induction
   c. discharging electrostatic force   d. distributing unlike charges.

8. _____ In charging by induction
   a. a charged object can be used to change the charge of another charged object
   b. a charged object can be used to charge a neutral object without touching it
   c. a neutral object can be used to separate like charges
   d. no charges are separated.

9. _____ The force that charge q exerts on charge q' is opposite and _____ the force that charge q' exerts on q.
   a. greater than   b. less than   c. equal to

10. _____ Electric force is a vector quantity because it has magnitude and
    a. direction   b. duration   c. frequency   d. strength.

11. _____ Which of the following statements is *not* true of a charged object?
    a. It may attract another charged object.   b. It may repel another charged object.
    c. It always attracts a neutral object.   d. It always repels a neutral object.

B. Applying Concepts

Answer the following questions in two or three complete sentences.

1. Which of the following would you use to prevent the spread of an electrical charge: copper, plastic, or graphite? Explain your answer.

2. How is the separation of charges involved in electrical interactions?

3. Why do socks and other pieces of clothing stick together after being tumbled in a dryer?

4. Distinguish between charging by conduction and charging by induction.

5. What kind of charging occurs during a thunderstorm? Explain.

6. Two positive charges are located 2 cm apart. Charge q is 2×10^{-9} C and charge q' is 3×10^{-9} C. Is the force between these charges attractive or repulsive? Explain your answer.

20 Evaluation

C. Understanding Concepts

1. A positive charge of 3.6×10^{-5} C and a negative charge of -2.4×10^{-5} C are 0.034 m apart. What is the force between the two particles?

2. The force between two objects is 64 N. One has a positive charge of 1.4×10^{-6} C while the other has a negative charge of 1.8×10^{-6} C. How far apart are the two objects?

3. Two negative charges of -4.2×10^{-8} C are separated by 0.46 m. What is the magnitude of the force acting on each object?

4. Two objects exert a force on each other of 4.2 N. The distance between the objects is 0.36 m. The charge on one object is 2.8×10^{-9} C. What is the charge on the second object?

5. Assuming the force exerted between two spheres is 64 N, what will be the magnitude of the force if the distance is doubled? Tripled?

D. Extending Concepts

1. Two objects, one having twice the charge of the other, are separated by 0.78 m and exert a force of 3.8×10^3 N. What is the charge on each object?

2. The drawing shown indicates the charges on three objects, and the distances between charges, **A** and **B** and between charges **B** and **C**. Charges **A** and **C** are 90° apart with respect to charge **B**. On the drawing, show the direction of the forces acting on charge **B**. Calculate the total charge acting on charge **B**.

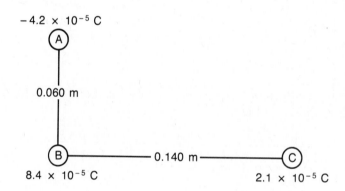

-4.2×10^{-5} C

Ⓐ

0.060 m

Ⓑ——————— 0.140 m ———————Ⓒ

8.4 × 10⁻⁵ C   2.1 × 10⁻⁵ C

3. What is the vector angle of the force acting on charge **B**? Add this vector to the drawing, showing its approximate position.

CHAPTER
21 Evaluation

ELECTRIC FIELDS

A. Testing Concepts

In the space to the left, write the letter of the answer to each question.

1. _____ An electric field is equal to
   a. force per unit mass   b. force per unit charge
   c. force per unit time   d. force times direction.

2. _____ The force on a test charge in an electric field is
   a. directly proportional to the magnitude of the field
   b. inversely proportional to the magnitude of the field
   c. inversely proportional to the square of the magnitude of the field
   d. unrelated to the magnitude of the field.

3. _____ The strength of the force on a charge in an electric field depends on
   a. the direction of the field   b. the magnitude of the field
   c. the size of the charge   d. both b and c.

4. _____ As an electric field becomes stronger the field lines should be drawn
   a. thicker   b. thinner   c. closer together   d. farther apart.

5. _____ The difference between an electric field and field lines is that
   a. electric fields do not really exist
   b. field lines are a method for measuring the force on a charge
   c. field lines are produced by more than one charge
   d. field lines are only a model of an electric field.

6. _____ The work done moving a test charge from one point to another is
   a. potential energy   b. kinetic energy
   c. electric potential   d. electric potential difference.

7. _____ In a uniform electric field, the potential difference between two points is found using the equation
   a. $V = Ed$ b. $E = Vd$ c. $V = E/d$ d. $E = V/d$

8. _____ Robert A. Millikan determined that
   a. each electron always carries the same charge   b. charges are quantized
   c. changes in charges are caused by one or more electrons being added or removed
   d. all of the above are true.

9. _____ Touching an object to Earth to eliminate excess charge is
   a. conduction   b. induction   c. grounding   d. friction.

10. _____ The charges on a hollow conductor are found
    a. on the outer surface   b. on the inner surface
    c. at the ends   d. on both the outer and inner surfaces.

11. _____ A capacitor is
    a. a device that stores a charge
    b. made up of two conductors separated by an insulator
    c. a device that measures electric potential differences   d. both a and b.

B. Applying Concepts

Answer the following questions in two or three complete sentences.

1. Compare an electric field with a gravitational field.

2. What is the direction of an electric field between a negative and a positive charge?

3. Explain why electric potential energy is larger when two like charges are closer together than when two unlike charges are closer together.

4. If a high-voltage wire falls on a car, will the people inside be safe from electrocution? Explain your answer.

5. What is the net charge on a capacitor? Explain your answer.

21 Evaluation

C. Understanding Concepts

1. A positive charge of 2.4×10^{-6} C is acted on by a force of 0.43 N at a certain distance. What is the electric field intensity at that distance?

2. What charge exists on a test charge that is acted on by a force of 3.60×10^{-6} N at a point where the electric field intensity is 1.60×10^{-5} N/C?

3. The electric field intensity between two charged plates is 2.80×10^4 N/C. The plates are 0.0640 m apart. What is the potential difference between the plates in volts?

4. A voltmeter connected between two plates registers 38.2 V. The plates are separated by a distance of 0.046 m. What is the field intensity between the plates?

5. How much work is done to transfer 0.47 C of charge through a potential difference of 12 V?

6. A 9.0-V battery does 1.0×10^3 J of work transferring charge. How much charge is transferred?

D. Extending Concepts

1. A force of 7.60×10^3 N acts on a charge of 1.60×10^{-2} C over a distance of 0.0440 m. What is the potential difference of this system?

2. How much work is done by a system in which the force is 6.8×10^4 N, the potential difference is 4.2 V, and the electric field intensity is 1.2×10^{-3} N/C?

3. How much energy is stored in a capacitor of 12.2 μF which has been charged to 4.26×10^2 V?

4. How much power is required to charge a capacitor of 9.4 μF to 5.4×10^2 V in 48 s?

CHAPTER
22 Evaluation

CURRENT ELECTRICITY

A. Testing Concepts

In the space to the left, write the letter of the answer to each question.

1. _____ In an electric circuit, charged particles
   a. flow around in a closed loop.   b. flow from higher potential to lower potential
   c. get energy from an external source   d. do all of the above.

2. _____ The energy carried by an electric current depends on which of the following?
   a. the charge transferred   b. the potential difference
   c. the total number of charges in the circuit   d. both a and b

3. _____ The rate at which energy is transferred is
   a. power   b. conventional current   c. resistance   d. electric current.

4. _____ The resistance of a conductor can be determined if _____ are known.
   a. energy and current   b. potential difference and current
   c. voltage and potential difference   d. current and amperes

5. _____ The scientist Georg Simon Ohm found that for most conductors
   a. current does not depend on resistance   b. resistance does not depend on voltage
   c. voltage does not depend on current   d. resistance and voltage depend on current.

6. _____ The current flowing in an electric circuit can be increased by
   a. increasing voltage or decreasing resistance
   b. decreasing voltage or increasing resistance
   c. increasing voltage and increasing resistance
   d. decreasing voltage and decreasing resistance.

7. _____ A device that measures the amount of current in a circuit is a(n)
   a. potentiometer   b. resistor   c. voltmeter   d. ammeter.

8. _____ Space heaters convert most of the electrical energy in a circuit into
   a. light energy   b. thermal energy   c. mechanical energy   d. sound energy.

9. _____ Energy from a battery is stored in the electric field of a capacitor when
   a. there is no potential difference across the resistor
   b. there is no more current flowing
   c. the voltage across the capacitor reaches the battery voltage
   d. all of the above are true.

10. _____ Electricity is carried long distances at high voltages because
    a. current can be kept low and less power is lost as thermal energy
    b. resistance can be kept low and less power is lost as thermal energy
    c. current cannot be changed to reduce thermal energy
    d. resistance cannot be changed to reduce thermal energy.

11. _____ Utility companies measure energy use in _____ because other units are two small.
    a. joules   b. kilowatt hours   c. watt-seconds   d. watts

B. Applying Concepts

Answer the following questions in two or three complete sentences.

1. What is the difference between an ampere and a volt?

2. Identify the parts of this schematic. Will current flow through the circuit? Explain your answer.

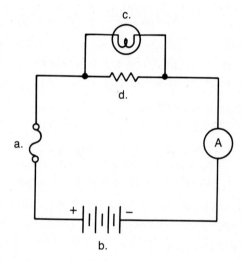

3. Could a voltmeter be substituted for the ammeter shown in the schematic? Explain your answer.

4. What would happen to current if both voltage and resistance were doubled?

5. Which has a greater effect on the amount of thermal energy produced in a heater, the current or the resistance of the heater? Explain your answer.

C. Understanding Concepts

1. A portable compact disc player receives its energy from a 9.0-V cell. The current used to operate the player is 135 A.
   a. How many joules of energy does the cell deliver to the CD player each second?

   b. How much power in watts does the CD player use?

   c. How much energy does the CD player use to play a selection 3.0 min long?

2. What voltage is applied to a 6.80-Ω resistor if the current is 3.20 A?

3. An electric buzzer is connected across a 4.2-V difference in potential. The current through the buzzer is 1.8 A.
   a. What is the power rating of the buzzer?

   b. How much electric energy does the buzzer convert in 1.5 min?

4. An electric blanket with a resistance of 8.6 Ω is connected to a 120-V source.
   a. What is the current in the circuit?

   b. How much heat is produced if the blanket is turned on for 15 min?

D. Extending Concepts

1. An electric motor operates an elevator the mass of which is 2.0×10^3. The elevator rises 120 m in 32 s. The motor has a resistance while operating of 34.0 Ω and is connected across a 2.4×10^3-V source. What percent of electric energy is converted to kinetic energy?

2. A three-pack of 1.5-V hearing aid batteries costs $4.26. Each battery puts out 8.0 mA of current. Each battery lasts for 15 days. What is the cost per kWh to operate the hearing aid with one battery?

3. While waiting for the school bus you keep your hands warm in a pair of electric gloves. The heating element in each glove has a resistance of 8.0 Ω. Each glove operates from a 12-V source. The thermal energy produced by each glove is 640 J. You wait for the bus for 3.0 min. When the bus arrives, are your hands warm or cold?

4. A model electric train makes one complete pass around a circular track every 15 s. The train's motor has a resistance of 6.0 Ω and is connected to a 70.0-V source. How much energy will the train use in 12 complete passes around the track?

CHAPTER

23 Evaluation

SERIES AND PARALLEL CIRCUITS

A. Testing Concepts

In the space to the left, write the letter of the answer to each question.

1. _____ If there are four electrical devices connected in a series circuit, then the number of current paths is equal to
   a. one   b. two   c. three   d. four.

2. _____ A series circuit contains a generator, an ammeter, and a lamp. The current in the lamp is
   a. equal to the current in the ammeter   b. less than the current in the ammeter
   c. equal to the current in the generator   d. a and c.

3. _____ A series circuit contains four resistors. The equivalent resistance of the circuit is equal to
   a. $4R$ b. $R_1 + R_2 + R_3 + R_4$ c. $\dfrac{R}{4}$ d. $\dfrac{R_1 + R_2 + R_3 + R_4}{4}$

4. _____ A 5-Ω resistor, a 20-Ω resistor, and a 25-Ω resistor are connected in series across a 90-V battery. The net change in potential going around this circuit is
   a. zero   b. 4 V   c. 50 V   d. 90 V.

5. _____ A series circuit has a 120-V generator but requires a 60-V potential source. To achieve the desired potential, a _____ can be used.
   a. photoresistor   b. sensor   c. voltage divider   d. semiconductor

6. _____ If three resistors are connected in parallel, there are _____ current paths in the circuit.
   a. one   b. two   c. three   d. four

7. _____ The equivalent resistance of a parallel circuit is always _____ the resistance of any resistor in the circuit.
   a. greater than   b. less than   c. equal to

8. _____ A 10-Ω resistor is connected in series with a 60-V battery. Two 15-Ω resistors are connected in parallel with the same battery. How many current paths are there?
   a. one   b. two   c. three   d. four

9. _____ An ammeter should have very low resistance because current would
   a. increase if the ammeter increased resistance in the circuit
   b. decrease if the ammeter decreased resistance in the circuit
   c. increase if the ammeter decreased resistance in the circuit
   d. decrease if the ammeter increased resistance in the circuit.

10. _____ Connecting a voltmeter across a resistor causes the potential across the resistor to
    a. double   b. decrease to one-half   c. remain about the same.

11. _____ An ammeter is connected in _____ and a voltmeter is connected in _____
    a. parallel, series   b. parallel, parallel   c. series, series   d. series, parallel.

12. _____ The first step in calculating the equivalent resistance in a combination circuit is to
    a. calculate the current in each resistor
    b. calculate the equivalent resistance of any resistors connected in parallel
    c. calculate the current in the whole circuit
    d. measure the voltage drop in the whole circuit.

B. Applying Concepts

Answer the following questions in two or three complete sentences.

1. A string of holiday lights has 15 bulbs connected in series. If one of the bulbs burns out, what happens to the other bulbs?

2. What happens to resistance when a resistor is added to a parallel circuit that already has two resistors?

3. How is it possible to use more than one electrical appliance at a time in a house?

4. A circuit has five identical resistors: **A, B, C, D,** and **E**. Resistors **A, D,** and **E** have the same potential difference across them. What kind of circuit is this? Explain your answer.

5. What would happen in a circuit if a voltmeter were substituted for an ammeter?

C. Understanding Concepts

1. Two resistors of 3.0 Ω and 8.0 Ω are connected in series across a 9.0-V battery.

   a. What is the equivalent resistance of the circuit?

   b. What is the current through the 3.0-Ω resistor?

   c. What is the current through the 8.0-Ω resistor?

   d. What is the voltage drop across each resistor?

2. A 15.0-Ω bell and an 8.0-Ω lamp are connected in parallel and placed across a difference in potential of 42 V.

   a. What is the equivalent resistance of the circuit?

   b. What is the current in the circuit?

   c. What is the current through each resistor?

   d. What is the voltage drop through each resistor?

D. Extending Concepts

1. Find the reading of each ammeter and each voltmeter in the following illustration.

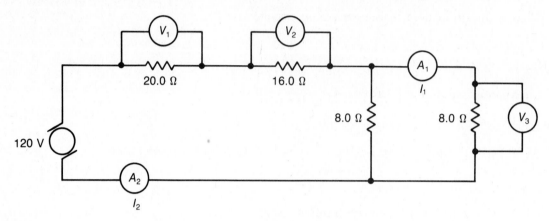

2. What is the power in watts used by each resistance in the illustration shown above?

CHAPTER

24 Evaluation

MAGNETIC FIELDS

A. Testing Concepts

In the space to the left, write the letter of the answer to each question.

1. _____ An object that is magnetic has
   a. a south-seeking pole   b. a north-seeking pole
   c. a magnetic field   d. all of the above.

2. _____ When iron filings are sprinkled around a bar magnet, the pattern that forms shows that field lines
   a. point straight out in all directions
   b. form closed loops that leave the north pole and enter the south pole
   c. leave the middle of the bar and enter the ends
   d. leave the ends of the bar and enter the middle.

3. _____ The strength of current-carrying wire is _____ to the magnetic field around a current.
   a. proportional   b. inversely proportional   c. equal   d. parallel

4. _____ Increasing the number of loops in an electromagnet causes the strength of the magnetic field to
   a. increase   b. decrease   c. remain the same.

5. _____ In a magnetic material the _____ act like tiny electromagnets.
   a. atoms   b. electrons   c. protons   d. neutrons

6. _____ The magnetic force on a current-carrying wire is _____ the direction of the current.
   a. opposite to   b. parallel to   c. perpendicular to   d. the same as

7. _____ The magnitude of the magnetic force on a current-carrying wire depends on
   a. the strength of the magnetic field   b. the current in the wire
   c. the length of wire in the magnetic field   d. all of the above.

8. _____ A device used to measure very small electric currents is a(n)
   a. ammeter   b. voltmeter   c. galvanometer   d. electric meter.

9. _____ A galvanometer consists of
   a. a small coil of wire placed in the magnetic field of a permanent magnet
   b. a straight wire connecting two electromagnets
   c. a small coil of wire connecting two electromagnets
   d. a small coil of wire attached to a source of potential difference and an electromagnet.

10. _____ In an electric motor
   a. several loops of wire rotate through 360°   b. current is reversed every half turn
   c. loops of wire rotate because of the force from a magnetic field   d. all of the above occur.

11. _____ The speed of an electric motor can be controlled by
   a. changing the direction of current flow   b. limiting the rotation of the wire loops
   c. varying the current flow   d. changing the direction of force on the wire loops.

12. _____ The force of a magnetic field on a single electron depends on
   a. the velocity of the electron   b. the strength of the field
   c. the angle between the directions of the velocity and the field   d. all of the above.

B. Applying Concepts

Answer the following questions in two or three complete sentences.

1. If all electrons create magnetic fields, why aren't all materials magnets?

2. How are the forces between charges similar to the forces between magnetic poles?

3. Suppose you have two bar magnets. Only one of the magnets has north and south poles labeled. How would you determine which are the south and north poles on the unlabeled magnet?

4. An electrical wire carries current in a straight line from east to west. What is the direction of the resulting magnetic field above the wire? What is the direction of the field below the wire?

5. If an electromagnet is used to pick up nails and other metal objects, what happens when the current is turned off?

6. If a permanent magnet is dropped or struck by a hammer, it may lose its magnetism. Explain why.

24 Evaluation

C. Understanding Concepts

1. A wire, 0.80 m long, carries a current of 6.0 A. The wire is at right angles to a uniform magnetic field the force of which is 0.62 N. What is the strength of the magnetic field?

2. A wire, 60.0 cm long, is at right angles to a uniform magnetic field of magnetic induction equal to 0.400 T. The current through the wire is 4.00 A. What is the force that acts on the wire?

3. A wire, 2.0 m long, carries a current of 12 A. The wire is at right angles to a uniform magnetic field the force of which is 0.50 N. What is the induction of the magnetic field?

4. A wire is at right angles to a magnetic field the force of which is 2.4 N. A current of 8.6 A flows through the wire. The induction of the magnetic field is 0.66 T. What is the length of the wire?

5. A high-speed electron travels at right angles to a magnetic field the induction of which is 0.420 T. The electron is traveling at 3.46×10^7 m/s. What is the force acting on the electron?

D. Extending Concepts

1. A particle that has a mass of 2.42×10^{-22} kg and a charge of 3.40×10^{-20} C is traveling through space at 2.50×10^{8} m/s when it encounters a magnetic field with an intensity of 2.40 T. The particle is moving perpendicular to the field. If the particle's velocity remains constant, what will be the radius of the curvature of its path?

2. A particle of unknown mass moves through a magnetic field intensity of 0.80 T at 1.4×10^{7} m/s. The charge on the particle is 2.8×10^{-16} C. The radius of the curvature of its path is 4.6 m. What is the mass of the particle?

3. Starting from a speed of 0 m/s, a proton is accelerated through a potential difference of 32 000 V. What is the proton's velocity?

4. The energy of a proton moving through a magnetic field of intensity 0.20 T is 4.4×10^{-15} J. What is the radius of the proton's path if it moves in a direction that is always perpendicular to the field?

CHAPTER

25 Evaluation

ELECTROMAGNETIC INDUCTION

A. Testing Concepts

In the space to the left, write the letter of the answer to each question.

1. _____ An electric current is generated in a wire when the wire is
   a. held stationary in a magnetic field   b. moved parallel to a magnetic field
   c. moved so that it cuts across magnetic field lines
   d. placed in a magnetic field of large intensity.

2. _____ Current can be made to flow in a stationary conductor by
   a. holding a magnet over the wire   b. moving a magnetic field across the wire
   c. moving a magnetic field parallel to the wire   d. touching the wire with a magnet.

3. _____ The electromotive force depends on
   a. magnetic field strength   b. the length of the wire in the magnetic field
   c. the velocity of the wire in the magnetic field   d. all of the above.

4. _____ An electric generator converts
   a. electrical energy to heat energy   b. electrical energy to mechanical energy
   c. mechanical energy to heat energy   d. mechanical energy to electrical energy.

5. _____ An electric motor is almost identical in construction to an electric generator, but the motor converts
   a. electrical energy to heat energy   b. electrical energy to mechanical energy
   c. mechanical energy to heat energy   d. mechanical energy to electrical energy.

6. _____ The power produced by a generator
   a. is the product of the resistance and the voltage   b. can be positive or negative
   c. has a lower average value for alternating currents than for direct currents
   d. is all of the above.

7. _____ According to Lenz's Law, the direction of induced current is such that the magnetic field resulting from the induced current _____ the change in flux that caused the current.
   a. opposes   b. strengthens   c. is perpendicular to   d. has no effect on

8. _____ If a generator produces only a small current, then the opposing force on the armature will be _____ and the armature will be _____ to turn.
   a. large, easy   b. large, hard   c. small, easy   d. small, hard

9. _____ As a motor begins to turn, a back-*EMF* is induced that _____ the current flow.
   a. opposes   b. is in the same direction as   c. is perpendicular to   d. has no effect on

10. _____ The size of the *EMF* generated by self-inductance is
    a. proportional to the rate at which current changes
    b. proportional to the rate at which flux lines cut through the wires
    c. zero when current reaches a steady value and magnetic flux is constant
    d. all of the above.

11. _____ In a step-up transformer, the primary voltage is _____ the secondary voltage.
    a. greater than   b. less than   c. equal to

25 Evaluation

B. Applying Concepts

Answer the following questions in two or three complete sentences.

1. A loop of wire is connected to a galvanometer. If a bar magnet is dropped through the loop, what happens to the galvanometer?

2. A bar magnet and a loop of wire are moving parallel to each other at the same velocity. What is the voltage induced in the loop? Explain.

3. What happens to induced *EMF* when magnetic field strength is doubled?

4. Compare the operation of an electric motor with that of an electric generator.

5. Why do the lights in a room dim momentarily when a large appliance is turned on?

6. What happens to the primary voltage when the number of turns on a secondary transformer coil is doubled?

C. Understanding Concepts

1. A wire 42.0 m long moves directly upward through a 6.20×10^{-4} T-magnetic field at a speed of 18.0 m/s. What *EMF* is induced in the wire?

2. An AC generator develops a maximum *EMF* of 620 V. What effective *EMF* does the generator deliver to an external circuit?

3. A step-up transformer has 125 turns on its primary coil. Its secondary coil consists of 1440 turns. The primary coil receives an AC current at 120 V.

   a. What voltage is across the secondary coil?

   b. The current in the secondary coil is 3.6 A. What current flows in the primary circuit?

   c. What is the power input and output of the transformer?

4. The primary coil of a transformer has 640 turns and is connected to a 240-V source. How many turns would be needed in the secondary coil to supply 8.0×10^2 V?

D. Extending Concepts

1. A wire 0.60 m long moves through a magnetic field of 0.48 T. The current flowing through the wire is 2.4×10^{-3} A. The wire is connected across a circuit of 8.0 Ω resistance. If the wire is moving perpendicular through the magnetic field, what is the velocity of the wire?

2. A space vehicle is sent to Jupiter to explore the planet's properties from orbit. The vehicle travels 1.0×10^3 km each minute. When in orbit, the probe deploys a horizontal antenna that is 120 m in length. Data received on Earth indicate that the probe is overflying a location of Jupiter where the magnetic field is 1.8×10^{-1} T. What voltage is induced between the antenna's tips?

3. An engineer can vary the rate at which water falls directly down through a generator at a hydroelectric power plant. The generator and its turbine can supply 268 MW of electric power when the rate at which the water supplies power to the turbine is 335 MW.

   a. What is the efficiency of the turbine/generator system?

   b. What is the change in the potential energy of the falling water per second?

   c. If the water falls 16 m to the turbine, what mass of water must be directed through the turbine per second to supply the power indicated above?

4. The secondary coil of a transformer has 8.00×10^2 turns while the primary coil has 2.40×10^2 turns. The input voltage is 24.0 V and the input current is 4.00 A. What is the output current?

CHAPTER

26 Evaluation

ELECTRIC AND MAGNETIC FIELDS

A. Testing Concepts

In the space to the left, write the letter of the answer to each question.

1. _____ In a cathode-ray tube, an electric field pulls electrons out of the _____ toward the _____
   a. negatively-charged cathode, positively-charged anode
   b. positively-charged anode, negatively-charged cathode
   c. negatively-charged anode, positively-charged cathode
   d. positively-charged cathode, negatively-charged anode.

2. _____ Electrons in a cathode-ray tube follow a straight path when the forces due to the electric and magnetic fields are
   a. equal in magnitude   b. in opposite directions
   c. in the same direction   d. both a and b.

3. _____ The masses of positive ions can be measured precisely using a
   a. Thomson tube   b. Bainbridge tube
   c. cathode-ray tube   d. mass spectrometer.

4. _____ James Clerk Maxwell postulated
   a. that accelerating charges produce electric and magnetic fields that move through space
   b. that changing magnetic fields produce changing electric fields
   c. that changing electric fields produce changing magnetic fields   d. all of the above.

5. _____ In an electromagnetic wave, the electric and magnetic fields are _____ to each other and _____ to the direction of wave motion.
   a. at right angles, perpendicular   b. at right angles, parallel
   c. parallel, at right angles   d. opposite, parallel

6. _____ Electromagnetic waves can be generated by
   a. oscillating fields produced by an AC generator
   b. oscillating fields produced by a coil and a capacitor connected in a series circuit
   c. vibrating quartz crystals   d. all of the above.

7. _____ A receiver consists of
   a. an antenna   b. a coil and capacitor circuit
   c. an amplifier   d. all of the above.

8. _____ In a microwave oven, the energy in electromagnetic waves is converted into _____ in food molecules.
   a. light energy   b. sound energy   c. thermal energy   d. chemical energy

9. _____ In a television antenna, the strength of a signal is increased by the constructive interference patterns of the _____ generated in the individual wires.
   a. electric fields   b. magnetic fields   c. electric currents   d. television waves

10. _____ When high-energy electrons crash into matter, their kinetic energies are converted into
    a. gamma rays   b. X rays   c. microwaves   d. radio waves.

11. _____ Which of the following frequencies is in the range of radio waves?
    a. 1×10^6 Hz   b. 1×10^{14} Hz   c. 1×10^{20} Hz   d. 1×10^{24} Hz

B. Applying Concepts

Answer the following questions in two or three complete sentences.

1. A scientist wishes to determine how much of a given pollutant is found in the air near a factory. Ordinarily, the pollutant is found in minute amounts. How can the scientist obtain this information?

2. What is piezoelectricity? How is it involved in producing an electromagnetic field?

3. Explain what is happening when you change the setting on your radio from one station to another.

4. If the orientation of the electric and magnetic fields generated by an electromagnetic wave are known, is it possible to determine the direction of the motion of the wave? Explain your answer.

5. Briefly explain how an electromagnetic wave is produced by the antenna from a television broadcast station.

6. What is the importance of finding the charge-to-mass ratio for an electron?

C. Understanding Concepts

1. An unknown particle having a mass of 2.4×20^{-27} kg and a charge of 3.2×10^{-19} C passes through a magnetic field of 5.6×10^{-1} T. The velocity of the particle is 6.8×10^3 m/s.

   a. What is the radius of its path?

   b. What is the circumference of the circle its path makes?

2. A particle with a mass of 4.1×10^{-27} kg and a charge of 6.4×10^{-19} C crosses a magnetic field that measures 2.6×10^{-2} T. The particle assumes a circular path the radius of which is 1.2×10^{-1} m. At what speed is the particle moving?

3. An object passes through a magnetic field of 6.2×10^{-2} T. The object's speed is 8.4×10^3 m/s. What is the electric field intensity?

4. A particle passing through a magnetic field has a mass of 6.5×10^{-27} kg and is moving at 3.2×10^4 m/s. The charge on the particle is determined to be 2.5×10^{-18} C and the radius of its circular path through the field is 4.1×10^{-2} m. What is the strength of the magnetic field?

5. A particle with a mass of 3.34×10^{-27} kg passes through a magnetic field of 3.8×10^{-3} T, which causes the nucleus to assume a circular path the radius of which is 0.060 m. A potential difference of what value accelerated the particle?

D. Extending Concepts

1. In an attempt to identify an unknown atom, a research team has narrowed down the possibilities to a few atoms. The nuclear composition (protons and neutrons) of each member of these atoms is shown. Note that each proton or neutron has a mass of 1.67×10^{-24} kg. Experiments have yielded the following data. The atom has a negative charge of 1.6×10^{-19} C. When passing through a magnetic field of 7.8×10^{-3} T at a speed of 7.9 m/s, the atom develops a circular path the radius of which is 8.3×10^{-4} m. What is the identity of the atom?

Atom	Protons	Neutrons
Chlorine	17	18
Argon	18	22
Bromine	35	44
Krypton	36	48
Iodine	53	74

2. Radon, Rn, is a radioactive element. As such it gives off certain particles. Assume you are a researcher attempting to identify the particle given off. It is known to have a charge of 3.2×10^{-19} C. When passing through a magnetic field of 2.0 T across a potential difference of 1.6×10^7 V, the particle is observed to follow a circular path the radius of which is 4.1×10^{-1} mg. What is the mass of the particle?

3. A particle possesses a charge of 5.8×10^{-17} C.

   a. How much energy is required to move it across a potential difference of 6.4×10^4 V?

   b. If the particle has a mass of 2.8×10^{-20} kg, what is its speed?

CHAPTER

27 Evaluation

QUANTUM THEORY

A. Testing Concepts

In the space to the left, write the letter of the answer to each question.

1. _____ In a star's spectrum, the frequency of the radiation emitted _____
   a. increases as the star's temperature increases
   b. decreases as the star's temperature increases
   c. increases as the star's temperature decreases
   d. increases as the wavelength increases.

2. _____ According to Planck's hypothesis,
   a. the energy of an incandescent body is quantized
   b. the variable *n* can have any real number value
   c. the frequency of vibration is indirectly proportional to the energy
   d. atoms radiate electromagnetic waves all the time that they vibrate.

3. _____ Einstein showed that the momentum of a photon is
   a. directly proportional to the speed of light
   b. indirectly proportional to the wavelength
   c. directly proportional to Planck's constant   d. all of the above.

4. _____ Compton's X-ray experiment showed that
   a. only photons behave like particles   b. only electrons behave like particles
   c. momentum and kinetic energy are conserved when photons collide with electrons
   d. photons have more mass than electrons.

5. _____ The wavelength of a particle is
   a. directly proportional to the particle's momentum
   b. indirectly proportional to Planck's constant
   c. directly proportional to the product of the mass and velocity of the particle
   d. indirectly proportional to the particle's momentum.

6. _____ To understand the nature of light, _____ properties of light need to be taken into consideration.
   a. wave   b. particle   c. both wave and particle

7. _____ The Heisenberg uncertainty principle is due to
   a. physicists not knowing whether to treat light as waves or particles
   b. not being able to detect the position and momentum of a particle at exactly the
   same moment   c. de Broglie's wavelength theory   d. the Compton effect.

8. _____ The work function is
   a. measured by the threshold frequency in the photoelectric effect
   b. the energy needed to free an electron from a metal
   c. the energy needed to free a proton from a metal   d. both a and b.

9. _____ The slope of a graph of the kinetic energy of ejected electrons versus the frequency of the
   incident radiation is equal to
   a. Planck's constant   b. the wavelength of the radiation
   c. the work function   d. none of the above.

B. Applying Concepts

Answer the following questions in two or three complete sentences.

1. What conditions must exist for a current to flow in a photocell? Does all radiation result in current flow? Explain your answer.

2. Differentiate between the electromagnetic wave theory and the photon theory.

3. What happens to the energy of a photon as it interacts with an electron of a metal?

4. How are the Compton effect and the photoelectric effect similar?

5. In the 1920s a scientist suggested that material particles have wave properties. What evidence was discovered that supports this suggestion?

6. Explain the Heisenberg uncertainty principle.

C. Understanding Concepts

1. The stopping potential of a photocell is 2.5 V. What is the kinetic energy given to the electrons by the incident light? Give your answer in joules and electron volts.

2. When a certain photoelectric surface is illuminated with light that has a wavelength of 5790 nm, the stopping potential is 0.24 V. What is the threshold frequency?

3. What is the photoelectric work function, in joules, of the surface in Problem 2?

4. What is the kinetic energy, in electron volts, of the electrons ejected from the surface in Problem 2?

5. What is the de Broglie wavelength of a 1.00-kg object traveling at 45.0 m/s?

6. An X ray traveling in a vacuum has a wavelength of 4.2×10^{-12} m. What is the momentum of the wave?

D. Extending Concepts

1. The emission of X rays can be described as an inverse photoelectric effect. What is the potential difference through which an electron must be accelerated in order to produce an X ray with a wavelength of 0.10 nm.

2. An electron is accelerated by a potential difference of 200 V. What is the de Broglie wavelength of the electron?

3. The threshold frequency of sodium is 5.6×10^{14} Hz. If sodium is illuminated by light at a frequency of 7.8×10^{14} Hz, electrons are emitted. How fast does one of these electrons travel?

CHAPTER

28 Evaluation

THE ATOM

A. Testing Concepts

In the space to the left, write the letter of the answer to each question.

1. _____ To determine the structure of the atom, Ernest Rutherford and his co-workers directed a beam of alpha particles at a sheet of metal a few atoms thick. The results indicated
   a. that all the negative charge of an atom is concentrated in a tiny, massive central core
   b. that all the positive charge of an atom is concentrated in a tiny, massive central core
   c. that an atom is mostly empty space   d. both b and c.

2. _____ According to the nuclear model of the atom, electrons
   a. are inside the nucleus but do not contribute a significant amount of mass
   b. are outside the nucleus and do not contribute a significant amount of mass
   c. have more mass than the nucleus   d. are packed together near the nucleus.

3. _____ Which of the following is *not* characteristic of the emission spectrum for a gas?
   a. a series of lines of different colors   b. a continuous band of colors from red through violet   c. light emitted at wavelengths characteristic of the atoms in the gas
   d. None of the above is characteristic of an emission spectrum.

4. _____ Unlike an emission spectrum, an absorption spectrum
   a. is created by passing white light through a cool gas
   b. shows which wavelengths of light are emitted by particular kinds of atoms
   c. shows which wavelengths of light are absorbed by particular kinds of atoms
   d. both a and c.

5. _____ Which of the following describes an electron in the ground state?
   a. It has the smallest allowable amount of energy.   b. It can emit energy.
   c. It can remain in the state for only a fraction of a second.
   d. It can make a transition to a lower energy level.

6. _____ The equation $r_n = \dfrac{h_2}{4\pi^2 Kmq} n^2$ can be used to calculate
   a. the radius of the second allowable energy level in a hydrogen atom
   b. the velocity of an electron at a given energy level   c. the wavelength of an electron
   d. the potential energy of an electron.

7. _____ The Bohr model of the atom is limited because
   a. it cannot be used to determine the energy levels of hydrogen
   b. it cannot be used to explain any of the chemical properties of elements
   c. it does not account for the wave properties of particles
   d. it cannot be used to calculate the ionization energy of a hydrogen atom.

8. _____ The region in which there is a high probability of finding an electron is called
   a. the Bohr orbit   b. the electron cloud   c. quantum mechanics
   d. none of the above.

9. _____ The light emitted by a laser
   a. is coherent   b. is the result of spontaneous emission
   c. is an avalanche of electrons   d. has many wavelengths.

28 Evaluation

B. Applying Concepts

Answer the following questions in two or three complete sentences.

1. Explain why line spectra can be thought of as "atomic fingerprints."

2. Distinguish between the ground state and excited state of an electron.

3. Explain why electrons in an atom do not fall into the nucleus.

4. How does the quantum model of the atom differ from the Bohr model?

5. Explain line spectra in terms of the quantum model of the atom.

6. Why is the word *avalanche* used when describing how a laser works?

C. Understanding Concepts

1. Calculate the radius of a hydrogen electron in the $n = 4$ orbital.

2. What is the energy of a photon emitted when a hydrogen electron drops from the $n = 3$ orbital to the $n = 2$ orbital?

3. What is the wavelength of the photon in Question 2?

4. An electric charge passed through a mercury vapor causes a spectral line of 245 nm. Calculate the energy of the photon emitted in electronvolts.

5. Which transition of a hydrogen electron emits a photon with the greatest amount of energy: $n = 5$ to $n = 3$, $n = 6$ to $n = 2$, or $n = 2$ to $n = 1$?

6. A photon has a wavelength of 6.00×10^2 nm. Find the frequency and the energy of the photon.

28 Evaluation

NAME ——————————————————————

D. Extending Concepts

1. A laser emits light with a wavelength of 633 nm. The laser pulses are 20 ms long. The power of the laser is 0.5 W.

   a. What is the energy of a photon emitted by the laser?

   b. How much energy is in the pulse?

   c. How many photons are in one pulse?

2. Calculate the velocity of an electron in the first Bohr orbit.

3. Given the angular momentum and wavelength of an electron, derive a formula to determine the electron's velocity.

CHAPTER
29 Evaluation

SOLID STATE ELECTRONICS

A. Testing Concepts

In the space to the left, write the letter of the answer to each question.

1. _____ When two atoms are brought together in a solid,
    a. the electric field of one atom affects the field of the other atom
    b. the energy level of one atom is raised while the level of the other is lowered
    c. the energy levels of the atoms are changed   d. all of the above occur.

2. _____ When a potential difference is placed across a wire,
    a. electron speeds decrease
    b. electrons drift slowly toward the positive end of the wire
    c. the conductivity increases as temperature increases
    d. electron collisions are more infrequent as temperature increases.

3. _____ Electrons in a(n) _____ have very high random speeds similar to the atoms in a gas.
    a. insulator   b. conductor   c. salt   d. nonmetal

4. _____ In a conductor, conductivity increases as
    a. resistance decreases   b. resistance increases
    c. temperature increases   d. electrons move from the valence band.

5. _____ In an insulator, the lowest energy level in the _____ band is between 5 eV and 10 eV above the highest energy level in the _____ band.
    a. ground state, conduction   b. completely filled, partially filled
    c. conduction, valence   d. valence, conduction

6. _____ In a semiconductor, the forbidden gap is _____ the forbidden gap in an insulator.
    a. larger than   b. smaller than   c. about the same size as

7. _____ In a(n) _____, impurity atoms are added to increase the conductivity of the material.
    a. conductor   b. insulator   c. intrinsic semiconductor   d. extrinsic semiconductor

8. _____ Dopants increase conductivity by _____ the material.
    a. increasing the electric field of   b. adding electrons or holes to
    c. decreasing the temperature of   d. causing donor electrons to escape from

9. _____ When dopants are added to a semiconductor, the net charge of the material
    a. becomes more positive   b. becomes more negative   c. does not change.

10. _____ In a _____ diode, the holes and free electrons are attracted toward the battery.
    a. forward-biased   b. reverse-biased   c. depleted   d. conventional-current

11. _____ In a silicon diode, if the applied voltage is positive,
    a. the diode acts like a small resistance   b. the diode is reverse-biased
    c. there is very high resistance   d. none of the above occurs.

12. _____ In a junction transistor, if the base is a p-type layer, then the emitter and collector regions must be
    a. forbidden gaps   b. n-type semiconductors
    c. p-type semiconductors   d. one n-type and one p-type semiconductor.

NAME ————————————————————————

29 Evaluation

B. Applying Concepts

Answer the following questions in two or three complete sentences.

1. Contrast conductors and insulators in terms of energy bands.

2. Why is silicon a good semiconductor?

3. Compare and contrast n-type semiconductors with p-type semiconductors.

4. Why does a diode conduct charges in only one direction?

5. How does a supermarket bar-code scanner work?

6. Use the figure to explain how a pnp transistor works. Use arrows and labels to show the emitter current, the collector current, and the hole flow.

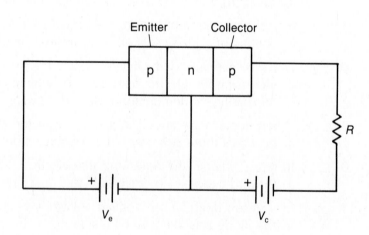

C. Understanding Concepts

1. Zinc has a density of 7.13 g/cm^3. Its atomic mass is 65.37 g/mole. If zinc has two free electrons per atom, how many free electrons are in a cubic centimeter of zinc?

2. Calculate the density of copper if each copper atom contributes one free electron and there are 8.49×10^{22} free e$^-$/cm^3 Cu. The atomic mass of copper is 63.54 g/mole.

3. How many silicon atoms are in one cubic centimeter of silicon? There are 1.00×10^{13} e$^-$/cm^3 at room temperature. The atomic mass of silicon is 28.09 g/mole and its density is 2.33 g/cm^3.

4. In a forward-biased silicon diode, the current is 22 mA and the voltage is 0.7 V. If the diode is connected to a battery through a 450-Ω resistor, what is the voltage of the battery?

5. A forward-biased silicon diode is connected to a 12.0-V battery through a resistor. If the current is 12 mA and the voltage is 0.7 V, what is the resistance?

D. Extending Concepts

1. A forward-biased silicon diode is connected to a 6.0-V battery. Also in the circuit are three 220-Ω resistors, connected in series. The voltage in the circuit is 0.7 V. What is the current?

2. There are 4.99×10^{22} silicon atoms/cm^3 in a doped silicon crystal. The silicon is doped with gallium so that one in every 10^7 silicon atoms is replaced by a gallium atom.

   a. If each gallium atom donates one electron to the conduction band, what is the density of free electrons in the resulting semiconductor?

   b. If there are 10^{13} free e$^-$ in pure silicon, what is the ratio of doped to pure silicon?

   c. Is conduction by thermally-freed electrons of the silicon or by the gallium-donated electrons? Explain your answer.

CHAPTER
30 Evaluation

THE NUCLEUS

A. Testing Concepts

In the space to the left, write the letter of the answer to each question.

1. _____ An atom's atomic number refers to the
   a. number of neutrons in a neutral atom b. number of protons in a neutral atom
   c. half the atom's atomic mass d. number of isotopes of the atom.

2. _____ The mass number of an atom is equal to
   a. the sum of its protons and electrons b. twice its number of neutrons
   c. half its atomic number d. the sum of its protons and neutrons.

3. _____ All nuclides of an element have
   a. different numbers of protons b. the same number of neutrons
   c. the same number of protons d. different numbers of electrons.

4. _____ The number of decays per second in a sample of radioactive material is its
   a. half-life b. activity c. gamma decay d. lepton.

5. _____ Which of the following types of radioactive decay occurs when a neutron is changed to a proton within the nucleus?
   a. alpha decay b. beta decay c. gamma decay d. both a and b

6. _____ The time required for half the atoms in any given quantity of a radioactive isotope to decay is the _____ of that element.
   a. half-life b. activity c. ionization rate d. weak interaction

7. _____ Which of the following is a type of accelerator?
   a. Geiger-Mueller tube b. Wilson cloud chamber
   c. synchrotron d. all of the above

8. _____ Photographic film can be used to detect
   a. alpha particles b. beta particles c. gamma particles d. all of the above.

9. _____ Physicists believe that quarks make up
   a. neutrons and electrons b. neutrinos and neutrons
   c. protons and electrons d. protons and neutrons.

10. _____ What is required to balance the following nuclear equation: $^4_2He + ^9_4Be \rightarrow$ _____ $+ ^1_0n$.
    a. $^6_{12}C$ b. $^{12}_6C$ c. $^{14}_6C$ d. $^8_{14}C$

11. _____ When a quark and its antiparticle collide, they annihilate each other and are transformed into
    a. photons b. mesons c. weak bosons d. gluons.

12. _____ Pair production results in a
    a. nucleus and an electron b. positron and an electron
    c. pair of protons d. pair of isotopes.

13. _____ In the quark model, the force that holds individual quarks together _____ as the quarks are pulled farther apart.
    a. becomes stronger b. becomes weaker c. remains the same

B. Applying Concepts

Answer the following questions in two or three complete sentences.

1. How can you find the mass of a nucleus?

2. Compare the energies with which the three different kinds of radiation are emitted.

3. Describe the effect gamma decay has on the mass number and atomic number of an atom.

4. Compare the number of protons, neutrons, and electrons found in two isotopes of the same element.

5. Since no nuclear particles are destroyed during a nuclear reaction, what must be true of an equation representing such a reaction?

6. Why is a linear accelerator unable to accelerate neutrons?

7. Use the quark model to explain why a proton has a positive charge and a neutron has no charge.

C. Understanding Concepts

1. The atomic mass of the most abundant isotope of bismuth is about 209 u. The atomic number of bismuth is 83. How many neutrons does an atom of this isotope of bismuth contain?

2. A radium atom, $^{224}_{88}Ra$, decays to radon, Rn, by emitting an alpha particle.

    a. Write a nuclear equation for this transmutation.

    b. What is the charge of the new nucleus?

3. An atom of plutonium, $^{243}_{94}Pu$, emits a beta particle when its nucleus decays to americium, Am.

    a. Write a nuclear equation for this transmutation.

    b. Indicate the number of protons and neutrons in the americium nucleus.

4. Complete the following equations.

    a. $^{253}_{99}Es + ^{4}_{2}He \rightarrow ^{256}_{101}Md +$ _____

    b. $^{238}_{92}U + 17\,^{1}_{0}n \rightarrow ^{255}_{100}Fm +$ _____

5. If a radioactive sample has an activity of 24 decays per second, what will the activity be after two half-lives have passed?

D. Extending Concepts

1. Geologists use the radioactive decay of $^{40}_{19}K$ to determine the ages of certain minerals. Assume that when the mineral is formed, $^{40}_{19}K$ is trapped in the mineral's crystalline structure but none of its decay products exist in the mineral at the time. The half-life of $^{40}_{19}K$ is 1.3×10^9 years. The decay products of $^{40}_{19}K$ are $^{40}_{18}Ar$ (12%) and $^{40}_{20}Ca$ (88%). An analysis of the mineral reveals that the ratio of $^{40}_{29}K$ to $^{40}_{18}Ar$ to $^{40}_{20}Ca$ is approximately 25:9:66.

   a. What is the approximate age of the mineral? Explain how you arrived at your answer.

   b. Write an equation that describes the transmutation of $^{40}_{19}K$ to $^{42}_{20}Ca$.

   c. Write an equation that describes the transmutation of $^{40}_{19}K$ to $^{40}_{18}Ar$.

2. The half-life of $^{33}_{17}Cl$ is 2.5 s. It decays to sulfur, S, through the emission of a positron.

   a. If the mass of a sample of $^{33}_{17}Cl$ is 16 g, how much will remain after 15 s?

   b. Write a complete equation to represent the decay of $^{33}_{17}Cl$.

3. The half-life of $^{52}_{25}Mn$ is 5.6 days. What was the original mass of $^{52}_{25}Mn$ if after 50.4 days 1.20 g are found?

4. In nature, $^{238}_{92}U$ decay continues through 14 steps until a stable nuclide is formed. The illustration shows these 14 steps. Some information is missing at each step. Fill in the missing subscripts and superscripts for each nuclide. Also label each arrow as alpha or beta decay.

$$^{238}_{92}U \xrightarrow{\alpha} \underline{\quad}Th \xrightarrow{\beta} \underline{\quad}Pa \rightleftharpoons ^{234}_{92}U \rightleftharpoons ^{230}_{90}Th \;\rceil\alpha$$

$$\beta\lceil \underline{\quad}Bi \xleftarrow{\beta} ^{214}_{82}Pb \rightleftharpoons ^{218}_{84}Po \rightleftharpoons \underline{\quad}Rn \xleftarrow{\alpha} \underline{\quad}Ra$$

$$\underline{\quad}Po \xrightarrow{\alpha} \underline{\quad}Pb \xrightarrow{\beta} \underline{\quad}Bi \rightleftharpoons ^{210}_{84}Po \rightleftharpoons ^{206}_{82}Pb$$

CHAPTER
31 Evaluation

NUCLEAR APPLICATIONS

A. Testing Concepts

In the space to the left, write the letter of the answer to each question.

1. _____ The range over which the strong force acts is about
   a. 13.0×10^{-15} m   b. 1.3×10^{15} m   c. 1.3×10^{-15} m   d. 1.3×10^{-15} cm.

2. _____ Binding energy refers to the amount of energy required to
   a. separate the nucleus into individual nucleons
   b. separate the nucleus into individual protons
   c. separate the nucleus into individual neutrons
   d. combine individual nucleons.

3. _____ The binding energy of the nucleus is
   a. negative   b. positive   c. neutral.

4. _____ The mass of the assembled nucleus is _____ the sum of the masses of the nucleons that compose it.
   a. greater than   b. less than   c. equal to

5. _____ In a nuclear reaction, the binding energy before the reaction is _____ it is after the reaction.
   a. greater than   b. less than   c. the same as

6. _____ Artificially produced radioactive isotopes can be formed by bombarding stable nuclei with
   a. protons   b. neutrons   c. gamma rays   d. all of the above.

7. _____ Radioactive isotopes are used in medicine to
   a. destroy cells   b. determine how well certain organs function
   c. provide maps of internal organs   d. do all of the above.

8. _____ If $^{226}_{88}$Ra emits an alpha particle the decay product is
   a. $^{234}_{90}$Th   b. $^{222}_{86}$Rn   c. $^{222}_{88}$Ra   d. $^{218}_{84}$Po.

9. _____ Nuclear fission refers to
   a. a chemical reaction in which an atom dissociates into ions
   b. the combining of two nuclei
   c. the division of a nucleus
   d. the separation of two atoms.

10. _____ A moderator in a nuclear reactor decreases the speed of
    a. neutrons   b. electrons   c. protons   d. none of the above.

11. _____ The rate of a chain reaction is changed by the use of
    a. moderators   b. control rods   c. nucleons   d. uranium rods.

12. _____ In the fusion process in the sun a helium nucleus is formed by
    a. the fusion of four hydrogen nuclei   b. the fusion of four neutrons
    c. the transmutation of a hydrogen nucleus   d. the fission of a beryllium nucleus.

13. _____ In controlled fusion, the plasma is confined by
    a. a layer of electrons   b. a layer of neutrons
    c. a metal container   d. a magnetic field.

B. Applying Concepts

Answer the following questions in two or three complete sentences.

1. Explain how the mass defect relates to the equation $E = mc^2$.

2. What circumstances must exist for energy to be released by a nuclear reaction?

3. How did Lise Meitner and Otto Frisch explain the production of small atoms, such as barium, from uranium atoms?

4. What is the function of a moderator in a nuclear reactor?

5. What is the Cerenkov effect and what causes it?

6. Compare the amount of energy released during chemical reactions to the amount of energy released during a fusion reaction.

7. Describe how a magnetic field can be used to produce controlled fusion.

C. Understanding Concepts

1. The human thyroid gland uses iodine to produce vital hormones. Based on this fact, scientists have devised ways of using radioactive $^{131}_{53}I$ to measure the functions of the thyroid.

    a. $^{131}_{53}I$ decays to xenon, Xe, by emission of a beta particle. What isotope of xenon is formed?

    b. Write the equation for this reaction.

    c. The half life of $^{131}_{53}I$ is 8.05 days. If a patient is given a 6.0-mg dose of $^{131}_{53}I$ at 6:00 P.M. on a Monday, how much $^{131}_{53}I$ will remain in the patient's body at 6:30 P.M. on the following Friday?

2. The nuclear mass of $^{101}_{44}Ru$ is 100.9 u.
    a. What is its mass defect?

    b. What is its binding energy in MeV?

3. Complete the following nuclear equations for beta decay.

    a. $^{94}_{43}Tc$ to ruthenium, Ru   b. $^{111}_{46}Pd$ to silver, Aq   c. $^{134}_{55}Cs$ to barium, Ba

4. Complete the following nuclear equations for alpha decay.

    a. $^{144}_{60}Nd$ to cesium, Ce   b. $^{147}_{63}Eu$ to promethium, Pm   c. $^{190}_{78}Pt$ to osmium, Os

5. Write equations for the changes described below.

    a. $^{174}_{73}Ta$ emits a positron, and forms hafnium, Hf.   b. $^{138}_{53}I$ emits a neutron.

6. When a nucleus of $^{235}_{92}U$ is struck by a neutron the products are $^{92}_{36}Kr$, $^{141}_{56}Ba$, and some neutrons.

    a. How many neutrons are produced?

    b. Write an equation to represent the reaction.

D. Extending Concepts

1. A sample of a pure isotope of berkelium, Bk, decays to produce an isotope of curium, $^{248}_{96}$Cm. In this process, the nucleus captures an orbiting electron.

   a. What was the original isotope of berkelium?

   b. Write an equation for this decay.

2. The energy released in the fission of one atom of $^{239}_{94}$Pu is 1.6 MeV.

   a. How many atoms are in 2.0 kg of pure $^{239}_{94}$Pu?

   b. How much energy would be released if all these atoms underwent fission?

3. An $^{252}_{99}$Es nucleus (mass = 252.0829 u) decays to $^{248}_{97}$Bk (mass = 248.0702 u) by emission of an alpha particle (mass = 4.0026 u) with a kinetic energy of 6.64 MeV. What is the kinetic energy of the berkelium nucleus?

4. If 1.806 × 10^{24} atoms of $^{235}_{92}$U undergo fission and the energy produced is 1.0 × 10^{13} J, how much energy per kg of $^{235}_{92}$U is produced?

MIDTERM

Evaluation

A. Testing Concepts

In the space to the left, write the letter of the answer to each question.

1. _____ In physics, a framework of explanations that explains experimental data and predicts new results is called a(n)
   a. law   b. theory   c. technology   d. analysis.

2. _____ When multiplying measurements, the number of significant digits in _____ is used.
   a. both factors   b. the least precise factor
   c. the most precise factor   d. the difference of the two factors

3. _____ The _____ of an object can be found from a position-time graph.
   a. slope   b. mass   c. scalar   d. velocity

4. _____ The change in the velocity of an automobile with time is its
   a. average velocity   b. instantaneous velocity
   c. average acceleration   d. instantaneous acceleration.

5. _____ If a net force acts upon an object, the object will
   a. remain at rest   b. accelerate   c. move at constant velocity.

6. _____ As the angle of an inclined plane increases, the acceleration of an object moving along the inclined plane
   a. increases   b. decreases   c. remains the same.

7. _____ The final horizontal velocity of a projectile depends on
   a. the final vertical velocity of a projectile   b. the initial vertical velocity
   c. the initial horizontal velocity   d. all of the above.

8. _____ As the distance between two bodies decreases, the force of attraction between the bodies
   a. increases   b. decreases   c. remains the same.

9. _____ In a closed, isolated system consisting of four balls, if the momentum of three of the balls decreases, the momentum of the fourth ball
   a. increases   b. decreases   c. remains unchanged.

10. _____ In an ideal machine
    a. efficiency is 100%   b. there is no friction
    c. work input equals work output   d. all of the above are true.

11. _____ As an object falls, the increase in its kinetic energy is equal to
    a. the increase in its velocity   b. its mass
    c. the decrease in its potential energy   d. its distance from the ground.

12. _____ If thermal energy is removed from ice at a temperature of $-10°C$,
    a. the temperature of the ice will increase   b. the temperature of the ice will decrease
    c. the ice will melt   d. the temperature of the ice will not change.

13. _____ If you squeeze one end of a tube of toothpaste, the other end will bulge outward. This is an example of
    a. Archimedes' principle   b. Bernoulli's principle
    c. Pascal's principle   d. cohesion.

NAME _____

Evaluation

B. Applying Concepts

Answer the following questions in two or three complete sentences.

1. Explain the importance of effective communication in scientific investigations.

2. Why does an automobile sometimes skid on a wet, slippery curve in the road?

3. A wagon is pulled up a hill and then allowed to roll down the hill, propelled only by its own weight. Sketch the forces acting on the wagon after it is released. What makes the wagon roll down the hill?

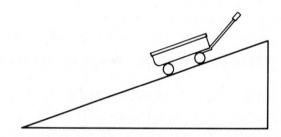

4. As a snowball rolls down a hill, it grows larger as new layers of snow build up on its surface. If the velocity of the snowball remains constant, what happens to its momentum? Explain your answer.

5. How are work and power related?

6. How is it possible to increase the thermal energy of a system without heating it? Give an example to illustrate your answer.

Evaluation

C. Understanding Concepts

1. Find the slope and y-intercept for the graph that shows the relationship $x = 4y - 8p$.

2. How long will it take a car starting from rest to travel 540.0 km if its acceleration is 2.00 m/s²?

3. A projectile is launched horizontally with a speed of 70.0 m/s. If the launch point is 1.8 m above the floor, how long would it take for the projectile to reach the floor?

4. How far from the launch position would the projectile in Problem 3 land?

5. A golf ball having a mass of 48.0 g is moving at a speed of 60.0 m/s. If the ball was initially at rest, how much work was done on the ball to give it this extra energy?

6. A metal object having a volume of 160 cm³ is suspended from a spring scale. When the object is completely immersed in water, the spring scale reads 1.1 N. How much does the object weigh in air? (Density of water = 1 g/cm³.)

NAME ――――――――――――――――――――――――――

Evaluation

D. Extending Concepts

1. The data shown represent the positions of two people as they moved relative to a fixed point. Find the velocity of person **A** relative to person **B**.

Time (s)	Position Person A (m)	Position Person B (m)
0.0	0.0	20.0
2.0	5.0	18.0
4.0	10.0	16.0
6.0	15.0	14.0
8.0	20.0	12.0

2. On the surface of the moon, a 3.0-kg mass would weigh about 4.9 N. The diameter of the moon is 3.476×10^3 m. Calculate the mass of the moon.

3. A construction worker carries a keg of nails up a ladder to a platform that is 12 m above the ground. The worker does 13 000 J of work on the keg. The bottom of the ladder forms an angle of 50° with the ground. Assume the efficiency of the machine (inclined plane) is 100%.

   a. What is the *IMA* of the ladder?

   b. How much force does the worker exert on the keg of nails?

   c. How much does the keg of nails weigh?

4. How much heat is needed to melt a 2.0-kg sample of iron that is at room temperature (20.0°C). The melting point of iron is 1535.0°C. The specific heat of iron is 450 J/kg·K. The heat of fusion of iron is 2.66×10^5 J/kg.

F I N A L

Evaluation

A. Testing Concepts

In the space to the left, write the letter of the answer to each question.

1. _____ When a trough from one wave meets a crest from another wave, _____ occurs.
   a. destructive interference   b. constructive interference   c. resonance   d. diffraction

2. _____ Because it allows light to be transmitted, water in most public swimming pools is described as
   a. transparent   b. translucent   c. opaque   d. none of the above.

3. _____ Which lens forms a real image in a microscope?
   a. concave   b. objective   c. eyepiece   d. none of the above

4. _____ In an electrical interaction there is an attraction between
   a. positive charges and negative charges   b. positive charges and positive charges
   c. negative charges and negative charges   d. all charged objects.

5. _____ If the electric field intensity and the force on a charge are known, the size of the charge may be found by
   a. dividing E by F b. dividing F by E
   c. multiplying E and F d. subtracting E from F.

6. _____ Ohm's law can be stated as
   a. $R = VI$ b. $I = VR$ c. $V = IR$ d. none of the above.

7. _____ If a 5-Ω resistor and a 9-Ω resistor are connected in parallel, the amount of current flowing through the 5-Ω resistor is _____ the amount of current flowing through the 9-Ω resistor.
   a. greater than   b. less than   c. equal to

8. _____ In a uniform magnetic field, the path of a charged particle is
   a. linear and opposite to the direction of the field   b. circular
   c. linear in the same direction as the field   d. linear and perpendicular to the field.

9. _____ In a step-down transformer, the current in the secondary circuit is _____ the current in the primary circuit.
   a. greater than   b. less than   c. equal to

10. _____ The energy of a photon depends on
    a. its mass   b. its velocity   c. the frequency of the light   d. all of the above.

11. _____ In a laser, when a photon strikes an electron in the excited state,
    a. the electron makes a transition to a lower state
    b. a total of two photons leave the atom
    c. photons leaving the atom strike other atoms and produce an avalanche of photons
    d. all of the above happen.

12. _____ In a semiconductor, conductivity _____ as the room temperature increases.
    a. increases   b. decreases   c. remains the same

13. _____ Which of the following is *not* a type of particle that transmits forces between particles?
    a. neutrino   b. graviton   c. photon   d. gluon

14. _____ The strong nuclear force overcomes the mutual repulsion between
    a. neutrons   b. protons   c. protons and neutrons   d. electrons.

Evaluation

B. Applying Concepts

Answer the following questions in two or three complete sentences.

1. What physical characteristic of sound waves causes timbre?

2. The moon is not a luminous body. Why then can we see it?

3. How is charging by induction different from charging by conduction?

4. How do series and parallel circuits differ? What is the effect on equivalent resistance and current if another resistor is added to each type of circuit?

5. Which antenna is longer, one designed to detect radio waves or one designed to detect microwaves? Explain your answer.

6. Explain why an insulator does not conduct electricity.

7. Explain why photographic film is sometimes used to detect radioactive particles and rays.

NAME ———————————————————————

Evaluation

C. Understanding Concepts

1. The speed of sound in water is 1498 m/s. A sonar signal has a frequency of 1.00×10^6 Hz. What is the wavelength of the signal in mm?

2. The index of refraction of quartz is 1.54. What is the speed of light in this material?

3. An object, 4.45 cm tall, is 1.0 m from a convex lens with a focal length of 8.0 cm.

   a. Where is the image?

   b. Is the image real or virtual? Explain your answer.

   c. What is the height of the image?

4. What is the distance to the screen from a double slit when light with a wavelength of 630.0 nm produces first order lines 65.3 mm from the central bright band? The slit separation is 9.66×10^{-6}.

5. A current of 7.0 A flows through a wire 1.2 m long. The wire lies perpendicular to a magnetic field the induction of which is 0.74 T. What force acts on the wire?

Evaluation

D. Extending Concepts

1. An air column at 25°C produces resonances spaced by 40.4 cm. What is the frequency of the tuning fork used to produce the sounds?

2. A current-carrying wire generates 4.86×10^5 J of thermal energy in 4.50 min. The resistance of the wire is 8.0 Ω. What is the potential difference across the wire?

3. A length of wire with a total resistance of 8 Ω is connected to the terminals of a galvanometer. The resistance of the galvanometer is 942 Ω. Part of the wire is exposed to a magnetic field of 1.6×10^{-3} T. The length of wire between the magnetic poles is 24 cm. If the wire is moved upward through the field at 2.0 m/s, what current will the galvanometer indicate?

CHAPTER

1 : Evaluation

WHAT IS PHYSICS?

A. Testing Concepts

In the space to the left, write the letter of the answer to each question.

__d__ 1. Which of the following are the results of the work of physicists?
a. lasers   b. calculators   c. computers   d. all of the above

__a__ 2. The BCS theory was developed to explain how
a. superconductors work   b. magnets attract matter
c. generators work   d. to build an atomic bomb.

__d__ 3. Absolute zero is the
a. highest possible temperature at which matter freezes   b. lowest possible temperature at which materials conduct electricity   c. highest possible temperature at which materials conduct electricity   d. lowest possible temperature for matter.

__c__ 4. Which of the following is called the language of physics?
a. biology   b. engineering   c. mathematics   d. chemistry

__d__ 5. Physics is the study of
a. matter and cells   b. energy and heat
c. energy and atoms   d. matter and energy.

__c__ 6. Why is the work of theoretical physicists in superconductivity not finished?
a. Superconductors have not yet been produced.   b. Absolute zero has not yet been reached.   c. There is no complete explanation of how new superconductors work.
d. Room-temperature superconductors have not yet been produced.

__c__ 7. Aristotle believed that all matter was composed of
a. atoms   b. energy   c. four elements   d. motion.

__b__ 8. Aristotle and his followers were mainly concerned with finding out
a. when specific events occur   b. why specific events occur
c. how specific events occur   d. all of the above.

__d__ 9. One of the first European scientists to claim publicly that knowledge must be based on observations and experiments was
a. Albert Einstein   b. Aristotle   c. Heike Kamerlingh Onnes   d. Galileo Galilei.

__a__ 10. A surprising aspect of physics is that its results can be described by a small number of relationships, or
a. laws   b. earthly elements   c. rules   d. theories.

CHAPTER

1 : Evaluation

B. Applying Concepts

Answer the following questions in two or three complete sentences.

1. What problem with early superconductors has been eliminated by the discovery of new superconductors that work at higher temperatures?

   Early superconductors worked at such low temperatures that they had to be cooled by liquid helium, which is very expensive and difficult to store. The new superconductors work at temperatures that are farther above absolute zero and as a result can be cooled with liquid nitrogen, which is much less expensive.

2. Explain the difference between an experimental physicist and a theoretical physicist.

   Experimental physicists perform experiments and interpret their results. Theoretical physicists use mathematics and computers to construct a framework of explanations to explain experimental data and predict new results.

3. What is the difference between a theory and a law in physics?

   In physics, a theory is an explanation of experimental data while a law describes a relationship between events.

4. What are some personality traits that aid physicists in their work?

   Physicists need to be inquisitive, knowledgeable, imaginative, and creative.

5. Why is an understanding of physics a benefit to all citizens?

   An understanding of physics helps all citizens make informed decisions about problems involving society. A knowledge of physics also helps people understand how common devices, such as electrical appliances, work.

6. Name two views held by Galileo that differed from those held by scientists who had gone before him.

   Galileo did not believe that Earth was the center of the universe. He also doubted Aristotle's idea that objects of large mass fall faster than objects of small mass.

7. How is the way all scientists study problems similar?

   All scientists study problems in an organized way. They combine systematic experimentation with careful measurements and analysis of results, and then draw conclusions.

CHAPTER

2 Evaluation

A MATHEMATICAL TOOLKIT

A. Testing Concepts

In the space to the left, write the letter of the answer to each question.

1. **c** ___ The fundamental SI unit for time is the
   a. minute   b. day   c. second   d. hour.

2. **a** ___ In scientific notation, a number between 1 and 10 is multiplied by
   a. a whole-number power of 10   b. a fraction   c. 10   d. any whole number.

3. **d** ___ The metric prefix that means 100 is
   a. pico   b. nano   c. centi   d. hecto.

4. **a** ___ When multiplying quantities expressed in scientific notation ($M \times 10^n$) that have different exponents, you multiply the values of M and ___ the exponents.
   a. add   b. multiply   c. subtract   d. divide

5. **a** ___ To avoid parallax errors, laboratory instruments should be read
   a. at eye level   b. from the side   c. below eye level   d. at all of these positions.

6. **b** ___ The degree of exactness to which the measurement of a quantity can be reproduced is called
   a. accuracy   b. precision   c. parallax   d. none of the above.

7. **c** ___ When adding or subtracting measurements, first perform the operation and then round off the result to correspond to the ___ value involved.
   a. most precise   b. largest   c. least precise   d. smallest

8. **b** ___ A variable that can be manipulated in an experiment is
   a. a dependent variable   b. an independent variable   c. a responding variable   d. none of the above.

9. **a** ___ When constructing a graph from data, the range of the x-axis is determined by the range of the
   a. independent variable   b. dependent variable   c. combined range of the independent variable and dependent variable   d. origin.

10. **c** ___ What is indicated by a smooth, upward curving line on a graph?
    a. a linear relationship between x and y   b. an inverse relationship between x and y   c. a direct relationship between y and with the square of x   d. No relationship between x and y is indicated.

11. **c** ___ The slope of a straight-line graph is the vertical change ___ the horizontal change.
    a. minus   b. added to   c. divided by   d. multiplied by

12. **a** ___ A graph that is a hyperbola represents ___ relationship.
    a. an inverse   b. a quadratic   c. a linear   d. no

13. **c** ___ To solve the equation $vt = d$ for t,
    a. multiply both sides of the equation by v b. add v to both sides of the equation   c. divide both sides of the equation by v d. divide both sides of the equation by t.

14. **c** ___ An equation is wrong if both sides contain
    a. different variables   b. the same variable   c. different units of measure   d. the same unit of measure.

CHAPTER

2 Evaluation

B. Applying Concepts

Answer the following questions in two or three complete sentences.

1. Describe the relationship between fundamental units and derived units.

   Fundamental units are units that can be used to describe other quantities. Derived units are combinations of fundamental units.

2. Which of the following length measurements are equivalent?
   a. 5687 nm   b. 568.7 km   c. 0.000 568 7 dag   d. 0.000 056 87 dm

   a and d

3. Which of the following is a more precise measurement, the length of a car measured to the nearest meter or measured to the nearest millimeter? Explain your answer.

   Since the millimeter is the smaller unit, it indicates a more precise measure of the car's length.

4. Explain the difference between accuracy and precision.

   Precision is the degree of exactness with which a quantity is measured. Accuracy is the extent to which the measured and accepted values of a quantity agree.

5. State the number of significant digits in each of the following measurements.
   a. 3809 m   b. 9.013 m   c. 0.0045 m

   a. four
   b. four
   c. two

6. Which of the following measurements contains zeros that are *not significant*? Explain your answer.
   a. 3.050×10.5 b. 0.0053 m   c. 45.020 cm   d. 101.20 g

   Answer b is the only measure that contains zeros that are not significant since they are used solely for spacing the decimal point. In all the other answers, the zeros after the decimal point are significant.

7. How are independent and dependent variables related? Identify the graph axis on which each type of variable would be plotted.

   The independent variable is a manipulated variable. Dependent variables are responding variables that change as a result of a change in an independent variable. On a graph, the independent variable is plotted on the x-axis and the dependent variable is plotted on the y-axis.

C. Understanding Concepts

1. Express the following measurements in scientific notation.
   a. 142 000 s   b. 0.008 09 kg   c. 501 000 000 m
   a. 142×10^5 s
   b. 8.09×10^{-3} kg
   c. 5.01×10^8 m

2. Solve the following problems. Express your answers in scientific notation using the correct number of significant digits.
   a. $(2 \times 10^6 \text{ m})(5 \times 10^5 \text{ m})$
   1×10^{12} m²
   b. $(12 \times 10^6 \text{ m})/(4 \times 10^2 \text{ s})$
   3×10^4 m/s
   c. $(5.06 \times 10^2 \text{ m}) + (8.124 \text{ km})$
   8.630×10^3 m or 8.630 km

3. Describe the relationship between the variables shown in the graph below. Identify the general equation that is used to represent this type of relationship.

   The graph shows that as time increases, speed decreases. It shows an inverse relationship between the variables.

   Speed vs Time

   (graph of Speed (m/s) vs Time(s))

4. Identify the slope and y-intercept of the equation $y = 3x + 6$.

   The slope is 3 and the y-intercept is 6.

5. Solve each equation for x.
   a. $p = rx$ c. $b = \dfrac{x - d}{y}$
   $x = \dfrac{p}{r}$ $x = by + d$
   b. $w = \dfrac{s}{x}$
   $x = \dfrac{s}{w}$

6. Write an equation using the variables M and P to represent the following sentence: "Twice Peter's age is equal to one-fourth Mary's age."

   $2P = \frac{1}{4} M$

7. If $v = 15.5$ m/s and $t = 12$ s, find d using $d = vt$. Include the correct units in your answer.
   $d = vt$
   = (15.5 m/s)(12 s)
   = 186 m
   = 190 m

D. Extending Concepts

1. The total mass of four containers is 5.000 kg. If the mass of Container **A** is 256 mg, Container **B** is 5117 cg, and Container C is 382 g, what is the mass of Container **D**?

   D = 5.000 kg − (A + B + C)
   = 5.000 kg − (0.000 256 kg + 0.051 17 kg + 0.382 kg)
   = 4.566574 kg
   = 4.567 kg

2. The results of a class experiment investigating the relationship between mass and acceleration are shown in the table below. The force applied to each mass remained constant.

Mass (g)	Acceleration (m/s²)
0.5	6.0
1.0	3.0
1.5	2.0
2.0	1.5
2.5	1.25
3.0	1.0

   a. Plot the values given and draw the curve that best fits the points.
   b. Describe the resulting curve.
      The graph is a hyperbola.
   c. What is the relationship between mass and the acceleration produced by a constant force?
      The relationship between the variables is an inverse relationship.
   d. What is the general equation for the relationship shown in the graph?
      The equation is
      $a = \dfrac{k}{m}$ or $a = \dfrac{f}{m}$

3. Manipulate the equation $v = \dfrac{d}{t}$ and find the answers to each problem. Express each answer in the correct unit.
   a. Find the distance a bike travels in 4.50 min if it is traveling at a constant speed of 20.0 km/h.
   $v = \dfrac{d}{t}$
   $d = vt$
   = (20.0 km/h)(4.50 min)(1 h/60 min)
   = 1.50 km
   b. How long would it take a car to travel 6.0×10^3 m if its speed is a constant 30.0 km/h?
   $v = \dfrac{d}{t}$
   $t = \dfrac{d}{v}$

   = $\dfrac{6.0 \text{ km}}{30.0 \text{ km/h}}$
   = 0.20 h

CHAPTER 3 : Evaluation

DESCRIBING MOTION: VELOCITY

A. Testing Concepts

In the space to the left, write the letter of the answer to each question.

1. __b__ A runner is 5.0 km east of another runner, who is 5.0 km east of a parking lot. Where is the first runner with respect to the parking lot?
  a. +5.0 km from the lot   b. +10.0 km from the lot   c. –5.0 km from the lot
  d. –10.0 km from the lot

2. __d__ The parking lot mentioned above is
  a. a distance between the two runners   b. a position separating the two runners
  c. the displacement between the two runners   d. a reference point for the runners.

3. __c__ Distance is a quantity that
  a. always needs a reference point   b. is always a vector   c. has only magnitude
  d. is always positive.

4. __a__ A cyclist finishes a 100-km race in 2.7 hours. The average velocity
  a. equals the displacement divided by the total time
  b. equals the time divided by the displacement
  c. equals the greatest speed divided by the total time.

5. __a__ If the average velocity of an object is the same for all time intervals, then the object moves at a(n)
  a. constant velocity   b. instantaneous velocity   c. changing speed   d. relative speed.

6. __c__ On a position-time graph, the velocity equals
  a. the x-intercept   b. the y-intercept   c. the rise divided by the run
  d. the run divided by the rise.

7. __c__ Using _____ rise and run will result in the most accurate slope on a position-time graph.
  a. an average   b. the smallest   c. the largest

8. __c__ A runner traveled 15 km east then backtracked 11 km before stopping. The displacement from the original position is
  a. +26.0 km   b. –4.0 km   c. +4.0 km   d. –26.0 km.

9. __d__ The _____ of any point on a velocity-time graph equals the instantaneous velocity at the time.
  a. slope of the tangent   b. displacement   c. horizontal value   d. vertical value

10. __b__ The area under the curve on a velocity-time graph equals the
  a. rise divided by the run   b. displacement from the original position to its position at time *t*
  c. relative velocity.   d. instantaneous velocity.

11. __c__ A child on a bicycle rides eastward past a house, as a car, also traveling eastward, slowly passes. Which of the following people would perceive the biker as having the greatest velocity?
  a. the biker   b. the driver of the car   c. a person in the house   d. all of the above

12. __d__ The slope of the tangent on a position-time graph equals the
  a. average speed   b. constant speed   c. average velocity   d. instantaneous velocity.

Acceleration vs Mass

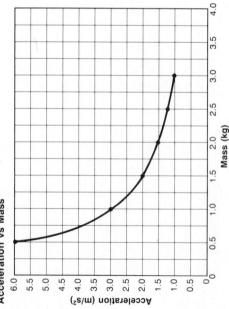

3 Evaluation

B. Applying Concepts

Answer the following questions in two or three complete sentences.

1. In terms of graphing, distinguish between average velocity and instantaneous velocity.

   Average velocity is the rise divided by the run of the curve on a position-time graph. Instantaneous velocity is the slope of the tangent to the curve at a given instant.

2. When does an object move at a constant velocity?

   An object moves at a constant or uniform velocity when the average velocity of the object is the same for all time intervals.

3. Show mathematically that an object can have a negative position but a positive velocity.

   Numbers will vary, but students should use the equation for average velocity to demonstrate that a more negative position minus a less negative position divided by (a positive) time equals a positive velocity.

4. On a position-time graph, compare the instantaneous velocities of an object when the tangent to the curve slopes upward to the right, when the tangent slopes downward to the right, and when the tangent is horizontal.

   If the tangent to the curve at a given point slopes upward to the right, the velocity is positive. If the tangent slopes downward to the right, the velocity is negative. At a point where the tangent is horizontal, the velocity is zero.

5. A stunt car is driven along a flat train car. The stunt car is moving toward the engine of the train. How would you calculate the velocity of the stunt car relative to Earth?

   The velocity of the car relative to Earth equals the velocity of the car relative to the train plus the velocity of the train relative to Earth.

6. Suppose a runner is running aboard an ocean liner at +12 km/h toward the southeast. What is the velocity of the ocean liner relative to the runner?

   The luxury liner is moving at −12 km/h relative to the runner.

---

3 Evaluation

C. Understanding Concepts

1. After 16.5 s, a jogger's displacement is 200.0 m. What is the average velocity in m/s? In km/h?

   $\bar{v} = \Delta d/\Delta t$
   $= +200.0 \text{ m}/16.5 \text{ s}$
   $= +12.1 \text{ m/s}$

   $\dfrac{(+12.1 \text{ m/s})(3600 \text{ s/h})}{1000 \text{ m/km}} = +43.6 \text{ km/h}$

2. The data shown represent a series of readings taken by a motorcyclist. Find the average velocity during each 2-second interval.

Time (s)	Position (m)
0.0	+0.0
2.0	+0.0
4.0	+2.0
6.0	+5.0
8.0	+10.0
10.0	+15.0
12.0	+20.0

   $\bar{v} = \dfrac{\Delta d}{\Delta t}$

   $\bar{v}_1 = (0.0 \text{ m} - 0.0 \text{ m})/(2.0 \text{ s} - 0.0 \text{ s}) = 0.0 \text{ m/s}$
   $\bar{v}_2 = (2.0 \text{ m} - 0.0 \text{ m})/(4.0 \text{ s} - 2.0 \text{ s}) = 1.0 \text{ m/s}$
   $\bar{v}_3 = (5.0 \text{ m} - 2.0 \text{ m})/(6.0 \text{ s} - 4.0 \text{ s}) = 1.5 \text{ m/s}$
   $\bar{v}_4 = (10.0 \text{ m} - 5.0 \text{ m})/(8.0 \text{ s} - 6.0 \text{ s}) = 2.5 \text{ m/s}$
   $\bar{v}_5 = (15.0 \text{ m} - 10.0 \text{ m})/(10.0 \text{ s} - 8.0 \text{ s}) = 2.5 \text{ m/s}$
   $\bar{v}_6 = (20.0 \text{ m} - 15.0 \text{ m})/(12.0 \text{ s} - 10.0 \text{ s}) = 2.5 \text{ m/s}$

3. Find the average velocity of the cyclist between 2.0 and 8.0 s.

   $\bar{v} = \dfrac{\Delta d}{\Delta t}$

   $= (10.0 \text{ m} - 0.0 \text{ m})/(8.0 \text{ s} - 2.0 \text{ s})$
   $= 1.7 \text{ m/s}$

4. Use the following data to make a velocity-time graph.

Time (s)	Velocity (m/s)
0	20
2	20
5	20
6	30
7	35
8	40
10	30
11	15
12	10

5. Describe the velocity of the object using the graph you made for Problem 4.

   For the first 5 s, the velocity is constant. The object then increases its velocity for 3 s before it decreases its velocity.

6. Use the graph to find the displacement in the first 5 s.

   $d = vt$
   $= (20 \text{ m/s})(5 \text{ s})$
   $= 100 \text{ m}$

NAME _____

D. Extending Concepts

1. A "moving sidewalk" in a busy airport terminal moves 1.0 m/s and is 200.0 m long. A passenger steps onto one end and walks, in the same direction as the sidewalk is moving, at a rate of 2.0 m/s relative to the moving sidewalk. How much time does it take the passenger to reach the opposite end of the walkway?

$v_{relative\ to\ Earth}$ = $v_{relative\ to\ walk}$ + $v_{walk\ relative\ to\ Earth}$

= (+2.0 m/s) + (+1.0 m/s)

= +3.0 m/s

$\Delta t = \dfrac{d}{v}$

= $\dfrac{200.0\ m}{3.0\ m/s}$

= 67 s

2. Suppose another passenger gets on one end of the same "moving sidewalk" and walks at a rate of 2.0 m/s relative to the moving sidewalk but in a direction opposite to that of the sidewalk. How much time does it take this passenger to reach the opposite end of the walkway?

$v_{relative\ to\ Earth}$ = $v_{relative\ to\ walk}$ + $v_{walk\ relative\ to\ Earth}$

= (+2.0 m/s) + (−1.0 m/s)

= 1.0 m/s

$\Delta t = \dfrac{\Delta d}{v}$

= $\dfrac{200.0\ m}{1.0\ m/s}$

= 2.0 × 10² s

3. If the two passengers step on the moving sidewalk at the same time, how far will the second passenger have moved, relative to the sidewalk, when the first passenger steps off the sidewalk?

$\Delta d = \bar{v}\Delta t$

= (2.0 m/s)(67 s)

= 134 m

4. The following data show velocity readings taken every 5 s. Prepare a position-time graph for the data.

Time (s)	Velocity (m/s)		Displacement (m)	Position (m)
0.0	0.0			
5.0	6.2			
10.0	12.4	$\Delta d = \bar{v}\Delta t$		
15.0	22.0			
20.0	22.0	d_1 = (0.0 m/s)(0.0 s) =	0.0	0.0
25.0	18.0	d_2 = (6.2 m/s)(5.0 s) =	31	31.0
30.0	18.0	d_3 = (12.4 m/s)(5.0 s) =	62	93
		d_4 = (22.0 m/s)(5.0 s) =	110	203
		d_4 = (22.0 m/s)(5.0 s) =	110	313
		d_5 = (18.0 m/s)(5.0 s) =	90	403
		d_6 = (18.0 m/s)(5.0 s) =	90	493

Section C, Question 4, Velocity vs Time

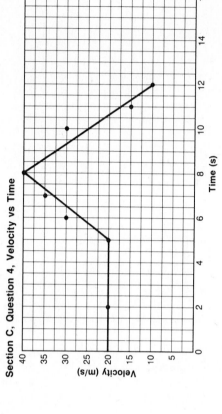

Section D, Question 4, Position vs Time

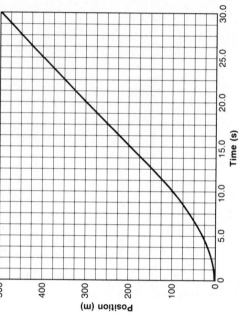

CHAPTER

4 Evaluation

ACCELERATION

A. Testing Concepts

In the space to the left, write the letter of the answer to each question.

1. c The change in a "runner's velocity with time is the runner's
    a. average velocity   b. instantaneous velocity   c. average acceleration
    d. instantaneous acceleration.

2. a A child lets go of a ball at the top of a driveway. The instantaneous velocity of the ball as the child lets go is
    a. zero   b. positive   c. negative.

3. d On a velocity-time graph, the slope of the tangent to the curve at a given point is the
    a. average velocity   b. average acceleration   c. instantaneous velocity
    d. instantaneous acceleration.

4. b Constant acceleration on a velocity-time graph produces a curve that is
    a. half a parabola   b. a straight line   c. parallel to the horizontal axis
    d. parallel to the vertical axis.

5. a The area under a curve on a velocity-time graph for an object moving with a uniform acceleration is the _____ of that object.
    a. displacement   b. position   c. velocity   d. acceleration

6. b The slope of a position-time graph is the _____ of an object.
    a. displacement   b. velocity   c. acceleration   d. mass

7. c Which of the following best describes the relationship between the final and initial velocities of a uniformly accelerating object?
    a. The final velocity increases as the initial velocity decreases.   b. The final velocity decreases as the initial velocity increases.   c. The final velocity increases as the initial velocity increases.

8. c Ignoring air resistance, if a 10-kg ball and a 200-kg crate were both dropped from the top of a building, the acceleration of the crate would be _____ the acceleration of the ball.
    a. greater than   b. less than   c. equal to

9. a In Greenland, the acceleration due to gravity is _____ the acceleration due to gravity at Earth's equator.
    a. greater than   b. less than   c. equal to

10. b A toy rocket is launched straight up into the air. When the rocket reaches its maximum height, its velocity is
    a. at its maximum   b. at its minimum   c. equal to its displacement multiplied by time.
    d. equal to its displacement divided by time.

11. a The total displacement of the toy rocket upon landing is
    a. zero   b. equal to the distance it traveled up   c. equal to the distance it traveled up multiplied by 2   d. equal to the difference between the final and initial velocities divided by the acceleration due to gravity.

CHAPTER

4 Evaluation

B. Applying Concepts

Answer the following questions in two or three complete sentences.

1. After making a delivery, a truck driver must maneuver the vehicle backwards down a narrow ramp. The speed of the truck increases with distance down the ramp. Describe the truck's acceleration.

Because the truck's velocity is backward, or negative, the acceleration is also negative even though the truck's speed is increasing.

2. How can you find the instantaneous acceleration of an object whose curve on the velocity-time graph is a straight line?

The instantaneous acceleration is the slope of the curve on such a graph.

3. Suppose an object starts at rest. Explain how the displacement of the object, which has a constant acceleration, can be determined from a velocity-time graph.

The displacement is the area under the curve on such a graph. The curve in this case is a straight line. The triangular area under the curve equals the displacement of the object.

4. Describe the curve on a position-time graph of an object with a constant velocity. How does the curve differ for an object that is accelerating constantly?

For an object with a constant velocity, the curve is a straight line. For an accelerating object, the curve is half of a parabola.

5. Derive an equation for determining displacement when velocity and acceleration are known.

By using $d = \frac{1}{2}(v_f + v_i)t$ and $(v_f - v_i)/a = t$ and substituting the second equation into the first, displacement can be calculated using the equation: $d = (v_f^2 - v_i^2)/2a$.

6. How is the acceleration of an object in freefall related to acceleration due to gravity?

For an object in freefall, $a = g$.

7. In your own words, state the first and last steps that are critical to solving any physics problem. Making a sketch could be helpful. Once the problem is solved systematically, the answer should be evaluated to determine whether or not the numerical value is reasonable.

The problem must first be carefully read and analyzed.

4 Evaluation

C. Understanding Concepts

1. A skateboard rider starts from rest and accelerates at a constant +0.50 m/s² for 8.4 s. What is the rider's displacement during this time?

$d = \frac{1}{2}at^2$

$= \frac{1}{2}(+0.50 \text{ m/s}^2)(8.4 \text{ s})^2$

$= 18 \text{ m}$

2. A sports car can move 100.0 m in the first 4.5 s of uniform acceleration. Find the car's acceleration.

$a = \frac{2d}{t^2}$

$= \frac{(2)(100.0 \text{ m})}{(4.5 \text{ s})^2}$

$= 9.9 \text{ m/s}^2$

3. A cyclist passes a race check point at +5.5 m/s and then accelerates at a constant rate of +0.55 m/s². The cyclist forgot to check in at the check point, and after 20.0 s turns around to head back. How far did the cyclist move from the check point to the point of turning back?

$d = v_i t + \frac{1}{2}at^2$

$= (+5.5 \text{ m/s})(20.0 \text{ s}) + \frac{1}{2}(+0.55 \text{ m/s}^2)(20.0 \text{ s})^2$

$= 220 \text{ m}$

4. A rolling ball has an initial velocity of −1.63 m/s.

a. If the ball accelerates at a constant rate of −0.33 m/s², what is its velocity after 3.6 s?

$v_f = v_i + at$

$= (−1.63 \text{ m/s}) + (−0.33 \text{ m/s}^2)(3.6 \text{ s})$

$= −2.82 \text{ m/s}$

b. If this acceleration occurs for another 2.8 s, what is the ball's final velocity?

$v_f = v_i + at$

$= (−1.63 \text{ m/s}) + (−0.33 \text{ m/s}^2)(6.4 \text{ s})$

$= −3.74 \text{ m/s}$

5. A construction worker drops a tool from a bridge and it hits the river 3.60 s later. What is the displacement of the tool?

$d = v_i t + \frac{1}{2}gt^2$

$= (0.0 \text{ m/s})(3.60 \text{ s}) + (\frac{1}{2})(−9.80 \text{ m/s}^2)(3.60 \text{ s})^2$

$= 0 + (−63.5 \text{ m})$

$= −63.5 \text{ m or } 63.5 \text{ m toward Earth}$

6. A jogger accelerates constantly to a velocity of 2.3 m/s in 6.5 s. After jogging 11 m, the jogger stops. What was the initial velocity of the jogger?

$v_i = \frac{2d}{t} − v_f$

$= \frac{(2)(11 \text{ m})}{6.5 \text{ s}} − 2.3 \text{ m/s}$

$= 1.1 \text{ m/s}$

4 Evaluation

D. Extending Concepts

1. A car is traveling with a velocity of +88.0 km/h. It accelerates at a constant rate of −20.0 m/s². If the acceleration lasts for 5.60 s, what is the final velocity of the car?

$v_i = (88.0 \text{ km/hr})(1 \text{ hr}/60 \text{ min})(1 \text{ min}/60 \text{ s})(1000 \text{ m/km})$

$= 24.4 \text{ m/s}$

$v_f = v_i + at$

$= +24.4 \text{ m/s} + (−20.0 \text{ m/s}^2)(5.60 \text{ s})$

$= −87.6 \text{ m/s}$

2. A toy rocket is shot straight up into the air with an initial speed of 45.0 m/s.

a. How long does it take the rocket to reach its highest point?

$t = v_f − v_i/g$

$= (0.0 \text{ m/s} − 45.0 \text{ m/s})/(−9.80 \text{ m/s}^2)$

$= 4.6 \text{ s}$

b. How high does the rocket rise above the ground?

$d = (v_f^2 − v_i^2)/2g$

$= \frac{(0.0 \text{ m/s})^2 − (45.0 \text{ m/s})^2}{(2)(−9.80 \text{ m/s}^2)}$

$= +103 \text{ m}$

3. A bird drops an acorn from a tree branch that is 8.00 m from the ground.

a. How long is the acorn in the air?

$t = \sqrt{2d/a}$

$= \sqrt{(2)(−8.00 \text{ m})/(−9.80 \text{ m/s}^2)}$

$= 1.28 \text{ s}$

b. What is its velocity when it reaches the ground?

$v_f = v_i + gt$

$= 0.0 \text{ m/s} + [(9.80 \text{ m/s}^2)(1.28 \text{ s})]$

$= −12.5 \text{ m/s or } 12.5 \text{ m/s toward Earth}$

4. Derive an equation to determine how long it takes a runner moving at 10.2 m/s on a circular track to go completely around the track once. The radius of the track is 25.0 m.

The distance around the track is 2πr. Velocity is distance traveled divided by time, t. Thus, the runner's velocity equals 2πr/t.

$t = 2πr/v$

$= (2)(π)(25.0 \text{ m})/10.2 \text{ m/s}$

$= 15.4 \text{ s}$

CHAPTER

5 : Evaluation

FORCES

A. Testing Concepts

In the space to the left, write the letter of the answer to each question.

1. __b__ The attractive force that acts between all objects is
   a. electromagnetic force   b. gravitational force
   c. strong nuclear force   d. weak nuclear force.

2. __c__ The strongest force is
   a. electromagnetic force   b. gravitational force
   c. strong nuclear force   d. weak nuclear force.

3. __a__ Metals such as copper can be pounded into thin sheets due to
   a. electromagnetic force   b. gravitational force
   c. strong nuclear force   d. weak nuclear force.

4. __a__ According to Newton's _____ law, an object with no net force acting on it remains at rest or in motion with a constant velocity.
   a. first   b. second   c. third

5. __b__ Newton's _____ law states that the acceleration of a body is directly proportional to the net force on it and inversely proportional to its mass.
   a. first   b. second   c. third

6. __b__ Losing speed as you ride your bike uphill demonstrates Newton's _____ law.
   a. first   b. second   c. third

7. __a__ Two teams in a tug of war exert the same amount of force on each other and the rope does not move. Newton's _____ law explains why the rope does not move.
   a. first   b. second   c. third

8. __c__ If you push against a wall, the wall pushes back against you with _____ force.
   a. no   b. less   c. equal   d. more

9. __a__ The gravitational force exerted by a large body, such as Earth, is
   a. weight   b. mass   c. acceleration   d. inertial mass.

10. __a__ Mass and weight are related by
    a. the force of gravity   b. newtons   c. friction   d. none of these.

11. __c__ Difficulty in pushing a large crate from rest involves
    a. gravity   b. sliding friction   c. static friction   d. balanced forces.

12. __c__ When the drag force on an object equals the force of gravity, _____ occurs.
    a. acceleration   b. inertial mass   c. terminal velocity   d. maximum mass

13. __b__ The effect of air resistance on the tail of a kite is _____ the effect of air resistance on the body of the kite.
    a. the same as   b. less than   c. more than

14. __a__ If the force of gravity on a balloon is 3000 N, and the lift force provided by the atmosphere is 3300 N, in which direction is the net force acting?
    a. upward   b. downward   c. toward the east   d. There is no net force.

CHAPTER

5 : Evaluation

B. Applying Concepts

Answer the following questions in two or three complete sentences.

1. Explain the relationship between mass and weight on Earth. Would this relationship change on Mars? Explain your answer.

   The weight of any object is proportional to the mass of the object. The force of gravity on Mars would be different from the force of gravity on Earth. Mass would not change, but weight would change. However, mass and weight would still be proportional.

2. Why is it easier to stop a compact car than a large station wagon when both are moving at the same speed?

   The station wagon is more difficult to stop because it has a greater mass.

3. An elevator is traveling from the lobby to the top of the building. As it stops on the top floor, in which direction is its acceleration? Explain.

   When an object slows down, its acceleration is in the direction opposite to the velocity of the object. The acceleration of the elevator is down.

4. In the drawing at right, use arrows to show the two horizontal and two vertical forces acting on the boat as it is pulled to the shore. Is there a net force on the boat?

   Yes, there is a net force on the boat in the direction of the person pulling it from the water.

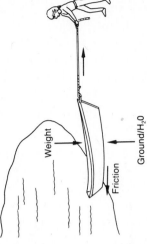

Weight

Friction

Ground/H₂0

5. Explain the difference between action-reaction forces and net forces. Using the boat shown in the figure, describe an example of each.

   Action-reaction forces act on different objects, and are equal in magnitude but opposite in direction. Several examples may be found. The girl pulling the boat demonstrates action-reaction pairs in that she pulls against the boat with the same force that the boat pulls against her. The forces, though, are in opposite directions. Net forces act on the same object and are not necessarily equal in magnitude. The pull of the girl on the boat is greater than the opposing pull of friction, so the boat moves in the direction of the girl.

6. What is the relationship between sliding friction and speed? Between sliding friction and normal force?

   Sliding friction is independent of speed. Sliding friction is proportional to normal force.

7. Suppose you try to pull a rope tied to a large carton. You cannot move the carton. What forces are acting on your hand?

   The forces acting on your hand are the forces exerted by your arm muscles and the force exerted by the rope.

C. Understanding Concepts

1. What force is required to accelerate a 6.0-kg bowling ball at +2.0 m/s²?

$F = ma$
$= (6.0 \text{ kg})(+2.0 \text{ m/s}^2)$
$= +12 \text{ N}$

2. What is the mass of a cat that weighs 30.0 N?

$W = mg \quad m = \dfrac{W}{g}$
$m = \dfrac{(30.0 \text{ N})}{(9.80 \text{ m/s}^2)}$
$= 3.06 \text{ kg}$

3. Acceleration due to gravity on Mars is 3.8 m/s².

a. Would a 5.0-kg watermelon weigh more on Earth or on Mars?

$W_E = mg_E \qquad W_M = mg_M$
$= (5.0 \text{ kg})(9.80 \text{ m/s}^2) \qquad = (5.0 \text{ kg})(3.80 \text{ m/s}^2)$
$= 49 \text{ N} \qquad = 19 \text{ N}$

It would weigh more on Earth.

b. How would the mass of the watermelon differ?

Mass would remain the same.

4. What is the inertial mass of a 75-N dog?

$F = ma \quad m = \dfrac{F}{a}$
$m = \dfrac{(75 \text{ N})}{(9.8 \text{ m/s}^2)}$
$= 7.7 \text{ kg}$

5. How much force is needed to keep a 78-kg box moving at a constant velocity across a warehouse floor if the coefficient of friction between the box and the floor is 0.21?

$F_N = W = mg \qquad\qquad F_f = \mu F_N$
$= (78 \text{ kg})(9.8 \text{ m/s}^2) \qquad\quad = (0.21)(760 \text{ N})$
$= 760 \text{ N} \qquad\qquad\qquad = 160 \text{ N}$

6. A 597-N cross-country skier is moving over packed snow. The coefficient of friction between the skis and the snow is 0.11. What force is required to keep the skier moving at a constant speed?

$F_A = \mu F_N$
$= (0.11)(597 \text{ N})$
$= 66 \text{ N}$

7. What is the coefficient of friction between a 65-kg roller skater and the floor of the roller rink if the skater moves at a constant speed with a force of 75 N?

$F_{normal} = W = mg$
$= (65 \text{ kg})(9.8 \text{ m/s}^2)$
$= 640 \text{ N}$

$\mu = \dfrac{F_f}{F_N}$
$= \dfrac{(75 \text{ N})}{(640 \text{ N})}$
$= 0.12$

D. Extending Concepts

1. An elevator has a mass of 1.10 × 10³ kg. Suppose it accelerates upward at 0.45 m/s². What is the force acting on the elevator's support cable?

$W = mg \qquad\qquad\qquad F_a = ma$
$= (1.10 \times 10^3 \text{ kg})(-9.80 \text{ m/s}^2) \qquad = (1.10 \times 10^3 \text{ kg})(+0.45 \text{ m/s}^2)$
$= -1.08 \times 10^4 \text{ N} \qquad\qquad\qquad = 4.95 \times 10^2 \text{ N}$

Net force is the sum of the force that causes acceleration (+4.95 × 10² N) and the upward force that balances the weight of the elevator (+1.08 × 10⁴ N)

$F_{net} = F_a + F_w$
$= (+4.95 \times 10^2 \text{ N}) + (+1.08 \times 10^4 \text{ N})$
$= 1.12 \times 10^4 \text{ N}$

2. A rocket weighs 2.0 × 10⁷ N. Its engines exert +25 × 10⁶ N of force at lift-off.

a. What is the mass of the rocket?

$m = \dfrac{W}{g}$
$= \dfrac{(2.0 \times 10^7 \text{ N})}{(9.8 \text{ m/s}^2)}$
$= 2.0 \times 10^6 \text{ kg}$

b. What is its acceleration when it lifts off?

$F_{net} = F_A + W \qquad\qquad a = \dfrac{F_{net}}{m}$
$= (+25 \times 10^6 \text{ N}) + (-2.0 \times 10^7 \text{ N}) \qquad = \dfrac{(+5.0 \times 10^6 \text{ N})}{(2.0 \times 10^6 \text{ kg})}$
$= +5.0 \times 10^6 \text{ N} \qquad\qquad\qquad = 2.5 \text{ m/s}^2$

c. The average acceleration of the rocket during its 7.0 minute launch is 10.0 m/s². What velocity does it reach?

$v = at$
$= (10.0 \text{ m/s}^2)(7.0 \text{ min})(60 \text{ s/min})$
$= 4200 \text{ m/s}$

3. A 47-N box is pulled along a horizontal surface by a 25-N weight hanging from a cord along a frictionless pulley.

a. What is the acceleration of the box and the weight?

$m_b = \dfrac{W}{g} \qquad\qquad m_w = \dfrac{W}{g} \qquad\qquad a = \dfrac{F}{m_b + m_w}$
$= \dfrac{(47 \text{ N})}{(9.8 \text{ m/s}^2)} \qquad = \dfrac{(25 \text{ N})}{(9.8 \text{ m/s}^2)} \qquad = \dfrac{25 \text{ N}}{(4.8 \text{ kg}) + (2.6 \text{ kg})}$
$= 4.8 \text{ kg} \qquad\qquad = 2.6 \text{ kg} \qquad\qquad = 3.4 \text{ m/s}^2$

b. What force is exerted on the cord?

$F_{cord} = ma$
$= (4.8 \text{ kg})(3.4 \text{ m/s}^2)$
$= 16 \text{ N}$

CHAPTER

6 Evaluation

VECTORS

A. Testing Concepts

In the space to the left, write the letter of the answer to each question.

1. __c__ A hiker moves 15 km due east then heads due north for 8 km. What is the direction of the resultant vector?
a. due east   b. due north   c. northeast   d. southwest

2. __c__ The downstream velocity of a river that flows south ____ a boat's eastward velocity.
a. slightly increases   b. slightly decreases   c. has no effect on

3. __b__ When adding vectors graphically, the direction and length of each vector must
a. be the same as the equilibrant   b. not be changed   c. be similar to the direction and length of the resultant   d. be reversed.

4. __a__ Knowing the magnitudes of the hypotenuse of a right triangle and the side opposite angle θ, you could compute the ____ of angle θ.
a. sine   b. cosine   c. tangent

5. __c__ The effect of the resultant vector is ____ the effect of the original vectors.
a. less than   b. greater than   c. the same as

6. __d__ Suppose you pull a wagon along a horizontal sidewalk. The force that pulls the wagon forward over the sidewalk is the ____ force.
a. resultant   b. vertical component   c. equilibrant   d. horizontal component

7. __c__ If the horizontal component of a force is positive, then, by convention, the force acts
a. upward   b. downward   c. to the right   d. to the left.

8. __b__ An object is in equilibrium when
a. the vertical component equals the horizontal component of force   b. the net sum of the forces is zero   c. the resultant force is the equilibrant.

9. __c__ The equilibrant force is ____ the resultant.
a. greater than and in the same direction as   b. less than but opposite in direction to
c. equal in magnitude but opposite in direction to
d. equal in magnitude and in the same direction as

10. __a__ To resolve a force vector into its components, a set of perpendicular axes is drawn. Then the ____ is drawn to scale at the correct angle.
a. resultant force   b. horizontal component   c. vertical component
d. the equilibrant

11. __a__ When vectors are resolved into components on an inclined plane, the ____ force is the one that acts along the incline.
a. parallel   b. perpendicular   c. original   d. weight

12. __d__ As the angle of an inclined plane increases, the parallel force ____ and the perpendicular force ____.
a. decreases, decreases   b. decreases, increases   c. increases, increases
d. increases, decreases

---

6 Evaluation

B. Applying Concepts

Answer the following questions in two or three complete sentences.

1. Is a plane traveling at a constant velocity in equilibrium? Explain your answer.

   Yes, an object does not have to be at rest to be in equilibrium. The weight of the plane is balanced by the lift produced by the flow of air over its wings. The drag on the plane is balanced by the thrust provided by the plane's engines.

2. There are four forces acting on the plane described above. Explain how you would add these vectors graphically.

   Vector addition is commutative. Each vector would be added head-to-tail. The resultant would be drawn from the tail of the first vector to the head of the last vector.

3. Describe how perpendicular vectors are added.

   The vectors would be added like all vectors—head-to-tail. The resultant would be drawn from the tail of the first vector to the head of the second vector.

4. Suppose the hill described above were frictionless. If a force of 150 N was needed to move the wagon uphill at a constant speed, what force is needed for the wagon to roll downhill at a constant speed?

   A force that is equal in magnitude but opposite in direction would be needed. The downhill force would be 150 N.

5. Suppose you are driving due north at 15 m/s in a severe thunderstorm. The wind is blowing due east at 30 km/h. How does the wind affect your northward movement?

   Because the vectors are perpendicular, they are independent of each other. The car is moving northward at 15 m/s.

6. Is a person standing still on a carpeted floor in equilibrium? Explain your answer.

   Yes, the person is in equilibrium. The weight exerts a downward force while the floor exerts an upward force on the person with the same magnitude as the weight. Because the net force is zero, the person is in equilibrium.

7. What is the relationship between the components of the weight of an object and the angle of an inclined plane on which the object rests?

   The parallel component of the object's weight is proportional to the sine of the angle the plane makes with the horizontal. The perpendicular component is proportional to the cosine of that angle.

CHAPTER

NAME _____

6 Evaluation

C. Understanding Concepts

1. A runner jogs 8.0 km due west, turns and jogs 10.0 km south, and then jogs 7.0 km due north at a constant speed. Graphically determine the magnitude and direction of the jogger's total displacement.

   8.5 km southwest or at 200° from east

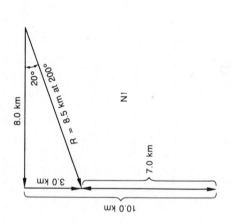

2. Trigonometrically determine the magnitude and direction of the velocity of a plane that is flying toward 180° at 100.0 km/h while the wind blows toward 90° at 65.0 km/h.

   $v_r^2 = v_p^2 + v_w^2$
   $= (100.0 \text{ km/h})^2 + (65.0 \text{ km/h})^2$
   $v_r = 199 \text{ km/h}$

   $\tan θ$ = opposite side/adjacent side
   = (65.0 km/h)/(100.0 km/h)
   = 0.65
   θ = **33° north of due west or 147° from east**

3. The force exerted on a rope pulling a wagon is 49.0 N. The rope is 35° above the horizontal. Find the force that pulls the wagon over the ground.

   $F_h = F \cos θ$
   $= (49.0 \text{ N})(0.819)$
   $= 40.1 \text{ N}$

4. A pilot wants to fly a plane at 500.0 km/h, directly north. The wind is blowing at 90.0 km/h from the east. Find the magnitude and direction of the course the pilot should fly.

   $R^2 = v_p^2 + v_w^2$
   $= (500.0 \text{ km/h})^2 + (-90.0 \text{ km/h})^2$
   $R = 508 \text{ km/h}$

   $\tan θ$ = opposite side/adjacent side
   = (500.0 km/h)/(90.0 km/h)
   = 5.56
   θ = **80.0° from east**

5. A net force of 125 N acts due east on an object. Find the single force that will produce equilibrium.

   A net force of 125 N due west (180° from east) will produce equilibrium.

6. A crate weighing 823 N is resting on a plank that makes a 25° angle with the ground. Find the components of the crate's weight parallel and perpendicular to the plank.

   $F_{parallel} = W \sin θ$
   $= (823 \text{ N})(0.423)$
   $= 348 \text{ N}$

   $F_{perpendicular} = W \cos θ$
   $= (823 \text{ N})(0.906)$
   $= 746 \text{ N}$

CHAPTER

NAME _____

6 Evaluation

D. Extending Concepts

1. Two people pull on a wagon using two ropes. One rope is exerting a force of 200.0 N at 5° from east. The other is exerting a force of 250.0 N at 120° from east. Assume that friction is negligible. What is the net force acting on the wagon?

   $F_x = F \cos θ$ $\quad F_y = F \sin θ$
   $F_{1x} = (200.0 \text{ N})(\cos 5.0°) = 199.2 \text{ N}$
   $F_{1y} = (200.0 \text{ N})(\sin 5.0°) = 17.44 \text{ N}$
   $F_{2x} = (250.0 \text{ N})(\cos 120.0°) = -125.0 \text{ N}$
   $F_{2y} = (250.0 \text{ N})(\sin 120.0°) = 216.5 \text{ N}$
   $F_{netx} = 199.2 \text{ N} + (-125.0 \text{ N}) = 74.2 \text{ N}$
   $F_{nety} = 17.44 \text{ N} + 216.5 \text{ N} = 233.9$

   $F_{net} = \sqrt{F_x^2 + F_y^2}$
   $= \sqrt{(74.2 \text{ N})^2 + (233.9 \text{ N})^2}$
   $= 245.4 \text{ N}$
   $\tan θ = F_y/F_x$
   $= (233.9 \text{ N})/(74.2 \text{ N})$
   $= 3.17$
   $θ = 72.5°$

2. A child weighing 29.0 kg is on a swing supported by two chains. Another child is pulling the swing back so that the chains make a 30° angle with the vertical. What force is exerted by each chain?

   $W = mg$
   $= (29.0 \text{ kg})(9.80 \text{ m/s}^2)$
   $= 284 \text{ N}$

   $F_{chains} = F_{weight} \cos 30°$
   $= (284 \text{ N})(0.866)$
   $= 246 \text{ N}$
   or 123 N on each chain

3. A 55-N force acts on an object at 25°. A second force of 63 N acts at 90°. What is the magnitude and direction of the equilibrant?

   sin θ = opposite/hypotenuse
   opposite = (sin θ)(hypotenuse)
   = (0.423)(55.0 N)
   0° component = 23.3 N at 0°
   cos θ = adjacent/hypotenuse
   adjacent = (cos θ)(hypotenuse)
   = (0.906)(55.0 N)
   90° component = 49.8 N at 90°

   $R^2 = (23.3 \text{ N})^2 + (49.8 \text{ N} + 63.0 \text{ N})^2$
   $R = 115 \text{ N}$
   tan θ = opposite/adjacent
   = (112.8 N)/(23.3 N)
   = 4.84
   θ = 78° from east
   equilibrant = 115 N 258° from east

4. A trunk with a mass of 200.0 kg is resting on a moving truck ramp that makes a 45° angle with the horizontal.

   a. Find the components of the weight of the trunk both parallel and perpendicular to the ramp.

   $W = mg$
   $= (200.0 \text{ kg})(9.80 \text{ m/s}^2)$
   $= 1960 \text{ N}$
   $F_{perpendicular} = W \cos θ$
   $= (1960 \text{ N})(\cos 45.0°)$
   $= 1390 \text{ N}$
   $F_{parallel} = W \sin θ$
   $= (1960 \text{ N})(\sin 45.0°)$
   $= 1390 \text{ N}$

   b. What is the acceleration of the trunk?

   $a = g \sin θ$
   $= (9.80 \text{ m/s}^2)(0.707)$
   $= 6.93 \text{ m/s}^2$ down the ramp

CHAPTER
7 **Evaluation**

MOTION IN TWO DIMENSIONS

A. Testing Concepts

In the space to the left, write the letter of the answer to each question.

1. __c__ For an object moving along a trajectory, the horizontal acceleration of the object _____ as the position changes.
   a. increases b. decreases c. is constant

2. __a__ The vertical change in position of an object that is dropped and that of an identical object that is thrown horizontally from the same height
   a. is the same b. is greater for the thrown object c. is less for the thrown object
   d. depends on the initial velocities of the objects.

3. __b__ Suppose an object is dropped from a moving train. The time it takes to fall
   a. will vary depending upon the observer's position relative to the train
   b. is independent of the observer's position c. depends upon the shape of the trajectory
   d. depends upon the speed of the train.

4. __c__ In trajectory motion, the initial horizontal velocity is _____ the final horizontal velocity.
   a. greater than b. less than c. equal to

5. __c__ In projectile motion, the rising and falling times of the object are equal if the launching position is _____ the landing position.
   a. above b. below c. at the same height as

6. __c__ Where would a pitcher have to aim a fast ball in order to have it pass at the height of the batter's chest?
   a. exactly at the height of the batter's chest b. slightly below the height of the batter's chest c. just above the height of the batter's chest d. at any height

7. __b__ For an object moving with circular motion, the direction of centripetal acceleration is
   a. tangent to the circle b. toward the center of the circle c. away from the center of the circle d. toward the circumference of the circle.

8. __c__ An object in circular motion travels a distance of _____ during its period.
   a. r b. $4\pi r^2$ c. $2\pi r$ d. v^2/r

9. __a__ When the displacement of an object with simple harmonic motion is greatest, the acceleration has a
   a. maximum value b. minimum value c. value between maximum and minimum.

10. __b__ The period of a simple pendulum depends upon
    a. the mass of the bob b. the length of the pendulum c. the amplitude of the swing
    d. the stiffness of the pendulum.

11. __a__ To produce mechanical resonance, the time between applied forces must equal the _____ of the object.
    a. period b. frequency c. length d. mass

---

7 **Evaluation**

B. Applying Concepts

Answer the following questions in two or three complete sentences.

1. Compare the distance a ball falls during the first second after it is dropped with the distance it falls during the second second.

   The ball accelerates as it falls. Each second its velocity increases so it falls a greater distance during the second second.

2. If the ball described in Problem 1 were thrown downward instead of being dropped from rest, would the average velocity for its downward motion be different? Would its being thrown affect the time required to fall to the ground? Explain both answers.

   The average velocity would be greater because the initial velocity was not zero. The time required for the fall would decrease because of the greater velocity.

3. Two people are on a carnival ride that uses centripetal and frictional forces to hold its riders in place inside a rotating drum. How do the velocity, acceleration, and force acting on the people differ if one person has twice the mass of the other?

   The velocity and the acceleration of the two riders are the same. The force required to hold the more massive person in place is greater than the force required to hold the other person.

4. Could the equations you learned in this chapter be used to calculate the height of a building from which paper confetti was thrown? Explain your answer.

   No, air resistance would be a very important factor in this case. Situations presented in the chapter were such that air resistance could be ignored.

5. On a certain game show, contestants spin a large wheel to determine the prize associated with correct answers. Explain how a contestant would apply force to get the wheel to spin as rapidly as possible.

   A contestant should apply as much force at the rim of the wheel as possible. The force should be applied to the wheel tangentially.

6. Hooke's law describes a relationship between force and the displacement from an equilibrium position for certain objects with simple harmonic motion. A proportionality constant k relates the other two quantities. Write an equation to represent Hooke's law. Identify the variables in the equation.

   $F = kx$, where F is the force that must be exerted on an elastic body to produce the displacement, x.

7. Explain the relationship among velocity, displacement, and acceleration of a mass suspended on a vibrating spring when the mass is at its equilibrium point.

   Before motion begins, the displacement, acceleration, and velocity are all zero. When the mass again reaches the equilibrium position, the acceleration is zero but the velocity is at its maximum.

8. Describe the force on the bob of a simple pendulum when it is pulled away from the vertical.

   The force that results is the gravitational force or the weight, which can be resolved into two components: a component parallel to the arm of the pendulum and a force perpendicular, or at right angles, to the arm of the pendulum.

9. Explain how you could use the physics you learned in this chapter to break a fine crystal glass without touching it.

   The glass can be made to vibrate by exposing it to sound at one of its natural frequencies. This phenomenon is resonance.

C. Understanding Concepts

1. A projectile is launched horizontally with a speed of 80.0 m/s. If the projectile is launched 1.5 m above the floor, how long does it take the projectile to hit the floor?

$y = v_y t + \frac{1}{2}gt^2$
$t = \sqrt{2y/g}$
$= \sqrt{\dfrac{2(-1.5 \text{ m})}{-9.80 \text{ m/s}^2}}$
$= 0.55$ s

2. A soccer ball is kicked into the air at an angle of 38° above the horizontal. The initial velocity of the ball is +30.0 m/s. How long is the soccer ball in the air?

$v_y = (v_i)(\sin\theta)$
$= (+30.0 \text{ m/s})(0.616)$
$= +18.5$ m/s
$t = -2v_y/g$
$= (-2)(+18.5 \text{ m/s})/(-9.80 \text{ m/s}^2)$
$= 3.78$ s

3. What is the horizontal distance traveled by the soccer ball in Problem 2?

$v_x = (v_i)(\cos\theta)$
$= (+30.0 \text{ m/s})(0.788)$
$= +23.6$ m/s
$R = v_x t$
$= (+23.6 \text{ m/s})(3.78 \text{ s})$
$= +89.2$ m

4. What is the maximum height reached by the soccer ball mentioned in Problem 2?

$y = v_y t + \frac{1}{2}gt^2$
$= (+18.5 \text{ m/s})(1.89 \text{ s}) + [(\frac{1}{2})(-9.80 \text{ m/s}^2)(1.89 \text{ s}^2)]$
$= +17.5$ m

5. A runner moving at a speed of 5.60 m/s rounds a curved track with a 60.0 m-radius. What is the runner's acceleration?

$a_c = v^2/r$
$= (5.60 \text{ m/s})^2/60.0 \text{ m}$
$= 0.523 \text{ m/s}^2$

6. A person with a mass of 75 kg sits at a distance of 1.5 m from the pivot point on a 4-m seesaw. Where would a person with a mass of 65 kg have to sit to balance the seesaw?

$d_2 = m_1 g d_1/m_2 g$
$= (75 \text{ kg})(1.5 \text{ m})/65 \text{ kg}$
$= 1.7$ m from the pivot point

7. What is the period of a simple pendulum that is 0.56 m in length?

$T = 2\pi\sqrt{l/g}$
$= 2\pi\sqrt{0.56 \text{ m}/9.80 \text{ m/s}^2}$
$= 1.5$ s

D. Extending Concepts

1. A coin rolls along the top of a 1.33 m-high desk with a constant velocity. It reaches the edge of the desk and hits the ground +0.25 m from the edge of the desk. What was the velocity of the coin as it rolled across the desk?

$t = \sqrt{2y/g}$
$= \sqrt{[(2)(-1.33 \text{ m})]/(-9.80 \text{ m/s}^2)}$
$= 0.52$ s
$v_x = x/t$
$= +0.25 \text{ m}/0.52 \text{ s}$
$= +0.48$ m/s

2. A 0.500 kg-object attached to the end of a 0.550 m-wire revolves uniformly on a flat, frictionless surface.

a. If the object makes three complete revolutions per second, what is the force exerted by the wire on the object?

$F_c = ma_c$
$= (0.500 \text{ kg})(197 \text{ m/s}^2)$
$= 98.5$ N inward

b. What is the speed of the object?

$v = 2\pi r/T$
$= (2)(\pi)(0.550 \text{ m})/0.333 \text{ s}$
$= 10.4$ m/s
$a_c = v^2/r$
$= (10.4 \text{ m/s})^2/0.550 \text{ m}$
$= 197 \text{ m/s}^2$

3. Earth's moon, which is 3.80 × 10⁸ m from the planet, is in freefall. Acceleration due to Earth's gravity acting on the moon is $2.70 \times 10^{-3} \text{ m/s}^2$.

a. What is the moon's speed?

$v = \sqrt{ar}$
$= \sqrt{2.70 \times 10^{-30} \text{ m/s}^2)(3.80 \times 10^8 \text{ m})}$
$= 1.01 \times 10^3$ m/s

b. How long does it take to complete its orbit?

$T = 2\pi r/v$
$= (2\pi)(3.80 \times 10^8 \text{ m})/1.01 \times 10^3/\text{s}$
$= 2.36 \times 10^6$ s or 27.3 days

4. The mass of the moon is 7.38×10^{22} kg. What is the centripetal force acting on the moon?

$F_c = m\left(\dfrac{4\pi^2 r}{T^2}\right)$
$= \dfrac{(7.38 \times 10^{22} \text{ kg})(4)(\pi^2)(3.80 \times 10^8 \text{ m})}{(2.36 \times 10^6 \text{ s})^2}$
$= 1.99 \times 10^{20}$ N

CHAPTER

8 Evaluation

UNIVERSAL GRAVITATION

A. Testing Concepts

In the space to the left, write the letter of the answer to each question.

1. __a__ During its orbital period, as a planet moves closer to the sun, the orbital velocity of the planet
   a. increases   b. decreases   c. remains the same.

2. __b__ According to Newton's law of universal gravitation, the force of attraction between any two masses is directly related to
   a. the distance between the masses   b. the product of the two masses   c. the velocity of the two masses   d. the sum of the two masses.

3. __b__ As the distance between two bodies increases, the force of attraction between the bodies
   a. increases   b. decreases   c. remains the same.

4. __b__ In his experiment, Cavendish was able to determine
   a. the mass of several lead spheres   b. the value of G c. the period of Io
   d. the mass of Io.

5. __a__ Astronauts in an orbiting space shuttle experience a sensation of weightlessness because
   a. the space shuttle is falling freely toward Earth   b. the space shuttle is not affected by Earth's gravity   c. the mass of the space shuttle decreases as the distance from Earth increases   d. the space shuttle is moving away from Earth.

6. __a__ According to Einstein's general theory of relativity
   a. mass causes space to be curved   b. gravity is a contact force   c. the gravitational force between two bodies is not affected by the distance between the bodies
   d. all of the above are true.

7. __c__ According to _____, an imaginary line from the sun to a planet sweeps out equal areas in equal time intervals.
   a. Newton's law of universal gravitation   b. Newton's third law of motion
   c. Kepler's second law of planetary motion   d. Cavendish's experiment

8. __c__ Anything that has mass is surrounded by
   a. a satellite in orbit   b. a magnetic field   c. a gravitational field   d. all of these.

9. __c__ The force of attraction will be equal between which two pairs of spheres?
   a. 1 and 2   b. 2 and 3   c. 1 and 3

(1) 32 kg ○ ── 20 cm ── ○ 25 kg

(2) 80 kg ○ ── 40 cm ── ○ 20 kg ── ○ 90 kg

(3) 90 kg ○ ── 15 cm ── ○ 5 kg

CHAPTER

8 Evaluation

B. Applying Concepts

Answer the following questions in two or three complete sentences.

1. Explain why Kepler was able to use Tycho Brahe's data about the positions of stars and planets to develop his laws of planetary motion, while Brahe was unable to use the same data successfully.

   Brahe believed in an Earth-centered universe. In formulating his laws of planetary motion, Kepler applied Brahe's data to the motions of planets in a sun-centered system.

2. Earth is closer to the sun in December than it is in July. What happens to the orbital speed of the planet between July and December? Explain your answer.

   The orbital speed of Earth increases between July and December. During this period, Earth is moving closer to the sun, and the closer a planet is to the sun, the faster the planet moves in its orbit.

3. What would happen to the magnitude of the gravitational force between two bodies if:

   a. the mass of one of the bodies were doubled?

      The gravitational force between them is doubled.

   b. the distance between the two bodies were doubled?

      The gravitational force between them is only one-fourth as great.

4. What information do you need to find the period of a planet?

   To find the period of a planet you need to know the period of another planet and the orbital radii of both planets.

5. The mass of Jupiter is approximately 318 times that of Earth. Yet, the surface gravity of Jupiter is less than three times the surface gravity of Earth. How do you account for this apparent discrepancy?

   The surface gravity of each planet is inversely related to the square of the radius of the planet. Jupiter's radius is much (almost 11 times) greater than Earth's radius.

6. How does an artificial satellite remain in orbit at a constant distance from Earth's surface?

   The satellite moves with uniform circular motion such that the curvature of Earth's surface exactly matches the curvature of the trajectory of the satellite. Earth's surface "falls away" from the satellite at the same rate that the satellite falls toward Earth.

7. How does Einstein's general theory of relativity account for the presence of "black holes" in the universe?

   According to Einstein's theory, light is deflected by the mass of a body. If an object is massive enough, light leaving the object will be bent back toward it. No light ever escapes the object, and the object appears as a black hole.

8 Evaluation

C. Understanding Concepts

1. Two spheres, each having a mass of 20.0 kg, are positioned so that their centers are 8.00 m apart. What is the gravitational force between the spheres?

$$F = G\frac{m_1 m_2}{d^2}$$
$$= \frac{(6.673 \times 10^{-11} \text{ N•m}^2/\text{kg}^2)(2.00 \times 10^1 \text{ kg})(2.00 \times 10^1 \text{ kg})}{(8.00 \text{ m})^2}$$
$$= 4.17 \times 10^{-10} \text{ N}$$

2. What will the force be if the spheres described in Problem 1 are positioned with their centers 4.00 m apart?

$$F = G\frac{m_1 m_2}{d^2}$$
$$= \frac{(6.673 \times 10^{-11} \text{ N•m}^2/\text{kg}^2)(2.00 \times 10^1 \text{ kg})(2.00 \times 10^1 \text{ kg})}{(4.00 \text{ m})^2}$$
$$= 1.67 \times 10^{-9} \text{ N}$$

3. If the mass of one of the spheres described in Problem 1 were doubled, how far apart would the spheres have to be placed in order to maintain the same gravitational force between them?

$$d^2 = \frac{Gm_1 m_2}{F}$$
$$= \frac{(6.673 \times 10^{-11} \text{ N•m}^2/\text{kg}^2)(2.00 \times 10^1 \text{ kg})(4.00 \times 10^1 \text{ kg})}{4.17 \times 10^{-1} \text{ N}}$$
$$d^2 = 1.28 \times 10^{-2} \text{ m}^2$$
$$d = 1.13 \times 10^{-1} \text{ m}$$

4. At Earth's surface a 1.0-kg mass weighs 9.8 N. How much would the same mass weigh on the surface of Mercury? (The mass of Mercury is 3.2 × 10²³ kg. Its mean radius is 2.43 × 10⁶ m. The mass of Earth is 5.979 × 10²⁴ kg. Its mean radius is 6.3713 × 10⁶ m.)

$$F = G\frac{m_1 m_2}{d^2}$$

where m_2 is the mass of Mercury and d is the mean radius of Mercury.

$$F = \frac{(6.673 \times 10^{-11} \text{ N•m}^2/\text{kg}^2)(1 \text{ kg})(3.2 \times 10^{23} \text{ kg})}{(2.43 \times 10^6 \text{ m})^2}$$
$$= 3.6 \text{ N}$$

---

8 Evaluation

D. Extending Concepts

1. The distance between Earth and the sun is often expressed as one astronomical unit (AU). Using this unit, find the distance between the sun and Mars, which has a period of approximately 686 Earth days.

$$r_m^3 = \left(\frac{T_m}{T_E}\right)^2 (1.0 \text{ AU})^3$$
$$= \left(\frac{686 \text{ days}}{365 \text{ days}}\right)^2 (1.0 \text{ AU})^3$$
$$r_m = 1.52 \text{ AU}$$

2. The mean distance between the center of Earth and the center of the moon is 3.84 × 10⁸ meters, and the moon has an orbital period of 27.3 days. Find the distance from Earth of an artificial satellite that has an orbital period of 9.1 days.

$$r_s^3 = \left(\frac{T_s}{T_m}\right)^2 r_m^3$$
$$= \left(\frac{9.1 \text{ days}}{27.3 \text{ days}}\right)^2 (3.84 \times 10^8 \text{ m})^3$$
$$r_s = 1.84 \times 10^8 \text{ m}$$

3. The gravitational force between two spheres is 2.50 × 10⁻⁸ N. Their centers are 105 cm apart. The larger sphere has a mass of 8.20 kg. Find the mass of the smaller sphere.

$$F = G\frac{m_1 m_2}{d^2}$$
$$m_2 = \frac{Fd^2}{Gm_1}$$
$$= \frac{(2.50 \times 10^{-8} \text{ N})(1.05 \times 10^2 \text{ m})^2}{(6.673 \times 10^{-11} \text{ N•m}^2/\text{kg}^2)(8.2 \text{ kg})}$$
$$= 5.03 \times 10^{-2} \text{ kg}$$

4. A body orbits the sun at a distance ten times the mean distance of Earth's orbit from the sun.

a. Find the period of the body in years.

$$T_b^2 = \left(\frac{r_b}{r_E}\right)^3 T_E^2$$
$$= \left(\frac{1.49 \times 10^{12} \text{ km}}{1.49 \times 10^{11} \text{ km}}\right)^3 (1 \text{ yr})^2$$

b. Determine the velocity of the body.

$$v = \sqrt{\frac{Gm_s}{r}} \quad \text{where } m_s = \text{mass of the sun}$$
$$v = \sqrt{\frac{(6.673 \times 10^{-11} \text{ N•m}^2/\text{kg}^2)(1.991 \times 10^{30} \text{ kg})}{1.49 \times 10^{12} \text{ m}}}$$
$$= 9.44 \times 10^3 \text{ m/s}$$

CHAPTER 9 Evaluation

MOMENTUM AND ITS CONSERVATION

A. Testing Concepts

In the space to the left, write the letter of the answer to each question.

1. __b__ Momentum can be calculated by multiplying mass by
   a. acceleration b. velocity c. impulse d. time.

2. __a__ If no net force acts on a body
   a. the velocity of the body is constant b. the body is accelerating
   c. the momentum of the body is zero d. the momentum of the body is increasing.

3. __a__ The greatest change in momentum will be produced by
   a. a large force acting over a long time b. a small force acting over a short time
   c. a large force acting over a short time.

4. __b__ If an object with a velocity of 50 m/s has the same momentum as that of a 10-kg mass having a velocity of 20 m/s, the mass of the object is
   a. greater than 10 kg b. less than 10 kg c. 10 kg.

5. __b__ Impulse can be represented by
   a. $\Delta v/\Delta t$ b. $F\Delta t$ c. mv d. none of these.

6. __a__ When a golfer hits a golf ball, the force exerted by the ball on the club is _____ that exerted by the club on the ball.
   a. equal to b. greater than c. less than

7. __b__ When a golf club hits a golf ball, the change in momentum of the ball is _____ the change in momentum of the club.
   a. equal to b. greater than c. less than

8. __b__ When a golf club hits a golf ball, the change in velocity of the ball is _____ that of the club.
   a. equal to b. greater than c. less than

9. __c__ A system is said to be closed if
   a. no net external force acts on it b. the momentum of each object in the system remains constant c. objects cannot enter or leave the system d. objects can enter, but not leave, the system.

10. __b__ If an object moving at a rate of 20 m/s collides with a stationary object and the two objects move away together, the velocity of the combined objects will be
   a. greater than 20 m/s b. less than 20 m/s c. 20 m/s.

11. __c__ An internal force _____ the total momentum of a system.
   a. increases b. decreases c. does not change

12. __a__ Two moving objects collide and move apart on paths that are 120° apart. The total momentum of the objects after the collision is _____ the total momentum before the collision.
   a. equal to b. greater than c. less than

CHAPTER 9 Evaluation

B. Applying Concepts

Answer the following questions in two or three complete sentences.

1. Explain how it is possible for a motorcycle to have the same momentum as a locomotive.

   Momentum depends on mass and velocity. The less massive motorcycle must have a proportionately greater velocity in order to have the same momentum as a locomotive.

2. In order to effectively "bunt" a baseball, at the instant the ball strikes the bat the batter moves the bat in the same direction as the moving baseball. What effect does this action have? Why?

   Moving the bat in the same direction as the moving ball has the effect of keeping the ball in contact with the bat for a longer period of time. This decreases the force produced by the collision of the bat and ball.

3. In the sport of curling, players slide large 19-kg masses called "stones" along the surface of the ice toward a target. If a stone traveling 3 m/s strikes a stationary stone directly, the first stone will stop moving. Using the concept of conservation of momentum, describe what happens to the second stone. Assume there is no friction.

   The second stone will move in the same direction and at the same speed as the first stone. Thus, momentum within the closed system is conserved.

4. Why does a fire hose recoil, or "kick" backward, when the water is turned on?

   Water under pressure in the hose exerts a force on the water leaving the hose. As the water leaves the hose, it exerts an equal and opposite force on the water that is still in the hose. This force produces the recoil of the hose.

5. Use impulse and momentum to explain why an empty pickup truck can change speed and direction more easily than an identical truck traveling at the same speed but carrying a load of gravel.

   The combined mass of the truck and gravel is greater than the mass of the empty truck. Thus the momentum of the loaded truck is greater than that of the empty truck. The greater the momentum, the greater the impulse required to change the momentum.

6. The drawing shows five identical metal spheres suspended from a support. What will happen if the elevated sphere is released and allowed to strike the ball adjacent to it? Explain your answer.

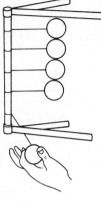

   The momentum of the moving sphere will be conserved. It will be passed from sphere to sphere, and the sphere at the end of the line will move away from the line at the same speed as the original sphere.

7. Suppose you were an astronaut drifting in space several meters from your spacecraft. The only thing you have with you is a sack filled with "moon rocks". How could you return to your ship?

   You could throw the rocks in the direction away from the ship. This would have the effect of exerting a force on your body equal to the force exerted on the rocks but in the opposite direction—toward your ship.

C. Understanding Concepts

1. Which has the greater momentum: a 145-g baseball traveling at 40.0 m/s or a 45-g golf ball traveling at 67.0 m/s? How much greater?

Baseball:
$p = mv$
$p = (0.145 \text{ kg})(40.0 \text{ m/s})$
$= 5.80$ kg·m/s

Golf Ball:
$p = mv$
$= (0.045 \text{ kg})(67.0 \text{ m/s})$
$= 3.0$ kg·m/s

$\quad 5.80$ kg·m/s
-3.0 kg·m/s
$\quad 2.8$ kg·m/s

The baseball has the greater momentum by 2.8 kg·m/s.

2. What impulse is needed to stop a 45-g mass traveling at 42 m/s?
$F\Delta t = m\Delta v$
$= (0.045 \text{ kg})(42 \text{ m/s})$
$= 1.9$ N·s

3. A force of 540 N is used to stop an object with a mass of 65 kg moving 175 m/s. How long will it take to bring the object to a full stop?
$F\Delta t = m\Delta v \qquad t = \dfrac{m\Delta v}{F}$
$= \dfrac{(65 \text{ kg})(175 \text{ m/s})}{540 \text{ kg·m/s}} = 21$ s

4. In hitting a stationary hockey puck having a mass of 180 g, a hockey player gives the puck an impulse of 6.0 N·s. At what speed will the puck move toward the goal?
$F\Delta t = m\Delta v \qquad v = \dfrac{F\Delta t}{m}$
$= \dfrac{6.0 \text{ N·s}}{0.180 \text{ kg}}$
$= 33$ m/s

5. A metal sphere with a mass of 80.0 g rolls along a frictionless surface at 20.0 m/s and strikes a stationary sphere having a mass of 200.0 g. The first sphere stops completely. At what speed does the second sphere move away from the point of impact?
$m_1v_1 = m_2v_2 \qquad v_2 = \dfrac{m_1v_1}{m_2}$
$= \dfrac{(0.080 \text{ kg})(20.0 \text{ m/s})}{0.200 \text{ kg}}$
$= 8.0$ m/s

6. A snowball with a mass of 85 g hits a snowman's top hat and sticks to it. The hat and the snowball, with a combined mass of 220 g, fall off together at 8.0 m/s. How fast was the snowball moving at the moment of impact?
$m_1v_1 = m_2v_2 \qquad v_1 = \dfrac{m_2v_2}{m_1}$
$= \dfrac{0.22 \text{ kg} \times 8.0 \text{ m/s}}{0.085 \text{ kg}}$
$= 21$ m/s

D. Extending Concepts

1. A ball with a mass of 12 g moving at +15.0 m/s collides with a second ball of mass 36 g moving at +5.0 m/s. After the collision, the 12-g ball moves at +6.0 m/s. What is the change in momentum of the 36-g ball?

$p_A + p_B = p'_A + p'_B$
$m_Av_A + m_Bp_B = m_Av'_A + m'_Bv'_B$
$v'_B = \dfrac{m_Av_A + m_Bv_B - m_Av'_A}{m_B}$
$= \dfrac{[(0.012 \text{ kg})(15.0 \text{ m/s})] + [(0.036 \text{ kg})(5.0 \text{ m/s})] - [(0.012 \text{ kg})(6.0 \text{ m/s})]}{0.036 \text{ kg}}$
$= +8.0$ m/s
$\Delta p_B = m_Bv'_B - m_Bv_B$
$= m_B(v'_B - v_B)$
$= (0.036 \text{ kg})(8.0 \text{ m/s} - 5.0 \text{ m/s})$
$= +0.12$ kg·m/s

2. A 24.0-kg dog running at a speed of 3.0 m/s jumps onto a stationary skateboard that has a mass of 3.6 kg. How long will it take an average force of 9.0 N to stop the skateboard and dog?
$m_1v_1 = m_2v_2 \qquad F\Delta t = m\Delta v \qquad \Delta t = \dfrac{m\Delta v}{F}$
$v_2 = \dfrac{m_1v_1}{v_2} \qquad\qquad\qquad\quad = \dfrac{m(v_f - v_i)}{F}$
$= \dfrac{(24.0 \text{ kg})(3.0 \text{ m/s})}{27.6 \text{ kg}} \qquad = \dfrac{(27.6 \text{ kg})(0 \text{ m/s} - 2.6 \text{ m/s})}{-9.0 \text{ N}}$
$= 2.6$ m/s $\qquad\qquad\qquad = 8.0$ s

3. A sphere of mass 5.00 kg moving at 4.00 m/s collides with an identical sphere that is at rest. If the first sphere moves off at an angle of 60° from its original path, what are the speeds of the two spheres as they separate? Assume frictionless conditions.

$p_A + p_B = p'_A + p'_B$
$p_A = m_Av_A$
$= (5.00 \text{ kg})(4.00 \text{ m/s})$
$= 20.0$ kg·m/s
$p = p_A + p_B = 20.0$ kg·m/s

$p_B = m_Bv_B$
$= (5.00 \text{ kg})(0 \text{ m/s})$
$= 0$ kg·m/s

Sphere A
$\cos 60° = \dfrac{p'_A}{p}$
$p'_A = p \cos 60°$
$= (20.0 \text{ kg·m/s})(0.500)$
$= 10.0$ kg·m/s
$p'_A = m_Av'_A$
$v'_A = \dfrac{p'_A}{m_A}$
$= \dfrac{10.0 \text{ kg·m/s}}{5.00 \text{ kg}}$
$= 2.00$ m/s

Sphere B
$\sin 60° = \dfrac{p'_B}{p}$
$p'_B = p \sin 60°$
$= (20 \text{ kg·m/s})(0.866)$
$= 17.3$ kg·m/s
$p'_B = m_Bv'_B$
$v'_B = \dfrac{p'_B}{m_B}$
$= \dfrac{17.3 \text{ kg·m/s}}{5.00 \text{ kg}}$
$= 3.46$ m/s

CHAPTER
10 Evaluation

WORK, ENERGY, AND SIMPLE MACHINES

A. Testing Concepts

In the space to the left, write the letter of the answer to each question.

1. **b** ___ Any object that has energy has the ability to
   a. burn   b. produce a change   c. fall   d. do none of these.

2. **c** ___ When a force is exerted on an object, work is done only if the object
   a. is heavy   b. remains stationary   c. moves   d. has no momentum.

3. **b** ___ In which of the following situations is no work done on a football?
   a. picking up the football   b. carrying the football down the field   c. dropping the football   d. all of the above

4. **a** ___ In which of the following situations is work done on the football by a person?
   a. picking up the football   b. carrying the football down the field   c. dropping the football   d. all of the above

5. **c** ___ In which of the following situations is work done on the football by gravity?
   a. picking up the football   b. carrying the football down the field   c. dropping the football   d. all of the above

6. **d** ___ How much work is done if you raise a 6.0-N weight 1.5 m above the ground?
   a. 0.0 J   b. 4.0 J   c. 7.5 J   d. 9.0 J

7. **a** ___ One definition of power is
   a. force exerted per unit distance   b. work done per unit time   c. the amount of energy expended   d. force applied multiplied by time interval.

8. **c** ___ A machine with a mechanical advantage greater than one
   a. increases friction   b. increases energy   c. increases effort force   d. does all of these.

9. **c** ___ For an ideal machine,
   a. the mechanical advantage is always greater than 1   b. input work is always less than output work   c. efficiency is always 100%   d. all of the above are true.

10. **a** ___ If the mechanical advantage of a machine is less than 1,
   a. effort force is greater than resistance force   b. output work is greater than input work   c. efficiency is greater than 100%   d. all of the above are true.

11. **a** ___ Using an ideal machine, a worker exerts an effort force of 5.0 N to move a 12.0-N weight a distance of 3.0 meters. The effort distance is
   a. greater than 3.0 meters   b. 3.0 meters   c. less than 3.0 meters.

12. **c** ___ Which of the following objects is not being used as a simple machine?
   a. a pulley used to lift a heavy object   b. a wedge used to split wood   c. a stick used to hold up a wilted plant   d. a screwdriver used to pry open a can of paint

13. **a** ___ Which of the following make up a complex machine?
   a. a lever and a pulley   b. a wheel and an axle   c. a pair of gears   d. All of the above are complex machines.

CHAPTER
10 Evaluation

B. Applying Concepts

Answer the following questions in two or three complete sentences.

1. Two students are moving 80-N cartons of books from the floor up onto a platform. One student moves 12 cartons in 7 minutes. The other student moves the same number of cartons in 5 minutes. Which student does more work? Explain your answer.

   Each student does the same amount of work because each exerts the same amount of force over the same distance. The difference in their performances is that the second student generates more power in getting the work done faster.

2. What type of simple machine is the handle of a pencil sharpener? How does it make work easier?

   The handle is a wheel and axle. Force applied at the perimeter of the "wheel" is transferred to the axle at the center of the system, where it is multiplied and used to do work.

3. Explain the following: When a screwdriver is used to drive a screw, the diameter of its handle is more important than its length, but when used to pry open a stuck window, its length is more important than the diameter of its handle.

   When used to drive a screw, a screwdriver is a wheel and axle, in which the handle is the wheel and the shaft is the axle. The larger the ratio of the diameter of the handle to the shaft, the greater the IMA of the machine. When used to pry off the lid, the screwdriver is a lever, in which the edge of the windowsill is the fulcrum. The longer the effort arm of the lever, the greater its IMA.

4. If a machine is used to increase force, what factor is sacrificed? Cite an example.

   Effort distance is sacrificed. Examples may vary, but should be machines in which a small effort force acts over a large distance to exert a large resistance force over a small distance.

5. Distinguish between work and power.

   Work is the transfer of energy by mechanical means. Power is the rate at which that energy is transferred. Power involves time; work does not.

6. Compare the size of the effort force to the size of the resistance force in a machine that has a mechanical advantage less than 1. What can be gained by using such a machine?

   In such a machine, the effort force is greater than the resistance. Such machines are used to multiply effort distance.

7. Use mechanical advantage to explain what happens when you shift the gears of a multi-speed bike.

   The gears in a bike are a type of wheel and axle machine in which the MA is the ratio of the "effort gear" attached to the pedals and the "resistance gear" attached to the rear wheel. Shifting gears changes this gear ratio, thus changing the MA of the wheel and axle machine.

C. Understanding Concepts

1. An adult and a child exert a total force of 930 N in pushing a car 15 m down their driveway. The adult exerts twice as much force as the child. How much work does each person do?

Total force, F = 930 N
Force exerted by adult, F = (930 N)(2/3) = 620 N
Force exerted by child, F = (930−620)N = 310 N

Work done by adult, $W = Fd$
$= (620 \text{ N})(15 \text{ m})$
$= 9300$ J

Work done by child, $W = Fd$
$= (310 \text{ N})(15 \text{ m})$
$= 4600$ J

2. An effort force of 200.0 N is applied to an ideal machine to move a 750.0-N resistance a distance of 300.0 cm.

a. Through what distance must the effort force act?

$F_e d_e = F_r d_r$

$d_e = \dfrac{F_r d_r}{F_e}$

$= \dfrac{(750.0 \text{ N})(300.0 \text{ cm})}{200 \text{ N}}$

$= 1125$ cm

b. What is the IMA of the machine?

$MA = \dfrac{F_r}{F_e}$

$= \dfrac{750.0 \text{ N}}{200.0 \text{ N}}$

$= 3.750$

3. How much power is developed by an electric motor that moves a 500-N load a distance of 20 m in 10 s?

$P = \dfrac{W}{t} = \dfrac{Fd}{t}$

$= \dfrac{(500 \text{ N})(20 \text{ m})}{10 \text{ s}}$

$= 1000$ W

4. How much work must be put into a machine that is 70.0 efficient in order to move a mass of 400.0 kg a distance of 12.5 m?

$W_i = \dfrac{W_o}{\text{efficiency}} \times 100\%$

$= \dfrac{(400.0 \text{ kg})(9.80 \text{ m/s}^2)(12.5 \text{ m})}{70.0\%} \times 100\%$

$= 7.00 \times 10^4$ N

5. How much power is generated by a machine in moving a 250-kg mass a distance of 150 m in 30.0 seconds?

$P = \dfrac{W}{t}$

$= \dfrac{(250 \text{ kg})(9.80 \text{ m/s}^2)(150 \text{ m})}{30.0 \text{ s}}$

$= 1.2 \times 10^4$ W = 1.2 kW

D. Extending Concepts

1. An adult pulls a child across the ice on a sled. The combined weight of the sled and the child is 26 N, and the adult pulls on a rope that joins the sled at an angle of 30° above horizontal. Ignoring friction, how much work is done in pulling the sled 390 m?

$W = (Fd)(\cos 30°)$
$= (26 \text{ N})(390 \text{ m})(0.866)$
$= 8800$ J

2. A grocer lifts an 8.0-kg carton from the floor to a height of 0.80 m, carries it 24 m across the store, and places it on a shelf 1.8 m above the floor. How much work does the grocer accomplish?

$W = Fd$
$= (8.0 \text{ kg})(9.8 \text{ m/s}^2)(1.8 \text{ m})$
$= 140$ J

Note: No work is done on the carton while it is carried horizontally.

3. At what rate (speed) can a 150-W motor lift a 2500-N load?

$P = \dfrac{W}{t} = \dfrac{Fd}{t} = F\left(\dfrac{d}{t}\right) = Fv$

$v = \dfrac{P}{F} = \dfrac{1.5 \times 10^2 \text{ W}}{2.5 \times 10^3 \text{ N}} = 6.0 \times 10^{-2} \dfrac{\text{W}}{\text{N}} = \dfrac{6.10^{-2} \text{ kg·m}^2/\text{s}^2/\text{s}}{1.0 \text{ kg·m/s}^2}$

$= 6.0 \times 10^{-2}$ m/s

4. A mover pushes a 260-kg piano on wheels up a ramp 7.0 m long onto a stage 1.75 m above the auditorium floor. The mover pushes the piano with a force of 680 N.

a. How much work does the mover do?

$W = Fd$
$= (680 \text{ N})(7.0 \text{ m})$
$= 4800$ J

b. What work is done on the piano by the machine?

$W = Fd$
$= (260 \text{ kg})(9.8 \text{ m/s}^2)(1.75 \text{ m})$
$= 4500$ J

c. What is the efficiency of the machine?

$\text{efficiency} = \dfrac{W_o}{W_i} \times 100\%$

$= \dfrac{4500 \text{ J}}{4800 \text{ J}} \times 100\%$

$= 94\%$

CHAPTER

11 Evaluation

ENERGY

A. Testing Concepts

In the space to the left, write the letter of the answer to each question.

1. __b__ The transfer of energy by mechanical means is
   a. momentum   b. work   c. effort   d. acceleration.

2. __c__ An object has energy caused by its motion. This is
   a. potential energy   b. chemical energy   c. kinetic energy   d. momentum.

3. __a__ Which of these is *not* needed to find the kinetic energy of an object?
   a. its shape   b. its mass   c. its velocity
   d. None of the above are needed to find kinetic energy.

4. __d__ When you throw a ball up into the air, the total energy of the ball at any point in its flight can be expressed as kinetic energy ——— potential energy.
   a. times   b. minus   c. divided by   d. plus

5. __b__ As an object falls towards Earth, the potential energy of the object
   a. increases   b. decreases   c. remains the same.

6. __b__ The kinetic energy of a boulder weighing 50.0 N perched on the edge of a cliff 25.0 m high is
   a. 750.0 J   b. 0 J   c. 2.0 J   d. 25.0 J.

7. __c__ The total amount of energy in an isolated, closed system
   a. is constantly increasing   b. is constantly decreasing   c. remains constant
   d. cannot be accurately measured.

8. __c__ A change in the kinetic energy of an object is equal to the
   a. force exerted on the object   b. velocity of the object   c. net work done on the object
   d. change in its mass.

9. __d__ The gravitational potential energy of an object close to Earth is directly related to
   a. the mass of the object   b. the height of the object   c. the velocity of the object
   d. both a and b.

10. __c__ If two bodies meet in an elastic collision, the total *KE* of the bodies before the collision is ——— the total *KE* of the bodies after the collision.
    a. greater than   b. less than   c. equal to

---

11 Evaluation

B. Applying Concepts

Answer the following questions in two or three complete sentences.

1. Describe the energy changes that take place when the spring of a toy car is wound up and then released.

   The work done in winding the spring is changed to potential energy. When the spring is released, the potential energy stored in the wound spring is changed to the kinetic energy of the moving car.

2. Why must the first hill of a roller coaster ride be the highest hill?

   The gravitational potential energy stored in the car at the top of the first hill is the source of energy, both kinetic and potential, for the entire ride. If any other hill were higher than the first one, the car would not have enough kinetic energy to reach the top of that hill.

3. When a golfer drives a golf ball, is the net work done on the ball positive or negative? Explain your answer.

   The net work done on the golf ball is positive. The ball moves in the direction of the force exerted on it.

4. Distinguish between an elastic collision and an inelastic collision.

   In an elastic collision, the kinetic energy of the colliding bodies after the collision is equal to their kinetic energy before the collision. In an inelastic collision, the kinetic energy of the bodies after the collision is less than the kinetic energy before the collision. In such a collision, some of the kinetic energy of the colliding bodies is changed into other forms of energy.

5. A ball is thrown up into the air. Describe the work done on the ball and the energy transformations that take place between the time the ball is released and the time it reaches its maximum height.

   Work is done when a force is applied to the ball through a distance. The work done on the ball is changed to kinetic energy as the ball travels through the air. As the ball travels away from Earth's surface, its speed decreases as kinetic energy is changed to gravitational potential energy. When the ball reaches its maximum height, its kinetic energy is zero and its gravitational potential energy is greatest.

6. When a pitcher throws a ball, the net work done on the ball is positive. Describe the net work done on the pitched ball when a batter strikes the ball with a bat and hits it back toward the pitcher.

   When a bat strikes a pitched ball, for a brief instant the work done on the ball is negative, in the direction opposite to the motion of the ball. As the ball moves back toward the pitcher, in the direction of the force applied to it by the bat, the work done on the ball is positive.

7. Under what condition will a marble and a baseball have the same gravitational potential energy? Under what condition will they have the same kinetic energy?

   A marble and a baseball have the same gravitational potential energy when the marble is at a greater height above Earth so that the product of the mass and height of the marble equals that of the baseball. They have the same kinetic energy when the product of the mass and the square of the velocity of the marble is equal to the product of the mass and the square of the velocity of the baseball.

C. Understanding Concepts

1. Find the kinetic energy of an airplane traveling at a speed of 648 km/h. The mass of the airplane is 5.00×10^3 kg.

$\dfrac{648 \text{ km/h}}{3600 \text{ s/h}} = 1.80 \times 10^{-1} \text{ km/s}$
$= 1.80 \times 10^2 \text{ m/s}$

$KE = \frac{1}{2}mv^2$
$= (\frac{1}{2})(5.00 \times 10^3 \text{ km})(1.80 \times 10^2 \text{ m/s})^2$
$= 8.10 \times 10^5 \text{ J}$

2. A diver, who has a mass of 48 kg, climbs up a ladder to a diving platform 5.0 m above the ground. How much potential energy does the diver gain?

$PE = mgh$
$= (48 \text{ kg})(9.8 \text{ m/s}^2)(5 \text{ m})$
$= 2.4 \times 10^3 \text{ J}$

3. How does the gravitational potential energy of a 550-g object, 20.0 m above the ground, compare with that of a 350-g object, 30.0 m above the ground?

$PE = mgh$
$= (0.55 \text{ kg})(9.8 \text{ m/s}^2)(20.0 \text{ m})$
$= 1.1 \times 10^2 \text{ J}$

$PE = mgh$
$= (0.35 \text{ kg})(9.8 \text{ m/s}^2)(30.0 \text{ m})$
$= 1.0 \times 10^2 \text{ J}$

The 550-g object has more potential energy.

4. An object with a mass of 10.0 kg moves toward the east along a frictionless surface at a velocity of 16.0 m/s. A net force of 20.0 N acts on the object and its velocity changes to 10.0 m/s toward the east.

a. In what direction is the net force applied?

Toward the west

b. How much does the kinetic energy of the object change?

$KE = \frac{1}{2}mv^2$
$= (\frac{1}{2})(10.0 \text{ kg})(16.0 \text{ m/s})^2$
$= 1.28 \times 10^3 \text{ J}$

$KE = \frac{1}{2}mv^2$
$= (\frac{1}{2})(10.0 \text{ kg})(10.0 \text{ m/s})^2$
$= 5.00 \times 10^2 \text{ J}$

The *KE* of the object decreases by 7.8×10^2 J.

5. A weightlifter lifts a 90.0-kg barbell from a stand 0.90 m high and raises it to a height of 1.75 m. What is the increase in the potential energy of the barbell?

$PE = mgh_2 - mgh_1 = mg\Delta h$
$= (90.0 \text{ kg})(9.80 \text{ m/s}^2)(1.75 \text{ m} - 0.90 \text{ m})$
$= 750 \text{ J}$

6. A child having a mass of 35.0 kg is on a sled having a mass of 5.0 kg. If the child and sled together have a kinetic energy of 260 J, how fast are they moving?

$KE = \frac{1}{2}mv^2 \qquad v = \sqrt{\dfrac{2KE}{m}}$
$= \sqrt{\dfrac{(2)(260 \text{ J})}{40.0 \text{ kg}}}$
$= 3.6 \text{ m/s}$

D. Extending Concepts

1. Two projectiles are launched horizontally at a point 1.0 m above the ground. Each has a mass of 40.0 g. One projectile lands 200.0 m away. The second projectile lands 220.0 m away. Find the potential and kinetic energy of each projectile at the time it is launched.

$PE = mgh$
$= (0.0400 \text{ kg})(9.80 \text{ m/s}^2)(1.0 \text{ m})$
$= 0.39 \text{ J}$

Kinetic energy of each projectile is calculated from the distance it travelled and the time it was in the air (the time it took to fall 1.0 m).

$KE = \frac{1}{2}mv^2 \qquad v = \dfrac{d}{t} \qquad t^2 = \dfrac{2d}{g}$

$KE = \frac{1}{2}m\left(\dfrac{d}{\sqrt{2d/g}}\right)^2$

$KE_1 = (\frac{1}{2})(0.0400 \text{ kg})\left(\dfrac{200.0 \text{ m}}{\sqrt{(2)(1.0 \text{ m})/(9.80 \text{ m/s}^2)}}\right)^2$
$= 3900 \text{ J}$

$KE_2 = (\frac{1}{2})(0.0400 \text{ kg})\left(\dfrac{220.0 \text{ m}}{\sqrt{(2)(1.0 \text{ m})/(9.80 \text{ m/s}^2)}}\right)^2$
$= 4700 \text{ J}$

2. A body with a mass of 5.0 kg has the same kinetic energy as a second body. The second body has a mass of 10.0 kg and is moving at a speed of 20.0 m/s. How fast is the first body moving?

$\frac{1}{2}m_1v_1^2 = \frac{1}{2}m_2v_2^2$
$v_1 = \sqrt{\dfrac{(m_2v_2^2)}{m_1}}$
$= \sqrt{\dfrac{(10.0 \text{ kg})(20.0 \text{ m/s})^2}{5.0 \text{ kg}}}$
$= 28 \text{ m/s}$

3. During a contest that involved throwing a 7.0-kg bowling ball straight up in the air, one contestant exerted a force of 810 N on the ball. If the force was exerted through a distance of 2.0 m, how high did the ball go from the point of release?

$W = Fd \qquad W = \Delta KE$
$\Delta PE = \Delta KE$
$mgh = Fd$
$h = \dfrac{Fd}{mg}$
$= \dfrac{(810 \text{ N})(2.0 \text{ m})}{(7.0 \text{ kg})(9.80 \text{ m/s}^2)}$
$= 24 \text{ m}$

CHAPTER
12 Evaluation

THERMAL ENERGY

A. Testing Concepts
In the space to the left, write the letter of the answer to each question.

1. a ___ Which form of thermal energy transfer is most effective in fluids?
   a. convection   b. radiation   c. conduction
   d. All of the above are equally effective in fluids.

2. c ___ The hotness of a body is its
   a. thermal energy   b. thermal equilibrium   c. temperature   d. specific heat.

3. c ___ The amount of heat needed to melt one kilogram of a substance is called that substance's
   a. melting point   b. specific heat   c. heat of fusion   d. heat of vaporization.

4. a ___ A heat engine converts
   a. thermal energy to mechanical energy   b. thermal energy to chemical energy
   c. mechanical energy to thermal energy   d. mechanical energy to chemical energy.

5. d ___ The disorder in a system is known as
   a. thermodynamic   b. fusion   c. equilibrium   d. entropy.

6. b ___ The energy that flows as a result of a difference in temperature is
   a. radiation   b. heat   c. temperature   d. vaporization.

7. d ___ On the Kelvin temperature scale, the freezing point of water is _____ K.
   a. -273.15 b. -100 c. 0   d. 273.15

8. c ___ When two objects are at thermal equilibrium,
   a. they contain the same amount of heat   b. they have the same thermal energy
   c. they are at the same temperature   d. they melt.

9. c ___ If thermal energy is added to equal masses of substances, they will show different changes in temperature because their _____ are different.
   a. heats of fusion   b. heats of vaporization   c. specific heats   d. volumes

10. c ___ If 25 g of hot water are added to 35 g of cold water, the heat lost by the hot water is _____ the heat gained by the cold water.
    a. greater than   b. less than   c. equal to

11. b ___ Unlike work, heat is energy transferred because of
    a. mechanical action   b. a difference in temperature   c. forces acting on matter
    d. accelerating particles.

12. a ___ The total increase in the thermal energy of a system is the work done on it _____ the heat added to it.
    a. plus   b. minus   c. multiplied by   d. divided by

13. b ___ If the average kinetic energy of the particles that make up a liquid increases,
    a. the liquid changes state   b. the temperature of the liquid increases
    c. the liquid loses heat to its surroundings   d. all of the above take place.

B. Applying Concepts
Answer the following questions in two or three complete sentences.

1. Define thermal energy in terms of the kinetic-molecular theory.

   According to the kinetic-molecular theory, matter is made up of tiny particles that are in constant motion. These particles have both kinetic and potential energy. The sum of the kinetic and potential energies of the particles that make up a sample of matter is the thermal energy of that sample.

2. Distinguish among thermal energy, temperature, and heat.

   The thermal energy of a sample of matter is the sum of the kinetic and potential energies of the particles of that sample. The temperature of the sample is determined by the average kinetic energy of its particles. Heat is the flow of thermal energy from a region of higher temperature to one of lower temperature.

3. What is absolute zero? What is its value on the Celsius scale?

   Absolute zero is the theoretical temperature at which all molecular motion ceases. On the Celsius scale, absolute zero is $-273.15°C$.

4. Equal masses of methyl alcohol and water are heated by the same heat source. How will the temperatures of these two substances compare after being heated for the same period of time? Explain your answer.

   The temperature of the alcohol will be higher than that of the water. Alcohol has a lower specific heat than water, so the temperature of a given mass of alcohol will increase faster than that of an equal mass of water when the same amount of heat is added to each substance.

5. A sample of iron at a temperature of 225 K is placed in a container of water at a temperature of 350 K. Describe what takes place in terms of heat transfer and temperature.

   Heat will be transferred from the warmer material to the cooler material—from the water to the iron. At equilibrium, the temperature of the two substances will be between 225 K and 350 K.

6. What is entropy? How does the entropy of a system change when heat is removed from the system?

   Entropy is the disorder in a system. When heat is removed from a system, the average kinetic energy of the particles is decreased, the particles slow down, and the system becomes more orderly. Thus, the entropy of the system decreases.

7. The term *latent* means "hidden." Why are heats of fusion and vaporization often referred to as latent heats?

   When heat is added to a substance that is undergoing a change of state, the energy is used to increase the potential energy of the particles. The kinetic energy of the particles does not increase, so the addition of heat does not produce an increase in temperature. Thus, the effect of adding heat to the substance is "hidden."

C. Understanding Concepts

NOTE: In these exercises, assume that no energy is transferred between the system described and its surroundings unless otherwise stated.

1. The boiling point of liquid helium is −267°C, which is the lowest boiling point of all the elements. Express this temperature in Kelvins.

$$K = °C + 273.15$$
$$= -267°C + 273.15$$
$$= 4 \text{ K}$$

2. How much heat must be added to 250 g of methanol to raise its temperature by 15°C? The specific heat of methanol is 2450 J/kg•K.

$$Q = mC\Delta T$$
$$= (0.25 \text{ kg})(2450 \text{ J/kg•K})(15 \text{ K})$$
$$= 9.2 \times 10^3 \text{ J}$$

3. How much heat must be absorbed by 2.0 kg of ice at −20.0°C to raise it to its melting point? The specific heat of ice is 2060 J/kg•K. The heat of fusion of ice is 3.34 × 10⁵ J/kg.

$$Q = mC\Delta T$$
$$= (2.0 \text{ kg})(2060 \text{ J/kg•K})(20.0 \text{ K})$$
$$= 8.2 \times 10^4 \text{ J}$$

4. How much more heat must be added to the ice in Problem 3 to change it to liquid water at 0°C?

$$Q = mH_f$$
$$= (2.0 \text{ kg})(3.34 \times 10^5 \text{ J/kg})$$
$$= 6.7 \times 10^5 \text{ J}$$

5. How much heat must be added to 1.5 kg of water at 95.0°C to change it to steam at 100.0°C? The specific heat of water is 4180 J/kg•K. The heat of vaporization of water is 2.26 × 10⁶ J/kg.

$$Q = mC\Delta T + mH_v$$
$$= [(1.5 \text{ kg})(4180 \text{ J/kg•K})(5.0 \text{ k})] + [(1.5 \text{ kg})(2.26 \times 10^6 \text{ J/kg})]$$
$$= 3.4 \times 10^6 \text{ J}$$

6. A 2.0-kg cube of iron at a temperature 300.0°C is placed on a 5-kg block of ice at 0.0°C. How much ice will change to liquid water at 0.0°C? The specific heat of iron is 450 J/kg•K.

$$Q = mC\Delta T$$
$$= (2.0 \text{ kg})(450 \text{ J/kg•K})(300.0 \text{ K})$$
$$= 2.7 \times 10^5 \text{ J}$$

$$Q = mH_f$$
$$m = \frac{Q}{H_f}$$
$$= \frac{2.7 \times 10^5 \text{ J}}{3.34 \times 10^5 \text{ J/kg}}$$
$$= 0.81 \text{ kg}$$

D. Extending Concepts

1. A 4.0-kg iron ball at a temperature of 225°C is placed in a container of water at 42°C. When the system reaches thermal equilibrium, its temperature is 45°C. What is the volume of water in the container? (1 kg of water = 1 L) The specific heat of iron is 450 J/kg•K. The specific heat of water is 4180 J/kg•K.

$$m_1C_1\Delta T_1 = m_2C_2\Delta T_2$$
$$m_1 = \frac{m_2C_2\Delta T_2}{C_1\Delta T_1}$$
$$= \frac{(4.0 \text{ kg})(450 \text{ J/kg•K})(183 \text{ K})}{(4180 \text{ J/kg•K})(3 \text{ K})}$$
$$= 26 \text{ kg} = 26 \text{ L}$$

2. How much heat is absorbed in changing 2.00 kg of ice at −5.0°C to steam at 110.0°C? The specific heat of ice is 2060 J/kg•K and of steam is 2020 J/kg•K. The heat of fusion of water is 3.34 × 10⁵ J/kg. The heat of vaporization of water is 2.26 × 10⁶ J/kg.

$$Q = mC\Delta T + mH_f + mC\Delta T + mH_v + mC\Delta T$$
$$= [(2.00 \text{ kg})(2060 \text{ J/kg•K})(5.0 \text{ K})] + [(2.00 \text{ kg})(3.34 \times 10^5 \text{ J/kg})]$$
$$+ [(2.00 \text{ kg})(4180 \text{ J/kg•K})(100.0 \text{ K})] + [(2.00 \text{ kg})(2.26 \times 10^6 \text{ J/kg})]$$
$$+ [(2.00 \text{ kg})(2020 \text{ J/kg•K})(10.0 \text{ K})]$$
$$= 60.8 \times 10^5 \text{ J}$$

3. The melting point of lead is 327.5°C. In order to change 50.0 g of lead at room temperature (20.0°C) to a liquid at its melting point, 3150 J of heat must be added. The specific heat of lead is 130 J/kg•K. What is the heat of fusion of lead?

$$Q = mC\Delta T + mH_f$$
$$H_f = \frac{Q}{m} - C\Delta T$$
$$= \left(\frac{3020 \text{ J}}{0.0500 \text{ kg}}\right) - [(130 \text{ J/kg•K})(307.5 \text{ K})]$$
$$= 2.04 \times 10^4 \text{ J/kg}$$

4. If 50.0 g of ice at 0.0°C is added to 150.0 g of water at 80.0°C, what will the temperature of the mixture be when it reaches thermal equilibrium?

Q gained by ice = Q lost by water

$$m_1H_f + m_1C(T_f - T_1) = m_1C(T_w - T_f)$$
$$T_f = \frac{m_2TC_w + m_2CT_1 - m_1H_f}{m_1C + m_2C}$$
$$= \frac{[(0.1500 \text{ kg})(4180 \text{ J/kg•C°})(80.0°C)] + [(0.0500 \text{ kg})(4180 \text{ J/kg•C°})(0.0°C)] - [(0.0500 \text{ kg})(3.34 \times 10^5 \text{ J/kg})]}{[(0.500 \text{ kg})(4180 \text{ J/kg•C°})] + [(0.1500 \text{ kg})(4180 \text{ J/kg•C°})]}$$
$$= 40.0°C$$

CHAPTER
13 Evaluation

STATES OF MATTER

A. Testing Concepts

In the space to the left, write the letter of the answer to each question.

1. c ___ At sea level, if the area of a surface increases, the pressure of the atmosphere on the surface
   a. increases   b. decreases   c. stays the same.

2. d ___ Pressure can be calculated as force ___ area.
   a. plus   b. minus   c. multiplied by   d. divided by

3. a ___ The SI unit of pressure is the
   a. pascal   b. atmosphere   c. millibar   d. newton.

4. d ___ According to Pascal's principle, any change on a confined fluid
   a. is directly proportional to the volume of the fluid
   b. is inversely proportional to the volume of the fluid
   c. depends on the shape of the container
   d. is transmitted unchanged throughout the fluid.

5. b ___ The buoyant force exerted on an object immersed in a fluid is equal to
   a. the volume of the immersed object   b. the weight of the displaced fluid
   c. the weight of the immersed object   d. the mass of the immersed object.

6. b ___ According to Bernoulli's principle, as the velocity of fluid increases,
   a. the density of the fluid decreases   b. the pressure exerted by the fluid decreases
   c. the buoyant force of the fluid increases   d. the buoyant force of the fluid decreases.

7. b ___ When heated, only matter in the solid state exhibits
   a. volume expansion   b. linear expansion   c. decrease in density   d. all of these.

8. a ___ The process by which matter changes state from a gas to a liquid is
   a. condensation   b. evaporation   c. sublimation   d. buoyancy.

9. b ___ As heat is applied to a sample of water at 1°C, the volume of the water
   a. increases   b. decreases   c. remains the same.

10. a ___ A crystal lattice is a characteristic of many
    a. solids   b. liquids   c. gases   d. solids and liquids.

11. c ___ An object that is deformed by a force and returns to its original form when the force is removed shows the property of
    a. buoyancy   b. expansion   c. elasticity   d. contraction.

12. d ___ The state of matter in which atoms become torn apart is
    a. solid   b. liquid   c. gas   d. plasma.

13. b ___ Surface tension is the result of ___ forces within a liquid.
    a. adhesive   b. cohesive   c. gravitational   d. buoyant

---

CHAPTER
13 Evaluation

B. Applying Concepts

Answer the following questions in one or two complete sentences.

1. Use the kinetic molecular theory of matter to explain the properties of gases.

   The particles that make up a gas are in constant, random motion and are widely separated. All collisions among particles or between gas particles and the walls of the container that holds them are perfectly elastic.

2. Most automobile brake systems are hydraulic systems. Explain how pressing on a brake pedal inside an automobile can cause pressure to be exerted on the brakes on all four wheels.

   The brake system of an automobile is a fluid-filled system. Pressure exerted on the brake pedal is transferred throughout the enclosed fluid of the brake system. The pressure causes the mechanical portions of the brakes to move, creating friction, which causes the car to slow down.

3. An iron cube weighing 5 N is suspended from a string and lowered into a container of water until it is completely immersed. Describe what happens to the weight of the cube. Explain your answer.

   The weight of the cube seems to decrease. The cube is buoyed up by a force equal to the weight of the water it displaces. This buoyant force acts in the opposite direction to gravity, thereby decreasing the weight of the object.

4. What properties can be used to distinguish between gases and liquids? What properties do gases and liquids have in common that allow them to be classified as fluids?

   A liquid has a definite volume; a gas takes the volume of the container that holds it. The particles of a liquid are much closer together than those of a gas. Therefore, a liquid is much less compressible than a gas. The properties that make liquids and gases fluids are the ability to flow and the ability to change shape easily under pressure.

5. How is matter in the plasma state similar to matter in the gas state? How is it different?

   The particles of matter in the plasma state are far apart and in rapid, random motion. The plasma state differs from the gas state in that the particles of a plasma are electrically-charged ions.

6. Explain the principle behind the operation of a bimetallic strip.

   A bimetallic strip operates on the principle that different materials have different coefficients of expansion. A change in temperature causes a bimetallic strip to bend, thereby breaking or completing an electric circuit.

CHAPTER
13 Evaluation

C. Understanding Concepts

1. Atmospheric pressure at sea level is about 1.0×10^5 Pa. How much force does the atmosphere exert on a driveway that is 15.0 m long and 5.0 m wide?

$p = \dfrac{F}{A}$

$F = pA$
$= (1.0 \times 10^5 \text{ Pa})(15.0 \text{ m})(5.0 \text{ m})$
$= 7.5 \times 10^6 \text{ N}$

2. Find the total force exerted by Earth's atmosphere on the top and sides of a rectangular can. The base of the can is 10.0 cm wide and 15.0 cm long, and the can is 12.0 cm high.

Total area $= 2\ hl + 2\ wh + wl$
$= 2[(15.0 \text{ cm})(12.0 \text{ cm})] + 2[(10.0 \text{ cm} \times 12.0 \text{ cm})] + (10.0 \text{ cm} \times 15.0 \text{ cm})$
$= 7.50 \times 10^2 \text{ cm}^2$

$F = pA$
$= (1.0 \times 10^5 \text{ Pa})(7.50 \times 10^2 \text{ cm}^2)$
$= 7.50 \times 10^7 \text{ N}$

3. A force of 400.0 N is exerted on a small piston, which has an area of 8.0 cm². How much weight can be lifted on a large piston, which has an area of 20.0 cm²?

$\dfrac{F_1}{A_1} = \dfrac{F_2}{A_2} \qquad F_2 = \dfrac{F_1 A_2}{A_1}$
$= \dfrac{(400.0 \text{ N})(20.0 \text{ cm}^2)}{8.0 \text{ cm}^2}$
$= 1.0 \times 10^3 \text{ N}$

4. The area of a small piston is 4.0 cm². A force of 150 N on the small piston will move a weight of 1200 N on a large piston. What is the area of the large piston?

$A_2 = \dfrac{F_2 A_1}{F_1}$
$= \dfrac{(1200 \text{ N})(4.00 \text{ cm}^2)}{150 \text{ N}}$
$= 32 \text{ cm}^2$

5. A cube of lead, 10.0 cm on each side, is suspended from a line and immersed in water. How much force is exerted on the line holding the lead cube? The density of lead is 11.3×10^3 kg/m³.

$F_{net} = mq - F_{buoyant} \qquad F_{buoyant} = V_{water}q$
$F_{net} = mq - V_{water}q$
$= [(1.00 \times 10^{-3} \text{ m}^3)(11.3 \times 10^3 \text{ kg/m}^3)(9.80 \text{ m/s}^2)] - [(1.00 \times 10^{-3} \text{ m}^3)(1.00 \times 10^3 \text{ kg/m}^3)(9.8 \text{ m/s}^2)]$
$= 101 \text{ N}$

6. An iron bar 1.6 m long at room temperature (20°C) is heated uniformly along its entire length until its temperature reaches 1250°C. How much longer is the bar at the higher temperature? The coefficient of linear expansion of iron is 12×10^{-6} °C⁻¹.

$L = L_1 \alpha \Delta T$
$= (1.6 \text{ m})(12 \times 10^{-6} \text{ °C}^{-1})(1230 \text{°C})$
$= 2.4 \times 10^{-2} \text{ m}$

CHAPTER
13 Evaluation

D. Extending Concepts

1. A cylindrical water tank 30.0 m high has a diameter of 14.0 m. The tank is two-thirds full of water. What is the pressure at the bottom of the tank?

$V = \pi r^2 h$
$= 3.12 \times (7.0 \text{ m})^2 \times 20.0 \text{ m}$
$= 3.1 \times 10^3 \text{ m}^3$

$W = Vpq$
$= (3.1 \times 10^3 \text{ m}^3)(1.0 \times 10^3 \text{ kg/m}^3)(9.8 \text{ m/s}^2)$
$= 3.1 \times 10^7 \text{ N}$

$p = \dfrac{F}{A}$
$= \dfrac{3.1 \times 10^7 \text{ N}}{\pi (7.0 \text{ m})^2}$
$= 2.0 \times 10^5 \text{ Pa}$

2. A rectangular solid measures 1.20 m × 0.80 m × 0.20 m. When the solid is standing on its smallest face, it exerts a pressure of 5.2×10^3 Pa.

a. How much does the solid weigh?

$P = \dfrac{F}{A}$

$F = PA$
$= (5.2 \times 10^3 \text{ N/m}^2)(0.80 \text{ m})(0.20 \text{ m})$
$= 8.3 \times 10^2 \text{ N}$

b. What is the density of the solid?

$P = \dfrac{m}{V} \qquad m = \dfrac{F}{q}$

$= \dfrac{F/q}{V}$

$= \dfrac{(8.3 \times 10^2 \text{ kg} \cdot \text{m/a}^2)/9.8 \text{ m/s}^2}{(1.20 \text{ m})(0.80 \text{ m})(0.20 \text{ m})}$
$= 4.4 \times 10^2 \text{ Pa}$

3. An open-top container with a capacity of 200.0 mL is filled to the brim with water at a temperature of 4°C. The container and its contents are heated to 95°C and then cooled. How much water is in the container when it returns to its original temperature? Explain your answer. Assume no change in the volume of the container. The coefficient of volume expansion of water is 210×10^{-6} °C⁻¹.

$V = V_1 - \beta V_1 \Delta T$
$= 200.0 \text{ mL} + [(210 \times 10^{-6} \text{ °C}^{-1})(200.0 \text{ mL})(91\text{°C})]$
$= 196.2 \text{ mL}$

As the water expands during heating, the water in excess of 200 mL will overflow the sides of the container. The final volume will be the volume that remains after 200.0 mL of water at 95°C contract during cooling to 4°C.

CHAPTER
14 Evaluation

WAVES AND ENERGY TRANSFER

A. Testing Concepts
In the space to the left, write the letter of the answer to each question.

1. __b__ A(n) ____ transmits energy without transferring matter.
   a. light particle   b. sound wave   c. electron   d. proton.

2. __a__ Waves on banjo strings are ____ waves.
   a. transverse   b. electromagnetic   c. longitudinal   d. surface

3. __a__ Dropping a stone into water will produce a(n)
   a. single wave pulse   b. standing wave   c. longitudinal wave
   d. electromagnetic wave.

4. __c__ Vibrating bells produce ____ waves.
   a. electromagnetic   b. surface   c. traveling   d. light

5. __b__ The shortest time interval during which wave motion repeats is the
   a. wave pulse   b. period   c. frequency   d. wavelength.

6. __c__ The number of complete vibrations per second is the
   a. wave pulse   b. period   c. frequency   d. wavelength.

7. __d__ The shortest distance between two points on a wave where the wave pattern is repeated is the
   a. amplitude   b. period   c. frequency   d. wavelength.

8. __a__ The speed of any mechanical wave depends on
   a. the medium through which it travels   b. its amplitude   c. its frequency
   d. its reflection.

9. __a__ When light from the air enters a body of water, some of the energy moves back into the air as a(n) ____ wave.
   a. reflected   b. incident   c. transmitted   d. sound

10. __c__ During constructive interference, the individual wave pulses
   a. change their shapes   b. change their sizes   c. retain their original sizes and shapes   d. change both their sizes and shapes.

11. __b__ A(n) ____ is produced during destructive interference of waves.
   a. antinode   b. node   c. higher crest   d. lower trough

12. __d__ The ____ states that the angle of incidence equals the angle of reflection.
   a. principle of superposition   b. law of standing waves   c. principle of refraction   d. law of reflection

13. __c__ The change in the direction of waves at the boundary between two different media is
   a. resonance   b. reflection   c. refraction   d. diffraction.

14. __d__ When waves spread out around the edge of a barrier, ____ occurs.
   a. resonance   b. reflection   c. refraction   d. diffraction

---

CHAPTER
14 Evaluation

B. Applying Concepts
Answer the following questions in two or three complete sentences.

1. Describe the relationship between the amplitude of a wave and the energy that is transferred by the wave.

   The greater the amplitude, the greater the amount of energy transferred. The rate at which energy is carried is proportional to the square of the amplitude.

2. Suppose two boats a few meters apart are subjected to passing ocean waves. Describe the motion of the boats. Will the oscillations of the two boats have the same amplitudes and frequencies?

   The boats will bob up and down as the waves pass. The repeated bobbing, or oscillations, will have the same amplitude and frequency, but the oscillations will differ in phase.

3. How do the reflected waves produced when a wave passes into a less dense medium differ from reflected waves produced when a wave passes into a more dense medium?

   A reflected wave is erect when a wave passes from a more dense medium into a less dense medium. When the second medium is more dense, however, the reflected wave is inverted.

4. What is the principle of superposition and how is it related to interference?

   The principle of superposition states that the displacement of a medium caused by two or more waves is the algebraic sum of the displacement caused by each wave. The result of the superposition of waves is interference.

5. Contrast the amount of energy transmitted by a wave passing through two similar media with that transmitted through two very different materials.

   When two consecutive media are similar, most of the energy of the incident wave will be transmitted. If the two materials differ enough, most of the energy will be reflected.

6. How do the speed of the transmitted wave and orientation of the reflected wave pulse change when a sound wave is transmitted from the air into water?

   The velocity of the wave increases as it passes from the air into water. Since the wave is passing from a less dense medium to a more dense medium, the reflected wave pulse is inverted.

14 Evaluation

C. Understanding Concepts

1. Middle C on a finely tuned piano vibrates 262 times per second. What is the period of the wave?

$T = 1/f$
$= 1/(262\ Hz)$
$= 3.82 \times 10^{-3}\ s$

2. Sound travels at 5600 m/s through a steel rod. If the frequency of the waves is 2480 Hz, what is the wavelength?

$\lambda = \dfrac{v}{f}$
$= \dfrac{5600\ m/s}{2480/s}$
$= 2.26\ m$

3. Suppose the steel rod mentioned in Problem 2 was fixed at one end but attached to a taut cord at its other end. What is the frequency of a wave that originated in the rod and traveled through the cord?

The speed and wavelength of the wave would differ, but the frequency would be the same because the wave in the rod generated the wave in the cord.

4. The wavelength of a sound produced by a tuning fork is 1.30 m. The fork has a frequency of 256 Hz. What is the wave velocity?

$v = df$
$= (1.30\ m)(256/s)$
$= 333\ m/s$

5. The wavelength of a water wave is 4.0×10^2 m. The wave is approaching land at 25 m/s. What is the period?

$f = \dfrac{v}{\lambda}$
$= \dfrac{25.0\ m/s}{400\ m}$
$= 0.06/s$
$T = 1/f$
$= 16\ s$

6. A beam of light strikes a mirror at an angle of 43°. What is the angle between the normal and the reflected ray?

The angle of incidence equals the angle of reflection; thus the angle is 43°.

---

14 Evaluation

D. Extending Concepts

1. You set a cup of coffee on the kitchen counter while the dishwasher is running. You notice that the vibration of the dishwasher causes standing waves in the coffee. The crests form four concentric rings, and the diameter of the cup is 6.0 cm. The speed of the wave in water is 1.5 m/s. What is the frequency of the vibrations coming from the dishwasher?

$f = \dfrac{v}{d}$
$= \dfrac{1.5\ m/s}{(3.0 \times 10^{-2}\ m)/4}$
$= 2.0 \times 10^2\ Hz$

2. The average distance between Earth and the moon is 384 790 km. If Earth's atmosphere were uniform and extended to the moon's surface, how many days would it take sound to travel to the moon?

seconds/day $= 60\ s/min \times 60\ min/h \times 24\ h/day$
$= 86\ 400\ s/day$

$t = \dfrac{d}{v}$
$= \dfrac{384\ 790\ km}{(343\ km/s)(86\ 400\ s/day)}$
$= 13.0\ days$

3. Waves traveling along a string have a wavelength of 2.4 m. When the waves reach the fixed end of the string, they are reflected. How far from the end are the first two antinodes?

The fixed end of the string is a node. Therefore, the first antinode is one-quarter of a wavelength, or 0.6 m, from the end. The second antinode is one-half a wavelength farther, or 0.6 m + 2.4 m/2 = 1.8 m, from the end.

4. Two springs are tied together. A transverse wave is started on the heavier spring. The wavelength is 0.20 m. When the wave reaches the point where the springs are tied together, a wave with a small amplitude travels back along the heavier spring at a speed of 5.0 m/s. A wave also passes along the lighter spring at a speed of 7.5 m/s. What is the wavelength of the wave in the lighter spring?

$f_L = f_H$
$\dfrac{v_L}{d_L} = \dfrac{v_H}{d_H}$
$d_L = \dfrac{v_L d_H}{v_H}$
$= \dfrac{(7.5\ m/s)(0.20\ m)}{(5.0\ m/s)}$
$= 0.30\ m$

DATE _____ PERIOD _____ NAME _____

CHAPTER
15 Evaluation

SOUND

A. Testing Concepts

In the space to the left, write the letter of the answer to each question.

__d__ 1. Echoes demonstrate _____ of sound waves.
a. refraction b. interference c. diffraction d. reflection

__b__ 2. Sound is a(n) _____ wave.
a. transverse b. longitudinal c. electromagnetic d. electron

__c__ 3. As an approaching ambulance passes a stationary observer, the frequency of the sound emitted by its siren
a. increases b. decreases c. stays the same.

__b__ 4. The frequency of the sound heard by the observer in Question 3 _____ as the approaching ambulance passes the observer.
a. increases b. decreases c. stays the same

__c__ 5. A detected change in the frequency of a sound due to a moving source or a moving observer is
a. refraction b. sonar c. the Doppler effect d. resonance.

__c__ 6. Which of the following *does not* describe the pitch of a sound?
a. frequency of vibration b. a note on a musical scale c. loud or soft d. high or low

__b__ 7. Two notes have frequencies the ratio of which is 2:1. The notes differ by a(n)
a. major third b. octave c. fifth d. fourth.

__d__ 8. A source with a sound level of 40 dB has a pressure amplitude that is _____ times greater than a source with a sound level of 20 dB.
a. 5 b. 10 c. 20 d. 100

__b__ 9. The sound heard from a record album is
a. sound that is stored on the vinyl disk b. produced by the needle vibrating against the record c. produced by vibrations within the turntable d. none of the above.

__d__ 10. Which of the following *is not true* of closed-pipe resonators?
a. Nodes are separated by one-half wavelength. b. The pressure wave is reflected from the closed end without inversion. c. A pressure wave is inverted when it is reflected from the open end. d. The open end of the pipe is a pressure antinode.

__b__ 11. Which of the following *is not true* of open-pipe resonators?
a. There are nodes at each end of the pipe. b. The resonances are spaced by quarter wavelengths. c. Some sound is transmitted at the open ends. d. Some sound is reflected at the open ends.

__d__ 12. The _____ of the human ear collects sound waves.
a. auditory canal b. eardrum c. inner ear d. pinna

__d__ 13. Sound quality of the human voice depends on
a. tongue movements b. nasal cavities c. throat movements d. all of these.

EVALUATION 29T

CHAPTER
15 Evaluation

NAME _____

B. Applying Concepts

Answer the following questions in two or three complete sentences.

1. How are molecules in air involved in producing sound from a trumpet?

   Sound is produced when the horn is blown. The vibrating instrument produces regular variations in air pressure. As the molecules in air collide, they transmit pressure oscillations away from the trumpet.

2. In terms of resonance, pitch, and frequency, describe how sound is produced in a trumpet.

   When the trumpet is played, air within the tube vibrates in resonance with the vibrating lips of the player. Pitch is varied by changing the length of the air column, which in turn determines the resonant frequencies of the vibrating air.

3. Tornadoes can develop in only an hour and they can cause much damage in only a few minutes. Describe how the Doppler effect could be used to warn against an oncoming tornado.

   Signals could be sent outward from weather stations to detect severe turbulence in precipitation, which could indicate an approaching tornado. The position, strength, wind speed, and direction of the storm could be determined and people could be forewarned.

4. Diagram the standing waves on plucked strings. The relationship between the length of the string and the wavelength of the note is shown for each example. Label nodes and antinodes.

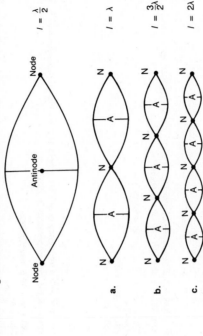

5. What is a beat and what produces it?

   A beat is an oscillation of the wave amplitude produced by two waves. When two waves are of slightly different frequencies, the amplitude of the resultant wave oscillates in intensity, producing a beat.

6. What are harmonics? Contrast the harmonics of open-pipe resonators with the harmonics of closed-pipe resonators.

   Pipe resonators produce sounds with more than one resonant frequency. The lowest frequency is the fundamental. Waves having frequencies that are whole-number multiples of the fundamental are harmonics. Open-pipe resonators with a fundamental frequency f, have frequencies f, $2f$, $3f$, and so on. Closed-pipe resonators have only odd-numbered harmonics.

EVALUATION 55

56 EVALUATION

C. Understanding Concepts

1. A sound wave traveling at a speed of 340 m/s has a wavelength of 1.25 m. What is the frequency of the sound?

$f = v/\lambda$
$= (340 \text{ m/s})/1.25 \text{ m}$
$= 270$ Hz

2. What would be the wavelength of the wave in Problem 1 if it were traveling through water at 1435 m/s?

$\lambda = v/f$
$= (1435 \text{ m/s})/(270/\text{s})$
$= 5.3$ m

3. An A on the piano has a frequency of 55 Hz. What is the frequency of the A three octaves higher?

The frequency for each octave is twice the given octave. Thus, 55 Hz × 2 × 2 × 2 is 440 Hz.

4. What is the wavelength of a sound made by a violin string vibrating at 640 Hz if the wave is traveling at 350 m/s?

$\lambda = v/f$
$= (350 \text{ m/s})/(640 \text{ Hz})$
$= 0.55$ m

5. What is the period of the sound wave in Problem 4?

$T = 1/f$
$= 1/640 \text{ s}^{-1}$
$= 1.6 \times 10^{-3}$ s

6. A 448-Hz tuning fork and a 444-Hz tuning fork are struck at the same time. What is the frequency of the beat produced?

$f = |f_2 - f_1|$
$= |448 \text{ Hz} - 444 \text{ Hz}|$
$= 4$ Hz

7. Two tuning forks are struck simultaneously to produce 2 beats/s. The frequency of one fork is 364 Hz. What are the possible frequencies of the other tuning fork?

$f_2 = f_1 \pm \Delta f$
$= 364 \text{ Hz} \pm 2 \text{ Hz}$
$= 362$ Hz or 366 Hz

D. Extending Concepts

1. The speed of sound through air depends on air temperature. Sound waves travel through 20°C air at 343 m/s. The velocity of sound in air increases 0.6 m/s for each increase of 1 Celsius degree. What is the temperature of the air if the speed of sound is 350 m/s?

Temp $= [(350 \text{ m/s} - 343 \text{ m/s})/(0.6 \text{ m/s/°C})] + 20°C$
$= 32°C$

2. A tuning fork has a frequency of 395 Hz. The fork causes resonances in an air column spaced at 45.6 cm. What is the velocity of the sound?

$v = (f)(\lambda)$

$\lambda = (2)(l)$
$v = (f)(2)(l)$
$= (365 \text{ Hz})(2)(0.456 \text{ m})$
$= 333$ m/s

3. A tuning fork with a frequency of 365 Hz is held above a closed pipe. What is the spacing between resonances if the air temperature is 15°C?

$v = 343 \text{ m/s} - (0.6 \text{ m/s/°C})(5°C)$
$= 340$ m/s
$\lambda = v/f$
$= 340 \text{ m/s}/365 \text{ s}^{-1}$
$= 0.93$ m
$l = \lambda/4$
$= \dfrac{v/f}{4}$
$= \dfrac{(340 \text{ m/s})/365 \text{ s}^{-1}}{4}$
$= 0.23$ m

4. The equation for the Doppler shift of a sound wave moving at a velocity v, approaching a moving detector, is: $f = f [(v + v_d)/(v - v_s)]$. If a whistle has a frequency of 545 Hz and the air temperature is 7°C, what frequency will you hear if you are approaching the whistle at 32 m/s?

$v = 343 \text{ m/s} - (0.6 \text{ m/s/°C})(13°C)$
$= 333$ m/s
$f = f[(v + v_d)/(v - v_s)]$
$= 545 \text{ Hz} [(333 \text{ m/s} + 32 \text{ m/s})/(333 \text{ m/s} - 0)]$
$= 597$ Hz

CHAPTER
16 Evaluation

LIGHT

A. Testing Concepts

In the space to the left, write the letter of the answer to each question.

1. a Light is a(n) ——— wave.
   a. electromagnetic b. mechanical c.compressional d. longitudinal

2. b Violet light has a wavelength of about
   a. 0.2 μm b. 0.4 μm c. 500 nm d. 700 nm.

3. d The wavelength of red light is
   a. 0.2 μm b. 0.4 μm c. 500 nm d. 700 nm.

4. b Putting your hand into the path of light from a flashlight illustrates
   a. that light is a mechanical wave b. that light travels in a straight line
   c. the refractive property of light d. the candela unit of measurement.

5. b The ——— of light is a defined value.
   a. wavelength b. speed c. frequency d. amplitude

6. a The rate at which light is emitted is the ——— of a light bulb.
   a. luminous flux b. illuminance c. candela d. luminous intensity

7. b Illuminance directly under a small light source is
   a. directly proportional to $4\pi d^2$ b. directly proportional to luminous flux
   c. indirectly proportional to luminous flux d. indirectly proportional to luminous intensity.

8. b Thin, white tissue paper can be described as
   a. transparent b. translucent c. opaque d. none of the above.

9. c Materials such as concrete that do not allow any transmission of light are described as
   a. transparent b. translucent c. opaque d. none of the above.

10. d Using primary colors of light to produce other colors is a(n) ——— process.
    a. secondary b. pigment c. subtractive d. additive

11. d When yellow light and blue light are combined, ——— light is produced.
    a. green b. black c. red d. white

12. a Which of the following is *not* true of primary pigments?
    a. They absorb all colors from white light. b. They are secondary light colors.
    c. They absorb light by the subtractive process.
    d. They absorb one and reflect two primary colors.

13. c The spectrum of colors produced by an oil film on water is due to the
    a. absorption of colors in a pigment b. separation of white light into its components
    c. constructive interference of light waves d. reflection of colors by a pigment.

14. d As the thickness of a film increases, the light that is least strongly reflected is ——— light.
    a. blue b. green c. orange d. red

15. c Only waves ——— to the polarizing axis of a polarizing filter can pass through.
    a. smaller than the opening b. larger than the opening
    c. vibrating parallel d. vibrating perpendicular

CHAPTER
16 Evaluation

B. Applying Concepts

Answer the following questions in two or three complete sentences.

1. What is a ray? How are rays used to study light?

A ray is a straight line that represents the path of a very narrow beam of light. Using rays ignores the wave nature of light, but rays can still be used to describe how light is reflected and refracted.

2. Contrast luminous flux, luminous intensity, and illuminance.

Luminous flux is the rate at which light is emitted from a source. Luminous intensity is the luminous flux that falls on one square meter of a sphere with a one meter radius. Illuminance is the amount of illumination displayed on a surface.

3. Mathematically describe the relationship between illumination on a surface and the distance the surface is from the light source.

Illumination is inversely proportional to the square of the distance from the light source.

4. Explain why a dandelion appears yellow. Is the process additive or subtractive? Why?

When a dandelion is illuminated by white light, the molecules that make up the flower act as dyes that reflect red and green light and absorb blue light. The brain interprets the color as yellow. The process is subtractive.

5. How is a dye different from a pigment?

Dyes are molecules that dissolve in liquids to form colored solutions. Pigments are larger than molecules and form suspensions.

6. How can you tell whether or not light is polarized?

Light can be passed through a polarizer. When the polarizer is rotated, polarized light will be blocked when the axis of the polarizing filter is perpendicular to the field of the light. As a result, the light will brighten and dim as the filter is rotated. The brightness of nonpolarized light entering the polarizer is independent of the orientation of the filter.

C. Understanding Concepts

1. What is the frequency of light with a wavelength of 7.00×10^{-7} m? What color is the light?

$f = c/\lambda$
$= (3.00 \times 10^8 \text{ m/s})/(7.00 \times 10^{-7} \text{ m})$
$= 4.29 \times 10^{14}$ Hz
The light is red.

2. What is the illumination on a piece of paper that is on a table 3.0 m from a light source producing 1600 lumens of flux?

$E = \dfrac{P}{4\pi d^2}$

$= \dfrac{1600 \text{ lm}}{(4\pi)(3.0 \text{ m})^2}$

$= 14$ lx

3. How much luminous flux must a light bulb produce if the bulb is positioned 4.1 m from the surface and the luminance required is 22 lx?

$P = E4\pi d^2$
$= (22 \text{ lm/m}^2)(4\pi)(4.1 \text{ m})^2$
$= 4600$ lm

4. What is the candle power of a bulb with 2.00×10^3 lm flux?

$I = \dfrac{P}{4\pi}$

$= 2.00 \times 10^3 \text{ lm}/4\pi$
$= 159$ cd

5. The light of a sodium vapor lamp emits light waves with wavelengths of 570 nm. What is the frequency of the electromagnetic waves?

$f = c/\lambda$
$= (3.00 \times 10^8 \text{ m/s})/(5.70 \times 10^{-7} \text{ m})$
$= 5.26 \times 10^{14}$ Hz

6. At what distance from a work area would the lamp in Problem 5 have to be placed in order to provide maximum illumination of the space?

$d = \sqrt{4\pi E/P}$

$= \sqrt{(4\pi)(25 \text{ lx})/(2000 \text{ lm})}$

$= 0.4$ m

D. Extending Concepts

1. The radius of Saturn's orbit is 1.43×10^9 km. How long, in minutes, will it take light to cross its orbit?

diameter $= (2)(1.43 \times 10^9 \text{ km})$
$= 2.86 \times 10^9$ km or 2.86×10^{12} m
$t = d/v$
$= (2.86 \times 10^{12} \text{ m})/(3.00 \times 10^8 \text{ m/s})$
$= 9.53 \times 10^3$ s $= 159$ min

2. On the average, one watt of electromagnetic energy produces about 500 lumens of luminous flux. What is the illumination of a 40-watt fluorescent bulb that operates at 20% efficiency if the bulb is placed 2.0 m from a book it is illuminating?

$P = (40 \text{ W})(0.2)(500 \text{ lm/W})$
$= 4000$ lm
$E = P/(4\pi d^2)$
$= 4000 \text{ lm}/(4\pi)(2.0 \text{ m})^2$
$= 80 \text{ lm/m}^2$

3. Use the data provided in Problem 2 to compare the fluorescent bulb with an incandescent lamp, which is only about 3% efficient.

$P = (40 \text{ W})(0.03)(500 \text{ lm/W})$
$E = P/(4\pi d^2)$
$= 600 \text{ lm}/(4\pi)(2.0 \text{ m})^2$
$= 12$ lx

4. Suppose a lamp were placed on a desk 0.33 m above a work area. How would the illumination compare with that provided by a ceiling light fixture, with the same luminous flux of 1500 lm, which is 2.0 m from the work area?

$I = P/4\pi$
$= 1500 \text{ lm}/4\pi$
$= 120$ lm
$E_{lamp} = P/4\pi r^2$
$= 120 \text{ lm}/(4\pi)(0.33 \text{ m})^2$
$= 88 \text{ lm/m}^2$
$E_{fixture} = P/4\pi r^2$
$= 120 \text{ lm}/(4\pi)(2.0 \text{ m})^2$
$= 2.4 \text{ lm/m}^2$

17 Evaluation

REFLECTION AND REFRACTION

A. Testing Concepts

In the space to the left, write the letter of the answer to each question.

1. __d__ According to the law of reflection,
   a. the normal is parallel to the angle of reflection   b. the incident ray and the reflected ray are in different planes   c. light rays are reflected in the same direction from a smooth surface   d. the angles of reflection and incidence are equal.

2. __b__ From which of the following surfaces would light rays undergo regular reflection?
   a. white construction paper   b. a telescope mirror
   c. a piece of black cloth   d. a concrete sidewalk

3. __a__ Refraction occurs when
   a. light travels through two adjacent media with different optical densities   b. light strikes the boundary of two media with the same optical density   c. the angle of incidence equals zero   d. the angle of reflection equals zero.

4. __a__ When light rays travel from an optically-dense medium into a less-dense medium,
   a. the rays travel more quickly   b. the angle of refraction is smaller than the angle of incidence   c. the refracted rays bend toward the normal
   d. the angle of incidence equals the angle of refraction.

5. __b__ Which of the following is *not* true of Snell's law?
   a. Light moving from a substance with a smaller n to a larger n is bent toward the normal.   b. Light rays traveling between any two media are related by a constant, n.   c. As the angle of refraction increases, the angle of incidence increases.
   d. The sines of the angles of refraction and incidence are inversely proportional to the indices of refraction of the two media.

6. __c__ The incident angle for which a refracted ray emerges tangent to the surface of a medium is the _____ angle.
   a. reflected   b. zero   c. critical   d. normal

7. __b__ The sine of the critical angle of a substance is
   a. directly proportional to the index of refraction of the substance   b. indirectly proportional to the index of refraction of the substance   c. indirectly proportional to the sine of 90°   d. directly proportional to the cosine of 90°.

8. __d__ A rainbow is a phenomenon caused by
   a. a mirage   b. refraction   c. total internal reflection   d. b and c.

9. __a__ In an optical fiber, the index of refraction of the core is _____ that of the outer layer.
   a. greater than   b. less than   c. equal to

10. __c__ The index of refraction of the mineral, beryl, ranges between 1.57 and 1.61. Transparent quartz has an index of 1.54. Which of the following statements is true?
   a. Both minerals will disperse the same amount of light.   b. Quartz will disperse more light than beryl.   c. Beryl will disperse more light than the quartz.
   d. Both minerals will disperse more light than diamond.

---

17 Evaluation

B. Applying Concepts

Answer the following questions in two or three complete sentences.

1. Explain the difference between regular and diffuse reflection.

   When light rays strike a rough surface, the rays are reflected in many directions. Such reflection is diffuse reflection. Regular reflection occurs when parallel rays of light strike a flat, smooth surface and the reflected rays are parallel.

2. Explain the relationship between the sine of the angle of incidence and the sine of the angle of refraction of light rays traveling from a vacuum into another medium.

   The sine of the angle of incidence divided by the sine of the angle of refraction is a constant called the index of refraction of the medium.

3. Mathematically express the relationship between indices of refraction for a light ray traveling from one medium into another.

   $$n_i \sin \theta_i = n_r \sin \theta_r$$

4. How does the angle of refraction change as a light ray passes from a medium with a higher index of refraction to one with a lower index of refraction?

   The greater the obliquity of the incident ray, the greater the angle of refraction.

5. What is total internal reflection?

   Total internal reflection occurs when light passes from a more optically-dense medium to a less optically-dense medium at an angle so great that there is no refracted ray. This incident angle is called the critical angle.

6. Why is the sun still visible over the horizon after sunset?

   Sunlight travels slower through the air than it does in space. Thus, the light is refracted. In the evening, sunlight is bent above the horizon by Earth's atmosphere.

C. Understanding Concepts

1. Light rays traveling through quartz enter the quartz at an angle of 35°. The index of refraction of quartz is 1.54. At what angle do the light rays leave the substance?

$\sin \theta_r = \dfrac{n_i(\sin \theta_i)}{n_r}$

$= (1.00)(0.574)/(1.54)$

$= 0.373$

$\theta_r = 22°$

2. A light ray enters a substance at an angle of 55°. The light is refracted inside the substance and leaves the substance at an angle of 35°. What is the index of refraction of the material?

$n_r = \sin \theta_i / \sin \theta_r$

$= 0.819/0.574$

$= 1.43$

3. Diamond has an index of refraction of 2.42. If it is immersed in water, which has an index of 1.33, and light rays in the water shine on the diamond at a 53° angle, what is the angle of refraction inside the diamond?

$\sin \theta_r = \dfrac{n_i(\sin \theta_i)}{n_r}$

$= (1.33)(0.799)/(2.42)$

$= 0.439$

$\theta_r = 26°$

4. The index of refraction of halite, or table salt, is 1.54. What is the speed of light in this mineral?

$v_s = c/n_s$

$= (3.00 \times 10^8 \text{ m/s})/(1.54)$

$= 1.95 \times 10^8 \text{ m/s}$

5. What is the index of refraction of a material if light travels through the material at 2.10×10^8 m/s?

$n_s = c/v_s$

$= (3.00 \times 10^8 \text{ m/s})/(2.10 \times 10^8 \text{ m/s})$

$= 1.43$

6. The mineral calcite, $CaCO_3$, has an index of refraction of 1.66. What is the critical angle of calcite?

$\sin \theta_c = \dfrac{1}{n_i}$

$= 1/1.66$

$= 0.602$

$\theta_c = 37°$

D. Extending Concepts

1. Flint glass has an index of refraction of 1.57 for red light and 1.59 for violet light. If the red light ray is refracted at 67°, what is the angle of incidence for the violet ray?

$\sin \theta_i = \dfrac{n_r(\sin \theta_r)}{n_i}$

$= (1.57)(\sin 67°)$

$= \dfrac{1.59}{}$

$= 0.909$

$\theta_i = 65°$

2. A light ray in a tub of water makes an angle of incidence of 52° at the surface. The index of refraction of air is 1.00 and of water is 1.33.

a. Prove that the ray undergoes total internal reflection.

$\sin \theta_r = \dfrac{n_w(\sin \theta_i)}{n_a}$

$= \dfrac{(1.33)(0.788)}{1.00}$

$= 1.05$

There is no angle with this sine value. The largest angle of refraction is 90° (sin = 1.000). Therefore, this ray undergoes total internal reflection.

b. What is the value of the angle of internal reflection?

The angle of reflection is 52°.

3. In some optical instruments, such as binoculars, 45°-prisms are used to produce total internal reflection at two surfaces. What is the minimum index of refraction needed for each prism?

$n_g = \dfrac{\sin 90°}{\sin 45°}$

$= \dfrac{1.00}{0.71}$

$= 1.41$

4. The index of refraction for borate flint glass is 1.57 for red light and 1.59 for violet light. When a ray of white light nears the surface of the glass at an angle of 60.0°, what are the angles of refraction for the two wavelengths?

For the red wavelength:

$\sin \theta_r = \dfrac{\sin \theta_i}{n}$

$= \dfrac{0.8666}{1.57}$

$\theta_r = 33.5°$

For the violet wavelength:

$\sin \theta_r = \dfrac{\sin \theta_i}{n}$

$= \dfrac{0.866}{1.59}$

$= 0.545$

$\theta_r = 33.0°$

CHAPTER
18 Evaluation

MIRRORS AND LENSES

A. Testing Concepts

In the space to the left, write the letter of the answer to each question.

1. **a** Which of the following is *not* true of plane mirrors and the images they form?
   a. The light rays intersect at a point behind the mirror to form a real erect image.
   b. The angles of reflection and incidence are equal.   c. A virtual image is formed at the same distance behind the mirror that the object is in front of the mirror.
   d. The virtual image that forms is the same size as the actual object.

2. **c** For very small angles, the focal length of a concave mirror is
   a. equal to the radius of the mirror   b. two times the length of the principal axis
   c. half the distance between the center of curvature and the mirror's surface
   d. equal to twice the radius of the mirror.

3. **b** Parabolic mirrors are often used in
   a. department store dressing rooms   b. certain types of astronomical equipment
   c. eyeglasses   d. all of the above.

4. **a** A real image is formed when
   a. light rays converge and pass through the image   b. light rays seem to diverge from behind the mirror   c. the image cannot be projected onto a screen
   d. rays farthest from the principal axis meet at the mirror's surface.

5. **c** If an object is located between the focal point and a concave mirror, the image formed will be _____ than the object.
   a. real and smaller   b. real and larger
   c. virtual and larger   d. virtual and smaller

6. **b** Which of the following is *not* true of a convex mirror?
   a. It reflects light from its outer surface.   b. It forms real images.   c. The focal point is behind the mirror.   d. The focal length of the mirror is negative.

7. **a** The image formed of an object located beyond the principal focus of a convex lens is _____ than the actual object.
   a. real and smaller   b. virtual and smaller
   c. virtual and larger   d. real and larger

8. **c** Which of the following is *not* true of a concave lens?
   a. It forms a virtual, erect, and reduced image.   b. The image is formed due to divergence of the light rays.   c. It has a positive focal length.
   d. It is thinner in the middle than at the edges.

9. **d** Chromatic aberration can be reduced by cementing _____ together to form a single lens.
   a. two converging lenses   b. two diverging lenses
   c. three converging lenses   d. a converging lens and a diverging lens

10. **a** The focal length of the objective lens in a telescope is _____ the focal length of the objective lens in a microscope.
    a. greater than   b. less than   c. about the same as

CHAPTER
18 Evaluation

B. Applying Concepts

Answer the following questions in two or three complete sentences.

1. What happens to a light ray that is parallel to the principal axis of a concave mirror after it is reflected from the mirror's surface? What happens to a ray that passes through the focal point of such a mirror before being reflected?

   A ray that is parallel to the principal axis passes through the focal point of a concave mirror. A ray passing through the focal point of the mirror is reflected parallel to the principal axis.

2. What causes spherical aberration?

   Parallel rays converge at the focal point of a spherical mirror only if the rays are close to the principal axis. Rays farthest from the principal axis will converge at a point closer to the mirror's surface than the other rays. Thus, the image formed in a large spherical mirror is a disk, rather than a point. This phenomenon is called spherical aberration.

3. Complete the diagram to show the size and location of the image of an object located beyond the center of curvature of a concave mirror.

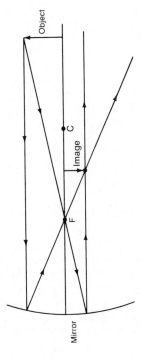

4. Contrast convex and concave lenses.

   A convex lens is thicker at the center than it is at its edges and refracts parallel light rays so that they meet. A concave lens is thinner in the middle than at the edges. A concave lens refracts light rays so that they diverge.

5. Contrast the image formed by a converging lens when an object is located beyond the principal focus of the lens with the image formed when the object is between the lens and the principal focus.

   If the object is outside the principal focus, the image is real, inverted, and reduced. If the object is between the principal focus and the lens, the object is virtual, erect, and enlarged.

6. Complete the diagram to show the size and location of the image produced by a concave lens.

EVALUATION   35T

C. Understanding Concepts

1. A thimble 2.5 cm high is 32.0 cm from a concave mirror. The curvature of the mirror is 22.0 cm. Where is the image located?

$f = (1/2)(r)$
$= (1/2)(22.0 \text{ cm})$
$= 11.0 \text{ cm}$

$d_i = \dfrac{fd_o}{d_o - f}$
$= \dfrac{(11.0 \text{ cm})(32.0 \text{ cm})}{(32.0 \text{ cm}) - (11.0 \text{ cm})}$
$= 16.8 \text{ cm from the mirror}$

2. What is the size and orientation of the thimble's image in Problem 1?

$h_i = \dfrac{-d_i h_o}{d_o}$
$= \dfrac{-(17.0 \text{ cm})(2.5 \text{ cm})}{32.0 \text{ cm}}$
$= 1.3 \text{ cm, meaning the image is inverted}$

3. What is the magnification of the mirror in Problem 1?

$m = h_i/h_o$
$= 1.3 \text{ cm}/2.5 \text{ cm}$
$= -0.52$

4. What is the size of the image produced by a child 1.1 m tall who is standing 6.0 m from a convex mirror if the location of the image produced is 0.40 m behind the mirror?

$h_i = \dfrac{-h_o d_i}{d_o}$
$= \dfrac{-(1.1 \text{ m})(0.40 \text{ m})}{6.0 \text{ m}}$
$= 0.073 \text{ m}$

5. What is the focal length of the mirror in Problem 4?

$1/f = 1/d_o + 1/d_i$
$= 1/(6.0 \text{ m}) + 1/(-0.40 \text{ m})$
$f = -2.3 \text{ cm}$
$= -0.43 \text{ m}$

6. An object is 5.00 cm from a convex lens with a focal length of 6.00 cm. Locate and describe the image.

$d_i = \dfrac{d_o f}{d_o - f}$
$= \dfrac{(5.00 \text{ cm})(6.0 \text{ cm})}{(5.00 \text{ cm}) - (6.00 \text{ cm})}$
$= -30.0 \text{ cm}$

The image is virtual.

7. What focal length concave lens is needed to form a virtual image 10 cm from the lens when the object is 35 cm from the lens?

$1/d = 1/d_o - 1/d_i$
$= 1/(35.0 \text{ cm}) - 1/(10.0 \text{ cm})$
$= 0.0714 \text{ cm}$
$f = 14.0 \text{ cm}$

D. Extending Concepts

1. If a flower 1.00 m high is to have an image 35 mm high when the flower is 10.0 m from the concave mirror, what must the radius of curvature of the mirror be?

$d_i = \dfrac{d_o h_i}{h_o}$
$= \dfrac{(10.0 \text{ m})(0.035 \text{ m})}{1.00 \text{ m}}$
$= 0.35 \text{ m}$

$r = 2f$
$= 2(0.33 \text{ m})$
$= 0.66 \text{ m or } 66 \text{ cm}$

$1/f = 1/d_o + 1/d_i$
$= 1/(10.0 \text{ m}) + 1/(0.35 \text{ m})$
$= 3.0 \text{ m}$
$f = 0.33 \text{ m}$

2. If a vehicle 2.0 m high is 4.6 m from your car's convex mirror, find the size and position of the image. The radius of curvature of the mirror is 80.0 cm. Is the image real or virtual? Explain.

$f = -(1/2r)$
$= -[(1/2)(0.800 \text{ m})]$
$= -0.400 \text{ cm}$

$d_i = \dfrac{d_o}{d_o - f}$
$= \dfrac{(4.6 \text{ m})(-0.400 \text{ m})}{(4.6 \text{ m}) - (-0.400 \text{ m})}$
$= -0.37 \text{ m}$

A negative image distance indicates a virtual image.

$h_i = \dfrac{-d_i h_o}{d_o}$
$= \dfrac{-(-0.37 \text{ m})(2.0 \text{ m})}{4.6 \text{ m}}$
$= 0.16 \text{ m}$

3. Two convex lenses are positioned 52 cm apart. The first lens has a focal length of 10.0 cm and the second has a focal length of 13.0 cm. An object 1.0 cm high is placed 13 cm from the first lens. What is the size of the image produced by the second lens? Is the image real or virtual?

$d_i = \dfrac{fd_o}{d_o - f}$
$= \dfrac{(10.0 \text{ cm})(13.0 \text{ cm})}{(13.0 \text{ cm}) - (10.0 \text{ cm})}$
$= 43.3 \text{ cm}$

$h_i = \dfrac{h_o d_i}{d_o}$
$= \dfrac{(1.0 \text{ cm})(43.3 \text{ cm})}{13 \text{ cm}}$
$= 3.3 \text{ cm}$

$d_i = \dfrac{fd_o}{d_o - f}$
$= \dfrac{(13.0 \text{ cm})(8.7 \text{ cm})}{(8.7 \text{ cm}) - (13.0 \text{ cm})}$
$= -26 \text{ cm}$

$h_i = \dfrac{h_o d_i}{d_o}$
$= \dfrac{(3.3 \text{ cm})(-26 \text{ cm})}{8.7 \text{ cm}}$
$= -9.9 \text{ cm}$

The image is virtual.

CHAPTER
19 Evaluation

DIFFRACTION AND INTERFERENCE OF LIGHT

A. Testing Concepts

In the space to the left, write the letter of the answer to each question.

1. __a__ The destructive and constructive interference of light that passes through two closely-spaced slits produces
   a. interference fringes   b. monochromatic light sources
   c. coherent light waves   d. diffraction gratings.

2. __a__ The bending of waves around the edges of barriers is
   a. diffraction   b. interference   c. refraction   d. reflection.

3. __d__ What happens when monochromatic light is passed successively through a single narrow slit and then through a double slit?
   a. The double slit acts as two sources of circular waves.
   b. The waves interfere destructively where crests and troughs overlap.
   c. The light waves interfere constructively where two crests meet.
   d. all of the above

4. __a__ The paths of the light waves that interfere to cause first-order lines
   a. differ in length by the wavelength of the light   b. are parallel lines
   c. are the same length   d. are curved lines.

5. __c__ The wavelength of light using double-slit interference patterns is
   a. directly proportional to the distance between the screen and the slits
   b. indirectly proportional to the distance between the two slits
   c. indirectly proportional to the distance between the slits and the screen
   d. directly proportional to the distance between the two slits.

6. __b__ When light passes through a single slit,
   a. a series of equally-bright bands appear
   b. a bright central band appears, with dimmer bright bands to the sides
   c. a dark central band appears, with bright bands to either side
   d. a single wide bright band appears.

7. __d__ Interference patterns of diffraction gratings
   a. form in a similar way to those formed by double slits
   b. have bright bands that are narrower than those produced by double slits
   c. allow wavelengths to be measured more accurately than with double slits
   d. do all of the above.

8. __b__ A binary star system can be misinterpreted as a single star because
   a. the telescope lens acts as a double slit
   b. the lens has a limited resolution
   c. the light is refracted as it enters Earth's atmosphere
   d. a binary star system contains only one star.

9. __a__ The effects of diffraction on the resolving power of the telescope can be reduced by
   a. increasing the size of the lens   b. decreasing the size of the lens
   c. magnifying the images being viewed   d. using yellow filters to view the objects.

---

19 Evaluation

B. Applying Concepts

Answer the following questions in two or three complete sentences.

1. Why are the edges of shadows not sharp? What is this phenomenon called?

The bending of light waves around the edges of barriers causes the fuzziness at the edges of shadows. This phenomenon is called diffraction.

2. Complete and label this geometric representation of Young's double-slit experiment. How can wavelength be determined from the drawing?

$$\lambda = \frac{xd}{L}$$

3. Explain the cause of the dark bands seen as a result of single-slit diffraction.

When the paths of two light waves differ in length by $\frac{1}{2}\lambda$, destructive interference occurs, and no light is seen.

4. Contrast the interference patterns formed by double slits with those formed by diffraction gratings.

The patterns are formed the same way. Bright bands are in the same locations, but are narrower when formed by diffraction gratings. The dark regions formed by gratings are broader than those formed by double slits. Thus, colors produced by the gratings are more easily distinguished from one another.

5. Can the values for white-light wavelengths be directly measured with a grating spectrometer? Explain your answer.

The wavelength cannot be measured directly, but it can be calculated. When a white-light source falls on a slit and then passes through a diffraction grating, a series of bright bands appears on either side of the central bright band. Each band of light is a spectrum. The spectrometer is moved until the desired line appears in the middle of a viewer. The angle θ is then read from the spectrometer. Once d is known and θ can be measured, the wavelength can be calculated.

C. Understanding Concepts

1. If the slit separation is 1.72 x 10⁻⁵ m and the screen is 0.650 m from the slits, how far from the central band will the violet light of the spectrum appear? The wavelength of violet light is 4.50 x 10⁻⁷ m.

$x = \dfrac{\lambda L}{d}$

$= \dfrac{(4.50 \times 10^{-7} \text{ m})(0.650 \text{ m})}{1.72 \times 10^{-5} \text{ m}}$

$= 1.70 \times 10^{-2}$ m

2. A red laser falls on two slits that are 1.95 x 10⁵ m apart. A first-order line appears 4.42 x 10⁻² m from the central bright line. If the screen is 1.25 m from the slits, what is the wavelength of the light?

$\lambda = \dfrac{xd}{L}$

$= \dfrac{(4.42 \times 10^{-2} \text{ m})(1.95 \times 10^{-5} \text{ m})}{1.25 \text{ m}}$

$= 6.90 \times 10^{-7}$ m

3. Monochromatic light of a sodium vapor lamp has a wavelength of 570 nm. If two slits are separated by 1.90 x 10⁻⁵ m and the slits are 0.800 m from the screen, what is the distance from the central line to the first-order yellow line?

$x = \dfrac{\lambda L}{d}$

$= \dfrac{(5.70 \times 10^{-7} \text{ m})(0.800 \text{ m})}{1.90 \times 10^{-5} \text{ m}}$

$= 0.0240$ m

4. Suppose the double slit in Problem 3 were replaced by a single slit 0.0900 mm wide. What is the distance from the center of the central band to the first dark band?

$x = \dfrac{\lambda L}{w}$

$= \dfrac{(5.70 \times 10^{-7} \text{ m})(0.800 \text{ m})}{9.0 \times 10^{-5} \text{ m}}$

$= 5.07 \times 10^{-3}$ m

5. A diffraction grating has 6.00 x 10³ lines per centimeter. The screen is 0.40 m from the grating. If a red line appears on the screen 12.9 cm from the central line, what is the wavelength of the red light?

$\lambda = \dfrac{xd}{L}$

$= \dfrac{(1.29 \times 10^{-1} \text{ m})(1.76 \times 10^{-6} \text{ m})}{0.40 \text{ m}}$

$= 539$ nm

D. Extending Concepts

1. The range of wavelengths for visible light is from about 400 nm to 700 nm. What is the angular breadth of the first-order visible spectrum produced by a grating that has 1.00 x 10⁴ lines per cm?

$d = 1/(1.00 \times 10^4 \text{ lines cm}^{-1})$

$= 1.00 \times 10^{-6}$ m

$\sin \theta = \dfrac{\lambda}{d}$

$= \dfrac{4.00 \times 10^{-7} \text{ m}}{1.00 \times 10^{-6} \text{ m}}$

$= 0.400$

$\theta = 23.6°$

$\sin \theta_r = \dfrac{\lambda}{d}$

$= \dfrac{7.00 \times 10^{-7} \text{ m}}{1.00 \times 10^{-6} \text{ m}}$

$= 0.700$

$\theta = 44.4°$

Thus, the first-order visible spectrum includes an angle of 44.4° – 23.6° = 20.8°.

2. A diffraction grating forms a number of spectra on either side of the normal. Using the equation

$$\sin \theta = (m\lambda)/d$$

spectra can be classified. Those that correspond to $m = 1$ are first order, those that correspond to $m = 2$ are second order and so on. Use this information to show that the violet of the third-order spectrum overlaps the red of the second-order spectrum. The wavelength for violet is about 400 nm; the wavelength for red light is about 700 nm.

The angle for the third-order violet is $\sin \theta = (3)(4.00 \times 10^{-7}$ m$)/d$. For second-order red, it is $\sin \theta = (2)(7.00 \times 10^{-7}$ m$)/d$. Since the first angle is smaller than the second angle, no matter what the distance between the lines on the grating, the third order will always overlap the second order.

3. Using the equation given in Problem 2, what is the longest wavelength that can be observed in the fourth order of a diffraction grating that has 5000 lines per cm?

$\lambda = \left(\dfrac{\sin \theta}{m}\right)(d)$

$= \left(\dfrac{\sin 90°}{4}\right)(2.00 \times 10^{-6} \text{ m})$

$= 500$ nm

CHAPTER
20 Evaluation

STATIC ELECTRICITY

A. Testing Concepts
In the space to the left, write the letter of the answer to each question.

1. __a__ Because charged objects can attract other charged objects upward, away from Earth, the upward acceleration due to the electrical charge must be _____ the acceleration downward due to gravity.
   a. greater than   b. less than   c. equal to

2. __b__ Rubbing two objects such as plastic and wool together creates a static charge because
   a. atoms are transferred from one object to another
   b. electrons are transferred from atoms in one object to atoms in the other object
   c. the electrons in one object are attracted to the nuclei in the other object
   d. electrons become more widely distributed in each object.

3. __a__ Bits of paper stick to a plastic comb that has been rubbed because of
   a. electrical charge   b. nuclear forces   c. gravity   d. kinetic energy.

4. __c__ When electrons are transferred from one object to another, positive and negative charges are
   a. created   b. reversed   c. separated   d. canceled.

5. __d__ An important difference between insulators and conductors is that in conductors
   a. electrons can be removed from atoms easily
   b. electrons are free to move around
   c. electrons carry electric charges   d. all of the above are true.

6. __d__ When an electroscope is charged, its leaves spread apart because
   a. like charges repel   b. charges exert force on other charges over a distance
   c. positive and negative charges spread over the metal surfaces
   d. of both a and b.

7. __a__ Touching an electroscope with a negatively-charged rod is an example of
   a. charging by conduction   b. charging by induction
   c. discharging electrostatic force   d. distributing unlike charges.

8. __b__ In charging by induction
   a. a charged object can be used to change the charge of another charged object
   b. a charged object can be used to charge a neutral object without touching it
   c. a neutral object can be used to separate like charges
   d. no charges are separated.

9. __c__ The force that charge q exerts on charge q' is opposite and _____ the force that charge q' exerts on q.
   a. greater than   b. less than   c. equal to

10. __a__ Electric force is a vector quantity because it has magnitude and
   a. direction   b. duration   c. frequency   d. strength.

11. __d__ Which of the following statements is *not* true of a charged object?
   a. It may attract another charged object.   b. It may repel another charged object.
   c. It always attracts a neutral object.   d. It always repels a neutral object.

CHAPTER
20 Evaluation

B. Applying Concepts
Answer the following questions in two or three complete sentences.

1. Which of the following would you use to prevent the spread of an electrical charge: copper, plastic, or graphite? Explain your answer.

   An insulator must be used to prevent the spread of electrical charge. Plastic is a good insulator; electrons (electric charges) do not move freely through plastic. Copper and graphite are good conductors.

2. How is the separation of charges involved in electrical interactions?

   An electrical interaction depends on the forces between either like or different charges. The separation of charges brings either like charges together or unlike charges together. The result is repulsive force between like charges or attractive force between unlike charges.

3. Why do socks and other pieces of clothing stick together after being tumbled in a dryer?

   As clothing is tumbled in the hot, dry air of a dryer, electrons are pulled off the atoms in some articles of clothing and added to the atoms in others. Clothing pieces with a net negative charge are then attracted to pieces with a net positive charge.

4. Distinguish between charging by conduction and charging by induction.

   In charging by conduction, electrons are transferred from one object to another simply by touching. In charging by induction, charges are redistributed within an object without direct contact between two objects.

5. What kind of charging occurs during a thunderstorm? Explain.

   During a thunderstorm, charging by induction occurs. The bottoms of clouds are negatively charged. They produce a positive charge on Earth's surface beneath them.

6. Two positive charges are located 2 cm apart. Charge q is 2×10^{-9} C and charge q' is 3×10^{-9} C. Is the force between these charges attractive or repulsive? Explain your answer.

   There is a repulsive force between the charges because they are both positive.

C. Understanding Concepts

1. A positive charge of 3.6 x 10⁻⁵ C and a negative charge of -2.4×10^{-5} C are 0.034 m apart. What is the force between the two particles?

$$F = \frac{Kqq'}{d^2}$$
$$= \frac{(9.0 \times 10^9 \text{ N·m}^2/\text{C}^2)(3.6 \times 10^{-5} \text{ C})(-2.4 \times 10^{-5} \text{ C})}{0.034 \text{ m}^2}$$
$$= -6.7 \times 10^3 \text{ N}$$

2. The force between two objects is 64 N. One has a positive charge of 1.4×10^{-6} C while the other has a negative charge of 1.8×10^{-6} C. How far apart are the two objects?

$$d = \sqrt{\frac{Kqq'}{F}}$$
$$= \sqrt{\frac{(9.0 \times 10^9 \text{ N·m}^2/\text{C}^2)(1.4 \times 10^{-6} \text{ C})(1.8 \times 10^{-6} \text{ C})}{64 \text{ N}}}$$
$$= 1.9 \times 10^{-2} \text{ m}$$

3. Two negative charges of -4.2×10^{-8} C are separated by 0.46 m. What is the magnitude of the force acting on each object?

$$F = \frac{Kqq'}{d^2}$$
$$= \frac{(9.0 \times 10^9 \text{ N·m}^2/\text{C}^2)(-4.2 \times 10^{-8} \text{ C})(-4.2 \times 10^{-8} \text{ C})}{0.46 \text{ m}^2}$$
$$= 7.5 \times 10^{-5} \text{ N}$$

4. Two objects exert a force on each other of 4.2 N. The distance between the objects is 0.36 m. The charge on one object is 2.8×10^{-9} C. What is the charge on the second object?

$$q' = \frac{Fd^2}{Kq} = \frac{(4.2 \text{ N})(0.36 \text{ m})^2}{(9.0 \times 10^9 \text{ N·m}^2/\text{C}^2)(2.8 \times 10^{-9} \text{ C})}$$
$$= 0.022 \text{ C}$$

5. Assuming the force exerted between two spheres is 64 N, what will be the magnitude of the force if the distance is doubled? Tripled?

$$\frac{64 \text{ N}}{4} = 16 \text{ N}$$
$$\frac{64 \text{ N}}{9} = 7.1 \text{ N}$$

D. Extending Concepts

1. Two objects, one having twice the charge of the other, are separated by 0.78 m and exert a force of 3.8×10^3 N. What is the charge on each object?

$$F = \frac{Kq(2q)}{d^2}$$
$$q = \sqrt{\frac{Fd^2}{2K}}$$
$$= \sqrt{\frac{(3.8 \times 10^3 \text{ N})(0.78 \text{ m})^2}{(2)(9.0 \times 10^9 \text{ N·m}^2/\text{C}^2)}}$$
$$= 3.6 \times 10^{-4} \text{ C}$$

2. The drawing shown indicates the charges on three objects, and the distances between charges, **A** and **B** and between charges **B** and **C**. Charges **A** and **C** are 90° apart with respect to charge **B**. On the drawing, show the direction of the forces acting on charge **B**. Calculate the total force acting on charge **B**.

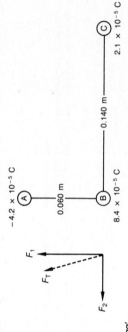

$$F_1 = \frac{qq'}{d^2}$$
$$= \frac{(9.0 \times 10^9 \text{ N·m}^2/\text{C}^2)(8.4 \times 10^{-5} \text{ C})(-4.2 \times 10^{-5} \text{ C})}{(6.0 \times 10^{-2} \text{ m})^2}$$
$$= -8.8 \times 10^3 \text{ N at } 0°$$
$$F_2 = \frac{(9.0 \times 10^9 \text{ N·m}^2/\text{C}^2)(8.4 \times 10^{-5} \text{ C})(2.1 \times 10^{-5} \text{ C})}{(1.4 \times 10^{-1} \text{ m})^2}$$
$$= 8.1 \times 10^2 \text{ N at } 270°$$
$$F_T^2 = F_1^2 + F_2^2$$
$$F_T = \sqrt{(-8.8 \times 10^3 \text{ N})^2 + (8.1 \times 10^2 \text{ N})^2}$$
$$= 8.8 \times 10^3 \text{ N}$$

3. What is the vector angle of the force acting on charge **B**? Add this vector to the drawing, showing its approximate position.

$$\tan \theta = \frac{\text{opposite}}{\text{adjacent}}$$
$$= \frac{8.8 \times 10^3 \text{ N}}{8.1 \times 10^2 \text{ N}}$$
$$= 10.9$$
$$\theta = 85°$$
$$\text{Vector angle} = 85° + 270° = 355°$$

CHAPTER
21 Evaluation

ELECTRIC FIELDS

A. Testing Concepts
In the space to the left, write the letter of the answer to each question.

1. __b__ An electric field is equal to
   a. force per unit mass   b. force per unit charge
   c. force per unit time   d. force times direction.

2. __a__ The force on a test charge in an electric field is
   a. directly proportional to the magnitude of the field
   b. inversely proportional to the magnitude of the field
   c. inversely proportional to the square of the magnitude of the field
   d. unrelated to the magnitude of the field.

3. __d__ The strength of the force on a charge in an electric field depends on
   a. the direction of the field   b. the magnitude of the field
   c. the size of the charge   d. both b and c.

4. __c__ As an electric field becomes stronger the field lines should be drawn
   a. thicker   b. thinner   c. closer together   d. farther apart.

5. __d__ The difference between an electric field and field lines is that
   a. electric fields do not really exist
   b. field lines are a method for measuring the force on a charge
   c. field lines are produced by more than one charge
   d. field lines are only a model of an electric field.

6. __d__ The work done moving a test charge from one point to another is
   a. potential energy   b. kinetic energy
   c. electric potential   d. electric potential difference.

7. __a__ In a uniform electric field, the potential difference between two points is found using the equation
   a. $V = Ed$ b. $E = Vd$ c. $V = E/d$ d. $E = V/d$

8. __d__ Robert A. Millikan determined that
   a. each electron always carries the same charge   b. charges are quantized
   c. changes in charges are caused by one or more electrons being added or removed
   d. all of the above are true.

9. __c__ Touching an object to Earth to eliminate excess charge is
   a. conduction   b. induction   c. grounding   d. friction.

10. __a__ The charges on a hollow conductor are found
   a. on the outer surface   b. on the inner surface
   c. at the ends   d. on both the outer and inner surfaces.

11. __d__ A capacitor is
   a. a device that stores a charge
   b. made up of two conductors separated by an insulator
   c. a device that measures electric potential differences   d. both a and b.

CHAPTER
21 Evaluation

B. Applying Concepts
Answer the following questions in two or three complete sentences.

1. Compare an electric field with a gravitational field.

   Both an electric field and a gravitational field act between bodies that are not in contact with each other. In a gravitational field, one mass exerts a force on another mass. In an electric field, one charge exerts a force on another charge. An electric field is the force per unit charge. A gravitational field is the force per unit mass.

2. What is the direction of an electric field between a negative and a positive charge?

   The field is away from the positive charge and toward the negative charge.

3. Explain why electric potential energy is larger when two like charges are closer together than when two unlike charges are closer together.

   Since like charges repel each other, more work is done bringing them together than bringing together unlike charges.

4. If a high-voltage wire falls on a car, will the people inside be safe from electrocution? Explain your answer.

   Yes. The car is a closed metal conductor that is hollow. Charges move to the external surface, shielding the interior from the electric field.

5. What is the net charge on a capacitor? Explain your answer.

   The net charge is zero since the two conductors have equal and opposite charge.

21 Evaluation

C. Understanding Concepts

1. A positive charge of 2.4×10^{-6} C is acted on by a force of 0.43 N at a certain distance. What is the electric field intensity at that distance?

$E = \dfrac{F}{q}$

$= \dfrac{4.3 \times 10^{-1} \text{ N}}{2.4 \times 10^{-6} \text{ C}}$

$= 1.8 \times 10^{5}$ N/C

2. What charge exists on a test charge that is acted on by a force of 3.60×10^{-6} N at a point where the electric field intensity is 1.60×10^{-5} N/C?

$q = \dfrac{F}{E}$

$= \dfrac{3.60 \times 10^{-6} \text{ N}}{1.60 \times 10^{-5} \text{ N/C}}$

$= 2.25 \times 10^{-1}$ C

3. The electric field intensity between two charged plates is 2.80×10^{4} N/C. The plates are 0.0640 m apart. What is the potential difference between the plates in volts?

$V = Ed$

$= (2.80 \times 10^{4} \text{ N/C})(6.40 \times 10^{-2} \text{ m})$

$= 1.79 \times 10^{3}$ V

4. A voltmeter connected between two plates registers 38.2 V. The plates are separated by a distance of 0.046 m. What is the field intensity between the plates?

$E = \dfrac{V}{d}$

$= \dfrac{38.2 \text{ V}}{0.046 \text{ m}}$

$= 830$ V/m

$= 830$ N/C

5. How much work is done to transfer 0.47 C of charge through a potential difference of 12 V?

$W = qV$

$= (0.47 \text{ C})(12 \text{ V})$

$= 5.6$ J

6. A 9.0-V battery does 1.0×10^{3} J of work transferring charge. How much charge is transferred?

$q = \dfrac{W}{V}$

$= \dfrac{1.0 \times 10^{3} \text{ J}}{9.0 \text{ V}}$

$= 1.1 \times 10^{2}$ C

---

21 Evaluation

D. Extending Concepts

1. A force of 7.60×10^{3} N acts on a charge of 1.60×10^{-2} C over a distance of 0.0440 m. What is the potential difference of this system?

$V = Ed \qquad E = \dfrac{F}{q}$

$V = \dfrac{Fd}{q}$

$= \dfrac{(7.60 \times 10^{3} \text{ N})(0.0440 \text{ m})}{1.60 \times 10^{-2} \text{ C}}$

$= 2.09 \times 10^{4}$ V

2. How much work is done by a system in which the force is 6.8×10^{4} N, the potential difference is 4.2 V, and the electric field intensity is 1.2×10^{-3} N/C?

$W = qV \qquad q = \dfrac{F}{E}$

$W = \dfrac{FV}{E}$

$= \dfrac{(6.8 \times 10^{4} \text{ N})(4.2 \text{ V})}{1.2 \times 10^{-3} \text{ N/C}}$

$= 2.4 \times 10^{8}$ J

3. How much energy is stored in a capacitor of 12.2 μF which has been charged to 4.26×10^{2} V?

$\Delta PE = W \qquad W = qV \qquad q = CV$

$W = CV^{2}$

$= (1.22 \times 10^{-5} \text{ F})(4.26 \times 10^{2} \text{ V})^{2}$

$= 2.21$ J

4. How much power is required to charge a capacitor of 9.4 μF to 5.4×10^{2} V in 48 s?

$P = \dfrac{W}{t} \qquad W = CV^{2}$

$P = \dfrac{CV^{2}}{t}$

$= \dfrac{(9.4 \times 10^{-6} \text{ F})(5.4 \times 10^{2} \text{ V})^{2}}{48 \text{ s}}$

$= 5.7 \times 10^{-2}$ W

CHAPTER
22 Evaluation

CURRENT ELECTRICITY

A. Testing Concepts

In the space to the left, write the letter of the answer to each question.

1. __d__ In an electric circuit, charged particles
   a. flow around in a closed loop.   b. flow from higher potential to lower potential
   c. get energy from an external source   d. do all of the above.

2. __d__ The energy carried by an electric current depends on which of the following?
   a. the charge transferred   b. the potential difference
   c. the total number of charges in the circuit   d. both a and b

3. __a__ The rate at which energy is transferred is
   a. power   b. conventional current   c. resistance   d. electric current.

4. __b__ The resistance of a conductor can be determined if ____ are known.
   a. energy and current   b. potential difference and current
   c. voltage and potential difference   d. current and amperes

5. __b__ The scientist Georg Simon Ohm found that for most conductors
   a. current does not depend on resistance   b. resistance does not depend on voltage
   c. voltage does not depend on current   d. resistance and voltage depend on current.

6. __a__ The current flowing in an electric circuit can be increased by
   a. increasing voltage or decreasing resistance
   b. decreasing voltage or increasing resistance
   c. increasing voltage and increasing resistance
   d. decreasing voltage and decreasing resistance.

7. __d__ A device that measures the amount of current in a circuit is a(n)
   a. potentiometer   b. resistor   c. voltmeter   d. ammeter.

8. __b__ Space heaters convert most of the electrical energy in a circuit into
   a. light energy   b. thermal energy   c. mechanical energy   d. sound energy.

9. __d__ Energy from a battery is stored in the electric field of a capacitor when
   a. there is no potential difference across the resistor
   b. there is no more current flowing
   c. the voltage across the capacitor reaches the battery voltage
   d. all of the above are true.

10. __a__ Electricity is carried long distances at high voltages because
    a. current can be kept low and less power is lost as thermal energy
    b. resistance can be kept low and less power is lost as thermal energy
    c. current cannot be changed to reduce thermal energy
    d. resistance cannot be changed to reduce thermal energy.

11. __b__ Utility companies measure energy use in ____ because other units are two small.
    a. joules   b. kilowatt hours   c. watt-seconds   d. watts

---

CHAPTER
22 Evaluation

B. Applying Concepts

Answer the following questions in two or three complete sentences.

1. What is the difference between an ampere and a volt?

An ampere is the rate of flow of electric charge, or charge per unit of time. A volt is a measure of the voltage, or potential difference, between charges.

2. Identify the parts of this schematic. Will current flow through the circuit? Explain your answer.

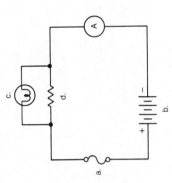

a. fuse   b. battery   c. bulb   d. resistor. Yes, current will flow because the circuit forms a closed loop.

3. Could a voltmeter be substituted for the ammeter shown in the schematic? Explain your answer.

No, the ammeter cannot be replaced by a voltmeter. The ammeter is connected in series. The voltmeter must be connected in parallel, not in series.

4. What would happen to current if both voltage and resistance were doubled?

The current would remain the same.

5. Which has a greater effect on the amount of thermal energy produced in a heater, the current or the resistance of the heater? Explain your answer.

The current has a greater effect because the amount of power dissipated (and heat produced) in a resistor is directly proportional to resistance, but it is also directly proportional to the square of the current.

C. Understanding Concepts

1. A portable compact disc player receives its energy from a 9.0-V cell. The current used to operate the player is 135 A.

a. How many joules of energy does the cell deliver to the CD player each second?

$P = VI$
$= (9.0\text{ V})(135\text{ A})$
$= 1.2 \times 10^3\text{ J/s}$

b. How much power in watts does the CD player use?

$P = 1.2 \times 10^3\text{ W}$

c. How much energy does the CD player use to play a selection 3.0 min long?

$E = Pt$
$= (1.2 \times 10^3\text{ J/s})(180\text{ s})$
$= 2.2 \times 10^5\text{ J}$

2. What voltage is applied to a 6.80-Ω resistor if the current is 3.20 A?

$V = IR$
$= (3.20\text{ A})(6.80\text{ Ω})$
$= 21.8\text{ V}$

3. An electric buzzer is connected across a 4.2-V difference in potential. The current through the buzzer is 1.8 A.

a. What is the power rating of the buzzer?

$P = VI$
$= (4.2\text{ V})(1.8\text{ A})$
$= 7.6\text{ W}$

b. How much electric energy does the buzzer convert in 1.5 min?

$E = PE$
$= (7.6\text{ W})(9.0 \times 10^1\text{ s})$
$= 6.8 \times 10^1\text{ J}$

4. An electric blanket with a resistance of 8.6 Ω is connected to a 120-V source.

a. What is the current in the circuit?

$I = \dfrac{V}{R}$
$= \dfrac{120\text{ V}}{8.6\text{ Ω}}$
$= 14\text{ A}$

b. How much heat is produced if the blanket is turned on for 15 min?

$Q = I^2Rt$
$= (14\text{ A})^2(8.6\text{ Ω})(9.0 \times 10^2\text{ s})$
$= 1.5 \times 10^6\text{ J}$

D. Extending Concepts

1. An electric motor operates an elevator the mass of which is 2.0×10^3 kg. The elevator rises 120 m in 32 s. The motor has a resistance while operating of 34.0 Ω and is connected across a 2.4×10^3-V source. What percent of electric energy is converted to kinetic energy?

$E_E = mgd$
$= (2.0 \times 10^3\text{ kg})(9.8\text{ m/s}^2)(120\text{ m})$
$= 2.4 \times 10^6\text{ J}$

$I = \dfrac{V}{R}$
$= \dfrac{2.4 \times 10^3\text{ V}}{34.0\text{ Ω}}$
$= 7.1 \times 10^1\text{ A}$

$E_m = IVt$
$= (7.1 \times 10^1\text{ A})(2.4 \times 10^3\text{ V})(32\text{ s})$
$= 5.5 \times 10^6\text{ J}$

$\% = \dfrac{E_E}{E_m} \times 100\%$
$= \dfrac{2.4 \times 10^6\text{ J}}{5.5 \times 10^6\text{ J}} \times 100\%$
$= 44\%$

2. A three-pack of 1.5-V hearing aid batteries costs $4.26. Each battery lasts for 15 days. Each battery puts out 8.0 mA of current. What is the cost per kWh to operate the hearing aid with one battery?

$P = IV$
$= (0.0080\text{ A})(1.5\text{ V})$
$= 0.012\text{ W} = 1.2 \times 10^{-5}\text{ kW}$
$E = Pt$
$= (1.2 \times 10^{-5}\text{ kW})(360\text{ h})$
$= 4.3 \times 10^{-3}\text{ kWh}$

$\dfrac{\text{cost}}{\text{kWh}} = \dfrac{\$1.42}{4.3 \times 10^{-3}\text{ kWh}}$
$= \$330$

3. While waiting for the school bus you keep your hands warm in a pair of electric gloves. The heating element in each glove has a resistance of 8.0 Ω. Each glove operates from a 12-V source. The thermal energy produced by each glove is 640 J. You wait for the bus for 3.0 min. When the bus arrives, are your hands warm or cold?

$t = \dfrac{E}{I^2R}$
$= \dfrac{640\text{ J}}{(1.5\text{ A})^2(8.0\text{ Ω})}$
$= 36\text{ s}$
Since the gloves produce heat for only 36 s, your hands will be cold after 3 min (180 s).

4. A model electric train makes one complete pass around a circular track every 15 s. The train's motor has a resistance of 6.0 Ω and is connected to a 70.0-V source. How much energy will the train use in 12 complete passes around the track?

$E = I^2Rt \qquad I = \dfrac{V}{R}$

$E = \dfrac{V^2}{R}Rt$

$E = \dfrac{V^2t}{R}$
$= \dfrac{(70.0\text{ V})^2(180\text{ s})}{6.0\text{ Ω}}$
$= 1.5 \times 10^5\text{ J}$

CHAPTER

23 Evaluation

SERIES AND PARALLEL CIRCUITS

A. Testing Concepts

In the space to the left, write the letter of the answer to each question.

1. **a** _____ If there are four electrical devices connected in a series circuit, then the number of current paths is equal to
   a. one   b. two   c. three   d. four.

2. **d** _____ A series circuit contains a generator, an ammeter, and a lamp. The current in the lamp is
   a. equal to the current in the ammeter   b. less than the current in the ammeter
   c. equal to the current in the generator   d. a and c.

3. **b** _____ A series circuit contains four resistors. The equivalent resistance of the circuit is equal to
   a. $4R$ b. $R_1 + R_2 + R_3 + R_4$ c. $\dfrac{R}{4}$ d. $\dfrac{R_1 + R_2 + R_3 + R_4}{4}$

4. **a** _____ A 5-Ω resistor, a 20-Ω resistor, and a 25-Ω resistor are connected in series across a 90-V battery. The net change in potential going around this circuit is
   a. zero   b. 4 V   c. 50 V   d. 90 V.

5. **c** _____ A series circuit has a 120-V generator but requires a 60-V potential source. To achieve the desired potential, a _____ can be used.
   a. photoresistor   b. sensor   c. voltage divider   d. semiconductor

6. **c** _____ If three resistors are connected in parallel, there are _____ current paths in the circuit.
   a. one   b. two   c. three   d. four

7. **b** _____ The equivalent resistance of a parallel circuit is always _____ the resistance of any resistor in the circuit.
   a. greater than   b. less than   c. equal to

8. **c** _____ A 10-Ω resistor is connected in series with a 60-V battery. Two 15-Ω resistors are connected in parallel with the same battery. How many current paths are there?
   a. one   b. two   c. three   d. four

9. **d** _____ An ammeter should have very low resistance because current would
   a. increase if the ammeter increased resistance in the circuit
   b. decrease if the ammeter decreased resistance in the circuit
   c. increase if the ammeter decreased resistance in the circuit
   d. decrease if the ammeter increased resistance in the circuit.

10. **c** _____ Connecting a voltmeter across a resistor causes the potential across the resistor to
    a. double   b. decrease to one-half   c. remain about the same.

11. **d** _____ An ammeter is connected in _____ and a voltmeter is connected in _____.
    a. parallel, series   b. parallel, parallel   c. series, series   d. series, parallel.

12. **b** _____ The first step in calculating the equivalent resistance in a combination circuit is to
    a. calculate the current in each resistor
    b. calculate the equivalent resistance of any resistors connected in parallel
    c. calculate the current in the whole circuit
    d. measure the voltage drop in the whole circuit.

CHAPTER

23 Evaluation

B. Applying Concepts

Answer the following questions in two or three complete sentences.

1. A string of holiday lights has 15 bulbs connected in series. If one of the bulbs burns out, what happens to the other bulbs?

   They go out because the flow of current in the series circuit has been interrupted.

2. What happens to resistance when a resistor is added to a parallel circuit that already has two resistors?

   As the number of parallel branches is increased, the overall resistance of the circuit decreases.

3. How is it possible to use more than one electrical appliance at a time in a house?

   The electric wiring uses parallel circuits so the current in one circuit does not depend on the current in any other circuit.

4. A circuit has five identical resistors: **A**, **B**, **C**, **D**, and **E**. Resistors **A**, **D**, and **E** have the same potential difference across them. What kind of circuit is this? Explain your answer.

   It is a combination series-parallel circuit. Resistors B and C are in series, and A, D, and E, which have the same potential difference across them, are in parallel.

5. What would happen in a circuit if a voltmeter were substituted for an ammeter?

   An ammeter is connected in series. Its low resistance does not affect the current. If a voltmeter were substituted for the ammeter the high resistance of the voltmeter would decrease the current.

C. Understanding Concepts

1. Two resistors of 3.0 Ω and 8.0 Ω are connected in series across a 9.0-V battery.

a. What is the equivalent resistance of the circuit?

$R = R_1 + R_2$
$= 3.0\ \Omega + 8.0\ \Omega$
$= 11.0\ \Omega$

b. What is the current through the 3.0-Ω resistor?

$I_1 = \dfrac{V}{R_1 + R_2}$
$= \dfrac{9.0\ V}{11.0\ \Omega}$
$= 0.82\ \Omega$

c. What is the current through the 8.0-Ω resistor?

$I_2 = I_1 = 0.82\ A$

d. What is the voltage drop across each resistor?

$V_1 = IR_1$ $V_2 = IR_2$
$= (0.82\ A)(3.0\ \Omega)$ $= (0.82\ A)(8.0\ \Omega)$
$= 2.5\ V$ $= 6.6\ V$

2. A 15.0-Ω bell and an 8.0-Ω lamp are connected in parallel and placed across a difference in potential of 42 V.

a. What is the equivalent resistance of the circuit?

$\dfrac{1}{R} = \dfrac{1}{R_1} + \dfrac{1}{R_2}$
$= \dfrac{1}{15.0\ \Omega} + \dfrac{1}{8.0\ \Omega}$
$= 5.2\ \Omega$

b. What is the current in the circuit?

$I = \dfrac{V}{R}$
$= \dfrac{42\ V}{5.2\ V}$
$= 8.1\ A$

c. What is the current through each resistor?

$I_1 = \dfrac{V}{R_1}$ $I_2 = \dfrac{V}{R_2}$
$= \dfrac{42\ V}{15.0\ \Omega}$ $= \dfrac{42\ V}{8.0\ \Omega}$
$= 2.8\ A$ $= 5.2\ A$

d. What is the voltage drop through each resistor?

$V_1 = I_1R_1$ $V_2 = I_2R_2$
$= (2.8\ A)(15.0\ \Omega)$ $= (5.2\ A)(8.0\ \Omega)$
$= 42\ V$ $= 42\ V$

D. Extending Concepts

1. Find the reading of each ammeter and each voltmeter in the following illustration.

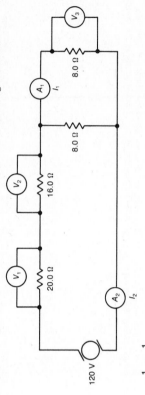

$\dfrac{1}{E} = \dfrac{1}{R_1} + \dfrac{1}{R_2}$
$= \dfrac{1}{8.0\ \Omega} + \dfrac{1}{8.0\ \Omega}$
$R = 4.0\ \Omega$

For the entire circuit, the equivalent resistance is:
$R = R_1 + R_2 + R_3$
$= 4.0\ \Omega + 20.0\ \Omega + 16.0\ \Omega$
$= 40.0\ \Omega$

$I_{TOTAL} = I_2 = \dfrac{V}{R}$
$= \dfrac{120\ V}{40.0\ \Omega}$
$= 3.0\ A$

$V_3 = IR$
$= (3.0\ A)(4.0\ \Omega)$
$= 12\ V$

$V_1 = I_2R$
$= (3.0\ A)(20.0\ \Omega)$
$= 6.0 \times 10^1\ V$

The voltage drop across each 8.0-Ω resistor is:

$I_1 = \dfrac{V}{R}$
$= \dfrac{12\ V}{8.0\ \Omega}$
$= 1.5\ A$

$V_2 = I_2R$
$= (3.0\ A)(1.6.0\ \Omega)$
$= 48\ V$

2. What is the power in watts used by each resistance in the illustration shown above?

For the 20.0-Ω resistor,
$P = I_2V_1$
$= (3.0\ A)(6.0 \times 10^1\ V)$
$= 120\ W$

For the 16-Ω resistor,
$P = I_2V_2$
$= (3.0\ A)(48\ V)$
$= 1.14 \times 10^2\ W$

In each of the 8-Ω resistors the power will be equal:
$P = I_1V_3$
$= (1.5\ A)(12\ V)$
$= 18\ W$

CHAPTER
24 Evaluation

MAGNETIC FIELDS

A. Testing Concepts

In the space to the left, write the letter of the answer to each question.

1. __d__ An object that is magnetic has
   a. a south-seeking pole   b. a north-seeking pole
   c. a magnetic field   d. all of the above.

2. __b__ When iron filings are sprinkled around a bar magnet, the pattern that forms shows that field lines
   a. point straight out in all directions
   b. form closed loops that leave the north pole and enter the south pole
   c. leave the middle of the bar and enter the ends
   d. leave the ends of the bar and enter the middle.

3. __a__ The strength of current-carrying wire is _____ to the magnetic field around a current.
   a. proportional   b. inversely proportional   c. equal   d. parallel

4. __a__ Increasing the number of loops in an electromagnet causes the strength of the magnetic field to
   a. increase   b. decrease   c. remain the same.

5. __b__ In a magnetic material the _____ act like tiny electromagnets.
   a. atoms   b. electrons   c. protons   d. neutrons

6. __c__ The magnetic force on a current-carrying wire is _____ the direction of the current.
   a. opposite to   b. parallel to   c. perpendicular to   d. the same as

7. __d__ The magnitude of the magnetic force on a current-carrying wire depends on
   a. the strength of the magnetic field   b. the current in the wire
   c. the length of wire in the magnetic field   d. all of the above.

8. __c__ A device used to measure very small electric currents is a(n)
   a. ammeter   b. voltmeter   c. galvanometer   d. electric meter.

9. __a__ A galvanometer consists of
   a. a small coil of wire placed in the magnetic field of a permanent magnet
   b. a straight wire connecting two electromagnets
   c. a small coil of wire connecting two electromagnets
   d. a small coil of wire attached to a source of potential difference and an electromagnet.

10. __d__ In an electric motor
   a. several loops of wire rotate through 360°   b. current is reversed every half turn
   c. loops of wire rotate because of the force from a magnetic field   d. all of the above occur.

11. __c__ The speed of an electric motor can be controlled by
   a. changing the direction of current flow   b. limiting the rotation of the wire loops
   c. varying the current flow   d. changing the direction of force on the wire loops.

12. __d__ The force of a magnetic field on a single electron depends on
   a. the velocity of the electron   b. the strength of the field
   c. the angle between the directions of the velocity and the field   d. all of the above.

CHAPTER
24 Evaluation

B. Applying Concepts

Answer the following questions in two or three complete sentences.

1. If all electrons create magnetic fields, why aren't all materials magnets?

   If the electrons within a particular object are not all generating magnetic fields in the same direction, then the domains cancel each other out.

2. How are the forces between charges similar to the forces between magnetic poles?

   Like charges repel and unlike charges attract. Like poles also repel and unlike poles attract.

3. Suppose you have two bar magnets. Only one of the magnets has north and south poles labeled. How would you determine which are the south and north poles on the unlabeled magnet?

   Hold the ends of the magnets near each other. The north pole of the labeled magnet will attract the south pole of the other magnet and repel the north pole. The south pole of the labeled magnet will attract the north pole of the unlabeled magnet and repel the south pole of the unlabeled magnet.

4. An electrical wire carries current in a straight line from east to west. What is the direction of the resulting magnetic field above the wire? What is the direction of the field below the wire?

   According to the right-hand rule, the direction of the field above the wire is south to north. The direction of the field below the wire is north to south.

5. If an electromagnet is used to pick up nails and other metal objects, what happens when the current is turned off?

   Without the current there is no magnetic force, therefore all the objects attracted by the electromagnet will be released.

6. If a permanent magnet is dropped or struck by a hammer, it may lose its magnetism. Explain why.

   Jarring the magnet may knock some domains out of alignment. If this happens their fields will cancel each other out.

CHAPTER
24 Evaluation

C. Understanding Concepts

1. A wire, 0.80 m long, carries a current of 6.0 A. The wire is at right angles to a uniform magnetic field the force of which is 0.62 N. What is the strength of the magnetic field?

$$B = \frac{F}{IL}$$
$$= \frac{0.62 \text{ N}}{(6.0 \text{ A})(0.80 \text{ m})}$$
$$= 0.13 \text{ T}$$

2. A wire, 60.0 cm long, is at right angles to a uniform magnetic field of magnetic induction equal to 0.400 T. The current through the wire is 4.00 A. What is the force that acts on the wire?

$$F = BIL$$
$$= (0.40 \text{ N/A·m})(4.00 \text{ A})(0.600 \text{ m})$$
$$= 0.960 \text{ N}$$

3. A wire, 2.0 m long, carries a current of 12 A. The wire is at right angles to a uniform magnetic field the force of which is 0.50 N. What is the induction of the magnetic field?

$$B = \frac{F}{IL}$$
$$= \frac{0.50 \text{ N}}{(12 \text{ A})(2.0 \text{ m})}$$
$$= 2.1 \times 10^{-2} \text{ T}$$

4. A wire is at right angles to a magnetic field the force of which is 2.4 N. A current of 8.6 A flows through the wire. The induction of the magnetic field is 0.66 T. What is the length of the wire?

$$L = \frac{F}{BI}$$
$$= \frac{2.4}{(0.66 \text{ N/A·m})(8.6 \text{ A})}$$
$$= 0.42 \text{ m}$$

5. A high-speed electron travels at right angles to a magnetic field the induction of which is 0.420 T. The electron is traveling at 3.46×10^7 m/s. What is the force acting on the electron?

$$F = Bqv$$
$$= (0.420 \text{ N/A·m})(1.6 \times 10^{-19} \text{ C})(3.46 \times 10^7 \text{ m/s})$$
$$= 2.33 \times 10^{-12} \text{ N}$$

CHAPTER
24 Evaluation

D. Extending Concepts

1. A particle that has a mass of 2.42×10^{-22} kg and a charge of 3.40×10^{-20} C is traveling through space at 2.50×10^8 m/s when it encounters a magnetic field with an intensity of 2.40 T. The particle is moving perpendicular to the field. If the particle's velocity remains constant, what will be the radius of the curvature of its path?

$$F = Bqv$$
$$= (2.40 \text{ T})(3.4 \times 10^{-20} \text{ C})(2.5 \text{ m/s})$$
$$= 2.04 \times 10^{-19} \text{ N}$$
$$F = \frac{mv^2}{r}$$
$$r = \frac{mv^2}{F}$$
$$= \frac{(2.42 \times 10^{-22} \text{ kg})(2.5 \times 10^8 \text{ m/s})^2}{2.04 \times 10^{-19} \text{ N}}$$
$$= 7.41 \times 10^{13} \text{ m}$$

2. A particle of unknown mass moves through a magnetic field intensity of 0.80 T at 1.4×10^7 m/s. The charge on the particle is 2.8×10^{-16} C. The radius of the curvature of its path is 4.6 m. What is the mass of the particle?

$$r = \frac{mv^2}{F} \qquad F = Bqv$$
$$m = \frac{rBqv}{v^2} = \frac{rBq}{v}$$
$$= \frac{(4.6 \text{ m})(0.80 \text{ T})(2.8 \times 10^{-16} \text{ C})}{1.4 \times 10^7 \text{ m/s}}$$
$$= 7.4 \times 10^{-23} \text{ kg}$$

3. Starting from a speed of 0 m/s, a proton is accelerated through a potential difference of 32 000 V. What is the proton's velocity?

$$E = (32\ 000 \text{ J/C})(1.6 \times 10^{-19} \text{ C})$$
$$= 5.1 \times 10^{-15} \text{ J}$$
$$E = \frac{1}{2}mv^2$$
$$v = \sqrt{\frac{2E}{m}}$$
$$= \sqrt{\frac{(2)(5.1 \times 10^{-15} \text{ J})}{1.67 \times 10^{-27} \text{ kg}}}$$
$$= 2.5 \times 10^6 \text{ m/s}$$

4. The energy of a proton moving through a magnetic field of intensity 0.20 T is 4.4×10^{-15} J. What is the radius of the proton's path if it moves in a direction that is always perpendicular to the field?

$$E = \frac{1}{2}mv^2$$
$$v = \sqrt{\frac{2E}{m}}$$
$$= \sqrt{\frac{(2)(4.4 \times 10^{-15} \text{ J})}{1.67 \times 10^{-27} \text{ kg}}}$$
$$= 2.3 \times 10^6 \text{ m/s}$$

$$F = Bqv$$
$$= (0.20 \text{ T})(1.6 \times 10^{-19} \text{ C})(2.3 \times 10^6 \text{ m/s})$$
$$= 7.4 \times 10^{-14} \text{ N}$$
$$r = \frac{mv^2}{F}$$
$$= \frac{(1.67 \times 10^{-27} \text{ kg})(2.3 \times 10^6 \text{ m/s})^2}{7.4 \times 10^{-14} \text{ N}}$$
$$= 1.2 \times 10^{-1} \text{ m}$$

CHAPTER
25 Evaluation

ELECTROMAGNETIC INDUCTION

A. Testing Concepts

In the space to the left, write the letter of the answer to each question.

1. __c__ An electric current is generated in a wire when the wire is
   a. held stationary in a magnetic field   b. moved parallel to a magnetic field
   c. moved so that it cuts across magnetic field lines
   d. placed in a magnetic field of large intensity.

2. __b__ Current can be made to flow in a stationary conductor by
   a. holding a magnet over the wire   b. moving a magnetic field across the wire
   c. moving a magnetic field parallel to the wire   d. touching the wire with a magnet.

3. __d__ The electromotive force depends on
   a. magnetic field strength   b. the length of the wire in the magnetic field
   c. the velocity of the wire in the magnetic field   d. all of the above.

4. __d__ An electric generator converts
   a. electrical energy to heat energy   b. electrical energy to mechanical energy
   c. mechanical energy to heat energy   d. mechanical energy to electrical energy.

5. __b__ An electric motor is almost identical in construction to an electric generator, but the motor converts
   a. electrical energy to heat energy   b. electrical energy to mechanical energy
   c. mechanical energy to heat energy   d. mechanical energy to electrical energy.

6. __c__ The power produced by a generator
   a. is the product of the resistance and the voltage   b. can be positive or negative
   c. has a lower average value for alternating currents than for direct currents
   d. is all of the above.

7. __a__ According to Lenz's Law, the direction of induced current is such that the magnetic field resulting from the induced current _____ the change in flux that caused the current.
   a. opposes   b. strengthens   c. is perpendicular to   d. has no effect on

8. __c__ If a generator produces only a small current, then the opposing force on the armature will be _____ and the armature will be _____ to turn.
   a. large, easy   b. large, hard   c. small, easy   d. small, hard

9. __a__ As a motor begins to turn, a back-*EMF* is induced that _____ the current flow.
   a. opposes   b. is in the same direction as   c. is perpendicular to   d. has no effect on

10. __d__ The size of the *EMF* generated by self-inductance is
    a. proportional to the rate at which current changes
    b. proportional to the rate at which flux lines cut through the wires
    c. zero when current reaches a steady value and magnetic flux is constant
    d. all of the above.

11. __b__ In a step-up transformer, the primary voltage is _____ the secondary voltage.
    a. greater than   b. less than   c. equal to

CHAPTER
25 Evaluation

B. Applying Concepts

Answer the following questions in two or three complete sentences.

1. A loop of wire is connected to a galvanometer. If a bar magnet is dropped through the loop, what happens to the galvanometer?

   The galvanometer shows that a current is produced in the loop of wire as the magnetic field of the magnet crosses the conducting wire.

2. A bar magnet and a loop of wire are moving parallel to each other at the same velocity. What is the voltage induced in the loop? Explain.

   The voltage is zero. No current is induced because the conductor is not moving through the magnetic field.

3. What happens to induced *EMF* when magnetic field strength is doubled?

   Since *EMF* is directly proportional to magnetic field strength, it doubles.

4. Compare the operation of an electric motor with that of an electric generator.

   The two devices are almost identical in construction. In an electric motor, a voltage is placed across an armature coil in a magnetic field. The voltage causes current to flow in the coil, and the armature turns. In a generator, mechanical energy turns an armature in a magnetic field.

5. Why do the lights in a room dim momentarily when a large appliance is turned on?

   The heavy current required when a motor is started causes a voltage drop across the wires that carry current to the motor. In turn, the voltage across the motor drops, along with the voltage of lights connected in parallel near the motor.

6. What happens to the primary voltage when the number of turns on a secondary transformer coil is doubled?

   Since primary voltage is inversely proportional to the number of turns on the secondary coil, doubling the turns cuts the primary voltage in half.

C. Understanding Concepts

1. A wire 42.0 m long moves directly upward through a 6.20×10^{-4} T-magnetic field at a speed of 18.0 m/s. What EMF is induced in the wire?

$EMF = Blv$
$= (6.20 \times 10^{-4}\ \text{T})(42.0\ \text{m})(18.0\ \text{m/s})$
$= 0.469\ \text{V}$

2. An AC generator develops a maximum EMF of 620 V. What effective EMF does the generator deliver to an external circuit?

$V_{eff} = 0.707(V_{max})$
$= 0.707(620\ \text{V})$
$= 440\ \text{V}$

3. A step-up transformer has 125 turns on its primary coil. Its secondary coil consists of 1440 turns. The primary coil receives an AC current at 120 V.

a. What voltage is across the secondary coil?

$\dfrac{V_p}{V_s} = \dfrac{N_p}{N_s}$ $\qquad V_s = \dfrac{V_p N_s}{N_p}$
$= \dfrac{(120\ \text{V})(1440)}{125}$
$= 1.4 \times 10^3\ \text{V}$

b. The current in the secondary coil is 3.6 A. What current flows in the primary circuit?

$V_p I_p = V_s I_s$ $\qquad I_p = \dfrac{V_s I_s}{V_p}$
$= \dfrac{(1.4 \times 10^3\ \text{V})(3.6\ \text{A})}{120\ \text{V}}$
$= 42\ \text{A}$

c. What is the power input and output of the transformer?

$V_p I_p = (120\ \text{V})(42\ \text{A})$
$= 5.0 \times 10^3\ \text{W}$
$V_s I_s = (1.4 \times 10^3\ \text{V})(3.6\ \text{A})$
$= 5.0 \times 10^3\ \text{W}$

4. The primary coil of a transformer has 640 turns and is connected to a 240-V source. How many turns would be needed in the secondary coil to supply 8.0×10^2 V?

$\dfrac{V_p}{V_s} = \dfrac{N_p}{N_s}$ $\qquad N_s = \dfrac{N_p V_s}{V_p}$
$= \dfrac{(640)(8.0 \times 10^2\ \text{V})}{240\ \text{V}}$
$= 2.1 \times 10^3$

D. Extending Concepts

1. A wire 0.60 m long moves through a magnetic field of 0.48 T. The current flowing through the wire is 2.4×10^{-3} A. The wire is connected across a circuit of 8.0 Ω resistance. If the wire is moving perpendicular through the magnetic field, what is the velocity of the wire?

$V = IR$ $\qquad EMF = Blv$ $\qquad v = \dfrac{IR}{Bl}$
$= \dfrac{(2.4 \times 10^{-3}\ \text{A})(8.0\ \Omega)}{(0.48\ \text{T})(0.60\ \text{m})}$
$= 6.7 \times 10^{-2}\ \text{m/s}$

2. A space vehicle is sent to Jupiter to explore the planet's properties from orbit. The vehicle travels 1.0×10^3 km each minute. When in orbit, the probe deploys a horizontal antenna that is 120 m in length. Data received on Earth indicate that the probe is overflying a location of Jupiter where the magnetic field is 1.8×10^{-1} T. What voltage is induced between the antenna's tips?

$EMF = Blv$ $\qquad v = d/t$ $\qquad EMF = \dfrac{Bld}{t}$
$= \dfrac{(1.8 \times 10^{-1}\ \text{T})(120\ \text{m})(1.0 \times 10^6\ \text{m})}{60\ \text{s}}$
$= 3.6 \times 10^5\ \text{V}$

3. An engineer can vary the rate at which water falls directly down through a generator at a hydroelectric power plant. The generator and its turbine can supply 268 MW of electric power when the rate at which the water supplies power to the turbine is 335 MW.

a. What is the efficiency of the turbine/generator system?

$Efficiency = \dfrac{Power\ out}{Power\ in} \times 100\%$
$= \dfrac{268\ \text{MW}}{335\ \text{MW}} \times 100\%$
$= 80.0\%$

b. What is the change in the potential energy of the falling water per second?

$335\ \text{MW} = 3.35 \times 10^8\ \text{J/s}$

c. If the water falls 16 m to the turbine, what mass of water must be directed through the turbine per second to supply the power indicated above?

$PE = mgh$ $\qquad m = \dfrac{PE}{gh}$
$= \dfrac{(3.35 \times 10^8\ \text{J})}{(9.8\ \text{m/s}^2)(16\ \text{m})}$
$= 2.1 \times 10^6\ \text{kg}$

4. The secondary coil of a transformer has 8.00×10^2 turns while the primary coil has 2.40×10^2 turns. The input voltage is 24.0 V and the input current is 4.00 A. What is the output current?

$\dfrac{V_p}{V_s} = \dfrac{N_p}{N_s}$ $\qquad V_s = \dfrac{V_p N_s}{N_p}$ $\qquad V_p I_p = V_s I_s$ $\qquad I_s = \dfrac{V_p I_p}{V_s}$
$= \dfrac{(2.40\ \text{V})(8.00 \times 10^2)}{2.40 \times 10^2}$ $\qquad = \dfrac{(24.0\ \text{V})(4.00\ \text{A})}{80.0\ \text{V}}$
$= 80.0\ \text{V}$ $\qquad = 1.20\ \text{A}$

CHAPTER

26 Evaluation

ELECTRIC AND MAGNETIC FIELDS

A. Testing Concepts

In the space to the left, write the letter of the answer to each question.

1. **a** ___ In a cathode-ray tube, an electric field pulls electrons out of the _____ toward the _____
   a. negatively-charged cathode, positively-charged anode
   b. positively-charged anode, negatively-charged cathode
   c. negatively-charged anode, positively-charged cathode
   d. positively-charged cathode, negatively-charged anode.

2. **d** ___ Electrons in a cathode-ray tube follow a straight path when the forces due to the electric and magnetic fields are
   a. equal in magnitude   b. in opposite directions
   c. in the same direction   d. both a and b.

3. **d** ___ The masses of positive ions can be measured precisely using a
   a. Thomson tube   b. Bainbridge tube
   c. cathode-ray tube   d. mass spectrometer.

4. **d** ___ James Clerk Maxwell postulated
   a. that accelerating charges produce electric and magnetic fields that move through space
   b. that changing magnetic fields produce changing electric fields
   c. that changing electric fields produce changing magnetic fields   d. all of the above.

5. **a** ___ In an electromagnetic wave, the electric and magnetic fields are _____ to each other and _____ to the direction of wave motion.
   a. at right angles, perpendicular   b. at right angles, parallel
   c. parallel, at right angles   d. opposite, parallel

6. **d** ___ Electromagnetic waves can be generated by
   a. oscillating fields produced by an AC generator
   b. oscillating fields produced by a coil and a capacitor connected in a series circuit
   c. vibrating quartz crystals   d. all of the above.

7. **d** ___ A receiver consists of
   a. an antenna   b. a coil and capacitor circuit
   c. an amplifier   d. all of the above.

8. **c** ___ In a microwave oven, the energy in electromagnetic waves is converted into _____ in food molecules.
   a. light energy   b. sound energy   c. thermal energy   d. chemical energy

9. **a** ___ In a television antenna, the strength of a signal is increased by the constructive interference patterns of the _____ generated in the individual wires.
   a. electric fields   b. magnetic fields   c. electric currents   d. television waves

10. **b** ___ When high-energy electrons crash into matter, their kinetic energies are converted into
    a. gamma rays   b. X rays   c. microwaves   d. radio waves.

11. **a** ___ Which of the following frequencies is in the range of radio waves?
    a. 1×10^6 Hz   b. 1×10^{14} Hz   c. 1×10^{20} Hz   d. 1×10^{24} Hz

---

CHAPTER

26 Evaluation

B. Applying Concepts

Answer the following questions in two or three complete sentences.

1. A scientist wishes to determine how much of a given pollutant is found in the air near a factory. Ordinarily, the pollutant is found in minute amounts. How can the scientist obtain this information?

   Tiny amounts of specific substances can be detected using a mass spectrometer. The ions that make up the pollutant can be separated and identified on the basis of their masses.

2. What is piezoelectricity? How is it involved in producing an electromagnetic field?

   Piezoelectricity is the ability of a substance to bend when a voltage is applied across it. It is also the ability of a substance to produce voltage when bent or deformed. When a quartz crystal vibrates, it generates an *EMF* at the same frequency as its vibration. The changing *EMF* generates an electromagnetic wave.

3. Explain what is happening when you change the setting on your radio from one station to another.

   The capacitance of the circuit is being adjusted so that the oscillation frequency of the circuit is equal to the frequency of the wave emitted by the desired radio station.

4. If the orientation of the electric and magnetic fields generated by an electromagnetic wave are known, is it possible to determine the direction of the motion of the wave? Explain your answer.

   Yes. The electric and magnetic fields are perpendicular to each other and to the direction of wave propagation.

5. Briefly explain how an electromagnetic wave is produced by the antenna from a television broadcast station.

   The antenna is connected to an alternating current source. The changing current in the antenna creates a changing electric field, which moves outward from the antenna. The changing electric field generates a changing magnetic field that also moves outward.

6. What is the importance of finding the charge-to-mass ratio for an electron?

   The mass of an electron is too small to be measured. However, if the charge-to-mass ratio is known, the mass of an electron can be calculated.

CHAPTER
26 Evaluation

C. Understanding Concepts

1. An unknown particle having a mass of 2.4×20^{-27} kg and a charge of 3.2×10^{-19} C passes through a magnetic field of 5.6×10^{-1} T. The velocity of the particle is 6.8×10^{3} m/s.

a. What is the radius of its path?

$$r = \frac{mv}{Bq}$$
$$= \frac{(2.4 \times 10^{-27} \text{ kg})(6.8 \times 10^{3} \text{ m/s})}{(5.6 \times 10^{-1} \text{ T})(3.2 \times 10^{-19} \text{ C})}$$
$$= 9.1 \times 10^{-5} \text{ m}$$

b. What is the circumference of the circle its path makes?

$$C = 2\pi r$$
$$= (2)(3.14)(9.1 \times 10^{-5} \text{ m})$$
$$= 5.7 \times 10^{-4}$$

2. A particle with a mass of 4.1×10^{-27} kg and a charge of 6.4×10^{-19} C crosses a magnetic field that measures 2.6×10^{-2} T. The particle assumes a circular path the radius of which is 1.2×10^{-1} m. At what speed is the particle moving?

$$V = \frac{Brq}{m}$$
$$= \frac{(2.6 \times 10^{-2} \text{ T})(1.2 \times 10^{-1} \text{ m})(6.4 \times 10^{-19} \text{ C})}{4.1 \times 10^{-27} \text{ kg}}$$
$$= 4.9 \times 10^{5} \text{ m/s}$$

3. An object passes through a magnetic field of 6.2×10^{-2} T. The object's speed is 8.4×10^{3} m/s. What is the electric field intensity?

$$E = Bv$$
$$= (6.2 \times 10^{-2} \text{ T})(8.4 \times 10^{3} \text{ m/s})$$
$$= 5.2 \times 10^{2} \text{ N/C}$$

4. A particle passing through a magnetic field has a mass of 6.5×10^{-27} kg and is moving at 3.2×10^{4} m/s. The charge on the particle is determined to be 2.5×10^{-18} C and the radius of its circular path through the field is 4.1×10^{-2} m. What is the strength of the magnetic field?

$$B = \frac{mv}{qr}$$
$$= \frac{(6.5 \times 10^{-27} \text{ kg})(3.2 \times 10^{4} \text{ m/s})}{(2.5 \times 10^{-18} \text{ C})(4.1 \times 10^{-2} \text{ m})}$$
$$= 2.0 \times 10^{-3} \text{ T}$$

5. A particle with a mass of 3.34×10^{-27} kg passes through a magnetic field of 3.8×10^{-3} T, which causes the nucleus to assume a circular path the radius of which is 0.060 m. A potential difference of what value accelerated the particle?

$$V = \frac{qB^2r^2}{2m}$$
$$= \frac{(1.6 \times 10^{-19} \text{ C})(3.8 \times 10^{-3} \text{ T})^2 (6.0 \times 10^{-2} \text{ m})^2}{(2)(3.34 \times 10^{-27} \text{ kg})}$$
$$= 1.2 \text{ V}$$

CHAPTER
26 Evaluation

D. Extending Concepts

1. In an attempt to identify an unknown atom, a research team has narrowed down the possibilities to a few atoms. The nuclear composition (protons and neutrons) of each member of these atoms is shown. Note that each proton or neutron has a mass of 1.67×10^{-24} kg. Experiments have yielded the following data. The atom has a negative charge of 1.6×10^{-19} C. When passing through a magnetic field of 7.8×10^{-3} T at a speed of 7.9 m/s, the atom develops a circular path the radius of which is 8.3×10^{-4} m. What is the identity of the atom?

Atom	Protons	Neutrons
Chlorine	17	18
Argon	18	22
Bromine	35	44
Krypton	36	48
Iodine	53	74

$$m = \frac{Bqr}{V}$$
$$= \frac{(7.8 \times 10^{-3} \text{ T})(1.60 \times 10^{-19} \text{ C})(8.3 \times 10^{-4} \text{ m})}{7.9 \text{ m/s}}$$
$$= 1.3 \times 10^{-25} \text{ kg/atom}$$

$$\text{Number of protons and neutrons} = \frac{\text{mass of atom}}{1.67 \times 10^{-24} \text{ kg}}$$
$$= \frac{1.3 \times 10^{-25} \text{ kg/atom}}{1.67 \times 10^{-27} \text{ kg/proton}}$$
$$= 78$$

The atom whose combined number of protons and neutrons approximated 78 is bromine, which has a total of 79 protons and neutrons.

2. Radon, Rn, is a radioactive element. As such it gives off certain particles. Assume you are a researcher attempting to identify the particle given off. It is known to have a charge of 3.2×10^{-19} C. When passing through a magnetic field of 2.0 T across a potential difference of 1.6×10^{7} V, the particle is observed to follow a circular path the radius of which is 4.1×10^{-1} mg. What is the mass of the particle?

$$m = \frac{qB^2r^2}{2V}$$
$$= \frac{(3.2 \times 10^{-19} \text{ C})(2.0 \text{ T})^2 (4.1 \times 10^{-1})^2}{(2)(1.6 \times 10^{7} \text{ V})}$$
$$= 6.7 \times 10^{-27} \text{ kg}$$

3. A particle possesses a charge of 5.8×10^{-17} C.

a. How much energy is required to move it across a potential difference of 6.4×10^{4} V?

$$KE = qv$$
$$= (5.8 \times 10^{-17} \text{ C})(6.4 \times 10^{4} \text{ V})$$
$$= 3.7 \times 10^{-12} \text{ J}$$

b. If the particle has a mass of 2.8×10^{-20} kg, what is its speed?

$$v = \sqrt{\frac{2qv}{m}} \qquad KE = qv$$
$$v = \sqrt{\frac{2KE}{m}}$$
$$= \sqrt{\frac{(2)(3.7 \times 10^{-12} \text{ J})}{2.8 \times 10^{-20} \text{ kg}}}$$
$$= 1.6 \times 10^{4} \text{ m/s}$$

CHAPTER
27 Evaluation

QUANTUM THEORY

A. Testing Concepts

In the space to the left, write the letter of the answer to each question.

1. **a** — In a star's spectrum, the frequency of the radiation emitted
   a. increases as the star's temperature increases
   b. decreases as the star's temperature increases
   c. increases as the star's temperature decreases
   d. increases as the wavelength increases.

2. **a** — According to Planck's hypothesis,
   a. the energy of an incandescent body is quantized
   b. the variable n can have any real number value
   c. the frequency of vibration is indirectly proportional to the energy
   d. atoms radiate electromagnetic waves all the time that they vibrate.

3. **b** — Einstein showed that the momentum of a photon is
   a. directly proportional to the speed of light
   b. indirectly proportional to the wavelength
   c. directly proportional to Planck's constant   d. all of the above.

4. **c** — Compton's X-ray experiment showed that
   a. only photons behave like particles   b. only electrons behave like particles
   c. momentum and kinetic energy are conserved when photons collide with electrons
   d. photons have more mass than electrons.

5. **d** — The wavelength of a particle is
   a. directly proportional to the particle's momentum
   b. indirectly proportional to Planck's constant
   c. directly proportional to the product of the mass and velocity of the particle
   d. indirectly proportional to the particle's momentum.

6. **c** — To understand the nature of light, _____ properties of light need to be taken into consideration.
   a. wave   b. particle   c. both wave and particle

7. **b** — The Heisenberg uncertainty principle is due to
   a. physicists not knowing whether to treat light as waves or particles
   b. not being able to detect the position and momentum of a particle at exactly the same moment   c. de Broglie's wavelength theory   d. the Compton effect.

8. **d** — The work function is
   a. measured by the threshold frequency in the photoelectric effect
   b. the energy needed to free an electron from a metal   d. both a and b.
   c. the energy needed to free a proton from a metal

9. **a** — The slope of a graph of the kinetic energy of ejected electrons versus the frequency of the incident radiation is equal to
   a. Planck's constant   b. the wavelength of the radiation
   c. the work function   d. none of the above.

CHAPTER
27 Evaluation

B. Applying Concepts

Answer the following questions in two or three complete sentences.

1. What conditions must exist for a current to flow in a photocell? Does all radiation result in current flow? Explain your answer.

   When no radiation falls on the cathode, current does not flow. Electrons are ejected only if the frequency of radiation is at or above the threshold frequency.

2. Differentiate between the electromagnetic wave theory and the photon theory.

   The electromagnetic theory cannot explain the photoelectric effect. This theory states that the more intense the radiation, regardless of the frequency, the stronger the electric and magnetic fields. The photon theory, on the other hand, explains the photoelectric effect by proposing that light and other forms of radiation consist of discrete bundles of energy called photons. The energy of each photon depends on the frequency of light.

3. What happens to the energy of a photon as it interacts with an electron of a metal?

   Only one photon interacts with one electron from the metal. Part of the photon's energy frees the electron from the metal. The remaining energy becomes the kinetic energy of the electron.

4. How are the Compton effect and the photoelectric effect similar?

   Both indicate that electromagnetic radiation has particle-like properties.

5. In the 1920s a scientist suggested that material particles have wave properties. What evidence was discovered that supports this suggestion?

   The strong reflections scattered from the atomic layers in a crystal proved that material particles have wave properties.

6. Explain the Heisenberg uncertainty principle.

   The principle states that measuring either a particle's momentum or its position changes the other variable. As a result, both variables—position and momentum—cannot be known precisely at the same instant in time.

C. Understanding Concepts

1. The stopping potential of a photocell is 2.5 V. What is the kinetic energy given to the electrons by the incident light? Give your answer in joules and electron volts.

$$KE = -qV_0$$
$$= -(-1.60 \times 10^{-19}\ C)(2.5\ J/C)$$
$$= +4.0 \times 10^{-19}\ J$$
$$\text{or}$$
$$= (+4.0 \times 10^{-19}\ J)(1\ eV/1.6 \times 10^{-19}\ J)$$
$$= 2.5\ eV$$

2. When a certain photoelectric surface is illuminated with light that has a wavelength of 5790 nm, the stopping potential is 0.24 V. What is the threshold frequency?

$$f = \frac{c}{\lambda}$$
$$= \frac{3.0 \times 10^8\ m \cdot s^{-1}}{5.79 \times 10^{-7}\ m}$$
$$= 5.2 \times 10^{14}\ Hz$$

$$f_0 = (qV_0 + hf)/h$$
$$= \frac{(-1.60 \times 10^{-19}\ C)(0.24\ J/C) + (6.6 \times 10^{-34}\ J/Hz)(5.2 \times 10^{14}\ Hz)}{6.6 \times 10^{-34}\ J\ Hz}$$
$$= 4.62 \times 10^{14}\ Hz$$

3. What is the photoelectric work function, in joules, of the surface in Problem 2?

$$\text{work function} = hf_0$$
$$= (6.6 \times 10^{-34}\ J/Hz)(4.62 \times 10^{14}\ Hz)$$
$$= 3.05 \times 10^{-19}\ J$$

4. What is the kinetic energy, in electron volts, of the electrons ejected from the surface in Problem 2?

$$KE = -qV_0$$
$$= -(-1.60 \times 10^{-19}\ C)(0.24\ J/C)$$
$$= (3.84 \times 10^{-20}\ J)(1\ eV/1.6 \times 10^{-19}\ J)$$
$$= 0.24\ eV$$

5. What is the de Broglie wavelength of a 1.00-kg object traveling at 45.0 m/s?

$$\lambda = \frac{h}{mv}$$
$$= \frac{6.6 \times 10^{-34}\ J \cdot s}{(1.00\ kg)(45.0\ m/s)}$$
$$= 1.47 \times 10^{-35}\ m$$

6. An X ray traveling in a vacuum has a wavelength of 4.2×10^{-12} m. What is the momentum of the wave?

$$p = \frac{h}{\lambda}$$
$$= \frac{6.6 \times 10^{-34}\ J \cdot s}{4.2 \times 10^{-12}\ m}$$
$$= 1.6 \times 10^{-22}\ kg \cdot m/s$$

D. Extending Concepts

1. The emission of X rays can be described as an inverse photoelectric effect. What is the potential difference through which an electron must be accelerated in order to produce an X ray with a wavelength of 0.10 nm.

$$f = \frac{c}{\lambda}$$
$$= \frac{3.0 \times 10^8\ m/s}{1.0 \times 10^{-10}\ m}$$
$$= 3.0 \times 10^{18}\ s^{-1}$$

$$V_0 = \frac{KE}{-q} = \frac{hf}{-q}$$
$$= \frac{(6.62 \times 10^{-34}\ J \cdot s)(3.0 \times 10^{18}\ s^{-1})}{-(-1.60 \times 10^{-19}\ C)}$$
$$= 1.2 \times 10^4\ V$$

2. An electron is accelerated by a potential difference of 200 V. What is the de Broglie wavelength of the electron?

$$v = \sqrt{2qV/m}$$
$$= \sqrt{\frac{2(1.6 \times 10^{-19}\ C)(200\ V)}{9.11 \times 10^{-34}\ kg}}$$
$$= 2.7 \times 10^8\ m/s$$
$$= h/mv$$
$$= \frac{6.6 \times 10^{-34}\ J\ s}{(9.11 \times 10^{-34}\ kg)(2.7 \times 10^8\ m/s)}$$
$$= 2.7 \times 10^{-9}\ m$$

3. The threshold frequency of sodium is 5.6×10^{14} Hz. If sodium is illuminated by light at a frequency of 7.8×10^{14} Hz, electrons are emitted. How fast does one of these electrons travel?

$$KE = \tfrac{1}{2}mv^2 \quad KE = hf - hf_0$$
$$\tfrac{1}{2}mv_2 = h(f - f_0)$$

$$v = \sqrt{\frac{2h(f - f_0)}{m}}$$
$$= \sqrt{\frac{(2)(6.6 \times 10^{-34}\ J/Hz)(7.8 \times 10^{14}\ Hz - 5.6 \times 10^{14}\ Hz)}{9.11 \times 10^{-34}\ kg}}$$
$$= 1.8 \times 10^7\ m/s$$

CHAPTER
28 Evaluation

THE ATOM

A. Testing Concepts
In the space to the left, write the letter of the answer to each question.

1. __d__ To determine the structure of the atom, Ernest Rutherford and his co-workers directed a beam of alpha particles at a sheet of metal a few atoms thick. The results indicated
   a. that all the negative charge of an atom is concentrated in a tiny, massive central core
   b. that all the positive charge of an atom is concentrated in a tiny, massive central core
   c. that an atom is mostly empty space   d. both b and c.

2. __b__ According to the nuclear model of the atom, electrons
   a. are inside the nucleus but do not contribute a significant amount of mass
   b. are outside the nucleus and do not contribute a significant amount of mass
   c. have more mass than the nucleus   d. are packed together near the nucleus.

3. __b__ Which of the following is *not* characteristic of the emission spectrum for a gas?
   a. a series of lines of different colors   b. a continuous band of colors from red through violet   c. light emitted at wavelengths characteristic of the atoms in the gas
   d. None of the above is characteristic of an emission spectrum.

4. __d__ Unlike an emission spectrum, an absorption spectrum
   a. is created by passing white light through a cool gas
   b. shows which wavelengths of light are emitted by particular kinds of atoms
   c. shows which wavelengths of light are absorbed by particular kinds of atoms
   d. both a and c.

5. __a__ Which of the following describes an electron in the ground state?
   a. It has the smallest allowable amount of energy.   b. It can emit energy.
   c. It can remain in the state for only a fraction of a second.
   d. It can make a transition to a lower energy level.

6. __a__ The equation $r_n = \frac{h_2}{4\pi^2 Kmq} n^2$ can be used to calculate
   a. the radius of the second allowable energy level in a hydrogen atom
   b. the velocity of an electron at a given energy level   c. the wavelength of an electron
   d. the potential energy of an electron.

7. __c__ The Bohr model of the atom is limited because
   a. it cannot be used to determine the energy levels of hydrogen
   b. it cannot be used to explain any of the chemical properties of elements
   c. it does not account for the wave properties of particles
   d. it cannot be used to calculate the ionization energy of a hydrogen atom.

8. __b__ The region in which there is a high probability of finding an electron is called
   a. the Bohr orbit   b. the electron cloud   c. quantum mechanics
   d. none of the above.

9. __a__ The light emitted by a laser
   a. is coherent   b. is the result of spontaneous emission
   c. is an avalanche of electrons   d. has many wavelengths.

CHAPTER
28 Evaluation

B. Applying Concepts
Answer the following questions in two or three complete sentences.

1. Explain why line spectra can be thought of as "atomic fingerprints."

   Each type of atom has a characteristic spectrum.

2. Distinguish between the ground state and excited state of an electron.

   In the ground state, an electron has the lowest amount of energy possible. An electron in the ground state can gain energy and move to a higher energy level known as an excited state. An electron can stay in an excited state for only a very short time.

3. Explain why electrons in an atom do not fall into the nucleus.

   Electrons in a stable orbit do not radiate electromagnetic energy, even though they are accelerating. Since total energy remains constant, an orbiting electron does not spiral into the nucleus.

4. How does the quantum model of the atom differ from the Bohr model?

   According to the quantum model, electrons have wave properties as well as particle properties. The wave properties explain how energy is quantized and why electron orbits do not decay.

5. Explain line spectra in terms of the quantum model of the atom.

   Since energy in an atom is quantized, energy emissions have discrete values (that is, particular frequencies and wavelengths). These discrete values are what are represented by line spectra.

6. Why is the word *avalanche* used when describing how a laser works?

   Avalanche refers to the process by which the photons that make up laser light are produced. Photons generated by stimulated emission can strike other atoms in the laser gas, generating more photons and starting the avalanche.

28 Evaluation

C. Understanding Concepts

1. Calculate the radius of a hydrogen electron in the $n = 4$ orbital.

$r_n = (0.053 \text{ nm})n^2$
$r_4 = (0.053 \text{ nm})(4)^2$
$\quad = 0.848 \text{ nm}$

2. What is the energy of a photon emitted when a hydrogen electron drops from the $n = 3$ orbital to the $n = 2$ orbital?

$E_n = -13.6 \text{ eV}/n^2 \qquad E_f = -13.6 \text{ eV}/2^2$
$E_i = -13.6 \text{ eV}/3^2 \qquad\quad = -3.4 \text{ eV}$
$\quad = -1.5 \text{ eV} \qquad\qquad \Delta E = E_i - E_f$
$\qquad\qquad\qquad\qquad\qquad = -1.5 \text{ eV} - (-3.4 \text{ eV})$
$\qquad\qquad\qquad\qquad\qquad = 1.9 \text{ eV}$

3. What is the wavelength of the photon in Question 2?

$f = \dfrac{(\Delta E)(1.6 \times 10^{-19} \text{ J/eV})}{h}$

$\quad = \dfrac{(1.9 \text{ eV})(1.6 \times 10^{-19} \text{ J/eV})}{6.63 \times 10^{-34} \text{ J/Hz}}$

$\quad = 4.6 \times 10^{14} \text{ Hz}$

$\lambda = \dfrac{c}{f}$

$\quad = (3.00 \times 10^8 \text{ m/s})/(4.6 \times 10^{14} \text{ Hz})$

$\quad = 6.5 \times 10^{7} \text{ m}$

4. An electric charge passed through a mercury vapor causes a spectral line of 245 nm. Calculate the energy of the photon emitted in electronvolts.

$E = \dfrac{hc}{\lambda}$

$\quad = \dfrac{(6.63 \times 10^{-34} \text{ J/Hz})(3.00 \times 10^8 \text{ m/s})}{254 \times 10^{-9} \text{ m}}$

$\quad = (7.82 \times 10^{-19} \text{ J})/(1.60 \times 10^{19} \text{ J/eV})$

$\quad = 4.9 \text{ eV}$

5. Which transition of a hydrogen electron emits a photon with the greatest amount of energy: $n = 5$ to $n = 3$, $n = 6$ to $n = 2$, or $n = 2$ to $n = 1$?

$E_n = -13.6 \text{ eV}/n^2$
$E_5 = -0.54 \text{ eV}, E_3 = -1.51 \text{ eV}; \Delta E = 0.97 \text{ eV}$
$E_6 = -0.38 \text{ eV}, E_2 = -3.4 \text{ eV}; \Delta E = 3.02 \text{ eV}$
$E_2 = -3.4 \text{ eV}, E_1 = -13.6 \text{ eV}; \Delta E = 10.2 \text{ eV}$
$\Delta E = E_i - E_f$
$\quad = (-13.6 \text{ eV}/n^2) - (-13.6 \text{ eV}/n^2)$
$\quad = (-13.6 \text{ eV}/5^2) - (-13.6 \text{ eV}/3^2)$
$\quad = 0.97 \text{ eV}$

6. A photon has a wavelength of 6.00×10^2 nm. Find the frequency and the energy of the photon.

$f = \dfrac{c}{\lambda}$

$\quad = (3.00 \times 10^8 \text{ m/s})(6.00 \times 10^{-7} \text{ m})$

$\quad = 5.00 \times 10^{14} \text{ Hz}$

$E = hf$

$\quad = (6.63 \times 10^{-34} \text{ J/Hz})(5.00 \times 10^{14} \text{ Hz})$

$\quad = 3.31 \times 10^{-19} \text{ J}$

28 Evaluation

D. Extending Concepts

1. A laser emits light with a wavelength of 633 nm. The laser pulses are 20 ms long. The power of the laser is 0.5 W.

a. What is the energy of a photon emitted by the laser?

$E = \dfrac{hc}{\lambda}$

$\quad = (6.63 \times 10^{-34} \text{ J/Hz})(3.00 \times 10^8 \text{ m/s})/(633 \times 10^{-9} \text{ m})$

$\quad = 3.14 \times 10^{-19} \text{ J}$

b. How much energy is in the pulse?

Power = 0.5 W = 0.5 J/s
Energy of pulse = power × time
$E = (0.5 \text{ J/s})(20 \times 10^{-3} \text{ s})$
$\quad = 0.01 \text{ J}$

c. How many photons are in one pulse?

Number of photons = energy of pulse/energy per electron
$N = (0.01 \text{ J})/(3.14 \times 10^{-19} \text{ J})$
$\quad = 3 \times 10^{16} \text{ photons}$

2. Calculate the velocity of an electron in the first Bohr orbit.

$r_n = (0.053 \text{ nm})(n)^2$
$r_1 = (0.053 \text{ nm})(1)^2$
$\quad = 0.053 \text{ nm}$

$v = \dfrac{nh}{mr2\pi}$

$\quad = \dfrac{(1)(6.63 \times 10^{-34} \text{ J/Hz})}{(9.11 \times 10^{-31} \text{ kg})(0.053 \times 10^{-9} \text{ m})2\pi}$

$\quad = 2.19 \times 10^6 \text{ m/s}$

3. Given the angular momentum and wavelength of an electron, derive a formula to determine the electron's velocity.

$mvr = \dfrac{hr}{\lambda}$

$v = \dfrac{hr}{\lambda mr}$

$v = \dfrac{h}{\lambda m}$

CHAPTER 29 Evaluation

SOLID STATE ELECTRONICS

A. Testing Concepts

In the space to the left, write the letter of the answer to each question.

1. __d__ When two atoms are brought together in a solid,
   a. the electric field of one atom affects the field of the other atom
   b. the energy level of one atom is raised while the level of the other is lowered
   c. the energy levels of the atoms are changed   d. all of the above occur.

2. __b__ When a potential difference is placed across a wire,
   a. electron speeds decrease
   b. electrons drift slowly toward the positive end of the wire
   c. the conductivity increases as temperature increases
   d. electron collisions are more infrequent as temperature increases.

3. __b__ Electrons in a(n) _____ have very high random speeds similar to the atoms in a gas.
   a. insulator   b. conductor   c. salt   d. nonmetal

4. __a__ In a conductor, conductivity increases as
   a. resistance decreases   b. resistance increases
   c. temperature increases   d. electrons move from the valence band.

5. __c__ In an insulator, the lowest energy level in the _____ band is between 5 eV and 10 eV above the highest energy level in the _____ band.
   a. ground state, conduction   b. completely filled, partially filled
   c. conduction, valence   d. valence, conduction

6. __b__ In a semiconductor, the forbidden gap is _____ the forbidden gap in an insulator.
   a. larger than   b. smaller than   c. about the same size as

7. __d__ In a(n) _____, impurity atoms are added to increase the conductivity of the material.
   a. conductor   b. insulator   c. intrinsic semiconductor   d. extrinsic semiconductor

8. __b__ Dopants increase conductivity by _____ the material.
   a. increasing the electric field of   b. adding electrons or holes to
   c. decreasing the temperature of   d. causing donor electrons to escape from

9. __c__ When dopants are added to a semiconductor, the net charge of the material
   a. becomes more positive   b. becomes more negative   c. does not change.

10. __b__ In a _____ diode, the holes and free electrons are attracted toward the battery.
    a. forward-biased   b. reverse-biased   c. depleted   d. conventional-current

11. __a__ In a silicon diode, if the applied voltage is positive,
    a. the diode acts like a small resistance   b. the diode is reverse-biased
    c. there is very high resistance   d. none of the above occurs.

12. __b__ In a junction transistor, if the base is a p-type layer, then the emitter and collector regions must be
    a. forbidden gaps   b. n-type semiconductors
    c. p-type semiconductors   d. one n-type and one p-type semiconductor.

CHAPTER 29 Evaluation

B. Applying Concepts

Answer the following questions in two or three complete sentences.

1. Contrast conductors and insulators in terms of energy bands.

   In conductors, the lowest band is only partially filled, and there are more spaces in the lowest band than there are electrons to fill them. Charges can move through a conductor. In insulators, all energy levels in the lowest band are filled. Charges in an insulator remain in place.

2. Why is silicon a good semiconductor?

   Silicon atoms have four valence electrons that are bound to an individual atom. These electrons form a band that is filled and the forbidden gap is so small that these valence electrons often reach the conduction band due only to their thermal energy.

3. Compare and contrast n-type semiconductors with p-type semiconductors.

   Both are materials doped with sources of either electrons or holes to increase the conductivity of the material. An n-type semiconductor conducts by means of negatively-charged particles or free electrons. The conductivity of a p-type semiconductor is increased by the addition of positively-charged holes.

4. Why does a diode conduct charges in only one direction?

   Free electrons on the n-side are attracted to the positively-charged holes on the p-side of the diode. Electrons and holes combine readily with one another. As a result of this flow, the n-side has a net positive charge and the p-side a net negative charge. The region around the junction then is depleted of charge carriers and is a poor conductor of electricity. If the diode is connected to a circuit one way, the depletion layer increases and very little current flows. If it is connected in the opposite way, the depletion layer is eliminated and current flows.

5. How does a supermarket bar-code scanner work?

   It contains reversed-biased pn-junction diodes that detect light reflected from the bar-codes. The light that falls on the junction creates pairs of free electrons and holes. These are pulled toward the ends of the diode, which results in a flow of current.

6. Use the figure to explain how a pnp transistor works. Use arrows and labels to show the emitter current, the collector current, and the hole flow.

   When V_e = zero, the current in the collector circuit is very small. When a potential V_e is applied between the emitter and the base, holes travel from the emitter to the base. When V_c is relatively large, most of the holes continue into the collector. The collector current, I_c, is controlled by the emitter current, I_e

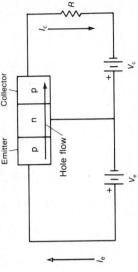

CHAPTER
29 Evaluation

NAME _____

C. Understanding Concepts

1. Zinc has a density of 7.13 g/cm³. Its atomic mass is 65.37 g/mole. If zinc has two free electrons per atom, how many free electrons are in a cubic centimeter of zinc?

$$\frac{\text{free } e^-}{cm^3 \; Zn} = \left(\frac{2 \text{ free } e^-}{1 \text{ atom}}\right)\left(\frac{6.02 \times 10^{23} \text{ atoms}}{1 \text{ mole}}\right)\left(\frac{1 \text{ mole Zn}}{65.37 \text{ g}}\right)\left(\frac{7.13 \text{ g}}{1 \text{ cm}^3 \; Zn}\right)$$

$$= 1.31 \text{ free } e^-$$

2. Calculate the density of copper if each copper atom contributes one free electron and there are 8.49×10^{22} free e^-/cm^3 Cu. The atomic mass of copper is 63.54 g/mole.

$$\rho = \left(\frac{8.49 \times 10^{23} \text{ free } e^-}{1 \text{ cm}^3 \; Cu}\right)\left(\frac{1 \text{ atom}}{1 \text{ free } e^-}\right)\left(\frac{1 \text{ mole}}{6.02 \times 10^{23} \text{ atoms}}\right)\left(\frac{63.54 \text{ g}}{1 \text{ mole}}\right)$$

$$= 8.96 \text{ g/cm}^3$$

3. How many silicon atoms are in one cubic centimeter of silicon? There are $1.00 \times 10^{13} \; e^-/cm^3$ at room temperature. The atomic mass of silicon is 28.09 g/mole and its density is 2.33 g/cm³.

$$\frac{\text{atoms}}{cm^3 \; Si} = \left(\frac{6.02 \times 10^{23} \text{ atoms}}{1 \text{ mole}}\right)\left(\frac{1 \text{ mole}}{28.09 \text{ g}}\right)\left(\frac{2.33 \text{ g}}{1 \text{ cm}^3 \; Si}\right)$$

$$= 4.99 \times 10^{22} \text{ atoms/cm}^3$$

4. In a forward-biased silicon diode, the current is 22 mA and the voltage is 0.7 V. If the diode is connected to a battery through a 450-Ω resistor, what is the voltage of the battery?

$$V = V_d + IR$$
$$= 0.7 \text{ V} + (2.2 \times 10^{-2} \text{ A})(450 \text{ }\Omega)$$
$$= 10.6 \text{ V}$$

5. A forward-biased silicon diode is connected to a 12.0-V battery through a resistor. If the current is 12 mA and the voltage is 0.7 V, what is the resistance?

$$V = V_d + IR$$
$$R = \frac{V - V_d}{I}$$
$$= \frac{12.0 \text{ V} - 0.7 \text{ V}}{1.2 \times 10^{-2} \text{ A}}$$
$$= 940 \text{ }\Omega$$

CHAPTER
29 Evaluation

NAME _____

D. Extending Concepts

1. A forward-biased silicon diode is connected to a 6.0-V battery. Also in the circuit are three 220-Ω resistors, connected in series. The voltage in the circuit is 0.7 V. What is the current?

$$V = V_d + IR$$
$$= \frac{V - V_d}{R}$$
$$= \frac{6.0 \text{ V} - 0.7 \text{ V}}{3(220 \text{ }\Omega)}$$
$$= 8.0 \text{ mA}$$

2. There are 4.99×10^{22} silicon atoms/cm³ in a doped silicon crystal. The silicon is doped with gallium so that one in every 10^7 silicon atoms is replaced by a gallium atom.

a. If each gallium atom donates one electron to the conduction band, what is the density of free electrons in the resulting semiconductor?

$$\frac{\text{free } e^-}{cm^3} = \left(\frac{\text{free } e^-}{\text{Ga atom}}\right)\left(\frac{\text{Ga atom}}{\text{Si atoms}}\right)\left(\frac{\text{Si atoms}}{cm^3}\right)$$

$$= \left(\frac{1 \text{ free } e^-}{1 \text{ Ga atom}}\right)\left(\frac{1 \text{ Ga atom}}{10^7 \text{ Si atoms}}\right)\left(\frac{4.99 \times 10^{22} \text{ Si atoms}}{cm^3}\right)$$

$$= 4.99 \times 10^{15} \text{ free } e^-/cm^3$$

b. If there are 10^{13} free e^- in pure silicon, what is the ratio of doped to pure silicon?

$$\text{ratio} = \frac{\text{free } e^-/cm^3 \text{ doped Si}}{\text{free } e^-/cm^3 \text{ pure Si}}$$

$$= \frac{4.99 \times 10^{15} \text{ free } e^-/cm^3}{\text{s} \times 10^{13} \text{ free } e^-/cm^3}$$

$$= 499/1$$

c. Is conduction by thermally-freed electrons of the silicon or by the gallium-donated electrons? Explain your answer.

Since there are about 500 gallium-donated electrons for every intrinsic silicon atom, the conduction is mainly by the gallium-donated electrons.

CHAPTER

30 Evaluation

THE NUCLEUS

A. Testing Concepts

In the space to the left, write the letter of the answer to each question.

1. b ___ An atom's atomic number refers to the
   a. number of neutrons in a neutral atom   b. number of protons in a neutral atom
   c. half the atom's atomic mass   d. number of isotopes of the atom.

2. d ___ The mass number of an atom is equal to
   a. the sum of its protons and electrons   b. twice its number of neutrons
   c. half its atomic number   d. the sum of its protons and neutrons.

3. c ___ All nuclides of an element have
   a. different numbers of protons   b. the same number of neutrons
   c. the same number of protons   d. different numbers of electrons.

4. b ___ The number of decays per second in a sample of radioactive material is its
   a. half-life   b. activity   c. gamma decay   d. lepton.

5. b ___ Which of the following types of radioactive decay occurs when a neutron is changed to a proton within the nucleus?
   a. alpha decay   b. beta decay   c. gamma decay   d. both a and b

6. a ___ The time required for half the atoms in any given quantity of a radioactive isotope to decay is the ___ of that element.
   a. half-life   b. activity   c. ionization rate   d. weak interaction

7. c ___ Which of the following is a type of accelerator?
   a. Geiger-Mueller tube   b. Wilson cloud chamber
   c. synchrotron   d. all of the above

8. d ___ Photographic film can be used to detect
   a. alpha particles   b. beta particles   c. gamma particles   d. all of the above.

9. d ___ Physicists believe that quarks make up
   a. neutrons and electrons   b. neutrinos and neutrons
   c. protons and electrons   d. protons and neutrons.

10. b ___ What is required to balance the following nuclear equation: $^4_2He + ^9_4Be \rightarrow$ ___ $+ ^1_0n$.
    a. $^6_{12}C$ b. $^{12}_6C$ c. $^{14}_6C$ d. $^8_{14}C$

11. a ___ When a quark and its antiparticle collide, they annihilate each other and are transformed into
    a. photons   b. mesons   c. weak bosons   d. gluons.

12. c ___ Pair production results in a
    a. nucleus and an electron   b. positron and an electron
    c. pair of protons   d. pair of isotopes.

13. c ___ In the quark model, the force that holds individual quarks together ___ as the quarks are pulled farther apart.
    a. becomes stronger   b. becomes weaker   c. remains the same

---

CHAPTER

30 Evaluation

B. Applying Concepts

Answer the following questions in two or three complete sentences.

1. How can you find the mass of a nucleus?

   The mass of a nucleus is approximately equal to its mass number multiplied by its atomic mass unit.

2. Compare the energies with which the three different kinds of radiation are emitted.

   Alpha particles and gamma rays are emitted with a specific energy that depends on the radioactive isotope. Beta particles are emitted with a wide range of energies.

3. Describe the effect gamma decay has on the mass number and atomic number of an atom.

   Since gamma radiation results from the redistribution of the charge within a nucleus, gamma decay does not change the mass number or the atomic number of an atom.

4. Compare the number of protons, neutrons, and electrons found in two isotopes of the same element.

   Two isotopes of the same element have the same number of protons and electrons, but different numbers of neutrons.

5. Since no nuclear particles are destroyed during a nuclear reaction, what must be true of an equation representing such a reaction?

   The sum of the superscripts on the right side of the equation must equal the sum of the superscripts on the left side of the equation.

6. Why is a linear accelerator unable to accelerate neutrons?

   Since neutrons do not have an electrical charge, they are not affected by an electric field. As a result, they cannot be used in a linear accelerator.

7. Use the quark model to explain why a proton has a positive charge and a neutron has no charge.

   The quark model describes a proton as a combination of three quarks, two up quarks and one down quark. The charge of the proton is the sum of the charges of the three quarks, which is positive. The quark model describes a neutron as a combination of one up quark and two down quarks. The sum of the charges of these three quarks is zero.

C. Understanding Concepts

1. The atomic mass of the most abundant isotope of bismuth is about 209 u. The atomic number of bismuth is 83. How many neutrons does an atom of this isotope of bismuth contain?

mass = $p + n$
n = mass − p
= 209 − 83
= 126

2. A radium atom, $^{224}_{88}$Ra, decays to radon, Rn, by emitting an alpha particle.

a. Write a nuclear equation for this transmutation.

$^{224}_{88}$Ra → $^{220}_{86}$Rn + $^{4}_{2}$He

b. What is the charge of the new nucleus?

The charge of the new nucleus is +86.

3. An atom of plutonium, $^{243}_{94}$Pu, emits a beta particle when its nucleus decays to americium, Am.

a. Write a nuclear equation for this transmutation.

$^{243}_{94}$Pu → $^{243}_{95}$Am + $^{0}_{-1}$e + $^{0}_{0}\bar{v}$

b. Indicate the number of protons and neutrons in the americium nucleus.

There are 95 protons and 148 neutrons.

4. Complete the following equations.

a. $^{253}_{99}$Es + $^{4}_{2}$He → $^{256}_{101}$Md + $\underline{\ ^{1}_{0}n\ }$

b. $^{238}_{92}$U + 17 $^{1}_{0}$n → $^{255}_{100}$Fm + $\underline{\ 8\ ^{0}_{-1}e\ }$

5. If a radioactive sample has an activity of 24 decays per second, what will the activity be after two half-lives have passed?

activity = (activity)$\left(\frac{1}{2}\right)^n$
= $(24/s)\left(\frac{1}{2}\right)^2$
= 6/s

D. Extending Concepts

1. Geologists use the radioactive decay of $^{40}_{19}$K to determine the ages of certain minerals. Assume that when the mineral is formed, $^{40}_{19}$K is trapped in the mineral's crystalline structure but none of its decay products exist in the mineral at the time. The half-life of $^{40}_{19}$K is 1.3×10^9 years. The decay products of $^{40}_{19}$K are $^{40}_{18}$Ar (12%) and $^{40}_{20}$Ca (88%). An analysis of the mineral reveals that the ratio of $^{40}_{19}$K to $^{40}_{18}$Ar to $^{40}_{20}$Ca is approximately 25:9:66.

a. What is the approximate age of the mineral? Explain how you arrived at your answer.

2.6 × 10⁹ years
At the time the mineral formed no $^{40}_{18}$Ar or $^{40}_{20}$Ca existed. After one-life, the mass of the $^{40}_{19}$K was one half of what it was when the mineral formed. The decayed 50% now consisted of $^{40}_{18}$Ar (0.12 × 50%, or 6% and 0.88 × 50%, or 44%). After two half-lives, these figures would be 25% $^{40}_{19}$K, 9% $^{40}_{18}$Ar, and 66% $^{40}_{20}$Ca.

b. Write an equation that describes the transmutation of $^{40}_{19}$K to $^{42}_{20}$Ca.

$^{40}_{19}$K → $^{40}_{20}$Ca + $^{0}_{-1}$e

c. Write an equation that describes the transmutation of $^{40}_{19}$K to $^{40}_{18}$Ar.

$^{40}_{19}$K + $^{0}_{-1}$e → $^{40}_{18}$Ar

2. The half-life of $^{33}_{17}$Cl is 2.5 s. It decays to sulfur, S, through the emission of a positron.

a. If the mass of a sample of $^{33}_{17}$Cl is 16 g, how much will remain after 15 s?

Number of half-lives = $\dfrac{15 \text{ s}}{2.5 \text{ s}}$ = 6

$m = m\left(\frac{1}{2}\right)^n$
= $(16 \text{ g})\left(\frac{1}{2}\right)^6$
= 0.25 g

b. Write a complete equation to represent the decay of $^{33}_{17}$Cl.

$^{33}_{17}$Cl → $^{33}_{16}$S + $^{0}_{1}$e + $^{0}_{0}\bar{v}$

3. The half-life of $^{52}_{25}$Mn is 5.6 days. What was the original mass of $^{52}_{25}$Mn if after 50.4 days 1.20 g are found?

$\dfrac{50.4 \text{ days}}{5.6 \text{ days/half-life}}$ = 9 half-lives

$m = m\left(\frac{1}{2}\right)^n$

$m_i = \dfrac{m}{\left(\frac{1}{2}\right)^n}$
= $\dfrac{1.20 \text{ g}}{\left(\frac{1}{2}\right)^9}$
= 614 g

4. In nature, $^{238}_{92}$U decay continues through 14 steps until a stable nuclide is formed. The illustration shows these 14 steps. Some information is missing at each step. Fill in the missing subscripts and superscripts for each nuclide. Also label each arrow as alpha or beta decay.

$^{238}_{92}$U $\xrightarrow{\alpha}$ $^{234}_{90}$Th $\xrightarrow{\beta}$ $^{235}_{91}$Pa $\xrightarrow{\beta}$ $^{234}_{92}$U $\xrightarrow{\alpha}$ $^{230}_{90}$Th

$^{214}_{83}$Bi $\xrightarrow{\beta}$ $^{214}_{82}$Pb $\xrightarrow{\alpha}$ $^{218}_{84}$Po $\xrightarrow{\beta}$ $^{222}_{86}$Rn $\xrightarrow{\alpha}$ $^{226}_{88}$Ra

$^{214}_{84}$Po $\xrightarrow{\alpha}$ $^{210}_{82}$Pb $\xrightarrow{\beta}$ $^{210}_{83}$Bi $\xrightarrow{\beta}$ $^{210}_{84}$Po $\xrightarrow{\alpha}$ $^{206}_{82}$Pb

DATE _____ PERIOD _____ NAME _____

CHAPTER

31 : Evaluation

NUCLEAR APPLICATIONS

A. Testing Concepts

In the space to the left, write the letter of the answer to each question.

1. __c__ The range over which the strong force acts is about
    a. 13.0×10^{-15} m   b. 1.3×10^{15} m   c. 1.3×10^{-15} m   d. 1.3×10^{-15} cm.

2. __a__ Binding energy refers to the amount of energy required to
    a. separate the nucleus into individual nucleons
    b. separate the nucleus into individual protons
    c. separate the nucleus into individual neutrons
    d. combine individual nucleons.

3. __a__ The binding energy of the nucleus is
    a. negative   b. positive   c. neutral.

4. __b__ The mass of the assembled nucleus is ____ the sum of the masses of the nucleons that compose it.
    a. greater than   b. less than   c. equal to

5. __b__ In a nuclear reaction, the binding energy before the reaction is ____ it is after the reaction.
    a. greater than   b. less than   c. the same as

6. __d__ Artificially produced radioactive isotopes can be formed by bombarding stable nuclei with
    a. protons   b. neutrons   c. gamma rays   d. all of the above.

7. __d__ Radioactive isotopes are used in medicine to
    a. destroy cells   b. determine how well certain organs function
    c. provide maps of internal organs   d. do all of the above.

8. __b__ If $^{226}_{88}$Ra emits an alpha particle the decay product is
    a. $^{234}_{90}$Th   b. $^{222}_{86}$Rn   c. $^{222}_{88}$Ra   d. $^{218}_{84}$Po.

9. __c__ Nuclear fission refers to
    a. a chemical reaction in which an atom dissociates into ions
    b. the combining of two nuclei
    c. the division of a nucleus
    d. the separation of two atoms.

10. __a__ A moderator in a nuclear reactor decreases the speed of
    a. neutrons   b. electrons   c. protons   d. none of the above.

11. __b__ The rate of a chain reaction is changed by the use of
    a. moderators   b. control rods   c. nucleons   d. uranium rods.

12. __a__ In the fusion process in the sun a helium nucleus is formed by
    a. the fusion of four hydrogen nuclei   b. the fusion of four neutrons
    c. the transmutation of a hydrogen nucleus   d. the fission of a beryllium nucleus.

13. __d__ In controlled fusion, the plasma is confined by
    a. a layer of electrons   b. a layer of neutrons
    c. a metal container   d. a magnetic field.

DATE _____ .... NAME _____

CHAPTER

31 : Evaluation

B. Applying Concepts

Answer the following questions in two or three complete sentences.

1. Explain how the mass defect relates to the equation $E = mc^2$.

The mass defect of a nuclear reaction refers to the difference between the masses of the reactants and the products. The sum of the masses of the products is less than the sum of the masses of the reactants. The energy equivalent of this mass defect can be calculated by using the formula $E = mc^2$.

2. What circumstances must exist for energy to be released by a nuclear reaction?

Energy will be released if the nucleus that is a product of the reaction is more tightly bound than the nucleus that decays.

3. How did Lise Meitner and Otto Frisch explain the production of small atoms, such as barium, from uranium atoms?

Meitner and Frisch proposed that uranium nuclei had been split by neutrons to form new products including barium nuclei.

4. What is the function of a moderator in a nuclear reactor?

Moderators collide with fast neutrons, slowing their motion. This increase in slow neutrons increases the probability of the fission of $^{235}_{92}$U nuclei present in the reactor which, in turn, produce more neutrons that can split other $^{235}_{92}$U nuclei. Thus, moderators help keep chain reactions going.

5. What is the Cerenkov effect and what causes it?

The Cerenkov effect is the production of a blue glow in water in which nuclear fuel rods have been placed. The glow is caused when high energy electrons and neutrons enter the water at speeds exceeding that of light in water.

6. Compare the amount of energy released during chemical reactions to the amount of energy released during a fusion reaction.

The energy released from one dynamite molecule during a chemical reaction is about 20 eV while that released by the fusion of one helium molecule is 25 MeV. Thus, in this case, the fusion reaction releases 1.25 million times more energy than the chemical reaction.

7. Describe how a magnetic field can be used to produce controlled fusion.

Magnetic fields can be used to confine charged particles which, because of the heat produced by them, could not be held in containers made of any known material. In addition, if the intensity of the magnetic field is suddenly increased, the pressure produced increases the temperature of the contained plasma to a point where fusion can take place.

31 Evaluation

C. Understanding Concepts

1. The human thyroid gland uses iodine to produce vital hormones. Based on this fact, scientists have devised ways of using radioactive $^{131}_{53}I$ to measure the functions of the thyroid.

   a. $^{131}_{53}I$ decays to xenon, Xe, by emission of a beta particle. What isotope of xenon is formed?

   $^{131}_{54}Xe$

   b. Write the equation for this reaction.

   $^{131}_{53}I \rightarrow \ ^{131}_{54}Xe + \ ^{0}_{-1}e$

   c. The half life of $^{131}_{53}I$ is 8.05 days. If a patient is given a 6.0-mg dose of $^{131}_{53}I$ at 6:00 P.M. on a Monday, how much $^{131}_{53}I$ will remain in the patient's body at 6:30 P.M. on the following Friday?

   $M = m\left(\frac{1}{2}\right)^n$
   $= (6.0 \text{ mg})\left(\frac{1}{2}\right)^{0.5}$
   $= 4.3 \text{ mg}$

2. The nuclear mass of $^{101}_{44}Ru$ is 100.9 u.

   a. What is its mass defect?

   44 p = (44)(1.007825 u) = 44.3443 u
   57 n = (57)(1.00865 u) = 57.49305 u
   Total = 101. 83735 u

   mass defect = $m_T - m_{Ru}$
   = 101.83735 u − 100.9 u
   = 0.9 u

   b. What is its binding energy in MeV?

   energy = (0.9 u)(931.5 MeV/u) = 8×10^2 MeV

3. Complete the following nuclear equations for beta decay.

   a. $^{94}_{43}Tc$ to ruthenium, Ru

   $^{94}_{43}Tc \rightarrow \ ^{94}_{44}Ru + \ ^{0}_{-1}e$

   b. $^{111}_{46}Pd$ to silver, Aq

   $^{111}_{46}Pd \rightarrow \ ^{111}_{47}Ag + \ ^{0}_{-1}e$

   c. $^{134}_{55}Cs$ to barium, Ba

   $^{134}_{55}Cs \rightarrow \ ^{134}_{56}Ba + \ ^{0}_{-1}e$

4. Complete the following nuclear equations for alpha decay.

   a. $^{144}_{60}Nd$ to cesium, Ce

   $^{144}_{60}Nd \rightarrow \ ^{140}_{58}Ce + \ ^{4}_{2}He$

   b. $^{147}_{63}Eu$ to promethium, Pm

   $^{147}_{63}Eu \rightarrow \ ^{143}_{61}Pm + \ ^{4}_{2}He$

   c. $^{190}_{78}Pt$ to osmium, Os

   $^{190}_{78}Pt \rightarrow \ ^{186}_{76}Oc + \ ^{4}_{2}He$

5. Write equations for the changes described below.

   a. $^{174}_{73}Ta$ emits a positron, and forms hafnium, Hf.

   $^{174}_{73}Ta \rightarrow \ ^{174}_{72}Hf + \ ^{0}_{1}e + \ ^{0}_{0}\bar{v}$

   b. $^{138}_{53}I$ emits a neutron.

   $^{138}_{53}I \rightarrow \ ^{137}_{53}I + \ ^{1}_{0}n$

6. When a nucleus of $^{235}_{92}U$ is struck by a neutron the products are $^{92}_{36}Kr$, $^{141}_{56}Ba$, and some neutrons.

   a. How many neutrons are produced?

   three

   b. Write an equation to represent the reaction.

   $^{235}_{92}U + \ ^{1}_{0}n \rightarrow \ ^{92}_{36}Kr + \ ^{141}_{56}Ba + 3 \ ^{1}_{0}n$

31 Evaluation

D. Extending Concepts

1. A sample of a pure isotope of berkelium, Bk, decays to produce an isotope of curium, $^{248}_{96}Cm$. In this process, the nucleus captures an orbiting electron.

   a. What was the original isotope of berkelium?

   The original isotope of Bk is $^{248}_{97}Bk$

   b. Write an equation for this decay.

   $^{248}_{97}Bk + \ ^{0}_{-1}e \rightarrow \ ^{248}_{96}Cm$

2. The energy released in the fission of one atom of $^{239}_{94}Pu$ is 1.6 MeV.

   a. How many atoms are in 2.0 kg of pure $^{239}_{94}Pu$?

   $n = \dfrac{(6.02 \times 10^{23} \text{ atoms/mole})(2 \text{ kg})}{0.239 \text{ kg/mole}}$
   $= 5.04 \times 10^{24}$ atoms

   b. How much energy would be released if all these atoms underwent fission?

   $E = (2.0 \text{ kg})\left(\dfrac{5.04 \times 10^{24} \text{ atoms}}{1 \text{ kg}}\right)\left(\dfrac{1.6 \text{ MeV}}{1 \text{ atom}}\right)\left(\dfrac{10^6 \text{ eV}}{1 \text{ MeV}}\right)\left(\dfrac{1.6 \times 10^{-19} \text{ s}}{\text{eV}}\right)$
   $= 2.6 \times 10^{12}$ J

3. An $^{252}_{99}Es$ nucleus (mass = 252.0829 u) decays to $^{248}_{97}Bk$ (mass = 248.0702 u) by emission of an alpha particle (mass = 4.0026 u) with a kinetic energy of 6.64 MeV. What is the kinetic energy of the berkelium nucleus?

   mass defect = (252.0829 u) − (248.0702 + 4.0026 u)
   = 0.0101 u
   KE = (0.0101 u)(931.5 MeV/u)
   = 9.41 MeV
   $KE_{Bk} = KE_T - KE_{He}$
   = (9.4 MeV) − (6.64 MeV) = 2.71 MeV

4. If 1.806×10^{24} atoms of $^{235}_{92}U$ undergo fission and the energy produced is 1.0×10^{13} J, how much energy per kg of $^{235}_{92}U$ is produced?

   $E = \left(\dfrac{1.0 \times 10^{13} \text{ J}}{1.806 \times 10^{24} \text{ atoms}}\right)\left(\dfrac{6.02 \times 10^{23} \text{ atoms}}{1 \text{ mole}}\right)\left(\dfrac{1 \text{ mole}}{0.235 \text{ kg}}\right)$
   $= 1.42 \times 10^{13}$ J

MIDTERM

Evaluation

A. Testing Concepts

In the space to the left, write the letter of the answer to each question.

1. __b__ In physics, a framework of explanations that explains experimental data and predicts new results is called a(n)
   a. law   b. theory   c. technology   d. analysis.

2. __b__ When multiplying measurements, the number of significant digits in _____ is used.
   a. both factors   b. the least precise factor
   c. the most precise factor   d. the difference of the two factors

3. __d__ The _____ of an object can be found from a position-time graph.
   a. slope   b. mass   c. scalar   d. velocity

4. __c__ The change in the velocity of an automobile with time is its
   a. average velocity   b. instantaneous velocity
   c. average acceleration   d. instantaneous acceleration.

5. __b__ If a net force acts upon an object, the object will
   a. remain at rest   b. accelerate   c. move at constant velocity.

6. __a__ As the angle of an inclined plane increases, the acceleration of an object moving along the inclined plane
   a. increases   b. decreases   c. remains the same.

7. __c__ The final horizontal velocity of a projectile depends on
   a. the final vertical velocity of a projectile   b. the initial vertical velocity
   c. the initial horizontal velocity   d. all of the above.

8. __a__ As the distance between two bodies decreases, the force of attraction between the bodies
   a. increases   b. decreases   c. remains the same.

9. __a__ In a closed, isolated system consisting of four balls, if the momentum of three of the balls decreases, the momentum of the fourth ball
   a. increases   b. decreases   c. remains unchanged.

10. __d__ In an ideal machine
    a. efficiency is 100%   b. there is no friction
    c. work input equals work output   d. all of the above are true.

11. __c__ As an object falls, the increase in its kinetic energy is equal to
    a. the increase in its velocity   b. its mass
    c. the decrease in its potential energy   d. its distance from the ground.

12. __b__ If thermal energy is removed from ice at a temperature of −10°C,
    a. the temperature of the ice will increase   b. the temperature of the ice will decrease
    c. the ice will melt   d. the temperature of the ice will not change.

13. __c__ If you squeeze one end of a tube of toothpaste, the other end will bulge outward. This is an example of
    a. Archimedes' principle   b. Bernoulli's principle
    c. Pascal's principle   d. cohesion.

Evaluation

B. Applying Concepts

Answer the following questions in two or three complete sentences.

1. Explain the importance of effective communication in scientific investigations.

   Effective communication is a vital ingredient in scientific investigations because groups of specialists often work collectively on a problem. It is also vital that scientists communicate their findings with the scientific community.

2. Why does an automobile sometimes skid on a wet, slippery curve in the road?

   The road surface furnishes friction through the tires. If the road is wet, friction is decreased and may not be strong enough to hold the automobile on the road. According to Newton's first law, the automobile will continue moving in a straight line and tend to skid off the road.

3. A wagon is pulled up a hill and then allowed to roll down the hill, propelled only by its own weight. Sketch the forces acting on the wagon after it is released. What makes the wagon roll down the hill?

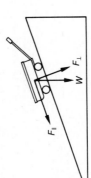

   The wagon rolls down the hill due to a component of its weight. The component is parallel to the surface of the hill.

4. As a snowball rolls down a hill, it grows larger as new layers of snow build up on its surface. If the velocity of the snowball remains constant, what happens to its momentum? Explain your answer.

   Momentum depends on mass and velocity. If the mass of the snowball increases and velocity remains constant, the momentum of the snowball increases.

5. How are work and power related?

   Power depends on the amount of work done. Power is work done per unit time. As the amount of work done in a given amount of time increases, power increases.

6. How is it possible to increase the thermal energy of a system without heating it? Give an example to illustrate your answer.

   The thermal energy of a system can be increased by doing work on it. The heating of a material due to friction is one example.

Evaluation

C. Understanding Concepts

1. Find the slope and y-intercept for the graph that shows the relationship $x = 4y - 8p$.

$x = 4y - 8p$

$y = \frac{1}{4}x + 2p$

The slope is $\frac{1}{4}$ and the y-intercept is $2p$.

2. How long will it take a car starting from rest to travel 540.0 km if its acceleration is 2.00 m/s²?

$t = \sqrt{2d/a}$

$= \sqrt{(2)(540.0\ km)(1000\ m/km)/(2.0\ m/s^2)}$

$= 735\ s$ or $0.204\ h$

3. A projectile is launched horizontally with a speed of 70.0 m/s. If the launch point is 1.8 m above the floor, how long would it take for the projectile to reach the floor?

$t = \sqrt{2y/g}$

$= \sqrt{\dfrac{2(-1.8\ m)}{-9.80\ m/s^2}}$

$= 0.61\ s$

4. How far from the launch position would the projectile in Problem 3 land?

$x = vt$

$= (70.0\ m/s)(0.61\ s)$

$= 43\ m$

5. A golf ball having a mass of 48.0 g is moving at a speed of 60.0 m/s. If the ball was initially at rest, how much work was done on the ball to give it this extra energy?

$W = \Delta KE = \frac{1}{2}mv_2^2 - \frac{1}{2}mv_1^2$

$= [(\frac{1}{2})(0.0480\ kg)(60.0\ m/s)^2] - [(\frac{1}{2})(0.0480\ kg)(0\ m/s^2)]$

$= 86.4\ J$

6. A metal object having a volume of 160 cm³ is suspended from a spring scale. When the object is completely immersed in water, the spring scale reads 1.1 N. How much does the object weigh in air? (Density of water = 1 g/cm³.)

$F_{buoyant} = Vpg \qquad W = F_{net} + F_{buoyant}$

$W = F_{net} + Vpg$

$= 1.1\ N + [(160\ cm^3)(1.0 \times 10^{-3}\ kg/cm^3)(9.8\ m/s^2)]$

$= 2.7\ N$

Evaluation

D. Extending Concepts

1. The data shown represent the positions of two people as they moved relative to a fixed point. Find the velocity of person **A** relative to person **B**.

Time (s)	Position Person A (m)	Position Person B (m)
0.0	0.0	20.0
2.0	5.0	18.0
4.0	10.0	16.0
6.0	15.0	14.0
8.0	20.0	12.0

$v_A = \dfrac{\Delta d_A}{\Delta t_A}$

$= \dfrac{20.0\ m - 0.0\ m}{8.0\ s - 0.0\ s}$

$= 2.5\ m/s$

$v_B = \dfrac{\Delta d_B}{\Delta t_B}$

$= \dfrac{12.0\ m - 20.0\ m}{8.0\ s - 0.0\ s}$

$= -1.0\ m/s$

$v_{REL} = v_A - v_B$

$= (2.5\ m/s) - (-1.0\ m/s)$

$= 3.5\ m/s$

2. On the surface of the moon, a 3.0-kg mass would weigh about 4.9 N. The diameter of the moon is 3.476 × 10³ m. Calculate the mass of the moon.

$m_M = \dfrac{Fd^2}{Gm_1}$

$= \dfrac{(4.9\ N)(1.738 \times 10^3\ m)^2}{(6.673 \times 10^{-11}\ N \cdot m^2/kg^2)(3.0\ kg)}$

$= 7.4 \times 10^{16}\ kg$

3. A construction worker carries a keg of nails up a ladder to a platform that is 12 m above the ground. The worker does 13 000 J of work on the keg. The bottom of the ladder forms an angle of 50° with the ground. Assume the efficiency of the machine (inclined plane) is 100%.

a. What is the IMA of the ladder?

$\sin 50° = \dfrac{\text{height of platform}}{\text{length of ladder}} \qquad IMA = \dfrac{\text{length}}{\text{height}}$

$l = \dfrac{h}{\sin 50°} \qquad\qquad\qquad = \dfrac{16\ m}{12\ m}$

$= \dfrac{12\ m}{0.766} \qquad\qquad\qquad = 1.3$

$= 16\ m$

b. How much force does the worker exert on the keg of nails?

$F = \dfrac{W}{d} = \dfrac{13\ 000\ J}{16\ m} = 810\ N$

c. How much does the keg of nails weigh?

$F_r = \dfrac{F_e d_e}{d_r} = \dfrac{(810\ N)(16\ m)}{12\ m} = 1100\ N$

4. How much heat is needed to melt a 2.0-kg sample of iron that is at room temperature (20.0°C). The melting point of iron is 1535.0°C. The specific heat of iron is 450 J/kg·K. The heat of fusion of iron is 2.66 × 10⁵ J/kg.

$Q = mC\Delta T + mH_f$

$= [(2.0\ kg)(450\ J/kg \cdot C°)(1515.0°C)] + [(2.0\ kg)(2.66 \times 10^5\ J/kg)]$

$= 1.9 \times 10^6\ J$

Evaluation

A. Testing Concepts

In the space to the left, write the letter of the answer to each question.

1. a When a trough from one wave meets a crest from another wave, _____ occurs.
a. destructive interference   b. constructive interference   c. resonance   d. diffraction

2. a Because it allows light to be transmitted, water in most public swimming pools is described as
a. transparent   b. translucent   c. opaque   d. none of the above.

3. b Which lens forms a real image in a microscope?
a. concave   b. objective   c. eyepiece   d. none of the above

4. a In an electrical interaction there is an attraction between
a. positive charges and negative charges   b. positive charges and positive charges
c. negative charges and negative charges   d. all charged objects.

5. b If the electric field intensity and the force on a charge are known, the size of the charge may be found by
a. dividing E by F b. dividing F by E
c. multiplying E and F d. subtracting E from F.

6. c Ohm's law can be stated as
a. $R = VI$ b. $I = VR$ c. $V = IR$ d. none of the above.

7. a If a 5-Ω resistor and a 9-Ω resistor are connected in parallel, the amount of current flowing through the 5-Ω resistor is _____ the amount of current flowing through the 9-Ω resistor.
a. greater than   b. less than   c. equal to

8. b In a uniform magnetic field, the path of a charged particle is
a. linear and opposite to the direction of the field   b. circular
c. linear in the same direction as the field   d. linear and perpendicular to the field.

9. a In a step-down transformer, the current in the secondary circuit is _____ the current in the primary circuit.
a. greater than   b. less than   c. equal to

10. c The energy of a photon depends on
a. its mass   b. its velocity   c. the frequency of the light   d. all of the above.

11. d In a laser, when a photon strikes an electron in the excited state,
a. the electron makes a transition to a lower state
b. a total of two photons leave the atom
c. photons leaving the atom strike other atoms and produce an avalanche of photons
d. all of the above happen.

12. b In a semiconductor, conductivity _____ as the room temperature increases.
a. increases   b. decreases   c. remains the same

13. a Which of the following is *not* a type of particle that transmits forces between particles?
a. neutrino   b. graviton   c. photon   d. gluon

14. b The strong nuclear force overcomes the mutual repulsion between
a. neutrons   b. protons   c. protons and neutrons   d. electrons.

Evaluation

B. Applying Concepts

Answer the following questions in two or three complete sentences.

1. What physical characteristic of sound waves causes timbre?

   The timbre, or sound quality, depends on the relative intensities of the frequencies of the sound.

2. The moon is not a luminous body. Why then can we see it?

   The moon is an illuminated body that reflects sunlight.

3. How is charging by induction different from charging by conduction?

   In charging by induction, charges are redistributed within an object without direct contact between two objects. In charging by conduction, electrons are transferred from one object to another simply by touching.

4. How do series and parallel circuits differ? What is the effect on equivalent resistance and current if another resistor is added to each type of circuit?

   In a series circuit there is only one path for current. In a parallel circuit the path branches, so there is more than one path for current. Adding a resistor to a series circuit increases the equivalent resistance and decreases the current. Adding another resistance in a parallel circuit decreases the equivalent resistance and increases the current.

5. Which antenna is longer, one designed to detect radio waves or one designed to detect microwaves? Explain your answer.

   The antenna designed to detect radio waves is longer. The antenna produces the greatest *EMF* if it is one-half the wavelength of the wave being received. Since radio waves have longer wavelengths than microwaves, they require a longer antenna.

6. Explain why an insulator does not conduct electricity.

   At room temperature, the average thermal energy is not enough to allow the electrons to cross the forbidden gap. If an electric field is placed across an insulator, almost no electrons gain enough energy to reach the conduction band, so no current flows.

7. Explain why photographic film is sometimes used to detect radioactive particles and rays.

   Photographic films become exposed when struck by radioactive particles and rays. This is because a collision with a high-speed particle will remove electrons from atoms. The ions produced take part in chemical reactions in the film.

Evaluation

C. Understanding Concepts

1. The speed of sound in water is 1498 m/s. A sonar signal has a frequency of 1.00×10^6 Hz. What is the wavelength of the signal in mm?

$$\lambda = \frac{v}{f}$$
$$= \frac{(1498 \text{ m/s})}{(1.00 \times 10^6/\text{s})}$$
$$= (0.00 \ 150 \text{ m})(100 \text{ cm/m})(10 \text{ mm/cm})$$
$$= 1.50 \text{ mm}$$

2. The index of refraction of quartz is 1.54. What is the speed of light in this material?

$$v_s = \frac{c}{n_s}$$
$$= \frac{(3.00 \times 10^8 \text{ m/s})}{1.54}$$
$$= 1.95 \times 10^8 \text{ m/s}$$

3. An object, 4.45 cm tall, is 1.0 m from a convex lens with a focal length of 8.0 cm.

a. Where is the image?

$$d_i = \frac{d_o f}{d_o - f}$$
$$= \frac{(100.0 \text{ cm})(8.0 \text{ cm})}{100.0 \text{ cm} - 8.0 \text{ cm}}$$
$$= 8.70 \text{ cm from the lens}$$

b. Is the image real or virtual? Explain your answer.

The image is real because d_i is positive.

c. What is the height of the image?

$$h_i = \frac{-d_i h_o}{d_o}$$
$$= \frac{(-8.70 \text{ cm})(4.45 \text{ cm})}{100.0 \text{ cm}}$$
$$= -0.39 \text{ cm}$$

4. What is the distance to the screen from a double slit when light with a wavelength of 630.0 nm produces first order lines 65.3 mm from the central bright band? The slit separation is 9.66×10^{-6}.

$$L = \frac{xd}{\lambda}$$
$$= \frac{(65.3 \times 10^{-3} \text{ m})(9.66 \times 10^{-6} \text{ m})}{6.30 \times 10^{-7} \text{ m}}$$
$$= 1.00 \text{ m}$$

5. A current of 7.0 A flows through a wire 1.2 m long. The wire lies perpendicular to a magnetic field the induction of which is 0.74 T. What force acts on the wire?

$$F = BIL$$
$$= (0.74 \text{ N/A·m})(7.0 \text{ A})(1.2 \text{ m})$$
$$= 6.2 \text{ N}$$

Evaluation

D. Extending Concepts

1. An air column at 25°C produces resonances spaced by 40.4 cm. What is the frequency of the tuning fork used to produce the sounds?

$$\lambda = (2)(l)$$
$$= (2)(0.404 \text{ m})$$
$$= 0.808 \text{ m}$$
$$v = 343 \text{ m/s} + (0.6 \text{ m/s/°C})(5°\text{C})$$
$$= 346 \text{ m/s}$$
$$f = v/\lambda$$
$$= \frac{346 \text{ m/s}}{0.808 \text{ m}}$$
$$= 428 \text{ Hz}$$

2. A current-carrying wire generates 4.86×10^5 J of thermal energy in 4.50 min. The resistance of the wire is 8.0 Ω. What is the potential difference across the wire?

$$Q = I^2Rt \qquad V = IR$$
$$I = \sqrt{\frac{Q}{Rt}}$$
$$V = \left(\sqrt{\frac{Q}{Rt}}\right)R$$
$$= \sqrt{\frac{4.86 \times 10^5 \text{ J}}{(8.00 \ \Omega)(2.70 \times 10^2 \text{ s})}}$$
$$= 1.20 \times 10^2 \text{ V}$$

3. A length of wire with a total resistance of 8 Ω is connected to the terminals of a galvanometer. The resistance of the galvanometer is 942 Ω. Part of the wire is exposed to a magnetic field of 1.6×10^{-3} T. The length of wire between the magnetic poles is 24 cm. If the wire is moved upward through the field at 2.0 m/s, what current will the galvanometer indicate?

$$EMF = BLv \qquad I = \frac{V}{R}$$
$$I = \frac{BLv}{R}$$
$$= \frac{(1.6 \times 10^{-3} \text{ T})(0.24 \text{ m})(2.0 \text{ m/s})}{8 \ \Omega + 942 \ \Omega}$$
$$= 8.1 \times 10^{-7} \text{ A}$$

Second Edition

The Reading/Writing Connection

Strategies for Teaching and Learning in the Secondary Classroom

Carol Booth Olson
University of California, Irvine

PEARSON
and

Boston • New York • San Francisco
Mexico City • Montreal • Toronto • London • Madrid • Munich • Paris
Hong Kong • Singapore • Tokyo • Cape Town • Sydney

Executive Editor: Aurora Martínez Ramos
Series Editorial Assistant: Lynda Giles
Executive Marketing Manager: Krista Clark
Editorial Production Service: Omegatype Typography, Inc.
Composition Buyer: Linda Cox
Manufacturing Buyer: Linda Morris
Electronic Composition: Omegatype Typography, Inc.
Interior Design: Carol Somberg
Cover Administrator: Joel Gendron

For related titles and support materials, visit our online catalog at www.ablongman.com.

Between the time website information is gathered and then published, it is not unusual for some sites to have closed. Also, the transcription of URLs can result in typographical errors. The publisher would appreciate notification where these occur so that they may be corrected in subsequent editions.

Library of Congress Cataloging-in-Publication Data

Olson, Carol Booth.
    The reading/writing connection : strategies for teaching and learning in the secondary classroom / Carol Booth Olson. — 2nd ed.
        p. cm.
    Includes bibliographical references and index.
    ISBN 0-205-49473-0 (paperback)
    1. Language arts (Secondary)   2. Language arts (Middle school)   I. Title

LB1631 .O55 2007
418.0071'2—dc22

                                                                    2006046022

Printed in the United States of America

10   9   8   7   6   5   4   3   2   1   11   10   09   08   07   06

Photo Credits   pp. i, 1, 18, 39, 68, 90, 116, 136, 166, 193, 236, 261, 287, 323, 352: top photo, Frank Siteman; middle photo, Ken Karp/Prentice Hall School Division; bottom photo, Comstock Royalty Free Division.

To Celia

Contents

Preface

The purpose of this book is to explore and reinforce the reading/writing connection and thus help teachers make visible to their students what it is that experienced readers and writers do when they make meaning from and with texts. Reading and writing have traditionally been thought of and taught as opposites—with reading regarded as receptive and writing as productive. However, researchers have increasingly noted the connections between reading and writing, identifying them as essentially similar processes of meaning construction. Especially compelling is the notion that both reading and writing are acts of composing and that the process of meaning construction is a process of drafting and redrafting.

Experienced readers and writers share a surprising number of common characteristics. For example, both readers and writers are actively engaged in the construction of meaning, go back to go forward in a recursive process, interact and negotiate with each other (i.e., the reader keeps the writer in mind and the writer keeps the reader in mind), use skills automatically, and are motivated and self-confident. Most importantly, experienced readers and writers are strategic. That is, they deliberately and purposefully access a common "tool kit" of cognitive strategies in order to make meaning from and with texts.

In order to help inexperienced readers and writers develop confidence and competence, we need to explicitly introduce them to and then provide them with guided practice in the habits of mind demonstrated by more engaged readers and writers. It is the teacher's job to clarify the cognitive strategies that underlie the reading and writing process so students know what strategies to access from their tool kits as well as how, why, and when to implement them. Using an instructional scaffolding model, teachers can develop student ownership in reading and writing, design appropriate reading and writing tasks, provide ample structure and opportunities for practice, encourage students to collaborate on their construction of and responses to texts, and help students internalize a repertoire of cognitive strategies so they can apply them independently. Research indicates that when reading and writing are taught together, they engage students in a greater use and variety of cognitive strategies than when they are taught separately.

After making a theoretical case for perceiving reading and writing as complementary processes involving the use of similar cognitive strategies, this book turns its attention to the application of theory to practice. It showcases the work of exemplary teachers who have intentionally and strategically made the reading/writing connection a reality in their classrooms in order to meet the needs of diverse learners. The chapters not only feature an array of individual reading/writing strategies, activities, and minilessons, but also carefully scaffold these strategies in more extended demonstration lessons.

The strategies profiled in this book for teaching students to learn are also strategies for learning to teach. In other words, in designing pedagogical strategies to help students become confident and competent readers and writers, teachers routinely access their own tool kit of cognitive strategies.

Think of your classroom as a text. You are always in the process of constructing meaning. As when an author writes a text, however, the meaning you construct is dependent upon your audience—your students. Your goal is not transmission but transaction; that is, you want not to make meaning for your students but rather to provide them with the tools to construct their own. So too, it is my hope that this book will serve as a tool for reflection as you draft and redraft your vision of what effective teaching is and what you want your students to know and be able to do. Use this book as a point of departure as you

- Plan and set goals for instruction
- Tap prior knowledge about effective teaching practices
- Ask questions about teaching and learning
- Make predictions about the impact of the pedagogical strategies you select to use to help students access their cognitive tool kits
- Organize, visualize, and construct the gist of your classroom
- Make connections with your students
- Monitor your instruction and adjust to revise meaning
- Step back to reflect and relate in order to understand the meaning being made by your students
- Evaluate both the products and the processes that demonstrate student learning in your classroom

Above all, remember that the teacher is also a learner and that there will always be new meaning to construct, new students to serve, new lenses from which to view what goes on in your classroom, and new strategies for teaching and learning.

SNAPSHOT OF MAIN FEATURES IN THIS TEXT

- **Practical demonstration lessons** in almost every chapter model how to scaffold guided practice activities into coherent lesson sequences, paving the way for teachers to implement theoretically sound, teacher-tested lessons in the classroom or modify the ideas to teach other texts.
- **Student models** at both the middle- and high-school levels in most chapters illustrate actual student responses to reading and writing activities.
- **"Learning Log Reflection"** section at the end of each chapter invites readers to take a step back and ponder what has been learned, providing teachers the opportunities to engage in the same cognitive strategies that readers and writers use when they compose.
- **Literary selections** give teachers easy access to the literature featured in the activities and demonstration lessons.

NEW TO THIS EDITION

- New literary selections, including the poem "The Voice You Hear When You Read Silently" by Thomas Lux and the short story "The War of the Wall" by Toni Cade Bambara (Chapter 2)
- A new chapter on introducing students to the cognitive strategies in their mental tool kits, including practical ideas for teaching metacognition through think-alouds (Chapter 2)

- Information on learning styles and language arts instruction in Chapter 5
- New strategies for interacting with a text—including Say Something, highlighting confusion, and book wheels—in Chapter 6
- An engaging Shakespearian insults activity in Chapter 7
- More emphasis on how to help struggling readers and writers and English language learners (ELLs) "beat the odds" in Chapter 8
- Academic vocabulary strategies in Chapter 12
- Specific ideas for teaching students to understand and analyze prompts and to perform well on timed writing assessments in Chapter 13
- A new Appendix demonstrating the efficacy of the scaffolded lessons and cognitive strategies approach through scientifically based research

RESOURCES ON THE COMPANION WEBSITE

In addition to the charts and graphic organizers that are referenced in this book and available on the companion website, the following resources are also included on the companion website (www.ablongman.com/olson2e):

- Lesson plans, including a new writing lesson plan for "The War of the Wall" in Chapter 2
- Student samples, including new student essays that are color coded to help students distinguish between plot summary, supporting detail, and commentary (Chapter 11)
- Activities, including new Shakespeare performance activities in Chapter 7
- Teaching sequences, including a new step-by-step sequence for teaching the multigenre research paper in Chapter 10
- Complete list of works of literature cited in this book
- Selected annotated bibliography of relevant resources on the reading/writing connection
- Addendum of technology resources for secondary language arts instruction that includes educational software, videos, and videodiscs; websites; English language arts standards; lesson plans; teaching resources for specific texts; online English writing classes; reading, writing, and grammar resources; and reference materials.

> **To access the website:**
> - Type www.ablongman.com/olson2e.
> - At the top left hand corner of the web page, click on the arrow next to the words "Jump to. . . ."
> - Scroll down to the chapter you want and click.
> - The table of contents for the chapter will appear on the far left.
> - Click on the desired material.

ACKNOWLEDGMENTS

More than twenty years ago, I arrived at the University of California, Irvine (UCI), fresh out of graduate school, to assume an academic position. Before I was even settled in, I returned to my alma mater, UCLA, to spend the day at the charter Summer Institute of the UCLA Writing Project. After participating in what Dick Dodge, one of the UCLA Writing Project founders, called (only partially in jest) "one-third seminar, one-third group therapy, and one-third religious experience," I was completely hooked! I must admit that it was hard not to wax evangelical about the spirit of community engendered by this inspiring teachers-teaching-teachers model. My plans for creating a Writing Project site at UCI began that day, and our own project was established one year later.

As the youngest member of the first UCI Writing Project Summer Institute, and having the dubious distinction of possessing the least amount of teaching experience, my biggest concern was how I could bluff my way through the five-week program without revealing how green I was. I quickly discovered that in a community of learners, no one person needs to have the "right" answer. Indeed, there is no one way to teach reading and writing. The point, we learned, is to have good questions about the dynamic processes of teaching and learning and to pursue inquiries and illuminate understandings collaboratively. For his extraordinary vision and leadership in creating this important professional development model, many thanks to Jim Gray, founder and original director of the Bay Area, California, and National Writing Projects, and to his successors, Mary Ann Smith, former executive director of the California Writing Project, and Richard Sterling, executive director of the National Writing Project, for supporting and strengthening the work of the Writing Project.

This book showcases the work of exemplary classroom teachers from my learning community, the UCI Writing Project. I am deeply grateful to the teacher/consultants who gave me permission to share their classroom strategies as well as to countless other Writing Project colleagues who have sparked my interest in the reading/writing connection and contributed to my thinking. Special thanks to Thelma Anselmi, Brenda Borron, Catherine D'Aoust, Kathleen Peterson, Carol Mooney, Maureen Rippie, Meredith Ritner, and Sharon Schiesl, who provided me with a wealth of materials and samples of student work; and to Pat Clark, who served as my response partner and cheerleader. I would also like to acknowledge the many students, from sixth graders to university students, who expressed their thoughts about the reading/writing process and shared their work in this manuscript.

Although the classroom teachers and students profiled in this book are primarily from California, the scholars whose work informs the book and the practices of these teachers are national and international in scope. We have benefited greatly and learned much from these scholars, many of whom are affiliated with other National Writing Project sites, firsthand during workshops at UC Irvine. The references cited in each chapter acknowledge the many scholars who have influenced the theory and practice espoused in this book.

For reviewing the manuscript for this edition, I thank Anna L. Bolling, California State University–Stanislaus; Kathy Bussert-Web, University of Texas–Brownsville; AnneMarie Francois, University of California–Los Angeles; Harry Noden, Kent State University; and Donna Uebler, Bradley University.

In addition, I would particularly like to thank the following individuals for providing special assistance: Janet Allen, Ruby Bernstein, Sheridan Blau, Rebekah Caplan, Joni Chancer, Fran Claggett, Harvey Daniels, Stephen Dunning, Peter Elbow, Jenée Gossard, George Hillocks, Carol Jago, Dan Kirby, Barry Lane, Judith Langer, Harry Noden, Gabriele Rico, Robin Scarcella, Jane Schaffer, Bill Strong, Irene Thomas, Gail Tompkins, Bob Tierney, Connie Weaver, and Jeff Wilhelm.

I could not have completed this manuscript without the technical assistance of Eric Chansy. Also, Aurora Martínez, my editor at Allyn and Bacon, was endlessly patient and helpful and shepherded my manuscript through its long journey.

Finally, I would like to express my gratitude to my husband, Todd, and my son, Tyler, who tolerated with remarkably good humor an absentee wife and mom for virtually every weekend for two years, who picked up the slack at home, and who provided ongoing encouragement. Most importantly, I dedicate this book to my sister, Celia. Throughout a courageous seven-month battle with cancer that she ultimately could not win, she never stopped asking me how the book was going and continually urged me to keep writing. I finished this book for you, C.

What Is the Reading/Writing Connection?

In *You Gotta BE the Book* (1997), Jeff Wilhelm describes an exchange between two middle school students. One could offer "absolutely nothing" about his experience in the "world" of a book; the other was highly articulate about his reading process. Wilhelm writes,

> After Ron shared . . . with his reading partner Jon, Jon said, "I can't believe you do all that stuff when you read! Holy crap, I'm not doing . . . like nothing . . . compared to you!"
>
> Ron responded that "I can't believe you don't do something. If you don't you're not reading man. . . . It's gotta be like wrestling, or watching a movie or playing a video . . . you've got to . . . like . . . *be* there." (p. 49)

How can we help all of our students *be* there as readers and writers? How can we cultivate in them both confidence and competence? The purpose of this book is to explore and reinforce the reading/writing connection and thus help teachers make visible to their students what it is that experienced readers and writers do when they make meaning from and with texts.

WHAT IS THE READING/WRITING CONNECTION?

Gail Tompkins (1997) notes that reading and writing have been traditionally thought of and taught as "flip sides of the coin—as opposites; readers decoded or deciphered language and writers encoded or produced written language" (p. 249). Since the early 1980s, however, researchers have increasingly noted the connections between reading and writing. In particular, through a technique called protocol analysis, researchers have studied what actually goes on in the minds of readers and writers during the act of meaning construction (Flower & Hayes, 1981a). During a protocol session readers or writers are asked to give on-the-spot, moment-by-moment reports of what is occurring in their minds by verbally thinking out loud as they make meaning from or with texts. As a result of analyzing these think-aloud protocols, researchers began to perceive and discuss reading and writing as complementary processes involving the use of similar cognitive strategies.

What is it about what mature, experienced, and engaged readers and writers do when they make meaning that has prompted researchers to focus on the parallels between these two acts of mind? The reflections of two of my students, Tim Titus and Cris Greaves, illustrate important features of the meaning-making processes of mature readers and writers. We will return to what Tim and Cris have to say as we review the research on the reading/writing connection. Tim describes his behavior as a reader:

■   Reading is a developmental process for me. It is a movie in my head which fleshes out as the story develops. I start by reading the first passage carefully and slowly; I have to get used to the author's style. The first passage colors the entire text in my mind. From there I go through the book slowly. I am a slow reader because I hate to not understand things. If I get stuck, I will go back as many pages as I have to in order to figure out the problem.

Because of the movie that a book triggers in my mind, I get very impatient with texts which don't adequately describe the scene. I want to *see* it. If I can't, I get frustrated and sometimes can't continue. When I'm engaged, it must be awful to be around me. It's all I can think of or talk about. I've left work early, shown up late, cut dates short and ignored my responsibilities in order to "find out what happens." I remember locking myself in the closet at the end of *The Two Towers* ("Lord of the Rings," part 2) because the situation was so intense. The last line, "Frodo was alive, but taken by the enemy," made me throw the book down and immediately reach for the next book. At the end of a book (except for *The Two Towers*), I always turn back and read the first paragraph again in an effort to fully understand the journey I have just finished.

—Tim

As an avid reader, Tim enters the text world and assumes the role of coconstructor as he interacts with the author and the words on the page to create his own mental movie. He constantly monitors his comprehension and is aware of how to solve a problem when he encounters one.

Cris analyzes her writing process:

■   How do I transform my thoughts into writing? Hmm. . . . I grasp on to one thing, a symbol, a moment, a color, a feeling. I feel and think with the camera eye. Then I mull and stew, compare it, contrast it, synthesize, humanize my symbol, hopefully twist it into a new shape or feeling, different from the trite. From there, I knock it out without thinking; then I go over and over and over it, rewrite. Mostly, if it is good, the guts are out on the page. My first write is 80% good or basic stuff; then a lot of throwing out goes on. Finally, I edit, but it is a two week process. I live inside of it. Sometimes, I go into great pain—and I know it because it is part of the process. But when I really write something good, the child in me feels a certain awe and wonder (I'm still a knobby-kneed little kid about it), and I am pleased. I feel as if I have shared or done something, so I trudge on willingly.

—Cris

Like Tim, Cris also is a strong visualizer, as she feels and thinks with the "camera eye." Her entry highlights the interplay between the affective and the cognitive in the process of meaning construction: She reaches deep into her feelings and then will "mull and stew" as she analyzes what to say and how to say it.

As students in the Teaching Credential Program at the University of California at Irvine (UCI) who have gone on to become successful secondary English teachers, both Tim and Cris are experienced and engaged readers and writers who are knowledgeable, thoughtful, and articulate about what it is that they do when they create meaning from or with texts. My job is easy. I get to prepare students like Tim and Cris—students who have a passion for literacy, who "live inside of" what they read and write—to become classroom teachers. The job they have is infinitely more challenging; for although they are certain to encounter some students who share their "awe and wonder" about literature and language, many more will have neither the commitment nor the capacity that Tim and Cris possess. In order to help inexperienced readers and writers develop confidence and competence, we need to explicitly introduce them to and provide guided practice in the habits of mind demonstrated by more engaged and experienced readers and writers.

CHARACTERISTICS OF EXPERIENCED READERS AND WRITERS

What are these common characteristics? Before reading on, you might want to generate your own knowledge and revisit your assumptions about the characteristics of experienced readers and writers by filling out the first and second columns of the K-W-L chart, a graphic brainstorming organizer, in Figure 1.1 (Ogle, 1986). An 8½-by-11 copy of Figure 1.1 is available on the companion website to this book; a detailed description of the K-W-L previewing strategy is included in Chapter 6. (See p. xiii for instructions for accessing the companion website.)

Active Engagement in Constructing Meaning from and with Texts

Jeff Wilhelm (1997) notes that "Once students have learned how to read, and move through middle school, reading is still regarded as a passive act of receiving someone else's meaning" (p. 13)—and often of proving that you "get it" by correctly answering the questions at the end of the text. This is perhaps why the General English students in Janet Allen's (1995)

Figure 1.1   **K-W-L Chart**   (*Source:* Ogle, 1986)

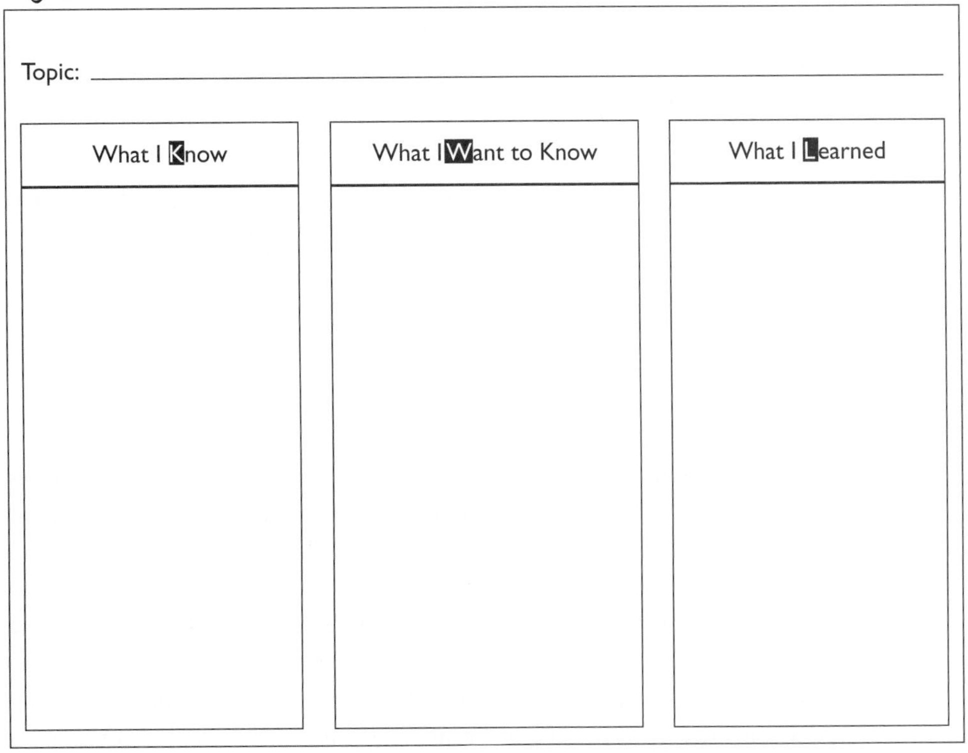

Topic: _____

What I Know	What I Want to Know	What I Learned

high school class—students identified and labeled as non–college bound—neither saw it as their responsibility nor felt they had the tools to interact with the author and the text to construct their own meaning. Instead, as Allen observes, they waited for reading to *happen* to them. For example, Janet quotes a student named Jennifer: "I thought if I just learned all the sounds and the syllables and stuff, I'd be able to read. And then I would open the book and it didn't happen" (p. 98). This is not unlike the beginning writer who sits, brows furrowed, in front of a blank sheet of paper waiting for inspiration to strike, or who is too focused on getting it right to get anything down. Reading and writing don't just happen. Experienced readers and writers are active, not passive; productive, not receptive. They interact with language, making movies in their heads, like Tim, or shaping and twisting language like so much clay, as Cris does, to produce the form they want. Robert Scholes (1985) points out that, first, we need to "perceive reading not simply as a consumptive but as a productive activity, the making of meaning in which one is guided by the text one reads"; second, "we need to perceive writing as an activity that is also sustained and guided by prior texts" (p. 8). Whether we are in the role of reader or writer, we make sense—either of or with print—and to make sense we activate our prior knowledge of the topic and the genre, our personal experiences, our reader/writer-based expectations as well as our culturally based expectations, and our contextual frames of reference (Tierney & Shanahan, 1991).

Tierney and Pearson (1983) have proposed that reading and writing are both acts of composing. These researchers make a case for reading not as a sequential series of stages but as a set of simultaneous processes that parallel what experienced writers do when they compose: processes that include planning, drafting, aligning, revising, and monitoring. Especially compelling is Tierney and Pearson's notion that readers create "drafts" of readings, refinements of meaning that evolve as the person continues reading or rereads, in much the same way as writers produce a first and second draft of a text. Experienced readers and writers know that ideas and interpretations grow over time as one pauses, reviews, rethinks, and revises. Inexperienced readers and writers often "get 'bogged down' in their desire to achieve a perfect text or 'fit' on their first draft" (p. 572). Tierney and Pearson's constructivist view of reading and their consideration of reading and writing as "essentially similar processes of meaning construction" (p. 568) have been echoed by other researchers and have received widespread acceptance within the education community.

The Recursive Process: Going Back in Order to Go Forward

Experienced readers and writers go back in order to go forward. That is, the process is recursive. One of the problems that inexperienced readers have is that they think good readers get it right the first time. Therefore, they plunge in and often proceed on "automatic pilot" as if on a race to the finish line, "oblivious" to what they don't understand (Duffy & Roehler, 1987). This may explain why Jan Horn, an instructor of reading at Irvine Valley College in Irvine, California, reports that her students will read straight down a column of text, reading right through print clearly set apart in a shaded sidebar as if it were a continuation of the unshaded column, with only the faintest glimmer that something is amiss. In contrast, experienced readers like Tim, who "hate to not understand things," will go back and work for as long as it takes "to figure out the problem."

Cris, our writer, also goes back, but for a different reason. She is "mulling and stewing" over what she has written. Sondra Perl (1990) notes that few writers she has observed write for long periods of time without going back to reread some or all of what they have previously composed. As she explains, "recursiveness in writing implies that there is a forward moving action that exists by virtue of a backward moving action" (p. 44). In other words, writers reconnect with the ideas they have already articulated in order to generate new ideas. Not only do readers and writers go back to bits of text in order to keep the process moving forward; they may also go back to clarify and refine their thinking. This is one of the reasons why Cris goes "over and over and over" her emerging text. In going back, we often discover new meaning and are prompted to reconstruct our mental or written draft. For example, Natalie Wilson, a ninth grader at Villa Park High School in Villa Park, California, writes, "There are many times when I started out to write something but discovered something along the way that made me go back and change the majority of what I wrote as well as change the direction of what I planned on writing. I love when this happens because it is like a 'breakthrough' to understand what you are really writing."

Interaction and Negotiation by Experienced Readers and Writers

When readers and writers go back to go forward, they are often attempting to respond to the text from a different perspective. In reading, this may mean trying to see the text through the author's eyes. In writing, this may involve trying to distance ourselves enough from our written words to encounter them as the readers may. Frank Smith (1988) notes that learning to read like a writer is a crucial step in learning to write like a writer:

> To read like a writer we engage vicariously with what the author is writing. We anticipate what the author is writing, so that the author is in effect writing on our behalf, not simply showing how something is done but doing it with us. . . . Bit by bit . . . the learner learns through *reading* like a writer to *write* like a writer. (p. 25)

Just as readers project themselves into the role of the writer, writers also project themselves into the roles of readers. Smith goes on to say that the author becomes an "unwitting collaborator" with the reader (p. 25). Perl (1990) would disagree with the term *unwitting*. She argues that experienced writers knowingly and deliberately attempt to take their readers' points of view in order to imagine what the reader might need to know for their words to communicate in a way that is clear and compelling. In other words, readers and writers interact and negotiate with their perceived counterpart in order to make meaning. Martin Nystrand (1986) calls the relationship between readers and writers a *condition of reciprocity*. The word *reciprocity* suggests how both parties depend on each other's understanding to ensure a meaningful interaction. The problem comes when there is a mismatch between the reader's and writer's expectations and understandings. For example, even an experienced reader like Tim can become "very impatient" with a text that doesn't meet his expectations and will abandon the collaboration if he can't adequately "make a movie" out of the writer's descriptions. Kim van der Elst, a 10th grader at Villa Park High School, has experienced the mismatch between what she meant to say and what her reader interpreted. She writes, "I usually write in one great metaphor that only I can really decipher. I guess it's because I am writing for myself and I don't think much about how someone else might interpret it. But then when I think I've written something wonderful, no one really understands it."

A Strategic Approach

When Tim visualizes the text he is reading, making "a movie in his head," or when he gets "stuck" and tells himself to go back and figure out the problem, he is being strategic. Tim's ability to visualize is probably so developmentally advanced that he can apply this strategy without consciously willing himself to do so (Paris, Wasik, & Turner, 1991); in the case of getting stuck, however, he deliberately accesses his capacity to monitor his comprehension and sends himself a message that there is a problem to be solved. In general, readers and writers purposefully select strategies to "orchestrate higher order thinking" (Tompkins, 1997, p. 143). According to Paris, Wasik, and Turner (1991), "Strategic readers are not characterized by the volume of tactics that they use but rather by the selection of appropriate strategies that fit the particular text, purpose and occasion" (p. 611). Similarly, Flower and Hayes (1981a) liken the use of strategies within the writing process to having "a writer's tool kit" (p. 376), which the writer can access, unconstrained by any fixed order, to solve the problem of constructing a text.

Because the use of cognitive strategies is such a crucial factor in the construction of meaning in both reading and writing, these powerful thinking processes will be discussed at length in the next section of this chapter. In general, both readers and writers plan and goal-set, tap prior knowledge, ask questions, predict, visualize, organize, formulate meaning, monitor, revise meaning, and evaluate (Flower & Hayes, 1981a; Paris, Wasik, & Turner, 1991; Tompkins, 1997). Block and Pressley (2002) indicate that there is a "plethora of research establishing the efficacy" (p. 385) of strategies instruction and emphasize the importance of providing modeling, scaffolding, guided practice, and independent use of strategies so that students can learn to internalize and self-regulate their cognitive and metacognitive processes.

Automatic Use of Skills, Allowing a Focus on Appropriate Strategies

Experienced readers and writers like Tim and Cris can attend to the higher-level cognitive demands of their respective composing processes because they are not bogged down with consciously executing the information-processing skills required to decode (translate the words on the page into mental or oral speech) or transcribe (put ideas into visible language). These skills are highly automated, allowing fluent reading and writing with minimal interference. This is not the case with young or inexperienced readers, who are often so focused on understanding individual words in print that they cannot attend to the overall meaning of the sentence or paragraph. Similarly, novice or poor writers must focus primarily on very low-level goals, such as correctly spelling a word or generating and transcribing their thoughts one sentence at a time, and thus cannot maintain a coherent sense of what they want to say.

Researchers agree that the degree to which the skills and subskills of reading and writing are automated affects the fluency with which language is processed. This fluency, in turn, influences the reader's or writer's ability to make meaning (Flower & Hayes, 1981a; La Berge & Samuels, 1974; Scardamalia, 1981; Stanovich, 1991). The more slowly readers and writers decode and transcribe, and the more their attention is directed toward the surface features of language, the less able they are to create coherent meaning (Anderson, Hiebert, Scott, & Wilkinson, 1985).

Motivation and Self-Confidence

There is a growing recognition that the development of strategic reading and writing is linked to personal motivation (Blau, 1997; Paris, Wasik, & Turner, 1991). In other words, reading and writing are affective as well as cognitive. This is why Tim will actually go so far as to lock himself in a closet in order to find out what happens in *The Two Towers* and why Cris is willing to "go into great pain" in order to produce a text she can feel proud of. Both individuals are highly motivated. Inexperienced readers and writers may be not only less able but also less willing to make the investment required for genuine engagement. In fact, they often adopt defensive tactics that deepen their sense of disenfranchisement. These avoidance behaviors apply equally to nonstrategic readers and to struggling writers: withdrawing participation, devaluing reading (or writing) as an activity, setting inappropriate goals, blaming external factors for their difficulties, avoiding challenging texts, and bypassing strategies that they perceive as requiring too much effort (Paris, Wasik, & Turner, 1991).

Janet Allen (1995) points out that if the two most powerful sources of motivation are achievement and recognition, as the research she cites by Wiener (1979) suggests, then it is no wonder that inexperienced readers and writers lack motivation. Allen's students could not tell her of any times they had felt successful or received social recognition for their academic achievements. In fact, they had been sent and, at some point, had even begun to send themselves numerous messages about their lack of achievement.

Strategic readers and writers regard themselves as competent to perform the tasks they undertake (Blau, 1997; Paris, Wasik, & Turner, 1991). Cris is able to "trudge on willingly," to stick with what she describes as a painstaking process, because she is confident in her ability to get the job done. She can also anticipate the sense of satisfaction she will feel when the text is completed. This anticipation, which is based upon previous success, fuels Cris's commitment to stay focused. Inexperienced readers and writers have no such history to sustain them. By making visible for inexperienced readers and writers what the cognitive strategies are that underlie the reading and writing process, particularly in a way that engages them affectively, we may be able to orchestrate incremental experiences of success for students and enable them to reconstruct their perceptions of themselves as learners.

COGNITIVE STRATEGIES THAT UNDERLIE THE READING AND WRITING PROCESS

Researchers agree that reading and writing are both complex acts of critical thinking. For example, La Berge and Samuels (1974) note that reading is probably one of the most complex skills in the repertoire of the average adult (p. 292); Flower and Hayes (1981b) identify writing as "among the most complex of all human mental activities" (p. 39). Underlying these mental activities are powerful cognitive strategies that are fundamental to the construction of meaning. This is the core of the reading/writing connection. Experienced readers and writers select and implement appropriate strategies and monitor and regulate their use in order to construct and refine meaning. Let's look at the strategies that underlie the reading and writing process. Figure 1.2 provides a graphic representation of the cognitive strategies that make up a reader's or writer's "tool kit." The list may give the impression that reading and writing are sequential stage processes in which meaning making progresses in a relatively predictable order. This may occasionally be the case—but only for some readers and writers, some of the time. Remember that experienced readers and writers go back in order to go forward and that they have the knowledge and motivation to access their tool kit of cognitive strategies when the need arises without being constrained by any fixed order.

Planning and Goal Setting

Readers and writers begin to plan even before they tap prior knowledge regarding the task they are about to undertake. In fact, tapping prior knowledge occurs as a result of planning. Readers and writers develop two types of plans—*procedural* plans and *substantive* plans

Figure 1.2 Cognitive Strategies: A Reader's and Writer's Tool Kit (*Source:* Adapted from Flower and Hayes, 1981a; Langer, 1989; Paris, Wasik, and Turner, 1991; Tierney and Pearson, 1983; and Tompkins, 1997)

Planning and Goal Setting
- Developing procedural and substantive plans
- Creating and setting goals
- Establishing a purpose
- Determining priorities

Tapping Prior Knowledge
- Mobilizing knowledge
- Searching existing schemata

Asking Questions and Making Predictions
- Generating questions re: topic, genre, author/audience, purpose, etc.
- Finding a focus/directing attention
- Predicting what will happen next
- Fostering forward momentum
- Establishing focal points for confirming or revising meaning

Constructing the Gist
- Visualizing
- Making connections
- Identifying main ideas
- Organizing information
- Expanding schemata
- Summarizing key information
- Forming preliminary interpretations
- Adopting an alignment

Monitoring
- Directing the cognitive process
- Regulating the kind and duration of activities
- Confirming reader/writer is on track
- Signaling the need for fix up strategies
- Clarifying understanding

Revising Meaning: Reconstructing the Draft
- Backtracking
- Revising meaning
- Seeking validation for interpretations
- Analyzing text closely/digging deeper
- Analyzing author's craft

Reflecting and Relating
- Stepping back
- Taking stock
- Rethinking what one knows
- Formulating guidelines for personal ways of living

Evaluating
- Reviewing
- Asking questions
- Evaluating/assessing quality
- Formulating criticisms

An 8½-by-11 copy of this figure is available on the companion website.

(Flower & Hayes, 1981a; Tierney & Pearson, 1983). Procedural plans are content-free plans regarding how to accomplish a task. These "how-to" plans provide a continuing structure for the composing process. For example, plans for generating ideas through brainstorming and outlining fall into this category. Substantive plans are content-based plans that focus more directly on the specific topic at hand. The following learning log reflection from one of my students, Frank Ashby, illustrates how he used a procedural plan to determine how he was going to go about meeting the requirements of the prompt and a substantive plan to explore the themes of unrequited love and isolation in two works of literature:

■   In writing my comparison/contrast paper about Tennyson's Mariana and Dickens' Miss Havisham, I first got out the prompt, studied it, and then wrote out what I was going to do. Then, I looked in a book of quotations and found a quote from Shakespeare about how one sorrow could lead to another that applied to both characters. In my opening paragraph, I also used the image of a snake and talked about how both women were "bitten by the serpent of unrequited love." I resolved to refer to both the image and the quote whenever it could help to explain the similarities between both women—as long as it wasn't too often or contrived.

Both procedural and substantive plans help a reader or writer to set goals. According to Flower and Hayes (1981a), the most important aspect of goals is that they are created by the learner. Whereas many plans are stored in and retrieved from long-term memory, goals are generated and revised by the reader or writer as part as the composing process. Both planning and goal setting *establish a purpose* for reading or writing as well as enabling the learner to *determine priorities*. Experienced readers and writers not only plan and goal-set more extensively than inexperienced readers and writers but also are more flexible about modifying their plans and goals and more apt to elaborate on and revise them as the text evolves (Faigley, Cherry, Jolliffe, & Skinner, 1985; Flower & Hayes, 1981a).

Tapping Prior Knowledge

The construction of meaning in both reading and writing "never occurs in a vacuum" (Tierney & Pearson, 1998, p. 88). Readers and writers tap prior knowledge; that is, they draw upon long-term memory to access a vast storehouse of background information. Knowledge is usually a resource; however it can be a limiting factor when there is little information to mobilize (Flower & Hayes, 1980). The reader/writer searches his or her *existing schemata* to make sense of information from or for a text. According to Tompkins (1997), "Schemata are like mental file cabinets, and new information is organized with prior knowledge in the filing system" (p. 13). One might have a personal experiences file cabinet, a cultural expectations file cabinet, a knowledge of topic file cabinet, a knowledge of genre file cabinet, and so forth. As the reader or writer composes, new information is added to these cabinets (i.e., schemata).

Asking Questions and Making Predictions

As the reader reads or the writer writes, she or he is constructing what Judith Langer (1989) calls an envisionment—a "personal text-world embodying all she or he understands, assumes, or imagines up to that point" (p. 2). In other words, an envisionment is the text you are creating in your mind as you read or write. It will continue to change and deepen as you continue to make meaning. In the early stages of reading or writing, Langer describes the learner as adopting a "stance" toward the text that she calls "being out and stepping into an envisionment" (p. 7). The reader or writer at this point may have a somewhat distant relationship with the text and may be trying to become more familiar with it. For example, Toni Lee, a ninth grader at Villa Park High School, observes that it's hard to get into a book at first because "it's like meeting a new friend. You don't really know much about him or her which makes it difficult to feel close to the person." As the reader or writer begins to tap prior knowledge, he or she will naturally start to ask questions and make predictions. The questions readers and writers generate about the topic, genre, author or audience, purpose, and so forth will help them to find a focus and to direct their attention while composing. The predictions readers and writers make about what will happen next foster their forward momentum and become a focal point for confirming or revising meaning. Experienced readers and writers continue to ask questions and make predictions throughout the reading/writing process.

Constructing the Gist

The initial envisionment that a reader or writer creates is, in essence, a first draft. In other words, he or she is constructing the *gist* of the text. An early step in creating a "personal text-world" (Langer, 1989, p. 2) is to visualize it. In studying the students in his middle school classroom, Jeff Wilhelm (1997) noted that his engaged readers mentally anticipated entering the story world even before curling up with a good book. For example, Wilhelm's student Ron said, "When I get ready to read I always think about what kind of story it is, you know, and what I'll have to do to get into it. I kind of imagine myself inside the story, even before I start reading and what it's going to be like in there" (p. 51). In a sense, then, experienced readers may begin to construct their envisionment by visualizing the act of entering the story world itself. Writers also conjure up a vision of what they want to create; but this perception, which Sondra Perl (1990) calls the "felt sense," is perhaps more kinesthetic than spatial. According to Perl, the felt sense is "anchored in the writer's body" (p. 46), and it is from the felt sense that the writer summons the images, words, ideas, and feelings that will be transformed into written words. Perl's description brings to mind Cris's musing: "How do I transform my thoughts into writing? Hmm. . . . I grasp on to one thing, a symbol, a moment, a color, a feeling. I feel and think with the camera eye." Christina Chang, a ninth grader at Villa Park High School, captures the power of tapping the felt sense when she remarks, "When writing something I really care about I feel as if I am exploding inside with emotion. Ideas come rushing out so fast I cannot even catch up with my writing."

Once inside the text world, readers and writers begin to create mental and/or linguistic images of the text landscape. Like Tim, many students describe the process of visualization with a movie-making metaphor, noting that they can use slow motion or flashback as well as fast-forward, "especially if it's really exciting" (Wilhelm, 1997, p. 63). Students also personalize what they are reading or writing about by making connections—drawing on their own real-world experiences to make meaning and enrich what they are constructing. For instance, Michelle Gajewski, an eleventh grader at Los Amigos High School in Garden Grove, California, reflects, "When a light goes on and something in a book touches my life it's scary in a way. But, then again, it's also nice because it can bring up old memories but help me see them with a new insight that is refreshing." As the reader or writer constructs the gist of this first draft, he or she will also identify main ideas and organize information, sequencing and prioritizing the events or ideas into main and supporting details; into beginning, middle, and end; from most to least important; or in some other structural format. In essence, the reader or the writer will be adding to his or her mental filing cabinets—that is, expanding his or her schemata.

As students move from being outside a text to stepping into a text, they will use personal experiences and knowledge as well as their perceptions of the text they have read or written thus far to "push their envisionments along" (p. 10)—in other words, to formulate meaning. Langer calls this next stance "being in and moving through an envisionment." Scholes (1985) notes that readers constantly shift from reading to interpretation and that writers construct certain texts to force this shift. This shift from reading to forming preliminary interpretations is activated when the reader senses that the text has levels of meaning and that to move beyond what is literally happening to what might be inferred at a deeper or more symbolic level of meaning, one must actively develop one's own conception of the text's significance. To illustrate, he comments that "we may *read* a parable for the story but we must *interpret* it for the meaning" (p. 22). When writers move from a summary of events to a discussion of meaning or theme, they are also shifting to interpretation. The preliminary interpretations readers and writers construct often evolve as the student continues to move through the envisionment and revisits the text to revise meaning.

Tierney and Pearson (1983) believe that adopting an alignment "can have an overriding influence on the composer's ability to achieve coherence" (p. 572). They define *alignment* as the reader's/writer's stance toward the author or audience and the degree to which the reader or writer adopts and immerses himself or herself in a variety of roles during the construction of meaning. They explain:

> A writer's stance toward her readers might be intimate, challenging or quite neutral. And, within the context of these collaborations she might share what she wants to say through characters or as an observer of events. Likewise, a reader can adopt a stance toward the writer which is sympathetic, critical or passive. And, within the context of these collaborations, he can immerse himself in the text as an eyewitness, participant or character. (p. 572)

Michelle Gajewski writes of her experience as a reader, "When I begin to feel a kinship for a character, I find that I begin to feel their emotions and begin to think the way they do." Michelle's classmate at Los Amigos High School, Qui Thinh, aligns herself even more closely. She notes, "There are times when a book speaks of me. I don't feel like I am there with the character; I am the character. Sometimes I get too emotional and it's not exactly the character I'm crying over but I am reminded of experiences I have had."

The alignment or perspective we assume shapes the images we visualize, the connections we make, the ideas and information we identify and organize, and the meaning we formulate. "Just as a filmmaker can adopt and vary the angle from which a scene is depicted in order to maximize the richness of a filmgoer's experience," Tierney and Pearson argue, "so too can a reader and writer adopt and vary the angle from which language meanings are negotiated" (p. 573).

Monitoring

Experienced readers and writers are able not only to select and implement appropriate cognitive strategies but also to monitor and regulate their use. The *monitor* has been called an executive function, a "third eye," and a strategist (Flower & Hayes, 1981a; Langer, 1986; Tierney & Pearson, 1983). In both reading and writing, the monitor, which is a metacognitive process, directs the reader's or writer's cognitive process as he or she strives to make meaning. In essence, it keeps track of the ongoing composing process and decides what activities should be engaged in and for how long. The monitor may send the reader or writer a signal confirming that he or she is on the right track and should proceed full steam ahead, or may raise a red flag when understanding or communication has broken down and the composer needs to apply fix-up strategies and clarify meaning. Experienced readers and writers are keenly attuned to their monitors. Tim is well aware when he gets "stuck" and immediately goes back as many pages as necessary to "figure out the problem." Cris instinctively knows if what she has "knocked out" is good stuff—if "the guts are out on the page." When her monitor approves, Cris is filled with pride like a "knobby-kneed little kid." Younger and less experienced readers and writers often have difficulty operationalizing their monitors, because they often are so focused on lower-level tasks that they don't have the resources or attention to monitor and regulate their process; they lack awareness of how to monitor their own cognitive activities; and/or they may fail to take action when the monitor does tell them they need to revise (Paris, Wasik, & Turner, 1991; Tompkins, 1997). Because monitoring is a "critical step in self-regulation" (Block & Pressley, 2002), it is not enough to teach students cognitive strategies. They must acquire the ability to use their monitors independently to determine when to use a strategy, which one to access, why, and for how long.

Revising Meaning: Reconstructing the Draft

Although the monitor sends readers and writers a variety of messages throughout the composing process, what often activates the monitor is a sense that there is a breakdown in the construction of meaning. This recognition will usually cause the reader or writer to stop and backtrack, to return to reread bits of text in order to revise meaning and reconstruct the draft. Less experienced readers and writers tend to plunge in and proceed from start to finish in a linear fashion; in contrast, experienced readers and writers "revise their understanding recursively" (Paris, Wasik, & Turner, 1991, p. 614). Tim comments that he only fully understands the "journey" he has just finished when he goes back and rereads the beginning of the text. His motivation for backtracking is not to repair a faulty understanding but to enhance his overall envisionment. Strategic readers and writers may also make several passes through the text to seek validation for their interpretations (Langer, 1986; Paris, Wasik, & Turner, 1991). Although ample research documents that experienced readers and writers go back in order to go forward as they move through an envisionment, studies of readers' think-alouds and writers' protocols also indicate that the "revision cycles" of individual readers and writers differ markedly (Tierney & Pearson, 1983). Some writers, like Cris, "mull and stew" during prewriting; then "knock out" a draft without thinking; then finally, painstakingly and repeatedly, revise the draft. Eleventh-grader Qui Thinh's writing process is similar to Cris's:

■ If I just dive in, I often write things that are irrelevant to the topic. Therefore, I plan ahead before I write. It's much easier if you plan but that doesn't mean you won't encounter problems along the way. I often get an idea and get fascinated and write like a mad dog. But then, I can also sit staring at my computer screen for the longest time just looking at the empty page. Then, surprisingly, something strikes me and I'll write like mad again.

Writing would be easier if people thought of it like drawing. We start with a sketch, then color it, and afterwards put on the final touches to make it stand out.

—Qui

Other writers who have very strong monitors mentally revise a draft even before putting pen to paper and, consequently, write very slowly. Still others progress in segments, writing and revising a chunk of text at a time.

Many inexperienced readers think the sign of a good reader is to read rapidly straight through a text with maximum recall (Schallert & Tierney, 1982); in fact, however, experienced readers pause, backtrack, reflect, and revise their initial "drafts" of texts just like writers do. Here again, the revision cycles of readers are widely divergent. Some readers may pause in midsentence, proceed page by page, or proceed chapter by chapter, clarifying and revising meaning as they go. Others, like Keri Kemble, a UCI teaching credential candidate, consciously read in drafts:

■   My reading process seems to me like going clamming. You go to the beach and, first of all, get to walk quickly over sand furthest away from the shore. As you reach the shoreline, you scan the surface of the sand to look for any slight bumps or bubbles. This is like my first read-through. I pick up the book and zoom through, enjoying the ride and the surface aspects of the story. Then it's time to start looking carefully for some clue, some little treasure. You bend closer to the sand, to see the telltale signs more clearly. When you catch those bubbles, or if you're lucky, the little hairs of the clam are waving like a flag in the receding water, you run over and dig quickly. This is exactly like when you stumble upon something in the text that gives you a starting point to explore a deeper theme. When you find the clue in the sand, you have to dig in order to get the clam. What's exciting about the process itself is that you never know whether the clam will be buried deep in the sand or near the surface, whether it will be so small that you should leave it there, or whether it will be a whopper! It's the same with the reading process. Both cause you to get a little uncomfortable before you reap the rewards.

—Keri

What's intriguing about Keri's clamming analogy is the idea of analyzing text closely and digging deeper—something that experienced readers and writers do: Readers dig deeper in the text to discover the pearls, often creating meaning beyond that suggested by the text (Wilhelm, 1997). Writers may reach into themselves, back into the felt sense, to move the text to a deeper level of complexity.

During the many cycles of revision, readers and writers may analyze and revise not only for content but also for style. The latter process involves taking a closer look at the author's or the writer's own craft to analyze how the nuances of language impact meaning.

Reflecting and Relating

As readers and writers begin to crystallize their envisionment of the meaning of a text, they are likely to ask the question *So what?* Langer (1986) calls this stance "stepping back and rethinking what one knows" (p. 13). In essence, the reader/writer who has been immersed in the text world steps back to ponder not just *What does it mean?* but *What does it mean to me?* When students make connections while constructing the gist, they are using their personal experiences and background knowledge to enrich their understanding of the text and make their own personal meaning. Wilhelm (1997) points out as one of his "key findings" that if students cannot do this—if they cannot bring "personally lived experience to literature"—then "the reverse operation, bringing literature back to life" (p. 70), will not take place. In this stance, which is more likely to occur in the latter stages of the meaning-making process, readers "use their envisionments to reflect on and sometimes enrich their real world" (Langer, 1989, p. 14). In other words, they reflect upon the significance of their growing understandings to their own lives. These metacognitive learning logs from ninth graders at Century High School in Santa Ana, California, in response to reading and writing about Amy Tan's "The Moon Lady" from *The Joy Luck Club,* demonstrate the important messages students elicited from the story, internalized, and applied to their own lives:

■   Stand your own ground. Don't let anybody intimidate you. If you feel lonely or confused, talk to someone. Let your feelings out. Don't keep them bottled up.

■ I don't want to feel lost anymore even though I am. I didn't get to know my father. So, I will try to make it up with my stepfather. I will from now on enjoy my family.

■ I can tell you that it's good to believe in your culture's way; but you should also believe in yourself and your own ideals. If you keep your desires hidden away and don't talk about them, no one will really know you as a person.

(See Chapter 8 for a demonstration lesson on Tan's "The Moon Lady.")

Ultimately, this type of stepping back, taking stock, and rethinking what one knows can help students to "gain heightened awareness of their personal identities and to formulate guidelines for personal ways of living" (Wilhelm, 1997, p. 70).

Evaluating

Evaluating means "stepping out and objectifying the experience" (Langer, 1989) of reading or writing. In this stance, readers and writers distance themselves from the envisionment they have been constructing. They review the mental or written text they have developed, ask questions about their purpose, and evaluate or assess the quality of their experience with the text and the meaning they have made.

When students evaluate either the process or the product of their reading or writing, or both, they do so against a set of criteria—internal or external—of what it means to read or write well. Judging how well one's reading or writing measures up to norms is an act of *criticism.* According to Scholes (1985), when we read (and, by analogy, when we write) we produce *text within text.* That is, we are constructing an initial understanding of the gist. When we interpret, we produce *text upon text.* We look closely, engage in a dialogue with the text, dig deeper, and formulate and revise our meaning, often adding new layers of meaning to our initial envisionment. When we criticize, we produce *text against text.* In other words, we exercise what Scholes calls "taste," which is never "a truly personal thing but a carefully inculcated norm" (p. 24). In the act of producing text against text, we turn, once again, to the monitor. The monitor may confirm that the reader's or writer's journey is complete and worthwhile; send the learner back into the text to redraft; or, occasionally, prompt the reader or writer to label the experience and/or the artifact as unsatisfactory but not worth revisiting.

THE POWER OF INTEGRATING READING AND WRITING INSTRUCTION

It is precisely because reading and writing access similar cognitive strategies that reading and writing make such a powerful combination when taught in connection with each other. Research suggests that using writing as a learning tool in reading instruction leads to better reading achievement, and that using reading as a resource for elaborating on ideas or for understanding opposing views leads to better writing performance (Tierney & Shanahan, 1991; Tierney, Soter, O'Flahavan, & McGinley, 1989). More importantly, reading and writing taught together engage students in a greater use and variety of cognitive strategies than do reading and writing taught separately (Tierney & Shanahan, 1991, p. 272). This exposure to and practice in an array of cognitive strategies promotes and enhances critical thinking. In fact, research indicates that "reading and writing in combination have the potential to contribute in powerful ways to thinking" (Tierney et al., 1989, p. 166).

MAKING THE READING/WRITING CONNECTION
VISIBLE THROUGH INSTRUCTIONAL SCAFFOLDING

Inexperienced readers and writers are simply that—inexperienced, not incapable. It is the teacher's responsibility to make visible what it is that experienced readers and writers do when they make meaning from or with texts, and to help students become aware that readers and writers draw from the same tool kit of cognitive strategies when they compose. In addition, teachers need to introduce these cognitive strategies to students in meaningful contexts and provide enough sustained, guided practice that students can internalize these strategies and, ultimately, perform complex reading and writing tasks competently and confidently on their own.

Langer and Applebee (1986) present *instructional scaffolding* as an especially effective model for planning and analyzing instruction in reading and writing. They credit the language acquisition and learning theories of Lev Vygotsky and Jerome Bruner as the foundation for their instructional scaffolding model. Vygotsky (1986) focuses on language as a social and communicative activity. He holds that children become literate by engaging in literacy activities that are mediated by adults, who provide youngsters with structure and guidance in tasks that they cannot yet perform independently. Vygotsky claims that children can exceed their "actual mental age" and work at the edge of their "zone of proximal development" in language learning if they are provided with this critical assistance (p. 187). Through the repeated modeling of adults and through successive opportunities to practice, children eventually internalize language structures and strategies that they can access and apply as autonomous learners. As Vygotsky says, "What a child can do in cooperation today he can do alone tomorrow" (p. 188). Bruner (1978) used the term *scaffolding* to describe the tutorial assistance provided by the adult that includes: reducing the size of the task and the "degrees of freedom in which the child has to cope"; concentrating the child's attention on something manageable; providing models of what is expected; extending the opportunities for practice; and ensuring that the child does not "slide back" but moves to the next "launching platform" (p. 254).

Building on Vygotsky's and Bruner's theories, Applebee and Langer (1983) propose a model in which "the novice reader or writer learns new skills in contexts where more skilled language users provide support necessary to carry through unfamiliar tasks" (p. 168). In this scaffolded approach, the teacher analyzes the language task to be carried out by the students, determines the difficulties the task is likely to pose when students undertake it independently, and provides guided practice in strategies that enable students to approach and complete the task successfully. Just as a real scaffold is a temporary structure that holds workmen and materials while a project is under construction, the ultimate goal of instructional scaffolding is the gradual withdrawal of that teacher-guided practice when students demonstrate they have internalized the strategies and can apply them independently.

In concluding their 1991 article "Research on the Reading–Writing Relationship: Interactions, Transactions and Outcomes," Tierney and Shanahan look to the future of reading/writing instruction and pose the "possibility" that students can be taught "to use reading and writing together in an intentional strategic fashion, based on the thinking operations required by the learner's goals" (p. 274). This book will showcase the work of exemplary teachers who have intentionally and strategically made the reading/writing connection a reality in their classrooms as a model for prospective teachers who are building their instructional repertoire and for existing teachers who wish to enhance their expertise. It will highlight the pedagogical strategies exemplary teachers have developed and/or adapted and implemented based upon the professional literature. Succeeding chapters will not only feature an array of individual strategies but also carefully scaffold these strategies in demonstration lessons. Teachers can use the demonstration lessons as a point of departure for developing their own curricula, appropriate for their own students' needs and interests.

To Sum Up

Reading and writing have traditionally been thought of and taught as opposites—with reading regarded as receptive and writing as productive. However, researchers have increasingly noted the connections between reading and writing, identifying them as essentially similar processes of meaning construction. Experienced readers and writers share a surprising number of common characteristics. Both readers and writers:

- Are actively engaged in constructing meaning from and with texts
- Go back to go forward in a recursive process
- Interact and negotiate with each other (i.e., the reader keeps the writer in mind and the writer keeps the reader in mind)
- Access a common tool kit of cognitive strategies, including planning and setting goals, tapping prior knowledge, asking questions and making connections, constructing the gist, monitoring, revising meaning, reflecting and relating, and evaluating
- Use skills automatically
- Are motivated and self confident

It is the responsibility of the teacher to make visible for students what it is that experienced readers and writers do when they compose; to introduce the cognitive strategies that underlie reading and writing in meaningful contexts; and to provide enough sustained, guided practice that students can internalize these strategies and perform complex independent tasks competently and confidently.

Learning Log Reflection

A learning log is a place to think out loud on paper—to explore, ask questions, make connections, organize information, dig deeper, and reflect on and assess what one is learning. As you read this book, you may want to keep a learning log to chronicle your reactions to and reflections about this text.

Begin by returning to the K-W-L chart (Figure 1.1). Fill out the What I Learned column to revisit what you have learned about the reading/writing connection. Then think about your own meaning-making process as you interacted with this text. You may want to take a look at Figure 1.2, Cognitive Strategies: A Reader's and Writer's Tool Kit, as you write your reflection.

The questions below may also serve as a point of departure as you explore the acts of mind you engaged in while reading this chapter. Do not feel compelled to answer them all; rather, use them to stimulate your thinking:

1. For what purpose did you read this chapter?

2. How much prior knowledge did you bring to the text, and to what degree did it help you to construct your own gist of what you were reading?

3. Given that the substance of the text was cognitively demanding, was it difficult to move from being outside the text to stepping in?

4. What kinds of questions did you ask yourself as you read?

5. Did your monitor ever say, *I don't get this* and cause you to backtrack?

6. What is the *So what?* of this chapter for you? What implications do you take away for yourself as a teacher?

Introducing Students to the Cognitive Strategies in Their Mental Tool Kits

> After Ron shared . . . with his reading partner Jon, Jon said, "I can't believe you do all that stuff when you read! Holy crap, I'm not doing . . . like nothing . . . compared to you!"
>
> Ron responded that "I can't believe you don't do something. If you don't you're not reading man. . . . It's gotta be like wrestling, or watching a movie or playing a video . . . you've got to . . . like . . . *be* there."

Let us return to Jeff Wilhelm's account in *You Gotta BE the Book* of an exchange between two middle school students, one who could offer "absolutely nothing" about his experience in the "world" of a book and the other who was highly articulate about his process. Jon's realization that "I'm not doing . . . like . . . nothing" in comparison with his partner Ron is an important first step in self-awareness. He now knows something that he didn't know—that reading doesn't just happen to you; you have to *do* something in order to *be* there. But this knowledge alone will not help Jon to be a more strategic learner.

DECLARATIVE, PROCEDURAL, AND CONDITIONAL KNOWLEDGE: FOUNDATIONS OF STRATEGIC READING AND WRITING

Jon will need to acquire three kinds of knowledge in order to read and write more strategically. First, Jon must develop *declarative knowledge:* He needs to know that experienced readers and writers deliberately access cognitive strategies to help them construct meaning from or with texts, and he needs to become familiar with what these strategies are. Second, Jon will need to have *procedural knowledge*—knowledge of how to apply these strategies. Finally, Jon will need to have *conditional knowledge*—knowledge of when to apply strategies and why they are effective (Paris, Lipson, & Wixon, 1983). Conditional knowledge is essential to create the motivation or disposition to use cognitive strategies. As Scott Paris (1985) observes, only when students are "convinced that the actions are reasonable, worth the extra effort, and functionally effective" (p. 135) will they be likely to implement these strategies on their own without being prompted or supervised by the teacher.

COGNITIVE STRATEGIES: A READER'S AND WRITER'S TOOL KIT

It is the teacher's job to make visible for students like Jon what it is that experienced readers and writers do. Borrowing a metaphor from researchers Flower and Hayes (1981a), I have likened a student's repertoire of cognitive strategies to having a tool kit. Most experienced readers and writers have a wide array of tools at their disposal. To be strategic means to be deliberate and purposeful about what tool you select and to know when, why, and for how long to apply that tool. Teachers can foster students' competence and confidence as readers and writers, incrementally over time, by building students' declarative knowledge about these and other strategies drawn from each teacher's own reading, experience, and reflection; providing students with guidance and with opportunities to develop procedural knowledge; and by engineering some successful interactions that will prompt students to act on conditional knowledge.

In Chapter 1, I proposed a model of the cognitive strategies that make up a reader's and writer's mental repertoire or tool kit, adapted from the work of Flower and Hayes (1981a); Tierney and Pearson (1983); Langer (1989); Paris, Wasik, and Turner (1991); and Tompkins (1997). To make the cognitive strategies that experienced readers and writers use when they construct meaning from and with texts more accessible to students, I developed the cognitive strategies sentence starters in Figure 2.1. These sentence openers are intended to model what goes on in the mind of a reader or writer engaged in the composing process.

Influenced by Robert Probst's (1988) focus questions in "Dialogue with a Text" (see Chapter 6), I also designed a more in-depth booklet with a range of questions related to each of the cognitive strategies. Figure 2.2 shows the questions from the Forming Interpretations and Revising Meaning page.

My cognitive strategies approach worked well for students like Ron who already have strong declarative, procedural, and conditional knowledge of reading and writing. But I quickly learned that I was expecting students like Jon to make a cognitive leap without providing enough instructional scaffolding.

Tierney and Pearson (1998, p. 85) argue that because teachers have more experience and expertise within the classroom community, they must participate as senior members of the community by sharing and modeling how they negotiate complex learning tasks, thereby making the use of cognitive strategies to construct meaning visible to inexperienced readers and writers. They advocate a cognitive apprentice model of learning (Brown, Collins, and Duguid, 1989) much like Langer and Applebee's (1986) instructional scaffolding model, in which the master learner/teacher takes on the tutorial task of showing the apprentice the "tricks of the trade while both are engaged in authentic learning tasks" (p. 85). In both the cognitive apprentice and scaffolding approaches, information is explained, modeled/demonstrated, practiced in meaningful contexts, and then applied in new contexts.

Researchers disagree as to whether teachers should introduce students to one cognitive strategy at a time or to multiple strategies. In *Mosaic of Thought,* Keene and Zimmerman (1997) advocate a one-strategy-at-a-time approach, especially with younger students, and Pressley (2002) concedes that there is a great deal of evidence that is consistent with this view. However, he proposes teaching a repertoire of strategies using what he call "transactional strategies instruction" (p.20) because highly accomplished learners "never use only one strategy but rather fluidly coordinate a number of strategies to make sense of text" (Pressley & Afflerback, 1995).

Figure 2.1   **Cognitive Strategies Sentence Starters**

Planning and Goal Setting

• My purpose is . . .
• My top priority is . . .
• To accomplish my goal, I plan to . . .

Tapping Prior Knowledge

• I already know that . . .
• This reminds me of . . .
• This relates to . . .

Asking Questions

• I wonder why . . .
• What if . . .
• How come . . .

Predicting

• I'll bet that . . .
• I think . . .
• If _____, then . . .

Visualizing

• I can picture . . .
• In my mind I see . . .
• If this were a movie . . .

Making Connections

• This reminds me of . . .
• I experienced this once when . . .
• I can relate to this because . . .

Summarizing

• The basic gist is . . .
• The key information is . . .
• In a nutshell, this says that . . .

Adopting an Alignment

• The character I most identify with is . . .
• I really got into the story when . . .
• I can relate to this author because . . .

Forming Interpretations

• What this means to me is . . .
• I think this represents . . .
• The idea I'm getting is . . .

Monitoring

• I got lost here because . . .
• I need to reread the part where . . .
• I know I'm on the right track because . . .

Clarifying

• To understand better, I need to know more about . . .
• Something that is still not clear is . . .
• I'm guessing that this means _____, but I need to . . .

Revising Meaning

• At first I thought _____, but now I . . .
• My latest thought about this is . . .
• I'm getting a different picture here because . . .

Analyzing the Author's Craft

• A golden line for me is . . .
• This word/phrase stands out for me because . . .
• I like how the author uses _____ to show . . .

Reflecting and Relating

• So, the big idea is . . .
• A conclusion I'm drawing is . . .
• This is relevant to my life because . . .

Evaluating

• I like/don't like _____ because . . .
• This could be more effective if . . .
• The most important message is . . .

An 8½-by-11 version of the cognitive strategies sentence starters is available on the companion website.

To help my students *learn by doing,* I designed a tutorial that introduces the cognitive strategies listed in Figure 1.2 (p. 8) in the context of a high-interest story by Toni Cade Bambara, "The War of the Wall," and enables them to practice implementing those strategies. Geared toward middle school readers but also appropriate for older ones, this story explores the reactions of children and adults in an urban neighborhood to a stranger who arrives unexpectedly and begins painting a wall in their community. A copy of the story is available at the end of this chapter (pp. 34–38).

The Cognitive Strategies tutorial is designed to introduce students to all of the cognitive strategies that are already in their mental tool kits. Because the teacher needs to stop repeatedly while reading aloud to explicitly point out what strategy might be appropriate to com-

Figure 2.2   **Sample Page from Cognitive Strategies Booklet**

Forming Interpretations and Revising Meaning

When we focus on what the text says, on what is literally happening or being said, we are reading. When we focus on what the text means, what its message is, we are interpreting. Interpretations are created by the reader in response to the writing of the writer. What is your interpretation of the meaning of the text you have just read?

For example:

- What is the message or BIG IDEA of all or part of this text, in your opinion?
- What in the text made you come up with the message or BIG IDEA that you did?
- Did your sense of the meaning of this text stay the same as you read or did your interpretation change? You might respond to this question by saying, "At first I thought _____, but then I _____."

When you read something that has a deeper meaning and you figure out what it means to you, how does that make you feel as a reader?

 A template for a complete booklet—with two parallel sets of questions so that 8½-by-11 sheets can be copied and cut in half to form two booklets—is available on the companion website.

prehend some aspect of the text, the process is anything but fluid. However, it helps to emphasize that this tutorial was designed for the purposes of demonstration and practice and that the reading (or writing) instruction in a language arts class generally will not be so stop-and-go. When I presented this lesson scaffold to forty-five secondary teachers in the Santa Ana Unified School District with whom I have been working for several years, I made sure to stress that what I developed should be considered as a model and not a script. To have ownership, the teachers themselves needed to improvise. Some adapted the concept to other stories. (Ray Bradbury's "All Summer in a Day" and Liliana Heker's "The Stolen Party," reprinted in this book, both lend themselves well to this tutorial approach.) Others decided that they would introduce some but not all of the cognitive strategies. Several brought actual tool boxes from home to class to make the tool kit analogy more concrete. A few mentioned that they interspersed teacher think-alouds with the more student participation–oriented activities to demonstrate some of the cognitive strategies. (See information on think-alouds elsewhere in this chapter.) During the tutorial, it is helpful if each student can refer to a copy of the Cognitive Strategies Sentence Starters in Figure 2.1.

THE COGNITIVE STRATEGIES TUTORIAL

Introducing Students to the Tool Kit Analogy

The first step in the tutorial is to help students understand that when we read, we have thinking tools or cognitive strategies inside our heads that we access to construct meaning. Researchers say that when we read, we're composing, just as when we write (Tierney & Pearson, 1983). What they mean is that while we read, we're creating our own draft of the story inside our heads and as we keep reading and come across something we didn't expect to happen or suddenly make a big discovery about what something means, we start on a second draft of our understanding. Tell students:

■   So, when you think of yourself as a reader or writer, think of yourself as a craftsman, but instead of reaching into a metal tool kit for a hammer or a screwdriver to construct tangible

Figure 2.3   **Cognitive Strategies: A Reader's and Writer's Tool Kit**

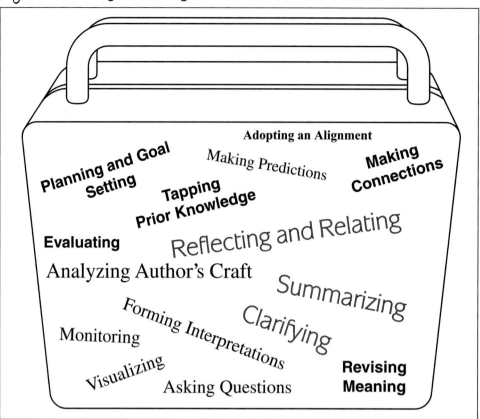

 An 8½-by-11 copy of this figure is available on the companion website.

objects, you're reaching into your mental tool kit for cognitive strategies like visualizing or making predictions to construct meaning from or with words.

Present students with copies of the tool kit graphic in Figure 2.3.

Planning and Goal Setting   An important characteristic of strategic readers and writers is that they set learning goals and make plans. Share with students the goal: for everyone in the class to become a strategic learner over the course of the year. Say that you plan to directly teach them what the cognitive strategies are so that they develop *declarative knowledge,* you will provide repeated opportunities to practice using those strategies as readers and writers so that they gain *procedural knowledge,* and you will sometimes challenge them to work on their reading and writing independently so they develop their *conditional knowledge* to make decisions about what strategies to use.

Tapping Prior Knowledge   Rather than just diving into a story, effective readers begin by seeing if the title will give them any clues about what they are about to read. A good strategy to access when one ventures into a text is tapping prior knowledge. Explain to students: "Think of prior knowledge as being stored in file cabinets in your head. You have a storehouse of knowledge based on all your life experiences, the cultural group you belong to, the area you live in, the school you go to, the books you have read, and so forth. That's why, when you read, the mental draft of the text you are creating in your head will be slightly different for each reader." When readers tap prior knowledge, they might say to themselves in-

Figure 2.4   **"The War of the Wall" Cluster**

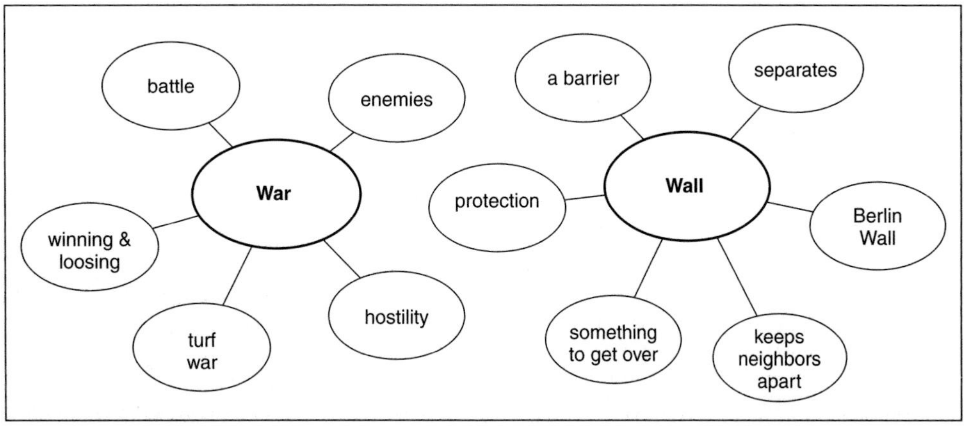

side their heads, "I already know that . . . ," "This reminds me of . . . ," or "This makes me think about. . . ." Invite students to notice what words and associations jump out at them as they consider the title "The War of the Wall." A sample cluster of students' responses might look something like the one in Figure 2.4.

Making Predictions   As readers tap prior knowledge, this naturally leads them to make predictions, educated guesses about what is going to happen. When people make predictions, they often use expressions like "I'll bet that _____ is going to happen," or "I think this story will be about _____ because. . . ." Ask students to make predictions based on the class discussion of the words in the title. They are likely to predict: a fight over turf; a misunderstanding; a wall gets built that shuts something out.

Introducing the Author   Ask students if anyone knows anything about the background of the author of the story. If so, encourage students to share. If not, explain that Toni Cade Bambara is an African American writer, and former teacher and social worker, who grew up in New York City and who often writes coming-of-age stories about kids and stories about human relationships. Then ask the class to add to their predictions. Students may speculate that the story: will involve gangs; be set in an inner city; possibly include an incident related to tagging/graffiti; or be about a symbolic wall of discrimination rather than be about a conflict over a literal wall.

Beginning the Story

Read the first three paragraphs, up to "And then we'd really be late for school." The opening of the story is reprinted below:

The War of the Wall
by Toni Cade Bambara

Me and Lou had no time for courtesies. We were late for school. So we just flat out told the painter lady to quit messing with the wall. It was our wall, and she had no right coming into our neighborhood painting on it. Stirring in the paint bucket and not even looking at us, she mumbled something about Mr. Eubanks, the barber, giving her permission. That had nothing to do with it as far as we were concerned. We've been pitching pennies against that wall since we were little kids. Old folks have been dragging their chairs out to sit in the shade of the wall for years. Big kids have been playing handball against the wall since so-called integration when the crazies 'cross town poured cement in our pool so we couldn't use it. I'd sprained my neck one time boosting my cousin Lou up to chisel Jimmy Lyons's name into the wall when we found out he was never coming home from the war in Vietnam to take us fishing.

"If you lean close," Lou said, leaning hipshot against her beat-up car, "you'll get a whiff of bubble gum and kids' sweat. And that'll tell you something—that this wall belongs to the kids of Taliaferro Street." I thought Lou sounded very convincing. But the painter lady paid us no mind. She just snapped the brim of her straw hat down and hauled her bucket up the ladder.

"You're not even from around here," I hollered up after her. The license plates on her old piece of car said "New York." Lou dragged me away because I was about to grab hold of that ladder and shake it. And then we'd really be late for school.

Source: "The War of the Wall," from *Deep Sightings and Rescue Missions* by Toni Cade Bambara, copyright © 1996, by The Estate of Toni Cade Bambara. Used by permission of Pantheon Books, a division of Random House, Inc.

Constructing the Gist, Summarizing, and Asking Questions   Say to students: "In creating the first draft in our heads of our understanding of the story, it's very important that we can follow what is literally happening. This is called constructing the gist. The word *gist* means 'the main point.' So, when we're constructing the gist, we're getting the basic point of what is happening and summarizing what we know so far." Ask students to turn to a partner and summarize the basic gist of the story. Continue to explain that as we begin to construct a draft of the story inside our heads, we often ask ourselves "I wonder why," "How come," or "What if" questions. Ask students to pose an internal question about what they've read so far and then to articulate it to a partner. Follow-up by asking some teacher-directed questions such as the following: Who do you think the narrator of the story is? Where does the story take place? What ethnicity do you think the characters are? When does the story take place? As students offer responses, continually ask, "What makes you think that?" to send them back into the text to search for evidence. For example, the reference to "integration" can be used as evidence that the characters are most likely African American. Since students may have a limited amount of prior knowledge of the Vietnam War era, the teacher may want to provide some historical background.

Making Connections   Experienced readers also make connections when they read. That is, they draw on personal experiences to relate to the text. Ask students: Was there a special place in your neighborhood when you were growing up where you hung out and where you felt like you had some ownership? Or, have you ever had someone that you viewed as an intruder invade your space? People often make connections by saying, "This reminds me of . . ." or "I can relate to this because. . . ." Encourage students to share their connections in a small group and then ask for volunteers to share with the whole class.

Further Reading

Read up to "Me and Lou definitely did not want to hear that. Why couldn't she set up an easel downtown or draw on the sidewalk in her own neighborhood." In this section of the story, the Morris twins bring dinner to the "painter lady" as she is mapping out her design for the mural she is planning to paint. She wags her head as if there is something terrible on the plate and tells them to thank their mother very much but she brought her own dinner along. Later, she shows up famished at the local diner and alienates the adults there by being extremely picky and indecisive about ordering her meal. However, the narrator's mother, who works in the restaurant, later regrets that she got impatient with her and rationalizes that the woman was probably just trying to follow a strict diet and that it's hard to be an artist and get recognition for one's work. This is exactly what the narrator and his friend, Lou, don't want to hear since they have declared war on the painter lady.

Adopting an Alignment   Ask students: "How is the story going so far? Are you into it? Why? Usually when you read something and you're so involved that you feel like you are there, you have tapped a cognitive strategy called *adopting an alignment.* This strategy involves the degree to which you indentify with the characters, are engrossed in the topic, or can relate to the author. Sometimes, people talk about adopting an alignment in terms of feeling a sense of kinship with the characters in a text or with the author or topic of the story. They say things like, 'The character I most identify with is . . . ,' or 'I can relate to this because. . . .' Of the characters we have met so far in the story, which one do you feel aligned with? Why? Which character is the hardest to relate to so far? Why?" Students can discuss this with a partner prior to some whole group discussion.

Monitoring, Analyzing Author's Craft, and Clarifying   Experienced readers and writers are able not only to select and implement appropriate cognitive strategies but also to monitor and regulate their use. Ask the class: "Has anyone been listening to the story so far and come across a word or phrase where you said to yourself inside your head, 'Wait. I don't get this?' If you have, you were using a cognitive strategy called *monitoring.* The monitor in our tool kit tells us if we are understanding what we're reading or if we need to go back to figure something out. When you are monitoring your reading process, you might say to yourself, 'I know I'm on the right track because . . .' or 'I need to go back and reread this because. . . .' For example, did anyone come to the description of the painter's eyes being 'full of sky' and think, 'Now, what in the heck does that mean?' Since the painter can't literally have sky in her eyes, we have to reach into our tool kits and clarify our understanding. In this case, we can use analyzing author's craft to understand this metaphor. What do you think the writer means?" Many students will assume that "eyes full of sky" is a reference to the painter having blue eyes. This can lead to an interesting discussion about the race of the painter lady. The majority of students are likely to picture this stranger as a white woman. Someone may suggest she is Jewish because she doesn't eat pork. A small contingent of the class may feel she is African American and Muslim and use as evidence the fact that mama calls her "sistuh" (sister) and that she is considered ill-mannered for not acknowledging the elders when she enters the restaurant. Encourage the class to continue to watch for evidence concerning the painter's race. Return to the "eyes full of sky" expression and ask students to consider that it could mean something else. Someone will notice the word "trance" in the following sentence and conclude that the expression may signify that the painter lady's mind is somewhere else; that is, she has her head in the clouds.

Further Reading, Predicting, and Evaluating   Read from "All weekend long" to "We spent our whole allowance on this." In this part of the story, the narrator and Lou see a news story on TV about kids spray painting subway trains in New York and they head off to the hardware store in search of the some paint of their own, leading most students to predict that the boys are planning to deface the mural the painter lady is creating. This is a good place to introduce the cognitive strategy of evaluating. Explain to students: "When you evaluate, you look carefully at something to judge its quality or worth by criteria, such as a rating scale of 1 to 10 in the Olympics signifying poor to excellent, or a set of values such as bad to good, or a moral scale of wrong to right. For example, if you think the boys are going to destroy the painter lady's artwork by putting graffiti on the wall, how would you evaluate their actions? Can this behavior be justified in any way?"

Finish the Story

When the boys return with their paint, they find most of their neighbors huddled in awe in front of the wall. To their surprise, along with important figures from African American history, they see themselves depicted on this "wall of respect," which is dedicated to the painter's cousin, Jimmy Lyons, who lived in the neighborhood and died in Vietnam.

Revising Meaning Sometimes as we read, we make certain predictions about what is going to happen and then the plot of the story goes in an unexpected direction and surprises us. This causes us to use another strategy in our tool kit—revising meaning. When we revise meaning, we work on our second draft of what we think the text means. Ask: "How many of you were surprised by the end of the story? Did it cause you to revise meaning?" Invite students to turn to a partner and complete this sentence, "At first I thought _____ but now I . . . ."

Visualizing When people visualize, they often talk about making a movie inside their heads or use expressions like " I can picture . . . " or "In my mind I see . . . ." Say: "You've probably been watching your own internal movie all along as we've been reading. What are some scenes you pictured?" After students share the scenes which stand out in their minds, give them time to do a quicksketch of the closing scene of the story—both the mural itself and of the characters who are awestruck by it.

Forming Interpretations and Reflecting and Relating After a reader finishes a text, it is time to stand back and ask the big question, *So what?* When readers use the cognitive strategies of forming interpretations and reflecting and relating, they use expressions like: "So, the big idea is . . . ," "A conclusion I'm drawing is . . . ," "This is relevant to my life because . . . ," "Something important I learned is . . . ." Ask students: "What do you think the big idea of this story is?" Encourage them to dig deeper to uncover the message or theme of the story. Because this story is so rich, it lends itself to multiple interpretations, including: don't rush to judgment; first impressions can be deceiving; strangers aren't necessarily enemies; it is important to communicate your intentions, especially when you could be misunderstood; what unites us is more powerful than what divides us; it is important to have pride in one's heritage.

Constructing a Wall of Respect As a culminating activity, students can create their own wall of respect, as Jeff Elsten's ninth graders did at Los Amigos High School in Garden Grove, California. After reading the story, students spontaneously asked to create their own class mural to depict: their national pride, represented by the Statute of Liberty and the Twin Towers; their cultural pride, represented by Emiliano Zapata, who said, "I would rather die on my feet than live on my knees"; and their school pride, represented by their mascot, the wolf. As a finishing touch, and as a way of symbolizing their growth as readers in confidence and competence from tapping the cognitive strategies in their tool kits, students also included their portraits inside flowers blooming across the border of their wall of respect. (See Figure 2.5.)

Figure 2.5   **Wall of Respect**   (Courtesy of Jeffrey S. Elsten.)

The Reading/Writing Connection

Because the point of the tutorial is to begin to build students' declarative knowledge and
provide some initial practice in implementing the strategies, teachers may want to limit their
focus, at first, to introducing cognitive strategies within the context of reading and to repeat
this process with several texts before guiding students through an integrated reading/writing
demonstration lesson sequence like the one described in Chapter 3. However, for teachers
who wish to use this tutorial to scaffold writing instruction as well, a prompt, planning activity, rubric, and student writing samples are available on the companion website.

THE ROLE OF METACOGNITION
IN COGNITIVE STRATEGIES INSTRUCTION

Explicitly introducing students to the cognitive strategies in their mental tool kits via
a teacher-directed tutorial is just the first step in a long-term enterprise. As Alexander and
Murphy (1998) point out, "To assume that one can simply have students memorize and
routinely execute a set of strategies is to misconceive the nature of strategic processing
or executive control. Such rote applications of these procedures represents, in essence,
a true oxymoron—nonstrategic strategic processing" (p. 3). To help students move beyond
awareness of what the strategies are to the point where they acquire the ability to fluidly implement those strategies will involve ongoing demonstration by the teacher followed
by opportunities for students to practice strategy use in a variety of contexts. Further,
to develop conditional knowledge, students will need independently to select which
strategies to employ and to monitor and regulate their use. In other words, students will need
to learn to become metacognitive. Baker and Brown (1984) define metacognition as follows:

> Metacognition is a term that is now widely used to refer to the knowledge and control
> we have of our own cognitive processes. The knowledge component of metacognition is

concerned with the ability to reflect on our own cognitive processes, and it includes knowledge about ourselves as learners, about aspects of the task, and about strategy use. The control component is concerned with self-regulation of our own cognitive efforts, and it includes planning our actions, checking the outcomes of our efforts, evaluating our progress, remediating difficulties that arise, and testing and revising our strategies for learning. (Quoted in Baker, 2002, p. 77)

Along with strategy use, students must be taught to think about their thinking. "Thinking about one's thinking is the core of strategic behavior" (Paris, Lipson, & Wixon, 1983, p. 295). Teaching students to think aloud is one method to promote metacognition.

USING THINK-ALOUDS TO FOSTER METACOGNITION

According to Kucan and Beck (1997), researchers originally focused on thinking aloud as a method of inquiry, then as a mode of instruction, and more recently, as a means for encouraging social interaction:

> As a method of inquiry, the analysis of verbal reports provided by readers thinking aloud revealed the flexible and goal-directed processing of expert readers. As a mode of instruction, thinking aloud was first employed by teachers who modeled their processing during reading, making overt the strategies they were using to comprehend text. Subsequently, instructional approaches were developed to engage the students themselves in thinking aloud. (p. 1)

This line of investigation in reading is paralleled by the use of think-aloud protocols in writing (Flower & Hayes, 1981a; Scardamalia, Bereiter, Steinbach, 1984).

In his book *Improving Comprehension with Think-Aloud Strategies,* Jeff Wilhelm (2001) describes the following procedure for implementing think-alouds in the classroom:

- Step 1: Choose a short selection of text (or a short text) that will be interesting to students which is challenging and could present some difficulty if read independently;

- Step 2: Decide on a few strategies to highlight and explain to students what a think-aloud is, why you are modeling, and how these strategies will be helpful to them;

- Step 3: State your purpose for reading the specific selection and ask students to pay attention to the strategies you select so they can explain what, why, how, and when you used them;

- Step 4: Read the text aloud to students and think-aloud as you do so;

- Step 5: Have students underline the words and phrases that helped you use a strategy;

- Step 6: Ask them to make a list of the strategies you used and the verbal cues that prompted strategy use;*

- Step 7: Ask students to use other situations (real world and reading situations) in which they could use these same strategies;

- Step 8: Reinforce the think-aloud with follow-up lessons. (pp. 42–51)

The activity sequence that I developed to introduce students to the think-aloud shares with Wilhelm's eight steps the goal of making strategic knowledge visible and available to students and heightening their emotional and cognitive engagement. However, my initial approach is somewhat more inductive and puts more emphasis on the reading/writing connection.

Note: In "The War of the Wall," the expression "eyes full of sky" is a character-interpretation cue that causes readers to infer that the painter lady's head is in the clouds. In "The Stolen Party" in Chapter 9, the repeated reference to the monkey is a cue that the animal is a symbol.

METACOGNITION WORKSHOP: TEACHING STUDENTS TO REFLECT ON THEIR MEANING-MAKING PROCESSES

I developed the following activity sequence after attending an informative three-day training session for California Writing Project Directors and Teacher/ Consultants presented by the Strategic Literacy Initiative (WestEd) and delivered by two of the authors of *Reading for Understanding* (1999), Christine Cziko and Cindy Greenleaf. The Play-Doh activity that initiates my workshops was adapted from the work of Christine Cziko, and Thomas Lux's poem "The Voice You Hear When You Read Silently" was shared during the training. The original Play-Doh activity is posted at www.wested.org/strategicliteracy (click on Resources tab/ Resources for Teachers/Making Thinking Visible with Animal Creations).

The Play-Doh Demonstration

Begin by explaining to the class that you are going to make a creature out of Play-Doh that will stand up independently, and that while you are constructing this creature you will be thinking out loud—not explaining to the class how to make the creature but just verbally articulating what is going on inside your head. Before beginning, ask a student to (or have a fellow teacher) write down some of your thinking-out-loud statements on a transparency. Set a kitchen timer for three minutes. Get ready. Go! The self-talk transcript might look something like this:

> I think I'm going to make one of those elephants with the big ears like Dumbo.
>
> Let's see, I'll need to break this up into three pieces for the head, body, and tail.
>
> Whoops! I forgot the trunk, so four pieces. I wonder why elephants are called
>
> pachyderms? Derm means skin. Hmm. Maybe it means
>
> thick skin. Geez. This guy is looking more like Mickey
>
> Mouse than Dumbo. Better try reshaping those ears.

And so forth.

After you have completed your Play-Doh creature, divide students into pairs. In two three-minute sessions, one student will make the creature while the other writes down what he or she says and vice-versa.

Introducing the Concept of Think-Alouds
Explain that what you were doing as you created your animal and shared what was going on inside your head is called a think-aloud. Teachers use think-alouds to make visible for students the thinking processes involved in solving a problem and/or constructing meaning.

Labeling the Cognitive Strategies
Draw students' attention to the fact that while you were thinking aloud you were

Mirella Fuentes, an eighth grader at McFadden Intermediate School in Santa Ana, California, constructs her Play-Doh creature.

tapping the cognitive strategies in your mental tool kit. Put Figure 2.3 of the tool kit up on a transparency and remind them of all of the strategies at their disposal. Then, put up the transparency of your think-aloud statements and working with input from the students, label them. You may want to use abbreviations, as in the examples below:

Planning and Goal Setting—PGS	Adopting an Alignment—AA
Tapping Prior Knowledge—TPK	Forming Interpretations—FI
Asking Questions—AQ	Monitoring—M
Making Predictions—MP	Analyzing Author's Craft—AAC
Constructing the Gist—CG	Clarifying Understanding—CU
Visualizing—V	Revising Meaning—RM
Making Connections—MC	Reflecting and Relating—RR
Summarizing—S	Evaluating—E

PGS   TPK   V MC
I think I'm going to make one of those elephants with the big ears like Dumbo. Let's
  PGS
see, I'll need to break this up into three pieces for the head, body, and tail. Whoops! I
   RM   AQ
forgot the trunk, so four pieces. I wonder why elephants are called pachyderms? Derm
  TPK   MP/FI   V/E
means skin. Hmm. Maybe it means thick skin. Geez. This guy is looking more like
        RM
Mickey Mouse than Dumbo. Better try reshaping those ears.

Schoenbach and colleagues (1999) note, "Once students have seen teachers model strategies, making them visible through the think-aloud process, they can begin to practice thinking aloud strategically themselves" (p. 77). Have student partners work together to review the notes that they have taken during the Play-Doh activity and to label the cognitive strategies tapped in each other's think-alouds. As Baker (2002) points out, social interaction, both between expert and novice and between peers, is an "important mediator of metacognitive development" (p. 78).

Reinforcing the Tool Kit Analogy   Reinforce the tool kit analogy by saying: "We have just constructed an animal out of Play-Doh and then labled the cognitive strategies we used to solve this problem. When we read and write we are also constructing something. We use the strategies in our mental tool kits to construct meaning either inside our heads as we read or on the page as we write."

Talking to Ourselves inside Our Heads   Explain that when we read and write, we often talk to ourselves inside our heads. This is not only normal, it is desirable. Read the poem, "The Voice You Hear When You Read Silently" by Thomas Lux, reprinted in Figure 2.6. If your students have little prior knowledge or schema for responding to the word "barn," you might want to ask what they picture when they think of a barn and read E. B. White's description of the barn Wilbur lives in from *Charlotte's Web,* which is reprinted in Prewriting Activity 2 of The Memory Snapshot Paper in Chapter 9.

From Think-Aloud to Write-Aloud

Tell students that it is important to tune in to the voices inside our heads. However, since we can't always talk out loud as we read and have someone record what we say, it's important to

Figure 2.6   **The Voice You Hear When You Read Silently** (*Source:* "The Voice You Hear When You Read Silently," from *New and Selected Poems, 1975–1995* by Thomas Lux. Copyright © 1997 by Thomas Lux. Reprinted by permission of Houghton Mifflin Company. All rights reserved.)

Is not silent, it is a speaking-
out-loud voice in your head: it is *spoken,*
a voice is saying it
as you read. It's the writer's words,
of course, in a literary sense
his or her *voice,* but the sound
of that voice is the sound of your voice.
Not the sound your friends know
or the sound of a tape played back
but your voice
caught in the dark cathedral
of your skull, your voice heard
by an internal ear informed by internal abstracts
and what you know by feeling,
having felt. It is your voice
saying, for example, the word barn
that the writer wrote
but the barn you say
is a barn you know or knew. The voice
in your head, speaking as you read,
never says anything neutrally—some people
hated the barn they knew,
some people love the barn they know
so you hear the word loaded
and a sensory constellation
is lit: horse-gnawed stalls,
hayloft, black heat tape wrapping
a water pipe, a slippery
spilled chirr of oats from a split sack,
the bony, filthy haunches of cows . . .
And barn is only a noun—no verb
or subject has entered into the sentence yet!
The voice you hear when you read to yourself
Is the clearest voice: you speak it
speaking to you.

learn to go through this process silently and to make our thinking visible by writing thoughts down on paper. We might call this a write-aloud. Explain that you will be combining the think-aloud and write-aloud strategies to demonstrate what goes on in your head as you read a poem.

Put "The Writer" up on a transparency. ("The Writer" is reprinted on the opening page of Chapter 9.) Read the entire poem out loud first to construct the gist. Then read the poem stanza by stanza verbally articulating your thoughts and recording them in marginal notations.

Figure 2.7 Sample Write-Aloud (*Source:* "The Writer" from *The Mind-Reader,* Copyright © by Richard Wilbur, reprinted by permission of Harcourt, Inc.)

The Writer
by Richard Wilbur

In her room at the prow of the house
Where light breaks, and the windows
    are tossed with linden,
My daughter is writing a story.
I pause in the stairwell, hearing
From her shut door a commotion of
    typewriter-keys
Like a chain hauled over a gunwale.

Young as she is, the stuff
Of her life is a great cargo, and some
    of it heavy:
I wish her a lucky passage.

> Nautical metaphor
> AAC

> So, it's about the writing process but also about parenting CG/FI

> What's linden?
> M/AQ

> More boat imagery
> AAC

> Like Sylvia Plath
> MC

> Only luck?
> E

> Life is a journey
> FI

After you have completed this process, invite students to help you label the cognitive strategies you have tapped. Figure 2.7 is a sample of the marginal notes and cognitive strategies that might be accessed for the first two stanzas.

Think Aloud/Write Aloud: After reading the poem through once this is a sample of self-talk you might model for the students:

> OK. So the poem is about the writing process and a girl who is composing in fits and starts but it also seems to be about parenting and the need to let your children learn life's lessons on their own. I'll read stanza by stanza to look deeper. "In her room at the prow of the house . . ." That's interesting. Wilbur is using a nautical metaphor, comparing the house to a boat. "Where light breaks and the windows are tossed with linden." I don't know what linden is. I should look it up. *(After looking in the dictionary . . .)* OK, it's a type of shade tree. So, I'm picturing dappled light filtering into the room. "My daughter is writing a story/ I pause in the stairwell, hearing/ From her shut door a commotion of typewriter-keys/ Like a chain hauled over a gunwale." I'm not entirely sure what a gunwale is but I know it's part of a boat. So, the author seems to be saying that the daughter is on some kind of journey. She must be writing something personal, because it says, "Young as she is, the stuff/Of her life is a great cargo, and some of it heavy." That reminds me of that poem "Tulips" by Sylvia Plath where she calls herself a thirty-year-old cargo boat. So, I guess the heavy cargo is the burdens of life. That's weird. I assume the speaker is her father. I would expect him to wish her more than luck as she grows up.

After the teacher models, it is time for the students to practice. "Old Horse," which is reprinted in *Strategic Reading: Guiding Students to Lifelong Literacy* (Wilhelm, Baker, & Dube, 2001; pp. 74–76), about a teacher and a student who are objects of teasing, lends itself well to this exercise, as does "The Stolen Party," which is reprinted in Chapter 9. For the initial practice with learning to write marginal notes and labeling cognitive strategies, I suggest that students combine the think-aloud and write-aloud and alternate every other page, having one talk and the other write down what is said. After the story is completed, they can go back and label their cognitive strategies.

Writing about Your Thinking

Once students have become familiar enough with the cognitive strategies that they can iden- tify what acts of mind they are engaging in, the term *metacognition* will make more sense to them. Explain that they have been engaging in metacognition—thinking about their thinking. Share Baker and Brown's (1984) definition of metacognition to emphasize the importance of not only reflecting on our own cognitive processes but also being able to monitor and regu- late their use. Propose that one way to think deeply about our thinking is to write about the process we go through and the cognitive strategies we tap as we make sense of a text we are reading or writing. Share a written model of the process you went through to understand and interpret the poem you modeled. My description of my process of making meaning from "The Writer" is available on the companion website.

Stress that each person's process is different and because each person brings diverse expe- riences to their interaction with the text, interpretations will also vary. Therefore, it is important for each student to write his or her metacognitive reflection independently. Here is a learning log entry by Czara Heath, a sixth grader at Thurston Middle School in Laguna Beach, Califor- nia, about what she had to think about in order to make sense of "The Stolen Party" (see Chap- ter 9). Notice how familiar and comfortable she is with the cognitive strategies in her tool kit.

■   I started out by asking a lot of questions like "I wonder why her mother is so mad?" and "What has the monkey got to do with the story?" The beginning of the story threw me off be- cause when it started Rosaura was at the party and then she was back at home with her mom. That was confusing. I had to use monitoring to figure out that the beginning was a flashback. I predicted that the mom wouldn't let Rosaura go the party but she surprised me and let her go. I adopted an alignment with Rosaura because her mom seemed so mean at first. Also, I've been to a party where there was a girl who was a big brat and was snobby to me. I really could visualize when Rosaura kicked that blonde girl in the shin. I predicted that the monkey would be stolen but I was wrong about that.

At first I thought it was a stupid story because I didn't understand what was going on. But then I started to form the interpetation that Rosaura was really at the party not to have fun but to work and help out. I didn't totally get that until the very end. I really could see that in my mind. Why did Señora Ines call Rosaura her pet? I'm also still not totally sure why the title is "The Stolen Party." But the big idea I got was that Rosaura was really at the party not to have fun but as more of a maid like her mother.

Much like our mature reader and writer, Tim and Cris, in Chapter 1, Czara is making visible for herself what her composing process is like as she makes meaning from a text. Be- coming aware of her process and the acts of mind she engages in will help Czara understand how she uses strategies to complete a task so that she can "take over control of the task" (Langer & Applebee, 1986, p. 188) from the teacher and apply what she knows to new situa- tions. Czara's important questions at the end of her entry should also tell her teacher, Chris Byron, that her job as an instructional scaffolder is not over. This student, and many others, could not grasp the full import of the story without help from the senior member of their in- terpretive community, the teacher, who can now guide the class in revisiting the text.

To Sum Up

Students need to acquire three kinds of knowledge in order to be strategic: declarative knowledge that experienced readers and writers tap cognitive strategies to make sense of and with texts and knowledge of what those strategies are; procedural knowledge of how to implement these strategies; and conditional knowledge of when to apply strategies and why they are effective. Teachers can introduce students to the cognitive strategies in their mental tool kits by designing a tutorial in which they explicitly introduce strategies and model their use within the context of a genuine meaning making activity such as reading a high interest text. Since conditional knowledge, which is metacognitive knowledge, is essential to create the motivation or disposition to use cognitive strategies, the teacher should provide opportunities for students to work together to think aloud, to write marginal notes, and to label the cognitive strategies they accessed. Writing independent metacognitive reflections about their processes of meaning construction will also help students to become attuned to themselves as learners and to internalize strategy use.

Learning Log Reflection

Block and Pressley (2002) note that the first step in becoming a strategic teacher is to develop declarative, procedural, and conditional knowledge of the role of cognitive strategies in your own process of meaning construction. Pick a challenging text and, with a partner, engage in the activity sequence described in this chapter. Then, write about your process and what you learned about strategy use. Pressley (2002) also asks, "How can we develop thought-filled adaptive teaching episodes so that strategies can be described sensibly and meaningfully to students?" (p. 6). How well do you think this chapter responds to Pressley's question?

Notes/Reactions

The War of the Wall

by Toni Cade Bambara

Me and Lou had no time for courtesies. We were late for school. So we just flat out told the painter lady to quit messing with the wall. It was our wall, and she had no right coming into our neighborhood painting on it. Stirring in the paint bucket and not even looking at us, she mumbled something about Mr. Eubanks, the barber, giving her permission. That had nothing to do with it as far as we were concerned. We've been pitching pennies against that wall since we were little kids. Old folks have been dragging their chairs out to sit in the shade of the wall for years. Big kids have been playing handball against the wall since so-called integration when the crazies 'cross town poured cement in our pool so we couldn't use it. I'd sprained my neck one time boosting my cousin Lou up to chisel Jimmy Lyons's name into the wall when we found out he was never coming home from the war in Vietnam to take us fishing.

"If you lean close," Lou said, leaning hipshot against her beat-up car, "you'll get a whiff of bubble gum and kids' sweat. And that'll tell you something—that this wall belongs to the kids of Taliaferro Street." I thought Lou sounded very convincing. But the painter lady paid us no mind. She just snapped the brim of her straw hat down and hauled her bucket up the ladder.

"You're not even from around here," I hollered up after her. The license plates on her old piece of car said "New York." Lou dragged me away because I was about to grab hold of that ladder and shake it. And then we'd really be late for school.

When we came from school, the wall was slick with white. The painter lady was running string across the wall and taping it here and there. Me and Lou leaned against the gum ball machine outside the pool hall and watched . . .

The Morris twins crossed the street, hanging back at the curb next to the beat-up car. The twin with the red ribbons was hugging a jug of cloudy lemonade. The one with yellow ribbons was holding a plate of dinner away from her dress. The painter lady began snapping the strings. The blue chalk dust measured off halves and quarters up and down and sideways too. Lou was about to say how hip it all was, but I dropped my book satchel on his toes to remind him we were at war.

Some good aromas were drifting our way from the plate leaking pot likker onto the Morris girl's white socks. I could tell from where I stood that under the tinfoil was baked ham, collard greens, and candied yams. And knowing Mrs. Morris, who sometimes bakes for my mama's restaurant, a slab of buttered cornbread was probably up under there too, sopping up some of the pot likker. Me and Lou rolled our eyes, wishing somebody would send us some dinner. But the painter lady didn't even turn around. She was pulling the strings down and prying bits of tape loose.

Side Pocket came strolling out of the pool hall to see what Lou and me were studying so hard. He gave the painter lady the once-over, checking out her painted-spattered jeans, her chalky T-shirt, her floppy-brimmed straw hat.

"Watcha got there, Sweetheart?" he asked the twin with plate.

"Suppah," she said, all soft and country-like. "For her," the one with the jug added, jerking her chin toward the painter lady's back.

Still she didn't turn around. She was rearing back on her heels, her hands jammed into her back pockets, her face squinched up like the masterpiece she had in mind was taking shape on the wall by magic. We could have been gophers crawled up into a rotten hollow for all she cared. She didn't even say hello to anybody. Lou was muttering something about how great her concentration was. I butt him with my hip, and his elbow slid off the gum machine.

"Good evening," Side Pocket said in his best ain't-I-fine voice. But the painter lady was moving from the milk crate to the stepstool to the ladder, moving up and down fast, scribbling all over the wall like a crazy person. We looked at Side Pocket. He looked at the twins. The twins looked at us. The painter lady . . . didn't even look where she was stepping. And for a minute there, hanging on the ladder to reach a far spot, she looked like she was going to tip right over.

"Ahh," Side Pocket cleared his throat and moved fast to catch the ladder. "These young ladies here have brought you some supper."

"Ma'am?" The twins stepped forward. Finally the painter turned around, her eyes "full of sky," as my grandmama would say. Then she stepped down like she was in a trance. She wiped her hands on her jeans as the Morris twins offered up the plate and the jug. She rolled back the tinfoil, then wagged her head as though something terrible was on the plate.

"Thank your mother very much," she said, sounding like her mouth was full of sky too. "I've brought my own dinner along." And then, without even excusing herself, she went back up the ladder, drawing on the wall in a wild way. Side Pocket whistled one of those oh-brother breathy whistles and went back into the pool hall. The Morris twins shifted their weight from one foot to the other, then crossed the street and went home. Lou had to drag me away, I was so mad. . . .

Later that night, while me and Lou were in the back doing our chores, we found out that the painter lady was a liar. She came into the restaurant and leaned against the glass of the steam table, talking about how starved she was. I was scrubbing pots and Lou was chopping onions, but we could hear her through the service window. She was asking Mama was that a ham hock in the greens, and was that a neck bone in the pole beans, and were there any vegetables cooked without meat, especially pork.

"I don't care who your spiritual leader is," Mama said in that way of hers. "If you eat in the community, sistuh, you gonna eat pig by-and-by, one way or t'other."

Me and Lou were cracking up in the kitchen, and several customers at the counter were clearing their throats waiting for Mama to really fix her wagon for not speaking to the elders when she came in. The painter lady took a stool at the counter and went right on with her questions. Was there cheese in the baked macaroni, she wanted to know? Were there eggs in the salad? Was it honey or sugar in the iced tea? Mama was fixing Pop Johnson's plate. And every time the painter lady asked a fool question, Mama would dump another spoonful of rice on the pile. She was tapping her foot and heating up in a dangerous way. . . . Me and Lou peeked through the service window, wondering what planet the painter lady came from. Who ever heard of baked macaroni without cheese, or potato salad without eggs?

When Mama finally took her order, the starving lady all of a sudden couldn't make up her mind whether she wanted a vegetable plate or fish and a salad. She finally settled on the broiled trout and a tossed salad. But just when Mama reached for a plate to serve her, the painter lady leaned over the counter with her finger all up in the air.

"Excuse me," she said, "One more thing." Mama was holding the plate like a Frisbee, tapping that foot, one hand on her hip. "Can I get raw beets in that tossed salad?"

"You will get," Mama said, leaning her face close to the painter lady's, "whatever Lou back there tossed. Now sit down." And the painter lady sat back down on her stool and shut right up.

. . . Me and Lou tried to get Mama to open fire on the painter lady. But Mama said that seeing as how she was from the North, you couldn't expect her to have any manners. Then Mama said she was sorry she'd been so impatient with the woman because she seemed like a decent person and was simply trying to stick to a very strict diet. Me and Lou didn't want to hear that. Who did that lady think she was, coming into our neighborhood and taking over our wall?

"Wellllll," Mama drawled, . . . "it's hard on an artist, ya know. They can't always get people to look at their work. So she's just doing her work in the open, that's all."

Me and Lou definitely did not want to hear that. Why couldn't she set up an easel downtown or draw on the sidewalk in her own neighborhood? . . .

All weekend long, me and Lou tried to scheme up ways to recapture our wall. Daddy and Mama said they were sick of hearing about it. Grandmama turned up the TV to drown us out. On the late news was a story about the New York subways. When a train came roaring into the station all covered from top to bottom, windows too, with writings and drawings done with spray paint, me and Lou slapped five. Mama said it was too bad kids in New York had nothing better to do than spray paint all over the trains. Daddy said that in the cities, even grown-ups wrote all over the trains and buildings too. Daddy called it "graffiti." Grandmama called it a shame.

We couldn't wait to get out of school on Monday. We couldn't find any black spray paint anywhere. But in a junky hardware store downtown we found a can of white epoxy paint, the kind you touch up old refrigerators with when they get splotchy and peely. We spent our whole allowance on it. . . .

When we reached the corner of Taliaferro and Fifth, it looked like a block party or something. Half the neighborhood was gathered on the sidewalk in front of the wall. I looked at the bag with epoxy and wondered how we were going to work our scheme. The painter lady's car was nowhere in sight. But there were too many people standing around to do anything. Side Pocket and his buddies were leaning on their cue sticks, hunching each other. Daddy was there with a lineman he catches a ride with on Mondays. Mrs. Morris had her arms flung around the shoulders of the twins on either side of her. Mama was talking with some of her customers, many of them with napkins still at the throat. Mr. Eubanks came out of the barber shop, followed by a man in a striped poncho, half his face shaved, the other half full of foam.

"She really did it, didn't she?" Mr. Eubanks huffed out his chest. Lots of folks answered right quick that she surely did when they saw the straight razor in his hand.

Mama beckoned us over. And then we saw it. The wall. Reds, greens, figures outlined in black. Swirls of purple and orange. Storms of blues and yellows. It was something. I recognized some of the faces right off. There was Martin Luther King, Jr. And there was a man with glasses on and his mouth open like he was laying down a heavy rap. Daddy came up alongside and reminded us that he was Minister Malcolm X. The serious woman with a rifle I knew was Harriet Tubman because my grandmama has pictures of her all over the house. And I knew Mrs. Fannie Lou Hamer 'cause a signed photograph of her hangs in the restaurant next to the calendar.

Then I let my eyes follow what looked like a vine. It trailed past a man with a horn, a woman with a big white flower in her hair, a handsome dude in a tuxedo seated at a piano, and a man with a goatee holding a book. When I looked more closely, I realized that what had looked like flowers were really faces. One face with yellow petals looked just like Frieda Morris. One with red petals looked just like Hattie Morris. I could hardly believe my eyes.

"Notice," Side Pocket said, stepping close to the wall with his cue stick like a classroom pointer. "These are the flags of liberation," he said in a voice I'd never heard him use before. We all stepped closer while he pointed and spoke. "Red, black, and green," he said, his pointer falling on the leaflike flags of the vine. "Our liberation flag. And here Ghana, there Tanzania. Guinea-Bissau, Angola, Mozambique." Side Pocket sounded very tall, as though he'd been waiting all his life to give this lesson.

Mama tapped us on the shoulder and pointed to a high section of the wall. There was a fierce-looking man with his arms crossed against his chest guarding a bunch of children. His muscles bulged, and he looked a lot like my daddy. One kid was looking at a row of books. Lou hunched me 'cause the kid looked like me. The one that looked like Lou was spinning a globe on the tip of his finger like a basketball. There were other kids there with microscopes and compasses. And the more I looked, the more it looked like the fierce man was not so much guarding the kids as defending their right to do what they were doing.

Then Lou gasped and dropped the paint bag and ran forward, running his hands over a rainbow. He had to tiptoe and stretch to do it, it was so high. I couldn't breathe either. The painter lady had found the chisel marks and had painted Jimmy Lyons's name in a rainbow.

"Read the inscription, honey," Mrs. Morris said, urging little Frieda forward. She didn't have to urge much. Frieda marched right up, bent down, and in loud voice that made everybody quit oohing and ahhing and listen, she read,

To the People of Taliaferro Street
I Dedicate This Wall of Respect
Painted in Memory of My Cousin
Jimmy Lyons

Source: Adapted from "The War of the Wall," from *Deep Sightings and Rescue Missions* by Toni Cade Bambara, copyright © 1996 by The Estate of Toni Cade Bambara. Used by permission of Pantheon Books, a division of Random House, Inc.

Integrating Reading and Writing Instruction through Scaffolded Demonstration Lessons

One of the early and influential researchers on thinking aloud as a mode of instruction, Beth Davey (1983) advises teachers, "After initial experience with these modeling activities, move to ample practice with daily school materials and tasks. Integrate these thinking strategies with selected reading lessons and content reading" (p. 46). Because, as we learned in Chapter 1, "reading and writing in combination have the potential to contribute in powerful ways to thinking" (Tierney et al., 1989, p. 166), this chapter will explore how to use instructional scaffolding to embed thinking strategies into integrated reading and writing instruction.

Langer and Applebee (1986) have argued that instructional scaffolding is an especially effective model for planning and analyzing instruction in reading and writing. In a scaffolded approach, the teacher analyzes the language task to be carried out by the students, determines the difficulties the task is likely to pose when students undertake it independently, and designs guided practice activities in strategies that enable students to complete the task successfully. Through repeated modeling and successive opportunities to practice, students eventually internalize the strategies so that they no longer rely on the teacher for guidance but can select, apply, and regulate the use of strategies as autonomous learners.

COMPONENTS OF EFFECTIVE INSTRUCTIONAL SCAFFOLDING

Langer and Applebee propose five components of effective instructional scaffolding. First, effective instructional scaffolding gives students *ownership* by providing "the room to say something of their own in their writing or in the interpretations they draw in their reading" (p. 185). Students must have a sense of why they are doing what they are doing and see "a point to the task, beyond simple obedience to the teacher's demands" (p. 185). Second, effective instructional scaffolding is characterized by *appropriateness.* It builds on the reading,

Figure 3.1   **Components of Effective Instructional Scaffolding** (*Source:* Adapted by permission from Langer and Applebee, 1986.)

> Effective instructional scaffolding involves:
>
> • Ownership: Providing students with a sense of purposefulness.
>
> • Appropriateness: Selecting tasks that build upon students' existing reading, thinking, and writing abilities and that will stretch students intellectually.
>
> • Structure: Making the structure of the task clear and guiding students through the specific task so that it can be applied in other contexts.
>
> • Collaboration: Promoting collaboration among students and between students and the teacher so that meaning can be constructed and shared collaboratively.
>
> • Internalization: Transferring control to the students as they gain competence and can apply the strategies independently.

thinking, and writing abilities students already have and stretches learners intellectually—prompting them to work in their zone of proximal development, "defined essentially as tasks that a learner can complete with appropriate help, but would be unable to complete unaided" (p. 186). Third, it is essential to make the *structure* of the task clear and to guide students through the specific task at hand in a way that enables them to apply the strategies in new contexts. Fourth, effective instructional scaffolding promotes *collaboration* among students and between students and the teacher so that knowledge can be constructed and shared interactively. Finally, the goal of the scaffolding approach is *internalization*—that is, the transfer of control from teacher to student as the students "gain competence in the new tasks" (p. 187). Figure 3.1 depicts the components of effective instructional scaffolding.

REDUCING THE CONSTRAINTS ON STUDENT READERS AND WRITERS

The purpose of instructional scaffolding and other guided practice models is to reduce the constraints on student readers and writers in order to make the task more manageable and increase the opportunities for success. Flower and Hayes (1980) have coined the term "juggling constraints" to capture the dynamics of composing. They envision the writer (and, by analogy, the reader) as simultaneously juggling "a number of demands being made on conscious attention" (p. 32). To depict the complexity of the composing process, they liken the cognitive demands on a writer to those of a busy switchboard operator:

• She has two important calls on hold. (Don't forget that idea.)
• Four lights just started flashing. (They demand immediate attention or they'll be lost.)
• A party of five wants to be hooked up together. (They need to be connected somehow.)
• A party of two thinks they've been incorrectly connected. (Where do they go?)
• And throughout this complicated process of remembering, retrieving, and connecting, the operator's voice must project calmness, confidence, and complete control. (p. 33)

For inexperienced readers and writers, juggling too many constraints can cause "cognitive overload" (p. 33). Under too much strain, students' intellectual circuits can shut down.

When designing and scaffolding guided practice activities, it is important to keep the following constraints in mind and to devise ways to reduce the cognitive strain on student readers and writers:

Cognitive Constraints. Students can be constrained by the knowledge they bring to the task—especially if that knowledge is limited. To lessen the cognitive constraints, the teacher must scaffold activities that help students tap and mobilize existing knowledge as well as construct new knowledge.

Linguistic Constraints. Students may not possess the language adequate to understand or produce text. To lessen these constraints, the teacher must design activities that create a language-rich environment for students to draw and build upon.

Communicative Constraints. Students are often constrained by the audience for whom they perceive they are reading or writing—which is, in most cases, the teacher. To reduce these constraints, the teacher can broaden the audiences students write to and for, downplay his or her role as assessor, enlist students as peer responders to give and receive feedback on each other's texts, and foster more self-monitoring and self-reflection on the part of the students.

Contextual Constraints. Contextual constraints involve the circumstances or context in which reading and writing take place. If students are to produce multiple-draft readings and writings, the teacher must adopt a "less is more" philosophy and allow for the extended time necessary for ideas to evolve. Further, rather than focusing exclusively on the finished product, the teacher should value all of the facets of the composing process.

Textual Constraints. Students bring to the mental or written texts they are composing the influence of the content and the form of all the prior texts they have read or written. These texts can powerfully influence the student's composing process. An experienced, well practiced student will have a wide array of options to choose from, whereas a less experienced student will work from a limited range of resources. To lessen textual constraints, the teacher should expose students to a rich array of models to enrich their textual repertoire. (Adapted from Frederiksen & Dominic, 1981, pp. 17–20)

Affective Constraints. Researchers tend to zero in on the cognitive constraints that readers and writers must deal with when they compose—but the affective constraints students face when they do not find school reading and writing tasks to be meaningful can loom just as large. Indeed, lacking the confidence, the willingness, or the motivation to undertake a challenging reading or writing task can be as debilitating as lacking the capacity to do so. To lessen these constraints, teachers must actively seek to make reading and writing instruction meaningful by building in as many concrete, personal, and interactive activities as possible and by helping to make the texts their students read and write accessible, relevant, and engaging.

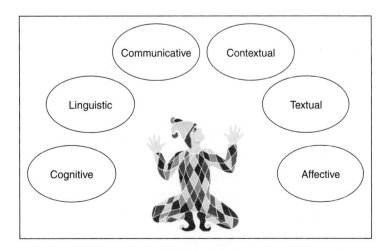

REINFORCING THE READING/WRITING CONNECTION THROUGH SCAFFOLDED DEMONSTRATION LESSONS

The aim of the full-length demonstration lessons showcased in this book is to reduce the constraints on students by taking them through a sequence of guided practice activities that make visible what it is that experienced readers and writers do when they compose. The term *demonstration* has been chosen with some care. One definition of the term is "a description or explanation, as of a process, illustrated by examples" (Random House, 1983, p. 531). Hence, the demonstration lessons are intended to offer a *model* for how to provide students with much-needed practice in the cognitive strategies experienced readers and writers use, not to present a rigid formula for what to do in what order. As Madeline Hunter (1989) rightly points out, "*There are no absolutes in teaching!* There is no substitute for a teacher's considered judgment . . . about *these* students in *this* learning situation at *this* moment in time" (pp. 17–18). The intent is that as you read through this book, you will use the individual strategies and the scaffolded lessons as a point of departure for developing your own curricula, suitable for your particular students and learning situation.

The format for the demonstration lessons is delineated in Figure 3.2. It integrates the reading and writing process rather than depicting them separately. This is not to imply that reading should always precede writing or that all writing should be based on an external text. Students need opportunities to read for the sake of reading and to write out of personal experience. However, in light of the fact that ample models of the reading process and of the writing process are available in the professional literature, this model attempts to reinforce the reading/writing connection. Further, it capitalizes on Tierney and Shanahan's (1991) work showing that reading and writing when taught together engage students in the use of a greater variety of cognitive strategies than when they are taught separately; and it aims to operationalize these researchers' suggestion that "students can be taught to use reading and writing together in an intentional strategic fashion" (p. 274). Many teachers conceptualize and design language arts lessons in fifty-minute or daily increments. The demonstration lessons in this book are more process-oriented and are constructed as a sequence of activities that might take several days or even several weeks. A copy of the UCI Department of Education's hourly/daily secondary lesson plan form is available on the companion website.

Flower and Hayes (1980) have observed that the stage process model (which progresses in a before, during, and after sequence) can make composing sound as if it can be accomplished in a "tidy sequence of steps," like baking a cake or filling out a tax return, whereas in reality composing is a complex act that involves juggling constraints and working on "cognitive overload" (p. 33). And it is true that the cognitive process model, in which any number of mental operations may be accessed at any time during composing, may be the most accurate representation of how readers and writers actually construct meaning from or with texts. However, the stage process model serves as a useful pedagogical tool for scaffolding guided practice activities. It provides students with a language with which to talk about the reading and writing process, and it helps break up a task into manageable increments that allow "think time" for ideas and expression to evolve. Given that the most experienced readers and writers make meaning recursively, it is incumbent upon the teacher to make the process from conception to completion less linear by building in time for students to pause, monitor, evaluate, and reflect—in other words, to go back to go forward.

Using the stage process model as a framework, the demonstration lessons provided here present an extensive lesson scaffold that moves through a sequence of guided practice activi-

Figure 3.2   **Demonstration Lesson Format**

<table>
<tr><td colspan="2" align="center">**Title**</td></tr>
<tr><td>**Overview:**</td><td>A brief abstract of the content of the lesson.</td></tr>
<tr><td>**Objectives:**</td><td>The reading, thinking, and writing tasks to be undertaken by the students.</td></tr>
<tr><td colspan="2" align="center">**The Process**</td></tr>
<tr><td>**Prereading:**</td><td>Activities that set the stage for reading, including setting purposes for reading, activating prior knowledge, and creating motivation.</td></tr>
<tr><td>**During Reading:**</td><td>Activities that guide students through the text, helping them to visualize, make connections, form preliminary interpretations, and revise meaning.</td></tr>
<tr><td>**Postreading:**</td><td>Activities that help students go back into the text to explore it more analytically, examine writer's craft, and deepen interpretations.</td></tr>
<tr><td>**Prewriting:**</td><td>Activities that create a knowledge base to make the writing task accessible to diverse learners, generate ideas and motivation, and provide practice in the key cognitive tasks and writing skills called for in the prompt.</td></tr>
<tr><td>**Prompt:**</td><td>A description of the specific writing task.</td></tr>
<tr><td>**Planning:**</td><td>Activities that provide a structure for accomplishing the writing task and that promote the formulation of a writing plan.</td></tr>
<tr><td>**Writing:**</td><td>The first draft, which aims for fluency—for discovery and expression of content rather than refinement of thought.</td></tr>
<tr><td>**Sharing:**</td><td>Giving and receiving feedback regarding the impact of the writing on a reader or readers.</td></tr>
<tr><td>**Revising:**</td><td>Rethinking, reseeing, reshaping the content and clarity of the first draft, incorporating the feedback from sharing.</td></tr>
<tr><td>**Editing:**</td><td>Proofreading the surface features of the writing to ensure that it conforms to the conventions of written English.</td></tr>
<tr><td>**Evaluation:**</td><td>Judging the writing to determine if it satisfies the writer and the reader and meets the criteria designated in the evaluation rubric.</td></tr>
<tr><td>**Reflection:**</td><td>An invitation to step back and think about the process of reading, thinking, and writing and the lessons learned.</td></tr>
</table>

ties from prereading through postreading and from prewriting through evaluation. The centerpiece of the scaffold is prompted writing—that is, writing that is framed by the teacher. Note that in the English classroom not all reading should be teacher-guided, nor all writing teacher-prompted. Self-selected reading and writing are essential to student growth and engagement (see Chapter 14). The point of scaffolding is to help students practice and internalize cognitive strategies and to expose them to a wide range of texts to read and write, thus expanding their options. Langer and Applebee (1986) make the point, based on their research on literacy instruction, that teachers often fall into two categories. The first group assumes that all that is necessary is to give students a text to read or a topic to write about and students will have the resources to proceed independently. The second group assumes that every component of a new task must be "taught from scratch" (p. 186) as if the students had no resources to bring to the task. In a scaffolded approach, the teacher builds on what students do know and provides support for what they don't know. Ideally, once the students acquire an accumulating repertoire of strategies, the teacher will gradually withdraw elements of the scaffold so that students can make independent decisions about how to negotiate a reading/thinking/writing task.

Paris, Wasik, and Turner (1991) remind us that strategic readers and writers are characterized not by "the volume of tactics that they use" (p. 611) but by their careful selection of what strategies to use and by knowing when, how, and why to use them. So too, strategic teachers must exercise their professional judgment about how much scaffolding is necessary and at what points in the reading/writing process teacher guidance will be most productive. Although the demonstration lessons offer a wide and varied array of activities at each stage of the reading/writing process, thus indicating the many options available, teachers are encouraged to decide which activities to use as is; which to modify, replace, or delete entirely; and which stages of the process to highlight during any given lesson.

A DESCRIPTION OF THE
READING/WRITING LESSON FORMAT

Before we turn to our demonstration lesson, a description of each of the stages in the integrated reading/writing lesson design format is in order. The *overview* contains a brief abstract of the content of the lesson. Some of these reading/writing tasks are very open-ended; others are more narrowly focused. However, all are intended to provide students with a sense of ownership and the latitude to develop their own interpretation and voices. The *objectives* delineate the reading, thinking, and writing tasks to be undertaken by the students. The terms used to identify and describe these tasks are taken from the list shown in Figure 1.2, Cognitive Strategies: A Reader's and Writer's Tool Kit, and from a UCI Writing Project adaptation of Bloom and colleagues' "taxonomy of the cognitive domain" (1956, pp. 201–207), shown in Figure 3.3.

Tompkins (1997) notes that "the reading process does not begin as readers open a book and read the first sentence. The first stage is preparing to read" (p. 250). The *prereading* section of the demonstration lessons provides activities that set the stage for the reading, whether they are designed to enhance students' prior knowledge, set purposes for reading, spark curiosity and question asking, generate a can-do attitude, or guide students toward making inferences and elaborations while reading. Teachers must make "considered judgments," to use Madeline Hunter's term, about how much prereading is necessary and useful as an entrée into a specific text. Research shows that previewing helps students generate a more positive attitude toward reading, that activating prior knowledge influences comprehension (Paris, Wasik, & Turner, 1991, p. 611), and that setting purposes assists students in monitoring their reading (Tompkins, 1997, p. 252). However, too much teacher-guided prereading may also infringe on a student's authentic individual response to a text. On the other hand, prereading activities can hook a student and keep the student reading a text he or she might otherwise abandon as being too difficult or uninteresting. *During reading* activities guide students through the text. The judicious use of activities during reading can help students visualize, make connections, adopt an alignment, form preliminary interpretations, revise meaning, begin reflecting and relating, and so forth. As Langer and Applebee (1986) suggest, activities must be appropriate: They should assist and not bog down or overburden a student as he or she is constructing meaning, and they should prompt the student to practice tasks that he or she would be reluctant or ill prepared to undertake alone. Some of these activities should be collaborative in nature and should encourage students to develop interpretations collectively. *Postreading* activities enable students to "go back into the text to explore it more analytically" (Tompkins, 1997, p. 259). Students reread and review sections of text, confirm previous predictions, examine author's craft, ask new questions, dig deeper to en-

Figure 3.3 **Reading, Thinking, and Writing Tasks** (*Source:* Adapted from "Bloom's Taxonomy of the Cognitive Domain, 1956," from C. B. Olson, Ed., 1992, *Thinking/writing: Fostering critical thinking through writing.* Copyright © by Pearson Education. Reprinted by permission of the publisher.)

Level	Cue Words	
Knowledge *Recall* Remembering previously learned material	Observe Repeat Label/name Cluster List Record Match	Memorize Recall Recount Sort Outline (format stated) Define
Comprehension *Translate* Grasping the meaning of material	Recognize Locate Identify Restate Paraphrase Tell Describe	Report Express Explain Review Cite Document/support Summarize Precis/abstract
Application *Generalize* Using the learned material in new and concrete situations	Select Use Manipulate Sequence Organize Imitate Frame	Show/demonstrate How to Apply Dramatize Illustrate Test out/solve Imagine (information known)
Analysis *Break Down/Discover* Breaking down material into its component parts so that it may be more easily understood	Examine Classify Distinguish/differentiate Outline Map Relate to Characterize Compare/contrast	Question Research Interpret Debate/defend Refute Infer Conclude Analyze
Synthesis *Compose* Putting material together to form a new whole	Propose Plan Compose Formulate Design	Criticize Emulate Imagine/speculate Create Invent
Evaluation *Judge* Judging the value of material for a given purpose	Compare pro/con Prioritize/rank Judge Decide Rate Evaluate Predict	Criticize Argue Justify Convince Persuade Assess Value

hance interpretations, evaluate the text and their own reading process, and sometimes go beyond the text to speculate about its broader implications or to relate it to their own lives.

Tompkins (1997) calls the culminating stage in the reading process "extending" (p. 263). Building on initial and exploratory responses to the text, students extend their understanding by expressing the meaning they have constructed through projects. These projects might involve further reading, writing, discussion, drama, art, or research. In our integrated reading/writing scaffold, the extending stage of the reading process leads to a prompted writing task. Therefore, postreading activities may not only encourage looking back but also set the stage for moving forward—to extend the lesson into prewriting. *Prewriting* activities develop a knowledge base that will make the writing task accessible to a range of learners, generate ideas and motivation for writing, and provide practice in the key cognitive strategies in the writing skills called for in the *prompt*. Although the words *prompt, writing task,* and *assignment* all have the same denotative meaning of written work that someone tells the student to accomplish, the connotation of the word *prompt* is to suggest or motivate. Well-scaffolded prewriting activities should generate affective buy-in so that the students feel both well grounded in what they are asked to undertake and receptive to it. Effective prompts not only clearly address the content of the writing task but also discuss form and correctness issues.

Flower and Hayes (1981b) note that writing is a complex problem-solving process and that "myths of inspiration to the contrary, writers do not simply receive ideas but, even as they gaze out of the window, they draw on a set of mental operations or *heuristics*" (p. 40). One of the most powerful of these heuristics is planning. In the English classroom teachers often spend large amounts of time helping students prewrite—that is, generate ideas for writing. They are often baffled and frustrated when, despite their best efforts, students still agonize over the blank page, perhaps even knowing what they want to say but at a loss as to how to say it. The *planning* stage of the writing process not only guides students in continuing to generate and narrow ideas that are specific to the prompt but also provides structure: an understanding of what a particular type of writing looks and sounds like. The presentation and study of models are crucial elements in the planning process. Before the writing stage, depending on the type of writing, it is also helpful for students to formulate a writing plan—not a rigid outline that shuts out the possibility of discovery but a rough road map of where each student is headed.

During the *writing* stage students draw on their prewriting and planning activities as resources to build and move their envisionments along. In the first draft, students should aim for fluency—for the discovery and expression of content rather than the refinement of thought. It is useful to write in drafts and to move to the *sharing* stage before the final draft is completed. Students are often more willing to revise an introduction, opening scene, or full-length rough draft based on feedback while their work is in progress than after they feel they have finished. Through collaborating with others, a writer receives feedback concerning how his or her words affect the reader. As with the other stages of the process, sharing activities must be scaffolded and modeled so that feedback is descriptive and detailed rather than evaluative and sparse.

In a certain sense, revision begins even before a writer puts pen to paper as thoughts are formulated, verbalized internally, and organized. Once the writer has generated a draft and received feedback, the *revising* stage allows time to reflect upon what has been written—to rethink, resee, and reshape words and ideas. "Revision can also be seen as a juggling of constraints. Demands a writer could not consciously attend to while drafting can be considered during revision" (D'Aoust, 1992, p. 19). Research indicates that inexperienced writers perceive revision as a "rewording activity" and focus on minor lexical changes because "economy is their goal," whereas experienced writers describe their primary objective as "finding the form or shape of their argument" (Sommers, 1980, pp. 381–382). Teachers need to guide students in reconceptualizing what revision is and to differentiate it from *editing*. Experienced writers who have automatized their editing skills draft and edit, for the most part, simultaneously. But inexperienced writers who pay too much attention too soon to getting surface features right often compose so slowly that they struggle to get their thoughts down on paper. In other words, they have trouble developing fluency or voice. Setting a separate stage aside for editing gives students permission early on to attend to the content of their writing over the conventions of written English. Teachers need to value students' thinking while still holding them accountable for correctness. Papers that are error-filled do not communicate well because they distract the reader from and often obscure what is being said.

Not all student writing can or should be taken to the *evaluation* stage. But evaluation by the teacher, by peers, and by the student himself or herself helps students take a critical stance toward their work. In his synthesis of research on writing, George Hillocks (1987) identifies what he calls scales (sets of criteria for judging and revising compositions) as a "powerful" instructional method for helping students "develop better control over and under-standing of discourse knowledge" (p. 77). It is important to share the criteria by which the students' work will be evaluated early on in the writing process. Once students have practice in writing with criteria in mind, involving them in generating class writing rubrics (or crite-ria) is an important step toward helping them internalize criteria to apply independently. Be-cause there is no one way to assess writing, the demonstration lessons will model different types of scoring rubrics rather than adopting a standard grading scale. Finally, *reflection* is an important part of the reading/writing process. To encourage students to take a step back and consider their reading, thinking, and writing and the lessons learned—not only about the process and product of meaning construction but about life—the demonstration lessons will conclude with an invitation to write a learning log reflection.

STANDARDS-BASED LANGUAGE ARTS INSTRUCTION

The demonstration lesson that follows and those that appear throughout this book are aligned with national and state English language arts content standards. *The IRA/NCTE Standards for the English Language Arts* in Figure 3.4 present the current consensus among literacy teach-ers and researchers about what students should know and be able to do across the grade levels based on an expanded definition of literacy addressing six language arts: reading, writing, speaking, listening, viewing, and visually representing. They stress that the language arts learning activities are "seldom wholly discrete—'just reading,' 'just writing,' or 'just view-ing,'"—because "each medium relates directly or indirectly to every other" (NCTE/IRA, 1997, p. 7). Further, they advocate that students develop language competencies "through meaningful activities and settings, such as reading and viewing whole texts, writing and creat-ing visual images for recognizable purposes, and speaking and listening to others both within and outside the classroom" (p. 7). The demonstration lessons are designed to foster the inte-grated language arts instruction promoted by the International Reading Association and Na-tional Council of Teachers of English. They are also informed by the more specific *California English-Language Arts Content Standards,* which specify grade-level competencies in: word analysis, fluency, and systematic vocabulary development; reading comprehension; literary response and analysis; writing strategies; writing applications (genres and their characteris-tics); and written and oral language conventions. The *California English Language-Arts Con-tent Standards* have become a model for the standards established in several other states. They may be accessed at www.cde.ca.gov/be/st/ss/engmain.asp. A link to these standards is avail-able in the technology resources section of the companion website.

Figure 3.4 IRA/NCTE Standards for the English Language Arts (Copyright 1996 by the International Reading Association and the National Council of Teachers of English. Reprinted with permission.)

The vision guiding these standards is that all students must have the opportunities and resources to develop the language skills they need to pursue life's goals and to participate fully as informed, productive members of society. These standards assume that literacy growth begins before children enter school as they experience and experiment with literacy activities—reading and writing, and associating spoken words with their graphic representations. Recognizing this fact, these standards encourage the development of curriculum and instruction that make productive use of the emerging literacy abilities that children bring to school. Furthermore, the standards provide ample room for the innovation and creativity essential to teaching and learning. They are not prescriptions for particular curriculum or instruction.

Although we present these standards as a list, we want to emphasize that they are not distinct and separable; they are, in fact, interrelated and should be considered as a whole.

- Students read a wide range of print and nonprint texts to build an understanding of texts, of themselves, and of the cultures of the United States and the world; to acquire new information; to respond to the needs and demands of society and the workplace; and for personal fulfillment.

- Students read a wide range of literature from many periods in many genres to build an understanding of the many dimensions (e.g., philosophical, ethical, aesthetic) of human experience.

- Students apply a wide range of strategies to comprehend, interpret, evaluate, and appreciate texts. They draw on their prior experience, their interactions with other readers and writers, their knowledge of word meaning and of other texts, their word identification strategies, and their understanding of textual features (e.g., sound-letter correspondence, sentence structure, context, graphics).

- Students adjust their use of spoken, written, and visual language (e.g., conventions, style, vocabulary) to communicate effectively with a variety of audiences and for different purposes.

- Students employ a wide range of strategies as they write and use different writing process elements appropriately to communicate with different audiences for a variety of purposes.

- Students apply knowledge of language structure, language conventions (e.g., spelling and punctuation), media techniques, figurative language, and genre to create, critique, and discuss print and nonprint texts.

- Students conduct research on issues and interests by generating ideas and questions, and by posing problems. They gather, evaluate, and synthesize data from a variety of sources (e.g., print and non-print texts, artifacts, people) to communicate their discoveries in ways that suit their purpose and audience.

- Students use a variety of technological and informational resources (e.g., libraries, databases, computer networks, video) to gather and synthesize information and to create and communicate knowledge.

- Students develop an understanding of and respect for diversity in language use, patterns, and dialects across cultures, ethnic groups, geographic regions, and social roles.

- Students whose first language is not English make use of their first language to develop competency in the English language arts and to develop understanding of content across the curriculum.

- Students participate as knowledgeable, reflective, creative, and critical members of a variety of literacy communities.

- Students use spoken, written, and visual language to accomplish their own purposes (e.g., for learning, enjoyment, persuasion, and the exchange of information).

An 8½-x-11 copy of these standards is available on the companion website.

DEMONSTRATION LESSON

A Letter from Margot: "All Summer in a Day"

Suppose that you were teaching Ray Bradbury's short story "All Summer in a Day" and decided to ask students to assume the persona of the main character, Margot, then project themselves into the future and write a letter to Margot's former classmates about how they treated her. How would you design an instructional scaffold that would provide students with guided practice in the key cognitive strategies they would need in order to analyze the text, make their own meaning, and respond successfully to the writing task? This lesson scaffold will bring together theory and practice by illustrating how to integrate a reading/writing lesson that makes visible for students what it is that experienced readers and writers do when they compose a mental or written text.

The lesson has been adapted from one written by Meredith Ritner, a teacher from Aliso Viejo Middle School in Aliso Viejo, California, for a unit entitled "Encounters with Prejudice" in the Scott Foresman/Addison Wesley textbook series *Literature and Integrated Studies* (1997).* Although it was intended for grade 7, this lesson has been implemented successfully in both middle and high school classrooms. Because this is the first demonstration lesson to be showcased in this book, the lesson scaffold will be annotated and will provide a detailed array of guided practice activities at each stage of the reading/writing process. The terms used to identify the cognitive strategies called for in each of these activities are taken from Figure 1.2, Cognitive Strategies: A Reader's and Writer's Tool Kit, and from a UCI Writing Project adaptation of Bloom and colleagues' "Taxonomy of the Cognitive Domain" (1956, pp. 201–207) seen in Figure 3.3. Demonstration lessons in subsequent chapters will be presented in a more truncated fashion. Teachers are always encouraged to add, modify, or delete activities to suit their instructional purposes. Further, the aim is for the strategies highlighted in the guided practice activities to be applicable to the teaching of other texts.

Overview

After reading and analyzing Ray Bradbury's short story, "All Summer in a Day," students will assume the persona of the main character, Margot; project themselves into the future; and write a letter to Margot's former classmates about how they treated her when she lived among them.

Objectives

Students will:

1. Tap prior knowledge of summer to make predictions about the title of the story
2. Visualize and interpret a picture to revise meaning and make further predictions
3. Make connections by bringing personal experiences to the text
4. Search existing schemata for knowledge about the author and the genre
5. Revise meaning before, during, and after being exposed to sections of the text
6. Practice a range of cognitive strategies by keeping marginal notes using sentence starters
7. Analyze writer's craft by playing the prediction/style game, Beat the Author

---

*Copyright © 1997. Reprinted by permission of Scott Foresman/Addison Wesley Educational Publishers, Inc.

8. Discuss the term *prejudice* and apply it to the story
9. Make inferences about why the children acted as they did
10. Visualize and make inferences about Margot's personality traits by creating a mandala
11. Adopt an alignment by assuming Margot's persona
12. Project Margot into the future
13. Compose a letter to her classmates exploring why the other children treated her as they did and explaining her feelings then and now.

The Process

This lesson takes between one to two weeks to implement. Teachers need to determine which activities are best suited to their students' needs and interests. The intent of the lesson scaffold is to facilitate the construction of meaning, not to bog down or overburden students, so some of the guided practice activities will not be necessary or appropriate for more experienced readers and writers. Some of the independent activities can be assigned as homework.

Prereading Activity

Easy as 1, 2, 3!

The Easy as 1, 2, 3! activity in Figure 3.5 was developed by Donna Moore, a teacher at Fitz Intermediate in Garden Grove, California, to spark her students' curiosity, to acquaint them with a text, and to build personal investment so that her students would be more likely to keep reading when they encountered unfamiliar words or a complicated story line.

1. *Title (Tapping Prior Knowledge and Making Predictions).* Ask students to think about the title in light of their own knowledge of and experiences during the summer and to use that background to jot down predictions regarding what the story will be about on the Easy as 1, 2, 3! form. Ask for volunteers to share and write students' predictions on the board.

2. *Picture (Visualizing and Revising Meaning).* Show students Robert Vickrey's picture *The Magic Carpet,* Figure 3.6. (It is important that the picture be presented without the title, because the title is very suggestive and will influence students' interpretations of what they see in the artwork.) Explain that although this painting was not created to illustrate "All Summer in a Day," it captures the mood of the story and the demeanor of the character. Ask students to examine the picture closely and to jot down what they see on the Easy as 1, 2, 3!

Figure 3.5   **Easy as 1, 2, 3!**   (Reprinted by permission of Donna Moore.)

What Do You Know about This Story?
1. This is what I think I know because of the **Title**
_____
2. This is what I think I know because of the **Pictures**
_____
3. This is what I know because of the **Words**
_____

 An 8½-by-11 copy of the Easy as 1, 2, 3! form is available on the companion website.

Figure 3.6 **The Magic Carpet** (Reprinted by permission of Robert R. Vickrey.)

 An 8½-by-11 version of this picture is available on the companion website.

form. Again, volunteers can share their perceptions. Once you have noted these ideas on the board, ask the students if anyone wants to revise their predictions about the title of the story. For example, students may have predicted that the story will be about cramming all of the exciting events of summer into one day. In examining the picture, they may notice the spareness of the surroundings, the girl's pensive expression, the patterns of light and shadow on the floor; they may sense the somber mood and feeling of entrapment. The class may at this point predict that the story will be troubling rather than light and happy.

3. *Words (Making Connections, Expanding Schemata, and Revising Meaning).* Before turning to the words, ask students if anyone has ever had to move from one place to another as a child and found the experience to be difficult. What was the experience like? Was it easy or hard to make friends in the new place? Volunteers can share their stories. Then ask if anyone ever had to move from one climate to a very different climate. Again, allow volunteers to describe their circumstances. At this point, explain to students that the story they are about to read is about a young girl who has to move to a new place where the weather is dramatically different.

Just before reading the opening scene of the story (below), ask what the students know, if anything, about the author, Ray Bradbury, and what experiences they have already had reading in this genre, science fiction. Based on their prior knowledge of this author, the characteristics of the science fiction genre, and the limited information they have about the story line thus far, see if they have any additional predictions to make.

Students should now be sufficiently curious about and motivated to read "All Summer in a Day." Read the opening lines aloud to the class:

> "Ready?"
> "Ready."
> "Now?"
> "Soon."
> "Do the scientists really know? Will it happen today, will it?"
> "Look, look; see for yourself!"
> The children pressed to each other like so many roses, so many weeds, intermixed, peering out for a look at the hidden sun.

It rained.

It had been raining for seven years; thousands upon thousands of days compounded and filled from one end to the other with rain, with the drum and gush of water, with the sweet crystal fall of showers and the concussion of storms so heavy they were tidal waves come over the islands. A thousand forests had been crushed under the rain and grown up a thousand times to be crushed again. And this was the way life was forever on the planet Venus, and this was the schoolroom of the children of the rocket men and women who had come to a raining world to set up civilization and live out their lives.

"It's stopping, it's stopping!"

"Yes, yes!"

Ask students to jot down their new or revised predictions after hearing the words. Have students turn to a partner and compare their speculations. Then add some of these partners' predictions to the board.

During Reading Activity 1

Reading Aloud ■ *Constructing the Gist*

Read "All Summer in a Day" aloud to the class up to the point where the children lock Margot in the closet and the sun is about to come out. Ask students to listen closely and to follow along in the text as you read. A copy of "All Summer in a Day" with a blank column for students to record marginal notes is available at the end of this chapter on pages 63–67.

During Reading Activity 2

Rereading Silently and Responding ■ *Visualizing, Making Connections, Revising Meaning, and So On*

Provide students with the cognitive strategies sentence starters in Figure 2.1 on page 20. Emphasize that in their previous activities, students have already tapped prior knowledge, made predictions, visualized, made connections, and revised meaning. Now have them reread the first part of the story silently, using the sentence starters as a resource for making marginal notations. Put a page of the text up on the overhead on a transparency with your own marginalia written in; or read a passage aloud and, using the think-aloud procedure described in Chapter 2, demonstrate the process of making these notations.

During Reading Activity 3

Beat the Author ■ *Making Predictions and Analyzing Author's Craft*

Students should be very curious about what happens in the remainder of the story. Capitalize on this by asking them to play a collaborative prediction game that is popular among UCI Writing Project teachers: Beat the Author. Have students form teams of four to six students. Tell them to put their heads together and speculate about what happens immediately after the line, "The sun came out." Their job is to write the next "chunk" of the text, about four to seven sentences. Be clear that the goal is not to finish the story but only to write the next few lines—which might be all one paragraph or might include dialogue. Give students ten minutes to decide on the most plausible content for their continuation of the story. Then explain that their versions of the story will be placed in competition with one another as well as with the real version. Whichever team most students vote for as the actual author (and which thereby "beats the author") will win the game; prizes also will go to any team that votes for Ray Bradbury's entry. This will necessitate a close textual analysis by each group to study the author's style. Give groups ten minutes to make a list of the author's stylistic traits; then have each group share their findings. These may include short bits of dialogue, often not identifying the speaker; lots of sensory details (sights and sounds especially); frequent use of similes; long sentences with commas followed by short sentences; strong verbs during action scenes. (Students may need more or less guidance in analyzing style, depending on their grade level. The minilesson on metaphor and simile on the companion website may be useful in some classrooms.) Stress to students that you will be photocopying either word-processed or handwritten versions of their entries unedited. Therefore, correctness is essential to competing well. A careless spelling error or run-on sentence will be easily spotted and cause the elimination of a team's efforts. Students will need approximately thirty minutes to compose their entries. The next class meeting, hand out a packet of the entries to each group. (If you distribute the Bradbury entry handwritten, do not copy it yourself, as students will know your handwriting.) Have students read the entries carefully, vote, and then explain their reasons, one group at a time.

Note that a team can vote for its own entry, pretending it is the real thing, to influence other teams to vote their way. Read the four sample entries in Figure 3.7, three of which were written by UCI teaching credential candidates during a game of Beat the Author. Which do you think is by Ray Bradbury?

Figure 3.7   Beat the Author

Which entry do you think was written by Ray Bradbury?

#1

The children stood immobilized and silent until the warmth and light of the sun encircled them in an orange glow.

"It's real," whispered one girl.

"And bright."

"Look at it."

"I can't!" one boy shouted as he covered his eyes.

#2

The jubilant children rushed through the open door to greet the glorious, long-awaited sun.

"It's warm," exclaimed William. "It does look like a flower."

"Margot was right," another child chimed in.

At this remark, the effusion ceased as the children remembered Margot. And in the silence, the children heard a faint pounding.

#3

The children blinked at the reflection of the sun glistening on the wet vegetation. As they watched, flowers thrust their stems into the sun, bursting into bloom. Released from the weight of the rain, the trees stretched out their branches as if in reverent prayer.

And then the children remembered.

#4

It was the color of flaming bronze, and it was very large. And the sky around it was a blazing blue tile color. And the jungle burned with sunlight as the children, released from their spell, rushed out, yelling, into the springtime.

"Now, don't go too far," called the teacher after them.

Postreading Activity 1

Completing the Story, Responding, and Making Marginal Notes ■ *Interpreting, Making Connections, Revising Meaning, and So On*

After playing Beat the Author, return to the reading of the text. Ask students to keep their predictions in mind as you read the final section of the story aloud. Because the conclusion of the story is emotionally wrenching, it is best to follow the reading of the story by asking an open-ended question like "What is your initial response to this story?" and inviting students to turn to a partner and just talk. Then direct students to continue making the marginal notes they have been keeping, again using the cognitive strategies sentence starters in Figure 2.1. Once these notes are complete, have students turn to a partner and take two minutes each to tell the story of their reading of the text—also referring to their Easy as 1, 2, 3! forms and the predictions on the board. Give students the phrase "At first I thought _____, but now I . . . " as a way to get started.

Postreading Activity 2

Grand Conversation ■ *Asking Questions and Formulating Interpretations*

Give each student a 3-by-5 card and ask the students to take five minutes to write an interpretive question about the story. Tell them an interpretive question is not factual in nature or designed to elicit a right or wrong answer. An interpretive question usually begins with "why," "how," or "what if . . . ?" After five minutes, have the students form a circle so the class members can see one another. Facilitate the discussion but encourage the dialogue to occur among the students. Depending on the class, a volunteer can ask the first question, you can get the ball rolling, or you can call on a student to begin. Allow fifteen to thirty minutes for the grand conversation. It is very likely that several students will have asked a question about the children's actions: "Why are the children so cruel to Margot?" or "What motivates the other children to lock Margot in the closet?" Such a question will enable you to unobtrusively introduce the terms *prejudice* (forming opinions without taking the time to judge fairly) and *discrimination* (a difference in attitude or treatment shown to a particular person, class, etc.) and to prompt students to discuss the intolerance the other children exhibit toward Margot. If the subject does not come up in the natural course of the discussion, pose the question and facilitate the discussion yourself. A good question with which to close the postreading activities is, "Do you think the children will treat Margot differently after what they did to her? Why or why not?" This question has no right answer, and it will evoke a range of responses. Some students will feel that the children's guilt will cause them to try to make it up to Margot. Others will speculate that the children will turn their guilt outward into anger toward Margot—the person who "made" them act badly—and will ostracize her even more.

Prewriting Activity

Interior Monologue ■ *Adopting an Alignment*

Tierney and Pearson (1983) report, "From our own interviews with readers and writers we have found that identification with characters and immersion in a story reported by our interviewees accounts for much of the vibrancy, sense of control and fulfillment experienced during reading and writing" (p. 573). They suggest having students "project themselves into a scene as a character, eye witness or object" (p. 573) as a way to develop and deepen engagement in reading and writing. To help students prepare for the key cognitive task in the upcoming prompt (speculating about the thoughts and feelings of Margot and assuming her persona), invite them to write an interior monologue in her voice. To create a bridge from the final prereading activity, you might want to introduce the task this way:

■ Although it is interesting to speculate about how the other children will treat Margot after they have locked her in the closet, it is even more compelling to consider how the trauma of being denied her moment in the sun will affect Margot. Become Margot and, in her voice, write an interior monologue, revealing her thoughts and feelings while she was locked inside the closet.

Allow ten minutes for this activity. Here is a sample from Thomas Mitchell, a sixth-grade student at Willard Intermediate in Santa Ana, California:

■ How could they do this to me! I sat crying in the closet. Soon, my sobbing stopped and my anger took over. I want to push William right into the acid rain. Suddenly, I was aware of the silence, how the obnoxious sound of beads dropping and the howl of darkness was fading. Soon, the noise stopped. Through the walls, I could hear the muted sound of rusting metal moving as the building door opened for the first time in seven years. "Let me out. Let me out!" I screamed into the emptiness. Then, I heard it, the heart-piercing sound of happiness the sun had brought into the lives of the children who destroyed me.

Have students share their interior monologues with a partner and then ask for two or three volunteers to read their quickwrites to the whole class. Now pose this final set of questions: "What do you think will happen when the children let Margot out of the closet? Will the same Margot who went into the closet come out again? Will she come out fighting, or will she have lost her spirit forever? What do you think her parents will do as a result of the incident?" Present a copy of the following prompt to each member of the class. An 8½-by-11 copy is available on the companion website.

Prompt

In Ray Bradbury's short story "All Summer in a Day," Margot's classmates deprive her of her long-awaited encounter with her much beloved sun, a sun she remembers so fondly from five years ago when she lived on Earth, by cruelly locking her in a closet. This is a devastating blow to Margot, because on Venus the sun comes out for only one day of summer every seven years. *Become* Margot and project yourself anywhere from five to ten years into the future. Write a letter to your classmates back on Venus exploring the treatment you received from them on the day the sun came out. Think about what Margot might say and how she might say it. Speak in her voice. Your letter should have a greeting, body, and closing.

1. After your greeting, begin your letter by reminding your classmates of who you are. Describe your present situation, including information about where you live now and what you are doing. (Remember, this story is science fiction. It is up to you to decide Margot's present location and circumstances.)
2. Go on to explain why you're writing. Review what happened on that fateful day and discuss why you think the others treated you as they did when you lived among them.
3. Explore the children's final act of cruelty and its impact on you.
4. Conclude your letter by expressing what you learned from the experience.

The best papers will go well beyond plot summary to examine not only *what* the children did to Margot but *why* they did it and *how* it affected Margot. Use concrete details from the story as you refer to the events of that day, and use rich descriptive and figurative language that will paint a picture for the reader as well as make you sound as if you *are* Margot. Your letter should follow the conventions of written English: spelling, punctuation, grammar (including correct use of pronouns), sentence structure, and so on. Use your imagination: This is your opportunity to speak to those who treated you unfairly.

Planning Activity 1

Clustering ■ *Organizing Information*

In order for students to project Margot five to ten years into the future, it is important for them to construct a personality profile of her at the time of the experience. Ask students to volunteer the personality traits that Margot exhibits. Students may, at first, list descriptive words—such as frail, depressed, and soft-spoken—that suggest that Margot is a very passive person. Ask them if they see any spark in Margot, any sign of passion or strength. You may wish to review the following passage:

> They surged about her, caught her up and bore her, protesting, and then pleading, and then crying, back into a tunnel, a room, a closet, where they slammed and locked the door. They stood looking at the door and saw it tremble from her beating and throwing herself against it. They heard her muffled cries. Then, smiling, they turned and went out and back down the tunnel, just as the teacher arrived.

Students may note how desperately Margot fights to keep herself from being deprived of the sight of her beloved sun.

Planning Activity 2

Creating a Sun–Shadow Mandala ■ *Visualizing*

Remind students that the Margot we see in the story has been subjected to five years of constant rain and has been set apart from the others at school because of her difference. We can only imagine the four-year-old who lived on Earth and remembers the sun so fondly as a flower, a penny, and a fire. One way to explore both sides of Margot's personality is to create a Sun–Shadow Mandala. The Sun–Shadow Mandala was popularized by Fran Claggett in her book *Drawing Your Own Conclusions* (1992). The ancient concept of the mandala is the idea of the circular shape as an archetype denoting the integration of various elements to make a whole. In its simplest form, a mandala is a circle with an uncomplicated design in it. The Sun–Shadow Mandala involves students in working with the dualities found within themselves or in other people, literary characters, character relationships, or concepts. In making a Sun–Shadow Mandala, students move from making metaphors, to choosing specific attributes for those metaphors, to integrating them in a circular design.

INSTRUCTIONS FOR THE SUN–SHADOW MANDALA

Selecting Sun Images:

In many works of literature, we are exposed to the character's sun side first; then the author slowly reveals the darker or shadow side. In "All Summer in a Day," we see the shadow side of Margot and can only intuit what her sun side could potentially be like. Looking at Margot, select images for what the sun side of Margot's character could be most like. To select sun images, answer these questions:

1. What animal is Margot most like on her sun side?
2. What plant?
3. What color?
4. What shape?
5. What number?
6. What mineral or gem?

Writing a Sun Sentence:

Next, write a sun sentence describing the specific image for each question. Example:

■   Margot is most like a butterfly because she wants to fly out of the prison of Venus into the sunlight.

Then, condense this to one word:

	Most like	Describing word
Animal	Butterfly	Free

Record this comparison on the chart in Figure 3.8. Then select shadow images. Think of shadow images and descriptive words (animal, plant, and so on) that are the opposites of the sun images; write a shadow sentence for each image; and record the comparisons on the chart.

Writing a Shadow Sentence:

■   On her shadow side, Margot is restrained in the cocoon of herself, unable to emerge into the sun and fly free.

Note: After students practice one sun and one shadow sentence, you may want to have them complete the chart without writing an individual sentence for each comparison.

	Most like	Describing word
Sun Image	Butterfly	Free

	Most like	Describing word
Shadow Image	Cocoon	Restrained

Drawing the Mandala:

Next, draw a circle. Inside the circle, arrange the sun and shadow images any way you like. Based on her chart in Figure 3.8, Heidi Schwabl, a UCI teaching credential candidate, created the mandala shown in Figure 3.9.

Writing a Framing Sentence:

Complete the mandala by composing one or two sentences that weave your sun and shadow images together and writing them on the outer circle of the mandala, as in Figure 3.9.

Figure 3.8   **Sun–Shadow Chart**

	Sun Symbol		Shadow Symbol	
	Most Like	*Word Describing the Sun Image*	Most Like	*Word Describing the Shadow Image*
Animal	Butterfly	Free	Cocoon	Restrained
Plant	Sunflower	Bright	Roots	Dull
Color	Green	Growing	Brown	Stagnant
Number	4	Wholesome	¼	Partial
Shape	Round	Full	Funnel	Empty
Gem or mineral	Topaz	Sunny	Lead	Overcast
Element (air, earth, fire, or water)	Air	Light	Earth	Heavy

 An 8½-by-11 copy of this chart that students can fill in is available on the companion website.

Figure 3.9   **Sun–Shadow Mandala** (Reprinted by permission of Heidi Schwabl.)

Example:

> The butterfly and sunflower thrive in the wholesome air and sunshine of Earth—a place she cannot see in her lead-like cocoon that pulls her into the empty darkness.

Planning Activity 3

Deciding Margot's Future ■ *Speculating and Making Predictions*

After exploring Margot's sun and shadow sides, students are now ready to make some decisions about the persona they will assume in their letters. First, they must choose to be anywhere from fourteen to nineteen years old. (The two options will give both middle and high school students a greater element of choice.) Then they must decide where Margot will be in five to ten years and how her location will influence her personality. To facilitate this decision, have students complete the following sentences:

- If Margot stays on Venus, she will be . . .
- If Margot returns to Earth, she will be . . .
- If Margot goes to _____, she will be . . .

Planning Activity 4

Charting Margot's Actions and Interactions ■ *Collecting Evidence*

Students will want to use concrete details about Margot's actions and her interactions with her classmates in order to make their discussion of her unjust treatment by them as specific and vivid as possible. Have students make a chart to organize these details. Revisiting the story will also enable them to review how Margot speaks.

What Margot says and does	How the children react	What I infer about their relationship from this
Writes a poem about the sun: *I think the sun is a flower That blooms for just one hour.*	William doubts that Margot wrote it herself.	Maybe William is jealous because Margot knows more about the sun than he does.

Students may notice as they dig deeper that Margot actually exhibits some behaviors that contribute to her estrangement from the others. They may or may not want to acknowledge this in their letters.

Planning Activity 5

Formulating a Writing Plan ■ *Organizing Information*

Students are now ready to organize their information into an informal writing plan that maps out what they intend to say. Revisit the prompt and pass out the scoring rubric included on the companion website, as will be described later in this demonstration lesson under Evaluation. Remind students that the best papers will go well beyond plot summary to examine not only *what* the children did to Margot but *why* they did it and *how* it affected Margot. To help students respond to the requirements in the prompt, ask them to plan their letters before starting to write. This four-part structure may be helpful as a rough road map for some students:

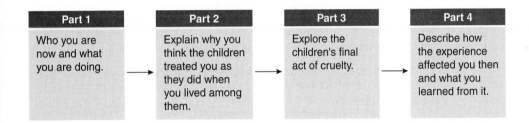

Part 1	Part 2	Part 3	Part 4
Who you are now and what you are doing.	Explain why you think the children treated you as they did when you lived among them.	Explore the children's final act of cruelty.	Describe how the experience affected you then and what you learned from it.

Note: Students who do not need so much structure should be encouraged to take a more individualized approach to planning their letters.

Writing ■ *Constructing the Gist*

Students have a variety of resources to draw from as they write their drafts, including their marginal notes on the text, Beat the Author entry, traits cluster, mandala, and writing plan. In this first draft, have them concentrate on getting their ideas down on paper. For students who are having trouble getting started, you might want to suggest the following:

- Introduce yourself by describing how you felt about life on Venus;
- Begin by reminding your classmates what they did to you the day the sun came out;
- Describe the weather where you are now as a hook to catch your readers' attention; or
- Begin by explaining why you decided to write.

Sharing Activity

A Letter to Margot Response Form ■ *Reviewing, Evaluating, Giving, and Receiving Feedback*

Teachers often spend hours writing copious notes on the final drafts of students' papers, only to find students giving them a quick glance and filing them away. If teachers want students to genuinely revise meaning and style, the most helpful time to provide feedback is at the draft stage. Moreover, students can be enlisted and trained as peer responders. Reading the work of other students at the draft stage not only will help the student internalize the criteria in the prompt and apply it to another's as well as to his or her own writing but also will enable him or her to see alternate models of how other students approached the writing task and solved the "problem." Because the writing task is a letter, the feedback form, which is available on the companion website, is also designed as a letter. As practice, the class as a group can review the student model by Mary Carol Ferguson, a seventh grader from Aliso Viejo Middle School in Aliso Viejo, California, shown in Figure 3.10.

Figure 3.10 **A Letter from Margot** (Reprinted by permission of Mary Carol Ferguson.)

October 8, 2032

Dear Classmates,

Lately I have been recalling that horrible day that happened nearly seven years ago. Since I know that you are approaching that day when the sun comes out for one hour, I thought I would write you a letter. Just in case some of you do not remember me, I am Margot, and I was in your third grade class. Since then, I have moved back to Earth because when I lived on Venus, it was like I was constantly looking for the lighthouse in the storm. It was the only thing I had to look forward to. But here on Earth, the sun is like a giant lemon hanging from the tree we call a solar system. I am currently in high school where I am on the swim team and have a boyfriend. But mostly, I just like hanging out with friends. I felt like I needed some closure on my old life from Venus, and so I thought I would drop you a note. Although I was young, I vividly remember my time on Venus and the way you all made me feel. I knew I was different, and you knew I was different, but it was the way you treated me that made the gap between us seem like it was growing by the minute.

Through my nine-year-old view, I remember that day when the scientists predicted that the sun would come out. I remember the closet door slamming in my face. I asked myself why you did such a thing to me. "Was it because I wouldn't play tag, or take a shower after gym? Was it because I constantly dreamed of the sun I so fondly remembered?" Then it was total darkness. Total and complete darkness. The only noise I could hear was that of the rain slowly, yet steadily, letting up. And then came another noise, one that not only echoed in the closet, but in my ears also. It was a noise that made my anger nearly tangible. It was the shrieks of laughter of children. But just not any children. It was the voices of those who had locked me in the closet only a few moments prior.

All of a sudden, I realized I was helpless. Not only helpless, but lonely, the kind of lonely that makes you sick to your stomach. I prayed that one of you would come and save me from this torture, but after some time, I knew it. I had just pushed the thought to the back of my mind until finally, I admitted it. No one was going to come and save me. Not one of you was going to rescue me, then take me up to where the sky shined so bright it hurt your eyes to look at it. I knew I had not one friend. Not one of you understood how much I had anticipated this. How much I had longed to have the sun on my face once more. And that is when it happened; my nine-year-old heart sank.

It sank so low I could have sworn I felt it in the bottom of my shoes. And as I sat there, I remembered you had never felt the sun on your face until this moment. You had never felt the same way I had about the sun. And you would never feel the same way again. I realized that when you got right down to it, the reason I was sitting all alone in a closet, and you were playing in the sun, was because I was different from the majority of you. And because of that difference, I had been tormented endlessly by others. A difference is like a gap. We all have gaps between us, but some of us have smaller gaps to fill, while other gaps seem to be as large as the Grand Canyon which, by the way, is a great big canyon here on Earth. Some are better at crossing these gaps. Still others seem to take the short cut and cross only the small gaps. When I lived on Venus the gaps between you and me were so great, I might as well have been back here on Earth. So I guess that is the reason my parents moved me back here. I didn't really have anyone I would be missing the way I missed Earth. So soon after that day, my parents moved me back to Earth. And I have never heard from any of you since. I hope your hour in the sun is a memorable one. And I do not want to "rain on your parade," but you see, here on Earth, the sun is like a fire in the middle of a storm. But I don't think you would understand what I am saying since on Venus you just have the storm.

Your friend,
Margot

Mary Carol Ferguson, 7th Grade

Revising Activity

Focus on Descriptive Language ■ *Revising Meaning and Analyzing Author's Craft*

Students will use the feedback from the teacher and/or their response partner or partners to reconstruct their first draft. Given that the response form focuses primarily on the content of the letter, the teacher should review with students the use of descriptive and figurative language.

Ask students to take a yellow highlighter and mark the descriptive words in the following passage:

> They stopped running and stood in the great jungle that covered Venus, that grew and never stopped growing, tumultuously, even as you watched it. It was a nest of octopi, clustering up great arms of fleshlike weed, wavering, flowering in this brief spring. It was the color of rubber and ash, this jungle, from the many years without sun. It was the color of stones and white cheeses and ink, and it was the color of the moon.

Note the use of metaphor in the passage, and review the metaphor and simile minilesson on the companion website. Encourage students to add descriptive words to their texts and at least one simile or metaphor.

Editing Activity

Focus on Pronouns ■ *Proofreading for Correctness*

Ask students to edit their papers in pairs, watching for errors in the conventions of written English: spelling, punctuation, grammar, and sentence structure. When they edit, students should also pay particular attention to a specific element of correctness that is relevant to the writing task at hand. Because this letter from Margot will necessitate using a number of different pronouns, pronoun reference is an appropriate editing strategy for a minilesson. A minilesson on pronouns is available on the companion website.

Evaluation

The Scoring Rubric ■ *Assessing Quality against Criteria*

The teacher, peers, or the student himself or herself can evaluate the final product using the full six-point holistic scoring rubric provided on the companion website. The criteria for a score of 6 are the following:

6 SUPERIOR

The 6 paper is clearly superior: well written, insightful, carefully organized, and technically correct. The 6 paper does all or most of the following well:

- Is written in standard letter form: greeting, body, closing
- Assumes the persona of Margot and impressively writes in her voice
- Begins by reminding classmates of who the writer is
- Clearly describes Margot's present situation, including where she lives now and what she is doing
- Thoughtfully explains why Margot is writing
- Reviews in detail *what* happened on the day the sun came out
- Uses concrete evidence from the text to make the letter specific
- Offers perceptive insights into *why* the children treated her as they did
- Explores the children's final act of cruelty and analyzes in depth *how* it affected Margot

- Concludes by articulately and thoughtfully expressing what she learned
- Uses rich, descriptive language to paint a vivid picture for the reader, including similes and/or metaphors
- Contains few, if any, errors in the conventions of written English

Learning Log Reflection

Quickwrite ■ *Monitoring, Reflecting, and Relating*

Think about what you learned from writing your letter as you answer these two questions in a quickwrite:

1. What did you have to think about in order to write your letter? Describe your process and the specific cognitive strategies you most relied on to become Margot and write a letter in her voice.
2. Have you learned anything about yourself while examining the actions and motives of both Margot and the other children? If so, what have you learned?

To Sum Up

Langer and Applebee (1986) have argued that instructional scaffolding is an especially effective model for planning and analyzing instruction in reading and writing. The five components of effective instructional scaffolding are ownership, appropriateness, structure, collaboration, and internalization. Scaffolding helps to reduce the cognitive, linguistic, communicative, contextual, textual (Frederiksen & Dominic, 1981), and affective constraints on student readers and writers. Taking students through some of the guided reading and writing practice activities in demonstration lessons such as the ones in "All Summer in a Day" will expose students to an array of cognitive strategies they can implement with a wide range of texts, thus expanding their options and capabilities when they undertake independent reading and writing tasks.

Learning Log Reflection

Revisit the integrated reading/writing demonstration lesson "All Summer in a Day" in light of the constraints faced by student readers and writers. How does the lesson scaffold help to reduce the cognitive, linguistic, communicative, contextual, textual, and affective constraints placed on student readers and writers? What aspect of the lesson did you find most helpful? What would you add to, modify, or delete from the lesson scaffold? Now think of a text you plan to teach in the near future. Which of the guided practice activities in the demonstration lesson lend themselves to that text?

All Summer in a Day

by Ray Bradbury

"Ready?"

"Ready."

"Now?"

"Soon."

"Do the scientists really know? Will it happen today, will it?"

"Look, look; see for yourself!"

The children pressed to each other like so many roses, so many weeds, intermixed, peering out for a look at the hidden sun.

It rained.

It had been raining for seven years; thousands upon thousands of days compounded and filled from one end to the other with rain, with the drum and gush of water, with the sweet crystal fall of showers and the concussion of storms so heavy they were tidal waves come over the islands. A thousand forests had been crushed under the rain and grown up a thousand times to be crushed again. And this was the way life was forever on the planet Venus, and this was the schoolroom of the children of the rocket men and women who had come to a raining world to set up civilization and live out their lives.

"It's stopping, it's stopping!"

"Yes, yes!"

Margot stood apart from them, from these children who could never remember a time when there wasn't rain and rain and rain. They were all nine years old, and if there had been a day, seven years ago, when the sun came out for an hour and showed its face to the stunned world, they could not recall. Sometimes, at night, she heard them stir, in remembrance, and she knew they were dreaming and remembering gold or a yellow crayon or a coin large enough to buy the world with. She knew they thought they remembered a warmness, like a blushing in the face, in the body, in the arms and legs and trembling hands. But then they always awoke to the tatting drum, the endless shaking down of clear bead necklaces upon the roof, the walk, the gardens, the forests and their dreams were gone.

All day yesterday they had read in class about the sun. About how like a lemon it was, and how hot. And they had written small stories or essays or poems about it:

I think the sun is a flower
That blooms for just one hour.

That was Margot's poem, read in a quiet voice in the still classroom while the rain was falling outside.

"Aw, you didn't write that!" protested one of the boys.

"I did," said Margot. "I *did*."

"William!" said the teacher.

But that was yesterday. Now, the rain was slackening, and the children were crushed in the great thick windows.

"Where's teacher?"

"She'll be back."

"She'd better hurry; we'll miss it!"

They turned on themselves, like a feverish wheel, all tumbling spokes.

Margot stood alone. She was a very frail girl who looked as if she had been lost in the rain for years and the rain had washed out the blue from her eyes and the red from her mouth and the yellow from her hair. She was an old photograph dusted from an album, whitened away, and if she spoke at all, her voice would be a ghost. Now, she stood, separate, staring at the rain and the loud, wet world beyond the huge glass.

"What're you looking at?" said William.

Margot said nothing.

"Speak when you're spoken to." He gave her a shove. But she did not move; rather, she let herself be moved only by him and nothing else.

They edged away from her; they would not look at her. She felt them go away. And this was because she would not play games with them in the echoing tunnels of the underground city. If they tagged her and ran, she stood blinking after them and did not follow. When the class sang songs about happiness and life and games, her lips barely moved. Only when they sang about the sun and the summer did her lips move as she watched the drenched windows.

And then, of course, the biggest crime of all was that she had come here only five years ago from Earth, and she remembered the sun and the way the sun was and the sky was when she was four in Ohio. And they, they had been on Venus all their lives, and they had been only two years old when last the sun came out and had long since forgotten the color and heat of it and the way it really was. But Margot remembered.

"It's like a penny," she said once, eyes closed.

"No, it's not!" the children cried.

"It's like a fire," she said, "in the stove."

"You're lying; you don't remember!" cried the children.

But she remembered and stood quietly apart from all of them and watched the patterning windows. And once, a month ago, she had refused to shower in the school shower rooms, had clutched her hands to her ears and over her head, screaming that the water mustn't touch her head. So after that, dimly, dimly, she sensed it, she was different and they knew her difference and kept away.

There was talk that her father and mother were taking her back to Earth next year; it seemed vital to her that they do so, though it would mean the loss of thousands of dollars to her family. And so the children hated her for all these reasons of big and little consequence. They hated her pale snow face, her waiting silence, her thinness, and her possible future.

"Get away!" The boy gave her another push. "What're you waiting for?"

Then, for the first time, she turned and looked at him. And what she was waiting for was in her eyes.

"Well, don't wait around here!" cried the boy savagely. "You won't see nothing!"

Her lips moved.

"Nothing!" he cried. "It was all a joke, wasn't it?" He turned to the other children. "Nothing's happening today. Is it?"

They all blinked at him and then, understanding, laughed and shook their heads. "Nothing, nothing!"

"Oh, but," Margot whispered, her eyes helpless. "But this is the day, the scientists predict, they say, they know, the sun . . . "

"All a joke!" said the boy, and seized her roughly. "Hey, everyone, let's put her in a closet before teacher comes!"

"No," said Margot, falling back.

They surged around her, caught her up and bore her, protesting, and then pleading, and then crying, back into a tunnel, a room, a closet, where they slammed and locked the door. They stood looking at the door and saw it tremble from her beating and throwing herself against it. They heard her muffled cries. Then, smiling, they turned and went out and back down the tunnel, just as the teacher arrived.

"Ready, children?" She glanced at her watch.

"Yes!" said everyone.

"Are we all here?"

"Yes!"

The rain slackened still more.

They crowded to the huge door.

The rain stopped.

It was as if, in the midst of a film concerning an avalanche, a tornado, a hurricane, a volcanic eruption, something had, first, gone wrong with the sound apparatus, thus muffling and finally cutting off all noise, all of the blasts and repercussions and thunders, and then, second, ripped the film from the projector and inserted in its place a peaceful tropical slide which did not move or tremor. The world ground to a standstill. The silence was so immense and unbelievable that you felt your ears had been stuffed or you had lost your hearing altogether. The children put their hands to their ears. They stood apart. The door slid back and the smell of the silent, waiting world came in to them.

The sun came out.

> **Students should read to here only, and
> then write the next few lines themselves if you
> want them to play Beat the Author. See page 52.**

It was the color of flaming bronze, and it was very large. And the sky around it was a blazing blue tile color. And the jungle burned with sunlight as the children, released from their spell, rushed out, yelling into the springtime.

"Now, don't go too far," called the teacher after them. "You've only two hours, you know. You wouldn't want to get caught out!"

But they were running and turning their faces up to the sky and feeling the sun on their cheeks like a warm iron; they were taking off their jackets and letting the sun burn their arms.

"Oh, it's better than the sun lamps, isn't it?"

"Much, much better!"

They stopped running and stood in the great jungle that covered Venus, that grew and never stopped growing, tumultuously, even as you watched it. It was a nest of octopi, clustering up great arms of fleshlike weed, wavering, flowering in this brief spring. It was the color of rubber and ash, this jungle, from the many years without sun. It was the color of stones and white cheeses and ink, and it was the color of the moon.

The children lay out, laughing, on the jungle mattress and heard it sigh and squeak under them, resilient and alive. They ran among the trees, they slipped and fell, they pushed each other, they played hide-and-seek and tag, but most of all they squinted at the sun until tears ran down their faces, they put their hands up to that yellowness and that amazing blueness and they breathed of the fresh, fresh air and listened and listened to the silence which suspended them in a blessed sea of no sound and no motion. They looked at everything and savored everything. Then, wildly, like animals escaped from their caves, they ran and ran in shouting circles. They ran for an hour and did not stop running.

And then—

In the midst of their running, one of the girls wailed.

Everyone stopped.

The girl, standing in the open, held out her hand.

"Oh, look, look," she said, trembling.

They came slowly to look at her opened palm.

In the center of it, cupped and huge, was a single raindrop.

She began to cry, looking at it.

They glanced quietly at the sky.

"Oh. Oh."

A few cold drops fell on their noses and their cheeks and their mouths. The sun faded behind a stir of mist. A wind blew cool around them. They turned and started to walk back toward the underground house, their hands at their sides, their smiles vanishing away.

A boom of thunder startled them and like leaves before a new hurricane, they tumbled upon each other and ran. Lightning struck ten miles away, five miles away, a mile, a half mile. The sky darkened into midnight in a flash.

They stood in the doorway of the underground for a moment until it was raining hard. Then they closed the door and heard the gigantic sound of the rain falling in tons of avalanches, everywhere and forever.

"Will it be seven more years?"

"Yes. Seven."

Then one of them gave a little cry.

"Margot!"

"What?"

"She's still in the closet where we locked her."

"Margot."

They stood as if someone had driven them, like so many stakes, into the floor. They looked at each other and then looked away. They glanced out at the world that was raining now and raining and raining steadily. They could not meet each other's glances. Their faces were solemn and pale. They looked at their hands and feet, their faces down.

"Margot."

One of the girls said, "Well . . . ?"

No one moved.

They walked slowly down the hall in the sound of cold rain. They turned through the doorway to the room in the sound of the storm and thunder, lightning on their faces, blue and terrible. They walked over to the closet door slowly and stood by it.

Behind the closet door there was only silence.

They unlocked the door, even more slowly, and let Margot out.

Source: Reprinted by permission of Don Congdon Associates, Inc. Copyright © 1954, renewed 1982 by Ray Bradbury.

Getting Started

Creating a Community of Learners

■ The first week sets the tone. If students leave school on Friday afternoon feeling serious and excited about themselves as writers and readers, and me as their teacher, we're halfway there.

—Nancie Atwell

The focus of this book is how to cultivate in students the habits of mind exhibited by experienced readers and writers. But what role does affect play in the use of cognitive strategies? Researchers point out that the development of strategic reading and writing is linked to personal motivation (Blau, 1997; Paris, Wasik, & Turner, 1991). Further, there is a strong correlation between a student's motivation and the degree to which the student (1) expects to perform successfully if he or she tries reasonably hard, and (2) values the available rewards for success (Good & Brophy, 1997). But what of students like Janet Allen's (1995), who had rarely, if ever, reaped those rewards of achievement and recognition? If we are to invite our students to become members of a learning community and motivate them to become "serious and excited about themselves as writers and readers," then, as Nancie Atwell suggests (1998, p. 118), we must "set the tone" from the moment students walk into our classrooms. Before we walk through that classroom door, however, let's take a look at the role of affect in learning.

THE ROLE OF AFFECT IN LEARNING

After spending a decade researching the attributes of influential and motivating literacy teachers, Robert Ruddell (1995) determined that across the grade levels, elementary through college, the most effective teachers guided their students through an intellectual discovery process and encouraged them to negotiate meaning as members of an interpretive classroom community. To create that community, the teacher must promote an affective investment on the part of his or her students. Tchudi and Mitchell (1999) note that "Too often the affective domain in secondary classrooms is pooh-poohed and dismissed as nonessential" (p. 118). However, research indicates that affect is just as critical a dimension of learning as cognition. As Krathwohl, Bloom, and Masia point out in their *Taxonomy of Educational Objectives: Affective Domain* (1964), nearly all cognitive objectives have an affective counterpart. These researchers liken the interdependence of the affective and cognitive domains to a man scaling a wall via two intertwining stepladders:

> The ladders are so constructed that the rungs of one ladder fall between the rungs of the other. The attainment of some complex goal is made possible by alternately climbing a rung on one ladder, which brings the rung of the next ladder within reach. Thus alternating between the affective and the cognitive domains, one may seek a cognitive goal using the attainment of a cognitive goal to raise interest (an affective goal). This permits the achievement of a higher cognitive goal, and so on. (p. 60)

One of the first and most essential rungs in the ladder is an affective one—attention. Within the affective domain, the student moves up the continuum from passively receiving information to actively attending to it; willingly responding and taking satisfaction in responding; valuing and making a commitment to the activity and/or the response; conceptualizing and internalizing beliefs and values; and, finally, organizing and creating a value system that integrates beliefs, ideas, and attitudes into a total philosophy or worldview (Krathwohl et al., 1964, pp. 176–185). How does one create a classroom environment that encourages students to actively attend to, take satisfaction in, and value what they are learning while developing what Jerome Bruner (1960) calls "an appropriate set of attitudes and values about intellectual activities in general" (p. 73)? Most researchers agree that it all begins with building a community of learners; and building a community involves, first, creating a shared sense of place.

HOW THE CLASSROOM ITSELF PROMOTES CLASSROOM COMMUNITY

The first step in promoting a sense of community in the classroom is to create a literate environment. From the moment students walk in the door, "everything in our classroom from the arrangement of the desks to the way we respond to children speaks loudly about who we are and how safe students can be in our class" (Tchudi & Mitchell, 1999, p. 118). If you're in Jeff Wilhelm's class (1997), he'll be at the door to greet you—and, when trust has developed between teacher and students, you can expect to receive a high five as you walk inside. Notice how welcome the atmosphere of Janet Allen's classroom (1995) made one student feel:

> Janet Allen's room was one of a kind. I don't believe that there was or ever will be one like it again. To me the room was filled with everything you could dream of. There was posters, pictures, papers, drawings, writings, and books. Books, everywhere you would look there would be books looking back at you. If you were an outsider coming in, I think that all you would see is a room with stuff on the wall, but if you would look closer, you would find a message. The message would not be right out in the open, you would have to read into whatever was on the wall. And when I started finding those little messages, I felt proud of myself and a lot better about myself. I mean, everywhere you would look the room would be telling you to keep going, don't stop, try harder, reach for your dreams, and many other things that would tell you things that would lift your spirits. And not only was the room inspirational, it was beautiful and it was made by us, the young adults. A lot of us were dreamers, I still am, and in Room 130 I could find my dreams, and in seeing them I would try harder to reach my dreams. (p. 28)

In California, where large class sizes are the norm and the physical logistics of accommodating students can be an obstacle, teachers have had to improvise. In her classroom at Century High, in Santa Ana, California, Pat Clark has arranged tables end to end around the perimeter of the classroom in a U shape, facing forward, with a smaller U of tables set within the larger one. When students participate in group work, those in the smaller U turn their chairs around and become partners with the students at the table behind them. In Sharon Schiesl's classroom at McFadden Intermediate, also in Santa Ana, where the teacher must make do with chairs with arm rests, she maintains straight rows for independent work, two rows turned inward to form surfaces for partner work, and four chairs pulled together to form a table for small groups. Common to both these classrooms, and to the classrooms of most UCI Writing Project teachers, are extensive classroom libraries where, during independent reading and book clubs, students make their own decisions about what books to read. Research indicates that the tangible presence of accessible books in the classroom promotes motivation to read and that self-selection of books increases reader engagement (Gambrell, 1994). Further, classroom environments that are physically comfortable positively influence motivation to read (Gambrell, 1994). While creating a nurturing environment within the secondary classroom, particularly in classrooms with large class sizes, is more difficult than in an elementary classroom, it is well worth the effort. For example, Meredith Ritner established a reading corner in her classroom at Aliso Viejo Intermediate, in Aliso Viejo, California. Soliciting donations of throw pillows from parents, she created an inviting place for sustained silent reading even though she had only a small space to work with. In a sense, this reading corner is symbolic as well as functional, because it sends a message about reading enjoyment. In a community environment, displaying students' writing also sends a message about what is valued. The students' own writings are celebrated, featured prominently on bulletin boards, and used as models for instruction and for pleasure reading right along with the works of professional writers.

WHAT IS A COMMUNITY OF LEARNERS?

Being in a community implies more than a shared sense of a physical place. It involves mutual interests as well as membership in a larger whole. Frank Smith (1988) stresses that membership in the classroom community or "literacy club" is the automatic right of each student and that it is the teacher's job to facilitate "admission" into the club (p. 11). There is an often repeated expression among teachers regarding student learners: "They don't care how much you know until they know how much you care." The foundation of the community is affective, and the building blocks revolve around the values and the demeanor of the teacher. In *Beyond Discipline* (1996) Alfie Kohn writes:

> In saying that a classroom or school is a "community," then, I mean that it is a place in which students feel cared about and are encouraged to care about each other. They experience a sense of being valued and respected; the children matter to one another and to the teacher. They have come to think in the plural: they feel connected to each other; they are part of an "us." And as a result of all this, they feel safe in their classes, not only physically but emotionally. (p. 101)

In such classrooms teachers actively encourage students to collaborate; they provide ongoing opportunities and thoughtful activities that invite students to engage in shared inquiry, keeping in mind that "what a child can do in cooperation today, he can do alone tomorrow" (Vygotsky, 1986, p. 188). Building a classroom community also involves collaboration between teacher and students that lets students develop a sense of ownership in the learning. Gail Tompkins (1997) compares this to the difference between owning and renting a home:

> In a classroom community, students and the teacher are joint owners of the classroom. Students assume responsibility for their own learning and behavior, work collaboratively with

classmates, complete assignments, and care for the classroom. In contrast, in traditional classrooms, the classroom is the teacher's and the students are simply renters for the school year. (p. 7)

In recalling the sense of wonder and possibility that one of his favorite teachers engendered in him, Jerome Bruner (1986) remarks, "Miss Orcutt was the rarity. She was a human event, not a transmission device" (p. 126). Fostering shared ownership in the classroom necessitates a shift in the teacher's role from "transmission device" to "senior member" of a community of learners (Tierney & Pearson, 1998, p. 85). This shift in the teacher's role means not that direct instruction is absent from the teacher's pedagogical repertoire but that information is shared, modeled, demonstrated, and practiced in meaningful contexts. In a classroom community the teacher's intention is to move from "sage on the stage" to "guide on the side." Robert Scholes (1985) acknowledges that "There is a bright little student inside most teachers, who wants to set the rest of the class straight, because he or she *knows* the 'right' answer. Still, the point of teaching interpretation is not to usurp the interpreter's role but to explain the rules of the interpretive game" (p. 30). In assuming the role of senior member, guide, or coach, the teacher must resist the temptation to make meaning for the students; instead, he or she must provide them with tools so that they can construct their own meaning, both collaboratively and independently, and truly become an interpretive community.

THE FIRST WEEK

Effective teachers take one to two weeks at the beginning of the school year to establish the physical, psychological, and social environment that will build a climate for learning (Atwell, 1998; Sumara & Walker, 1991). Creating an affective tone and enabling the students to get to know both you and one another and "to come together as a corps of writers and readers" (Atwell, 1998, p. 118) is essential to establishing a spirit of community. However, it is equally important to communicate that the work of the class is serious business and to put in place consistent and predictable structures for accomplishing the task of learning (Sumara & Walker, 1991). Making students feel that learning can be exciting and fun while, at the same time, making clear that succeeding academically will also require organization and hard work can take a great deal of planning. In fact, Atwell (1998) admits, "I plan the first days in more detail than any other week of the school year" (p. 118).

Classroom Rules

One of the items on most teachers' "To Do" list for the first day of class is to establish the classroom rules. The way those rules are communicated can heavily influence students' affect. The best advice is, don't begin with *don'ts*. As Janet Allen (1995) observes, "Students who have found so much joy in breaking rules don't need a list of don'ts" (p. 42). One way to begin immediately to create a community is to enlist students as coconstructors of the rules. Here's how Bob Tierney, a teacher/consultant from the Bay Area Writing Project, described in a workshop presentation his initial teacher-centered approach and his transformation to a more collaborative, student-centered approach to establishing the rules in his high school classroom:

> My master teacher, a long time ago, admonished me, "Do not smile the first three weeks of school. The students need to know you're in control." At the time, it sounded like sage advice.
> 　　The first day of school, after the faculty meeting and the "inspirational" address from the superintendent, I began by handing out a seating chart and telling the students to print

their name in the space indicating their seat. This was followed by handing out the classroom rules. The administration required that each teacher have a set of classroom rules, in writing, with a copy to the vice principal. I read the rules to the students and indicated I would be a strict enforcer of the same. The first day ended with a brief discussion of how important the subject matter was and what my expectations were. The only questions the students asked were: "Are you going to grade on a curve? Do we have to keep notebooks? Is it true your tests are hard?" Their reactions indicated most of them thought I was out to get them. It was not a good way to start, but that's what I did for the first few years.

I came to understand that learning best takes place in an atmosphere of trust where teacher and student are partners in the educational experience. I also understood it was all right to smile, or even laugh, during the first three weeks. Forsaking my master teacher's advice, I decided to design something into the first week of school that would build a bond of trust between myself and the students—something that might make them look forward to learning.

If I could somehow give the students some of the ownership, they would have to accept some of the responsibility for class conduct. The old way of dealing with classroom rules put the total responsibility on my shoulders. Early in the first week, the students, working in groups of three, are asked to make a list of 10 characteristics of a good student. They roll their eyes, mumble, and reluctantly get out a sheet of paper. When I ask them to make another list of the 10 characteristics of a good teacher, their eyes widen and flash with a glimmer of excitement. No one has ever asked them to do that before.

The lists from all my classes are collected and condensed into two separate lists. Each list will contain about 30 characteristics. I make copies and distribute them to the students the following day. The original lists will have suggestions for good teacher traits like: Does not give homework; lets us eat in class; lets us out early, etc. Any time you go from a teacher-centered classroom to a student-centered one, you are taking a risk. I bite my lip and proceed by asking them to choose the 10 they really believe in. Letting them leave class early and other similar suggestions disappear after everyone has a laugh.

The characteristics of a good student list will contain everything a teacher might desire, like: brings materials to class; respects other students. The first three items on the teacher list most likely will be: fair; listens, and knows his stuff. Placing the results of the voting on large sheets of butcher paper, I inform the students they have just made the classroom rules. Later, some of the students will volunteer to change the butcher sheet scribbling to attractive, artistic signs.

My students understand I will be a strict enforcer of *their* rules. Pointing to the teacher list, I inform them I do not know if I can be that good of a teacher, but will try. I grade them. They grade me. Each month, the students are given a 4x6 card and told to give me, anonymously, a letter grade based upon the criteria of the list. They write a paragraph explaining why they gave me the grade they did. This is the best evaluation I ever get.

After going through the process of sharing ownership of the classroom rules and participating in a number of get-acquainted activities together during the first week of school, I get to know my students as individuals and they get to know me. They realize that I am not out to get them. We have created an atmosphere of trust that provides my students with the motivation to engage in the serious work of learning in my classroom.

Expectations

As Kirby and Kuykendall (1991) note, "In creating a climate for thinking, there's no getting around our expectations: Rarely do we get more than we expect" (p. 24). Good and Brophy (1997) explain that teachers' expectations can affect the way they teach their students and that this, in turn, affects what and how much students learn. They conclude, "In this sense, then, expectations are self-fulfilling: teachers with high expectations attempt to teach more, and teachers with low expectations attempt to teach less. As a result, both groups of teachers tend to end up with what they expected . . ." (p. 70). So teachers' expectations should be high for *all* students; but they should also be realistic. The work of the class should be challenging, yet accessible.

Because there is a strong correlation between students' motivation and the degree to which they expect to perform successfully if they try reasonably hard (Good & Brophy, 1997), it is also important to orchestrate incremental experiences of success for students early in the school year—especially for those who have internalized "I can't" and "I'm not good at" messages. In the first few weeks of school, this may mean inviting students to read, write, and talk about what they already know. For example, one of Janet Allen's (1995) introductory activities is to ask students to complete a series of sentence starts such as "Today I feel . . ."; "I'm at my best when . . ."; "I wish people wouldn't . . ."; "I look forward to . . ."; and so forth (p. 187). It may also mean providing feedback but withholding evaluation on initial learning tasks. In order to build a learning community, before becoming the assessor the teacher is well advised to assume the role of response partner. This way, students have the experience and the validation of being heard and acknowledged before they submit work that is evaluated for a grade.

KNOW YOUR STUDENTS

" 'Know the children.' How trite a statement, yet it is one that gets more short shrift than is realized" (Graves, 1983, p. 22). So said Donald Graves as he challenged first himself and then a group of teachers in a workshop to (1) write down the names of their students from memory; (2) write next to teach student's name something unique to that person—an experience or a hobby, for example; and (3) to make a check mark if they had personally confirmed their information with the student. Graves had it easy. He had only the names of twenty-three graduate students to recall. Yet he could remember only about fourteen on the first try. Graves's task of recalling all your students' names from memory is a daunting one for secondary teachers—never mind eliciting and confirming a specific detail about each student's life. But to build rapport and a sense of community, it is important to get to know your students and to invite them to know you. When Glenn Patchell was gracious enough to let me try out a two-week assignment with his eleventh-grade students at Irvine High School in Irvine, California, I needed a quick way to make a connection with students. So I passed out five-by-seven-inch cards and asked the students to tell me a little bit about themselves, being sure to include one thing that I wouldn't know just by looking at them. The other side of the card was folded in half to become the name tag for the day. At the end of class, I collected these name tags and read through them. I learned who was on the football team, who aspired to be an actress, and who kept tropical fish as a hobby; in addition, a few students surprised me by disclosing very personal information, such as the boy who confided that he was having trouble concentrating on his studies because his parents were in the middle of divorce. Several students also took the opportunity to warn me not to expect much of them during our time together, saying they were "not any good at English." I now had a window into the class—who might need special attention or encouragement, who would have to be won over, and so on. I wrote brief comments on the back of each name tag—"What position do you play?" "What an interesting hobby," "I'm sorry to hear this and I understand why you're distracted," or "Maybe this assignment will surprise you and you'll find out you are better at this than you think"—so everyone would know they had been heard.

GET-ACQUAINTED ACTIVITIES

In Glenn Patchell's class, I only had two weeks with the students, period. This is about the amount of time Sumara and Walker (1991) observed that effective teachers devote at the beginning of the year to getting acquainted and building a climate for learning. During this time the teacher will not only want to get to know the students but enable them to connect with one another. Here are just a few of the many activities one might use to get acquainted and begin to build a classroom community.

How I Learned to Read and Write

In order to help students move forward as readers and writers, it is important to know what their past experiences have been and to determine how those experiences have affected their present attitudes. Many teachers ask their students to write a short history of themselves as readers and writers. I pose the question this way:

Prompt

Learning Log Reflection: How I Learned to Read and Write
Sift through your memories of learning to read and write. Are they mostly positive or negative? Are they vivid or murky? What are your earliest memories? What people come to mind? Are they relatives or teachers? Explore your own learning process and paint a picture so that I can experience your memories with you.

These narratives not only help me understand where my individual students are coming from but also serve as valuable reminders of the conditions, both at home and at school, that facilitate or hinder students' learning. In the following passage Hetty Jun, a UCI teaching credential candidate, explores her trials and tribulations as well as her successes in becoming a confident and very competent reader and writer:

■ When I think of how I learned to read and write, responses such as frustration, pulling hair, blurred vision, and headaches are the things I remember. Mastering skills in reading and writing were difficult. In retrospect, I believe I have struggled with reading and writing ever since my immigration to the United States.

I was reading, but I did not understand the deep structure of the text. I did not realize the connection, but my writing suffered as a consequence of my poor abilities in reading comprehension. Many of my answers in junior high school were superficial responses. When I tried to analyze or think critically, my head felt clogged with "stuff." Although I was able to verbalize my thoughts, my writing was incoherent and without fluidity. Oftentimes, writing was an excruciating and emotionally draining process where empty gratification awaited what seemed like my "best" efforts. I recall comments such as "awkward sentence structure," "how does this relate or support your topic?" "are you sure this is what the author meant?" or "a better word would be. . . ." My improvements did not happen overnight. It was a gradual process. I pondered the teacher's remarks and made changes. Many of the changes were guesses. I tried to guess what she wanted from me. I was always asking, "Is this what the teacher wanted?" rather than asking, "What did I not communicate or how can I write this statement so that it has clarity?" I stopped the guessing game in graduate school.

Ironically, I entered the graduate program in education. When I entered graduate school, reading and writing became all important. Simply put, I wanted and I needed to be smart if I wanted to continue in my new community of graduate colleagues. In order for me to possess and maintain credibility and reliability, I needed to become an expert reader and writer. I took a course on metacognition which led me to closely reexamine and investigate the gaps in my learning. Also, my professor provided detailed, constructive feedback that helped me see how to improve. I am still amazed that I had the capability to write effectively. More importantly, I am astonished that someone in my academic life took the time to critique and highlight my writing strengths and needs, rather than attack and bleed on my paper with unclear and cryptic remarks. With determination, many opportunities to write, work in groups, and time to examine and review "good" pieces of writing, my writing improved. As my writing improved, my anxiety and frustration began to subside.

I cannot say that I do cartwheels when I am asked to write a 10-page paper. But, over time and with practice, the act of reading and writing became an automatic and natural process.

Although Hetty is a second language learner, her reminiscence has much to teach us about any student who struggles. Because her teachers did not make explicit what it is that experienced readers and writers do, Hetty had to resort to guessing. She struggled, fell short, and became anxious. Her anxiety, in turn, clouded her thinking, further affecting the coherence of her reading and writing. What is remarkable, and perhaps is atypical, is that although she could not count on performing successfully if she tried reasonably hard, Hetty did not give up. Because she is so bright and intrinsically motivated, Hetty persevered until she found an influential teacher who made visible for her what it is that "expert" readers and writers do, offered detailed, constructive feedback regarding how to improve her work, and repeatedly provided occasions to practice. Neither Hetty nor any other student should have to wait until graduate school for this opportunity to arise. Hetty's illustration (Figure 4.1) of her state of mind before and after taking her metacognition class clearly demonstrates the way affective confidence and cognitive competence are inextricably related.

Four Corners and Personality Collage Doll

While the "How I Learned to Read and Write" activity is primarily a learning tool for the teacher, the four corners and personality collage doll activity is intended to help students get

Figure 4.1   **How I Learned to Read and Write** (Reprinted by permission of Hetty Jun.)

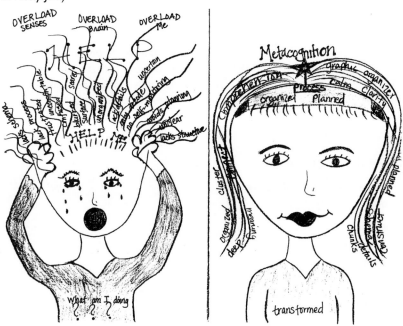

to know one another. Developed by Kerri Whipple, a former teacher at Laguna Hills High School in Mission Viejo, California, this activity enables students both to explore their own personality traits and to step outside the cliques they may already belong to and discover they have things in common with a range of class members. The four corners part of the activity may necessitate moving chairs to make walking space to and from corners and talking space at the corners. Prior to the activity, which will take a full class period (fifty minutes), the teacher needs to photocopy a class roster for each student, decide what questions and corner options to present, and create and post large signs for these corner options in the four corners of the room. For example, the teacher might ask, "Which animal do you think you are most like in terms of your personality style—a panther, dolphin, monkey, or flamingo? You might choose a monkey if you're mischievous, or a flamingo if you're colorful or exotic." Students then head off to the corner of their choice, check off the students they meet there on their roster, and explain why they have chosen to come to this corner. After five minutes, ask students to stop and write one descriptive word or phrase about themselves on their roster (see Figure 4.2), such as "fun loving" or "wise," before presenting the next corner option. A second corners question might be, "What kind of car best fits the type of person you are—a VW bug, sport utility vehicle, Porsche, or Lexus?" Again, students go to the corner of their choice. Subsequent corner options such as travel destinations, current movies, favorite leisure-time activities, and so on can be tailored to the teacher's student population and geographical area. A final corner activity that works well is, "Go to the corner posted oldest, middle, youngest, or only. These indicate your place in the birth order of children in your family. Together with the other students there, come up with three personality traits that you all share in common." For instance, "oldest" groups will typically come up with terms like *leader* and *responsible,* whereas "youngest" groups will more likely choose *fun loving* and *risk taker.*

After students have spent about twenty minutes in corners, have them return to their seats and begin their personality collage dolls. For this part of the activity, you will need magazines, scissors, glue, and precut doll figures. Provide written directions for the students, as shown here.

> **Prompt**
>
> **Directions for Personality Collage Doll**
> After thinking about your personality traits, look through magazines and cut out and paste on to your doll some or all of the following:
>
> 1. Pictures that are symbolic of who you are (for example, if you have a bubbly personality, you might put bubble bath or a bottle of champagne on your collage)
> 2. Pictures that illustrate things that you like to do (for example, cook, garden, ski, etc.)
> 3. Pictures of things you value (for example, family, reading, friendship, etc.)
> 4. Words to accompany your pictures

Figure 4.2   Class Roster

Name	Descriptive Word	Animals	Cars	Travel Destinations	Birth Order
Alongi, Anna					
Alvizures, Cecilia					
Bettini, Michael					
Bhathal, Surjit					
Bowers, Lori					
Brock, Matthew					

Because it is important for the students also to get to know you, you might consider making your own doll and using it as a model. Figure 4.3 shows the doll I made to introduce myself to my class. I point out that I'm a teacher (hence the picture of Kermit on the left leg) who happens to be sentimental and a little corny (hence the picture of the ear of corn on the doll's right leg). In general, I'm a dreamer who lives inside my head. I've chosen the pictures of a bird, floating balloons, and a castle to symbolize this quality. I tend to be pretty upbeat, so I've chosen the sun to represent my sunny disposition. And I'm crazy about my two cats, Spanky and Darla. Therefore, I've written "cat lover" on my doll.

With your doll as an example, students fully grasp the task and go straight to work. Encourage them to spread out, sitting on the floor if they need to, and to feel free to chat while they construct their dolls. Students should also feel free to ask others to keep an eye out for a desired picture, such as a computer for the student who is hooked on e-mail. Save the last ten minutes of the period (or more, if possible) for students to share their dolls. You can have them pair off to share their dolls; then each person can use their partner's doll to introduce that person to a small group or the whole class. Or students can use their own dolls to introduce themselves in small groups or to the whole class.

Object Exchange

A variation on the personality collage doll activity is the object exchange. Both activities not only help students get acquainted but build interpretive skills that will be useful in the study of literature. Later, students can create personality collage dolls for literary characters or se-

Figure 4.3   Personality Collage Doll

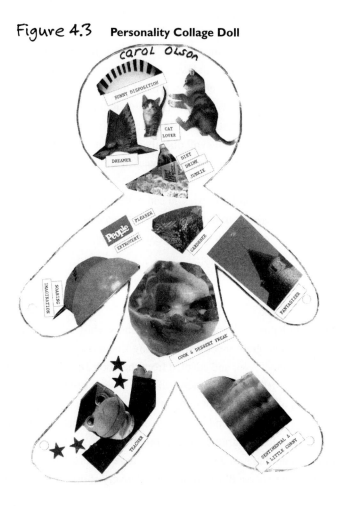

lect objects to symbolically represent characters. In the object exchange, students are asked to bring an object to school that is significant to them and that symbolically says something about who they are or what they value. As the students enter the classroom, have each person place his or her object anonymously on a table designated by you; number the tables 1 through 4 or 1 through 6, depending on the size of the class. Every important object also has a story behind it. Ask the students to take fifteen minutes to tell the story of how and why they came to acquire and value their object in a brief narrative.

Some students may need a model of how one tells such a story, so you might want to bring in an object from your home to share and reminisce about. Steve Dutcher, a teacher at El Dorado High School, in Placentia, California, told one of the more memorable object stories I've heard at the UCI Writing Project one summer. As a boy, Steve was always getting into things—he found the word *don't* an irresistible temptation. At Boy Scout Camp, after being told not to wander off or get into trouble, Steve did just that. Hiking alone through the forest, he came upon an unbelievable treasure: a heavy, rusted, round metal object that was not quite big enough to fit over a boy's head. Or was it? Steve had to know. So he slipped the iron circle over his head, forcing it past his ears, and wore it proudly as a necklace as he continued on his rambles. But it was heavy. Too heavy. As he tried to rid himself of this burden, Steve realized that his iron necklace was not going anywhere. Struggle as he might, he could not slide it back over his head. Returning to camp, Steve paraded around for a while showing off his iron necklace. But ultimately he had to admit to the Boy Scout leader, his dad, that he was in a jam. Several hours and jars of vaseline later, Steve was finally freed from his acquisition. But he kept this object, and to this day it represents for him his irrepressible spirit of curiosity and how this often gets him into trouble.

Have students write their stories and conclude by reflecting upon what their object might say about them to others. Then ask the students to go to their numbered tables and select an object that is not their own. Have them take a few minutes to analyze the object they have chosen, guess whose it might be, and consider what it might represent about that person. Students now form small groups according to their table numbers. One person should start by showing the object they have selected, sharing why they think it might be significant to someone in the group, and what it might symbolically represent about that person. The student then takes a guess as to whose it is. The real owner acknowledges the object and reads his or her object story.

After students have shared in small groups, you can collect the object narratives to read and enjoy. This is a perfect opportunity to help students feel successful: You can read for the story and respond as a partner while privately noting issues of craft and correctness that you will want to teach the class later.

Personal Brochure

Sharon Schiesl and Meredith Ritner, two middle school teachers whose classrooms we looked at earlier in this chapter, have had great success with having students create a personal brochure—a concept they learned about and adapted from the book *Did You Really Fall into a Vat of Anchovies?* (Armstrong, 1993). This activity will take several weeks, because each panel of the brochure can highlight a different topic. It is ideal either at the beginning of the year as a get-acquainted project or at the end of school year as a culminating activity.

Begin by bringing in samples of various types of brochures—from travel agencies, computer companies, political candidates, and so forth. After students peruse these brochures and discuss how brochures intersperse illustrations and relatively short bits of text to get a

Figure 4.4   **Personal Brochure** (Reprinted by permission of Tyler Olson.)

A Brochure about Tyler
Everything you always wanted to know but were afraid to ask!

Just the Facts
1. I'm in the 8th grade at South Lake Middle School.
2. I play forward and halfback for the Irvine Lasers soccer team.
3. The best book I've read lately is *The Bourne Identity* by Robert Ludlum.
4. When I get home from school, I inhale macaroni and cheese and ice cream sandwiches.
5. I'm a Bruin fan and I hope to go to UCLA in the future.

point across, explain that students will get to create a brochure on a subject that is of great interest to them—themselves (Armstrong, 1993, p. 78). Schiesl and Ritner require two topics recommended in the *Anchovies* book, "Me in a Nutshell," in which the students briefly describe who they are, their hobbies and interests, and so forth, and "The Future," which involves looking ahead and discussing goals and dreams. But the remainder of the brochure is up to the students. It could include their "How I Learned to Read and Write" reminiscence, an excerpt from their object piece, a paragraph describing their personality traits, lists of likes and dislikes, poetry, or other elements. Instructions for how to design the brochure and what to include are available on the companion website. Figure 4.4 displays the front page of a brochure created by Tyler Olson, an eighth grader at South Lake Middle School in Irvine, California. Janet Allen (1995) observes that "for students who really believe that they're not very good at spelling, writing, and reading, the opportunities to feel proud in English are often limited" (p. 26). The personal brochure may be just what these less experienced and more reluctant student learners need in order to invest themselves in something to be proud of. If the brochure is completed in stages, the teacher can help students edit a draft so that the final product is something that will make students feel "professional."

DEMONSTRATION LESSON

My Name, My Self: Using Name to Explore Identity

Tchudi and Mitchell (1999) note, "Working hard at the beginning of the year to learn each other's names" can save students "the embarrassment of having to ask someone his or her name after they have been in the class two or three months. It can also save them from feeling unimportant or not valued when no one knows their names" (p. 122). This demonstration lesson has been adapted from one written by Brenda Borron, an instructor of English at Irvine Valley College in Irvine, California, and published in a book by UCI Writing Project teacher/consultants entitled *Reading, Thinking and Writing about Multicultural Literature* (Olson, 1996b).* It encourages the students not only to learn one another's names but also to

---

*Adapted by permission of Brenda Borron.

look at the significance of names and how names relate to one's self-concept. The rich stories students write about their names also provide the teacher with an in-depth opportunity to get to know students and how they perceive themselves. Although Borron originally wrote the lesson for students at Saddleback High School in Santa Ana, California, it has been used successfully with students from middle school through college. Terms used to identify and describe the reading, thinking, and writing tasks in the lesson are taken from Figure 1.2 (Cognitive Strategies: A Reader's and Writer's Tool Kit) and from Figure 3.3 (the UCI Writing Project's adaptation of Bloom's "taxonomy of the cognitive domain").

Overview

After reading "My Name" from *The House on Mango Street* by Sandra Cisneros, students will analyze and reflect on the meaning of their names and write a personal essay exploring how their name has affected them.

Objectives

Students will:

1. Analyze the short story "My Name" from *The House on Mango Street* by Sandra Cisneros
2. Tap prior knowledge about or research how they got their names
3. Create metaphorical equivalents for their names
4. Visualize by illustrating a coat of arms with symbols reflecting their names
5. Speculate about how their names have helped shape them
6. Examine and reflect on their feelings about their names and how their names have affected them
7. Compose a personal essay about their names

The Process

This lesson will take approximately one week to implement. If it is intended as a get-acquainted activity during the early weeks of school, the teacher may decide not to take the lesson through the evaluation stage. Suggested supplementary readings for this lesson are "Kizzy" from *Roots* by Alex Haley and "A Pair of Tickets" from *The Joy Luck Club* by Amy Tan.

Note: The first two activities (prereading) may be skipped or modified if the teacher has already had students introduce themselves.

Prereading Activity 1

Name Tags ■ *Tapping Prior Knowledge*

Provide students with materials to create name tags. Use colored card stock for the tags so that they can be folded to sit on students' desks. While students are making the name tags, ask them to think about their names: the origin of their first or last name, how they came to get their name, their thoughts and feelings about their name, and so on. Provide a model by sharing details about your own name. An example:

■   I am the daughter of an English professor, and both my sisters and I are named after works of literature. My oldest sister, Barbara Allen, is named after an old English ballad. My middle sister, Celia, is named after the poem "To Celia" by Ben Jonson. When I arrived in the middle of Christmas dinner, my father could not resist naming me after Charles Dickens's "A Christmas Carol." (My father was a Victorian scholar.) I've never really felt like a Carol. My middle name, Lee, has more spunk and feels more like the real me. But when I looked Carol up in the *Name Your Baby* book and saw it meant "a song of joy," I began to appreciate it.

Prereading Activity 2

Lining Up ■ *Making Connections*

Ask students to take their completed name tags and to line up along one wall of your classroom according to the month and day they were born—January through December. Pair students up and ask each set of two to share their stories, thoughts and feelings about their names. Now break the line into two groups and ask each group to form a circle. As each student holds his or her name tag, partners should introduce each other to the larger group.

During Reading Activity 1

Reading Aloud ■ *Constructing the Gist*

Read "My Name" aloud to the class.

Prompt

My Name

In English my name means hope. In Spanish it means too many letters. It means sadness, it means waiting. It is like the number nine. A muddy color. It is the Mexican records my father plays on Sunday mornings when he is shaving, songs like sobbing.

It was my great-grandmother's name and now it is mine. She was a horsewoman too, born like me in the Chinese year of the horse—which is supposed to be bad luck if you're born female—but I think this is a Chinese lie because Chinese, like Mexicans, don't like their women strong.

My great-grandmother I would've liked to have known her, a wild horse of a woman, so wild she wouldn't marry until my great-grandfather threw a sack over her head and carried her off. Just like that, as if she were a fancy chandelier. That's the way he did it.

And the story goes she never forgave him. She looked out the window all her life, the way so many women sit their sadness on an elbow. I wonder if she made the best with what she got or was she sorry because she couldn't be all the things she wanted to be. Esperanza, I have inherited her name, but I don't want to inherit her place by the window.

At school they say my name funny as if the syllables were made out of tin and hurt the roof of your mouth. But in Spanish my name is made out of a softer something like silver, not quite as thick as my sister's name Magdalena, which is uglier than mine. Magdalena, who at least can come home and become Nenny. But I am always Esperanza.

I would like to baptize myself under a new name, a name more like the real me, the one nobody sees. Esperanza as Lisandra or Maritza or Zeze the X. Yes. Something like Zeze the X will do.

Source: The House on Mango Street. Copyright © 1984 by Sandra Cisneros. Published by Vintage Books, a division of Random House, Inc., and in hardcover by Alfred A. Knopf in 1994. Reprinted by permission of Susan Bergholz Literary Services, New York. All rights reserved.

During Reading Activity 2

Rereading Silently and Responding ■ *Tapping Prior Knowledge, Asking Questions, Making Connections, and So On*

Ask students to reread the vignette silently and, using a yellow marker, to highlight the golden lines—words and phrases that are memorable for them. After students finish highlighting, ask them to take two minutes to write a *text-based response* about Esperanza or some aspect of the text and two minutes to write a *personal response,* which might be about their own name or about something or someone the text reminds them of. (Note: You may want to hand out the cognitive strategies sentence starters from Figure 2.1 to help students generate their responses.) Then ask students to take two minutes to share their responses in partners.

Postreading Activity

Clustering Esperanza ■ *Organizing Information, Analyzing Text Closely, and Forming Interpretations*

Ask students to look over their golden lines and to share facts about Esperanza or her grandmother, feelings Esperanza has about her name or that the students have about Esperanza, and the fanciful and imaginative expressions Esperanza uses to describe people and situations. A sample cluster is illustrated in Figure 4.5. As students volunteer facts and ideas to add to the cluster, encourage them to dialogue about Esperanza's character and what she has and hasn't inherited from her grandmother.

Figure 4.5 Cluster

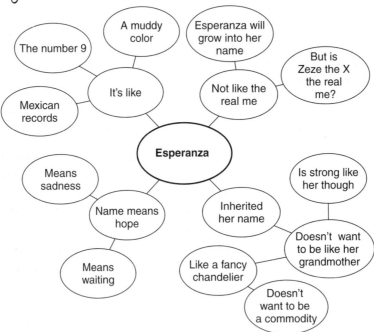

Prewriting Activity

Clustering One's Own Name ■ *Organizing Information, Making Connections, Reflecting, and Relating*

Ask students to cluster their own names. They should think of facts, feelings, and fanciful explorations of their names. Explain that exploring their name will also entail listing personality traits. You may want to cluster your own name on the board while students are clustering theirs. Useful resources are a book like *The Mother of All Baby Name Books* (Lansky, 2003) and the Chinese zodiac on the companion website. Students can also obtain information about their names online by accessing the websites www.babynamesword.com and www.behindthename.com. These sites are particularly useful if the students are culturally diverse. While baby-name books for English-speaking parents tend to focus on "Anglo" names, these sites are comprehensive and include a wide range of nationalities and cultures. My students felt surprised and validated to find their names listed.

Prompt Introduce students to the following prompt. An 8½-by-11 copy of the prompt is available on the companion website.

A name is just a word. Yet it is more than a word. Names have feelings, memories, meanings, and histories associated with them.

We can find meanings for our names in dictionaries, but our names are more than their dictionary meanings. Our names contain our families, our pasts, our feelings, our memories, our dreams. When we explore our names, we are exploring ourselves.

In a personal essay, explore your name. Include facts, personal experiences, fanciful explorations of your name, and an analysis of how your name has affected you.

Here are some suggestions for you to think about as you explore your name. Look at your name as other things. If it were a time of day, what would that time be? Why? A color? A musical instrument? A plant?

Begin your paper with an interesting title and hook (a beginning that captures your reader's attention). Help your ideas flow by carefully structuring your sentences and your paragraphs. Make your paper come full circle; end it so that it feels finished.

Check your spelling, punctuation, and usage to make your work as error-free as possible.

The best papers will move beyond a factual and/or personal exploration of names to a fanciful and imaginative analysis of the relationship between name and identity. They will engage the reader with lively writing that employs figurative language.

Planning Activity 1

Character Frame and Coat of Arms for Esperanza ■ *Forming Interpretations for Esperanza and Visualizing*

Pass out a blank character frame for Esperanza and a blank coat of arms to students. (Note: A blank character frame for Esperanza and a blank coat of arms are available on the companion website.) Ask them to form small groups and, collaboratively, to think of Esperanza's name in terms of various metaphors. Example: "If Esperanza's name were an animal, it would be a _____ because. . . ." Give them ten minutes to fill out as many items on the frame as they can. It is not necessary to complete 1 through 10 in order or to have a response for every item. After ten minutes, ask students to take ten more minutes to transfer the written metaphors into visual images, as in Figure 4.6. While students participate in this activity, they will be dialoguing about the significance of Esperanza's name, interpreting her character, and translating their interpretations into written and visual images. The following frame was completed by Brenda Borron's eleventh-grade class at Saddleback High School:

1. If Esperanza's name were an animal, it would be a *turtle* because *she's always ducking back into her shell.*
2. If Esperanza's name were a plant, it would be a *weeping willow* because *she sways with the wind; because she is not sure what she will be but she wants to be strong.*
3. If Esperanza's name were a season, it would be *autumn* because *she is too old for her age; she is brooding.*
4. If Esperanza's name were a time of day, it would be *dusk* because *she is waiting uneasily; she feels the dark coming.*

Figure 4.6   **Coat of Arms**

5. If Esperanza's name were a word, it would be *rust* because *she is colored by the name and life of another.*

6. If Esperanza's name were a musical instrument, it would be a *phonograph* because *it plays the Mexican records that are her name.*

7. If Esperanza's name were an object, it would be an *open window* because *she doesn't want to inherit her great-grandmother's place by a closed one.*

8. If Esperanza's name were a song, it would be *"Seventeen"* because *even though she is not really seventeen, the song captures her personality.*

9. If Esperanza's name were an emotion, it would be *melancholy* because *everything she feels about her name is melancholy, aching with sadness.*

10. If Esperanza's name were a color, it would be *blue* because *she seems like she's in a blue mood.*

Ask various groups to volunteer their responses for each of the ten questions on the frame. Choose different groups for each question to ensure full participation by the class. It is helpful to elicit more than one response per item to highlight how interpretations can differ across groups. What's important is the group's rationale for their choice. For instance, in the model, Esperanza is compared to a weeping willow because she sways with the wind, not sure of what she wants to be. Another group might argue that she is more like a cactus. She appears to be hard and prickly on the outside but she is capable of producing a spectacular bloom.

Planning Activity 2

Character Frame and Coat of Arms for the Student ■ *Forming Interpretations and Visualizing*

Collaboratively filling out the character frame and coat of arms for Esperanza provides the scaffolding for students independently to complete a character frame and coat of arms for their own names. This activity will help students generate comparisons that they can draw on when writing to the prompt. (A blank "If my name were a _____" character frame is available on the companion website.) Have students share and interpret their coats of arms with partners, relating them to their character frame, before moving on to do the next activity.

Planning Activity 3

Quickwrite ■ *Tapping Prior Knowledge, Generating Ideas, and Forming Preliminary Interpretations*

In preparation for writing their personal essays, have students do a ten-minute quickwrite about their initial feelings, associations, memories, and metaphors (or similes) about their names. Cecilia Alvizures, a UCI teaching credential candidate, had this story to tell about her name:

■   In my former country, Guatemala, people use two names: the first and the middle name. I remember how proud I felt to say, "My name is Cecilia Esperanza." But when I came to the United States, all that was changed. Here, most of the time, the first name is only used and the middle initial. This American tradition prompted me to investigate and learn more about my middle name. According to my mother, I was not going to be born at all. Her labor was so difficult that the doctors did not think she and I were going to make it. But she never gave up hope. She told me that when she saw me for the first time, she was crying with happiness and promised to herself that I was going to be named "Esperanza." Now that I am older, I am beginning to realize the sacrifice and the love that this name represents. When I think about my name, I think about a butterfly or perhaps sometimes the smell of flowers in spring. I picture myself listening to a romantic song . . . a song that could represent my personality and my name. I have always thought about it and I think the title of the song will be a song from the sixties titled "Cecilia" . . . "Cecilia, you are breaking my heart. . . ." Yes, I think that song will be the one.

Writing

Constructing the Gist

Have students use their clusters, coats of arms, and quickwrite to write a draft about their names and their selves.

WRITING THE HOOK

You may want to help them get started by providing the following information about a hook:

Hook: Writers use the term *hook* when they are talking about the first few lines of a piece. A hook is a bit of dialogue, an unusual statement, an exciting moment from the story, a question, an especially vivid description, or another attention-getting device that will make the reader want to read on.

Here is the opening of a paper by Rachelle, an eleventh grader in Brenda Borron's class at Saddleback High:

■ UNIQUELY RACHELLE

The R stands tall at the beginning of my name—the R that makes my name unique, unusual and different. "If I could just change that 'Ra' to a 'Mi,' " I would say as a child, "then I could be normal." The theory is people whose names begin with R give selfless service, have a gift of structured communication and are full of brotherly love. I believe this is true of me, and so it is, there is a reason for this R.

Sharing Activity 1

Practice Responding to Sample Student Essay ■ *Analyzing Author's Craft*

Refer students to the model essay "Flower from God" by eleventh grader Parichat Smittipatana, also from Brenda Borron's class at Saddleback High, in Figure 4.7. Use the essay

Figure 4.7   **Student Model Essay** (Reprinted by permission of Parichat Smittipatana.)

Flower from God

Parichat is like silk, a very nice gentle sound which flows through your mouth. If you pronounce it right, Parichat sounds very pretty. It's not too hard, just three simple syllables. You pronounce Par like a pear that you eat, ri with a short i, and then chat like chart without saying the r.

My name means "flower from God" in Thailand. Also, it is the name of a flower you can smell only in the early morning. Most people present this flower to the monks because of its meaning and sweet smell. Only this flower is allowed to decorate the monk's temples.

The flower represents a virgin by its sweet smell and the purity of a lady by its white petals.

It is a tradition in Thailand that when a baby is born, its name is given by the monks who are said to know what the child is going to be like in the future. But my parents weren't just going to settle for any name the monks thought up. My dad wanted to call me "Little Brat" because he knew I was going to be spoiled. My mom wanted to call me "Little Angel" because I was a cute baby. They couldn't decide, so they went to the monks.

When I was born, I weighed seven and a half pounds, so my parents brought seven and a half pounds of parichat flowers to the monks when they took me to be named. That is how I got my name, Parichat, as pure as a baby.

I was born in the Chinese year of the ox; that sounds dangerous and wild, but I think it fits me better than "flower from God." I should be sweet, nice, polite, or in other words, ladylike—which I'm not.

Even my nickname was a problem. My dad wanted to call me "Cherry" because when I was born, our cherry tree gave its first fruit. It was small like me and red like my fat cheeks. My mom wanted to call me "nonk" which means "little sister" because I have three older sisters and one older brother. So it was both names for me. I call myself "little sister" and everybody else calls me little sister Cherry. When I turned thirteen years old, Cherry began to sound childish to me, so I changed my nickname to Sherrie because it sounded more mature and it is easier for people pronounce than my real name.

I used to want to change my name to "Patricia" because I'm an American citizen now. I thought I wanted to have an American name that wouldn't take everyone ten minutes to say. But doing things like Americans, like eating steaks and salad, dressing and talking American makes me homesick sometimes. I want to speak Thai which I can no longer remember. I want to preserve my culture and traditions; that makes me think twice about changing my name. Parichat is unique, one-of-a-kind. It reminds me that part of me is still Thai.   —*Parichat Smittipatana*

response sheet on the companion website to evaluate the effectiveness of the model. As you go through the items on the response sheet with your class, model the kinds of responses you want them to use for one another's papers in peer response.

Sharing Activity 2

Responding to a Partner's Essay ■ *Analyzing Author's Craft, Giving and Receiving Feedback*

After students have responded to Parichat Smittipatana's paper as a whole group, have them form partners and respond to each other's drafts.

Revising Activity 1

Applying the Scoring Guide ■ *Reviewing and Assessing Quality*

Refer students to the scoring rubric provided on the companion website and review the twelve criteria for an effective essay. Ask students to mentally replace the word *your* in the criteria with *my,* as in "My paper is interesting and informative," and to use the scoring guide as a self-checklist for revision.

Revising Activity 2

Minilesson on Similes and Metaphors ■ *Analyzing Author's Craft*

Remind students that the prompt and scoring guide call for students to include fanciful explorations of their names, using figurative language to compare their names to other things. Remind them about the definitions of a simile and a metaphor:

- A simile states a comparison using the terms *like* or *as:*
  > It is *like the number nine.*
- A metaphor is a direct comparison of two things on the basis of a shared quality—as if the one thing were the other:
  > My great-grandmother I would've liked to have known her, a *wild horse* of a woman, so wild she wouldn't marry until my grandfather threw a sack over her head and carried her off.

Now ask the students to take out yellow highlighters and to find the similes and metaphors in this quickwrite by Keri Kemble, a UCI teaching credential candidate:

■   "Keri" is bright, almost blinding, like stepping out from a Las Vegas casino into the blistering heat and light of the sun. "Keri" is fire-engine red, or perhaps an astrobright shade of lime green. Nothing about "Keri" is difficult to grasp—to comprehend, much like an advertisement. There is no subtlety, no mystery. "Keri" is vivacious and an open book. "Keri" is a yellow daisy.

I am everything that "Keri" is not, although I can become "Keri" at the drop of a hat, on cue like a circus animal. I am soft and quiet, like the Irish rain falling upon an impossibly green field. I am the periwinkle blue of pre-dawn, when the world is still asleep and the street lights look odd shining in the boulevard. I am a calla lily, seeming smooth and strong, with a thick, moist base, but ever so fragile. I am a cup of English Breakfast tea and a book on a rainy winter's day, sitting by the fire with a warm throw.

I am nothing like "Keri." We are diametrically opposed. I am a Sarah, a Madeline, a Beatrice, but not a "Keri." How will I ever be able to live up to my name?

After they share with a partner the lines they have highlighted and discuss the effectiveness of Keri's use of figurative language, have students highlight figurative language in their own papers. If they cannot find examples, or if similes and metaphors are few and far between or uninteresting, students can create additional comparisons and insert them at this time.

Revising Activity 3

Evaluating the Title ■ *Reviewing and Assessing Quality*

Remind students that the first thing a reader of their text will encounter is the title. You may want to review the following information about titles:

> *Title:* Your title gives the reader his or her first impression of you and your paper. Good titles pique the reader's interest. They cause readers to ask questions, to predict, to make associations. Good titles pull the reader into the paper.

After discussing why Parichat selected "Flower from God" as her title, ask students to rethink their own titles as they revise. Will their titles capture the reader's attention and convey something essential about the paper's focus? Remind students not to underline or put quotation marks around their titles.

Editing Activity

Correctness/Editing Guide ■ *Monitoring and Proofreading for Correctness*

Working in partners, students can use the correctness/editing guide on the companion website to check each other's papers for correctness.

Evaluation

The Scoring Rubric ■ *Assessing Quality against Criteria*

The scoring rubric on the companion website can be used to evaluate students' papers. This is a weighted trait scale that can be modified by the teacher to include fewer criteria or to give more weight to some criteria than others.

   If this is a beginning-of-the-year activity, however, you may wish to bypass the evaluation stage of the lesson. Students could also put their drafts in their portfolios and opt to revise them for evaluation later in the year.

Postwriting Activity ■ *Making Connections*

Students' "My Name" pieces and their coats of arms can be displayed on a bulletin board, along with a photograph of each student if possible, to help students to get to know one another and to feel proud of what they have accomplished.

Learning Log Reflection ■ *Monitoring, Reflecting, and Relating*

Ask students to write a five- to ten-minute quickwrite using these two sentence starters:

   Before I was asked to write about my name, I . . .
   Now that I've explored my name, I . . .

This will enable them to think out loud on paper about how the act of writing about their name has affected them.

To Sum Up

Although some teachers may insist that content is paramount in a secondary classroom and that creating an affective climate is inconsequential, research indicates that affect is just as critical a dimension of learning as cognition. One of the most effective ways to encourage students to actively attend to, take satisfaction in, and value what they are learning is to create a community of learners. Effective teachers take at least two weeks at the beginning of school to build a climate for learning and cultivate a spirit of community (Sumara & Walker, 1991). In order to set the tone, the teacher must engage students in a variety of get-acquainted activities to help them get to know one another while at the same time establishing rules, communicating expectations, and putting in place consistent and predictable structures in which learning will take place. To establish trust and to help students feel invested in the goals of the class and in themselves as learners, it is important to have students read and write early on about things they already know—most importantly, themselves. Activities like the My Name, My Self demonstration lesson can enable students to explore the significance of their names while giving the teacher an in-depth opportunity to get to know his or her students and how they perceive themselves. During the early weeks of school, the teacher should model, demonstrate, and practice along with the students to establish himself or herself as a senior member of the community of learners (Tierney & Pearson, 1998).

Learning Log Reflection

As you think about building a climate for learning in your classroom and fostering a spirit of community, what activities do you plan to use during the early weeks of school to set the tone? Construct a plan for the first week that will prompt students to feel "serious and excited" (Atwell, 1998, p. 118) about themselves as readers and writers—and about you as their teacher—by the time they leave school on Friday.

A Multiple Intelligences Approach to Language Arts Instruction for Mainstream and English Language Development Classrooms

"I bet somebody is having a party. Look! There's candles and a balloon," Jose says.

But Marisa is not so sure. "Wait a minute. That balloon is all wilted and sad looking. And the birthday candle is in an onion. Whoever heard of a birthday onion?"

"Makes you cry," Tran mumbles.

"What?" everyone asks.

"An onion makes you cry. You know, when you cut it. It must have been a pretty sad birthday."

The eighth-grade students in Transitional ELD (English language development) at McFadden Intermediate School in Santa Ana Unified School District, a large urban district in Southern California with the highest percentage of limited-English-speaking students in the state, have been working in groups to examine tangible items that have symbolic significance in the story "Eleven" by Sandra Cisneros. Some items, like a set of nested dolls and a Band-Aid box filled with pennies, are literally named in the text. Others, like the "birthday onion," are more interpretative in nature. After the groups speculate amongst themselves for about ten minutes, Sharon Schiesl, their teacher, calls them to order.

"Okay, class. You've all had a chance to examine these mystery items, which we will encounter again when we read 'Eleven.' Based on these items and the title, what do you predict the story will be about?" Hands go up immediately.

"What do you think, Jose?"

"Well, our group thought it would be about a birthday, and we think the person will get money because there's pennies in that Band-Aid box."

As she writes this prediction on the board, Schiesl responds, "A Band-Aid box is a pretty curious place to put money, don't you think? What do you make of that?"

"Oh, oh." Michelle is waving her hand vigorously to get the teacher's attention. "Band-Aids are for cuts and scratches and stuff. I think someone gets hurt."

"So, do you think someone physically gets hurt—like breaks an arm or something?"

Michelle ponders. "No, but maybe it's like a hurt inside. Maybe that's why there's an onion with a candle instead of a birthday cake."

"Okay. Good idea, Michelle."

Michelle's comment turns on a light for Cao. "Wait. Everything is inside something else—the Band-Aid box, dolls inside dolls, all those tree rings, even the onion. Everything has layers."

"Great insight, Cao. Let's all keep our eyes out for how this idea of layers will apply to the story. I notice that no one has mentioned the red sweater. What about that?"

The class is silent for a long minute as they reexamine the very red and very bedraggled sweater sitting in a heap on the desk. Then Juan pipes up, "Boy, that would be a crummy present. Do you suppose it belongs to a poor girl?"

"Why would you say a girl?" Imelda asks.

"Because no boy would wear a sweater like that. That's a *girl's* sweater."

"Do you think it's important that it's a red sweater?" Schiesl probes. "What does the color red say to you?"

From around the class, students yell out, "Hot. Angry. Blood. Excitement. Explosion."

"Okay. We have lots of good clues for the story we're about to read. Let's get to it."

MULTIPLE INTELLIGENCES THEORY IN THE CLASSROOM

Sharon Schiesl has been taking a multiple intelligences approach to teaching reading and writing in her classroom based upon her collaboration with other UCI Writing Project teacher/consultants on a teacher research grant for which I served as principal investigator. Drawing upon the research of Howard Gardner (1983), Schiesl and her colleagues designed an interactive, integrated reading/writing curriculum that would appeal to students with a variety of intellectual comfort zones and would build upon each student's strengths to bolster their linguistic competence. This chapter explores how a multiple intelligences approach can enrich language arts instruction in both mainstream and ELD classrooms.

Frames of Mind: The Theory of Multiple Intelligences (1983)—even the title of Gardner's book may take some people aback. After all, "intelligence," as we all know, is a singular noun in the dictionary. However, Gardner's book questions the notion that human beings have a "unitary dimension called intelligence" (Ellison, 1984, p. 26) that can be measured and quantified. According to Gardner, studies of cognition and neurobiology suggest that we may have several different intellectual strengths, or domains of intelligence—each located in discrete parts of the brain; each responsible for a particular human ability; each relatively autonomous from other human faculties; and each progressing through Piagetian-like stages or levels (novice, apprentice, expert, or master) at rates that are influenced not only by heredity but by cultural values. In *Frames of Mind* Gardner offers a provisional list and profiles of seven intelligences that have the "capacity to solve problems or to fashion products that are valued in one or more cultural settings" (Gardner & Hatch, 1989, p. 5). These intelligences are briefly described below.

Linguistic Intelligence   The most widely and democratically shared intellectual competence across all human beings, *linguistic intelligence* involves a sensitivity to the sounds, rhythms, and meanings of words, as well as to the functions of language. Four aspects of linguistic knowledge have "proved of striking importance in human society" (Gardner, 1983, p. 78): (1) *rhetorical aspect*—ability to use language to convince and persuade others of a course of action or point of view; (2) *mnemonic aspect*—ability to use language as a tool for remembering; (3) *explanation aspect*—ability to use language to convey instructions and information, both orally and in writing; and (4) *metalinguistic aspect*—ability to use language to reflect upon language.

Musical Intelligence   Often viewed as a "gift" rather than as a form of thinking, *musical intelligence* calls for a keen auditory sense; a feel for patterns and rhythms, pitch and tonality; and an appreciation for the forms of musical expression. Whereas there is a considerable emphasis in school on linguistic attainment, music "occupies a relatively low niche in our culture" (p. 109). In some other cultures, however—those of China, Japan, and Hungary, for example—musical intelligence is highly prized.

Logical–Mathematical Intelligence   Linguistic and musical capacities have their origins in the auditory–oral sphere, but *logical–mathematical intelligence* "can be traced to a confrontation with the world of objects" (p. 129). That is, it involves the ability, first, to recognize, group, and assess material objects and, later, to manipulate abstract symbols. Logical–mathematical thought requires sensitivity to and the ability to discern logical or numerical patterns, memory of and the capacity to handle long chains of reasoning, an appreciation of the links between propositions, and a love of abstraction and problem solving. Whereas linguistic intelligence is the most democratically shared of all the intelligences, logical–mathematical intelligence is very unequally spread across the population. Influenced largely by Piaget, who perceived logical thought as the "glue that holds together all cognition" (p. 134) and whose theories have been a driving force behind intelligence testing, the educational community has long placed a high premium on logical–mathematical intelligence.

Spatial Intelligence   Spatially intelligent people have a heightened capacity to perceive the visual–spatial world and to mentally recreate aspects of visual experience—even in the absence of physical stimuli. Three components of *spatial intelligence* are the ability to recognize the identity of an object when it is seen from different angles; the ability to imagine movement or internal displacement among the parts of a configuration; and the ability to think about spatial relations. Psychologist Rudolph Arnheim (1969) has argued that the most important operations of thinking come directly from our perceptions of the world; because unless we can conjure up a visual image of a concept, we will be unable to think about it clearly. Albert Einstein, who derived many of his insights from spatial models, is a case in point. As Einstein once said,

> The words of my language, as they are written and spoken, do not seem to play any role in my mechanisms of thought. The psychical entities which seem to serve as elements in thought are certain signs and more or less clear images which can be voluntarily reproduced or combined. . . . The above mentioned elements are, in my case, of visual and some of muscular type. (Quoted in Gardner, 1983, pp. 190–191)

Bodily–Kinesthetic Intelligence   *Bodily–kinesthetic intelligence* involves a well-honed sense of timing, an ability to anticipate what is coming next, expertise in control of one's body movements, overall smoothness of performance, and an automaticity of certain reflexes or activities. Athletes, like basketball great Michael Jordan, or "Air Jordan" as he is called, clearly possess the qualities described above; actors, too, rely on bodily–kinesthetic intelligence for a successful performance, for the delivery of their lines has no authenticity or power without the communication that comes from body language. Further, bodily–kinesthetic intelligence is critical to the skill of surgeons, who literally have people's lives in their hands.

The Personal Intelligences   Two forms of intelligence that are almost virtually ignored by students of cognition are intrapersonal and interpersonal intelligence. It is easy to understand how those who see a clear division between thought and emotion would relegate both *intrapersonal intelligence* (access to one's own feeling life) and *interpersonal intelligence* (ability to read the intentions and desires of others) solely to the affective domain. Gardner, however, sees the personal intelligences as information-processing abilities. Intrapersonal intelligence, the capacity to know oneself, involves directing information inward and relating it to inner states of being. Interpersonal intelligence, the capacity to know others, involves processing external information by reading the intentions of others and discerning the relationship of the self to the outside community. The integration of these two intelligences, which leads to a firmly developed sense of self, "appears as the highest achievement of human beings" (p. 279). It is important to note that just as it takes the integration of the personal intelligences to foster a well-developed sense of self, so too it is the interaction and integration of the intelligences functioning together that enable us to engage in and execute intricate human activities. The companion website contains a chart that graphically depicts each intelligence and the characteristics of learners who favor that intelligence.

Naturalist Intelligence   Gardner takes great pains to emphasize that what he postulates is a theory only; that there will never be "a single, irrefutable and universally accepted list" of "three, seven, or three hundred intelligences" (p. 60); and that what he proposes are not "physically verifiable entities" but "useful scientific constructs" (p. 70). In recent years he has been developing a profile for an intelligence he calls the naturalist (Checkley, 1997). The *naturalist intelligence* involves the human ability to discriminate among living things, a sensitivity to other features of the natural world such as clouds or rock formations, and the ability to recognize cultural artifacts (Checkley, 1997). According to Gardner, "Darwin is probably the most famous example of a naturalist because he saw so deeply into the nature of living things" (Checkley, 1997, p. 9).

Gardner's work has given rise to more than a few "Ahas" for Schiesl and the other teachers in the research group—and for me as well. As English teachers, we had all tended to favor our own intellectual comfort zone, the medium of words. We tended to lead with our own strong suit, often leaving certain "players" in our classrooms out of the game. It didn't immediately occur to us that art, drama, music, or even mathematics could provide pathways into the world of print. When students didn't understand our writing assignments, we often read them again to the class—only louder. We also had to nod our heads and say *mea culpa* to Gardner's observation that teachers tend unconsciously to be drawn to those students who share their own intellectual preferences. How often have we all passed over the student who was staring intently into the grain of his or her desk, to call on the student whose body language said, "I like this!"?

Our second "Aha" was about students. Not only do students all have different kinds of minds and ways of learning, they all have areas of intellectual strength—some of which are more or less valued and accessed in school. Gardner points out that although the intelligences "may be rooted in biology . . . vast and highly instructive differences in their constructions can be discerned across cultures" (Gardner, 1983, p. 268). Robin Scarcella (1990) notes that the organization of most classrooms "tends to reflect the style which is characteristic of mainstream schooling" (p. 121). That is, middle-American schools rely heavily on linguistic and logical–mathematical intelligence and tend to promote intrapersonal over interpersonal intelligence. This emphasis privileges certain students while raising barriers for others. Given that teachers have an obligation to provide children of all cultural backgrounds with an opportunity to learn and to feel successful, it is vital to tap, identify, and capitalize on students' strengths and to use those intellectual competencies as a bridge to reach and foster their less developed or less practiced intelligences. In *A Place Called School* (1994), John Goodlad notes that when he and a team of researchers studied more than 1,000 classrooms throughout the United States, they did not see "much opportunity for students to become engaged with knowledge so as to employ the full range of intellectual abilities" (p. 231). Certainly, all students deserve this opportunity.

WHY A MULTIPLE INTELLIGENCES APPROACH WORKS WITH ENGLISH LANGUAGE LEARNERS

Sharon Schiesl and I experienced another "Aha" as we reflected upon Howard Gardner's multiple intelligences (MI) theory: That is, English language learners (ELLs) who do not yet have the linguistic competence in the target language to adequately comprehend information or express themselves, even if they are innately linguistic learners, naturally access other intelligences in order to understand or make themselves understood. If you have ever been to a foreign country where you had little or no knowledge or command of the language, you may vividly recall how quickly you resorted to throwing yourself upon the mercy of strangers and using sign language and crude drawings in order to communicate. Armstrong (1994) remarks that "MI theory makes its greatest contribution to education by suggesting that teachers need to expand their repertoire of techniques, tools, and strategies beyond the typical linguistic and logical ones predominantly used in American classrooms" (p. 48). MI theory legitimizes the use of a range of approaches to teaching and learning and, for ELLs, increases the amount of comprehensible input the student is exposed to. It is especially important for teachers to address the learning needs of ELLs because K–12 ELLs are the fastest growing school-age population in the United States, projected soon to exceed more than five million students (USDOE Office of Language Acquisition, 2004). While the general school-age population in the United States is only 12 percent greater than it was in 1991, the number of students classified as limited English proficient (LEP) has skyrocketed by 105 percent (Kindler, 2002).

According to Stephen Krashen (1981), the most essential component of second language learning is comprehensible input. This is the input in which "the focus is on the message and not the form" (p. 9). Similarly, Tracy Terrell (1977) observes that the most effective way to promote "communicative competence" (p. 325) is to engage students in classroom activities that focus on content and in which the principles of grammar are absorbed through genuine experiences of communication using the second language. As part of this more meaning-centered or "natural approach" (Terrell, 1977)—which has replaced models of education of the skill and drill variety "that sometimes see minority children as deficient in their abilities simply because they do not speak English" (Urzúa, 1989, p. 35)—second language teachers have adopted a variety of strategies compatible with MI theory. For example, James Asher (1966) developed total physical response (TPR), a kinesthetic approach to language learning, based on his research finding that dramatically acting out commands in the target language is "vastly more effective as a learning format than merely a sedentary kind of observation" (p. 81). This active approach to language learning, in which one literally learns by doing, enhances retention, increases motivation, and sustains interest. Scarcella (1997) advocates the use of visual aids such as pictures, diagrams, charts, gestures, and items from the outside world to develop the concepts, vocabulary, and structures students will encounter in reading. Au (1993) proposes that reading/writing programs for students of intermediate fluency should extend the exploration of themes in literature into the expressive arts: creative dramatics, arts and crafts, readers' theater, musical accompaniment, jazz chants, creative movement, dance, puppetry, and movie making using filmstrip and TV boxes with written scripts (p. 152). A panel of distinguished researchers convened by The Education Alliance and the Annenberg Institute for School Reform concurs with Au that "ELLs are most successful when teachers employ a variety of strategies to help students understand challenging language, texts, and concepts. These may include linguistic simplification, demonstrations, hands-on activities, mime and gestures, native language support, use of graphic organizers, and learning logs" (Coady et al., 2003). In other words, these educators advocate helping ELLs to "use the combination of their intelligences to be successful in school," as Gardner would say (Checkley, 1997, p. 10) and to enhance language acquisition.

Krashen (1981) suggests that the key to the language acquisition process is understanding language structures that are "just beyond the acquirer's current level of competence" (p. 101). Targeting for what Krashen calls "i+1" (p. 103) involves not only simplifying language structures and using MI approaches to providing comprehensible input but also taking students' cultural backgrounds into account. Carrasquillo and Rodriguez (1995) comment that "Teachers often underestimate the importance that culture plays in reading comprehension. Students must have knowledge and understanding of the world around them as they interact with a text or attempt to write about a topic" (p. 85). Scarcella and Oxford (1992) explain that cultural relevance is "directly related to schema theory" (p. 105). Even when the language in a text is accessible to ELLs, if there are cultural references the students don't understand, those "cultural gaps" will interfere with the student's comprehension.

Many second language scholars advocate cooperative learning as a means of increasing comprehensible input. They emphasize the importance of integrating ELLs and native speakers in cooperative groups so that they can work together on meaningful tasks (Rigg & Allen, 1995; Coady et al., 2003). Carrasquillo and Rodriguez (1995) recommend interactive collaborative groups to ensure oral participation before, during, and after reading and writing. They point out that large group discussions "tend to intimidate LEP students, and this lack of confidence and intimidation often translates into silence" (p. 87). Scarcella (1990) observes that whereas "competition is the primary method among middle Americans of motivating members of a group" (p. 125), research indicates that interpersonal intelligence is more highly valued among African Americans, Mexican Americans, and some Asian groups (p. 123); thus, collaborating on group or family goals is more strongly linked to achievement. For ELLs, and for many native speakers as well, cooperation can increase the students' sense of being part of a community of learners. This community spirit, in turn, can positively influence a student's attitudes toward learning, toward the teacher and the other students, and toward himself or herself as a learner. Krashen (1981) explains that when students like the teacher and feel a level of comfort in the classroom, they are more receptive to comprehensible input. Additionally, because research indicates that there is a direct relationship between attitude and language acquisition, Krashen concludes "that attitudinal factors and motivational factors are more important than aptitude" (p. 5) in second language acquisition. For a concise review of the research on second language learning and practical guidelines for teaching, see Robin Scarcella's article, "English Learners and Writing: Responding to Linguistic Diversity" on the companion website.

INTEGRATING MULTIPLE INTELLIGENCES THEORY AND COGNITIVE STRATEGIES THROUGH INSTRUCTIONAL SCAFFOLDING

Two National Research Council (NRC) reports (August & Hakuta, 1997; Snow, Burns, & Griffin, 1998) point out the paucity of research on how best to teach English to ELLs, particularly in secondary schools. The NRC committee identified the following attributes of effective schools and classrooms that benefit all learners, especially ELLs: curriculum that balances basic and higher order skills; explicit skills instruction for certain tasks, particularly in acquiring learning strategies; instructional approaches to enhance comprehension; articulation and coordination of programs and practices within and between schools. Like the NCR reports, Fitzgerald (1995), in her analysis of effective reading instruction for ELLs, argues that both native and nonnative English-speaking children benefit from the same types of balanced reading approaches—approaches that include explicit strategy instruction. She states that there is "virtually no evidence that ESL learners need notably divergent forms of instruction to guide or develop their cognitive reading process" (p. 184), and advises that ". . . at least with regard to the cognitive aspects of reading, U.S. teachers of ESL students should follow sound principles of reading instruction based on current cognitive research done with native English speakers" (p. 184). In a similar vein, Wong Fillmore and Snow (2003) argue that all children need to learn cognitive strategies. Jiménez, García, and Pearson (1994), who studied the reading strategies of bilingual Latino/a students who are successful readers, concur that cognitive strategies might help ELLs develop academic literacy. Other researchers such as Wong

Fillmore (1986), members of The Education Alliance (Coady et al., 2003), and Anderson and Roit (1994), emphasize a cognitive strategies approach to link reading and writing instruction.

Although the term *instructional scaffolding* appears rarely in second language scholarship, the principles of many second language pedagogies are theoretically compatible with the scaffolding model. For example, Krashen's (1981) theory of comprehensible input is grounded in the same research on first language acquisition and "caretaker speech" (p. 102) that Bruner (1978) cited when he used the term "instructional scaffolding" (p. 254). Further, Chamot and O'Malley (1994) stress that teachers of ELLs should focus instruction on cognitive, metacognitive, problem solving, and social/affective learning strategies, and their description of the cognitive academic language learning approach (CALLA) parallels the practices of effective instructional scaffolding delineated by Langer and Applebee (1986): preparation—tapping prior knowledge; presentation—explanation and modeling of new information; practice—hands-on experimentation with the teacher as facilitator; evaluation—self-monitoring; expansion—real-world application extending to a new situation; and the ultimate goal, internalization as autonomous learners (pp. 120–122). Our experience at the UCI Writing Project has been that ELLs often need more instructional scaffolding than their English-speaking peers to develop as confident and competent readers and writers and that multiple intelligences approaches can be used as a tool to help them achieve that goal.

INTRODUCING STUDENTS TO MI THEORY

Howard Gardner was asked in an interview, "A popular activity among those who are first exploring multiple intelligences is to construct their own intellectual profile . . . what do you think of this activity?" (Checkley, 1997, p. 10). He replied,

> My own studies have shown that people love to do this. Kids like to do it, adults like to do it. And, as an activity, I think it's perfectly harmless. I get concerned, though, when people think that determining your intellectual profile—or that of someone else—is an end in itself. You have to use the profile to understand the ways in which you seem to learn easily. And from there, determine how to use those strengths to help you become successful in other endeavors. (pp. 10–11)

We agree with Gardner on both counts. Students do enjoy exploring their intellectual comfort zones and avoidance areas. Further, like Gardner, we'd like them to use this self-awareness to build on their strengths so as to become confident and competent learners in a range of intelligences. Armstrong (1994) usually begins introducing students to MI theory by asking them, "How many of you think you're intelligent?" Interestingly enough, he has discovered that there "seems to be an inverse relationship between the number of hands that go up and the grade level that he's teaching" (p. 38). This has caused him to wonder—if students enter the school system believing they're smart, "What do we do in the intervening years to convince children that they're not intelligent?" (p. 38). We begin our introduction of MI theory more indirectly by involving students in a corners activity much like the one described in Chapter 4.

Corners Activity

This corners activity was adapted from *History Alive!,* a publication of the Teachers' Curriculum Institute (Bower, Lobdell, & Swenson, 1999), by the UCI Writing Project MI Research Team (Gloria Austin, Carolee Dunn, Holly Feldt, Cathie Hunsberger, and Julie

Simpson). Create a chart to give to students similar to the one shown in Figure 4.2 on page 76. Replace the categories (e.g., animals, cars) with the letters *A* through *G*. Then, post signs for *A–G* in seven locations throughout the room. Initiate the activity by saying:

> I will ask you five questions. Choose the answer most suited to you and go to the appropriate section of the room. Find out the names of everyone who has chosen the same area as you and put a check by each name on your chart. Explain to one another why you chose that answer instead of the others. After talking to others, think of one word to describe why you chose that particular corner and record it in the far right column on your chart. You have one minute to move to a corner, four minutes to talk with the people you meet there, and one minute to record a word that comes to mind—such as "loner," "athlete," "organized," "dramatic," and so forth.

Then present students with the four forced-choice scenarios below, allowing six minutes for each interaction:

1. Which method could best help you memorize facts for a test?
   A. Rephrase the facts in your own words so they make sense to you
   B. Create a kind of jingle to sing the facts to yourself
   C. Arrange the facts in logical categories
   D. Sketch shapes or objects that will help you recall the facts
   E. Pace around your room or house while you memorize
   F. Study each fact long enough to make a personal connection to it
   G. Work with a study partner to practice the details

2. If you had one free afternoon and had to choose one of the following activities, which would you be most likely to do?
   A. Read a good book
   B. Listen to music
   C. Figure out a new computer program
   D. Play a sport, dance
   E. Draw, play a video game, do a jigsaw puzzle
   F. Spend time by yourself, thinking or daydreaming
   G. Get a group together to go on a picnic

3. If your senior high school class decided to create a project to leave for future students at their school, which task would you feel most comfortable working on?
   A. Writing letters to local businesses, asking for donations of materials or money
   B. Creating musical ads to sing over the morning announcements to lure other seniors to help
   C. Calculating the materials needed and what the costs would be
   D. Drawing the plans for the project
   E. Constructing the project
   F. Reflecting upon what kind of project might send a significant message to future students
   G. Visiting businesses to solicit donations

4. Which career most interests you as you look forward to the future?
   A. Journalist, writer, lawyer
   B. Singer, songwriter, musician, choral director
   C. Computer programmer, mathematician, accountant, scientist

D. Painter, graphic artist, cartoonist, interior designer

E. Actor, sculptor, dancer, construction worker, athlete

F. Poet, philosopher, self-employed businessperson

G. Teacher, counselor, activities director

Ask students to remain in their question 4 groupings for question 5.

5. *Taking a Fair Share.* Present students with the following word problem from Larry Chrystal, a lecturer in mathematics in the UCI School of Physical Sciences, and ask them to take five minutes to work together to solve the problem. Ask them to pay special attention to the different or common methods people in the group use to arrive at the solution, and to record those on the chart when you call time:

> Jack, Sue, and Steve were given a plate of cookies to share after finishing their homework. Jack finished first, took a third of the cookies, and returned to his room. Then Sue, who did not know that Jack had already finished, took a third of the cookies on the plate and returned to her room. Then Steve, certain that he had finished before Jack and Sue, took a third of the cookies on the plate and returned to his room. If there were eight cookies left on the plate, how many cookies were there originally?

As they select their various corners options, students may find that they meet many of the same classmates at each of the corners. This is because, unbeknownst to them, the corner options A–G have been arranged according to the intelligence categories (A = linguistic; B = musical; C = logical–mathematical; D = spatial; E = bodily–kinesthetic; F = intrapersonal; G = interpersonal). Once they take the multiple intelligences survey, students will discover the relevance of the corners activity.

Multiple Intelligences Survey

After students have participated in the corners activity, pass out the multiple intelligences survey, also adapted from *History Alive!* (Bower, Lobdell, & Swenson, 1999) by the UCI Writing Project MI Research Team. The survey, which is available on the companion website, asks students to mark *yes, no,* or *yes and no* to such statements as:

• I'd rather draw a map than give someone verbal directions.

• I like to work with calculators and computers.

• I like to gather together groups of people for parties or events.

• I can usually find my way around unfamiliar places.

I often find that the teaching credential candidates in my classes take this survey too seriously, even becoming disappointed if they score low on certain intelligence categories. So I take time to explain that the survey is *unscientific,* that we are taking it for fun, and that their own intuition is as good a predictor of their intellectual comfort zones and avoidance areas as this pencil-and-paper test (which Howard Gardner would probably abhor, by the way). I also counsel them to choose yes *or* no rather than yes *and* no as much as possible, because "yes and no" responses will lower their overall score.

Once students complete questions 1 through 49 on the survey, they can total up their scores and shade in a grid that will graphically illustrate their intellectual strengths and the areas in which they are less dominant. Some students are stumped as to what to do when they arrive at this point in the survey. I usually joke that if they can't figure it out, they probably won't score high in the logical and spatial arenas and that they should turn to a partner for help.

Expert Groups Using the results of the MI survey, place students in one of the seven groups (A–G) based on their strengths. Ask them to talk among themselves to figure out what they might have in common that would explain why they have been grouped together. Once they have discovered the intellectual strength they share in common, small groups should then make a brief presentation to the larger group about the attributes of that particular intelligence. If time permits, the small groups can create an artifact (poster, tangible object, formula, etc.) to illustrate their respective traits. During or after the group presentations, the teacher should augment students' statements with background on MI theory.

There is a saying among proponents of MI theory, "It's not how smart you are, but how you are smart." The gist of the expression is that all students have intellectual strengths. It is the teacher's job to identify and build on those strengths, create bridges between students' intellectual strengths and those intelligences which are most highly valued in school, and to enhance students' self-esteem. Teaching students about MI theory can also expand their notion of what it means to be smart. The National Research Council Report *How People Learn* (Donovan, Bransford, & Pellegrino, 1999) notes, "Students' theories of what it means to be intelligent can affect their performance. Research shows that students who think intelligence is a fixed entity are more likely to be performance oriented—they want to look good rather than risk making mistakes while learning. These students are especially likely to bail out when tasks become difficult. In contrast, students who think intelligence is malleable are more willing to struggle with challenging tasks; they are more comfortable with risk" (p. 20).

Learning Log Reflection To help students begin to explore what significance MI theory has for them as learners, ask them to respond to the following informal prompt and to write a one-page reflection.

Prompt

Learning Log Reflection

1. In which intelligence(s) do you most prefer to operate? What is it about this area (or these areas) that creates a comfort zone for you? Explain how you use this intelligence (or these intelligences) as a learning tool.

2. In which intelligence (or intelligences) do you feel least confident or able? Explain what you do as a learner when a task calls for you to use this intelligence (or these intelligences). How might you strengthen this area (or these areas)?

DEMONSTRATION LESSON

"Not Mine!" Interpreting Sandra Cisneros's "Eleven"

Robin Scarcella (1997) observes, "Exposing learners to comprehensible input in the writing classroom is not enough. For example, they can be given the right type of comprehensible reading material; but to get them to learn from it, teachers need to have them interact meaningfully with it and to use it in their writing" (p. 88). This is true of both ELLs and native speakers. As Urzúa (1989) remarks, "All of us, first- and second-language readers alike, bring to a literary task the expectation to construct meaning" (p. 29). Multiple intelligences approaches to language arts instruction can be an effective tool in facilitating the process of meaning construction.

Sharon Schiesl and I (1996) originally developed this lesson for her eighth-grade transitional ELD class at McFadden Intermediate School in Santa Ana, California. However, it has been implemented successfully in mainstream middle and high school classrooms as well. Terms used to describe the reading, thinking, and writing tasks are taken from Figure 1.2 (Cognitive Strategies: A Reader's and Writer's Tool Kit) and from Figure 3.2 (the UCI Writing Project's adaptation of Bloom's "taxonomy of the cognitive domain"). Additionally, within the narrative that describes the activities, we identify the types of intelligences accessed. Note that in this lesson we did not attempt to tap all eight of the intelligences identified by Gardner but focused on the ones that lent themselves well to providing additional windows into the text.

Because this lesson was originally geared for ELD students, the written product it calls for is a letter. We have also had success with an essay as the end product; teachers interested in focusing on the essay will find the prompt, the scoring rubric, and a sample student paper on the companion website. Most of the lesson activities can be used for both domains of writing. For essay writing, however, the planning activities in the Chapter 8 demonstration lesson on Amy Tan's "The Moon Lady" also will be helpful.

Overview

After reading, visualizing, and interpreting Sandra Cisneros's short story "Eleven," students will assume the persona of Rachel and write a letter to another character in the text, using similes and metaphors to describe their thoughts and feelings about the incident that occurred in class because of the red sweater.

Objectives

Students will:

1. Make predictions about the story based on an examination of tangible items that have symbolic significance in the story
2. Kinesthetically dramatize and visualize the story through performing a reader's theater
3. Practice a range of cognitive strategies using marginal notes stemming from sentence starters
4. Work in groups to visualize and interpret the incident with the red sweater by spatially rendering the imagery and symbolism in the story
5. Make personal connections with the text by creating similes and metaphors for themselves
6. Create an original simile or metaphor to represent the experience of Rachel
7. Adopt an alignment by assuming Rachel's persona
8. As Rachel, compose a letter to another character in the text to communicate thoughts and feelings about the incident with the red sweater.

The Process

This lesson will take approximately one week to implement. The time frame may be condensed for older students and mainstream learners or expanded for ELLs.

Prereading Activity 1

Mystery Items ■ *Analyzing and Making Predictions*

Bring to class the following items: a Band-Aid box with pennies inside it; an onion with a birthday candle inserted in one end; a set of nested dolls; a partially deflated balloon; tree rings (for example, thin slices cut from a thick tree branch or Christmas tree trunk); and the most objectionable red sweater you can find. Tell students that the mystery items you have brought in have symbolic significance in the story "Eleven," by Sandra Cisneros, which the class will be reading shortly. (A copy of the story is available at the end of this chapter.) Some of these items are literally identified in the text; others represent the teacher's interpretation of certain references in the story. As students sit in groups, circulate these items from table to table. As students kinesthetically manipulate these items, ask them to discuss what meaning they might represent in the text and to begin to make predictions about what will happen in the story. Discussions will proceed along the lines of the group dialogue at the beginning of this chapter.

Prereading Activity 2

Prediction/Confirmation Chart ■ *Analyzing and Making Predictions*

After all of the items have been analyzed and discussed by each group, call the whole group together and ask for predictions about the story. Be sure to probe for elaboration by asking questions like "What makes you think that?" If students do not mention the red sweater, be sure to bring it up and engage the class in discussion. Record the students' predictions on a chart such as the one on the left-hand side of Figure 5.1.

During Reading Activity 1

Readers' Theater ■ *Visualizing*

Once the prediction activity has set the stage for the story and students are curious about what happens, select eight students to dramatize the story kinesthetically by performing the text as a readers' theater. In a readers' theater, students take on the roles of the narrator and various characters and act out the story as if it were a play. Scarcella (1997) notes that having students "perform actions in a story" is an important way to "ensure that students understand the English used in their lessons" (p. 88). ELLs will need to rehearse their parts, with assistance from the teacher, whereas mainstream students can probably just read their parts through once or twice before the performance. (It is helpful to highlight each actor's part in the original story or in the story typed up as a script.) It is also helpful to put the red sweater on a hanger and to have some schoolbooks and a ruler up at the front desk to serve as props during the performance. Take care not to select a shy student to play the part of Rachel; the

Figure 5.1   **Prediction/Confirmation Chart, Completed**

Predictions	Confirmations
• It's about a birthday party.	• It's about a birthday, but the party will come later and it has been spoiled.
• The gift will be money.	• This prediction did not pan out.
• Someone is sad.	• Yes, Rachel ends up sad.
• Something bad will happen.	• Mrs. Price embarrasses her.
• It's a poor girl's birthday.	• We don't really know if Rachel is poor or not.
• Someone is going to cry.	• Yes, Rachel cries like she's three.
• Red means attention, so someone will get all the attention.	• She gets attention all right, but it's negative.
• There's something about layers.	• We all have all the years we are inside of us like layers of who we are.

part has few speaking lines, but it does call for some kinesthetic dramatics (such as crying). The following excerpt demonstrates how the readers' theater is delivered:

Rachel's Narrator: Except when math period ends Mrs. Price says loud and in front of everybody,

Mrs. Price: "Now, Rachel, that's enough."

Rachel's Narrator: Because she sees I've shoved the red sweater to the tippy-tip corner of my desk and it's hanging all over the edge like a waterfall, but I don't care.

Mrs. Price: "Rachel—"

Mrs. Price's Narrator: Mrs. Price says. She says it like she's getting mad.

Mrs. Price: "You put that sweater on right now and no more nonsense."

Rachel: "But it's not—"

Mrs. Price: "Now!"

Mrs. Price's Narrator: Mrs. Price says.

Rachel's Narrator: This is when I wish I wasn't eleven, because all the years inside of me—ten, nine, eight, seven, six, five, four, three, two and one—are pushing at the back of my eyes when I put one arm through one sleeve of the sweater that smells like cottage cheese, and then the other arm through the other and stand there with my arms apart like if the sweater hurts me and it does, all itchy and full of germs that aren't even mine.

During Reading Activity 2

Prediction/Confirmation Chart ■ *Confirming and Revising Meaning*

After completing the readers' theater, draw students' attention to the predictions they made before reading. Discuss which predictions were accurate and which predictions were inaccurate or need to be modified. Complete the confirmation side of the prediction/confirmation chart (Figure 5.1).

During Reading Activity 3

Rereading and Responding ■ *Visualizing, Making Connections, Interpreting*

After checking the actual events in the story against their predictions, students should reread the text closely and make marginal notes using the cognitive strategies sentence starters in Figure 2.1 on page 20. The complete story, with a column for notes and reactions, is printed at the end of this chapter. Mainstream students can reread the story silently and use the complete list of response starters; with ELD students, however, it is important for the teacher to reread the story aloud and to narrow the response options to starters like "This reminds me of . . . ," "I wonder why . . . ," "I can picture . . . ," and "I think this represents . . ." Allen (1989) notes that "second language learners need to have the opportunity to hear familiar stories read again and again" (p. 62). Schiesl found that it was necessary to reread the story to her class in manageable chunks, to model how to analyze a text closely, and to model making marginal notes, as in Figure 5.2.

Postreading Activity 1

What's with That Red Sweater? ■ *Analyzing Symbols and Forming Interpretations*

Explain to students that a symbol is a word, object, or action that literally is one thing but that suggests or stands for something other than itself. For example, an American flag is literally a piece of cloth with stars and stripes on it, but it represents or stands for the United States and its democratic ideals. Some symbols are commonly interpreted one way. For

Figure 5.2 **Marginalia**

| **"Eleven" by Sandra Cisneros**

What they don't understand about birth-days and what they never tell you is that when you're eleven, you're also ten, and nine, and eight, and seven, and six, and five, and four, and three, and two and one. And when you wake up on your eleventh birth-day you expect to feel eleven, but you don't. You open your eyes and everything's just like yesterday, only it's today. And you don't feel eleven at all. You feel like you're still ten. And you are—underneath the year that makes you eleven. | *So, you really are like a set of nesting dolls, with the person you were last year inside the person you are this year. I feel this when it's my birthday too. It takes a while to feel like you're the next year old. This reminds me of what Cao said about layers.* |

example, on Valentine's Day we give hearts to signify love and affection. Other symbols are open to interpretation. Even the symbol of the American flag means something different to those countries or people who see the United States as an adversary. In literature, authors often use a symbol repeatedly in a text—and they expect the reader to do some detective work, to read the clues as it were, to figure out what a symbol means.

Direct the students' attention to the red sweater. Why does the red sweater figure so prominently in the story? What might this object symbolize? Students' answers may vary but will probably include embarrassment (you turn red when you're embarrassed); a wound (red signifies blood, and Rachel's pride is symbolically wounded by Mrs. Price); shame (shame burns like fire and fire is red); and so on. The students may also bring up the role of power in the story and discuss how, by forcing Rachel to put on the sweater, Mrs. Price exerts her power. The teacher may also want to go through the significance of the other objects he or she brought in—for example, the deflated balloon as a symbol of a deflated ego and the birthday onion as a symbol of the inevitable tears.

Postreading Activity 2

Hibbing and Rankin-Erickson (2003) remark, "We have noticed that the strategic use of visual material can enhance reading experiences for reluctant and low-ability readers, and indeed, can help them become more proficient creators of internal visual imagery that supports comprehension" (p. 759). This is also true of ELLs whose understanding may surpass their ability to linguistically articulate what they know. This is why the *California Teaching Performance Expectations* (California Commission on Teacher Credentialing, 2001) call for ELL teachers to "select instructional materials and strategies, including activities in the area of visual and performing arts, to develop students' abilities to comprehend and produce English" and to "allow students to express meaning in a variety of ways" (p. A-8). Engaging ELLs in collaborative art activities also encourages a deep level of talk about texts as the students negotiate regarding the artifact they are creating and its meaning.

Illustrated Group Work ■ *Visualizing*

Ask students to form groups of three to four and to illustrate and explicate their understanding of the story using one of the following four graphic activities. As students interact to render the imagery and symbolism in the story, they will be accessing their interpersonal, spatial, and linguistic intelligences.

Figure 5.3   **Storyboard**

STORYBOARD

The storyboard activity involves dividing a piece of paper into six squares; envisioning the story cinematically, as if it were a movie; sketching the most crucial scenes, in order; and inserting pertinent lines from the text. While the storyboard primarily taps spatial intelligence, the sequencing part of the activity also involves logical–mathematical abilities. A template for the storyboard is available on the companion website. Two sample storyboard scenes from Sharon Schiesl's ELD class are displayed in Figure 5.3.

OPEN MIND

The open mind activity allows students to get into the minds of the characters they are studying and to depict their thoughts and feelings both graphically and verbally. We originally assigned a split open mind, in which students would use half the open mind to capture Rachel's thoughts and feelings before the red sweater incident and the other half to illustrate her sense of self after the incident. But Schiesl's students found the limited space too restricting, so we adopted a double open mind structure as in Figure 5.4. (A template for the split open mind is available on the companion website.)

Figure 5.4   **Open Mind**

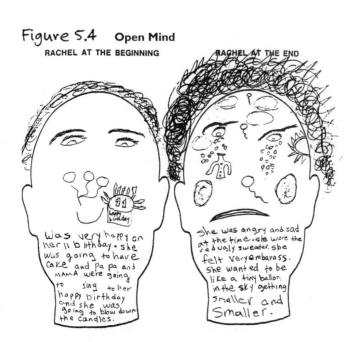

Figure 5.5 **Literature Portrait**

LITERATURE PORTRAIT

In literature portraits, students are asked to conceptualize a story as if it were a painting. First, they create a border or frame for their portrait and decorate it with words or images from the story. Second, they have to draw the Big Idea, or theme, of the story in the center of the portrait. Third, in their own words, they write down the theme of the story. Finally, they select a quote from the story that best illustrates this theme, as in Figure 5.5. (Instructions for the literature portrait are available on the companion website.)

CHARACTER FRAME AND COAT OF ARMS

Students could also choose to create a coat of arms for Rachel. See Planning Activities 1 and 2 in the Chapter 4 "My Name, My Self" demonstration lesson for an explanation of the character frame and the coat of arms. A blank character frame and coat of arms for Rachel are available on the companion website.

Prewriting Activity

Quickwrite as Rachel ■ *Adopting an Alignment*

After students have explored Rachel's thoughts and feelings in small groups, ask them to become Rachel and, in her voice, to write for five minutes about how she felt during the incident:

■ I remember that ugly big, red mountain she put on my desk and accused me of it being mine. She believed Sylvia Saldivar when she said it was mine! But we both knew it wasn't. She didn't even care of what I was going to say.

—Karina

 Prompt Introduce students to the following prompt. An 8½-by-11 copy of the prompt is available on the companion website; an alternative prompt that culminates in an essay is also included on the website.

 Pretend you are Rachel in the story "Eleven" by Sandra Cisneros. Become Rachel and, in her voice, write a letter to another character in the story describing how you felt about what happened to you in class with Mrs. Price and the red sweater. You may write as Rachel at the time of the incident, or you may project yourself into the future (i.e., be Rachel at an older age). As you express your thoughts and feelings about the incident, describe yourself (Rachel) through at least one simile or metaphor that comes directly from the story and at least one simile or metaphor of your own.

Your letter should be in standard letter form—greeting, body, and closing.

1. Begin by addressing your audience and explaining why you are writing.
2. Go on to describe the incident with the red sweater and how you felt about what happened to you, using at least one simile or metaphor from the text and one simile or metaphor of your own.
3. Bring the body of your letter to a close with a final remark about the incident or parting words to the person you are writing.
4. Remember to write "Sincerely," "Yours truly," or (if you are writing to your mother or father) "Love," before you sign Rachel's name.

Be sure to use correct spelling, punctuation, and sentence structure to make your letter impress your audience.

Planning Activity 1

Character Chart ■ *Analyzing and Digging Deeper*

To help students decide whom to write to, hand out the character chart provided on the companion website so that students can closely examine each character mentioned in the story, what that character did, and Rachel's response—and can reflect on what the student would do if he or she were in Rachel's place.

Planning Activity 2

Minilesson on Similes and Metaphors ■ *Analyzing Author's Craft*

Remind students that the prompt calls for them to use at least one simile or metaphor from the text in their letter and then to compose an original simile or metaphor to include in their letter. Introduce or revisit the definitions of a simile and metaphor:

- A simile states a comparison using the terms *like* or *as*:

    I want to be far away already, far away *like a runaway balloon* . . .

- A metaphor is a direct comparison of two things on the basis of a shared quality—as if one thing were the other:

    I put my head down on the desk and bury my face in my stupid *clown-sweater arms.*

Have students take a yellow highlighter and mark the similes and metaphors they find. Tell them that although Cisneros relies almost exclusively on similes in her text, they can feel free to use metaphors in theirs.

Planning Activity 3

Similes for Self ■ *Analyzing and Interpreting*

Sharon and I had hoped that ELD students would be able to make the cognitive leap from finding figurative language in the text to creating similes or metaphors of their own. However, they had such difficulty with this task that we had to backtrack and ask them to create a set of similes for themselves. Schiesl's students came up with examples such as the following:

■ What animal are you most like?
I am like a bird because I love to sing.

- What plant are you most like?

  I am like a dandelion because I am strong and hard to get rid of.

- What shape are you most like?

  I am like a circle because I keep going and going.

Once students had created figures of speech to represent themselves, they were able to grasp how to do the same for Rachel.

Planning Activity 4

Original Simile or Metaphor for Rachel ■ *Visualizing and Forming Interpretations*

Before students create their own simile or metaphor to represent Rachel's experience, you may want to provide a model as in Figure 5.6. Suggest that students use their spatial intelligence to draw their simile or metaphor, then freewrite about it as in the model. Ask students to underline the simile in the model ("like she's in a lineup") and the metaphor ("the red sweater criminal") to remind them once again of the two figures of speech.

Then ask students to work on their own comparisons. Here are some examples from Sharon's class:

- Rachel is no red sweater. She is cashmere and silk!

  —Kathleen

- Rachel feels like a warm Coke after someone shakes it.

  —Susan

- Rachel feels like the winter, cold and rainy.

  —Susana

Writing

■ *Constructing the Gist*

Have students use their marginal notes, illustrated group work, character chart, and drawing and quickwrite original for their simile or metaphor to write their letter to their chosen audi-

Figure 5.6   Original Simile and Metaphor

I bet Rachel feels like she's in a lineup with the bright lights beating down on her and the perspiration running down her neck. "You," Mrs. Price says, "number 11. Step forward. That's her. That's the red sweater criminal. She's the one."

ence. Before they begin writing, remind them of the letter format: greeting, body, and closing.

Sharing Activity 1

Practice Responding to Sample Student Essay ■ *Analyzing Author's Craft*

Refer students to the sample letter by Karina Alejo from Schiesl's eighth-grade ELD class in Figure 5.7. With Karina's letter on an overhead, ask the class to help you to do the following:

- Underline the date, greeting, and closing in green. (Point out the appropriate punctuation for the date, greeting, and closing.)
- Underline why the author is writing in blue.
- Underline the similes and metaphors taken directly from the text in red.
- Underline the original similes and metaphors in orange.
- Underline the final remark in purple.

Ask the students to volunteer some specific details about the student model that they particularly like. For example, they may think it's clever that Karina put herself in the sixth grade (the grade Rachel would be in, in the story) and wrote to Mrs. Price eleven years later. They might also note how naturally she weaves the figures of speech from "Eleven" into her letter or admire the way she compares herself to the fall leaves.

Sharing Activity 2

Responding to Each Other's Letters ■ *Analyzing Author's Craft*

Have students trade papers with a partner and use the sharing sheet on the companion website, which replicates what the students did with the model, to respond to each other's

Figure 5.7 Student Model (Reprinted by permission of Karina Alejo.)

November 30, 2007

Dear Mrs. Price,

   Do you remember me? I am Rachel. I was in your 6th grade class in 1996. I was the skinny little girl that was shy and was a loner. Now I am 22 years old. I am in college now studying to be a teacher.

   It was eleven years ago today when you embarrassed me in front of all of my classmates. Today is my birthday! Also, eleven years ago you made me the most unhappy eleven-year-old in the world. It all started with that ugly red sweater.

   You remember that ugly, big, red mountain you put on my desk and accused me of it being mine. You believed Sylvia Salvidar when she said it was mine! But we both know now that it wasn't mine. You didn't even care of what I was going to say. You didn't say you were sorry when Phyllis Lopez admitted it was hers. Also, when I cried in front of all of my classmates you just turned to page 32 and math problem number 4. The sweater was "not mine, not mine, not mine!" I wanted to be invisible like when a balloon gets away from you and looks like a little tiny "o" in the sky. You close your eyes to see it and it's gone. That's what I wanted to be.

   I guess I am like the fall season. Every year I change my leaves and every year I am a different color of leaves. I have changed and learned a lot since 6th grade. I am studying to be a teacher to help all the other Rachels in the 6th grade and help them not go through what you made me go through.

   Well, now it's goodbye because I have no more to say. I am just happy that I got that out of me.

Sincerely,
Rachel
(Karina Alejo)

An 8½-by-11 copy of Karina's letter that can be made into a transparency is available on the companion website. An 8½-by-11 copy of a model student essay is also on the website.

papers. Note that the color coding gives students a visual/spatial way to see if they have fulfilled the requirements of the prompt.

Revising Activity 1

Applying the Scoring Rubric ■ *Reviewing and Assessing Quality*

Refer students to the scoring rubric on the companion website. Scarcella (1997) notes that teachers may need to give "intermediate and advanced English learners one grade for grammar and another for content and organization" (p. 90). Therefore, this lesson uses a primary and secondary trait scoring system. Refer students to the primary trait scoring rubric and review the criteria. Students can also use the content checklist on the website to double-check that they have met all the requirements of the prompt.

Revising Activity 2

Reconstructing the Draft ■ *Revising for Meaning*

After students complete their content checklist, they can revise their letters accordingly. Note: The ELD teacher may wish to conference with students, using their draft and checklist as a conversation piece, before students revise.

Editing Activity

Form and Correctness ■ *Proofreading for Correctness*

Have students consult the secondary trait scoring rubric and, working together in partners, check each other's papers for the following:

- Letter format—date, greeting, body, closing
- Proper paragraph form (indentation for each paragraph)
- Complete sentences
- Proper punctuation (comma between day and year; comma after greeting and closing)
- Correct spelling
- Proper usage/grammar

Before students begin this editing activity, the teacher should point out the words taken directly from the text, like "balloon," that students are spelling incorrectly in their illustrated group work and quickwrites. Also review words not in the text that students have used and misspelled, such as "embarrass" or "humiliate." You may also want to review the minilesson on pronouns on the companion website (Chapter 3). Depending on the level of the class, the teacher may want to point out that when Karina says, "You didn't even care of what I was going to say," the proper usage is "You didn't even care *about* what I was going to say." The teacher should be available as a technical consultant so students can double-check when they are uncertain about spelling, sentence construction, and so forth.

Evaluation

The Scoring Rubric ■ *Assessing Quality against Criteria*

The teacher can evaluate the final product using the full six-point primary trait and four-point secondary trait scoring rubric available on the companion website. (Note: The rubric for the essay is also on the companion website.) The criteria for a 6, the maximum score possible for the primary trait, and for a 4, the maximum score possible for the secondary trait, are provided below. Note that the rubric gives a higher weight to content than to form and correctness.

Primary Trait ■ *Content*

SUPERIOR

The 6 letter is clearly superior: well written, insightful, and creative. The 6 paper does all or most of the following well:

- Assumes the persona of Rachel and impressively writes in her voice
- Addresses the person to whom the letter is written and clearly explains why Rachel is writing
- Describes in depth Rachel's thoughts and feelings during the incident with the red sweater
- Skillfully weaves at least one simile or metaphor from the text into the letter
- Uses at least one simile or metaphor that is original, creative, and/or insightful
- Includes a thoughtful or significant final remark about the incident or parting words to the person

Secondary Trait ■ *Form and Correctness*

SUPERIOR

A 4 letter has few, if any, errors in form and correctness. The 4 paper will contain the following:

- Proper letter form: date, greeting, body, closing
- Proper paragraph form
- Complete sentences and correct sentence structure
- Few if any, errors in the conventions of written English, including spelling, usage, grammar, and punctuation

ELD teachers may also want to have the revised drafts turned in so the teacher can review them and mark remaining problem areas before students finalize their drafts.

Postwriting

Designing Stationery ■ *Visualizing and Interpreting*

An optional culminating activity is to have the students use their spatial and kinesthetic intelligence to design their own stationery, which they can decorate with symbols relevant to the text, and copy their letters neatly in handwriting. Letters can be displayed on a class bulletin board so students can appreciate one another's similes and metaphors.

Learning Log Reflection

Quickwrite ■ *Stepping Back, Monitoring, and Reflecting*

Present the following learning log quickwrite prompt to students:

Review the activities you participated in as you prepared to write your letter. Which activities helped you the most to understand the story and to interpret the symbols Sandra Cisneros uses to depict Rachel's experience? Which activities helped you the most to create your own similes and metaphors to compare Rachel's thoughts and feelings to other things? Describe which of the multiple intelligences these activities tapped and what the experience of using these intelligences as a learning tool was like for you.

MI THEORY AND LEARNING STYLES

The term *learning style* refers to the preferred way that an individual acquires, processes, and retains information. Silver, Strong, and Perini (2000) point out that while MI theory is a model concerned primarily with the content or *what* of learning, learning styles pertain to the *how* of learning—in other words, to an individual's preferences for certain types of thinking processes and how those preferences affect learning. Learning styles and MI theory are often presented to students in tandem. The most traditional description of learning styles focuses on three learning preferences: *Visual learners* learn best by seeing things and are most engaged when reading, looking at pictures and charts, and watching films, videos, and demonstrations; *auditory learners* prefer attending lectures over reading texts because they learn best when they can hear information being imparted; *kinesthetic learners* gravitate toward hands-on experiences where they can learn by doing (Von Blerkom, 1997, pp. 80–81.)

Another model of learning styles, based on the Myers-Briggs Type Indicator (MBTI, Briggs-Myers 1993) and designed by Barbara Soloman at North Carolina State University, identifies four dimensions of learning, each of which has two opposing styles:

> *Active/reflective.* Active learners learn best by experiencing knowledge through their own actions. Reflective learners understand information best when they have had time to reflect on it on their own.
>
> *Factual/theoretical.* Factual learners learn best through specific facts, data, and detailed experimentation. Theoretical learners are more comfortable with big-picture ideas, symbols, and new concepts.
>
> *Visual/verbal.* Visual learners remember best what they see: diagrams, flowcharts, time lines, films, and demonstrations. Verbal learners gain most learning from reading, hearing spoken words, participating in discussion, and explaining things to others.
>
> *Linear/holistic.* Linear learners find it easiest to learn material presented step by step in a logical, ordered progression. Holistic learners progress in fits and starts, perhaps feeling lost for a while, but eventually seeing the big picture in a clear and creative way. (Carter, Bishop, & Kravits, 1998, p. 41)

Students in college study skills courses are often asked to take both MI and learning style inventories to develop their study strategies.

In *Integrating Learning Styles and Multiple Intelligences,* Silver, Strong, and Perini (2000) propose four learning styles that are also influenced by the Myers-Briggs Type Indicator: *Sensing-thinking learners* or *mastery learners* who are action- and results-oriented, need structured environments, and prefer closed-ended tasks; *intuitive-thinking learners* or *understanding learners* who are concerned with objective truth more than fact and like challenging tasks that cause them to think critically and to interpret; *intuitive-feeling learners* or *self-expressive learners* who prefer to use their imaginations rather than to undertake rote assignments, look for creative and unique ways to express themselves, and tend to multi-task, something appearing scattered or chaotic; and *sensing-feeling learners* or *interpersonal learners* who take a personal approach to learning, like to collaborate, tend to be spontaneous, and look for connections between what they are learning and personal experiences (pp. 24–28). Silver, Strong, and Perini have integrated MI theory and learning styles by mapping each of the four learning style preferences onto Gardner's eight intelligences to demonstrate how each type of learner would exercise that intelligence, matching vocations and real world applications to each intelligence-style profile, and listing products that learners demonstrating those intelligence-styles might create in a performance assessment (pp. 42–43). All of these approaches acknowledge that there are different pathways to learning. This is why the National Research Council commissioned a report synthesizing *How People Learn* (Donovan, Bransford, & Pellegrino, 1999) to determine how best to educate today's students. In addition to MI theory and learning styles, there are many recent books on brain-based learning. Popular texts among UCI Writing Project teachers are *Brain Matters: Translating Research into Classroom Practice* (Wolfe, 2001) and the brain-compatible learning strategies of Eric Jensen (1997; 1998).

EPILOGUE

The students in Sharon Schiesl's ELD class are sitting in groups examining a square cage with a small towel inside it and a sign on the side that says "Algernon."

"I don't see anything moving," Jose says. "She's just tricking us."

"Well, what is an Algernon anyway?" Lihn asks.

"It's a name. Get it? Like for a rat or something," Jose retorts. "But I don't see it moving, like I said. Maybe it's under that towel though, sleeping or something."

"We'll just have to wait and see what Mrs. Schiesl does next," Jesus chimes in. "I bet we're going to read something good. And I bet that cage will have something to do with it."

To Sum Up

Howard Gardner's theory of multiple intelligences (1983) encourages teachers to move beyond the linguistic and logical–mathematical domains that currently predominate in U.S. schools and to broaden their instructional repertoire to reach and engage *all* learners in their classrooms. It legitimizes the use of a range of approaches to teaching and learning. In addition, for ELLs, MI approaches increase the amount of comprehensible input the student is exposed to. The most essential and important ingredient in second language learning is comprehensible input, in which the focus is on the message being communicated or received and not on the form (Krashen, 1981). Second language scholars advocate enhancing comprehensible input by using visual aids such as pictures, diagrams, and charts; acting things out; using gestures; and adding musical accompaniment, jazz chants, creative movement, dance, puppetry, and more—because when students are acquiring a new language, even the innately linguistic learners do not yet have enough command of the language to understand fully what is being communicated to them or to make themselves completely understood. MI approaches to language arts instruction, such as the kinesthetic, spatial, and cooperative learning activities illustrated in the demonstration lesson on "Eleven," provide ELLs and mainstream students alike with an accessible way to develop their interpretive abilities. The goal in helping students access their individual intellectual strengths is to position them to use those strengths to gain confidence and competence in their multiple intelligences. Integrating MI Theory into the language arts classroom enables teachers to lower students' affective filters, making them more receptive to language learning, and to help students use their multiple intelligences and learning styles as tools to become more accomplished readers and writers.

Learning Log Reflection

Think of a text you teach that would lend itself to a multiple intelligences approach. Which of the intelligences would fit best with this text? How could you design MI activities and scaffold them in a way that would make the text more accessible to students? How can you use the nonlinguistic intelligences as a springboard to enhance your students' linguistic competence?

Notes/Reactions

Eleven

by Sandra Cisneros

What they don't understand about birthdays and what they never tell you is that when you're eleven, you're also ten, and nine, and eight, and seven, and six, and five, and four, and three, and two and one. And when you wake up on your eleventh birthday you expect to feel eleven, but you don't. You open your eyes and everything's just like yesterday, only it's today. And you don't feel eleven at all. You feel like you're still ten. And you are—underneath the year that makes you eleven.

Like some days you might say something stupid, and that's the part of you that's still ten. Or maybe some days you might need to sit on your mama's lap because you're scared, and that's the part of you that's five. And maybe one day when you're all grown up maybe you will need to cry like if you're three, and that's okay. That's what I tell Mama when she's sad and needs to cry. Maybe she's feeling three.

Because the way you grow old is kind of like an onion or like the rings inside a tree trunk or like my little wooden dolls that fit one inside the other, each year inside the next one. That's how being eleven years old is.

You don't feel eleven. Not right away. It takes a few days, weeks even, sometimes even months before you say Eleven when they ask you. And you don't feel smart eleven, not until you're almost twelve. That's the way it is.

Only today I wish I didn't have only eleven years rattling inside me like pennies in a tin Band-Aid box. Today I wish I was one hundred and two instead of eleven because if I was one hundred and two I'd have known what to say when Mrs. Price put the red sweater on my desk. I would've known how to tell her it wasn't mine instead of just sitting there with that look on my face and nothing coming out of my mouth.

"Whose is this?" Mrs. Price says, and she holds the red sweater up in the air for all the class to see. "Whose? It's been sitting in the coatroom for a month."

"Not mine," says everybody. "Not me."

"It has to belong to somebody," Mrs. Price keeps saying, but nobody can remember. It's an ugly sweater with red plastic buttons—and a collar and sleeves all stretched out like you could use it for a jump rope. It's maybe a thousand years old and even if it belonged to me I wouldn't say so.

Maybe because I'm skinny, maybe because she doesn't like me, that stupid Sylvia Saldivar says, "I think it belongs to Rachel." An ugly sweater like that, all raggedy and old, but Mrs. Price believes her. Mrs. Price takes the sweater and puts it right on my desk, but when I open my mouth nothing comes out.

"That's not, I don't, you're not. . . . Not mine," I finally say in a little voice that was maybe me when I was four.

"Of course it's yours," Mrs. Price says, "I remember you wearing it once." Because she's older and the teacher she's right and I'm not.

Not mine, not mine, not mine, but Mrs. Price is already turning to page thirty-two, and math problem number four. I don't know why but all of a sudden I'm feeling sick inside, like the part of me that's three wants to come out of my eyes, only I squeeze them shut tight and bite down on my teeth real hard and try to remember today I am eleven, eleven. Mama is making a cake for me for tonight, and when Papa comes home everybody will sing Happy birthday, happy birthday to you.

But when the sick feeling goes away and I open my eyes, the red sweater's still there like a big red mountain. I move the red sweater to the corner of my desk with my ruler. I move my pencil and books and eraser as far from it as possible. I even move my chair a little to the right. Not mine, not mine, not mine.

In my head I'm thinking how long till lunchtime, how long till I can take the red sweater and throw it over the schoolyard fence, or leave it hanging on a parking meter, or bunch it up into a little ball and toss it in the alley. Except when math period ends Mrs. Price says loud and in front of everybody, "Now, Rachel, that's enough," because she sees I've shoved the red sweater to the tippy-tip corner of my desk and it's hanging all over the edge like a waterfall, but I don't care.

"Rachel," Mrs. Price says. She says it like she's getting mad. "You put that sweater on right now and no more nonsense."

"But it's not—"

"Now!" Mrs. Price says.

This is when I wish I wasn't eleven, because all the years inside of me— ten, nine, eight, seven, six, five, four, three, two and one—are pushing at the back of my eyes when I put one arm through one sleeve of the sweater that smells like cottage cheese, and then the other arm through the other and stand there with my arms apart like if the sweater hurts me and it does, all itchy and full of germs that aren't even mine.

That's when everything I've been holding in since this morning, since when Mrs. Price put the sweater on my desk, finally lets go, and all of a sudden I'm crying in front of everybody. I wish I was invisible but I'm not. I'm eleven and it's my birthday today and I'm crying like I'm three in front of everybody. I put my head down on the desk and bury my face in my stupid clown-sweater arms. My face all hot and spit coming out of my mouth because I can't stop the little animal noises from coming out of me, until there aren't any more tears left in my eyes, and it's just my body shaking like when you have the hiccups, and my whole head hurts like when you drink milk too fast.

But the worst part is right before the bell rings for lunch. That stupid Phyllis Lopez, who is even dumber than Sylvia Saldivar, says she remembers the red sweater is hers! I take it off right away and give to her, only Mrs. Price pretends like everything's okay.

Today I'm eleven. There's a cake Mama's making for tonight, and when Papa comes home from work we'll eat it. There'll be candles and presents and everybody will sing Happy birthday, happy birthday to you, Rachel, only it's too late.

I'm eleven today. I'm eleven, ten, nine, eight, seven, six, five, four, three, two and one, but I wish I was one hundred and two. I wish I was anything but eleven, because I want to be far away already, far away like a runaway balloon, like a tiny *o* in the sky, so tiny-tiny you have to close your eyes to see it.

Strategies for Interacting with a Text

Using Reading and Writing to Learn

In his article "Dialogue with a Text," Robert Probst (1988) tells about a battle of wills he once observed between a teacher and her students in a secondary English class. It seems that the students were so troubled by a story they were reading—"So Much Unfairness of Things" by C. D. B. Bryan, in which a student succumbs to the temptation to cheat on an exam—that they repeatedly evaded the teacher's question, "What techniques does the author use to reveal character in this story?" The students talked instead about the moral complexities of the story and its relationship to their own lives. Reacting to the pressures that cause students to cheat, one girl blurted out, "My father has warned me what medical school is going to be like, and I'm not sure I can get through it—I'm not even sure I want to be a doctor. . . ." Another boy muttered under his breath, "I *did* cheat once, on a test, and I was scared to death, but no one turned me in." The teacher "tolerated the outpouring for a few brief moments." But, bound and determined to steer the class back toward her own agenda, the teacher finally ordered the class to answer her question: "What techniques does the author use to reveal character in this story? We've had them before," she insisted. "You studied them last year, you know what they are, there are only three—*now what are they?*" Stunned into submission, the students, now slumped in their chairs, quietly volunteered, "Well, the author can just tell you about somebody's character. . . . He can show how the character acts. . . . He can show other characters reacting to him or talking about him." Breathing a sigh of relief, the teacher, having finally achieved her objective, said, "Good . . . now let's go on. . . ."

When Probst later inquired why the teacher had felt so compelled to focus on her question rather than on the students' genuine responses, she explained that she had to move on:

> There were other stories to cover, other skills and techniques to be learned, and there was to be a test that Friday. They had to be ready for the test. It had to do with the techniques of characterization and it was important. Those kids . . . would be under a great deal of pressure to pass it, one way or another. They might even be tempted to cheat. (Probst, 1988, pp. 32–33)*

Source: R. Probst (1988), "Dialogue with a Text," *English Journal 77*(1), pp. 32–38. Copyright © 1988 by the National Council of Teachers of English. Reprinted with permission.

THE GUIDED TOUR PROBLEM

Probst's reminiscence struck a chord with me. It vividly brought to mind my experience as a graduate student teaching composition and literature at UCLA. In those days, I thought it was my job to guide students toward an "accepted" interpretation of each text. So, yellow highlighter in hand, I went through each line or page of a poem, story, or novel, carefully framing questions that would enable us all to arrive at a reading predetermined by my previous experience with the text, the readings of my professors culled from old class notes, and the insights of literary critics. I will even admit to occasionally taking a look at that old standby, *Cliffs Notes,* for an annotation of some obscure textual reference or for a second opinion on an interpretation that I myself felt rather uncertain about. I did a lot of fishing in those days—fishing for the right answers to what were sometimes ill-framed questions. When the class didn't bite, I would often just answer the question myself so that we could move on. As it was to the teacher in Probst's story, moving on was very important to me in those early days of teaching, although I can't recall precisely why. It was often, although not always, a laborious journey. But, as I think back, the journey may have been more laborious for me than for my students. After all, I was the one who was painstakingly trudging through each text, giving the guided tour, as it were. Like the teacher in Probst's story, I also did not trust the students' own instinctive responses to texts; nor did I see student collaboration on a shared interpretation of a text as a legitimate goal of the English classroom. In fact, on more than one occasion, I assigned the paper on a work of literature to be due the day before the class discussion so no one could "borrow" any of their classmates' ideas.

Research suggests that the dominant teacher practices used to promote reading comprehension are not unlike my own practice as a beginning teacher described above. That is, a teacher asks students questions about selections they have just read, and students complete worksheets and other exercises on their own at the end of the selection (Durkin, 1978–79; Paris, 1985). I must assume that, like me, most teachers are well meaning in this endeavor. Robert Scholes (1985) perhaps accounts for our behavior when he says, "There is a bright little student inside most teachers who wants to set the rest of the class straight because he or she knows the 'right' answer" (p. 30). Like the teacher in Probst's story, I didn't understand that clinging to one's own agenda and one's own reasoning prevents students from interacting with and thinking deeply about what they read. As Dan Kirby (1997) says, "If you're presenting the central tenets of your content as issues already settled, as truth already known and uncontested, then your students aren't going to be inclined to interact with that content and raise questions of their own. They're going to feel locked away from that content" (p. 169). Further, research indicates that instruction focused primarily on teacher-directed questioning can cause students to become so reliant on the teacher for understanding text material that they may become unable to go beyond constructing the gist at the literal level to form interpretations on their own (Searfoss & Readence, 1989).

Scholes (1985) emphasizes that "the point of teaching interpretation is not to usurp the interpreter's role but to explain the rules of the interpretive game" (p. 30). In order to help students construct their own meanings, we must enable them to gain access to the cognitive tool kit that experienced readers and writers use. But it is not enough to make them aware that experienced readers and writers tap prior knowledge, ask questions, make predictions, visualize, construct the gist, monitor their comprehension, revise meaning, and so forth. As Scott Paris (1985) advises, "Knowing about reading strategies will not insure that students use them while they read. Teaching is more than telling; the information must be supplemented with a rationale for using strategies" (p. 135). Additionally, the rationale must be supplemented with repeated occasions to practice, apply, and internalize the strategies.

USING PEDAGOGICAL STRATEGIES TO FOSTER COGNITIVE STRATEGIES

Paris, Wasik, and Turner (1991) define *strategies* as "actions selected deliberately to achieve particular goals." *Skills,* in contrast, are "information processing techniques" that are automatic and "applied to text unconsciously" (pp. 610–611). Gail Tompkins (1997) elaborates:

> Readers and writers use both skills and strategies when they read and write. They use skills automatically, such as sounding out an unfamiliar word when reading, or capitalizing the first letter of a name when writing. In contrast, strategies are problem-solving procedures that students choose and use consciously. Readers, for example, use fix-up strategies when they're reading and realize they don't understand something. Writers use clustering to organize ideas before writing, and use proofreading to identify mechanical errors. (p. 30)

As I have discussed before, one of the key differences between experienced and inexperienced readers and writers is that experienced readers and writers are strategic: They purposefully select and implement strategies in order to construct meaning. To become strategic, inexperienced readers and writers need both the knowledge and the motivation to select, apply, and monitor their use of strategies. Until students are motivated to be—and capable of being—strategic on their own, it is the teacher's job to build their declarative knowledge, provide them with guidance and with opportunities to develop procedural knowledge, and engineer some successful interactions that will prompt them to act on conditional knowledge. To this end, teachers themselves must be strategic. They must deliberately select actions from their instructional repertoire designed to achieve particular goals. In other words, the teacher must use pedagogical strategies that enable students to practice cognitive strategies. Pearson and Leys (1985) propose, only "partially in jest," that the model for teaching should be "planned obsolescence" (p. 6). Like Langer and Applebee (1986), whose model of instructional scaffolding informs this book (see Chapters 1–3), they believe the ultimate goal of instruction is for students to internalize the strategies and to accept "100 percent of the responsibility" (p. 6) for selecting and applying them independently.

THE CONCEPT OF READING AND WRITING TO LEARN

In Chapter 4, as she described the painful and emotionally wrenching process of learning to read and write as a second language learner, Hetty Jun noted how she spent most of her time pondering the teacher's cryptic remarks and playing a guessing game—"Is this what the teacher wanted?" Students ask this question because they have been trained to do so. More often than not, in their assigned reading and writing activities, they have been expected to show what they have learned and to respond to questions for which there is a "right" or at least an appropriate answer. An important step in exposing students to cognitive strategies and motivating them to embrace them is to introduce the concept and practice of reading and writing to learn.

In 1975, James Britton and a team of researchers with the Schools Council Project on Written Language in England released an important study, *The Development of Writing Abilities (11–18),* that had a significant influence on U.S. educators. In this three-year study of sixty-five secondary schools in England, Britton and his associates examined more than 2,000 writing samples from students aged eleven to eighteen, in an attempt to classify the types of writing tasks students were asked to undertake across the curriculum and to draw conclusions about the development of writing abilities in the secondary school. Setting aside the traditional rhetorical categories of narration, description, exposition, and argument, Britton and colleagues designated three function categories—transactional, expressive, and poetic—within which to ask or answer the question, "Why are you writing?" (Britton et al., 1975, p. 5). Britton defines *transactional writing* as the use of language "to get things done: to inform people (telling them what they need or want to know or what we think they ought to know), to advise or persuade or instruct people" (p. 88). In other words, transactional writing is writing to instruct or to show what you've learned. As opposed to transactional writing, *poetic writing* is intensely personal writing in which it is "taken for granted that 'true or false?' is not a relevant question at the literal level" (Martin et al., 1976, p. 25). The poems, stories, and reminiscences that constitute poetic writing use "language as an art medium" (Britton et al., 1975, p. 90) to create an imaginative text world that the reader will experience rather than use as a "guidebook or map" (Martin et al., 1976, p. 25). Finally, whereas transactional and poetic writing both culminate in finished products, *expressive writing* is writing in process—"the kind of writing that might be called 'thinking aloud on paper'" (Britton et al., 1975, p. 89). Expressive writing lends itself to exploration and discovery because it is intended as a learning tool for the writer's own use. Because expressive writing is "free of external demands," it is useful "in developing a provisional first draft of ideas . . . " (Britton et al., 1975, p. 145).

Britton and his colleagues (1975) were disappointed to discover that only 5 percent of the writing samples they analyzed could be classified as expressive and that these samples came almost exclusively from English classes. As expected, transactional writing was the dominant form of writing in school, making up 64 percent of all school writing (p. 164). Further, of the various audiences that students might write to (self, trusted adult, teacher as partner in dialogue, teacher as assessor, peers, or unknown audience), the majority of the transactional writing (which was primarily informative in purpose) was written to the teacher as examiner (p. 175). Poetic writing accounted for 18 percent of the writing samples—and again came primarily from English classes. However, the percentage of poetic samples went down as the grade level went up. In short, there was "three times as much transactional writing as the other two functions put together. And thirteen times as much transactional writing as expressive" (p. 163).

Particularly when Arthur Applebee, with Anne Auten and Fran Lehr, published *Writing in the Secondary School* (1981), which involved a two-year observation of ninth- and eleventh-grade classes in two schools and a national survey of secondary school teachers, the notion of including more expressive writing or writing to learn in the curriculum began to gain currency with U.S. educators. Applebee and his colleagues found that students spent an average of 44 percent of all class time involved in writing tasks of some kind (p. 93). However, the majority of those activities involved mechanical uses of writing, such as responses to short-answer, multiple-choice, and fill-in-the blank questions. Further, during the brief 3 percent of the time that students were involved with writing activities of paragraph length or longer, the writing was often used "merely as a vehicle to test knowledge of specific content, with the teacher functioning primarily in the role of examiner" (p. 101). Although he acknowledges that writing to show what you've learned is a "legitimate use of writing" (p. 101), Applebee points out that writing can also be "a powerful process for discovering meaning rather than just transcribing an idea that is in some sense waiting fully developed in the writer's mind" (p. 100). Therefore, he calls for "more situations in which writing can serve as a tool for learning rather than as a means to display acquired knowledge" (p. 101).

THE STRATEGIC APPROACH TO INTERACTING WITH A TEXT

Provided in the following section is a range of pedagogical strategies teachers can purposefully implement in the classroom to help students interact with a text and with each other in order to make meaning. These reading/writing strategies are *expressive* in nature. That is, they are designed to serve as "a tool for learning rather than as a means to display acquired knowledge" (Applebee, 1981, p. 101) and are useful in helping students develop "a provisional first draft of ideas" (Britton et al., 1975, p. 145). The strategies highlighted in this chapter are primarily linguistic in nature, linking reading and writing as tools for discovery and interpretation. Other strategies that provide more spatial or kinesthetic routes to interpretation are discussed elsewhere in the book—particularly in Chapters 5 and 14. Although most of these teaching/learning strategies are flexible and can be implemented at various and multiple stages of the reading/writing process, I have made an attempt to sequence them in the order a teacher might initially introduce them in scaffolded instruction. The cognitive strategies each pedagogical strategy taps, which appear in italics, are discussed in Chapter 1 and are listed in Figure 1.2, Cognitive Strategies: A Reader's and Writer's Tool Kit.

Because the focus of these strategies for interacting with a text is on reading and writing to learn rather than to show what you've learned, it is important that the teacher respond as a partner in dialogue rather than as an assessor, perhaps giving credit to initial drafts of ideas through a point system rather than assessing in-process work as if it were a finished product.

Before-Reading Strategies

Easy as 1, 2, 3!   When asked to read independently, inexperienced readers can be quick to abandon a text when they encounter unfamiliar words or a complicated story line. Donna Moore, a teacher at Fitz Intermediate School in Garden Grove, California, developed a strategy called Easy as 1, 2, 3! to spark students' curiosity, to acquaint them with the text, and to build personal investment—to make her students less likely to tell themselves "I can't" or "I won't" and more willing to read further. A graphic organizer for the Easy as 1, 2, 3! strategy is available in Chapter 3 under Prereading Activity.

The first step in Easy as 1, 2, 3! is to prompt students to *tap prior knowledge* and *make predictions* by asking them to think about the title of a text in light of their own background knowledge and experiences and to write down and then discuss their predictions of what the text will be about based on the title. For example, in responding to Ray Bradbury's short story "All Summer in a Day," students often predict that the story will focus on all the exciting events of summer crammed into just one short day. The next step is to select a significant picture that accompanies the text or to take a picture walk through the text and to "read" the pictures by *visualizing*. Students then record their predictions about the context of the text based on the pictures they have *interpreted*. If there is a disparity between their predictions based on the title and the picture they have analyzed, students are also prompted to *revise meaning*. These thoughts are recorded on the Easy as 1, 2, 3! sheet before the class discusses them in partners or as a whole group. In "All Summer in a Day," for instance, the picture by Robert Vickrey that the publisher selected to accompany the text creates a mood of isolation and entrapment. Students are quick to "read" the somber expression on the child's face, revise their original prediction of a fun-filled adventure, and anticipate a much gloomier outcome than they had initially expected. Finally, the teacher reads a selection from the text, if possible stopping at a spot that leaves the students in suspense. Students jot down their new or revised predictions based on how they received the words and then turn to a partner or to the whole class to compare their speculations.

The Easy as 1, 2, 3! strategy is designed to convince students that interacting with a text is as easy as making predictions about the title, "reading" the pictures through visualization, and responding to the words. While she's getting her students hooked and ready to read on, Moore is also fostering the cognitive strategies she wants her students to access and practice.

Tea Party   Tea party is another strategy that can hook students and create buy-in before students launch into a text. Developed by Sue Perona (1989), a teacher/consultant from the South Coast Writing Project at the University of California, Santa Barbara, tea party engages students as active participants as they circulate around the room sharing phrases from a text they are about to read and then make predictions in small groups. To prepare for tea party, the teacher should select key sentences and phrases from the text the class is about to read and write them on 3-by-5 cards, being careful to give just enough information to spark interest but not to give away the plot. For example, for "Eleven" by Sandra Cisneros in Chapter 5, the teacher might record:

- "What they don't understand about birthdays and what they never tell you is that when you're eleven, you're also ten, and nine, and eight, and seven, and six, and five, and four, and three, and two, and one."
- "Because the way you grow old is kind of like an onion . . ."
- "Only today I wish I didn't have only eleven years rattling inside me like pennies in a tin Band-aid box."
- "Because she's older and the teacher and she's right and I'm not."

Students circulate around the room, and as they share their sentences and phrases, they are piecing the fragments of information together, *developing schema* for and *constructing the gist* of the text.

K-W-L   Donna Ogle (1998) remarks, "As teachers we need to employ classroom instructional strategies that facilitate students' construction of their own meanings" (p. 270). The K-W-L strategy she developed (1986) is designed to help students *tap prior knowledge; make connections* between what they know and the information that will be presented in the text; *ask questions* about what they want to know; and later, after the text has been read, *step back, rethink what they know,* and *reflect* upon what they have learned. The letters in K-W-L stand for Know, Want to know, and Learned.

Before reading, the teacher introduces the K-W-L strategy by briefly explaining the topic to be addressed in the text. Then, collectively, the students brainstorm what they already know about that topic while the teacher records their ideas on a chart like the one in Figure 1.1 on page 3.

It has been my experience that students often need a prompt of some kind to jog their memories and enable them to tap prior knowledge. For example, Courtney Martz, a teacher at El Toro High School in El Toro, California, was preparing her students to read John Hersey's *Hiroshima.* She told the class they were going to be reading this nonfiction text and asked students to tell her what they already knew about Hiroshima. Complete silence ensued: The students searched for something to unlock the schemata in their mental file cabinets and came up empty. But Martz had a key. "Hey, didn't anybody see *Saving Private Ryan?*" At the mention of Steven Spielberg's movie, the class suddenly came alive.

"Oh, you mean World War !I?" one student asked.

"That's when the holocaust took place," another volunteered.

"Oh, yeah, and the Japanese bombed Pearl Harbor."

The second step of the K-W-L process is to ask students to generate what they want to know. Having students write down their questions independently, before whole class discussion, "provides a concrete way for all students to participate in thinking about the topic even when not talking" and creates a "more personal commitment" to the reading (Ogle, 1998, p. 274). In Martz's class, for example, students wanted to know why Japan entered the war, when and why the Americans dropped the atomic bomb on Hiroshima, and what the short- and long-term effects were on the country and its inhabitants. For Martz, the K-W-L was what she called a "launch point"—a way into the text. She then assigned the students in each of the six rows in her class to follow one of the six central characters in the book (for example, Reverend Tanimoto or Miss Sasaki). The students' job was to take note of where the characters were when the bomb dropped; the immediate and long-term effects of the bomb on their lives, physically and emotionally; and what their lives were like forty years after the devastation. After each group collectively organized their notes, they presented their character's experience to the whole class in a peer group-teaching approach. Subsequently, for closure, the students returned to column three of the K-W-L chart to reflect upon and record what they had learned about this significant historical event.

Anticipation Guides   The anticipation guide (also known as the anticipation/reaction guide) operates much like the K-W-L strategy. Developed by Readence, Bean, and Baldwin (1989), it is designed to help students to *tap prior knowledge, make predictions,* and *ask questions* before beginning to read and to *step back* after reading, *rethink what they know,* and perhaps *revise meaning* by identifying initial misconceptions. Before reading a text, students are asked to respond, typically in a yes/no or agree/disagree fashion, to a series of statements about the topic that is to come. "These statements are carefully worded so as to challenge the students' beliefs, which are based upon their past experiences with the subject" (Head & Readence, 1998, p. 228). For example, Figure 6.1 shows an anticipation guide that Charlie AuBuchon, a teacher from McFadden Intermediate in Santa Ana, California, developed for her eighth-grade class in preparation for their reading of *Anne Frank: The Diary of a Young Girl.* Notice that AuBuchon does not "fall into the trap of writing what amounts to true–false statements" (Head & Readence, 1998, p. 232) but aims to stimulate divergent responses that will be controversial and prompt discussion. Searfoss and Readence (1989) note that the role of the teacher during the class discussion after students complete the Before Reading section of the anticipation guide is crucial. They point out, "Because the statements used in the guide are experience based, and because a mismatch may be created between the children's experiences and the concepts to be learned, a variety of responses, both supporting and rejecting the statements, may be elicited" (p. 273). But even if some of these statements may be blatantly wrong, all responses should be accepted. The point of the anticipation guide is to set the stage for the students to modify their own misconceptions while and after they read. During the reaction portion of the process, students return to the anticipation guide, reassess their prereading responses, and compare them to their reactions after reading. This is an excellent opportunity for students to take ten to fifteen minutes to think out loud on paper in a piece of expressive writing that explores how their preconceptions may have changed. The process culminates with a whole class discussion about what has been learned.

Figure 6.1 **Anticipation Guide: Anne Frank: The Diary of a Young Girl** (Reprinted by permission of Charlie AuBuchon.)

Below are eight statements dealing with the world Anne knew as a teenager growing up in Holland during World War II and facing the onslaught of German tyranny. Before you read Anne's diary, tell whether you agree or disagree with each statement by marking a YES or NO next to each statement. After you read the diary, mark YES or NO again and see if you have changed your perceptions.

Statement	Before Reading	After Reading
1. When problems arise, family members become close to one another.		
2. Strangers are always afraid to help those in need.		
3. Facing tragedy makes you grow up more rapidly.		
4. People find it easy to change their habits when they need to survive.		
5. Teenage daughters often find it difficult to get along with their mothers.		
6. When survival is the primary concern, romantic love cannot evolve.		
7. When you live with many people, you never feel alone.		
8. Friendship means sharing your thoughts with another person.		

Clustering   Gabriele Rico (1983), who developed the concept of clustering, describes it as a "non-linear brainstorming process akin to free-association" (p. 28) that makes invisible mental processes visible. In Figure 6.2 one of Rico's students presents a more graphic definition of this strategy.

Teachers use clustering primarily as a prereading/prewriting strategy (and sometimes during reading and writing activity) in which students *tap prior knowledge, ask questions, make predictions,* and *make connections.* The process involves providing a stimulus word—such as a topic for writing, the title of a book, the name of a character, a specific historical period, or an abstract concept—and then generating ideas, images, and feelings around that

Figure 6.2 **Clustering a Topic** (*Source:* Rico, 1997. Reprinted by permission of Gabriele Rico.)

I believe that clustering is a natural process we do unconsciously in our mind. It is more helpful to do it on paper, though. Our mind clusters many ideas and thoughts, but it is unable to sort and sift the ideas into a reasonable order around one main focus. When we cluster on paper, we can visually look at our ideas and choose which ones we want to use. The thoughts in our mind are all piled together, and we see only one or two at a time. On paper, through clustering, we can see all our thoughts at once as a whole.

word until a pattern becomes discernible. Rico explains that as students cluster around a stimulus word, "the encoded words rapidly radiate outward until a sudden shift takes place, a sort of 'Aha!' that signals a sudden awareness of a sensitive whole that allows students to begin writing" (p. 15).

Although clustering is most often used as a brainstorming activity, it can also be an excellent way to *organize information.* For example, before writing an interpretive essay on a work of literature, such as the character analysis of Ying-ying from Amy Tan's "The Moon Lady" in *The Joy Luck Club* (discussed in Chapter 8), students can use clustering to generate the main points they will make. These clusters can then be numbered in the order the ideas will be introduced. Further, students can search for quotes as evidence to support each main idea, which can in turn be clustered off existing clusters. Susan Starbuck, language arts coordinator for the Long Beach Unified School District in Long Beach, California, has also had great success with clustering as a *reviewing* strategy: Students cluster all the items they *predict* will be on an upcoming exam, then cluster further around specific test questions.

During-Reading Strategies

Dialectical Journals/Reader Response Logs   As described by Ann Berthoff in *The Making of Meaning* (1981), the dialectical journal is a double-entry note-taking/note-making process students can engage in while reading a text. It provides students with two columns that are in dialogue with each other, enabling them to conduct "the continual 'audit of meaning' that is at the heart of learning to read and write critically" (p. 45). In the left-hand column, students select and copy down a passage that they find intriguing, puzzling, or illuminating in some way. In the right-hand column, they record thoughts and feelings that come to mind, thinking out loud on paper and working toward that "provisional first draft of ideas" mentioned by Britton and colleagues (1975, p. 145). Figure 6.3 contains a dialectical journal from a student in a composition class taught by Sheila Koff at Orange Coast College in Costa Mesa, California.

The dialectical journal can be an excellent way for students to access all of the cognitive strategies in their tool kit—*tapping prior knowledge, asking questions, making predictions, making connections, revising meaning, evaluating,* and so forth. However, if the students have little training in accessing these strategies, and particularly if the dialectical journal is routinely assigned as homework (never discussed but instead treated as "proof" that students have done the reading), my experience is that many students will simply go through the motions on autopilot, retelling the plot rather than sharing their perceptions or deepening their understanding.

Figure 6.3   **Dialectical Journal** (*Source:* Koff, 1997. Reprinted by permission of Sheila Koff.)

Note Taking: What the Text Says	Note Making: What the Text Means to Me
"I stood there with my hand on a box of Hi-Ho crackers, trying to remember if I rang it up or not." (p. 12)	The sight of the three bathing suited girls is enough to make Sammy lose his concentration?!
"The sheep pushing their carts down the aisle . . ." (p. 190)	What makes him refer to people as sheep? Is he bored with people, seeing them day after day shopping? Is he mad at them?
"Stoksie's married with two babies chalked up on his fuselage already . . ." (p. 190)	Sammy sees Stoksie as already tied up, in this town, this job, this life. He's already caught.

For students who have not had much previous practice with responding to literature, UCLA Writing Project teacher/consultant Jenée Gossard (1997b) suggests reading key passages aloud to the class and providing examples of a range of common reader responses to help expand and guide students' responses:

Common Responses from Readers
Feelings (boring, sad, exciting, weird)
Questions (I wonder why the author put in the boring parts?)
Images (pictures in the mind, with full sensory response)
Favorite (or detested) words and phrases
Echoes (of other books, movies, television shows, headlines, songs, or poems)
Reaction to characters or events ("That Templeton is such a rat! Ha, ha.")
Memories (people, events, places you've known)
Connections (to other ideas, people, feelings, books) (p. 213)

These categories can become a springboard for students' responses to whatever text they are reading.

Dialectical journals/reader response logs can also become a springboard for students' interactions with one another. Koff (1997) suggests that students highlight two or three of their favorite selections from their dialectical journals; form groups of four or five; read their journals aloud; discuss their interpretations; and elicit an important connection, insight, or question to share in whole group discussion. Gossard (1997b) asks students to review their reader response logs at the end of each week and to select one entry for further reflection. They might

- expand a response;
- relate an image or idea to their own lives;
- recall a memory;
- explore a new idea; or
- play around with an idea or structure. (p. 215)

After writing, students form groups, read their new entry aloud, and listen to the responses of others while asking themselves, "How is it like mine? How is it different? What do I like about it?" (p. 215). After hearing all of the reflections, each group discusses common themes that emerged or issues that prompted divergent responses and then report on this discussion to the whole group.

Reciprocal Teaching In contrast to dialectical journals and reader response logs, which students keep independently as they are reading and then may share in small or large groups, reciprocal teaching involves students in making meaning collaboratively from the outset as they read and discuss a text in small increments. Palincsar and Brown (1985) note, "Theories of learning suggest that efficient learning from text requires flexible use of a repertoire of comprehension-fostering and monitoring activities" (p. 157). In the reciprocal teaching model, these researchers identify four complementary strategies that address problems in text comprehension: *summarizing,* or self-review; *question generating,* or self-testing; *predicting,* or setting the stage for further reading; and *demanding clarity,* or noting when a breakdown in comprehension has occurred (p. 158).

The term *reciprocal* refers to the back-and-forth interchange that takes place as the teacher and students engage in a dialogue about a section of the text they have just read together or independently, using these four cognitive strategies. Initially, the teacher provides "expert modeling" as well as orchestrating the "structured practice" (p. 157) while students rehearse in order to acquire and refine the strategies. In time, the teacher's aim is to back out of the process and enable a selected student to act in the teacher's role.

One of the short stories often used in in-service workshops to introduce reciprocal teaching to teachers is "Two Were Left" by Hugh B. Cave. A copy of "Two Were Left" is available on the companion website. The teacher (or the student who assumes the role of the teacher) might read only the first two sentences of this text to open the dialogue:

> On the third night of hunger, Noni thought of the dog. Nothing of flesh and blood lived upon the floating ice island except those two.*

Palincsar and Brown prescribe no specific order for using the strategies but do offer rough guidelines—for example, that predicting often comes last, as the students are preparing to read on. After reading the sentences above out loud, the teacher might model as follows:

- From what we've read so far, I can tell that Noni, the main character, and Noni's dog have been stranded and haven't eaten for three days. Who can add to my summary? (Students add to the teacher's summary.)
- The teacher should model asking a variety of questions that are both literal and interpretive. For example, a knowledge-level question might be, How many were left, how long had they been there, and where were they? An analysis-level question calling for inference might be, Who can tell me what they think happened that left Noni and the dog stranded? (Students then attempt to answer the teacher's question as well as add questions of their own.)
- I need some clarification about what a floating ice island is. I am guessing it is an iceberg. Does anyone have a different idea or know what I should do to verify my idea? (Students help clarify and/or provide advice as to how to proceed.)
- Based on the title of the story and what I have read so far, I predict Noni and the dog will be pitted against each other as they begin to starve. Who else thinks my prediction will come true? Who has a different prediction? (Students validate the teacher's prediction or provide a different perspective.)

Students then read on and link their existing knowledge with the next section of the text.

Palincsar and Brown readily acknowledge, "While we have been delighted with the progress students can make toward becoming active readers who look for and construct meaning . . . this can be a slow and tedious procedure" that requires at least twelve successive days of instruction before students "demonstrate stable improvement in comprehension" (p. 154). One way to vary the process is to have students read some sections of the text independently; then write up their summary, a question, one idea or word they found difficult and needed clarification on, and their prediction; and then share these in small groups. (Note: Please see Chapter 11 for a detailed description of literature circles, another structure for small group discussion.)

Say Something   Another strategy that helps students tune in when they are reading and tap cognitive strategies but is less structured than reciprocal teaching is Say Something. Developed by Harste, Short, and Burke (1988) and popularized by Kylene Beers (2003), this strategy involves having students, in pairs or small groups, pause frequently as they are reading out loud to one another to respond to the text. Beers' rules for say something are as follows:

1. With your partner, decide who will say something first.

---

*Copyright © 1942 by the Crowell-Collier Publishing Co. for *American Magazine.* Reprinted by permission of the author.

2. When you say something, do one or more of the following:
   • Make a prediction
   • Ask a question
   • Clarify something you had misunderstood
   • Make a comment
   • Make a connection
3. If you can't do one of those five things, then you need to reread. (p. 107)

Note that this strategy allows students independently to access their mental took kits to select the cognitive strategy that is most appropriate for that section of the text. Beers encourages two-way interaction by giving the partner a job—to respond to what was said.

Highlighting Confusion   Say Something enables students to articulate what they know, but sometimes students get stuck and struggle with what to say. Cris Tovani (2000) advises students to look for six signals of confusion: the voice inside the reader's head isn't interacting with the text; the camera inside the reader's head shuts off; the reader's mind begins to wander; the reader can't remember what has been read; clarifying questions asked by the reader aren't answered; and the reader reencounters a character and has no recollection when that character was introduced (p. 38). To reinforce the concept of *monitoring* comprehension, she asks students to read a challenging text with a pink and yellow highlighter in hand. They must highlight in pink any portion of the text they feel they understand well enough to explain to someone else, and in yellow portions they don't understand. After students highlight, the teacher asks everyone to hold up their pink and yellow copies, noting that each person's copy looks somewhat different. She then rereads the text aloud, stopping occasionally for those who highlighted that portion in pink to *clarify* the text for those who marked it in yellow. This strategy brings home to students that knowing when you are confused is a sign of a strategic learner and will enable them to apply fix-up strategies. In fact, Sheridan Blau (2003) is fond of saying, "Confusion is an advanced state of understanding" (p. 21).

Showing, Not Telling   Like clustering, "showing, not telling" is well known to most Writing Project teachers. As Bay Area Writing Project teacher/consultant Rebekah Caplan (1997) explains, the assumption behind showing, not telling is that students have not been trained to show what they mean. "By training, I do not mean the occasional exercises from composition textbooks. . . . What I mean by training is the performing of constant mental warm-up, short and rigorous, which is not unlike the training routines of musicians, dancers and athletes" (p. 39). Showing, not telling encourages students to dramatize their writing with specific details that paint pictures in the reader's mind. It involves giving students a "telling sentence" such as *The room was vacant* or *The student was bored* and challenging students to "show" the statement in a detailed paragraph without using the telling sentence. That is, they must show that *The student was bored* through rich, concrete description rather than making the claim directly. For example, a student might write, "Lugging his backpack as if it were a thousand-pound weight, the student trudged into the classroom, shoved the pack under his desk unopened, and slumped into his chair in preparation for catching a little shut-eye. As the teacher droned on about photosynthesis, the student yawned audibly and sank deeper into his seat. His head began bobbing like a yo-yo as he drifted off to sleep."

Caplan's strategy has worked so well as a tool for helping students be more specific and detailed in their writing that teachers have begun applying showing, not telling to the study of literature. For example, Bill Burns (1997), a teacher at Sonora High School in La Habra, California, has had great success with having students show, not tell about literature by providing them with telling sentences throughout the reading of a novel or play. When teaching William Golding's *Lord of the Flies,* Burns gave students sample sentences like the ones below and asked them to show the statements, using descriptive language and evidence from the text in a well-developed paragraph.

> *Setting:* The island was a paradise.
> *Character:* Ralph and Jack were different kinds of leaders.
> *Plot:* Life on the island wasn't as much fun as the boys imagined it would be.
> *Writing Techniques:* Golding uses fire as a symbol.

Notice how Karissa Pacheco, a ninth grader in Bill Burns's class, uses showing, not telling to begin an essay on *Great Expectations:*

The Eccentric and Vengeful Miss Havisham

A log crackled in the fireplace, and candles provided the only source of light. For the windows were covered with thick drapes. Even with all the candles in the room there was a drafty chill. Sitting by the fireplace in a high-backed chair, an old woman sat straight up with a stiff proudness. Her hair was made up in a messy arrangement of dead flowers. Her gown looked like it could have once been worn by a happy bride, but it now was reduced to a faded yellow, wrinkled mess.

Down the hall there was a door that led into a great banquet room. On the great table were silver bowls, fine china, and glass cups—all rusted, dusty and dirty. The table was so heavily covered in cobwebs you could hardly tell what it was. The food that was laid out to be eaten was covered in bugs, from maggots to roaches to ants. The greatest splendor of them all was the towering wedding cake. White frosting was now yellow and growing mold. Spiders, beetles, and mice had carved little tunnels and homes on each level of the cake. The room itself seemed to grow like a black fungus.

In the book *Great Expectations,* you are introduced to a character unlike any other, a character whose heart was broken at twenty minutes to nine, and from then on lived her life in a depressed "time warp" that could never be broken. This is the eccentric and vengeful Miss Havisham.

Occasionally, as an alternative to a multiple-draft interpretive essay on a work of literature, Burns allows students to hand in a packet of show, not tell paragraphs written at intervals throughout the reading of a work of literature. He reflects, "I am just beginning to discover how to use telling sentences to help students be more explicit, to help their reading, and to enhance their understanding of both reading and writing. . . . Isn't it curious how simple concepts turn out to be so subtle?" (1997, p. 55).

After-Reading Strategies

Dialogue with a Text   In analyzing the battle of wills between the teacher and her students described at the beginning of this chapter, Robert Probst (1988) writes, "I'm sure that all of the pressures the teacher felt were real, almost as real as those her students felt and wanted to talk about" (p. 33). However, "She saw her job as the teaching of skills and terms and techniques. The students wanted to discuss the moral dilemmas presented in the story" (p. 33). Probst would argue that the students' response was the more authentic and significant one. He perceived in the discussion that spontaneously erupted the potential for a powerful opportunity to make meaning as a collaborative learning community. Influenced by the work of Louise Rosenblatt (1983), Probst defines the process of meaning construction as follows:

> Meaning is the product of the transaction between active minds and the words on the page—
> it does not reside in the ink, to be ferreted out, unearthed, uncovered. Rather, it is created,
> formed, shaped, by readers in the act of reading, and thus it is *their* meaning. (p. 34)

Building on the principles of reader response espoused by Rosenblatt, Probst has developed his "dialogue with a text" strategy. The goal is to help students engage in the kind of dialogue that will yield a rich literary experience rather than a recitation of what they think the teacher wants to hear.

The dialogue with a text strategy involves providing partners or small groups of students with copies of a booklet containing a series of questions "designed and arranged to encourage reflection on several aspects of the act of reading" (p. 35). After students have read a short text, for example a poem or short story, they receive the booklets, which begin with the following instructions:

> Please read the text and take a moment or two to reflect on it. Then turn to the next page and begin. Take a few minutes—as much time as you need or want—with each question. Please reflect on each question for a moment or two, perhaps jotting down brief notes, before discussing it. Some may be more productive than others for you, and you may wish to give those more time. There is no rush, no need to finish them all. Please don't glance ahead in the booklet.

Figure 6.4 contains the complete list of questions provided by Probst—although he suggests selecting five to ten, depending on the maturity of the readers and the time available. Notice that the focus questions begin with the reader's initial response and gradually move toward a consideration of the author, other readings, and other readers. Cognitive strategies tapped include *visualizing, making connections, analyzing author's craft, forming preliminary interpretations, adopting an alignment, revising meaning,* and *evaluating.* After students dialogue with one another and with the text, Probst reconvenes them to discuss their reactions to the activity in a whole group. He poses such questions as "Did your understanding of the text or your feelings about it change as you talked? If so, how and why did your understanding or feelings change?" Although Probst intends these questions to be posed orally, this is an ideal opportunity to invite some independent, expressive writing before the large group discussion.

Plus/Minus Time Line   At first glance, developing a time line might appear to be a simple *reviewing* activity in which students would reconstruct in sequence what happened in a text. However, Joni Chancer, a teacher/consultant for the South Coast Writing Project at UC Santa Barbara, added a twist to this activity that involves students in *analyzing, reflecting,* and *evaluating.* She suggests that students work in small groups and write above the time line events that they interpret to be positive (+) and below the time line events they interpret as negative or problematic (–). The example shown in Figure 6.5 is part of a time line from the demonstration lesson on Amy Tan's "The Moon Lady," from *The Joy Luck Club,* in Chapter 8.

This task can potentially elicit a great deal of animated discussion if the significance of events is subject to interpretation. For example, students are asked to construct their time line for Ying-ying, the main character in Tan's story, beginning with her retelling of the incident in the seventh paragraph of the story: "In 1918, the year that I was four. . . ." When they arrive at the opening paragraphs of the story, in which Ying-ying reflects on her present life as an adult and her relationship with her daughter, a good deal of healthy disagreement erupts. Has Ying-ying found herself? Has she had an epiphany? Or is she just as lost and voiceless as ever? Students return to the text, argue their positions, and negotiate as they decide where to place events on the time line. Emphasize that there is no right or wrong answer; it is a matter of interpretation.

Figure 6.4   **Dialogue with a Text**   (*Source:* R. Probst, 1988. "Dialogue with a Text," *English Journal 77*, 1, pp. 32–38. Copyright © 1988 by the National Council of Teachers of English. Reprinted with permission.)

Focus	Questions
First reaction	What was your first reaction or response to the text? Describe or explain briefly.
Feelings	What feelings did the text awaken in you? What emotions did you feel as you read the text?
Perceptions	What did you see happening in the text? Paraphrase it; retell the major events briefly.
Visual images	What image was called to mind by the text? Describe it briefly.
Associations	What memory does the text call to mind—of people, places, events, sights, smells, or even of something more ambiguous, perhaps feelings or attitudes?
Thoughts, ideas	What idea or thought was suggested by the text? Explain briefly.
Selection of textual elements	On what, in the text, did you focus most intently as you read—what word, phrase, important idea?
Judgments of what is important	What is the most important word in the text? What is the most important phrase in the text? What is the most important aspect of the text?
Identification of problems	What is the most difficult word in the text? What is there in the text or in your reading that you had the most trouble understanding?
Author	What sort of person do you imagine the author of this text to be?
Patterns of response	How did you respond to the text—emotionally or intellectually? Did you feel involved with the text or distant from it?
Other readings	How did your reading of the text differ from that of your discussion partner (or the others in your group)? In what ways were they similar?
Evolution of your reading	How did your understanding of the text or your feelings about it change as you talked?
Evaluations	Do you think the text is a good one? Why or why not?
Literary associations	Did this text call to mind any other literary work (poem, play, film, story—any genre)? If it did, what is the work and what is the connection you see between the two?
Writing	If you were asked to write about your reading of the text, on what would you focus? Would you write about some association or memory, some aspect of the text itself, something about the author, or some other matter?
Other readers	What did you observe about your discussion partner (or the others in your group) as the talk progressed?

Figure 6.5   **Plus/Minus Time Line**   (Reprinted by permission of Joni Chancer.)

+	Delights over idea of Moon Festival	Sees restless shadow	Rides to Moon Festival on rickshaw with mother		
−	Chided by Amah while being dressed	Learns it is selfish to think of own needs	Wanders off and soils her clothes	Scolded by Amah	Falls into water

Book Wheels for Book Talks   While students create plus-minus time lines for whole texts, book wheels (Huck, 1992) are often use to recall the narrative sequence in an episode of a longer text. An episode is a developed situation in a work of fiction that is part of the continuous narrative, the larger whole, but which may be identified and discussed separately because it has its own distinct beginning, middle, and end. Students are asked to *identify main ideas/events* in their episodes in a text they are reading and select one to give an oral book talk on, *organize information* into a sequence, *summarize* using key words, and *visualize* by choosing appropriate images and pictures to display in a tangible book wheel that the writer turns while delivering the book talk.

The book wheel is formed by placing two paper circles together, connected, at the center point by a brad fastener. The bottom circle is divided like a pie, each slice containing key words and visuals from the episode in sequential order. The top circle has a "window" the size of one book wheel segment, which is cut out to reveal one scene in the episode (see Figure 6.6).

When he was at Thurston Intermediate School in Laguna Beach, California, Todd Huck required his students to create both a "backlist" of complete sentences describing each event in the episode and a "frontlist" of key words and phrases, as in the example below from *The Adventures of Tom Sawyer*:

Backlist	**Frontlist**
1. On a beautiful Saturday morning, Tom is depressed because he must whitewash the fence as punishment.	1. Saturday, Tom depressed, whitewash
2. Tom begins working, but he is soon discouraged by the long stretch of fence left to paint.	2. Tom begins, discouraged
3. Jim, the slave, passes by and Tom tries to bribe him with a marble to paint the fence.	3. Jim arrives, Tom bribes

Students then used both their front and backlists as notes for their book talk.

Figure 6.6   **Book Wheel**

Book talks also work well with nonfiction. Figure 6.6 is a book wheel I created after reading *Seabiscuit* by Laura Hillenbrand. My model combines a summary sentence and key words as well as combines the book wheel with the plus/minus time line. Directions for how to construct the book wheel are available on the companion website.

Story Maps   Whereas plus/minus time lines and book wheels tend to focus on the sequence of events, story maps deal with *identifying* and *organizing* the elements of fiction: character, setting, plot, and so forth. Story maps grow out of Bartlett's (1932) contention that memory is reconstructive and that readers have an internal schema or grammar that influences story comprehension. A simple story map might move from setting (characters, time, place), to problem, to goal, to action, to outcome (Davis & MacPherson, 1989). Another popular version of a simple story map is the framework "Somebody wanted but so" (MacOn, Bewell, & Vogt, 1991). In SWBS, students *summarize* the story elements by recounting the character or characters (somebody), the plot (wanted), the conflict (but), and the resolution (so). Story maps can also look at story elements in depth, as in Figure 6.7, or they can be narrowly focused on cause and effect, problem and solution, facts and inferences, and so forth.

Venn Diagram/Double Bubble   Like story maps, the Venn diagram is a predominantly graphic strategy that enables students to *step back, analyze text closely, form preliminary interpretations,* and *seek validation for interpretations.* Venn diagrams are overlapping circles, often used in mathematics to show relationships. In language arts instruction, Venn diagrams

Figure 6.7   Story Grammar/Story Maps (*Source: Reading Instruction that Makes Sense,* by Mary Tarasoff. Copyright © 1996. Reprinted by permission of Mary Egan.)

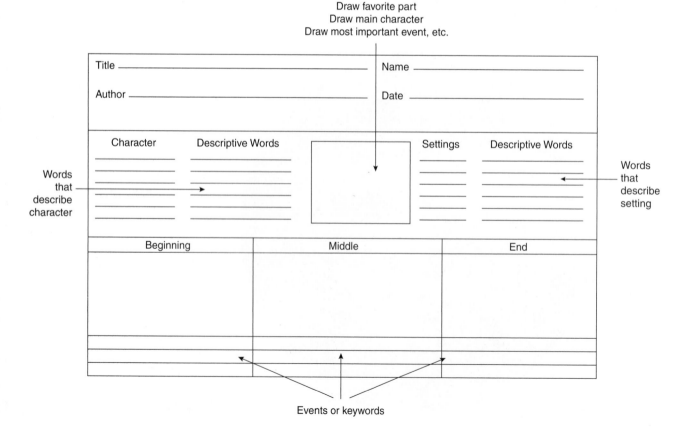

Figure 6.8 **Venn Diagram** (Reprinted by permission of Tyler Olson.)

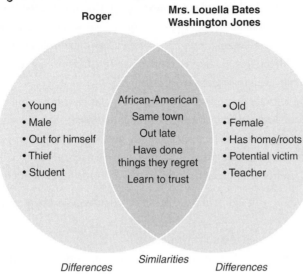

Roger

Mrs. Louella Bates Washington Jones

• Young
• Male
• Out for himself
• Thief
• Student

African-American
Same town
Out late
Have done things they regret
Learn to trust

• Old
• Female
• Has home/roots
• Potential victim
• Teacher

Differences   *Similarities*   *Differences*

Both Roger and Mrs. Jones are African-American and they live in the same town. They're also both out late at night. But Roger has no business being out that late whereas Mrs. Jones is on her way home from work. I was surprised that she didn't call the cops. Instead, she took Roger home and kind of became his teacher. She didn't give him a big lecture about being a thief. Rather, she said, "I have done things, too, which I would not tell you, son, I neither tell God if He didn't already know." She's saying that we all make mistakes. I think Roger will turn a corner because she trusted him.

are useful for examining similarities and differences. Students find them especially helpful in comparing and contrasting characters, settings, and themes in literature. As with clustering, teachers often stop at the graphic analysis, but Venn diagrams can lead naturally into expressive writing. Figure 6.8, by Tyler Olson, an eighth grader at South Lake Middle School in Irvine, California, compares and contrasts the characters of Roger and Mrs. Louella Bates Washington Jones from Langston Hughes's short story "Thank You, Ma'am."

An alternative to the Venn diagram is the double bubble, a comparison/contrast strategy illustrated in Figure 6.9 by Cecilia Hong, a sixth grader at Los Flores Middle School in Los Flores, California. Cecilia uses the expanded graphic organizer to analyze the similarities and differences between ancient Egypt and India graphically and linguistically.

Learning Logs and Exit Slips   A learning log is a chronicle of the student's experience as a learner in your class. It is distinct from a journal, which usually deals with personal

Figure 6.9 **Double Bubble** (Reprinted by permission of Cecilia Hong.)

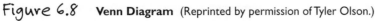

experience; it is a broader and more open-ended tool for reflection than a dialectical journal or reader response log, both of which are solely text-based. Cognitively, the learning log is a place for students to think out loud on paper—to *ask questions,* sort through and *organize information, monitor* their understanding, *rethink what they know,* and *reflect* upon and *assess* what they are learning. Affectively, the log is a safe place for students to express how they are feeling about learning, even to express frustration.

Typically, learning logs are completed by students regularly—for example, at the end of each class period, school week, or unit of study—to enable students to reflect and comment on what they have learned. Some teachers occasionally give students a prompt around which to focus their reflection. For example, Mindy Moffatt (1997), a teacher at Davidson Middle School in San Rafael, California, posed the following tasks for her eighth graders:

- Write about everything you did in class; then share your feelings about and reactions to the activities.
- What is something you want to know more about?
- If your parents had been watching this class through a one-way mirror, what would they have seen today?
- What do you like about our class? (p. 80)

Other times, the learning log topic is the student's choice. Moffatt observes, "This activity provides insight for a teacher to keep in touch with the development of students. . . . The students were anxious to get their logs back; not only did they look for my remarks, but also they reread their entries to see what they had written the week before" (p. 79).

Students have a habit of closing up shop mentally, and sometimes even physically, five to ten minutes before the bell rings. For teachers who are hesitant to take on the paper load of an ongoing learning log, or who collect logs weekly or monthly and want a window into where the students are on a given day, an exit slip can be a revealing substitute. Popularized by Bay Area Writing Project teacher/consultant Bob Tierney, an exit slip is a student's ticket out of the class. For the last five or ten minutes of a class period, students are asked to *reflect* on what they learned that day and to *summarize* their understanding, write down a *question,* explore a puzzlement, or share an Aha! As students write, the teacher stands at the door to collect each slip as the students file out of class. Exit slips can offer the teacher an important perspective on and an opportunity to monitor the learning taking place in his or her class. They can provide the signal to move full steam ahead—or send a teacher back to the drawing board when the students have clearly missed the boat. Both learning logs and exit slips also send a message to students that what they have to say about their own learning matters to the teacher.

LETTING GO OF THE GUIDED TOUR

According to Dan Kirby (1997), "Reforming your teaching to nurture thinking involves more than dreaming up new activities or offering students more decision-making freedom. At the heart of this reform is a new attitude toward knowledge and how it is acquired." This new view of knowledge "does not mean you have nothing to teach students or that textbooks are no longer valuable." What it does mean is that teachers must plan for and structure their classes in such a way that students "construct their own versions of knowledge in new and personal ways" (p. 168). And allowing students to construct their own versions of knowledge in more personal ways means that you as a teacher have to allow students to embark on their own journeys through texts and possibly arrive at destinations that may be unfamiliar to you.

As I watch students interacting with the texts and with one another, using the expressive reading and writing strategies surveyed in this chapter as a springboard for reflection, I find their own fresh questions and concerns replacing my prepackaged ones. I no longer lead the guided tour through the text. My students' own responses lead the way.

To Sum Up

To help students construct their own meaning, we must enable them to gain access to the cognitive tool kit that experienced readers and writers use. But it is not enough to make them aware that experienced readers and writers tap prior knowledge, ask questions, make predictions, visualize, construct the gist, monitor their comprehension, revise meaning, and so forth. Teachers must deliberately select and scaffold pedagogical strategies from their respective instructional repertoires that will provide students with opportunities to practice and eventually internalize cognitive strategies. An important step in exposing students to cognitive strategies and motivating them to embrace them is to introduce them to the concept of reading and writing to learn. In particular, by using expressive reading and writing as learning tools for exploration and discovery while interacting with a text, students can develop first drafts of ideas that can evolve and deepen with further reflection. As students engage in reading and writing to learn, the teacher can capitalize on this guided practice to build on students' declarative, procedural, and conditional knowledge so that they understand what cognitive strategies are and when, how, and why to use them.

Learning Log Reflection

Try the dialogue with a text strategy for a dialogue with a chapter. Interact with the ideas presented in this chapter, using the focus questions below as a point of departure for some expressive writing about your reading.

	Focus Questions
First reaction	What is your first reaction to the chapter? Describe or explain briefly.
Thoughts, ideas	What key ideas or thoughts were suggested by the chapter? Explain briefly.
Selection of textual elements	On what strategy or strategies for interacting with the text presented in this chapter did you focus most intently as you read?
Pedagogical associations	Did the interactive strategies discussed bring to mind any other expressive reading/writing strategies you know of or are currently using?

Teaching Literature

From Reading to Interpretation

■ There are readings—of the same text—that are dutiful, readings that map and dissect, readings that hear a rustling of unheard sounds, that count grey little pronouns. . . . There are personal readings, which snatch for personal meanings . . . full of love, or disgust, or fear. . . . There are—believe it—impersonal readings—where the mind's eye sees the lines move onwards. . . .

Now and then there are readings that make the hairs on the neck . . . stand on end and tremble, where every word burns and shines hard and clear and infinite and exact, like stones of fire, like points of stars in the dark—readings when the knowledge that we *shall know* the writing differently or better or satisfactorily, runs ahead of our capacity to say what we know, or how. In these readings, a sense that the text has appeared to be wholly new, never before seen, is followed, almost immediately, by the sense that it was *always there,* that we the readers, know it was always there, and have *always known* it was as it was, though we have now for the first time recognized, become fully cognizant of, our knowledge.

—A. S. Byatt

A. S. Byatt's powerful reflection (from her novel *Possession*) reminds us that there are many kinds of reading. Some people read for information, some for pleasure. Some people read for what they can carry away from a text; others read to be carried away by the text. As Charlotte Huck (1987) observes, "Literature has the power to take us out of ourselves and return us to ourselves a changed self" (p. 69).

EFFERENT AND AESTHETIC READINGS

Byatt's description recalls Louise Rosenblatt's (1976) discussion of efferent and aesthetic readings. Derived from the Latin *efferre,* to carry away, the term *efferent,* in the context of reading, involves paying attention to the information that will "remain as the residue *after* the reading" (p. 23). In an *aesthetic* reading, on the other hand, the primary focus is on the experience during the reading event—on what the reader is "living through *during* his relationship with a particular text" (p. 24). Both Byatt and Rosenblatt acknowledge that one can adopt either an efferent or an aesthetic stance with the same text, or can even alternate these stances. The problem arises when, through both words and actions, teachers send students mixed messages about why we read literature. Most of us who teach English/language arts have experienced that shock of recognition when a text speaks to us and articulates something we recognize as being profound and true. Our fondest hope is that something in our classrooms will enable our students to share in the exhilaration of this discovery. And yet we often ask students to count the "grey little pronouns," leaving students like Ron, the middle schooler in Jeff Wilhelm's (1997) class whom we met in Chapter 1, to conclude, "You can read something good and the teacher ruins it by asking you questions that you already know, that don't matter, that you disagree with . . ." (p. 26). The teacher in Robert Probst's story in Chapter 6 is a case in point. She was so consumed with getting the correct answer to her question, "What techniques does the author use to reveal character in this story?" and moving on that she failed to notice that she had completely appropriated the students' discussion and actually interfered with their process of meaning construction.

The teacher in Probst's story was not malicious. She simply saw her job as "the teaching of skills and terms and techniques" (Probst, 1988, p. 33). Apparently, she confused one limited means of teaching literature with an end in and of itself. But how we conceive of the teaching of literature can significantly affect how our students perceive reading, so it is essential that we carefully consider what our goals are as teachers of literature and how we plan to go about achieving them.

WHY TEACH LITERATURE?

If the end of literature instruction is not to teach skills, terms, and techniques, then why do we teach literature? Eloquent testimonials addressing this question abound in professional books and journals. Here are just three perspectives:

> If literature existed only to be comprehended, we could regard "response to literature" as merely a subclass of "reading comprehension," since literature is only one kind of reading matter. But literature exists not only to be understood but to be undergone. . . . Serious fiction, plays, and poetry, or certain essays and true stories are meant to act on our whole being—to astonish, decondition, purge, exhilarate, or dismay us, for example. (Moffett, 1990, p. 302)

> Whatever the form—poem, novel, drama, biography, essay—literature makes comprehensible the myriad ways in which human beings meet the infinite possibilities that life offers. (Rosenblatt, 1976, p. 6)

> All literature—the stories we read as well as those we tell—provides us with a way to imagine human potential. In its best sense, literature is intellectually provocative as well as humanizing, allowing us various angles of vision to examine thoughts, beliefs, and actions. (Langer, 1995, p. 5)

Moffett, Rosenblatt, and Langer all share an aesthetic perspective on the goal of reading: Literature is meant not just to be understood but to be experienced, not just to teach us but to move us, not just to be accepted but to be reflected upon and sometimes even resisted.

If we want students to perceive literature as something that can be richly rewarding, both intellectually and emotionally, and not merely a chore imposed by the teacher, we must find ways to promote and value the students' own process of meaning construction. Although current teaching practices may have changed somewhat with the widespread acceptance of reader response theory, Arthur Applebee's description of the typical literature lesson still holds true in many classrooms today. In his research study *Literature in the Secondary School* (1993), Applebee reports that instruction in teaching literature is a "relatively traditional enterprise," consisting of seatwork focusing on "what is happening" in the text, whole class discussion in which the teacher tries to "meld the individual understandings into a commonly agreed-upon whole" (p. 194), and individual postreading questions in which a correct answer is expected.

Applebee notes that constructivist approaches to the teaching of English/language arts have been "particularly appealing" to scholars because "in such a tradition, understanding a work of literature does not mean memorizing someone else's interpretations but constructing and elaborating upon one's own within the constraints of the text and the conventions of the classroom discourse community" (p. 200). However, for students to move from reading to interpretation, they must have access to skills and strategies. Robert Scholes (1985) reminds us that when we read we construct the gist of what is happening and produce *text within text.* He suggests that we invite students to retell the story, to summarize and expand on it as ways of reinforcing reading. But to truly experience a text aesthetically, we must move beyond reading to construct our own meaning, producing interpretation or *text upon text,* exploring the significance of what we have read (pp. 21–35). Scholes stresses that to move students from following a narrative—"It's about a soldier in a trench" *(text within text)* to thematizing—"It's about fear—or shame, or betrayal, or hypocrisy, or human frailty" *(text upon text),* the teacher must teach interpretation (p. 31). "Still," he cautions, "the point of teaching interpretation is not to usurp the interpreter's role but to explain the rules of the interpretive game" (p. 30). This brings us back to skills and strategies. In order to construct their own interpretations, readers must access certain skills and cognitive strategies. In the interest of teaching the rules of the interpretive game, the teacher may need to occasionally take an efferent approach to teaching as a means of helping students engage with texts aesthetically. This may mean directly teaching students about the cognitive strategies experienced readers use to make meaning from texts (tapping prior knowledge, visualizing, monitoring, etc.) or drawing their attention to the use of these strategies during guided practice activities. It may also mean teaching the elements of plot, setting, character, and theme or introducing literary terms (simile, metaphor, personification, etc.), to give students tools with which to understand and appreciate author's craft and on which to build their own interpretations. Occasionally, the teacher will also want to contextualize a work of literature for students by providing relevant biographical or historical background. The trick is to avoid sending students mixed messages: Keep them informed about *why* you are providing a particular type of instruction or background or asking them to engage in a certain type of guided practice, and clearly distinguish between the end of literature and the means to achieve this end.

Langer (1985) would argue that the end of literature instruction is to create lifelong envisionment builders. As we have discussed previously, an envisionment is an evolving text world in the mind that develops as individuals "use their past experiences with literature, literacy, and life as threads from which to weave new understandings" (p. 58). Envisionments go beyond reading and interpretation to include reflecting, relating, and evaluating or criticism *(text against text).* Langer stresses that "envisionment building is not just a literary activity; we build envisionments all the time when we make sense of ourselves, of others, and of the world" (p. 9). From this perspective, our goal is to help all of our students to become not just confident and competent readers and writers but independent, critical thinkers and decision makers as well.

CRITICAL APPROACHES TO LITERATURE

Deborah Appleman (1993) notes that too often, teachers relegate the reading of a text—determining what it says—to students while predetermining the interpretation—what it means—by selecting a particular critical approach with which to view the text and either providing "a single reified interpretation for the students" or allowing students only to "create interpretations within the context of that singular critical approach" (p. 159). The various schools of literary criticism can offer students different lenses through which to view a work of literature. However, these approaches are rarely explicitly taught in secondary school; instead, one literary theory tends to "dominate the teaching of literature until it is replaced by another" (p. 156). For several decades the approach called *New Criticism* (Richards, 1929) shaped the teaching of literature in both secondary schools and colleges. In New Criticism the text was regarded as an artifact to be read, analyzed, and appreciated independent of the personal history of the author, the social context, or what the reader brings to the text. Eliciting the meaning of a text was thought to be bound up in a "trained appreciation of its form" (McCormick, 1994, p. 34)—tone, point of view, imagery, metaphor, symbolism, irony, and so on—and only mature readers with an "educated sensibility" were thought to be able to conduct the kind of "close reading" that would allow them to arrive at a correct or ideal interpretation of the text. This approach definitely puts teachers in the driver's seat, charting the course through the text and pointing out landmarks along the way so that students (who occupy the backseat in this process) can all arrive safely at the same predetermined destination.

In the 1970s teachers began to embrace the work of Louise Rosenblatt, begun in the 1930s, which reacts against the study of texts in isolation apart from the existence of a reader. Kathleen McCormick (1994) notes, "The importance of the reader-response movement in democratizing the teaching of literature cannot be underestimated" (p. 38). *Reader response criticism* offers an alternative to the more objective approach of New Criticism, maintaining instead that the reading of literature is essentially subjective. As Rosenblatt (1976) observes,

> There is no such thing as a generic reader or a generic literary work; there are only the potential millions of individual readers of the potential millions of individual literary works. A novel or poem or play remains merely ink spots on paper until a reader transforms them into a set of meaningful symbols. The literary work exists in the live circuit set up between reader and text: the reader infuses intellectual and emotional meanings into the pattern of verbal symbols, and those symbols channel thoughts and feelings. Out of this complex process emerges a more or less imaginative experience. (p. 25)

According to Rosenblatt, meaning resides neither exclusively in the text nor in the reader but in the transaction (negotiation) between the reader and the text; the reader draws upon his or her "past experiences with life and language as the raw materials out of which to shape the new experience symbolized on the page" (p. 26). Because every reader is unique, there is no such thing as an ideal reading in reader response. The teacher's job is no longer to lead the guided tour but rather "to foster fruitful interactions or, more precisely, transactions" (p. 26) that allow readers to embark on their own journeys through texts and sometimes arrive at diverse destinations.

Arthur Applebee (1993) notes that today's teachers "seem caught between constructivist and earlier traditions" (p. 200). That is, while there is widespread acceptance of reader response and an emphasis on student-centered instruction, students are often invited to respond to the teacher's questions rather than to generate their own, and the presumption in many classrooms is still that students' experiences "should *begin* from the teacher's knowledge of correct interpretations, toward which everyone should be led" (p. 201). I recently witnessed the tension that can arise when teachers are (often unconsciously) trying to juggle these critical approaches. One of my student teachers, an especially talented and well-intentioned young man, resolved to take a risk in the classroom by taking students out of rows, forming a circle, and having a student-led discussion about *To Kill a Mockingbird* in which he planned simply to participate as one more respondent. The day before, to prepare for the discussion, he had modeled how to ask an interpretive question (i.e., a question for which there is no right or wrong answer and that invites multiple perspectives); and for homework he had asked each student to bring one question to the circle. In the circle, although the students were somewhat uncomfortable about speaking up without raising their hands and being called on, they were managing to keep the conversation going. About ten minutes into the discussion, the student teacher took a turn, drew the students' attention to the passage in *Mockingbird* in which the rabid dog comes into the neighborhood and Atticus has to shoot it, and asked, "What does this remind you of?" The students' faces went blank; they didn't have a clue. The student teacher then asked, "What time of year do dogs usually go mad, and what month was this?" The students dutifully searched through the text. When they found the answers (August; February), he probed further: "Now that's curious, isn't it? What does that suggest to you?" Again, blank faces. Fifteen minutes and several attempts later, the student teacher, now visibly frustrated, abandoned his fishing expedition and explicitly said, "Doesn't it seem to you like the dog is a symbol of the town of Maycomb?" More blank faces. Students stared hard at the armrests on their desks and hoped that someone else would figure out what the teacher wanted them to say.

When we debriefed after class, I asked the student teacher why he couldn't just let go of his agenda and return to the students' questions. He confessed that although he had actually missed the symbolism of the rabid dog himself when reading the text, a fellow student teacher had learned this as a high school student. This interpretation struck him as such an important revelation that he just couldn't resist continuing to fish long after it was clear that the students were not ready to make this particular connection. We discussed how, once they had read farther into the novel, he might try inviting them to create a coat of arms for Maycomb (see Chapter 3) and to develop their own similes or metaphors. For example, in response to the frame, "If Maycomb were an animal it would be a _____ because _____," they might write, "Maycomb would be a snake because the prejudice there is poisonous." Once they had developed their own interpretations, students might be ready to revisit the rabid dog scene—perhaps in conjunction with the remark Atticus makes several pages earlier, "Why reasonable people go stark raving mad when anything involving a Negro comes up is something I don't understand"—and discuss its significance.

Just as New Criticism has its critics, so does reader response. Although New Criticism privileges the text over the reader, some scholars question whether reader response gives too much authority to the reader, privileging the reader over the text. Leila Christenbury (1994) stresses, "A reader's response must be intelligent, thoughtful, and have some tie to the text, however tenuous that might first appear. To consider a discussion where students do not have to pay any attention to what they have read is not reader response—it's irresponsible" (p. 105). Several critics have pointed out that readers are also shaped by their culture. Kathleen McCormick (1994) points out that the different discourse communities in education today "have not adequately re-theorized the reader as a social subject and the text as a social production" (p. 47). She argues that not only do students need to learn how to analyze how texts are culturally constructed but also how they themselves are shaped by their culture. Bruce Pirie (1997), whose book *Reshaping High School English* discusses the implications of *cultural studies criticism* for the teaching of literature at the secondary level, adds that only after we recognize how our culture shapes our values and how our "values shape our readings" are we in the position "to criticize those values, measure them against the values of others, and celebrate or revise our values as appropriate" (p. 44).

Jack Thomson (1993) suggests that students be trained to ask themselves the question, "What is it that I am bringing to the text that causes me to respond as I do?" (p. 153). Once they become conscious that there are not only a reader and a text but also contexts (both the reader's and the writer's) that influence the process of meaning construction, students can move beyond interpretation to evaluation or criticism *(text against text)*. Thomson (p. 153) suggests that in order to identify one's own ideology as well as to avoid being manipulated by the text, it is important to take a step back and ask oneself these questions:

- How am I being positioned by the author and by my culture to read this text?
- What is the author's ideology?
- Can I relate to it/refute it with my own?

Because all of these critical approaches (and others, such as feminist, Marxist, and psychoanalytic criticism) have contributions to make to the teaching of literature, focusing the lens through which a student views a text according to the teacher's preferred approach seems somewhat limiting. If we want to broaden the lenses through which our students move from reading to interpretation, then we should make them aware of all of the factors that shape their processes of meaning construction—the reader; the text; and the context (of the reader, of the writer and of the text), which might include social, cultural, historical, political, and even psychological background. For a comprehensive review of literary criticism, from precritical approaches through reader response, see *A Handbook of Critical Approaches to Literature* (Guerin et al., 1992).

ORGANIZING THE CURRICULUM

According to Arthur Applebee (1993), if you are a beginning teacher, the curriculum for your secondary English/language arts class will already have been decided for you in large part by your department, taking into consideration district and state recommended courses of study and individual teacher preferences. Although there are a variety of ways to organize classroom instruction—chronologically, by author, by genre, by theme, and so on—there is a 75 percent chance that the curriculum you inherit will focus on the study of individual major works, most likely grouped by genre or possibly by theme, sequenced chronologically, or representing the literature of a specific group (pp. 49, 51). At a high school you can expect to teach certain core works. Figure 7.1 contains a list of the most popular titles of book-length works for grades 9 through 12 in public schools. This list remained relatively stable from 1963 to 1993, so there is little reason to suspect it has changed dramatically in the last fifteen years.

Bruce Pirie (1997) suggests that to read critically we should notice not only what is included in a text but also what is excluded. If we apply a critical lens to the list in Figure 7.1, we will notice significant omissions—for example, of female authors (with one exception), of authors of color, and of authors not of European or European American heritage. One might also consider whether the interpretive road has been so well traveled with these texts that students will be reluctant to develop interpretations of their own. Still, these are important works that have stood the test of time; students should not only be exposed to

Figure 7.1   **Most Popular Titles of Book-Length Works, Grades 9–12** (*Source:* Applebee, 1993. *Literature in the secondary school: Studies of curriculum and instruction in the United States,* p. 65. Urbana, IL: National Council of Teachers of English.)

Romeo and Juliet	*To Kill a Mockingbird*	*Hamlet*
Macbeth	*The Scarlet Letter*	*The Great Gatsby*
Huckleberry Finn	*Of Mice and Men*	*Lord of the Flies*
Julius Caesar		

but encouraged to interact with such works. It is the teacher's job to bring fresh approaches to the study of canonical works as well to supplement the departmental curriculum with other material that will expand his or her students' textual repertoire. In addition to including multicultural literature (see Chapter 8), the teacher might also incorporate popular young adult literature into the curriculum. According to Leila Christenbury (1994, p. 121), the genre of young adult literature is characterized by:

- A teenage (or young adult) protagonist
- A stripped-down plot with few, if any, subplots
- A limited number of characters
- A compressed time span and a restricted setting
- An approximate length of 125–250 pages

Young adult literature makes ideal reading for book clubs and literature circles, but Tchudi and Mitchell (1999) advocate also pairing YA literature with core literature. Figure 7.2 features some suggested pairings. (See Chapter 14 and the companion website for a more in-depth discussion of and a list of titles of YA literature.)

Applebee's research (1993) confirms that literature occupies a central place in the English/language arts classroom, with 50 percent of class time devoted directly to the study of literature and about 75 percent devoted to literature-related activities. Of the writing that takes place in the English/language arts classroom, approximately 75 percent is about literature (p. 159). Further, the most typical writing assignment is the formal text-based essay. As Chapter 6 stressed, it is essential to provide ongoing opportunities for students to interact with texts and to use expressive writing as a tool for learning. However, it is also clearly the teacher's obligation to scaffold instruction that enables students to learn how to write the interpretive literature-based essay. Through integrating reading and writing instruction, the teacher can guide students in developing interpretive abilities while constructing meaning both from and with texts.

Figure 7.2   **Pairing Young Adult Literature with Core Texts** (*Source:* Tchudi and Mitchell, 1997. *Exploring teaching and the English language arts,* p. 189. New York: Addison Wesley Longman.)

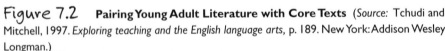

Young Adult Literature		Core Text
Walter Dean Myers, *Fallen Angels*	⟷	Stephen Crane, *The Red Badge of Courage*
Rodman Philbrick, *Freak the Mighty*	⟷	John Steinbeck, *Of Mice and Men*
Mildred Taylor, *The Road to Memphis*	⟷	Harper Lee, *To Kill a Mockingbird*
Philip Pullman, *Ruby in the Smoke*	⟷	Charles Dickens, *Great Expectations*
Stephanie Tolan, *The Plague Year*	⟷	Arthur Miller, *The Crucible*
Lois Lowry, *The Giver*	⟷	Aldous Huxley, *Brave New World*

DEMONSTRATION LESSON

Setting and Character in Tennyson's "Mariana": Teaching Literary Interpretation

This lesson (Olson, 1984; 1997b) provides a variety of strategies for helping students interact with poetry and for teaching students the art of literary interpretation. Tchudi and Mitchell (1999) note that "even experienced teachers who seem to have no problems dealing with other genres often ask, 'What do I do with a poem besides read it?'" (p. 176). Actually, poetry offers teachers rich opportunities to help students move from reading to interpretation. Robert Probst (1988) points out that because "the language of poetry is compressed, with each word carrying a heavy burden of meaning" (p. 92), poets tend to suggest rather than state. This leaves students to turn the words over in their minds, painting their own mental pictures and forming their own impressions.

The focus of this demonstration lesson is on paying close attention to the landscape or setting of a narrative poem by Alfred, Lord Tennyson and determining the relationship between the external environment described in the poem and the state of mind of the persona, Mariana, who inhabits the setting. The scaffolded activities purposefully point students in this direction and thus focus the lens through which they view the poem, perhaps closing the poem off to other perspectives. However, as early as 1835, John Stuart Mill commented on Tennyson's remarkable ability, in early poems such as "Mariana," to use descriptive language to create powerful scenery "in keeping with some state of human feeling so fitted to it as to be the embodied symbol of it, and to summon up the state of feeling itself, with a force not to be surpassed by anything but reality" (quoted in Abrams et al., 1968, p. 820). Each line of "Mariana" abounds with images to be analyzed, interpreted, and commented on.

The text-based essay the scaffolded activities lead to might be perceived as fairly traditional, dealing as it does with a discussion of setting, character, and theme through the interpretation of images and symbols. I believe we do students a disservice if we do not expose them to the "standard" literary interpretation paper. Our job is to provide them with the tools to say something of significance based on their own perceptions and reflections.

The terms used to identify the cognitive strategies called for in each of the guided practice activities are taken from Figure 1.2 (Cognitive Strategies: A Reader's and Writer's Tool Kit) and from Figure 3.2 (the UCI Writing Project's adaptation of Bloom's "taxonomy of the cognitive domain").

Overview

After reading and analyzing Alfred, Lord Tennyson's poem "Mariana," students will write an interpretive essay in which they explore the relationship of the setting of the poem to the state of mind of the character.

Objectives

Students will:

1. Analyze and interpret setting as it applies to television and to their own lives
2. Create a fictionalized setting based on a telling sentence
3. Visualize the setting of "Mariana" through drawing
4. Analyze the poem individually and collaboratively
5. Examine specific images and symbols and interpret their significance

6. Make inferences about the relationship between the external landscape and the state of mind of a character

7. Identify and draw conclusions about themes in "Mariana"

8. Write an interpretive essay that conveys a predominant feeling, impression, or message about the poem

The Process

This lesson will take one to two weeks, depending on the level of sophistication of the class.

Prereading Activity 1

Clustering ■ *Analyzing and Making Inferences*

To generate interest in the idea that the external environment or setting can sometimes provide us with clues regarding the personality traits or state of mind of characters who inhabit that setting, start with the familiar. Select a popular television show that takes place in a distinctive setting and initiate a discussion that focuses on *where* the show takes place, *why* it takes places where it does, and *what* the environment potentially tells us about the character or characters.

Be sure to look for a series with a distinctive setting that speaks to the viewer about the inhabitants. The living room in *Frasier,* a long-running sit-com which may still be in reruns, comes to mind. Positioned squarely in the center of a room that could otherwise be on the cover of *Architectural Digest* or *House Beautiful* (tasteful art, baby grand piano, a Zen-like sprig of orchid in an expensive vase) is a dumpy, threadbare brown Barcalounger, patched with electrician's tape, just five feet from a television and on which Eddie, the dog, is sprawled. At a glance we can see the tension between two lifestyles: that of Frasier, the effete psychiatrist, and that of the unpretentious ex-cop father who is living with him. Frasier's distaste for the Barcalounger and his many attempts to remove it were the focus of several hilarious episodes.

Prereading Activity 2

Applying Setting to Your Own Character ■ *Analyzing and Making Inferences*

After planting the seed about how the setting of a "text" can potentially provide us with clues about the character who inhabits that setting, turn students' attention to the ways in which their own environment defines who they are. Pass out a blank chart (see Figure 7.3) with these instructions:

1. List in Column 1 four items in or around your home that have some meaning for you. (Be as descriptive as possible.)

2. Think about what these items might say about you to others, and record your ideas in Column 2.

3. Fold Column 1 to the right so that it covers Column 2, and pass your chart to another student. That student should read the list in Column 1, interpret the significance of these items, and record in Column 3 what the items say to him or her about you.

4. Refold Column 1 to the right so that it now covers Columns 2 and 3, and pass the chart to a new responder.

5. Repeat the interpreting and commenting activity until three responders have had a chance to react.

Figure 7.3   **Student Sample of a Setting Chart** (Reprinted by permission of James Curry.)

Column 1	Column 2	Column 3	Column 4	Column 5
Items in or around My Home (a brief description)	*What I Think These Items Say about Me to Others*	*What These Items Do Say about Me to Others (response #1)*	*What These Items Do Say about Me to Others (response #2)*	*What These Items Do Say about Me to Others (response #3)*
1. A pool with a diving board & spa. Kept clean & taken care of, often heated.	1. I like to go swimming a great deal. I swim all year round but I like it to be warm.	1. You are someone who enjoys the water a lot.	1. You enjoy swimming & being in the water	1. Very neat & organized or your parents are neat & clean. Maybe *you* have to clean it on weekends. Like to swim, do tricks on diving board. Like to relax, often cold. Use it a lot or daily.
2. A new computer that was bought as soon as it came out & is top of the line. Kept clean & organized.	2. I like to keep up to date with technology. I enjoy using computers & could be called a "computer geek."	2. You like to have new things. You like to keep in touch with modern technology.	2. You probably have a lot of money. You enjoy having state-of-the-art tech. You are organized.	2. One of your parents works on a computer. Maybe bought & given to you as a gift because you like to type a lot & play computer games/use AOL daily?
3. A young dog, a beagle, very clean, doesn't like people, very wild. All black with a little brown.	3. I like animals as long as they are small & easy to care for. I never took the time to really train him.	3. You like animals in your house.	3. You like animals. You are probably like your dog, clean, & maybe distrustful of people.	3. Your dog? Maybe very special to you & your family. Very neat, probably a perfectionist. Maybe a lot like you or symbolizing something special.
4. A large, comfortable bed with lots of pillows & a giant heating blanket.	4. I love to sleep! I like to be comfortable & feel safe including being warm.	4. You like large spaces & warm places.	4. You enjoy sleeping. You also like open space.	4. Like to relax after school. Maybe TV in room.

Before students begin filling out their charts, to help them get the idea of the importance of providing their reader with enough detail, give them one or two examples. For instance, if I say I have carrots in my refrigerator, the reader might assume I am health conscious. However, if I add that these carrots have been in the refrigerator so long that they are oozing and moldy and have begun to take on a life of their own, the reader might assume that I have been too busy to cook lately. Again, if I say I have lots of CDs, the reader can only infer that I like music; but if I include that the CDs are by the Beatles, the Doors, Joni Mitchell, and Crosby, Stills, Nash and Young, students might conclude that I probably was a teenager in the late 1960s or early '70s and might have been a flower child. Figure 7.3 contains an example by twelfth grader James Curry of Villa Park High in Villa Park, California, of what a filled-in chart looks like. A blank chart is available on the companion website. Demonstrate how to fold the chart before passing it on to the next person, and point out that in Column 1 you write your items from the top to the bottom of that column, not from left to right across the whole chart.

Students enjoy the kinesthetic aspect of this activity as well as the focus on the personal. Once students have passed their charts three times, they should be returned to their owners. A certain chaos will ensue as charts find their way back to the authors. Silence will follow rather quickly, occasionally interrupted by bursts of laughter. Students should be given ample time to review the input they receive from their peers.

Depending on the level of sophistication of the class, you may want to explain that when students were just comprehending the list of items in Column 1, they were *reading*—that is, attending to what it says. But when they moved to the other columns, they began analyzing—that is, closely examining what it says to make an inference and form an *interpretation* about what it means. When we make an inference, we arrive at an assumption or draw a conclusion based on logical reasoning. We then draw on our inferences to express our own conception or interpretation of the meaning of what we have just read. Ask students how accurate their three responders were in interpreting what the items said about them. Were the three responses consistent? Did any response come as a surprise? Were there some items that elicited standard interpretations while others gave rise to divergent responses? Discuss why this might be the case. James Curry remarked that he was surprised that "one person really recognized that my dog is very similar to me."

Prereading Activity 3

Showing, Not Telling about Character through Setting ■ *Visualizing and Synthesizing*

After students have applied setting to their own lives and have practiced making inferences, interpreting, and commenting about the settings of others, give them an opportunity to synthesize this information by creating their own characters and settings. Introduce the concept of showing rather than telling with sentences like "The blind woman was terrified of unfamiliar places" or "The amusement park was run down and depressing." Demonstrate writing paragraphs that exemplify the telling sentences without repeating the statements themselves. (See Chapter 6 for more information on showing, not telling.) Once students have discussed the models, give them the following telling sentence:

> The state that her house was in made it clear that she had long since ceased to care about herself.

Have students underline in the sentence what it is that they will have to show about the character through a description of setting, and discuss this as a group. Give students ten minutes to write their descriptive paragraphs. Jack Thomson (1993) and Bruce Pirie (1997) both point out how ironic it is that we want students to interact with literature aesthetically yet always ask them to write about it efferently. Thomson writes, "Only in English have we traditionally set up a portrait-gallery model of the curriculum as opposed to a workshop model. We have expected our students to walk through the gallery of great writers and admire what they see, but not to touch the works or create any of their own" (p. 132). This activity enables students to create their own literature in anticipation of encountering the work of a professional author.

When students have completed their "showing paragraphs," ask them what they had to think about in order to get started. Some will have to visualize—to construct a mental picture of the surroundings—before they write. Others will need to conjure up a memory out of which to weave an imaginary character. For some students, establishing a point of view will be the prerequisite; others must begin by describing a room in the house (very often the kitchen) before widening the camera lens to take in the complete panorama. Allow at least as much time for students to share their thinking and writing process as for the written products themselves. Most students have rarely thought about their own writing process, and they are often intrigued by this discussion. Asking if people got stuck in their writing, why this happened, and how they were able to move forward again also elicits important insights about composing. Finally, ask for volunteers to share what they have written. Here are two sample student quickwrites:

■ "Come on down!" the voice from the television shouted. She reached for the remote control but missed—sending a spaghetti-stained plate and four empty beer cans clattering to the floor. No matter. No real need to change the channel. After all, one voice was as good as another. *I wonder what day this is,* she thought to herself.

■ The dripping faucet made greasy rivulets on the mounds of dirty dishes piled high in the sink. Flies buzzed in and out of the open mayonnaise jar, which had turned into a yellowish, sour-smelling custard. A cockroach darted across the floor as I made my way through the kitchen and yelled toward the bedroom, "Is anyone home?"

As the pieces are shared, listen for differing approaches to showing as well as for memorable words and phrases. Comment about what each student did particularly well, capitalizing on students' own techniques to teach concepts like imagery, foreshadowing, personification, point of view, and so forth. This approach will enable you to begin to introduce students to the tools of literary analysis in a personally meaningful context. As Bruce Pirie (1997) suggests, we should let the introduction of literary labels "grow naturally out of the meaning-making processes of the reader, rather than beginning with lists of terms and drills in the hunting and labeling of metaphors" (p. 69).

During Reading Activity 1

Reading the Text Aloud ■ *Visualizing and Constructing the Gist*

Read the poem "Mariana" aloud to the class. Ask students to close their eyes as you read and to try to picture what they hear. (An additional copy of the poem is available on the companion website.)

Mariana

Mariana in the moated grange (Measure for Measure)

With blackest moss the flower-plots
Were thickly crusted, one and all:
The rusted nails fell from the knots
That held the pear to the gable-wall.
The broken sheds looked sad and strange:
Unlifted was the clinking latch;
Weeded and worn the ancient thatch
Upon the lonely moated grange.
She only said, "My life is dreary,
He cometh not," she said;
She said, "I am aweary, aweary,
I would that I were dead!"

Her tears fell with the dews at even;
Her tears fell ere the dews were dried;
She could not look on the sweet heaven,
Either at morn or eventide.
After the flitting of the bats,
When thickest dark did trance the sky,
She drew her casement-curtain by,
And glanced athwart the glooming flats.
She only said, "The night is dreary,
He cometh not," she said;
She said, "I am aweary, aweary,
I would that I were dead!"

Upon the middle of the night,
Waking she heard the night-fowl crow:
The cock sung out an hour ere light:
From the dark fen the oxen's low
Came to her: without hope of change,
In sleep she seemed to walk forlorn,
Till cold winds woke the gray-eyed morn
About the lonely moated grange.
She only said, "The night is dreary,
He cometh not," she said;
She said, "I am aweary, aweary,
I would that I were dead!"

About a stone-cast from the wall
A sluice with blackened waters slept,
And o'er it many, round and small,
The clustered marish-mosses crept.
Hard by a poplar shook alway,
All silver-green with gnarled bark:
For leagues no other tree did mark
The level waste, the rounding gray.
She only said, "My life is dreary,
He cometh not," she said;
She said, "I am aweary, aweary,
I would that I were dead!"

And ever when the moon was low,
And the shrill winds were up and away,
In the white curtain, to and fro,
She saw the gusty shadow sway.
But when the moon was very low,
And wild winds bound within their cell,

The shadow of the poplar fell
Upon her bed, across her brow.
She only said, "The night is dreary,
He cometh not," she said;
She said, "I am aweary, aweary,
I would that I were dead!"

All day within the dreamy house,
The doors upon their hinges creaked;
The blue fly sung in the pane; the mouse
Behind the mouldering wainscot shrieked,
Or from the crevice peered about.
Old faces glimmered through the doors,
Old footsteps trod the upper floors,
Old voices called her from without.
She only said, "The night is dreary,
He cometh not," she said;
She said, "I am aweary, aweary,
I would that I were dead!"

The sparrow's chirrup on the roof,
The slow clock ticking, and the sound
Which to the wooing wind aloof
The poplar made, did all confound
Her sense; but most she loathed the hour
When the thick-moted sunbeam lay
Athwart the chambers, and the day
Was sloping toward his western bower.
Then, said she, "I am very dreary,
He will not come," she said;
She wept, "I am aweary, aweary,
Oh God, that I were dead!"

—Alfred, Lord Tennyson (1830)

During Reading Activity 2

Responding to the Text ■ *Constructing the Gist, Making Connections, Formulating Preliminary Interpretations*

After reading the text aloud, ask students to complete three two-minute quickwrites using these focus questions adapted from Robert Probst (1988):

- *First reaction.* What is your first reaction or response to the poem after hearing it for the first time?
- *Feelings.* How does this poem make you feel?
- *Ideas.* What idea or thought was suggested by the poem?

Give students five minutes to share their responses with a partner.

During Reading Activity 3

Rereading Silently and Responding ■ *Making Connections, Forming Interpretations, Revising Meaning*

Hand out a copy of the poem to students and ask them to read it silently. As they read, ask them to use Peter Elbow's (1973) pointing technique of underlining words and phrases that seem especially vivid, memorable, surprising, or puzzling. (See Chapter 11 for more on

Elbow's response strategies.) Then ask them again to do three two-minute quickwrites using focus questions adapted from Probst (1988):

> *Second reaction.* What is your second reaction to the text after reading the poem silently?
>
> *Selection of textual elements.* On what word, phrase, image, or ideas in the poem did you focus most intently during this reading?
>
> *Patterns of response.* How did you react to the text emotionally or intellectually? Was it the same or different from your first reaction?

Postreading Activity

Vocabulary Building ■ *Expanding Schemata*

Some students may find that they have difficulty responding to "Mariana" because they are unfamiliar with certain words that are central to the understanding of the text. Ask the class to list words they are unfamiliar with and discuss their definitions. These words might include:

gable	the triangular part of the end of a building formed by the sides of the roof sloping from the ridgepole down to the eaves
latch	a catch that holds a door or gate closed
thatch	plant material (such as straw) for use as roofing
marish	marsh; wet soft land; swamp
moat(ed)	(having) a deep, wide, usually water-filled trench around the rampart of a castle
grange	a farm or farmhouse with its various buildings
trance	daze; stupor; a prolonged and profound sleeplike condition (as in deep hypnosis); a state of mystical absorption
casement	a window sash that opens like a door; also, a window having such a sash
flats	level surfaces of land; plains
sluice	an artificial passage for water with a gate for controlling the flow; also, the gate so used; a channel that carries off surplus water; an inclined trough or flume for washing ore or floating logs
gnarl(ed)	(having) a hard enlargement with twisted grain
mouldering	crumbling; decaying
wainscot	a usually paneled wooden lining of an interior wall of a room; the lower part of an interior wall when finished differently from the rest
mote(d)	(composed of) small particle(s)
athwart	across; in opposition to
bower	a shelter of boughs or vines; arbor*

Because these vocabulary words are not words that are likely to be used by students in other contexts, I would not suggest devising a strategy to help students memorize them.

Prewriting Activity

Drawing ■ *Visualizing*

Ask students to think about the setting they pictured as they listened to "Mariana" with their eyes closed and again as they read the text silently. Now ask them to take ten to fifteen minutes to draw the picture they have in their minds. This may take the form of one

*Adapted from *The Merriam Webster Dictionary* (1974). Springfield, MA: G. & C. Merriam.

complete pictorial scene (for example, a sketch of her yard and the farmhouse) or be a less representational collage of images and symbols that the text conjures up for them. Figure 7.4 is a drawing rendered by Ryan Kataoka, a student in the UCI Teaching Credential Program. Figure 7.5 is a sketch by a sixth-grade student from Thurston Middle School in Laguna

Figure 7.4   Drawing of "Mariana"   (Reprinted by permission of Ryan M. Kataoka.)

Figure 7.5   Dungeon Drawing of "Mariana"

Beach, California. When we used this poem in a research study, sixth through eighth graders struggled with both the content and the language. (We had not thought through how little schema younger students would have to bring to the task.) However, several of these younger students surprised us with their insights. I retrieved Figure 7.5 from the wastebasket in Lynne Watenpaugh's sixth-grade classroom. I went back to the boy's desk and asked him why he had thrown his drawing away. He said, "Well, at first I thought Mariana was in a prison, so I drew her in a dungeon. But now I realize she's just in her house—so my drawing is wrong!" I asked him if there was any way living in her house could be like being in a prison for Mariana. His eyes lit up and, with a grin on his face, he began on a new sketch. I happily pocketed this one (after asking him if I could keep it).

Prompt

Introduce students to the following prompt. An 8½-by-11 copy of the prompt is available on the companion website.

When we read a work of literature, the external environment the author depicts can sometimes give us clues about the feelings, thoughts, and overall state of mind of a character whose story is unfolding. In other words, setting can serve as a reflection or mirror of character. Analyze what the text says in the poem "Mariana," think about what it means to you, and present an interpretation of the poem, paying special attention to the relationship between the external environment and the state of mind of the character who inhabits that setting. Refer to specific images and symbols in the landscape of the poem that reveal something to you about the state of mind of Mariana and interpret their significance.

Questions you might want to consider include:

- What does Mariana's environment say to you about the way she is living her life?
- What themes emerge for you as you explore the world Mariana lives in?
- After analyzing "Mariana" closely, what predominant feeling, impression, or message about this poem would you like to convey to another reader?

Your paper should be written in standard expository form (introduction, main body, conclusion), with logically developed ideas and smooth transitions. Be sure to include specific references to and quotes from the text to support what you have to say. Use precise, apt, and descriptive language to show and not just tell about setting as a mirror of character and to present your interpretation as vividly as possible.

Please consult the scoring guide for the criteria by which your paper will be evaluated.

Planning Activity 1

Textual Analysis ■ *Digging Deeper, Revising Meaning, Analyzing Author's Craft*

Ask students to choose at least four images associated with the setting of the poem to analyze closely. On a chart similar to the one they filled out during prewriting (Figure 7.3), students can list the items in the external landscape that they highlighted earlier as being especially vivid, memorable, surprising, or puzzling; examine these items literally; form an interpretation about what they might suggest symbolically; and step back to consider how they might represent a larger theme in the poem (see Figure 7.6). You may need to review with students that a *theme* is a central or dominant (and often recurring idea) of a work of literature, which extends beyond the story and can often be applied to the reader's life and/or to other contexts. The theme often grows out of the relationships of the setting, the events, and the characters.

Ask students to meet in groups of four and share their charts. Students may have listed some of the same images, but with different interpretations. Encourage them to write down one another's interpretations and questions in a different color of ink as well as to add new items to the list. After groups have had ample time to meet, call the class back together and

Figure 7.6   Interpretations of Textual References

What the Text Says	What the Text Means to Me	The Big Picture
Items in the external land-scape that say something about Mariana	*My interpretation of the significance of what the text says*	*Themes that emerge for me as I look at images and symbols in the larger context of the poem*
Rusted nails, broken shed, weeds	Mariana has let things fall apart. She no longer cares about appearances.	Neglect (the by-product of her grief is neglect)
Unlifted latch	No one comes but also Mariana doesn't go out.	Isolation
Lonely moated grange	Not a real moat—not on a farm.	Mariana builds a moat of isolation
Sluice with blackened waters	Instead of being a symbol of life, water is a symbol of death-in-life. Even her tears are not cleansing. So her grief is not natural.	Stagnation
(Etc.)	(Etc.)	(Etc.)

A blank chart is available on the companion website.

have each group report back, highlighting their most interesting item of discussion. This group report might feature an interpretation they arrived at collaboratively, or a puzzlement.

Planning Activity 2

Introducing Literary Terms ■ *Analyzing Author's Craft*

After students have analyzed the text closely, you can, if you wish, either introduce or review literary terms that students might use to understand and appreciate author's craft and/or to discuss author's craft in their essays. Provided on the companion website are definitions for various figures of speech and sound devices. Students can go into the text and look for examples of these literary conventions if you feel this will be a productive exercise. Because this is a very lyrical poem, you may want also to use it to introduce meter; you can note how Tennyson deviates from iambic tetrameter toward the end of the poem to slow the poem down and then bring it to a standstill.

Students are usually taught to look for similes and metaphors in literature. They will notice that these two figures of speech are conspicuously absent in this poem. Rather, the poem works through imagery and personification. You might ask students to speculate about why this might be the case. This may also be a good occasion to explain the allusion to Shakespeare: In *Measure for Measure,* the lady Mariana is betrothed to Angelo. However, when Mariana's dowry is lost in a shipwreck on the high seas, Angelo rejects Mariana. In order to extract himself from the engagement, Angelo spreads a rumor that Mariana has been involved in some impropriety. She retires to the "moated grange," her reputation stained, abandoned by her fiancé.

Planning Activity 3

Prove It! Showing, Not Telling ■ *Collecting Evidence*

After student groups have shared and discussed the images on their charts and noted the interpretations of others as well as questions that may arise, ask them to develop a telling sentence about Mariana, based on their analysis of the setting, for another group to write a showing paragraph about. To refresh their memories about showing, not telling, refer back to the telling sentence the students wrote to during prewriting: *The state her house was in made it clear that she had long since ceased to care about herself.* Telling sentences student groups might come up with could include:

- While Mariana waits for someone who will not come, life passes her by.
- Mariana is imprisoned by her own grief.
- Mariana leads a monotonous life in which everything decays.
- The dreary landscape reflects Mariana's weariness with life.

Ask each group to write their telling sentence and to pass it to another group. That group's task is to write a descriptive paragraph that "shows" the telling sentence through references to the poem's setting, including direct quotes from the text. Allow about fifteen minutes for this activity. Then ask each group to read their telling sentence and showing paragraph. Point out that each group has just made a claim about the character of Mariana that might serve as a thesis statement or lead them to a thesis—the key proposition or argument to be supported, advanced, or defended by the writer—for the essays they are about to write.

Planning Activity 4

Quickwriting ■ *Formulating Interpretation and Drawing Conclusions*

Based on the preceding activities, which emphasize a close analysis of the text, ask students to quickwrite individually for ten minutes in response to this question: *After analyzing "Mariana" closely, what predominant feeling, impression, or message about this poem would you like to convey to another reader?*

Planning Activity 5

The Microtheme: Formulating a Writing Plan ■ *Organizing Information*

Students are now ready to organize their ideas and information about the relationship of setting to character into a writing plan. Enable them to think ahead by asking them to create a "microtheme" (Bean, Drenk, & Lee, 1982). On a piece of notebook paper, have students write three categories: Introduction, Main Body, and Conclusion. Under Introduction, ask them to describe three different ways they might begin their paper: quote, anecdote, thesis statement, description, and so on. (Note: You may want to refer to the packet How to Structure Analytical/Expository Writing, included on the companion website for Chapter 9, for examples of different types of introductions and conclusions.) Under Main Body, ask them to refer back to their charts and look for patterns and then to brainstorm a list of main points they intend to make, noting the specific references from the text they will use to support those points. Under Conclusion, suggest that they write a sentence based on their freewrite describing the predominant feeling, impression, or message with which they would like to leave the reader of their essay. This microtheme should be viewed only as a point of departure for writing—as a guideline for how students will communicate their ideas rather than an outline of precisely what they are going to say. (Figure 7.7 illustrates the microtheme format.)

Writing

Constructing the Gist

Students will draft their interpretive essays, using their chart, quickwrite, and microtheme as points of departure. Before they begin writing, ask students to put the main points they listed in their microtheme into a logical sequence.

Figure 7.7   **Microtheme**

Introduction: *I could begin my paper one of the following three ways . . .*
• _____
• _____
• _____

Thesis: The claim I want to make and support in my essay is as follows: _____
_____
_____

Main Body:

Main points I want to make:

• _____

• _____

• _____

Specific references from the text to support
my main point:

• _____
• _____
• _____
• _____
• _____

Conclusion: *A predominant feeling, impression, or message that I want to leave my reader with is . . .*

An 8½-by-11 copy of the microtheme form is available on the companion website. (Jump to Chapter 2.)

Sharing Activity 1

Responding to Peers' Essays ■ *Analyzing Author's Craft and Assessing Quality*

Ask students to find a partner. Each set of partners will trade their papers with another set of partners. Each pair can read and respond to the papers written by the other pair using the response sheet on the companion website; they may also give the papers an in-progress score (which the teacher will not see) based on the scoring rubric (see Evaluation).

Sharing Activity 2

Color-Coding for Commentary ■ *Analyzing Author's Craft*

If your students have had previous experience writing interpretive essays, you may want to look at the section in Chapter 9 on helping students distinguish between retelling (or plot summary), supporting detail, and commentary. You could have students color-code the two essays on "The Stolen Party" provided in Figure 9.7, Chapter 9, as practice for color-coding their own or their partner's draft of this paper. (It is problematic to color-code a model essay on the same topic at the draft stage, because students may be tempted to abandon their own interpretations and adopt those of the featured writer.) If students are new to writing interpretive essays, providing support for interpretations from the microtheme should be enough for them to attend to.

Revising Activity

Applying the Scoring Rubric ■ *Reviewing and Assessing Quality; Revising Meaning*

Students have used the scoring rubric to give a set of two classmates an in-progress score, and they have also received an in-progress score themselves. Students should compare their response sheets against the rubric and then recheck their microtheme statement to see if the message they intended to get across was received by their readers. (If students participated in the color-coding activity described in Sharing Activity 2, they will also have visual evidence of whether they need to add more interpretation/commentary to their papers.)

Editing Activity

Focus on Quotations ■ *Proofreading for Correctness*

Students should now edit their papers for correctness, paying particular attention to the rules for quoting from the text that are provided on the companion website.

Evaluation

The Scoring Rubric ■ *Assessing Quality against Criteria*

The teacher and/or the student himself or herself can evaluate the final, edited draft based on the complete six-point rubric on the companion website. The criteria for a score of 6 follow, as well as a sample 6 paper in Figure 7.8. This paper is especially remarkable because it was written by a tenth-grade honors student as a fifty-minute timed writing, with no guided

Figure 7.8 Student Model Essay

"Lasciate ogni speranza, voi ch'entrate"

"Abandon hope, all ye who enter here," a quote from Dante, should be the sign posted above Mariana's door with the rusted nail. Mariana, the main character in Alfred, Lord Tennyson's "Mariana," has hope, but should abandon it, for it only makes her victim to more disappointment and depression. Looking at the environment and objects around her, one can see there is hardly hope of saving her from destruction.

Probably the most obvious aspect of Mariana that can be seen through the setting is that of decay and depression. Most of this is symbolized through objects in Mariana's environment. Like "the flower-pots [that] were thickly crusted . . . with the blackest moss" and the "sluice with blackened waters," Mariana's mind has been poisoned and polluted by pity for herself. Likewise, the "rusted nails," "the mouldering wainscot," and the "weeded and worn" thatch represent the decay of Mariana's life as a result of this pity and depression. These themes are confirmed by "Her tears [which] fell with the dews at even," and the words from her own mouth, "My life is dreary . . . I am aweary, aweary / I would that I were dead."

The previous quote, which is repeated in the last four lines of each stanza, introduces the theme of monotony which is prevalent in Mariana's life, and this theme is supported by other items in Mariana's life. Ever since her depression began, her life has been the same day after day, waiting for a person who "cometh not." "She could not look on the sweet heaven, / Either at morn or eventide," for due to the repeated disappointments, she has lost faith in God, and herself. "All day . . . / The doors upon their hinges creaked" because the sound has become so commonplace that she has ceased to care about it, and obviously the life that she leads. This theme of monotony is further accentuated by "the slow clock ticking." It has a steady pace which, like Mariana's life, is "without hope of change," unless someone were to break through to the source.

There are many obstacles to overcome in order to reach Mariana, for she is isolated from the outside world. It has evidently been a long time since "Old faces glimmered through the doors,/ Old footsteps trod the upper floors, / [and] Old voices called her from without." There is no one in the world left to care for her which is symbolized by the fact that "unlifted was the clinking latch" of the gate. Living "Upon the lonely moated grange" signifies that she has chosen to be isolated and has built a barrier around herself, preventing others to enter. Mariana is much like the "poplar . . . all silver-green with gnarled bark," because "no other tree did mark / the level waste," representative of Mariana's lonely life.

Each aspect of Mariana's dreary, lonely, and monotonous life is a result and a cause of the other aspects. It has become a never-ending cycle of hope and depression. Unless she can abandon the hope she has for the person who will not come, then there will be no hope for her. She must break through her own barrier and realize how she can change, or else she, like everything around her, will decay away.

—Tenth-Grade Honors Student, Irvine High School

---

prereading or prewriting activities. The student's thesis—that in order to save herself from destruction, Mariana must abandon all hope—is intriguing and admirably argued.

6 SUPERIOR

A 6 paper is clearly superior: well-written, insightful, clearly organized, and technically correct. A 6 paper does all or most of the following well:

- Analyzes the way setting is a mirror of character in the poem "Mariana" especially carefully and critically
- Makes inferences about Mariana based on the setting and offers numerous insights into the state of mind of Mariana and into what the environment tells the reader/writer about the world Mariana lives in
- Refers to several specific images and symbols from the text to reveal Mariana's state of mind and clearly interprets their significance
- Thoroughly discusses themes that emerge as the reader/writer explores the world Mariana lives in
- Displays standard expository form:

  —Has a clear introduction

  —Has a well-developed main body with specific references to the text and adequate transitions

  —Has a logical and impressive conclusion that leaves the reader with a predominant feeling, message, or impression about "Mariana"

- Uses especially precise, apt, and descriptive language to enrich expository writing, to make interpretation vivid, and to show and not just tell about the relationship between setting and character
- Generates a lot of interest and keeps the reader engaged
- Exhibits few, if any, errors in the conventions of written English; quotes from the text accurately

Learning Log Reflection

Quickwrite ■ *Reflecting and Relating*

Present the following learning log quickwrite prompt to students:

> Reflect on the predominant feeling, impression, or message about the poem "Mariana" that you expressed in your interpretive essay. Relate your interpretation of the poem to your own life. How might your interpretation influence the way you respond to rejection, setbacks, or a traumatic event in the future?

Extension Activity 1

Comparing/Contrasting Mariana with Miss Havisham ■ *Analyzing*

Tennyson's portrait of Mariana can readily be paired with Dickens's depiction of Miss Havisham in *Great Expectations*. (A sample prompt and an excerpt from *Great Expectations* are included on the companion website.) Although the circumstances of the two women are very similar, the way they deal with their grief is quite different. The points of comparison and contrast lend themselves to rich discussion.

Extension Activity 2

From Interpretation to Criticism ■ *Text against Text*

Students usually produce impressive writing about this poem, but they often grow "aweary, aweary" of Mariana's whining; they may even become angry with her, blaming her for succumbing to her grief as if she were a real person. But Mariana is a construction of Alfred, Lord Tennyson, a British poet laureate and a product of the Victorian period. Although in 1830, when this poem was written, women in Britain were no longer required to provide a dowry in order to get married, there was still intense pressure to find a suitable match by one's twenties; women who failed to do so were labeled spinsters. Invite students to stand back and ask:

- How am I being positioned by the author and by my culture to read this text?
- What is the author's attitude toward his subject?
- Can I relate to it/refute it with my own perspective?

As a counterpoint, students might be interested in reading "Story of an Hour" by Kate Chopin, an American writer at the turn of the twentieth century who was rebuffed in her own time because of the public reaction against her strong, independent female heroines. In "Story of an Hour" Mrs. Mallard, the protagonist, experiences what is at first a shocking and then a welcome sense of liberation when she learns of her husband's death—because now she is free and does not need to bend her will to the whims of her spouse.

TEACHING LONGER WORKS OF FICTION

Like Tchudi and Mitchell (1999), I have found that beginning teachers can sometimes be insecure about how to go about teaching poetry. Additionally, although teaching short stories is well within their comfort level, my students tend to view the task of teaching longer works of fiction as a bit daunting. Let's explore some questions student teachers have posed to me and to one another on an e-mail listserv during their student teaching experience.

Do We Have to Read the Whole Thing Out Loud in Class?

Sometimes a teacher fears that the reading won't get done at home. There is certainly much to be said for reading aloud in class; but it can also be a bottleneck in the reading process, slowing down the pace. Further, if you assume students can't or won't read independently, you will train them to fulfill your expectations. Be judicious about how much of a text to read in class, and choose passages that are especially engaging or thought-provoking, or that call for further explanation. Most teachers tend to read to the end of the scene, episode, or chapter. Consider stopping at a point that leaves the students in suspense—anxious to find out what happens next—and then asking them to continue reading independently.

Students can also participate in reading aloud in ways that don't conjure up that old familiar dread of being called on. For example, in a *jump-in reading,* one student volunteers to start and reads as much or little of the text as he or she wants, making sure to read through to the end of a sentence. The next student who feels comfortable simply jumps in and keeps reading. Students can select when they want to jump in and therefore can attend to the text without worrying about whether they will be called on and forced to read.

In a *readers' theater* (see Chapter 5), students assume the roles of characters and the narrator and read the text interactively, as if it were being performed, as in the example from Sandra Cisneros's "Eleven" given in Chapter 5. It is not necessary to have scripted the text to participate in a readers' theater, but it does help to have highlighted each reader's part.

Another type of participatory reading is a kind of *choral reading* in which students first individually preview the selection to be read and select vivid or memorable phrases or sentences. As the teacher reads aloud, students join in when their own golden lines come up. Sometimes a lone voice joins the teacher's; at other times, lines resonate for the entire class.

If students are given an engaging activity to complete during or after reading—such as the graphic strategies described in Chapter 5 (coat of arms, storyboard, literature portrait, open mind, split open mind, etc.) and Chapter 6 (clustering, time line, etc.)—they also will have a purpose for a reading and a creative way to express their understanding and interpretation of the text.

What Do I Do with English Language Learners and Inexperienced Readers in My Class?

Mifanwy Patricia Kaiser was faced with this challenge when she resolved to teach the same literature to her inexperienced readers and second language learners in the "remedial" track at Costa Mesa High School in Costa Mesa, California, as her colleague Michelle Lindfors, the advanced placement teacher, was discussing. Kaiser and Lindfors were reacting against the "monotonous stream of worksheets and grammar lessons" (1997, p. 105) that students in classes like Kaiser's are traditionally subjected to. They felt that all students should have access to significant works of literature. Still, Kaiser was concerned that her students would have difficulty negotiating texts like *The Scarlet Letter, Heart of Darkness,* and *Death of a Salesman*—all of which were on Lindfors's syllabus. So, rather than purchase watered-down versions of these texts, Kaiser devised what she called a "budget tour." She did not plan to guide her students toward accepted interpretations of the texts, but she did plan to orchestrate their reading to the extent that they all would comprehend "what is happening." In a budget tour the teacher, rather than an editor removed from the classroom, previews the text and determines what sections of the reading will be beyond the students' frustration threshold and which sections can be read and understood—that is, with guidance from the teacher. For example, in *The Scarlet Letter,* she decided to detour around the Custom House section.

Although the AP class read the full-length version of *The Scarlet Letter* and Kaiser's class read a shortened budget tour version, the activities for both classes were the same: reader response logs; drawing key scenes; dramatic reading; writing interior monologues from the point of view of different characters; and show, not tell paragraphs. When the students wrote an essay about who was the greatest sinner in the novel, both teachers were surprised to find that the ideas expressed by the students in the two classes were "remarkably similar" (p. 107), even though Lindfors's students were far more articulate and fluent. Kaiser noted that her students' self-esteem was heightened when they were assigned to read the same literature as the high-achieving students, and the careful scaffolding and storytelling she did to weave the stops on the budget tour into a coherent journey helped them negotiate this difficult literature successfully. She comments, "The beauty of the budget tour is that the student still uses the original work and is not singled out" (p. 107) as needing a dumbed-down version.

Note that although instructional scaffolding can enable students to read at their instructional level—with the teacher's guidance—it is also important to provide ample opportunities for them to read and feel successful at their independent level. As Leila Christenbury (1994) observes, "While we have a contractual obligation to adhere to what the school system and our English language arts department encourage or mandate that we 'cover,' we also need to remember that we have a similar obligation to our students to give them reading to which they can truly respond" (p. 116). Pairing young adult literature with the classics, providing a wide array of options for self-selected reading, and organizing book clubs (see Chapter 14) will enable students to gain confidence and competence at their independent reading level.

What If Students Get Bored and Tune Out?

Throughout the demonstration lessons showcased in this book, and particularly in Chapters 5, 6, and 14, you will find a wide array of pedagogical strategies designed to keep students from losing interest and tuning out. Here are five additional approaches to promoting reader engagement. Tierney and Gee (1990) note that very few researchers have studied the affective dimension of readers' involvement in text worlds. They observe, "It's as if engagement has been viewed as peripheral when it may be at the very heart of our understanding of the meanings readers negotiate" (p. 204). All of the strategies described here are exercises in *adopting an alignment*—immersing oneself in a text to identify with the author and/or the characters as part of the process of meaning construction.

Symbolic Story Representation   To help his students enter the world of texts and understand the wonder of reading, Jeff Wilhelm developed a strategy called the symbolic story representation. In the SSR (1997), students reenact important scenes in the story using cutouts, objects, or special props to represent characters, settings, motifs, and key ideas. They must also describe how they managed to "step in" to the text, to use Langer's term (1989). Wilhelm's students began by using pieces of colored paper to recount their experience of the story. But they soon graduated to more sophisticated representations, such as dice to show risk taking or a tortilla to signify that a character was "all wrapped up" (p. 44) in himself.

Figure 7.9 illustrates my rendition of the scene in the barn in Toni Morrison's *Beloved* in which the schoolteacher allows his sons to force themselves on Sethe and take her milk while he looks on, taking notes. I made the floor of the barn red with an X in the center marked by bandages. This is where the violation occurs, creating a wound as deep as the scars on Sethe's back that will occur as a repercussion from this event. The background is black; a white lightning bolt is shedding milky tears. In the hayloft is a broken heart, because Halley sees all yet remains silent. And I am the small eye way up on a hayloft beam, wincing; hence the Band-Aid that says "Ouch." Because this scene spirals in on itself and we construct it like a puzzle, in bits and pieces, Morrison keeps the reader on the periphery, trying to make sense. The SSR is valuable as an individual activity, yet it is in the small group sharing of each reader's experience that the text is illuminated and comes alive.

Figure 7.9   **Symbolic Story Representation**

Hot Seat/Talk Show   Hot seat and talk show are both role-playing activities. In the hot seat, one student (or the teacher) assumes the persona of a character, sits in a chair at the front of the class, and answers questions posed by the other students. For instance, when her students at Irvine High School in Irvine, California, began to grow aweary of Mariana, Sue Ellen Gold arrived in class wearing a costume based on a painting of Mariana by Dante Gabriel Rossetti. In character, she answered queries from the class about who rejected her and why, when it happened, and why she decided to close up shop on life.

In the talk show format, a panel of students comes up front, in character, with an Oprah–type emcee and a theme such as "Women Who've Been Jilted." The audience poses questions to individual panel members, and the characters respond. Collaborative groups can take turns performing the talk show, and the opening banter and sample questions can be scripted. (A talk show script for *To Kill a Mockingbird* is included on the companion website.)

Literary Scrapbook   A literary scrapbook is a project that can be sustained throughout the reading of a longer work of fiction. Students assume the identity of one of the characters and keep a scrapbook of mementos from various events that occur or might have occurred in the story. For example, when her seventh-grade class at South Lake Middle School in Irvine, California, was reading *Flowers for Algernon,* student teacher Leslie Baldwin asked her students to "become" Charlie and create literary scrapbooks at least ten pages in length. They included: three writing samples from Charlie at different points during the experiment; a letter from another character to Charlie; and a newspaper article written about the experiment. The prompt for this assignment is available on the companion website.

I had an opportunity to visit Baldwin's class and thumb through her students' scrapbooks. I was struck by how thoughtful they were, how personalized. Additionally, students decorated their pages with the extra-credit images from the sixties, downloaded from the Internet. The scrapbook project also enabled students to write in several domains both in the voice of their character and in the third person (for the newspaper article).

Literary Newspaper   Like the literary scrapbook, the literary newspaper can be an ongoing project that evolves throughout the reading of a longer work of fiction. While the literary scrapbook is usually an individual effort, the literary newspaper lends itself to small group collaboration. Students become reporters for the town newspaper and, stepping into the text world, create a news article, feature, editorial, column, advice column, cartoon, illustrations with captions, an advertisement—and, in the case *of Romeo and Juliet,* an obituary. The project enables the teacher to provide instruction in the components of journalism and gives the students an opportunity to create their own fictional artifact. Figure 7.10 shows *The Verona Voice,* produced by Kimberley Harris's ninth graders at Sunny Hills High School in Fullerton, California.

Shakespearian Insults   Students know that they are supposed to *love* Shakespeare, so they are often loath to admit that they just don't get it. Carol Mooney at Villa Park High in Villa Park, California, helps her ninth grade students warm up to Shakespeare by getting into character. Adapting ideas from Hill and Ottchen (1995), she begins by asking them to say "Where have you been?" in an angry, frightened, suspicious, excited, and shy tone of voice. Next, she asks them to stand up and deliver the same questions using physical gestures. After describing the theater in Shakespeare's day and explaining that the often unruly groundlings who watched the plays in the Old Globe standing up in the pit had a high need for bawdy humor in the early acts of the play in order to stay entertained, she introduces the idea of hurling insults. Students form two lines on either side of the room and take turns stepping forward and saying, "Thou art a _____," choosing appropriate descriptive language from three columns of

words—for example, "Thou art a paunchy, ill-natured harpy!" or "Thou art a scattering, clay-brained malt-worm!" A list of insults is available on the companion website. My student teachers used this strategy and their students were completely engrossed with hurling their insults (all in fun, of course). Mooney makes the point that Shakespeare's plays were intended to be performed, not read in a classroom. The Shakespearian insult activity is an icebreaker of

sorts to prepare students for a variety of performance activities as they read. Mooney's Shakespeare in Performance activities for *Romeo and Juliet* are available on the companion website.

Figure 7.10 Literary Newspaper (Reprinted by permission of Kimberley Lathrop-Harris.)

THE VERONA VOICE

Thursday, July 11, 1596 No. 123 35 Lira

NEWS
Mercutio, Tybalt die

**By Beverly, Diane,
Linda and Roger**

VERONA—Two men were killed and another banished after hot days spur more bloodshed in the already feud-torn streets.

According to witness Benvolio, Tybalt was looking to brawl with Romeo.

After Romeo declined the fight, Benvolio said that Mercutio was "ashamed of Romeo's refusal" and took up the fight with Tybalt.

Witnesses said Tybalt gave Mercutio a fatal blow during the congenial rough housing. "Tis not so deep as a well, nor so wide as a church door," said Mercutio after being stabbed. "But tis enough, ask for me tomorrow and you shall find me a grave man."

Tybalt fled the scene only to return after Romeo called for him. Upon their meeting, a duel took place which resulted in the death of Tybalt by Romeo.

"They were both pretty stupid," said one witness. "Tybalt should have kept walking and Romeo should have kept his mouth shut."

According to law, Romeo could have been sentenced to death. But due to special circumstances, he received the reduced sentence of banishment.

Some townspeople, however, still support the idea of vengeance.

"We must allow our friends to avenge our death," said one Montague. "We need some sense of order and civilization."

Brian Montague and Eric Capulet refuse to heed the Prince's warning.

FEATURE
Families in Grief Look for Answers

By Anna, Hoppy and Sela

The church's six-foot wide aisle separates women dressed in black, but the division between these families is as vast as the English Channel.

Attempting to mend personal and political wounds, Montagues and Capulets attended a joint memorial service for the late Romeo and Juliet.

"It was quite a gesture on the paterfamilias' part," said the Prince. "This will do more good than any edict about feuding I could make."

Friar Lawrence, who married the lovers, led the service.

"I'm glad to see that perhaps some good will come out of all of this," Lawrence said.

Despite the superficial unity, many felt the tension between the two families.

Of course the real purpose was not forgotten.

"It's a shame that the quarrel between these families has caused such a tragic loss of young lives," lamented one townsperson in attendance at the church services.

Some observers, however, found little sympathy for the victims of double suicide.

A visitor from the Middle East commented, "They deserved their fate, for if they had followed in their families' traditions this would not have happened."

EDITORIAL
Romeo, Stop Snivelling!

There can be no justification for your excessive whimpering. Two men are dead as a result of your meddling, without which they might have lived, while you are merely banished.

The Prince could have sentenced you to death. You should be thankful.

In our opinion, you are a provocative, rabble-rousing hoodlum who has caused turmoil in Verona while corrupting the innocent daughter of one of our city's most notable families.

If it were up to us, your head would be struck off and displayed in the plaza for everyone to see the wretch you are.

By Kristen, Rene and Stuart

The laws must apply to all equally. Well, almost. THE COMMON PEOPLE MONTAGUE CAPULET
The fair and just prince of Verona

COLUMN
Blood Feud in the Palazzo

By Barbara, Jeff and Stephanie

"Not again," I thought, as I rode from the barracks. Prince Eschalus had called our regiment to accompany him to palazzo to stand between Verona's favorite feuding families.

For the umpteenth time, we had to quell the chaotic violence that erupted.

As I arrived, the crowds parted for the Prince.

There lay on the cobblestones the bodies of Tybalt Capulet and Mercutio, cousin to the Prince and Verona's leading wit.

Swordproof Vests

"Yes, I, Romeo, am wearing my swordproof vest. Mercutio would still live if he had paid the 2,000 lire for a No-Points Vest."

**Vests 'R' Us
303 Appian Way
Rome, Italy**

This item is not guaranteed against injuries to the back, groin, armpits, or other uncovered areas.

OBITUARY
Lovers Surrender to Suicide

By Carol, Carrie and Renate

VERONA—It was a sad day for the Montagues and the Capulets when their teenage children, Romeo and Juliet, were found dead in the Capulet family tomb.

The victim of suicide, Romeo consumed a toxic poison, in grief over a mistaken belief that Juliet was dead.

Upon discovering Romeo's still-warm body, Juliet stabbed herself with Romeo's dagger.

Friar Lawrence expressed his regret by saying, "Such an untimely event has befallen these two star-crossed lovers. We will mourn them eternally."

Romeo and Juliet are survived by their parents, who have vowed to end the feud.

ADVICE COLUMN
Star-Crossed, Lonely in Mantua

Dear Abby,
I am the star-crossed husband of the daughter of one of the most prestigious families in Verona. Neither of our parents know we were married yesterday. As luck would have it, I was the unwitting participant in a murder on my wedding day, and through no fault of my own killed my wife's cousin.

Now banished by the Prince of Verona, I reside in Mantua and if I return to Verona will be killed immediately.

I love and miss my wife desperately and want to be reunited with her but I don't know how. Please advise me how to proceed.

Lonely in Mantua

Dear Lonely:
You have definitely got yourself into a royal mess. As difficult as it is, you need to let both parents know that you are married. Although they will be initially upset, they will come around when they see that your intentions are honorable. With marriage comes responsibility, and you must begin now.

God speed.
By Candy, Catherine, JoAnne

How Do I Hold Students Accountable for Their Reading?

To hold students accountable, most teachers I know provide study guide questions (which they themselves construct) and resort to the pop quiz on rare occasions. But they intermix these accountability measures with more engaging activities that enable students to demonstrate that they are indeed doing the reading. These include dialectical journals, storyboards, open minds, literature portraits, and other strategies discussed in Chapters 5, 6, and 14. Described below are two additional ways to let students show that they are keeping up with the reading.

Figure 7.11   **Paragraph Quiz**

In the trial sequence in *To Kill a Mockingbird,* Atticus raises several points in Tom's defense that suggest that Tom is not guilty of the crime of which he is accused. Select three key issues in Atticus's defense, and in a paragraph, explain them and comment on their significance.

Topic Sentence _____ .

Key Idea #1 _____ .

Specific Example/Quote #1 _____ .

Follow-Up Comment on Significance #1 _____ .

Key Idea #2 _____ .

Specific Example/Quote #2 _____ .

Follow-Up Comment on Significance #2 _____ .

Key Idea #3 _____ .

Specific Example/Quote #3 _____ .

Follow-Up Comment on Significance #3 _____ .

Paragraph Quiz   In an attempt to get more mileage out of the literature-based quiz, Todd Huck, an instructor of composition and literature at Santa Ana College in Santa Ana, California, poses a question to the class about a text and then frames their response as if it were the body paragraph in an essay. Students are free to consult their books, because the quiz format requires them to quote from the text. Further, the question posed invites students to think critically and to formulate an interpretive response. Figure 7.11 illustrates the paragraph quiz format for Harper Lee's *To Kill a Mockingbird.*

Jeopardy!   If you want students to be able to answer factual questions about a text, try making a game of it to give students an incentive to master names, dates, places, memorable quotes, and other bits of specific information. The familiar television show *Jeopardy!* can easily be adapted to the classroom. When Heather Ko was student teaching at Costa Mesa High School in Costa Mesa, California, she devised *Julius Caesar* Jeopardy! to encourage her students to become well acquainted with Shakespeare's play. She developed five categories—Terms, Characters, Quotes, Action, and Vocabulary—and created a series of questions that varied in difficulty. While one student served as the recorder and tabulator of points, Ko played game show host Alex Trebek and called on students, who were separated into two competing teams. Each person on a side had to volunteer to take a turn before any person on one side could volunteer twice. Depending on their level of confidence, students selected a category worth from 100 to 500 points. Here are some samples of the *Julius Caesar* Jeopardy! cards:

Quotes for 100	**Terms for 200**	**Characters for 300**
He said, "Beware the Ides of March."	This term from the play means "brave."	He tried to hand Caesar a letter of warning on the day of the conspiracy.
Who was the soothsayer?	**What is valiant?**	**Who is Artemidorus?**

As in the real game of Jeopardy!, if a student got the answer wrong, the scorer deducted the question's point value from the team's total.

I have observed students playing Jeopardy!; it never fails to generate a lively exchange! The prospect of the competition provides an incentive to get to know the literary work in detail. The competition itself is highly engaging, with students fairly leaping out of their desks when they know the answer and a classmate answers incorrectly. While students are having fun, they are also learning new vocabulary words, internalizing memorable quotes, getting clear who the characters are, and so forth.

What Do I Do Before, During, and After Teaching a Novel?

Although I like to think that my students have been exposed to a wealth of pedagogical strategies during their participation in my Methods for Teaching English in the Secondary School class, they still ask questions about how one weaves these strategies together to help students interact with and make meaning from a longer work of fiction. Provided on the companion website are a sequence of guided practice activities that one might implement before, during, and after the reading of Harper Lee's *To Kill a Mockingbird*. They demonstrate how a teacher can interweave a variety of activities, discussed in this chapter, to keep students engaged as learners, even with a novel-length work.

WHAT ABOUT NONFICTION?

Stephanie Harvey (1998) points out, "Although most of the reading people do in life is non-fiction, most classroom reading programs focus heavily on fiction" (p. 69). This is why, when students arrive in Jan Horn's remedial reading class at Irvine Valley College in Irvine, California, they tend to read the nonfiction texts she gives them straight through from beginning to end as if they were narratives, including reading the information in shaded sidebars as if they were part of the unshaded column, often without a glimmer that something is amiss. If we want students to develop a textual repertoire, we need to expose them to a wide range of texts—both fiction and nonfiction. We also need to make students aware that when we read an expository text from an efferent stance (i.e., with the purpose of carrying away information), we approach it differently than when we read a narrative from an aesthetic stance (to be carried away by the story). As Harvey notes, "We read fiction primarily for enjoyment, to connect the text with our lives, to let our imagination carry us away, to hear the sound of narrative language, and to explore age-old themes. We read nonfiction to learn. If we lose ourselves too far in the language or mood of a nonfiction piece, meaning may be disrupted, comprehension can suffer, and learning may go up in smoke" (p. 70). This is not to say that we don't learn from literature or that some informational texts can't be so engaging that we can experience them aesthetically. But in general, when we read a work of fiction, we rarely preview the chapters or look at the ending—for fear we might spoil the reading experience. In contrast, when we read an informational text, especially a complex one, it behooves us to get the lay of the land by reviewing the headings and subheads, sidebars, graphics, print in special fonts, and end material in order to have a sense of where we're going. We don't really want the destination to be a surprise.

Paris, Wasik, and Turner (1991) remark that *previewing* a text (by skimming, looking at pictures, and examining the title and subheadings) is the mark of a strategic reader and increases students' comprehension of both explicit and implicit information. Additionally, *identifying the main idea* has been described as the essence of reading comprehension (Johnston & Afferbach, 1985), because the reader must understand what has been read, make decisions about what is important, and consolidate information. But according to Paris, Wasik, and Turner, young and inexperienced readers have difficulty distinguishing relevant from irrelevant information in nonfiction passages. Ann Kaganoff, a certified educational therapist, has designed a previewing checklist for student readers to use before beginning a chapter or unit in a textbook; it is available on the companion website.

Students also need to know that expository texts are organized in identifiable text structures. Figure 7.12, taken from Gail Tompkins's *Literacy for the 21st Century* (1997), defines the five most common text structures, provides cue or signal words one might find associated with each structure, suggests the most useful type of graphic organizer to map this structure, and gives an example. According to Tompkins, "researchers have confirmed that when students use the five expository text structures to organize their reading and writing, they are more effective readers and writers" (p. 221). I have created a version of Tompkin's chart that contains only the pattern and description columns (see the companion website). I

Figure 7.12 **The Five Expository Text Structures** (*Source: Literacy for the 21st Century: A Balanced Approach* by Tompkins, Gail, © 1997. Reprinted by permission of Prentice-Hall, Inc., Upper Saddle River, NJ.)

Pattern	Description	Cue Words	Graphic Organizer	Sample Passage
Description	The author describes a topic by listing characteristics, features, and examples.	*for example* *characteristics are*		The Olympic symbol consists of five interlocking rings. The rings represent the five continents—Africa, Asia, Europe, North America, and South America—from which athletes come to compete in the games. The rings are colored black, blue, green, red, and yellow. At least one of these colors is found in the flag of every country sending athletes to compete in the Olympic games.
Sequence	The author lists items or events in numerical or chronological order.	*first, second, third* *next* *then* *finally*	1. _____ 2. _____ 3. _____ 4. _____ 5. _____	The Olympic games began as athletic festivals to honor the Greek gods. The most important festival was held in the valley of Olympia to honor Zeus, the king of the gods. It was this festival that became the Olympic games in 776 B.C. These games were ended in A.D. 394 by the Roman Emperor who ruled Greece. No Olympic games were held for more than 1,500 years. Then the modern Olympics began in 1896. Almost 300 male athletes competed in the first modern Olympics. In the games held in 1900, female athletes were allowed to compete. The games have continued every four years since 1896 except during World War II, and they will most likely continue for many years to come.
Comparison	The author explains how two or more things are alike and/or how they are different.	*different* *in contrast* *alike* *same as* *on the other hand*	Different — Alike / Different	The modern Olympics is very unlike the ancient Olympic games. Individual events are different. While there were no swimming races in the ancient games, for example, there were chariot races. There were no female contestants and all athletes competed in the nude. Of course, the ancient and modern Olympics are also alike in many ways. Some events, such as the javelin and discus throws, are the same. Some people say that cheating, professionalism, and nationalism in the modern games are a disgrace to the Olympic tradition. But according to the ancient Greek writers, there were many cases of cheating, nationalism, and professionalism in their Olympics, too.
Cause and Effect	The author lists one or more causes and the resulting effect or effects.	*reasons why* *if . . . then* *as a result* *therefore* *because*	Cause — Effect #1 / Effect #2 / Effect #3	There are several reasons why so many people attend the Olympic games or watch them on television. One reason is tradition. The name *Olympics* and the torch and flame remind people of the ancient games. People can escape the ordinariness of daily life by attending or watching the Olympics. They like to identify with someone else's individual sacrifice and accomplishment. National pride is another reason, and an athlete's or a team's hard-earned victory becomes a nation's victory. There are national medal counts and people keep track of how many medals their country's athletes have won.
Problem and Solution	The author states a problem and lists one or more solutions for the problem. A variation of this pattern is the question-and-answer format in which the author poses a question and then answers it.	*problem is* *dilemma is* *puzzle is* *solved* *question . . .* *answer*	Problem — Solution	One problem with the modern Olympics is that is has become very big and expensive to operate. The city or country that hosts the game often loses a lot of money. A stadium, pools, and playing fields must be built for the athletic events and housing is needed for the athletes who come from around the world. And all of these facilities are used for only 2 weeks! In 1984, Los Angeles solved these problems by charging a fee for companies who wanted to be official sponsors of the games. Companies like McDonald's paid a lot of money to be part of the Olympics. Many buildings that were already built in the Los Angeles area were also used. The Coliseum where the 1932 games were held was used again and many colleges and universities in the area became playing and living sites.

have then copied the original chart and cut up the cue words, graphic organizers, and sample passages into squares and placed them in envelopes. Students are then asked to work in pairs to reconstruct the chart without the teacher's assistance. After we compare the students' charts to the original, I give them a nonfiction text such as one about Hurricane Katrina and ask them to identify the text structures the author has used. This activity helps students to internalize the text structures as they learn by doing.

Although readers and writers of fiction and nonfiction read and write these types of texts for different reasons and using different approaches, they still access the same tool kit of cognitive strategies. Harvey (1998) lists key strategies for comprehending nonfiction: activating background knowledge, questioning, determining important ideas, monitoring and repairing comprehension, drawing inferences, synthesizing, and visualizing (p. 72). Almost all of the pedagogical strategies for using cognitive strategies to interact with literary texts can be used profitably in reading and writing about nonfiction. For good resources on reading nonfiction at the secondary level, see *Content Area Literacy* by Readence, Bean, and Baldwin (1998); *Tools for Teaching Content Literacy* by Janet Allen (2004); and *Subjects Matter: Every Teacher's Guide to Content Area Reading* by Daniels and Zemelman (2004). Additionally, *Write for Insight: Empowering Content Area Learning, Grades 6–12,* by William Strong (2006), has a wide range of writing to learn strategies geard toward nonfiction.

To Sum Up

Louise Rosenblatt (1978) reminds us that some people read efferently, to carry away information after the reading, and some people read aesthetically, to be carried away by the experience that is lived through during the reading. Teachers have an obligation to provide students with guided practice to enable them to become competent and confident efferent and aesthetic readers. The problem arises when teachers send students mixed messages, professing to read for aesthetic appreciation and then assigning tasks that cause a text to be viewed as a body of information to be dissected rather than meaningfully interacted with. If we want students to perceive literature as something that can be richly rewarding, both intellectually and emotionally, and not just a chore imposed by the teacher, we need to find ways to value the process of meaning construction. This will involve providing students with the strategies to move from *reading* (what the text says) to forming their own *interpretations* (what the text means). In order to move students to thematizing, we may need to take an efferent approach to teaching them the interpretive game and providing them with the tools to understand, appreciate, and discuss author's craft. But we must be explicit about why we're doing what we're doing. We must also make students aware that meaning resides neither exclusively in the reader nor solely in the text but in the reader, the text, and the context. Exposing students to a wide range of texts—both fiction and nonfiction—will develop students' textual repertoire and enable them to put into practice the cognitive strategies that experienced readers and writers use.

Learning Log Reflection

Return to A. S. Byatt's quote at the beginning of this chapter. Write about a time when you experienced a text that deeply moved you, where the words burned and shone "like points of stars in the dark." What was it about the text that drew you in aesthetically, took you out of yourself, and returned you to yourself a changed self?

Reading, Thinking, and Writing about Multicultural Literature in Culturally Diverse Classrooms

■ California's changing face is visible in the workplaces, streets, and communities of the state. But nowhere is California's changed population more prevalent than in the public schools—and nowhere is the need to acknowledge the changes more critical.

—Laurie Olsen

Twelfth graders in Introduction to Multicultural Literature at Woodrow Wilson High School in Long Beach, California.

As Laurie Olsen stated so well in the report *Crossing the Schoolhouse Border* (1988), California is in the midst of a wave of immigration that is dramatically transforming its cultural and ethnic makeup. Back at the time of Olsen's report, white students still made up 50 percent of the K–12 public school population, and Hispanic or Latino students made up 30 percent of the total. But the demographics of the state have been changing so rapidly that by 2004–05 the percentage of Hispanic/Latino students had increased to 47 percent as the percentage of white students fell slightly below 32 percent (California Basic Educational Data Systems, 2004–05). Depending on the geographic region of California, the ethnic breakdown of K–12 students may differ. For example, Asian students make up 13 percent of the total county enrollment in Orange County, where the University of California is located, but they represent 8 percent of the total state enrollment. African American students are underrepresented in Orange County, at 2 percent of the K–12 population, but make up approximately 8 percent of students statewide. The point is that in virtually no region of California can a teacher simply assume that he or she will serve predominantly white, mainstream youngsters. Overall, white students no longer represent the majority in K–12 schools in California.

The situation in California is by no means unique. Although coastal and border states have experienced more rapid increases and dramatic demographic shifts than other states, population trends point to an increase in students of diverse cultural backgrounds across the nation. In 1982 nearly 3 out of 4 American youths ages 0 to 17 were European American (Pallas, Natriello, & McDill, 1989), but by 2020 this proportion will change to 1 out of 2 (Au, 1993). Furthermore, while the general school age population in the United States is only 12 percent greater than it was in 1991, the ELL population nationwide has skyrocketed, increasing 105 percent. (Kindler, 2002).

Compiling statistics is one thing. Meeting the needs of an increasingly diverse student population on a day-to-day basis is another. As we in the UCI Writing Project saw the changing face of California in the changing faces in our classrooms, we began to ask ourselves: How can we, as teachers, be responsive to these changes and responsible about finding ways to recognize, validate, and motivate all of the students we serve? Diane Pollard (1989) states,

> We need to honor pluralism. We need not only to recognize the existence of other cultures but to incorporate them into the classroom everyday. Non-European cultures must be presented not just as an adjunct to the "regular" classroom but as a part of the total curriculum presented to the child. This is necessary in classrooms that are culturally heterogeneous but also in classrooms composed primarily or solely of White students. (pp. 74–75)

Because literature is the stock in trade of the English/language arts teacher, integrating multicultural literature is one of the most natural ways to "honor pluralism" in the classroom.

WHAT IS MULTICULTURAL LITERATURE? DEFINING TERMS

In order to talk about what multicultural literature is we first need to define the terms *race, culture,* and *ethnicity.* This task might seem clear-cut; but in fact there is some confusion about these terms, because the labels are often used interchangeably. For instance, when we are asked to indicate our "ethnicity" on forms by checking the appropriate box, the choices may include race based on color (white), ethnicity (African American), language (Hispanic), and geography (Pacific Islander). Moreover, political concerns about what is the proper label (is it American Indian or Native American?) or even generational differences (is it Chicano or Mexican American?) add to the confusion.

According to Banks and Banks (2003), the term *race* refers to the attempt by anthropologists to classify human beings into groups based on physical characteristics and genetic markers. Because modern societies are highly mixed physically, "different and often conflicting typologies exist" (p. 434). *Culture* can be defined as a group's "program for survival in and adaptation to its environment" (p. 434). It includes the symbols, behaviors, values, and beliefs that are shared by a group. Culture is socially constructed and learned; it is created by human beings in interaction with one another. In a large, pluralist nation like the United States, the overarching culture that all individuals and groups within the nation share is called the *macroculture*. Within the macroculture are many smaller cultures called *microcultures*. Individuals within a culture or microculture usually interpret the meanings of symbols, artifacts, and behaviors in the same or similar ways. *Ethnicity* involves membership in a group that shares cultural characteristics. Banks and Banks point out that "an ethnic group is not the same as a racial group"(p. 434). In fact, some ethnic groups, such as Puerto Rican Americans, include individuals of different races. A sense of peoplehood is one of the most important characteristics of an ethnic group. An *ethnic minority* group is an ethnic group with distinctive characteristics, which may be behavioral, racial, or cultural, and which make the group members easily identifiable. For instance, Jewish Americans are differentiated on the basis of cultural and religious characteristics. African Americans, Mexican Americans, Japanese Americans, and other groups are differentiated on the basis of both biological and cultural characteristics. Ethnic minority groups are usually a numerical minority within their societies and are often marginalized.

The overriding point is that every human being is cultural. As Banks and Banks note,

> to put it more bluntly, within U.S. society White people are just as cultural as are people of color (indeed the terms *White* and *people of color* represent cultural categories that are socially constructed). Moreover, White Anglo-Saxon Protestants (WASPs) are just as cultural as Jews or Catholics; men are just as cultural as women; adults are just as cultural as teenagers; northerners are just as cultural as southerners; English speakers are just as cultural as the speakers of other languages; and native-born Americans are just as cultural as immigrants or citizens who reside in other countries.

However, within the macroculture, not all cultures are valued equally.

Because in the United States some cultures have been marginalized relative to white mainstream culture, *multicultural literature* has come to refer to literature by and about members of groups considered to be outside the political mainstream of this country (Bishop, 1992); literature representative of the perspectives of people of color (Harris, 1992); and literature dealing with people of diverse backgrounds within the United States, including African Americans, Asian Americans, Hispanic Americans, and Native Americans (Au, 1993). However, although it is essential to right the imbalance in the K–12 curriculum, which has focused almost exclusively on the works of European American and European writers, it is also important for students to know that in a nation of immigrants, we are all multicultural. White students are also of diverse backgrounds—Anglo-Saxon Protestant, Italian American, Irish American, Russian American, and so on. They need to know that they, too, are members of ethnic groups. Junko Yokota (1993) offers a broader and more inclusive definition in describing multicultural literature as "literature that represents *any* distinct cultural group through accurate portrayal and rich detail" (p. 157).

WHY TEACH MULTICULTURAL LITERATURE?

Of the many reasons to integrate multicultural literature into the English/language arts curriculum, here are some of the most compelling:

- *To be responsive to the changing demographics of the nation and responsible to the increasing number of culturally diverse students we serve.* Demographers predict that students of color will make up 46 percent of the nation's school-age population by the year 2020 (Banks & Banks, 2003). These students already represent large majorities in urban school districts in many states. Given these trends, the current curriculum, which is geared toward predominantly white mainstream students, may no longer be well suited to the students of the twenty-first century. As Bruce Pirie (1997) notes, "The multicultural realities of English-speaking countries make it hard for us to hold up reverentially a model of culture that was designed in another age for purposes that no longer seem so commanding, including imperialistic and moralistic purposes" (p. 3).

- *To help level the playing field between mainstream students and students of other cultural backgrounds.* In K–12 schooling in America, most curriculum design and instructional materials are Eurocentric. That is, they reflect the "middle-class experiences, perspectives, and value priorities" of European Americans and, as such, are likely to be more relevant to mainstream students than to students of color (Banks & Banks, 2003). As Chapter 5 indicated, cultural relevance is directly related to schema theory (Scarcella & Oxford, 1992). If students do not have the schema to understand what they are reading, the cultural gaps will interfere with their comprehension and with the information retained after reading (Desai, 1997). Arthur Applebee (1991) suggests that the school literacy achievement of nonmainstream students might be improved if students of diverse backgrounds were exposed to literature that was more relevant to their own experiences.

Banks and Banks (2003) point out that the longer students of color remain in school, the farther their achievement lags behind that of white mainstream students. Jim Cummins (1986) notes that the relative lack of success of various "crusades against underachievement" and what he calls the "disabling" of students of color have resulted, in part, from the reductionist, drill-oriented curriculum students have been exposed to—curriculum that is frequently rationalized on the basis of responding to these students' "needs" (p. 30). While analyzing research data on the academic language learning of limited-English-proficiency students, Lily Wong Fillmore (1986) made this discovery:

> I came to realize that what these LEP children generally get in school does not add up to a real education at all. Much of what they are being taught can be described as "basic skills" rather than as "content." Instruction in reading, for example, is mostly focused on developing accuracy in reading rather than on understanding or appreciating textual materials. Writing focuses on accuracy in spelling, punctuation, the niceties of grammar rather than on communicating ideas in written form or on the development of sustained reasoning and the use of evidence in supporting written arguments. (p. 478)

But the reductionist curriculum is not reserved exclusively for ELLs. Jeannie Oakes's (1985) research on tracking also reveals that minority and poor students receive instruction that emphasizes low-level literacy; white and affluent students receive more of what seems to be effective teaching, with more focus on higher-level thinking than other groups. As she remarks, "There is no presumption that high-status knowledge is equally appropriate for all" (p. 74).

In addition to curriculum, the predominant mode of instruction advantages white mainstream students. That is, instruction in American schools is designed to promote individual achievement, and "competition is the primary method among middle-Americans of motivating members of a group" (Scarcella, 1990, p. 125). But there is evidence that African American, Mexican American, Asian American, and Native American students place a strong value on cooperative work and experience "a mismatch between home/culture values on one side and school/culture values on the other" (Kagan, 1989, 3.6–3.7).

Incorporating more multicultural literature into the English/language arts curriculum—not just as a nod to Martin Luther King Jr.'s birthday or Asian American Studies Week but as an ongoing and integral part of what constitutes a quality literature program—will not redress all of the inequities in the current educational system. But enabling students of all cultures to form interpretive communities and to explore high-quality literature in meaningful ways that are cognitively demanding, and providing them with the instructional scaffolding to develop the tools to negotiate these tasks successfully, is an important step in helping to level the playing field between white mainstream students and students of color.

- *To give culturally diverse students access to the "codes of power" and develop academic literacy so they can "beat the odds."* Academic English, defined by Scarcella (2003) as a variety or register of English used in professional books and characterized by specific linguistic features associated with academic disciplines, is probably one of the surest, most reliable ways of attaining socio-economic success in the United States today. Expertise in academic literacy involves mastery of a writing system and its particular academic conventions as well as proficiency in reading, speaking, and listening. In addition, academic literacy involves the development of certain habits of mind such as curiosity and the ability to see other points of view that enable students to engage in broad intellectual practices (ICAS, 2002). A recent study of prototype test items for high school exit exams (Wong Fillmore & Snow, 2003) reveals the degree of academic literacy expected of all secondary students, including ELLs, who are assessed on their ability to do the following, and more: summarize texts, using linguistic cues to interpret and infer the writer's intentions and messages; analyze texts, assessing the writer's use of language for rhetorical and aesthetic purposes; evaluate evidence and arguments presented in texts and critique the logic of arguments made in them; compose and write extended, reasoned text that is well developed and supported with evidence and details.

  Many teachers of struggling students, culturally diverse students, and ELLs avoid teaching and requiring students to read and interpret complex texts or write analytical essays because they feel the skills required (strategic reading, development of a meaningful thesis, control of organization, effective use of evidence and supporting details, sentence variety, and command of the conventions of written English) are too sophisticated for the population they serve. Yet, these are the very abilities assessed on high stakes exams.

  In the interest of determining what the features of instruction are of schools, teachers, and classrooms "that strive to increase student performance and, despite obstacles and difficulties serving the poor, beat the odds on standardized tests in reading and writing, that is, gain higher literacy, beyond comparable schools," Judith Langer (2000, p. 8) conducted a five-year study of forty-four teachers in twenty-five schools in four states. Schools with diverse student populations predominated in the study. Overall, she observed that in high-performing schools, students were engaged in quality, "minds-on" (p. 20) activities involving high literacy accompanied by carefully planned lessons on grammar, spelling, vocabulary, and organizational structure, taught in context but also including activities that focus directly on the structure and use of language. Lisa Delpit (1995) would argue that to have command of the skills of academic English is to have access to the codes of power. Like Langer, she believes that students "must be *taught* the codes needed to participate fully in the mainstream American life, not by being forced to attend to hollow, inane, decontextualized subskills but rather within the context of meaningful endeavors" (p. 45).

Figure 8.1 summarizes Langer's findings regarding six issues that distinguish beating-the-odds schools from typical schools and teachers. According to Langer, "The overriding contributor to success was the attention to students' higher literacy needs and development throughout the curriculum" (p. 46). These schools and classrooms also exuded caring and went the extra mile to create a "culture of community" that exhibited respect for cultures within school and for community knowledge and learning outside school. Teachers also went beyond superficial treatments of multicultural literature or acknowledging students' cultures such as having them write stories about their home lives and collecting them into a book, instead making diversity a fundamental part of the fabric of instruction "to explore possibilities and reach deep understandings" and to promote "intercultural as well as content understanding" (2004, p. 80).

- *To empower students of culturally diverse backgrounds by enabling them to see themselves reflected in the literature that they study in school.* As we saw in Chapter 4, affect is just as critical a dimension of learning as cognition. Learning requires paying attention, being willing to respond, taking satisfaction in responding, and developing an appropriate set of values about intellectual activities (Bruner, 1960; Krathwohl, Bloom, & Masia, 1964). Most researchers agree that the first step in creating a classroom environment that encourages students to actively attend to, respond to, and value what they are learning is to build a community of learners. But being in a community involves a shared sense of membership. When students of color are consistently exposed to a curriculum that excludes differing perspectives, they begin to feel disenfranchised. Lisa

Figure 8.1   **Six Issues that Distinguish Beating-the-Odds Schools and Teachers** (*Source: Beating the Odds: Teaching Middle and High School Students to Read and Write Well*, p. 21, by Judith Langer. Copyright © 2000 by the National Research Center on English Learning and Achievement. Reprinted by permission of Judith Langer.)

Issue	Beating-the-Odds Schools and Teachers	Typical Schools and Teachers
Approaches to skills instruction	Systematic use of separated, simulated, and integrated skills instruction	Instruction dominated by one approach (which varies among schools and teachers)
Test preparation	Integrated into ongoing goals, curriculum, and regular lessons	Allocated to test prep; separate from ongoing goals, curriculum, and instruction
Connecting learnings	Overt connections made among knowledge, skills, and ideas across lessons, classes and grades, and across in-school and out-of-school applications	Knowledge and skills within lessons, units, and curricula typically treated as discrete entities; connections left implicit even when they do occur
Enabling strategies	Overt teaching of strategies for planning, organizing, completing, and reflecting on content and activities	Teaching of content or skills without overt attention to strategies for thinking and doing
Conceptions of learning	When learning goal is met, teacher moves students beyond it to deeper understanding and generativity of ideas	When learning goal is met, teacher moves on to unrelated activity with different goals/content
Classroom organization	Students work together to develop depth and complexity of understanding in interaction with others	Student work alone, in groups, or with the teacher to get the work done, but do not engage in rich discussion of ideas

Delpit (1995) remarks, "In part, the problems we see exhibited in school by African-American children and children of other oppressed minorities can be traced to this lack of curriculum in which they can find represented the intellectual achievements of people who look like themselves. . . . Our children of color need to see the brilliance of their legacy too" (p. 177).

Frank Smith (1988) has insisted that admission to the "literacy club" is the automatic right of each student. One way to help all students feel like members of the classroom community is to select literature that highlights the experiences of the cultural groups they represent. When students are validated in this way, they learn to take pride in their identity and their heritage and feel more empowered in school (Cummins, 1986; Harris, 1992).

- *To celebrate diversity and to foster awareness, understanding, tolerance, and mutual respect among students, regardless of their cultural backgrounds, by exposing all students to literature from cultures that are different from their own.* Jimmy Baca, author of *Martin & Meditations on the South Valley,* once said,

  > It's much better to celebrate and acknowledge one's culture than to censor and ignore. One's culture is part of the seasons of America. They make America blossom. It is truest democracy giving to future generations its most important gift via language through literature and poetry. Literature is the tree through which we pass on the most important fruits of culture, nourish the soul, and give it sustenance to dream of a world more humane and loving. (Quoted in Olson, 1996b, p. xiii)

  Multicultural literature can be a mirror in which students of culturally diverse backgrounds can see themselves reflected and from which they can develop pride in their heritage. But it can also be a window into cultures that are unlike our own (Cox & Gadda, 1990). Multicultural literature can offer students a lens through which to view the similarities and differences between their own culture and the cultures of others. By not only validating and celebrating the uniqueness of each individual and culture but also surfacing the commonalties that unite us all as Americans and human beings, we work to engender "a world more humane and loving."

- *To enrich the literary canon for all students.* Arthur Applebee (1991) remarks that we are "failing in a fundamental way to open the gates of literacy" (p. 235) to our young African American, Hispanic, and Asian students and our young women of any ethnic background by focusing exclusively on the canon that we presently offer. (See Chapter 7 for a list of the ten book-length works of literature most widely taught in U.S. public schools.) But white male mainstream students are also being shortchanged, because a wealth of high-quality literature by and about people of color is available. This literature is often particularly relevant to secondary students, because much of it is related to issues that revolve around growing up and embracing one's identity.

THE TEACHER'S ROLE IN THE MULTICULTURAL CLASSROOM

The percentage of students of culturally diverse backgrounds may be increasing dramatically, but the percentage of teachers of color is actually on decline. In 1980 teachers of color made up 12.5 percent of the nation's K–12 certificated workforce; twenty years later they represented only 6 percent of the teaching population (Banks & Banks, 2003). Because the probability that teachers will serve students who share their cultural heritage is low, it is more incumbent than ever on teachers to learn something about the cultural, linguistic, and social backgrounds of the students in their classrooms. As Tchudi and Mitchell (1999) warn us, "Not being aware of who our students are, how they are culturally situated, what knowledge is privileged, and what our own cultural background predisposes us to view as right or good could work to deprive some of our students of educational opportunities in our classrooms" (p. 126).

The first step in enfranchising students is affective. The central tenet of Jim Cummins's (1986) work is that students from "dominated" societal groups can be either "empowered" or "disabled" as a direct result of their interaction with educators in the schools (p. 21). Teachers who "celebrate, not merely tolerate" diversity in the classroom (Delpit, 1995, p. 67) have a powerful impact on students' motivation and on their performance. After extensively interviewing students of color who achieved academic success, Sonia Nieto (2003) observed that "In case after case, students remembered those teachers who affirmed them, either through their language, their culture, or their concerns" (p. 298). For example, students can be invited to become the experts in the class and teach one another about aspects of their culture. The teacher can also value the literacy students bring from home by asking them to investigate, write about, and share their home talk. Valuing the linguistic forms students bring from home—forms that are "intimately connected with loved ones, community, and personal identity" (Delpit, 1995, p. 53)—instead of labeling those forms as incorrect or wrong can do much to help generate an atmosphere of acceptance in the classroom. In a sense, the teacher is creating the culture of the classroom, orchestrating experiences that motivate students to become personally invested as learners and to feel a sense of membership.

SETTING THE STAGE FOR MULTICULTURAL LITERATURE

As we saw in Chapter 4, in any classroom where a teacher hopes to create a shared sense of values, beliefs, and belonging—that is, to create a classroom culture—it is important to spend time building an affective community. If the teacher also wants to foster in students an awareness of and appreciation for their own culture and a tolerance and respect for the cultures of others, it is important to engage the students early on in activities designed to highlight issues of culture and multiculturalism and to set a positive tone.

Human Cultural Bingo

One get-acquainted activity that will immediately involve students in thinking and learning about culture is human cultural bingo. A sample bingo template adapted by Suzanne Charlton, director of UC Irvine's CLAD (Crosscultural, Language Academic Development) Program is illustrated in Figure 8.2. Charlton notes, "Out of 25 cultural squares, only one is related to food. This is the way multicultural education in your classrooms should be, too!" It is important to modify the game with your own students in mind so that every student can be an "expert" on at least one square. The object of the game is for students to circulate around the room, find someone who knows the answer to one of the squares, encourage that individual to tell them a personal story about how he or she knows the answer, and write that person's name in the square. Allow about fifteen to twenty minutes for this activity. Because students enjoy trying to get bingo, have them yell out when they have a row of squares filled in horizontally, vertically, or diagonally. But encourage the students to keep playing. The point is not to win but to learn as much as you can about the people in the room and the information on the bingo card.

Figure 8.2   **Human Cultural Bingo Game**   (Reprinted by permission of Suzanne Charlton.)

Directions: Walk around the room and ask various people which square they can sign. As they sign, ask them to tell you their "personal story" related to that square. Sometimes they will only need to tell you an answer, but try to encourage the telling of personal stories.

Can you find someone who . . . ?

. . . knows what *nisei* means	. . . has had a name mispronounced	. . . has an abuela	. . . knows what Rosa Parks did	. . . has seen a step show
. . . knows who Steven Biko was	. . . listens to ethnic music	. . . speaks a language other than English	. . . knows who Susan B. Anthony was	. . . knows what a *lumpia* is
. . . knows what an eagle feather symbolizes	. . . has been discriminated against	. . . knows who Cesar Chavez was	. . . knows what date Juneteenth is	. . . is from a mixed heritage background
. . . knows what the Trail of Tears was	. . . knows what a goy is	. . . knows what "comparable worth" is	. . . knows what a *quinceañera* is	. . . has read something by Amy Tan

An 8½-by-11 copy of the bingo game is available on the companion website.

After you call time, ask students to form groups of six to eight and help one another fill in any empty squares with students' names and their stories. If all students in the group have a blank square that no one can address, they can send a "runner" to another group or, as a last resort, to the teacher to find the answer. After ten to fifteen minutes, call time. Now ask the group to create a definition of the term *culture*. Students will come up with varied responses and ideally will note that culture includes history, knowledge, behaviors, symbols, and so forth. You may want to point out that culture is not the same as race; that we all belong to one or more microcultures but also share certain characteristics and values as members of the macroculture of America (hence the terms Hawaiian American, Jewish American, African American, etc.); and that thus we are all multicultural.

Biopoem

Although we are all members of one or more microcultures and of the macroculture, we are also unique individuals with distinctive characteristics. Asking students to write a biopoem is an effective way to turn their attention inward. The biopoem is a form of pattern writing in which students complete a frame that is provided for them, as in the example below:

Biopoem

Name
Son/daughter of
Lover of (3 things)
Who feels (3 things)
Who needs (3 things)
Who fears (3 things)
Who gives (3 things)
Who would like to see (3 things)
Resident of
Last name

The student responses to the biopoem could be the basis for completing the personality collage doll activity described in Chapter 3. Either the poems or the personality collage dolls and poems could be shared and displayed on a bulletin board as a way of affirming each student.

Sure You Can Ask Me a Personal Question: Dispelling Stereotypes

Lisa Delpit (1995) writes,

> We live in a society that nurtures and maintains stereotypes: we are all bombarded daily, for instance, with the portrayal of the young black male as a monster. When we see a group of young black men, we lock our car doors, cross to the other side of the street, or clutch our handbags. We are constantly told of the one out of four black men who is involved with the prison system—but what about the three of four who are not? During a major storm this past winter, a group of young black men in my neighborhood spent the day freeing cars that were stuck in the ice. When do we see their lives portrayed on the six o'clock news? (p. xiii)

In order to create a classroom culture in which everyone has a stake and a sense of belonging, we need to leave the stereotypes we may have brought with us outside the classroom door. But this is easier said than done. In her Introduction to Multicultural Literature class at Woodrow Wilson High School in Long Beach, California, Maureen Rippee confronts this issue head on. Rippee's students represent a mix of different microcultures—30 percent Latino, 25 percent Asian, 20 percent white, 20 percent African American, 5 percent other (Pacific Islander, Middle Eastern, etc.)—and within the wider community these groups sometimes come into conflict. Rippee feels that it's important to surface the prejudices and preconceptions students have so that they can let go of them.

Rippee begins by asking her students to write a personal definition of what a stereotype is. Students come up with a variety of definitions such as the following:

- Ideas based on ignorance
- When people think you are bad based on how you look
- Making judgments about an entire race without really knowing anyone of that race

Rippee then invites the class to think about stereotypes associated with teachers. She is quick to point out that stereotypes are both positive and negative and that the class is generating ideas about the stereotype of teachers in general, rather than about her in particular, so that they won't feel uncomfortable. A typical list usually looks like this:

Teacher Stereotypes

Positive	Negative
Intelligent	Poor
Educated	Too demanding
Caring	Out of touch with kids
Likes kids	Control freak
Good listener	Disorganized

Rippee happens to have long blond hair, so she also asks students to share stereotypes of blondes (e.g., "have more fun"; "are airheads"). She then encourages the students to ask her any personal questions they might have, such as What kind of car do you drive? Are you married? What do you do besides grade papers?

Once she has broken the ice by making herself vulnerable, Rippee introduces the poem "Sure You Can Ask Me a Personal Question" by Diane Burns, who is of Anishinabe and Chemehuevi heritage:

Sure You Can Ask Me a Personal Question

How do you do?
   No, I am not Chinese.
No, not Spanish.
   No, I am American Indi—uh, Native American.
No, not from India.
   No, not Apache.
No, not Navajo.
   No, not Sioux.
No, we are not extinct.
   Yes, Indian.
Oh?
   So that's where you got those high cheekbones.
Your great grandmother, huh?
   An Indian Princess, huh?
Hair down to there?
   Let me guess. Cherokee?
Oh, so you've had an Indian friend?
   That close?
Oh, so you've had an Indian lover?
   That tight?
Oh, so you've had an Indian servant?
   That much?
Yeah, it was awful what you guys did to us.
   It's real decent of you to apologize.
No, I don't know where you can get peyote.
   No, I don't know where you can get Navajo rugs real cheap.
No, I didn't make this. I bought it at Bloomingdales.
   Thank you. I like your hair too.
I don't know if anyone knows whether or not Cher is really Indian.
   No, I didn't make it rain tonight.
Yeah. Uh-huh. Spirituality.
   Uh-huh. Yeah. Spirituality. Uh-huh. Mother
Earth. Yeah. Uh-huh. Uh-huh. Spirituality.
   No, I didn't major in archery.
Yeah, a lot of us drink too much.
   Some of us can't drink enough.
This ain't no stoic look.
   This is my face.

Source: Songs from the Earth on Turtle's Back edited by Joseph Bruchac. Copyright © 1983 by Strawberry Press. Reprinted by permission of Strawberry Press.

Lisa Delpit (1995) makes the point that to ignore certain students in our classrooms under the guise of being "sensitive" is to render them invisible. In talking about this poem, therefore, it is important to acknowledge students in your class of American Indian heritage if you know who they are (or to ask if you don't know). Invite them to respond to the poem with a personal experience if they wish to. Ask if any other students have been approached by a complete stranger and questioned about their heritage, and encourage volunteers to share. You may wish to add that English teachers, with their folders full of student papers, are a dead giveaway—and that after confirming that yes, we *are* English teachers, we repeatedly have to hear about how English was the stranger's "worst" subject and how he or she is afraid to say *who* or *whom* in front of us.

As a class, Rippee's students next make a T chart of the positive and negative stereotypes in the poem:

Native American Stereotypes

Positive	Negative
High cheekbones	Poor
Beautiful hair	Alcoholic
Spiritual	Into drugs
Close to nature	Losers
Supernatural powers	

Then, Rippee asks her students to break up into groups consisting of classmates with whom they feel they share cultural characteristics and to make a T chart for their own group. It is important that the groups self-select and that the stereotypes they generate, both positive and negative, are generated by each group about their own group. Each group will then make a poster, which they can illustrate if they wish to, and present their stereotype chart to the class as in the photograph from Rippee's twelfth-grade Introduction to Multicultural Literature class in Figure 8.3.

Next, Rippee asks the students to each write their own "Sure You Can Ask Me a Personal Question" poem in imitation of Diane Burns. Sample poems by Woodrow Wilson High Students Salin Kim and Tamara Mitchell are included in Figure 8.4.

The activity culminates with the casting aside of negative stereotypes. Each student receives a 3-by-5 card on which he or she fills in the sentence frame, "Just because I'm _____ doesn't mean _____." Students line up in front of the class and, one by one, as is depicted in the photo at the beginning of this chapter, read their sentence and deposit their cards in the trash can. A few examples:

- Just because I'm Asian doesn't mean I eat rice all the time.
- Just because I'm Mexican doesn't mean I'm a border hopper.
- Just because I'm white doesn't mean I'm rich.
- Just because I'm African American doesn't mean I'll grow up to be on welfare.
- Just because I'm German doesn't mean my family are Nazis.

With these stereotypes aired and rejected, the students can move on and begin to build a classroom community. This is the first and last time Rippee's students will be grouped by culture rather than heterogeneously mixed within her classroom.

Figure 8.3   Students Presenting Their Stereotype Chart

Figure 8.4 **Sure You Can Ask Me a Personal Question** ("What Do You Want to Know" is reprinted by permission of Salin Kim. "I Like My Caramel Skin Too" is reprinted by permission of Tamara Mitchell.)

What Do You Want to Know	**I Like My Caramel Skin Too**
Hi, how are you?	How do you do?
No, I am not Japanese.	Thank you, I like my caramel skin too.
No, not Spanish.	What am I?
No, I am Khm—uh, Asian American.	Yes, I have high cheekbones.
No, not from Cambodia.	No, not Indian.
No, not Khmer Rouge.	No, not from the Caribbean.
No, not a Refugee.	No, not native African.
No, we are not dirty.	Yes, I'm a proud African-American woman.
Yes, Khmer.	I'm black and beautiful.
Oh, so that's why you're short.	I have a bright future ahead of me.
Are all Khmer or Cambodian people short?	Oh?
Are they?	So, that's why you style your hair like that.
Let me guess. Buddha?	Your great, great grandfather was a slave?
So, food any good?	He escaped, huh?
Oh, so why do you guys run away from home?	Bought his freedom, you say?
Very strict parents, huh?	Oh, so you know the experience of prejudice?
Yeah, it's good to know you care.	A lot of Black friends?
How big of you.	Yeah, it's awful what they did to us.
No, all Cambodians are not short.	It's decent of you to apologize.
Yes, we have a great variety of foods.	No, I don't hate White people.
No, we do not eat dogs.	No, I don't eat chitterlings, black-eyed peas, or
No, I don't own a hair and nail salon.	pickled-pigsfeet.
I don't know.	I prefer a nice pasta dish.
Our parents just care for our safety.	No, I don't make voodoo dolls.
Do yours?	I'm a Christian.
No, we don't meditate at home everyday.	No, I'm not a gangbanger or a rapper.
Yeah, we are spiritual.	No, I don't know where you can get a quick fix.
Uh-huh, yeah, spiritual.	Yeah. Uh-huh.
No, I didn't major in being a doctor.	Does it matter if this isn't my real hair?
Yeah, we drive horribly.	No, I'm not considered an at-risk student.
Some of us can't even drive.	I'm an Honors student.
This isn't an acrimonious look.	Thank you, I've worked hard for my grades.
This is my face.	Believe it or not, I get to places on time.
—Salin Kim	Yeah. Uh-huh. Stereotypes.
	Uh-huh. Racism. Uh-huh. Affirmative Action.
	Yeah. Uh-huh. Ebonics.
	Stereotypes.
	No, superiority.
	Yeah, a lot of us are made to feel inferior.
	I have always been taught to believe in myself.
	Do you prefer to be called Black
	or African-American?
	I prefer to be called by my name.
	—Tamara Mitchell

The Heritage Quilt

In Chapter 4, Sandra Cisneros's vignette "My Name" from *The House on Mango Street* is the focus of the demonstration lesson in which students write a personal essay reflecting on the significance of their names and the relationship between their names and their sense of identity. This lesson works well as a get-acquainted activity and as an introduction to multicultural literature. Another way to set the stage for thinking about cultural roots is to engage students in making a quilt that reflects their heritage.

Patricia Polacco's children's book *The Keeping Quilt* (see the reading list on the companion website) is a great point of departure for this activity. The book recounts the story of the immigration of Polacco's Russian Jewish great-grandparents to America and traces the passing down of a family quilt, made from items from back home like Great-Gramma Anna's babushka and her brother Vladimir's shirt, from one generation to the next. As time goes by and members of the family intermarry, we see traditions changing and symbols from different cultures, like gold, bread, salt, and wine blending together to enrich the family's heritage. Patricia's daughter, Tracie Denise, is of Russian/Italian American heritage.

UCI Writing Project teacher/consultant Dale Sprowl (1996) has designed a demonstration lesson based on *The Keeping Quilt.* She begins by asking students to share their knowledge, associations, and personal memories about quilts as she creates a class cluster. They also discuss other types of heirlooms that are passed down in their families. After reading aloud *The Keeping Quilt,* she invites students to add information to the cluster and to talk about what they think the quilt symbolizes for Polacco.

For high school students, you may want to introduce a second piece of literature at this point, "My Mother Pieced Quilts," by Teresa Palomo Acosta, shown in Figure 8.5. Ask the students to make a T chart on which they record facts and inferences about the poem, as in the example below:

Fact	Inference
dime store velvets	Maybe they shopped where their money would go far
michigan spring faded curtain pieces/santa fe work shirt	They moved around a lot and it sounds like they had working class jobs. (Migrant workers?)
corpus christi noon	Corpus Christi could be just the name of a town. But it could be a religious reference.

Discuss what we learn about Acosta's family and her heritage through her poetic evocation of the quilt. Consider what the quilt symbolizes for Acosta and whether this is like or unlike what the quilt symbolizes for Polacco.

Sprowl asks students to go back into Polacco's book and create a family tree. An example of a family tree for *The Keeping Quilt* is available on the companion website. Students are then encouraged to construct their own family tree in any graphic form they choose to. Sprowl notes that the family tree can bring up sensitive issues for some students and that teachers may want to broaden the definition of what a family is. Then, after filling out a family interest inventory that asks for information about family traditions, favorite vacation spots, symbols related to country of origin, family activities, heirlooms, and so on, students create their own quilt square either out of cloth (if the teacher is feeling ambitious) or out of

construction paper. Sprowl allows students to choose three to five symbols based upon their family interest inventory. I have adapted her lesson and provided the instructions on the companion website as a point of departure for creating the quilt square.

Once students have completed their squares, the teacher, parents, or members of the class can piece together the individual squares into a class quilt. A paper quilt can easily go up on a bulletin board with pushpins, but some teachers prefer tying the squares together

Figure 8.5   My Mother Pieced Quilts (Reprinted by permission of Teresa P. Acosta.)

My Mother Pieced Quilts

they were just meant as covers
in winters
as weapons
against pounding january winds

but it was just that every morning I awoke
    to these
october ripened canvases
passed my hand across their cloth faces
and began to wonder how you pieced
all these together
these strips of gentle communion cotton
    and flannel nightgowns
wedding organdies
dime store velvets

how you shaped patterns square and
    oblong and round
positioned
balanced
then cemented them
with your thread
a steel needle
a thimble

how the thread darted in and out
galloping along the frayed edges, tucking
    them in
as you did us at night
oh how you stretched and turned and
    rearranged
your michigan spring faded curtain pieces

my father's santa fe work shirt
the summer denims, the tweeds of fall

in the evening you sat at your canvas
—our cracked linoleum floor the
    drawing board

me lounging on your arm
and you staking out the plan:
whether to put the lilac purple of easter
    against the red plaid of winter-going-
into-spring
whether to mix a yellow with blue and white
    and paint the
corpus christi noon when my father held
    your hand

whether to shape a five-point star from the
somber black silk you wore to grandmother's
    funeral

you were the river current
carrying the roaring notes . . .
forming them into pictures of a little
    boy reclining
a swallow flying
you were the caravan master at the reins
driving your threaded needle artillery across
    the mosaic cloth bridges
delivering yourself in separate testimonies
oh mother you plunged me sobbing
    and laughing
into our past
into the river crossing at five
into the spinach fields
into the plainview cotton rows
into tuberculosis wards
into braids and muslin dresses
sewn hard and taut to withstand the
    thrashings of twenty-five years
stretched out they lay
armed/ready/shouting/celebrating
knotted with love
the quilts sing on

—Teresa Paloma Acosta

with yarn. The heritage quilt can lead to a personal essay interpreting one's symbols, or to a comparison/contrast paper. If you use it as a get-acquainted activity, you may wish to have students share their squares in triads and complete this simple quickwrite:

Our quilt squares show that each of us is unique in the following ways: _____

_____

Although each of us is unique, we all share some things in common: _____

_____

What we've learned from this is _____

_____

RECOMMENDED WORKS OF MULTICULTURAL LITERATURE FOR THE SECONDARY CLASSROOM

Provided on the companion website is an annotated list of more than thirty-five recommended readings representing the work of African American, Asian American, European American, Mexican American, and Puerto Rican American writers, as well as a world literature section, which have been suggested by UCI Writing Project teachers. It is not intended to be a comprehensive list of quality multicultural literature (for example, Alice Walker's Pulitzer Prize–winning novel *The Color Purple* does not appear). Rather, it reflects the literature currently being taught in our area that has been particularly engaging to students of all cultural backgrounds. Scholars of multicultural education advocate selecting literature that is "culturally conscious" (Sims, 1982)—that is, literature that accurately reflects the history, beliefs, and values of a culture "without perpetuating stereotypes" (Tompkins, 1997). In most cases, though not all, the culture represented in the recommended literature reflects the cultural background of the author and, as such, is portrayed from an insider rather than an outsider perspective. Michael Smith (1998) makes the point that if teachers select primarily works of literature by people of color that they feel they will be accessible to white audiences, they will be depriving students of "experiencing the uncomfortable growth that can occur when they have to face a character whose life is much different from their own" (p. 134). Part of what fosters growth may involve dealing with discrimination, prejudice, identity, and human dignity.

Teachers need to keep the students in their classrooms in mind when selecting appropriate literature and should plan ahead regarding how to deal sensitively with the harsh realities depicted in some literary works. The language used to lend authenticity to a text may also be of concern to some parents, and teachers need to consider whether it is advisable or necessary to obtain parents' permission. Ironically, many multicultural works that are often deemed controversial and are subject to censorship in some school districts (whether they are by mainstream authors or by authors of color) are often taught in honors classes. Because the students I have been discussing in this chapter are often underrepresented in honors classes, they are unfortunately excluded from reading and responding to literary works that might resonate with them and make their experience in school more meaningful.

DEMONSTRATION LESSON

Character and Culture in Amy Tan's "The Moon Lady"

This demonstration lesson has been adapted* from a lesson that Pat Clark, from Century High School in Santa Ana, California, and I wrote for the UCI Writing Project's publication *Reading, Thinking and Writing about Multicultural Literature* (Olson, 1996b). It has been used successfully with students from middle school through college. "The Moon Lady," from Amy Tan's *The Joy Luck Club* (see the list on the companion website) is the story of a young Chinese girl who becomes lost, both literally and symbolically, and sacrifices her sense of self to conform to society's expectations. Dealing as it does with issues of age, gender, class, and cultural values, it lends itself well to an exploration of the influence of culture on character. It also fosters academic literacy by culminating in an interpretive essay. (For information on the impact of the scaffolded multicultural lessons in this book on students of

*Adapted by permission of Addison Wesley Educational Publishers, Inc., and Patricia A. Clark.

culturally diverse backgrounds, see the Appendix.) Terms used to describe the reading, thinking, and writing tasks in the lesson are taken from Figure 1.2 (Cognitive Strategies: A Reader's and Writer's Tool Kit) and from Figure 3.3 (the UCI Writing Project's adaptation of Bloom's "taxonomy of the cognitive domain").

Overview

After reading and analyzing "The Moon Lady" from *The Joy Luck Club,* students will write an interpretive essay in which they describe how the incident at the Moon Festival affects the main character, Ying-ying, taking into consideration the degree to which Ying-ying's culture contributes to her transformation.

Objectives

Students will:

1. Analyze the literal and symbolic implications of the word *lost*
2. Interpret Ying-ying's experience at the Moon Festival in a found poem
3. Trace the changes in Ying-ying's character before and after the incident at the Moon Festival
4. Pose interpretive questions about the story
5. Visualize Ying-ying's character by illustrating a coat of arms with symbols that represent her
6. Speculate about how and why Ying-ying changes
7. Compose an interpretive essay about how the incident at the Moon Festival affects Ying-ying, taking into consideration the degree to which her culture contributes to her transformation

The Process

This lesson requires students to immerse themselves in a variety of reading and writing activities that help them elicit meaning from literature. It familiarizes the students with interpretive writing and with standard expository form. The activities should help students not only to perceive the character of Ying-ying metaphorically but also to weave figurative language into analytical writing. If taught in conjunction with an Asian unit in history classes, this lesson lends itself well to a cross-curricular study of cultural values. In the form presented here, the lesson will take approximately three weeks to complete. Teachers under time constraints should condense as needed.

Prereading Activity

Clustering ■ *Tapping Prior Knowledge*

To set the stage for the reading of the story, ask students individually to cluster the word *lost* on a piece of paper; then cluster the word *lost* on the board with the class. Ask students to suggest anything that comes to mind. Feelings? Associations? Circumstances?

During Reading Activity

Reading Aloud and Highlighting ■ *Constructing the Gist*

Read "The Moon Lady" from *The Joy Luck Club* out loud to the class. (Note: You may want to break up the story into two parts and read it over two class periods.) As you read, have students underline any words, phrases, or sentences that particularly appeal to them.

Postreading Activity 1

Quaker Reading ■ *Identifying Main Ideas and Making Connections*

Have students read aloud any words, phrases, or sentences they underlined while reading the story. In a "Quaker reading," anyone may speak at any time and important lines may be repeated. This continues until all the students who wish to share have done so. This technique often brings out the most important ideas in a story. As the Quaker reading proceeds, students will begin to make connections between certain images and symbols. For instance, after one person says, "I loved my shadow, this dark side of me that had my same restless nature," another student may quickly jump in with a choice such as "I once again saw my shadow. It was shorter this time, shrunken and wild looking."

Postreading Activity 2

Clustering ■ *Organizing Information and Forming Preliminary Interpretations*

Ask students to return to their *lost* cluster and add new ideas, levels of meaning, images and symbols, etc., stimulated by their reading of the story, using a different color of ink. A sample cluster might look like Figure 8.6.

Have students in pairs share their clusters and discuss how hearing "The Moon Lady" and participating in the Quaker reading gave them an additional perspective on the word *lost*. Ask several pairs to share their new cluster words and to name which words, phrases, or events from the story brought these cluster words to mind. This discussion should bring out the fact that there are two kinds of *lost*—literal and symbolic. The many levels of lostness in the story students usually identify include loss of illusion, loss of innocence, loss of identity, loss of status, loss of restless shadow, loss of family, loss of self-respect. (Note: If students do not point out the phrase from the story, "We are lost, she and I, unseen and not seeing, unheard and not hearing, unknown by others," the teacher might want to bring it to the attention of the class and elicit comments about its meaning.)

Prewriting Activity 1

Quickwrite ■ *Making Connections*

In order to help students relate Ying-ying's plight to their own lives, particularly if they don't share her cultural background, ask them to do a quickwrite about a time when they felt lost,

Figure 8.6   Sample "Lost" Cluster

not literally but symbolically, because people did not know them or see them for who they really are. Point out that Ying-ying most often uses the image of the shadow to describe herself. Ask them what image, if any, they associate with how they felt. Allow fifteen to twenty minutes for this activity. Once students have completed their quickwrites, ask them to share what they have written in triads; any students who feel uncomfortable sharing should be given the option to pass, however. The example below by Chris Welle, from Century High School, illustrates one of the big issues for ninth graders—fitting in.

■ I Felt Lost

The first day in my new school, I desperately tried to be accepted into a group. Drastically, trying far too hard, I attempted to make my way into the popular "clicks," not letting them into my past, protecting it from the clever, attractive, and husky teenagers the same way a mother cat hides her young from predators. I answered their questions the best way I could, hiding the real me, but hoping I was predestined to be in the group. Feeling a subtle pressure from the teenagers, I began to believe that they were toying with me. Finally, the time came for the word that would deliver me from the alleys of the disliked to the skyscrapers of the approved. I felt myself hurled off the tallest structure. I was rejected, quickly and surely, excluded because no one knew me. Finding out that I was not predestined for popularity was a major fall in my life.

—Chris Welle, Grade 9

After the quickwrites have been shared and discussed, ask students to comment in their groups on whether their experience was like or unlike Ying-ying's and why.

Prewriting Activity 2

Textual Analysis ■ *Analyzing Text Closely and Seeking Validation for Interpretations*

Now ask the students to look back at what they underlined in their Quaker reading and to locate and write down at least four quotes from the text through which Amy Tan shows that Ying-ying felt lost. These quotes might include:

- "All these years I kept my true nature hidden, running along like a small shadow so nobody could catch me."
- "I did not lose myself all at once. I rubbed out my face over the years washing away my pain, the same way carvings on stone are worn down by water."
- "In one small moment, we had both lost the world, and there was no way to get it back."
- "On the dock, with the bright moon behind me, I once again saw my shadow. It was shorter this time, shrunken and wild-looking. We ran together over to some bushes along a walkway and hid."

Prewriting Activity 3

Found Poetry ■ *Synthesizing and Forming Interpretations*

One way to help students examine the imagery and symbols in a work of literature is to ask them to translate what they read into another genre. In found poetry, students "find" a poem that is embedded in a work of literature by rearranging the words, phrases, and images that resonate for them.

Ask students to examine both the words they underlined during the Quaker reading and those they wrote down in the textual analysis activity above. Have them make these images their own by "finding" a poem of at least six lines. They should feel free to add new words or change words if they seem cumbersome, but they must base their poem on actual words and phrases in Tan's story. Allow approximately twenty minutes for this activity. If time permits, students will enjoy meeting in groups and combining their efforts into a composite found poem that includes at least one line from each student. These poems can be posted around the room for students to read.

Found Poetry Example for "The Moon Lady"

Innocence, trust and restlessness,
Wonder, fear and loneliness.
A boy can run and chase dragonflies,
But a girl should stand still,
Unseen and not seeing, unheard and not hearing.
And then, I ceased to be amazed.
I kept my true nature hidden.
If I stood perfectly still,
No one would notice.
For woman is yin, the darkness within,
And man is yang,
Bright truth lighting the mind.
And, I discovered my shadow,
My shadow, this dark side of me.
And I, running along like a small shadow.
But I remember now how I lost myself,
How the Moon Lady looked at me and became a man,
And I remember my wish.
I wished to be found.

Prompt

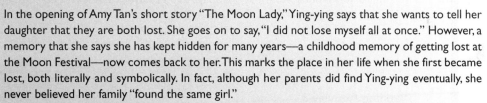

Review the following prompt with the class. An 8½-by-11 copy of the prompt is available on the companion website.

In the opening of Amy Tan's short story "The Moon Lady," Ying-ying says that she wants to tell her daughter that they are both lost. She goes on to say, "I did not lose myself all at once." However, a memory that she says she has kept hidden for many years—a childhood memory of getting lost at the Moon Festival—now comes back to her. This marks the place in her life when she first became lost, both literally and symbolically. In fact, although her parents did find Ying-ying eventually, she never believed her family "found the same girl."

In a well-organized essay, describe how the incident at the Moon Festival affects Ying-ying.

• How and why did she change?
• How did Ying-ying's culture contribute to her transformation?
• How did she allow herself to become lost symbolically?

The best papers will move beyond a factual account of the story to a true analysis of Ying-ying's character, the change in the way she perceives herself, and the way her culture perceives her role in society. Refer to specific images and symbols in the text to support your character analysis. Use direct quotes when applicable. Your paper should be written in standard expository form (introduction, main body, conclusion). Be sure to use precise, apt, descriptive, and figurative language to show and not just tell about how the incident in Ying-ying's life affected her character. In other words, make your writing as vivid as possible for your reader. Your paper should also correctly follow the conventions of written English, including the rules for accurately quoting from a text.

Please consult the scoring guide for the criteria by which your paper will be evaluated.

Planning Activity 1

Time Line ■ *Organizing Information and Evaluating*

Have students reread the story as they create a time line of the significant events in "The Moon Lady," placing events they feel are positive above the line and those that strike them as more negative below the line, as in the example below:

	Delight over idea of Moon Festival	Sees restless shadow
+		
−	Chided by Amah while being dressed	Learns it is selfish to think of own needs

Have students begin their time line where Ying-ying's retelling of the incident begins: "In 1918, the year that I was four" (seventh paragraph). They should return to the beginning of the story only after charting the narrative through the fifth paragraph from the end (when the Moon Lady becomes a man). Partners will most likely agree about whether events are positive or negative up to the conclusion of the story; they may have some healthy disagreement about the opening of the story, however. Stress that there is no right or wrong answer in creating the time line.

Planning Activity 2

Dialectical Journal ■ *Analyzing Text Closely and Forming Interpretations*

Have students write down six quotations from the text—two from the time between Ying-ying's hearing about the Moon Festival and the point when she becomes lost, two from the time she's lost, and two from the time she is found. Then have them respond to each quote. Use the first two columns of the following dialectical journal format as a model:

Quotation from Text	*Personal Response*	*Further Reflection*
"We are lost, she and I, unseen and not seeing, unheard and not hearing, unknown by others."	After hiding her true feelings even from herself, Ying-ying finally realizes that she has lived as a shadow.	

Planning Activity 3

Grand Conversation ■ *Asking Questions*

After completing their dialectical journal, partners should go back through the text and write down any questions they have on 3-by-5 cards. Tell them their questions will probably be interpretive. That means there will be no right or wrong answers, although there may be evidence in the story to back up different viewpoints. Interpretive questions usually begin with words like *why, how,* or *what if.* Students' questions will be used for class discussion. Some examples follow:

- Why must girls be quiet while boys can be noisy and run and play?
- What was the thing that squeezed Ying-ying and tossed her in the boat?
- Why is woman yin, the darkness within, and man yang, bright truth?
- Why did the Moon Lady turn into a man?
- Why did Ying-ying still wish to be found after her parents found her?

Ask students to form a circle. Start the discussion by asking, "Who would like to begin?" Gradually, call on students to ask one of their questions. To encourage answers, stress the fact that no answer can be wrong. Also, ask the students to look for and quote textual evidence in order to lend authenticity to a particular interpretation.

Planning Activity 4

More Dialectical Journaling ■ *Digging Deeper and Revising Meaning*

After a thorough discussion of the interpretive questions, students can go back to their dialectical journals and reflect further about their entries. They can look for connections between entries, expand upon their original responses, add some new insight that has emerged, and/or look for what their quotes and responses tell them about Ying-ying's character and her culture.

Quotation from Text	*Personal Response*	*Further Reflection*
"We are lost, she and I, unseen and not seeing, unheard and not hearing, unknown by others."	After hiding her true feelings even from herself, Ying-ying finally realizes that she has lived as a shadow.	Ying-ying has now "found" herself, but is it too late? And what about her daughter? She doesn't know she's invisible.

Planning Activity 5

Character Frame and Coat of Arms ■ *Forming Interpretations and Visualizing*

Have students fill out a character frame and then draw a coat of arms for Ying-ying; see Chapter 4, Planning Activity 1 for a description and model of the character frame and coat of arms. A character frame and coat of arms for Ying-ying are available on the companion website. (Note: An alternative is to have students complete a split open mind with images that reflect Ying-ying's thoughts, feelings, and character traits before and after the Moon Festival. See Chapter 5, During Reading Activity 3 for a description and model of a split open mind.) The point here is to give students an opportunity to think metaphorically about Ying-ying's character. A sample coat of arms by ninth grader Nina Alexander from Century High is provided in Figure 8.7. Nina is also the author of the model student paper in the Sharing Activity on page 190, "Wild Mustang to Work Horse."

Planning Activity 6

Analyzing Ying-ying's Culture ■ *Analyzing, Comparing and Contrasting, and Evaluating*

Explain to students that culture is something that is socially constructed by members of a group in interaction with one another. It includes the behaviors, value systems, beliefs, and symbols that are shared by a group. Ask students to analyze the attributes of Ying-ying's Chinese culture using these questions as a point of departure:

- How does Ying-ying's age and the order in which she is born into her family affect how she is treated and expected to behave?
- How does Ying-ying's gender affect how she is treated and expected to behave? What are some of those expectations?
- How does Ying-ying's social class affect how she is treated and expected to behave and how she treats others?
- What are some of the traditions and symbols in Ying-ying's culture, what do they represent, and how do they relate to Ying-ying?

Figure 8.7   **Coat of Arms for Ying-ying** (Reprinted by permission of Nina Alexander.)

I see Ying - ying as a wild mustang who is encumbered by the ropes of society's expectations and transformed into a work horse.

- What are some words you would use to describe Ying-ying's character and her behavior before and after the Moon Festival? How did the incident at the Moon Festival affect her?
- How did Ying-ying's culture contribute to her transformation?
- To what degree is Ying-ying responsible for allowing herself to become lost symbolically?

Planning Activity 7

Considering Culture ■ *Making Connections and Comparing and Contrasting*

Once students have explored Ying-ying's culture, ask them, again in pairs, to respond to these questions:

- How am I being positioned by the author to read this text?
- How am I being positioned by my culture to respond to this text?
- How is Ying-ying's culture like or unlike my own?

In considering this last question, one of the female students in Pat Clark's ninth-grade class at Century High wrote:

■   Her culture like my Mexican culture basically goes by the same rules. Women can't be in charge or be the more powerful, dominant creature. They "have" to be in the kitchen, barefoot and pregnant. In my culture, supposedly the man has a major case of "machismo." BULL. What they have is a major case of cowardice. They are afraid to show their feelings.

If they wish to, students can then complete a Venn diagram (see Figure 6.8, Chapter 6) to examine the similarities and differences between Ying-ying's culture and their own.

Planning Activity 8

Quickwrite ■ *Stepping Back and Rethinking What One Knows*

To help students clarify their ideas before writing, ask them to quickwrite for fifteen minutes on this topic: *How did the Moon Festival experience affect Ying-ying? How and why did she change?* A student model follows:

■ Student Model

It is a world of confusion and beauty, a place where hidden passions lie. This is the Ying-ying zone. It's hard to say why Ying-ying changed her ways. Was it her culture? Was it her attitude? The mystery of Ying-ying remains unsolved. She is like a set of tinted windows, able to look out, but it is impossible to look in.

Ying-ying at first did not see herself as being lost. She did not even think she had changed all that much. But, as the seasons changed, so did Ying-ying. Like the leaves falling slowly from the autumn trees, she said, "I did not lose myself all at once. I rubbed out my face over the years washing away my pain. . . ." These words may be a clue as to why Ying-ying transformed from a sweet little girl to a lost old woman.

Ying-ying's culture is something that contributed to her confusion and her reasons for hiding from herself. When Ying-ying was young, before the experience at the Moon Festival, she frolicked and played like a boy. But her culture said she should have been really serious and sedate, acting like a "lady." The old ways of the Chinese culture are set in stone. No one tries to change them. But Ying-ying was out to alter that. Unfortunately, she was thwarted, and in later life she paid the price of loneliness.

—Matt Carr, Grade 9

Planning Activity 8

The Microtheme: Formulating a Writing Plan ■ *Organizing Information*

Students are now ready to organize their ideas and information about the influence of culture on character into a writing plan. Enable them to think ahead, to consider how they will proceed, by asking them to create a "microtheme" (Bean, Drenk, & Lee, 1982). For detailed instructions on the microtheme activity, see the Chapter 7 demonstration lesson, Planning Activity 5. A graphic of the microtheme format is included in the Chapter 7 activity as well, and a template for the microtheme is available on the companion website.

Writing

Constructing the Gist

Students will now write their essays, using the dialectical journal, coat of arms, quickwrite, microtheme, and so on as points of departure. Review the scoring rubric (see Evaluation) before students begin composing. Encourage them to weave into their essays some of the metaphorical language with which they have previously described Ying-ying.

Sharing Activity

Responding to Peers' Essays ■ *Analyzing Author's Craft and Assessing Quality*

Using the response sheet for essays on "The Moon Lady" that is available on the companion website, have the class as a group critique the student model essay that follows. Then partners or small groups can critique one another's work, also using the response sheet.

■ Wild Mustang to Work Horse

As a small child, Ying-ying was like a wild mustang, free to roam, her spirit undaunted. As she became older, her mother, Amah, and the Chinese culture broke her spirit and put the reins of society upon her. Ying-ying became more of a cart horse with blinders than an independent mustang. Instead of ropes, the traditional Chinese culture bound her down. Ying-ying was first encumbered by the heavy ropes of society's expectations when she was six, at the all important Moon Lady Festival. This was the first time that she lost herself.

Before Ying-ying became entangled by the ropes of expectations, she was a carefree, happy child. She would run after dragonflies, explore unknown places, and peer wide-eyed at new marvels. Ying-ying was defiant toward the social pressures and didn't worry about what others thought. She did not worry about her place in society. She did not worry about "careless desires" or being subdued and subservient. She did not worry because she was Ying-ying, the wild mustang.

For the first six years of her life, there were often many cowboys trying to lasso Ying-ying into the corral. Amah was always rushing around and scolding Ying-ying for not acting ladylike and running around like a boy. Her mother told her, "A boy can run and chase dragonflies, because that is his nature, but a girl should stand still. If you are still for a very long time, a dragonfly will no longer see you. Then, it will come to you and hide in the comfort of your shadow." And society said, "A woman is yin, the darkness within, where untempered passions lie. A man is yang, bright truth lighting our minds." Ying-ying resisted their ropes until she met the Moon Lady.

When Ying-ying saw the sorrowful tale of the Moon Lady, she began to weep. Ying-ying said, "Even though I did not understand the entire story, I understood her grief. In one small moment we had both lost the world, and there was no way to get it back." While watching the tale, Ying-ying saw all the things that Amah, her mother, and society had warned her about, the careless desires and the untempered passions of mankind. For those few moments, she became the Moon Lady, and her spirit was broken.

As the broken-spirited work horse followed the Moon Lady, the Moon Lady "became a man." To Ying-ying's shock, the wig and dress were carelessly thrown away, along with Ying-ying's independence. The lady she had identified with, who was "flung from the earth by her own wantoness," was a man. This put the final blinders on Ying-ying. The transformation from mustang to work horse was complete.

—Nina Alexander, Grade 9

Revising Activity

Reconstructing the Draft ■ *Revising Meaning and Enhancing Author's Craft*

Students should compare the group response sheet they received from peers with their microtheme statement to see whether the message they intended to get across was received by the readers. They can then revise their essays according to the responses they received on each evaluation criterion. Additionally, they can enrich their papers with descriptive and figurative language if they received an OK or Needs Work on that item.

Editing Activity

Focus on Quotations ■ *Proofreading for Correctness*

Students should now edit their papers for correctness, paying particular attention to the rules for quoting accurately from the text, which are included on the companion website.

Evaluation

The Scoring Rubric ■ *Assessing Quality against Criteria*

The teacher or the students can evaluate the final draft based on the complete six-point rubric on the companion website. The criteria for a score of 6 are as follows:

6 SUPERIOR

A 6 paper is clearly superior: well written, insightful, carefully organized, and technically correct. A 6 paper does all or most of the following well:

- Carefully analyzes the way the incident at the Moon Festival affects Ying-ying
- Offers insights into the character of Ying-ying and how and why she has changed
- Refers to several specific images and symbols from the text to show Ying-ying's transformation
- Considers how Ying-ying's culture contributes to her transformation
- Considers how Ying-ying allows herself to become symbolically lost
- Is written in standard expository form

    —Has a clear introduction that has a "hook"

    —Has a well-developed main body with specific references to the text and adequate transitions

    —Has a logical and impressive conclusion that leaves the reader with a predominant feeling, message, or impression about Ying-ying

- Uses especially precise, apt, descriptive, and figurative language to enrich expository writing, to make interpretation vivid, and to show and not just tell about Ying-ying's character
- Maintains a high level of interest and keeps the reader engaged
- Has few, if any, errors in the conventions of written English; quotes from the text accurately

Learning Log Reflection

Quickwrites ■ *Stepping Back and Formulating Guidelines for Personal Ways of Living*

The following metacognitive questions will provide closure to your students' study of "The Moon Lady":

1. At the opening of "The Moon Lady," Ying-ying says that she wants to tell her daughter that they are both lost. Think about what you have learned about Ying-ying and possibly about yourself because of reading "The Moon Lady." If you could convey a message to another person that summarized what you learned, what would that message be?
2. What did you learn about the ways in which Ying-ying's culture contributed to her feeling of being "lost"?
3. How is Ying-ying's culture like or unlike your culture in its treatment of girls?
4. Is there anything that you see differently, think differently about, or will do differently as a result of reading this story?

Please see the *Reflecting and Relating* section under Cognitive Strategies in Chapter 1 for sample learning log reflections from Pat Clark's students at Century High School.

Extension Activity

Comparing and Contrasting Ying-ying with Mariana ■ *Analyzing*

Tan's Ying-ying and Tennyson's Mariana (see Chapter 7) are from distinctly different cultures. Yet both women experience a traumatic event that shatters their sense of self-worth. Additionally, both authors use rich, imagistic language to symbolize their characters' states of being. You may wish to teach these two works in tandem.

To Sum Up

Demographers predict that students of color will make up 46 percent of the nation's school age population by the year 2020 (Banks & Banks, 2003). Given these trends, the current curriculum, which is geared toward serving predominantly white, mainstream students, may no longer be well suited to the students of the twenty-first century. We must ask ourselves: How can we, as teachers, be responsive to our increasingly culturally diverse classrooms and responsible about ways to recognize, validate, and motivate all of the students whom we serve? Because literature is the stock in trade of the English/language arts teacher, teaching multicultural literature is a natural vehicle to honor pluralism in the classroom.

Of the many reasons to integrate multicultural literature in the classroom, some of the most compelling are:

- To be responsive to the changing demographics of the nation and responsible to the increasing number of culturally diverse students we serve
- To help level the playing field between mainstream students and students of color
- To give culturally diverse students access to the "codes of power" and develop academic literacy so they can "beat the odds"
- To empower students of culturally diverse backgrounds by enabling them to see themselves reflected in the literature that they study in school
- To celebrate diversity and to foster mutual cultural awareness, understanding, tolerance, and respect among students, regardless of their cultural backgrounds
- To enrich the literary canon for all students by integrating high-quality multicultural literature into the curriculum

Although teaching multicultural literature, in and of itself, may affect the attitude and the achievement of some nonmainstream students, the greatest impact will come from carefully scaffolding activities for reading, thinking, and writing to reveal to students of all cultures the strategies experienced readers and writers use. For information regarding how the cognitive strategies approach to instruction and carefully scaffolded multicultural literature lessons in this book have helped students of culturally diverse backgrounds beat the odds, please see the Appendix to this book.

Learning Log Reflection

Think about the literature that made up the canon when you were a secondary and a college student. How much multicultural literature is part of your textual repertoire? Review the companion website's list of recommended readings to see how many works you recognize or have read. Make it a point to read something on the list . . . and enjoy!

Teaching Writing

Helping Students Play the Whole Range

The Writer

In her room at the prow of the house
Where light breaks, and the windows are tossed
   with linden,
My daughter is writing a story.
I pause in the stairwell, hearing
From her shut door a commotion of typewriter-keys
Like a chain hauled over a gunwale.

Young as she is, the stuff
Of her life is a great cargo, and some of it heavy:
I wish her a lucky passage.

But now it is she who pauses,
As if to reject my thought and its easy figure.
A stillness greatens, in which

The whole house seems to be thinking,
And then she is at it again with a bunched clamor
Of strokes, and again is silent.

I remember the dazed starling
Which was trapped in that very room, two years ago;
How we stole in, lifted a sash

And retreated, not to affright it;
And how for a helpless hour, through the crack of the door,
We watched the sleek, wild, dark

And iridescent creature
Batter against the brilliance, drop like a glove
To the hard floor, or the desk-top,

And wait then, humped and bloody,
For the wits to try it again; and how our spirits
Rose when, suddenly sure,

It lifted off from the chair-back,
Beating a smooth course for the right window
And clearing the sill of the world.

It is always a matter, my darling,
of life or death, as I had forgotten. I wish
What I wished you before, but harder.

—Richard Wilbur

Source: "The Writer" from *The Mind-Reader*, copyright
© by Richard Wilbur, reprinted by permission of
Harcourt, Inc.

Several years ago at the opening session of Writing Project II, a monthly after-school staff development program in which interested teachers from the UCI Writing Project met to explore the reading/writing connection, we began by reading, thinking, and writing about the process of meaning construction. Using Richard Wilbur's poem "The Writer" as a point of departure, we explored the acts of mind we engaged in as readers to make meaning from the poem and discussed whether our respective processes as writers were like or unlike the writer's in the poem. However, although our discussion was valuable, the poem seemed to will us in another direction—away from examining how we construct meaning and toward exploring the meaning of the poem itself. For many of us, of course, the poem brought to mind our roles as parents; yet we couldn't read this poem without thinking of our roles as teachers of writing. When someone posed the question of whether, as teachers, we could metaphorically open the window or lift the sash in our classrooms, step back, and get out of the way, the response from the group was a spontaneous shaking of heads and a unanimous "No!" We admitted that, unlike the father in the poem, we were not convinced that our students had the commitment or the competence to go it alone. Now thoroughly embroiled in the analogy of the starling, we talked about how we would repeatedly stair-step our students up to the sill and encourage them to take some trial flights, perhaps with a safety net, for starters. Our job, as we saw it, was not only to motivate our students to care about writing but also to provide them with the tools to ultimately negotiate this complex task with confidence and grace.

According to the 2002 report of the National Assessment of Education Progress, our student writers are not yet ready to "clear the sill of the world." In the *NAEP 2002 Writing Report Card for the Nation and the States* (Persky, Daane, & Jin, 2002), about 54 percent of the students tested at the fourth, eighth, and twelfth grades demonstrated "basic" skills, defined as a partial mastery of fundamental writing techniques and a rudimentary ability to convey an idea or point. About 18 percent of the students in the national sample fell below even the basic level. Just over 25 percent were classified as "proficient," defined as being able to produce an effective response that is organized; makes use of details and elaboration; and shows evidence of analytical, evaluative, or creative thinking. (Please note that this definition sets a relatively high standard for "proficiency.") Only 2 percent of the students sampled were rated as "advanced," the highest classification. In California, 57 percent of students tested fell into the "basic" category, and 20 percent scored below the basic level of minimal competence (Cooper & Groves, 2002). It might be convenient to attribute the mediocre performance of the students in the NAEP sample to large class sizes, the rise in the number of LEP students, the number of students classified at the poverty level, the level of parents' education, the lack of books in the home, and so forth; nevertheless, we need to take a hard look at what it is that we teach when we teach writing.

In his intensive study *Writing in the Secondary School* (1981), as I discussed in Chapter 6, Arthur Applebee reported that across all the content areas, 44 percent of all class time was devoted to writing activities of some sort. The vast majority of that writing, however, involved short-answer and fill-in-the-blank tasks or note taking. Only 3 percent of the writing was of paragraph length or longer. Even in the English classroom, only 10 percent of class time was spent on more extensive writing tasks (p. 58). Further, even when students were being asked to write at some length, the writing was usually a page or less and most often used "as a vehicle to test specific content" (p. 101). In other words, students were writing to show what they had learned rather than using writing itself as a tool for learning. Although we certainly hope this situation has improved over the last twenty-plus years, the conclusion Applebee and Langer (1987) arrived at after reviewing six consecutive NAEP reports still holds true today: "Put simply . . . American children do not write frequently enough, and the reading and writing tasks they are given do not require them to think deeply enough" (p. 4).

Tchudi and Mitchell (1999) begin their chapter on teaching writing with a letter from a student, Scott Bates, in his own handwriting that begins:

I would like to start out by saying "I hate wrighting."

Apparently Scott is not alone. In the 1990 NAEP writing report card, the last assessment in which attitudinal data were collected, Applebee and his colleagues noted that as students progress up the grade levels, their enthusiasm for writing diminishes. The research team was "disappointed" to find students expressing relatively negative attitudes toward writing at the secondary level, especially given that research indicates a strong correlation between a positive attitude toward writing and writing proficiency (p. 32). We must ask ourselves whether there is also a correlation between students' attitudes toward writing and what they are asked to write. Thomas Newkirk (1989) points out that when children move from the elementary level, they leave behind them most "creative" discourse forms—because high school is a place "to put aside childish things" (p. 5). This approach, which Newkirk terms the Great Divide, transitions students into writing in almost exclusively nonnarrative modes when "no groundwork has been laid for this new demand." No wonder secondary students come to see writing as a chore one does simply to satisfy the teacher! In *Active Voice* (1981) James Moffett proposed a very thoughtful sequence of writing activities, moving from inner speech to dialogue and from narrative to essay, that he envisioned continuing across grade levels as an "*accumulating repertory* from which nothing is ever really dropped" (p. 10). This sequence was not linear but a spiral. Its point was not to enable students "to come out on top" but, as Moffett put it, to help them "play the whole range" (p. 12). For both cognitive and affective reasons, teachers need to provide students with the opportunity and the guidance to write both short and extended pieces in a variety of domains or modes, for diverse audiences, and for different purposes. Teachers need to help students "play the whole range." We need to lead students up to the "sill of the world" and help them to see what their options are.

WHY WRITE?

In *The English Teacher's Companion* (1999), Jim Burke observes, "Writing is exciting because it's productive and creative; it's where the rubber hits the road. You can't write and not think. There are no *Cliffs Notes* for writing. Written expression is one of our primary means of reflecting on what we think and what we know" (p. 72). As novelist E. M. Forster (1927) once said, "How do I know what I think until I see what I say?" (p. 157). In order to create a written text, writers must generate ideas, plan both for the process of writing and for the written product itself, translate thought into print, revise what they have articulated, and evaluate the effectiveness of their efforts. While moving from conception to completion, writers must juggle all of the constraints that affect the composing process, such as the knowledge we have for constructing and expressing meaning, the language we have for communicating what we know, the audience and purpose for writing, the context in which writing occurs, and the form and lexical demands of the text itself. In short, as Flower and Hayes (1981a) point out, "Writing is among the most complex of all human mental activities" (p. 39).

Langer and Applebee (1987) suggest that "written language not only makes ideas more widely and easily available, it changes the development and shape of the ideas themselves"; writing "shapes" thinking (p. 3). For example, note taking, short-answer comprehension questions, and summarizing tasks prompt students to focus on specific items of information and lead to short-term recall but foster little analysis of the material. Analytical writing tasks, on the other hand, prompt students to think more about smaller amounts of information and to reconstruct and link ideas in complex ways (p. 135). Additionally, when students are writing to show what they have learned and submitting their products for evaluation, they focus on presenting their ideas carefully and sequentially but tend to play it safe and to stay "close to the known and familiar" (p. 71). In contrast, when they are writing expressively to learn, perceiving their writing as part of an ongoing instructional dialogue that is not subject to assessment by the teacher, their thinking and writing is more exploratory and they are more apt to take risks in form and content. However, Langer and Applebee report that *any* of the many sorts of writing they studied led to better learning than activities involving reading and studying only. In their words, there is "clear evidence" that "writing assists learning" (p. 135).

So far, we have looked at the cognitive dimension of the question, Why write? Writing is a tool for learning that heightens and refines thinking. But what about the affective domain? What of Christina Chang, the ninth grader at Villa High School who says, "When I write about something I care about I feel as if I'm exploding inside with emotion"? Or Cris Greaves, our graduate student in Chapter 1, who's a "knobby-kneed little kid" filled with "awe and wonder" when she writes something good? Surely, if we read both efferently and aesthetically—to carry something away from the text or to be carried away by the text—we must also write efferently and aesthetically, to transmit or to transport. Calling upon our "felt sense" (Perl, 1990), we must write to explore feelings as well as thoughts.

Louise Rosenblatt (1978) notes that the same text can be read efferently or aesthetically. The same holds true for writing. Teachers often complain that students who write vivid narratives, full of personal voice, often simply disappear off the page when writing an essay. Yet the reverse can also happen: Narrative writing can be communicated efferently ("first this happened, and then . . . and then . . . and then"), and analytical writing (like Nina Alexander's essay "Wild Mustang to Work Horse" in Chapter 8) can be rich and evocative. The first step is to motivate students to become personally invested in what they have to say, regardless of the writing task. But caring about what they have to say is not enough if students lack the competence to consciously craft their writing. Nina Alexander deliberately infused elements of narrative writing into her analytical essay. She created the metaphor of a wild mustang that is transformed into a workhorse, complete with blinders, so that her argument would be not only compelling but also aesthetically engaging. In so doing, Nina was being strategic. The teacher's job is to help all students to become strategic—that is, to be able to purposefully select tactics to achieve particular goals. Until students are capable of being strategic on their own, the teacher must scaffold instruction to build students' declarative knowledge of *what* it is that experienced writers do, provide opportunities for students to develop procedural knowledge of *how* to engage in these behaviors, and foster the conditional knowledge of *when* to apply certain strategies and *why* they are effective (Paris, Lipson, & Wixon, 1983). In short, the teacher must provide both the guidance and the opportunities for less experienced writers to think and act like more experienced writers.

INFORMING THE TEACHING OF WRITING WITH PREMISES ABOUT THINKING

Researchers agree that writing is a complex cognitive process; so it stands to reason that the following key premises about thinking, derived from learning theory, should inform the teaching of writing:

Thinking Is Developmental   As Lev Vygotsky (1986) and Jerome Bruner (1978) have observed, thinking develops over time. It is not a static but an evolving capacity; it grows with experience, with maturity, and with guidance from more experienced learners, who provide structure and assistance for tasks that children cannot yet perform independently. Vygotsky claims that children can exceed their "actual mental age" and work at the edges of their "zone of proximal development" if they are provided with this critical modeling and with opportunities to practice (p. 187). In the writing classroom, teachers must begin by assessing where their students are, developmentally, and by creating learning experiences that are challenging yet attainable. That is, they must keep instruction within their students' zone of proximal development but push them to stretch intellectually, expanding their competence.

Thinking Is Progressive   The developing mind progresses from the ability to operate at the most concrete levels to thought at the most abstract levels. Jean Piaget (1930) identified the sensorimotor, concrete operational, and formal operations stages. Howard Gardner (1983) introduced the notion that thinking may entail not just one but several intellectual stage processes, all progressing simultaneously but at different rates from novice to apprentice to master. If the mind is better able to make cognitive leaps when it moves from concrete to abstract, then a progressive writing curriculum will also move from concrete to abstract. For example, it might sequence the domains of writing from descriptive to narrative to expository, it might move from known to unknown audiences, or it might progress in another fashion according to the teacher's design. Within any given writing task, the teacher can focus on something concrete, or what Hillocks (1995) calls a "gateway" activity, as a point of departure. For example, in teaching students to think analogically and create similes or metaphors, the teacher might begin by bringing in a concrete object, such as a seashell, and asking students to observe it closely and compare it to other things.

Flower and Hayes (1980) have observed that the stage process model of composition can make composing sound like it can be accomplished in a "tidy sequence of steps," like baking a cake or filling out a tax return, whereas in reality, as we saw in Chapter 3, "a writer caught in the act looks like a busy switchboard operator," juggling constraints and working on "cognitive overload" (p. 33). However, although there is no one description of the writing process—because different writers have different processes—the stage process model can serve as a teaching tool: It provides students with the language to talk about writing, and it builds in "think time" for ideas and expression to evolve.

Thinking Is Cumulative and Recursive   Linda Flower (1981) makes the case that writing is a problem-solving process and that if we were to look at it as a psychologist might, "we would see that it has much in common with other problem-solving processes that people use in carrying out a wide range of tasks" (p. 3). Good chess players, for example, bring to the current game they are playing a "great deal of knowledge and a repertory of powerful strategies" (p. 3) based on their cumulative experiences playing chess. In other words, thinking experiences build on one another. So too, in writing, when a writer attempts to solve the problem of writing a short story, for instance, he or she brings to that task not only all the prior narratives he or she has written but the cumulative knowledge gained from reading narratives. Although thinking experiences build on one another, the pathway to complex thought is not a linear one. Researchers have noted that writing, in particular, is a recursive process (Flower & Hayes, 1981a; Perl, 1990). Writers often go back in their thinking in order to move forward in their writing.

Given these premises about thinking, a writing curriculum should be designed with a sequence in mind, and that sequence should enable students to build on what they are learning so as to develop an "accumulating repertory" of strategies, to use Moffett's term (1981, p. 10). Because the goal, again, is not to "come out on top" but to "play the whole range" (p. 12), the idea is to invite students to continually revisit their prior learning and incorporate that learning into the new task. For example, suppose a teacher focuses one week on having students describe a place so vividly that another reader can draw that place. Next week he or she might move to writing a personal narrative about an event—but frame the narrative task to incorporate vivid description of the setting so that the reader can visualize where the event took place. Bruner has advocated what he calls a spiral curriculum (Good & Brophy, 1995, p. 187), in which students are brought back to the same general topics but are encouraged to address these topics at different levels of knowledge and analysis.

Thinking Takes Practice   Because one of the primary modes for learning is discovery, thinking cannot simply be taught like facts from a textbook. Maturity, experience, and practice all play a role in the development of a range of thinking abilities. Hilda Taba (1964) acknowledged the crucial role the teacher plays in this process when she concluded, "How people think may depend largely on the kinds of 'thinking experience' they have had" (p. 25). Teachers are providers of experiences that facilitate cognitive growth. Writing is one of the most complex and challenging thinking experiences the teacher can provide. As Langer and Applebee (1986) point out, the practice provided by teachers must allow for student ownership; be appropriately geared at the students' developmental level while prompting them to stretch intellectually; have a clear structure; promote collaboration; and facilitate internalization, transferring the control from teacher to students as students gain competence.

WHAT TO TEACH AND WHY

Anyone who turns to this section of this text expecting to find a handy "To Do" list of exactly what to teach in a writing curriculum in what order will come away disappointed. As Madeline Hunter (1989) once said, "*There are no absolutes in teaching. . . . There is no substitute for a teacher's considered judgment . . . about these students in this learning situation at this moment in time*" (pp. 17–18). What I can offer is my own considered judgment and the advice of several scholars concerning the scope and sequence of writing instruction. Ultimately, as George Hillocks (1995) points out, making the decisions about what texts, writing tasks, instructional strategies, and levels of instructional scaffolding will be appropriate for a given class "remains an art" (p. 61) and not a science. Further, if we, as teachers, wish to continue to grow as learners, our curriculum should be subject to experimentation, scrutiny, and change.

Integrate Reading and Writing Instruction

The central premise of this book is that reading and writing should be integrated. Research indicates that using writing as a learning tool while reading leads to better reading achievement, and using reading as a vehicle for elaborating on ideas and understanding opposing views leads to better writing performance (Tierney & Shanahan, 1991; Tierney, Soter, O'Flahavan, & McGinley, 1989). More importantly, as discussed in Chapter 1, reading and writing, when taught together, engage students in a greater use and variety of cognitive strategies than do reading and writing taught separately (Tierney & Shanahan, 1991, p. 272). This does not mean that all writing instruction should be literature-based, although research suggests that the majority of student writing in the English/language arts class is in response to literary texts (Applebee, 1993). Because writing is recursive and writers go back to reread bits of text in order to keep the process moving forward, reading is a natural and essential component of the writing process. In addition, when responding to classmates' writing, students gain insights into the composing process and into the author's craft of their peers, thus expanding their own options as writers. Robert Scholes (1985) describes the reading/writing connection this way:

> Reading and writing are complementary acts that remain unfinished unless completed by their reciprocals. The last thing I do when I write a text is to read it, and the act that completes my response to a text I am reading is my written response to it. Moreover, my writing is unfinished until it is read by others as well, whose response may become known to me, engendering new textualities. We have an endless web here, of growth, and change, and interaction. . . . (pp. 20–21)

Make Cognitive Strategies Visible

Because teaching reading and writing in an integrated fashion engages students in a greater use and variety of cognitive strategies than do reading and writing if taught separately, teachers have an increased opportunity to make visible for students what it is that experienced readers and writers do. Acting as a "senior member" in a community of learners (Tierney & Pearson, 1998, p. 85), teachers can explain what cognitive strategies are, model how to use them, and provide opportunities for students to practice. Nancie Atwell (1998) notes, "We need to find ways to reveal to students what adult, experienced writers do—to reclaim the tradition of demonstration that allows young people to apprentice themselves to grown-ups" (p. 369). One pedagogical strategy used by Atwell and many others (e.g., Murray, 1982a; Romano, 1987; Wilhelm, 2001) is to think aloud and write in front of students on an overhead projector. Atwell explains,

> Most importantly, I take off the top of my head and write out loud in front of them on overhead-projector transparencies. I show them how I plan, change my mind, confront problems, weigh options, make decisions, use conventions to make my writing sound and look the way I want it to and my readers will need it to, and generally compose my life. (p. 25)

Asking students to step back and reflect on their process as a writer after completing a paper, and to write a learning log entry describing what they had to think about in order to produce a particular text, will also prompt them to become more conscious of the strategies they access in their reader's and writer's tool kit.

Give Students Writing Practice in a Variety of Domains

In order to help students "play the whole range," teachers need to provide students with opportunities to write in a variety of domains or modes. Although in reading there seems to be a general consensus on what to call the kinds of texts people read (the various genres), the same does not hold true for what students write. Nancie Atwell (1998) uses the common-sense approach of referring to the kinds of writing her students produce by standard genre designations, but in most classrooms teachers tend to use more global terminology. The problem is that scholars disagree about how to categorize and label writing. The most common, and most criticized, classification of writing has been in terms of the discourse modes:

narration (to tell a story); description (to describe a person, place, or thing); exposition (to give information); and argumentation (to persuade) (Applebee, 1981).

Applebee, Hillocks (1995), and many others complain that these categories overlap far too much to be useful. Britton and colleagues' (1975) separation of writing into three function categories—poetic (personal/creative writing), expressive (writing to learn), and transactional (writing to inform, advise, and persuade)—is significant because it reminds teachers that an important and neglected use of writing is to think out loud on paper. However, these categories are not particularly helpful in describing the wide range of writing tasks we want students to experience in school. Applebee attempted to expand on Britton's function categories by creating labels for the uses of school writing: mechanical uses (multiple-choice, fill-in-the-blank, and short-answer items, etc.); informational uses (note taking, recording, reporting, summary, analysis, theory, persuasive or regulatory uses); personal uses (journal, diary, keeping-in-touch letters); imaginative uses (stories, poems, play scripts, etc.). Moffett's (1981) system is organized by a progression of speaker–subject relationships—from drama (recording what is happening), to narrative (reporting what happened), to exposition (generalizing what happened), to logical argumentation (inferring what will, may, or could be true).

Numerous other schemes for categorizing writing also exist. Regardless of what terminology we use to categorize writing, however, the point is to make sure that students have rich and repeated opportunities to read and to write all kinds of texts—to "play the whole range." The teacher must help students expand and enhance their textual repertoire.

In my secondary English methods class at UCI, I introduce my students both to the concept of *writing domains,* adapted from Los Angeles Unified School District's composition program (McHugh, 1997), and to *writing types,* taken from the California Learning Assessment System *Writing Assessment Handbook* (Tempes, 1993). The LAUSD model establishes four broad domains of writing: sensory/descriptive, imaginative/narrative, practical/informative, and analytical/expository. To me, these categories roughly follow a developmental progression from more concrete to more abstract; and the fact that the categories overlap, rather than necessarily posing a problem, can highlight that most effective writing shares certain common features. A description of the domains:

Sensory/descriptive writing is based on concrete details. Writers gather information through all five senses and use those details to present a word picture of a person, place, object, or event. The goal is to provide vivid, concrete details that will allow the listener or reader to recapture the author's perceptions. It is within this domain that students learn to focus and sharpen their powers of observation and to choose precise words to convey the sensory description. The skills developed in this domain provide a foundation for writing in the remaining three domains.

Imaginative/narrative writing tells a story. It requires students to focus on events, actual or imaginary, and to arrange the parts in a time/order frame. Here, students learn about ordering, beginning and ending, transition and balance, and suspense and climax. The action of an event, placed in proper sequence, is embedded with "observed" sensory details, thus enriching the story.

Practical/informative writing provides clear information without much interpretation or analysis. Working in this domain, students learn accuracy, clarity, attention to facts, appropriateness of tone, and conventional forms. Because the goal of practical/informative writing is to inform, instruct, or tell "how to," writing in this domain tends to be very literal to avoid being misinterpreted by the reader.

Writing in the *analytical/expository* domain explains, interprets, persuades, and influences. It emphasizes analysis, organization, and development. The goals are for students to examine closely, see relationships, and build logical arguments. They should support their claims with evidence and sometimes use figurative language to make their case more compelling.

It would be a serious mistake to view these four domains as completely separate or sequential realms of writing. Research and practice show that these categories are interdependent and that they combine elements in varying proportions. Narration frequently utilizes description; exposition often incorporates aspects of all writing domains. A practical/informative letter of complaint, for example, might lean heavily on description and narration to make its point. A successful analytical/expository editorial may employ precise description, narrative ordering, and informative presentation of facts in order to convince the reader.

Finally, it is clear that the levels of complexity in the domains of writing vary according to the thinking and writing skills being practiced, as well as to the sophistication of the subject matter. Cartoon captions, dialogues, autobiographies, and allegories suggest the wide range of difficulty possible within the imaginative/narrative domain. Analytical/expository writing can be a single-paragraph definition or a multipage research paper. Figure 9.1 contains examples of different types of writing that fall within each domain. Note that some writing types are repeated in more than one column, because they cross domains.

Figure 9.1   Types of Writing within and across Domains (*Source:* Adapted from McHugh, 1997.)

Sensory/Descriptive	Imaginative/Narrative	Practical/Informative	Analytical/Expository
Journal entry	Journal or diary entry (real or fictional)	Learning log	Learning log reflection
Diary entry	Anecdote	"How to" instructions	Single-paragraph analysis
Description of an object	Vignette	Recipes	Letter to the editor
Description of a place	Autobiographical incident	Lecture/class notes	Editorial
Description of an event	Memoir	Meeting minutes	Speech
Description of a specific sight, sound, taste, touch, or smell	Biographical sketch	Thank-you notes	Book review
Description of a process	Eyewitness account	Sympathy cards	Movie/TV review
Character sketch	Monologue	Friendly letters	Application (to be selected for something)
Nature writing	Dialogue	Business letter (complaint, order, request)	Grant proposal
Monologue	Historical fiction	Summary/précis	Comparison/contrast essay
Dialogue	Comic	Encyclopedia-type report	Observational essay
Poems (haiku, diamante, cinquain, acrostic, biopoem, etc.)	Short story	Accident report	Interpretive essay
Advertising copy	Play script	Interview	Controversial issue essay
Personal brochure	Movie/TV script	Newspaper article	Speculation on causes and effects essay
Travel brochure	Folk tale/fairy tale	Newsletter	Persuasive essay
Observational essay	Fable	Commercial	Evaluation essay
	Narrative/epic poem	Brochure	Reflective essay
	Myth	Résumé	I-search paper
	Allegory	Application	Research paper
	Parody	Memorandum	
	Letters from a character	Prospectus	
	Feature article	Observational essay	
	Reflective essay		

In 1986, for the first time, California launched a large-scale direct writing assessment of students in grade 8. This led to the establishment of the California Learning Assessment System (CLAS) in 1993 and to the development of an integrated reading/writing assessment for students at grades 4, 8, and 10. Influenced by the work of James Britton and his associates (1975), teams of California teachers and special consultants—among them Professor Charles Cooper from the University of California, San Diego—identified eight types of writing to be assessed at the high school level, which derive in part from James Moffett's "assignment" sequences in *Active Voice* (1981). They are as follows:

Autobiographical incident. The autobiographical incident is a narrative about an occurrence in a writer's life. It takes place during a specific period of time, includes sensory detail, and has a clear sequence of action. The significance of the incident to the writer is apparent, either from the narrative itself or through the interpretation that the writer gives.

Report of information. An effective report of information conveys information accurately and convincingly. Writers of reports of information collect, synthesize, and organize the results of their investigation to increase readers' knowledge of a subject, to help readers better understand a procedure or a process, or to provide readers with an enhanced comprehension of a concept or an idea.

Observation. Observational writing records a person's perceptions of an object, a person, a place, an animal, or an event. Like autobiographical incident, observational writing is grounded in personal experience. However, the stance of the observational writer is that of an eyewitness rather than of a participant. The observational essay presents a singular perspective on the subject observed and communicates that perspective through the selection and ordering of details and the angle from which the subject is viewed.

Interpretation. Interpretation involves taking a text, an event, or a phenomenon and trying to explain its meaning in the writer's own words. A writer must name the subject to be interpreted, provide a context for the interpretation, make claims about his or her understanding of the subject, and provide specific support for those claims.

Controversial issue. A controversial issue essay is a position paper on a substantive matter about which people disagree. In addressing a controversial issue, writers examine an issue thoughtfully, establish a position on the issue, and develop a carefully reasoned, well-supported argument for their position. Writers often address counterarguments, accommodating valid ones and refuting invalid ones, while forcefully arguing for their own position.

Speculation about causes and effects. Speculation about causes and effects requires writers to conjecture about causes or to predict the effects of a given situation, event, or trend for which there is inconclusive or uncertain evidence. Writers describe the situation, speculate confidently about the causes or effects of the situation, and present a fully developed, convincing argument for the speculations. These papers may have an if . . . then or why . . . because pattern of development.

Reflective essay. Writing a successful reflective essay requires moving from a personal experience to an exploration of its more universal significance. The writer's focus is the search for a meaning applicable to the human condition. Although the essay's subject is often stimulated by a small incident, its reasoning is analytical and its intentions philosophical.

Evaluation. In evaluation, the writer presents a judgment based upon a critical assessment of a particular subject and supports that judgment with a convincing, well-reasoned discussion with the use of evidence. In an effective evaluation, the writer speaks with authority on the subject (adapted from Tempes, 1993).

Note: Sample prompts for each of the eight writing types as well as the commonly taught comparison/contrast paper, are available on the companion website.

Although it was short-lived for various reasons, most of which were political, the CLAS direct reading/writing assessment had a positive impact in some respects: It brought writing into the forefront of English/language arts classrooms in California; and, for many teachers, it expanded the range of writing instruction. However, the types identified tended to deepen the Great Divide (Newkirk, 1989) between elementary, middle, and high schools. For example, the majority of high school writing types tend to fall into the analytical/expository domain. Additionally, English departments tended to divide up the types—autobiographical incident in grade 9, reflective essay in grade 10, and so forth.

At the college level, writing is often organized according to rhetorical modes or strategies: narration (recounting events), description (portraying people, places, and things), illustration (explaining with examples), process analysis (explaining how something works or is done), comparison and contrast (showing similarities and differences), classification and division (explaining categories and parts), definition (explaining the meaning of something), cause and effect (using reasons and results to explain), and argumentation (making a claim and offering reasons and evidence in support of a claim as well as anticipating opposing viewpoints). Although college composition courses tend to focus on essay writing, students who are well versed in all of the domains of writing are better able to bring voice and style into exposition. In fact, students are often encouraged to use description and narration "to illustrate abstract ideas, to make information memorable, or to support an argument" (Axelrod & Cooper, 2004, pp. 627 and 643).

Balance Teacher-Prompted and Student-Selected Writing Tasks

Another debate among language arts professionals concerns whether or not to assign writing. Some scholars (Atwell, 1987; Graves, 1983; Romano, 1987) argue that students should select their own writing topics so that they will have more of a stake in their learning. However, much of the academic writing students will undertake in college and even the workplace writing they will do as adults will be specified by the audience for whom the writing is addressed. For example, as an English educator, I routinely write grant proposals in which I must follow a strictly prescribed format or risk being disqualified. I write in the language of the grantor, sequence my responses to their questions exactly as they are laid out (even if this means being redundant), and never go one line past the maximum length allowed. Learning to work within the constraints set by others is an important life skill. Therefore, it benefits students to have the experience of writing to a few tightly framed assignments that call for specific types of writing the students are unlikely to select on their own.

More often, teachers can ask students to do prompted writing that allows them some element of choice. For example, some literature-based prompts specify the writing task but give students options about how to go about approaching the task. Other teacher-prompted assignments can offer a broad frame around a task, as in the memory snapshot demonstration lesson in this chapter. In this lesson students are free to select and write about any tangible or mental snapshot that they associate with a specific memory; but the teacher will guide the writing experience, teaching the students important elements of author's craft. In her revised version of *In the Middle* (1998), Nancie Atwell describes how some of her ideas about her role as a teacher have evolved over time. She writes, "I have become a teacher with a capital T. This does not mean I've reverted to playing God and making all the decisions from behind my desk. But it does mean I'm no longer willing to withhold suggestions and directions from my kids when I can help them solve a problem, do something they've never done before, produce stunning writing, and ultimately, become more independent of me" (p. 21). Although Atwell is still a strong advocate of a student-centered writing workshop classroom, she does occasionally assign the same writing task to the whole class. She explains why she believes the assignment will serve an important purpose and, writing to the assignment along with her students, she models effective ways to approach the task. Students also need to have opportunities to select their own texts and to engage in writing tasks of their choice. If they have been introduced to different types of writing through prompted writing tasks, they should be more aware of their options when they make independent choices regarding what to write. Each teacher will have to make a professional decision about how and to what degree to balance teacher-prompted writing with student-selected writing. But it is important to keep in mind that research suggests a correlation between student choice, enhanced motivation, and a positive attitude (Gambrell, 1994). Because we do not want students to perceive writing as a chore that one does simply to appease the teacher, it is also important to engage students in expressive writing that is not evaluated by the teacher—and sometimes to let students have a say regarding what piece or pieces of their writing will be submitted for evaluation.

Focus on Process *and* on Products

Despite the fact that most researchers agree that there is no such thing as "the writing process" and that the cognitive processes writers engage in during composing are complex, recursive, and sometimes simultaneous, taking a stage process approach to teaching writing has become the "conventional wisdom" in most English classrooms (Langer & Applebee, 1987). The process-oriented approach has survived more than two decades of educational reform for several reasons. First, it demystifies composing. Students learn that good writers don't just produce perfectly articulate texts in one sitting. Experienced writers ponder, plan, draft, talk to themselves inside their heads, reread, revise, polish surface features, and so on. As Nancie Atwell (1998) says of her process, "It means false starts, page after page that goes nowhere, enough bravado to confront a blank piece of paper, enough self-confidence to fill the page with writing that is stupid, pompous or off-the-wall, and enough patience to go back and think about it, again and again, and try to revise toward something like intelligence and maybe, if I'm lucky, grace" (p. 332). Second, when teachers break up composing into manageable chunks and ask students to create opening scenes, first drafts, revised drafts, and the rest, it gives the students "think time." On rare occasions, good writing just boils over inside of us and we are surprised as it spills out onto the page, capturing precisely what we wanted to convey. But more often, good writing gets better if we can put it on simmer—leave it to sit until we're ready to come back to it and add a few more ingredients. The process approach also opens up opportunities for feedback. Rather than waiting until the final draft, when the students have already mentally said "The end," the teacher and classmates can provide responses at the draft stage, when students are more apt to act on suggestions to improve their writing. Although the majority of the writing that is assessed by the teacher should include time to generate ideas, plan for both the process and the product, receive feedback, revise, and edit, students will also benefit from timed writing experiences—

first for practice only and then for a score. Being able to mobilize and express one's ideas under time constraints is another important ability students should develop. If students have been trained to let their thinking and writing percolate gradually and then suddenly must perform for an assessment such as the NAEP, many are likely to have unfinished papers when the proctor calls time.

Advocates of the stage process approach have been criticized for emphasizing process over products; this emphasis has been interpreted by some to mean that correctness is not perceived as important. However, within the National Writing Project, which is often associated with the process approach, there have always been three goals: fluency, form, and correctness. Notice that these goals are depicted in a triangle:

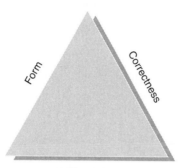

No one facet of this triangle is more important than another. Fluency is at the base of the triangle, however, because once students begin to feel comfortable with expressing their thoughts and feelings, they are better able to attend to concerns of form and to the task of editing for correctness.

Students need to know that finished products submitted for assessment or for being displayed, published, or sent to the intended audience should be proofread to ensure that no errors in the conventions of written English will interfere with the writer's intended message. The role of the teacher is to provide instruction and guided practice that includes all three facets of composing a written text. If the teacher values writing as a process, he or she is also well advised to consider the process as part of the product. That is, anything from initial clusters to first drafts to editing sheets can be handed in with the final draft and accorded some type of credit. Students need to understand that if thinking is cumulative, every product, and the process that underlies it, expands their textual repertoire.

EXPLORING THE DOMAINS

As was mentioned previously, Figure 9.1 lists some of the many and varied types of writing that fall within the four domains and sometimes cross one or more domains. Let's look at four successful classroom lessons, each highlighting a type of writing in one domain. The second of these lessons is the demonstration lesson for this chapter.

Seashells and Similes: Sensory/Descriptive Observational Poetry

Poetry is often left off the list when scholars categorize writing because it's difficult to pigeonhole. Depending upon its purpose, poetry can fit in any of the domains. Atwell (1998) points out that some teachers avoid teaching poetry because they feel "intimidated by it" (p. 416). Others may have students read poetry and write interpretive essays about it but are reluctant to spend time having students write poetry themselves, because this type of writing is hard to evaluate and will not show up on assessment tests. But, as Atwell notes, "Poetry changes us: it makes us think, look, hear, and wonder in ways that we never would have otherwise" (p. 427).

One lesson that encourages students to do just that—to look closely and imagine in ways that they never would have otherwise—is "Seashells and Similes," designed by Susan Starbuck, a language arts consultant at Long Beach Unified School District in Long Beach, California. Susan originally developed this introduction to poetry and to figurative language when she inherited a very tough class (the kind of students teachers sometimes identify as the "teach me if you dare") her first year at Jordan High School in Long Beach and immediately began exploring ways to invest those students in school and in themselves as writers. Her lesson has since been repeated successfully with students from grades 2 through college, from remedial to advanced placement. (For other successful poetry lessons, see the sections on I Remember and Facade poems in Chapter 14.)

The hook, or what Hillocks (1995) would call the "gateway activity," for "Seashells and Similes" involves the close observation of a seashell by the whole class. Select a large, interesting-looking shell with distinctive coloration or a unique shape. Begin by passing the shell around the class. As students examine the shell closely, ask them to volunteer a word or phrase that comes to mind when they look at the shell. This can be a single descriptive word, or a phrase physically describing the shell or describing what the shell reminds them of. Record their responses as the shell moves around the room, as in the cluster in Figure 9.2.

Draw students' attention to the fact that some words and phrases are clustered in circles and others in squares. Ask students to confer in pairs and discuss what is different about the two sets of words and phrases—namely, that some words are literal descriptions and others involve figurative comparisons. You may want to point out that most of the comparisons are similes, because they use *like* or *as*. If you have some metaphors, like "zebra-striped," you may wish to distinguish between similes and metaphors (which compare unlike things without using any words of comparison).

The next step is for each student to select his or her own shell (collections could also include sea urchins, starfish, and other types of marine life) and to create an individual cluster,

Figure 9.2 Sample "Seashell" Cluster

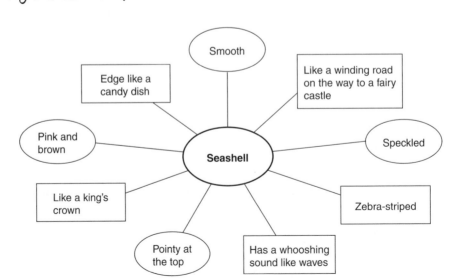

using the class cluster as a model. After about ten minutes, ask students to stop and to draw their object from two different angles—the second of which must put the object in a position that is unexpected or surprising. As students draw, they will naturally compare their objects to other things. Have them add their new literal descriptions and figurative comparisons onto their clusters.

The inspiration for Starbuck's lesson is a meditation on a shell written by Anne Morrow Lindbergh in *Gift from the Sea* (1975). After reviewing unfamiliar vocabulary, share the following excerpt:

> This is a snail shell, round, full and glossy as a horse chestnut. Comfortable and compact, it sits curled up like a cat in the hollow of my hand. Milky and opaque, it has the pinkish bloom of the sky on a summer evening, ripening to rain. On its smooth symmetrical face is penciled with precision a smooth spiral, winding inward to the pinpoint center of the shell, the tiny dark core of the apex, the pupil of the eye. It stares at me, this mysterious single eye—and I stare back.
>
> Now it is the moon, solitary in the sky, full and round, replete with power. Now it is the eye of a cat that brushes noiselessly through long grass at night. Now it is an island, set in ever-widening circles of waves, alone, self-contained, serene. (pp. 39–40)

Students who have not had much experience looking closely at an object through an imaginative eye may have trouble perceiving their shell as other things. Read the excerpt a second time; then ask those who hear a line that relates to their shell to demonstrate for the class. For example, students could model how their shell is "curled up like a cat" in the palm of their hand. The prompt for Starbuck's lesson is as follows:

Prompt ▶

Seashells and Similes

Write a meditation on your shell, connecting the shell with all the images—sights, sounds, tastes, textures, and smells—it suggests to you. Your first attempt does not have to be logically connected. Let your fancy free. Try to create at least *six comparisons of your shell with other things.* You may write your results as a paragraph or as a poem. One possible pattern is presented below. You can use this pattern to start your meditation and, if you choose, you may then use the line beginnings of each of the lines in a poem. Add or delete anything from the lines to make them fit your ideas. Or begin a completely different poem of your own with six comparisons arranged in your own way.

Some teachers may object to giving students a pattern such as at the one below to use as a point of departure for their poems. But my experience has been that those students who need the structure of the frame or pattern will feel more successful if they follow it. Those who find the frame or pattern limiting can simply ignore it and create their own form. An 8½-by-11 frame is available on the companion website.

Seashell Frame
As I gaze into the . . . of the shell
First it is . . .
And then it is like . . .
And then I look into . . .
And then it becomes . . .
And now it is . . .
And now it is . . .
And now it is . . .
And now I am . . .

Starbuck models both the poetry frame and a free verse poem so students have a clear sense of how both look and sound:

As I gaze into the pink hollow of the shell
First it is the sunrise above dark desert mountains
And then it is like the stretched wrinkled freckled skin of an ancient woman
And then I look into a pink kaleidoscope rimmed with purple
And now it is a whirling star
And now I am a starrider.

—Susan Starbuck*

Gift From the Sea
It's moonlight
            And rainbows
                              A seraph's wings
      Silvery satin
              Rippling waters
                    Saturn's rings
Everything you are, and meant to be . . .
          I smile and caress my gift from the sea.

—Susan Starbuck*

After composing and sharing their rough drafts, revising to make their comparisons more unique, and editing for correct spelling, students can mount their poems on a bulletin board, along with their seashell drawings, if they choose to.

After composing and sharing their rough drafts, revising to make their comparisons more distinctive, and editing for correct spelling, students can mount their poems on a bulletin board, as well as their seashell drawings, if they choose to.

I have yet to see this lesson fail to engage students or to elicit rich descriptive writing. Even students who are bound and determined to let you know beforehand that they don't have a creative bone in their body and that they "suck" at writing poetry surprise themselves and find some golden line among their comparisons to feel good about. Figure 9.3 contains a poem by Tyrone Jenkins, a tenth grader at Jordan High School, who chose a sea horse as his object.

Figure 9.3   **Sea Horse Poem** (Reprinted by permission of Tyrone Jenkins.)

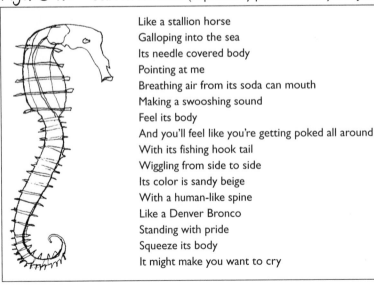

Like a stallion horse
Galloping into the sea
Its needle covered body
Pointing at me
Breathing air from its soda can mouth
Making a swooshing sound
Feel its body
And you'll feel like you're getting poked all around
With its fishing hook tail
Wiggling from side to side
Its color is sandy beige
With a human-like spine
Like a Denver Bronco
Standing with pride
Squeeze its body
It might make you want to cry

DEMONSTRATION LESSON

The Memory Snapshot Paper: Imaginative/Narrative Autobiographical Writing

Autobiographical incident writing is a form of narrative writing commonly taught at both middle and high school. The autobiographical incident focuses on a specific event in the writer's life and often shows rather than directly tells why that event was significant. I designed the memory snapshot lesson after reading Barry Lane's book *After THE END* (1992).* I found Lane's technique of using "snapshots" and "thoughtshots" in narrative writing especially helpful. Using the snapshot and thoughtshot techniques, the memory snapshot is designed to move students away from the *First this happened . . . and then . . . and then . . . and then* style of narration to a more dramatic, more sensory/descriptive rendering that creates a *You are there* feeling in the reader. I use this lesson as a get-acquainted activity at the UCI Writing Project Summer Institute. Teachers at all grade levels have taken the idea back to their classrooms, and I've had consistent reports that students enthusiastically embrace the task and invest themselves in producing rich and thoughtful texts. The terms used to identify the cognitive strategies in the demonstration lesson activities are taken from Figure 1.2 (Cognitive Strategies: A Reader's and Writer's Tool Kit) and from Figure 3.3 (the UCI Writing Project's adaptation of Bloom's "taxonomy of the cognitive domain").

Overview

Students will select a tangible photograph or a mental snapshot that they associate with a significant memory and will write an autobiographical account showing what happened by dramatizing the incident.

Objectives

Students will:

1. Tap prior knowledge to generate memories associated with a tangible photograph or mental snapshot
2. Make connections with the memories of others
3. Organize information by clustering sensory details
4. Visualize their thoughts and feelings by creating an open mind
5. Visualize impressions "beyond the Kodak" by drawing their memory
6. Step back and analyze why their memory is significant
7. Compose an autobiographical account dramatizing a significant incident and creating a *You are there* feeling in the reader.

The Process

This lesson will take one to two weeks to implement. Before you introduce students to the concept of snapshots and thoughtshots, I suggest they spend several weeks practicing writing showing, not telling descriptions. An activity to acquaint students with showing, not telling is included in the lesson scaffold. It can be skipped if students are already familiar with this strategy.

---

*Adapted by permission. Visit Barry Lane's website: www.discoverwriting.com.

Prereading Activity

Showing, Not Telling: Setting the Stage for the Memory Snapshot ■ *Organizing Information and Elaborating*

For several weeks before introducing the memory snapshot lesson, have students practice writing descriptive paragraphs that "show" a telling sentence. As explained in Chapter 6, showing, not telling was popularized by Bay Area Writing Project teacher/consultant Rebekah Caplan (1997). It is a technique to help students to show what they mean by dramatizing their writing with concrete details that paint pictures in the reader's mind. For example, for a "telling sentence" such as *The student was bored,* Russ Frank (1992), a regional Title I coordinator for San Bernardino County in California, teaches the concept by actually role-playing a bored student while one of his students pretends to be the teacher. As the "teacher" reads a lengthy description of photosynthesis, Frank bursts into the room after the tardy bell, slumps into his chair, yawns loudly, makes paper airplanes, winks at girls, and eventually pretends to fall asleep. After this performance the class constructs a showing paragraph based on the telling sentence. If the class begins with something like "The student walked into the room and sat down," the teacher immediately asks, "Is this showing or telling?" If the students respond, "It's telling," he counters with, "So, how can we show that?" Line by line, the class constructs a showing description, which might commence as follows:

> Bobby shuffled into class and slumped into his seat. Before he was even settled, he stretched his arms out, tilted his head back and let out a weary yawn that sounded like the roar of a tired lion. As the teacher began to drone on about photosynthesis, Bobby yawned again but louder this time. Both students sitting next to him stopped taking notes and frowned at him disdainfully. (Frank, 1992, p. 65)

Getting the hang of using concrete details to show rather than tell takes some practice. For the first ten minutes of class several times a week, or for homework, give students a choice of telling sentences to write showing paragraphs about. A few examples of sentences:

The birthday party was fun.	The fight was action-packed.
The kid acted weird.	The landscape was beautiful.
The roller-coaster ride was awesome.	She looks nervous.
The meal was delicious.	

Prereading Activity 2

Introducing Snapshots and Thoughtshots ■ *Visualizing*

SNAPSHOTS

Once students are familiar with the concept of showing, not telling, you can introduce the notion of "snapshots." Barry Lane (1992) is especially adept at talking about writing in language that is accessible to students. Share the following analogy with students:

> Writers are like photographers with giant zoom lenses, observing life in incredibly fine detail, pulling back to make sweeping generalizations, then zooming in again to make those generalizations come alive with detail. . . .(p. 32)

Explain that Lane developed a concept called a "snapshot" to teach writers to observe closely and portray their subjects with sharp concrete detail. Snapshots are a form of showing, not telling. For example, Lane notes that Laura Ingalls Wilder could have written, "Ma put the kids to bed and did some sewing until they fell asleep" (p. 35)—which is a telling sentence—but instead she uses the telephoto lens to describe her subject:

Ma kissed them both, and tucked the covers in around them. They lay there awhile, looking at Ma's smooth, parted hair and her hands busy sewing in the lamplight. Her needle made little clicking sounds against her thimble and then the thread went softly, swish! through the pretty calico that Pa had traded furs for.

One of my favorite examples of snapshot writing comes from E. B. White's *Charlotte's Web* (1952):

The barn was very large. It was very old. It smelled of hay and it smelled of manure. It smelled of the perspiration of tired horses and the wonderful sweet breath of patient cows. It often had a sort of peaceful smell—as though nothing bad could happen ever again in the world. It smelled of grain and of harness dressing and of axle grease and of rubber boots and of new rope. And whenever the cat was given a fish-head to eat, the barn would smell of fish. But mostly it smelled of hay, for there was always hay in the great loft up overhead. And there was always hay being pitched down to the cows and the horses and the sheep.

The barn was pleasantly warm in winter when the animals spent most of their time indoors, and it was pleasantly cool in summer when the big doors stood wide open to the breeze. The barn had stalls on the main floor for the work horses, tie-ups on the main floor for the cows, a sheepfold down below for the sheep, a pigpen down below for Wilbur, and it was full of all sorts of things that you find in barns: ladders, grindstones, pitch forks, monkey wrenches, scythes, lawn mowers, snow shovels, ax handles, milk pails, water buckets, empty grain sacks, and rusty rat traps. It was the kind of barn that swallows like to build their nests in. It was the kind of barn that children like to play in. And the whole thing was owned by Fern's uncle, Mr. Homer L. Zuckerman. (pp. 13–14)

I ask students to take a yellow highlighter and mark the snapshot's details. Then they turn to a partner and discuss what elements of author's craft E. B. White uses to create a vivid picture in the reader's mind. Students usually note that he begins with the sense of smell, then moves to touch and finally sight. He also offers a wealth of concrete details, literally filling the barn up with "stuff." By the time he says, "It was the kind of barn swallows like to build their nests in," we know exactly why.

Because the purpose of White's prose at this point in his story is simply to describe, we as readers are content to look at still photographs or slides, as it were. But when a writer's goal is to dramatize what happens or to convey action, a video approach is more in order. Lane notes that writers "have a magic camera that they can point at the world and create snapshots that contain smells and sounds as well as colors and light" (p. 35). I suggest to students that they think of narrative writing as turning on the video camera, making sure to record sound and movement as well as sights.

THOUGHTSHOTS

Lane points out that "Writers can go deeper into minds than cameras" (p. 47). He coined the term *thoughtshot* to describe how writers can get inside their characters to reveal their thoughts and feelings. Lane gives the following example of a thoughtshot:

Brad wondered if Sarah ever loved him. There was a knot in his stomach as he walked up to the door. (p. 44)

I point out to students that the first part of the thoughtshot, "Brad wondered if Sarah ever loved him," is telling; "There was a knot in his stomach as he walked up to the door" is showing. Although in narrative writing you need to tell as well as to show to move the story along, I suggest to students that interior monologue can convey showing thoughtshots. I also suggest to students that they use italics to highlight a character's internal thoughts:

I wonder if she ever loved me, Brad thought to himself. There was a knot in his stomach as he walked up to the door.

Thoughtshots often create frames around snapshots and provide the reader with a glimpse of the big picture, the *So what?* of the overall experience.

Prereading Activity

Clustering Memories ■ *Tapping Prior Knowledge*

Put the term "memories" in the center of a cluster on the board and ask students to help you cluster types of memories that members of the class have experienced. Students may come up with some of the following: Childhood adventures, family vacations, injuries, funny moments, firsts (day at school, date, first time driving), personal victories, and so on.

Now ask students to turn to a partner and answer the question, "What makes a memory stick in your mind? What makes it significant?" Answers may vary, but the hope is that students will recognize that a significant memory is one that makes a lasting impression for some specific reason.

Using the general categories of memories from the cluster, ask students to create their own clusters of personal memories. For example, off the category "family vacations," students can write down specific locations that their family has visited.

During Reading Activity

Modeling a Memory Snapshot Paper ■ *Constructing the Gist and Analyzing Author's Craft*

There are many models of autobiographical incident writing by professional writers, as in the examples listed on the companion website. However, I suggest that you take this opportunity to write and share a model of your own. James Gray, founder of the Bay Area and National Writing Projects, has always maintained that teachers of writing must write themselves in order to confidently teach writing and convey how satisfying it can be. Tom Romano (1987) and Nancie Atwell (1998) insist that teachers must write along with and even in front of their students. As Romano notes, "Most students have seen teachers in art, woodworking, or music demonstrate their composing techniques. They've seen teachers mold wet clay at a potter's wheel, shape wood at a lathe, and make music with a saxophone. But few students have seen English teachers write anything more than hall passes or homework assignments" (p. 41). In that spirit, I wrote my first memory snapshot paper along with my students, keeping just one step ahead of them. Now I share a completed memory snapshot to begin the lesson and also embark on a new one with the class. Figure 9.4 includes a memory snapshot paper I wrote about a family trip to Costa Rica.

Postreading/Prewriting Activity

Revisiting the Memory Cluster ■ *Making Connections*

After students have heard your memory snapshot paper, ask them to return to the cluster they created of their own memories. Explain that they will have an opportunity to write a paper about a significant memory and that the springboard for their writing should either be an actual photograph or a vivid mental picture. Have them star all of the categories on their cluster for which they actually have a photograph and put two stars by memories for which they have no tangible snapshot but have a vivid mental one. Put students in triads and give them five minutes each to describe several of their memories and get a sense from their partners of which one might make a compelling narrative.

Present a copy of the prompt to each member of the class. (An 8½-by-11 copy is available on the companion website). As homework, ask students to select the photograph (or mental snapshot) they wish to write about and to bring it to class the following day.

Figure 9.4   Teacher Model: Memory Snapshot

The Intrusion

The insects were humming dreamily as our horses plodded along the muddy trail in Costa Rica. Their incessant song, the squish of the horses' hooves, and the chattering of the birds were the only melodies playing as we journeyed in silence. More tourist than rider, I just sat there soaking in the scenery. On either side of the trail, giant pothos, their broad leaves like elephant ears, clung to the gnarled tree trunks and wound their way ever upwards. Above me, the trees formed a lacy patchwork in the dappled sunlight. As I brushed aside an occasional fern and marveled at sprays of delicate purple orchids suspended among the creepers, I thought to myself, *This really is paradise!*

The sweeping vistas of verdant green, the steamy heat rising from the trail, and the rocking rhythm of the horse's gait had almost lulled me to sleep when I heard the swishing of the tree branches. Leaves rasped and rattled as something scampered unseen along the branches. Then, in a clearing, I saw our traveling companion swing leisurely from branch to branch like some acrobat on the flying trapeze, soaring high above us. Suddenly, in an act of daring, it vaulted across the trail to what looked like an awaiting vine—black, drooping and shiny. As its arm grasped the "vine," I heard a crackling sound followed by a harsh buzzing. *Oh, no!* We all winced as the monkey writhed in the clutches of the lethal wire and the smell of seared flesh permeated the air. The monkey froze for a second and, before our eyes, patches of its black fur standing on end turned to gray. Then, it fell to the ground like a dead weight.

Our guide, Raul, jumped down from his horse and scooped its limp body into his arms. We followed, feeling helpless to do more than look on. I peered into that face, which looked for all the world like a premature human baby. *Poor thing. It was a cruel trick, wasn't it?*

"Is it muerto?" we asked in our pitiful Spanish. "Nada? No más?"

"Do something, Mom," my nine-year-old son implored.

"I can't, Tyler. But maybe it's not dead after all. Look at its chest . . . there. See. It's still breathing." Suddenly, the monkey's head rolled back, its mouth opened and a tiny noise emerged. "Woo, woo," it muttered from a hazy sleep. The guide wrapped it up in his bandanna, cradled it in his arms, and remounted his horse. "We take him to the animal hospital," he said in broken English. Relief flooded our collective faces.

As we rode along the trail, the wounded monkey gradually began to awaken from its electric slumber. Emerging from the confines of the bandanna, it staggered this way and that on the horse as it watched the world spin by. And then, all of a sudden, it seemed to realize. . . . HORSE!!! HUMANS!!! Startled, it leaped up and, baring its teeth, attacked, viciously biting the horse on the neck. The horse screamed in pain, reared, and shook its head furiously, trying to rid itself of the unwanted guest.

Our guide made several futile attempts to recapture our injured friend who was still attached to his wrist by a loop of the rein about its neck, a loop that now threatened to become a hangman's noose. Since it was possible to injure the monkey even more while trying to come to its aid—not to mention getting bitten by those savage fangs—Raul thought better of it and cut the leather loop, setting the monkey free. It sprang from the horse's back, sat dazed for a moment on the ground, and then scampered off into the rain forest, swerving this way and that, like a drunken sailor on a swaying deck.

"I sure hope it's going to be OK," Tyler said.

"Me too, Ty."

"We all do," my husband chimed in.

And, with that, we resumed our ride. But as we plodded up the narrow jungle trail, I couldn't help noticing the lethal black wire that seemed to be following us, weaving in and out of the branches, a dark intrusion in the treeline. A current of guilt made me shudder. *Yeah, I hope the little guy makes it.*

Prompt

Select a photograph that you associate with a significant memory. It can be a picture of you at any age, of another family member (or the whole family) or other significant person, of a vacation, or of an important event, a special place, and so on. (If you have a vivid mental snapshot inside your head that you do not have a photograph of but that you very much want to bring to life, this is OK.) Think about why you chose your snapshot—tangible and/or mental. How and why did the experience it depicts make a lasting impression on you?

Your task will be to create a written mental snapshot that captures your photograph in words and creates a *You are there* feeling in the reader. Use the magic camera of your pen to zoom in on your subject and pinpoint rich sensory details (sight, sound, smell, taste, touch, and movement). Remember that you can make your snapshot a "moving picture" by adding action and dialogue. Also, give the reader more panoramic views of thoughts, feelings, and big ideas to create a frame for your specific details.

You will be writing an autobiographical incident account about your memory/snapshot. An autobiographical incident focuses on a specific time period and a particular event that directly involves you. Your goal is not to tell about your event but to show what happened by *dramatizing* the event. You may write in the present tense, as if your event were happening now, or in the past tense, to describe your incident as a recollection.

Your memory snapshot paper will have a setting that conveys to the reader a dominant visual impression, a plot or story line, and characters. However, the nature of your memory may cause you to place your emphasis on one of these elements over the others. Throughout your paper, and particularly in your conclusion, you should show—not tell—the reader why this memory is so significant for you.

See the Evaluation section of this lesson for a list of the criteria for the most effective papers.

Planning Activity 1

Clustering by the Senses ■ *Organizing Information*

Ask students to reread your memory snapshot paper and to highlight the words and phrases that create a vivid picture in their minds. Listen carefully and organize their responses on the board as in Figure 9.5.

Figure 9.5   **Sample Sensory Cluster**

Ask students what is different about how you organized this cluster. When they note that most of the words are organized by the senses, encourage them to rely on all of their senses, not just sight, when they write their papers. To help students recreate the snapshots for their memory, pass out the blank senses cluster available on the companion website. The website also includes an extensive list of descriptive words for each of the senses.

Planning Activity 2

Open Mind ■ *Visualizing Thoughts and Feelings*

While students are generating ideas for snapshots by creating their sensory clusters, draw an open mind (see Chapter 5) for your memory snapshot paper, as in Figure 9.6 below, graphically depicting your thoughts and feelings during the event. The open mind allows students to get into the minds of characters or to revisit what was going on in their own minds during an event. A blank open mind outline is available on the companion website. When students are ready to begin working on their open minds, interpret your own illustrations and any words you have written as a model. For example, "As I was riding along, I heard the sounds of nature in this harmonious melody, so I drew some musical notes. And I thought to myself, *This really is paradise;* so I drew the sun streaming through the trees . . ." and so forth.

Students should take ten to fifteen minutes to create their open minds. When they are finished, they should meet in triads or partners and share their sensory clusters and open minds.

Planning Activity 3

Beyond the Kodak: Showing and Telling ■ *Visualizing, Stepping Back, and Evaluating*

Some students feel that they have to confine their narratives to the tangible photograph they have selected. I explain that the nice thing about our memories is they go "beyond the Kodak" and ask them to draw on their remembrance of the incident, going beyond the frame of the photograph. For example, my photograph is of our guide, Raul, and the injured

Figure 9.6   **Open Mind**

monkey when it was still very groggy. But my memory really begins with the dreaminess of the humming insects and the harmony I felt with nature. After students finish their drawings, I ask them to complete this sentence at the bottom of the page: "This memory is significant to me because . . . " For instance, I wrote, "This memory is significant to me because it disrupted the serenity of the day and showed me how much man intrudes upon nature." Explain to students that this is their *telling* sentence. Their job will be to *show* this in the paper rather than coming right out and saying it directly.

Planning Activity 4

Reviewing Dialogue ■ *Examining Author's Craft*

Remind students that one effective way to dramatize what happened rather than to relate things secondhand is to use dialogue and to let characters directly speak for themselves. Using your memory snapshot as a model, or using a page copied from a short story or novel, have students work in pairs to review the technical rules for using dialogue.

Rules for Dialogue

- Indent a new paragraph for each speaker. Example:

    "Do something, Mom," my nine-year-old son implored.

    "I can't, Tyler. But maybe it's not dead after all. Look at its chest . . . there. See. It's still breathing."

- Use quotation marks around speech.
- Inside the quotation marks, characters usually speak in the present tense.
- Commas and periods go inside quotation marks. Semicolons and colons go outside.
- Question marks go inside if the speaker is asking the question.
- Dialogue may be introduced with narration or completed with narration. The narration often identifies the speaker or adds descriptive detail. Example:

    "We all do," my husband chimed in.

- In general, use a comma to set off narrative that either introduces or follows the dialogue. Example:

    Looking at me imploringly, my nine-year-old son said, "Do something, Mom."

    Or

    "Do something, Mom," my nine-year-old son implored.

Students may want to practice writing some remembered dialogue before they begin writing their papers.

Writing Activity 1

Writing the Hook and Opening Scene ■ *Constructing the Gist*

Explain to students that their first task is to write the opening scene of their memory snapshot paper. Their goal will be to open with an engaging hook and to set the stage. Explain that writers use the term *hook* when talking about the first few lines of a piece. A hook is a bit of dialogue, an unusual statement, an exciting moment from the story, an especially vivid description, or another device that will make the reader want to read on to find out what happens. Share the following hooks with students, and discuss how each writer creates a compelling beginning.

■ I still remember that humid summer in Florida—that broken-down house with the old man, his pruney fingers clenching my shoulder, the heavy weight atop my head, and the blinding flash of the camera. Oh how I wish some traditions were never started. . . .

—Rachel Willey, Grade 7, Rancho Santa Margarita Middle School

■ I was leaving the only house I had ever known. Not just to the next town, but to the other side of the country. *Will my fish make the long drive in her old beat-up cooler? What about my dog? Will it get too hot for him in the desert?* All these questions filled my brain. I was moving. My heart felt like a sinking ship.

—Michael Lower, Grade 7, Rancho Santa Margarita Middle School

■ "Amanda, come sit over here with me, I have something I need to tell you," Grandma softly called from across the room at the dining room table. Reluctantly, I made my way through my little cousin's litter of Barbies to the smoke-filled dining room. Holding my breath, trying not to breathe in the cloud of smoke that surrounded my cancer-ridden grandmother, I asked her what she needed.

"I just need to tell you something. Sit down, this is important," she ordered. "It's about your father."

My breath caught in my throat when she mentioned my father, and I suddenly felt as if I had to get out of the room, but I couldn't move.

—Amanda Savory, Grade 12, Villa Park High School

Sharing Activity 1

Job Cards ■ *Reviewing, Giving and Receiving Feedback, Asking Questions*

I have found that if students give and get feedback early on in the writing process and make additions or changes that they are pleased with, they have a sense of being off to a good start and continue their writing with greater confidence. Have students share their opening scenes in groups of four. Give each of the three response partners the following job cards:

Reader 1

> Has the writer got your attention? If so, tell the writer what hooked you. If not, give suggestions as to what would draw you into the paper more.

Reader 2

> Do you feel like you are there? If so, tell the writer why. If not, make suggestions as to how to make the piece more vivid.

Reader 3

> Has the writer chosen a significant event to dramatize? Summarize to the writer what you think his or her piece is going to focus on.

After each of the three readers has responded to their respective job, the other partners should add their comments and suggestions. Before moving on to the next paper and rotating the job cards, each reader should write at least one question about the opening scene on a sticky note and hand it to the writer to affix to his or her paper. Lane notes that "strong leads often leave questions in the reader's mind. Questions that make the reader want to read on" (1992, p. 18).

Writing Activity 2

Creating the First Draft ■ *Constructing the Gist*

Most students will use the feedback from their groups to revise their opening scene before moving on. Then they should be given ample time to complete a rough draft of their paper.

Sharing Activity 2

Peer Partner Scoring of the Memory Snapshots ■ *Reviewing, Evaluating, Giving and Receiving Feedback*

At the draft stage students can break into partners and trade their papers with another set of partners to get feedback and an in-progress score on their paper. This score gives the student an idea of where he or she is at the draft stage but is not seen by the teacher. As practice, students can apply the response sheet on the companion website to the student model by Jennifer Pera, a twelfth grader from Villa Park High School in Villa Park, California (see Figure 9.7). The response sheet gives students guidelines for writing directly on the draft, derived from Peter Elbow (1973), as well as a separate form to fill out. The criteria for a score of 6 are listed under Evaluation. A copy of the complete six-point memory snapshot rubric is available on the companion website.

Revising Activity

Focus on Snapshots and Thoughtshots ■ *Revising Meaning and Analyzing Author's Craft*

Ask students to reread their drafts with an eye to polishing their snapshots and thoughtshots. Provide a sample from the rough draft of your memory snapshot and show students what words you revised to make your piece more vivid, as in this example:

■ The insects were humming dreamily as our horses plodded along the ~~muddy~~ trail in Costa Rica. Their incessant song, the squish of the horses' hooves, and ~~the~~ chattering of the birds were the only melod~~y~~ies playing as we journeyed in silence. I just sat there soaking in the scenery. On either side of the trail, giant pothos, their broad leaves looking like elephant ears, clung to the *gnarled* tree trunks and wound their way ever upwards. Above me, the trees formed a lacy patchwork in the dappled sunlight. As I brushed aside an occasional fern and marveled at the ~~tropical flowers~~ *sprays of delicate purple orchids* suspended among the creepers, I thought to myself, ~~This is the life!~~ *This really is paradise!*

[margin annotations: "More tourist than rider,"]

Editing Activity

Focus on Dialogue Form ■ *Proofreading for Correctness*

Refer students back to the rules of dialogue listed under Planning Activity 4. Have them work in pairs to make sure their dialogue is technically correct.

Figure 9.7   **Student Model: Memory Snapshot**   (Reprinted by permission of Jennifer Pera.)

A Treasured Memory

I had been waiting for this day as long as I could remember. The lists were made, the house was set up, the food was ordered; there was no turning back. The thousands of butterflies that lay dormant in my stomach fluttered to life, beating their wings at what seemed like a hundred miles per hour. My mind was racing with hundreds of questions about that night. *Will they come? If they do, will they have fun? Who will show up?* After months of planning, the night was finally here and all of my questions were to be answered.

"Today is going to be hectic!" I said to my mom. She nodded her head in agreement reassuring me that she would take care of the preparations at the house while I was at my soccer game. At the game, I tried hard to concentrate, but my sixteenth birthday party shoved its way to be top priority in my head. It was an ongoing battle, but ultimately the idea of me turning sixteen took first place. The referee blew the final whistle of the game and we were victorious! *Great. Another reason to celebrate!*

After showering, I headed to the salon to get my hair done in a pretty up do. If I was to be the center of attention, I was going to have to look *good!* My mind was thinking about a million different things at once. Almost everyone that I knew was invited, including adults. No one had RSVP'd their regrets, but I assumed there were some who wouldn't show up. *Who will and won't come? Gee, I sure hope everyone has a good time?* There was just too much pressure with throwing a party!

"Jennifer, how do you like your hair?" interrupted my hair dresser, Colleen. She was young and tall, with red and blond highlights in her hair. I gazed into the mirror. My hair was done up in delicate ringlet curls all bunched together. They were each pinned down carefully and looked like a huge bun of curls. Two pieces of hair framed my face.

I watched my face twist into a smile. "I love it," I said softly, "I absolutely love it."

At home, I was greeted by an unfamiliar house flourishing with activity. The sweet aroma of Mexican food immediately found its way to my nostrils. There, lined neatly on the dining room table were three gleaming canisters containing the evening's delicacies. A stream of smoke flowed from the top of each canister and vanished into the air.

"Checking, one . . . two . . . three. Checking, one . . . two . . . three." My heart skipped a beat as I recognized the deep and slightly husky voice of the DJ. He was about six feet tall, had bleached blond hair, and huge dark brown eyes. He was incredibly attractive and very lively; I immediately liked him the first time I had met him. I self-consciously stepped down the wide set of stairs toward the living room. I wasn't quite sure if I looked okay in my new shiny, short black dress. As I rounded the corner, the DJ and his assistant immediately looked up, and for a moment were at a loss for words. I stood there awkwardly, the wooden dance floor cold beneath my bare feet, while they scrambled for something to say.

"You look great," the DJ said and his assistant nodded in agreement. My cheeks flushed with color and I shyly muttered a thank you. As I turned to find my mom, I could no longer keep the broad smile from forming on my face. My self-consciousness had completely disappeared.

I found my mom in the backyard, finishing off the last of the preparations. To the right was a table covered with liter bottles of every soda imaginable. A bowl of ice was placed in the far left corner, and to the right was a seven-layer dip. Gazing to my left, my eyes fell upon six large, round tables surrounded by ten chairs each. Each was covered in a forest green table cloth, and in the center lay a burgundy flower candle floating in a bowl of water. Each flame danced in the bowl of water, casting moving shadows over the center of the table. The metallic silver confetti sprinkled around each candle glimmered in the slowly falling sun. The pool also flickered to life with large floating white candles. White lights were strung all around the tables and delicately twinkled in the darkness of evening. The dull concrete backyard had been transformed into a perfect, romantic party atmosphere.

Finally, the slamming car doors signaled the arrival of my first guests. *Uh oh. . . . Here goes!* They walked in, wearing cute dresses or nice shirts. A video camera was immediately shoved in their face, waiting for them to say something about the birthday girl. Soon, enough groups of people wandered in, and the music drowned out the gentle hum of the numerous

(continued)

conversations taking place. People slowly migrated down to the dance floor and chatted in small groups. No one was dancing yet and my stomach began twisting into knots. *If no one dances my party will turn into a complete disaster!* My fears were quieted as people started to get their grooves on. The beat of the music slowly took hold and the pulsating lights beckoned everyone to the dance floor. A layer of dense, pina colada smelling fog (courtesy of the DJ) engulfed the crowd. . . . The music blasted into my eardrums and beat in my chest. Everywhere I turned there were people. It no longer mattered whether you knew a person or not; we had all become one. Despite our sweaty foreheads and our sweat-soaked shirts, we continued to dance hour after hour. I never left the dance floor for more than five minutes, and the smile on my face never left the entire night.

"Say Cheese!" shouted my friend's mom, Kathy. "I'm getting as many pictures as possible so you will always remember tonight." My friends Nicole, Kenny, Danny, Ryan, and Chris quickly put their arms around my shoulder and grinned for the camera. I tried my hardest not to laugh as Nicole's hair gently tickled my bare shoulder. *Kathy is right; I want to remember this night forever.* Just as quickly as it had come, even quicker it was gone. Now I only have the pictures as reminders of what was one of the best nights of my life.

—*Jennifer Pera*

Evaluation

The Scoring Rubric ■ *Assessing Quality against Criteria*

The teacher, classmates, or the student himself or herself can evaluate the final product based on the full six-point rubric provided on the companion website. The criteria for a 6 is provided below:

SUPERIOR

The 6 paper is clearly superior—well written, vivid, carefully narrated, and technically correct. The 6 paper will do all or most of the following well:

- Open with a strong and compelling hook that draws the reader into the incident and makes him or her want to read on
- Use a consistent "I" point of view
- Contain especially rich sensory/descriptive details (i.e., written snapshots, including sight, sound, taste, smell, touch, and movement)
- Effectively portray a clear sequence of events (not necessarily in chronological order) that helps the reader follow the story line
- Use particularly strong, interesting verbs to express action that keeps the reader engaged
- Include well-described characters (unless the writer is alone; in this case, the writer may want to use flashbacks to bring characters in) and effective dialogue to show characters interacting
- Insightfully reveal the character's inner thoughts through interior monologue or thoughtshots
- Leave the reader with a dominant visual impression—even if the writer uses a focused "photo album" technique (i.e., a series of snapshots) rather than just one snapshot
- Use all of the above elements especially effectively to create a *You are there* feeling in the reader
- Come to a satisfying conclusion that effectively shows, doesn't just tell, why the memory is significant
- Correctly follow the conventions of written English (spelling, grammar, punctuation, and sentence structure) with few, if any errors

Note: An anchor set of student-written memory snapshot papers representing a range of scores can be found on the companion website for Chapter 13.

Postwriting

The Gallery Walk ■ *Celebrating Author's Craft*

Most writing experiences end with the evaluation stage of the process. But student writing also needs to be celebrated and put on display. Have students print out or copy an unmarked version of their paper and bring it to class. Give students a class period (or a homework assignment) to frame their memory snapshots with brightly colored construction paper, stickers, glitter, felt, and so on. Arrange the framed memory snapshots on the wall as if they are hanging in an art gallery. Now begins the gallery walk. Each student should take a stack of brightly colored sticky notes. Roaming the room, they should read several of their peers' memory snapshots. For each one they should write a "kind comment" on a sticky note and put the compliment directly on the student's framed memory snapshot. The collage of the gallery walk in Figure 9.8 was sent to me by Kathy Kliewer, who teaches at Rancho Santa Margarita Middle School in Rancho Santa Margarita, California, when her seventh graders displayed their memory snapshot papers. She wrote,

■　The kids really had fun in class the day I got out the glue and construction paper to make our frames (even though they turned my room into an absolute disaster with all of the art supplies!). We did a Gallery Walk the next day. I gave them each three sticky notes to use to put on each other's pieces. While many of the comments were vague ("I liked your story"), some of the comments the kids wrote touched my heart and were strong evidence that writing can connect our lives: "Jessica, your story made me sad because my grandma died from cancer too"; "Warren, I liked your story a lot. From Aaron. P.S. I'm Jewish too." . . . We did Author's Chair today and it was the most incredibly empowering experience for these writers. I've never had so many kids volunteer to read their work aloud before. It didn't even feel like "real" school because it was so much fun for all of us. . . .

Figure 9.8 **Gallery Walk**

Learning Log Reflection

Quickwrite ■ *Making Connections and Drawing Conclusions*

As you read your classmates' memory snapshot papers, what connections, if any, did you see between their memories and yours? If you found no commonalties, what do you think made your memory unique? The word "significant" can mean many things. In your opinion, what was significant about the memories you and your classmates brought to life through writing?

The Saturation Report: Practical/Informative Report of Information

There are many types of practical/informative writing: "how to" instructions, letters, reports, articles, brochures, and so forth. The purpose of this type of writing is to inform or instruct, giving attention to the accuracy of details. One assignment that introduces students to the practical/informative report of information—and which draws upon students' sensory/descriptive and narrative strengths while also preparing them for more complex, analytical research writing—is the saturation report. Popularized by Bay Area Writing Project teacher/consultant Ruby Bernstein (1997), the saturation report draws from Tom Wolfe's concept of "new journalism" and encourages students to practice observing, interviewing, separating fact from opinion, and conducting both first- and sometimes secondhand research as they report on real people, places, or events. Bernstein describes the key features of a saturation report as follows.

A saturation report involves:

- Writing about some place, some event, some group, or some individual that you know well or can get to know well firsthand. You "saturate" yourself with your subject.
- Writing a nonfiction article, using fictional techniques. There will be scenes, characters and characterizations, dialogue, and a subtle, rather than overt statement.
- The appeal of information and facts. You are writing nonfiction, and the reader will want to "know" about your subject; in short, be sensitive to this thirst for facts on the part of your reader.
- Author identification. Your point of view can be quite flexible. You can be an active participant in the action; you can remove yourself; or you can come in and then move out.
- Microcosm. You are focusing on some particular subject, but in so doing you are saying something more. As you capture an isolated segment of today's world, you say something about the total world.
- Implication. Much of what you attempt to "say" in your article (because of your use of fictional techniques) will be said through implication—through dialogue and through your manipulation of details.
- Reporting. You will observe your subject with a keen eye. You will note interesting "overheard" conversations. You might want to interview someone.
- Form. You might write your article in pieces—conversations, descriptions, interviews, facts—and then piece it together, finding the best form for your subject (time sequence and so forth). A "patchwork"—working sections together with no transition—can be quite acceptable.
- Choice of subject. You can pick some subject from the present or recreate some subject from your past. (p. 137)

Using Bernstein's criteria as a foundation, I designed the following sequence of activities to guide students through writing a saturation report:

- Step 1. Explain to students several weeks in advance (so they have some "think time") that they will have opportunities to immerse themselves in a person, place, or event and bring their subject to life by presenting factual information scene by scene, using description, characterization, dialogue, and so forth. Pass out the list of key features of a saturation report, as outlined by Ruby Bernstein.

- Step 2. Provide students with a model of a saturation report and a list of criteria on which their papers will be evaluated. (This rubric should be created by each teacher to fit his or her objectives and classroom situation.) I usually begin by reading to the class a paper I wrote about the Christmas "spirit" exhibited by frantic shoppers at a shopping mall on Christmas Eve day. Then I hand out one of my favorite student samples, a report on female mud wrestling written by Dave Meltzer in a class I taught at Irvine Valley College in Irvine, California. A copy of "Female Mud Wrestling" is available on the companion website. Like the memory snapshot paper, a good saturation report will create a *You are there* feeling in the reader.

- Step 3. Once students have a clear idea of what the saturation report entails, ask them to brainstorm topics they could write about and to place the names on a chart with categories for people, places, and events. Then have them write "GI" next to the topics they are genuinely interested in and "MC" by the topics they are mildly curious about. After eliminating all the MCs from their lists, students can set priorities for their GIs and select the most promising topic.

- Step 4. Enable/require students to begin planning early by asking them to write a one-page abstract that explains what their topic is, why they selected it, and how they intend to go about getting the information they need. Review these abstracts while students share their ideas and get feedback from their peer groups. Meet with any students who still need to narrow their focus.

- Step 5. The students are now ready to go out and observe their person, place, or event. Encourage them to record everything they hear, see, touch, smell, taste, and so on and to note their own impressions and reactions. Allow a week for the information-generating stage of the process. You may find the accompanying chart here helpful for showing your students how the data they collect can relate to each of the four domains of writing.

Sensory/Descriptive	*Imaginative/Narrative*
RECORD: Sights, smells, tastes, textures, sounds, action words, character description	RECORD: Dialogue, time frame, ideas for scenes, transition words, dramatic effects, mood
Practical/Informative	*Analytical/Expository*
RECORD: Historical background, interesting facts and statistics, "how to" information, interview questions and responses	RECORD: First impressions, reactions, afterthoughts, opinions, judgments, criticisms

- Step 6. When students come back to class with their notes, help them organize their ideas by asking them to think of themselves as photographers or cinematographers. If they were filming this, what kind of camera angles would they use? What focus? What kind of lighting? How often would they change the scene? Then ask them to create a scene-by-scene cluster of their report. Walk around the room to review these and offer suggestions.

- Step 7. Finally, to make sure that the students are off to a good start, have them write their opening scene and bring copies to class for sharing. Jenée Gossard's (1997a) read-around technique works particularly well for bringing to the students' attention opening scenes that look particularly promising. (See Sharing Activity 1 in the Saturation Research Paper demonstration lesson in Chapter 10 for a description of the read-around technique.) The scenes can be read aloud to the whole group (in addition to being read silently by all) and discussed in terms of their special merits. Students can then go back to their own papers with a fresh perspective on their own writing, some new ideas gained from seeing other students' work, and the motivation of writing for their peers.

Like memory snapshot papers, saturation reports are actually fun to grade, because they are as diverse as students are. They give the teacher interesting insights into how his or her students perceive the people, places, and events in the world around them.

Analytical/Expository Compositions

Analytical/expository compositions are the dominant form of writing in the English/language arts classroom at the secondary level. According to Arthur Applebee (1993), 75 percent of writing in the English class is literature-based, and the most typical literature-based assignment is the formal essay. Because the demonstration lessons in Chapters 7 and 8 provide the scaffolding for teaching a literature-based analytical/expository essay, this chapter will not include a full-length lesson.

A TRAINING PROGRAM TO HELP STUDENTS DEVELOP CRITERIA FOR AN EFFECTIVE ESSAY

One of the best ways to make visible for students what the elements of an effective essay are is to enable them to read student models and to derive the criteria for themselves. The following training session, which focuses on student papers written about Liliana Heker's "The Stolen Party," has had a significant impact on the writing abilities of second language learners whose teachers I work with in Santa Ana Unified School District in Santa Ana, California. The training session will be more beneficial if students have their own literature-based essay *on a different work of literature* at the rough draft stage before being taken through this guided practice. I suggest having students write an essay on "Eleven." (See the companion website for Chapter 5.)

Reading "The Stolen Party"

The steps in the reading phase of this lesson are as follows.

1. Ask students to tap prior knowledge by clustering the term "party." After they cluster for a few minutes, tell them the main character in the story is nine years old. Continue clustering for a minute.
2. Now, tell students that the title of the story is "The Stolen Party." Ask them to speculate about the meaning of the title. Record their predictions to come back to later.
3. Read "The Stolen Party" up to the line "I'll die if I don't go." A copy of "The Stolen Party" appears at the end of this chapter. Then ask students to stop and react to the text. For example, students can

   —Make connections—*This reminds me of* . . .

   —Make predictions—*I bet that* . . .

   —Ask questions—*Why does* . . . ?

   —Generalize—*Rich people always* . . .

   —Evaluate—*I don't like how this character is acting because* . . .

   They can write directly in the margins of the story or on a separate piece of paper. The cognitive strategies sentence starters in Chapter 2, Figure 2.1, can provide students with a point of departure for their marginalia.

4. Read to the line "Thank you very much, my little countess"; again, have the students do marginalia or a second quickwrite.

5. Repeat this process, stopping at "But she never completed the movement."

6. Finish the story and have students react a final time.

7. Break students into groups and have them share their marginalia or quickwrites. Tell them to focus on sharing the history of their process as readers. Did their understanding and interpretation of what was going on in the story change over time? Ask them to discuss how they revised meaning as they read.

8. Close by asking a few volunteers to share with the whole group. Go back and check their changing predictions and reactions against their original predictions based on the title. You may want to ask them to underline any portion of the story they are puzzled about; you could then discuss and clarify these passages.

9. (Optional.) If you have the time, this would be a place to break into literature circles with groups of four—Questioner, Illustrator, Literary Luminary, and Connector—instead of the whole group discussion suggested above. (See the Chapter 11 material on the companion website for the literature circle role sheets.) An alternative would be to use the booklets discussed in Chapter 2 (see Figure 2.2).

Evaluating Sample Essays

Steps for the evaluation phase begin with the following prompt:

Prompt > **The Stolen Party**
In the story "The Stolen Party," Liliana Heker describes a birthday party that makes a strong impression on the main character, Rosaura. Think about what happens to Rosaura and how she feels about the incident. How does it affect the way she feels about herself?

Write an essay in which you explain how you think Rosaura views herself at the party. Consider why she sees herself as she does, what has affected her view, and if her feelings about herself change as a result of her experience. How does the author show us Rosaura's feelings, and how do we know if those feelings change? Be sure to use specific details from the text to show why you think the way you do. While writing your paper, remember to use standard written English.

1. You may want to have students quickwrite to the prompt or discuss how they respond to it in small groups.

2. Ask students to read papers 22115 and 50142 in Figure 9.9 and decide which of the two papers is stronger and why. (Both papers are available on the companion website.) Explain that both papers were written by secondary students in Santa Ana Unified School District as a fifty-minute timed writing and that the authors were not given an opportunity to write a second draft. They are reproduced in Figure 9.9 unedited.

3. Take a vote on which paper is stronger. If all goes well, everyone will recognize that 50142 is stronger. Now ask for students to volunteer what it is about the paper that makes it stand out. They should say any or all of the following—although, depending on their exposure to analytical/expository writing, they may not have the vocabulary to point out the paper's strengths using these exact terms.

- Clear thesis
- Good organization—introduction, main body, conclusion
- Interesting opening (i.e., hook)
- Good use of quotes
- Ample use of transition words

Figure 9.9 **Student Models: Analytical Essays**

Paper 22115

I think Rosaura feels excited about going to the party. Rosaura's mom doesn't really want Rosaura to go to the party because she thinks only rich people are going. Rosaura is very excited about seeing the monkes. Rosaura's mom thinks monkeys at a party is nonsense. Rosaura's mom scrath her Christmas dress so she could wear it. Rosaura thought she looked terribly pretty with her white and glossy dress and glossy hair. When Rosaura got to the part Señora Ines also seemed to notice how pretty she looked. Señora Ines wanted Rosaura to serve the drinks because she was the only one who wasn't boisterous at the party. I think Rosaura felt angry with Rosaura's cousin because she was saying that she wasn't Luciana's friend. I also think Rosaura was feeling a little nervous because all the questions she was asking. When Rosaura was passing the cake out and she was giving big slices of cake and give Luciana a thin piece that you could see thrue. Rosaura feels a little nervous when the magician chosed her to help him. Rosaura feels happy when the magician tells her thank you. When Rosaura was going home Señora Ines wanted to giver money. Rosaura felt sad because she though she was going to the party because she was a friend not because she was going like a slave. Rosauras feelings change a lot at the end because at the beginning she's excited about going to the party and at the end she's sad.

Paper 50142

"It's a rich people's party," was what her mother told her, but Rosaura could not understand the differences between the rich and the non-rich. After all, she was invited by the family and was a friend of their daughter, Luciana. So, despite her mother's protest in the beginning, Rosaura attended the party with wonderful enthusiasm. She seemed proud to be able to help out with the drinks, the cake, and even the magic act; for the first time in her life, she felt special. However, Rosaura's view of herself was quickly and callously shattered by Señora Ines's small token of thanks.

Rosaura considered herself a good friend of Luciana because "they would both finish their homework while Rosaura's mother did the cleaning" everyday after school. They would have tea in the kitchen and even told each other secrets. It was only natural that Rosaura was beguiled by the nature of the invitation. "I'm going because it will be the most lovely party in the whole world," she had said.

Indeed, it was a lovely party. Dressed up in her Christmas dress, Rosaura felt "terribly pretty." She was made even more proud by Señora Ines's compliment, "How lovely you look today, Rosaura." As she stepped into the galla event, she did not consider herself as "the maid's daughter," but as a guest. She felt uniquely special to be chosen to serve drinks and pass out cakes. She won the sack race, nobody caught her while playing tag, and her instant popularity while playing charades made her beam with happiness. Her proudest moment came when the magician picked her out of the crowd to assist him in his magic trick. She was fantastic and very brave. The heavy applause won her over and made her feel like she truly belong.

The only sour incident during the party occurred in the beginning when the girl with the bow grilled her about her identity, but Rosaura was prepared for it. However, she was not prepared for what occured at the end of the party. Feeling as high as a kite, Rosaura greeted her mother at the front entrance. "I was the best behaved at the party," she told her mother with pride. Then Señora Ines came over and bestowed a great compliment on her that made both her and her mother proud. Rosaura waited anxiously for her little gift, but instead, she was handed two bills by Señora Ines.

Rosaura's ego was destroyed. She came to the party thinking she was a welcome guest, but discovered that she was used as a maid. Her view toward herself changed at this moment as well as her view toward rich people, especially Señora Ines. "Rosaura's eyes had a cold, clear look that fixed itself on Señora Ines's face." She feels less important now, and not special at all. Señora Ines, someone whom she loved and respected, made her feel like a servant instead of a friend. After that incident, Rosaura didn't feel that great about herself or about Señora Ines. The last paragraph in the story described a sort of barrier between the rich and the non-rich. "An infinitely delicate balance" is the line that separates Rosaura from Señora Ines's world. Rosaura finally realized that she could not, and would not be allowed, to cross that perfectly drawn line.

- Use of figurative language
- Insights and interpretation (goes far beyond plot summary)
- Strong conclusion

If students don't bring all of these aspects, you may want to point out the missing items. Students also may recognize the mature vocabulary and sentence variety.

4. It would be helpful if students have highlighters or colored pencils for this step. Ask them to highlight the following things in paper 50142. Review each one first if you need to.

- *Introduction, main body, conclusion.* Analytical/expository compositions are designed to explain, analyze, interpret, speculate, evaluate, persuade, or reflect. But regardless of what they are about or their intent, these essays usually have a three-part structure consisting of introduction, main body, and conclusion. The *introduction* orients the reader to the writer's purpose and focus as well as indicating something about what the reader can expect to find in the remainder of the essay. In the *main body,* the writer explores and develops the controlling idea or ideas point by point by providing examples, details, and facts; giving reasons; and relating incidents. The *conclusion* reminds the reader of the essay's main point; it may summarize, come full circle, explore the significance of something, ask a question, offer a new insight, and so on. Ask students to number the introduction (#1), main body (#2), and conclusion (#3).

- *Interesting opening, or hook.* A *hook* is an anecdote, a bit of description, an interesting quote, a question, or another attention-getting opening. Hooks are often just as effective in analytical/expository writing as in imaginative/narrative writing. Ask students to put a star by the hook in paper 50142 ("It's a rich people's party . . . ").

- *Thesis.* The thesis is the key proposition, claim, or argument to be supported, advanced, or defended by the writer. Ask students to underline the thesis ("Rosaura's view of herself was quickly and callously shattered by Señora Ines's small token of thanks").

- *Good use of quotes.* In most analytical/expository essays, whether or not they are literature-based, it is customary to quote from the text or other source material to support one's argument. Effective papers weave relevant quotes into the writers' own prose smoothly and logically. Ask students to put a wavy line under the quotes the writer used.

- *Ample use of transition words.* Transition and signal words and phrases emphasize the connections between sentences and paragraphs and guide the reader through the text. These words help readers follow sequences (*first, next, finally*), comprehend place and direction (*above, below, across from*), identify cause and effect (*accordingly, as a result, hence*), anticipate examples (*for instance, to illustrate, namely, etc.*). Ask students to circle the transition words in paper 50142.

- *Figurative language.* Although the majority of the prose in an analytical/expository essay should be literal and straightforward, a well-turned figurative expression can have a powerful effect on the reader. When we speak figuratively, we identify or compare one thing in terms of another. Ask students to put a bracket around the figurative expression used by the writer ("feeling as high as a kite").

- *A strong conclusion.* A well-written conclusion will not only reinforce the main point of an essay but add to the power of its message. Ask students to identify what type of conclusion the writer of 50142 uses. (Most will say, "Comes full circle" and/or "Closes with an Aha.")

 A packet entitled How to Structure Analytical/Expository Writing is available on the companion website and can be duplicated and handed out to students. It deals with the elements of analytical/expository writing in greater detail.

Color-Coding: Helping Students Distinguish between Plot Summary, Supporting Detail, and Commentary

After you have reviewed the strong paper, turn students' attention to the marginal paper—22115. Ask them to tell you why it is a much weaker paper than 50142. Students should note that this paper simply retells the story, whereas the strong paper includes the writer's interpretation of the events.

The next step in this training builds on Jane Schaffer's (1995) work in helping students to understand what commentary is and to add more commentary to their writing. Schaffer is chair of the English Department of Grossmont High School in San Diego, California.* Through extensive experience assessing Advanced Placement essays for the Educational Testing Service, she determined that to achieve a high score, student essays generally need to have a *minimum* of two parts commentary to one part summary or concrete detail. Schaffer identifies concrete detail as the *what* in an essay and commentary as the *so what?* In a literature-based essay, concrete details are the examples from the text; commentary consists of the reader's/writer's opinion, interpretation, insight, analysis, explication, evaluation, and reflection. I have adapted Schaffer's model and introduced students to three terms instead of two: plot summary, supporting detail, and commentary. *Plot summary* reiterates what is obvious and known in the text. *Supporting detail* is the evidence from the text that supports what the reader has to say; it can be used to elaborate on plot summary or substantiate commentary. *Commentary,* as described above, involves moving from literal comprehension to interpretation and sharing our thoughts, opinions, perceptions, and insights. Commentary goes a step beyond summary and support to remark on the significance of something.

1. Have students practice writing commentary by giving them this sentence:

■ Although Rosaura thinks she is going to get both a bracelet and a yo-yo, Señora Ines hands her two bills instead.

Note that this sentence is plot summary. Students now need to interpret the significance of the action:

■ Although Rosaura thinks she is going to get both a bracelet and a yo-yo, Señora Ines hands her two bills instead. *Suddenly it hits her like a slap in the face; her mother was right!*

Now ask students to elaborate on their remark by adding a further comment:

■ Although Rosaura thinks she is going to get both a bracelet and a yo-yo, Señora Ines hands her two bills instead. *Suddenly it hits her like a slap in the face; her mother was right! All along, she has been considered the hired help and not a party guest.*

2. Once students have practiced writing commentary, review the distinction between plot summary, supporting detail, and commentary with the class again, using the following paragraph as an example:

[1]At the end of the party, Rosaura is expecting to receive a present of either a yo-yo or a bracelet, like all the other party guests. [2]In fact, because she was the most helpful and "the best-behaved at the party," serving the cake and performing with the magician, Rosaura secretly believes she will be given both presents. [3]Instead, Señora Ines hands her two dollar bills. [4]This is a slap in the face of Rosaura. [5]Señora Ines has treated Rosaura like hired help instead of like a guest. [6]To make matters worse, [7]Señora Ines says, "Thank you for all your help, my pet." [8]This is a second slap that adds insult to injury. [9]Rosaura is no better than the trained monkey who performs at the party. [10]Señora Ines treats her like she is less than human. [11]What a devastating blow!

[1]Plot summary; [2]Supporting detail; [3]Plot summary; [4]Commentary; [5]Commentary; [6]Commentary; [7]Supporting detail; [8]Commentary; [9]Commentary; [10]Commentary; [11]Commentary

*Adapted by permission. Visit Jane Schaffer's website: www.curriculumguides.com or call 1-800-471-8844.

Designate a color for each of the three types of sentences that make up an essay. I tell students plot summary is *yellow,* because it's kind of superficial and lightweight: We sometimes need some plot summary to orient our reader to the facts, but we want to keep plot summary to a minimum. Commentary is *blue,* because it goes beneath the surface of things to look at the deeper meaning. Supporting detail is *green,* because it's what glues together plot summary and commentary. In writing a successful essay, it is especially important to quote from the text to provide evidence for your ideas.

3. Photocopy student papers 22115, and 50142, provided on the companion website, and hand out yellow, green, and blue colored pencils to students. Starting with 22115, go through the papers sentence by sentence, color-coding the essays as a class. Students often have trouble coding the opening sentence "I think Rosaura feels excited about going to the party," which most students will identify as commentary. Ask the class if it is obvious and known to us that Rosaura is excited about going to the party. Most will agree that indeed it is obvious. Ask, "How do we know this?" Students will note that Rosaura announces, "It will be the most lovely party in the whole world" and goes so far as to say, "I'll die if I don't go." Once students have color-coded the sentence in yellow, explain that just because a student puts "I think" in front of a sentence doesn't make it commentary. The remainder of the essay is primarily yellow with a little green until the writer says, "Rosaura felt sad because she though[t] she was going to the party because she was a friend not because she was going like a slave." Here is a genuine piece of commentary that could very well be brought up to the introduction of the essay as its thesis.

As students color-code essay 50142, they will note the vast difference in sophistication between papers 22115 and 50142. Particularly as they near the conclusion of 50142, students will be color-coding almost exclusively in blue. They can visually see how the writer skillfully builds to an insightful and powerful conclusion. (Note: Color-coded versions of the two essays are available on the companion website.)

Revising One's Own Essay

After color-coding the student models, students can return to their own rough draft essays on a different work of literature and, individually or in partners, color-code their own sentences to determine to what degree they used plot summary, supporting detail, and commentary in their writing. This is usually a very eye-opening experience for students. They can concretely see their thinking laid out on the page; they now have a solid point of departure for revising.

Our experience has been that engaging students in reviewing the criteria for an effective essay through color-coding practice with both marginal and strong model papers has a significant impact on students' understanding of how to construct a successful essay and improves their performance as writers. When students I work with in Santa Ana Unified School District who were trained in the color-coding techniques were asked to read their own pretests and posttests, assess their growth over time, and discuss what influenced their growth, they made comments such as the following:

■ The color-coding of my essay and all of the revising we did helped me see the difference between my drafts. Each time really pushed me forward.

■ My first paper wasn't that good but the second one had a hook, thesis, transitions, quotes, and commentary.

■ The yellow–green–blue thing helped me write a better essay.

■ I went from summary (90%) to using comments—my own personal opinions.

WHAT ABOUT WRITING ACROSS THE CURRICULUM?

Although writing about literature may well be the focal point in the English/language arts classroom, "playing the whole range" also means reading and writing about other kinds of texts. Chapter 10 will highlight two demonstration lessons that take students beyond the confines of the traditional English curriculum into a content area that sparks their curiosity. Further, many of the expressive writing strategies for interacting with a text described in Chapter 6 can help enhance student learning in all content areas. Langer and Applebee (1987) acknowledge that "because writing and thinking are so deeply intertwined . . . students need broad-based experiences in which reading and writing tasks are integrated with their work throughout the curriculum" (p. 4).

To Sum Up

If we want to help our students negotiate the complex task of writing with confidence and competence, we need to think carefully about what it is that we teach when we teach writing. For both cognitive and affective reasons, teachers need to expose students to a variety of domains or modes of writing, enable them to practice writing different types of papers within and across those domains, and provide them with the declarative, procedural, and conditional knowledge of author's craft to move from conception to completion. In expanding our students' textual repertoire, we will be helping them to "play the whole range" as writers, to use James Moffett's (1981) term. Effective teachers of writing:

- Apply what they know about thinking to writing instruction
- Integrate reading and writing
- Make cognitive strategies visible
- Expose students to a variety of domains and encourage them to practice different types of writing
- Provide a balance of teacher-prompted and student-selected writing tasks
- Scaffold tasks that are appropriate, create ownership, include structure, encourage collaboration, and foster internalization
- Focus on process *and* products

Learning Log Reflection

Return to Figure 9.1, which identifies types of writing within and across domains. Keeping in mind that thinking is developmental, progressive, cumulative, recursive, and fostered by practice, design a sequence of writing activities that will engage your students' interest and develop their craft as writers.

The Stolen Party

by Liliana Heker

As soon as she arrived she went straight to the kitchen to see if the monkey was there. It was: what a relief! She wouldn't have liked to admit that her mother had been right. *Monkeys at a birthday?* her mother had sneered. *Get away with you, believing any nonsense you're told*! She was cross, but not because of the monkey, the girl thought; it's just because of the party.

"I don't like you going," she told her. "It's a rich people's party."

"Rich people go to Heaven too," said the girl, who studied religion at school.

"Get away with Heaven," said the mother.

The girl didn't approve of the way her mother spoke. She was barely nine, and one of the best in her class.

"I'm going because I've been invited," she said. "And I've been invited because Luciana is my friend. So there."

"Ah yes, your friend," her mother grumbled. She paused. "Listen, Rosaura," she said at last. "That one's not your friend. You know what you are to them? The maid's daughter, that's what."

Rosaura blinked hard: she wasn't going to cry . . . then she yelled: "Shut up! You know nothing about being friends!"

Every afternoon she used to go to Luciana's house and they would both finish their homework while Rosaura's mother did the cleaning. They had their tea in the kitchen and they told each other secrets. Rosaura loved everything in the big house, and she also loved the people who lived there.

"I'm going because it will be the most lovely party in the whole world, Luciana told me it would. There will be a magician and he will bring a monkey and everything."

The mother swung around to take a good look at her child, and pompously put her hands on her hips.

"Monkeys at a birthday?" she said. "Get away with you, believing any nonsense you're told!"

Rosaura was deeply offended. She thought it unfair of her mother to accuse other people of being liars simply because they were rich. Rosaura too wanted to be rich, of course. If one day she managed to live in a beautiful palace, would her mother stop loving her? She felt very sad. She wanted to go to that party more than anything else in the world.

"I'll die if I don't go," she whispered, almost without moving her lips.

And she wasn't sure whether she had been heard, but on the morning of the party she discovered that her mother had starched her Christmas dress. And in the afternoon, after washing her hair, her mother rinsed it in apple vinegar so that it would be all nice and shiny. Before going out, Rosaura admired herself in the mirror, with her white dress and glossy hair, and thought she looked terribly pretty.

Señora Ines also seemed to notice. As soon as she saw her, she said:

"How lovely you look today, Rosaura."

Rosaura gave her starched skirt a slight toss with her hands and walked into the party with a firm step. She said hello to Luciana and asked about the monkey. Luciana put on a secretive look and whispered into Rosaura's ear: "He's in the kitchen. But don't tell anyone, because it's a surprise."

Rosaura wanted to make sure. Carefully she entered the kitchen and there she saw it: deep in thought, inside its cage. It looked so funny that the girl stood there for a while, watching it, and later, every so often, she would slip out of the party unseen and go and admire it. Rosaura was the only one allowed into the kitchen. Señora Ines had said: "You yes, but not the others, they're much too boisterous, they might break something." Rosaura had never broken anything. She even managed the jug of orange juice, carrying it from the kitchen into the dining-room. She held it carefully and didn't spill a single drop. And Señora Ines had said: "Are you sure you can manage a jug as big as that?" Of course she could manage. She wasn't a butterfingers, like the others. Like that blonde girl with the bow in her hair. As soon as she saw Rosaura, the girl with the bow had said:

"And you? Who are you?"

"I'm a friend of Luciana," said Rosaura.

"No," said the girl with the bow, "you are not a friend of Luciana because I'm her cousin and I know all her friends. And I don't know you."

"So what," said Rosaura. "I come here every afternoon with my mother and we do our homework together."

"You and your mother do your homework together?" asked the girl, laughing.

"I and Luciana do our homework together," said Rosaura, very seriously.

The girl with the bow shrugged her shoulders.

"That's not being friends," she said. "Do you go to school together?"

"No."

"So where do you know her from?" said the girl, getting impatient.

Rosaura remembered her mother's words perfectly. She took a deep breath.

"I'm the daughter of the employee," she said.

Her mother had said very clearly: "If someone asks, you say you're the daughter of the employee; that's all." She also told her to add: "And proud of it." But Rosaura thought that never in her life would she dare say something of the sort.

"What employee?" said the girl with the bow. "Employee in a shop?"

"No," said Rosaura angrily. "My mother doesn't sell anything in any shop, so there."

"So how come she's an employee?" said the girl with the bow.

Just then Señora Ines arrived saying Shh Shh, and asked Rosaura if she wouldn't mind helping serve out the hot-dogs, as she knew the house so much better than the others.

"See?" said Rosaura to the girl with the bow, and when no one was looking she kicked her in the shin.

Apart from the girl with the bow, all the others were delightful. The one she liked best was Luciana, with her golden birthday crown; and then the boys. Rosaura won the sack race, and nobody managed to catch her when they played tag. When they split into two teams to play charades, all the boys wanted her for their side. Rosaura felt she had never been so happy in all her life.

But the best was still to come. The best came after Luciana blew out the candles. First the cake. Señora Ines had asked her to help pass the cake around, and Rosaura had enjoyed the task immensely, because everyone called out to her, shouting "Me, me!" Rosaura remembered a story in which there was a queen who had the power of life or death over her subjects. She had always loved that, having the power of life or death. To Luciana and the boys she gave the largest pieces, and to the girl with the bow she gave a slice so thin one could see through it.

After the cake came the magician, tall and bony, with a fine red cape. A true magician: he could untie handkerchiefs by blowing on them and make a chain with links that had no openings. He could guess what cards were pulled out from a pack, and the monkey was his assistant. He called the monkey "partner." "Let's see here, partner," he would say, "Turn over a card." And, "Don't run away, partner: time to work now."

The final trick was wonderful. One of the children had to hold the monkey in his arms and the magician said he would make him disappear.

"What, the boy?" they all shouted.

"No, the monkey!" shouted back the magician.

Rosaura thought that this was truly the most amusing party in the whole world.

The magician asked a small fat boy to come and help, but the small fat boy got frightened almost at once and dropped the monkey on the floor. The magician picked him up carefully, whispered something in his ear, and the monkey nodded almost if he understood.

"You mustn't be so unmanly, my friend," the magician said to the fat boy.

"What's unmanly?" said the fat boy.

The magician turned around as if to look for spies.

"A sissy," said the magician. "Go sit down."

Then he stared at all the faces, one by one. Rosaura felt her heart tremble.

"You, with the Spanish eyes," said the magician. And everyone saw that he was pointing at her.

She wasn't afraid. Neither holding the monkey, nor when the magician made him vanish; not even when, at the end, the magician flung his red cape over Rosaura's head and uttered a few magic words . . . and the monkey reappeared, chattering happily, in her arms.

The children clapped furiously. And before Rosaura returned to her seat, the magician said:

"Thank you very much, my little countess."

She was so pleased with the compliment that a while later, when her mother came to fetch her, that was the first thing she told her.

"I helped the magician and he said to me, 'Thank you very much, my little countess.'"

It was strange because up to then Rosaura had thought that she was angry with her mother. All along Rosaura had imagined that she would say to her: "See that the monkey wasn't a lie?" But instead she was so thrilled that she told her mother all about the wonderful magician.

Her mother tapped her on the head and said: "So now we're a countess!" But one could see that she was beaming.

And now they both stood in the entrance, because a moment ago Señora Ines, smiling, had said: "Please wait here a second."

Her mother suddenly seemed worried.

"What is it?" she asked Rosaura.

"What is what?" said Rosaura. "It's nothing: she just wants to get the presents for those who are leaving, see?"

She pointed at the fat boy and at a girl with pigtails who were also waiting there, next to their mothers. And she explained about the presents. She knew, because she had been watching those who left before her. When one of the girls was about to leave, Señora Ines would give her a bracelet. When a boy left, Señora Ines gave him a yo-yo. Rosaura preferred that yo-yo because it sparkled, but she didn't mention that to her mother. Her mother might have said: "So why don't you ask for one, you blockhead?" That's what her mother was like. Rosaura didn't feel like explaining that she'd be horribly ashamed to be the odd one out. Instead she said:

"I was the best-behaved at the party."

And she said no more because Señora Ines came out into the hall with two bags, one pink and one blue.

First she went up to the fat boy, gave him a yo-yo out of the blue bag, and the fat boy left with his mother. Then she went up to the girl and gave her a bracelet out of the pink bag, and the girl with the pigtails left as well.

Finally she came up to Rosaura and her mother. She had a big smile on her face and Rosaura liked that. Señora Ines looked down at her, then looked up at her mother, and then said something that made Rosaura proud:

"What a marvelous daughter you have, Herminia."

For an instant, Rosaura thought that she'd give her two presents: The bracelet and the yo-yo. Señora Ines bent down as if about to look for something. Rosaura also leaned forward, stretching out her arm. But she never completed the movement.

Stop here and ask students to react in writing before finishing the story.

Señora Ines didn't look in the pink bag. Nor did she look in the blue bag. Instead she rummaged in her purse. In her hand appeared two bills.

"You really and truly earned this," she said handing them over. "Thank you for all your help, my pet."

Rosaura felt her arms stiffen, stick close to her body, and then she noticed her mother's hand on her shoulder. Instinctively she pressed herself against her mother's body. That was all. Except her eyes. Rosaura's eyes had a cold, clear look that fixed itself on Señora Ines's face.

Señora Ines, motionless, stood there with her hand outstretched. As if she didn't dare draw it back. As if the slightest change might shatter an infinitely delicate balance.

Source: "The Stolen Party" by Liliana Heker, © 1982, which appeared in *Other Fires: Short Fiction by Latin American Women*, edited and translated by Alberto Manguel, © 1985. Reprinted by permission of Westwood Creative Artists, Ltd.

Alternative Approaches to the Research Paper

Picture this: It's nearing the end of the semester and those research papers you felt honor bound to assign are about to come due. Weeks ago, you sent your students off to the library (or on to the Internet), 3-by-5 cards in hand, and they have been busily collecting and organizing data on topics they feel befit the seriousness of something as lofty and formal as the Research Paper. Ahead of you, you have twenty-two or thirty-six or sixty-eight of these products to respond to.

Now, be honest. How do you *really* feel as you face the thought of an entire weekend—and then some—consumed by student discussions of such questions as "Should we legislate gun control?" and "What is the impact of television on American society?"

WHAT ARE WE TEACHING STUDENTS WHEN WE TEACH THE RESEARCH PAPER?

Why is it that we have come to dread reading and responding to our students' research papers almost as much as they have come to dread writing them? Perhaps the answer to this question is rooted in the answer to another: *Is what we are asking the students to do in the name of "research" really research?* I think not. My sense is that when students compose what Carol Jago (1997), a UCLA Writing Project teacher/consultant, calls the Termpapersaurus Rex, they are conducting research on research. That is, instead of being actively engaged in a genuine problem-solving and discovery process, many students merely analyze and restate the results of someone else's intellectual inquiry, an inquiry in which they may have no personal investment.

This picture of students who are passively summarizing someone else's investigation or experimentation gives rise to another question: *What are we teaching when we teach research on research?* If our goal is to foster critical thinking in our students and to encourage them to take a "speculative or questioning stance toward knowledge and experiences" (Petrosky, 1986, p. 3), then we may be doing students a disservice by teaching research on research. The nature and scope of most research topics that students elect to pursue, their lack of ownership in those topics, and the strict time constraints under which they must operate relegate many students to "strip mining" for "verifiable information and facts" (p. 3), to use Petrosky's metaphor. There is little opportunity or incentive for reflection and interpretation. In fact, students often are not expected or encouraged to make their own meaning. The students' assumption, and sometimes the teacher's as well, is that the answers to their questions reside in something that is external to them, in the "findings" of someone else.

In "Reforming Your Teaching for Thinking," Dan Kirby (1997) remarks, "If you're going to develop your students as thinkers, you must begin to look at knowledge and knowing in new ways." He goes on to say, "This new view of knowledge doesn't mean you have nothing to teach students or that textbooks are no longer important or that old knowledge is no longer valuable. What it does mean is that we have to plan for and structure our classrooms in such a way that students construct their own versions of old knowledge in new and more personal ways" (p. 168). If the traditional research paper, as it is commonly taught, does not promote a spirit of reflection or foster our students' ability to construct their own versions of knowledge and to respond interpretatively to people, events, books, and ideas, then we must ask ourselves, How can we frame assignments that enable and encourage students to select topics for research and inquiry in which they have a genuine personal stake and from which they can make their own meaning?

The saturation research paper and the I-search paper, presented in the two demonstration lessons in this chapter, are two assignments that encourage active research that students conduct out of genuine interest. I agree with Ken Macrorie (1988) that the dictionary definition of research as "patient study and investigation in some field of knowledge, undertaken to establish facts and principles" leaves out "the basic motivation for the whole effort" (p. 162). My students are rarely patient about anything. I would rather have them get so involved in a topic that they launch their hunt for information in several different directions simultaneously than have them, bored before they begin, dragging their bodies down to the library or sitting at home surfing the Internet, simply going through the motions of research. It seems to me that the point of having students conduct research is not just to teach them how to systematically collect, organize, and report data to establish facts and principles, but to let them experience some of the excitement of hunting for and grappling with that information to make their own connections and discover new insights. What we're after, then, is not just transmission but transaction. We want students to interact with the information they are compiling—not just to search but to research, to see anew.

The saturation research paper and I-research paper offer students just such an opportunity. The saturation research paper calls on students to make their own meaning out of a historical incident: to assume the persona of the key figure involved and to speculate on and articulate what that person might have done, thought, felt, and said. The word *might* is important here, because although the student engages in a research process in order to write this paper and must weave in factual information, the product of the research is historical fiction. The writer's goal, simply put, is to bring history to life by turning it into literature.

Ken Macrorie's "I-search" paper (1988), grows out of a student's intense need to know about a topic that has immediate relevance for him or her. Macrorie (1997) uses the term *I-search* rather than *research* "not to convey that this paper is written to search an I or me, to come to 'know oneself' but rather to remind the reader or writer that there is an *I* doing the searching and writing who affects the bend and quality of the truth in the work"(p. 153). Although the I-search is closer to a traditional expository research paper in its intent and form than is a saturation research paper, writers often adopt a narrative style as they tell the story of their search for answers to their inquiry question. In so doing, they produce serious, well-organized, amply documented, insightful research in engaging prose that retains their own voices as writers.

DEMONSTRATION LESSON

The Saturation Research Paper

The idea for the saturation research paper comes from my colleague Catherine D'Aoust (1997), codirector of the UCI Writing Project and coordinator of instructional services for Saddleback Valley Unified School District in Mission Viejo, California. It meets an eleventh- and twelfth-grade California English-Language Arts Content Standard: Students write and orally deliver historical investigation reports after analyzing several historical records of a single event "using narration, description, argumentation, exposition or some combination of rhetorical strategies" (O'Malley, *Reading/Language Arts Framework for California Public Schools,* p. 212). This demonstration lesson has been adapted from an article I wrote for a book called *The Critical Writing Workshop* (Capossela, 1993).* Terms used to describe the reading, thinking, and writing tasks in the lesson are taken from Figure 1.2 (Cognitive Strategies: A Reader's and Writer's Tool Kit) and from Figure 3.3 (the UCI Writing Project's adaptation of Bloom's "taxonomy of the cognitive domain").

Overview

Students will research and saturate themselves in a historical figure; select a significant event from that person's life; assume the persona of that person; and, weaving together factual information and fictional techniques, dramatize the event, showing why it is significant.

Objectives

Students will:

1. Tap prior knowledge regarding famous historical figures
2. Select a "famous" historical figure to research and identify a significant event in his or her life
3. Organize information gleaned from research
4. Adopt an alignment by becoming the person or a witness to the event
5. Speculate about what their chosen person might have done, thought, felt, and said
6. Compose a research-based narrative portraying the person and dramatizing the event

The Process

This lesson took three weeks when I implemented it with eleventh graders at Irvine High School in Irvine, California. However, it only occupied six class meetings over those three weeks; students used time between sessions to think, research, write, and revise.

Prereading Activity

Introducing the Saturation Research Paper ■ *Creating and Setting Goals and Mobilizing Knowledge*

Let students know at least a week in advance that they will have an opportunity to saturate themselves in the life of a historical figure who is of interest to them; choose a significant

---

*From "Saturation Research: An Alternative Approach to the Research Paper" by Carol Booth Olson. In *The Critical Writing Workshop: Designing Writing Assignments to Foster Critical Thinking* edited by Toni-Lee Capossela. Copyright © 1993 by Boynton/Cook Publishers, Inc. Published by Boynton/Cook Publishers, Inc., a subsidiary of Reed Elsevier, Inc., Portsmouth, NH.

event in that person's life; and bring that event to life, either by becoming the person and speaking through his or her voice or by becoming a witness to the event. I stress that although the paper must be based on and weave in factual information derived from research, students will be writing historical fiction. Students are to approximate what might have happened based on the resources available and on their own best speculative and reflective thinking. For example, much less is known about Harriet Tubman's escape from slavery than about the assassination of John F. Kennedy. In either case, however, the writer cannot know with any certainty what Harriet Tubman was thinking as her song rang out among the slave quarters to signal the hour of her escape, or what ran through Jacqueline Kennedy's mind when an assassin's bullet caught her husband in the temple and sent him reeling into her lap, his blood splattering her pink suit. What the writer can do is to create an interior monologue for the character that is plausible, given what *is* known factually. Ask students to let the idea of this assignment percolate and to jot down any good ideas they have for subjects throughout the week.

During Reading Activity

Reading Aloud and Highlighting ■ *Constructing the Gist*

Read aloud to the class the student model in Figure 10.1 (pages 240–241), written by UCI teaching credential candidate Alyse Rome. Ask students to follow along and, using highlighters, to mark any words, phrases, or sentences that particularly appeal to them and make history come to life for them.

Postreading Activity

Reviewing the Student Model ■ *Analyzing Author's Craft*

Ask students to turn to a partner and review the golden lines they have highlighted. Then ask the class, "What literary techniques does the author use to bring this historical event to life and create a *you are there* feeling in the reader?" Students are likely to cite some of the following as techniques the author uses to draw the reader into the story: authentic-sounding dialect; good use of dialogue so that characters interact directly; effective use of the point of view of the elderly Tubman looking back; interesting flashback to dramatize the escape; vivid sensory/descriptive language and concrete details; good use of figurative language; facts woven in naturally; and symbolic title. Ask students to keep these techniques in mind as they continue thinking of historical figures to write about.

Prewriting Activity

Clustering to Find a Topic and Quickwriting ■ *Tapping Prior Knowledge, Finding a Focus, and Evaluating*

One good way to help students identify a historical figure who is of genuine interest to them is to ask them to cluster the names of people they can recall from their history classes, from independent reading, from current events, or from conversations with friends, and then to do quickwrites about the names they come up with. These activities often help students not only to recall names of historical figures but also to get in touch with their own values and preoccupations.

For example, through the cluster in Figure 10.2 (page 242), Alyse Rome found out early on that she was attracted to individuals of culturally diverse backgrounds who have fought against oppression and to strong women who can serve as positive role models. She combined these interests in her choice of Harriet Tubman (asterisked). Rome's comments follow the cluster.

Figure 10.1   **Student Model: Saturation Research Paper** (Reprinted by permission of Alyse Rome.)

Through Freedom's Gate

It was 1849, the year I got my freedom. Mind you, it wasn't given to me. The only thing Master Ed and Miss Susan ever give me was a sore whippin', an' I's got scars an' callouses all over my stocky black body to show for it (Petry, 1995, p. 5). It weren't many a poor Negro slave that got freedom given to him. Lord no. He had to go on out and run to catch his freedom. Run faster and farther than he ever did from master's whip. Faster and farther than he'd ever pray he'd run agin. And that's just what I did, that night in 1849 (Humphreville, 1967, p. 129).

I had reasoned this out in my mind, after hearin' those forbidden stories whispered agin and agin, quietly around the fire—stories of the slave revolt brought on by Nat Turner (Jackson, 1985, p. 121; Stoddard, 1970, p. 422) and of the runaways ridin' to freedom on the Underground Railroad. I figured they was one of two things I had a right to: liberty or death. If I could not have one, I would have the other. No man should take Harriet Tubman alive. I should fight for my liberty as long as my strength lasted; and when the time came for me to go, the Lord would let them take me (Sterling, 1954, p. 60).

It was my visions and my faith in the Lord that got me through that first time, and the times after (Heidish, 1976, p. 305). The gash on my forehead, from the two-pound weight that nasty overseer done throw at me when I was fifteen, may have counted for somethin' after all (Jackson, 1985, p. 12). My sleepin' spells, when I'd black out and see my visions were a 'cause of that gash. Mebbe it was the Lord's way of speakin' to me.

1849. . . . I'd been brewin' in my head how I's to get out. Brewin' an' thinkin' till I thought I'd bust. My brothers, Benjamin and William knew what I was schemin' (Sterling, 1954 p. 59). It was only at the very last minute that they changed their plannin' to come with me. The very last minute. . . .

> "I's bound for de Promised Land.
> Friends, I's gwine to leave you.
> I'm sorry, friends, to leave you.
> Farewell oh, farewell" (Sterling, 1954, p. 63).

My hoarse-soundin' voice floated through the still night air softly signalin' to the cabins in the slave quarter that this was the time, the time I'd told em' all about. The time Harriet Tubman was finally gwine to leave them and catch the freedom train.

"Shh, William. Listen! . . . That'd be Hatt. You ready?" Benjamin stuffed the last bit of ashcake and salt herring in his makeshift satchel while he waited for brother Will to answer (Heidish, 1975, p. 96).

William stood for a piece, as if he was waitin' for a sign from God. Finally, he grunted. "Uh ya. I's read."

They pulled their satchels over their shoulders and slipped silently out of their cramped cabin into the shadowless black of the moonless night. The sparklin' stars above were the only light they had to lead their way to Freedom's door. They reached the meetin' place in the boneyard, between the meadow and the swamplands (p. 132). I slipped out of the thick shelter of nearby trees and demanded, "Le's move it! They's no time to waste" (Heidish, 1976, p. 12).

Silently, we ran through the cool, damp grass of the pasture til we reached the thickened stand of trees which signaled the beginning of the forest land. William was the first to break the silence, as his thoughts turned from freedom to danger. "Ssst! Hold on," he whispered hoarsely. "I thinks I hears somethin'."

Benjamin and I stopped, an' turned to face William. We listened, specktin to hear the hoofbeats of the patroller's horses comin' at us from behind. We heard nothin' but the cool breeze rattlin' the leaves around us.

"Will" I gritted through my teeth. "We can't be stoppin' every minute to be listenin' to your fool 'maginins. Now le's move!"

But William didn't budge none. He stood motionless, as if frozen by the frost of an early winter.

"Will? What's the matter with you?" Benjamin asked. William stayed frozen another moment, then rasped, "I cain't do it, Hatt. I knows I told you different. But I just cain't."

I went to shake him. But Benjamin came between us. "No, Hatt. S'no good. Le's go back. We'll try agin next Satyday."

I shook my head defiantly and declared quietly, but with all my passion for freedom boilin' up from my inner being, "I'm agoin on. With or without you."

Benjamin know'd better than to fight me. My hunger for freedom was gnawin' at me stronger than ever now, an' it lit up a fire burnin' in my eyes.

"Then the Lawd see you gets to Freedom's gate safely, Hatt."

"Thank you, kindly, Ben."

"I's terrible sorry, Hatt," Will murmured, head lowered. It was plain he was feelin' a touch ashamed but, nevertheless, was resolved to stay.

"Sawright now, Will. Don't you think on it none. I best be on my way."

My eyes filled to over-flow'n blurrin' my vision—just like happens at the beginnin' of one of my sleepin' spells. I quickly turned before they could see the glistenin' in my eyes and I was gone (Humphreville, 1967, p. 130).

Benjamin and Will scat quickly, dartin' like dragonflies, back to the safety of their straw pallets on the earthen floor of their cabin—returnin' to only dreams of freedom, such as we'd all dreamed for so many countless nights gone by.

That night was the beginning of my long journey on the Underground Railroad—a journey that lasted ten years after that first time I made it safely through Freedom's gate, over sixty years ago. The Railroad was a network of houses, barns, and people, mostly Quakers, German farmers and freed Negroes that hid runaways and helped them make their way North. They were known as "stationmasters" (Petry, 1955, p. 100). I worked as a "conductor" on the Railroad, goin' back nineteen times to lead over three hundred of my people to the Promised Land in the North (Smith & Jeffers, 1968, p. 41); and I'm proud to say, I never lost a passenger (Jackson, 1985, p. 4). An though I be an ol' woman today, achin' and such with rheumatism, I'd go back south today n' do it agin if Mr. Lincoln hadn't given my people our freedom in 1863, at the end of the Civil War (Harding, 1981, p. 232).

Ventually, my brothers did come North with me, as did Ol' Rit an' Ben, my mama n' papa, even though by then, they was well into their eighties (Smith & Jeffers, 1968, p. 41).

I worked for the Northern army durin' the war, as both a spy an' a nurse, on account of I knew the Southern territory better than most of the commandin' generals. I's been told I was the first Negro to be allowed to join the army, and I was the only woman to fight on the battlefield. I guess I did all right. The only thing that bothered ol' Hatt was my long skirts gettin' in the way, as we marched Southward into battle (Petty, 1955, p. 227). Lord, sometimes I thinks I was meant to be a man 'riginally.

This here house I lives in now, I built from money I got workin' as a cleanin' woman (Harding, 1981, p. 53) and I brought Ol' Rit n' Ben here to Auburn, New York, to live out their last years. It shore was a blessin' from God, them livin' their final days here in peace, knowin' they was free at last. An' Lord willin', I 'spect that is 'xactly what I'm a goin' to do here, too.

—Alyse Rome

List of Works Cited

Harding, V. (1981). *There is a river.* New York: Harcourt Brace Jovanovich.

Heidish, M. (1976). *A woman called Moses.* Boston: Houghton Mifflin.

Humphreville, F. T. (1967). *Harriet Tubman, flame of freedom.* Boston: Houghton Mifflin.

Jackson, G. F. (1985). *Black women makers of history: A portrait.* Oakland: Jackson.

Petry, A. (1955). *Harriet Tubman, conductor on the underground railroad.* New York: Crowell.

Smith, Senator M. C. & Jeffers, H. P. (1968). *Gallant women.* New York: McGraw-Hill.

Sterling, D. (1954). *Freedom train.* New York: Doubleday.

Stoddard, H. (1970). *Famous American women.* New York: Crowell.

Figure 10.2 **Sample Cluster of Historical Figures**

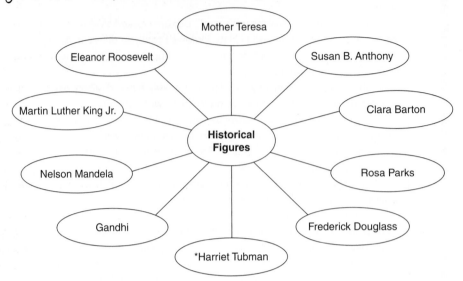

The idea of exposing students to cultures and races other than that of the white Anglo Saxon Protestant majority of Middle America really appeals to me. Especially because of the current emphasis on multicultural education in the classroom, it's important to know how all the cultures represented here in America contributed to our history. So, I guess I'm getting clear that it's someone who figures in U.S. history that I want to focus on.

Equally important to me is the concern I share with many others about the lack of historical data on great women leaders and shapers of history. I feel it is necessary to offer more positive role models (not simply more of the proverbial victim) for girls and women of the world to emulate. I think maybe Harriet Tubman, from what little I know about her, is the kind of strong woman whose story all the kids in the classes I'll be teaching could learn from.

Be aware that students' idea of a "famous" historical figure may not be the same as yours. You must decide ahead of time if personalities such as Lance Armstrong or George Lucas meet your criteria. Because students' personal investment is a real key to the success of the assignment, I personally don't set limits. However, the teacher needs to reserve the right to disapprove of a student's choice if it is inappropriate. If you require students to submit an abstract stating who they have selected, why they made this choice, the incident they intend to focus on (if they know this before they have started their research), and at least three sources they will consult, you have a better basis for making a decision to approve or deny their selection. For example, one student of mine chose to research Charles Manson because he wanted to understand the psyche of a sociopath. This was acceptable in my classroom, but it might not be elsewhere.

Prompt Provide students with the following prompt. An 8½-by-11 copy of the prompt is available on the companion website.

Choose a historical figure that you can saturate yourself in through library research (and firsthand sources, if available). Select one significant event in that person's life, and dramatize it either by becoming the person and speaking through his or her voice or by becoming a witness to the event. Weave together factual information with fictional techniques, and use your best speculative and reflective thinking to bring history to life. Your goal is to create a *You are there* feeling in the reader.

The most effective saturation research papers will:

- Demonstrate that the writer has genuinely "saturated" himself or herself in the historical figure
- Highlight an event in that person's life that is clearly significant
- Adopt a discernible "I" point of view that is consistent throughout the narrative
- Capture the event as if it were happening now, using the present tense, or as a recollection, using the past tense
- Display insight into and critical thinking about the person and convey judgments and opinions about the person through showing rather than telling
- Weave accurate, factual information derived from library research together with sensory/ descriptive details about setting, characterization, and plot in order to create a *You are there* feeling in the reader
- Reveal the person's thoughts and feelings through such techniques as dialogue; interior monologue; use of showing, not telling description; use of symbolism; and other fictional/cinematic techniques, such as flashback
- Document at least three sources, including one book, using in-text citations and a list of works cited
- Vary sentence structure and length
- Use the conventions of written English effectively (spelling, punctuation, grammar, sentence structure, dialogue form, etc.)

Planning Activity 1

Conducting the Research ■ *Mobilizing Knowledge, Expanding Schemata, and Organizing Information*

EVALUATING SOURCES

Either as a whole class or in homework assignments, students need time to conduct library and online research. By 2013, many educators predict that 100 percent of students will have access to the World Wide Web (AT&T, 1998) and that students must learn how to analyze sources and data critically because "credentialing, as a method of judging credibility, is becoming obsolete in Web-based reading" (Block & Pressley, p. 5). To determine credibility, students should identify the authors of the website, examine the authors' qualifications or the legitimacy of the organization sponsoring the website, and explore the authors' reasons or purpose for producing the site. The book *Reading & Learning Strategies: Middle Grades through High School* (Lenski, Wham, & Johns, 2003) has a useful set of questions students can use as they assess the accuracy, objectivity, recency, and coverage of websites, as well as a website evaluation questionnaire.

DOCUMENTING SOURCES

As students conduct their research, remind them to take notes of relevant facts that will be useful to weave into their papers and to record their references for documentation purposes. Some teachers may require MLA (Modern Language Association) format for research papers. However, MLA in-text citations are made with a combination of signal phrases and parenthetical references; for example,

> Harding notes that Harriet Tubman built a house in Auburn, New York, with the money she got working as a cleaning woman (153).

Because the saturation research paper writer wants to embed the citation into the narrative and thus to make the documentation as unobtrusive as possible, APA (American Psychological Association) format works better:

> This here house I lives in now, I built from money I got workin' as a cleanin' woman (Harding, 1981, p. 153).

The APA format for works cited is as follows:

> Harding, V. (1981). *There is a river.* New York: Harcourt Brace Jovanovich.

Students doing online searches will find the following sources on the Internet particularly useful:

- Dogpile.com: This is a multisearch engine that accesses a large variety of search engines, newsgroups, and use groups. Students can type in their topic and dogpile.com will list resources and offer buttons to go to the specific search engine site for further exploration.
- Ask.com: This is a single search engine that uses natural language. Students can type in a topic or pose a question.
- Thomas.gov: This is the Library of Congress website and will be useful for biographical searches on historical figures on whom the Library of Congress has information.

The APA format for electronic works cited is as follows:

> Gibson, B. E. (1995). Still going on exhibit. *Still going on: An exhibit celebrating the life and times of William Grant Still.* Retrieved July 14, 1997, from http://scriptorium.lib.duke.edu/sgo/home.html

The Chicago Manual of Style (2003) provides a comprehensive overview of current style, technology, and professional practices.

Planning Activity 2

Showing, Not Telling ■ *Adopting an Alignment*

After students have conducted some or all of their research, ask them to review their notes and to write a series of telling sentences (i.e., main points) that capture central messages they plan to convey about their historical figure. Then ask them to select one sentence and, in the voice of their character, to show their telling sentence. For Alyse Rome, it was Harriet Tubman's determination to secure her freedom that stood out:

Telling sentence: *Harriet Tubman was determined to gain her freedom.*

    I slipped out of the cabin into the shelter of darkness, my teeth clamped so tightly in my jaws, they set my ears to ringing. The whisper-like sound of the wind sweeping through the branches of the cypresses stirred my nerves, but my mind refused to hear the echoes of fear which rattled the nerves shook loose in my body. . . . I could feel my desire for freedom stronger than ever now, for I knew that each step forward meant one step closer to that great Promised Land in the North. Couldn't stop now. . . . I could almost feel my hand pushing open Freedom's gate. . . .

These show, not tell descriptions often provide students with the focus and the point of departure they need to begin writing their papers.

Planning Activity 3

Creating a Storyboard ■ *Visualizing and Organizing Information*

Remind students that their job is to bring history to life—to create a movie for TV, as it were. Cinematographers actually use storyboards to block out the scenes they plan to film. Ask students to create a storyboard for their saturation research paper, mapping out the sequence of events they will develop. Provide students with the storyboard template on the companion website and tell them to sketch the dominant visual impression for each key scene. (Chapter 5, Figure 5.8, shows sample storyboard squares.) Review the rules for dialogue listed in Chapter 9 under Planning Activity 4 of the memory snapshot demonstration lesson. As an alternative, you might want to have students return to Alyse Rome's paper, work in partners to note how she uses dialogue, and tell you what the rules for dialogue are. Students should write key bits of dialogue onto their storyboard squares. To practice interior monologue, they can also write phrases their character might be thinking, using italics or bubbles. (Note that you can use the memory snapshot papers in Chapter 9, Figures 9.4 and 9.7, to demonstrate how to write interior monologue.)

Writing Activity 1

Writing the Opening Scene ■ *Constructing the Gist*

Students who are accustomed to writing impersonal expository reports may find historical fiction to be unfamiliar territory. To get into the persona of their character and to strategize about how to get started can be challenging and may involve several preliminary attempts. Therefore, I always require students to write and share an opening scene that sets the stage for their significant event before going further. Before students start to write, it is helpful to have them read and discuss how other students approached the task of drawing the reader into their text. Provided below are two opening scenes by eleventh graders at Irvine High School.

I am sitting in the front row, right on the hardwood floor. A basketball court looks really huge from down here. It's also very exciting watching an NBA game. Thump, thump, thump, right in front of me . . . swish . . . three point basket. Awesome! Most kids would give their sisters away for a chance to get these seats. I've been here before though, because my dad is Earvin "Magic" Johnson. . . . His large size makes it seem ironic that his movements look so fluid, almost like a dancer in a stage production. Every gesture seems choreographed. However, you know those moves are spontaneous because of the effect those slam dunks have on the opposing team. Sitting here watching my dad, I am so proud that I could burst.

"Oh God, there it goes again!"
"I hear it."
"But this is the third time, Mr. Frank. What do you think is going on? Maybe we should answer it."
"No! Are you crazy? That's what they want; it's a trick."
"I wasn't speaking to you Van Daan! Mr. Frank, something is very wrong; Miep hasn't been here for three days, no one has come to work today, and now the telephone!" . . .

The fear has gotten worse lately. It seemed in the spring that the war would soon be over. But time, which seemed to be our friend, is now our enemy. The longer we wait, the more we suspect that things are not going well for the Allies. I've begun to write in this journal because I see how Anne's diary helps her get through times when all seems lost. It's funny what parents learn from their children. *Oh, no. There goes the ringing again!*

Sharing Activity 1

Read-Around ■ *Reviewing, Analyzing Author's Craft, and Evaluating*

After students write their opening scenes, have them participate in a read-around (Gossard, 1997a). On the day of the read-around, they should bring a draft of their opening scene that has the last four digits of their phone number, rather than their name, in the upper right-hand corner of the paper. Each student also should give his or her opening scene a working title before the read-around begins. Place students in groups of four. Have them collect their opening scenes and pass them on to the next group. Explain that they will be reading each scene for two minutes. As they read, they are to look for which of the four papers seems to be off to the best start. Then give the signal to start. Every two minutes, call time and tell students to pass the papers to the right. When each group has read all four papers, it has two minutes to choose the paper it liked best, record the code number and title, and write down a reason for the selection (e.g., grabbed our attention; started with action; had good setting description; began with interesting dialogue, etc.). Students have an attention span for—and class time will permit—about four read-arounds. After the groups have read sixteen papers (not their own set), ask each group to list the code numbers, titles, and reasons for their choices of favorites. Record the reasons on the board. Inevitably, some code numbers will appear more than once. Call for the two opening scenes with the greatest number of votes and read them aloud to the class. Compare the top papers with the list of criteria for an effective opening scene. Ask students to write down the traits of an effective opening scene and to use them to revise their initial drafts.

Writing Activity 2

Completing the First Draft ■ *Revising Meaning and Constructing the Gist*

Students can use the criteria discovered during the read-around as a point of departure for re-seeing their opening scene and making revisions. They should then build on their opening scene to complete their rough draft, using their storyboards as a guide.

Sharing Activity 2

Peer Partner Scoring of the Saturation Research Paper Draft

At the draft stage, students can break into partners and trade papers with another set of partners to get feedback and an in-progress score. A copy of the guidelines for responding to the draft and an 8½-by-11 copy of the saturation research paper response form are available on the companion website. Explain to student partners that they should go beyond simply marking the appropriate boxes: They should give classmates specific written feedback explaining why they marked the box they did. After students have given the in-progress score and filled out the form, reunite the four readers as a peer group. Allow five minutes per student for an oral discussion of each writer's draft.

Revising Activity

Focus on Dialogue ■ *Revising Meaning and Enhancing Author's Craft*

Students can use the feedback they received from their peer partners to revise their draft. Additionally, ask them to look for places in their texts where they can insert dialogue or convert telling into showing. Students have a tendency to report what their characters said to one another rather than to let their characters speak directly for themselves. Draw their attention to these two examples:

1. William told me that he just couldn't go through with the escape. That made me so angry that I wanted to shake him. But William stopped me and tried to convince me to wait another week. However, I was set on going ahead with our plan, with or without my brothers.

2. William stayed frozen another moment, then rasped, "I cain't do it, Hatt. I knows I told you different. But I just cain't."

I went to shake him. But Benjamin came between us. "No, Hatt. S'no good. Le's go back. We'll try again next Satyday."

I shook my head defiantly and declared quietly, but with all my passion for freedom boilin' up from my inner being, "I'm agoin on. With or without you."

Ask students to say which version creates a *You are there* feeling in the reader. This concrete example of how to convert telling into showing helps them go back to their own papers and make additions and changes.

Editing Activity

Focus on Verb Tenses ■ *Proofreading for Correctness*

Students should edit their final drafts for correctness. Ask them to pay particular attention to verb tenses and to see if they have consistently stayed in either the past tense or the present tense, unless they have a legitimate reason for switching tenses. For example, Alyse Rome concludes her paper in the present tense ("This here house I lives in now") because she is portraying Harriet Tubman as an old woman looking back on her life. The present tense can make a saturation research paper much more immediate. But students often have trouble keeping their verbs in the present tense. Give them an excerpt like the one below on missionary Elisabeth Elliot, and have them practice making tenses consistent:

"Elisabeth, they're here," Rachel whispered ^{whispers}, almost choking on the words. Bronze bodies appeared silently, stealthily, along the jungle's edge. The guides hail a polite greeting in the Huaorani language and the Huaorani reply with friendly gestures. Suddenly, a scene from four years ago fills my head—flying lances, machetes, and the awful screams of our husbands amidst it all. I instinctively take a step backward, but Rachel grabs my hand as if to say, *Remember why we're here.*

Rachel turned ^{turns} to block my fearful gaze with her determined eyes. "They want to talk to us, remember? They want to explain the massacre. We will finally know why. We came all this way. And we can reach them, Elisabeth. You know we can."

Evaluation

The Scoring Rubric ■ *Assessing Quality against Criteria*

The teacher or the students can evaluate the final draft based on the full six-point scoring rubric on the companion website. The criteria for a score of 6 appear in the Prompt section of this demonstration lesson.

Learning Log Reflection

Thinking about Your Thinking ■ *Stepping Back, Monitoring, and Evaluating*

Ask students to do a ten-minute quickwrite in response to the following miniprompt: "What did you have to think about in order to become the historical figure you selected and bring a significant event to life? Describe your process." In the metacognitive log entry Alyse Rome wrote after completing her paper, she said the following:

I had to think about how a black slave woman in the mid-nineteenth century would have sounded, appeared, thought, felt, lived, and acted. I not only thought about what it would be like to be the person, Harriet Tubman, but about the history and the setting. I tried to imagine the time and place, the plantation grounds in Maryland, the feel of the air, the lighting, the sounds, the smells, the danger. . . .

In order to include the relationship between Harriet and her brothers, I had to learn as much as I could about the slaves' family lives in general, as I found little specific reference to Harriet's family in my research. From there, I created the relationship between Harriet and her brothers for the purpose of writing my flashback. Since I could find nothing written about the circumstances of the escape but I did find evidence that Harriet came back to help her brothers escape, I had to invent my scene, making it as lifelike as possible.

DEMONSTRATION LESSON

Personalizing Research in the I-Search Paper

This lesson is an adaptation of Ken Macrorie's (1988) innovative "I-search" paper. Because it is somewhat more structured than Macrorie's notion of the I-search, I called it the personalized research paper (Olson, 1992) when I wrote the original version of this lesson. Nevertheless, Macrorie's work remains a key source for what follows. The terms used to describe the reading, thinking, and writing tasks in the lesson are taken from Figure 1.2 (Cognitive Strategies: A Reader's and Writer's Tool Kit) and from Figure 3.3 (the UCI Writing Project's adaptation of Bloom's "taxonomy of the cognitive domain").

This lesson taps all four domains of writing. It reinforces sensory/descriptive skills such as using precise, vivid language and rich sensory detail; stresses imaginative/narrative elements such as story line, sequence events, transitions, first person point of view, and so on; draws on the clarity and coherence of practical/informative writing as well as calling for facts and information; and involves a thoughtful analysis of what the student has learned. Like the saturation research paper, this lesson takes about three weeks to complete but may not require more than six or eight sessions of in-class time.

Overview

Students will research a topic based on a genuine need to know and write up the process of their search in a three-part format: What I Know, Assume, or Imagine; The Search; What I Discovered.

Objectives

Students will:

1. Tap prior knowledge regarding issues they genuinely need to know about and evaluate which one merits pursuing
2. Speculate about what they know, assume, or imagine about their topic
3. Conduct research and organize information
4. Compose a narrative account of their hunt for facts and information
5. Step back, reflect on, and evaluate what they learned in the process of their search
6. Comment on their discoveries

Prereading Activity

Discovering Your Topic ■ *Mobilizing Knowledge and Reflecting*

Explain to students that, as opposed to producing a standard research paper (in which the writer assumes a detached and objective stance), they will be writing a personalized research paper based on their own genuine desire to know something. The cardinal rule in an I-search paper is to select a topic that is of keen personal interest and that you really feel a need to know more about. Sample titles have included:

> "Should I Invest in the Silver Market?"
> "Procrastination: How Can I Get Over It?"
> "Diabetes: What's the Prognosis?"
> "Understanding and Resolving Tension in Stepfamilies"
> "Should I Become a Firefighter?"
> "Auuugghhh! An Exploration of Stress and Burnout"
> "Computers: What's the Best Buy for the Money?"

In order to get students thinking, provide a list of questions like the ones below.

- Is there something you would like to do in your free time (e.g., skydiving, gourmet cooking, playing racquetball, volunteer work) that you need to know more about?
- Are you saving up to buy anything (e.g., camera, home computer, motorcycle) that you need to learn more about in terms of what your options are?
- Are you beginning to think about what you want to do when you graduate (go to college, get a particular job, travel, etc.) and about which you need more information to make a decision?
- Do you think you might like to move to another city or country someday? How much do you know about where you would like to relocate?
- Do you have any concerns about health (e.g., pros and cons of popular diets or exercise routines; dangers from smoking, drinking, or drugs; the individual risks when a disease runs in the family) that you would like to explore?
- What do you fear the most? Would you like to know why?

Give students time to "discover" their topic. Ask them to keep a pocket notebook handy for a week and to record every question they have during that week that they genuinely need to know the answer to.

During Reading Activity

Reviewing the Student Model ■ *Analyzing Author's Craft*

Read aloud to the class the student model in Figure 10.3, "A Matter of Identity" by Intisar Najd. Although Najd wrote this paper as an undergraduate student at UCI, the question she poses—whether to have cosmetic surgery—has great appeal for high school students. Ken Macrorie liked it so much that he requested permission to reprint it in *The I-Search Paper* (1998, pp. 197–202). (Macrorie's book includes several model I-search papers, most written by college students. An additional paper written by one of my students, Caren Rice, about a disease called canine parvovirus, which nearly killed her puppy, is available on the companion website.) As they listen to Najd's paper, ask students to make a list of what they think the requirements of this type of research paper are. You may want to stop reading right after Intisar's interview with Marcia, a woman who underwent the cosmetic surgery that Intisar is contemplating in her paper, and ask the students to speculate about what they think Intisar is going to decide before reading the final two paragraphs.

Figure 10.3 **Student Model: Personalized Research Paper** (Reprinted by permission of Intisar Najd.)

A Matter of Identity

"Just relax and be yourself. Keep looking at the camera. When you are not talking to the guest, you must be looking at the camera. You can look at the monitor and fix your makeup before you start, if you like. But, afterwards, you must address the camera. That's your audience."

I stare at the camera. *What a responsive audience!* I reflect sarcastically to myself; but I nod my head approvingly. The atmosphere is encouraging. I am supposed to interview a Lebanese musician whom I greatly respect and whose work I enjoy. So, too, the director and the camera man are old friends of mine. As a matter of fact, it doesn't seem like an audition at all. It's more like a rehearsal session.

I look at the monitor and my dark eyes, enhanced by the black Arabic eyeliner on them, look back at me assuringly. My eyes have always given me confidence in my appearance. I run my fingers through my hair, fluffing it over my ears. It looks great—soft, thick and healthy. My hair has never failed me. Every hairdresser who has touched it has commented on its quality. My mouth looks fine although it feels heavier than usual with this much lipstick on. Ordinarily I lick it off; I cannot do that now. I concentrate on my mouth for a couple of seconds. I've been told "it's too big," especially when I laugh. But I don't care. I have a beautiful set of teeth that compensate for that.

Having given my self the "once-over," I practice one of my best camera-ready smiles. As my lips curve, the tip of my Arabic nose dips down right into the middle of my smile. *I knew it,* I muse to myself, constricting my smile, *I knew my nose would get into it!* I study my nose; it sits there otherwise unobtrusively. But when I smile again, I can only watch as it dominates my face. Feeling uneasy, I take the tip of my nose between my fingers and press it back and then up. I peer askance at myself in the mirror, considering the adjustment, and reevaluate my smile, then my head to check my profile. *Of course it looks better ... or maybe it doesn't,* I think ambivalently. It's as though I've seen my nose for the very first time. Yet I cannot remember ever not seeing it. I feel ridiculous because here I am manipulating it as if it were some newly discovered piece of my anatomy—and not a very attractive one at that. *Don't make too much of it,* I tell myself.

Momentarily, I try to think of some of the positive remarks that people have made about this nose of mine: "It is distinctive" (*so is a rhino's horn*); "It's got character" (*maybe it is a character*); "It suits your face" (*perhaps it should be wearing a suit*); "It's ... er, ... typically Arabic" (*sure, just like a camel's hump*); "At least it's not bigger than a breadbox!" (*but it couldn't fit inside a bread box either*). Nothing seems reassuring, as I force it closer to my face.

"You surely would look gorgeous that way," says the director who has been watching me all this time. I burst into laughter.

"You really think so? I'm not so sure. I think I like my nose the way it is," I respond, trying to conceal my ambivalence.

"C'mon, Intisar, I don't think you like it *that* much. Look at your profile. It would make a lotta difference if your nose were a little shorter and lacked that Arabic bump. You know, TV is a helluva sensitive medium. People out there focus on your face continuously. And the nose seems to be a focal point, you know what I mean? Now, a nose like yours could ... er ... kind of get in the way, you know what I mean? You could have them focus on your eyes instead by getting an ordinary nose. I got an idea: why don't you consider having a nose job for this opportunity?"

"I really don't know. I am not sure," I reply candidly as I turn to start the interview.

". . . You did wonderfully, Intisar. Presence, personality, voice, diction—all in all just fine. But like I said last time, your nose, at some point, gets all the attention. You been thinking about my suggestion? I'm telling you, it would be a guaranteed opportunity." I manage to give a diplomatic but noncommittal response to his query; and we end up discussing everything *but* my nose.

I have to admit to myself that I have been thinking about what the director said, but not without lots of ambivalence. My nose has been functioning well, except for the usual colds and sinuses. It has never affected my confidence, nor has it interfered with my activities. The truth is, however, that I do not like it. I have been always sarcastic about it, wishing I could change it. Yet the idea of nose surgery—cutting bones and removing cartilage, and I don't know what else, frightens me. I wish there were some kind of physical exercise that could fix it up—pressing, pushing, rubbing, molding, anything but surgery.

The job as a hostess on a cultural program for Arab-American TV is still available to me in January, just six months from now. I must make a decision: cosmetic surgery, a new opportunity, perhaps a new career or my life (including my nose) as it is.

A week passed after the telephone call, and I was still reflecting on the psychological aspect of cosmetic surgery and consulting with my closest friends. Although I have not been completely satisfied with the look of my nose, I have accepted it as part of my personal as well as my ethnic identity. Would my decision now, in favor of cosmetic surgery, offend my sense of identity and stigmatize me as an inferior person who's complying with other people's aesthetic criteria? One friend, who thinks that my nose is "distinctive," does not favor unnecessary cosmetic surgery. He argues that Asian girls who have operations on their eyes to make them look bigger and "rounder" are only deceiving themselves. And black women who straighten their hair are admitting a sense of inferiority.

I think, if that is the case, then we should question the validity of our use of makeup, our interest in fashions or hair styles, and anything we do that may change our very natural appearance. But in doing so, would we be denying every culture part of its aesthetic, its standards of beauty? And would we also be denying human beings the right to share their aesthetic standards? Certainly, undergoing cosmetic surgery shouldn't require or be accompanied by any special apologies; it should be accepted as a means to improve an individual's appearance when she/he has the choice. Nevertheless, when it comes to cosmetic surgery, there is a great deal of risk, and one should take into consideration the possibilities of an unsuccessful surgery, the potential hazards associated with the surgical procedure. Accordingly, I started my research for reliable and factual information, even though I was still ambivalent about surgery.

Dr. Michael J. Watanabe, a plastic surgeon at Saddleback Medical Center, recommended that I start my inquiry by reading his group's medical publications, which answer the most frequently asked questions about nasal surgery. He also recommended that I plan on a consultation visit whereby an appraisal for my case would be specific and personal.

According to *Cosmetic Surgery* (1977) one of the medical booklets, aesthetic rhinoplasty is performed to reduce the overall size of the nose: to reshape a tip or remove a nasal hump or to improve a poor angle between the nose and the upper lip. One or all of these changes can be made during a single operation. This booklet had an encouraging and realistic tone. While not denying the overall risk of undergoing any surgery, it assures the reader that the surgical procedures have been repeated successfully thousands of times and are dependable when executed by experienced, competent cosmetic surgeons. It attributes the yearly increase in the number of individuals who undergo cosmetic surgery to the social and economic influences which place emphasis upon appearance. This includes "younger people seeking peer acceptance and older people facing their own challenge in maintaining positive attitudes for an extended time" (p. 8). In my case, I am a college student and would be risking a perfectly well-functioning nose for the sake of a new career opportunity! Would it be worth it? Well, I didn't know. I hadn't learned enough about the surgical procedures yet. I might be more decisive if I did.

Surgery of the Nose (1984) another medical booklet, exemplifies and illustrates the procedures of the different kinds of rhinoplasty. I examined the illustrations casually, with a mirror in my hand, comparing them to my nose, trying to appraise my own case. But as I started reading, I became more apprehensive:

> On the surgeon's recommendation, the patient may be operated on in the surgeon's office, in an outpatient facility, or may be admitted to a hospital. The surgery may be performed under a local or general anesthetic. . . . In most nasal surgery an incision is made inside the nostrils, through which the surgeon can cut, trim, and manipulate the cartilage and bone to reshape the nose and alter its external appearance. A hump is removed by using a sawing instrument or a chisel and then bringing the nasal bones together to form a narrower bridge." (p. 6)

> *This is frightening!* I tell myself, staring down the words—cut . . . trim . . . sawing . . . instrument . . . chisel . . . bridge. . . . This sounds more like carpentry, with my nose being the project.

(continued)

I touch my entire nose—protectively. The "hump" that I found so offensive in the monitor three weeks ago is hardly there now. It's not big at all. I grab the mirror and peer into its magnifying side. Even that side agrees with me. *Well,* I ponder to myself, *why a hump removal? I don't need that. Maybe what I need is just reducing the size of the nasal tip and improving the angle between the nose and my upper lip!* I continue reading.

> Removing cartilage reduces the size of a nasal tip and provides better contour. . . . To improve the angle between the nose and the upper lip, the nasal tip is elevated by trimming the septum through the incisions in the nostrils. . . . Following surgery, a splint composed of tape and a plastic or plaster overlay is applied to the nose to maintain bone and cartilage in the new shape. Nasal packs are inserted to protect the septum. (p. 6)

This sounded less frightening to me. But I became anxious to find out about the postoperative recovery. The medical publications were too general. I felt I needed a firsthand narrative from someone who had actual experience. So I called Marcia Smith, one of Dr. Watanabe's patients, who agreed to share her experience.

Although she is not completely recovered yet, Marcia believes she has had a satisfactory result. Her surgery consisted of correction of a deviated septum, hump removal, reduction of tip, and angle improvement. All this was done in the surgeon's office, and under local anesthetic. Marcia, thirty-eight years old now, regrets the fact she did not benefit from cosmetic surgery fifteen years ago.

"I always thought about it," she told me, "but never knew it was so easy. I went into the office at 7:00 AM and at 12:30 PM I was home. I had the packing in my nose for one day. I stayed at home one week. The second week I went back to work."

"You sound like you just had fun, Marcia! What about the cast and the pain?" I inquired with astonishment.

"Oh, the cast was on for two weeks. But it is not as uncomfortable as you might think, and the medication takes care of all the pain. However, it is *very* important to adhere to the postoperative instructions. I was restricted from activities that raise the blood pressure like jogging, swimming, or even bending, for about four weeks."

"Didn't the swelling bother you? They say it persists for months?" I asked.

"Yes, this is the hard part of it. As a matter of fact, it has been three months now and my nose still feels numb and is a little swollen, but it is not noticeable after the first two weeks; besides, I had no bruising around the eyes," she answered assuringly.

Despite the fact that Marcia's story was—and still is—heartening, the particulars of her case are different from mine. She apparently never accepted her nose and was, in that sense, convinced that she should undergo surgery. As for me, even as ambivalent as I am, I don't think I rejected my nose. Whether it is viewed as socially acceptable or not, it remains *my* nose. It does what it's supposed to do. And the more I've thought about cosmetic surgery, the more I equate it with a violation of the unique characteristics of my nose. Noses such as mine may someday become fashionable—even ideal. I think I'll just accept my own standards which means accepting *all* of me.

That week, the director called to know what my final decision was. With a new found confidence resulting from my search, I said, "No nose job—opportunity or not." He groaned but was unsurprised: "I knew it. I knew you wouldn't go for that. But I thought I'd give it a shot. Anyway, come over next week and bring your nose with you for rehearsal."

—*Intisar Najd*

Works Cited

Cosmetic surgery. (1977). Newark, NJ: Plastic Surgery Publications.

Surgery of the nose, rhinoplasty. (1984). Chicago, IL: American Society of Plastic and Reconstructive Surgeons.

Personal interview with Dr. Michael J. Watanabe, Saddleback Medical Center, Mission Viejo, CA., June 8, 1985.

Telephone interview with Marcia Smith, patient of Dr. Watanabe, Mission Viejo, CA., June 12, 1985.

After hearing the student model, students may list some of the following as requirements of the personalized research paper:

- The writer needs to tell what he or she wants to know and explain why.
- What the writer wants to know revolves around some kind of question.
- The writer needs to consult both first- and secondhand sources to answer the question.
- The writer uses "I" in describing the process he or she went through to answer the question.
- The paper includes what the writer intends to do with the information he or she learned.

Prewriting Activity

Selecting a Topic ■ *Reviewing and Evaluating*

Ask students to take out the ongoing lists of questions they have been compiling over the past week. Have them label the questions according to two categories:

GN: genuinely need to know
MC: mildly curious about

The students should eliminate all the MCs, then prioritize the remaining GNs according to importance.

Prompt The following prompt will give students the guidelines to make the final selection for their personalized research paper. An 8½-by-11 copy of the prompt is available on the companion website.

Description

The I-search paper is designed to teach both the writer and the reader something valuable about a chosen topic and about the nature of searching and discovery. Unlike the standard research paper, in which the writer usually assumes a detached and objective stance, this paper allows you to take an active role in your search, to experience some of the hunt for facts and truths firsthand, and to create a step-by-step record of the discovery process.

Topic

The cardinal rule in the I-search paper is to select a topic that genuinely interests you and that you need to know more about. The important point is that you choose the topic rather than having the instructor select a topic or a choice of topics.

Format

The I-search paper should be written in three sections. These can be organized either explicitly, with subheadings, or implicitly. The sections are:

I. What I Know, Assume, or Imagine
II. The Search
III. What I Discovered

I. What I Know, Assume, or Imagine

Before conducting any formal research, write a section in which you explain to the reader what you think you know, what you assume, or what you imagine about your topic. For example, if you decided to investigate teenage alcoholism, you might want to offer some ideas about the causes of teenage alcoholism, give your estimate of the severity of the problem, create a portrait of a typical teenage drinker, and so on. This section can tell the story of how you came to be interested in your topic.

(continued)

II. The Search

Test your knowledge, assumptions, or conjectures by researching your paper topic thoroughly. Conduct firsthand activities like writing letters, making telephone calls, initiating face-to-face interviews, and going on field trips. Also consult useful secondhand sources such as books, magazines, newspapers, films, tapes, electronic sources, and so forth. Be sure to record all the information you gather. For a search on teenage alcoholism, for example, you might want to do some of the following: make an appointment to visit an alcohol rehabilitation center, attend a meeting of Al-Anon or Alcoholics Anonymous, consult an alcoholism counselor, or interview your peers; you would also need to check out a book on the subject, read several pertinent articles, and perhaps see a film.

Write your search up in a narrative form, relating the steps of the discovery process. Do not feel obligated to tell everything, but highlight the happenings and facts you uncovered that were crucial to your hunt and contributed to your understanding of information; use documentation when appropriate.

III. What I Discovered

After concluding your search, compare what you thought you knew, assumed, or imagined with what you actually discovered; assess your overall learning experience; and offer some personal commentary about the value of your discoveries and/or draw some conclusions. For instance, after completing your search on teenage alcoholism, you might learn that the problem is far more severe and often begins at an earlier age than you formerly believed. Perhaps you assumed that parental neglect was a key factor in the incidence of teenage alcoholism but have now learned that peer pressure is the prime contributing factor. Consequently, you might want to propose that an alcoholism awareness and prevention program, including peer counseling sessions, be instituted in the public school system as early as sixth grade.

Documentation

Include in-text citations and a list of works cited to document the research sources you consulted.

Planning Activity

Planning for the Process and the Product ■ *Creating Procedural and Substantive Plans*

After the students have selected their topic and checked to make sure research sources are available, they should write up an abstract (not to exceed one page in length), in which they explain *what* their topic is, *why* they have chosen it, and *how* they intend to go about searching and writing. A sample abstract:

Abstract for I-Search Paper on Procrastination

For almost as long as I can remember, I've had this nasty habit of procrastinating— postponing until tomorrow what could easily be completed today. This is especially true of the way I handle written work (like papers for this class, for instance) which has established due dates and a reader with high expectations. I'd like to take a close look at why I procrastinate and suffer all the anxiety caused by putting things off until the last minute. Maybe I can learn something that will not only make my behavior more understandable, but will enable me to *do something about it!* Then I'll hire myself out as a consultant to all my fellow procrastinators.

Speaking of fellow procrastinators, I'll start by interviewing my friends and also try to make an appointment with a counseling psychologist. Maybe talking to a time management consultant would be useful too. I've checked at the library in the reader's guide to periodicals, and it looks like *Psychology Today* is my best bet for secondary sources. I didn't see any entire books on the subject, but maybe I can also find a chapter in a couple of books.

Have students share these abstracts in peer groups so that they can exchange ideas about their topics. Students are good at helping each other clarify and refine their ideas about what they're planning to do and why; in addition, they also serve as valuable resources. A student wishing to investigate careers designing video game software, for example, may find that another student knows someone in that field and can arrange for an interview.

While they are sharing, call students up for individual conferences. The main thing on which students seem to need help from the teacher at this point is narrowing their scope. During the same class session, pass out the rubric for the assignment (see the Evaluation section of this lesson) so students have a list of the criteria for the I-search paper.

Writing Activity 1

Section I—What I Know, Assume, or Imagine ■ *Constructing the Gist and Speculating*

Ideally, students should write the What I Know, Assume, or Imagine section of their papers before they conduct their research, because this section helps them to pose their question and articulate what it is they want to know.

Sharing Activity 1

Read-Around/Response Form ■ *Reviewing, Analyzing Author's Craft, and Evaluating*

Because this paper is written in stages, it is important to enable students to receive both oral and written feedback on their work throughout the writing process. To ensure that they are off to a good start, students can do a read-around, as described in Sharing Activity 1 of the saturation research paper lesson earlier in this chapter; or they can form partners, exchange their papers with another set of partners, and fill out the Section I response form on the companion website. Encourage students to write comments on the form, not just check the boxes. Also, allow time for the groups of four to meet and discuss whether each of them is off to a good start and how to improve.

Writing Activity 2

Section II—The Search ■ *Organizing Information*

Once students have completed the What I Know, Assume, or Imagine section of their paper, they should begin collecting data for the search. The abstracts they wrote to explain the *what, why,* and *how* of their topic can be used as an action plan. To enable students to make maximum use of firsthand sources, you may want to role-play an interview or have students brainstorm interview questions. Also, remind students to record information from their research to use when documenting their sources in the paper. Information on documentation is available under Planning Activity 1 in the lesson on the saturation research paper.

Before students begin writing the Search portion of their papers, ask them to retrace their data collection journey by creating an outline, clustering, or designing a storyboard.

Sharing Activity 2

Job Cards ■ *Reviewing, Giving and Receiving Feedback, Asking Questions*

Have students reconvene in the groups of four who worked together on Section I. This time, rather than splitting up into partners to read each other's work, they will remain together as a response group. As each writer reads the Search section of his or her paper aloud, the other three members of the team will listen carefully and provide feedback related to one of the three job cards on the companion website. (See Chapter 9, Sharing Activity 1, for a sample of a job card.)

Writing Activity 3

Section III—What I Learned ■ *Stepping Back, Reflecting, and Evaluating*

Ask students to do a ten-minute quickwrite about what they learned from their search, then to draft the final section of their paper. These questions may be helpful in generating the quickwrite phase:

- How accurate were your original assumptions?
- What new information did you acquire?
- Overall, what value did you derive from the process of searching and discovery?

Students may want to share these reflections in small groups before completing their draft.

Revising Activity

Self-Reflection Checklist ■ *Reviewing, Assessing Quality against Criteria*

Because students are getting ongoing feedback on their paper, they will most likely be revising as they go. Direct their attention now to the total product. The self-reflection checklist on the companion website will help students assess how well they have met the requirements of the prompt.

Editing Focus

Focus on Dialogue ■ *Revising Meaning and Enhancing Author's Craft*

The I-search paper involves consulting firsthand sources, so most writers will include a question-and-answer-type dialogue in their paper. Refer students to the technical rules for dialogue under Planning Activity 4 in the demonstration lesson in Chapter 9, or have them review Intisar Najd's paper "A Matter of Identity" in Figure 10.2 and derive the rules for using dialogue. In partners, students can check to see that they have followed the conventions for using dialogue appropriately.

Evaluation

The Scoring Rubric ■ *Assessing Quality against Criteria*

The teacher or the students can evaluate the final draft of the personalized research paper based on the full six-point rubric on the companion website. The criteria for a score of 6 are provided below.

6 SUPERIOR

A 6 paper is clearly superior—well written, clearly organized, insightful, and technically correct. The writer of a 6 paper does all or most of the following:

- Provides a a genuine learning experience for the writer and the reader
- Displays evidence of critical thinking and offers special insight into the topic discussed
- Focuses on a topic well adapted to investigation and discovery
- Writes the paper in three sections (format may be explicit or implicit):
    I. What I Know, Assume, or Imagine (prior to the search)
    II. The Search (testing knowledge, assumptions, or conjecture through documented research)
    III. What I Discovered (including commentary and conclusions)
- Takes an active rather than a passive role in the search
- Uses research effectively as a supplement to, but not as a substitute for, his or her own ideas
- Conveys a clear sense of his or her own "voice" or style
- Uses precise, apt, and descriptive language
- Carefully supports the main points of the essay with examples
- Uses ample transitions between ideas, paragraphs, and sections
- Varies sentence structure and length
- Documents the Search portion of the essay with citations in correct form
- Includes references to a minimum of two primary and two secondary research sources
- Includes a works cited page
- Generally uses effectively the conventions of written English (spelling, punctuation, grammar, sentence structure, etc.)

Learning Log

Analyzing Process and Product ■ *Stepping Back, Reviewing, Reflecting, and Evaluating*

Ask students to take a step back and to analyze both the process of their search and the actual product they generated. To do this, have them complete a quickwrite in response to these questions:

- What aspect of your process of searching and writing was the most interesting, valuable, or worthwhile?
- What do you like best about your personalized research paper in terms of its author's craft?

READING SATURATION RESEARCH PAPERS AND I-SEARCH PAPERS

Picture this: It's nearing the end of the semester, and those saturation research and/or I-search papers that you decided to assign as an experiment are about to come due. Weeks ago, you sent your students off to the library (or on to the Internet), 3-by-5 cards in hand. They have been busily collecting, reflecting on, interpreting, and constructing their versions of the data as they have figured out how to assume the persona and consciousness of another human being during a pivotal time in that person's life, or how to narrate their pursuit of an answer to an important personal question. Ahead of you, you have twenty-two or thirty-six or sixty-eight of these products to respond to.

As you face the thought of an entire weekend consumed in reliving significant moments in the lives and minds of famous historical figures, or reliving with students their process of searching and discovery about a topic they genuinely need to learn about, you find yourself actually looking forward to receiving these papers and taking them home to read and evaluate.

Although I am aware of how powerful the saturation and I-search approaches to research are, I never cease to be amazed by the richness, depth, and quality of my students' thinking and writing; and I never cease to grow as a learner as a result of my students' inquiries. Why is it that these alternative approaches to the research paper are so engaging for students and teachers alike? It strikes me that what prompts students to stretch intellectually and inspires them to produce some of their finest work is as much affective as cognitive in nature. Anthony Petrosky (1986) points out that "reflective thinking has its source in our interpretive encounters with experiences" (p. 2). The saturation research paper and the I-search paper are, indeed, interpretive encounters. Students must take what they learn from research and look within to make their own meaning. In the process, they make personal connections with the subjects of their research that often leave lasting impressions on them.

Multigenre Papers

Multigenre papers are another popular alternative to the traditional research paper. The idea for the multigenre paper came to Tom Romano (2000) when he read a book by Michael Ondaatje (1984) called *The Collected Works of Billy the Kid* in which he blended genres (songs, thumbnail character sketches, a comic book excerpt, stream of consciousness passages, newspaper articles, photographs and drawings) to capture both the factual and imaginative world of this famous outlaw. Intrigued by this approach, Romano challenged his students to write research papers in Ondaatje's multigenre style. They rose to the occasion. To prepare students to explore and write about their own topics, Romano suggests giving them an encyclopedia entry about a historical figure (for example, Count Basie) and asking them to write a summary of what they learned. Then he gives them a poem about Count Basie and again, has them write about what they learned. Students immediately recognize that the encyclopedia conveys facts while the poem goes beyond facts to create "a visceral scene" (p. 20) of the man and his art. Romano points out that each genre "does different work" (p. 22). Multigenre papers give students the opportunity to look at a topic through different lenses and to "mold the cognitive with the emotional" (p. 24).

 Inspired by a workshop Tom Romano conducted at UCI, and by reading his book *Blending Genre, Blending Style: Writing Multigenre Papers* (2001), Becky Aten, an English teacher at Valley High School, and Katie Berger, an English teacher at Sergerstrom High School, both in Santa Ana, California, designed the multigenre assignment on the companion website.

Multimedia Projects

The multigenre paper lends itself to experimenting with various forms of expression, including text messages, blogs, and other means of communication that reflect popular culture. While some teachers may want to discourage students' use of these types of texts or dismiss them as trivial or even problematic (since rules of correctness are often ignored), our perception of what constitutes literacy is constantly evolving. Underwood and Pearson (2004) note, "Many scholars and teachers have been at work trying to expand our notion of what counts as texts, extending the construct to imaginal texts, electronic texts" (p. 157). PowerPoint presentations have become a staple in most classrooms and students are usually better versed in designing web pages than their teachers are. For a good resource on multimedia projects, see *Multimedia Learning* by Richard Mayer (2001). A list of websites for videography and web design is on the companion website.

WHAT ABOUT THE TRADITIONAL RESEARCH PAPER?

A decade after Carol Jago (1989) called for the extinction of Termpapersaurus Rex, she admitted to regretting her earlier stand and stated emphatically, "We need to resuscitate the beast" (1999, p. 23). Former students who stopped by to visit Jago at Santa Monica High School in Santa Monica, California, over the years after she abandoned the "term paper," told her they felt lost when they were assigned research papers in college.

Jago's own compromise with the traditional research paper was to link the literature students were studying in her class with a research project. For example, after her students finished reading Maxine Hong Kingston's *The Woman Warrior,* she met the class in the library and asked them what was still puzzling to them about the novel. She writes,

> These tenth graders were bursting with questions about the novel; and, as fast as I could write, I charted them on a large piece of paper we could save as a reference. They wanted to know more about Chinese superstitions; they wanted to know if the attitudes toward girls had changed in contemporary China; they wondered how the combination of science and magic worked in hospitals. We filled the sheet with possible research questions—all theirs. (1997, p. 164)

Because their questions all grew out of the same text, students could collaborate on identifying good research sources, including interviewing "experts" like Chinese grandmothers. Further, the findings of each student illuminated the understanding of the entire class.

What Jago's approach has in common with the saturation research paper, the I-search, and the multigenre paper is that it fosters a personal investment on the part of the students. However, the product can be written in the third person and structured in standard essay format, with an introduction, main body, and conclusion.

Students might also benefit from rereading their saturation research or I-search papers to generate a thesis, then converting these alternative research papers into traditional research papers—making a claim at the beginning and then proceeding to support and elaborate on the claim with evidence from research.

Dealing with Plagiarism

The alternative approaches to the research paper described in this chapter discourage students from plagiarizing because the approach to research involves creative and critical thinking that can't simply be downloaded off a computer. Nevertheless, it is important to clarify for students that plagiarism, which derives from the Latin work for "kidnapping," does not occur only when another's exact words are used; it is the unacknowledged use of another's words, ideas, or information (Axelrod & Cooper, 2004). Teaching students how to paraphrase a source will help them to avoid the appearance of plagiarism. (A strategy used by Todd Huck at Santa Ana College is available on the companion website.) A useful website instructors can access to determine whether a student has plagiarized is www.plagiarism.com.

To Sum Up

If what we're after when we teach the research paper is not just transmission but transaction, then we need to find ways to engage students actively in responding interpretively to people, events, books, and ideas. The point of conducting research is not only to learn how to systematically collect, organize, and report data to establish facts and principles, but also to experience some of the excitement of hunting for and grappling with information to make personal connections and discover new insights. Therefore, it is essential, whether a class is taking an alternative approach to the research paper or writing a more traditional research paper, that students have a personal investment in their learning. Langer and Applebee (1986) remind us that *ownership* is one of the five principles of effective instructional scaffolding. If we want students to have confidence in themselves as speculative and reflective thinkers, we must encourage them to make their own meaning rather than simply to report the results of someone else's intellectual inquiry.

Learning Log Reflection

Develop an implementation plan for a research paper assignment. Your goal is to enable and encourage students to participate actively in researching a topic in which they have a genuine personal stake and from which they can make their own meaning. You can explore how you might adapt either the saturation research paper, the I-search paper, or the multigenre paper for your classroom; or consider how Carol Jago's concept of literature-based research might apply to a text or texts you are teaching. Leila Christenbury (1994) has had great success asking students to research the day of their birth—national and local events of the day, movies playing, the costs of goods and items, the weather, sports scores, car ads, reactions from family interviews, and so forth. Whatever approach you decide to take, design the assignment to engender a spirit of inquiry in students. Give your students the opportunity to experience some of the excitement of hunting for and grappling with information so they can make their own connections and discover new insights.

Sharing Our Responses to Texts as Readers and Writers and Revising Meaning

In presenting their expanded vision of literacy, authors of the NCTE/IRA Standards for the English Language Arts (1997; see Chapter 3) stress the interconnectedness of the six areas: "Learners' repertoires of words, images, and concepts grow as they read, listen, and view; new words, images, and concepts then become part of their written, spoken, and visual language systems" (p. 6). They also broaden the notion of "texts" to refer not only to written texts but to spoken and visual forms of expression and the concept of "reading" to include listening and viewing in addition to print-oriented reading. This is the listening/speaking/reading/writing/viewing connection through which individuals construct meaning. Given this integrated and expanded vision of literacy, sharing our responses to "texts" is one of the best ways to move beyond first draft understanding and to revise meaning.

THE ROLE OF LISTENING IN THE LANGUAGE ARTS CLASSROOM

Listening is "the most used and perhaps the most important of the language (and learning) arts" (Devine, 1982, p. 1). Yet even though children and adults spend as much time listening as they do reading, writing, and talking combined (Werner, 1975), listening is often taught in the classroom as a "pay attention tool" (Tompkins, 2002, p. 281) rather than as a process of thinking and constructing meaning. Gail Tompkins stresses that students need to be taught three kinds of listening: aesthetic, efferent, and critical. Each type of listening involves the use of many of the same cognitive strategies that students use when reading and writing (Pinnell & Jaggar, 1991). As was mentioned in Chapter 7, *aesthetic reading* involves focusing on the experience during the reading event for pleasure or appreciation—with the intention of being carried away by the text rather than carrying information away. Aesthetic listening involves listening not for specific information but for emotional impact. The cognitive strategies that are especially important for aesthetic listening are predicting, visualizing, making connections, revising meaning, analyzing author's craft, and summarizing. Having students listen for golden lines (memorable words and phrases) while listening to a story that is being read aloud is an example of aesthetic listening.

Efferent listening, the most common form of listening taught in school, involves understanding and retaining important facts and information. Cognitive strategies accessed when listening efferently are organizing, identifying main idea, summarizing, monitoring, and applying fix-up strategies such as asking questions and clarifying. Asking students to keep a double-entry Note Taking/Note Making log (see Chapter 6) as they are listening to an informational lecture, in which they ask questions, make connections, form interpretations, and so forth, on the note-making side, will assist them in efferent listening. Teachers also need to pause during lecturing or to put the videotape or other method of delivery on pause occasionally, to allow students to process.

Critical listening means evaluating the message that is being delivered and assessing its effectiveness, validity, appeal, and possible bias. When listening critically, students tap cognitive strategies such as visualizing, monitoring, analyzing author's craft, reflecting and relating, and evaluating. Having students listen to and evaluate television ads or media campaigns for or against specific voter issues for bias will foster students' critical listening. Students can also be taught oral language structures, such as "While I understand your point that _____, I must disagree because _____" to respond to a controversial issue being presented by a classmate. This will help to keep them focused on the argument being presented. (Adapted from Tompkins, 1997, pp. 278–325.)

THE ROLE OF SPEAKING IN THE LANGUAGE ARTS CLASSROOM

■ Talk is essential in a writing class. Writers need to share their writing and hear others, particularly a sensitive teacher, talking about it with interest, asking genuine questions it has raised. And, just as important, writers need opportunities to talk about their own writing, to elaborate on information, discuss plans, verbalize dilemmas or problems they face. From such talk student writers begin to think critically about what they're saying and how they're saying it. In turn, when students speak, teachers learn things about them that will affect instruction. Teaching and learning will not be deaf; they will be based upon oral response, with all its potential for clear, immediate communication and the development of warm rapport.

—Tom Romano

Tom Romano's (1987, p. 85) comment about the power of talk in the writing class could have been made just as easily and aptly about the power of talk in the reading class. After all, our responses to writing are the responses of readers, even if we are rereading our own text in the midst of writing it. Whether we are constructing the gist of a text inside our heads as we read or on the page as we write, sharing those texts and our responses helps us to move beyond first draft thinking and to revise meaning. Although these responses may be written as well as oral, there is much to be said for a face-to-face discussion in which readers and writers illuminate a text together by asking questions, making connections, clarifying interpretations, challenging or defending points of view, and rendering and justifying judgments.

Dudley-Marling and Searle (1991) contend that "our ability to think depends upon the many previous dialogues we have taken part in—we learn to think by participating in dialogues" (p. 60). Further, engaging in large group and especially small group dialogues can foster the "warm rapport" Romano speaks of—rapport that is essential to establishing a community of learners. Within that community, ongoing *collaboration* among students and between students and the teacher enables knowledge to be constructed and shared interactively. This, in turn, creates a sense of *ownership,* because students feel there is "room to say something of their own in their writing or in the interpretations they draw in reading" (Langer & Applebee, 1986, p. 185). These are two of the principles of effective instructional scaffolding. As students share their responses to texts, they are expanding their concept of audience and their understanding of how writer's craft impacts reader response. Research indicates that in classrooms that are more collaborative and where students frequently interact as readers and writers, students not only develop a keener awareness of audience but read and respond to their own writing with more objectivity and with more understanding of how to revise than do students in noncollaborative settings (Graves & Hansen, 1983; Newkirk, 1982).

WHAT IS A CLASS DISCUSSION?

According to Arthur Applebee (1993), when English teachers in a national survey were asked to rate the importance of a variety of specific instructional techniques in the study of literature, the single most highly rated technique was "organizing class discussions" (p. 127). Within these teachers' classrooms, regardless of the genre being taught, whole class discussion on the meaning of texts was the primary means of instruction (p. 131). But what do we mean when we label something a class discussion? When trained observers went into case study schools to see class discussions in action, they reported seeing highly structured, teacher-centered instruction in which the students were clearly dependent on the teacher's questions and engaged in few, if any, free exchanges of expression. As one observer put it, "The prevailing approach I saw was a lecture/recitation process in which the teachers, rarely sharing control, would intersperse explanations of the text with questions about what happened and why" (Applebee, 1993, p. 126). Art Costa (1991a) would call the interaction taking place in these classrooms a recitation and not a discussion. Citing the work of Dillon (1984), Costa notes that a recitation is characterized by a recurring sequence of teacher questions in which students recount what they already know or are learning through the teacher's line of questioning. In a discussion, in contrast, students explore what they do not know, usually by considering a subject from multiple points of view. As the discussion leader, the teacher's role is not to have the "right" answers for prepackaged questions already in mind but to promote conversation by "creating an atmosphere of freedom, clarity and equality" (p. 194).

Realistically, inexperienced readers and writers may need just as much teacher modeling and guided practice in sharing their responses to texts as they do in learning how to be strategic in reading and writing texts. The teacher should use question asking as a teaching tool that leads to authentic dialogue and prepares students to become independent inquirers.

THE ROLE OF QUESTION ASKING IN TEACHER-LED CLASS DISCUSSION

Costa (1991a) points out, "Teachers have awesome power. Through the careful and selective use of questions or statements, they prompt students to perform cognitive behaviors" (p. 196). In other words, thought-provoking questions on the part of the teacher can foster critical thinking in students. Research indicates that even the syntax a teacher uses to structure a question will influence not only how a student responds but also the type of thinking he or she will access (Cole & Williams, 1973). Therefore, teachers can use the questions that initiate and orchestrate a whole class discussion as a means of modeling not just how to ask questions but the habits of mind underlying those questions. If the goal of instructional scaffolding is *internalization,* the teacher's ultimate aim should be to motivate and prepare students to shape and articulate questions of their own.

Good and Brophy (1997) stress that effective questions are purposeful, clear, briefly worded, phrased in natural language, thought-provoking, and sequenced in such a way as "to help students develop connected understandings" rather than posed in isolation from one another. Many educators have drawn from Bloom and colleagues' (1956) "taxonomy of the cognitive domain" to fashion questions that call for different levels of cognitive response from students. A chart adapted by UCI Writing Project teacher/consultants from Bloom's model is presented in Chapter 3, Figure 3.3. We do not use the chart to "level" questions, as we agree with Moffett (1981) that the teacher's goal is not to prompt students to reach the top of any hierarchy but to encourage them to "play the whole range" (p. 10). But we do recognize in Bloom a rough progression from *what,* to *how,* to *why,* to *so what?* that makes sense to us and that is useful to keep in mind when posing questions and scaffolding instruction. Students will be hard pressed to evaluate a text at the *so what?* level if they have not constructed the gist and if they do not literally comprehend what is happening. But if a discussion never gets beyond marching through the plot, students never have a chance to reflect on the significance of the text. In this instance, one should legitimately ask, what then is the point?

Building on Bloom's taxonomy and Guilford's "structure of the intellect" concept (Guilford, 1967), Costa (1991) has developed a model of human intellectual functioning based on how individuals process information: (1) getting information through the senses or memory, (2) comparing that information with what we already know, (3) drawing meaningful relationships, (4) applying and transferring those relationships to hypothetical or novel situations, and (5) evaluating what we have done (p. 195). Many teachers in California use Costa's method of sequencing questions according to the stages of input, processing, and output.

Input questions draw from information, concepts, feelings, or experiences students have stored in short- or long-term memory. Cognitive behaviors accessed include listing, describing, recalling, matching, naming, counting, selecting, identifying, and completing. *Processing* questions are designed to prompt students to draw relationships between information they have generated or gathered and to see cause and effect. Processing includes cognitive objectives like synthesizing, analyzing, categorizing, explaining, classifying, comparing/contrasting, stating causality, inferring, experimenting, organizing, distinguishing, sequencing, summarizing, grouping, or making analogies. *Output* questions require students to go beyond processing information to use the concept or principle in novel or hypothetical situations. They invite students to think creatively and speculatively, to apply, and to make judgments. Output questions foster cognitive objectives like applying, imagining, speculating, generalizing, forecasting, inventing, hypothesizing, judging, and evaluating (Costa, 1991, pp. 195–196). A sample sequence of questions for Sandra Cisneros's "Eleven" (see Chapter 5) might proceed as follows:

Input

- What happens at school on Rachel's eleventh birthday with Mrs. Price and the red sweater? (Recall/Recount)
- How does what happens between Rachel and Mrs. Price make Rachel feel? (Describe)

Processing

- What does Rachel mean when she says, "What they don't understand about birthdays and what they never tell you is that when you're eleven, you're also ten, and nine, and eight, and seven, and six, and five, and four, and three, and two, and one"? (Explain/Interpret)
- Rachel compares the red sweater to "a big mountain" and a "waterfall" and associates it with the smell of cottage cheese and the look of a clown. What do the things Rachel associates the red sweater with tell you about how she perceives it and what it represents for her? (Make inferences)

Output

- If you could become Rachel and write a letter to Mrs. Price about how her treatment of you on your eleventh birthday made you feel, what would you say to her? (Imagine/Speculate)
- Do you feel that Mrs. Price's actions were justified, that she acted out of ignorance, or that she was malicious in her treatment of Rachel? Support your response with evidence from the text. (Evaluate/Justify)

Costa's point, like Good and Brophy's, is that there should be an order to the teacher's questioning that leads students to deeper levels of thinking.

Tchudi and Mitchell (1999) caution teachers not to jump immediately to the *so what?* or output questions but to try to sequence questions according to the way readers read. Their idea of scaffolding questions according to Judith Langer's (1989) stances of envisionment is especially intriguing because Langer's research on the process of understanding literature has had such a profound impact on English/language arts instruction. Langer defines an envisionment as a reader's "personal text-world embodying all she or he understands, assumes or imagines up to that point" (p. 2). This envisionment continues to evolve as the reader reads, constructs the gist, and revises meaning. A description of Langer's stances is included in Chapter 1. Sample questions that correlate with the stances are provided on the companion website. Langer would maintain that because the process of literary understanding is recursive and not linear, the stances need not necessarily proceed in a specified order to enhance meaning construction.

The idea of carefully scaffolding a sequence of teacher-generated questions may sound as if it contradicts the notion of genuine class discussion that encourages dialogue and multiple points of view. But consider your questions as a point of departure to model the habits of mind that get at the deeper meaning of a text. Keep input or recall questions to a minimum, and do your best to get out of the way once you ask a good, open-ended question. That is, if your question sparks a dialogue between students rather than generates a response directed exclusively toward you, be flexible enough to let the discussion evolve as the students converse. Your discussion questions are just that—aimed at sparking discussion. If you have achieved your goal, your questions can be put on the back burner.

Some Don'ts and Dos of Question Asking

The professional literature abounds with advice about what not to do and what to do when asking questions. Figure 11.1 lists several of the most relevant tips.

RESPONDING TO STUDENTS DURING CLASS DISCUSSION

The actions a teacher takes after a student answers a question actually influence student behavior more than what the teacher asks or tells students to do (Lowery & Marshall, 1980).

Figure 11.1   **Don'ts and Dos When Asking Questions**

Don't	Do
• Ask yes/no, one-word, or fill-in-the-blank questions. Nothing can make a discussion more deadly than questions that cannot go anywhere. Christenbury (1994) notes that this can make your classroom interaction seem like an interrogation rather than a discussion (p. 209).	• Ask open-ended questions beginning with words like *why, how,* or *to what extent?*—questions that lend themselves to multiple responses and points of view.
• Fish for a specific answer that you have in mind to a question. If you can't resist fishing, avoid casting the same line out in different phrasing if the students don't bite.	• Pay attention to students' responses rather than promoting your own. Look for the rationale behind student responses to questions. Extend the discussion by asking, "What in the text caused you to think that?"
• Ask isolated questions that are disconnected from one another and don't lead anywhere.	• Develop a sequence of scaffolded questions that lead students to a deeper level of meaning construction—even if you don't end up asking them all.
• Answer the question yourself if you don't see a hand go up immediately.	• Practice wait time so that students have an opportunity to generate thoughtful responses to your questions. Research indicates that longer wait time leads to more active participation by a larger number of students as well as to higher-quality responses (Rowe, 1986).
• Be the center of the discussion in such a way that your questions generate dialogue only between you and the person who is responding.	• Orchestrate opportunities for students to respond to classmates' comments without the teacher mediating every exchange. Asking students to turn to a partner to discuss an issue and then reconvening the whole group can also get the teacher out of center stage.
• Expect to have a meaningful, interactive discussion when students are all sitting in straight rows facing forward and able to see only the teacher.	• Arrange the seating so that students can see one another. Sitting in a circle or placing the desks in a U shape will help foster genuine dialogue.
• Call on the same four or five students repeatedly. Also, avoid focusing on only one side of the room.	• Make it a goal to engage everyone in the discussion. Interspersing talk between partners may increase the number of students who volunteer to share their ideas in the large group. Some teachers also find giving participation points an incentive.

According to Costa (1991), some teacher response behaviors tend to terminate or close down student thinking; others open up or extend student thinking.

Behaviors That Close Down Student Thinking

Criticism   When the teacher responds to a student's performance with negative words like "poor," "incorrect," or "wrong," students tend to "give up and stop thinking" (Costa, 1991, p. 200). Additionally, sarcasm and other put-downs tend to affect not just the individual student involved but the learning environment of the whole class. Christenbury (1994) suggests that responding with "I'm not sure" or "No, I don't think so" are more effective ways of handling a student response that is misguided or mistaken.

Praise   Nothing brings a class discussion to a screeching halt faster than saying "very good" or "excellent" in response to the first volunteer. Students assume that their lucky classmate got the answer the teacher was looking for and are not willing to risk a second place or wrong answer. Research on praise indicates that it tends to make students depend on others for their worth (Costa, 1991, p. 200). Costa notes that authentic praise may be useful with reluctant, unmotivated, and inexperienced learners as well as with younger students; but he cautions to use it sparingly.

Behaviors That Open Up Thinking

Silence   In her research on wait time, Mary Rowe (1986) found that the teachers she observed waited less than one second after asking a question before calling on someone to respond and often answered their own questions themselves if they did not see a hand go up immediately. But complex, open-ended questions need to be processed and reflected on. Good and Brophy (1997) suggest that a teacher communicates his or her expectations of students through silence. Observing moments of silence signifies that a question is worth pondering and that the teacher believes students are capable of generating a thoughtful response. Giving students two minutes to do some expressive writing in response to a question before initiating class discussion will also allow time for ideas to percolate.

Accepting Responses   Perhaps we should have added to the Don'ts and Dos list (Figure 11.1), don't be evaluative or judgmental; do be descriptive and accepting. An alternative to responding with "wrong" or "excellent" is to acknowledge student response, either passively or actively. In *passive acceptance,* the teacher can nod, write the student's response on the board, or respond with "Um-hmm," "That's a thought," or "I understand." These responses signal that the teacher has heard the student's message but leaves room for others to add their ideas and opinions. *Active acceptance* involves restating the student's response in different words, ("So, what you're saying is . . .") to affirm, summarize, or build on what has been said. *Empathetic acceptance* demonstrates that the teacher not only hears and understands the student's ideas but empathizes with the emotions underlying the ideas. Statements like "I had trouble relating to that part of the text too" or "I can tell by your response that you're feeling frustrated. What can I do to help clarify things?" convey to the student that the teacher is responding on an affective level. When students feel accepted, they are much more willing to take risks in the classroom (Costa, 1991, p. 202).

Clarifying   Whereas acceptance signifies that the teacher comprehends the student's response, asking for clarification means that the teacher does not fully understand and needs more information. Teachers clarify by asking students to explain their answer or describe how they arrived at their particular point of view. Phrases like "Can you elaborate on that idea?" or "Go over that one more time, please" let students know that the teacher is genuinely concerned about understanding the full meaning of their response. Research indicates that clarifying contributes to the development of students' metacognitive ability, because in talking about their thinking they became more attuned to their cognitive processes (Whimbey, 1980).

Facilitating the Acquisition of Data   When students demonstrate a need for information, the teacher's role is to facilitate the acquisition of data. This may involve directing students to source materials where they can access information themselves—or simply providing an answer to a question (such as the meaning of a word) when it is advantageous to have a quick response. The teacher can also draw students' attention to the kind of questions they are answering or asking as well as to the cognitive strategies they are using. Students also need data about their progress as learners. When the teacher provides timely feedback and orchestrates opportunities for students to obtain feedback from classmates or check their own work against a teacher's model, students' intrinsic motivation is likely to increase (Deci, 1976).

All of the positive response behaviors identified by Costa (1991, pp. 201–203) combine to create a climate in the classroom that is conducive to learning. These behaviors also model for students the types of thinking we want them to engage in as independent learners in student-centered situations.

OTHER FORMATS FOR WHOLE CLASS DISCUSSION

Although teacher-led whole class discussion is the most common means of instruction in the secondary English language arts classroom, several pedagogical strategies promote whole classroom interaction that is more student-centered.

Socratic Seminar

■   Socrates had no syllabus. He wanted Athenians to think for themselves. No wonder the local authorities were disturbed. That's the way it is with authorities. They love a syllabus and they get very upset when learning goes on without one. Inevitably, they decided that Socrates was subversive.

—Dennis Gray

As Dennis Gray (1987, p. 2) points out, Socrates believed in teaching students to think for themselves by engaging in intense dialogues about ideas, values, issues, and moral dilemmas. Rather than searching for "right" answers, in the Socratic approach individuals arrive at the truth "through doubt and systematic questioning" in conversation with others (Tredway, 1995, p. 26). Described by Mortimer Adler (1982) in his *Paideia Proposal,* Socratic seminars aim to enlarge students' understanding of intellectual complexities by focusing in depth on demanding texts. Seminars are typically offered weekly in fifty- to eighty-minute time blocks. Because the aim of the seminar is for students to interact with one another directly rather than through the teacher and to engage in an authentic dialogue, UCLA Writing Project teacher/consultant Jenée Gossard passes out these guidelines:

- Don't raise hands (it's a conversation).
- Talk to each other.
- Help each other out.
- Take a risk—be willing to think out loud; explore a new idea with the group.
- Be willing to stick with another person's idea until it becomes clear. Ask follow-up questions, locate a supporting passage from the text, offer an example, and so on.
- Refer to the text.
- Speak loudly enough that everyone can hear.
- Be respectful of the members of the group.

The Socratic seminar begins with a teacher-posed open-ended question that is designed as a springboard for discussion and is based on a brief text (or an excerpt from a text) that has been read aloud several times. For example, in Chapter 6 I told Robert Probst's (1988) story about a teacher who repeatedly and stubbornly clings to the question "What techniques does the author use to reveal character in this story?" when her students clearly want to talk about the moral complexities of cheating in C. D. B. Bryan's "So Much Unfairness of Things." The teacher's question is closed-ended and calls for recitation. Open-ended questions to initiate a seminar on this same story might include:

- Are there circumstances in a school environment in which the act of cheating can be excused?
- What are the pressures at school that cause students to cheat?
- If a school has a strict honor code calling for expulsion for cheating, should this penalty be enforced equally no matter what the circumstances surrounding the cheating are?

In one model of the Socratic seminar, half of the students are seated in an inner circle and the other half sit in an outer circle. As the members of the inner circle discuss the opening question—which, in turn, should prompt additional questions, requests for clarification, examples, elaborations, and so on—the members of the outer circle are charged with observing the group dynamics. In another model, the whole class sits in the circle with the exception of five to eight observers. In either case, the observers need to be clear about their task and held accountable in some way or their interest will wane. Margaret Metzger (1998) gives her students in the outer circle instructions such as the following:

- Take notes on the major questions that are asked.
- Take notes on the differences between boys and girls in the seminar.
- Take notes on the group's reactions to the loudest and the quietest members.
- Figure out what derails and what propels the discussion. (p. 242)

Metzger has also gone a step farther by asking the members of the outer circle to identify reading strategies they see students in the inner circle using, such as visualizing or making connections. This is an effective way to help students internalize the cognitive strategies effective readers use.

Grand Conversation

A grand conversation (Eeds & Wells, 1989) is very much like a Socratic seminar, except that the teacher's role in initiating the dialogue is to ask a question like "Who would like to begin?" "What did you think?" or "Who would like to share?" (Tompkins, 1997). In other words, it is the students' responsibility to come to the circle with questions. When Pat Clark and I implemented a grand conversation on Amy Tan's "The Moon Lady" (see Chapter 8), we asked students to write down their interpretive questions on 3-by-5 cards ahead of time. Interpretive questions have no right or wrong answer and usually begin with "Why," "How," or "What if." Students asked questions such as the following:

- Why must girls be quiet while boys can be noisy and run and play?
- What was the thing that squeezed Ying-ying and tossed her in the boat?
- Why is woman yin, the darkness within, and man yang, bright truth?
- Why did the Moon Lady turn into a man?

As in the Socratic seminar, the teacher, acting as a senior member of the group, may want to guide the discussion subtly by asking for elaboration or clarification or by encouraging students to respond to what has been said.

Hot Seat

As described in Chapter 7, the hot seat activity enables students to use their imagination to dialogue with a "character" from the text. Usually the teacher models first by role-playing a character—perhaps even arriving in costume, as Sue Ellen Gold did when she entered her eleventh grade British Literature class at Irvine High School in Irvine, California, in the guise of Alfred, Lord Tennyson's Mariana. (She used Rossetti's painting of Mariana for fashion tips.) The students were then encouraged to ask "Mariana" any questions that they had about the character, setting, plot, and symbolism of the narrative poem. For instance:

- Why have you shut yourself up in that stuffy old house?
- What old faces glimmered through the doors?
- What's with the poplar tree? Why is it the only green thing in the landscape?
- If your life is so dreary, why don't you do something about it instead of moaning, "Oh God, that I were dead"?

Students may also wish to give advice to the person in the hot seat. To encourage all students to interact with the character, the teacher can give participation points. After the teacher's modeling, other students can volunteer to take the hot seat. With *To Kill a Mockingbird,* for example, students could role-play a different character each day.

Talk Show

If the teacher has already modeled the hot seat role, there will be no need to model how talk show works. After all, students have many episodes of *Oprah* or *The Ellen Degeneres Show* under their belts and understand the talk show format. (Students may also have internalized some of the behavior of *The Jerry Springer Show,* so it is important to set firm ground rules about what types of language and actions are suitable for the classroom.) In talk show, as de-scribed in Chapter 7, students usually work in collaborative groups to create the talk show script and to designate the host and guest characters. All members of the class then engage in querying the panelists as groups take turns role-playing in front of the audience. Sometimes the teacher may give students a point of departure for the talk show by supplying an opening and/or closing script. See the sample talk show script for *To Kill a Mockingbird* on the com-panion website for Chapter 7.

Other times, students in the talk show are responsible for supplying an opening and closing script, and students in the audience must turn in questions they have prepared. After the talk show, the whole class can debrief about the talk show process and the perspectives shared during the dialogue between the "characters" and the audience. I have observed stu-dents who are otherwise reluctant to participate—or uninterested—in class discussions rise to the occasion in the more imaginative hot seat and talk show discussion formats.

SMALL GROUP FORMATS FOR SHARING RESPONSES TO TEXTS

As I have often emphasized, research indicates that when students interact frequently as read-ers and writers in collaborative groups, they not only develop a keener understanding of audi-ence and an appreciation of how writer's craft influences reader response but also can respond to and revise their own writing with more objectivity. Enabling students to participate in small groups as readers of texts by professional writers provides important practice in looking at and discussing texts closely; it also paves the way for talking about student-generated texts with more precision. Leila Christenbury (1994) makes the point that students need to read and respond to a range of texts produced by more and less experienced writers. She ponders, "I often wonder what effect it has on students to read only and see only the polished, analyzed, credentialed work of the great whom we know can write: Annie Dillard, Lewis Tomas, Henry David Thoreau, Martin Luther King, Jr. Letting students see and work with the writing of those like themselves who are learning to write can be a heartening experience" (p. 185).

A variety of small group discussion formats can promote cooperate learning among students and facilitate the active participation of every member of the class. Although small groups take the teacher out of center stage, he or she will still need to set the stage for what transpires—by establishing a clear purpose, providing whatever level of structure the task calls for, modeling if necessary, roaming from group to group as a coach, occasionally sitting in as a group member, and troubleshooting any problems that arise.

Reciprocal Teaching

Reciprocal teaching is a highly structured approach to involving students in making meaning collaboratively as they read and discuss a text in small increments. Each small group has someone who serves in the role of the teacher. Palincsar and Brown (1985) advocate "flexible use of a repertoire of comprehension-fostering and monitoring activities" (p. 157). In the reciprocal teaching model, these researchers identify four complementary strategies: *summarizing,* or self-review; *question generating,* or self-testing; *predicting,* or setting the stage for further reading; and *demanding clarity,* or noting when a breakdown in comprehension has occurred (p. 158).

The term *reciprocal* refers to the interchange that takes place as the teacher and students engage in a dialogue about a text, using these four cognitive strategies. Initially, the teacher models and orchestrates the strategies. In time, the teacher's aim is to back out of the process and enable a selected student in each small group to act in the teacher's role. A model of how the teacher orchestrates discussion using reciprocal teaching, using the story "Two Were Left" by Hugh B. Cave, is included in Chapter 6.

Literature Circles

Harvey Daniels (1994) remarks, "For too long we've treated school reading as a solitary, internal, somewhat lonely act. We haven't provided opportunities for kids just to read, just to react, to behave like normal real-world readers who read to express, effuse, emote, think, and weigh during and after reading. We've asked kids to bottle up their responses and in doing so we have blocked the pathway that leads upward from responding to analyzing and evaluating" (p. 9). Although reciprocal teaching makes strides toward having students interact with each other as they read, the nature of that interaction is intended to be teacher-centered—even when a student is performing the role of the teacher. That is, one person is orchestrating the dialogue as others respond to the questions he or she poses. In contrast, literature circles engage every member of a small group as an equal and active partner in "sharing ideas and constructing interpretations" (p. 10). Further, reciprocal teaching can be a "slow and tedious procedure," as Palincsar and Brown acknowledge (1985, p. 154); but students in literature circles can set their own pace in terms of how much they wish to read in a day or week, because they are reading independently, often for homework, rather than in class, silently or aloud, as a group. Daniels points out that the role of the teacher is to "*not teach,* at least in the traditional sense of the term" (p. 25), but rather to serve as a facilitator: to provide good books to choose from, help groups to form, visit and observe group meetings, become a fellow reader, orchestrate sharing sessions, confer with students who are struggling, and assess the process (p. 26).

Although it was Harvey Daniels who popularized literature circles, Daniels credits Karen Smith, a fifth-grade teacher at Lowell School in Phoenix, Arizona, as the source for the ideas and structures for this collaborative instructional strategy. Daniels describes literature circles as follows:

Literature circles are small, temporary discussion groups who have chosen to read the same story, poem, article, or book. While reading each group-determined portion of the text (either in or outside of class), each member prepares to take specific responsibilities in the upcoming discussion, and everyone comes to the group with the notes needed to help perform that job. The circles have regular meetings, with discussion roles rotating each session. When they finish a book, the circle members plan a way to share highlights of their reading with the wider community; then they trade members with other finishing groups, select more reading, and move into a new cycle. Once readers can successfully conduct their own wide-range, self sustaining discussions, formal discussion roles may be dropped. (p.13)

Groups are formed and function according to the following key principles:

1. Students *choose* their own reading materials.
2. *Small, temporary groups* are formed, based on book choice.
3. Different groups read *different books*.
4. Groups meet on a *regular, predictable schedule* to discuss their reading.
5. Kids use written or drawn *notes* to guide both their reading and their discussions.
6. Discussion *topics come from the students*.
7. Group meetings aim to be *open, natural conversations about books*, so personal connections, digressions, and open-ended questions are welcome.
8. In newly forming groups, students play a rotating assortment of task roles.
9. The teacher serves as a *facilitator*, not a group member or instructor.
10. Evaluation is by *teacher observation and student self-evaluation*.
11. A spirit of *playfulness and fun* pervades the room.
12. When books are finished, *readers share with their classmates,* and then *new groups form* around new reading choices. (p. 18)

Each member of the literature circle assumes a role—Questioner, Literary Luminary, Illustrator, Connector, Summarizer, Word Wizard, Scene Setter, or Researcher. The roles and the role sheets, "which are designed to enact key principles of collaborative learning and to initiate a genuine, kid-led, self-sustaining discussion" (p. 75), are an ideal way for students to practice the cognitive strategies used by experienced readers and writers. Four roles I have found particularly productive are those of the Questioner, which prompts students to tap prior knowledge, ask questions, make predictions, form preliminary interpretations, revise meaning, and evaluate; the Literary Luminary, which leads students to analyze text closely, seek validation for interpretations, and analyze author's craft; the Connector, which calls for the students to make connections between this text and their own lives or the world outside or between this text and other literary works; and the Illustrator, which fosters visualization as the artist shares his or her rendering of a key scene without comment and the group members speculate about the meaning of the visual and its connection to the themes in the text. The role sheets for these four roles are available on the companion website. Although he does not use the term, Daniels (1994) clearly perceives the role sheets as an instructional scaffold that provides support and structure for inexperienced readers but which the teacher should gradually withdraw as students can generate meaningful conversations on their own. (Note: As an alternative to the literature circle role sheets, teachers may want to implement the cognitive strategies booklets I designed that are described in Chapter 2 and available on the companion website for Chapter 2.)

Dialogue with a Text

Influenced by the work of Louise Rosenblatt (1983), Robert Probst (1988) defines the process of meaning construction as "the transaction between active minds and the words on the page. . . . [Meaning] is created, formed, shaped, by readers in the act of reading, and thus it is *their meaning*" (p. 34). Probst builds on the principles of reader response espoused by Rosenblatt in envisioning and developing a strategy for assisting students in engaging in the kind of dialogue that will yield a rich literary experience rather than a recitation of what they think the teacher wants to hear. His dialogue with a text strategy, described in Chapter 6, involves providing partners or small groups of students with copies of a booklet in which a series of questions "encourage reflection on several aspects of the act of reading" (p. 35).

TURNING READING GROUPS INTO WRITING GROUPS

Providing students with ongoing and varied opportunities to share their responses to the texts of professional writers as well as helping students have meaningful discussions about those texts can also serve as scaffolding for writing groups. That is, the strategies used in reading groups to discuss the great works heighten and refine the abilities of students to talk about one another's writing. As noted in Chapter 7, Jack Thomson (1993) writes that English/language arts educators "have expected our students to walk through the gallery of great writers and admire what they see, but not to touch the works or create any of their own" (p. 132). Students need to see their own writing as being worthy of close textual analysis and discussion, whether they have written a personal narrative or an analytical essay. They also need to see the audience for their writing as extending beyond the teacher. James Moffett (1981) makes the important point that "the teacher alone cannot process the quantity of writing students need to do to be good at it": The teacher can become a "bottleneck—an awful thought for any serious teacher" (p. 8) if he or she is the only source of feedback.

Introducing Students to Writing Groups

When I explain to my students at UCI that the reason we are participating in writing groups is to get feedback on how our words communicate to other readers at the rough draft stage and that our goal is to find ways to improve the final draft of every student's paper, my students often respond with puzzled looks. They are so used to competing with one another that the idea of cooperating is somewhat alien. They're not sure, at first, if they want to help others improve their writing—and, consequently, their grades. They also don't trust the capabilities of their peers to give valid feedback. The teacher is the ultimate arbiter, after all. However, I find that they warm up to the concept of writing groups rather quickly. I make it a point to convene groups frequently, even for the sharing of nongraded quickwrites in class. First and foremost, I want students to experience the satisfaction of sharing their responses to others' texts and receiving responses to their own. As noted previously, this collaboration will affect their own objectivity about their work and will give them tools to revise their writing—whether they write for pleasure or for evaluation.

Although students have already had plenty of practice responding to the work of professional writers through whole class discussion and reading groups, it is important to enable them to practice responding to less accomplished writing before convening writing groups. Occasionally I have written a rough draft of something right along with the class and passed out copies for my students to respond to. I might read the piece and invite the whole class to respond, or I might ask for three or four volunteers to come up front and model a writing group with me in fishbowl fashion. Students are comfortable making "I liked the way you . . ." comments, but you'll find they are a bit reluctant to provide constructive criticism to the teacher. You may need to ask for ideas about how to improve a specific passage or phrase you had trouble with.

STRATEGIES TO GUIDE PEER RESPONSE

Finding the Golden Lines

Because sharing their work in a writing group is actually quite risky for most students, I normally introduce the concept of finding the golden lines as a positive, nonthreatening way to get started. This strategy, which I learned from Bay Area Writing Project teacher/consultant Bob Tierney, involves reading the draft with a yellow highlighter and marking the words or phrases that are especially memorable, vivid, thought-provoking, or touching. As readers explain why they highlighted the lines they did, we can talk about effective elements of author's craft. I make it a practice to routinely read all student writing I collect, whether for evaluation or not, with a yellow highlighter and to find something in each paper to mark. Even the experienced students I teach at the university always look for the golden lines I've highlighted when their writing is returned. Even if the highlighting is not accompanied by a detailed explanation, it's an encouraging graphic signal of what is noteworthy in their writing.

The Elbow Method

Once students are comfortable with finding the golden lines in each other's texts and making what we call "kind comments," we are ready to practice more specific feedback techniques. Although many of the small group reading strategies described earlier in this chapter can also be used to discuss student writing, my preference is to use the guidelines Peter Elbow developed in *Writing without Teachers* (1973) and further elaborated in *Writing with Power* (1986). Elbow stresses that "Learning to make use of a class that depends heavily on students' responses to each other's writing is a struggle" (1997, p. 197). To create the commitment necessary to make writing groups work, it is important to meet frequently and to keep the same members in a group over time. Students also need training in how to convey their responses to one another's writing. Without some guidance and specific response strategies, students may play it safe and stick with superficial comments such as "I liked it" and "It was pretty good." Elbow offers four strategies for interacting in writing groups:

Pointing. Like finding golden lines, pointing involves indicating which words or phrases stick in one's mind as being especially vivid or memorable. However, it also includes sharing those sections of the text that don't ring true or seem weak or ineffective.

Summarizing. Respondents can summarize by zeroing in on the key ideas or main feelings—what Elbow (1997) calls "centers of gravity" (p. 199). They can also summarize the text in a single sentence, choose one word that best summarizes it, or choose a word that is not in the text but that captures its essence.

Telling. When readers tell the writer what happened in their heads or hearts as they read, or, as Elbow describes it, give "movies" of their minds (p. 198), they recount their experience of the text, usually in the form of a story: what happened first as they were reading; what happened next; what they understood; what was confusing; what touched them emotionally; where they lost interest; and so forth. Elbow cautions that in telling what happened, the reader needs to avoid departing too much from the text and drifting off into personal narrative.

Showing. Showing is difficult for student writers until they feel comfortable with one another in the group. In showing, readers compare the writing to something else—music, weather, motion, color, a body part (heart, head, hands, etc.), an animal, a type of art, and so forth. Elbow notes that "Telling is like looking inside your head to see what you can report. Showing is like installing a window in the top of your head and then taking a bow so the writers can see for themselves" (1997, p. 201).

The companion website contains a handout I adapted from Elbow's guidelines that my students use when meeting in writing groups. I stress that students should always make "I" statements when they comment on their peers' writing. Some of Elbow's best advice is that there is no right or wrong in writing; there is only what communicates and what doesn't. And what does or doesn't communicate to each reader will be subjective. Therefore, writers should receive the feedback and weigh it seriously but not be "tyrannized" by it (p. 201). (Note: Elbow and Belanoff [2000] have a handy and concise monograph entitled *Sharing and Responding* that builds on Elbow's earlier work.)

Job Cards

If students are working on prompted writing, or if they are all writing a piece in the same genre, it can be useful to give students specific attributes of author's craft to look for and respond to. Job cards are somewhat like Harvey Daniels's (1994) role sheets for literature circles, in that each member of the group has a different task as a respondent. These cards need to be tailored to fit the type of writing students are engaged in. For an example of job cards, see Sharing Activity 1 in the memory snapshot paper demonstration lesson in Chapter 9.

Read-Around Groups

Developed by Jenée Gossard (1997), read-around groups enable students to read a sampling of the drafts of the whole class while discussing their merits in small groups. Detailed instructions for read-arounds appear in Sharing Activity 1 in the saturation research paper demonstration lesson in Chapter 10.

I have found that read-around groups are particularly useful for making visible for students all the options a writer has in drafting a paper. For example, in sharing opening scenes of the saturation research paper (see Chapter 10), students saw their classmates using flashbacks, beginning with dialogue, starting in the middle of the action, and using other attention-getting techniques they themselves hadn't considered. Because the read-around occurs at the draft stage or earlier, students have an opportunity to go back and apply new ideas to their own writing.

Response Forms and Sharing Sheets

The peer response strategies I have discussed so far involve providing relatively immediate feedback after having heard a writer's paper read aloud and rereading it silently, or simply after reading it silently. But sometimes peer responders need time to read a classmate's paper silently and to talk it over among themselves before dialoguing with the author. In those instances it is helpful to develop some sort of response form on which students can record their thoughts and feelings. This form can then be used as a point of departure for discussion and will also serve as a written record for the writer. Some mechanism for sharing responses to texts is provided in each of the demonstration lessons in this book.

Sometimes the type of writing dictates the form of the response (e.g., a letter response form for letter writing); other times, the scoring rubric for the writing will play a role in how the response form is developed. The companion website contains numerous examples of response forms and sharing sheets for the demonstration lessons that are highlighted in this book.

HOW PEER RESPONSE HELPS STUDENTS TO REVISE MEANING

Sheridan Blau (1997) notes that the act of revising meaning is both affective and cognitive:

> If we reflect on the kind of thinking that is entailed in revising, in any of its modes or stages—that is, in the early stage of revising to discover one's ideas, in the later stage of amending a text to suit the needs of one's readers, or even in the stage of copy editing and proofreading—we will see that two apparently opposite acts of mind are required. These are *commitment* and *detachment*. (p. 240)

Affectively, students need to have a commitment to the completion of the writing task. This requires two "underlying acts of will—one finding value in the completion of the writing task and the other, consisting of faith (despite feelings to the contrary) in one's capacity to meet the challenge of the task" (p. 241). At the same time, writers need cognitive detachment, the ability to step back and view their work objectively with an eye to clarifying their meaning and adjusting their discourse to the needs of readers. Peer response groups help foster both the commitment and the detachment writers need in order to develop competence in revision. By participating in reading and especially in writing groups, students move from competition to cooperation as they learn to collaborate on the construction of meaning as a community of learners. Constructive, empathetic feedback from other students, and from the teacher, can convince a student that his or her work is valuable and hence worthy of reshaping; and it can encourage the writer to stick with the often difficult process of revision. It can also help the writer to develop a sense of readership—that is, to see what in his or her text needs to be refashioned for the sake of a reader.

Linda Flower (1990) would describe this aspect of revision as learning to convert one's text from writer-based prose to reader-based prose. Donald Murray (1982a) has identified two classes of revision—internal and external. As writers generate, review, and amend their own emerging texts in the act of discovering what they want to say, they revise internally, for themselves. In this stage, when constructing the gist and revising meaning as they go along, writers often use a style of writing Flower calls writer-based prose. In writer-based prose a writer writes to himself or herself, often associatively, and often in code words. The difference between inexperienced and experienced writers is that inexperienced writers cannot distinguish writer-based prose from reader-based prose, whereas experienced writers use writer-based prose only strategically—to explore and express an idea. In other words, they may purposely "ignore the reader, but only for a while" (Flower, 1990, p. 149). Experienced writers know how to transform texts from writer-based prose to reader-based prose and then move to what Murray would call external revision. But inexperienced writers have difficulty making this shift; in addition, they don't fully understand or appreciate what it means to revise. Peer response groups can help enable a writer to assume the perspective of a reader, identify the gaps in his or her thinking and writing, and truly revise meaning at the semantic as well as at the lexical level.

WHAT IS REVISION?

Murray (1982a) also points out that revision is the "least researched, least examined, least understood and—usually—least taught" (p. 72) stage of the writing process. Students often confuse revision with proofreading for correctness and assume that copying over a paper neatly or printing a second copy of a paper on the computer after running it through spellcheck will suffice. But revision is an ongoing process of discovering and refining meaning that one chooses to engage in. It begins with "the writer's evaluative review of either written text, mental text, or a writing plan" (Flower, Hayes, et al., 1986, p. 22) and his or her decision to make the text communicate better. Research shows that inexperienced writers tend to see revision as having to do with lexical as opposed to semantic or conceptual matters (Sommers, 1980). That is, they see revision as a rewording activity. As one student said, "I read what I have written and I cross out a word and put another word in, a more decent word or a better word" (Sommers, 1980, p. 381). Experienced writers, on the other hand, view revision more globally and take a more whole-text approach to reseeing and reshaping their argument. In the words of an experienced writer, "It is a matter of looking at the kernel of what I have written, the content, and then thinking about it, responding to it, making decisions, and actually restructuring it" (p. 383).

THE ROLE OF THE TEACHER IN REVISING MEANING

As a senior member of the community of learners, the teacher, even more than the peer group, can provide modeling, feedback, structure, and instruction that will help students to revise their concept of revision. Nancie Atwell (1998) remarked, "I'm no longer willing to withhold suggestions and directions from my kids when I can help them solve a problem, do something they've never done before, produce stunning writing, and ultimately, become more independent of me" (p. 21). The teacher has not only a unique opportunity but also an obligation to show students what the process of constructing the gist of a piece of writing and then revising meaning looks like—to provide structure, guidance, and strategies to help students transition from writer-based to reader-based prose.

Modeling through Think-Alouds

In a cognitive apprentice model of learning (Brown, Collins, & Duguid, 1989), the teacher takes on the tutorial task of introducing the apprentice to the "tricks of the trade while both are engaged in authentic learning tasks" (Tierney & Pearson, 1998, p. 85). In his ninth-grade English Class at Irvine High School in Irvine, California, Jerry Judd (Huck & Judd, 1992) often composes aloud on the overhead while his students are working on their own pieces at their desks. They have the option of listening in on his process or tuning him out. Judd explains,

> The cardinal rule in the thinking/writing aloud demonstration is that students can listen in but cannot interrupt the teacher's process with questions or comments. As they sit back in their chairs, you can almost hear the students saying to themselves, *Let's see how he gets himself out of this one.* And, after observing you in this process, the students will come to see you not just as the teacher, but as a fellow writer—as someone who shares the same frustrations and triumphs as they do. (p. 410)

Nancie Atwell (1998) would call this kind of modeling taking off the top of your head (p. 332). As you let students in on how you generate ideas, the questions you ask yourself as you compose, what happens when you get stuck, the process you go through as you reread a chunk of text and then revise what you have written to make it clearer or more vivid, they begin to create a working model for themselves of what effective writers do, a model they can imitate. Borrowing from Jerome Bruner (1986), Atwell calls the understandings that emerge as a more experienced learner demonstrates for a less experienced learner "hand-over" (p. 10)—the ultimate goal of which is *internalization* (Langer & Applebee, 1986). Modeling the strategies an experienced writer uses to craft a text can expand a student's sense of the writer's options and what it means to compose.

Feedback

The teacher also plays a major role as a provider of both oral and written feedback on student writing. In either case, the timing of the feedback is crucial. A comment from Nancie Atwell (1998) will probably strike a chord with most English teachers: "Any English teacher who has ever spent a Sunday writing comments on a class set of compositions has harbored the unsettling suspicion that she is shouting down a hole" (p. 220). If those copious comments you have labored over are on final drafts of student papers, you are probably doing just that. It is unrealistic to expect that students will take to heart, retain, and apply to the next writing task feedback on writing they perceive as finished. James Moffett (1981) reminds us that providing helpful feedback to the student writer "in mid-task is the key" (p. 22). Feedback on work in progress is much more likely to be acted on by the writer and to improve the final product. Further, if the student has received ample constructive response from peers and from the teacher at the draft stage, the final draft should not necessarily require more than a score. Given the realities of time constraints and student workload, teachers need to allocate their time in ways that will have maximum impact on their students.

Oral Conferences Many teachers choose to provide their feedback at the draft stage in an oral one-on-one conference with the student. Donald Murray (1982b) suggests that such meetings should be short and frequent. He has developed a repertoire of questions that will facilitate his interaction with the students, such as:

> What did you learn from this piece of writing?
> What do you intend to do in the next draft?
> What surprised you in the draft?
> What do you like best in a piece of writing?
> What are you going to do next?
> What questions do you have of me? (p. 159)

However, because Murray always invites the student to begin the conference, he often has no need to pose these questions. Often just asking "How's it going?" or "How can I help you?" is enough to get the ball rolling.

Written Feedback Although I conference with my students, I prefer to read and comment on their papers before we meet. This is obviously a more time- and labor-intensive method than reading the paper on the spot or asking the student to read it aloud. Nevertheless, I feel it is important for students to receive a written response to their texts. In general, when I provide written feedback on student writing, I try to do the following:

- Treat any paper I respond to as work in progress, even if it is a final draft. (My students have an open invitation to revise final drafts.)

- Make "I" statements like "I got confused here"; "I could really relate to this part"; "I see what you mean."
- Focus my comments so as not to overwhelm the student. For example, if we've been working on showing, not telling, I may focus my comments on the quality of descriptive writing and elaboration.
- Avoid making comments like "Awkward," which simply leave students baffled. If they had been able to "hear" awkwardness, they would have written differently in the first place.
- Reward the student for what he or she has done well. Golden lines; phrases like "Well put," "Wow," and "Great line"; and even happy faces adorn the pages of student writing after I've perused it.
- Give direct suggestions: "How about adding some dialogue here?" "Convert some of these bland verbs into action verbs." "A flashback might work here." "Great commentary." "Move this up in the paper and make it your thesis." Some teachers may feel this type of feedback is too directive. But I find that students appreciate receiving specific advice even if they don't always take it.
- Look for patterns in errors and mark them judiciously. Usually I do not do a student's editing work for him or her. I'll simply say, "Find the run-on sentence in this paragraph." However, if I see a recurring error that's worth zeroing in on, such as neglecting to double a consonant when adding "ing," I'll explain either in writing or in person.
- Close with words of encouragement that make a student want to revise: "A very promising first draft. I can't wait to see the revised version." "This paper has lots of potential. Adding dialogue will bring the characters to life and make your narrative even more vivid." Although praise may be detrimental in a whole group discussion (Costa, 1991), I find that a little praise or encouragement shared individually with a student helps strengthen his or her commitment to sticking with the task. And some of my more directive suggestions help students take a step back and develop the detachment they need in order to experience their papers through another reader's perspective.

 The two student essays on "The Stolen Party" that are discussed in Chapter 9 are included on the companion website for Chapter 11 with my marginal notes and commentary as an illustration of how one might give feedback to the writer of a less than successful paper to motivate the student to reshape the paper—and to a more experienced writer to challenge him or her to keep thinking and revising.

Electronic Feedback   Please see Chapter 12 for a discussion of online writing assessment. Teachers in the UCI Writing Project have found that the use of electronic writing assessment motivates students to revise.

PROVIDING STRUCTURE AND DIRECT INSTRUCTION ON STRATEGIES FOR REVISING MEANING

Langer and Applebee's (1986) research indicates that most students write little and that when they do write, "the writing usually involves a first-and-final draft of a page or less, produced in one class period" (p. 187). Along with frequent opportunities to revise, the modeling of what revision looks like, and feedback on students' initial drafts, teachers need to provide structure for specific revision activities and guide students through the activities so that they can apply them in other contexts.

Breaking the Task of Drafting and Redrafting into Manageable Chunks

Although this may not sound like a strategy for revising meaning, I have found that breaking the task of drafting and redrafting into manageable chunks with deadlines for sharing can have a dramatic impact on students' willingness to revise—and on the quality of their revisions. In my class, students submit a kernel of an idea; then draft an opening section on which they receive feedback; then write a rough draft, again shared with others; and finally complete a draft for evaluation, which can be revised for extra credit. I tell my students that good writing is like soup: It usually gets better if you put it on simmer. Research on the revising strategies of twelfth graders corroborates my finding. According to Lillian Bridwell (1980), "The longer a student was able to explore his or her ideas, the more likely he or she was to add, delete, or substitute extended segments of discourse" (p. 210).

Minilessons

Teachers need to provide students with direct instruction in the form of minilessons to help them practice the three key operations of revision—adding to, deleting from, or rearranging text for clarity, for impact, or for style. These minilessons may be introduced at the prewriting, planning, drafting, or revising stage of the composing process but should be reinforced as the writer is revising meaning to meet the needs of a reader. The companion website includes a chart of all the minilessons in this book that are aimed at helping students improve their writing to make a text communicate better. And because a properly edited paper also contributes to the clarity of the message, some editing minilessons are also included on the chart.

WIRMIs and Believing and Doubting

Earlier in this chapter, we explored a variety of formats for responding to texts and strategies for peer group and teacher responses that facilitate revision. Two specific strategies for helping students to revise meaning at the conceptual level are WIRMI statements and Elbow's (1973) "believing and doubting" approach.

WIRMI Statements   At the rough draft stage, before a student submits his or her draft to another student or to the teacher, it is helpful to write a WIRMI statement (Flower & Hayes, 1981b). In a WIRMI (What I Really Mean Is) statement, the writer tries to capture in a sentence or two the central message he or she intends to convey in the draft. The reader then reads the text without the benefit of seeing the writer's WIRMI statement, and writes back his or her own "What You Really Meant to Say Was" statement summarizing the message the reader received from the writer. A sample set of WIRMIs:

■   **What I Really Mean Is** . . .

More than anything I've read in the field of psychology, the study of birth order has given me some insight into the interactions of siblings within the family and how birth order affects their later lives. This awareness has helped me understand myself better.

■   **What You Really Meant to Say Was** . . .

What I got was that birth order theory has helped you understand why you are different from your older sister and also why your firstborn mom tends to favor her over you. What I wonder is what you will do with what you've learned. Do you plan to talk to your mom about this?

WIRMIs can be eye-opening for the writer. They can confirm that the writer has indeed communicated his or her message effectively, help the writer see where he or she needs to convert writer-based prose into reader-based prose, and identify areas that need elaboration or questions the writing has raised in the reader's mind.

Believing and Doubting   Developed by Peter Elbow (1973), the believing and doubting strategy is especially useful for revising writing in which the author makes an assertion or takes a stand. The idea is to look at the thesis or claim the writer makes from two perspectives—affirming what one finds to be valid while at the same time looking for counterarguments. It is important that the same reader be both believer and doubter. Elbow stresses that the reader should start with believing and look for good ideas or examples to back up the writer's point of view. Doubting should be expressed only when the writing process is farther along and the writer is ready for a reader with a critical eye. This gives the writer an opportunity to beef up his or her premise or to directly address and refute counterarguments within the text. For example, I might say to the student who wrote paper number 50142, the well-written essay on "The Stolen Party" in Chapter 9:

■   I believe that Rosaura does, indeed, realize that she cannot cross class lines, but I doubt that "Rosaura's ego was destroyed." At the end of the story, her eyes have a "cold, clear look." This doesn't strike me as defeat, however devastating the incident was to her at the time. What do you think?

The student can then weigh this feedback, leave his or her assertion as is, add more supporting detail, or amend what has been said.

Color-Coding: Visual Feedback for Revising for Meaning

In Chapter 9, I described a process for revising interpretive essays that involves pairing students and having them code the sentences in their essays as either yellow (plot summary), green (evidence and quotations), or blue (interpretation/commentary). This had been one of the most successful revising strategies used by UCI Writing Project teachers because it enables students to visually see if they are simply retelling the story or offering the thoughtful, thorough interpretation called for in California's new High School Exit Exam. The best way students can practice is to write an on-demand essay to a prompt, color-code that essay, revise their timed writing into a multiple-draft essay, and then write another on-demand essay to a similar prompt to determine their growth. The companion website includes a matched pre/post on-demand reading/writing assessment, prompts, scoring guide, and two color-coded on-demand essays written by the same sixth-grade English language learner in October and again in May. The student's progress is a testimony to the power of the color-coding approach.

REVISING FOR STYLE

In addition to revising for meaning and clarity, students may also want to revise their papers to enhance their style and the aesthetic impact of their words. Several of the minilessons in this book and on the companion website address how to make writing more vivid. Two helpful strategies help students develop more interesting, mature, and fluid sentence patterns: sentence combining and copy–change.

Sentence Combining

Sentence combining is a strategy built on the generative principle that every compound or complex sentence is derived from two or more simple sentences. In *Errors and Expectations,* Mina Shaughnessy (1977) points out,

> The practice of consciously transforming sentences from simple to complex structures helps the student cope with complexity in much the same way as finger exercises in piano or bar exercises in ballet enable performers to work out specific kinds of coordination that must be virtually habitual before the performer is free to interpret or execute a total composition. (p. 77)

Sentence combining provides these practice exercises at the bar to improve students' syntactic fluency, broaden their sense of sentence options, and enhance their style. Many sentence-combining exercises are taught out of workbooks, but the teacher can also select exercises thematically related to subject matter that is relevant to his or her class. Consider, for example, the sentence-combining exercise here, which was developed by Bill Strong (1984) for use in conjunction with C. D. B. Bryan's short story "So Much Unfairness of Things." The story concerns a boy who gets caught for cheating.

Prompt →

Value Judgment

1.1 Carol was working on her test.	5.1 Everyone had made a pledge.
1.2 Sue slipped her a note.	5.2 The pledge was not to cheat.
2.1 She unfolded the paper carefully.	6.1 Carol didn't want to go back on her word.
2.2 She didn't want her teacher to see.	6.2 Sue was her best friend.
3.1 The note asked for help on a question.	7.1 Time was running out.
3.2 The question was important.	7.2 She had to make up her mind.
4.1 Carol looked down at her paper.	8.1 Her mouth felt dry.
4.2 She thought about the class's honor system.	8.2 Her mouth felt tight.

Source: From *Sentence Combining: A Composing Book,* 3rd ed., by William Strong. Copyright © 1994 by McGraw-Hill. Reproduced with permission of The McGraw-Hill Companies and William Strong.

The teacher can also create his or her own sentence-combining exercises by taking a sentence or passage from a work of literature and breaking it down. Students work in groups to reformulate the sentence or sentences, share their collaborative efforts on the overhead to see different groups' versions of the exercise, then compare their prose with the author's.

In his meta-analysis of research on composition, George Hillocks (1984) found that sentence combining is twice as effective in improving student writing as freewriting and that practice in sentence combining does have transfer effect on student writing. As a result of practice building more complex sentences from simpler ones, students wrote with greater syntactic fluency and higher quality (Hillocks, 1987, p. 79). Hillocks suggests that sentence combining also may have "a positive effective on revision" (p. 79). To reinforce the impact of sentence combining, teachers can direct students to find sections in their own rough drafts where the sentences are short and choppy and to use sentence combining to create longer, more complex sentences. Requiring students to combine at least two or three sentences in a revised draft and to attach the original draft and underline the sentences they combined will ensure that students apply this strategy to their own texts.

Using Copy–Change for Stylistic Imitation

In Chapter 3, I discussed a prediction and style game, Beat the Author, in which groups of students anticipate what will happen next in a literary selection and compose the next chunk of text in the author's style. Each group's entry will be placed in competition with the work of the real author, and a group will "beat the author" if their selection receives the most votes as the authentic/original piece of writing. So it behooves students to imitate the author; and this, in turn, enhances their command of style. Another practice activity that expands students' command of author's craft and can enhance revision is copy–change. At the UCI Writing Project we were introduced to the concept of copy–change by former NCTE president Stephen Dunning (Dunning & Stafford, 1992). He suggests that students will first benefit from actually copying down lines of poetry or a prose passage to understand kinesthetically how a writer manipulates language. Then, after studying the structure of the language, students practice author's craft by imitating the writing, structure for structure, but plugging in their own words to fit their own topic, occasionally borrowing words directly from the original. Dunning and Stafford (1992) remark, "We imitate not so much to be like someone else as *to learn what she/he has already learned. When we know enough about how a poem's made, we are free to put our own stamp on things*" (p. 86).

Dunning starts out by giving students individual sentences to copy–change, such as the following:

- If he saw the winter birds scuffling in the cinders, if he felt this was the dawn of a new day, he didn't let on. (Philip Levine)
- Red, white and blue banners; crowds of people cheering and booing; candidates with tired eyes, smiling and shaking hand after hand: this is a political rally. (Joan Didion)
- He was one of the barefooted, shambling, overage, shaggy-haired, snaggle-toothed, dull-eyed cracker boys who always came to school in overalls and never took a bath. (George Garrett)

After students practice copy–changing sentences, they can move to longer passages of text by authors such as Twain, Hemingway, or Faulkner. I find that although students can copy–change sentences structure for structure, they often have difficulty trying to imitate a longer passage of text so closely. Therefore, I tell students to capture the flavor of the author's style but not to get bogged down in imitating word for word. Provided below is a copy–change exercise from UCI teaching credential candidate Grace Lim, which happens to be about her process as a writer.

■   It is a rule of nature that taking a day off school work sets a person back at least a week. I had been keeping up with my daily readings and reflections and letting everything else slide. With the mounting pressure of pending assignments, I made myself sit still for the entire morning, concentrating on the writing tasks before me. With over ten years experience, I still considered myself new enough at writing. I had written enough papers to fill filing cabinets, yet beginning each blank page still challenged me. I knew that with each paper I wrote the process should become pretty well mechanical—but it didn't. I struggled with the need to complete my assignments, and the need to pause, to marvel at the challenge of written expression before I continued on to perfect my writing.

—By Grace Lim with thanks to Jane Hamilton

Notice that Grace concludes her piece "with thanks to." Dunning stresses that the apprentice writer should always acknowledge the work of the master he or she is building on. Here's the model Grace worked from: a passage from *A Map of the World* by Jane Hamilton.

■ It is a rule of nature that taking a day off on a farm sets a person back at least a week. I had been keeping up with morning and evening chores and letting everything else slide. In the early hours, on Monday before the girls woke, I mustered the energy to kill the lamb that was half-dead. With five years experience I still considered myself new enough at killing. I was clumsy. I stunned the lamb with a blow to its head and then quickly slit its throat. I had killed the lambs and the chickens for food, and occasionally I had to kill something as a kindness. I knew that each time I slaughtered an animal I thought less about it, and that if I let it, the process might become pretty well mechanical. I struggled between wanting to numbly get on with the job, and the need to pause, to offer thanks to the breathing animal, to wonder at its essence before I knocked the life out of it.

One of the most ambitious and successful copy–change projects I've observed occurs in Sue Willett's (1992) eleventh-grade American Literature class at Tesoro High School in Mission Viejo, California. In order to help students internalize Walt Whitman's style and learn the art of writing free verse, Willett invites her students to write an autobiographical narrative poem in imitation of Whitman's "There Was a Child Went Forth." Students are to copy the first four lines of the poem verbatim:

There was a child went forth every day,
And the first object he look'd upon, that object he became,
And that object became part of him for the day or a certain part of the day,
Or for many years or stretching cycles of years.

Starting with line 5, students are to substitute their experience for Whitman's but to follow his style, structure for structure, culminating with the line, "These became part of that child who went forth every day, and who now goes, and will always go forth every day." At the revising stage, Willett provides students with a revision frame guide to see if they have retained Whitman's form and asks them to share their content, in partners, section by section, to determine if their own personal voice comes through and if they have made the poem their own. A copy of "There Was a Child Went Forth," the revision frame guide, and a student model are available on the companion website. (For more on sentence combining and sentence imitation, see also Teaching Sentence Sense and Sentence Craft in Chapter 12.)

THE IMPACT OF COMPUTERS ON THE PROCESS OF REVISING MEANING

The recent *NAEP 1998 Writing Report Card for the Nation and the States* (Greenwald et al., 1999) found that students who reported using computers for writing drafts and final versions of papers once or twice a month had higher scores on the NAEP writing assessment than those who reported never or hardly ever using computers (p. xiv). I believe that the advent of computers has made revision more palatable to many students who were reluctant to make substantive changes in their writing because of the time and the motor skills involved in recopying or typing something over. Now, with the press of a key, students can add, delete, or rearrange at will. As Jim Burke (1999) observes, "Students are willing to revise more since there is less effort involved in doing so" (p. 117). He also finds that students are much more likely to act on his comments and suggestions when they have access to the computer. Indeed, research indicates that when composing on the computer, students took a more integrated approach to producing and revising texts and appeared more willing to make significant changes while the text was in progress rather than waiting until an entire draft was produced (Golderg, Russell, & Cook, 2002). In a meta-analysis of research studies from 1992 to 2002 of twenty-six studies comparing K–12 students writing with computers versus pencil and paper, researchers found that "on average, students who use computers to learn to write are not only more engaged and motivated in their writing, but they produce written work that is of greater length and higher quality" (Goldberg, Russell, & Cook, 2002).

REVISING INDEPENDENTLY: QUESTIONS TO CONSIDER

Ultimately the teacher's goal is to equip students with the means to respond to their own texts and to revise independently throughout the writing process with the reader in mind. A list of questions students can use to reflect on their process and their product at each stage of composing is included on the companion website.

To Sum Up

Whether we are constructing the gist of a text inside our heads as we read or on the page as we write, sharing our texts and our responses to texts helps us to move beyond first draft thinking and to revise meaning. Research indicates that when students collaborate frequently as readers and writers in small groups, they not only develop a keener sense of audience and an appreciation of how writer's craft influences reader response, but also can respond to and revise their own writing with more objectivity. In so doing, they are exercising their listening and speaking skills, which are also forms of constructing meaning. Guided practice in small reading response groups can provide instructional scaffolding for interaction in writing groups. As students give and receive feedback on one another's writing, it helps them develop the commitment to stick with the task of refining their writing and the detachment to step back and view their words from the perspective of a reader. As the senior member in the community of learners and the most experienced reader and writer in the class, the teacher can play a crucial role in facilitating student response and revision. Through modeling, feedback, and direct instruction, the teacher makes visible what it is to share responses to texts and to revise meaning. This visibility helps students develop confidence and competence as they provide feedback on their classmates' writing and revise their own texts.

Learning Log Reflection

Try using the Elbow method (1973) to respond to this chapter:

1. Begin by *pointing* to specific sections of the chapter that you found especially memorable or perplexing.
2. Then see if you can *summarize* three to four big ideas presented in this chapter.
3. If you have the opportunity to meet in a small group, *tell* about your reactions to some of the strategies for responding to texts or revising meaning discussed in the chapter. What guided practice activities might you implement in your own classroom?
4. Finally, see if you can *show* by comparing the process of composing (including revision) to something else—such as gardening, cooking, sculpture, painting, playing an instrument, dance, or embarking on a journey.

Correctness Can Be Creative

Errorwocky

'Twas class time, and the eager youths
    Did squirm and wriggle in their seats:
All ready were their fresh ideas,
    And their paper was clean and neat.

"Beware the Error beast, my friends!
    The jaws that bite, the claws that rend!
Beware the Run-on bird, and shun
    The frumious frag(a)ment."

They took their eraser tips in hand;
    Long time the maxome foe they sought—
Then rested they from the Error hunt,
    And wrote awhile in thought.

And, as in uffish thought they wrote,
    The Error beast, with eyes of flame,
Came whiffling through their ballpoint pens,
    And burbled as it came!

One, two! One, two! And back and forth
    The eraser tips went snicker-snack!
They left it dead, and to their teach,
    They went galumphing back.

"And have you slain the Error beast?
    You'll pass this year, victorious youths!
O frabjous day! Callooh! Callay!"
    She chortled then, in truth.

'Twas class time, and the stunted youths
    Did slouch and huddle in their seats;
All shortened were their sentences,
    And their words had met defeat.

—Connie Weaver

Reprinted from *Teaching Grammar in Context* by Constance Weaver.
Copyright © 1996 by Constance Weaver. Published by Heinemann,
a division of Reed Elsevier Inc., Portsmouth, NH. All rights reserved.

I must admit that I was one of those kids who slouched and huddled in their seats when it came time for lessons on grammar and the hunt for error. As those drill and kill worksheets were passed down the row, I'd dash off the final bits of daily gossip in my note to Linda, a friend who sat in the same seat during third period, and tape my missive to the underside of the desk. Although I was an avid reader who had an innate sense of how language should sound, the logic of grammar eluded me. My branches on those tree diagrams often sprouted in wildly erroneous directions. Then, one day, Miss Singleton passed out a copy of Lewis Carroll's "Jabberwocky" and read the poem aloud to us with great seriousness of expression. (A copy of "Jabberwocky" is available on the companion website.) She then challenged us to identify the parts of speech in the nonsense poem and to create our own poem in imitation of the original. I dove into the task.

■   "'Twas brillig, and the slithy toves / Did gyre and gimble in the wabe." OK, "'Twas brillig." It was. . . .Could be a time of year or a time of day; so it must be a noun. Of course, it could be an adjective like hot or sunny. But my bet's on the noun. So, like, "'Twas Christmas, and the . . . slithy toves." OK, adjective . . . noun. You can tell slithy is an adjective because lots of adjectives end in "y" like "happy" or "busy" and, of course, it's modifying a noun. "'Twas Christmas, and the frantic shoppers" did "gyre and gimble," verb and verb, "in the wabe," preposition, article, noun. "Did push and shove in the mall."

I was off and running, my mind racing with ideas. As I sift through what are mostly murky remembrances of my encounters with grammar, this memory stands out vividly and still brings a smile to my face. It was fun; it took ingenuity; it inspired me to take ownership. Although identifying the parts of speech and constructing the imitation might have been even more engaging and informative if we had collaborated on this activity in small groups, I still tip my hat to Miss Singleton. She was ahead of her time. Imagine my surprise and delight when I turned a page in *Teaching Grammar in Context* (1996) to discover Constance Weaver's rendition of "Errorwocky."

THE ROLE OF AFFECT IN THE TEACHING AND LEARNING OF GRAMMAR

In Chapter 4 we saw that affect is just as critical a dimension of learning as cognition. In fact, attention, the affective ability of concentrating the mind, is a prerequisite to the acquisition of all cognitive objectives. Citing the research of psychologist Mihaly Csikszentimihaly, who studied the affective responses of people as they participated in a variety of daily activities, Brosnahan and Neuleib (1995) maintain that "humans need more than anything to be engaged with significant tasks" and that "learning as well as meaningful experience declines" when "schools ignore this need or set up circumstances that occupy rather than engage" (p. 207). The way schools occupy rather than engage students in the study of grammar is a case in point. Brosnahan and Neuleib write,

> In our own research we have observed junior high school teachers who move quickly through a classroom hour in which they and their collaboratively grouped students discussed stories and wrote about them with warmth and enthusiasm. We have then stayed on to the next class hour to observe the same teachers grimly ask students to open their grammar books and do the exercises on relative clauses or subject–verb agreement up and down the aisles for the entire class period. We have asked those teachers why they do not teach grammar in the same exciting and engaging way that they teach literature. The answers vary from "I hate teaching grammar" to "the school administration demands that we do it this way." (p. 207)

Why is it that even English teachers find the teaching of grammar unappealing? Perhaps the answer lies lurking within Weaver's poem. If both teachers and students alike perceive the purpose of grammar instruction as the conquest of the "Error beast" (Weaver, 1996, p. 100), then the focus in the classroom is always on ferreting out what is wrong with writing rather than on celebrating what communicates.

Many years ago at UCI, the composition program used to have a policy called the deep six. In essence, as soon as a student made six errors—in sentence structure, usage, punctuation, spelling, and so on—he or she was "deep-sixed"; that is, failed the composition. The result was that students became so intimidated by the error beast that they wrote as little and as simplistically as possible. Gone were the big ideas and the risk taking. As with the students in "Errorwocky," "All shortened were their sentences / And their words had met defeat." The composition faculty wisely deep-sixed the deep six rule when they realized the negative impact it was having on student writing. But many teachers still take this kind of punitive approach. Art Costa (1991a) points out that when a teacher responds to a student's performance during class discussion with negative words like "poor," "incorrect," or "wrong," students tend to "give up and stop thinking" (p. 200). The same is true for written communication. The expression "bleeding all over the paper" is trite for a reason. When students repeatedly receive what for them is confirmation, via the dread red pen, that they cannot write, they begin to believe it. No wonder these students not only fail to pay attention during the rote-level grammar exercises the teacher grimly assigns but also do what they can to avoid writing altogether.

Brosnahan and Neuleib stress that "fear of punishment must be replaced with an anticipation of success and enjoyment if future teachers are to be successful in their grammar classrooms" (p. 212). This chapter will offer a selection of strategies and activities teachers have implemented in the classroom to help students turn an affective corner and see that correctness can be creative. The point of the guided practice is both to involve students in the study of grammar in ways that are engaging and memorable and to help students apply what they are learning about how the language works to their own writing.

THE GREAT GRAMMAR DEBATE

Harry Noden (1999) remarks, "Discussing grammar in the teachers' lounge is a little like stepping in between two opposing 350-pound NFL linemen just after the ball is snapped" (p. vii). On the one side there's Mrs. McLarken, a thirty-three-year veteran, proudly flying the flag of grammar, who thinks college professors "don't have a clue what public teaching is all about" and that research is a lot of "hokey" (p. vii). On the opposite side of the field is Delaney, a relatively young teacher who champions "research-based" teaching and who believes that "teaching traditional grammar takes valuable time away from writing and reading" (p. vii). This familiar battle has been waged both in teachers' lounges and in the research community for more than half a century. Constance Weaver (1996) points out that as long ago as 1936, the Curriculum Commission of the National Council of Teachers of English recommended that "all teaching of grammar separate from the manipulation of sentences be discontinued . . . since every scientific attempt to prove that knowledge of grammar is useful has failed" (as quoted in H. A. Greene, 1950, p. 392). In 1963 another landmark study, by Braddock, Lloyd-Jones, and Schoer, came to a similar conclusion:

> In view of the widespread agreement of research studies based upon many types of students and teachers, the conclusion can be stated in strong and unqualified terms: the teaching of formal grammar has a negligible or, because it usually displaces some instruction and practice in actual composition, even a harmful effect on the improvement of writing. (pp. 37–38)

George Hillocks's (1986) often-quoted reflections in his 1986 study *Research on Written Composition* are equally adamant:

> In short, the findings of research on the composing process give us no reason to expect the study of grammar or mechanics to have any substantial effect on the writing process or on writing ability as reflected in the quality of written products. Experimental studies show that they have little or none. (p. 228)

> School boards, administrators, and teachers who impose the systematic study of traditional grammar on their students over lengthy periods of time in the name of teaching writing do them a gross disservice which should not be tolerated by anyone concerned with the effective teaching of good writing. (p. 248)

Clearly, the preponderance of evidence in the Great Grammar Debate falls on the side of our young teacher, Delaney, rather than with Mrs. McLarken; so why does the debate rage on? Researchers in the 1990s noted that the majority of the studies on which the above conclusions were based focused on the teaching of grammar in isolation, apart from students' own writing (Hunter & Wallace, 1995; Noguchi, 1991; Weaver, 1996). Many argue, as Rei Noguchi does, "Just because formal instruction in grammar proves generally unproductive in improving writing does not necessarily mean that we should discard all aspects of grammar instruction" (p. 3).

WHY TEACH GRAMMAR?

So why teach grammar? Before we consider this question, it may be useful to try to define the term *grammar.* I say *try* because the term means different things to different people. To parents, grammar is a collection of Nevers—"Never Split an Infinitive, Never End a Sentence with a Preposition, Never Begin One with *And* or *But,* Never Use a Double Negative or the Pronouns *I* and *You* . . . etc." (Brodie, 1996, p. 77)—all culled from the dos and don'ts they learned when they were in school. Daniel and Murphy (1995) define one component of grammar as a "set of conventions collectively known as usage" (p. 226)—the conscious application of rules that govern written discourse.

For both practical and political reasons it is important that we attend to this aspect of grammar in the classroom. On the political side, R. Baird Shuman (1995) notes that "because the public is a harsh judge of surface errors in writing, teachers and school administrators would be remiss if they did not encourage students to write in ways that avoid the displeasure and reproach of those whose judgments about such matters lead them to reach erroneous conclusions about people based upon such judgments" (p. 116). To drive this point home to his students, Harry Noden (1999) created the Grammar Income Test. This test from the "University of Mottsburgh" purports to predict with 80 percent accuracy the future income of an individual based on his or her ability to determine whether twenty sentences are grammatically correct. (A copy of the Grammar Income Test is available on the companion website.) Only after students take the test does Noden confess that there is no University of Mottsburgh and that the income prediction is fabricated. Nevertheless, he stresses that people really *do* assume that others are unintelligent, illiterate, or incompetent if they make grammatical errors. For both pragmatic and academic reasons, it is our job as teachers to acquaint students with the conventions of grammar and to help them become competent editors of their own writing. It is also important for political reasons that teachers help students acquire the conventions of standard written English—because, like it or not, the performance of teachers is often assessed by how well their students have mastered applied grammar.

Research suggests, however, that the mastery of applied grammar, which deals with the correctness and appropriateness of usage, has little to do with grammar in a sophisticated sense (Shuman, 1995, p. 115). At this more complex and more fundamental level, grammar is "the unconscious command of syntax that enables us to understand and speak the language" (Weaver, 1996, p. 2). Daniel and Murphy (1995) point out that in terms of this second definition of grammar, "the linguistic truth is that all normal humans have full control of the grammar they use every day" (p. 226). Although we may unconsciously know the constructions of mature syntax and can converse fluently, we may not have enough command of the syntax of written discourse to communicate as effectively as we might want. In her essay "Why I Write," Joan Didion (1976/1992) remarks,

> Grammar is the piano I play by ear, since I seem to have been out of school the year the rules were mentioned. All I know about grammar is its infinite power. To shift the structure of a sentence alters the meaning of that sentence, as definitely and inflexibly as the position of the camera alters the meaning of the object photographed. Many people know about the camera angles now, but not so many know about sentences. The arrangement of the words matters, and the arrangement can be found in the picture in your mind. (p. 139)

Students who are widely read may have acquired the linguistic structures to play the grammar piano by ear, as the research of Stephen Krashen (1993) indicates. But students who are less well read may lack the ability to manipulate syntax consciously to evoke style. Therefore, in the same way that it is essential for the teacher to make visible for inexperienced readers and writers the cognitive strategies that experienced readers and writers use when they make meaning from and with texts, it is important for the teacher to

- make students consciously, linguistically aware of the grammatical repertoire they already possess;
- provide them with a vocabulary to talk about writing from a technical standpoint;
- help them understand how sentences are constructed and empower them to manipulate language and to make stylistic choices;
- expand their awareness of the grammatical and stylistic options that are available to them as writers; and
- assist students in the revision and editing of their writing. (Noguchi, 1991; Ross, 1995; Shuman, 1995; and Weaver, 1996)

WHEN, WHAT, AND HOW TO TEACH GRAMMAR

When

Most researchers agree with Constance Weaver (1996) that teachers should "teach needed terms, structures, and skills when writers need them, ideally when they are ready to revise at the sentence level or to edit" (p. 141). However, we know that mature writers who play the grammar piano by ear have mastered the conventions of grammar as well as syntactical structures and have rendered them automatic to a certain extent. These writers don't wait until they have completed the act of composing to revise or to edit but make some changes as they go along. This is why Nancie Atwell (1998) wants her students not to perceive creativity and correctness as two completely separate stages of the writing process but to pay some attention to the conventions as they compose (p. 250). If students are writing a memoir that calls for rich descriptive language, action, and dialogue, it makes more sense to provide a minilesson on the uses of adjectives, similes and metaphors, strong verbs, or the conventions of dialogue form before the students begin to draft. However, these aspects of author's craft should be revisited during revision. Note that I used the term *author's craft*; therein may lie the distinction. If a teacher is focusing on the use of grammar or mechanics to further author's craft, it may be appropriate to provide guided practice early on in the writing process. But if the goal is editing for the correction of errors only, it is best to wait until the composing—the meaning construction—is complete and the goal is proofreading for correctness rather than revising meaning for clarity or polish.

What

There seems to be almost as much disagreement about what to teach as there is about whether to teach grammar at all. One scholar will see no point in teaching the parts of speech; another sees this as an absolute necessity. One scholar steadfastly maintains that students must know what a predicate is; another feels the concept isn't particularly useful. Nevertheless, there does seem to be general agreement that the amount of grammar taught should be minimized and that grammar should be addressed as a tool for writing improvement rather than as an academic subject (Noguchi, 1991, p. 17). Constance Weaver's (1996) "minimum of grammar for maximum benefits" (pp. 142–144) zeroes in on five key grammatical areas:

1. Teaching concepts of subject, verb, sentence, clause, phrase, and related concepts for editing
2. Teaching style through sentence combining and sentence generating
3. Teaching sentence sense and style through manipulation of syntactic elements
4. Teaching the power of dialects and the dialects of power
5. Teaching punctuation and mechanics for convention, clarity, and style

Rei Noguchi's (1991) minimalist approach is to clarify what differentiates a sentence from a nonsentence by teaching the concepts of subject, verb, and modifier. This more limited approach to grammar will, he feels, help students "make grammar connect better to writing" (p. 34).

How

The *Reading/Language Arts Framework for California Public Schools* (O'Malley, 1999), calls for second graders to be able to identify and correctly use various parts of speech, including nouns and verbs, in writing and speaking (p. 79). Because the framework requires an increasing command and control of grammar at each grade level, and because standardized tests include items related to writing conventions, teachers will continue to teach concepts like the parts of speech over and over and over again, regardless of whether scholars feel this is an effective instructional practice. So, given that most students can recite definitions like "a noun is a word that refers to a person, place, or thing" in their sleep, why is it that grammar doesn't seem to stick? My colleague Catherine D'Aoust, codirector of the UCI Writing Project, would maintain that the reason students have such a limited grasp of grammar, despite being bombarded with exercises year in and year out, has to do less with *what* is being taught than with *how* instruction is delivered. That is, teachers provide students with abstract definitions to memorize rather than connecting their instruction with what students intuitively know about the language. In her view, what will help students move from short-term rote learning to long-term acquisition is a foundation, or what she calls "mental Velcro," to which to anchor these abstract concepts. For her, the context for grammar instruction should be the texts that students are reading and writing.

Let us return to Brosnahan and Neuleib's (1995) observation that instruction that tends to occupy rather than engage is not memorable. To establish mental Velcro and help new concepts to stick, we need learning experiences that are both affectively and cognitively engaging. As Brosnahan and Neuleib point out, "Grammar both at its theoretical and at its applied level in editing and usage tends to be cerebral and unemotional" (p. 206) and boring. But teaching grammar can actually be—dare I say it—fun! Teachers need to experiment with new approaches to traditional grammar instruction so that the pursuit of style and correctness can indeed be a creative endeavor.

When researchers talk about grammar taught in isolation, they are referring to grammar taught from worksheets disconnected from students' own reading and writing. But grammar is also traditionally taught in another kind of isolation—the isolation of one student from another. It is often considered "cheating" to collaborate on those drill-and-kill worksheets. When students work as an interpretive community, however, they construct knowledge together. Weaver (1996) suggests that a constructivist approach to learning is "especially relevant for the teaching of grammar" (p. 26) because when students receive guidance that enables them to form their own hypotheses about concepts by analyzing a wide range of examples that are appropriate for their level of readiness, they *own* their own learning and hence retain it better than when concepts are simply handed to them. In short, the principles of instructional scaffolding—*ownership, appropriateness, structure, collaboration,* and *internalization*—(Langer & Applebee, 1986) all apply as much to the teaching of grammar as they do to the broader arenas of reading and writing instruction.

PEDAGOGICAL STRATEGIES AND ACTIVITIES TO MAKE GRAMMAR MEMORABLE

Provided on the pages that follow is a selection of pedagogical strategies and classroom lessons, minilessons, and activities designed to make grammar instruction memorable, engaging, and creative. By *strategy* I mean a deliberate teacher-selected pedagogical approach aimed at achieving a specific outcome—for example, making a particular grammatical concept accessible to students. Strategies are not lesson dependent; they can be applied in different contexts. An *activity,* on the other hand, has a more limited scope. Using these definitions, graphic grammar is a spatial strategy for helping students grasp grammatical concepts, whereas *Cloudy with a Chance of Meatballs* and the Dada poem are lessons/activities that operationalize the graphic grammar strategy. This strategy and several others draw from Gardner's theory of multiple intelligences (1983) and take spatial, kinesthetic, musical, logical–mathematical, and interpersonal and intrapersonal routes to enhancing linguistic intelligence. (See Chapter 5 for a discussion of MI theory.) Some of the activities described include steps that call for students to apply the concept directly to their own writing. Others foster linguistic awareness, building a cumulative bridge to the students' own texts.

Graphic Grammar: A Spatial Approach to Teaching Parts of Speech

I have learned a great deal about how to make grammatical concepts accessible to students by observing Viviana Bro's second-grade classroom at Concordia Elementary School in San Clemente, California. After immersing her students in a variety of poems, stories, and songs about spring, Bro brought her students up to the rug and invited them to generate as many words as they could think of that related to spring. The next day she returned with all of *their* words neatly written on 3-by-5 cards and introduced three labels: adjectives—which she also called *describing words;* nouns—which she also called *naming words;* and verbs—which she also called *doing or action words.* She then created three categories on the board, each designated by a specific color: for example, red for adjectives, blue for nouns, and green for verbs. One by one she drew the cards out of a basket and asked for volunteers to tape them to the board under the appropriate color and label. When a child was confused, as when one boy could not decide if "warm" was an adjective or a noun, she engaged the class in a discussion about how we use the word *warm*—warm sun, warm day, and so on—and then asked whether *warm* is a word that describes or names.

Once their word bank was established, the students turned to a pocket chart where their teacher had introduced the first lines of a yet-to-be-composed class poem followed by a color-coded pattern:

I know it's spring when

| Red | Blue | Green |

| Red | Blue | Green |

She explained that words from the red, blue, and green categories on the board could be used to fill in the pattern. Each set of red, blue, and green words would make a sentence, and the important thing was that it had to make sense. The children eagerly volunteered to select a word from the board and place it in the appropriate spot in the pocket chart:

I know it's spring when
Blue birds chirp
Yellow tulips bloom
Green grass grow

"Green grass grow?" As she looked at their puzzled faces, Bro said, "Now that sounds funny, doesn't it? What would we have to do to make it make sense?" "Add an s," the students chimed in.

Once the class poem was complete, the children set to work on creating their own individual poems. They could borrow any words they wished to use from the class word bank, but Bro encouraged them to choose new words of their own as well. After drafting, conferencing individually with the teacher, and meeting with a partner, the students were ready to return to the rug to share their creations. Many went far beyond the pattern:

I know it's spring when
Colorful rainbows fill the sky
Blue sunglasses cover your eyes
Somebody wears pink shorts at the beach.

"Somebody wears pink shorts at the beach?" All contributions, including the line from the divergent thinker who departed from the frame, received a rousing round of applause. Students scurried back to their desks for the editing stage—which they accomplished in partners, as their poems were to become part of a class anthology they would get to take home and show to their parents.

I have described Viviana Bro's lesson at length not only because it inspired me but because it is such a masterful example of instructional scaffolding. She created a rich literature base, provided structure at a level that was appropriate for her students, enabled them to practice as a whole group, engendered their ownership, and then empowered them to work independently with the support of a partner and of the teacher, who was always "on call." If second graders could do this, I thought, then perhaps this approach would strike a chord with secondary students.

Cloudy with a Chance of Meatballs

Although I was inspired by Viviana Bro's lesson, I could not picture middle school boys writing poems about spring with great enthusiasm. So I adopted as my text a whimsical story called *Cloudy with a Chance of Meatballs* by Judi Barrett (1982), about a town called Chewandswallow where "it never rained rain. It never snowed snow. And it never blew just wind. It rained things like soup and juice. It snowed mashed potatoes and green peas. And sometimes the wind blew in storms of hamburgers." With the goal of getting students to review and internalize the parts of speech and to purposefully use strong verbs in their own writing, I designed the following lesson steps.

Step 1   Ask students to tell you names of types of weather. Write these on the board in blue. For example:

rain	hail
snow	twister
sunshine	hurricane
tornado	

Occasionally, students will say "rainy," "warm," "stormy," and so on. Do not add these words to the list but write them down on the side. When the students are done volunteering, ask them why you didn't accept these words. Secondary students will recognize that they are adjectives and don't fit with the list in blue, which is composed of nouns. Ask someone to remind the class what nouns do. Write "nouns" and "naming words" above the list.

Step 2   Next, ask for words that describe weather and ask what part of speech "describing words" are. Write these all in red.

Step 3   Now, what about the "doing words"—the verbs? Ask students what they would say if they were assigned to report on what the weather did. Write these in green. Students may come up with some verbs of being as well as doing verbs; you may wish to point these out. Additionally, it is helpful to mention that sometimes the same word will change parts of speech depending on where it is in the sentence, as in "rainy," "rain," and "rained."

Steps 4 and 5   Ask for a list of words that modify verbs and tell how the action is done—that is, adverbs. Most adverbs that serve this function end in *ly*. But adverbs can also tell where, when, and to what extent. Record in brown the adverbs people can think of that relate to weather. Then turn to prepositions, those small words that show how one thing relates to something else. The key part of the word in *preposition* is *position;* prepositions indicate position, especially in time (amid, during, throughout), or space (below, next, over, under). Prepositions are always part of a phrase that ends in a noun form or a pronoun. Prepositional phrases can tell how, when, where, under what conditions, to what extent, which one, what kind, and how many. (Remember that any words that tell how, when, etc., that are not followed by a noun or pronoun are adverbs.) Ask students to brainstorm a list of prepositional phrases relating to weather, and record them in orange. The board might now look something like this:

Adjectives (describing words)	Nouns (naming words)	Verbs (doing words)	Adverbs (how/ly words)	Prepositional phrases (position words)
dense	rain	pelted	menacingly	throughout California
blustery	snow	pummeled	loudly	into the night
torrential	sunshine	ripped	ferociously	over the mountains
ferocious	tornado	poured	powerfully	by the river
gray	hail	surged	quickly	during the storm
rainy	twister	erupted	fiercely	across the plains
sunny	hurricane	rained	mercilessly	along the gulf stream

Step 6   Create a sentence from the categories on the board.

      adj.   noun   verb   adv.   prep   noun

Torrential rain poured mercilessly throughout California.

Step 7   Ask students to look back at the verbs on the list and see what they notice about them. Most likely, someone will mention that the majority of the verbs are strong action words. (In fact, many reporters use sports metaphors to talk about weather so their word choices pack a punch.) Ask students if they think a reporter could get an article on the weather onto the front page of the *Los Angeles Times* with the lead below:

> Mendota, Calif.—The San Joaquin River overflowed on Saturday and spilled over farm levees, putting towns along its length in danger as state officials got ready for new flooding.

Ask students to work in partners to underline the verbs in green, then replace the weak or bland verbs with stronger, more attention-getting ones. After students volunteer their rewrites, pass out a copy of the real *L.A. Times* lead and ask students to work in partners to color-code the entire sentence.

Los Angeles Times
January 5, 1997

San Joaquin River Endangers Town as Crisis Builds

Mendota, Calif.—The placid San Joaquin River erupted in a rampage Saturday that burst through farm levees and threatened towns along its length as state disaster officials braced for new flooding.

Students can compare the real lead with the "watered-down" version and discuss why the authentic lead made the front page. Note how words like "placid," "rampage," and "disaster" also lend a sense of urgency to the sentence.

Step 8   Now ask students to volunteer a couple of their favorite foods. Write a whimsical sentence such as

■   A dense fog of whipped cream with intermittent bursts of maraschino cherry hail pelted passersby in Munchtown last Thursday.

Step 9   Read *Cloudy with a Chance of Meatballs* aloud to the class.

Step 10   Ask students to bring in food items the next day (such as uncooked macaroni, red hots, Hershey Kisses, spaghetti, lemon drops, baby marshmallows) that can be glued. (No broccoli, please.) They should then form groups of four; one member of each group needs to volunteer to bring a shoe box, gift box, or other type of box top to class.

Step 11   The initial goal of each student foursome is to construct a diorama that can serve as a kinesthetic illustration for a newspaper article about an imaginary town being assaulted by consumable weather. They must give their town a food-related name, create a one-sentence caption to accompany the diorama, and color-code the parts of speech in the caption before pasting it to the box top. Before they get started, you might want to have students read the excerpt from *Cloudy with a Chance of Meatballs* that is available on the companion website and color-code the parts of speech for practice. You might also take time to generate some weather phrases with the class—"partly cloudy with," "low fog throughout," "intermittent showers followed by," and the like. A diorama and caption from a group of my teaching credential candidates is depicted in Figure 12.1.

Step 12   If you choose to take the lesson further, students can collaborate on a whimsical newspaper article to accompany their caption. This will give them a more sustained opportunity to deliberately employ parts of speech in writing. A prompt for the complete activity is available on the companion website. Some teachers may want students to color-code their entire articles instead of just the caption for the diorama.

Step 13   At this point students can select a piece of their own writing and color-code it to analyze how they use parts of speech in their writing (as will be illustrated in the demonstration lesson on the Dada poem); or they can just focus more narrowly on converting weak or bland verbs into stronger, more interesting verbs in a text they are drafting or revising.

Former students (now teachers) who have tried out this lesson tell me that the kids not only have fun (and, yes, some do eat the leftover candy with their sticky, glue-stained

Figure 12.1   Weather Diorama

fingers) but also *get it*! In other words, the knowledge of the parts of speech sticks, just as it did with me when Miss Singleton challenged me with the "Jabberwocky" assignment. They have also applied the concept to teaching more sophisticated works of literature, creating columns of words and writing color-coded sentences about *Beowulf,* for example.

The *Cloudy with a Chance of Meatballs* lesson takes a spatial approach to grammar but engages students' kinesthetic intelligence when they construct their dioramas. One book that takes a kinesthetic approach to teaching the parts of speech is *The Amazing Pop-Up Grammar Book* (Maizels & Petty, 1996). Each page in the book invites students to interact with the concept being taught by opening doors, turning dials, sliding flaps, pulling tabs, and so on. Of the pages of the book, the one that my teaching credential students have applied in the secondary classroom is the page on prepositions. As you turn the pages, a garden unfolds, complete with a gate that opens, a pool to swim in, a bridge to cross, a fence to go over, a hole to go through, and a tree to climb. In front of this garden is a doghouse where you can find Pip, the dog, attached by a long string. The point is to take Pip for a walk in the garden to experience what prepositions do. During their student teaching my students have engaged their second language learners in English Language Development classes in creating and displaying their own preposition pop-up books. Students pick their own subject and object (airplane/cloud, rabbit/hill, teenager/mall, etc.). They enjoy the creative aspect of the task and internalize prepositions along the way. A nice extension would be to have these learners visit an elementary school and use their pop-up books to teach this grammatical concept to a "little buddy."

 The companion website contains four additional activities related to teaching parts of speech. The titles: Teaching Parts of Speech and Alliteration through *Animalia;* Adjective Picture; MADDOG: Choosing Nouns to Create a Dominant Impression; and Musical and Kinesthetic Approaches to Prepositions, including "The Preposition Song."

DEMONSTRATION LESSON

The Dada Poem: A Creative Approach to Internalizing Parts of Speech

I have adapted this lesson from a lesson developed by Kathleen Peterson, a teacher at MacArthur Fundamental Intermediate School in Santa Ana, California, who, in turn, got the idea from Arlene Brown (1993) in *Booklinks.* The primary objective is to help students identify and understand the functions of the parts of speech. The lesson activates spatial, kinesthetic, and linguistic intelligences as students construct their own meaning by "finding" a grammar-based poem in a memorable way that will help them internalize what they are learning. As an extension to the Dada poem, students can color-code their own writing to explore how their selection and placement of the parts of speech inform their own style and relates to purpose in writing. Terms used to describe the reading, thinking, and writing tasks are taken from Figure 1.2 (Cognitive Strategies: A Reader's and Writer's Tool Kit) and from Figure 3.2 (the UCI Writing Project's adaptation of Bloom's "taxonomy of the cognitive domain").

Overview

After reading and analyzing an excerpt from Bebe Moore Campbell's autobiography, *Sweet Summer,* students will color-code the text to identify the parts of speech used and then "find" a grammar-based poem in the text that conveys a predominant theme, impression, or message.

Objectives

Students will:

1. Make connections between their own lives and Campbell's childhood reminiscence
2. Find the golden lines in the text and cluster the sensory details
3. Identify the parts of speech in the sensory cluster and analyze the author's craft
4. Color-code the excerpt for the parts of speech
5. Determine a theme, impression, or message they would like to convey
6. Select a limited number of words according to parts of speech
7. Manipulate these words to compose a Dada poem
8. Apply the color-coding strategy to their own writing to determine how their selection and placement of the parts of speech inform their own style and relate to purpose in writing

The Process

This lesson takes approximately one week to implement. The time frame may be condensed for older students or expanded for those who need a thorough review of the parts of speech. Although it is important to model the Dada poem process with the whole class, the text can be less or more sophisticated, depending on the learners. Ideally, the model lesson not only will become a springboard for students to explore their own linguistic choices but also can lead to the creation of additional Dada poems based on students' self-selected texts in reading workshop.

Prereading Activity 1

Reminiscing ■ *Tapping Prior Knowledge*

Ask students to get out a piece of paper and simply jot down any ideas that pop into their heads as you read the following questions. Read slowly so that students have some think time.

- Think of a place that reminds you of your childhood. Where does your memory take you back to?
- Think about a time when you went on a trip to visit a person you hadn't seen in a long time or to a place you hadn't been to for a while. What memories and specific sights, smells, tastes, sounds, and so forth come to mind as you think about being en route and as you mentally revisit your arrival?
- Think about a person, place, or event that made a lasting impression on you. What was it about that person, place, or event that stands out vividly in your mind?

Invite students to turn to a partner and share one of their memories in as much detail as they can remember.

During Reading Activity

Reading Aloud and Responding ■ *Constructing the Gist and Making Connections*

As I mentioned previously, any text can be used to model the process of constructing a Dada poem. Both Kathleen Peterson and I have had success with Bebe Moore Campbell's *Sweet Summer.* I have also used a passage from "All Summer in a Day" (see Chapter 3); two passages from *The Grapes of Wrath;* and a contemporary text by Rebecca Wells, *The Divine*

Secrets of the Ya-Ya Sisterhood. More advanced students can be given a selection of texts to choose from, or the teacher can model the process with a literary text he or she is reading for pleasure while each student selects his or her own text to work with.

Read aloud to the class the excerpt from *Sweet Summer* (Figure 12.2) or another literary selection of your choice. After reading the excerpt, ask students to write two two-minute responses. The first will be a *text-based response:* Students should focus on what aspects of Bebe Moore Campbell's reminiscence were especially vivid or memorable either in terms of the event and the relationship she describes or in terms of her use of author's craft. Then they should write a *personal response* in which they make a connection between the text and their personal lives. Sentence starters like "This reminds me of" or "I remember when" might serve as points of departure for students to relate to the text.

Figure 12.2   Excerpt from *Sweet Summer* (*Source: Sweet Summer* by Bebe Moore Campbell, copyright © 1989 by Bebe Moore Campbell. Used by permission of G. P. Putnam's Sons, a division of Penguin Group (USA) Inc.)

We drove for hours, eating chicken wings and thighs, nibbling on the cake and the Baby Ruth and drinking cold sodas as well as the lemonade in the thermos Nana had packed. After a while I took off my shoes and socks and tossed them onto the floor in the back. Daddy unbuttoned his top two shirt buttons, pulled a rag from behind his seat and began swiping at his damp neck. I read aloud to Daddy from *The Story of Harriet Tubman,* and then we listened to the radio until the station started crackling like dried-up fall leaves. As the day wore on, the June breeze turned silky; it was like a gentle pat across our faces. All the while we drove, Daddy and I had our hands on each other. My daddy's arm rested on my shoulder; I held his wrist. We were on the edge of summer.

It was almost dusk when we reached Route 17. I could smell summer on that road. The lush, heavy oak trees on either side of the one-lane highway grew so thick their branches stretched across the road to each other in an embrace, making a dark leafy tunnel of the road. "Look, Daddy, the trees are kissing," I said. He laughed. To our far right, beyond the dense leaves and branches, the murky waters of Dismal Swamp lay still and foreboding. Grandma once told me that before the Civil War slaves swam across the swamp to escape north, and I thought of the runaways as the stronger night breeze whistled and rattled against our windows. Maybe their ghosts came out at night, as haunting as the Turtle Lady, the green phantom who lurked in North Philly looking for children to eat. But I didn't see any ghosts, just water. The night air held a chill and Daddy and I rolled our windows all the way up. The trees loomed alongside us as tall as dark giants. All of a sudden I saw fading daylight again as the kissing trees thinned out. There in the clearing the words, "Welcome to North Carolina" and below that, in smaller letters, "The Tar Heel State" blazed out in blue and red. Almost summer. My bladder filled immediately.

"I gotta, I have to go to the bathroom."

"Can't you wait? We'll be there in fifteen or twenty minutes."

"I gotta go now, Daddy."

The car slowed and he pulled over to the side of the road near a deserted picnic table surrounded by a grove of pine trees. "Lookahere. Go duck behind that first tree. And Bebe, uh, uh, you better pull your shorts, I mean your panties, else you're gonna wet yourself." He laughed a little. His eyes crinkled up. From the prickly, thin sound of his laughter I knew he was embarrassed. I went behind a tree, about twenty feet away from the car. I heard Daddy yelling. "Lookahere. Watch where you step. Might be a snake in there." I peed fast. When I got back to the car I could hear a trickling sound. . . . "Might as well go too," he said.

The sky turned inky and crickets began to sing their brittle nighttime lullaby. Route 17 went right into Route 58, the heart of South Mills. The town was a collection of a few houses, a post office, and a justice of the peace. My cousin Ruby, Aunt Lela's daughter, and her family lived there. We stopped at her house for a split second, long enough for my plump, pretty cousin to hug me and for Daddy to shoot the breeze with her husband, Snoodlum, and drink a great big glass of water while I raced around the yard in the dark with their two sons, Johnny and Jimmy. Then we had to go, because I was getting antsy. Summer was up the road apiece, waiting for me.

From Ruby's I could have walked to Grandma's blindfolded, the land around me was so familiar. I could have followed the smell of the country night air so weighted with watermelons, roses and the potent stench from the hog pens. We crossed the bridge running over the canal that bordered South Mills. A sign announced that we had entered Pasquotank County. On either side of us, spread out like an open fan, were fields of corn, soybeans, peanuts and melons. White and brick frame houses broke up the landscape. Some belonged to white folks, some to colored. We reached Morgan's Corner and my stomach started quivering. It was where I bought my Baby Ruths and comic books! As my father's car slowed, my eyes scanned the fields of corn and soybeans for the opening to Grandma's. There it was! The car nearly stopped and we slowly turned into the narrow dirt lane. We jostled and bounced over the muddy ruts, the motor churning and sputtering as the tires attempted to plod through waterlogged ditches, a result of the last rain. Daddy drove slowly and carefully. "Sure don't wanna get stuck up this lane," he muttered. My stomach was churning just as desperately as the wheels on my father's Pontiac. We lurched out of a deep gulley and glided into the front yard. Finally it was summer.

Grandma Mary was sitting on the porch waiting for us, as I knew she would be. She could outwait anybody. She told me having babies gave you patience. Grandma had had twelve children; one baby died at birth; "You have to wait for the pains to start, then wait for them to go, all that waiting with nothing but a rag to bite down on," she said. She stood up when we drove into the yard. "Hey," she called, walking toward us. My father had barely parked before I was scrambling out of the car and Grandma caught me up in her fat ole arms, hugging and squeezing me. She had a smell, deep in her bosom, like biscuits and flowers and I don't know what all else. That's what washed over me. I turned around to see my daddy pulling his wheelchair out of the back of the car and placing it between his open car door and his seat. He gave a huge lunge and hopped from the driver's seat into the chair. Then he pulled out the pillow he sat on, hoisted up his body and stuffed the pillow under his behind. He rolled over to the ramp in front of the house, pulled himself up and went inside, yelling, "Hey," to Mr. Abe, Grandma's second husband, and "Hey there, girl," to Bunnie, my Aunt Susie's teenage daughter; Aunt Susie had died a few years earlier. I heard Mr. Abe answering back. Mr. Abe had been singing, some old gospel song that only he sang and nobody else. I hadn't heard that song in a year, a whole year. As soon as he answered my father, he started up with his song again. I stood on the porch with Grandma, soaking up Mr. Abe's song, trying to hear it not as last year's song, but as a song of this summer. I stood on Grandma's porch and listened hard. Mr. Abe's song was my bridge; if I could cross that bridge I was back home. I started humming.

After Reading Activity 1

Finding the Golden Lines and Clustering ■ *Analyzing Author's Craft and Organizing Information*

Ask students to reread the excerpt and to underline with yellow highlighters memorable words and phrases that strike them as particularly precise or vivid. Then call on students to volunteer some of their words and phrases. As they volunteer, record these words on the board in a cluster—but organize them into categories of sight, smell, taste, touch, sound, and movement. See Planning Activity 1 in Chapter 9 for a sensory cluster for the memory snapshot paper, "The Intrusion."

After Reading Activity 2

Class Discussion ■ *Analyzing Author's Craft and Forming Interpretations*

Draw the students' attention to the author's careful choice of words by using the following questions.

- As you listened to this piece and then reread it silently, did you feel like you were there with Bebe in the car and at Grandma's house? If so, what was it about the author's use of language that helped you to enter the scene? Students will point to the wealth of concrete detail, to the richness of sensory impressions, and to Campbell's use of figurative language (for example, the way she describes the static on the radio "crackling like dried-up fall leaves").

- How old do you think Bebe was at the time? Students will guess anywhere from about five to twelve. It is important to ask them why they have this impression. They may point to the fact that she refers to her father as "Daddy," that she's wearing socks and shoes, that she can't wait to get to a bathroom, that she gets "antsy," and so on.

  At this point, you might want to explain that Bebe was seven at the time and that every summer her father came north to Philadelphia, where she lived with her mother, to take her back south to North Carolina. Because Bebe's parents were divorced, her encounters with her father were limited by custody agreements and distances, and she says that this separation left her "lopsided and lonely." At that age, nine months can seem like a lifetime. And so, when Bebe's father would come for her, there was great anticipation but also some anxiety on both sides. The drive south in Daddy's green car was always a time and place to reconnect.

- How does Bebe show us instead of tell us how she feels? Students will mention her getting "antsy" and having a full bladder, her stomach's "churning just as desperately as the wheels on my father's Pontiac," and how she hums when she's finally home.

- Can you feel a sense of organization in this excerpt? For example, what would you identify as the opening hook? Students will point to the line "We were on the edge of summer," and how that metaphor is used throughout the piece.

- What gives you a sense of closure? Depending on their level of sophistication, students may point to the bridge metaphor at the end of the episode and the statement that Uncle Abe's song is the bridge that leads her home.

- Why has this place made a lasting impression on Bebe, and what is the most important message you take away with you? Students will point out that it's more than just a place or time of year; it's a time of belonging, connecting. They will also point out the love that surrounds this childhood memory.

Prewriting Step 1

Parts of Speech Review and Application ■ *Tapping Prior Knowledge and Expanding Schemata*

If students have participated in other lessons on the parts of speech, they can immediately begin identifying the parts of speech in the *Sweet Summer* cluster. If not, you will need to review the terminology. For example:

Noun: a word that names a person, place, thing, or idea
Pronoun: a word that takes the place of a noun and functions in the same way that nouns do
Verb: a word that shows action or occurrence
Adverb: a word that describes or modifies verbs, adjectives, other adverbs, or phrases or clauses
Adjective: a word that describes or modifies a noun, a pronoun, or a word group functioning as a noun
Preposition: a word that conveys a relationship, often of space or time, between the noun or pronoun following it and other words in the sentence

Conjunction: a word that connects or otherwise establishes a relationship between two or more words, phrases, or clauses (Troyka, 1995)

You may also want to discuss the parts of speech with user-friendly labels such as "naming words," "doing words," "how/ly words that tell how the action is done," "describing words," "position words," and "connecting words." (See the *Cloudy with a Chance of Meatballs* lesson earlier in this chapter.)

Ask students to apply their knowledge of the parts of speech by taking five minutes to work with a partner to attach the names of the parts of speech to as many of the words in a text-based sensory cluster as they can. For example, under the category of touch, they might write "silky breeze" and then identify "silky" as an adjective and "breeze" as a noun. Under movement, they might list "jostled" and "bounced" and identify these words as verbs.

After five minutes, ask students to volunteer their findings and also anything they noticed about Campbell's use of language. They may notice that she uses lots of verbs to describe action; that she gives us a catalogue of nouns to help us *be* with her in the car, eat what she ate, and see what she saw; that she uses adjectives like "silky" and "inky" so that we can feel what she felt, and so forth.

Prewriting Step 2

Introducing the Dada Poem and Color-Coding the Parts of Speech ■
Organizing Information and Visualizing

Ask if any students have ever experimented with magnetic poetry and composed poems or other sayings on their refrigerators. Tell students that they will have an opportunity to "find" a poem by color-coding the parts of speech in the *Sweet Summer* excerpt and fashioning those words into a verbal collage much as one does with magnetic poetry. The product will be a Dada poem. Explain that Dadaism was an artistic and literary movement that flourished between 1916 and 1922. Much of Dada art was playful and highly experimental. Dadaists saw art in accidental happenings and believed art need not depend on established rules or craftsmanship but could be evoked out of random combinations. Collages of colored paper pieces arranged according to chance and word collages were popular with the Dadaists. Students often have a difficult time visualizing what the Dada poem will look like. You may want to construct a Dada poem of your own to help them picture the final product; in fact, it is important to experience the process yourself first. Or you can show them the Dada poem I constructed from the opening pages of Chapter VI in *Charlotte's Web,* which appears on the companion website.

Students have an attention span of about twenty minutes for this color-coding activity. We have found that it is useful to have students work in groups of three, with each student searching for two parts of speech; but students can work alone if the teacher assigns the color-coding task as homework. The advantage of the group work is that students pool their collective knowledge and continually consult one another about the words in context. Making dictionaries and grammar resources available is a good idea. Students voluntarily refer to them!

Give students colored pencils and the following color-coding system:

Nouns—dark blue	Adjectives—red
Pronouns—light blue	Prepositions—orange
Verbs—green	Conjunctions—black
Adverbs—brown	

(Note that I have kept the color-coding system consistent across lessons so that students can associate one color with a part of speech. I have also refrained from using yellow because it is hard to see.)

Ask students to read the selection through once more to get a feel for the theme before beginning to color-code. Tell them not to underline every word, as this would become cumbersome, but to mark interesting nouns, verbs, or whatever parts of speech they are responsible for in their groups. Remind them that they can use a class cluster to get some of their words. Students should then transfer these words onto a piece of paper in list form by part of speech, in the appropriate color. For a twenty-one word Dada poem, they generally should have at least:

12 verbs	5 adjectives
3 adverbs	3 pronouns
10 nouns	2 conjunctions

The number of words can be adjusted up or down by the teacher, however, and parts of speech can be added or taken away. For example, some text selections may not contain as many as three adverbs.

> **Prompt**
>
> "Find" a twenty-one-word poem in the excerpt from Bebe Moore Campbell's *Sweet Summer* by color-coding the parts of speech in the text and fashioning those words into a verbal collage much as one does with magnetic poetry. Your product will be a Dada poem. Like the Dadaists, you will manipulate your collection of words until they form a pattern or theme. You must use *all* of the words that you write into the grid that is provided for you and compose your poem. Each word used must be color-coded and used appropriately for that part of speech.
>
> Be creative and have fun. You can say a lot in a few words. If you wish to, you can illustrate your poem before pasting down the words from your grid; or you can illustrate the perimeter of your paper after your poem is completed. An 8½-by-11 copy of the prompt is available on the companion website.

Planning Activity 1

Selecting Words for the Dada Poem ■ *Analyzing Author's Craft and Constructing the Gist*

If students are working in groups, they need to find a space to spread out all of their lists of words. Each student must select from the words compiled by his or her group to fill in on the grid that can be found on the companion website. Remind students to think carefully about the theme, impression, or message they want to convey before they select their words. The grid instructs them to choose a certain number of verbs, adverbs, nouns, and so on. This formula can be adjusted by the teacher. I also allow students to make minor adjustments because I do not want them to get stuck on counting words instead of constructing meaning. Each word transferred to the grid must be written in the appropriate color to designate its part of speech.

Writing Activity

Manipulating the Parts of Speech ■ *Organizing Information and Constructing the Gist*

Students should use scissors to cut up their grids and then should manipulate the individual word slips until a pattern emerges. Because there are so few words to work with, the poem is not intended to make perfect sense but rather to convey an impression.

Sharing and Revising Activity

Response Partners ■ *Analyzing Author's Craft and Revising Meaning*

Students can share their poems with partners before pasting them down. Partners can make suggestions regarding how rearranging certain words might convey a stronger impression. The reader can also let the writer know what communicates in his or her poem and what doesn't. Students may want to illustrate a backdrop for their poem before pasting down the words. Students will also want to complete the next phase of the lesson—editing—before gluing their words into final position.

Editing Activity

Reviewing for Parts of Speech ■ *Monitoring and Proofreading for Correctness*

Have students work in partners to look at how they have used their words in the poem in terms of their function and color. Students may find that they have actually used a green word (verb) in the place of blue word (noun) or turned a blue word (noun) into a red word (adjective). This happened to me in my Dada poem (which appears on the companion website). I color-coded "love" as a verb but used it as a noun and "lilac" as a noun but chose to use it as an adjective. In the original Dada poem I was introduced to, students were required to use all their words according to the parts of speech as they were originally coded. But this task is actually very difficult. I allow students to change words from one part of speech to another and encourage them to recolor their words (blue on top of green or red over blue) rather than to make a new slip. That way, as a class, we can see that the language is fluid and that words change depending on their purpose. Because our goal is to be creative but also correct, students may also modify a word by adding or deleting an ending such as *s* or *ed*. A sample *Sweet Summer* Dada poem by Kathleen Peterson's seventh-grade student Maria Soto is illustrated in Figure 12.3.

Learning Log Reflection

Applying the Color-Coding System to One's Own Writing ■ *Analyzing Author's Craft and Making Connections*

Students are now ready to apply what they have learned to their own writing—to see what their own linguistic choices are and how these choices inform their style. Ask students to select one of their own texts to analyze. If the literature used for practice was a narrative, it would be best if the student writing is also a narrative, such as the memory snapshot paper described in Chapter 9. Have students color-code a chunk of their own writing, or an entire text if it is relatively short, either in class or for homework. Then ask them to respond to the following questions in a learning log.

- What did you notice about the frequency with which you used certain parts of speech and their placement in your sentences? Did any one part of speech predominate? Can you link this to your purpose and your content?
- Did you have certain expectations about what you would find as you color-coded your own writing? Did anything surprise you?
- To what degree, if any, has color-coding your own writing made you more aware of or informed about your own craft as a writer?

Figure 12.3 **Dada Poem** (Reprinted by permission of Maria Soto.)

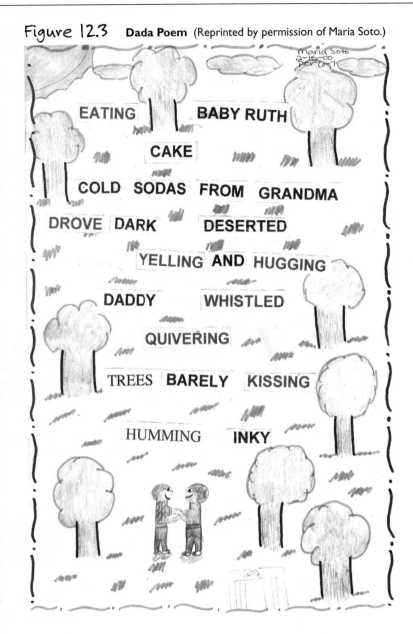

Eleventh graders in the UCI Young Writers' Project had this to say after color-coding a self-selected piece from their portfolios:

■ I used a lot of nouns, meaning that I get to the point without being complicated or overly descriptive.

■ I saw that nouns and verbs dominate my writings. I think I need to start using more adjectives to help the reader see what I'm talking about.

■ I found I used some adjectives but mainly used nouns. This might not be important because I chose to color-code a report and it was meant to be informative and straightforward.

Students also mentioned that the color-coding helped them "visualize" how words go together, that they found the artistic approach to grammar "intriguing," and that they felt more aware of the choices available to them as writers.

Evaluation

The Scoring Rubric ■ *Assessing Quality against Criteria*

Teachers may elect not to evaluate the Dada poems at all; they may want to accord credit or no-credit points; or they may elect to use a weighted straight scale such as the scoring guide on the companion website.

Extension Activity

Celebrating Author's Craft ■ *Analyzing Author's Craft and Forming Interpretations*

Students may also want to exchange papers with a partner and to celebrate their classmate's text by creating a Dada poem.

Teaching Sentence Sense and Sentence Craft

Linguist Francis Christensen wrote,

> If the new grammar is to be brought to bear on composition, it must be brought to bear on the rhetoric of the sentence. (1963, p. 155)

Many scholars acknowledge Christensen for inspiring teachers to move beyond teaching sentences only "as specimens for dissection" and to present them instead as "models for imitation" (Kilgallon, 1998, p. 181) and as keys to style. According to Christensen, "The best grammar is the grammar that best displays the layers of structure of the English sentence" (1963, p. 157). In order to develop a mature style, he says, students need to become "sentence acrobats, to dazzle by their syntactic dexterity" (1967, p. 137). Christensen also stresses that good writing is generative. That is, experienced writers are able to elaborate on their ideas. He praises novelist John Erskine for articulating this important principle: "When you write, you make a point, not by subtracting as though you sharpened a pencil, but by adding" (quoted in Christensen, 1963, p. 159). Provided on the pages that follow are a variety of strategies to teach students sentence sense and sentence craft through lessons in which they manipulate, imitate, and generate rather than dissect.

Sentence Expanding   The concept of a sentence is actually tricky to teach. Rei Noguchi (1991) notes that many students have difficulty grasping this notion because teachers present the definition of a sentence to them semantically, saying that a sentence is "a complete thought." The next question from students invariably is "What's a complete thought?" Further, people converse daily in incomplete or ungrammatical sentences that still effectively communicate as complete thoughts. Because the language is organized according to certain rules or syntactical structures, it may be easier for students if sentences are defined not in terms of meaning (semantics) but in terms of structure (syntax). There is disagreement about the most effective way to communicate what a sentence is. This definition gleaned from Constance Weaver (1996) suggests just how difficult it is:

> Sentence—A group of words called an independent clause that contain a subject that tells who or what is doing the action or existing in a state of being and a predicate, the part of the clause which contains the verb which shows the action or state of being and anything that completes or modifies the verb, plus any dependent clauses or phrases attached to the independent clause or embedded within it.

No wonder this concept is hard for students to grasp!

Scott Peterson (1998, pp. 78–81) has developed a simple yet engaging way of making the concept of subject and predicate accessible to students. He begins with a simple two-word sentence: "Cats slept." He tells students that a sentence consists of a subject (the who or what part of a sentence) and a predicate (the action or what they did) part of the sentence. Students can then identify the subject and verb in the sentence.

Although "Cats slept" is indeed a complete sentence, it doesn't create much of a picture in our minds. Peterson begins by asking students questions about the subject. For our example, we might ask:

- How many cats were sleeping?
  What color were they?
  Were they large or small?
  Did they have long or short fur?

Students then expand upon the subject. Example:

- Two plump black-and-white cats with long fur slept.

Peterson now turns his attention to the predicate and asks students to think about what the subject is doing. For our model, one might ask: Can you picture how the cats are sleeping? Where are they? What else is going on around them? Students then expand the predicate:

- Two plump black-and-white cats with long fur slept soundly, curled up like spoons, on a lawn chair in the backyard, as a pair of robins twittered right under their noses.

After practicing with the whole class model, students are ready to select their own two-word subject and predicate and begin expanding. When they are satisfied with the results, they take two sheets of 8½-by-11 paper and lay them side by side. They write (1) the subject on one page and the predicate on the other; (2) the expanded subject with the one-word predicate below that; and (3) the expanded subject and the expanded predicate across the bottom. Students then illustrate their sentence, using both sheets of paper, as in Figure 12.4 by Jazmine Diaz, an eighth grader at St. Columban School in Garden Grove, California. Thelma Anselmi, the teacher who experimented with the strategy, reports that her students got very involved in this activity, grasped the concept quickly, and asked to expand the subject and predicate one more time—hence number 4 in Figure 12.4.

Sentence Unscrambling   Not all sentences begin with the subject followed by the predicate. Once students grasp the roles of the subject and predicate, it is time for them to manipulate the parts of a sentence and experiment with word order. Don Kilgallon (1998) has developed sentence unscrambling to provide students with practice "in moving sentence parts for variety in style" (pp. 173–174).

The teacher can draw from the works of professional writers and disassemble their sentences, compose and scramble sentences of his or her own, or challenge groups of students with the task of composing and then taking apart sentences for others to reconstruct. For example, the following sentence parts can be unscrambled in a variety of ways:

at the mall	hanging out
the boys	the girls
whistled appreciatively	trying to look cool
and	made comments
checked out	about them

Figure 12.4 **Sentence Expanding** (Reprinted by permission of Jazmine Diaz.)

- Trying to look cool, the boys checked out the girls hanging out at the mall, made comments about them, and whistled appreciatively.
- The girls checked out the boys hanging out at the mall, made comments about them, and, trying to look cool, whistled appreciatively.
- At the mall, the girls checked out the boys hanging out, trying to look cool, made comments about them, and whistled appreciatively.

The original sentence: "Hanging out at the mall, trying to look cool, the boys checked out the girls, made comments about them, and whistled appreciatively."

Kilgallon maintains that "Subliminally, sentence unscrambling teaches the grammatical constructions—words, phrases, and clauses with all their variety—that make up the sentence parts in the scrambled list" (p. 173).

Sentence Combining   Like Don Kilgallon, Rei Noguchi (1991) argues that sentence combining, another form of sentence manipulation, succeeds because it relies upon the intuitive knowledge students already have about the structure of the language. In Chapter 11 I discussed sentence combining as a revision strategy to enhance style. Irene Thomas (1997) points out that it can also be used to showcase specific grammatical constructions and to help students eliminate errors. When presenting the technique for this purpose, the teacher will need to use the appropriate signal words in parentheses to aid the students in practicing specific constructions. Here are just a few examples from Thomas (1997, pp. 263–264):

Fragments beginning with adverbial conjunctions

These combining words (I like to call them "because" words since they all behave exactly like *because)* are just that: they connect two complete sentences that are related. If students have practice uncovering the original sentences and the combining word in model sentences or sentences from student writing, they have a better chance of catching those combining words—and potential fragments—in their own writing. Words like *because, since, although* can begin a sentence that is the result of combining two simple sentences:

The NASA budget has been cut.

The space program has been reduced. (Because . . .)

Resulting sentence: *Because the NASA budget has been cut, the space program has been reduced.*

When students associate words like *because* with a class of combining words, they are less likely to make fragments beginning with those words. If you wish, you can suggest the combining word or process to be used by putting it in parentheses, as I have above. Students should notice that *because* words can appear either initially or medially in a sentence.

Relative clauses and appositives

Relative clauses, both restrictive and nonrestrictive, are natural in students' speech; but when students write, they often overlook the fluency that structure adds to their sentences. If you select choppy sentences from students' writing that could be improved by combining with a relative pronoun, you have the perfect material to work with. Additionally, the question of whether to use *that* or *which* can be addressed in this context, as well as when *who* is more appropriate than *that* in referring to human subjects.

Notice how sentence combining clarifies the identity of the referents and displays the multiple possibilities:

Marge is the oldest member of a family. (who)

This family came to America on the *Mayflower.* (who, that, which)

Marge now teaches new Americans to read English.

One resulting sentence: Marge, who is the oldest member of a family that came to America on the *Mayflower,* now teaches new Americans to read English.

Reducing to an appositive and a noun phrase: Marge, the oldest member of a *Mayflower* family, now teaches literacy to new Americans.

Human Sentences   This activity helps students who have difficulty manipulating word order linguistically to grasp how sentence combining can enhance style. The students work collaboratively and literally stand up and move around to construct different versions of the same sentence.

Have students form groups of four to six. Give each group a series of envelopes, one for each sentence that will be combined into one human sentence, and one envelope of punctuation marks. Challenge each group to stand up, pick up the cards, pass them out to the group members, and begin moving around to arrange the words in the way that sounds best. The number of words that must be arranged and the punctuation marks necessary for different sentence constructions will cause students to use both hands, possibly their teeth, or tape cards on a pocket. As students stand up in front of the class to model their human sentence, members of the audience can ask them to change positions to see if the sentence might work better another way. As the students reconfigure, the rest of the class can literally see what difference reordering their positions makes to the sentence. These changes, in turn, may cause punctuation marks to have to be moved.

One of my favorite sentence-combining exercises comes from Bill Strong (1996), director of the Utah Writing Project:

Tucker was a trucker.

He was out of luck.

He was stuck in the muck.

He was in Winnemuca. (p. 179)*

---

*From *Writer's Toolbox: A Sentence-Combining Workshop* (McGraw-Hill, 1996) by William Strong. Reprinted by permission of William Strong.

This exercise lends itself to so wide a range of sentence combinations that Strong offers $100 to anyone who can replicate the version he has written down and stashed away in his pocket. (They never do.) Students definitely enjoy using their minds and their bodies actively to combine sentences. For students who learn by physically doing, this is a great way to engage them in experiencing how to vary sentence structure.

Sentence Sorting   Sentence sorting was developed by UCI Writing Project codirector Catherine D'Aoust, who is the coordinator of K–12 instructional services for Saddleback Valley Unified School District in Mission Viejo, California. Sentence sorting is a hands-on grammar activity that fosters understanding and appreciation of sentence structure and sentence variety. In a workshop, D'Aoust shared the sentence sorting process:

> In sentence sorts students group sentences which are given to them on strips of paper into piles based on some criterion or contrast. Students must analyze the sentences, working individually or in groups, to decide which sentences are similar or different. Initially, the sentences used in the sorts are chosen by the teacher from literature which the students are reading. In further sorts, sentences are included from students' writing along with literature sentences. Students gradually take a more active role in creating the sorts, finding sentences in both their writing and reading.
>
> Sentence sorts can be syntactic or semantic based, open or closed. Syntactic sorts focus on sentence structure [e.g., a sort contrasting simple and complex sentences, as in the sort taken from *From the Mixed-Up Files of Mrs. Basil E. Frankweiler* available on the companion website]. A semantic sort focuses on sentence meaning; e.g., a sort distinguishing between factual and interpretive sentences. A closed sort is one in which the two categories for the sort are known ahead of time by the students. In an open sort, students receive the 10–12 sentence strips and must determine the categories themselves. An example of an open, syntactic sort for twelfth graders would be a contrast between sentences with and without noun clauses and no information prior to the sort about the categories.
>
> Sentence sorting is active and fun. Students learn most when they sort with other students in groups of three or four. They discuss and analyze sentences. They learn the important connection between form and meaning in sentences and the variety of options they have in their grammatical knowledge. They use this information when they write to enhance meaning. Grammar becomes purposeful.

Participle Pantomime   Students need to go beyond manipulating sentences composed by others; they need to generate and experiment with sentences of their own. Harry Noden (1999) likens writing to painting with words and notes that "just as a painter combines a wide range of brush stroke techniques to create an image, the writer chooses from a repertoire of sentence structures" (p. 4).

One of the brush strokes that Noden teaches is the concept of the participle and participial phrase. To simplify this concept, Noden tells his students that a participle is an *ing* verb tagged on to the beginning or the end of a sentence and that a participial phrase is a participle along with any modifiers that complete the image. He provides the following examples:

- Original sentence: "The diamond-scaled snakes attacked their prey."
- Participle: "*Hissing, slithering, and coiling*, the diamond-scaled snakes attacked their prey."
- Participial phrase: "*Hissing their forked red tongues* and *coiling their cold bodies*, the diamond-scaled snakes attacked their prey." (pp. 4–5)

Bay Area Writing Project teacher/consultant Rebekah Caplan has developed an interactive approach to engaging students in writing sentences with participles and participial phrases. In essence, after sharing numerous models of *ing*-verb sentences, she dramatizes a scene through pantomine for students to write about. Imagine the gestures Caplan might have pantomimed to elicit these two sentences:

■ Chewing on the end of her pencil, frowning, mumbling something to herself, and finally taking a deep breath, Ms. Caplan opened the test booklet and began to write.

■ Bouncing the ball, once, twice, three times, concentrating, winding up for the serve, the tennis player raised her racket and slammed the ball with all her might, jumping into the air when she realized she had served an ace.

Caplan then invites her students to volunteer to think up their own pantomimes for the other students to describe.

Once students are comfortable with "painting with participles" (Noden, 1999, p. 4), Noden introduces the concept of absolutes, defined simply as a noun combined with an *ing* participle. The pantomime strategy can also lend itself to practicing this structure:

■ Heart palpitating, hands sweating, Ms. Caplan opened the test booklet, breathed deeply, and began to write.

All of the exercises described for teaching sentence sense and sentence craft foster the "syntactic dexterity" that Christensen (1967, p. 137) speaks of. Through appropriate practice, structure, and the engendering of ownership, students can begin to apply the concepts learned to their own writing. To encourage the incorporation of new syntatic structures into student writing, the teacher should ask students to underline something new they have tried in a revised text. The teacher should also provide recognition of some sort—be it extra credit points, reading the sentence aloud, or displaying the student's work on a bulletin board as the sentence of the week.

Punctuation Mythology

Pat Cordeiro (1998) remarks, "Punctuation is a persistent and troublesome aspect of writing because of our misconception of it as a mechanical skill that can be routinized and made subliminal. It is forever open to negotiation, and represents a semiotic transaction between the writer and reader" (p. 60). Perhaps students have trouble "getting" certain aspects of punctuation because writers often take certain licenses with the rules depending on what they are writing—for example, a narrative, an informal letter, or a formal business proposal. Punctuation helps readers to make sense of what they are reading. It tells us where and when to stop; it notifies the reader of "how much text must be retained in short-term memory" (p. 56); and it "distinguishes between the ambiguities that are built into the language" (p. 56) by helping us identify issues like possession.

Because punctuation actually helps students to make meaning, it is important that they know the rules before they can consciously break them to create some intended effect. As with teaching the parts of speech, traditional approaches to teaching these rules often don't stick even though they are taught and retaught across the grade levels. In *In the Middle* (1998), Nancie Atwell has a whole range of minilessons about the uses of various forms of punctuation that are well worth perusing. Bill Burns, a teacher at Sonora High School in Fullerton, California, created his "Punctuation Mythology" (found on the companion website) to help students grasp some of the punctuation rules that are generally thought to give people the most trouble (Shuman, 1995, p. 119). His story begins as follows:

Punctuation Mythology

In the Beginning . . . all was in chaos.

And the great god of Language, Verbos, saw that language needed some help. It needed organization. It needed a sign. Since Verbos, being a god, was good at signs, he created the first punctuation mark:

(Roll of drums, flourish of horns) . . . The Period ●

Now the period added strength and control to language and Verbos was pleased . . . for a while. Soon Verbos could see that the Period was lonely and needed something to help him bring language together, rather than separating it. So Verbos thought and thought and reached down and took a part of the Period and made another mark:

(Flourish of horns) . . . The Comma ❩

Burns concludes his tale by inviting his students to participate in the creation myth by continuing his story and accounting for the genesis of the exclamation point and question mark. Burns's "Punctuation Mythology" predates but is reminiscent of *Safari Punctuation* (Risso, 1990), in which a band of cartoon figures travel through the land of the commas, the periods, the question marks, and so on. Teachers can also share a model cartoon for punctuation marks from *Safari Punctuation* and engage students in creating their safari for another punctuation mark or work in groups to create a complete booklet. Earlier, I talked about the idea of "mental Velcro" and how students need a memorable foundation that will enable the knowledge of grammar and mechanics to stick. Involving students in creating their own narrative accounts of how language structures work can help to establish this mental Velcro.

A FEW WORDS ABOUT VOCABULARY AND SPELLING

It will come as no surprise that, as with the teaching of grammar, students learn vocabulary and spelling better when they are immersed in working with words in meaningful contexts, engaged in actively making connections between words and experiences and in determining how words work, invited to personalize word learning, introduced to well-modeled strategies and given opportunities to practice, and encouraged to apply what they have learned to texts they are reading and writing (Bear et al., 2000; Blachowicz & Fisher, 1996). As Blachowicz and Fisher (1996) point out, "As in all learning situations, having learners attempt to construct their own meanings is a hallmark of good teaching" (p. 7).

School-age students learn, on the average, 3,000 to 4,000 words per year (Nagy & Anderson, 1984). Clearly, this number far exceeds what students can be taught through direct instruction. In other words, a significant amount of vocabulary and spelling learning is acquired through wide reading, through environmental exposure to print and media, through discussion, and so forth (Blachowicz & Fisher, 1996; Krashen, 1993). Although this incidental learning is very powerful, it does not guarantee the learning of specific words. And "to be fully literate," students need knowledge of specific words as well as knowledge about the English spelling system so as to be able to recognize the regularities, patterns, and rules of orthography in the written language system (Bear et al., 2000). The more students can master the recognition, spelling, and meaning of specific words, the better their reading comprehension (Davis, 1968) and the broader their repertoire for writing.

Most students receive their vocabulary and spelling instruction via lists that they are expected to memorize. Research on direct spelling instruction actually indicates that words studied in lists are learned more quickly, remembered longer, and transferred more readily to new contexts (Horn, 1952). (It should be noted that lists need not be arbitrary and that vocabulary and spelling can be linked with texts students are reading in class and/or grouped according to some semantic or orthographic principle.) However, as Janet Allen (1999) stresses, "it takes more than definitional knowledge to know a word" (p. 8). As with the teaching of grammar, a multimodal approach to the teaching and learning of vocabulary and spelling may have the best chance of providing the mental Velcro that enables new knowledge to stick in a student's long-term memory. Richard Gentry's (1987) observation that effective spelling instruction should involve opportunities for "visual inspection, auditory inspection, kinesthetic reinforcement, and recall" (p. 32) may hold true for vocabulary as well.

Vocabutoons and Vocabulary Story

Blachowicz and Fisher (1996) note that one way to involve students in constructing word meaning is to make vocabulary visible by having students draw a picture or create a graphic memory organizer like a map or cluster, accompanied by sharing and discussion (p. 8). They also suggest, as a way to personalize meaning and assist memory, creating one's own mnemonic (such as ROY G. BIV for the spectrum colors red, orange, yellow, green, blue, indigo, violet). When I asked Thelma Anselmi, an eighth-grade teacher at St. Columban School in Garden Grove, California, and an inveterate vocabulary buff, what her single most successful classroom strategy was for teaching vocabulary, she identified vocabutoons, which use both pictures and mnemonic methods.

Vocabutoons are humorous cartoons that introduce vocabulary words through mnemonics, associating the new word with a memory trigger the student is already familiar with. For example, for the word *parry* (to ward off a blow; to turn aside; to avoid skillfully, to evade"), the mnemonic link in *Vocabutoons* (Burchers, 1999) is "pear." Below the definition are two plump pears, dressed in shoes and socks and sporting fencing gloves, illustrating the sentence "The PEARS PARRIED each other's fencing movements." Beneath the mnemonic are three additional sentences using the word *parry* in different contexts (p. 283). Anselmi challenges her students, individually or with a partner, to select vocabulary words and create Vocabutoons of their own. Figure 12.5 illustrates eighth grader Brittany New's vocabutoon for the word *raucous*. Students then teach the class the vocabulary word they have chosen. Anselmi remarks,

> The usual response to vocabulary is a concert of groans. Not so with this strategy. The students are often eager to work with a partner so the responsibility is shared. I couldn't begin to engineer the conversations about the vocabulary word, possible links, and what graphic to present. On polling the class after the vocabulary test, I was thrilled to discover that no words that had been taught by the students to each other were missed on the test. It was also exciting to see a couple of tests with sketches on them from the classroom demonstrations or to hear conversations between the students after the test: "Cherie and Tom did engulf; remember the golf ball in the hole?"

To use Bear and his colleagues' book title, Anselmi's students were learning *words their way.*

Another strategy I have observed in the classroom of Courtney Martz at El Toro High School in El Toro, California, generated a great deal of investment and excitement: the vocabulary story. Martz gives the students a list of vocabulary words drawn either from the current literature the class is reading or from Greek and Latin roots. The students study the words in fairly traditional ways—for example, looking up a definition, finding a synonym, writing the word in a sentence, and illustrating. On the day of the vocabulary story, the whole class reviews the words and definitions on the list. Then, after evening out the rows,

Figure 12.5 **Vocabutoon** (Reprinted by permission of Brittany New.)

Brittany New
Language Arts   Vocabulary Word

Raucous
(RAW•cus)
hoarse; harsh sounding

Link: Rock us

"The raucous beat of the radio will rock us."

★ Christopher-John's whistling increased to a RAUCOUS, nervous shrill, and grudgingly I let the matter drop and trudged along in silence, my brothers growing as pensively quiet as I.

★ The violin player, who did not play that well, performed a RAUCOUS tune.

★ I shrieked a RAUCOUS scream as my brother jumped out and scared me.

the class begins the vocabulary story. The first person in each row writes the opening sentence of a story, using and underlining one vocabulary word in the sentence. He or she then passes the paper to the next student in the row, who must continue the story and use a second vocabulary word. One rule is that the story must make sense—even if it is rather whimsical—and the words must be used correctly in the context of the sentence. (Students may not correct one another's sentences.) So students seated toward the end of the row have a challenging job. If a row uses all of the words on the list, which may necessitate some students' integrating more than one word into their sentence, the group receives extra credit points.

When Martz calls time (about fifteen minutes), either each row must present their contribution on a transparency or one reader from each row must read that row's story aloud, slowly, sentence by sentence. It is up to the whole class to determine if the words in each vocabulary story are used appropriately. Martz deducts one point for any vocabulary word used incorrectly. Hearing five vocabulary stories, which are often quite funny and imaginative, reinforces the use of the vocabulary words in context. Students pay close attention because it is they who must judge whether the words in the stories are accurately used.

A sample vocabulary story from Martz's class, using the Latin roots *aqua, arm,* and *art,* is depicted in Figure 12.6.

Building Academic Vocabulary

In their book *Building Academic Vocabulary,* Marzano and Pickering (2005) note, "Given the importance of academic background knowledge and the fact that vocabulary is such an essential aspect of it, one of the most crucial services that teachers can provide, particularly for

Figure 12.6 **Vocabulary Story** (Reprinted by permission of Courtney Martz.)

Row 5

The drunk sea captain, Bob, sailed the <u>aqueous</u> ocean with fierceness, ready to destroy! His crew sailed into a big bay, where they were met by their enemy, the Hawaiian <u>armada</u>. When they landed on shore, the crew found many precious <u>artifacts</u>. The captain was an <u>artisan</u>, skilled in crafts, and knew he could trade these goods and make lots of money. So, the captain pretended to make an <u>armistice</u> with the natives on the island to keep the peace. But it was all <u>artifice</u>. The natives figured out he really wanted to conquer them and so they speared him, right through his <u>armature</u>.

students who do not come from academically advantaged backgrounds, is systematic instruction in important academic terms" (p. 3). Their book contains a list of 7,923 terms across eleven subject areas and offers a six-step process for teaching the terms (2005, pp. 14–15):

Step 1: Provide a description, explanation, or example of the new term.
Step 2: Ask students to restate the description, explanation, or example in their own words.
Step 3: Ask students to construct a picture, symbol, or graphic representing the term.
Step 4: Engage students periodically in activities that help them add to their knowledge of the terms in their notebooks.
Step 5: Periodically ask students to discuss the terms with one another.
Step 6: Involve students periodically in games that allow them to play with the terms.

Spelling/Academic Vocabulary Charts

In his English Language Development classroom at Century High School in Santa Ana, California, Bob Bolander helps students to internalize academic vocabulary by teaching them vocabulary chants. Here is one stanza from a chart focusing on fifteen words involving critical thinking terms:

Critique, you say, critique—aha!
That's something you review
And then discuss quite critically,
For it's all up to you.

A copy of Bob's spelling vocabulary chant is available on the companion website.

Visual Approaches to Spelling

One of the differences between expert spellers and poor spellers is that expert spellers visualize. According to Richard Gentry and Jean Gillet (1993), "They have the ability to store and retrieve the visual form of the word in their brain. These spellers seem literally to see the word in their mind's eye" (p. 52). When asked to spell an unfamiliar word, less able spellers, instead of trying to visualize, revert to a lower-level strategy of trying to spell the word the way it sounds. Research indicates that the single most important component of spelling instruction is the self-corrected pretest, in which the teacher dictates the words, the students have a go at spelling them, and then the teacher presents the correct spelling while the students self-correct (Fitzsimmons & Loomer, 1980; Horn, 1954). As the teacher spells each word correctly out loud, the student touches each letter in the word with his or her pencil. This focuses visual, aural, and tactile attention simultaneously on the words misspelled as well as on the correction. Following the pretest, students are directed to:

1. Look at the correctly spelled word carefully.
2. Say the word.
3. With eyes closed, visualize the word.
4. Cover the word and then write it.
5. Check the spelling.
6. If the word is misspelled, repeat steps 1 through 5. (Fitzgerald, 1951)

Teachers in the UCI Writing Project also have students sketch the word to imprint a visual associated with the word in their minds, something also advocated by Marzano and Pickering (2005).

Word Trees and Word Sorts

To help students see the relationships between a group of words that grow from the same base and root words, students can work as a whole class, in pairs, or individually to create a word tree, as in Figure 12.7. Bear and colleagues (2000) suggest laminating a base and

Figure 12.7 **Word Tree** (*Source:* Bear, Invernizzi, et al., *Words Their Way: Word Study for Phonics, Vocabulary and Spelling Instruction*, 2nd edition. Copyright © 2000. Reprinted by permission of Prentice-Hall, Inc., Upper Saddle River, NJ)

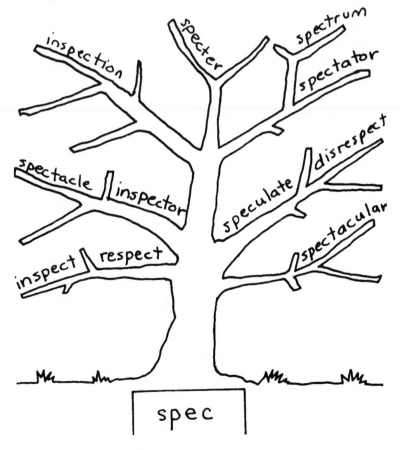

Figure 12.8   **Word Sort**

Open Sort				
chateau	shamble	sheer	shadow	shingle
chandelier	chauffeur	shoal	chiffon	chivalry

branches and writing with water-based overhead pens. That way, after the tree has been up for a week or so, it can be erased and a new word tree created. This activity helps students to grasp the spelling–meaning relationship: that is, the fact that words related in meaning are often related in spelling as well, despite changes in sound (Chomsky, 1970; Templeton, 1983; cited in Bear et al., 2000, p. 251).

Teachers in the UCI Writing Project, across the grade levels, have also looked to *Words Their Way* (Bear et al., 2000) for ideas for word sorts. Like sentence sorts, word sorts give students "hands-on opportunities to manipulate word features in a way that allows them to generalize beyond isolated, individual examples to entire groups of words that work the same way" (pp. 3–4). Word sorts help students to "find order, to compare and contrast, and to pay attention to what remains the same despite minor variations" (p. 2). Like sentence sorts, word sorts can be closed (i.e., with categories specified by the teacher) or open (in which students can construct their own hypotheses). The teacher designs or selects word sorts after assessing the students' developmental level and instructional needs. For example, Figure 12.8 contains an open word sort for high school students developed by UCI Writing Project codirector Catherine D'Aoust. In this open sort, students are asked to put the words in the sort into two categories and then to make a generalization about why they placed the words in the categories they did. In this case, students will notice that although the words fall into *sh* and *ch* categories, both sets of words make the \sh\ sound. Students may notice— or the teacher may have to explain—that the *ch* words are all derived from French.

WHAT TO DO ABOUT ERROR

What to do about error? That is the question! What and how much to mark as incorrect on student papers is a matter of considerable debate. The freshman composition students at UCI during the implementation of the deep six policy described at the beginning of this chapter probably felt like they were writing their way through a veritable minefield every time they put pen to paper. They could make syntactic errors (sentence fragments, run-ons, nonparallel structure, etc.), morphological errors (tense and number agreement errors), semantic and pragmatic errors (diction errors, wrong tone, etc.), and graphological errors (faulty punctuation, misspelling, etc.) (Noguchi, 1991, p. 18). These errors might be competence errors, meaning that they resulted from a lack of knowledge or ability; or performance errors, meaning that they derived from a mistake in language processing in student's heads (Murdick, 1996, p. 42). As Constance Weaver (1996) reminds us, whose writing growth wouldn't be "stunted" under the specter of the error beast (p. 81)? Yet, as Lisa Delpit (1995) emphatically points out, we do our students a grave disservice if we do not make clear to them that command of standard written English is one of the codes of power (pp. 24–25). How do we, as teachers, cope with this dilemma? Matching the findings of Connors and Lunsford (1988) on the frequency of errors committed by college students and the findings of Hairston's (1981) attitudinal survey of people in sixty-three occupations other than English teaching who ranked errors from most serious to least serious, Rei Noguchi (1991) concludes that it makes sense to place the greatest emphasis on those errors that occur most frequently *and* that seriously bother people in positions of power and hence may have social or socioeconomic consequences (p. 31). These include sentence boundary errors, subject–verb agreement errors, and punctuation errors (especially involving the use of commas) (pp. 33–34).

In responding to student writers as an editor, I try to:

- Encourage multiple-draft writing so that students who need to can attend to composing first and focus on editing in a later draft
- Pay attention to students' ideas and let them know when errors interfere with my understanding and/or appreciation of the meaning of the text
- Resist the temptation to mark everything (although it can be difficult to see an error and bypass it)
- Hold students accountable for the conventions I have taught in relation to the writing task and then expect students to develop an accumulating repertoire of skills over time
- Refrain from doing the corrections for the students (which gives me practice but not them) but rather mark a problem area and invite students to find and correct the problem
- Avoid making proofreading marks students don't understand (the student of one of our Writing Project teachers thought for an entire year that the teacher was putting happy faces on her papers when he tried to show her that periods go inside quotation marks ")
- Recognize that when students are taking a risk and tackling a topic that makes them stretch cognitively, or taking a risk linguistically by experimenting with style, their surface errors may increase
- Engage students in collaborating on editing their work and provide editing checklists delineating what to look for
- Look for patterns in students' errors and conference with them one-on-one to talk about what I notice
- Praise students when they do something correctly that they have had trouble with in the past—and express appreciation for stylistically apt sentences
- Provide an incentive for students to correct their errors by awarding extra credit points for editing done after final drafts have been graded
- Encourage students to keep track of their problems and their progress through a personalized error log

Provided below are just a few ideas to help students self-correct their own errors.

Yes Twice, Comma Splice

Of all the errors my students make at the university level, by far the most common is the comma splice. I have tried a variety of strategies to teach students to detect this type of sentence error, but this is one that seems to work best. Developed by Todd Huck, an instructor of English at Santa Ana College in Santa Ana, California, "yes twice, comma splice" is a simple and effective method for detecting comma splices. Students peruse their own writing for sentences that have a comma roughly in the middle. They then take a sticky note or 3-by-5 card and cover up the part of the sentence that comes after the comma:

- ■ We ate pizza, it tasted good.

- ■ We ate pizza, ▭

Students then check to see if the first part of the sentence has a subject and a verb.

$\qquad$ **s   v**
■   We ate pizza, ⬚⬚⬚⬚⬚⬚⬚

They then cover up the first part of the sentence to check the words after the comma, and follow the same procedure.

$\qquad$ **s   v**
■   ⬚⬚⬚⬚⬚⬚⬚ , it tasted good

Huck's rule is that if you can say yes twice (to whether you have a subject and verb in each of the two parts separated by commas), and if there is no conjunction after the comma (as in "We ate pizza, and it tasted good"), you have written a comma splice—which may be corrected as follows:

- We ate pizza. It tasted good.
- We ate pizza, and it tasted good.
- We ate pizza; it tasted good.

I have found that it takes about a five-minute conference and two or three examples before the student I'm working with says, "Oh, I get it." The teacher can also pull sentences with comma splices from a class set of papers and have students correct them in partners.

Sentence Drafts

Todd Huck also swears by the sentence draft. This strategy involves having students start at the end of their paper and, working from the bottom up, hit the return key on the computer after each sentence. This results in each individual sentence being printed on its own line. When students read their papers backward, line by line, with sentences divorced from their intended meaning, they can see the problems in their syntax more easily. If they read each sentence aloud, they can also hear where sentences have gone awry.

Job Cards

Just as students benefit by working collaboratively to respond to the content of one another's writing, they can enhance their skills as editors by working jointly on issues of correctness. Many teachers avoid engaging students in writing groups for editing purposes because they believe it's like the blind leading the blind. However, it is the teacher's job to train students in what to look for. It is also important to separate editing groups from writing groups: students need to hear first about what communicates in their writing before they are presented with a list of mistakes. Job cards, tailored by the teacher to the specific writing task, can be as useful for editing as they are for revision. The companion website contains some sample editing job cards designed by UCI teaching credential candidate Jenny Hussa for an essay on *Antigone*. They include Run-On and Fragment Fixers, Spelling Champions, Verb Victors, and Quotation Inspectors.

Editing Checklist

Ultimately, our goal is for students to be able to edit their own writing with confidence and competence. Providing students with a correcting/editing checklist like the one in Figure 12.9 to use when doing the final proofreading of their paper can be useful.

Figure 12.9   **Editing Checklist**

	Yes	No
• I remembered not to punctuate my title either by underlining it or by enclosing it in quotations.		
• I indicated new paragraphs by indenting.		
• I used "yes twice, comma splice" to look for sentence errors and also examined my sentences from the bottom up. I have also read the whole paper aloud to myself.		
• I kept the same verb tense throughout my essay unless the content dictated a change.		
• When I used pronouns, I made sure the noun each pronoun referred to was clear.		
• When I used prepositional phrases and modifying clauses, I made sure they were adjacent to the words they modified.		
• I have followed the conventions for quoting from the text.		
• I have looked up in the dictionary every word I was uncertain of how to spell.		

CELEBRATING CORRECTNESS

Constance Weaver (1996) observes that when teachers first give up the security of traditional grammar books, they may find it "reassuring" (p. 172) to teach a commercially prepared set of minilessons such as *Daily Oral Language* (Vail & Papenfuss, 1989/1990). However, her observation is that the sentences teachers put up on the board daily for students to correct are often not representative of the kinds of errors that the students themselves make most frequently. In addition, many of the teachers in our Writing Project are concerned about the focus on the hunt for error rather than the modeling of correctness. As an alternative, our teachers use the age-old strategy of dictation. Through dictation, students can listen carefully to language structures delivered orally and practice transcribing oral speech into written language. When the teacher puts the dictation excerpt on the overhead, what the students see modeled in front of them is technically correct. They can then look for discrepancies in their own writing, and the class can discuss where differences represent mistakes on their part and where certain elements of correctness, such as the use of an exclamation point, are matters of preference.

Further, in the interest of celebrating correctness rather than always rooting out and penalizing error, teachers develop Wall of Fame and Sentence of the Week bulletin boards. They are constantly on the lookout, while reading students' papers, for exemplary work to immerse the students in. When students see the work of their classmates as well as their own work held up as models to emulate, right alongside of the words of professional writers, they are more likely to attend to issues of style and correctness in their own writing.

To Sum Up

For both pragmatic and academic reasons, it is the teacher's job to acquaint students with the conventions of applied grammar as well as to help them develop sentence sense and sentence craft. In the same way that it is essential for the teacher to make visible for inexperienced readers and writers the cognitive strategies that experienced readers and writers use when they make meaning from and with texts, it is important for the teacher to:

- make students consciously, linguistically aware of the grammatical repertoire they already possess;
- provide them with the vocabulary to talk about writing from a technical standpoint;
- help them understand how sentences are constructed and empower them to manipulate language and make stylistic choices;
- expand their awareness of grammatical and stylistic options that are available to them as writers; and
- assist them in the revision and editing of their writing.

Although there is considerable disagreement about how to define grammar and what to teach when one teaches grammar, there does seem to be a consensus that grammar should be taught as a tool for writing improvement rather than as an academic subject. Further, researchers advocate delivering a "minimum of grammar for maximum benefits" (Weaver, 1996, p. 142) in a much more interactive and affectively engaging manner. Research indicates that students learn grammar, vocabulary, and spelling better when they are immersed in using language in meaningful contexts; involved in actively making hypotheses about how language works; invited to experiment with language not only linguistically but spatially, kinesthetically, musically, and so on; and encouraged to personalize learning by creating their own memory links. When learning is challenging and fun, students remember better. Through appropriate structure, practice, the engendering of ownership, and opportunities to collaborate, students can internalize grammatical concepts and apply them to their own writing. In short, all of the principles of instructional scaffolding (Langer & Applebee, 1986) are as relevant to the teaching of grammar as to the broader arena of reading and writing instruction.

Learning Log Reflection

Brosnahan and Neuleib (1995) postulate that most English teachers "enter the profession because they love literature, both reading and writing it," and that they find "linguistics and stylistics the least appealing part of the English curriculum because both have no 'life' in them" (p. 206). Think about how you felt about the teaching of grammar before reading this chapter. Has it generally been an aspect of the curriculum you look forward to teaching, dread, or just feel apprehensive about? Have your ideas about grammar itself or about how you might go about teaching it been influenced by the pedagogical strategies showcased in the chapter? How do you plan to keep the error beast at bay and make correctness creative?

Assessing Students' Reading and Writing in the Classroom

Dan Kirby, a frequent guest consultant to the UCI Writing Project Summer Institute on the topics of memoir writing and portfolios, is fond of speaking in metaphors. Here are two of my favorites from his presentations:

■ Education is like planting a seed, nurturing it and watching it grow. But the educational testers keep pulling the plants up out of the ground to see how the roots are doing.

■ Education is like making soup. You assemble all the essential ingredients and then put the pot on to simmer so the flavors will mature slowly. But the educational testers keep lifting up the lid and asking, "Is it done yet? Is it done yet?"

TEACHING AND TESTING: PROCESS VERSUS PRODUCT

Kirby's comparisons point out the discrepancy between a process approach to teaching and a product approach to testing. If we want to be "about the business of growing thinkers," as Kirby and Kuykendall (1991, p. 201) suggest, we want to create a climate for learning in which students are encouraged to take risks, in which it is OK to make mistakes, and in which it is desirable to construct one's own understandings in collaboration with others. Contrast this with an educational testing system in which the pressure to perform and to come out on top is so great that in one midwestern school district all kindergartners begin each day by trying to correctly fill in such test practice items as "Today is . . . ❏ sunny ❏ cloudy ❏ windy ❏ snowy— and in which these students (and struggling readers throughout all the grades) are referred to as "bubble children" (Calkins, Montgomery, & Santman, 1998, p. 5).

Students are not oblivious to the discrepancy between what we educators say we value and what we do. I often tell my students that embedded in the word "learn" is the word "earn." "What you earn," I tell them, "your reward for committing yourself to your education, is what you learn." But this idea—that a person's growth as a learner is its own reward—is often a hard sell to students who have faced a battery of two thousand test items per year in the K–12 system (Tierney,

Carter, & Desai, 1991). Test-weary students have already experienced what it's like to be transformed from "normal students into stressed-out adolescents" (Strickland & Strickland, 1998, p. 207) over taking the SAT exam, on which a matter of points can affect a student's chances of being accepted to a good college. "Sure," students agree, "lifelong learning is really important. Now, how long does that essay you were describing have to be, and how many points will it take to get an A?"

Students can't help but feel ambivalent about the goals of education in the face of so many mixed messages, throughout their schooling, about what is important. In fact, Elliot Eisner (1992) detects "more than a little ambivalence" about test scores on the part of educators themselves. "We have a strong tendency to proclaim the educational poverty of test scores and then turn around and use them as indices of our own success, thus legitimating the validity of the public's concerns about the quality of education," he remarks. "If test scores in their conventional form do not reveal what really matters in schools, we should not use them to judge our 'success' " (p. 4).

Zemelman, Daniels, and Hyde (1998) acknowledge that, in the end, teachers are just another group of Americans and that we have "acquired the evaluation fixation just as deeply, and in much the same way, as other citizens" (p. 249). But the keen interest of teachers in the dilemmas of testing has given rise to a movement toward exploring new forms of assessment, evaluation, grading, and reporting student progress, particularly in the areas of reading and writing. Many of these newer approaches focus on the process as well as the products of learning and may actually assist teachers in "growing thinkers" in their classrooms.

RESPONSE, ASSESSMENT, EVALUATION, GRADING: DEFINING TERMS

A committee of the National Council of Teachers of English was charged with investigating alternatives to grading students on writing—ways to evaluate progress that would be more sensitive to the needs of students. The NCTE group began by distinguishing among four concepts: response, assessment, evaluation, and grading (Tchudi, 1997). Because, first and foremost, students "need coaches, not judges" (Holaday, 1997, p. 35), it is essential that they receive a *response* on their first draft thinking that stems directly from the teacher's reaction to the students' individual texts and that is richly descriptive, personalized, and independent from any rating system. When responding, teachers assume the role of a partner in learning rather than an evaluator. As Holaday (1997) points out, "Coaches are friendly; judges are aloof. Coaches want you to do well; judges don't care" (p. 41). Responders focus on providing readers and writers with positive reinforcement so that they will be motivated to continue to compose and to revise meaning.

The term *assessment* refers to the deliberate use of many methods to gather evidence that the reader or writer is meeting his or her learning goals. Assessment is an ongoing part of instruction. It goes beyond response to offer formative, in-progress, here-and-now feedback to both the student and the teacher about how a reading or writing project is turning out or how the learner is progressing. Assessment is descriptive rather than evaluative, but it keeps an achievement target in mind—that is, "the extent to which the desired results are on the way to being achieved and to what extent they have been achieved" (Wiggins & McTighe, 2005, p. 6). Assessment data can be used to construct the criteria or benchmarks for evaluation. In this sense, assessment can be analytic (focused on developing specific criteria) as well as descriptive. Students use the in-progress data from assessment to monitor and adjust their performance; teachers use this data to monitor and adjust their instruction.

Whereas assessment is formative in nature, evaluation is more final or summative. Dan Kirby points out to his students that the word *evaluation* has the word *value* in it and that evaluation involves making value judgments about how the student work compares to certain fixed criteria. Even though evaluation lends itself to rating or ranking, this need not be the end of the learning process. Students often perceive evaluation as punitive, but effective evaluation should provide students with necessary constructive information and the impetus to improve in the future.

Strickland and Strickland (1998) note, "No matter how we assess and evaluate, for most of us, there comes a day when the Scantron sheets arrive in our mailbox and we have to report grades" (p. 129). *Grading* reduces a student's performances over time to one single symbol—a symbol that often doesn't communicate "descriptive information of any significance" (Tchudi, 1997, p. xv). Douglas Reeves (1998) makes the case that "saying that Matilda's math performance is a 'D+' suggests that she has some work to do this summer, but also suggests that she passed and is ready for the next grade. In fact, the 'D+' could mean one of several things. . . ." Reeves enumerates (1998, pp. 72–73):

- Matilda received average grades of 76 on all of her homework assignments and tests.
- Matilda does not understand the material at all, but she tries very hard, behaves well in class, and her earnestness has impressed the teacher so that a passing grade is appropriate. The "D+" is the teacher's attempt to provide Matilda with some self-esteem, which the teacher understands is important for "slow" children like Matilda.
- Matilda excels at math and is perhaps the brightest student in class. But she repeatedly turns in her homework assignments late and is missing some assignments.
- "Matilda is just not responsible," the teacher concludes; "Perhaps getting a 'D+' will teach her a lesson."
- Be honest, the teacher simply does not like Matilda, and Matilda makes it quite clear that the feeling is mutual.

In other words, Matilda's grade could be a measure of her achievement, ability, effort, growth, or even behavior. If a teacher has criteria, it is often invisible to the students. Yet end-of-term grades from different teachers at different schools in different geographical areas are used to calculate grade point averages that colleges use to compare students against one another "without substantial questioning about their intended meaning" (Reeves, 1998, p. 73). The companion website includes a chart delineating the characteristics of response, assessment, evaluation, and grading.

WHERE TO START: BEGIN WITH THE END IN MIND

Quoting Stephen Covey (1989), Jim Burke (1999) reminds us to "begin with the end in mind" (p. 171). In other words, we need to ask ourselves, What is the goal of instruction? What do we want our students to know and be able to do? Wiggins and McTighe (2005) argue that rather than thinking like activity designers, who focus on what resources, activities, and assignments will be interesting and engaging in relation to a specific topic, teachers should think like assessors and work backwards: identify desired results; determine acceptable evidence; and then plan learning experiences and instruction. In the backward design model, assessment is not only something that occurs at the end of instruction but also is a tool for planning from the beginning.

What Do We Want Students to Know and Be Able to Do?

What do we want our students to know and be able to do? To answer this question, many scholars suggest that we look first to the national, state, and local standards for English language arts. *Content standards* like the 1996 IRA/NCTE Standards for the English Language Arts, shown in Chapter 3 describe the general expectations for what a student should know and be able to do in specific disciplines. Most state standards, such as the 1997 California Content Standards for English Language Arts, go beyond the generic knowledge and skills belonging to particular disciplines to specify the benchmarks or expectations of students at critical levels of schooling. *Performance standards* such as the New Standards Performance Standards (1998), which are aligned with the IRA/NCTE Content Standards, delineate the levels of task performance (e.g., exceeds the standard, meets the standard, proficient, basic, and limited) that students must reach to demonstrate that they have met or are on their way toward meeting the content standards. Performance standards consider the question "How good is good enough?"

Determining Where Your Students Are on the Road to Meeting the Standards

In order to design curriculum, instruction, and assessment based on what students need to know and be able to do, you need not only to determine what standards you are working toward but also to assess where your students currently are as learners. Early in the semester, it is important to gather multiple sources of data rather than a single piece of evidence about what students can do as readers and writers.

Standardized Tests   Although teachers have access to standardized test scores, most teachers I know rarely consult these scores early on. They may not wish to prejudge their students; they may be distrustful of how valid the scores are as an indicator of ability; the scores may not be available in a timely fashion; and teachers may not have the time to pore over more than one hundred student files before the start of school. Tierney, Carter, and Desai (1991) point out that current standardized testing procedures reflect a limited view of reading and writing. These procedures test reading and writing separately; a predetermined response is the only acceptable answer; reading tests are based on snippets of texts that often lack a story line; writing tests often do not include having the students write—or, if writing is involved, students are given a topic and purpose designed by someone else and are expected to work by themselves; and, in most cases, student performance is summed up in a single numerical score, which is then translated into a grade level equivalent, stanine, or percentile rank. In short, standardized tests "do not reflect what we teach in our classrooms" and are not "representative of the kind of work that students do daily" (p. 27).

One promising use of standardized achievement tests in the classroom that could positively inform instruction involves the conversion of test scores into Lexile measures. Originally developed under the auspices of National Institute of Child Health and Human Development, the Lexile Framework for Reading from Metametrics (www.lexile.com) is the only educational tool currently available that can link texts and readers on a common scale (called a Lexile) and provide an empirical method of ability and performance.

Teacher Observations   Most teachers learn a lot about their students early on in the semester simply by "kid-watching" (Goodman, 1978). Through observing students as they read, write, talk, and listen to others, we can tell who is fully present and engaged in the class and who is only going through the motions, distinguish between the quiet and the reluctant learners, visibly see the indicators of who "gets" what's going on and who is lost, tell who likes to collaborate and who doesn't, and so forth. Everything we observe constitutes data. Whether we keep anecdotal notes or simply record impressions in our heads, we need to become "mindful" (Claggett, 1996) about how to use these data to improve the learning environment for all students. If we are doing all the talking in the classroom, it is much harder to focus on what's going on in the hearts and minds of the students. Strickland and Strickland (1998) note that teachers need to come out from behind their lecterns and observe their students participating in genuine learning experiences in order to be able to conduct assessment by observation.

Informal Reading Inventories   Most of the secondary English teachers I have surveyed feel they are on solid ground collecting and analyzing a range of writing samples to diagnose and respond to their students' needs as writers. They admit to being far less confident, however, about how to assess students' needs as readers and how to design appropriate reading instruction—particularly for students who appear to be struggling. In fact, it is these teachers' observations of students who are having difficulty in the act of reading, talking about their reading, or responding to reading in writing that often cause them to consult the standardized test scores, more or less to confirm their suspicion that a student is indeed a "low" reader. But what to do next?

Much of this book focuses on how to make visible for inexperienced readers the strategies that experienced readers use when interacting with texts. But research suggests that the aspects of meaning construction that give students trouble vary depending on their level of reading acquisition (Leslie & Caldwell, 1995); so some teachers may want to administer an informal reading inventory to examine students' reading behavior and to diagnose conditions under which individual students can identify and comprehend texts successfully or unsuccessfully. Informal reading inventories (IRIs) are nonstandardized, individually administered tests that consist of a series of graded passages, each with accompanying comprehension questions. Generally, the assessment will include reading aloud, reading silently, and listening to a text being read by the assessor. Teachers can use IRIs to determine students' independent, instructional, and frustration reading levels, to match students to appropriate texts, and to assess specific reading behaviors as a guide to intervention instruction.

Two IRIs used in California are the *Qualitative Reading Inventory–III* (Leslie & Caldwell, 2000) and the *Bader Reading and Language Inventory* (Bader, 2004). The former is geared for primary through middle school, the latter for primary through high school. Because IRIs are administered one-on-one and the process is time-consuming, however, it is unrealistic for the teacher to use this type of assessment with more than a small selection of students.

Teachers in the UCI Writing Project, especially middle school humanities teachers, have also made use of an assessment strategy developed by educational therapists Ann Kaganoff and Brenda Spencer called the prediction–knowledge relationship (PKR) task. In a personal communication (2000) Kaganoff explained:

> The Prediction–Knowledge Relationship works very well with books like the social studies text or health, because the pages are usually rich in readers' aids such as titles and subtitles, margin notes and question boxes, pictures and captions, etc.
>
> You select four facing pages, usually the first four pages of a lesson or chapter. Try to select a lesson or chapter that has a title that gives some information about the general topic. You then cut out a plain paper mask that covers all of the text but reveals the remainder of

the page information (titles, subtitles, etc.), holding the mask in place with Post-it tape. You then show the masked pages to the student, telling the student to inspect the pages so that he/she can then tell you what he/she thinks the lesson is going to be about. You have a blank sheet of paper on which you write what the student thinks (predicts) the lesson will be about, using the available page information. To get a good feel for the student's performance level, you try to elicit 3–6 predictions. The task is individually administered, and the whole process takes 5–7 minutes.

The PKR provides teachers with information related to the following three questions:

- Is the student effectively using text clues and relevant print information before reading?
- What prior knowledge background does the student bring to the meaning-making task, and how well is it activated and utilized?
- Is the student developing the necessary frameworks for understanding how knowledge is ordered in the specific area we are reading about?

Students are scored by the teacher as Novice, Emergent, or Advanced, based on their areas of knowledge about text, relevant background knowledge, and frameworks for organizing knowledge. The teacher can then use the information to shape both individualized and whole class instruction. A more in-depth explanation of the PKR and the scoring guide are available on the companion website. For teachers who are interested in assessing students' textual reading/study aids, vocabulary knowledge, and comprehension but wish to conduct a whole class assessment, *Content Area Literacy* (Readence, Bean, & Baldwin, 1998, pp. 66–70) contains instructions for how to select text material and develop a content reading inventory to administer to the whole class.

Student Surveys and Self-Assessment   Student themselves are a great source of data around which to design curriculum, instruction, and assessment. Further, asking students for their input helps to foster class climate and build ownership. Janet Allen's book *It's Never Too Late* (1995) includes an integrated reading/writing fall survey that asks students to describe what they have liked most and least about previous English classes, rate how important they consider reading to be in their lives, decide whether they feel they are a better readers or writers, fill out a checklist of the genres of reading they like best, circle what types of writing they have engaged in in the last six months, and so on (pp. 183–185). Nancie Atwell's 1998 revision of *In the Middle* contains separate beginning-of-the-year reading and writing surveys that are similar to Allen's but include some additional interesting questions, such as "If you had to guess, how many books would you say you owned? How many books would you say there are in your house? How many books would say you say you've read in the last twelve months?" (p. 495) and "What does someone have to do or know in order to write well?" (p. 494). Although teachers are free to copy these surveys from these professional resources and administer them, the surveys can also serve as point of departure for the teacher's own individually designed survey or set of learning log entries. The important point is for teachers to avail themselves of the rich data that the student can directly provide about where they are as readers and writers.

Teachers in the UCI Writing Project have enjoyed using Fran Claggett's (1996, pp. 15–16) task "What Kind of Reader Are You?" Available on the companion website along with a sample student response, this survey uses the metaphor of food (anorexic reader, perpetual diet reader, fast food reader, etc.) as a jumping-off point for students to assess their "literary palate." After a lively group discussion about students' literary tastes, favorite books, and memories of reading experiences, the journal entries students write for this task can be used by the teacher to assess where students are as both writers and readers.

Figure 13.1   **Learning Log**

> **Learning Log Reflection: How I Learned to Read and Write**
>
> Sift through your memories of learning to read and write. Are they mostly positive or negative? Are they vivid or murky? What are your earliest memories? What people come to mind? Are they relatives or teachers? Explore your own learning process and paint a picture so that I can experience your memories with you.

Assessing Attitude   James Popham (1995) remarks, " I personally regard affective variables as far more significant than cognitive variables. How many times, for example, have you seen people who weren't all that 'gifted' intellectually still succeed because they were highly motivated and hard working? Conversely, how many times have you seen truly able people simply veer away from challenges because they did not consider themselves worthy?" (p. 180). Although the surveys and the self-assessment activity described previously indirectly provide a lot of data about student affect, I find that the learning log reflection in Figure 13.1, which I describe in Chapter 4 in connection with a reminiscence by my student Hetty Jun, gives me a more direct window into the hearts and minds of my students. These log entries help me pinpoint the students who have emotional baggage they carry with them as readers or writers—as a result of, for example, being put into the "low" reading group or receiving papers covered in red ink—and who will need extra encouragement along with constructive feedback. They also help me target the students who love to read but "hate" writing *(the situation is almost never the reverse)* and whom I will have to win over.

For teachers interested in both qualitative and quantitative measures of student attitudes, the BJP Middle/Secondary Reading Attitude Survey (Baldwin, Johnson, & Peer, 1980) or the Daley/Miller Writing Apprehension Survey (Daley & Miller, 1975) can be administered and scored on a Scantron form. Such information is most useful in a pre/post design through which the teacher can assess change in attitude over time.

CRITERIA FOR EFFECTIVE ASSESSMENT

Once teachers have a grasp of where their students are as readers and writers and have determined what they want their students to know and be able to do, it is important to design a long-term assessment plan that will guide "the timing and use of a variety of assessment procedures" (Tierney, Carter, & Desai, 1991, p. 35). The following guidelines for effective assessment can inform the development of a long-term plan:

- Begin with a vision of success and delineate what the benchmarks are for achieving success in your classroom.
- Make assessment part of the ongoing instructional process; base it on the reading/writing experiences in which students are routinely engaged in the classroom.
- Define the overall purposes of assessment for yourself, for your students, and for the parents.
- Stress that assessment is formative, not summative.
- Clearly articulate and provide written criteria for success on assessment tasks.
- Make sure the type of assessment you select matches the task that is being assessed.
- Assess the process as well as the product.
- Provide timely feedback that is descriptive and analytic rather than judgmental.

- Make sure students are active participants; involve them in providing input for assessment design, in taking part in peer assessment, and in conducting self-assessment.
- Triangulate data to provide multiple sources of data for determining progress.
- Spend a moderate amount of time on assessment, promote collaboration, and avoid competition when possible.
- Use assessment to inform instruction and teacher effectiveness as well as to determine student progress. (Spandel & Stiggins, 1997; Tierney, Carter, & Desai, 1991; Zemelman, Daniels, & Hyde, 1998)

ASSESSMENT OR EVALUATION?

Distinguishing between assessment and evaluation is easier said than done. The difference between the two seems to lie not in the type of measure (e.g., multiple-choice or short-answer test, essay exam, composition, portfolio) but in when and why students and teachers are undertaking and/or reviewing the work. For example, when assessing how their portfolio is progressing in a formative way, students might conduct weekly "audits" (Kirby & Kuykendall, 1991) of the contents to document how their work is going. The responses to questions such as *"What's in stock? How many pieces do you have in your portfolio and in what shape are they?"* or *"What's on back order? What is still in your head? What pieces are you thinking about and planning to write?"* (p. 217) help a student go back and revisit prior learning and accomplishments in order to revise meaning or to go forward to a new challenge. These responses also give the teacher windows into students' minds and a sense of who needs teacher guidance. Or, in a school operating on trimesters, that same portfolio might be submitted three times a year, along with a student self-evaluation, for evaluation by the teacher according to a set of clearly delineated criteria.

The intent is what differentiates assessment and evaluation more than whether the product (or process) receives a score. Although evaluation tends to rely more on numerical scoring than does assessment, some assessments are also submitted for a score. Assessment scores generally place student progress on a horizontal continuum (e.g., limited, developing, capable, strong, exemplary) based on criteria related to what the student should know and be able to do at each level of performance. In evaluation the rating is more vertical, from best to worst (e.g., superior, commendable, adequate, barely adequate, little evidence of achievement), and is based on set criteria for what the final product should contain.

Wiggins and McTighe (2005) make the point that the evidence of learning that teachers collect in their classrooms should include observations and dialogues, traditional quizzes and tests, and performance tasks and projects, as well as students' assessments gathered over time. They divide assessment (or evaluation, depending on the intent) into three categories: quizzes and test items; academic prompts; and performance tasks and projects. *Quizzes* and *test items* are designed to help the teacher assess or evaluate factual information, concepts, and discrete skills. They use selected response formats (in which students select their response from a set of possible answers provided by the teacher, as in multiple-choice testing) or short-answer formats. These assessments/evaluations are easy to score, because the answers are convergent rather than divergent. *Academic prompts* require constructed responses; that is, students construct answers in their own words to open-ended questions for which there is no single right answer. These tasks call on the student to think critically rather than to rely on recall and typically require an explanation or defense of the answer given. Academic prompts lead to products like a response to an essay exam or the composition of an original essay, or to behaviors like the presentation of a speech or a one-act play. *Performance*

Figure 13.2 **Assessments Continuum** (*Source:* G. Wiggins and J. McTighe, *Understanding by Design,* second edition, p. 152. Copyright 2005 Association for Supervision and Curriculum Development. Reprinted by permission. To learn more, visit ASCD at www.ascd.org.)

tasks and *projects* are longer-term, multistaged projects that require a production or performance. They differ from prompts in that they typically require the student to address a specified audience; are based on a specific purpose that relates to that audience; involve a setting that realistically approximates experiences or challenges an adult would encounter in a similar situation; and allow students opportunities to personalize the task (p. 14).

James Popham (1995) observes that "performance assessment typically requires students to respond to a small number of more significant tasks rather than respond to a large number of less significant tasks" (p. 143). These tasks often have individual scoring guides for each task within the larger project. For example, the International Performance Assessment System (Reeves, 1998) describes a research project for language arts in grades 9 through 12 that includes standards/performance-based scoring guides for seven distinct tasks: Select a research topic; decide what resources you will research; read your sources; interview an expert; outline your paper; write the first draft; write the final paper; create an oral presentation (pp. 191–205). This is a good example of a *process-based performance.*

In designing assessment and evaluation tasks, the teacher must determine what the purpose of the assessment is. If the intent is to check for comprehension, quizzes and tests may be a perfectly appropriate tool. If the goal is to foster higher-level thinking through a focused task that is framed by the teacher and has a somewhat limited scope, then academic prompts will fit the bill. If the aim is to challenge students to embark on a personalized multistaged project in which they can demonstrate their process of meaning construction over time, then performance assessment is called for. Wiggins and McTighe (2005, p. 152) suggest that teachers consider scaffolding their assessments on a continuum. The design they offer is shown in Figure 13.2.

USING RUBRICS TO ASSESS AND/OR EVALUATE STUDENT WORK

Some types of assessment and most forms of evaluation of academic prompts, performances, or projects involve the application of a rubric, scale, or scoring guide delineating the criteria on which the student work is being measured. In his metanalysis of experimental treatment studies in the field of composition, George Hillocks (1984) observes that the use of scales, which he defines as a "set of criteria embodied in an actual scale or set of questions for application to pieces of writing" (p. 153), have a "powerful effect" (p. 161) on enhancing quality in writing. Hillocks stresses that scales "must be manifest in some concrete form, not simply existing in the mind of the teacher" (p. 153).

Often called rubrics or scoring guides, scales, if they are well designed and articulated, not only help teachers assess or evaluate student work but clearly delineate for students what they need to be able to do in order to achieve success and/or meet a performance standard.

Spandel and Stiggins (1997) stress that the most effective criteria are clearly written in language that is easy for students to understand; focus on significant aspects of the task or performance; clearly distinguish between the levels of performance that will achieve certain scores; use positive language, even for the beginning performance levels; and can be used as a teaching tool. Ideally, when used for assessment purposes, scoring guides are, at the very least, shared with students; often they may be developed collaboratively between students and the teacher. Rubrics are sometimes withheld from students during summative evaluation; Hillocks's research (1984), however, demonstrates that students "internalize criteria and bring them to bear in generating new material even when they do not have the criteria in front of them" (p. 161) if they receive the rubric early on and are engaged in applying the specific criteria to their own writing, to that of their peers, and to models supplied by the teacher.

Types of Scoring Rubrics

In *How Writing Shapes Thinking* (1987), Langer and Applebee observe that the most successful instruction occurs when the students and the teacher have a "shared understanding of specific goals of the instructional activity" (p. 140). Scoring rubrics are one vehicle for developing that shared understanding. As Strickland and Strickland (1998) point out, "Rubrics can do something grades alone never do: They can define quality. They give students the criteria and terminology to respond to their own and others' work" (p. 77). There are several different types of scoring rubrics that teachers can design, individually or in collaboration with their students, depending on what they wish to value and, hence, evaluate in students' reading and/or writing performance. The companion website provides a chart of the types of scoring rubrics included in this book. Almost all are task-specific rubrics—that is, they are tailored to a particular demonstration lesson, activity, or performance—as opposed to generic rubrics, which are applicable to a broad writing domain or type (e.g., the essay), regardless of the prompt. However, the task-specific prompts can be used as a springboard for designing rubrics for other reading or writing tasks.

Holistic Scoring   According to Spandel and Stiggins (1997), "Holistic scoring is based on the premise that the whole is more than the sum of its parts and that the most valid assessment of writing will consider how all the components—ideas, mechanics, voice, and so forth—work in harmony to achieve an overall effect" (p. 32). Based on a set of specific criteria for what constitutes a certain score, readers give students' papers a single general impression mark for the overall quality of the paper. (See, for example, the holistic rubric for the interpretive essay on Tennyson's "Mariana" in Chapter 7.) In situations in which students' papers are being evaluated by more than one person, readers routinely score a set of anchor papers before rating individual student work in order to internalize the criteria for scoring and to achieve some consensus on the levels of performance necessary for each score point. When holistic scoring is used for large-scale evaluation purposes, raters score but do not comment on the papers. However, I have rarely seen classroom teachers use any of the various types of scoring rubrics in lieu of making notations on the papers themselves, unless they are reading a set of final drafts that they have already commented on at the rough draft stage.

Analytical Scoring   Whereas holistic scoring focuses on the quality of the paper as a whole, analytical (or analytic) scoring involves determining separate scores for each of the prominent characteristics or traits of writing—usually of a particular domain or writing type. Spandel and Stiggins (1997) argue that analytical scoring offers the most complete picture of a student's writing, because the scoring system provides detailed information about areas of strength and areas that need improvement. This enables students to target their efforts during revision or when composing future papers. Based on the key qualities of writing that teachers in school districts across the country have most often identified as significant, Spandel and Stiggins have constructed a generic analytical trait scoring guide that focuses on the six traits shown in Figure 13.3. For each of the six traits, they provide a scoring guide with specific criteria for achieving anywhere from a 5, which is the highest possible score, to a 1, which is the lowest score. Students receive a separate score for each of the six traits, so an exemplary paper receiving a 5 on all six traits would receive a score of 30 points.

Weighted Trait Scoring Weighted trait scoring is a type of analytical scoring that allows the teacher to give extra weight to certain components or traits of a paper relative to the others. That is, rather than rating all the traits on the same scale, as Spandel and Stiggins do, teachers may allocate more points to certain traits than others. Teachers may signify the extra weight by putting a multiplication sign at the end of certain traits on the scoring guide. For instance, 5 4 3 2 1 × 3 would indicate that this trait is worth up to fifteen points instead of five. Figure 13.4 contains a weighted trait scale developed by Thelma Anselmi, an eighth-grade

Figure 13.3 **Six Key Traits of Quality Writing Identified by Classroom Teachers** (*Source:* Excerpted from pp. 49–50 of *Creating Writers: Linking Writing Assessment and Instruction,* 2nd ed., by Vicki Spandel and Richard J. Stiggins. Copyright © 1997, 1990 by Pearson Education. Reprinted by permission.) See pp. 51–57 in *Creating Writers* for the five-point analytical scoring rubric for each of the six traits and p. 70 for a sample scoring grid.

Ideas	**Organization**	**Voice**
Clear—makes sense	An inviting lead that pulls me in	Sounds like a person wrote it, not a committee
Writer has narrowed idea or story line to manageable proportions	Starts somewhere and goes somewhere	Sounds like *this* particular writer
Writer has plenty of information	Even when the writer seems to drift from the topic, everything's connected	Brings topic to life
A fresh, original perspective	I have the feeling it's building *to* something	Makes me feel part of it
Details that capture a reader's interest or make ideas understandable	A welcome surprise now and then	Makes me feel connected with the writer—maybe even want to meet the writer
	Doesn't just stop	Makes me respond, care what happens
	Doesn't end "Then I woke up and it was all a dream"	Writer seems involved, not bored
	Doesn't end with a redundant, banal, or preachy summary: "Now you know the three reasons why we must all join in the war on drugs"	Brims with energy
	A strong sense of resolution or completion	

Word Choice	**Sentence Fluency**	**Conventions**
Memorable moments	Easy to read aloud	Looks clean, edited, polished
Words and phrases I wish I'd thought of myself	Inviting, playful rhythms	Most things done correctly
Word pictures	Well-built sentences	Easy to decipher and follow
Every thought is crystal clear	Varied sentence length and structure	Free of distracting errors
Strong verbs	Cadence	Designed to make reading easy and pleasant
Simple language used well		Attention given to spelling, punctuation, grammar and usage, capitalization, and indentation
Words used precisely		
Minimal redundancy		
The writer is *speaking* to me— not trying to impress me		

teacher at St. Columban in Garden Grove, California, to rate oral presentations rather than written work. Note that some of the traits are rated on a five-point scale, whereas others are weighted double and worth up to ten points. Anselmi and a rotating group of three students use the scoring guide to evaluate oral presentations delivered in class.

Primary Trait Scoring When the teacher wishes to focus on a particular component of the writing quality in a specific writing type or context, he or she may wish to use primary trait scoring. Developed by the National Assessment of Educational Progress, primary trait scoring is designed to "focus the rater's attention on just those features of a piece which are relevant to the kind of discourse that it is: to the special blend of audience, speaker role, purpose, and subject required by that kind of discourse and by the particular writing task" (Cooper & Odell, 1977, p. 11). For example, in a persuasive letter designed to convince the intended audience to make some sort of concession, primary traits might be stating clearly what is wanted, using a tone suited to the audience, giving logical reasons, and using persuasive language. However, it is difficult to isolate such traits from the other elements of effective writing. For instance, if the piece of persuasive writing were riddled with errors, the errors would necessarily detract from the power of the prose. Therefore, most teachers create two holistic scales—a primary trait scale and a secondary trait scale. In the example of the persuasive letter, the letter format and conventions of written English might be listed as criteria for the secondary trait. The teacher would then give more weight (or points) to the primary trait than to the secondary trait—as shown in the primary/secondary trait scoring guide under Evaluation in the Chapter 5 demonstration lesson for the letter from Rachel to Mrs. Price (or other audience) in Sandra Cisneros's "Eleven." The intent there was to value content over form and correctness.

Rhetorical Effectiveness Scoring The California Subject Matter Projects provides a link to the California Writing Project website, where teachers can find the CWP/CAP online at http://csmp.ucop.edu/cwp/index.php and download from the California Assessment Program (CAP) *Writing Assessment Handbook* for grades 8 and 12. These handbooks contain a comprehensive set of scoring guides for each of the eight types of writing (and more) described in Chapter 9. Each writing type has a separate six-point scoring guide based on the key rhetorical features of that type of discourse. For example, whereas the autobiographical incident is scored according to criteria focused on incident, context, and significance, the controversial issue scoring guide focuses on issue, position, and support—and so forth. These scoring guides are useful as teaching tools to help students identify how rhetorical features can vary depending on the purpose of the writing. The *New Standards English Language Arts Reference Examination* (1998) also uses rhetorical effectiveness scoring to assess the on-demand independent writing portion of the exam and includes five-point rubrics for different writing types at specific grade levels. Both CAP and New Standards materials include a separate rubric for the scoring of conventions.

A Rubric for Assessing Achievement in Reading Fran Claggett (1996) makes the point that most scoring systems are designed to assess the process of reading through a product—for example, through a writing sample generated by the student following the reading of a literary work. Although it is certainly possible to ascertain much about a student's ability to move from reading to interpretation to criticism based upon a written essay, Claggett feels that this form of assessment doesn't give us much insight into the student's reading behaviors while interacting with a text. She advises using a separate rubric to assess

Figure 13.4 **Weighted Traits Scoring Rubric** (Developed by Thelma Anselmi, English Teacher, St. Columban School, Garden Grove, CA. Reprinted with permission.)

Oral Presentation: Contributions of a Famous Person

Title _____ Date _____

Presenter _____ Time _____

Content

Introduction has an engaging hook that orients the audience to "famous" person and accomplishments

| 5 | 4 | 3 | 2 | 1 |

Interest is generated through appropriate choice of anecdotes

| 10 | 8 | 6 | 4 | 2 |

Information is accurate and informative—judicious selection of details that support topic

| 10 | 8 | 6 | 4 | 2 |

Conclusion sums up the key points

| 5 | 4 | 3 | 2 | 1 |

Presentation is cohesive, focused, and easy to follow

| 10 | 8 | 6 | 4 | 2 |

Displays are balanced, colorful, attractive, and carefully crafted

| 5 | 4 | 3 | 2 | 1 |

Answers to questions are helpful, detailed and fluent

| 10 | 8 | 6 | 4 | 2 |

Time frame is within given limits—5 to 7 minutes

| 5 | 4 | 3 | 2 | 1 |

Notecards are printed, numbered, quotations only are in sentences and bibliography is included

| 5 | 4 | 3 | 2 | 1 |

Delivery

Eye contact, facial expressions, and gestures engage audience

| 5 | 4 | 3 | 2 | 1 |

Poised—displays confidence—stands, moves easily

| 5 | 4 | 3 | 2 | 1 |

Cue cards and visual aids are effectively used

| 5 | 4 | 3 | 2 | 1 |

Tone of voice is conversational, animated, clear, and loud enough for classroom setting

| 10 | 8 | 6 | 4 | 2 |

Delivery rate and volume are appropriate for classroom setting

| 5 | 4 | 3 | 2 | 1 |

Diction used is specific and accurate—avoids filler (*uh, and, you know, etc.*)

| 5 | 4 | 3 | 2 | 1 |

POINTS FOR CONTENT _____

POINTS FOR DELIVERY _____

TOTAL POINTS ACHIEVED: _____

COMMENTS: _____
_____
_____
_____
_____
_____

EVALUATED BY:

_____
Signature

the reading process, and she provides a detailed narrative description of reading performances scored from 6 to 1. The companion website includes Claggett's scoring guide. Another source of reading rubrics is the *New Standards English Language Arts Reference Examination* (1998). Recognizing, as Claggett does, that one individual writing sample is not enough to assess reading performance, the New Standards Project constructed a two-part exam that includes both an independent writing sample and an integrated reading and writing task.

Standards-Based Dimensional Scoring   With the exception of Claggett's rubric for exemplary reading performance discussed above, the rubrics described thus far are most often used to evaluate single sample writing (or reading) performances that are specified beforehand by the teacher or by the assessment and are usually produced within certain time constraints. But teachers are finding the need for more open-ended scoring systems designed to assess multiple samples that the students themselves select in order to show they have attained "the knowledge, abilities or habits of mind" (Murphy, 1999, p. 121) encompassed within certain dimensions of learning. Sandra Murphy (1999) defines *dimensions of learning* as the "essential elements of a particular kind of work, action or deed" (p. 121). Curriculum or performance standards that delineate what students are expected to know and be able to do in a specific discipline lend themselves to dimensional scoring.

An important feature of dimensional scoring is that students make their own decisions about what types of evidence, artifacts, or samples to compile and submit to illustrate that they have met a certain standard or dimension of learning. Whereas many teachers provide students with a menu of what to include in an assessment such as a portfolio (introductory preface, autobiographical incident, persuasive letter, literary analysis essay, self-assessment reflection, and so forth), a dimensional approach might challenge students to consider how to demonstrate that they

- Write for a variety of purposes
- Write for a range of audiences
- Write in a range of styles and formats (New Standards Project, 1994a, p. 14)

As Murphy (1999) notes, one student might include an essay in response to *Macbeth,* a personal narrative about Christmas, or a letter to President Truman about the atomic bomb; another student might include a reflective essay about the death of the father of a friend, a narrative written in emulation of Edgar Allan Poe, or a poem with biblical allusions, and more (pp. 124–125).

Within a portfolio or other type of multifaceted performance or project, students might be rated on a five-point scale (representing a continuum from beginning to developing, promising, accomplished, or exemplary) on several distinct dimensions of learning. For instance, in the same portfolio for which students are asked to demonstrate their ability to write for a variety of purposes to a range of audiences in a range of styles and formats, they might also be encouraged to think metacognitively and to assess their own performance as writers. Within this dimension of learning, students might be asked to provide evidence to "show us you can"

- Recognize the strengths and weaknesses of your writing
- Review your progress and set goals for improvement
- Explain the strategies you have used to make your writing better (New Standards Project, 1994b, p. 15)

To respond to this challenge, students might write a preface to their portfolio containing a reflective analysis of their growth as writers over the school year and citing specific texts that demonstrate improvement; they might include and discuss self-evaluation/goal-setting sheets; and/or they might include multiple drafts of a paper with a metacognitive process essay describing the specific strategies they used to move from initial idea to completed final draft.

Overall, dimensional scoring enables teachers and their students to focus on "important dimensions of learning and performance which have not been tapped by methods for assessing individual pieces of writing" (Murphy, 1999, p. 122).

Electronic Scoring   There are a number of online assessment tools that enable students to submit their papers and receive a score and limited diagnostic feedback on the dimensions of writing organization, mechanics, and so forth. One such tool that is used in many schools in California is My Access! (www.vantagelearning.com), a portfolio-based writing instruction program to allow teachers and students to track their progress over time. This program includes a customization feature that allows teachers to align assessments with their state rubrics. UCI Writing Project teachers whose schools have My Access! programs report that the advantage of the online scoring is its immediacy rather than the quality or accuracy of the feedback. This immediate feedback is a strong motivation for students who will instantly begin revising to see if they can receive a higher score on the next draft.

Using Rubrics as a Teaching Tool

Although rubrics are an effective and often efficient means of assessment and evaluation, their real power lies, as George Hillocks (1984) points out, in how they can be used in the design of curriculum and the delivery of instruction—in other words, as a teaching tool. For example, I usually introduce the memory snapshot autobiographical incident paper described in Chapter 8 by reading a model paper written by a former student to the class. As I read aloud, I ask the students to listen for what makes the paper memorable. They will normally point out the attention-getting opening; the interesting story line that engaged them as readers; pictorial/descriptive language that helped them visualize and be there with the writer; the use of dialogue; and so forth. I often follow up by passing out a memory snapshot paper I have composed and ask students to highlight the golden lines for homework as well as to bring a snapshot they want to write about to our next class. As described in earlier chapters, the students then share golden lines, cluster their photos, do quickwrites followed by a read-around, and vote for the most memorable quickwrites. We list the qualities that made these papers stand out. This list can serve as the beginning of a rubric for the memory snapshot paper. As a class, we can then compare the class rubric with one previously prepared by me; or I can opt to use the class rubric as my evaluation tool.

A six-point holistic rubric and set of four memory snapshot papers with a key indicating the scores my students gave these papers and their reasons why are available on the companion website. This practice with holistic scoring prepares students to break into partners, trade their set of two papers with another two partners, give each other a confidential in-progress score not shared with the teacher, and provide detailed written feedback via comments directly on the paper and on a response sheet. The fact that both readers have to come to consensus on their scores helps them internalize the criteria for a top-quality autobiographical incident paper. When they get ready to revise their own papers, students have a clearer sense of what effects they are striving for in the next draft. This is just one example of how a rubric can become an instrumental part of classroom instruction rather than something imposed after the fact by the teacher.

THE PORTFOLIO APPROACH TO ASSESSMENT AND EVALUATION

In the language arts classroom, a portfolio is a collection of works or artifacts deliberately selected and arranged with an audience or reader in mind to document progress over time. Tierney, Carter, and Desai (1991) stress that a portfolio should be viewed not as an object but as a vehicle for ongoing assessment; not as a product but as a process to illustrate and analyze the student's growth as a learner. One of the most compelling aspects of the portfolio is its element of student choice. That is, within certain guidelines specified by the teacher or collaboratively generated by teacher and students, students are free to select what artifacts or works they wish to present as evidence of their accomplishments and learning.

Tierney, Carter, and Desai (1991) warn that the "robust concept" of a portfolio can be undermined if teachers are "overly prescriptive" about what must be included in each student's portfolio. When portfolios allow for at least some degree of student choice, they engender ownership—one of the key factors of instructional scaffolding (Langer & Applebee, 1986).

Types of Portfolios

Within the classroom, students usually keep a *process* or *formative* portfolio throughout the semester or school year (depending upon the duration of the class) from which they complete an *exemplary* or *showcase* portfolio at the end of a period of learning. According to Claggett (1996), "The process portfolio, unlike the showcase portfolio, shows the author's process of working in a given area over time, along with all of the deadends, frustrations and moments of satisfaction, pride and relief that come along with achieving growth" (pp. 113–114). The process portfolio is likely to include many false starts; both unfinished and finished pieces of writing; and clusters, quickwrites, various graphic artifacts, and the like. As opposed to the process portfolio, the showcase portfolio "strives to show mastery of things taught and learned during a given period" (Claggett, 1996, p. 113) and is more likely to highlight the author's best works or works specifically included to show evidence of growth and/or achievement.

What's in a Portfolio?

The contents of a portfolio will differ according to the type of portfolio it is and the degree of choice students are given in selecting their artifacts. However, most portfolios have a table of contents; a cover letter, preface, or other piece of reflective writing describing the contents of the portfolio and what they are intended to demonstrate about the learner's progress or achievement; the artifacts or work samples themselves—often accompanied by metacognitive reflections; and sometimes an end-letter including a student self-assessment or statement of future goals. Students are often asked to show their completed portfolios to an audience such as parents or peers and to include their responses in the portfolio when submitting it to the teacher. The companion website includes two sample sets of portfolio requirements— one for Meredith Ritner's seventh-grade English class at Aliso Viejo Middle School in Aliso Viejo, California, and one for Carol Mooney's twelfth-grade Advanced Placement English class at Villa Park High School in Villa Park, California.

The Portfolio Process: Collect, Select, Reflect, Project, Affect

Jane Hansen (1998) has a helpful motto to describe the role of student learners in the portfolio process: collect, select, reflect, project, and affect (p. 51). Students need lots of work samples and artifacts to draw from in order to cull out those that are the most meaningful. As Hansen points out, "We learned that *selection* is impossible until a *collection* exists from which to select" (p. 51). Collections might include items generated in school and out of school; reading logs, book club projects; poems; song lyrics; diary entries; cartoons; clusters and quickwrites; rough and final drafts of papers; photographs; artwork; PowerPoint presentations, HyperStudio stacks, QuickTime movies or student-created websites; and so forth. For a showcase portfolio, students revisit their collections to select representative samples to create a portrait of themselves as learners. Hansen notes, "From the various possibilities of how we might portray ourselves, we select the items that give us the public face we want" (p. 52).

Most teachers and scholars agree that reflection is the heart of the portfolio process. Dictionary definitions of the term *reflection* include serious thought; contemplation; a turning or bending back upon itself; a mirroring—giving back an image or likeness. When students revisit the collections in their portfolios and select work samples to showcase themselves as learners, they are, in a sense, turning back upon themselves to explore their reading, thinking, and writing processes. As they contemplate how they came to produce each artifact and the lessons learned, and as they articulate these discoveries in reflective commentaries, students are actually "seeing their learning processes in action" (Claggett, 1996, p. 123). In a sense, the portfolio is indeed a mirror into which students can look and, if they look carefully and thoughtfully, see themselves as learners.

Most portfolios include reflections about individual work samples as well as more global reflections about the student's progress as a learner over time. Tierney, Carter, and Desai (1991) offer sample questions to invite students to think about individual artifacts and the portfolio as a whole. Among them:

A Single Piece of Writing

Why did you select this piece of writing?
What do you see as the strengths?
What was especially important to you when you were writing this piece?
What things did you wrestle with?
If you could work on this further, what would you do?
What were some of the reactions you received?
How is this the same or different from your other pieces?

Thinking about Your Portfolio

What kinds of material have you included in your portfolio?
In what ways are they different? The same?
What does your portfolio reveal about you as a reader, writer, person?
What does your portfolio suggest about how you have changed?
What do you think people will learn about from your portfolio?
How do you plan to use your portfolio? (p. 116)

Anthony Dickson's description of what he learned from writing his first saturation research paper (see Chapter 10), from his eighth-grade portfolio at St. Columban School, is a rich example of a single-work reflection:

■   When I first started thinking about the Saturation Research Paper, I was almost certain I wouldn't be able to find anything exciting or worthwhile to write about. But once I understood the concept that I could actually create a story with my own imagination rather than develop a strictly informative piece, I was hooked. This tampering with history can be partly pretty fun, huh?

I choose to write about Thurgood Marshall and I came to know him as a man, not just a historical figure. Even though some of the details in my paper were fictional, I feel that through giving my character thoughts and feelings he was becoming more than a subject to write about; he was becoming a human being.

When I completed my first draft, I honestly didn't think that I had left anything out and that I had an automatic final draft. Boy was I wrong! Before this piece, I didn't know about how to use interior monologue. I went back and interspersed his thoughts into my story, making it more interesting. During the course of this draft, I also found more information and added more facts to make my historical account more accurate.

One important thing I learned is that whenever I'm feeling distant from a historical figure or even someone closer to me, I should simply write a piece like this to get rid of the distance. I'm also proud that I broadened the boundaries of my writing! I look forward to another project of this type but after living and breathing this one for two weeks, I hope it won't be too soon!

Kay Leonard candidly assessed her growth as a reader after reviewing the contents of her semester portfolio in twelfth-grade AP English at Villa Park High School, offering a more global reflection about her growth over time:

■ As a reader, I have definitely matured since September. I came into AP English thinking I was well read, as I had just read two novels, two dramas, and two sets of poetry over a three-month period. Oh, how wrong I was. Now after reading Ibsen, Camus, Austen, *and* Shakespeare in second quarter alone, I feel like I'm but at the foot of the literary mountain. I have a nasty habit of reading only what is assigned during the school year, which makes reading somewhat of a monotonous task for me. I'd like to be able to sit down and read a novel without worrying that it is being read for a grade or for classroom knowledge. Outside of class, I've started reading J. K. Rowling's *Harry Potter* and so far, I'm enjoying it. It's nice to regress to "children's literature" every once in a while, though I suppose "fun stuff" is a better name for it—no offense to Ibsen and Shakespeare! I've also kept up with my *Rolling Stone* magazines and *People Weekly*. As far as other periodicals go, I try to read the newspaper every day (and not just the "Show Section") and I am going to give an honest effort to start reading *Time* and *Newsweek*. I want to be well-informed of worldly issues and not just who's going to be playing a concert when, and I know magazines of the like would be the remedy for that. This I consider to be real and honest development as a reader.

One purpose of assembling the portfolio is to look back and assess progress. Another is to look ahead—*project*—and to set goals for the future. In her twelfth-grade AP English class at Villa Park High School, Carol Mooney facilitates the recursive process of going back to go forward by having students submit portfolios four times a year, at quarters and semesters. In each portfolio she asks students to complete a goal sheet. Here are the instructions for the semester portfolio.

• Assess the goal you set for yourself this quarter. Reread your assessment of your first quarter goal; consider your progress toward your second quarter goal. Did you achieve your goal? Why or why not? Please be specific.

• Now, set a new goal for yourself third quarter. Consider your achievements; realistically assess your needs. Think about your progress in reading/thinking/writing thus far. Please be specific.

In her seventh-grade classroom at Aliso Viejo Middle School, Meredith Ritner asks students the following questions to help them project: "How would like to grow as a writer? What would you still like to learn? What type of writing do you intend to pursue?" She also gives them an additional audience to write to by asking them, "What advice would you give to my students next year to assist them with their writing?" After expressing her desire to learn more about the basics of writing children's books and setting a long-term goal of pursuing a career as a writer, student Anne Mayeres gave some very practical and astute advice to Mrs. Ritner's future seventh graders:

■   I have some simple advice to give next year's students. First of all, my best advice is to type almost every assignment; it will be easier to complete the portfolio at the end of the year. Secondly, always listen to Mrs. Ritner. She gives hidden tips for the writing and she gives the guidelines at the same time. Also, I know this doesn't have to do with writing, but it needs to be said: never EVER tip back in your chair; you'll pay for it!

Hansen (1998) takes the portfolio process one step farther by adding the dimension of affect. In other words, after all is said and done—after students collect, select, reflect, and project—how does the portfolio process *affect* them in their learning? In the direction of their lives? In their growth as a person? (p. 55). In Kay Leonard's twelfth-grade AP English portfolio, it was her mother, Anne, looking in from outside and thoughtfully reviewing her daughter's work samples and her reflections, who could see how much the portfolio process had affected her and remarked on it to her teacher, Carol Mooney:

■   Thank you for this opportunity to go over this assignment with Kay. What a fantastic idea! I like the Portfolio format as it gave her a chance to choose works that were meaningful to her, to engage in some reflection and introspection, and to set goals for her 3rd quarter.

I appreciate the time you obviously take going over her assignments. I enjoy your notes and happy faces in the margins almost as much as her work!

Kay has always been very strong in her verbal and writing skills and I feel you have brought so much more out of her. You must be terrifically organized to accomplish what you do in less than 5 hours a week of class time.

Ironically, she was in your freshman class when her grandmother died and in your senior class when her grandfather died. Since we had lived with them since she was 2 years old and they were like second parents to her, their deaths had quite an impact on her. I'm thankful she had you each time as I'm sure her journals, writing assignments and the other entries generated and shared in her portfolio were a much needed and valuable release and chance for expression.

Assessing and Evaluating Portfolios

Methods for scoring or marking portfolios are as diverse as the teachers implementing the portfolios. Kathleen Blake Yancy (1992) urges teachers to defer the grading of portfolios for as long as possible. She advocates formative assessment while the portfolio is in progress: the teacher assumes a posture of "inquiry reading" (p. 111) in which the goal is to understand and respond as a reader rather than as an evaluator and to generate questions that will help the writer move the piece or pieces forward. For summative evaluation, some teachers read the portfolio holistically, giving a general impression score; others take a more analytical approach, scoring the individual pieces. Still other teachers convene to "blind rate" (p. 112) each other's student portfolios. Tierney, Carter, and Desai (1991) stress that the values that underlie the portfolio process should also be present in the teacher's assessment and evaluation system. That is, assessment and evaluation should take into consideration: "(1) the processes readers, writers, problem solvers, and learners enlist; (2) the products they develop; (3) the improvements they achieve; (4) the effort they put forth; as well as (5) how these features vary across a range of reading and writing" (p. 41).

GRADING AND ALTERNATIVES TO THE TRADITIONAL GRADING SYSTEM

As Strickland and Strickland (1998) point out, "Grading doesn't exactly fit in a transactional classroom with authentic assessment and evaluation, yet teachers need to grade" (p. 129). Jim Burke (1999) concurs: "No matter what your philosophy or your attitude about grades, there comes a time when you get those scantron sheets, and must bubble in those magic letters" (p. 187). Most scholars seem to uniformly condemn the giving of grades. But, in reality, the problem is not so much the grade but the fact the grade is not accompanied by criteria delineating what differentiates an A from a B, C, or D performance. This is why we can't tell whether Matilda's D+, discussed earlier, reflects achievement, ability, effort, growth, or even behavior. Ideally, just as teachers have rubrics for individual learning tasks within the classroom, they should develop criteria for how final grades are determined. As Jim Burke stresses, "Whatever you do, you need a system that is efficient but offers students the information they need to understand why they got the grade and how they can improve in the future" (p. 186). Burke's students consistently said they preferred a rubric to letter grades, points, or percentages, as long as they received it ahead of time and the descriptors were specific. A final grading rubric would enable the teacher to reinforce what he or she values in a classroom. If issues like attendance, on-time completion of work, class participation, or positive attitude are valued and taken into account, students should be made aware of this. If the teacher places a premium on growth over time, this too should be part of the rubric. Making these criteria visible for students might even give some who have written themselves off as C or D students a clearer idea of how to work toward higher marks.

In the interest of making grading systems visible, some teachers have moved to growth-based, outcomes-based, achievement-based, or contract-based grading (Tchudi, 1997). Although these systems differ slightly, all involve making it clear exactly what is required to attain a certain grade and letting students decide whether to put in the amount of effort necessary to achieve a higher mark or to do less and receive a lower mark. For instance, to earn a B in Stephen Adkison's composition class at the University of Nevada, students need to do the following (1997, p. 197):

- Attend class regularly and come prepared
- Maintain an informal writing journal, responding to all assigned reading and other tasks
- Complete several field trips, which form the basis of in-class activities
- Complete five formal essays during the course of the semester
- Develop a final portfolio consisting of further revisions

For an A in the same class, students must develop an independent project that they propose and pursue. In most of these systems, to guard against quantity over quality, students' work must be deemed "acceptable" or worthy of "credit" based on a set of criteria tailored to the different tasks. Student work that is not considered "creditable" occasions a conference with the teacher and an opportunity to revise and resubmit.

This approach seems like a very promising one. Adkison and Tchudi (1997) note of their experiment with this alternative to traditional grading, "Given the prospect of a set of tasks to accomplish rather than a teacher to satisfy, students often discover motivation within themselves to work that does not exist when they perceive themselves pursuing a grade rather than getting the work done" (p. 199). Further, discouraged students who have previously felt that it was impossible to get an A no matter how hard they worked can now strive to make this goal a reality. Adkison and Tchudi found that students who had to write "acceptable" papers but received either "credit" or "no credit" rather than letter grades on these papers spent less time worrying about what the teacher wanted, took more risks, and wrote in a more authentic voice with greater clarity.

WHAT ABOUT STANDARDIZED TESTS?

In many ways standardized tests have little to do with response, assessment, evaluation, or grading in the language arts classroom. As Tierney, Carter, and Desai (1991) point out, current standardized testing procedures "do not reflect what we teach in our classrooms" and "are not representative of the kind of work that students do daily" (p. 27). But the reality is that standardized test scores are viewed by the media, and thus the public, as our educational report card—and bemoaning the "crisis" in education sells more newspapers than reports of successes. Citing the research of Berliner and Biddle (1995), Strickland and Strickland (1998) point out that despite the sensational news about disastrous test scores circulated in the media, SAT scores are on the rise, more students than ever are staying in school, and the dropout rate for students aged sixteen to twenty-four is declining. In short, although we certainly need to improve our schools, "Public education is serving the public" (p. 182).

Even if the media were reporting the data less selectively and more accurately, standardized tests are norm-referenced tests, which means that they are designed to produce scores on a bell curve. Test questions are purposely structured so that there are only a few questions that most students will be able to answer; the bulk of the questions are designed so that only some, but not many, of the students can answer correctly. In other words, the norm-referenced tests are designed to "discriminate among people" (Hill, 1992). When you rank-order test takers, some will, of necessity, be at the bottom, because they are being sorted and ranked against one another rather than on the basis of what they know and are able to do.

An additional concern has to do with how and on whom tests are normed. Calkins, Montgomery, and Santman (1998) had this to say after reviewing standardized reading tests:

> When reading tests assess a student's knowledge, there is often a risk of bias because the content the test makers expect all children to know will usually be content that is especially prevalent in the lives of middle class children. And test bias is not limited to the *content* of the passages. As we looked over sample test questions from a variety of nationally used standardized tests, we found questions on grammar and language use that present extra challenges for children who come from culturally and linguistically diverse backgrounds. Often the questions offered response options that were wrong but that could seem correct to children whose first language was not English. (p. 17)

Recognizing that "taking standardized tests will be part of American life for the next few generations at least" and that "no matter how invalid we think the test scores are" (p. 7) they have powerful implications for the nation, for states, for school districts, schools, teachers, and especially for students, Calkins and her colleagues decided to become more test wise as educators so that they could train their students in methods of standardized test preparation. They resolved that in knowledge there is power: "If our students do well on tests, we are in a far stronger position to be critical of those same tests. If we want people to listen to us when we say that alternative means of assessment need to replace or stand alongside tests, we will be heard better if our kids' scores are high" (p. 7). So Calkins and a cadre of teachers actually took a standardized reading test, not without some trepidation, to understand the test format from a test taker's perspective and to assess and learn from their own test-taking strategies.

Based on experience, Calkins and the other educators offer the following practical strategies to classroom teachers:

- Orient your students to the test not by telling them about the formats they will encounter but by letting them peruse a test, preferably with a partner, to see what they notice about the test layout and how the questions are constructed.
- Make sure students know they should read all the directions carefully so they are sure not to miss anything.
- Familiarize students with the language of the test—not just the individual words and phrases that might trip them up (like *predicate*) but the overall tone of the academic English used on standardized tests.
- Compare the test-taking process to a scavenger hunt in which the list of items to find is in the questions at the end of the passage.
- Use an overhead projector and model a think-aloud so students can see the kinds of questions you ask yourself and what you pay special attention to when reading the directions, the questions, or the passage.
- Before the test, build students' stamina for reading difficult texts; teach them strategies like reading in chunks, pausing and noticing key facts, making mental notes summarizing what they've read before going on, or reading with a finger under the text to keep their eyes and mind focused.
- Make sure that students have exposure to a variety of genres: not only fiction but also poetry, memos, scientific books, instruction manuals, and so on. Magazines are a good source of high-interest nonfiction. Game rules, simple assembly instructions, and recipes offer practice in following instructions in formats that are similar to test instructions.
- Retype familiar texts to look as daunting and dense as the test passages, to give kids confidence in reading texts that physically appear complex on the page.
- Help students learn how to move between the test booklet and the answer sheet without losing their place by showing them how to fill in the answers on the test booklet page before filling in the corresponding bubbles in the answer sheet. Also, show them how to use an index card to block out distracting print or mark their place. Advise them to do a quick check to match the question numbers with the bubbled answers every five minutes or so.
- Advise students to go back into the passage and confirm they have the correct answer rather than work from memory. To prevent their needing to reread the entire passage, teach them to mark the passages by circling items or writing key words in the margins as they read so this information is easier to relocate. (Calkins et al., 1998, pp. 58–64, 86–93, 94–104)

Essentially, Calkins and her colleagues are making visible for students what strategies effective test takers use and are providing guided practice in how to approach a standardized test. Although they in "no way advocate making reading instruction" in overall classroom practice more like standardized tests, they do recognize that if students' achievement is to be measured by such tests, then students deserve to be "acclimated to the genre of standardized tests" (p. 68). Further, rather than treating students as "islands, with eyes on their own papers, hands to themselves, with little conversation" (p. 70)—that is, replicating the conditions that occur on the actual test-taking day—they engaged the whole class as a community of learners in exploring this new genre called the standardized test.

Preparing Students for On-Demand Writing

Throughout this book I have advocated a process approach to integrating reading and writing, in which the teacher scaffolds instruction and guides students through a sequence of activities to ensure their success as learners. However, we do students a disservice if we do not also provide practice in planning and executing single-draft timed writing. Gere, Christenbury, and Sassi (2005) point out that in an on-demand writing test students know that the natural recursive nature of writing is compressed. "Most writing sample tests do not allow students the time to draft and change significantly. Therefore, planning writing through prewriting and reviewing writing at the end are vital tasks for successful on-demand writing" (p. 49). Becky Aten, an English teacher at Valley High School, and Katie Berger, an English teacher at Segerstrom High School, both in Santa Ana, California, have had success helping students to prepare for on-demand writing by using the "ABC" strategy developed by Kelly Gallagher, the author of *Reading Reasons: Motivating Mini-Lessons for Middle and High School* and *Deeper Reading: Comprehending Challenging Texts, 4–12*. Their description of how they have implemented Gallagher's strategy is provided below:

Prompt Dissection   To help students understand the expectations of a writing assignment, give them practice dissecting or carefully reading the prompt. In his writing workshops, Kelly Gallagher of Anaheim Unified High School District in Anaheim, California, has shared the ABC strategy, which is quite effective in teaching students to carefully read the prompt and quickly organize their ideas. By dividing prompt dissection into three easy steps (reading the prompt, brainstorming, and organizing), students are more able to remember and complete this task. According to Gallagher, the entire process should take no more than seven minutes.

A = Attack the Prompt   The first step asks students to attack the prompt either verbally or graphically, identifying the "to do" words and dissecting or "unwrapping" the question. A sample prompt follows:

> Rules and regulations are a part of everyone's life. Some are necessary; others seem unfair and in need of change. Choose a specific rule or regulation that you had to deal with in school, work, or elsewhere. Write an essay in which you describe the rule or regulation and discuss how it affected you. Explain why you endorse the rule or why you think it should be changed.

Verbal Approach

Circle the "to do"/action words:
choose, write, describe, discuss, explain
Unwrap the question by rewriting it:
- *choose one rule or regulation*
- *write an essay describing this one rule or regulation*
- *describe the rule*
- *discuss how this rule affected you*
- *explain whether you think the rule is good, or how it should be changed*

Graphic Approach

"to do" words	task
choose	rule
write	an essay
describe	the rule
discuss	how it affected you
explain	whether good or bad and how should it be changed

Figure 13.5 **Sample Brainstorm Cluster**

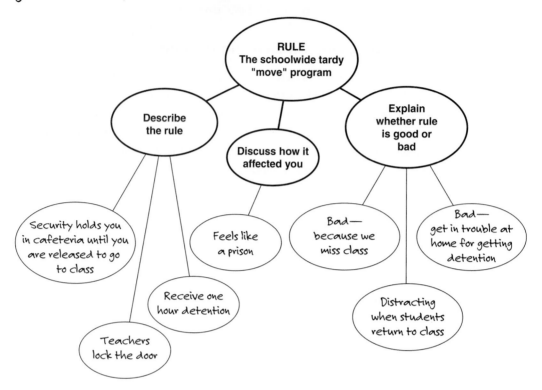

B = Brainstorm Possible Answers The second step asks the students to brainstorm possible ideas/responses for their essay. This may be done as a cluster or list. The brainstorm in Figure 13.5 was completed for the prompt above.

C = Choose the Order of Your Response After brainstorming, students should quickly choose the order in which they will discuss each idea or response. This step in the process is completed below.

1. Describe the rule of the schoolwide "move" tardy program
   - Security holds you in cafeteria until you are released to go to class
   - Teachers lock the door
   - Receive one hour detention

2. Tardy program "move" is a bad idea
   - Miss too much class
   - Get in trouble at home for receiving detention

3. How it affected me
   - Makes me feel that school is like prison
   - It is distracting when other students return to class

Teaching the ABC Strategy

Teachers should begin by modeling the strategy on an overhead in front of the class. An overhead for teachers to use in this process is available on the companion website. As students have more practice, they will be much more efficient in dissecting the prompt, completing these steps quickly and almost effortlessly on their own.

Practicing prompt dissection does not have to culminate in a written essay. Teachers may simply have students stop at the charting or brainstorming stage of the ABC strategy, or have them take the prompt to the outlining stage. You might want to have one student present his or her ABC strategy to the class on an overhead transparency. The selection of one student keeps all students "on their toes" because they don't know whether they will be selected or not. Another option is, after students have dissected a number of prompts, to have them choose one to take to the writing stage. These options will allow teachers to assign prompt dissection without worrying about being inundated with essays to grade. Note: Students who are taking the SAT writing assessment will not have time to complete a detailed ABC organizer during that test. After reading the prompt carefully, these students should simply highlight or underline key word/tasks.

INVOLVING STUDENTS IN ASSESSMENT, EVALUATION, AND GRADING

■   The foremost goal of evaluation is self-evaluation, that is, the analysis of our own attitudes and processes so that we can use the information to promote continued growth and learning. The purpose of self-evaluation is the purpose of education—to enable an individual to function independently, intelligently, and productively.

—Regie Routman

If, as Regie Routman (1991) argues so eloquently, the purpose of education is self-evaluation so that students can take charge of their own learning and function "independently, intelligently, and productively" (p. 342), then students must be given opportunities to participate as coassessors, coevaluators, and even cograders of their products as well as of their processes as readers, thinkers and writers. For example, in Thelma Anselmi's eighth-grade language arts class at St. Columban School, students begin the year by responding to a qualitative attitude survey in which they assess themselves as readers and writers and set individual goals for the year. Daily, they are given the last five minutes of class to complete exit cards in which they describe something they learned or relearned that day and pose one question that is on their minds. At the end of each week, they complete a weekly progress report in which they discuss the concept that they valued most that particular week; pose any questions that still remain unanswered; rate themselves as a learner that week on a scale of 1 to 5 and explain why; and discuss any problems they encountered, along with possible solutions. (Copies of Anselmi's exit cards and weekly progress report are available on the companion website.)

Throughout the year, Anselmi's students coconstruct rubrics for evaluating their papers along with the teacher by extrapolating criteria from models. They also collaborate in writing groups and not only give each other feedback and in-progress scores, on occasion, but also assess the dynamics of their writing group. And along with each final draft, students submit a metacognitive essay describing what they had to think about and what strategies they used in order to write in that particular domain.

Throughout the school year, Anselmi enlists the help of students as coevaluators of student performances. For instance, taking turns, three students at a time join the teacher in evaluating the oral presentations of their classmates, using the scoring guide in Figure 13.4. They also share the power to evaluate when students give book talks based on their independent reading. At the first and second trimesters, students conduct formative assessments of themselves as readers and writers in relation to the goals they set for themselves. At the end of the third trimester, they generate a showcase portfolio containing a summative self-evaluation (including their proposed letter grades for themselves in writing, reading, listening, speaking, attitude, and effort). This summative self-evaluation includes a parent assessment form. Anselmi writes to parents, "I believe the best assessment of student writing begins with the students themselves but must be broadened to include the widest possible audience. I encourage you to be part of that of audience."

In terms of instructional scaffolding (Langer & Applebee, 1986), Anselmi engenders *ownership* in her students by empowering them to participate as coevaluators of their own reading, thinking, and writing processes and products. She presents them with *appropriate* learning tasks that build on their abilities but stretch them intellectually. She provides a careful *structure* (through direct instruction, modeling, guided practice, etc.) not only for how to accomplish each task but for how to assess or evaluate the task. Students also *collaborate* with each other in writing groups, book clubs, and literature circles; provide feedback and in-progress scores on one another's work; and even collaborate with the teacher in evaluating student presentations. The goal of instructional scaffolding is *internalization*.

Will repeated opportunities to self-evaluate enable a student to function "independently, intelligently and productively" (Routman, 1991, p. 342)? As a culminating activity, Anselmi asks her students to conduct an in-depth analysis of two interpretive essays composed, respectively, in October and May. Without the benefit of a rubric, students are to look for indicators of their growth over time, specifically describe the changes they see in their author's craft, pinpoint what factors they believe contributed to their growth, and assess any changes they see in their attitude toward reading and writing. These excerpts from Anselmi's students' learning log reflections demonstrate how confidently and competently they assume the role of self-evaluator and how clearly they have internalized the criteria for effective reading and writing:

■   I think my progress is due to the practice we had with writing a thesis and conclusions. To me, these aspects of the essay must have priority over all else because these are the forces that guide the essay. It's like trying to hit a target with an arrow. The thesis is the arrow. It has to be focused, sharp and strong in order to hit its mark, or make your point. So, your conclusion is the target. That's where it all has to come together

—Romeo Ancheta

■   My view of myself as a reader has changed this year. I used to think I was a good reader because I could read quickly and understand the words. Now, I think I can read well because I look deeper into the characters' minds and am able to tell what they're thinking. I used to think I was a good writer because I have a natural ability to spell and think of ideas. Now, I think am a good writer because I know how to use commentary and supporting detail.

—Jenny Clement

■   I realized that there are more things to being a good reader and writer than I thought— some of those being determination, perseverance, a good imagination, and good revision skills. I also learned that reading and writing can be for everyone if you just practice.

—*Nick Mastroianni*

INFORMING INSTRUCTION THROUGH ASSESSMENT AND EVALUATION

As I described earlier, after Lucy Calkins (1998) and twenty-nine colleagues became acquainted firsthand with a fifth-grade standardized reading test by taking it themselves, they assessed the similarities and differences between the strategies they used to approach the test, paying special attention to the strategies employed by those teachers who identified themselves as good test takers. Subsequently, these teachers identified and observed the students in their classes who were star test takers and compared them with the more successful adult learners. Successful test takers in both age groups, it turned out, approached the test as a game they intended to win.

Through a careful process of analyzing both successful test strategies and the processes of less skilled test takers, Calkins's group arrived at a repertoire of guided practice activities to help students implement the beneficial strategies. In other words, they used multiple sources of assessment data to inform instruction. Teachers need to be aware that assessment and evaluation offer them rich sources of data regarding not only how their students are doing but also whether they have met their instructional objectives as teachers.

ASSESSING TEACHER EFFECTIVENESS

■ At its best, good teaching, which necessarily includes effective assessing, is about paying attention. This is what we should all strive for in our teaching and testing: to invite particular attention to worthy subjects, and use tests to measure the depth and accuracy of that attention. But let's not stop here: let every test be an invitation for us to pay specific attention to our own teaching, let students' portfolios be *our* portfolios and reflect not only what they accomplished but what we, their teachers, accomplished as evidenced by their progress, their pleasure, and their pride in their work.

—Jim Burke

As we assess, evaluate, and grade our students' reading and writing, we need to be mindful of the degree to which their work reflects "not only what they accomplished but what we, their teachers, accomplished as evidenced by their progress, their pleasure, and their pride in their work" (Burke, 1999, p. 171). Although assessments of student work are the most tangible sources of data regarding whether teachers have met their instructional objectives, they tell us more about the end of instruction than about the means of instruction. In other words, teachers need to be just as concerned about their processes of getting to a product (i.e., improving student learning as evidenced by their work) as their students are.

In California, the California Commission on Teacher Credentialing and the California Department of Education have set forth six standards for professional teaching practice that represent a "developmental, holistic view of teaching and are intended to meet the needs of diverse students and teachers" (1997, p. 1). The companion website provides a condensed version of these *California Standards for the Teaching Profession* (CSTP). The full-length document, which can be downloaded from the Beginning Teacher Support and Assessment website, www.btsa.ca.gov (under publications), contains a narrative description of each standard followed by key elements or examples of an accomplished level of teaching. Each element contains a list of helpful questions teachers can ask themselves to explore different aspects of their classroom practice. In addition, the California Commission on Teacher Credentialing (CCTC), the California Department of Education (CDE), and Educational Testing Service (ETS) have taken the CSTP one step farther by creating a companion document called *California Standards for the Teaching Profession: Resources for Professional Practice* (1999). This handbook contains detailed descriptions of the key elements under each teaching standard and descriptions-of-practice scales at four developmental levels: Practice Not Consistent with Standard Expectations, Developing Beginning Practice, Maturing Beginning Practice, and Experienced Practice That Exemplifies the Standard.

In view of the fact that we are increasingly assessing students' performances against standards, it certainly makes sense to do the same for teachers' performances. Nationwide, teachers with at least three years of experience have the opportunity to apply for national board certification from the National Board for Professional Teaching Standards (NBPTS). The NBPTS standards, as well as descriptions of the certification process in a variety of fields and for students in different age groups, are available on the website www.nbpts.org.

The NBPTS is raising the bar for U.S. teachers. Teachers in the UCI Writing Project who have received NBPTS certification all concur that they have never looked so closely at what they do, how they do it, and why they do it. However, teachers need not wait for official validation from an outside source to begin looking at classroom practice and collecting evidence of student learning. This process of assessing one's own effectiveness, however informal or formal, can provide teachers with a rich opportunity to enhance their instructional repertoire and to grow as teachers and learners.

Electronic Teaching Portfolios

Increasingly, preservice teachers, beginning teachers, and sometimes veteran teachers are asked to compile electronic teaching portfolios to document their professional practice. According to Lee Shulman (1998), a teaching portfolio is a "structured documentary history of a set of coached or mentored acts of teaching, substantiated by samples of student portfolios, and fully realized only through reflective writing, deliberation, and conversation" (p. 37). It is intended as a learning tool for the teacher as well as a place to demonstrate professional competence. Kilbane and Milman (2003) have compiled a handy booklet entitled *What Every Teacher Should Know about Creating Digital Portfolios* that walks teachers through the digital portfolio process.

To Sum Up

In the classroom, a teacher assumes the roles of responder, assessor, evaluator, and grader. Because, first and foremost, students need "coaches, not judges" (Holaday, 1997, p. 35), it is essential to provide students with a *response* to their reading and writing that is individualized, is descriptive rather than evaluative, focuses on first draft thinking, and motivates them to continue to compose and revise meaning. *Assessment* is an ongoing process teachers engage in to determine what students know and are able to do. The rich data from assessment can inform teachers' instruction; it can also enable them to provide students with here-and-now, in-progress, formative feedback about how to improve to meet an achievement target. *Evaluation* usually occurs at the end of a period of learning, is more final or summative in nature, and values or judges student work based on external criteria. Finally, *grading* reduces a student's performance over time to one single symbol, usually a letter grade.

Most researchers agree on the following:

- Teachers should think like assessors instead of activity designers: Begin with the end in mind; determine what they want students to know and be able to do; decide what would constitute acceptable evidence that students have achieved these outcomes; then plan learning experiences and instruction with these goals in mind.
- Teachers should look to national, state, and district content and performance standards for general expectations as to what students should know and be able to do in different disciplines and at different levels of schooling.

- Teachers should provide written criteria (or rubrics) that clearly delineate for students what is necessary to achieve success. Those criteria should be used not only for assessment and evaluation but also as a teaching tool.
- Teachers should focus on students' processes of reading, thinking, and writing as well as on their products.
- Teachers should involve students in self-evaluation. This process should include collecting, selecting, and reflecting on work samples/artifacts that create a portrait of themselves as learners, as well as projecting how they will use what they have learned in the future and pondering how their learning has affected them as human beings. Teachers need to be mindful of the degree to which student progress is a reflection of teacher performance. To enhance their instructional repertoire and to continue to grow as teachers and learners, teachers should continually assess their own effectiveness.

Learning Log Reflection

Keeping Langer and Applebee's principles of instructional scaffolding in mind, consider the following questions:

1. To what degree have I fostered student *ownership* of their own learning by involving them in self-assessment and self-evaluation? What evidence do I have that reflects my students' participation in the assessment/evaluation process?
2. In what ways have I used formative assessment of what students know and are able to do to design instruction that is *appropriate* for the learners in my classroom? What evidence do I have that I am assessing student work to design, monitor, and adjust instruction?
3. What type of *structure* have I provided to make my learning goals and expected outcomes clear to students? What evidence do I have that I have generated clearly delineated criteria for individual reading and writing tasks? For periods of learning? For my entire course?
4. In what ways have I engaged students in *collaboration* as assessors and evaluators? What evidence do I have of their working collectively on peer response, in-progress scoring, or final peer evaluation?
5. How can I determine whether students have *internalized* the criteria for what they should know and be able to do in English language arts at my grade level? What evidence can I collect to check the degree to which they have become strategic readers and writers?

Cultivating Motivated, Independent Readers and Writers through Reading and Writing Workshop

■ Time for independent writing and reading isn't the icing on the cake, the reward we proffer the senior honors students who survived the English curriculum. Writing and reading *are* the cake. When we fight for time, giving students one of the basic conditions for writing and reading, we begin to make writers and readers.

—Nancie Atwell

Much of this book has been devoted to making the strategies that experienced readers and writers use visible for students through carefully scaffolded teacher-guided demonstration lessons. The goal of these lessons is to provide modeling and practice in the cognitive strategies that are fundamental to the processes of meaning construction so that students will internalize these acts of mind and gradually apply them as independent readers and writers. As Nancie Atwell (1998) makes clear, independent reading and writing should not be viewed as the "icing on the cake" (p. 98); they are the cake. That is, they are the goal of scaffolded language arts instruction. Effective teachers create a balance of teacher-guided and student-selected reading and writing activities, often using the teacher-guided activities as a learning tool to establish the structure necessary for independent practice.

WHAT IS A WORKSHOP APPROACH?

Donald Graves (1981) was among the first scholars to liken the workshop classroom to an artist's studio. His mentee, Nancie Atwell (1998), expands on the metaphor:

> The artist sets up her studio so it has everything she needs, arranged to suit her and her art. In the midst of the messy and unpredictable act of creating, the artist knows where to find the right palette knife, brush, or tube of color. The studio exists for the convenience of the artist at work, just as the writing–reading classroom should exist for the convenience—and productivity—of young readers and writers. (p. 98)

In a workshop approach, students self-select the texts they read and write and work independently at their own pace while collaborating with peers and their teacher on their visions and revisions of texts under construction. Kirby and Kuykendall (1991) stress that the role of the teacher is to "stay out of the kids' way, but not too far out of the way" (p. 214). Like a master artist, the studio teacher models processes and products in front of the class and then coaches students individually while they experiment and practice as apprentice learners.

APPLYING THE PRINCIPLES OF INSTRUCTIONAL SCAFFOLDING TO READING AND WRITING WORKSHOP

Although Nancie Atwell points out that "a workshop is a different kind of ship" (p. 90), it is headed toward the same destination as the more teacher-prompted approaches explored in this book—that is, toward developing confident and competent independent readers and writers. A tightly run workshop "ship" exemplifies and reinforces all of the principles of instructional scaffolding (Langer & Applebee, 1986).

Ownership   Although all of the teacher-prompted reading and writing tasks in this book strive to give students "the room to say something of their own in their writing or in the interpretations they draw in their reading" (Langer & Applebee, 1986, p. 185), the teacher is still selecting the texts the students will read and write and framing the reading and writing tasks. Reading and writing workshop is based on student choice. Research indicates that there is a strong correlation between choice and the development of intrinsic motivation (Paris & Oka, 1986). Motivation, in turn, has been linked to the development of strategic reading and writing (Blau, 1997; Paris, Wasik, & Turner, 1991)—because in order to make strategic decisions, the learner must have both the knowledge and the motivation to select and apply appropriate tactics.

Appropriateness   In reading and writing workshop, teachers start with students where they are, developmentally, allowing them to select texts to read at their independent level (rather than at their instructional or frustration level) and inviting them to write about personal topics that are close to home. However, to extend Atwell's metaphor of the ship, while teachers are enabling students to cruise in safe waters, reading *Goosebumps* or writing about favorite vacations, they are carefully assessing what students know and are able to do. They then build on the reading, thinking, and writing abilities students already possess and provide the instruction and the encouragement to lead students into deeper waters, stretch intellectually, and meet new challenges.

Structure   Although it might appear that every student does his or her own thing in workshop, a workshop environment is actually highly structured and involves specific expectations, rules, predictable routines, time frames, and accountability measures. Additionally, the teacher's minilessons introduce students to new genres and to the specific cognitive strategies that effective readers and writers use.

Collaboration   Collaboration among the students and between the students and the teacher is the centerpiece of reading and writing workshop. Students continuously interact as a community of learners to give and receive feedback on the texts they are reading and writing. The teacher, acting in the role of senior member of this community, resists the temptation to make meaning for the students; instead, he or she provides them with tools and opportunities with which to construct their own meaning.

Internalization   Internalization is the transfer of control from the teacher to the students as they "gain competence in the new tasks" (Langer & Applebee, 1986, p. 187). The workshop environment offers students a safe place to experiment with and practice on their own the strategies they are learning in the more teacher-guided components of the language arts class. This is the ultimate opportunity to think and act strategically: Students are deliberately selecting which tactics to use and deciding when and why to implement them, and they are doing so independently.

Many teachers feel that, philosophically, one must choose to adopt either a teacher-guided or a student-centered approach to language arts instruction. Not so. The exemplary teachers identified by researchers Sumara and Walker (1991) moved fluidly between adopting authoritative and "learning" stances; and the students readily accepted their dual roles, recognizing when they were assuming the position of Teacher with a capital T and when they were participating as a partner in the classroom community. Students need teachers to prompt them to work at the edges of their zone of proximal development (Vygotsky, 1986) so as to undertake tasks that they initially can complete with "appropriate help, but would be unable to complete unaided" (Langer & Applebee, 1986, p. 186). They also need opportunities to chart their own course and to set sail for destinations they select for themselves.

CREATING A WORKSHOP ENVIRONMENT

As Kirby and Kuykendall (1991) point out, there's more to creating a studio classroom than just interior decorating; the aim is to create a psychological environment in which the students and the teacher share certain common values (p. 214). However, from the moment students enter the door, the physical setting does send students a message about whether they are renters in the teacher's classroom for the year or whether they are joint owners of the learning environment (Tompkins, 1997, p. 7). In her description of the artist's studio, Atwell mentions that the artist needs to have access to everything she needs from the right palette knife to the appropriate tube of color. So too, a workshop classroom will need paper, scissors, sticky notes, colored markers, a three-hole punch, file folders, glue sticks, index cards, and so forth—in short, all the supplies necessary for the construction of meaning from and with texts. And don't forget books! Research indicates that the tangible presence of accessible books in the classroom is a "significant factor in literacy development" (Gambrell, 1994, p. 3). There should be texts written not only by published authors but also by the students themselves, signaling that the output of the authors in the classroom is valued and valuable reading material.

The logistics of the desks and chairs are also an issue. It is difficult to create a community of learners when students are seated at individual desks in straight rows, facing forward. Teachers who do not have the luxury of tables can arrange chairs in a U shape or pull four chairs together for collaborative workspace. Research findings show that motivation to learn is high when students have environments that are nurturing and comfortable (Gambrell, 1994). Although constructing such an environment is more difficult in secondary than in elementary school, teachers can create reading corners with throw pillows or an easy chair or make space for a writing and publication center with all the necessary supplies and one or more computers.

In Chapter 4 we saw how welcome the atmosphere of Janet Allen's classroom (1995) made her students feel. As one student recalled, "I mean, everywhere you would look the room would be telling you to keep going, don't stop, try harder, reach for your dreams, and many other things . . . that would lift your spirits" (p. 28). Although Allen has her share of motivational quotes and posters on display and she fills the room with enticing books, the bulletin boards belong to the students. She invites them to take ownership of the space to reflect their community and their creations. Gail Tompkins (1997) would say that Allen's students are not renting a furnished classroom; they're "moving in" as co-owners for the year.

If students are more motivated in a setting that is comfortable, nurturing, and print rich, they also thrive in an environment whose predictable structures and routines let them experience a "sense of continuity" (Atwell, 1998, p. 97) from week to week. Atwell proposes two options for structuring reading and writing workshop for teachers whose schedules are based on fifty-minute periods.

Option 1: When a Workshop Approach Is the Curriculum
- Writing workshop on four regular, consecutive days (e.g., Monday–Thursday)
- Reading workshop on one regularly scheduled fifth day (e.g., Friday) but with booktalks and literary minilessons throughout the week
- A half hour's worth of independent reading as homework every night
- An hour's worth of writing as homework, done at the student's discretion between Thursday night and Monday morning

Option 2: When a Required Curriculum Must Be Covered
- Writing workshop four days a week (e.g., Monday–Thursday) for one semester, with an hour's worth of writing as homework between Thursday night and Monday morning
- The required curriculum four days a week for the alternate semester
- Reading workshop on one regularly scheduled fifth day (e.g., Friday) throughout the entire school year, and frequent booktalks and literary minilessons
- A half hour's worth of independent reading as homework every night (pp. 97–98)

Particularly since the release of the new content standards and the renewed emphasis on standardized testing, I have seen few teachers in the UCI Writing Project devote as much time exclusively to workshop as Atwell suggests. But teachers who have integrated reading and writing workshop into their classrooms to whatever degree their schedules will permit keep the spirit of workshop alive throughout their language arts curriculum. That is, whether the task is teacher-guided or student-selected, the class remains a community of learners operating in an environment in which the contributions of all members are valued and respected.

READING WORKSHOP

At the core of reading workshop is students' reading of self-selected fiction and nonfiction material.

The Power of Free Voluntary Reading

On the subject of reading, Nancie Atwell (1998) writes,

> There's nothing better for you—not broccoli, not an apple a day, not aerobic exercise. In terms of the whole rest of your life, in terms of making you smart in all ways, there's nothing better. Top-ranking scientists and mathematicians are people who read a lot. Top-ranking historians and researchers are people who read a lot. It's like money in the bank in terms of the rest your life, but it also helps you escape from the rest of your life and live experiences you can only dream of. Most important, along with writing, it's the best way I know to find out who you are, what you care about, and what kind of person you want to become. (p. 139)

Researcher Stephen Krashen (1993) would definitely agree that reading is good for you. And he would be quick to add that although assigned reading has a positive impact on literacy development and can expose students to a wide variety of books and genres, free voluntary reading "is one of the most powerful tools" (p. 1) in language arts education. He writes,

> My conclusions are simple. When children read for pleasure, when they get "hooked on books," they acquire, involuntarily and without conscious effort, nearly all of the so-called "language skills" many people are so concerned about: They will become adequate readers, acquire a large vocabulary, develop the ability to understand and use complex grammatical constructions, develop a good writing style, and become good (but not necessarily perfect) spellers. Although free voluntary reading alone will not ensure attainment of the highest levels of literacy, it will at least ensure an acceptable level. Without it, I suspect that children simply do not have a chance. (p. 84)

Research suggests that the amount of independent silent reading students do is directly related to gains in reading achievement (Allington, 1984). Avid readers do almost twenty times more independent reading than less motivated readers (Fielding, Wilson, & Anderson, 1990). Furthermore, there is a strong correlation between the amount of out-of-school pleasure reading students do and their success on measures of reading competency (Fielding et al., 1990). In-school free voluntary reading programs can ignite our students' passion for reading, motivating them to pursue reading more frequently in school as well as outside of school.

There are basically two kinds of in-school free voluntary reading programs. One is sustained silent reading (SSR), in which students and teachers (and sometimes the administrators and even the custodians) drop everything and read (hence the name DEAR time, used in some schools) for approximately fifteen minutes. SSR usually takes place at a specified time each day across subject areas. The other program, self-selected reading in some form of reading workshop, occurs during language arts class for a sustained period of time. Research indicates that free voluntary reading programs are consistently effective in promoting reading achievement and that the longer students participate in self-selecting books and reading for pleasure, the more consistent and the more positive the reading achievement results (Krashen, 1993, p. 3).

Principles of Reader Engagement

Drawing from the work of psychologist Mihaly Csikszentimihaly (1991), the National Reading Research Center defines an engaged reader as someone who

- chooses to read;
- reads widely, for both pleasure and information;
- possesses a repertoire of strategies for understanding and interpreting texts; and
- uses reading to develop a better understanding of self, others, and the world. (Gambrell, 1994, p. 2)

Linda Gambrell, principal investigator for the National Reading Research Center, and several colleagues spent two years interviewing students who fit this description of an engaged reader to learn what factors influenced their motivation to read. They identified five key principles of reader engagement and offer research-based suggestions for creating classroom environments that foster reading engagement. The principles and suggestions outlined by Gambrell (1994, pp. 3–5) can provide a strong foundation on which to establish reading workshop in the classroom:

1. *Engaged readers thrive when the classroom is "book rich."* As mentioned previously, the presence of books "is a significant factor in literacy development" (p. 3). Teachers should create high-quality classroom libraries to provide students with wide access to books.

2. *Engaged readers like to choose their own books.* Eighty percent of the students Gambrell and her colleagues interviewed indicated that they "most enjoyed" books they had selected themselves. This finding has been substantiated by other researchers. For example, Paris and Oka (1986) correlate choice and the development of intrinsic motivation; Turner (1992) suggests that self-selection promotes students' independence and versatility as readers.

3. *Engaged readers like books that provide familiar characters, settings, and story structures.* Hence, books written in a series are especially compelling. Students are also motivated to read books recommended by their peers. This finding has been documented both for upper elementary school students (Wendelin & Zinck, 1983) and for high school readers (Appleby & Conner, 1965).

4. *Engaged readers interact with others about their reading.* In addition, students who engage in frequent discussions about their reading are more motivated and have higher reading achievement scores than students who do not interact with others about books (Mullis, Campbell, & Farstrup, 1993). Providing opportunities for students to share with other readers their experiences with and responses to books is "an important factor in developing enthusiastic, engaged readers" (Gambrell, 1994, p. 4).

5. *For engaged readers, books are the best reward.* Students are often given prizes such as coupons to the local pizza parlor as an incentive to read books. Although this practice initially increases motivation to read, research demonstrates that in the long term, such rewards actually impair motivation (Fawson & Fawson, 1994). Gambrell (1994) concludes that in a climate in which books themselves are regarded as valuable and intrinsically satisfying rather than the means to the gold star, candy treat, or other token, the best reward for reading should be access to more books.

Goals and Expectations for Reading Workshop

Although students self-select what books to read in reading workshop, most teachers have specific goals and expectations that encourage students to read widely and deeply. These include the following; adapted from Atwell (1998, pp. 113–114 and 203–204):

Goals	Expectations
• To learn how to choose books	• Maintain a chronological record of the books you read, including those you abandon.
• To become lifelong readers	• Read books by a variety of authors; books on different subjects; books in diverse genres; and books for different purposes.
• To become more fluent and proficient readers	• Read for at least thirty minutes seven nights a week. Set and work toward specific individual reading goals, and assess your progress each trimester or semester.
• To read with greater understanding	• Keep reading logs in which you practice the strategies that experienced readers use (tapping prior knowledge, asking questions, making predictions, revising meaning, etc.) in written responses to texts.
• To collaborate with others to share responses to and interpretations of books	• Participate in some form of interactive dialogue about books in small groups at least once a week for a sustained period of time. Collaborate as a whole class on constructing the meaning of shared texts to interact as a community of learners.
• To learn what experienced writers do through reading good books	• Study author's craft through independent reading and through the teacher's minilessons. Write about author's craft in reading workshop. Practice applying the principles of author's craft to your own writing in both teacher-prompted and self-selected writing.

Getting Acquainted: Getting to Know Students and Getting Students to Know Books

At the beginning of the year, several activities can help introduce students and teacher to one another—and to a selection of books.

Literature Book Bingo   Meredith Ritner, a seventh-grade teacher at Aliso Viejo Middle School in Aliso Viejo, California, introduces her version of reading workshop to students with a round of literature book bingo. She puts a small bowl of M&Ms and one grid with sixteen squares for each student at the table. She then puts up on a transparency a list of twenty book titles, names of authors, characters, and so on; and she instructs students to insert fifteen of these "answers" into the squares of their bingo card, making one square a free square.

When everyone is ready, she reads a clue like "What is the name of the pig Fern took care of in *Charlotte's Web*?," "This boy attends Hogwart's School of Wizardry," or "Who wrote the *Goosebumps* series?" Students place their M&Ms on the bingo square that correctly responds to the clue while simultaneously eating the extra candy in the bowl. (A complete copy of the questions and answers for this game of bingo is available on the companion website.) The first four students to call "Bingo" when they get four squares in a row vertically, horizontally, or diagonally are given first dibs at selecting the book of their choice from the classroom library in Ritner's self-selected reading program. Thus, Ritner immediately establishes that knowledge about books is valuable and that the opportunity to select books for independent reading is something to be coveted. The bingo winners also receive one of Ritner's famous Pillow Passes (Figure 14.1). These passes enable students to select a pillow from Ritner's pillow collection and to find a comfortable spot in the classroom to lie on their pillow and read during independent reading time.

Dear Student Letter and Reading Reminiscence   In order to determine how her students feel about reading as well as to gauge their level of experience (or inexperience) with pleasure reading, Ritner writes her students a letter in which she shares some of her own memories about her early exposure to books, poses some questions for them to consider as they sift through their memories, and invites them to explore their own reading life and write her back. (An alternative to this activity is the How I Learned to Read and Write learning log reflection described in Chapter 4.) The companion website includes a copy of Ritner's letter to her class.

Receiving honest and open letters back from her students enables Ritner to assess where her students are developmentally and attitudinally as readers and to steer them toward books

Figure 14.1   **Pillow Pass** (Reprinted by permission of Meredith D. Ritner.)

that will be at their independent reading level, at which they can experience some success—rather than at their frustration level, at which they are likely to feel deficient and send themselves messages that they are "slow." She is now in a position to give a little extra encouragement and guidance to students who need it, thus giving all the students in her class an equal opportunity to become lifelong readers.

At Utt Middle School in Tustin, California, Barbara Valentine, a sixth-grade teacher, also launches her independent reading program by asking students to write a reminiscence about their history as a reader. In addition to composing a written recollection, students represent their reading life artistically. Figure 14.2 illustrates Tiffany Chung's reading life. Sitting under a tree of knowledge, she is surrounded by three-dimensional re-creations of the covers of her favorite books. Valentine's students use their artwork to introduce themselves as readers to one another in small collaborative groups.

Reading Survey   In lieu of or in addition to soliciting a student reminiscence about reading, some teachers like to give students a survey to fill out to indicate what they know and how they feel about reading. Both Janet Allen (1995) and Nancie Atwell (1998) have reading surveys in their books for teachers to copy. Thelma Anselmi, an eighth-grade teacher at St. Columban School in Garden Grove, California, adapted questions from Allen and Atwell as well as from Rief (1992) to create the survey shown on the companion website. Anselmi also has students assess their literary palate using Fran Claggett's (1996) "What Kind of Reader Are You?" exercise (see the website for Chapter 13), which uses the metaphor of food and asks students to decide if they are diet readers, fast food readers, omnivorous readers, and so forth.

Reading Territories   It is important to ascertain and honor what students already know about books when they come into your language arts classroom. But it is equally important to expand their horizons by introducing them to new reading territories. As a way of helping

Figure 14.2   **My Reading Life Poster** (Reprinted by permission of Tiffany Chung.)

her students get to know her as a passionate reader while also acquainting them with a wide variety of reading materials and domains, Nancie Atwell (1998) stands at the overhead and maps out her reading territories on a transparency. She launches into fiction, citing her favorite authors and titles and what types of topics draw her in; moves on to poetry and the way certain poets make her work or amaze her; describes plays, essays, magazines, newspapers, works of young adult literature, and children's picture books; and includes daily life reading such as correspondence, bills, instructions, catalogues, warranties, and the like. She even has a "guilty pleasures" category—*People Weekly,* various gossip columns, and so forth. She is careful to include works of student writing in her list, validating student work as a source of her reading pleasure. As she surveys her reading landscape, Atwell invites students to begin charting their own reading territories whenever something she says rings a bell. After she has completed her comprehensive self-portrait, she invites students to add to their reading territories any categories or titles from her list or to come up with additional items of their own. The students then review their lists and star a few items that are particularly interesting, surprising, or revealing. Students bring their reading territories lists to a whole group circle to share one reading territory or text on their list, thus establishing the class as a community of readers. This sets the stage for an invitation to browse among the texts in Atwell's classroom library and to select something to begin reading independently.

Providing Access to Books

■   It is certainly true that "you can lead a horse to water but you cannot make him drink." But first we must be sure that water is there.

—Stephen Krashen

Stephen Krashen's (1983, p. 33) metaphor is particularly apt. As he says, "The most obvious step is to provide access to books" (p. 33). Research indicates that students who live close to public libraries read more than students who do not (p. 35) and that students take more books out of school libraries that have more books and stay open longer (Houle & Montmarquette, 1984). The teacher has no influence on his or her students' access to reading outside of school and little to no influence on the size of the holdings in the school library. The teacher does, however, have control over the acquisitions in his or her own classroom library.

Creating a Classroom Library   If the tangible presence of books in the classroom promotes literacy development, then establishing a classroom library is a must. Some teachers receive school or district allocations to buy books for their classrooms, but many more will be left to their own resources. Meredith Ritner has had success appealing to parents on back-to-school night to donate books to her classroom library that their children have already read. At McFadden Intermediate School in Santa Ana, California, which is located in a low socioeconomic area, Sharon Schiesl conducts a recycled book drive and encourages parents and students to collect any types of used books they or their neighbors have. She then sells these books to a local used book store and spends the proceeds at the Friends of the Library shop at the public library, buying young adult literature and classics at reduced rates, or at the bargain books sections of Barnes & Noble or Borders bookstores. Schiesl also takes advantage of the credit she receives when students order books from Scholastic and purchases books for the classroom library. Before she had a wide array of books in her own classroom, Schiesl routinely took her whole class to the school library to check out books for independent reading. She also encourages students and their parents to get library cards at the Santa Ana Public Library, providing them with application forms.

Text Selection Because the students in any classroom will possess a range of reading backgrounds and abilities, it is important to have a wide array of books for them to choose from. Some students with a rich reading background and an academic bent may choose to read classics that are above their grade level. For example, I have seen seventh graders at South Lake Middle School in Irvine, California, enjoying *Wuthering Heights, The Crucible,* and *Lord of the Flies.* Other students may gravitate toward best-selling authors like John Grisham, Tom Clancy, or Michael Crichton or toward contemporary writers of culturally diverse backgrounds—Sandra Cisneros, Amy Tan, Alice Walker, or Sherman Alexie, to name a few. Students who wish to keep abreast of award-winning adult literature can download updated lists from the following websites:

- National Book Award—www.powells.com/prizes/national.html
- The Booker Critics Circle Award—www.powells.com/prizes/booker.html
- The Pulitzer Prize—www.powells.com/prizes/pulitzer_fiction.html

Many students at the middle school level (and at the high school level as well) may find that young adult literature best meets their needs and interests—especially at the beginning of reading workshop. As discussed in Chapter 7, Leila Christenbury (1994) describes the genre of young adult fiction as characterized by:

- A teenage (or young adult) protagonist
- A stripped-down plot with few, if any, subplots
- A limited number of characters
- A compressed time span and a restricted setting
- An approximate length of 125–250 pages

Figure 7.2 in Chapter 7 includes a list of recommended pairings of YA literature with core texts to be taught to the whole class. Young adult literature also makes ideal independent reading. The companion website provides a list of over twenty-five YA titles compiled by Alex Uhl, owner of A Whale of a Tale Bookstore in Irvine, California; these books have been best-sellers among her secondary school patrons. Nancie Atwell (1998) also has student-generated recommendations of favorite YA literature in Appendix L of *In the Middle.* An additional source that is continually updated is the Berkeley Public Library Teens Services Booklists: www.infopeople.org/bpl/teen/booklist.html.

Secondary students who struggle as readers and are reading well below grade level are often frustrated when they try to read books that are suitable in content for their level of maturity but are too difficult in terms of reading level. But books that are written for a much younger audience are equally off-putting for these students. Whether such students are second language learners or native speakers, Donna Moore, an English Language Development teacher at Fitz Intermediate in Garden Grove, California, recommends the publishers listed in Figure 14.3 as sources of engaging high-interest texts written at a lower reading level for secondary students.

Lots of big kids of all ages (including me) relish reading a good children's book now and then. Teachers can download current lists of award-winning children's books, including some works that cross over into young adult literature, from the following websites:

- Caldecott Medal—www.ala.org/alsc/caldpast.html
- Newbery Medal for Best Children's Books—www.amazon.com/exec/obidos/subst/lists/awards/newbery.html

Stephen Krashen (1983) observes, "Perhaps the most powerful way of encouraging children to read is by exposing them to light reading, a kind of reading that many children, for

Figure 14.3 **High-Interest Texts for Teens Written at a Lower Reading Level** *(Note: Northwest Regional Educational Laboratories—www.nwrel.org/learns/resources/publishers/#high— has a list of publishers of high-interest/low reading level books)*

Publisher	Series	Reading Level	Contact Information
• Saddleback Educational, Inc.	Disaster, sports, mystery, and adventure	Grades 3 through 5	(949) 860-2500 (888) SDL-BACK
• Kids In Between	Timely Topics for Teens	Grades 5 through 6	(800) 481-2799
• Harcourt • Steck-Vaughn	Mystery, adventure, and science fiction	Grades 2 through 4	(800) 531-5015
• Globe Fearon	Hopes and Dreams	Grades 1 through 3	(800) 848-9500

economic or ideological reasons, are deprived of" (p. 48). He also counsels teachers not to underestimate comic books, because research shows that comic books are at least as beneficial for students as other types of reading (p. 55). And it pays to have teen and adult magazines on hand, as there are studies that correlate magazine reading with increases on measures of teen reading achievement (Rucker, 1982).

Displaying Books When library corners have "attracting features"—posters, bulletin boards, displays—students show more interest in books (Morrow, 1982). Some teachers display books alphabetically by author and by genre (poetry, fiction, drama, nonfiction) and feature a "new titles" bookcase such as one would find in a bookstore. Other teachers color-code bookshelves from easier-to-read to harder-to-read books so that students can select a book at their comfort level. (Note that if you color-code the shelves rather than putting colored dots on the book spines, there's no stigma about who is reading what level book.) Still other teachers invite students to write brief recommendations on index cards for the "best-selling" books in the classroom library; they display the cards beneath the books so students can browse and read the recommendations of their peers. The cards might even include student commentaries about stories written by classmates that are available in the library. Posters with sayings like "Open a book and open your mind" or "Reading is not a spectator sport" also contribute to establishing a hooked-on-books environment in the classroom.

Getting Students Hooked on a Book To use Stephen Krashen's metaphor, once you've led the horse to water, it's time to make him drink. Having a wide array of high-interest books available for students, displaying them attractively, and prompting students to think of themselves as readers and to generate possible reading territories for themselves are all important steps in setting the stage for book selection. Before having students self-select their books, teachers can read a brief excerpt that sparks the students' curiosity and leaves them hanging, such as this one from Ivy Ruckman's 1984 book *Night of the Twisters:*

> The roaring had started somewhere to the east, then came bearing down on us like a hundred freight trains. Only that twister didn't move on. It stationed itself right overhead, making the loudest noise I'd ever heard, whining worse than any jet. There was a tremendous crack, and I felt the wall shudder behind us. I knew then our house was being ripped apart. Suddenly chunks of ceiling were falling on our heads.
>   We'll be buried! was all I could think. (p. 54)

On completing the excerpt, the teacher can ask, "OK, who wants to read this book?"

One method of exposing students to a substantial number of books in a short period of time is to initiate a book pass. Before starting the book pass activity, Donna Moore models how to look at the cover of the book, turn the book over and scan the blurb on the back cover, flip through the book for chapter headings and pictures, and select one page to read at the beginning of any chapter. She tells students to use the five finger rule—that is, when reading their page, to count all words they stumble over on their fingers. If they use up five fingers on one page, then the book is probably beyond their independent reading level. Every student then gets a book from the classroom library to peruse for three minutes and one minute to record on a sheet of paper the author of the book; the title; a rating from 1 to 5; and a reason for the rating, such as "lively action" for a 5 or "boring" for a 1. Depending on the class, allow fifteen to thirty minutes for this activity. Moore cautions that with inexperienced readers it is best to have students select the book they actually want to read immediately after the book pass, as they often lose interest by the following day.

Keeping Track   Once students select a book, the teacher needs to design an accountability system to monitor students' progress in their reading. Creating some form of reading chart with a daily or weekly reading requirement (usually thirty minutes a day or three hours a week) that is verified by a parent or guardian will help you keep track of where your students are.

Often the charts are a simple record as in this example:

Date	*Title*, Author	Pages Read	Minutes Read	Parent Signature
10/7	*The Hobbit*, J. R. R. Tolkein	57–89	40	K. Nelson

Alternatively, even though students are usually keeping a separate reading log or completing activities for literature circles or book clubs, some teachers want a more detailed record of their students' daily reading. Donna Moore provides students with a weekly "Step by Step through My Book" form, which is available on the companion website, that prompts them to practice their summarizing skills and to dig deeper to ask questions about what they have read. Copies of both types of reading records are available on the companion website.

Once the reading of self-selected texts is under way, the teacher can occasionally conduct "interrupted book reports" to monitor students' reading and to cultivate interest in books throughout the class. To initiate interrupted book reports:

1. Ask one student to be timekeeper.
2. Model the activity: In just thirty seconds, tell the class everything you can about a book you are reading. (Remind the timekeeper to interrupt you by calling time.)
3. Call on students at random to share where they are in their books and their current responses.

Like the status-of-the-class activity in writing workshop (see Writing Workshop later in this chapter), the interrupted book report gives students a taste of one another's texts, creates a sense of community, and generates interest in present and future reading.

Students need permission to abandon books that they simply cannot get into or connect with. Encourage them to stick with a text for the first few chapters; many stories take time to draw you in. But give students the option of selecting a new book if they really have encountered a dead end. Some teachers require students to submit a 3-by-5 card explaining why they wish to abandon their book before they opt for a new title. For example, Donna Moore recommended one of the high-interest books for inexperienced teen readers (see Figure 14.3) to a Mexican American student in her class. Because the book was about his favorite sport, basketball, she assumed he would be highly invested in reading it. She was puzzled when her student abandoned the text almost immediately. When he turned in his 3-by-5 card, Moore learned that he could not keep the characters, who were African American, straight because they had Muslim names that were unfamiliar to him. After Moore helped him plot the characters out on a character chart, he resumed reading and enjoyed the book immensely.

The Teacher's Role in Reading Workshop

The teacher's role in reading workshop is both affective and cognitive. Especially with inexperienced or struggling readers, the teacher will need to act as a cheerleader to create an environment in which students are willing to invest their time and energy to get hooked on books. But students will also need a coach who can make visible what it is that experienced readers do by introducing them to the cognitive strategies in a reader's tool kit. Within reading workshop, teachers may want to consider the following approaches.

Teach Core Texts Nancie Atwell (1998) advocates that when a required curriculum must be covered, teachers devote one semester to workshop and then one semester to the core curriculum. Other options are to integrate the teaching of core texts into reading workshop or to alternate weeks focused on core texts and workshop. The advantage of an integrated approach is that the teacher can use the instruction surrounding the reading of a common text as a model for students to practice independently with their self-selected books.

Read Aloud One of the clearest predictors of early reading ability is the amount of time children spend reading with parents (Mason & Allen, 1986). Further, when teachers read aloud to children and discuss the reading with the class, children read more (Morrow & Weinstein, 1982). There is ample evidence that reading aloud to students promotes literacy development (Krashen, 1993); in one study, for example, college students who were read works by Twain, Salinger, Poe, and Thurber one hour per week for thirteen weeks read more books and did better on their final essays than students in comparable classes that were not read to (Pitts, 1986). Yet few teachers read aloud at the secondary level. Janet Allen (1995) remarks that many of her students thought being read to was "stupid"; over time, however, she won them over. Allen acknowledges, "I learned that reading aloud was a risk-free way to turn many individuals into one group and share literature with students who believed they hated to read" (p. 4). She adds that "a bond is created during a read aloud that is unrivaled in terms of literacy" (p. 45).

To that end, Nancie Atwell (1998) pulls out all the stops when she reads. She writes,

> When reading aloud I go for it, changing my inflection for the different characters and moods of a text. I change my face, too—smile, frown, show anger or surprise or the effects of suspense or enlightenment—and I modulate the volume, louder or softer, to match the mood. I read slower than I speak, and I pause before and after parts I want to stress, to let things sink in. I ask questions: "What do you think might happen next? What do you already know about the main character? Is this character an antagonist or protagonist? What do you think the author is trying to get at here? Does this remind you of anything else you've read? Does this remind you of anything that's happened to you?" I show the illustrations. Before I read, I page ahead to get a sense of how much of a text I can read in ten or fifteen minutes, so the stopping point comes at a natural break. And I only read aloud from literature I like. The absolute worst thing I could demonstrate when reading to my kids is boredom. Literature I read with genuine pleasure is the only literature students will be able to listen to with genuine pleasure. (p. 145)

Make Strategies Visible   When Nancie Atwell is reading aloud and she pauses to ask, "What do you think might happen next?" (1998, p. 145) and so forth, she is modeling the cognitive strategies that experienced readers use to make meaning from texts. I would advocate going one step farther and naming those strategies, thereby giving students language with which to talk about their processes of meaning construction. Many of the teachers in the UCI Writing Project are experimenting with the booklet I designed, "Sharing Your Responses to Texts: A Cognitive Strategies Approach," which is discussed in Chapter 2 and included on the companion website for Chapter 2. In addition to implementing the booklets in collaborative groups as an alternative to literature circles, these teachers have used the booklets one page at a time to introduce and practice tapping prior knowledge, asking questions, predicting, visualizing, making connections, adopting an alignment, monitoring, forming interpretations and revising meaning, analyzing author's craft, reflecting and relating, and evaluating. They may utilize the booklets with a specific text, such as a short story like "All Summer in a Day" (see Chapter 3) or "The Stolen Party" (see Chapter 9); or they may employ it while reading several texts over time.

The teacher can also help students transfer the strategies applied to reading a shared text to their independent reading by doing a "think-aloud" (see Chapter 2). The process is similar to what Atwell models when she reads aloud and pauses, except that the teacher is delivering a monologue to make visible the tactics that effective readers use rather that attempting to engage class members in a dialogue.

Keene and Zimmerman (1997) point out that before engaging in a think-aloud, the teacher should clearly explain to the students the distinction between reading aloud and thinking aloud. He or she should also explain why readers use a specific strategy or strategies while reading. For example, in regard to the strategy of asking questions, the teacher might communicate the following key ideas:

- Proficient readers spontaneously generate questions before, during, and after reading.
- Proficient readers ask questions to
  - clarify meaning;
  - speculate about text yet to be read;
  - determine an author's intent, style, content, or format; and/or
  - locate a specific answer in text *or* consider rhetorical questions inspired by the text.
- Proficient readers use questions to focus their attention on important components of the text; they understand that they can pose questions critically.
- Proficient readers understand that many of the most intriguing questions are not answered explicitly in the text but left to the reader's interpretation.
- However, when an answer is needed, proficient readers determine whether it can be answered by the text or whether they will need to infer the answer from the text, their background knowledge, and/or other text.
- Proficient readers understand how the process of questioning is used in other areas of their lives, both academic and personal.
- Proficient readers understand how asking questions deepens their comprehension.
- Proficient readers are aware that as they hear others' questions, new ones are inspired in their own minds. (Keene & Zimmerman, 1997, p. 119)

After modeling a cognitive strategy through the think-aloud approach, the teacher can invite students to return to their self-selected texts, to generate questions, and to share them in small groups or with the teacher in a conference or in writing.

Teach Minilessons   Within my description of the think-aloud above, I have embedded a minilesson on asking questions courtesy of Keene and Zimmerman (1997). Minilessons consist of direct instruction designed to impart information about strategies, concepts, or techniques that help readers and writers to develop competence and confidence. As Atwell (1998) says, "The minilesson is a forum for sharing my authority—the things I know that will help readers and writers grow. I have experiences as an adult that my students have not had, and it's my responsibility to share the knowledge that I do have—and seek the knowledge that I don't—that will help them move forward" (p. 150). However, the best minilessons will move beyond creating declarative knowledge (knowing what a strategy is) to instilling procedural knowledge (knowing how to implement a strategy) and conditional knowledge (knowing when and why to use one strategy as opposed to another). To empower students with all three levels of knowledge, one can design a pedagogical strategy that provides guided practice in a specific cognitive strategy. Chapter 6, Strategies for Interacting with a Text, contains a wide range of pedagogical strategies that provide practice in the cognitive strategies effective readers use. For example, the Easy as 1, 2, 3! pedagogical strategy described in Chapter 6 (and shown in Figure 3.5 in Chapter 3), invites students to tap prior knowledge, make predictions, visualize, revise meaning, and make new predictions. The teacher can draw the students' attention to the cognitive strategies they have used in the Easy as 1, 2, 3! activity after they have interacted with the text and with one another.

Communicate with Individual Students Both Orally and in Writing   Much of reading workshop focuses on the interactions among students in small collaborative groups as they discuss the texts they are reading. But it is also important for the teacher to dialogue with students one-on-one about their responses to texts. While students are reading independently, the teacher can call individual students up for a brief conference about their books. The teacher might ask students several of the following questions, depending on where they are in the process of reading their book:

- What book are you reading, and what is it about?
- Why did you select this book to read?
- What character do you most identify with, and why?
- Is there anything about this book that reminds you of your own life?
- Does this book remind you of other books you have read?
- Do/did you find reading this book easy? Difficult? Challenging? Why?
- What do you think will happen next in your book?
- Would you recommend this book to your friends? Why or why not?

These brief discussions have both affective and cognitive implications. Affectively, they enable the teacher to communicate interest in each student's reading experience, thus motivating the student to keep reading. Cognitively, the teacher can assess whether students have selected appropriate books for their reading level, determine if they are progressing through the text satisfactorily, troubleshoot any difficulties they may be encountering, determine if and how well they are using cognitive strategies to construct meaning, and so forth. Donna Moore of Fitz Intermediate in Garden Grove sometimes focuses her conferences on questions that provide practice in some area of reading instruction the class has been working on. For example, to determine if they have a grasp on the elements of plot, she might ask:

"Who were the characters? What was the problem? What was the solution?" To reinforce sequencing skills, she might say "Tell me what happened first in your book? Next? After that? Finally?"

The teacher can also maintain written correspondence with students about their books. Once students self-select books, the teacher can invite them to drop him or her a line about their reading, using the questions previously listed for oral conferences as a point of departure, if needed. The role of the teacher as a correspondent is quite different from the role of the teacher as an evaluator. To engage in a genuine dialogue, the teacher should not write comments *on* the student's letter but actually write *back.*

Collaborating on Responses to Reading through Book Clubs

Research suggests that students who engage in frequent discussions about their reading are more motivated, have higher reading achievement, read more widely, and read more frequently than students who do not (Gambrell, 1994). In other words, social collaboration is an important factor in developing confidence and competence as readers. Two vehicles for facilitating interaction as students read self-selected books are literature circles and book clubs. The key difference in the way that these two small-group dialogue strategies are being used by teachers in the UCI Writing Project is that in literature circles, groups of four to six students have selected the same book to read, whereas in book clubs each individual in the group may be reading a different text. Literature circles are described at length in Chapter 11.

Most adult book clubs operate more like literature circles, in the sense that members of the group are all reading and discussing the same book—although the talk of mature readers may alleviate the need for roles. Student book clubs can also be formed according to this model. However, most teachers that I know use book clubs as a mechanism to form small heterogeneous groups of students of all ability levels who can share the different books they are reading as equal partners. Instead of assuming roles to engage in discussion, students write "lit. letters" to their book clubs, keeping the group posted on their progress through responses to their books. Further, most book clubs revolve around an activity (or a choice of activities), which is usually modeled beforehand by the teacher with a core text the class is reading in common.

Activities for Reading Workshop

Numerous classroom activities can enhance the reading workshop experience.

Book Cover Activity   Whether students participate in literature circles or book clubs, they need to have a place to collect their role sheets, lit. letters, and other materials. Although they could set aside a section of their portfolio for this purpose, I prefer that they keep their reading workshop materials in a separate manila folder. To help them personalize this folder, I designed the book cover activity described on the next page.

To model the activity, I created for myself the sample book cover in Figure 14.4. As with the personality collage doll activity and the "My Name, My Self" demonstration lesson in Chapter 4, students enjoy thinking about themselves metaphorically and using a tangible object to introduce themselves and become better acquainted with one another.

Prompt

Get-Acquainted Activity: Book Covers

Ed Ramirez, an eleventh-grade student at Century High School in Santa Ana, California, chose the metaphor of a book to describe himself:

A Book

I am a book stationed at a huge library, lost among many. My cover is not exciting, beautiful, or ugly. My cover is boring. I am a book, quiet, stationed on the shelves until someone picks me up. I am a book, and if you open me up, you'll find out I'm interesting, full of fiction and non-fiction material. I am a book in that I'm going through different stages or chapters as my life goes on. I am a book in that if you judge me by my cover you may never find out how interesting I am. I am a book in that one day there will be an end.

As I sit on the shelves, I see the rest of the books and magazines. It's incredible. I sit and gather dust while people won't let the other more "popular" better-looking reading material alone. I just sit, relax, wait, and wait, until a person comes and picks me up. This person doesn't flip through my pages for pictures; he reads page by page, day after day, and when he finishes, he is satisfied. He has read my material. He didn't judge my cover. He has found out I'm a pretty good book.

I feel happiness after opening my pages and flipping them for this person who has read me. But the sadness comes back. He puts me back on my old dusty shelf. Once again, people ignore me and pass me by. They go directly to the magazines and books with pictures, my more attractive peers. Yet, somebody discovered me. Perhaps, someday, I'll be discovered again.

Like Ed Ramirez, and like books, we all have many layers and are filled with stories to tell about the chapters in our lives. We also may have one kind of cover on the outside and another set of qualities on the inside.

Book Covers

As a way to get acquainted with your book club, please create a book cover for yourself. You may wish to write . . .

> On the outside, I'm . . .
> but on the inside, I'm . . .

Fill the outside and inside of your book cover with words and images (from magazines or hand sketched) that you think say something about you.

P.S. If you're not a person who is comfortable with "opening yourself up" to others right away, please feel free to decorate your outside cover only.

Enjoy!

An 8½-by-11 copy of the book cover activity is available on the companion website.

Writing Your First Lit. Letter Earlier, I discussed how the teacher can generate a genuine exchange of ideas about and responses to texts by conversing with students through letters. Although this correspondence is extremely valuable and can provide the teacher with windows into the hearts and minds of his or her students, the lit. letters students write to one another about the literature they are reading play an even more important role in creating a community of learners. Atwell (1998) notes, "However widely and sympathetically I've read their books, kids need and trust each other's advice. They're more playful with each other,

Figure 14.4 **Teacher's Book Cover Sample**

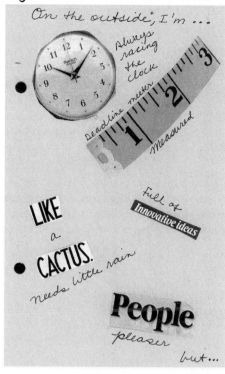 

Outside   **Inside**

joking and teasing as they couldn't with an adult. And they write more and longer letters than when I'm the sole audience" (p. 279). In writing to classmates about their reading in advance of the book club meeting, students have an opportunity to reflect on the specific texts they are reading, on the reading process in general, and on themselves as readers. Lit. letters provide readers with an audience for their reading: In the letters students both keep their peers updated on what's going on in their texts and go beyond comprehension to form interpretations, make predictions, discover connections with their own lives, and so forth.

In their first lit. letter, usually students introduce themselves to their book club as a reader; describe the book they are reading; explain why they selected it; and summarize and perhaps also interpret and comment on the plot, setting, and characters they have encountered thus far. Alexis Wagner's introductory letter to her seventh-grade book club at South Lake Middle School in Irvine, California, is a good example (Figure 14.5).

Writing about Reading: Dialectical Journals and Reader Response Logs As an alternative to using literature circle role sheets and/or lit. letters, as a point of departure for discussion, or as the next step after students are well acquainted with responding to texts in this manner, students can write and share open-ended dialectical journal entries or reader response logs. As described in Chapter 6, a dialectical journal is a double-entry note-taking/ note-making process students can engage in while reading a text. It provides students with two columns that are in dialogue with each other, enabling them to conduct "the continual 'audit of meaning' that is at the heart of learning to read and write critically" (Berthoff, 1981, p. 45). In the left-hand column, students select and copy down a passage they find intriguing, puzzling, or illuminating. In the right-hand column, they record thoughts and feelings that come to mind, thinking out loud on paper. A sample dialectical journal entry is available in Figure 6.3 in Chapter 6. Reader response logs also emphasize a close reading of

Figure 14.5 **Student Lit. Letter** (Reprinted by permission of Alexis Wagner.)

Dear Book Club,

Ever since I was little, I have always felt the love and joy of reading. It has influenced me throughout my entire life. As a toddler, reading could take me into the world of fantasy, with visions of pretty princesses and strong knights. As a young child, reading took me away from the cruel and harsh reality of my parents' divorce. And now, reading is just a simple pleasure that helps relieve the stress after a long day at school. Throughout my life, reading has had a great impact on me. Both parents read to me as I was growing up, and I have read a great number of books myself. I can still remember the nights when my parents came to tuck me in and read me a story so that I could fall asleep. My favorite story at the time was "Love You Forever." As long as I can remember, I have been reading that story when I feel sad and lonely. As I got older, my reading expanded, and I was going to the bookstore and library about five times a week. By fourth grade, I was at a sixth grade reading level.

At this time, I continue to read and enjoy books a great deal, trying with each one to challenge myself. In Book Club, I have started the book *A Tree Grows In Brooklyn,* by Betty Smith, an overall heartwarming story about Francie Nolan, a young girl growing up in the poverty of Brooklyn at the turn of the century. So far, the book has intrigued me to keep reading. The setting, Brooklyn, New York, is a harsh landscape for the imaginative eleven-year-old character. The author says that there's a tree that grows in Brooklyn. "Some people call it the Tree of Heaven." No matter where its seed falls, it makes a tree which struggles "to reach the sky." It grows out of cellar gratings. It is the only tree that grows out of cement. It grows "lushly" . . . survives without sun, water, and seemingly without earth. It would be considered beautiful except that there are too many of it. Francie reminds me of the tree, struggling to grow despite concrete and poverty. Her imagination reaches for the sky.

I hope to continue enjoying this book and all the challenges it holds for me. I feel connected with this character.

Your truly,
Alexis

the text. The student selects a passage that elicits feelings, questions, images, memories, connections, reactions, and so forth. The student then responds to sentence starters provided by the teacher such as "I wonder," "I began to think of," "If I had been," "I was reminded by," or writes an original response of his or her own. As students respond independently to texts, the teacher can also provide questions designed to correlate with Judith Langer's (1989) stances of envisionment, as discussed in Chapters 1 and 10, to use as a point of departure before, during, and after reading their book.

As a way of reinforcing students' declarative, procedural, and conditional knowledge about the tactics they use as competent readers, I have also asked them to identify which cognitive strategy they have selected from their tool kit when responding to a text. For example, Brett King, a teaching credential candidate, chose a series of passages from *Farewell to Manzanar* and wrote about the strategies he employed when reading them. A sample passage and strategy discussion appear in Figure 14.6.

Note that students can also use the cognitive strategies sentence starters in Figure 2.1 in Chapter 2, which are organized according to the cognitive strategies, to respond to passages in their texts.

Figure 14.6   Identifying Cognitive Strategies in Reader Response Logs (Reprinted by permission of Brett King.)

"He watched her for a moment and said he was sure he couldn't pay more than seventeen-fifty for that china. She reached into the red velvet case, took out a dinner plate and hurled it at the floor right in front of his feet. Mama took out another dinner plate and hurled it at the floor, then another and another, never moving, never opening her mouth, just quivering and glaring at the retreating dealer, with tears streaming down her cheeks. He finally turned and scuttled out the door, heading for the next house. When he was gone she stood there smashing cups and platters until the whole set lay in scattered blue and white fragments across the wooden floor."	**Forming Interpretations** *What I'm getting from this is that the culmination of pain and indignity Mama has had to suffer is now coming out when this scavenger offers to buy the family china. The only way to maintain any sense of control in this situation is to ensure that <u>nobody</u> will be able to have the china; the dealer (or anyone else for that matter) will not have the opportunity to pawn off her memories for a fast buck and cheapen the profound history and meaning behind these heirlooms. I saw this passage as Mama fighting back with the only thing she had left: her pride. It is a powerful passage, and I can envision the scenario perfectly. There is a cinematic quality to it that has really stayed with me since I read it.*

Constructing Graphic Responses to Texts   Throughout this book, you will find a wide variety of activities that elicit graphic responses to enable students to construct meaning from texts. Almost all of these activities combine the visual with the verbal: Students either expand on or interpret their graphic illustration through written expression.

Teachers from the UCI Writing Project have had success with five additional activities for constructing graphic responses to texts:

Bookmark Activity   After students have read a few chapters of their book, they can make a bookmark to share during small group discussion that will also serve a functional purpose while they continue reading. Directions are shown in the box here.

Bookmark Activity
Create a bookmark that corresponds with the book you are currently reading.

- Begin by selecting the shape of your bookmark. You might choose a traditional rectangle, or some shape that reflects a symbol or character from your reading.
- Design the front of your bookmark by illustrating a scene or a quotation from your reading that symbolizes an important moment in your book.
- On the back of your bookmark, write:
  "This bookmark belongs to (your name, class period)." You can also use this space to write a summary of your book or to quote a golden line.
- Somewhere on your bookmark, you need to include the title of your book (<u>underlined</u>) and the author.
- You are welcome to decorate your bookmark with a medium of your choosing. You could draw, use your computer, paint, cut out of a magazine, etc.

An 8½-by-11 copy of the bookmark activity is available on the companion website.

Figure 14.7 includes the front and back cover of a bookmark by Jeannette Su, a twelfth grader at Villa Park High School in Villa Park, California.

Figure 14.7   **Student's Bookmark** (Reprinted by permission of Jeanette Su.)

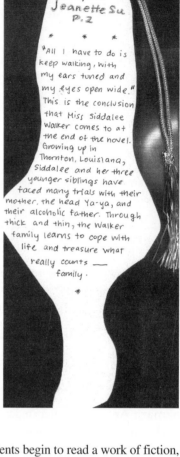

Stickman Activity   When students begin to read a work of fiction, they encounter and construct mental models of characters early on in their reading. Janet Allen (Allen & Gonzales, 1998) suggests that a graphic organizer is "a starting place for helping students visualize characters" (p. 51). Her coauthor in *There's Room for Me Here,* Kyle Gonzales, took Allen's advice and implemented the stickman activity, given to Allen by a teacher at a conference, as a way to help students analyze Georgie in *The Lottery Rose.* At first students struggled with filling out this organizer, providing Gonzales with an important learning experience: Teaching the strategy first "in the context of something with fewer challenges—a short story, video clip, or television sitcom—allows students to transfer the strategy to shared and independent reading" (p. 53). Teachers in the UCI Writing Project who have attended workshops led by Allen have found the stickman to be a useful conversation piece in reading workshop. They have adapted the original, adding the category of personality traits. Figure 14.8 includes their version of the stickman—which can be used to describe an individual or a group of people.

Flip Chart Activity   Like storyboards, flip charts are good ways for students to sequence the main events in their books and make decisions about which events are "key" and why. The teacher may need to model how to fold the paper to create the layered cascade of the scenes. The student model of the flip chart in Figure 14.9 is by Katelyn Alessi, a sixth grader at Foothill Ranch K–6 School in Foothill Ranch, California. Each page of the activity can be flipped up to reveal an illustration.

Figure 14.8 **Stickman Activity**
(Adapted from *There's Room for Me Here: Literacy Workshop in the Middle School* by Janet Allen and Kyle Gonzales. Copyright © 1998. Reprinted by permission of Stenhouse Publishers, Portland, ME.)

An 8½-by-11 copy of the stickman is available on the companion website.

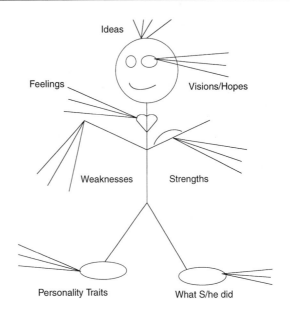

Figure 14.9 **Student Model of Flip Chart Activity** (Reprinted by permission of Katelyn Alessi.)

Fabrizio and his master were sent back to the castello because the King's daughter is being haunted. The King wants Mangus (master) to get rid of the ghost. The King thinks Mangus is a magician.

Fabrizio has seen this so called ghost with his own eyes. Princess Teresina had asked Fabrizio to lead Mangus to the niche (where the ghost comes) to see the ghost himself.

Mangus finds out the truth about the ghost, revealing what a horrible person the count Scarazoni is. Mangus, together with the queen, princess, prince, and Fabrizio plan to get rid of him.

Flip Chart Activity
First, layer two pieces of paper over each other as in Figure A. Then hold the two pieces of paper in place and fold them again so the pages are offset as in Figure B.

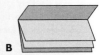

You now have four pages. On page one, write the name of your book and the author. Include a symbol from your novel.

In your most recent reading of your novel, what are some of the key events that have occurred? In sequence, illustrate three key events from your reading on the remaining pages of your flip chart. Write a brief sentence or explanation for each drawing.

An 8½-by-11 copy of the flip chart activity is available on the companion website.

Postcard Activity   Students can practice adopting an alignment by assuming the persona of a character from the book they are reading, then writing a postcard as if they were that character. Students can be given the instructions shown on page 375.

Figure 14.10 includes an illustration for a *Harry Potter and the Sorcerer's Stone* post-card by Monica Herrera and a *Harry Potter* letter written by Mike White, both ninth graders at Villa Park High School in Villa Park, California.

Framed Found Poetry Activity   Framed found poetry lends itself to analyzing author's craft, forming interpretations, reflecting, and relating. In found poetry students move

Figure 14.10   **Postcard Activity** (Front side of postcard reprinted by permission of Monica Herrera. Letter side of postcard reprinted by permission of Mike White.)

Front Side

Harry Potter & the Sorcerer's Stone
by
J.K Rowling

Letter Side

July 22, 1992

Hermione,
I hope that Hedwig gets this to you. I have been locked in my room ever since I returned from school. I guess this is to be expected though because the Dursleys hate magic and me. I was lucky to get this letter out to you for they also locked Hedwig in her cage, but I was able to set her free for this letter. Please tell Ron I got his call, but it would be advisable not to try again. I will see you on September 1, but I hope to see you before. Maybe we can meet at Diagon Alley for supplies?
Love

Hermione Granger
(You know where she is Hedwig)

Harry Potter

Postcard Activity

For this book club activity, you need to create a postcard.

First, illustrate a scene, line, or image from your book on the "picture" side. Include the title of the book (underlined) and the author's name.

On the other side, you need to write a letter. In your letter, mention where you are (the setting) as well as a significant event. Create a stamp (you might consider a symbol from the story), an address, and a postmark. For your letter, you could:

- Pretend that you're a character in the story and write a letter to your book club; or
- Pretend that you're a character in the story and write to another character in the story.

An 8½-by-11 copy of the postcard activity is available on the companion website.

beyond the text to create a literary artifact of their own by selecting golden lines from the original text and manipulating them to create a poem; the poem should communicate a theme that is significant to the reader. Leslie Baldwin, a former UCI teaching credential candidate, developed the concept of framing found poetry when she was student teaching at South Lake Middle School in Irvine, California. Baldwin designed the task shown here.

Framed Found Poem

For this book club activity, you will create a *found poem* based on the book you have been exploring these past few weeks. A *found poem* is a poem that is constructed by combining meaningful phrases from the book you are reading. It gives you an opportunity to share some of your favorite words or phrases from the story—words that create vivid pictures or express significant ideas. Your poem should reflect your interpretation of the theme or mood of your book.

- First, find passages in your book that are particularly interesting or well written, or that you just really like.
- Jot down the words and images that are strongest for you—words that are emotionally charged, or the most essential to the feeling of the story. Generate a long list of phrases.
- Now begin to play with these words and images, rearranging them until you find an order that appeals to you.

Some ideas to consider:

- Place the words that you think are most important at the ends of the lines.
- Set off powerful single words on lines by themselves.
- Use a repetitive refrain.
- Create a pattern: For example, start all of your lines with prepositions, *ing* words, or onomatopoetic words.
- Allow yourself to add, subtract, or change words to fit your poem.

Give your poem a title (it may or may not be different from your book title). Be sure to give credit to the author and the book (underlined, if handwritten; italicized, if word-processed or typed) that inspired your poem.

Now that you have your poem, it's time to design and create a frame for it. The frame should reflect your visual interpretation of your book, either symbolically or literally. Be creative, both in your design and in construction materials. Anything goes. In your frame, I am looking for:

- Choices that illustrate your comprehension of the larger themes of your book
- Creativity
- Evidence of time and thought expended

Have fun with this project!

An 8½-by-11 copy of the framed found poem activity is available on the companion website.

Figure 14.11   **Framed Found Poem** (Reprinted by permission of Kristen Davenport.)

Figure 14.11 contains the complete framed found poem of a text by Kristin Davenport, a seventh grader at South Lake Middle School.

Culminating Projects for Reading Workshop

Whether students are participating in literature circles, book clubs, or some other version of reading workshop, they usually embark on some sort of culminating project at the end of a book or to bring closure to the reading of several books. Here are just a few possibilities.

Read All About It! Book Promotion   In her seventh-grade classroom at Aliso Viejo Middle School in Aliso Viejo, California, Meredith Ritner culminates her book clubs with a project called Read All About It! in which students develop a flyer to adver-tise their favorite book, create a visual aid to accompany their flyer, and deliver a book talk in front of the class describing their book and explaining why they recommend it. The instructions for Read All About It! are included on the companion website. This project inspires the existing class members to keep reading and provides them with a wealth of titles to choose from; in addition, the flyers become part of "Recommended Readings for Book Clubs" notebooks in the classroom and school library for future students. Rinter's culminating projects for litera-ture circles are also available on the companion website.

Multiple Intelligences Literature Book Project   In Chapter 5, I discussed Howard Gardner's (1983) theory of multiple intelligences and its implications for and application to language arts instruction. As a way of helping my students in the UCI Teaching Credential Program to internalize MI theory, I ask them to create a three-dimensional symbolic representation of the book they are reading in their book clubs and to write a reflective paper interpreting their artifact. They, in turn, have implemented this project with remarkable success with students in both middle and high school classrooms. The companion website contains a description of the instructions for the project, the weighted trait scoring guide, a sample student reflective paper, and a photograph of a student project.

The Drop Everything and Read Day   Meredith Ritner culminates reading workshop in all of her classes each year with a celebration called the Drop Everything and Read Day. "Drop everything and read" (DEAR) is a common practice in elementary schools, where students literally read for the entire day. Ritner's version lasts a full class period. She reserves the school library for this occasion and places signs around the library for each class. The day before the Drop Everything and Read Day, she sets the tone by bringing in examples of what she intends to bring with her to the library—fuzzy slippers, a stuffed bear, a pillow, a sleeping bag, and an assortment of books—to create a sleep-over atmosphere. As students arrive at school in the morning, they drop off their provisions in the library under the sign for their class. A week in advance, Ritner holds a commemorative bookmark contest and presents each student with a laminated copy of the winning entry with a Jolly Rancher taped to the back. Students receive points for arriving at the library, setting up their "stuff," opening a book, and settling in to read. Usually the principal will join in, and several parents generally drop by as well. Ritner notes, "My students are beginning to grow up in so many different ways, but they relish this opportunity to just be a kid again." Figure 14.12 (page 378) contains a series of reading workshop photos from Ritner's classes, including visuals from the Drop Everything and Read Day.

WRITING WORKSHOP

Reading and writing workshop go hand in hand. As Frank Smith (1988) says, we need to learn to "read like a writer" (p. 25) in order to confidently and competently construct our own meaning from texts. As we come to understand, appreciate, and analyze author's craft, we can use what we learn to begin to *write like a writer*" (p. 25). Writing like a writer means that we write with a reader in mind and develop the capacity to convert writer-based prose into reader-based prose (Flower, 1990)—to speak to an audience.

Using Reading Workshop as a Bridge to Writing Workshop

Several of the teachers in the UCI Writing Project have found that launching a reading workshop program slightly in advance of implementing writing workshop can help prepare students for the transition from self-selected reading to self-selected writing. Thelma Anselmi, an eighth-grade teacher at St. Columban School in Garden Grove, California, writes,

■   I have had good luck using Reading Workshop as a way to ease students into Writing Workshop. Although my students are not reticent at all about choosing their own books, I find that they look to me to tell them what to write about and how long it needs to be. It takes a great deal of relearning for them to accept that the student seated right next to them might be writing something entirely different from what they're working on and that it's OK for that to happen.

Figure 14.12 **Reading Workshop in Meredith Ritner's Seventh-Grade Classroom** (Reprinted by permission of Meredith D. Ritner.)

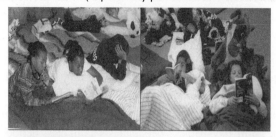

I use writing about their reading as a way to thaw their frozen pens. We find and celebrate the author's golden lines, practice writing showing paragraphs about telling sentences I have constructed about plot, setting or characters, assume the persona of a character and write diary entries or interior monologue, take sides and pass sheets of paper back and forth to debate controversial issues, play Beat the Author, and so forth. We also read a variety of genres to identify the elements of good writing that are present in all literature but also to see how writing takes many forms.

Once they are convinced that they have something of value to say about the stories of published authors, I slowly begin to have them tell their own stories, first orally and later in writing. It takes several months before we can blend reading and writing into Reading/Writing Workshop but the careful cultivation of my students as independent readers makes it safer and more comfortable for them to risk and succeed as independent writers.

Goals and Expectations for Writing Workshop

Just as teachers have specific goals and expectations for students in reading workshop, so too they have aspirations for their students as writers. These include the following; adapted from Atwell (1998, pp. 111–112):

Goals	Expectations
• To learn how to self-select topics for writing that are of personal significance	• Keep a writer's notebook to generate ideas and sources for writing.
• To become more fluent, proficient, and versatile as writers	• Maintain a portfolio of works in progress as well as finished pieces.
• To write with a greater awareness of author's craft	• Through the study of author's craft in both reading and writing workshops, apply specific strategies to enhance your own writing, both initially and during revision.
• To collaborate with others to share responses to one another's texts and facilitate the process of revision	• Meet in writing groups and provide specific, constructive feedback to help the writer communicate effectively with the reader.
• To develop command of the conventions of written English	• Through minilessons, peer editing, and individual self-correction, practice proofreading and editing your own writing. Develop an error log to keep track of and eliminate common mistakes.
• To become reflective about your own process as a writer	• Use expressive/metacognitive writing as a vehicle to explore the acts of mind you engage in as a reader as well as the role of affect in writing.

Getting Started: Cultivating Student Interest in Writing

A variety of activities will help "thaw the frozen pens" of students.

Writing Reminiscence   When I ask students to sift through their memories and recount "How I Learned to Read and Write" as discussed in Chapter 4, students often write fondly of their remembrances of reading, evoking images of sitting on a parent's lap and using words like *warm* and *cozy* to describe the experience. Reflections on learning to write, however, are sometimes clouded with images of the "bleeding" of red ink on the page. My student Hetty Jun especially recalled being caught up in the guessing game of "Is this what the teacher wanted?" This is not to say that some students don't bear the scars of being in the low reading group (the Buzzards instead of the Bluebirds, for example) and being forced to read aloud. But, as a rule, my experience has been that more students have unpleasant memories of learning to write than of learning to read. Perhaps this is because most of the learning-to-write memories are about being "corrected" at school rather than about being nurtured at home. At any rate, it is helpful to invite students to explore these early memories of learning to read and write in a piece of writing to clear the air. If students carry old baggage with them into class, it is easier to help them let go of it if you know who is reticent or anxious about their literacy and why.

Writing Survey   Another way to get at students' feelings, experiences, needs, and interests as a writer is to conduct a writing survey. As mentioned previously, Nancie Atwell (1998) has a writing survey that teachers can copy; so do Lane and Green (1994) and other authors. But teachers can easily develop their own questionnaire. For example, a writing survey that Thelma Anselmi developed for her eighth graders at St. Columban School in Garden Grove, California, is available on the companion website. Notice that the survey not only provides information for the teacher but also is revisited by students at the second and third trimester to help them assess their progress over time.

Writing Territories   Many teachers feel that they are intruding on student choice if they steer students toward particular kinds of writing. But the truth is that students cannot write in genres they are unfamiliar with. It is the teacher's job to make students aware of their options as well as to teach them the craft involved in writing in specific genres. A good place to start is for the teacher to share his or her writing territories, as Nancie Atwell (1998) does in her classroom. As with her exploration of her reading territories, Atwell stands at the overhead and reproduces a running jot list. She includes genres she has written in or would like to try, topics she has focused on or plans to address in the future, audiences she has written to or potential audiences she has in mind, projects she'd like to undertake, dreams or goals she has as a writer, and so forth. Her intent is to create a "self-portrait as a writer" (p. 120) and, in so doing, to motivate her students to begin their own writing territories jot list when anything she says rings a bell. When she has exhausted her writing territories, or when she can tell that her students' "wells have run dry" (p. 128), she pairs them up in partners. Classmates then share their lists—and add to them, if their partner has something interesting that they hadn't thought of.

Writing Warm-Ups   In the Writing Project, we often tell teachers who haven't written anything for pleasure in a long time that they shouldn't be surprised if they are rusty. We encourage them to turn the faucet on and to realize that it may take a while before what comes out of the tap runs clear. But less experienced writers in the secondary classroom aren't even rusty: They may have had little or no practice developing writing fluency. Sometimes teachers expect their students to feel liberated when they are set free to write about anything they choose—and therefore feel puzzled when some class members respond to this opportunity with moans and groans. Just as dancers need to do some warm-up exercises at the bar before they go on stage, it's helpful to conduct some low-stress whole class writing activities as a rehearsal and a training exercise before students embark on their solo writing experience. The My Name, My Self demonstration lesson in Chapter 4 and the memory snapshot paper in Chapter 9 both provide students with a teacher-guided, scaffolded experience with personal writing in an environment in which it is safe to take risks.

Pattern poetry, like the seashells and similies lesson featured in Chapter 9, is another type of activity that can build confidence in student writers. Some variations of pattern poetry are as follows:

Dialogue Poetry   This activity is especially helpful for students who are blocked as writers and protest that they simply don't have anything to say. Based on a concept developed by poet Toby Lurie (1978), dialogue poetry involves presenting students with a poem line by line and inviting them to have a conversation with the author. The teacher should read a line from the text slowly while students write it down. Then he or she should allow time for each reader to compose a line in response. The teacher then reads the next line; the students write it down, compose a line in response, and so forth. The idea is that the two voices will blend and create a new poem. Figure 14.13 contains a dialogue poem by Chris Populus from our seventh-through-eighth-grade UCI Young Writers' Project in response to Carl Sandburg's poem "Summer Grass."

I Am Poem   The I Am poem has been popularized by the California Reading and Literature Project and is frequently used as an initial writing activity by teachers across the grade levels. The poetry frame in Figure 14.14 is often modified. For instance, middle school boys often change the verb in the "I cry" line in the second stanza to something less emotional.

I Am poems can also be used in reading workshop and written in the voice of a literary character.

Figure 14.13 **Student Model of Dialogue Poetry** ("Summer Grass" from *Good Morning, America,* copyright © 1928 and renewed 1956 by Carl Sandburg, reprinted by permission of Harcourt, Inc. Student dialogue poem is reprinted by permission of Chris Populus.)

> *Summer grass aches and whispers*
> > Aching for the rain; whispering its prayers
> *It wants something:*
> > It desires the cool touch of water
> *It calls and sings*
> > Crying for mercy from the sun's rays
> *It pours out wishes*
> > Wishing for life.
> *To the overhead stars.*
> > Yet never listening
> *The rain hears;*
> > The plea of the grass
> *The rain answers;*
> > The prayers of the grass
> *The rain is slow coming;*
> > Not betraying its friend
> *The rain wets the face of the earth*
> > And cries of thanks ring out.

Figure 14.14 **I Am Poem**

> **I Am**
>
> I am
> I wonder
> I hear
> I see
> I want
> I am
>
> I pretend
> I feel
> I touch
> I worry
> I cry
> I am
>
> I understand
> I say
> I dream
> I try
> I hope
> I am

An 8½-by-11 copy of the I Am poetry frame is available on the companion website.

Facade Poem   This poem has a deceptively simple frame—"I seem to be . . . but really I'm." However, it can lead students to create some very insightful poems about themselves. In Figure 14.15, Megan Pike, a sixth grader at Los Flores Middle School in Los Flores, California, illustrated her facade poem with a mandala. Directions for creating a mandala are included in Chapter 3.

Figure 14.15 **Facade Poem** (Reprinted by permission of Megan Pike.)

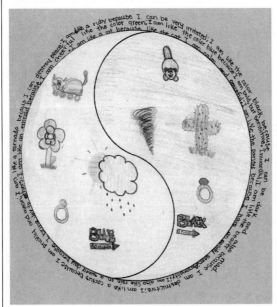

Facade Poem

I seem to be a bird, talkative and sweet
But really I'm a cat, aggressive and caring.
I seem to be an emerald, peaceful and calm
But really I'm a ruby, fiery mad.
I seem to be a laughing hyena, laughing and talking
But really I'm a turtle, shy inside its shell.
I seem to be a tornado, destructive and mad
But really I'm a sunny day, calm, and peaceful.
I seem to be a computer that knows everything
But really I'm a book looking everything up.
I seem to be a cactus jumping out to poke
But really I'm a pansy with great personality.
I seem to be a raging river
But really I'm a peaceful stream.

Megan Pike

But What Do I Write About?

Once students have done a little limbering up, they are ready to select their own topics. But teachers may still need to prime the pump with activities designed to help students generate topics for writing.

Circle Time   In circle time students sit in a circle to engage in oral storytelling. The teacher is usually the first to begin, sharing a memory of a specific event, person, place, and so on. For example, Ann Jones, a fifth-grade teacher at Ruby Drive Elementary School in Placentia, California, likes to tell this anecdote about a memorable birthday:

■   Happy Birthday to you
Happy Birthday to you
Happy Birthday dear Ann
Happy Birthday to you!

This was the fifth time this song had been sung to me. I just sat there basking in glory, watching the movement of multicolored, pastel balloons bobbing in bunches from strings everywhere in the patio. My birthday presents had been opened and my wish list had been answered: a baby doll with extra clothing, a china tea set, and a book of paper dolls, complete with a pair of sharp, shiny, silver scissors. Even the cake and ice cream were my favorites—chocolate.

The day had gone perfectly, until shortly after cleanup, when my parents adjourned to the living room with their friends, leaving me and my eight guests alone on the patio. Being the first-born child in my family, and naturally gifted with the talents of a leader and entrepreneur, I successfully convinced all eight partygoers that they were in need of a haircut; and for a promissory nickel, I used my new birthday scissors to do the job. My guests were delighted with their new looks, but not so their parents—or mine.

I spent the remainder of that day in my room with several clear imprints of my mother's hand on my back end. It was a memorable birthday, but not in the way I had expected.

After telling the story, Jones asks if her memory has brought to mind any stories for students in the circle. The teacher's reminiscence usually elicts an array of haircut stories as well as memories of birthdays or other events that didn't end up the way the teller expected. The teacher can also bring in a work of professional writing, like Gary Soto's "The Haircut" in *A Summer Life,* to augment the telling of the tale. As people tell their stories to the circle, the ideas snowball; pretty soon everyone has thought of something to write about. In a class of less experienced writers, circle time might last several weeks, as people gradually get comfortable with the idea that they have a rich repository of stories other people would like to hear.

Blueprint Exercise   Deanice Dreibus-Trytten, a fourth-grade teacher at Lomarena Elementary School in Laguna Hills, California, has had great success with the blueprint exercise, both in her classroom and with teachers in our Writing Project. She begins by drawing a "blueprint" (a plan) of her childhood home on a transparency at the overhead projector: front yard, first story, second story, backyard, etc. She then proceeds to give a tour of the house—which room was hers, which belonged to her sibling, Mom and Dad's room, where the cat slept, which room was the TV room, and so on. Students then draw their own blueprint of their childhood home, the house they have lived the longest in, or their favorite home, and provide an oral "walking tour" for a partner. Once students are acquainted with the layout of the teacher's and a partner's home, the teacher goes back through the house, room by room, sharing memories that she associates with different places: the day she first learned to ride a bike (driveway); a special Christmas (living room); the time the cat had kittens in the hall closet, and so forth. Students then explore their homes and their memories and generate topics for future writing.

The I Remember Poem   Dreibus-Trytten's blueprint exercise focuses students' memories on a specific place; Susan Leming's I Remember poem, in contrast, helps students generate a wider array of autobiographical incidents to write about. Drawing from Larry Fagin's (1995) book *The List Poem,* Leming, a tenth-grade teacher at Esperanza High School in Anaheim, California, begins by asking students to brainstorm categories that come to mind when they think of memories. Leming clusters the categories, then takes a category, such as "Injuries," and clusters her own personal memories off the category heading: the scar from skateboarding she got as a kid, the time she broke her nose in a car accident, the burn mark from putting her hand on the stove, and so forth. She then gives students ten minutes to cluster their specific memories off all of the cluster categories as well as to add new categories of their own.

Once students complete their cluster, they put a check mark by the two or three memories they recall most vividly and share those memories with a partner. The partner can indicate which of the stories he or she would most like to know more about.

Students then take another ten minutes to write "capture" sentences about as many of their memories as they can in the time allotted. The "capture" sentence must begin with "I remember" and include vivid language so the listener can picture the scene. For example, the teacher might offer a model such as *I remember the smell of rotten eggs at Yellowstone and how we all jumped back a little when Old Faithful erupted, sending a plume of sizzling spray into the air.*

At the end of the class period, students can write their favorite capture sentences on 3-by-5 cards for a class poem; Figure 14.16 shows the poem created by Leming's tenth graders. They should also complete their own I Remember poem of at least fifteen to twenty capture sentences. Students will return to this poem as a hot topics list for writing workshop.

Figure 14.16   Class-Generated I Remember Poem (Reprinted by permission of Susan Leming.)

I Remember...

I remember when I was on my uncle's farm all alone and I left the corral gate open and every animal got loose.

I remember when my friend told a boy I liked him and I was standing right there and I turned as red as a beet.

I remember my dog, Patches, who always drilled holes in the lawn looking for bones.

I remember a dream of being eaten by a puppet.

I remember when I forgot my lines in a kindergarten play and just stared at the audience in a daze.

I remember the first time I went out on our boat and I only put one engine in gear and we spun around in circles.

I remember when I pretended that my pillow was a flying saucer and I fell down the stairs with a giant thud and broke my arm.

I remember when I was over at my grandma's house and I was riding my bicycle with my eyes closed and, when I opened them, I was lost.

I remember a dream where my mother slammed the car door on my foot and it came off. When I woke up, my foot was hanging off the side of the bed.

I remember when I ran away from home and I packed an enormous suitcase with all my stuff that was so heavy that I turned back.

I remember when I cut my leg open with a point of a compass and then I had to walk 15 blocks home in agony.

I remember slipping and having my feet dangle over the side of the Grand Canyon and looking down at the jagged rocks below.

I remember a dream that I was two inches tall and a stick of butter was trying to kill me.

I remember gorging myself on plump red strawberries and then puffing up like a blowfish because I was allergic.

I remember being selected for the national touring show of "Annie" and how I was so proud I could burst!

Keeping a Writer's Notebook

■ Notebooks can become a habit of life, one that helps us recognize that our lives are filled with materials for writing. "Look at the world," the notebooks seem to say. "Look at the world in all its grandeur and all its horror. Let it matter."

—Lucy Calkins

All of the writing warm-up and getting started activities thus far can be kept in a writer's notebook and mined for potential extended writing workshop pieces. In *Living Between the Lines* (1991), Lucy Calkins stresses that the notebook should be a safe place where students can collect bits and pieces of ideas, impressions, scrawlings, entries, notes, lists, observations, and "ramblings on millions of topics and on no particular topic at all" (p. 38). It should serve as an ongoing record of the students' life experiences and help them develop a "lens to appreciate the richness that is already there in their lives" (p. 35).

Teachers usually model this process by keeping a notebook of their own with lots of room for a variety of jottings and by sharing various pieces with the class from time to time. To be a genuine resource, the notebook needs to be taken outside the classroom to become the writer's constant companion. As Calkins writes, the goal is for notebooks to be become a "habit of life" (p. 43). As students revisit their notebooks, they rediscover kernels of ideas that can be fleshed out and shared in writing workshop and compiled in their portfolios.

 The companion website contains a writer's notebook activity called Monday Musings, which Carol Mooney uses to challenge her Advanced Placement English students at Villa Park High School in Villa Park, California, to generate topics for writing workshop. Students submit Monday Musings from their writer's notebook along with a metacognitive reflection about what they wrote. Figure 14.17 contains a musing from twelfth grader Catherine Stocker.

Figure 14.17 **Monday Musing** (Reprinted by permission of Catherine Stocker.)

Monday Musing

Rage consumes me,
Shaking from head to toe.
She was supposed to be my friend,
She was supposed to know.
Betrayal.
The word stings the tongue.
Burns.
Bile tight in my throat, threatening to escape.
Like sisters, we said, always and forever.
With deceit, she lead,
Oh so very clever.
He's mine.
She knows it.
Still she,
She goes for it.
All that I've done for her.
All that we've been through.
Suddenly a knife.
I wouldn't have turned if I knew.

Meta

This is a pretty basic "vent" piece. I played around with a tiny bit of imagery and rhyme scheme . . . but nothing big. You probably recognize the knife reference as an allusion to the expression "stabbed in the back." I actually wrote this a couple of weeks ago. I like it, kinda, only cause it's weird. Please comment.

Keeping Track: Status of the Class

Some teachers take Kirby and Kuykendall (1991) literally and stay entirely "out of the kids' way," leaving them solely responsible for selecting their own topics and working at their own pace. But it's important not to stay "too far out of the way" (p. 214). Students benefit from a structured environment in which to write, predictable routines to follow, and an expectation that over the course of a semester they will take several pieces from conception to completion. Students need to be held accountable for using their workshop time wisely, and teachers need to monitor their progress. Many UCI Writing Project teachers have adopted Nancie Atwell's (1998) method of checking the status of the class as a way of keeping track and motivating students to stay focused. On a daily basis Atwell notes each student's plans for writing workshop when she calls roll. On a status-of-the-class record sheet, she notes down the topic; the genre; what the writer intends to do; whether the writer is starting a new piece, continuing a work in progress, or at the publication stage; and so forth. Deanice Dreibus-Trytten has developed the following coding system in her fourth-grade classroom at Lomarena Elementary School to streamline her status-of-the class record keeping:

Status-of-the-Class Record

Name	Monday	Tuesday	Wednesday	Thursday	Friday

P—Prewriting   R—Revising   C—Computer

D—Drafting   PS—Peer Sharing   FD—Final Draft

E—Editing   TC—Teacher Conference   WG—Writing Group

Teachers who conduct writing workshop once a week instead of daily can check on student progress on a weekly basis. Students should also be keeping track of their own progress with some type of writing record kept inside of their portfolios. Most teachers I know require students to submit a certain number of finished pieces for teacher feedback at regular intervals throughout the year.

The Teacher's Role in Writing Workshop

Just as with reading workshop, the teacher needs to be a cheerleader, a coach, and sometimes a Teacher with a capital *T*. Nancie Atwell conducts each workshop session in a predictable order:

1. Reading and discussion of a piece of writing
2. Writing minilesson
3. Status-of-the class conference
4. Independent writing and conferring
5. Read-aloud

Many teachers close writing workshop with author's chair, the activity in which one writer comes to the front of the class and reads his or her writing in progress while other class members comment.

In essence, the teacher's role is to foster *ownership;* to create expectations that are *appropriate;* to provide ample *structure* through modeling his or her own writing process and through minilessons that focus on author's craft and make strategies visible; to engage students in *collaboration* to improve one another's work; and, by delivering teacher feedback that is descriptive and instructive rather than exclusively evaluative, to help students develop and *internalize* a repertoire of effective writing strategies. The website for Chapter 11 contains a chart of the minilessons offered in this book to help students develop their craft as writers and gain skill in revising meaning. Chapter 11 also provides guidelines for the teacher to consider when conferencing with students and when providing written feedback.

Turning Reading Groups into Writing Groups

As mentioned previously, providing students with ongoing and varied opportunities to share and discuss their responses to the texts of professional writers in reading workshop can serve as scaffolding and pave the way for looking at author's craft in writing workshop. Chapter 11 discusses strategies to guide peer response—finding the golden lines; using Peter Elbow's response techniques of pointing, summarizing, telling, and showing; job cards, read-around groups; various forms for written reactions; WIRMI statements; and believing and doubting. In order to monitor the quality of her students' participation in writing groups and to stimulate them to reflect on the process of sharing and responding to their written products, Thelma Anselmi has developed a writing group assessment form for her eighth graders at St. Columban School. Included on the companion website, the form may be useful for other teachers.

Culminating Projects in Writing Workshop: Portfolios and Anthologies

In most classrooms students keep a *process* or *formative* portfolio throughout the semester or school year from which they create an *exemplary* or *showcase* portfolio at the end of a period of learning. As explained in Chapter 13, a portfolio is a collection of works or artifacts deliberately selected and arranged with an audience or reader in mind to document progress over time. An important aspect of the portfolio is student ownership. Because students select the artifacts, there is no set formula for what goes in a portfolio. However, most portfolios have a table of contents; a cover letter or piece of reflective writing describing the contents of the portfolio and what they are intended to demonstrate; the artifacts or work samples themselves, often accompanied by metacognitive reflections; sometimes a letter including the student's self-assessment and statement of future goals; and a parent response section. Chapter 13 explores middle and high school portfolios in more detail.

Portfolios enable students to *collect* artifacts that document their processes and products as learners, *select* those items that are particularly noteworthy from the collection to create a portrait of themselves as learners, *reflect* upon the significance of individual artifacts and the collection as a whole, and to look ahead and *project* by setting goals for the future. Teachers often have portfolio parties to culminate the school year and invite parents to drop in and respond to the students' accomplishments.

Another way to validate and celebrate student work is to create a class anthology that contains a favorite piece of writing from each member of the class. Meredith Ritner holds a contest to select the cover art for her seventh-grade class anthology at Aliso Viejo Middle School and has invested in a binder so that the anthology has a professional appearance and the pages are easy to turn. This anthology can then become a part of the classroom library and be checked out by future students as well as kept as a memento by its authors.

Publication in the Writing Workshop Classroom

"Publication" in the writing workshop classroom can take many forms. For example, a Wall of Fame bulletin board can display a student sentence of the week; golden lines from several students; whole pieces of students' writing (which can be framed as in the memory snapshot paper described in Chapter 9); or artifacts generated by students who have traded papers with a partner and have celebrated their partner's paper by creating a framed found poem, storyboard, or literature portrait; and so on. The classroom library is also a great place to "publish" and circulate the work of class members. In elementary classrooms it is a routine practice for students to create covers for their writing workshop products, insert an About the Author page and sometimes a Comments page, and place student work in the library for checkout. But secondary students also enjoy having access to their classmates' writing.

Beyond the classroom, students can send work to the school newspaper or literary magazine or submit feature articles or letters to the editor of the local paper. Nancie Atwell (1998) has established a publication center in her classroom to make her students aware of their options for professional publication. It includes rules for various writing contests, a file of information about magazines and journals that publish student writing, and resource books such as *Market Guide for Young Writers* (1996) by Kathy Henderson. Additionally, websites for children's online publishing (see the companion website for a list) are springing up and are extending the opportunities for writing and sharing.

ASSESSING AND EVALUATING READING AND WRITING IN READING/WRITING WORKSHOP

Ideally, given that the goal of reading and writing workshop is to cultivate intrinsically motivated, independent readers and writers, it would be best to find a way to acknowledge student work and assess the students' progress without evaluating each of their products. Most teachers I know tend to give credit of some kind for participation in reading and writing workshop, usually in the form of points. It is difficult to construct and implement the same type of evaluation or grading system for all students, however—particularly if students are reading and writing different kinds of texts and selecting their own forms of meaning making. As a general rule, reading and writing workshop offers students a rich opportunity to accumulate a body of work in a portfolio that represents their growth as a learner over time. This empowers them with the authority to select which pieces they will compile as evidence of their competence as readers and writers as well as the power to abandon some texts they couldn't get into as readers or get "out" as writers.

Students' Reactions to Reading and Writing Workshop

Because student ownership and reflection is such a crucial dimension of the portfolio process, many teachers engage students in determining and presenting their own self-evaluation score, developmental or achievement level, letter grade, or other form of evaluation of their entire body of work. Teachers then take the student's evaluation into account when arriving at their evaluation and often write detailed statements agreeing with the student or explaining why and on what points they differ. In *Seeking Diversity: Language Arts with Adolescents,* Linda Rief (1992) presents a very extensive year-end self-evaluation form for reading and writing workshop that several of the middle school teachers in our project have adapted as an evaluation tool. Carol Mooney has a much simplified form (reproduced on the companion website) for her twelfth-grade AP English class at Villa Park High School, which also elicits insightful student self-evaluation.

If we want to cultivate motivated, independent readers and writers in our classroom, we need to nurture students by giving them "the room to say something of their own in their writing or in the interpretations they draw in their reading" (Langer & Applebee, 1986, p. 185)—by creating a climate that encourages them to grow. Students at all grade levels tend to flourish in this type of environment if there are appropriate models, structures, and expectations to support their autonomy. Provided below are reflections about reading and writing workshop from students at the middle and high school levels.

Eighth Graders at St. Columban School in Garden Grove

■ Reading and Writing Workshop was different than what we did in my other language arts classes because we got to figure things out on our own instead of the teacher standing over our shoulders giving us all the answers. It was harder, but it was worth it.

—Krystle Dalton

■ Through Reading Workshop, I have become better able to voice my comments and ask questions to help myself and my classmates learn new strategies and better understand what I read. A lot of adults don't talk to children about books in a regular conversation because they think we have nothing to say. Give us a chance and we can show you what we think! In Writing Workshop, the teacher isn't a judge who decides whether your writing is right or wrong. I am better able to express my feelings, thoughts, opinions, and interpretations.

—Kelly Anne Klein

Twelfth Graders in AP English at Villa Park High School

■ I find it really tragic that some AP classes concentrate the bulk of their curriculum around drilling students on question answering and formal essay writing. Reading and Writing Workshop can help shape a student's lifelong thinking, creativity and communication skills. We do not just analyze the footsteps of writers gone before. We learn to critique our own footprints as we slowly become comfortable and then bold with our personal means of expression.

—Brian Wood

■ This year, I've seen myself develop into a mature participant of the language, willing to evolve to the point that I have left behind the student I was who read/wrote to only a superficial degree. Book Clubs and Writing Workshop encouraged each of us to take risks, expressing ourselves through *our* words, encouraging each other along the way. For the first time, I felt genuine pride and triumph in my English work. I did not just conform to the class to receive a good grade, I was able to take command and control over a portion of my life through writing.

—Michele Blanchard

To Sum Up

Independent reading and writing are the goal of scaffolded language arts instruction. A well-orchestrated workshop will engender student ownership by allowing students to self-select the texts they will read and write; build on the reading, thinking, and writing abilities students already possess and present appropriate challenges to help them stretch intellectually; provide structure through specific expectations, predictable routines, modeling, and mini-lessons; promote collaboration between students as they interact with one another and with texts; and foster internalization of the cognitive strategies effective readers and writers use to enhance command of author's craft. Many teachers feel that, philosophically, one must choose to adopt a teacher-guided or a student-centered approach to language arts instruction. Not so. Effective language arts teachers create a balance of teacher-guided and student-selected reading and writing activities, often using the teacher-guided activities as a learning tool to establish the structure necessary for independent practice.

Learning Log Reflection

In the spirit of self-selection, choose an activity described or referred to in this chapter to use as a vehicle to respond to the concept of reading and writing workshop. For example, you might want to write your own version of a lit. letter, describing this chapter to another teacher; you might experiment with using a graphic strategy like your own modified version of the stickman to analyze the contents of this chapter; or you might prefer an open-ended writer's notebook or Monday Musing entry to reflect on the potential that reading and writing workshop holds for you in your classroom. As Nancie Atwell (1998) says, choose your own palette knife, brush, or tube of color to explore and illustrate what you think about the workshop approach.

Appendix

Scientifically Based Research on the Scaffolded Lessons and Cognitive Strategies Approach to Instruction

There is no doubt about it. The process-based, integrated reading/writing lessons in this book take time. And time is a precious commodity in the secondary language arts classroom. Moreover, the cognitive-strategies approach must be introduced, stressed, and constantly reinforced in order for students to become confident and competent readers and writers of complex texts. However, our research supports the instructional scaffolding model presented in this book and indicates that these lessons and this approach provide the ownership, appropriateness, structure, and opportunities for collaboration that enable students to internalize the strategies in their mental took kits and apply them as independent learners. Two studies demonstrating the efficacy of this approach to reading and writing instruction are summarized below.

SCAFFOLDING MULTICULTURAL LITERATURE: A RESEARCH PROJECT

In fall 1992 the UCI Writing Project initiated a yearlong program called Writing Project II: Teaching Writing and Literature in the Multicultural Classroom. Of the thirty UCIWP Fellows attending this ten-session inservice program, which was held monthly throughout the school year, ten elected to participate in a research study during winter/spring 1993 to determine the impact of scaffolded multicultural literature-based curriculum materials on students in grades 7 through 9. The students these teachers serve represent the cultural spectrum of Orange County, from Santiago Middle School in the Orange Unified School District, with a slight majority of white students (53 percent), to Sunny Hills High School in the Fullerton Joint Union School District, which serves a large percentage of Asian and Pacific Islander students (47 percent), to McFadden Intermediate School in the Santa Ana Unified School District, where the students are predominantly Chicano and Latino (90 percent).

In February and again in May, teachers who were participating in the research component administered a fifty-minute timed pretest and posttest to their students. Students wrote to interpretive prompts focusing on "Eleven" by Sandra Cisneros or the "The Stolen Party" by Liliana Heker (see Chapter 5 and Chapter 9). Both prompts called for character analysis and dealt with the theme of being "put in one's place" as well as the consequent disillusionment and loss of innocence that comes with that experience. These two prompts were mixed so that half the students wrote about each work. The control teachers' students wrote to the same pretest and posttest prompts in the same order as the experimental teachers' students.

Between March and May, the teachers in the experimental group taught three scaffolded multicultural literature-based lessons that had been developed by UCIWP teacher/consultants. Each lesson—one using Sandra Cisneros's "My Name" (see Chapter 4) as a springboard, one analyzing Amy Tan's "The Moon Lady" (see Chapter 10), and one based on Alice Walker's "Everyday Use"—focused on literary interpretation. (See Olson, 1996, for a copy of this lesson.)

Students wrote several drafts of each paper and received feedback from both a peer response group and the teacher. Additionally, each student wrote a metacognitive log that contained both cognitive and affective comments about each work of literature and about the writing task itself. The entire body of this work (including copies of the pretest and posttest) was kept in individual portfolios; students were asked to revisit their portfolios at the end of the study to assess and comment on their own growth over time.

During the summer of 1993, we randomly sampled 14 pretests and posttests per teacher from both the experimental and control groups, a total of 560 papers, and scored them using a six-point rubric. Papers were scored by two readers for a composite score of anywhere from 2 [1+1] to 12 [6+6]. Papers that received scores that diverged by two or more points were read by a third reader. The overall growth from pretest to posttest in the experimental group was 0.971, the equivalent of half a letter grade. The growth of the control group students was a marginal .0193. Therefore, the difference between the gains by the experimental and control groups was 0.788. The probability of this gain occurring by chance alone was 8 in 1,000. Further, while the numbers of most of the ethnic groups were too small to draw any conclusions based on ethnicity, we did find that the two largest groups in the study—students who identified themselves as "Hispanic" and students who identified themselves as "White"—grew comparably.

When reviewing the growth in writing ability, Writing Project teachers remarked on the progress they saw in the students' reading and thinking ability. They noticed that many students who had initially relied on summary and retelling developed, over the seventeen-week period, more analytical strategies for responding to texts. Overall, teacher/consultants noticed the following shifts in the students' texts:

Reliance on summary and retelling ⟶	More evidence of analysis and interpretation
Emphasis on literal level of the text ⟶	Ability to discuss symbolic implications of the texts; evidence of inferential reasoning
Frequent tentativeness about taking a stance and making a claim ⟶	More confidence about taking a stance and making a claim
Little evidence of command of essay form ⟶	Evidence of planning and organizing; more structured essay format (introduction, main body, conclusion)
Lack of fluency in word choice and sentence structure ⟶	More control of and ease with language; syntactic maturity; some use of figurative language; stronger sense of personal voice

Our report on our research on scaffolding multicultural literature-based lessons won the Outstanding Education Research Award from Caddo Gap Press (the publishers of *Multicultural Education* and *Teacher Education Quarterly*) in 1994 and was commended in *The 1994 Yearbook of California Education Research* (Tierney, 1994) for describing "a powerful curricular tool for providing English language learners and other diverse learners with the academic skills needed to be successful in advanced educational settings" (p. 8). A copy of this article is available on the companion website.

THE COGNITIVE STRATEGIES APPROACH TO INSTRUCTIONAL SCAFFOLDING

Between 1996 and 2004, the UCI Writing Project conducted an eight-year longitudinal study of a reading and writing intervention in Santa Ana Unified School District, a large urban, low SES district where 93% of the students speak English as a second language and 60% are designated as Limited English Proficient (LEP). With funding from the U.S. Department of Education, Office of English Language Acquisition (OELA), secondary teachers who were engaged in ongoing professional development implemented a cognitive strategies approach to reading and writing instruction, making visible for students the thinking tools experienced readers and writers access in the process of meaning construction via tutorials, minilessons, and scaffolded demonstration lessons, many of which are in this book. In this longitudinal study, students progressed as a cadre up the grade levels (6–12) into the classes of teachers participating in the project. The aim of the Pathway Project was to help students to develop the academic literacy necessary to succeed in advanced educational settings. Students receiving cognitive strategies instruction significantly out-gained peers on holistically scored assessments of academic writing for seven consecutive years. Treatment group students also performed significantly better than control group students on GPA, standardized tests, and high stakes writing assessments. Findings reinforce the importance of having high expectations for English language learners (ELLs); exposing them to a rigorous language arts curriculum; explicitly teaching, modeling, and providing guided practice in a variety of strategies to help students read and write about challenging texts; as well as involving students as partners in a community of learners as they explore their own growth as readers and writers. Underwood and Pearson (2004) acknowledged the Pathway Project for "extending beyond declarative and procedural knowledge into conditional knowledge (the why and when of strategy use)" (p. 146) and note that the data supporting the project's effectiveness are "impressive" (p. 147). For further information on the Pathway Project study see Olson and Land (in press), "A Cognitive Strategies Approach to Reading and Writing Instruction for English Language Learners in Secondary School" in *Research in the Teaching of English,* a publication of the National Council of Teachers of English (www.ncte.org/pubs/journals/rte?source=gs).

References

Abrams, M. H., Talbot, D. E., Smith, H., Adams, R. M., Monk, S. H., Ford, G. H., & Daiches, D. (1968). *The Norton Anthology of English literature* (Vol. 2). New York: Norton.

Adkison, S., & Tchudi, S. (1997). Grading on merit and achievement: Where quality meets quantity. In S. Tchudi, *Alternatives to grading student writing*. Urbana, IL: National Council of Teachers of English.

Adler, M. (1982). *Paideia Proposal*. New York: Macmillan.

Alexander, P. A., & Murphy, P. K. (1998). The research base for APA's Learner-Centered Psychological Principles. In N. M. Lambert & B. L. McCombs (Eds.), *How students learn: Reforming schools through learner-centered education* (pp. 25–60). Washington, DC: American Psychological Association.

Allen, J. (1995). *It's never too late: Leading adolescents to lifelong literacy*. Portsmouth, NH: Heinemann.

Allen, J. (1999). *Words, words, words: Teaching vocabulary in grades 4–12*. York, ME: Stenhouse.

Allen, J. (2004). *Tools for teaching content literacy*. Portland, ME: Stenhouse.

Allen, J., & Gonzales, K. (1998). *There's room for me here: Literacy workshop in the middle school*. York, ME: Stenhouse.

Allen, V. G. (1989). Literature as a support to second language acquisition. In P. Rigg & V. G. Allen (Eds.), *When they don't speak English: Integrating the ESL student into the regular classroom* (pp. 55–64). Urbana, IL: National Council of Teachers of English.

Allington, R. L. (1984). Oral reading. In P. D. Pearson (Ed.), *Handbook of reading research* (pp. 829–864). New York: Longman.

Anderson, R. C., Hiebert, E. H., Scott, J. A., & Wilkinson, I. A. G. (1985). *Becoming a nation of readers: The report of the Commission on Reading*. Washington, DC: The National Institute of Education.

Anderson, V., & Roit, M. (1996). Linking reading comprehension instruction to language development for language-minority students. *The Elementary School Journal, 96*, 295–309.

Applebee, A. N. (1981). *Writing in the secondary school: English and the content areas*. NCTE Research Report No. 21. Urbana, IL: National Council of Teachers of English.

Applebee, A. (1991). Literature: Whose heritage? In E. H. Hiebert (Ed.), *Literature for a diverse society: Perspectives, practices, and policies* (pp. 228–233). New York: Teachers College Press.

Applebee, A. (1993). *Literature in the secondary school: Studies of curriculum and instruction in the United States*. NTCE Research Report No. 25. Urbana, IL: National Council of Teachers of English.

Applebee, A. N., with Auten, A., & Lehr, F. (1981). *Writing in the secondary school*. Urbana, IL: National Council of Teachers of English.

Applebee, A., Barrow, K., Brown, R., Cooper, C., Mullis, I., & Petrosky, A. *Reading, thinking and writing: Results from the 1979–80 National Assessment of Reading and Literature*. Denver, CO: National Assessment of Educational Progress, Report No. 11-L-01.

Applebee, A. N., & Langer, J. A. (1983). Instructional scaffolding: Reading and writing as natural language activities. *Language Arts, 60*, 168–175.

Applebee, A., & Langer, J. (1987). *How writing shapes thinking: A study of teaching and learning*. NCTE Research Report No. 22. Urbana IL: National Council of Teachers of English.

Applebee, A. N., Langer, J. A., Jenkins, L. B., Mullins, I. V. S., & Foertsch, M. A. (1990). *Learning to write in our nation's schools: Instruction and achievement in 1998 at grades 4, 8, and 12*. Washington, DC: U.S. Department of Education, Office of Educational Research and Improvement. National Center for Education Statistics.

Appleby, B., & Conner, J. (1965). Well, what did you think of it? *English Journal, 54*, 606–612.

Appleman, D. (1993). Looking through critical lenses: Teaching literary theory to secondary students. In S. B. Shaw and D. Bogdan (Eds.), *Constructive reading: Teaching beyond communication* (pp. 155–171). Portsmouth, NH: Boynton/Cook.

Armstrong, C. (1993). *Did you really fall into a vat of anchovies? And other activities for language arts*. Fort Collins, CO: Cottonwood Press.

Armstrong, T. (1994). *Multiple intelligences in the classroom*. Alexandria, VA: Association for Supervision and Curriculum Development.

Arnheim, R. (1969). *Visual thinking*. Berkeley: University of California Press.

Asher, J. (1966). The learning strategy of total physical response: A review. *Modern Language Journal, 50*, 79–84.

AT&T. (1998, May). *Classrooms of the future. Research conference report and videotaped demonstration*. AT&T Communication Systems, Atlanta, GA.

Atwell, Nancie (1987). *In the middle: Writing, reading, and learning with adolescents*. Portsmouth, NH: Heinemann.

Atwell, N. (1998). *In the middle: New understandings about writing, reading and learning.* Portsmouth, NH: Heinemann.

Au, K. H. (1993). *Literacy instruction in multicultural settings.* New York: Harcourt Brace Jovanovich.

Au, K. H., & Jordan, C. (1981). Teaching reading to Hawaiian children: Finding a culturally appropriate solution. In H. Trueba, G. P. Guthrie, & K. H. Au (Eds.), *Culture and the bilingual classroom: Studies in classroom ethnography* (pp. 139–152). Rowley, MA: Newbury House.

August, D., & Hakuta, K. (Eds.) (1997). *Improving schooling for language-minority children: A research agenda.* Washington, DC: National Academy Press.

Axelrod, R., & Cooper, C. (1998). *A writer's guidebook.* New York: St. Martin's Press.

Axelrod, R. B., & Cooper, C. R. (2003). *The St. Martin's guide to writing* (7th ed.) Boston: Bedford/St. Martin's.

Bader, L. A. (2004). *Bader reading and language inventory.* Upper Sadder River, NJ: Prentice-Hall.

Baker, L. (2002). Metacognition in comprehension instruction. In C. C. Block & M. Pressley (Eds.), *Comprehension instruction: Research-based best practices* (pp. 77–95). New York: Guilford.

Baker, L., & Brown, A. L. (1984). Metacognitive skills in reading. In P. D. Pearson, M. Kamiel, R. Barr, & P. Mosenthal, *Handbook of research in reading* (pp. 353–395). New York: Longman.

Baldwin, R. S., Johnson, D., & Peer, G. G. (1980). *Bookmatch.* Tulsa, OK: Educational Development Corporation.

Banks, I. A., & Banks, C. A. M. (2003). *Multicultural education: Issues and perspectives* (5th ed.). Boston, MA: John Wiley & Sons.

Barrett, J. (1982). *Cloudy with a chance of meatballs.* New York: Aladdin Books.

Bartlett, F. C. (1932). *Remembering: A story in experimental and social psychology.* Cambridge, England: Cambridge University Press.

Bean, J. C., Drenk, D. & Lee, F. D. (1982). Microtheme strategies for developing cognitive skills. In C. E. Griffin (Ed.), *New directions for teaching and learning* (pp. 27–38). San Francisco, CA: Jossey-Bass.

Bear, D. R., Invernizzi, M., Templeton, S., & Johnston, F. (2000). *Words their way: Word study for phonics, vocabulary and spelling instruction.* Upper Saddle River, NJ: Prentice-Hall.

Beers, K. (2003). *When kids can't read; What teachers can do.* Portsmouth, NH: Heinemann.

Berliner, D. C., & Biddle, B. J. (1995). *The manufactured crisis: Myths, fraud, and the attack on America's public schools.* Reading, MA: Addison Wesley.

Bernstein, R. (1997). Writing the saturation report: Using fictional techniques for nonfiction writing. In C. B. Olson (Ed.), *Practical ideas for teaching writing as a process at the high school and college levels* (pp. 135–138). Sacramento, CA: California Department of Education.

Berthoff, A. (1981). *The making of meaning: Metaphors, models and maxims for writing teachers.* Upper Montclair, NJ: Boynton/Cook.

Bishop, R. (1992). Multicultural literature for children: Making informed choices. In V. Harris (Ed.), *Teaching multicultural literature in grades K–8* (pp. 37–53). Norwood, MA: Christopher-Gordon.

Blachowicz, C., & Fisher, P. (1996). *Teaching vocabulary in all classrooms.* Englewood Cliffs, NJ: Prentice-Hall.

Blau, S. (1997). Competence for performance in revision. In C. B. Olson (Ed.), *Practical ideas for teaching writing as a process at the high school and college levels* (pp. 239–246). Sacramento, CA: California Department of Education.

Blau, S. (2003). *The literature workshop: Teaching texts and their readers.* Portmouth, NH: Heinemann.

Block, C. C., & Pressley, M. (Eds.). (2002). *Comprehension instruction: Research-based best practices.* New York: Guilford.

Bloom, B., Englehart, M. D., Furst, E. S., Hill, W. H., & Krathwohl, D. (1956). *Taxonomy of educational objectives: Handbook 1: Cognitive domain.* New York: David McKay.

Borron, B. (1996). My name, my self: Using name to explore identity. In C. B. Olson (Ed.), *Reading, thinking and writing about multicultural literature* (pp. 597–615). Glenview, IL: Scott Foresman.

Bower, B., Lobdell, J., & Swenson, L. (1999). *History alive! Engaging all learners in the diverse classroom* (2nd ed.). Palo Alto, CA: Teachers' Curriculum Institute.

Braddock, R., Lloyd-Jones, R., & Schoer, L. (1963). *Research in written composition.* Urbana, IL: National Council of Teachers of English.

Bridwell, L. S. (1980). Revising strategies in twelfth grade students' transactional writing. *Research in the Teaching of English, 14*(8), 197–222.

Briggs, K., & Myers, I. B. (1993). *Introduction to type* (5th ed.). Palo Alto, CA: Consulting Pyschologists Press.

Britton, J., Burgess, T., Martin, N., McLeod, A., & Rosen, H. (1975). *The development of writing abilities (11–18).* Urbana, IL: National Council of Teachers of English.

Brodie, P. (1996). Never say never: Teaching grammar and usage. *English Journal 85*, 77–78.

Brosnahan, I., & Neuleib, J. (1995). Teaching grammar affectively: Learning to like grammar. In S. Hunter and R. Wallace (Eds.), *The place of writing in grammar instruction: Past, present, and future* (pp. 204–212). Portsmouth, NH: Heinemann.

Brown, A. (1993). *Booklinks: Writing connections to children's literature.* San Antonio, TX: ECS Learning Systems.

Brown, J. S., Collins, A., & Duguid, P. (1989). Situated cognition and the culture of learning. *Educational Researcher, 18*, 32–42.

Bruner, J. (1960). *The process of education.* Cambridge, MA: Harvard University Press.

Bruner, J. (1978). The role of dialogue in language acquisition. In A. Sinclair, R. J. Jarvella, & W. J. M. Levelt (Eds.), *The child's conception of language* (pp. 241–256). New York: Springer.

Bruner, J. (1986). *Actual minds, possible worlds.* Cambridge, MA: Harvard University Press.

Burchers, S. (1999). *Vocabutoons: Vocabulary cartoons.* Punta Gorda, FL: New Monic Books.

Burke, J. (1999). *The English teacher's companion: A complete guide to classroom, curriculum and the profession.* Portsmouth, NH: Heinemann.

Burns, W. (1997). Writing about literature with showing, not telling. In C. B. Olson (Ed.), *Practical ideas for teaching writing as a process at the high school and college levels* (pp. 53–55). Sacramento, CA: California Department of Education.

California Commission on Teacher Credentialing. (1997). *California standards for the teaching profession.* Sacramento, CA: Author.

California Commission on Teacher Credentialing. (2001). Teaching performance expectations. In *Standards of quality and effectiveness for professional teacher preparation programs* (Appendix A). Sacramento, CA: Author.

California Department of Education. (1999). *Reading and language arts framework for California public schools, kindergarten through grade twelve.* Sacramento, CA: Curriculum Development and Supplemental Materials Commission.

California Department of Education. (1998–99). *CBEDS: California Basic Educational Data System.* Sacramento, CA: Educational Demographic Unit.

California standards for the teaching profession: Resources for professional practice: Element descriptions and descriptions of practice. (1999). Oakland, CA: Educational Testing Service.

Calkins, L., with Harwayne, S. (1991). *Living between the lines.* Portsmouth, NH: Heinemann.

Calkins, L., Montgomery, K., Santman, D. (1998). *A teacher's guide to standardized reading tests: Knowledge is power.* Portsmouth, NH: Heinemann.

Cambourne, B. (1988). *The whole story.* New York: Scholastic.

Caplan, R. (1997). Showing, not telling: A training program for student writers. In C. B. Olson (Ed.), *Practical ideas for teaching writing as a process at the high school and college levels* (pp. 39–45). Sacramento, CA: California Department of Education.

Capossela, T. (1993). *The critical writing workshop: Designing writing assignments to foster critical thinking.* Portsmouth, NH: Heinemann.

Carrasquillo, A. L., & Rodriguez, V. (1995). *Language minority students in the mainstream classroom.* Bristol, PA: Multilingual Matters.

Carter, C., Bishop, J., & Kravits, S. L.(1998). *Keys to college studying: Becoming a lifelong learner.* Upper Saddle River, NJ: Prentice Hall.

Chamot, V. C., & O'Malley, J. (1989). The cognitive academic language learning approach. In P. Rigg & V. G. Allen (Eds.), *When they don't speak English: Integrating the ESL student into the regular class-room* (pp. 108–125). Urbana, IL: National Council of Teachers of English.

Chamot, A. U., & O'Malley, J. M. (1994). *The CALLA handbook: Implementing the Cognitive Academic Language Learning Approach.* New York: Longman.

Charles, C. M. (1996). *Building classroom discipline* (5th ed.). New York: Longman.

Checkley, K. (1997). The first seven . . . and the eighth intelligence: A conversation with Howard Gardner. *Educational Leadership, 55*(1), 8–13.

Chomsky, C. (1970). Reading, writing, and phonology. *Harvard Educational Review, 40*(2), 287–309.

Christenbury, L. (1994). *Making the journey: Being and becoming a teacher of English language arts.* Portsmouth, NH: Heinemann.

Christensen, F. (1963). A generative rhetoric of the sentence. *College Composition and Communication, 14,* 155–161.

Christensen, F. (1967). *Notes toward a new rhetoric.* New York: Harper and Row.

Claggett, F. (1996). *A measure of success: From assignment to assessment in English language arts.* Portsmouth, NH: Heinemann.

Claggett, F., with Brown, J. (1992). *Drawing your own conclusions: Graphic strategies for reading, writing, and thinking.* Portsmouth, NH: Heinemann.

Coady, M., Hamann, E. T., Harrington, M., Pacheco, M., Pho, S., & Yedlin, J. (2003). *Claiming opportunities: A handbook for improving education for English language learners through comprehensive school reform.* Providence, RI: Brown University.

Cole, R. A., & Williams, D. (1973). Pupil response to teacher questions: Cognitive level, length and syntax. *Educational Leadership, 31,* 142–145.

Connors, R. J., & Lunsford, A. (1988). Frequency of formal errors in current college writing, or Ma and Pa Kettle do research. *College Composition and Communication, 39,* 395–409.

Conroy, J. (1999). *A teacher handbook for examining student work in relation to standards.* Irvine, CA: Irvine Unified School District.

Cooper, C., & Odell, L. (1977). *Evaluating writing: Describing, measuring, judging.* Urbana, IL: National Council of Teachers of English.

Cooper, R. T., & Groves, M. (1999, September 19). Just 1 in 4 students in U.S. now shows writing proficiency. *Los Angeles Times,* pp. A1, A15.

Cordeiro, P. (1998). Dora learns to write and in the process encounters punctuation. In C. Weaver (Ed.), *Lessons to share: On teaching grammar in context* (pp. 39–66). Portsmouth, NH: Heinemann.

Costa, A. (1991a). Teacher behaviors that enable student thinking. In A. Costa (Ed.), *Developing minds: A resource book for teaching thinking* (pp. 194–206). Alexandria, VA: Association for Supervision and Curriculum Development.

Costa, A. (1991b). *The school as home for the mind.* Palatine, IL: Skylight.

Costa, A. L., & Garmston, R. J. (1994). *Cognitive coaching: A foundation for renaissance schools.* Norwood, MA: Christopher-Gordon.

Covey, S. (1989). *The seven habits of highly effective people.* New York: Simon & Schuster.

Cox, S., & Gadda, L. (1990). Multicultural literature: Mirrors and windows on global community. *The Reading Teacher, 43,* 582–589.

Csikszentimihaly, M. (1991). Literacy and intrinsic motivation. In S. R. Graubard (Ed.), *Literacy: An overview by fourteen experts.* New York: Farrar, Straus & Giroux.

Cummins, J. (1986). Empowering minority students: A framework for intervention. *Harvard Educational Review, 56*(1), 18–36.

Daigon, A. (1990). Toward righting writing. In T. Newkirk (Ed.), *To compose: Teaching writing in high school and college* (pp. 3–14). Portsmouth, NH: Heinemann.

Daley, J. A., & Miller, M. D. (1975). The empirical development of an instrument to measure writing apprehension. *Research in the Teaching of English, 9,* 242–248.

Daniel, N., & Murphy, C. (1995). Correctness or clarity? Finding answers in the classroom and professional world. In S. Hunter & R. Wallace (Eds.), *The place of grammar in writing instruction: Past, present, future.* Portsmouth, NH: Heinemann.

Daniels, H. (1994). *Literature circles: Voice and choice in the student-centered classroom.* York, ME: Stenhouse.

Daniels, H. (2002). *Literature circles: Voice and choice in book clubs and reading groups.* Portland, ME: Stenhouse.

Daniels, H., & Bizar, M. (1998). *Methods that matter: Six structures for best practice classrooms.* Portland, ME: Stenhouse.

Daniels, H., & Zemelman, H. (2004). *Subjects matter: Every teacher's guide to content area reading.* Portsmouth, NH: Heinemann.

D'Aoust, C. (1992). Writing as a process. In C. B. Olson (Ed.), *Thinking/writing: Fostering critical thinking through writing* (pp. 17–19). New York: HarperCollins.

D'Aoust, C. (1997). The saturation research paper. In C. B. Olson (Ed.), *Practical ideas for teaching writing as a process at the high school and college levels* (pp. 142–144). Sacramento, CA: California Department of Education.

Davey, B. (1983). Think-aloud—Modeling the cognitive processes of reading comprehension. *Journal of Reading, 27*(1), 44–47.

Davis, F. B. (1968). Research on comprehension in reading. *Reading Research Quarterly, 3,* 499–545.

Davis, Z. T., & McPherson, M. S. (1989). Story map instruction: A road map for reading comprehension. *The Reading Teacher, 43*(3), 232–240.

Deci, E. L. (1976). *Intrinsic motivation.* New York: Plenum Press.

Delpit, L. (1995). *Other people's children: Cultural conflict in the classroom.* New York: The New Press.

Desai, L. E. (1997). Reflections on cultural diversity in literature and in the classroom. In T. Rogers & A. O. Soter (Eds.), *Reading across cultures: Teaching literature in a diverse society* (pp. 161–177). New York: Teachers College Press.

Devine, T. G. (1978). Listening: What do we know after fifty years of theorizing? *Journal of Reading, 21,* 296–304.

Dias, P. (1990). A literary response perspective on teaching reading comprehension. In D. Bogdan & S. B. Straw (Eds.), *Beyond communication: Reading comprehension and criticism* (pp. 283–299).

Didion, J. (1976/1992). Why I write. In C. Anderson, *Free/style: A direct approach to writing* (p. 139). Boston: Houghton Mifflin.

Dillon, J. (1984). Research on questioning and discussion. *Educational Leadership, 42,* 50–56.

Donovan, S. M., Bransford, J. D., & Pellegrino, J. W. (Eds.). (1999). *How people learn: Bridging research and practice.* Washington, DC: National Academy Press.

Dudley-Marling, C., & Searle, D. (1991). *When students have time to talk.* Portsmouth, NH: Heinemann.

Duffy, G., & Roehler, L. (1987). Improving classroom reading instruction through the use of responsive elaboration. *The Reading Teacher, 40,* 514–521.

Dulay, H., and Burt, M. (1977). Remarks on creativity in language acquisition. In M. Burt, H. Dulay, & M. Finnochiaro (Eds.), *Viewpoints on English as a second language* (pp. 95–126). New York: Regents.

Dunning, S., & Stafford, W. (1992). *Getting the knack: 20 poetry writing exercises.* Urbana, IL: National Council of Teachers of English.

Durkin, D. (1978–79). What classroom observations reveal about reading comprehension instruction. *Reading Research Quarterly, 14,* 481–533.

Eeds, M., & Wells, D. (1989). Grand conversations: An exploration of meaning construction in literature study groups. *Research in the Teaching of English, 23,* 4–29.

Eisner, E. (1992). The reality of reform. *English Leadership Quarterly, 14*(3), 2–5.

Elbow, P. (1973). *Writing without teachers.* New York: Oxford University Press.

Elbow, P. (1986). *Writing with power: Techniques for mastering the writing process.* New York: Oxford University Press.

Elbow, P. (1997). Some guidelines for writing—response groups. In C. B. Olson (Ed.), *Practical ideas for teaching writing as a process at the high school and college levels* (pp. 197–201). Sacramento, CA: California Department of Education.

Elbow, P., & Belanoff, P. (2000). *Sharing and responding* (3rd ed.). New York: McGraw-Hill.

Ellison, J. (1984). Howard Gardner: The seven frames of mind. *Psychology Today, 6,* 21–26.

Emmer, E. T., Evertson, C. M., Clements, B. S., & Worsham, M. E. (1997). *Classroom management for secondary teachers.* Boston: Allyn & Bacon.

English–language arts content standards for California public schools: Kindergarten through grade twelve.

(1997). Sacramento, CA: California Department of Education.

Enright, D. S., & McCloskey, M. L. (1988). *Integrating English: Developing English language and literacy in the multicultural classroom.* Reading, MA: Addison Wesley.

Fagin, L. (1995). *The list poem: A guide to teaching and writing catalogue verse.* New York: Teachers & Writers Collaborative.

Faigley, L., Cherry, R. D., Jolliffe, D. A., & Skinner, A. M. (1985). *Assessing writers' knowledge and processes of composing.* Norwood, NJ: Ablex.

Fawson, P. C., & Fawson, C. (1994). *Conditional philanthropy: A study of corporate sponsorship of reading incentive programs.* Paper presented at the International Reading Association, May, Toronto, Canada.

Fielding, L., & Pearson, D. (1994). Reading comprehension: What works? *Educational Leadership,* 51, 62–67.

Fielding, L. G., Wilson, P. T., & Anderson, R. C. (1990). A new focus on free reading: The role of trade books in reading instruction. In T. E. Raphael & R. Reynolds (Eds.), *Contexts of literacy.* New York: Longman.

Fillmore, L. W. (1986). Research currents: Equity or excellence? *Language Arts,* 63(5), 474–481.

Fitzgerald, J. (1995). English-as-a-second-language learners' cognitive reading processes: A review of research in the United States. *Review of Educational Research,* 65(2), 145–190.

Fitzgerald, J. A. (1951). *The teaching of spelling.* Milwaukee, WI: Bruce.

Fitzsimmons, R. J., & Loomer, B. M. (1980). *Spelling: The research basis.* Iowa City: The University of Iowa, Project Spelling.

Flower, L. (1981). *Problem-solving strategies for writing.* New York: Harcourt Brace Jovanovich.

Flower, L. (1990). Writer-based prose: A cognitive process for problems in writing. In T. Newkirk (Ed.), *To compose: Teaching writing in high school and college* (pp. 125–152). Portsmouth, NH: Heinemann.

Flower, L., & Hayes, J. R. (1980). The dynamics of composing: Making plans and juggling constraints. In L. W. Gregg & E. R. Steinberg (Eds.), *Cognitive processes in writing* (pp. 31–50). Hillsdale, NJ: Erlbaum.

Flower, L., & Hayes, J. R. (1981a). A cognitive process theory of writing. *College Composition and Communication,* 32, 365–387.

Flower L., & Hayes, J. R. (1981b). Plans that guide the composing process. In C. H. Frederiksen & J. H. Dominic (Eds.), *Writing: The nature, development and teaching of written communication* (Vol. 2, pp. 39–58). Hillsdale, NJ: Erlbaum.

Flower, L., Hayes, J. R., Carey, L., Schriver, K., & Stratman, J. (1986). Detection, diagnosis, and the strategies of revision. *College Composition and Communication,* 37, 16–55.

Forster, E. M. (1927). *Aspects of the novel.* New York: Harcourt Brace Jovanovich.

Frank, R. (1992). Bobby-B-Bored: Introducing showing writing with role playing. In C. B. Olson (Ed.), *Thinking/writing: Fostering critical thinking through writing* (pp. 55–68). New York: HarperCollins.

Frederiksen, C. H., & Dominic, J. F. (1981). *Writing: The nature, development and teaching of written communication* (Vol. 2, pp. 17–20). Hillsdale, NJ: Erlbaum.

Gambrell, L. (1994). What motivates children to read? *Scholastic Literacy Research Paper* (Vol. 2, pp. 1–6). Jefferson City, MO: Scholastic.

Gardner, H. (1983). *Frames of mind. The theory of multiple intelligences.* New York: Basic Books.

Gardner, H., & Hatch, T. (1989). Multiple intelligences go to school: Educational implications of the theory of multiple intelligences. *Educational Researcher,* 18, 4–10.

Gentry, R. (1987). *Spel . . . is a four letter word.* Portsmouth, NH: Heinemann.

Gentry, R. J., & Gillet, J. W. (1993). *Teaching kids to spell.* Portsmouth, NH: Heinemann.

Gere, A. R., Christenbury, L., & Sassi, K. (2005). *Writing on demand: Best practices and strategies for success.* Portsmouth, NH: Heinemann.

Gersten, R. M., & Jiménez, R. T. (1998). *Promoting learning for culturally and linguistically diverse students: Classroom applications from contemporary research.* New York: Wadsworth.

Goldberg, A., Russell, M., & Cook, A. (2003, March 10). The effect of computers on student writing: A meta-analysis of studies from 1992 to 2002. *The Journal of Technology, Learning, and Assessment,* 2(1). Retrieved December 15, 2003, from www.bc.edu/research/intasc/jtla/journal/pdf/v2n1_jtla.pdf

Good, T. L., & Brophy, J. (1995). *Contemporary educational psychology.* New York: Longman.

Good, T. L., & Brophy, J. E. (1997). *Looking in classrooms* (4th ed.). New York: Longman.

Goodlad, J. (1994). *A place called school: Prospects for the future.* New York: McGraw-Hill.

Goodman, Y. (1978). Kid-watching: An alternative to testing. *National Elementary Principals Journal,* 57, 41–45.

Gossard, J. (1997a). Using read-around groups to establish criteria for good writing. In C. B. Olson (Ed.), *Practical ideas for teaching writing as a process at the high school and college levels* (pp. 231–235). Sacramento, CA: California Department of Education.

Gossard, J. (1997b). Reader response logs. In C. B. Olson (Ed.), *Practical ideas for teaching writing as a process at the high school and college levels* (pp. 212–214). Sacramento, CA: California Department of Education.

Graves, D. (1981). Presentation at National Council of Teachers of English Annual Convention, November, Boston, MA.

Graves, D. (1983). *Writing: Teachers and children at work.* Portsmouth, NH: Heinemann.

Graves, D. (1984). *A researcher learns to write: Selected articles and monographs.* Portsmouth, NH: Heinemann.

Graves, D., & Hansen, J. (1983). The author's chair. *Language Arts,* 60, 176–182.

Gray, D. (1987). Breaking the rules and loving it. *Basic Education,* 80, 1–4.

Greene, H. A. (1950). English—language, grammar, and composition. In W. S. Monroe (Ed.), *Encyclopedia of educational research* (Rev. ed., pp. 383–396). New York: Macmillan.

Greenwald, E. A., Persky, H. R., Campbell, J. R., & Mazzeo, I. (1999). *NAEP 1998 writing report card for the nation and the states.* Washington, DC: U.S. Department of Education, Office of Educational Research and Improvement, National Center for Education Statistics.

Guerin, W. L., Labor, E., Morgan, L., Reesman, J. C., & Willingham, J. R. (1992). *A handbook of critical approaches to literature.* New York: Oxford University Press.

Guilford, J. P. (1967). *The nature of human intelligence.* New York: McGraw-Hill.

Hairston, M. (1981). Not all errors are created equal: Nonacademic readers in the professions respond to lapse in usage. *College English,* 43, 794–806.

Hansen, J. (1998). *When learners evaluate.* Portsmouth, NH: Heinemann.

Harris, V. (Ed.). (1992). *Teaching multicultural literature in grades K–8.* Norwood, MA: Christopher-Gordon.

Harste, J. C., Short, K. C., & Burke, C. (1998). *Creating classrooms for authors: The reading-writing connection.* Portsmouth, NH: Heinemann.

Harvey, S. (1998) *Nonfiction matters: Reading, writing and research in grades 3–8.* York, ME: Stenhouse.

Harvey, S., & Goudvis, A. (2000). *Strategies that work: Teaching comprehension to enhance understanding.* York, ME: Stenhouse.

Head, M., & Readence, J. E. (1998). Anticipation guides: Using prediction to promote learning from text. In J. E. Readence, T. W. Bean, & R. S. Baldwin (Eds.), *Content area literacy: An integrated approach* (6th ed.) (CD-ROM, pp. 227–233). Dubuque, IA: Kendall/Hunt.

Henderson, K. (1996). *Market guide for your writers: Where and how to sell what you write* (5th ed.). Cincinnati, OH: Writer's Digest Books.

Hibbing, A. N., & Rankin-Erickson, J. L. (2003). A picture is worth a thousand words: Using visual images to improve comprehension for middle school struggling readers. *The Reading Teacher,* 56(8), 758–770.

Hildebrand, L., & Hixon, J. (1991). Video assisted learning of study skills. *Elementary school guidance and counseling,* 26, 121–129.

Hill, C. (1992). *Testing and assessment: An ecological approach.* New York: Teachers College Press.

Hill, W. F., & Ottchen, C. J. (1995). *Shakespeare's insults: Educating your wit.* New York: Crown Publishing Group.

Hillocks, G., Jr. (1984). What works in teaching composition: A meta-analysis of experimental treatment studies. *American Journal of Education,* 93, 133–170.

Hillocks, G., Jr. (1986). *Research on written composition: New directions for teaching.* Urbana, IL: ERIC Clearinghouse on Reading and Composition Skills and the National Conference on Research in English. Distributed by the National Council of Teachers of English.

Hillocks, G., Jr. (1987). Synthesis of research on teaching writing. *Educational Leadership,* 44, 71–82.

Hillocks, G., Jr. (1995). *Teaching writing as a reflective practice.* New York: Teachers College Press.

Holaday, L. (1997). Writing students need coaches, not judges. In S. Tchudi (Ed.), *Alternatives to grading student writing* (pp. 35–46). Urbana, IL: National Council of Teachers of English.

Horn, E. (1954). Phonics and spelling. *Journal of Education,* 136, 233–235, 246.

Horn, T. (1952). That straw man: The spelling list. *Elementary English,* 29, 265–267.

Houle, R., & Montmarquette, C. (1984). An empirical analysis of loans by school libraries. *Alberta Journal of Education Research,* 30, 107–114. Retrieved March 1, 2000, from www.lexile.com/faq/lx_faq.html

Huck, C. (1977). Literature as the content of reading. *Theory into Practice,* 16(5), 363–371.

Huck, T. (1992). Book wheels: A book reporting activity involving reading, writing, listening, speaking, and art. In C. B. Olson (Ed.), *Thinking writing: Fostering critical thinking through writing* (pp. 40–50). New York: Harper Collins.

Huck, T., & Judd, J. (1992). Thinking and writing about thinking/writing. In C. B. Olson (Ed.), *Thinking/writing: Fostering critical thinking through writing* (pp. 403–410). New York: HarperCollins.

Hunter, M. (1989). Madeline Hunter in the English classroom. *English Journal,* 78, 17–18.

Hunter, S., & Wallace, R. (Eds.). (1995). *The place of grammar in writing instruction: Past, present, future.* Portsmouth, NH: Heinemann.

Jago, C. (1989). Death comes to the term paper: The extinction of Termpapersaurus Rex. *The Outlook.* Santa Monica, CA.

Jago, C. (1997). The extinction of Termpapasaurus Rex: The rise of text-based research. In C. B. Olson (Ed.), *Practical ideas for teaching writing as a process at the high school and college levels* (pp. 163–165). Sacramento, CA: California Department of Education.

Jago, C. (1999). The term paper revisited. *English Journal,* 89, 23–25.

Jensen, E. (1997). *Brain compatible strategies.* San Diego, CA: The Brain Store.

Jensen, E. (1998). *Introduction to brain compatible learning.* San Diego, CA: The Brain Store.

Jiménez, R. T., García, G., & Pearson, P. D. (1994). Three children, two languages, and strategic reading: Case studies in bilingual/monolingual reading. *American Educational Journal, 32,* 67–98.

Johnson, P., & Winograd, P. N. (1985). Passive failure in reading. *Journal of Reading Behavior, 17,* 279–301.

Johnston, P., & Afferbach, P. (1985). The process of constructing main ideas from text. *Cognition and Instruction, 2,* 207–232.

Kagan, S. (1989). *Cooperative learning: Resources for teachers.* San Juan Capistrano, CA: Resources for Teachers.

Kaiser, M. P., & Lindfors, M. (1997). Getting on track: Core literature for all students. In C. B. Olson (Ed.), *Practical ideas for teaching writing as a process at the high school and college levels* (pp. 104–109). Sacramento, CA: California Department of Education.

Keene, E. O., & Zimmerman, S. (1997). *A mosaic of thought: Teaching comprehension in a reader's workshop.* Portsmouth, NH: Heinemann.

Kilbane, C. R., & Milman, N. B. (2003). *What every teacher should know about creating digital portfolios.* Boston: Allyn & Bacon.

Killgallon, D. (1998). Sentence composing: Notes on a new rhetoric. In C. Weaver (Ed.), *Lessons to share on teaching grammar in context* (pp. 169–183). Portsmouth, NH: Heinemann.

Kindler, A. (2002). *Survey of states' limited English proficient students and available educational programs and services, 2001–2002.* (Summary Report). Washington, DC: National Clearinghouse for English Language Acquisition.

Kirby, D. (1997). Reforming your teaching for thinking: The studio approach. In C. B. Olson (Ed.), *Practical ideas for teaching writing as a process at the high school and college levels* (pp. 168–173). Sacramento, CA: California Department of Education.

Kirby, D., & Kuykendall, C. (1991). *Mind matters: Teaching for thinking.* Portsmouth, NH: Heinemann.

Koff, S. (1997). What the text says—what the text means to me. In C. B. Olson (Ed.), *Practical ideas for teaching writing as a process at the high school and college levels* (pp. 187–191). Sacramento, CA: California Department of Education.

Kohn, A. (1996). *Beyond discipline: From compliance to community.* Alexandria, VA: Association for Supervision and Curriculum Development.

Krashen, S. D. (1981). *Second language acquisition and second language learning.* New York: Pergamon Press.

Krashen, S. (1984). *Writing: Research, theory and applications.* Oxford: Pergamon Institute of English.

Krashen, S. (1993). *The power of reading: Insights from research.* Eaglewood, CO: Libraries Unlimited.

Krathwohl, D. R., Bloom, B. S., & Masia, B. B. (1964). *Taxonomy of educational objectives: Book 2. Affective domain.* New York: Longman.

Kucan, L., & Beck, I. (1997). Thinking aloud and reading comprehension research: Inquiry, instruction,

and social interaction. *Review of Educational Research, 67*(3), 271–299.

La Berge, D., & Samuels, S. J. (1974). Toward a theory of automatic information processing in reading. *Cognitive Psychology, 6,* 293–323.

Lane, B. (1992). *After THE END: Teaching and learning creative revision.* Portsmouth, NH: Heinemann. (See also Lane's website—www.discoverwriting.com)

Lane, B., & Green, A. (1994). *The portfolio source book: How to set up, manage and integrate portfolios into the reading/writing classroom.* Shoreham, VT: Vermont Portfolio Institute.

Lange, K. (1997). *Novel works: To kill a mockingbird* (teacher's resource book). Glenview, IL: Scott Foresman.

Langer, J. A. (1986). Reading, writing, and understanding: An analysis of the construction of meaning. *Written Communication, 3,* 219–267.

Langer, J. A. (1989). *The process of understanding literature* (Report No. 2.1). Albany, NY: Center for the Learning and Teaching of Literature.

Langer, J. A. (1991). Literacy and schooling: A sociocognitive perspective. In E. H. Hiebert (Ed.), *Literacy for a diverse society: Perspectives, practices and policies.* New York: Teachers College Press.

Langer, J. (1995). *Envisioning literature: Literary understanding and literature instruction.* New York: Teachers College Press.

Langer, J. A. (2000). *Beating the odds: Teaching middle and high school students to read and write well* (Report No. 12014). Albany, NY: National Research Center on English Learning & Achievement.

Langer, J. A. (2004). *Getting to excellent: How to create better schools.* New York: Teacher's College Press.

Langer, J. A., & Applebee, A. N. (1986). Reading and writing instruction: Toward a theory of teaching and learning. In E. Z. Rothkopf (Ed.), *Review of research in education* (Vol. 13, pp. 171–197). Washington, DC: American Educational Research Association.

Langer, J. A., & Applebee, A. N. (1987). *How writing shapes thinking: A study of teaching and learning.* NCTE Research Report No. 22. Urbana, IL: National Council of Teachers of English.

Lansky, B. (2003). *The mother of all baby name books.* New York: Meadowbrook Press.

Lazear, D. (1991). *Seven ways of knowing: Teaching for multiple intelligences.* Palatine, IL: Skylight.

Lenski, S. D., Wham, M. A., & Johns, J. L. (2003). *Reading and learning strategies: Middle grades through high school* (2nd ed.). Dubuque, IA: Kendall/Hunt.

Leslie, L., & Caldwell, J. (2000). *Qualitative reading inventory—II.* New York: HarperCollins.

Lexile framework for reading. "Frequently Asked Questions." 1997.

Lowery, L., & Marshall, H. (1980). *Learning about instruction: Teacher initiated statements and questions.* Berkeley, CA: University of California.

Lurie, T. (1978). *Conversations and constructions.* (Available from the author, 150 Seal Rock Drive, San Francisco, CA 94121)

Macon, D., Bewell, D., & Vogt, M. (1991). *Responses to literature.* Newark, DE: International Reading Association.

Macrorie, K. (1988). *The I-search paper: Revised edition of searching writing.* Portsmouth, NH: Heinemann.

Macrorie, K. (1997). The rewakening of curiosity: Research papers as hunting stories. In C. B. Olson (Ed.), *Practical ideas for teaching writing as a process at the high school and college levels* (pp. 152–155). Sacramento, CA: California Department of Education.

Maizels, J., & Petty, K. (1996). *The amazing pop-up grammar book.* New York: Dutton Children's Books.

Martin, N., D'Arcy, P., Newton, B., & Parker, R. (1976). *Writing and learning across the curriculum 11–16.* Upper Montclair, NJ: Boynton/Cook.

Marzano, R. J., & Pickering, D. J. (2005). *Building academic vocabulary.* Alexandria, VA: Association for Supervision and Curriculum Development.

Mason, J., & Allen, J. (1986). A review of emergent literacy with implications for research and practice in reading. In E. Rothkopf (Ed.), *Review of research in education* (Vol. 13, pp. 3–47). Washington, DC: American Educational Research Association.

Mayer, R. (2001). *Multimedia learning.* London: Cambridge University Press.

McCormick, K. (1994). *The culture of reading and the teaching of English.* New York: Manchester University Press.

McHugh, N. (1997). Teaching the domains of writing. In C. B. Olson (Ed.), *Practical ideas for teaching writing as a process at the high school and college levels* (pp. 112–118). Sacramento, CA: California Department of Education.

Metzger, M. (1998). Teaching reading: Beyond the plot. *Phi Delta Kappan, 80,* 240–256.

Moffatt, M. (1997). Learning logs. In C. B. Olson (Ed.), *Practical ideas for teaching writing as a process at the high school and college levels* (pp. 78–81). Sacramento, CA: California Department of Education.

Moffett, J. (1981). *Active voice: A writing program across the curriculum.* Upper Montclair, NJ: Boynton/Cook.

Moffett, J. (1990). *Ways of teaching literature.* In D. Bogdan & S. B. Straw (Eds.), *Beyond communication: Reading comprehension and criticism* (pp. 301–317). Portsmouth, NH: Boynton/Cook.

Morrow, L. (1982). Relationship between literature programs, library corner designs, and children's use of literature. *Journal of Educational Research, 75,* 339–344.

Morrow, L., & Weinstein, C. (1982). Increasing children's use of literature through program and physical changes. *Elementary School Journal, 83,* 131–137.

Mullis, I. V., Campell, S., & Farstrup, A. E. (1993). *NAEP 1992 reading report card for the nation and the states.* Washington, DC: Office of Educational Research and Improvement.

Murdick, W. (1996). What English teachers need to know about grammar. *English Journal, 85,* 38–45.

Murphy, S. (1999). Assessing portfolios. In C. R. Cooper & L. Odell (Eds.), *Evaluating writing: The role of teachers' knowledge about text, learning, and culture* (pp. 114–135). Urbana, IL: National Council of Teachers of English.

Murray, D. (1982a). Internal revision: A process of discovery. In *Learning by teaching: Selected articles on teaching and learning* (pp. 72–87). Upper Montclair, NJ: Boynton/Cook.

Murray, D. (1982b). The listening eye: Reflections on the writing conference. In *Learning by teaching: Selected articles on teaching and learning* (pp. 157–164). Upper Montclair, NJ: Boynton/Cook.

Nagy, W. E., & Anderson, R. C. (1984). How many words are there in printed school English? *Reading Research Quarterly, 19,* 303–330.

National Council of Teachers of English & International Reading Association. (1996). *Standards for the English language arts.* Urbana, IL: National Council of Teachers of English.

New Standards Project. (1994a). *Draft rubric for high school English language arts.* Washington, DC: National Center on Education and the Economy; Pittsburgh: University of Pittsburgh, Learning Research and Development Center.

New Standards Project. (1994b). *Student portfolio handbook: Middle school English language arts field version.* Washington, DC: National Center on Education and the Economy; Pittsburgh: University of Pittsburgh, Learning and Development Center.

New Standards English language arts reference examination. (1998). San Antonio, TX: Harcourt Brace Educational Measurement.

New Standards performance standards: Volume 3: High school. (1998). Pittsburgh, PA: National Center on Education and the Economy and the University of Pittsburgh.

Newkirk, T. (1982). Young writers as critical readers. *Language Arts, 59,* 451–547.

Newkirk, T. (1989). *More than stories: The range of children's writing.* Portsmouth, NH: Heinemann.

Nieto, S. (2003). *Affirming diversity: The sociopolitical context of multicultural education* (4th ed.). New York: Allyn & Bacon.

Noden, H. R. (1999). *Image grammar: Using grammatical structures to teach writing.* Portsmouth, NH: Heinemann.

Noguchi, R. (1991). *Grammar and the teaching of writing: Limits and possibilities.* Urbana, IL: National Council of Teachers of English.

Nystrand, M. (1986). *The structure of written communication: Studies in reciprocity between writers and readers.* Orlando, FL: Academic Press.

Oakes, J. (1985). Tracking, inequality, and the rhetoric of school reform: Why schools don't change. *Journal of Education, 168,* 61–80.

Ogle, D. (1986). K-W-L: A teaching model that develops active reading of expository text. *The Reading Teacher,* 39, 564–570.

Ogle, D. (1998). K-W-L in action: Secondary teachers find applications that work. In J. E. Readence, T. W. Bean, & R. S. Baldwin (Eds.), *Content area literacy: An integrated approach* (6th ed.) (CD-ROM, pp. 270–275). Dubuque, IA: Kendall/Hunt.

Olsen, L. (1988). *Crossing the schoolhouse border: Immigrant students in the California public schools.* San Francisco: California Tomorrow.

Olsen, L. (1992). *Programs for secondary limited English proficiency students: A California study.* San Francisco: California Tomorrow.

Olson, C. B. (1984). Fostering critical thinking skills through writing. *Educational Leadership,* 42(3), 28–39.

Olson, C. B. (Ed.). (1992). *Thinking/writing: Fostering critical thinking through writing.* New York: HarperCollins.

Olson, C. B. (1993). Saturation research: An alternative approach to the research paper. In T. Capossela (Ed.), *The critical writing workshop: Designing writing assignments to foster critical thinking* (pp. 178–192). Portsmouth, NH: Heinemann.

Olson, C. B. (1996a). *Applying the theory of multiple intelligences in English/language arts classrooms: Grades 7–12.* Unpublished report to the University of California, Office of the President for the Presidential Grants for Teacher Research in Education.

Olson, C. B. (Ed.). (1996b). *Reading, thinking and writing about multicultural literature.* Glenview, IL: Scott Foresman.

Olson, C. B. (1997). *Using the thinking/writing model to enhance reading, thinking and writing about literature.* Berkeley, CA: Office of the President, University of California.

Olson, C. B., Borron, B., Clark, P., & Land, R. (1994). Reading, thinking and writing about culturally diverse literature. In D. S. Tierney (Ed.), *1994 Yearbook of California education research* (pp. 13–32). San Francisco: Caddo Gap Press.

Olson, C. B., & Clark, P. (1996). Living in life's shadow. In C. B. Olson (Ed.), *Reading, thinking and writing about multicultural literature* (pp. 496–516). Glenview, IL: Scott Foresman.

Olson, C. B., & Land, R. (in press). A cognitive strategies approach to reading and writing instruction for English language learners in secondary school. *Research in the Teaching of English.*

Olson, C. B., & Schiesl, S. (1996). A multiple intelligences approach to teaching multicultural literature. *Language Arts Journal of Michigan,* 12(1), 1–14.

O'Malley, E. (Ed.). (1999). *Reading/language arts framework for California public schools, kindergarten through grade twelve.* Sacramento, CA: California Department of Education.

Ondaatje, M. (1984). *The collected works of Billy the kid.* New York: Penguin.

Palincsar, A. S., & Brown, A. L. (1985). Reciprocal teaching: Activities to promote "reading with your mind." In T. H. Harris and E. L. Cooper (Eds.), *Reading, thinking and concept development: Strategies for the classroom* (pp. 147–159). Newark, NJ: College Entrance Examination Board.

Pallas, A. M., Natriello, G., & McDill, E. L. (1989). Changing nature of the disadvantaged population: Current dimensions and future trends. *Educational Researcher,* 18(5), 16–22.

Paris, S. G. (1985). Using classroom dialogues and guided practice to teach comprehension strategies. In T. H. Harris & E. L. Cooper (Eds.), *Reading, thinking, and concept development: Strategies for the classroom* (pp. 133–145). Newark, NJ: College Entrance Examination Board.

Paris, S. G., Lipson, M. Y., & Wixon, K. K. (1983). Becoming a strategic reader. *Contemporary Educational Psychology,* 8, 293–316.

Paris, S. G., & Oka, E. R. (1986). Self-regulated learning among exceptional children. *Exceptional Children,* 53, 103–108.

Paris, S. G., Wasik, B. A., & Turner, J. C. (1991). The development of strategic readers. In R. Barr, M. L. Kamil, P. Mosenthal, & P. D. Pearson (Eds.), *Handbook of reading research* (Vol. 2, pp. 609–640). New York: Longman.

Pearson, P. D., & Leys, M. (1985). "Teaching" comprehension. In T. H. Harris & E. L. Cooper (Eds.), *Reading, thinking and concept development: Strategies for the classroom* (pp. 3–21). Newark, NJ: College Entrance Examination Board.

Perl, S. (1990). Understanding composing. In T. Newkirk (Ed.), *To compose: Teaching writing in high school and college.* Portsmouth, NH: Heinemann.

Perona, S. (1989, Jan./Feb.). The tea party: Into, through and beyond a piece of literature. *The Writing Notebook: Creative Word Processing in the Classroom,* 30–31.

Persky, H. R., Daane, M. C., & Jin, Y. (2002). *The Nation's Report Card: Writing 2002.* Washington, DC: U.S. Department of Education, Institute of Education Sciences, National Center for Education Statistics.

Peterson, S. (1998). Teaching writing and grammar in context. In C. Weaver (Ed.), *Lessons to share: On teaching grammar in context* (pp. 67–94). Portsmouth, NH: Heinemann.

Petrosky, A. (1986). Critical thinking: Qu'est-ce que c'est? *The English Record,* 37(3), 2–5.

Piaget, J. (1930). *The child's conception of physical causality.* New York: Harcourt Brace Jovanovich.

Pinnell, G. S., & Jaggar, A. M. (1991). Oral language: Speaking and listening in the classroom. In J. Flood, J. M. Jensen, D. Lapp, & J. R. Squire (Eds.), *Handbook of research on the teaching of the English language arts* (pp. 691–742). New York: Macmillan.

Pirie, B. (1997). *Reshaping high school English.* Urbana, IL: National Council of Teachers of English.

Pitts, S. (1986). Read aloud to adult learners? Of course! *Reading Psychology: An International Quarterly,* 7, 35–42.

Pollard, D. S. (1989). Reducing the impact of racism on students. *Educational Leadership, 47*(2), 74–75.

Popham, W. J. (1995). *Classroom assessment: What teachers need to know.* Boston: Allyn & Bacon.

Pressley, M. (2002). Comprehension strategies instruction: A turn-of-the-century status report. In C. C. Block & M. Pressley (Eds.), *Comprehension instruction: Research-based best practices* (pp. 11–27). New York: Guilford.

Pressley, M., & Afflerbach, P. (1995). *Verbal protocols of reading: The nature of constructively responsive reading.* Hillsdale, NJ: Erlbaum.

Probst, R. (1988). *Response and analysis: Teaching literature in junior and senior high school.* Portsmouth, NH: Heinemann.

The Random House dictionary of the English language. (1983). New York: Random House.

Readence, J. E., Bean, T. W., & Baldwin, R. S. (1998). *Content area literacy: An integrated approach* (6th ed). Dubuque, IA: Kendall/Hunt.

Reeves, D. B. (1998). *Making standards work: How to implement standards-based assessments in the classroom, school, and district.* Denver, CO: Center for Performance Assessment.

Richards, I. A. (1929). *Practical criticism.* New York: Harcourt, Brace & World.

Rico, G. L. (1983). *Writing the natural way: Using right-brain techniques to release your expressive powers.* Los Angeles: J. P. Tarcher.

Rico, G. L. (1997). Clustering: A prewriting process. In C. B. Olson (Ed.), *Practical ideas for teaching writing as a process at the high school and college levels* (pp. 14–17). Sacramento, CA: California Department of Education.

Rief, L. S. (1992). *Seeking diversity: Language arts with adolescents.* Portsmouth, NH: Heinemann.

Rigg, P., & Allen, V. G. (Eds.). (1995). *When they don't speak English: Integrating the ESL student into the regular classroom.* Urbana, IL: National Council of Teachers of English.

Risso, M. (1990). *Safari punctuation.* Lincolnwood, IL: Passport Books.

Ritner, M. (1997). Encounters with prejudice: Writing workshop. In A. C. Purves, C. B. Olson, C. E. Cortés, J. A. Brough, & E. N. Brazee (Senior Consultants), *Scott Foresman literature and integrated studies, Grade 7* (pp. 319–324). Glenview, IL: Scott Foresman/Addison Wesley.

Romano, T. (1987). *Clearing the way: Working with teenage writers.* Portsmouth, NH: Heinemann.

Romano, T. (2000). *Blending genre, blending style: Writing multigenre papers.* Portsmouth, NH: Boynton/Cook.

Rosenblatt, L. (1976). *The reader, the text, the poem: The transactional theory of the literary work.* Carbondale, IL: Southern Illinois University Press.

Rosenblatt, L. (1983). *Literature as exploration* (4th ed.). New York: Modern Language Association.

Ross, G. (1995). The 1945 NCTE Commission on the English Curriculum and teaching the grammar/ writing connection. In S. Hunter & R. Wallace (Eds.), *The place of grammar in writing instruction: Past, present, future* (pp. 71–86). Portsmouth, NH: Heinemann.

Routman, R. (1991). *Invitations: Changing as teachers and learners.* Portsmouth, NH: Heinemann.

Rowe, M. B. (1986). Wait time: Slowing down may be a way of speeding up! *Journal of Teacher Education, 37,* 227–232.

Rucker, B. (1982). Magazines and teenage reading skills: Two controlled field experiments. *Journalism Quarterly, 59,* 28–33.

Ruddell, R. (1995). Those influential literacy teachers: Meaning negotiators and motivation builders. *The Reading Teacher, 48,* 454–463.

Scarcella, R. (1990). *Teaching language minority students in the multicultural classroom.* Englewood Cliffs, NJ: Prentice-Hall.

Scarcella, R. (1997). Teaching writing in the culturally and linguistically diverse classroom. In C. B. Olson (Ed.), *Practical ideas for teaching writing as a process at the high school and college levels* (pp. 85–91). Sacramento, CA: California Department of Education.

Scarcella, R. (2003). *Accelerating academic English: A focus on English language learners.* Oakland: Regents of the University of California.

Scarcella, R., & Oxford, R. L. (1992). *The tapestry of language learning: The individual in the communicative classroom.* Boston: Heinle & Heinle.

Scardamalia, M. (1981). How children cope with the cognitive demands of writing. In C. H. Frederiksen & J. F. Dominic (Eds.), *Writing: The nature, development and teaching of written communication* (Vol. 2, pp. 81–103). Hillsdale, NJ: Erlbaum.

Scardamalia, M., Bereiter, & C., Steinbach, R. (1984). Teachability of reflective processes in written composition. *Cognitive Science, 8*(2), 173–190.

Schaffer, J. (1995). *Teaching the multiparagraph essay: A sequential nine-week unit.* San Diego, CA: Jane Schaffer Publications. (See also Schaffer's website: www.curriculumguides.com)

Schallert, D., & Tierney, R. J. (1982). *Learning from expository text: The interaction of text structure with reader characteristics.* Final Report: National Institute of Education.

Schoenbach, R., Greenleaf, C., Cziko, C., & Hurwitz, L. (1999). *Reading for understanding: A guide to improving reading in middle and high school.* San Francisco, CA: Jossey-Bass.

Scholes, R. (1985). *Textual power: Literary theory in the teaching of English.* New Haven, CT: Yale University Press.

Searfoss, L. W., & Readence, J. E. (1989). *Helping children learn to read* (2nd ed.). Englewood Cliffs, NJ: Prentice-Hall.

Shanahan, T. (1988). The reading–writing relationship: Seven instructional principles. *The Reading Teacher, 41,* 636–647.

Shaughnessy, M. (1977). *Errors and expectations: A guide for the teacher of basic writing.* New York: Oxford University Press.

Shulman, L. (1998). Teacher portfolios: A theoretical activity. In N. Lyons (Ed.), *With portfolios in hand: Validating the new teacher professionalism* (pp. 23–37). New York: Teachers College Press.

Shuman, R. B. (1995). Grammar for writers: How much is enough? In S. Hunter & R. Wallace (Eds.), *The place of grammar in writing instruction: Past, present, future* (pp. 114–128). Portsmouth, NH: Heinemann.

Silver, H. F., Strong, R. W., & Perini, M. J. (2000). *Integrating learning styles and multiple intelligences.* Alexandra, VA: Association for Supervision and Curriculum Development.

Sims, R. B. (1982). *Shadow and substance.* Urbana, IL: National Council of Teachers of English.

Smith, F. (1983). *Essays into literacy.* Portsmouth, NH: Heinemann.

Smith, F. (1988). *Joining the literacy club: Further essays into education.* Portsmouth, NH: Heinemann.

Smith, M., & Rabinowitz, P. J. (1998). *Authorizing readers.* Urbana, IL: National Council of Teachers of English and Teachers College Press.

Snow, C., Burns, S., & Griffin, P. (Eds.). (1998). *Preventing reading difficulties in young children.* Washington, DC: National Academy Press.

Sommers, N. (1980). Revision strategies of student writers and experienced writers. *College Composition and Communication, 31,* 378–389.

Spandel, V., & Stiggins, R. J. (1997). *Creating writers: Linking writing assessment and instruction* (2nd ed.). New York: Longman.

Sprowl, D. (1996). The class quilt: A multicultural experience. In C. B. Olson (Ed.), *Reading, thinking and writing about multicultural literature* (pp. 99–122). Glenview, IL: Scott Foresman.

Stanovich, K. E. (1991). Word recognition: Changing perspectives. In R. Barr, M. L. Kamil, P. B. Monsenthal, & P. D. Pearson (Eds.), *Handbook of reading research* (Vol. 2, pp. 418–452). New York: Longman.

Strickland, K., & Strickland, J. (1998). *Reflections on assessment: Its purposes, methods & effects on learning.* Portsmouth, NH: Heinemann.

Strong, W. (1984). *Practicing sentence options.* New York: Random House.

Strong, W. (1996). *Writers toolbox: A sentence-combining workshop.* New York: McGraw-Hill.

Strong, W. (2006). *Write for insight: Empowering content area learning, grades 6–12.* Boston: Allyn & Bacon.

Sumara, D., & Walker, L. (1991). The teacher's role in whole language. *Language Arts, 68,* 276–285.

Taba, H. (1964). *Thinking in elementary school children.* U.S. Department of Health, Education and Welfare, Cooperative Research Project No. 1571.

Tarasoff, M. (1996). *Reading instruction that makes sense.* Victoria, BC: Active Learning Institute.

Tchudi, S. (Ed.). (1997). *Alternatives to grading student writing.* Urbana, IL: National Council of Teachers of English.

Tchudi, S., & Mitchell, D. (1999). *Exploring and teaching the English language arts* (4th ed.). New York: Longman.

Tempes, F. (1993). *CLAS writing assessment handbook: High school.* Sacramento, CA: California Department of Education.

Templeton, S. (1983). Using the spelling/meaning connection to develop word knowledge in older students. *Journal of Reading, 27*(1), 8–14.

Terrell, T. (1977). A natural approach to second language acquisition. *Modern Language Journal, 61,* 325–337.

Thomas, I. (1997). Some basics that really do lead to correctness. In C. B. Olson (Ed.), *Practical ideas for teaching writing as a process at the high school and college levels* (pp. 260–264). Sacramento, CA: California Department of Education.

Thomson, J. (1993). Helping students control texts: Contemporary literary theory into classroom practice. In S. B. Straw and D. Bogdan (Eds.), *Constructive reading: Teaching beyond communication* (pp. 130–154). Portsmouth, NH: Heinemann.

Tierney, R. J., Carter, M. A., & Desai, L. E. (1991). *Portfolio assessment in the reading–writing classroom.* Norwood, MA: Christopher-Gordon.

Tierney, R., & Gee, M. (1990). Reading comprehension: Readers, authors, and the world of text. In D. Bogdan & S. B. Straw (Eds.), *Beyond communication: Reading comprehension and criticism* (pp. 197–209). Portsmouth, NH: Heinemann.

Tierney, R. J., Leys, M., & Rogers, T. (1986). Comprehension, composition, and collaboration. In T. Raphael (Ed.), *The contexts of school-based literacy.* New York: Random House.

Tierney, R. J., & Pearson, P. D. (1983). Toward a composing model of reading. *Language Arts, 60,* 568–580.

Tierney, R. J., & Pearson, D. (1998). A revisionist perspective on "Learning to learn from text: A framework for improving classroom practice." In J. E. Readence, T. W. Bean, & R. S. Baldwin (Eds.), *Content area literacy: An integrated approach* (6th ed.) (CD-ROM, pp. 82–85). Dubuque, IA: Kendall/Hunt.

Tierney, R. J., & Shanahan, T. (1991). Research on the reading–writing relationship: Interactions, transactions, and outcomes. In R. Barr, M. Kamil, P. Mosenthal, & P. D. Pearson (Eds.), *Handbook of reading research* (Vol. 2, pp. 246–280). New York: Longman.

Tierney, R. J., Soter, A., O'Flahavan, J. O., & McGinley, W. (1989). The effects of reading and writing upon thinking critically. *Reading Research Quarterly, 24,* 134–173.

Tompkins, G. E. (1997). *Literacy for the 21st century: A balanced approach.* Upper Saddle River, NJ: Prentice-Hall.

Tompkins, G. E. (2002). *Language Arts: Content and teaching strategies* (5th ed.). New York: Merrill.

Tovani, C. (2000). *I read it, but I don't get it: Comprehension strategies for adolescent readers.* Portland, ME: Stenhouse.

Tredway, L. (1995). Socratic seminars: Engaging students in intellectual discourse. *Educational Leadership, 53,* 26–29.

Troyka, L. Q. (1995). *Simon and Schuster quick access reference for writers.* New York: Simon & Schuster.

Turner, J. C. (1992). *Identifying motivation for literacy in first grade: An observational study.* Paper presented at the American Educational Research Association, April, San Francisco, CA.

Underwood, T., & Pearson, P. D. (2004). Teaching struggling adolescent readers to comprehend what they read. In T. L. Jetton & J. A. Dole (Eds.), *Adolescent literacy research and practice* (pp. 135–161). New York: Guilford.

University of Chicago. (2003). *Chicago manual of style: The essential guide for writers, editors, and publishers.* Chicago: University of Chicago Press.

U.S. Department of Education. Office of English Language Acquisition. (2004). www.ed.gov/about/offices/list/oela/index.html

Urzúa, C. (1989). I grow for a living. In P. Rigg & V. G. Allen (Eds.), *When they don't speak English: Integrating the ESL student into the regular classroom* (pp. 15–38). Urbana, IL: National Council of Teachers of English.

Vail, N. J., & Papenfuss, J. F. (1989–90). *Daily oral language.* Levels 1–12. Evanston, IL: McDougal, Littel.

Von Blerkom, D. L. (1997). *College study skills: Becoming a strategic learner* (2nd ed.). Belmont, CA: Wadsworth.

Vygotsky, L. S. (1986). *Thought and language.* Cambridge, MA: MIT Press.

Weaver, C. (1996). *Teaching grammar in context.* Portsmouth, NH: Heinemann.

Wellington, B. (1991). The promise of reflective practice. *Educational Leadership, 48,* 4–5.

Wendelin, K., & Zinck, R. A. (1983). How students make book choices. *Reading Horizons, 23,* 84–88.

Werner, E. K. (1975). *The study of communication time.* Unpublished master's thesis, University of Maryland, College Park.

Whimbey, A. (1980). Students can learn to be better problem solvers. *Educational Leadership, 37,* 56–65.

Wiener, B. (1979). A theory of motivation for some classroom experiences. *Journal of Educational Psychology, 71,* 3–25.

Wiggins, G., & McTighe, J. (2005). *Understanding by design* (2nd ed.). Alexandria, VA: Association for Supervision and Curriculum Development.

Wilhelm, J. (1997). *You gotta BE the book: Teaching engaged and reflective reading with adolescents.* New York: Teachers College Press.

Wilhelm, J. D. (2001). *Improving comprehension with think-aloud strategies.* New York: Scholastic.

Wilhelm, J. D., Baker, T. N., & Dube, J. (2001). *Strategic reading: Guiding students to enjoy literacy, 6–12.* Portsmouth, NH: Boynton Cook.

Willett, S. R. (1992). Your romantic childhood: A stylistic imitation of free verse. In C. B. Olson (Ed.), *Thinking/writing: Fostering critical thinking through writing* (pp. 174–195). New York: HarperCollins.

Wolfe, P. (2001). *Brain matters: Translating research into classroom practice.* Alexander, VA: Association for Supervision and Curriculum Development.

Wong Fillmore, L. (1986). Research currents: Equity or excellence. *Language Arts, 63,* 474–481.

Wong Fillmore, L., & Snow, C. (2003). What teachers need to know about language. In C. J. Adger, C. E. Snow, & D. Christian (Eds.), *What teachers need to know about language* (pp. 10–46). McHenry, IL: The Center for Applied Linguistics.

Yancey, K. B. (1992). *Portfolios in the writing classroom.* Urbana, IL: National Council of Teachers of English.

Yokota, J. (1993). Issues in selecting multicultural children's literature. *Language Arts, 70,* 156–167.

Zemelman, S., Daniels, H., & Hyde, A. (1998). *Best practice: New standards for teaching and learning in America's schools.* Portsmouth, NH: Heinemann.

Index